Requires-

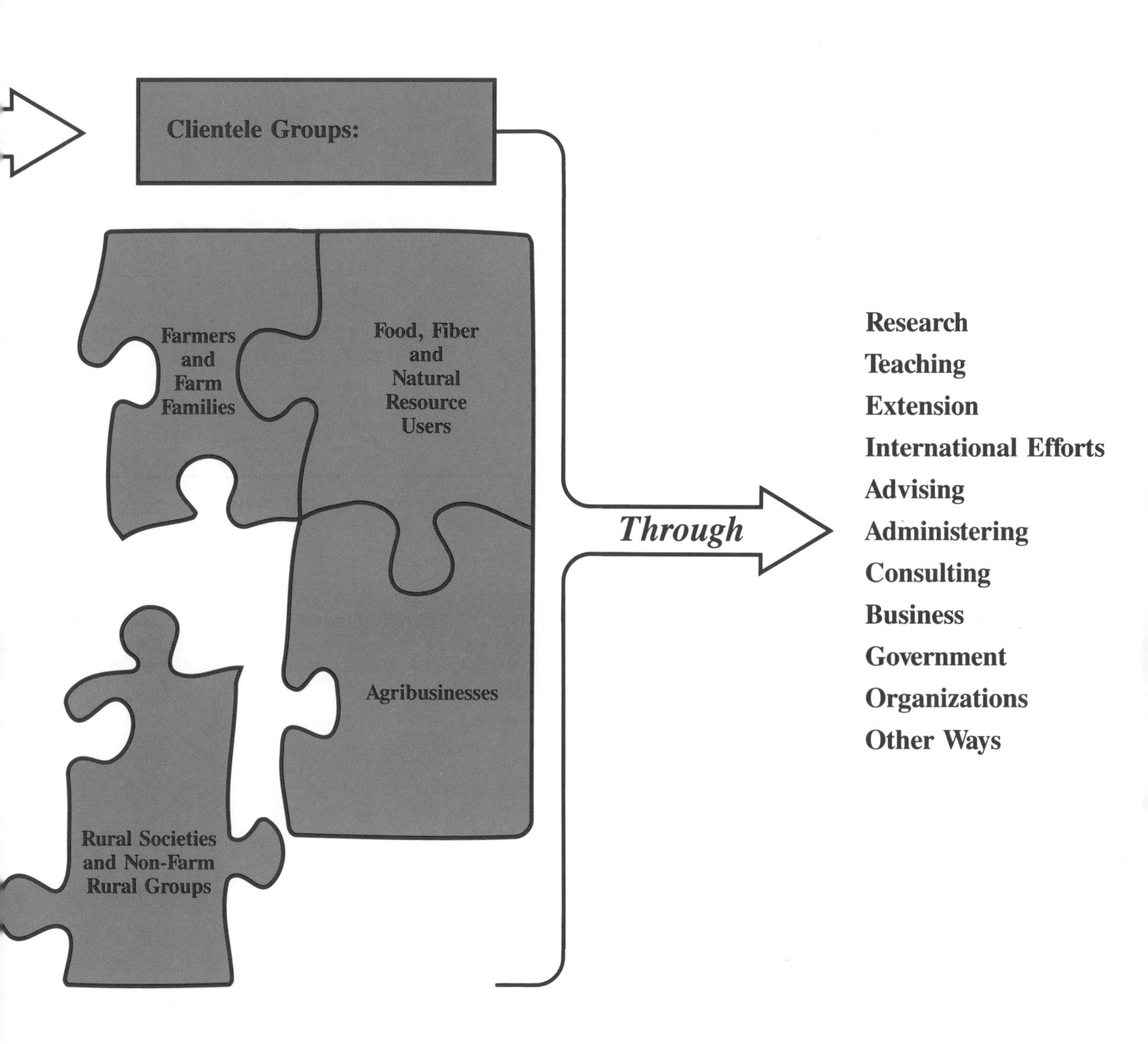
Clientele Groups:
Farmers and Farm Families
Food, Fiber and Natural Resource Users
Agribusinesses
Rural Societies and Non-Farm Rural Groups
Through
Research
Teaching
Extension
International Efforts
Advising
Administering
Consulting
Business
Government
Organizations
Other Ways

Social Science Agricultural Agendas and Strategies

Social Science Agricultural Agendas and Strategies

Edited by
Glenn L. Johnson and James T. Bonnen,
with Darrell Fienup, C. Leroy Quance, and Neill Schaller

Michigan State University Press
East Lansing
1991

Printed in the United States of America

Michigan State University Press
East Lansing, Michigan 48823-5202

The paper used in this publication meets the minimum requirements of American National Standard for Information Sciences — Permanence of Paper for Printed Library Materials ANSI Z39.48-1984

Library of Congress Cataloging-in-Publication Data

Social science agricultural agendas and strategies
edited by Glenn L. Johnson and James T. Bonnen, with Darrell Fienup, C. Leroy Quance, and Neill Schaller.
p. cm.
Includes bibliographical references and index.
ISBN 0-87013-289-X: $20.00
1. Rural development. 2. Sociology, Rural. 3. Agriculture — Social aspects — United States. 4. Agriculture — Economic aspects — United States. 5. Social sciences. I. Johnson, Glenn Leroy, 1918- . II. Bonnen, James T.
HT435.S63 1991
306.3′49′0973 — dc20 90-50847
CIP

CONTENTS

PART I
Introduction

PART II

Introduction to Domestic Farm, Agribusiness, and Consumer Work and All International Agricultural Development Work

Section 1 Domestic

Section 2 International

PART III
The Four Driving Forces For Development: Institutional Change, Human Development, Natural Resource Enhancement and Growth In Manmade Capital, and Technical Advance

Section 1
Institutional Change

Section 2
Human Development

Section 3
Resource Enhancement

Section 4 Technical Advance

PART IV
Three Crosscutting Concerns

Section 1
Databases and Information Systems

Section 2
Basic Social Sciences

Section 3
Ethics, Decisions, and Public Choices

PART V
Administration and Funding: Needed Research and Strategies

LIST OF FIGURES

LIST OF TABLES

PREFACE

For over a century, our public agricultural research, extension, and educational investments have been focused mainly on technology while farm and rural people and societies have been benignly neglected. Thus, the researchable, teachable, and actionable problems now facing agriculture and rural society fall increasingly, if not predominantly, into the domains of the social sciences. The relevance and capacities of the rural social sciences are not well understood or well supported today—even in our agricultural institutions where such support might be most expected. Several of the humanities are also relevant but generally missing from this arena.

The Social Science Agricultural (and Rural) Agenda Project (SSAAP) is a response to this failure. It focuses on the major farm and rural subjects and problems at issue today and attempts to identify where social science capability is relevant and necessary to alleviate or solve rural and agricultural problems and issues. SSAAP's case for the social sciences is not made at the expense of the biological and physical sciences. Because most of the sciences and humanities are necessary (but individually insufficient) in doing applied problem solving and even in doing some basic disciplinary work, the social sciences cannot be emphasized at the expense of the biological and physical sciences. In making the social sciences' case, SSAAP's leaders have been acutely aware of the narrow line they attempt to tread between unjustified advocacy and the objective case for the social sciences.

There are several products from SSAAP; one of these is this volume. In addition, an executive summary and a popular pamphlet are available as introductions to and summaries of both this large volume and the project. Important intermediate products of SSAAP were the interactions and learning that took place between social scientists and others from different disciplines and fields before, during, and after the large (250-plus participants) SSAAP March 1988 conference near Houston.

This volume is more than just a proceedings from the agenda-setting conference near Houston, Texas, and an earlier (June 1987) Spring Hill, Minnesota, planning conference. In addition to the papers commissioned for distribution before these two conferences and the agenda and strategy statements developed in Houston, additional papers were commissioned to fill subsequently identified gaps. Some of these additional papers were specially commissioned while others are reprinted from sources not readily available to many rural social scientists and administrators. Further, the editors of this volume have written introductory and concluding chapters for the five parts of this volume and their nine sections described below. The first chapter in each section, or part that is unsectioned, introduces the section involved and provides a brief review and update of the relevant literature. These reviews, done after the Houston conference, helped reveal gaps and deficiencies in the coverage and output from the Houston conference, which the editors then attempted to remedy with additional papers and their own post-Houston efforts. The concluding chapter of each section of Parts II through IV and of the unsectioned Part V in this volume contain abridged versions of the agendas produced at the Houston conference followed by a clearly identified set of additional agenda or strategy items for each area. Part I is introductory to the entire volume.

During the course of SSAAP's work, it became clear that a major reorientation of social scientists, the organizations in which social scientists work, and of their administrators was needed for better addressing the problems and issues of farmers; rural society; food, fiber, and resource consumers and users; and agribusinesses. It also became clear that such a reorientation calls for (1) rural social science agendas that indicate the important work the rural and basic social scientists can do in our reoriented public, semipublic, and private agricultural institutions sometimes referred to, collectively, as the agricultural establishment (AE) and (2) a set of strategies to facilitate the needed reorientation.

For SSAAP to have generated a few priority areas for social science funding and implementation would have been to let social scientists and administrators "off the hook" too easily; instead, SSAAP calls for a reorientation of both social scientists and administrators of the institutions of the AE. To this end, SSAAP challenges both groups with (1) ten agenda sets and (2) detailed, as well as overall, administrative and funding strategies.

The ten agenda sets should be useful inputs in setting priorities in an administratively reoriented AE. These agendas should not be regarded as either shopping lists or priorities. In presenting SSAAP's early tentative results to administrative, policy-setting, and funding bodies, SSAAP's leadership came to realize it would be arrogant for SSAAP to try to tell responsible administrators what their priorities should be when (1) those administrators had not delegated that responsibility to SSAAP, and (2) SSAAP lacked essential knowledge of budgetary and political limitations in the different, specific contexts within which different organizations must establish their location- and situation-specific priorities. Priorities are best set, federal agency by federal agency, state agency by state agency, academic organization by academic organization, business by business, parastatal agency by parastatal agency, interest organization by interest organization, problem by problem, and issue by issue. Priorities should be set by those with legislative, administrative and/or funding responsibilities for policies, programs, and projects rather than by a temporary, national organization of scientists and professionals, such as SSAAP.

SSAAP's agendas and strategies are not limited to research; they deal also with the complex and practical roles social scientists play as educators, extension workers, consultants, advisors, and administrators and in the business world.

SSAAP is concerned with multidisciplinary subject-matter and problem-solving work as well as specialized disciplinary work. SSAAP recognizes that the proper peers for evaluating and establishing the relevance and priority of different social science efforts extend well beyond researchers and academicians to the individuals, organizations, and agencies facing problems and issues. The opinions of legislators, institutional leaders, and individual students, farmers, agribusiness people, nonfarm rural residents, and consumers are to be considered.

In putting this volume together, the editors have given the outputs from the Spring Hill and Houston conferences a substantially different organization than those used at those conferences. This organizational shift, explained in the first chapter of Part 1, provides a more integrated synthesis of these materials into abridged agendas, interlinked related subjects, and a framework for and transitions from one agenda set to another. This volume of nine sections is organized into five parts. Part I introduces and explains the volume. Part II develops agendas in two separate sections, one for *domestic* agriculture and rural society and the other for *international* farm and rural development. The four sections of Part III present agendas for social science work on the four driving forces of rural and agricultural development: institutional change, human development, natural resource enhancement and growth in manmade capital, and technical advance. The three sections of Part IV present agendas that cut across the substantive agendas of Parts II and III, namely, for: the information systems that sustain the data bases for decision making; the basic social sciences upon which the rural social sciences depend; and knowledge of ethics, private decision making and public choices. Finally, Part V presents administrative and funding *strategies* and *agendas for needed research on administration and funding*. It also includes a summary chapter for the entire book that is practically the same as the separately published "Executive Summary." It is important to note that the pages are numbered separately within each of the book's five parts and that each part has its own index. (See Table of Contents for details.) It is hoped that this way of organizing the book will assist anyone interested in a specific subject by providing easy access to the relevant literature and identifying important agendas in that subject for which rural and basic social science capabilities are highly relevant.

Responsibility for the direction of SSAAP has been borne by SSAAP's Executive Committee and its Advisory Board with the Executive Secretary acting as SSAAP's day-to-day executive. They planned and executed the two conferences. Responsibility for the content and shape of this volume is mainly that of the editorial group. SSAAP's reports and work are independent of SSAAP's funders and sponsors.

Although SSAAP has sought and used information and advice from many persons in its funding and sponsoring agencies, SSAAP's reports have not been specifically and formally cleared through or approved by any of those agencies; hence, no agency other than SSAAP should be held responsible for the contents of this book and its accompanying executive summary and popular pamphlet. Responsibility for their contributions to this volume is borne by (1) the authors of the peer-reviewed, signed, original chapters and (2) members of various SSAAP work groups who developed the agendas and strategic statements reported in this book and identified with those work groups. Many peer reviewers were used, most of whom are unnamed herein. SSAAP's editorial group bears responsibility for the unsigned portions of SSAAP reports. The editorial group was directed by Glenn L. Johnson and James T. Bonnen. It also included Darrel Feinup, Leroy Quance, and Neill Schaller, who worked on specific portions of the manuscript at different times.

The Advisory Board was active up through the Houston conference and has, along with Spring Hill and Houston conference participants, been kept informed periodically by newsletter since then. During the planning period, reports from the Executive Committee kept the Advisory Board informed periodically between its meetings. Members of the Advisory Board have at one time or another included:

Agricultural History Society Presidents and dates:
- David B. Danbom, North Dakota State University, 1990–91
- Wayne Fuller, University of Texas at El Paso, 1989–90
- Trudy Peterson, National Archives, 1988–89
- Donald L. Winters, Vanderbilt University, 1987–88
- Thomas Wessell, Montana State University, 1986–87

American Agricultural Economic Association Presidents and dates:
- Warren Johnston, University of California, 1990–91
- Sandra S. Batie, Virginia Polytechnic Institute and State University, 1989–90
- Lester V. Manderscheid, Michigan State University, 1988–89
- Daniel Padberg, Texas Agricultural and Mechanical University, 1987–88
- Joseph Havlicek, The Ohio State University, 1986–87
- William Tomek, Cornell University, 1985–86

Peggy Barlett, Department of Anthropology, Emory University
Charles Benbrook, Executive Director, Board of Agriculture, National Research Council, Washington, D.C.
Sue S. Coates, representing the American Association of State Colleges of Agricultural and Renewal Resources, Chair of Department of Consumer Resources & Technology, Western Michigan University
Gary Comstock, Religious Studies Program, Iowa State University
James Cowan, representing the National Association of State Universities and Land-Grant Colleges, Washington, D.C.
Experiment Station Committee on Organization and Policy Chairpersons and dates:
Charles R. Krueger, Pennsylvania State University, 1990–91
James M. Davidson, University of Florida, 1989–90
Robert G. Gast, Michigan State University, 1988–89
Clive W. Donoho, University of Georgia, 1987–88
C. C. Kaltenbach, University of Wyoming, 1986–87
Extension Committee on Organization and Policy Chairpersons and dates:
Richard E. Fowler, University of Delaware, 1990–91
Patrick Borich, University of Minnesota, 1989–90
Chester D. Black, North Carolina State University, 1987–89
Roy S. Rauschkolb, University of Arizona, 1986–88
Kenneth R. Farrell, Vice President, Agriculture and Natural Resources, University of California
W. R. Freudenburg, Department of Rural Sociology, University of Wisconsin, Madison
Mitch Geasler, Director, Cooperative Extension Service, Virginia Polytechnical Institute and State University
R. James Hildreth, Managing Director, Farm Foundation
International Committee on Organization and Policy Chairpersons and dates:
J. Lawrence Apple, North Carolina State University, 1990–91
Harold R. Matteson, New Mexico State University, 1989–90
D. Woods Thomas, President, 1988–89
Erwin Johnson, Farmer and Farm Leader, Charles City, Iowa
Roberta Miller, Director, Division of Social and Economic Science, National Science Foundation, Washington, D.C.
Michel Petit, President, International Association of Agricultural Economists, Department of Agriculture and Rural Development, World Bank
Michael Phillips, Food and Renewable Resources, Office of Technology Assessment, Washington, D.C.
Resident Instruction Committee on Organization and Policy Chairpersons and dates:
Joseph E. Kunsman, University of Wyoming, 1990–91
Paul D. Hummer, Oklahoma State University, 1989–90
Gerald L. Zachariah, University of Florida, 1988–89
W. Keith Wharton, University of Minnesota, 1987–88
G. E. Rossmiller, Director, National Center for Food and Agricultural Policy, Resources for the Future
Rural Sociological Society Presidents and dates:
Frederick H. Buttel, Cornell University, 1990–91
Gene Summers, University of Wisconsin, 1989–90
William D. Heffernan, University of Missouri, 1988–89
Cornelia Flora, Kansas State University, 1987–88
James A. Christensen, University of Kentucky, 1986–87
Vernon W. Ruttan, Department of Agriculture and Applied Economics, University of Minnesota
G. Edward Schuh, Dean, Hubert H. Humphrey Institute of Public Affairs, University of Minnesota
Susan Sechler, Director, Rural Policy Program, Aspen Institute, Washington, D.C.
Barbara S. Stowe, Dean, College of Human Ecology, Kansas State University
Kenneth Terfertiller, Vice President for Agricultural Affairs, University of Florida
T. T. Williams, Director, Human Resource Development Center, Tuskegee University
James J. Zuiches, Director, Washington Agricultural Experiment Station, College of Agriculture and Home Economics, Washington State University.

The original Executive Committee of SSAAP was composed of Glenn L. Johnson (Executive Secretary), Michigan State University; Kenneth Farrell, Director of the National Center for Food and Agriculture Polity of Resources for the Future, and John E. Lee, Administrator of the Economic Research Service, U.S. Department of Agriculture. Seconds were James Bonnen (for Johnson), Ed Rossmiller (for Farrell), and John Miranowski (for Lee). As Executive Secretary, Johnson served as SSAAP's day-to-day executive with Bonnen playing a very important role comparable to that of Joint Executive Secretary. When Farrell moved to his current position of Vice President for Agriculture at the University of California, his second Ed Rossmiller replaced him as Director of the National Center and on SSAAP's Executive Committee.

The Social Science Agricultural Agenda Project would not have been possible without the cooperation and support of many people and organizations. Institutions that provided funding, in kind services, and/or unpaid editorial and administrative services for SSAAP include:

Aspen Institute
Farm Foundation
Ford Foundation
Michigan State University
National Science Foundation
National Center for Food and Agriculture Policy, Resources for the Future
U.S. Agency for International Development
U.S. Department of Agriculture: The Economic Research Service and The Cooperative State Research Service

Other organizations sponsored and provided valuable organizational support for SSAAP's effort. These organizations included:

Agricultural History Society
American Agricultural Economics Association
American Association of State Colleges of Agriculture and Renewable Resources
Caribbean Agro-Economics Association
Experiment Station Committee on Organization and Policy
Extension Service Committee on Organization and Policy

International Association of Agricultural Economists
International Bank for Reconstruction and Development
International Committee on Organization and Policy
National Association of State Universities and Land Grant Colleges
Rural Sociological Society
Social Science Research Council

Approximately 400 people participated in various SSAAP activities over a five-year period. More than 250 attended the 1988 Houston conference while 50 or so participated in the 1987 Spring Hill, Minnesota, planning conference. The Experiment Station and Extension Committees on Organization and Policy urged that state directors finance the travel of participants to the Houston conference, making it possible for many to attend.

All invited or commissioned papers in this volume were peer reviewed on a multidisciplinary basis by an average of three reviewers per page. Many other social scientists, agriculturalists, and others were used to review the introductory and concluding chapters of each section of the volume. Help was also used in producing, critiqueing, and reviewing SSAAP manuscripts, in making decisions for SSAAP on agendas and strategies, and in editing and checking the accuracy of SSAAP's work. Although any merit this volume may have is a cooperative product, the editors are responsible for all deficiencies except those in signed papers.

Much appreciated editorial assistance was provided by Julia McKay, Beverly Weber, and Romona Erickson. Romona Erickson was particularly helpful as an editorial assistant while Julia McKay provided editorial and accounting assistance in addition to her main duties as secretary to SSAAP's Executive Secretary. Beverly Weber filled in between Julia McKay and Romona Erickson to provide both secretarial and editorial assistance. Technical editing was provided by Dawn Martin from the Michigan State University Press under the direction of Julie L. Loehr, Editor-in-Chief, Michigan State University Press.

Part I

Introduction

CHAPTER 1

INTRODUCTION TO PART I AND, IN TURN, THIS BOOK

This introductory part of the book explains the origin, purpose, and anticipated uses of the papers and reports contained in it. It presents and/or covers (1) the origins, objectives, and scope of the Social Science Agricultural Agenda Project (SSAAP), (2) background papers and work shop reports that indicate in an overall way the need for SSAAP and how SSAAP was structured to develop agendas for the work of rural and basic social sciences relevant for U.S. agriculture and rural America, and Third-World-country rural development, (3) the contents of various SSAAP reports and presentations and the functions they play, and (4) the organization of the rest of the book including its relationship to a separately published executive summary (Chapter 9).

ORIGINS, OBJECTIVES, AND SCOPE OF THE SOCIAL SCIENCE AGRICULTURAL AGENDA PROJECT (SSAAP)

The Social Science Agricultural Agenda Project (SSAAP) grew out of the relative neglect of the rural social sciences (RSSs) in such agricultural research priority-setting exercises as the World Food and Nutrition Study (WFNS) and the Commission on World Hunger (CWH).

President Ford created the World Food and Nutrition Study (National Academy of Sciences 1977) to establish priorities whereby U.S. agricultural research capacity could make its best contribution to the solution of problems involving hunger and malnutrition. As has been pointed out elsewhere (Johnson 1977a), that study examined a broad range of research opportunities for the biological and physical agricultural sciences and established priorities among them. The rural social sciences were allocated a mere three-tenths of one percent of the recommended budgets, despite the fact that world hunger is caused primarily by failures in social organization, especially with respect to income distribution.

The Presidential Commission on World Hunger established by President Carter (1980) had a broader base inasmuch as it included political and agricultural leaders as well as agricultural scientists and researchers. Its final recommendations were somewhat more balanced than those of the World Food and Nutrition Study, but nonetheless placed primary emphasis on technology to the neglect of research on (1) improvements in policies, programs, and institutions (including social reforms) and (2) investments in human capacities and skills (Johnson 1977b).

There have been two international crop productivity conferences to develop research priorities; one took place eleven years ago (Brown et al. 1975) and another more recently (Gibbs and Carlson 1986). Both placed primary emphasis on research and development to generate new technologies for producing crops. The technical agricultural scientists in charge of these conferences were interested in what social scientists could do to prove the importance of technical research and to get that research into use. There was little interest displayed in research on policies, programs, and institutions including social reforms or research on human development to help attain balance among the four driving forces that have proven crucial for success time and again. Nonfarm rural resources and disadvantaged rural groups, whether farm or nonfarm, received little emphasis.

There has also been a conference to set research priorities with respect to animal agriculture (Pond et al. 1980). Again, the emphasis was on technological needs.

A conference on agricultural research was held in the spring of 1986 at the University of Minnesota. As usual, the emphasis was mainly on technological research for production agriculture. One group at the Minnesota conference was concerned with the research institutions of the U.S. Department of Agriculture, the agricultural experiment stations, and the international research centers with a focus on biological and physical research. Little consideration was given to research on agricultural policies and programs and rural institutions, in general. Research on human development and disadvantaged rural groups was hardly considered, though some attention was given to the development of biological and physical science expertise for staffing the technical research institutes and agencies.

Research on community and rural nonfarm development, the current farm financial crisis, and disadvantaged nonfarm rural groups received little consideration.

The International Association of Agricultural Economists (IAAE) devoted its ten-day, 1982 triennial meeting in Jakarta, Indonesia, to papers on agricultural "Growth and Equity" (Johnson 1983) that make useful contributions to our understanding of needed social science agendas.

The American Agricultural Economics Association conducted a postconference seminar in the summer of 1985 on "Critical Issues Facing American Agriculture for the 21st Century." Somewhat similar exercises have been conducted by the rural sociologists and home economists. These commendable exercises provide very useful input for the present attempt to deal with the whole of the rural social sciences and related basic disciplines.

When Vannevar Bush (1945) made the case after World War II for much greater investments in United States research, he argued for a balance between applied and basic research. The National Academy of Science and National Science Foundation have pushed hard toward basic disciplinary research in the biological and physical sciences. Even for agriculture, the emphasis since Bush advanced his argument has been placed on basic disciplinary research in the "hard" sciences to the neglect of applied research, partly as a result of the Pound report (National Academy of Sciences, 1972). This was unfortunate for important needed subject-matter (SM) and problem-solving (PS) research on the food system, community and resource development, and for general welfare (Bonnen 1986a). It was also unfortunate for the social sciences, because much applied research is necessarily multidisciplinary in a way that includes the social sciences, whereas social science is not nearly so relevant for the disciplinary research of the physical and biological sciences. Concentration on the basic disciplinary research of the biological and physical sciences, at the expense of multidisciplinarity, has contributed to the neglect of the rural social sciences by the agricultural research establishment. It has also resulted in the disenchantment of public and private decision makers with the agricultural research establishment—SM and PS results, as well as improvements in academic disciplines, are expected by legitimate clientele groups of the agricultural establishment. With respect to the research establishment, neglect of the practical has been noted recently by Shapley and Roy's book entitled *Lost at the Frontier* (1985), an obvious sequel to Vannevar Bush's post-World War II document entitled *Science: The Endless Frontier* (1945).

The current need for applied research does not, of course, justify reduced attention to disciplinary research in either (1) the basic biological and physical sciences or (2) the basic social sciences and the humanities. Our society (with its increasingly complex technologies, policies, institutions, and programs, and the concomitant demands for high-level human skills and capabilities) needs much more relevant disciplinary research across the social, biological, and physical sciences to support its applied research. SSAAP seeks to define the appropriate places in the agricultural and general research establishment for both the rural SM and PS sciences and basic social science research, teaching, consulting, extension, advising, and administrative work.

As the underemphasis on the rural social sciences in the exercises described above became more and more apparent, and as the need grew for social science work on agricultural technologies, rural institutions, human capital formation, and the generation of biological and physical capital, Kenneth Farrell of the National Center for Food and Agricultural Policy (NCFAP) and Glenn Johnson of Michigan State University (MSU) perceived the need for an exercise to establish working agendas and administrative strategies for the rural social sciences, including those basic social science disciplines (BSSDs) concerned with agricultural issues and problems. To this end, NCFAP provided a small amount of "seed money" that was used to explore the possibility of establishing a national project to deal with research priorities and administrative strategies vis-à-vis the rural social sciences and basic social science disciplines concerned with rural and agricultural issues and problems (broadly conceived).

This seed money was used to assemble a group of persons to explore the idea. Eight persons were provided, four by NCFAP and four by MSU. Representing NCFAP were Kenneth Farrell, Ed Rossmiller, and, borrowed from the U.S. Department of Agriculture, Gene Wunderlich and David Brown. From MSU came Marvin Olsen, Eileen vanRavenswaay, James Bonnen, and Glenn Johnson. The first meeting of this exploratory planning group was held on the day of the Challenger shuttle disaster, January 28, 1986. The morning of that meeting was very productive, but momentum and productivity were lost on receipt of the news of the shuttle disaster at lunchtime. Subsequent work by Kenneth Farrell and Glenn Johnson led to a reconvening of the workgroup on March 11, 1986. At this meeting momentum was regained and a prospectus outlining the work of the Social Science Agricultural Agenda Project was developed. The prospectus went through many iterations in the hands of the planning group and particularly in the hands of what later evolved into an Executive Committee for SSAAP. The prospectus established the objectives and scope of SSAAP as follows:

OBJECTIVES OF SSAAP

1. To enhance the quality and effectiveness of research and related activities in the rural social sciences and in the basic social science disciplines for improving farm and agribusiness productivity, farm and nonfarm rural-area development, nonfarm rural-resource development, and related aspects of general welfare by:
   a. Developing a strategic agenda and set of broad priorities for U.S. and international rural social science research, extension, consulting, advising, and related activities, and
   b. Clarifying the different roles that both *applied* rural social scientists and *disciplinary* social scientists should play to make effective contributions to the agricultural establishment of the United States and the world.
2. To develop wide support in funding, administrative, and user communities for the strategic research agenda and priorities to be developed.

SCOPE OF SSAAP, ITS FINANCIAL SUPPORT AND THREE BROAD KINDS OF WORK CONSIDERED

The scope of SSAAP includes:

1. Concern about the roles of the rural social sciences and the basic social science disciplines as they pertain to

research, teaching, extension, and related consulting; and advisory, entrepreneurial, and administrative work done on problems and issues important:

a. To farms and farmers.
b. To agribusinesses.
c. To consumers—including the malnourished and inadequately clothed.
d. To nonfarm rural residents including disadvantaged groups.
e. To organizations servicing farmers, agribusinesses, consumers, and people in rural areas.
f. To state and federal legislative and executive agencies.
g. For natural resources and the environment.
h. For rural communities and infrastructure.
i. For international trade and monetary/fiscal developments as they interrelate with agricultural and rural affairs.
j. To U.S., international, and non-U.S. agricultural research establishments.
k. To other international agencies serving the above.

2. Agricultural economics, rural sociology and anthropology, geography, agricultural history, the social science aspects of home economics, agricultural law, agricultural political science, and the like.
3. The basic social science disciplines—sociology, economics, geography, anthropology, human ecology, history, political science, law, and psychology.
4. The main related or ancillary disciplines—statistics, mathematics, and philosophy.
5. The work of physical and biological agricultural departments such as agronomy, animal husbandry, and agricultural engineering contribute, along with the work of rural social science departments, to applied agricultural research efforts.

Funding and other support for SSAAP was obtained using a prospectus including the above statement of scope and other material presented in this chapter. Enough money was committed to SSAAP to provide the financial resources needed to attain its objectives. In addition to monetary resources, SSAAP received the valuable sponsorship of the Social Science Research Council (SSRC), the Experiment Station Committee on Organization and Policy (ESCOP), the Resident Instruction Committee on Organization and Policy (RICOP), the International Committee on Organization and Policy (ICOP), the Extension Committee on Organization and Policy (ECOP), the International Association of Agricultural Economists (IAAE), and the U.S. associations representing rural sociologists, agricultural historians, and agricultural economists. SSAAP also has the valuable sponsorship of the National Association of State Universities and Land Grant Colleges (NASULGC) and American Association of State Colleges of Agriculture and Renewable Resources (AASCARR). As support and sponsorship were mobilized for SSAAP, an Advisory Board was established including representatives of those agencies funding and sponsoring SSAAP. The multidisciplinary and multiagency composition of the Advisory Board is indicated in the preface pages of this volume that list all sponsors and funders. The Advisory Board participated actively in the development of SSAAP's program.

Three broad kinds of work done by rural social scientists (RSSs) and basic social science disciplines (BSSDs) also indicated the nature of SSAAP's work vis-à-vis agriculture and rural communities. The academic, administrative, and entrepreneurial work of the agricultural sciences, including that of the rural social sciences, ranges across a spectrum stretching from problem-solving work at one extreme to work in such parent basic disciplines as history, economics, cell microbiology, sociology, genetics, and anthropology (Johnson, 1986). SSAAP is concerned with the roles of the rural and basic social sciences across this entire range of work.

As defined here, *problem-solving* (PS) work is work on a specific practical problem of a real-world decision maker in either the public or private sector. In using this definition, it is important to note that the phrase "practical problem" does not include answering the questions (sometimes called problems) that disciplinarians encounter in trying to improve the theories, techniques, and basic measurements of their disciplines.

At the other end of the spectrum is the *disciplinary* (DISC) work that rural social scientists do, defined here as work to improve the theories, basic measurements, and techniques of a specific discipline, such as chemistry, anthropology, genetics, or sociology.

Between these two extremes is *subject-matter* (SM) work, defined here as work on multidisciplinary subjects that is useful to rather well-defined sets of decision makers addressing rather well-defined problems.

FOUR DRIVING FORCES THAT INCREASE RURAL PRODUCTIVITY BROADLY DEFINED

SSAAP regards agricultural and rural productivity broadly to include the attainment of broad, private and social, monetary and nonmonetary objectives of rural society and the production of more products and services for public use and sale. Increasing rural and agricultural productivity turns on our ability to improve four basic driving forces: (1) technical advance, (2) institutional and policy improvements, (3) the development of human capacity, and (4) the enhancement and conservation of both natural and manmade resources. SSAAP treats all of these forces as individually *essential but insufficient* for increased rural and farm productivity and does not concentrate on one or more of them at the expense of those remaining. SSAAP seeks balanced consideration of all four driving forces.

ADMINISTRATION OF RSSs AND BSSDs

The rural social sciences are typically administered in subject-matter (SM) departments of the agricultural establishment that stress multidisciplinary subjects and sometimes the solution of specific practical problems. The RSS departments are typical of the other multidisciplinary departments of colleges of agriculture (professional colleges, generally) and other agricultural institutions; as such, they are more like multidisciplinary institutes than the basic social science disciplinary departments in arts, sciences, and humanities of traditional universities or parts of less traditional universities.

An RSS department is typically a multidisciplinary one drawing not only on a parent basic discipline but also on such other basic social science disciplines as political science, sociology, geography, and history. The basic biological and physical science disciplines necessary to understand technical agriculture and several of the other technical, multidisciplinary, agricultural subject-matter areas such as agronomy and animal husbandry are also included. Thus, the RSSs are organized into multidisciplinary–subject-matter departments designed to furnish bodies of multidisciplinary knowledge to rather well-defined sets of decision makers (their clientele) addressing rather well-defined sets of problems.

The basic social science disciplines and their ancillaries, on the other hand, stress disciplinary work including applications of specific disciplines. Like SM work, PS work is almost always multidisciplinary.

The above views of the work and administration of agricultural and rural social scientists make it clearly appropriate that the rural social sciences stress SM and PS work. At the same time, it is extremely important for the RSSs that DISC work go forward in the BSSDs that are relevant to their SM and PS work. Basic social science disciplinary work also includes work in such ancillary disciplines as statistics, mathematics, and philosophy. Ever since the so-called Pound Report (National Academy of Science 1972), agriculturalists have been sensitive to the complementarity that exists between the biological and physical agricultural sciences and their *basic disciplines* of chemistry, physics, genetics, microbiology, and the like. There is a similar high degree of complementarity or synergism between the SM and PS work of the RSSs, on one hand, and the disciplinary work of the BSSDs, on the other, that has been given careful consideration by SSAAP.

SSAAP'S THREE-STAGE PROGRAM OF WORK

SSAAP's work proceeded in three stages. The first stage was devoted to developing and conducting a work shop to provide guidance for subsequent SSAAP work. Meeting at the Spring Hill Conference Center near Minneapolis in June of 1987, participants in the first work shop included leading social scientists, educators, biological and physical agricultural scientists, administrators concerned with the agendas of the rural social sciences, agribusiness people, farmers, and policy and program officials. An unedited "working" proceedings volume was produced for subsequent use mainly within SSAAP.

After successful completion of the Stage I workshop, a second-stage, four-day conference was planned. The second conference was held in the Woodlands Conference Center near Houston in March of 1988 and drew upon and extended the Stage I effort with additional commissioned and invited papers. It included about 300 participants more fully representing some of the groups identified as under-represented at the Stage I work shop. Emphasis in selecting and encouraging participants for the second conference was on working social scientists doing problem-solving, subject-matter, and disciplinary research and related activities important in the list of areas suggested at the first work shop for additional investigation as that list was subsequently modified by the SSAAP Executive Committee and Advisory Board. The second conference established agendas and administrative and funding strategies for the different rural social science disciplines concerned with agriculture, again broadly defined, to help rural and basic social scientists contribute more effectively to (1) multidisciplinary SM and RSS work pertaining to agriculture and rural communities, and (2) basic disciplinary social science work relevant for agriculture.

The book introduced by this part reports on and integrates the Stage I and Stage II papers and reports the exchanges that took place, and the conclusions reached at the two conferences. After featuring the work agendas and the funding and administrative strategies that emerged from the Stage II conference, the book also presents agendas and conclusions reached by SSAAP's editorial group as it commissioned additional papers and assembled additional reports to fill omissions in, reduce inconsistencies of, and address questions unanswered at the SSAAP Houston conference. A condensed "executive summary" for administrators, priority setters, and funders is also being published to accompany this volume.

With the advice of SSAAP's Advisory Board, SSAAP's Executive Committee modified its plans for Stage III to consist of (1) presentations and meetings with such groups as the Experiment Station Committee on Organization and Policy, the Extension Committee on Organization and Policy, the Resident Instruction Committee on Organization and Policy, the International Committee on Organization and Policy, the Professional Agricultural Workers Conference (PAWC) at Tuskegee, the Joint Council on Food and Agricultural Sciences, the Congressional Reference Service, and the like, (2) the further development of SSAAP's agendas, recommendations, and administrative and funding strategies with additional meetings, commissioned papers, and work by SSAAP's editorial group, and (3) the preparation, publication, and distribution of this book, executive summary, and a public relations pamphlet.

HISTORICAL AND GEOGRAPHIC PERSPECTIVES

Much valuable perspective can be gained with respect to past and potential contributions of the rural social science areas and social science disciplines to the study of agricultural advance and rural improvement by examining experiences in different parts of the world at different times with attention to roles played by the presence of or lack of improvements in (1) technology, (2) policies, programs, and institutions, (3) the development of human skills and capacities, and (4) growth in the quantity of natural and manmade biological physical resources.

In the agricultural history of the United States and geographically around the world, one finds examples of instances in which agricultural sectors have been or are severely constrained by inappropriate policies and institutions, by lack of investments in human development, and by the absence of appropriate technologies. The continued existence of such instances attests to the difficulty and complexity of the task of getting all of the parts in place, and hence, of the need for social science research. Technology, alone, does not do it. Neither do policies and institutions, alone. Also, substantial investments in human development without appropriate institutions, policies, and technologies do not lead to success. Inflows of external capital without human skills, appropriate technologies, and supporting policies, programs, and institutions contribute little. Contributions to the general welfare have often depended in part on social and land reforms as prerequisites for developing the necessary supporting policies, programs, and institutions. The rural social sciences and the social science disciplines have much to contribute.

Repeatedly throughout this book, it will be noted that these four driving forces are individually necessary but individually insufficient for progress. Because of this individual necessity, it often appears that one of them is more important than the others, especially when that particular one is in short supply relative to the others.

PAST RESEARCH AGENDAS FOR AGRICULTURE AND FOOD AND THE SOCIAL SCIENCES

There is increased pressure on the agricultural establishment to devote more attention and research to the ethical aspects of agriculture. This pressure calls into question our agricultural research and science policies, as well as our price support, production control, surplus storage and disposal, international trade, poverty alleviation, rural development, resource utilization, waste disposal, energy, and other related policies. Over the past several years, at least ten major conferences have been held on agricultural ethics, some of which have been published (Haynes and Lanier 1982; Knowles 1983; Dahlberg 1986; Edens et al. 1985). These have considered problems involving environmental pollution, food chain contamination, malnutrition and starvation, erosion and soil conservation, water quality, gender inequality, family farming, family stress, appropriate technology, off-farm migration, regenerative agriculture, the demise of the family farm, multinationals, corporate farming, and the like. In the late 1960s and the early 1970s, food shortages were a central concern. Predictably, that concern was replaced with concern over the current "farm crisis" and surpluses. Agro-ethical conferences have dealt with social issues but have not led to delineation of priorities for social science research. Such conferences have sometimes been more activist than academically objective. An interesting development is a joint National Association of State Universities and Land Grant Colleges (NASULGC) and American Association of State Colleges of Agriculture and Renewable Resources (AASCARR) project which is developing undergraduate teaching materials to be used in colleges with agriculture courses involving agro-ethical issues and problems.

A part of the neglect of the social sciences in agricultural research priority-setting exercises is attributable to the dominance of logical positivism, the philosophy which finds its most appropriate applications in the work of the physical and biological sciences (Johnson 1985). Logical positivism represses research on values, which in turn constrains prescriptive research on policies, programs, and institutions and indeed, for that matter, on technology assessment (Collin 1985). After World War II, normativistic philosophies lost respectability in scientific circles. So did pragmatism, the philosophy that so often undergirds teaching and research methods in colleges of education, agricultural extension, and vocational agriculture. This brief mention of important philosophies undergirding agricultural research (and other related activities) serves to stress the importance of being philosophically eclectic enough in setting social science research agendas to deal with the full range of activities and subjects of concern to society in agriculture.

THREE COMMON CRITICAL ISSUES FOR THE WORK OF SSAAP

Three assertions have surfaced repeatedly as the work of SSAAP has progressed. These pertain to (1) an alleged lack of past accomplishments of social scientists, (2) underinvestment in the social sciences, and (3) the need for balanced pursuit of technical advance, better policies and institutions, human development, and improvement in our stocks of natural and manmade resources. In its work, SSAAP has addressed these issues and kept them before administrators, funders, and the academic and practical worlds so often that it is appropriate to include them in this introductory chapter of Part I.

ISSUE 1: DESPITE COMMON ASSERTIONS TO THE CONTRARY THERE HAVE BEEN SUBSTANTIAL PAST ACCOMPLISHMENTS BY RURAL AND BASIC SOCIAL SCIENTISTS

One commonly hears it asserted that the social sciences have not produced recognizable, useful products such as those produced by the biological and physical agricultural sciences—this despite the two rural social scientists who are Nobel laureates—one for research on human capital formation (T. W. Schultz) and the other for research on development of Third World countries (Arthur Lewis). In addition, several other basic social scientists have nobel laureates for basic social science research regularly used by rural social scientists. In addition and ironically, many who do not recognize the contributions of rural social scientists commonly use the U.S. federal agricultural databases built mainly by social scientists. The rural social scientists of the United States have led the world in objectively measuring economic, social, and political activity—by world standards, the United States has excellent price, yield, income, expenditure, consumption, utilization, and trade data on agriculture created for the most part by rural social scientists working closely with their colleagues from the ancillary discipline of statistics. Agricultural businesses and public policy makers could not function effectively today without these databases. Those who fail to see the accomplishments of the rural social sciences also use policy, price, technology assessment, and cost/benefit analyses done by social scientists, not to mention farm management, demographic, embargo, community, international trade, and productivity studies. Also ironically, the earliest social science contribution to agriculture—farm management—was pioneered by a few agronomists and animal scientists who saw the need for a management science to inform farmers of decisions involving complex combinations and interactions of technologies, enterprises, farm resources, people, and markets. Social scientists have also helped design and organize institutions and institutional changes such as cooperatives, farm credit and crop insurance programs, land reforms, zoning regulation, social security, and fairer, more equitable taxation laws. Also, there are tax, social security, family, marketing margin, minority, estate management, gender, and other social science studies whose results are so commonly used that those critical of social scientists are something like urban consumers who "don't know that milk comes from cows."

Some administrators argue that research on governmental programs, policies, and organizations is unproductive.

They point to the difficulties being experienced with present rural and agricultural programs, policies, and institutions that were designed with rural social science help to substantiate their position. In doing so, they forget that organizations,policies, and programs are rather similar to rust or pest resistant varieties of crops. There seems to be a sort of "social plasmid" in which resistances to and ways of circumventing organizations, policies, and program develop. A consequence is that the rural social scientists (like biological scientists) have to do "maintenance research, advising, and consulting" just to maintain viable institutional structures for farming and agribusiness, rural societies, and consumers. It should also be pointed out that the need for social science research on institutions cannot be avoided by turning problems and issues "over to the market" for resolution. Markets operate best when institutional arrangements support them with appropriate conditions *including regulations*. Presently our rural, agricultural, and food systems are stressed by conflicting demands for both deregulation and regulation. Clearly, social science efforts are required to assess these demands. Unwise regulation and deregulation now threaten the important contributions farmers and agribusinesses make to society.

Such disregard for the accomplishments of social scientists allows the biological and physical agricultural scientists to claim credit for all of the increased productivity and improved human welfare in agriculture—a demonstrably erroneous claim, as is the public R&D institution's habit of claiming all increased agricultural productivity for technology, thereby ignoring the private sector and, more importantly, the contributions of human capital formation; better policies, programs, and social infrastructure; and investments to enhance both natural and manmade resources (Bonnen 1987). We fail in the social sciences to establish a justified significant and relevant role for ourselves.

At the same time it must be noted that the blame does not fall entirely on social scientists. Most administrators and many leaders of the agricultural establishment are trained as biological and physical scientists. Their training, backgrounds, and imaginations do not tell them whether problems can or cannot be addressed by social science capability since social science knowledge and methods differ so greatly from those of the biological and physical sciences. Thus, they frequently respond to societal problems and issues with something based on biological and physical technologies or fall back on a positivistic science belief that science, including the social sciences, cannot address societal problems. In some instances, there are active administrative biases against the social sciences, i.e., they are often viewed as unobjective nonsciences. Fortunately, there are also many other administrators and leaders who are sympathetic and do understand the social sciences reasonably well.

ISSUE 2: UNDERINVESTMENT IN THE SOCIAL SCIENCES

As one surveys current problems and issues in rural areas and agriculture, one of the major conclusions that has to be drawn is that in agriculture and rural affairs we have underinvested in the social sciences relative to the biological and physical sciences. Specifically, as you go down the list of new or unsolved problems we now face, a large and growing proportion of these fall into the domain of the social sciences or have major social science dimensions. Many of these problems are the consequence of earlier pursuit of technical advances with inadequate concern for social, political, and environmental side effects. Many of our environmental and social structure problems are clearly due to this. We have created great technical changes in agriculture over the last seven to eight decades—unfortunately there have been many unanticipated and undesired side effects. We now face needs for assessment of technical advances, institutional innovations, and related investments in human capacities, all of which require research on ethics and values. These are fundamentally responsibilities for the social sciences as well as for some of the humanities for which we have also failed to provide adequate resources.

We can only list a sample of the many diverse issues on the current rural agenda for which the social sciences should have the funding required to bear major responsibility. We have been experiencing the largest financial crisis in agriculture since the "Great Depression." In the United States, farmers and rural businesses are in trouble, as are rural financial institutions and the agricultural credit system. We face complex and as yet poorly understood national and international macroeconomic impacts on agriculture and on rural communities here and abroad. We still do not fully understand the impacts of national deregulation of finance, banking, energy, and transportation on agriculture and rural community welfare.

Globalization of agricultural markets and growing international economic and political interdependence have created a new policy context and severely constrained national policy options. We face international issues ranging from protectionism and an immense trade deficit to the impact of obsolescent international monetary institutions on exchange rates and market stability. Indeed, excess production capacity, retaliatory protectionism, and competition in export subsidies have turned the agricultural policy crisis of individual industrial nations into a single, worldwide international trade crisis—which is now beyond the reach of policy actions of any nation acting alone. Only international cooperation and the creation of new international institutions hold much promise. These problems all fall primarily in the domain of social science knowledge. The list of difficulties goes on.

The institutional structure supporting science in agriculture, and in society generally, is in transition to some new configuration with almost no research on the issues involved—such as on alternative research funding systems, or on the means for interlinking and coordinating the various R&D actors and users. "Institution" means "rules of the game," organizations and, for that matter, the facilities and staffs of organizations, with emphasis on how individuals and groups relate to each other is governed by society. Organizations include the public agencies, nongovernmental agencies, private firms, families, and other decision-making entities of society. Rules of the game range from formal to informal rules: from the U.S. Constitution, state and federal law, local ordinances, regulatory and administrative rules to voluntary industrial standards, accounting conventions, standard industry operating procedures, social conventions, and cultural habits. Facilities include equipment, buildings, land, staffs, and the techniques embodied in organizations.

U.S. science policy is in disarray and contested. Except in agriculture and medicine, U.S. science policy was reshaped after World War II to support basic science. An emerging practical national objective is to sustain the development of the United States, a goal agricultural research has long addressed (Bonnen 1986a) but may now be abandoning by joining a national trend to disciplinary as opposed to more directly practical subject-matter and problem-solving efforts.

The new genetic technologies are beginning to change the way agricultural science is funded and managed. They are raising new institutional issues about property rights to genetic material, as well as societal control of the processes for genetic manipulation.

The nation's farm policy is obsolescent but continues without the political will to constrain either its costs or the chronic excess capacity that gave it rise and to which it makes additional contributions. Issues concerning the structure of agriculture must be faced, including the future performance of a farming and agribusiness sector that will be much more highly concentrated and vertically integrated.

Information-age electronics are changing the way we receive, process, store, and use information, not only in farm and agribusiness decision making but in government and general business. Near-real-time interactions and consequences are changing our problems and social options (Dillman 1985; Bonnen 1986b). Adapting agricultural and rural social institutions and policies to these and other new communication methods and facilities presents a substantial research and education challenge to the social sciences.

The fragility of the ecosystem and related environmental issues cry out for social science work on new institutions and policies. Both groundwater contamination and air pollution are serious and growing problems. Waste disposal and toxic chemicals affect health, degrade the environment, and threaten the biosphere. All of these are national and international problems.

Rural as well as urban poverty in the United States has increased at record rates since 1978 (Porter and Greenstein 1988). Problems of rural community decline and development accumulate in all the industrial nations (Barkley).

As a consequence of the rising economic value of time, issues in human capital formation have become more important determinants of local community and national welfare. In the past, most human capital has been formed in the family, but increasing disorder and instability in the American family suggest a reduced capacity for forming effective human beings. Social and economic issues surrounding the family and institutional substitutes are increasingly urgent problems, not only in the United States but in many lesser developed countries (LDCs). We have only touched upon the social science problems on our national agenda. Addressing these issues requires more than the expertise of any one social science discipline: sociology, political science, human ecology, economic, and legal knowledge are necessary, as well as the disciplines of geography, social psychology, cultural anthropology, and social work.

As for the humanities, the lack of systematic historical perspective disorders the understanding of policy makers, analysts, and USDA and land grant administrators. One cannot understand current institutional and functional disorders if one does not understand their origins and the long-term forces at work. The growing set of ethical issues and value-related problems in rural policy and in science require philosophic attention. The involvement of social science and agricultural professionals in world trade, aid, and development, as well as service in various kinds of international institutions and forums, requires a far better command of foreign languages and cultures than a typical college education now provides in the United States. Thus, not only the social sciences but also the related humanities are needed in addressing agriculture and rural problems. While the need for social science and humanistic knowledge has grown, funding and organizational support has not. Why?

The agricultural establishment now has a window of opportunity. But it will pass us by if social scientists and the administrators of the agricultural establishment do not exert themselves. The agricultural establishment needs a better grasp of what the social sciences have to offer in addressing society's important agricultural and rural problems, what the most urgent problems are, and what is required for the rural and basic social sciences to be effective. SSAAP is a cooperative effort to tell the social science story better and in a forthright, even aggressive, manner.

ISSUE 3: IMBALANCE IN THE AGRICULTURAL ESTABLISHMENT'S EFFORTS TO IMPROVE THE FOUR PRIME MOVERS FOR AGRICULTURAL AND RURAL PROGRESS

We need to be far more concerned about balance in our efforts to improve the four individually necessary but individually insufficient prime movers for growth and development of agriculture and our rural societies: (1) enhancement of biological and physical resources (both natural and manmade) that constitute the physical infrastructure of agriculture, (2) technical methods of production, (3) the improvement and creation of institutions, policies, and social infrastructure, and (4) human development.

In the last two-thirds of the twentieth century, the broad nineteenth-century U.S. rural policy focus on institution building was narrowed to promoting technical advances and their adaption to ecological and social systems in agriculture, and to policies that create specific financial benefits for farmers, such as in the farm programs of today. Today, the U.S. agenda of rural problems is dominated by unintended externalities, the consequences of obsolescent and failed institutions (including failed policies that need modification or replacement), the need for new institutions, and the need for higher quality human capital. We have failed to achieve an appropriate balance in the four complementary investments in these four forces when balance is necessary for successful development. Unfortunately, we are repeating these mistakes abroad in many of our LDCs' development efforts.

What constitutes an appropriate "balance" in the four prime movers differs among contexts and times. Also, there is usually no way of knowing beforehand the precisely correct mix of investments in the four prime movers. Rather, societies are faced with iterative, interactive learning processes and searches in which the problems, failures, and political responses encountered in development provide signals as to the direction in which balance lies. We can learn from experience about balance, and our recent experience indicates we are out of balance.

DIMENSIONS IN THE WORK OF THE RURAL SOCIAL SCIENCES (RSSs) AND BASIC SOCIAL SCIENCE DISCIPLINES (BSSDs)

The scope of agricultural research and related activities carried out by rural and basic social scientists has many dimensions that should not be omitted or distorted. These concern:

1. Different kinds of knowledge (value-free, value, and prescriptive) necessary to solve problems.
2. Appropriate domains of the various rural and disciplinary social sciences whose research capability must be brought to bear on problems.
3. The administrative structures of colleges of social sciences or of arts and sciences that are important in the organization of social science research for agriculture and related aspects of society.
4. Different ways of changing the real world and improving our capacity to solve or ameliorate the problems one wishes to address including the creation, through research and other scholarly activity, of new human capability; improved technology; new institutional policies, programs, and practices; and more or better use of existing natural and manmade capital.
5. Accountability for and other administrative aspects of the use of resources by social scientists required that SSAAP recognize the relevant, legitimate stakeholders whose priorities and perceptions partially determine the fundable agendas of rural and basic social scientists—stakeholders range from scientists and researchers, themselves, to the groups affected by those solutions to problems that are accepted as a basis for action.

SSAAP has tried to keep this rather substantial number of dimensions in focus in developing agricultural agendas and strategies for the rural social sciences.

KINDS OF KNOWLEDGE

In his 1956 book *The Image*, Kenneth Boulding examined the kinds of knowledge necessary to solve problems. In doing this, he considered three of what SSAAP treats as the four driving forces for increasing societal capacity. His discussion identifies production techniques, institutions, and people as important. Today, when referring to human development, economists often use T. W. Schultz's term "human capital formation" rather than Boulding's "people."

In dealing with kinds of knowledge, Boulding argued we create and hold two images or kinds of knowledge about these three aspects of reality. He characterized one image as value-free knowledge about technology, people, and institutions. The other image is of the values we attach to human capability, technology, and institutions. In the case of value knowledge, it is noted that there have been at least ten national conferences in recent years focused on the value and ethical aspects of issues and problems currently important for agriculture.

Boulding's conception can be advantageously extended to include improvement of manmade and natural biological and physical resources that also increase societal capability. In agriculture, for example, improved soil fertility, new buildings, and larger and better herds and orchards all increase capability to produce the means of solving problems. Thus, there are four of these primary sources of change (see Figure 1) to be studied by social scientists concerned with improving the agricultural and rural-related aspects of society. These are, of course, what were referred to as driving forces earlier in this chapter when the need for balanced treatment of them was discussed as one of the three major issues SSAAP has encountered in dealing with the proper role of the rural social sciences in the agricultural establishment.

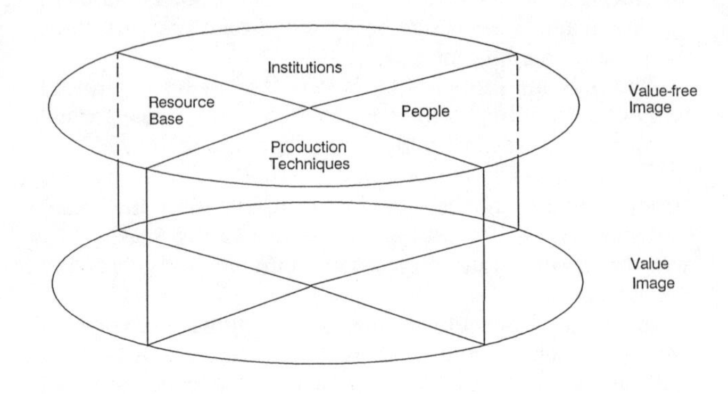

Figure 1. Boulding's Images with a Modification

The importance of recognizing Boulding's three (we added a fourth, the resource base made up of natural and manmade resources, in Figure 1) dimensions of society can be seen in the fact that the major structural problems of society create a need for some combination of new human capital, production techniques, institutions, and biological and physical capital to use in the resolution of those problems. Typically, governments and social units act when individual and market forces do not elicit needed structural changes. Such actions often impose losses and gains on different groups, thereby raising severe measurement problems for social scientists assessing welfare.

Though some problems may appear primarily technical in nature, practically all such problems also have human capability, institutional, and/or resource dimensions that must be recognized if they are to be successfully resolved. In the long run, almost all production techniques and even some institutions are embodied to some degree in conventional biological and physical capital and natural resources, or less conventional institutional and human capital, i.e., they are expressed through objects and arrangements in the real world.

All four of the broad sources of change considered herein have been studied by social scientists in the past and are likely to need further study in the future. Examples of past social science research on the four driving forces include T. W. Schultz's Nobel Prize-winning research on human capital formation, Ruttan's and Hayami's (1984) research on induced technical change and related work on induced institutional change. Sociologists, political scientists, agricultural historians, and human ecologists have also made significant contributions to the study of these driving forces that have been both more and less specialized than the "induced change" approach of economists. Investigation of specific problems and issues usually suggests specific sets of knowledge, lines of inquiry, and kinds of research that may be needed with respect to each of the four driving forces.

Some philosophers perceive two distinctly different forms of normative knowledge. C. I. Lewis, in his book entitled *The Ground and Nature of Right*, distinguishes knowledge *about values* from the *prescription knowledge* necessary for solving a problem. When a decision or choice is made, a conclusion is reached about what "should" be done. Should or "ought" statements are prescriptive. So are "should not" and "ought not" statements. Prescriptions are based on both value-free and value knowledge. The latter is about goodness and badness which is different from oughtness and oughtnotness or rightness and wrongness. When one has to minimize net losses, it may be right to do that which is bad. However, when one can maximize net gain, it is wrong to do that which is good if it is possible to do something still better with the same resources. The decision rules used to transform value-free and value knowledge into prescriptive knowledge involve distributions of power. Political scientists and historians study the distribution of political, military, and police power in the making of decisions important to agriculturalists. Among other things, sociologists study social and religious power while economists study market power. Such studies make important contributions to the solution and resolution of agricultural and rural-related problems and issues.

Thus, it is important in setting agendas for the social sciences to recognize not only the need for value-free knowledge but also the equal need to acquire, teach, and use value knowledge; the roles both play in generating prescriptions as to which actions "should be" taken to solve a problem also come into play. Failure of SSAAP to consider any of the three different kinds of knowledge discussed above would have biased the agendas it has established.

In developing agendas for social science research and related efforts, SSAAP has extended Boulding's notions by adding a dimension dealing with the three fundamentally different kinds of work as noted and discussed earlier. The three kinds of work are: disciplinary and multidisciplinary subject matter and problem solving.

ACCOUNTABILITY AND PEER REVIEW OF RURAL AND BASIC SOCIAL SCIENCE WORK

SSAAP participants have recognized that research and other agriculturally related activities must be accountable. Various groups in society and in agricultural institutions have a stake in the solutions of problems, and their voices are necessary for the support and evaluation of different types of work. If doing *disciplinary work,* the relevant peer group to judge that work is appropriately limited to the informed members of the discipline and those who fund disciplinary work though, even in this case, practical peers may be useful in judging its practical relevance. By contrast, appropriate groups for evaluating *subject-matter work* are substantially broader and include not only disciplinarians from the various relevant disciplines but also workers in other multidisciplinary, rural-related fields such as agronomy and animal husbandry, as well as members of other groups that have a stake in or who are affected by the problems addressed and their solutions. In the case of *problem-solving work*, the appropriate peer-review group involves not only the multidisciplinary problem-solving researchers but also, very importantly, those affected by actions based on solutions to the problems addressed. Thus, the SSAAP participants have ranged *from* disciplinarians *through* workers in multidisciplinary–subject-matter agricultural departments and agencies; administrators of academic, governmental and private agencies; the political leaders who fund RSS and BSSD work; and the various critics of agricultural institutions *to* more ultimate users *and* those who bear the consequences of the work. We must recognize that our work has both favorable *and* unfavorable impacts on the welfare of various groups in society. Our work is rarely neutral—generally it has negative and/ or favorable impacts. Experience proves it wise to pay attention to affected groups, and there is an obligation to do so in an agenda-setting process such as SSAAP.

THE REMAINDER OF PART I

For its first meeting at the Spring Hill Conference Center near Minneapolis, SSAAP commissioned a number of overview papers, as well as more specialized papers dealing with broad subjects of general interest across the rural and basic social sciences. Several of these papers are presented in Part I. These include:

Richard S. Kirkendall's paper entitled "A History of American Agriculture from Jefferson to Revolution to Crisis" is a very useful historical overview paper. It helps both basic and rural social scientists understand the natures of the agricultural industry and rural communities and societies.

Frederick H. Buttel's chapter entitled "Social Science Institutions, Tools, and Knowledge to Address Problems and Issues" is also a useful overview paper that leads us to a better understanding of the contributions rural and basic social scientists can make to resolve the institutional aspects of problems and issues important for agriculture and agricultural and rural communities.

Lester C. Thurow's paper entitled "Agricultural Institutions and Arrangements Under Fire" also serves a useful role. It is particularly valuable in broadening and balancing the views of rural as opposed to basic social scientists. Rural social scientists, like other agriculturalists, tend to be oriented so closely to agriculture and rural communities that they often have a somewhat less than objective view of how their work fits into the national picture—farm versus nonfarm, urban versus rural. Thurow brings some critical views of the performance of the agricultural establishment into focus and assesses them.

James C. Hite's paper entitled "Assessing the Capabilities of the Social Sciences in Rural Development and Natural Resource Management" is relevant and should be mentioned here even though it is presented in Part III. Some of what that paper has to say about community resources is closely related to Frederick H. Buttel's paper. On the other hand, part of Hite's paper deals with natural resources—the conservation and enhancement of natural resources—part of another of the driving forces for development. A paper not included in this part which should also be mentioned here is Dale Adams' paper entitled, "On Farm Capital Formation and Rural Financial Markets: Research Issues." This paper is presented later in this book in Part II, Section 2, dealing with international rural development. Much of what Adams has in his paper provides perspective on the generation, saving, and use of manmade resources that is useful here in Part I. It is suggested that readers seeking perspective on manmade resources (capital) as a driving force read his chapter in Part II, Section 2 (Chapter 9). Readers wanting to go further afield are advised to read a section on "capital" under agriculture, page 229 in the *International Encyclopedia of the Social Sciences* (Johnson 1968).

In addition to the June 9-11, 1987, Spring Hill Conference papers (and discussions) listed above, Part I contains papers commissioned for the Woodlands Conference, March 14-18, 1988. These are:

Vernon W. Ruttan's paper entitled "The Role of the Social Sciences in Rural Development and Natural Resource Management" deals with one of the four driving forces described earlier in this introductory chapter. While there is probably much more to institutional change and development than can be explained and predicted with what is known as the induced institutional change hypothesis, the hypothesis has much to contribute. Ruttan's paper makes this potential known to the noneconomists associated with the SSAAP enterprise.

G. Edward Schuh's paper entitled "Science and Technology Policy for the 21st Century: The United States in a Global Economy" discusses science and technology policy in the context of the broad forces now at work in the U.S. economy and the critical factors that will influence our development in the future. He presents information on a research agenda for sustaining our performance in the future. That agenda, of course, gives attention to the role of the social sciences in determining science and technology policies for the next century.

In turn, **Wallace E. Huffman's paper entitled "Human Capital for Future Economic Growth"** deals with another of the four driving forces—the creation and improvement of human beings, and is presented as Chapter 2 of Section 2, Part III: The Four Driving Forces. In his paper, he covers the contributions of T. W. Schultz and his colleagues to an induced change hypothesis with respect to human capital. Here again, there is probably much more to human development and improvement than can be explained and handled by induced human capital formation; nonetheless, the contribution of the hypothesis is important, and Huffman's paper makes an understanding of this line of work available to the noneconomists in the SSAAP project.

Richard J. Sauer's paper is written "From the Perspective of Users and Affected Persons." Sauer brings to the first part of this book extensive experience as an agricultural administrator. His background is in the biological and physical agricultural sciences. He is keenly aware of criticisms leveled at the agricultural establishment, what's right about the establishment, and the factors which complicate improving the situation. He addresses challenges for the future and then presents ideas on a new agricultural agenda. His paper helps set the tone for this book.

Because the agricultural establishment has placed so much emphasis on technological advance, SSAAP did not commission an overview paper on technological advances. Among the available references with respect to technology are the World Food and Nutrition Study (National Academy of Sciences 1977), the Presidential Commission on World Hunger (1980), the two Crop Productivity Studies (Brown 1975; Gibbs and Carlson 1986), and the Study of Livestock Productivity (Pond et al. 1980); all of the extensive literature on induced technological change plus the estimates of returns to investments and technical agriculture that stem from the original works of Zvi Griliches, Bob Evenson, and others are also included. More recently, Glenn Johnson (1988) has questioned the estimated returns to technological advance and human capital formation. There is extensive literature on induced technological change that was readily available to those participating in SSAAP activities (Ruttan 1971; Ruttan and Hayami 1984).

Part I is completed with Chapters 8 and 9. Chapter 8 summarizes the Stage I workgroup reports that structured SSAAP's Stage II conference. Chapter 9 relates SSAAP's Stage II Conference to the organization of the remaining parts of this book.

REFERENCES

Bonnen, James. 1986a. A century of science in agriculture: Lessons for science policy. *American Journal of Agricultural Economics* 68, no. 5: 1065-80.

_____1986b. Agriculture in the information age. Michigan State University Agricultural Economics staff paper no. 86-78. Keynote address to the Agricultural Institute of Canada, 7 July, Saskatoon, Canada.

_____1987. U.S. agricultural development: Transforming human capital, technology and institutions. In *U.S.-Mexico relations: Agricultural and rural development.* Edited by Bruce F. Johnson, Cassio Luiselli, Celso Cartas Conteras, and Roger D. Norton, 267-300. Stanford, Calif.: Stanford University Press.

Boulding, Kenneth. 1956. *The Image.* Ann Arbor: University of Michigan Press.

Brown, A. W. A., et al. 1975. *Crop productivity—Research imperatives.* East Lansing: Michigan State University, Agricultural Experiment Station. Yellow Springs, Ohio: The Charles F. Kettering Foundation.

Bush, Vannevar. [1945] 1960. *Science: The endless frontier. Reprint.* Washington, D.C.: National Science Foundation.

Collin, Finn. 1985. *Theory and understanding—A critique of interpretative social science.* New York: Basil Blackwell.

Dahlberg, Kenneth A., ed. 1986. *New directions for agriculture and agricultural research: Neglected dimensions and emerging alternatives.* Totowa, N.J.: Rowman & Littlefield.

Dillman, Don A. 1985. The social impacts of information technologies in rural North America. *Rural Sociology* 50, no. 1: 1-26.

Edens, Thomas C., Cynthia Fridgen, and Susan L. Battenfield, eds. 1985. *Sustainable agriculture and integrated farming systems: 1984 conference proceedings.* East Lansing: Michigan State University Press.

Evenson, Bob. 1967. The contribution of agricultural research to production. *Journal of Farm Economics* 49 (December): 1415-25.

Gibbs, Martin, and Carla Carlson, eds. 1986. Crop productivity-research imperatives revisited. An international conference held at Boyne Highlands Inn, 13-18 October 1985, and Airlie House, 11-13 December 1985. East Lansing: Michigan State University, Agricultural Experiment Station.

Griliches, Zvi. 1963. Estimates of the aggregate agricultural production function from cross-section data. *Journal of Farm Economics* 45:419-28.

Haynes, Richard, and Ray Lanier, eds. 1982. *Agriculture, change and human values: Proceedings of a multidisciplinary conference.* 2 vols. Gainesville: University of Florida, Humanities and Agriculture Program.

Johnson, Glenn L. 1968. Agriculture: Capital. *International Encyclopedia of the Social Sciences.* New York: The Macmillan Company and The Free Press. (See pages 229-36.)

_____1977a. Recent U.S. research priority assessments for food and nutrition: The neglect of the social sciences. Proceedings of the annual meeting, Canadian Agricultural Economics Society, 76-89.

_____1977b. Contributions of economists to a rational decision-making process in the field of agricultural policy. *Decision-making and agriculture.* Edited by T. Dams and K. E. Hunt. Oxford, England: Oxford Agricultural Economics Institute.

_____1983. Synoptic view. *Growth and equity in agricultural development.* Edited by Allen Maunder and Kazushi. Westmead, England: Gower Publishing Co.

_____1985. Agricultural ethics in the research agenda of agricultural experiment stations. *Research perspectives—Proceedings of the Symposium on the Research Agenda for the State Agricultural Experiment Stations.* Edited by Janet Pierce Frye. College Station: The Texas A&M University System, Texas Agricultural Experiment Station, Experiment Station Committee on Organization and Policy (ESCOP).

_____1986. *Research methodology for economists.* New York: Macmillan.

_____1988. *Agriculture and rural areas approaching the 21st century: Challenges for agricultural economics.* Edited by R. J. Hildreth, K. L. Lipton, K. C. Clayton, and C. C. O'Connor, 82-108. Ames: Iowa State University Press.

Knowles, Louis L., ed. 1983. *To End Hunger.* Washington, D.C.: National Council of Churches of Christ in the U.S.A.

Lewis, W. Arthur. 1949. *Overhead Costs.* London: Allen and Unwin.

Lewis, C. I. 1955. *The ground and nature of right.* New York: Columbia University Press.

National Academy of Sciences. 1977. *World food and nutrition study: The potential contributions of research.* Washington, D.C.: National Research Council, Commission on International Relations.

Pond, Wilson G., et al. 1980. *Animal agriculture—Research to meet human needs in the 21st century.* Boulder, Colo.: Westview Press.

Porter, Kathryn H., and Robert Greenstein. 1988. Welfare reform in rural areas. Toward rural development policy for the 1990's: Enhancing income and employment opportunities. Symposium sponsored by the Congressional Research Service and the Joint Economic Committee of the U.S. Congress, 29-30 September, Washington, D.C., 101st Cong., 1st sess. Senate Print 101-50:35-40.

Pound, Glen. 1972. *Report of the Committee on Research Advisory to the U.S. Department of Agriculture.* Washington, D.C.: National Academy of Sciences.

Presidential Commission on World Hunger. 1980. *Overcoming world hunger: The challenge ahead.* Washington, D.C.

Ruttan, Vernon W. 1971. Toward a theory of technical and institutional change. In *Agricultural development: An international perspective.* Baltimore: Johns Hopkins University Press.

Ruttan, Vernon W., and Yujiro Hayami. 1984. Toward a theory of institutional innovation. *The Journal of Development Studies* 20, no. 4: 203-23.

Schultz, T. W. 1960. Capital formation by education. *The Journal of Political Economy* 67, no. 6: 571-83.

Shapley, Deborah, and Rustum Roy. 1985. *Lost at the frontier: U.S. science and technology policy adrift.* Philadelphia.: ISI Press.

CHAPTER 2

A HISTORY OF AMERICAN AGRICULTURE FROM JEFFERSON TO REVOLUTION TO CRISIS

Richard S. Kirkendall[1]

INTRODUCTION

To define the agenda for the agricultural and rural social sciences, we must understand the present situations in agricultural and rural life and the ways in which they are moving, but to accomplish that, we must first comprehend the forces and decisions that brought us to the present and that are influencing the future. We must, in other words, gain historical perspective. We must go back as far as the beginning of the nation and the emergence of an American version of ideas about the fundamental importance of farming. We must also explore the "Great American Agricultural Revolution," the sense of power that it, along with the needs of other nations, gave some American leaders, and the consequent sense of great opportunities that emerged among farm people in the 1970s. Only then will we be able to interpret the present, the sense of crisis that now pervades American rural life, and the possibilities that lie ahead. The social sciences should, I assume, explore, clarify, and define those possibilities, providing bases for new decisions.

AMERICAN AGRARIANISM

Farming and farm people have always occupied special positions in American thought. The belief that they deserve high status and that the nation should be based upon them was part of the American heritage from Europe, running back to ancient Rome, the Renaissance, English writers of the seventeenth and eighteenth centuries, and the French physiocrats and other continental writers of the eighteenth century (Johnstone 1937, 1938). This heritage maintained that farming was the best way of life and the most important economic activity, that it conferred psychological as well as economic benefits, and that it produced the best citizens and soldiers. These ideas encouraged people to believe that America was a superior place for it supplied more and better opportunities to farm than did Europe (Eisenger 1947a, 1947b, 1949, 1954).

Americans both accepted and reshaped these ideas. In this development, Thomas Jefferson was especially important (Griswold 1948). The greatest "agrarianizer,"[2] he tried to construct a nation with a rural and agricultural base. He took ideas that had not been identified with democracy, at least not exclusively, and democratized them, arguing that to be democratic a nation must have a farm foundation. Although a planter himself, Jefferson emphasized the political value of the family farm—a farm owned and worked by members of one family and large enough to supply their needs. In his view, such a farm conferred independence, since the people on it worked for themselves, not others, and it required self-reliance and hard work. Its most important product was the personality type required for a democracy, rather than the debased type that appeared to grow out of European urban conditions. With family farms as democracy's essential foundation, farming's importance transcended the economic good produced by farmers.

Jefferson did not advocate fully self-sufficient, noncommercial farms. He saw value for the United States in Europe's need for food. It meant that there would be many good opportunities to farm in America. To prosper, American farmers should produce a surplus; they should grow more than farm families needed and more than the nation needed. Thus, the agrarian politician opposed obstacles to American trade with Europe, including the protective tariff and French control of the mouth of the Mississippi River (Appleby 1982, 1984; McCoy 1980).

Jefferson and other American agrarianizers saw western lands as even more valuable than the European market—more perhaps than any other feature, the western lands distinguished the United States from Europe. They had to be available to farmers, free of control by Indians and Europeans, and sold at a low price or given away. Their importance justified the purchase of Louisiana, for, by greatly enlarging the land possessed by the United States, the purchase guaranteed the success of American democracy and the continuation of American superiority (Pearce 1965, 56, 67, 70, 153; Berkhofer 1978, 157; Henry Nash Smith 1950, prologue, Chapter 11).

Jefferson came to accept manufacturing but within narrow confines. Fascinated by technology and fearful of overdependence on Europe, he also feared an urban proletariat. Thus, he insisted that American factories must be small and placed in rural settings and must employ only a small percent of the total American population. Farmers must continue to be the American majority (Bender 1975, 21–28).

Jefferson's democratic agrarianism achieved its most spectacular victory in 1862 with passage of the Homestead Act. Giving 160 acres to those who would make farms out of them, this land policy seemed to be a way of making the lands truly valuable and the nation healthy and strong. And giving the lands away seemed beneficial to urban workers as well as farmers, for it offered those workers a "safety valve." Giving them a way of escaping or avoiding oppression, it enabled them to develop a personality that differed from that of the European proletariat and was compatible with democracy. Or so it seemed to American agrarians (Smith 1950, Chapters 15, 20).

SURPLUS PEOPLE

One of the major features of American agrarianism was the idea that farmers must comprise a very large proportion of the total American population but, well before the end of the nineteenth century, farmers lost their status as the American majority, and the Great Depression of the 1930s encouraged a number of people in the agricultural colleges, the U. S. Department of Agriculture (USDA), and other places to argue that there were too many people in agriculture. This, it was argued, rather than other factors, such as class exploitation and racial discrimination, explained the large volume of poverty among farm people. The proposed solution was the substitution of technology for people. Such a change would permit the operation of larger farms, increase efficiency, reduce costs, and make farming profitable for the people who remained in it (Fite 1981; 1984, 143, 148, 151–52, 161).

The Secretary of Agriculture, Henry A. Wallace, had become an especially significant proponent of the theory of the surplus farm population. Earlier, as a participant in the battle over farm policy in the 1920s, he had embraced the old agrarian theory about the need for a large farm population and had issued warnings about the consequences of further urbanization of the American people (Kirkendall 1983, 1984). By the late 1930s, however, he was arguing that the solution to the nation's farm problem depended heavily on expanded industrial production, low industrial prices, full urban employment at high wages, and the migration of large numbers of people to the cities (Kirkendall 1967). "There is a normal excess of births over deaths of from 400,000 to 500,000 on the farms of America every year," he advised Eleanor Roosevelt in 1939. "When the nation was expanding, this increase in population had opportunity either on new land or in the growing cities. The closing of opportunity in those two directions has resulted in damming up on the farms of millions of people who normally would have been taken care of elsewhere."[3] This intellectual change on the highest level in farm politics was an important part of the preparation for a revolution. On other levels and in different places—in colleges and corporations and on farms—other preparations were also being made.

THE GREAT AMERICAN AGRICULTURAL REVOLUTION

Before another decade passed, the revolution had begun and gained momentum, making the nation very different from the one Jefferson had envisioned (Shover 1976, Introduction and Chapter 5; Fite 1981, Chapters 6–13). One of the most spectacular and significant events in American history, this revolution—the "Great American Agricultural Revolution"—had both technological and demographic dimensions. It substituted technology for people in farming and moved millions of people from farms to cities and towns.

Long-established agencies of change promoted the technological dimension of the revolution. They included the agricultural colleges, the experiment stations, and the extension services (Kirkendall 1986, 15–21). Corporations such as John Deere, Pioneer, and Monsanto also functioned as revolutionaries. (Broehl 1984; Browne 1983; Williams 1987; Lee 1984; Kloppenburg 1988; Paarlberg 1988.)

The technological side had several components. The most obvious was the mechanical: the substitution of the gasoline engine for animal and human power (Rasmussen 1962). By 1970, farmers employed nearly 5 million tractors, well over one for each American farm. Corn pickers increased from 110,000 in 1940 to 792,000 in 1960; grain combines rose from 190,000 to 1 million in the same period. Other components included hybrid corn, which completely displaced its competition, and chemical fertilizer, the consumption of which increased from 9.4 million tons in 1940 to 39.6 million in 1970 (*Historical Statistics*... 1975, 469). American farms were also electrified. Few had electricity in the early 1930s; virtually all farms had it soon after World War II.

These spectacular technological changes made the people who worked on farms much more productive of food and fiber for human consumption.[4] The number of people served by one farm worker rose from fewer than 11 in 1940 to more than 47 three decades later (*Historical Statistics*... 1975, 498).

As the technology of American agriculture changed at a revolutionary pace, rural America also experienced a demographic revolution. People moved in massive numbers from farm to city with the volume—over 30 million—similar in size to the movement of Europeans to the United States from 1815 to 1914. This time the pace was much more rapid for only a third of a century was required to accomplish the shift that earlier had taken a full century.

The technological changes supplied much of the force behind the movement of people. They cut farming's need for people, and as the new machines and other new technologies were more expensive than the ways they displaced, pressure was placed on farmers to expand their land holdings so as to capture the full potential of the technology. Consequently, farmers who could do so sought to buy out their neighbors, and many farmers chose to sell their land for they could not hope to match the capital requirements of a modernized farm.[5]

Off-farm job opportunities also had much to do with this migration. Unusually abundant most of the time from 1941 to 1969, they pulled people off the land by offering, or at least appearing to offer, better opportunities than the land supplied.

Thus, the farm population dropped sharply. The number of people on American farms dropped from 30.5 million in

1940 to 9.7 million in 1970. In 1940, the farm population made up 23.1 percent of the total; by 1970, the percentage had dropped to 4.8 (*Historical Statistics*... 1975, 457). As people moved off of farms, the country church declined, and the one-room school house surrendered to the forces of consolidation (Madison 1986; Fuller 1982, 245).

In the South, the transformation was especially large (Fite 1984, Chapters 9–10; Daniel 1985, Book 4). Farms dropped from 3 million in 1940 to 1.16 million in 1969, the southern farm population fell from 16.4 million to 4 million. By comparison, in the Middle West, farms moved from 2.1 million to 1.15 million, the number of farm people from 9.3 million to 4.5 million (*Historical Statistics*... 1975, 458–59).

The region long dominated by cotton became a very different place. Only 11.7 percent of the cotton farms had tractors in 1945; 73 percent had them in 1970. Mechanical cotton pickers harvested only 5 percent of the cotton in 1949; 96 percent was harvested by them 20 years later (Fite 1980, 1984). By then the South had fewer mules, fewer croppers, fewer blacks, and more wage laborers. Plantations, which had been fragmented in the sharecropper era, were integrated once again, although with machines and day-laborers rather than the gangs of slaves now doing the work (Kirby 1983). And the region raised much less cotton than before as much of it was shifted west to flatter lands. In its place, Southern farmers grew grass, hay, corn, soybeans, wheat, and timber and raised livestock and poultry (Daniel 1984).

In spite of this mass movement off farms, the United States did not become totally urban. Instead, the rural population remained quite large, declining only from 57.2 million to 53.9 million between 1940 and 1970, a decline of less than 7 percent that left the nation more than 26 percent rural (*Historical Statistics*... 1975, 11). Many rural communities survived and prospered by changing their economic base, shifting from agriculture to manufacturing, trade, services, and government. The number of rural counties dependent on farming declined from over 2,000 to about 700 between 1950 and 1970. Thus, many farm people moved into towns rather than cities, and some, including some farm women, continued to live on farms while taking jobs in town as a consequence of industrialization and other economic changes in rural areas. The industrialization of rural areas and increased participation in the paid labor force by farm women raised the standard of living and reduced the amount of poverty among farm people.[6] Many rural communities, however, did not reduce their dependence on agriculture and thus declined, as did the farm population (Korsching 1987).

THE CONTRIBUTIONS OF GOVERNMENT

Government policies contributed both negatively and positively to the "Great American Agricultural Revolution." In spite of the rapidly shrinking number of farmers, the federal government remained actively involved with agriculture (Cochrane and Ryan 1976; Shover 1976, Chapter 7; Fite 1981, Chapters 6–11). This was so, in part, because farmers had effective organizations in Washington, such as the American Farm Bureau Federation, the National Farmers Union, and various commodity groups. Furthermore, skillful and well-placed representatives of farmers served in Congress and helped shape policy. Also, agrarianism remained a part of the scene, helping farmers get government programs.

Government policies had a somewhat ambiguous relationship with the demographic dimension of the revolution. There was a strong tendency to regard planning as "un-American" during much of the period, and Congress, pressured by the Farm Bureau, destroyed the main agricultural planning agency, the USDA's Bureau of Agricultural Economics (Kirkendall 1982, Chapters 9–13). So the migration went forward in an unplanned way.

The federal government also scrapped efforts, begun during the 1930s, to hold the rural poor on the land by improving conditions (Baldwin 1969). There continued to be talk but little action about the problems of the rural poor.

The nation relied mainly on economic forces to solve the problems of the rural poor. There was not even a substantial effort to train rural people for urban life. Thus, the migration advanced without much guidance, regulation, or assistance and contributed to major riots in American cities in the second half of the 1960s.

The federal government tried but failed to eliminate the cost-price squeeze. National policy makers maintained the price-support system that had been established by the New Deal. Some politicians, most notably Ezra Taft Benson, the Secretary of Agriculture during most of the 1950s, talked of getting the government out of agriculture (Schapsmeier 1975; Peterson 1979), but the real debate focused on the level of price supports. Washington also tried to enlarge demand, making use of Public Law 480, the school lunch program, and the food stamp plan, to move American farm products into foreign and domestic markets. But, despite such efforts, the cost-price squeeze remained a problem and was especially severe in the mid–1950s.

Government policy had a clearly positive relationship with the technological dimension of the revolution. As Don Hadwiger argues, the "special interests" that dominate the shaping of agricultural policy have been "firmly committed to a developmental strategy," one that encourages the "trend toward large efficient farms" and aims at "a productive and efficient U.S. agriculture" (1986). "The support of Farm Bureau regional commodity interests and co-ops helped to make technology a reality in agriculture," another political scientist, William P. Browne observed. "It was hardly imposed from the outside."[7] National agencies supported prices and made payments and loans to farmers who frequently used the resulting resources to buy technology and land. The government supplemented what farmers could obtain from the market and from private credit agencies and made the largest payments and loans to the largest farmers, thereby helping them to expand their operations still more (Cochrane 1985, 1005–6). And policy makers rejected proposals to place a low cap on payments, to eliminate subsidies to the largest farmers, and give special funds to smaller operators. In addition, the federal government conducted and financed research that contributed in basic ways to the revolution, and the research that received federal funding was dominated by the interest in making farming productive and profitable, not holding people on the land (Hightower 1973; Hadwiger 1982; Newby 1982, 130–32, 138–39).

THE AGRICULTURAL SYSTEM

With Washington making important contributions, the agricultural revolution moved forward, and as it moved, it reconstructed the agricultural system. Although often called "agribusiness," the system included government agencies and public educational and research institutions as well as urban, town, and farm businesses (Fusonie 1986; Rasmussen 1975, 3408–13; McGovern 1967, 496–518; Shover 1976, Chapter 6; Merrill 1976; Goldschmidt 1986). Except for the number of farms and farmers, all parts of the system including the farms grew larger, and the farmers grew more dependent on the system's other parts.

The revolution reduced the number and enlarged the size of American farms. The number dropped 56 percent in 30 years, moving from 6.1 million in 1950 to 2.7 million in 1969. The average size expanded from 175 acres to 373 acres. By 1960, 23,000 farms grossed over $100,000 per year and produced and sold 17 percent of the total farm output. A decade later, although the price rise had been small, 53,000 farms grossed over $100,000, and they, although only 2 percent of the farms, produced and sold 34 percent of the national farm product (Cochrane 1985, 1002–3).

The revolution cut the number of family farms but did not destroy the type. The system also included plantations and industrialized corporate farms, both of which employed the latest technology and people who worked for salaries and wages (Newby 1982, 148–53). Another type, parttime farms, were worked by families who often used the new technology but depended heavily on income earned from nonfarm jobs. Owner-operated farms had reached a peak of 3.96 million in 1945, but dropped to 3.92 million by 1950 and 2.95 million in 1959. A decade later, the number had fallen to 2.37 million. Yet the owner-operated family farm continued to be the most numerous type. In fact, it became a larger part of the total than ever before. In 1945, owners operated 67 percent of the farms. By 1969, they operated 87 percent. Tenancy dropped from approximately 40 percent of the total in 1940 to about 15 percent three decades later, and sharecropping in the South virtually disappeared (Rhodes 1978; Rasmussen 1975, 3474–83; *Historical Statistics*... 1975, 465).

The revolution had not substituted industrialized corporate farms for family farms. Instead, nearly all of the family farms that had gone out of existence had been absorbed by other farms of the same type. Capable because of the new technology of farming larger units, some family farmers had expanded their operations by buying their neighbors' land. As one critic of the process, Wendell Berry, suggested, "farmers became convinced that it would be better to own a neighbor's farm than to have a neighbor..." (1977).

The revolution also enlarged the size and importance of the off-farm components of the agricultural system (Newby 1982, 146–48). They included all of the businesses involved in the production and distribution of food and fiber, such as the feed, seed, chemical, and farm machinery companies and the firms that processed and distributed farm products. As the revolution moved forward, it shifted functions, such as the production of energy, seed, and fertilizer, off farms making farmers more dependent on the market—and on corporations and cooperatives—than ever before for they now not only sold on the market but bought more things, including more food. And off-farm corporations also shifted risks and management away from some farms by developing contract farming.

Performing a wide variety of functions, the off-farm firms in the agricultural system obtained most of their income from the market place. Better than half of the dollars consumers spent on food and fiber went to the processors and distributors, while the firms that supplied commodities to farmers obtained most of the rest, leaving much less than half of the dollars spent by consumers on agricultural products for the people on the farms.

Farmers, of course, did not depend solely on the market. They received some income from another important part of the system, the federal government.

AGRIPOWER, THE FOOD CRISIS, AND THE BOOM

By the 1970s, the United States had developed a new and enormously productive agricultural system, and during the decade, that system seemed unusually valuable for the world as well as the nation. It seemed to give the United States substantial power. Thus, once again, as in the world wars, the federal government encouraged American farmers to put all of their land into production and farmers enjoyed a boom.

The idea that agriculture supplied a power base that could be used to accomplish political objectives had a long history, but it was now given a new name: "agripower" (Weber 1978). The idea had been expressed in such slogans as "King Cotton" and "Food Will Win the War." Former Secretary of Agriculture Earl Butz, among others, expressed it with great clarity. "Food is power," he insisted. "Agripower will be more important than petropower. Food is a tool in the kit of American diplomacy."

Applying to international affairs the belief in the superior importance of agriculture, especially American agriculture, agripower was influenced by new worries about American power. The nation had failed to manage the Vietnam War successfully and then encountered pressure from oil-producing states. The Arab nations in the Organization of Petroleum Exporting Countries (OPEC) embargoed the export of oil to the United States late in 1973 to protest against American support for Israel. The argument assumed that food was of basic importance, more vital than oil or weapons, and the American agricultural system was vastly superior to all others, and the theorists suggested that the United States could become once again the most powerful nation, capable of influencing others, including the Arabs and the Soviets. Even before the oil embargo, Washington employed this argument in its dealings with the Soviet Union, which faced a number of agricultural problems. The Nixon administration, hoping for detente as well as the expansion of exports, negotiated a large grain deal in 1972. Using agripower in a positive way, the United States sold the Soviets 19 million tons of grain, one-fourth of the American crop, at low prices.

Talk of a world food crisis contributed to the developing sense of power from American agriculture (Shover 1976, Chapter 8). The crisis seemed especially severe in 1973–74 when widespread drought and soaring fertilizer prices dropped food supplies and resulted in millions of deaths in Asia and Africa. Some students of such matters maintained that the new crisis was long-term rather than a temporary phenomenon, resulting from a "population explosion" and inadequate agricultural systems. To some, it seemed that the predictions of Thomas Malthus about the inevitable pressure of population on food supplies had come true. And the crisis existed in spite of the "Green Revolution." Represented most prominently by an American agricultural scientist, Norman Borlaug, who had worked in Mexico and Asia and received the Nobel Peace Prize for his contribution to the expansion of world food production in the late 1960s, that revolution now seemed to be faltering.

The idea of a food crisis generated various proposals, including agricultural development. It depended on help from the already developed nations and also the oil-rich countries. Those groups had to supply capital and technology on a massive scale. The United States had to contribute some of the capital, much of the "know-how," and most of the emergency supplies of food. To do the last, the United States needed to stop limiting farm production and store and distribute grain.

In 1973, leaders in the United States Department of Agriculture responded to the idea of the food crisis by promoting full production. Then headed by Earl Butz, an agricultural economist from Purdue University, the department relaxed controls on production and urged farmers to plant fence row to fence row. Farmers, most of whom had never liked government controls, welcomed the advice. To participants in the agricultural system, it seemed unlikely that foreign markets would disappear or that surpluses would reappear.

U.S. agricultural exports soared to a record high, 70 percent above the 1970 level by 1976. With grain exports especially large, the nation became the leading grain exporter, supplying more than half the world's exports of grain compared with a third in the late 1960s and a fourth in the mid 1950s. The farm exports compensated for the increased cost of oil imports, chiefly from the Middle East, and of expensive items from Japan and Europe. Although the new agricultural system had some critics, these results seemed to prove its great value (Cochrane 1978, Chapter 8; Fite 1981, Chapter 11).

The exports pleased farmers but alarmed some consumers, creating a difficult situation for the Ford administration which wanted good relations with the Soviet Union and looked upon grain as capable of serving that end. Selling 10.3 million tons of grain to the Soviets in 1975, the administration encountered protests from consumer and labor groups. In late summer/early fall of that year, Washington used agripower negatively, embargoing grain as a means of pressuring the Soviets into a long-term agreement and responding to domestic forces, but farmers; the Farm Bureau; leading Democrats; rural congressmen, including Republicans from farm states; and the grain companies howled in protest. In these circumstances, the administration worked out an agreement to sell to the Soviet Union at least 6 million tons of grain per year from 1976 to 1980 as long as supplies at home were adequate.

Political leaders had backed further away from the negative use of agripower. The Ford administration considered a grain embargo early in 1976 as a means of pressuring the Soviet Union to withdraw Cuban troops from Angola, but rejected the idea and then joined the Democrats in criticizing negative use of agricultural resources. Jimmy Carter, the Democratic candidate for the presidency, promised that he would not embargo grain as Ford had done. All of this suggested that agripower would be used only in positive ways, ones that would enlarge rather than reduce the market for American farm products and thus make use of the great productive capacity of American agriculture.

Viewed as enormously important in the foreign relations of the United States, American farmers enjoyed a boom similar to those they had experienced during the world wars. It began with a doubling of the world prices for wheat, rice, feed grains, soybeans, and other products from 1972 to 1974 and continued with smaller increases in 1975. Per capita income from farming rose above the off-farm level in 1973, reaching 110.2 percent, more than 35 points above the levels of the 1960s. Although net farm income dropped from the high of $33.3 billion in 1973, it remained quite high in 1974 ($26.1 billion) and 1975 ($24.5 billion) compared with the 1969 figure ($14.3 billion).

The farm situation weakened in 1976–77 as farm prices dropped while the costs of commodities, such as fuel and fertilizer, rose, thus triggering a new episode in farm protest. Net farm income fell to $17.8 billion by 1977, and a new farm organization, the American Agricultural Movement (AAM), emerged. The AAM staged a series of demonstrations from 1977 to 1979, often with farmers (obviously modern farmers) mounted on their tractors in Washington, D.C., and other places of political importance (Browne 1983). They criticized established farm programs, demanded 100 percent of parity, and threatened farm strikes, seeking to take advantage of the great importance of farmers by refusing to plant crops or buy city-produced goods. The AAM did attract attention and the government did expand its help to farmers in 1977–78, but the strike threat failed and the movement did not get a law guaranteeing parity prices at the desired level. Most commercial farmers and the established farm organizations refused to support the movement, and consumer groups and their political representatives opposed it.

The farm situation improved in 1978 and 1979. Net income from farming rose from $17.8 billion to $26.1 billion, and then $31 billion. And, the per capita income of farmers compared with nonfarmers rose from 87.1 percent to 102.4 percent.

The boom enhanced the value of land ownership. As farmers continued to substitute technology for people, the farm population dropped 38 percent during the decade, which exceeded the percentage drops of the 1940s and the 1950s and equaled that of the 1960s. Moving from 9.71 million to 6.05 million, the farm population fell below three percent of the American total by 1980. The increase in yield per acre for most crops slowed so farmers expanded output mainly by increasing the acres devoted to crops and livestock. In these circumstances, land values soared, rising over 200 percent during the decade (Cochrane 1985, 1003), and the ownership of land provided a rich resource on which farmers borrowed to buy technology and additional land. Credit organizations, including government agencies, promoted the borrowing, even raising credit limits as land values rose.[8]

The boom slowed, but did not halt, the decline in the number of farms. This number had dropped 30 percent in the 1950s and 26 percent in the 1960s, but it fell only 18 percent in 1970s, and nearly all of that took place in the first half of the decade. The numbers suggest that the desire and ability to hold onto a farm had increased, but they also indicate that the desire and ability to expand holdings still had considerable strength.

The figures also meant that production for the market was concentrating on fewer and fewer farms. The farms grossing over $100,000 per year, 11 percent of the total number, now produced and sold 66 percent of the total farm output (Cochrane 1985, 1003). This development aroused the concern of a liberal secretary of agriculture, Bob Bergland, in 1979–80, but this was rather late to express such a concern for the new structure of American farming had been taking shape for many years.

The boom contributed to what some observers called a "rural renaissance," as rural America, in spite of the continued decline in the farm population, had grown more rapidly than urban America. But agricultural prosperity was not the main factor responsible for the renaissance, because in places like Iowa, where many rural counties still depended chiefly on agriculture, those counties lost population during the decade. Obviously, even during the farm boom, rural counties needed to industrialize or reduce their dependence on agriculture in other ways in order to enjoy growth (Korsching 1987).

For many farmers, the 1970s was a relatively good time, one in which they could operate their businesses at a profit. Being highly productive, they were encouraged to produce even more and received praise as people who could save the world from starvation and once again make the United States the most powerful nation. As a consequence, farmers' basic resource—the land—seemed unusually valuable. Government officials and bankers urged them to farm all the land they had, expand their land holdings, update their technology to become more efficient and productive, and borrow money for these purposes. Thus, farm debt mounted. Farmers with a sense of history might have recalled that similar circumstances from 1915 to 1920 had ended in disaster, but many farmers—and many people who advised farmers—believed they had entered a new situation that would continue indefinitely (Cochrane 1978, Chapter 8; Fite 1981, Chapters 11–12; Fite 1984, Chapter 11; Soth 1987).

THE NEW CRISIS

In 1981, however, the boom of the 1970s ended, and a new farm crisis emerged. This crisis was especially severe for those farmers heavily in debt. For them, the crisis threatened their survival as farmers; many faced disaster, even though in most ways they were good farmers who owned substantial farms and the latest products of technology. They had participated in the revolution and in the efforts to feed the world and to increase American power.

Several forces produced the new crisis (Harl 1987; Stanley Johnson 1986; Gratto 1986),[9] one being the enormous productivity of American farmers. What had seemed a blessing now felt like a curse. Inflation also contributed to the crisis. It had begun with the nation's fiscal policy during the Vietnam War, had worsened as a result of the sharp increase in energy costs after 1972, and had become an anticipated part of life by the late 1970s. Decisions made by many people assumed that prices would continue to rise at a rapid pace. Another factor in the crisis was the huge debt burden of many farmers. Older farmers, eager to bring young family members into farming, had some of the debt, but young farmers shouldered most of the burden. The decisions that these different groups of farmers had made raised the farm debt in the nation from less than $50 billion in the early 1970s to over $200 billion by the early 1980s.

The debt situation made farmers highly vulnerable to any difficulties that might emerge in the farm economy. This was especially dangerous for those with debts equal to or above 40 percent of assets. In the nation as a whole, 20 percent of the farmers were in those circumstances; in the Middle West, the percentage was even higher, as high as 38.3 percent in Iowa in 1986 (Harl 1987).

Two moves by the national government hit and harmed these farmers. Beginning in October 1979, the Federal Reserve Board attacked inflation by forcing interest rates to rise sharply. Then in 1981, President Ronald Reagan proposed a sharp cut in taxes, and Congress responded with the Economic Recovery Act. One major consequence of those actions was massive deficits in the federal budget.

These policies had several important results for farmers, including cutting exports by strengthening the dollar and raising costs of production by pushing up interest rates.

Other factors contributed to the worsening of the situation. Of these, the expansion of food production in the countries that competed with American farmers and in the developing countries was especially important. Although starvation continued to be a problem in some places, the "world food crisis" now appeared to be a myth. World corn production in 1986–87 was more than 40 percent higher than it had been a decade before while soybean production had risen 61 percent and wheat output had expanded 20 percent (Harl 1987). Furthermore, economic troubles in countries that had been major purchasers of American farm products reduced their ability to import food.

The various forces came together to produce a large drop in American agricultural exports, which fell from $43.8 billion in 1981 to $26.3 billion in 1986. Exports of corn and wheat dropped by especially large amounts; those of cotton and rice decreased by smaller quantities. These trends indicated that American agriculture was not as important as had been assumed in the 1970s and that alternatives had more strength than had been believed.

The Carter administration's negative use of agripower has often been blamed for this crisis. Responding to the Soviet invasion of Afghanistan in 1979, the administration embargoed grain sales to the Soviet Union. In doing so, Carter violated the agreement that had been made four years before. According to critics, this not only slashed the Soviet market for American grain but generated doubts throughout the world about the United States as a reliable supplier of farm commodities. A recent report by the Economic Research Service indicates, however, that U.S. losses of international market share were not caused principally by the embargo.[10] As Lauren Soth summarized the report, the embargo as well as earlier ones did not affect U.S. exports "significantly." "Grain exports declined after 1981, to be sure, due to world recession, the high-valued dollar and increased production of grain in other countries," Soth writes. "The embargo evidently didn't persuade importers that the United States was unreliable, though of course they claimed it did in their trade bargaining."

The crisis hit agriculture throughout the country but struck the Middle West the hardest blows. The prices of agricultural commodities dropped, although not as sharply as they had in 1920–21, 1929–33, and 1953,[11] and did so while prices of most other goods and services rose, although more slowly than they had a short time before. The prices of farm land also fell. Grain prices, which were so important in the Middle West, dropped farther than farm prices in general. In Iowa, the price of the average acre of farm land plummeted from $2,147 in 1981 to $787 in 1986 (*Des Moines Register*, December 19, 1986).

Net farm income fell and would have dropped farther if government payments had not been raised. Income, which had reached $31 billion in 1979 and $33 billion in 1973, moved close to $24 billion in 1986. Government payments to farmers, which had been less that $1 billion in 1975 and not far above $1 billion in 1980, rose to $9.3 billion in 1983 and $10 billion in 1986. The average per farm, which had been only $320 in 1975, was $3,922 in 1983 (*Statistical Abstract*, 646). Writing of Iowa, a state heavily dependent on the export market and increasingly dependent on grain as beef shifted out of the state, an agricultural economist, Stanley R. Johnson, observed in the mid–1980s: "We used to have crops *and* livestock. Now we have crops and government payments!" There had been, in other words, a significant increase in the farmers' dependence on one part of the agricultural system: the federal government.

The crisis had a number of consequences. More than a normal number of farmers lost their farms through foreclosure. Many had to spend their savings, cash their insurance policies, sell some of their land and machinery, reduce health care for themselves and their families, and take off-farm jobs. And many of those hit hardest were among the most productive farmers.

The crisis reached beyond the farms and farmers. It affected entire rural communities (*Des Moines Register*, February 10, 1987). Their businesses lost sales as farmers cut purchases and activities sharply, and their governments lost tax money and were forced to cut back on budgets for schools, health facilities, and other public services. The crisis damaged larger communities also, places such as Waterloo, Iowa, where John Deere operated large facilities for the manufacture of farm machinery. Many of the firms that emphasized sales to farmers could not find customers for their products, could not obtain payments for goods they had sold earlier, and obtained assets of low value when they foreclosed. "Many of the industries that support agriculture—fertilizer, farm chemicals, and machinery—overexpanded right along with their customers during the boom years of the 1970s," a writer for the Des Moines newspaper commented recently. "And with agriculture itself, they've been struggling in the last several years to adjust to much leaner times" (*Des Moines Register*, February 9, 1987).[12] Iowa, which depends heavily on agriculture, suffered an estimated loss of 33,000 people from 1981 to 1986 (Korsching 1987).

The crisis resulted in serious distress for financial institutions. The Farm Credit System lost $2.7 billion in 1985; 68 agricultural banks failed that year. The circumstances persuaded the institutions to charge high interest rates compared with those outside the farm areas, thereby forcing farmers who were not in financial difficulty to pay for those who were. The difficulties generated pressure for actions to help both borrowers and lenders, debate over how to do so, and fear that the crisis would last so long that both the farming and the finance sectors of the system would be severely damaged (Brake et al. 1986).

The crisis had psychological as well as economic dimensions. Stress levels rose, there was more tension between farm husbands and wives, farm children had more problems in school, rural neighbors clashed more frequently with one another, and optimism gave way to pessimism among many farm people (Lasley 1986).

Unlike earlier periods of farm crisis, this one did not generate a mass uprising of farmers (Goodwyn 1978). Perhaps the demographic revolution is the key. It not only reduced the number of farmers capable of engaging in rallies and demonstrations, but by doing so, it may have given the remaining farmers a sense of powerlessness. On the other hand, the role of government in agriculture, especially the government payments, so much larger now than in earlier crises, may explain why farmers did not rebel as they had earlier.

THE FINAL CRISIS

There was some protest during the crisis, much of it on behalf of farmers rather than by farmers themselves. The protest revealed that agrarianism has survived, for that is the ideology expressed by the protesters. One theme seems especially significant: the prediction that this may be the final crisis of the family farm. It may be displaced by the industrialized corporate farm owned by stockholders and worked by employees. "Rural Crisis spawning new corporate owners as family farms fade," a headline in the *Des Moines Register* proclaimed on February 8, 1987. ". . . the farm crisis has become a fundamental force in hastening the end of a society built on independent farms, small towns, and an economic equality that made the rural Midwest a special part of America," the article reported. "It was not in Thomas Jefferson's native Virginia, but in places such as O'Brien County [Iowa], where the Jeffersonian vision of an agrarian nation came closest to reality. . . . To many observers," the journalist added, "it seems evident that the next decade or two may wring the last shred of meaning from the term 'family farm.'"

Although there are people inside and outside agriculture who maintain that farming is valuable only as a source of food and fiber or an opportunity to succeed or fail, that farms must continue to grow larger, and that farmers who cannot get big must get out, other participants in present-day farm politics find other values in farming that must be preserved, have not been, and are now threatened with extinction. These agrarians include Wendell Berry, a Kentucky farmer and writer; Jim Hightower, a writer and the Texas Commissioner of Agriculture; Senator Tom Harkin of Iowa; the National Catholic Rural Life Conference and the Catholic bishops; the Rev. David Ostendorf of the United Church of Christ and Prairiefire Rural Action; and groups like the Iowa Farm Unity Coalition, the North American Farm Alliance, and the Center for Rural Affairs. Such individuals and organizations offer a way of interpreting the crisis that makes it appear to be much more than trouble in one sector of the American business system (Comstock 1987; *Agriculture and Human Values* 1985).

These agrarians express a number of old themes. They speak and write of the great value of close contact with nature. They protest that big business and big government, including parts of the agricultural system—the Farm Bureau, the land-grant colleges, the agribusiness corporations—are insensitive and oppressive. They argue that many farmers are treated unfairly and that threats to family farmers are threats to the nation. They talk of returning power to the people and of a farmer-labor alliance, and they insist that government should supply more help to *real* farmers: family farmers. In this view of things, the "cost-price squeeze" is a mythical version of the crushing of family farmers between giant corporations allied with and aided by the government. The results are large profits for the corporations and concentration of land ownership.

Above all, these Jeffersonians of the late twentieth century warn that if the situation is not changed, family farms will disappear and all farming will be done by corporations. "Since World War II, corporate power and government programs have combined to eliminate three million small farms and accelerate big-business domination of farming," Hightower has written. "But until now, the family farmers have persisted, hunkered down, and become more efficient. Reaganculture promises to finally drive them to the suburbs and the factories." According to Maurice J. Dingman, recently retired as the Catholic bishop of Des Moines: "A corporate takeover is imminent. Family farms are disappearing. A national policy should be adopted stating clearly and forcibly that the ideal type of farm is that of family farming." People such as this repeat the argument that family farms are important for democracy for they distribute power and shape strong personalities; they insist that family farms are highly efficient, more so than large corporate farms, and they maintain that family farms guarantee better care of land and animals, reasonable prices for and a continuous supply of food, and superior communities (e.g., *Des Moines Register*, February 10, 11, March 8, 1987).

Is there any justification for the prediction that this may be the final crisis of the family farm? There are some supporting facts, including the survival during the crisis of the big operators, those with gross annual sales of over $500,000 per year. Seldom family-owned and family-worked farms, they obtained over one-third of the farm income and kept their expenses under control more satisfactorily than mid-sized farmers. Because of their size, they could work out good deals on purchases and credit and could finance much of their operations (*Des Moines Register*, March 3, 1987). Furthermore, they obtained higher payments from government. While the average payment in 1983 was under $4,000, the average for farms with these large sales was nearly $47,000 (*Statistical Abstract*... 1985, 646).

There are other bases for the prediction. The farm population has continued to drop, falling from 6.05 million in 1980 to 5.75 million in 1984; the number of farms has continued to decline, moving from 2.43 million in 1980 to 2.285 million in 1985 (*Statistical Abstract*... 1985, 633, 635). And the decline has taken place mostly among the middle-sized farms in acres and sales, those that are, in most cases, owned and operated by families, while big farms have survived and even increased in number. By 1985, less than 5 percent of the farmers produced and sold nearly one-half of the total farm product while 70 percent of the farmers contributed 13 percent of the total. As Cochrane points out, "the restructuring of the farm sector continues at a rapid pace in the direction of fewer and fewer and larger and larger farms," (Cochrane 1985, 1003–4).

Yet, other facts pose difficulties for the prediction. Even after the great decline in farms from 1940 to 1980, only a tiny fraction of the remaining farms were genuine corporate farms, owned by stockholders and worked by people who were paid wages and salaries. In 1982, there were only 1,143 corporate farms that were not owned by families and were owned by 11 or more stockholders. Nearly all corporate farms (over 50,000) were essentially family farms, owned by families and fewer than 11 stockholders (*Statistical Abstract*... 1985, 638). And, as has been true since the beginning of the revolution, nearly all recent farm purchases have been made by other farmers, not by corporations or other urban investors (*Des Moines Register*, February 9, 1987; *Farmline* April 1987, as reported in the *Ames Tribune*, April 27, 1987).

Furthermore, farms are not declining rapidly enough for family farms to disappear in the near future. While the number of farms dropped six percent in the first half of the 1980s and this exceeds the four percent decline from 1975 to 1980, the rate is far below that of each five-year period from 1950 to 1975. Then, the percentage was never below 12 and reached as high as 15. Even in Iowa, where the rate of decline in the 1980s is above the national average, the decline is slower than it was in the 1960s, the decade in which the number of farms in the state fell most rapidly (*Des Moines Register*, February 8, 1987). Some of the people who are alarmed now distinguish between the present decline and ones during the revolution, suggesting that most of the earlier migrants from farm to town and city were incompetent farmers while those who are leaving now are good ones and most of those who left before the 1980s did so voluntarily while those leaving during the crisis are being forced out. As Senator Tom Harkin from Iowa has put this: "What is happening in rural America is nothing less than the greatest forced migration in our nation's history." Perhaps these assumptions are correct, although many of the earlier decisions to migrate were made under heavy pressure and bad business decisions by farmers in the late 1970s and early 1980s contributed to the loss of farms in the 1980s. Perhaps the pace of change will accelerate, but it will need to do so very substantially for the prediction to be fulfilled.

In addition, there are several social, economic, and political factors working for the survival of family farms as the main type of American farm. These include the efficiency of the wisely capitalized, well-managed family farm. There is also the desire of some people to farm, a desire that is so strong with them that they are willing to accept a relatively low rate of return on their investment and labor (Newby 1982, 144, 148). Another factor is the poor investment opportunity that farming offers as compared with other prospects open to corporations and those who would build them. Here, the tax reforms of 1986 made a contribution by attacking tax-loss farming. And that change in policy suggests another possibility that could help family farms survive. Government policies, and also corporate policies, could be developed that would serve this goal, perhaps more effectively than it was served in the past (*Des Moines Register*, February 15, 1987).

Even the weather favors family farms. In the Middle West, at least, corporate farming appears to be advancing only in areas like poultry and livestock, areas that are not affected significantly by normal changes in weather. Thus, their work forces can be employed each day and for regular hours. Work on crops is, however, affected by weather and best done by people with flexible schedules. As a family farm combines a home and a business, the people on it are able to work long hours when the weather permits, cut back when it does not.[13]

CONCLUSIONS

The trend toward fewer and fewer farms continues and seems certain to persist, yet it seems unlikely that the current situation is the final crisis of the family farm.

Perhaps the prediction that it is "final" is only an effort to continue to derive political benefits from Jeffersonian agrarianism. But if this is the final crisis, or if a new technological revolution featuring biotechnology and new information systems finally destroys family farming (Office of Technology Assessment 1986), should the nation as a whole be upset by such a turn of events? Is not the present too late to become concerned? Now that the number of farms and the size of the farm population have become so small, what difference does it make to the nation whether our farms are plantations, corporations, or family units? Certainly, one can no longer argue convincingly that the survival of democracy depends upon the survival of the family farm. If that political system must have such a base, then democracy in America must have perished long ago! We have only a few family farmers now—and had only a few before the current crisis hit. In 1980 as well as in 1987, farm people constituted less than three percent of the total American population.

The only way to make family farms significant from a democratic point of view would be to increase the number substantially. That would involve a large-scale program of land reform emphasizing redistribution so that many more people would own land, live on it, and depend on it for their livelihoods. It would require that large farms be broken into small units and that the resulting structure of small-farm agriculture be preserved.

Although there are advocates of land reform of that type,[14] there seems little possibility of such a change. Surely, few of the existing family farmers favor it. Furthermore, some analysts argue that it would move America as a whole in an undemocratic direction for it would mean higher food prices, a factor of great importance in the lives of all people and especially those with low incomes that must be devoted to the necessities of life. In addition, the theory of the surplus farm population has reemerged in American thinking about agriculture, providing a rationale for yet more reduction in the number of farms and farmers, although also stimulating suggestions for more intelligent management of migration this time (Guither et al. 1986). There is, of course, a large problem confronting this solution to farm problems: the nonfarm economy is not producing jobs as abundantly as it did earlier.

In the circumstances that now exist, the farm policy debate seems more likely to focus, as it has since the 1920s, on the issue of strengthening farming as a business than on the question of building a base for democracy. The circumstances are basically those created by the "Great American Agricultural Revolution": a complex and highly productive agricultural system that includes within it a small number of farms and farmers compared with what existed only a half-century ago. The debate over how to make those farms profitable businesses has developed three major sides.[15] One emphasizes more effective government control of production to balance supply and demand at a higher level of prices. A second group advocates recapturing the world market for America's highly productive farmers by lowering prices and improving marketing opportunities. And, the third option is reliance on science and technology to develop additional crops and improved livestock and poultry and to devise alternative uses for farm products and farm land.

These proposals, unlike the one for land redistribution, accept the agricultural system that history has produced thus far. Although people can break with the past, as the concept of revolution implies, the possibility of doing so does not seem large at this juncture. The would-be revolutionaries appear to have little strength. There seems little possibility of anything more than modifications in the system, perhaps a reduction, or redesign of the role of government for the costs of the farm programs have become enormous, much of the money goes to farmers who are not in financial difficulties, and the programs have not prevented farms and farmers from declining in number and have even contributed to the decline, "...helping," as Willard Cochrane puts it, "one group of farmers do in another group." (Cochrane 1985, 1006–9) Even proposals for change of this magnitude would surely encounter, and are encountering, strong opposition from general farm and commodity organizations who are responsive to the larger, more financially secure farmers. Fearing loss of price support funds, they dislike proposals to target benefits to the weaker farmers.[16]

Strengthening the farm business is not the same as guaranteeing the survival of family farms. The American historical experience during the past half-century makes that point. Thus, if one of the policy options triumphs and works to make farming more profitable, we can expect that family farms will continue to decline in number as new mergers are worked out. This need not mean, however, that corporate farms, owned by stockholders and operated by employees, will become the major type of farm in the United States.

If we wish, we can maintain the system in which most of the farms are owned and operated by families. Champions of the 1890 land-grant universities and Tuskegee University, those that were exclusively Black institutions in the past, maintain they have much of value to teach the other land-grant schools for while the latter were encouraging migration out of farming by small farmers, the Black schools were working with such farmers, helping them survive. And these schools have been strengthened by federal legislation in the 1980s supplying more adequate financial support for research and planning efforts (Williams and Williamson 1987, 8–17).

Further decline in the number of family farms need not mean that small communities must continue to decline and die (Guither et al. 1986). Instead, they could develop new bases, depend less on agriculture and agricultural policies, more upon industrial and cultural policies, including ones that provide full- or part-time off-farm opportunities for members of farm families and others that help elderly people who have returned to rural communities from the cities (Williams and Williamson 1987, 15–16). Reducing rural America's dependence on agriculture would not be a new move. Instead, it would continue a trend that has been underway for a number of years, and thus planners and policy makers could draw upon available experiences. Those experiences need to be explored and analyzed, as do the implications for communities that do depend on agriculture of proposed agricultural policies, such as those that would take acres out of crop production (Korsching 1987).

To be useful now, the agencies of change in rural America, especially the land-grant universities, must have a broad outlook. They must serve all rural interests, not only the interest in making the farm business more productive and profitable, and seek to enrich rural society in various ways. To do so, the universities must have strength in both the basic and the applied sciences and in the social sciences and humanities as well (Bonnen 1986). Efforts to orient these universities in these ways seem certain to generate conflict of the sort that was so prominent in the early years of the land-grant system (Glenn L. Johnson 1984).

The agricultural system faces several serious challenges. The decline of the number of farms has alienated some people as has pollution of the environment and the food supply by modern farming's heavy use of chemicals. The production of surpluses has also suggested to some that expenditures on the system, especially its research branch, should be slashed. Its economic troubles, along with the small number of people raised on farms in recent years, threaten the system from yet another angle: it may not attract the "human capital," including the supply of well-trained scientists, needed for continued development (Hadwiger, 1986; RICOP 1983; Allan T. Smith 1987).

The entire agricultural system, not just the farming sector, may decline, but working for its survival is the long-recognized importance of the commodities it produces. This element of agrarianism, if no other, still seems to have some ability to build support for American agriculture. It may persuade the appropriate people that they must do what they can to make or maintain a superior agricultural system.

The quality of the system depends in large part upon the quality of its intellectual life. It depends upon its science, including its social science, which has the capacity to sort out myth and reality in agriculture and explore, develop, and evaluate ways of making the system function more effectively (Bonnen 1986).[17] And the need for evaluation of both proposals for change in the system and the system itself points to a significant role for the humanities (Glenn L. Johnson 1982; Comstock 1987; Haynes and Lanier 1982; Billington 1986). These conclusions do no more than suggest topics for social science research, but I have not assumed that spelling them out was my responsibility or even within my realm of competence. Rather, my task has been to supply insights into the present situation by exploring how it has come to be. The definition of next steps in research as well as policy must rest upon a realistic appraisal of what exists.

NOTES

1. Richard S. Kirkendall was the Henry A. Wallace Professor of History, Iowa State University when this article was written. He is now the Bullitt Professor of American History, University of Washington.

2. My colleague, Gary Comstock, suggested this term, offering it as the opposite of "modernizer" and preferable to "traditionalist."

3. June 7, 1939, Eleanor Roosevelt Papers, F. D. Roosevelt Library.

4. Willard W. Cochrane to author, April 13, 1987.

5. Kenneth L. Deavers clarified my thinking on these and other parts in a letter of April 24, 1987.

6. Deavers's letter was especially helpful on these points.

7. Letter to author, April 21, 1987.

8. Conversation with William G. Murray, April 19, 1987.

9. In addition to these articles, remarks by Dennis Starleaf, Robert Wisner, Gene Futrell, William Meyers, Daniel Otto, Michael Duffy, Charles Gratto, and Neil Harl at the Agricultural Leaders Conference, Iowa State University, February 25, 1987; regular reading of the *Des Moines Register*, frequent conversations with William G. Murray; and participation in the Kellogg-funded workshops at Iowa State in 1985 and 1986 have influenced my understanding of the crisis.

10. Deavers to author, April 24, 1987.

11. Willard W. Cochrane to author, April 13, 1987.

12. Firms on the other end of the system—those that processed and sold farm products—did not suffer similar difficulties (*Des Moines Register*, March 8, 1987).

13. Conversation with William G. Murray, May 20, 1987.

14. For example, John Hart of Carroll College (Montana), advisor to the Catholic bishops, author of *The Spirit of the Earth*, and participant in a conference entitled "Is There a Conspiracy Against Family Farmers?" held at Iowa State University, February 27, 1987.

15. I am grateful to colleagues in the College of Agriculture, Iowa State University, especially Neil Harl, Stanley Johnson, Robert W. Jolly, William Meyers, and Donald G. Woolley, for helping me understand the alternatives that are being considered. The national participants in the Agricultural Leaders Conference, *Midcourse Corrections in Agricultural Policy*, February 25, 1987, also contributed.

16. Neil E. Harl to author, April 14, 1987. Cochrane 1985, 1007–8.

17. William P. Browne to author, April 21, 1987.

REFERENCES

Agriculture and Human Values (Spring)1985.

Appleby, Joyce. 1982. Commercial farming and the "agrarian myth" in the early republic. *Journal of American History* 68 (March): 833–49.

_____1984. *Capitalism and a new social order: The republican vision of the 1790s*. New York: New York University Press.

Baldwin, Sidney. 1969. *Poverty and politics: The rise and decline of the farm security administration*. Chapel Hill: University of North Carolina Press.

Bender, Thomas. 1975 *Toward an urban vision: Ideas and institutions in nineteenth century America*. Lexington: University Press of Kentucky.

Berkhofer, Robert F., Jr. 1978. *The white man's Indian: Images of the American Indian from Columbus to the present*. New York: Oxford University Press.

Berry, Wendell. 1977. *The unsettling of America; culture and agriculture*. San Francisco: Sierra Club Books.

Billington, Monroe. 1986. Teaching agricultural history at land grant institutions. *OAH Newsletter* 14 (August): 12–13.

Bonnen, James T. 1986. A century of science in agriculture: Lessons for science policy. *American Journal of Agricultural Economics* 68, no. 5: 1065–80.

Brake, John, Mike Boehlje, and Warren Lee. 1986. *Short-term transition policies to ease the financial crisis*. Cooperative Extension Service, Iowa State University, May.

Broehl, Wayne S. 1984. *John Deere's company: A history of Deere and Company and its times*. New York: Doubleday.

Browne, William P. 1983. Mobilizing and activating group demands: The American agriculture movement. *Social Science Quarterly* 64 (March): 19–34.

Cochrane, Willard W. 1978. *The development of American agriculture: A historical analysis*. Minneapolis: University of Minnesota Press.

_____1985. The need to rethink agricultural policy in general and perform some radical surgery on commodity programs in particular. *American Journal of Agricultural Economics* 67 (December): 1002–9.

Cochrane, Willard W., and Mary E. Ryan. 1976. *American farm policy, 1948–1973*. Minneapolis: University of Minnesota Press.

Comstock, Gary. 1987. *Is there a moral obligation to save the family farm?* Ames: Iowa State University Press.

Daniel, Pete. 1984. The crossroads of change: Cotton, tobacco, and rice cultures in the twentieth century south. *Journal of Southern History* 50 (August): 429–56.

_____1985. *Breaking the land: The transformation of cotton, tobacco, and rice cultures since 1880*. Urbana: University of Illinois Press.

Eisenger, Chester E. 1947a. The freehold concept in eighteenth century American letters. *William and Mary Quarterly* 4 (January): 42–59.

_____1947b. The influence of natural rights and physiocratic doctrines on American agrarian thought during the revolutionary period. *Agricultural History* 21 (January): 12–13.

_____1949. Land and loyalty: Literary expressions of agrarian nationalism in the seventeenth and eighteenth centuries. *American Literature* 21 (May): 160–78.

_____1954. The farmer in the eighteenth century almanac. *Agricultural History* 28 (July): 107–12.

Fite, Gilbert C. 1980. Mechanization of cotton production since World War II. *Agricultural History* 54 (January): 190–207.

_____1981. *American farmers: The new minority*. Bloomington: Indiana University Press.

_____1984. *Cotton fields no more: Southern agriculture 1865–1980*. Lexington: University Press of Kentucky.

Fuller, Wayne E. 1982. *The old country school: The story of rural education in the middle west*. Chicago: University of Chicago Press.

Fusonie, Alan E. 1986. John H. Davis: His contributions to agricultural education and productivity. *Agricultural History* 60 (April): 97–110.

Goldschmidt, Walter. 1978. *As you sow: Three studies in the social consequences of agribusiness*. Montclair, N.J.: Allanheld, Osmun.

Goodwyn, Lawrence. 1978. *The populist moment: A short history of the agrarian revolt in America*. New York: Oxford.

Gratto, Charles. 1986. U.S. agricultural exports: Waiting for something to happen. *Iowa State University's Policy Update* no. 34, 15 October.

Griswold, A. Whitney. 1948. *Farming and democracy*. New York: Harcourt Brace.

Guither, Harold D., J. Paxton Marshall, and Paul W. Barkley. 1986. *Policies and programs to ease the transition of resources out of agriculture*. Cooperative Extension Service, Iowa State University.

Hadwiger, Don F. 1982. *The politics of agricultural research*. Lincoln: University of Nebraska.

_____1986. The politics of agricultural abundance. *Agriculture and Human Values* 3 (1986), 99–107.

Harl, Neil E. 1987. The people and the institutions: An economic assessment. *Understanding of public problems and policies—1986*. Oak Brook, Ill.: Farm Foundation.

Haynes, Richard, and Ray Lanier, eds. 1982. *Agriculture, change and human values. Proceedings of a multidisciplinary conference*. 2 vols. 18–21 October. Humanities and Agriculture Program, University of Florida, Gainesville.

_____1987. *The two problems in U.S. agriculture: Debt and overproduction*. Cooperative Extension Service, Iowa State University, February.

Hightower, Jim. 1973. *Hard tomatoes, hard times*. Cambridge: Schenkman Publishing Co.

Historical statistics of the United States: Colonial times to 1970. 1975. Washington, D.C.: U.S. Government Printing Office.

Johnson, Glenn L. 1982. Agro-ethics: Extension, research, and teaching. *Southern Journal of Agricultural Economics* 14 (July):1–10.

_____1984. *Academia needs a new covenant for serving agriculture*. Mississippi Agricultural and Forestry Experiment Station.

Johnson, Stanley R. 1986. Midwest agriculture and the food security act of 1985. *Agricultural distress in the midwest, past and present*. Edited by E. Gelfand and Robert J. Neymeyer. Iowa City: Center for the Study of the Recent History of the United States.

Johnstone, Paul H. 1937. In praise of husbandry. *Agricultural History* 11 (April): 80–95.

_____1938. Turnips and romanticism. *Agricultural History* 12 (July): 224–55.

Kirby, Jack Temple. 1983. The transformation of southern plantations ca. 1920–1960. *Agricultural History* 57 (July): 257–76.

Kirkendall, Richard S. 1967. Commentary on the thought of Henry A. Wallace. *Agricultural History* 41 (April): 139–42.

_____1982. *Social scientists and farm policies in the age of Roosevelt*. Ames: Iowa State University Presss.

_____1983. The mind of a farm leader. *The Annals of Iowa* 47 (Fall): 138–53.

_____1984. Corn huskers and master farmers: Henry A. Wallace and the merchandising of Iowa agriculture. *The Palimpsest* 65 (May/June): 82–93.

_____1986. The agricultural colleges: Between tradition and modernization. *Agricultural History* 60 (Spring): 3–21.

Kloppenburg, Jack R., Jr. 1988. *First the seed. The political economy of plant biotechnology*, 492–2000. Cambridge: Cambridge University Press.

Korsching, Peter F. 1987. Shutting down the plant: Social impacts. Agricultural Colloquium '87, Excess Capacity in Agriculture: The Next Challenge, 19 April, Iowa State University, Ames, Iowa.

Lasley, Paul. 1986. The human toll of the farm crisis. Unpublished manuscript.

Lee, Harold. 1984. *Roswell Garst: A biography*. Ames: Iowa State University Press.

McCoy, Drew R. 1980. Jefferson and Madison on Malthus: Population growth in Jeffersonian political economy. *Virginia Magazine of History and Biography* 88 (July): 259–76.

McGovern, George, ed. 1967. *Agricultural thought in the twentieth century*. Indianapolis, Ind.: Bobbs-Merrill.

Madison, James H. 1986. Reformers and the rural church, 1900–1950. *Journal of American History* 73 (December): 645–68.

Merrill, Richard, ed. 1976. *Radical agriculture*. New York: Harper and Row.

Newby, Howard. 1982. Rural sociology and its relevance to the agricultural economist: A review. *Journal of Agricultural Economics* 33 (May): 124–66.

Office of Technology Assessment (OTA). 1986. *Technology, public policy and the changing structure of American agriculture*. Washington, D.C.: U.S. Government Printing Office.

Paarlberg, Don. 1988. *Toward a well-fed world*. Ames: Iowa State University Press.

Pearce, Roy Harvey. 1965. *Savagism and civilization: A study of the Indian and the American mind*. Baltimore: Johns Hopkins University Press.

Peterson, Trudy Huskamp. 1979. *Agricultural exports, farm income and the Eisenhower administration*. Lincoln: University of Nebraska Press.

Rasmussen, Wayne. 1962. The impact of technological change on American agriculture. *Journal of Economic History* 22 (December): 578–91.

Rasmussen, Wayne, ed. 1975. *Agriculture in the United States: A documentary history*. New York: Random House.

Resident Instruction Committee on Organization and Policy (RICOP). 1983. *Human capital shortages: A threat to American agriculture*. Division of Agriculture, National Association of State Universities and Land Grant Colleges (NASULGC).

Rhodes, Richard. 1978. The American farm: Still family, still the wonder of the world. *American Heritage* 29 (February-March): 18–27.

Schapsmeier, Edward L., and Frederick Schapsmeier. 1975. *Ezra Taft Benson and the politics of agriculture: The Eisenhower years, 1953–1961*. Danville, Ill.: Interstate Printers and Publishers.

Shover, John L. 1976. *First majority-last minority: The transforming of rural life in America*. DeKalb: Northern Illinois University Press.

Smith, Allan T. 1987. Science and technology the 4-H way. 4-H Extension Service, United States Department of Agriculture. Unpublished draft, 9 January.

Smith, Henry Nash. 1950. *Virgin land: The American west as symbol and myth*. Cambridge: Harvard University Press.

Soth, Lauren. 1987. Farmers were misled by economists, government. *Des Moines Register*, 7 April.

Statistical abstract of the United States. 1985. Washington, D.C.: U.S. Government Printing Office.

Weber, William T. 1978. The complexities of agripower: A review essay. *Agricultural History* 52 (October): 526–37.

Williams, Robert C. 1987. *Fordson, Farmall, and Poppin' Johnny: A history of the farm tractor and its impact on America*. Urbana: University of Illinois Press.

Williams, Thomas T., and Handy Williamson, Jr. 1987. Teaching, research and extension programs at historically Black (1890) land-grant institutions. Unpublished manuscript.

CHAPTER 3

SOCIAL SCIENCE INSTITUTIONS, KNOWLEDGE, AND TOOLS TO ADDRESS PROBLEMS AND ISSUES

Frederick H. Buttel[1]

INTRODUCTION

A colleague once suggested to me, in only partial jest, that the only thing the social science departments in his college of agriculture had in common was they shared a common heating system and parking problem. One of the major contributions of the Social Science Agricultural Agenda Project (SSAAP) has been to make the case that land-grant administrators and social scientists should conceive of the land-grant social science effort in a more integrated way—as a cadre of "rural social scientists" with related missions and a purposive division of labor. In this paper I wish to make some preliminary notes about the prospects and problems of this conception of the role of the social sciences in colleges of agriculture. More specifically, I will attempt to provide an overview of several rural social science disciplines, their historic and potential future contributions, their strengths and limitations, and their institutional environments.

The initial portion of the paper will be devoted to laying out a framework for understanding the role of and challenges facing the rural social (as well as biological and physical) sciences. I will then provide an overview of disciplinary, subject-matter, and problem-solving research in the two major or "mainline" rural social sciences, agricultural economics and rural sociology. The next section discusses the contributions of the rural social sciences to problem solving, which is followed by a brief treatment of the state of the rural social sciences as disciplines. I will consider six disciplines other than my own: agricultural economics, history, anthropology, political science, geography, and philosophy, the last five of which are treated in a major section entitled "Nontraditional Rural Social Sciences." Two caveats should be stressed at the outset. First, what follows is a *personal perspective* on the rural social sciences and their future role in solving agricultural problems, and others will no doubt view the issues quite differently. Second, for reasons of space the coverage of actual or prospective rural social science disciplines is only partial. For example, I have not treated home economics (or human ecology) and education at all. I will also not treat the communication sciences as a separate "discipline" because of the inherent multidisciplinary character of departments of communication, agricultural journalism, and so on. Persons in these departments have typically been trained in such a wide range of disciplines (including sociology, psychology, journalism, and the humanities) that it is impossible to examine such programs as a single discipline. I will also not treat community development as a discipline. Community development, like the communication sciences, is inherently multidisciplinary. Further, community development has a very small research base in the land-grant system outside of rural sociology, agricultural economics, and home economics. I then turn to some major issues pertaining to the rural social sciences and the information delivery system. My concluding comments provide a set of suggestions for enhancing the role of the rural social sciences in the future.

A PERSPECTIVE ON THE SOCIAL, POLITICAL, AND ECONOMIC STRUCTURE OF U.S. AGRICULTURAL RESEARCH INSTITUTIONS: A BRIEF STATEMENT

Agricultural research (which, in a first approximation[2] will be defined as a biological or engineering research that increases agricultural productivity and output) exhibits a paradox, the analysis of which is central for understanding the role of the rural and agricultural social sciences. The paradox is that agricultural research, an activity from which so many are said to benefit, has such a limited base of political support at the federal level. Why, given the benefits of agricultural research to farmers, consumers, agribusiness, the rural or nonmetro population, and so on, has it been difficult to sustain agricultural research appropriations, especially at the national or federal level?

At this level of first approximation we can provide several answers to this paradoxical question. First, and perhaps most important, is the fact that agricultural research is not unambiguously of benefit to farmers as a whole, taken as a national aggregate of producers whose principal markets are national. This argument has, for example, been made in direct fashion by T. W. Schultz and inferentially by others (such as Willard W. Cochrane). The logic of the argument is that agricultural research, by increasing productivity and especially agricultural output, tends to reduce agricultural product prices and to set in motion a technological treadmill that results in some fraction of farmers being forced out of business or attracted to higher paying, nonfarm employment. This tendency is largely accounted for by the fact that most agricultural commodities have low price and income elasticities of demand; accordingly, farmer benefits from research are least and ambivalence about research is greatest for commodities with the lowest price and income elasticities of demand (i.e., the "basic," staple food commodities). Some fraction of farmers does, to be sure, benefit from productivity-increasing agricultural research—namely, early adopters of technology who receive innovator's rents until a point at which a certain proportion has adopted the technology and caused declining product prices and precipitated a technological treadmill. Nonetheless, these early adopters are a minority of the agricultural population, while those who receive little or no benefit are generally a majority. Also, given the tendency for agricultural productivity increase to place continual downward pressure on product prices, farmers' political interests tend to be far more that of product price maintenance than of research and new technology (Browne 1987).

Thus, it is not surprising that at the federal level farmers have tended not to be a strong, dependable voice in support of agricultural research appropriations. This is not so much because many—let alone a majority of—farmers actively oppose research. It is probably more accurate to say that the rank-and-file of farmers tends to be ambivalent about research, neither actively opposing nor actively supporting research (Gillespie and Buttel 1989). While there is some modest farmer support of research at the federal level, this support has tended to come from farmer groups in which early adopters of technology (i.e., potential recipients of innovator's rents) are numerically predominant. Historically, these groups have principally been the American Farm Bureau Federation and commodity groups, though it should be noted that in this time of farm crisis and deteriorating commodity prices the soybean commodity group has begun to oppose some types of research on their commodity for the reason alluded to earlier—that productivity-increasing research, especially if it can be transferred to foreign countries, will lead to expanded supply, lower product prices, and further financial stress for soybean producers.

Second, it is generally said that consumers have historically been the major beneficiary of agricultural research in the United States and elsewhere. Some critics of American agricultural research have challenged this notion, typically by arguing, with some justification, that raw agricultural product is increasingly a small component of retail food prices and that the increased processing, transportation, and merchandizing component of the food bill has kept food prices higher than they should be. Nonetheless, as a general historical proposition the notion of consumer benefit from agricultural research has a strong level of validity.

Why, then, have consumers not actively supported agricultural research at the federal level? The answer lies in two aspects of the "consumer posture" on productivity-increasing agricultural research. The general posture—that of the rank-and-file of citizens who benefit from cheaper food to a greater or lesser degree each year—is such that consumers receive benefits that are far too diffuse or intangible to cause citizens to mobilize in support of federal research appropriations. Each consumer each year receives benefits that are far too small to be part of the "policy consciousness," even though small gains each year have resulted in big gains over the decades. The more specific posture—that of "consumer groups"—is even less favorable to federal appropriations for research, since these groups have often been critics of the agricultural research establishment on the grounds that this research has resulted in the use of potentially harmful pesticides and food additives and in too high a level of food processing and merchandizing cost for the consumer. Thus, consumers, while historically the single most important category of agricultural research beneficiaries, have tended to offer very little support for federal agricultural research appropriations.

Third, organized groups of nonfarm-rural or nonmetropolitan residents rarely have actively supported federal agricultural research appropriations. This is likely due to a complex combination of factors. One is that to the degree to which agricultural research has improved rural community conditions, the benefit to any one rural or nonmetro resident in any year is small and diffuse, much like that observed above for consumers. Another is that productivity-increasing research, by putting downward pressure on commodity prices and causing labor displacement and a decline in the farm population, has been detrimental to rural communities that are heavily dependent on agriculture (Swanson 1988). Also, the USDA has historically never had a major rural development program; the vast bulk of rural development activity is typically identified with the land-grant system (especially extension) and with federal agencies other than the USDA, state government agencies, and private, voluntary rural development groups. The small base of the USDA rural development effort makes it such that federally funded agricultural research (construed broadly to include rural development and home economics) is rarely viewed by persons interested in rural development as a locus for benefiting the interests of the nonfarm rural population.

Thus, the historical experience of the political support base of agricultural research at the federal level has been that there have been two major groups of supporters: agricultural research administrators and agricultural researchers themselves, for obvious reasons, and agribusiness firms, for the reason that they might benefit from plant, animal, engineering, or social science research. This support base has been small, and federal appropriations modest, especially funds that support the research of the land-grant system, the cornerstone of the U.S. agricultural research effort.

Yet the American agricultural research establishment by world standards is quite large despite this modest base of support at the federal level. The reason for the large scope of the national agricultural research system despite a modest base of political and financial support at the federal level is, of course, the relatively high level of state government appropriations for agricultural research at their state agricultural experiment stations (SAESs). For most SAESs state funds exceed, by several-fold, those from federal sources. At the larger SAESs, state funds tend to be 10- to 20-fold, or more, those from the federal government. Over the past 25 years the stagnation of federal agricultural research funding and the expansion of state appropriations (which were related to general state university expansion in response to the "baby boom," but which began to stagnate in the late 1970s when the baby boom expired) have led to an SAES system in which the funding backbone is state government dollars.

Indeed, the federal-state partnership in research has led to a largely beneficent resolution of the problem of a lack of political support for agricultural research. Its basic logic is that, on one hand, states have an interest in at least matching federal funds in order to obtain these federal resources, and on the other, that it is in the interest of farmers in any state to support research at "their" SAES that helps them compete with farmers in other states. (A similar logic pertains to higher education in agriculture and extension—particularly the latter, since extension should ideally be an instrument for expanding a land-grant university's clientele and generating political support for the university as well as transferring technology.) In particular, farmers, rather than being ambivalent about research as they have largely been at the federal level, can be induced to be dependable supporters of research at the state level. This has been the organizational genius of the American agricultural research system, which has made it the largest and among the most productive in the world. This is also, in a sense, an important explanation of the expansion of the Agricultural Research Service (ARS), which has been based partly on the creation of decentralized research stations that do what the SAESs have historically been quite good at doing: creating locally adapted knowledge, materials, and technologies that benefit farmers in a particular region over farmers in others.

It is important to recognize the strengths and limitations of this research structure in relation to ongoing trends in agricultural science and the agribusiness industries. The raison d'etre of this decentralized SAES system whose funding backbone derives from state legislatures rather than the Congress or the White House is to conduct *applied, locally adapted research*, the benefits from which are at least partially capturable by localized groups of farmers and other rural residents. The status of applied, locally adapted research as the organizing principle for sustaining the SAES and larger land-grant system is, however, in some doubt. This is due to several reasons. First, it is widely recognized that the cutting edge of modern agricultural research lies increasingly in biotechnology (based on molecular and cell biology and biochemistry)—that is, in relatively basic or fundamental research—and that applied researchers and their agendas have become less important over the past decade. Second, the SAESs have rapidly expanded their full-time equivalent (FTE) biotechnology research positions, roughly from 4 percent of FTEs in 1982 to 8 percent in 1986, a rather startling reallocation of research resources at the margin. Third, biotechnology researchers will, at least for the foreseeable future until these new scientific exemplars have become routine in the agricultural research system, tend to produce *generic* technology (i.e., technology of broad, national-scale applicability) rather than locally adapted technology. Fourth, the dominant thrust of recent federal politics relating to research has been to urge the land-grant system to move more toward basic biology (to assist the U.S. effort in global technological competition) and to deemphasize applied, problem-solving (and, some would say, routine or low-quality) research. Fifth, there has been a significant increase in industrial funding of SAES research (though, it should be noted, to a lesser extent than was widely anticipated in the early 1980s; Buttel et al. 1986); accordingly, industry has become a more important clientele and, at least de facto, local farmer groups less so.

Sixth, industry has become the major performer of agricultural research and development (R&D), accounting for perhaps as much as two-thirds of annual agricultural R&D expenditures (Ruttan 1982), while the public sector has increasingly become a minority component of the national research system. Indeed, it could perhaps be said that industry research, rather than SAES and ARS research, is now most predominant in inducing new technological directions in American agriculture (broadly construed to include the larger food system). Finally, several SAESs have found themselves under pressure because of this new constellation of research activities and clientele. A few SAESs, for example, have been pressured by farmers concerning bovine growth hormone (BGH), which is a good example of a biotechnology produced in cooperation with industry (including industrial funding of SAES research) and of a generic technology that farmers in a particular state are not in a privileged position to benefit from (Buttel and Geisler 1989). At the same time, several SAESs have received countervailing pressures—for example, from financially strapped farmers who want their SAES to provide them with locally adapted research that will help them reduce their input costs. These new trends and pressures have enormous implications for the future role of agricultural researchers, including social as well as biological scientists. These implications will be discussed below.

What, then, do these observations have to tell us about the roles of the rural social sciences (other than the fact that a social science analysis undergirds this assessment)? One obvious implication is that the rural social sciences will largely rise or fall depending upon the viability of the land-grant and SAES systems. Second, we all know that the first approximation of the content of agricultural research employed above is too narrow. The agricultural research system performs many activities other than directly or indirectly increasing agricultural productivity. A partial list of these other activities includes research on the environmental consequences of agricultural technologies, nutrition, home economics, rural development, environmental resources, and so on. Social and nonsocial research also provide essential contributions to teaching, extension, international development, and "institution building." Each of these activities serves one or more of the following functions: (1) providing an *inherently necessary* adjunct to productivity increase (which I now define broadly to include the reduction of input usage and socioeconomic and environmental sustainability of production systems as well as output expansion), and (2) maintaining or building the political support base for a land-grant system.

Third, the very processes which generate farmer ambivalence about research at the federal level—differential benefits from research and the technological treadmill—have combined to create a startlingly diverse farmer clientele. In a sense, it is no longer accurate to speak of "farmers" as a particular group, since the profound differentiation among farmers has, at a minimum, generated three "agricultures" in the United States (Office of Technology Assessment [OTA] 1986). These three agricultures include: (1) very large — typically "larger-than-family" or "industrial"— farmers who primarily rely on a hired labor force, (2) medium-sized, largely full-time "family" farmers who rely principally on family labor, and (3) small, often part-time, farmers who rely heavily on off-farm earnings. Very large and very small farms have recently increased in prevalence (in terms of the level of sales accounted for and proportion of farm numbers, respectively), while the medium-sized, full-time, family farmer category has probably been in relative as well as absolute decline for 15 years. Each is an important clientele, but most importantly each has several distinctive technical/information needs. The land-grant system can no longer[3] serve the farming community by producing a single constellation of technologies intended for use by some imagined entity of "farmers as a whole," which for all practical purposes no longer exists.

Fourth, the SAESs and the larger land-grant system have a number of other nonfarmer clienteles, some of which it must serve to fulfill its land-grant mission (e.g., farm laborers, state and local officials, environmental groups, state-level agribusinesses, rural communities and their residents), others of which it must serve to ensure transfer of technology and information (e.g., out-of-state agricultural input and output industries), and still others of which are of key importance in maintaining and building the political support base (e.g., rural youth, consumer groups desiring nutritional information). Fifth, the interests of these diverse clientele groups are not necessarily consistent, and may in fact be in opposition. For example, farm workers and their industrial farmer employers are an obvious case in point. Thus, sixth, the SAES and larger land-grant portfolio are, intentionally or not, a mix of activities in which benefits (and costs) are distributed across the clientele groups, which can have major implications for clientele perceptions of the system and for its political support base.

A final—and, in many respects, uncomfortable—implication of the foregoing is that while, on one hand, we and our nonsocial science colleagues as trained scientists are most comfortable with matters technical and scientific, there is an irreducible political element to agricultural (and nonagricultural) research institutions. The very structure of these institutions is derivative of some basic parameters of the political demand structure of agricultural research. Their future structure and prospects depend upon what are, for all practical purposes, political strategies for maintaining and expanding upon the clienteles that we can serve well and for dealing with the differences of interest and opinion among these clienteles.

THE ESTABLISHMENT OF THE RURAL SOCIAL SCIENCES AND THEIR CONTRIBUTIONS TO THE SOLUTION OF AGRICULTURAL AND RURAL-RELATED PROBLEMS

THE DEVELOPMENT OF THE RURAL SOCIAL SCIENCE DISCIPLINES

With this background, let us turn to the historical development of the rural social sciences, focusing primarily on agricultural economics and rural sociology. It is useful to begin by noting that the founding of the land-grant system essentially predated the agricultural and rural social sciences as we know them today. The purpose of the Morrill Act was largely educational, and in 1862 it could be said that agricultural science scarcely existed. Indeed, the origins of agricultural research were in the large colonial empires of the several preceding centuries (Busch 1981), and since the United States was not a colonial power, it had a very small research establishment. At the time of the passage of the Morrill Act, agricultural research in the United States was limited to the work of a few agricultural chemists in Ivy League universities and state governments and to the importation and distribution of seeds by the federal government. The passage of the Hatch Act and the implicit modeling of the SAES system on the German agricultural experiment stations and research universities signaled a slow but significant reorientation of the land-grant system. Though hampered by the lack of trained scientists and a lack of knowledge in agricultural biology and genetics, research activities increased in prominence by the turn of the century. Then, with the "rediscovery" of Mendelian genetics shortly after the turn of the century, the subsequent invention of hybrid corn in the 1920s and 1930s, and continued soil fertility and crop nutrition research in the tradition of Liebig, the momentum of research increased decisively.

Just as in the early decades of the land-grant system when trained scientists in the conventional sense were hardly to be found, the social sciences as we currently understand them were essentially not present at all. If land-grant personnel were neither agricultural nor social scientists, what were their backgrounds and activities? In the main, they were clerics, engineers, former farmers who had received higher education, and so on. Indeed, with the exception of economics, the social science disciplines as we know them today—especially sociology and political science—did not exist in American universities.

The roots of the social-science presence in land-grant and SAES institutions resided in problems experienced by the land-grant system in encouraging farmers to use new technology and to improve their management practices. Agricultural economics emerged as farm management economics in the first decade of this century and was oriented to assisting farmers in allocating their resources more effectively and profitably. Rural sociology largely emerged about a decade later, in the aftermath of the Country Life Commission, which recommended that the SAESs engage in social science research to assist in the transfer of technology while at the same time preserving the social and moral fabric of rural communities (Danbom 1979). At many land-grant universities, rural sociology programs were established before sociology departments.

After the passage of the Smith-Lever Act in 1914, the progress of the rural social sciences until World War II occurred more through extension and through USDA funding than because of formula-funded research. For example, to the best of my knowledge rural sociology received essentially no Hatch funding until after World War II, and the most active rural sociology research programs were in the U.S. Department of Agriculture, especially during the "Depression." Much the same could probably be said about agricultural economics, except that I am not familiar with the history of its funding sources. Nonetheless, at the land-grant level the activities of the rural social sciences at this time were heavily oriented to extension and public service activities (in addition to teaching) and were only modestly directed to research activities.

Before proceeding, it is useful to make some preliminary comments on the rural social sciences as "disciplines." The two "mainline" rural social science disciplines (i.e., the two with the closest connections with the liberal arts social sciences) are agricultural economics and rural sociology. Each can be considered a discipline in a certain sense (i.e., each includes a number of subject-matter areas, involves a clear identity among its practitioners, has its own scholarly organizations and journals, and has some common core of theories and methods). Yet agricultural economics, for example, could as readily be considered a subdiscipline of a larger discipline: economics. Likewise, rural sociology could be seen as a subdiscipline of sociology. Moreover, there are several land-grant rural sociology programs (e.g., Michigan State University, Iowa State University, North Carolina State University, Colorado State University, Utah State University, Washington State University, University of Kentucky, Montana State University, University of Georgia, Louisiana State University) that are integral parts of larger sociology departments. (There are, to the best of my knowledge, only two agricultural economics programs [Iowa State and North Carolina] that are part of larger departments of economics.)

Nonetheless, the land-grant social sciences (as well as the biological and physical science departments) are disciplines in a particular sense—that is, they involve the institutionalization of a set of subject-matter foci into a discipline in a somewhat arbitrary way. The source of this arbitrariness, of course, is the land-grant system. That is, the rural social science disciplines are essentially coterminous with the mode in which these scientists are organized into land-grant departments. The logic of land-grant funding and departmental organization has caused them to be perceived—and, in most respects, to function—as disciplines.

But, as will be stressed below, agricultural economists and rural sociologists conduct disciplinary research in two different, though overlapping, ways: One is for an agricultural economist or rural sociologist to do work on problems that are seen to be of broad importance to her or his agricultural economics or rural sociology colleagues, to employ the theories and methods that are seen to be at the cutting edge by large numbers of these colleagues, and to direct this work largely or entirely to professional colleagues. The second is similar to that of the first, except that the referent is the larger discipline (economics or sociology).

Agricultural economics and rural sociology historically exhibited quite different routes to their current status as disciplines. Agricultural economics was largely born outside of the larger discipline of economics. This apparently was because the impetus for and early nature of agricultural economics was highly applied and public service oriented—namely, farm management. Agricultural economics has largely remained relatively isolated from the larger discipline with only a few exceptions, though, as I will suggest below, this has begun to change. The vast majority of its practitioners have received Ph.D.s in agricultural economics rather than economics; relatively few agricultural economists are active in the American Economics Association; and very few agricultural economists, other than a handful of development economists, have been widely known in the basic discipline.

Rural sociology has had a considerably different history. Its institutional roots were less immediately applied (in the sense of generating information to be of direct use to specific clientele groups). Rural sociology was very closely integrated into the larger discipline until the 1930s, when the rural sociology section of the American Sociological Society broke away in 1937 to form the Rural Sociological Society. Even so, rural sociology has retained relatively close ties to sociology. Several prominent rural sociologists have served as presidents of the American Sociological Association. Often, as noted earlier, rural sociologists are members of departments of sociology. Perhaps one-half or more of contemporary rural sociologists received their Ph.D.s in sociology (rather than rural sociology). Probably two-thirds or more of land-grant rural sociologists belong to the American Sociological Association. Many rural sociologists publish routinely in "general" sociological journals and participate in national or regional sociological associations.

DISCIPLINARY, SUBJECT-MATTER, AND PROBLEM-SOLVING RESEARCH IN AGRICULTURAL ECONOMICS AND RURAL SOCIOLOGY

Before proceeding to a discussion of the contributions of the major rural social sciences to solving agriculture- and rural-related problems, it is useful to discuss briefly the nature of research in the two major rural social sciences. It is most convenient to begin with subject-matter research foci, since these foci have a major influence on the basic research questions that are emphasized and the types of problem-solving activity that are typically undertaken.

Agricultural economics' major subject-matter areas are: (1) farm management/production economics, (2) demand (or price or commodity) analysis, (3) marketing (other than demand-price-commodity analysis), (4) resource economics, (5) domestic rural-community development, (6) international development, (7) agricultural finance, (8) policy, and (9) farm and agribusiness labor economics (though this last area is small relative to the preceding eight). The major subject-matter areas in rural sociology are: (1) sociology of agriculture, (2) sociology of natural resources, (3) domestic rural-community development, (4) international development, (5) demography and population studies, (6) youth, careers, and rural labor markets, and (7) family and rural household studies. These two lists suggest a striking degree of overlap in the subject-matter foci of agricultural economics and rural sociology. Indeed, given this overlap, it is, in a sense, surprising that there has not been more interdisciplinary problem-solving research involving agricultural economists and rural sociologists who are interested in comparable subject-matter areas. This issue will be addressed below.

There is a clear division of labor between agricultural economics and rural sociology that is belied by the apparent similarity in subject-matter foci; agricultural economists have placed greater emphasis on agriculture and farming, and rural sociologists have placed greater emphasis on rural communities and rural development. This historic division of labor probably has declined significantly recently as a result of a rather substantial shift of rural sociology toward greater emphasis on the sociology of agriculture over the past decade (Buttel et al. 1990). Nonetheless, this division of labor largely remains intact and, in particular, continues to have a major impact on the disciplinary and problem-solving research done by agricultural economists and rural sociologists.

Disciplinary research in agricultural economics and rural sociology is quite disparate. It would appear that the predominant thrust of disciplinary research in agricultural economics is methodological in nature—that is, the incorporation of new analytic, mathematical, and computational tools from the larger discipline of economics. This is, in large part, due to the close identity of theory and method in economics in the mathematical-quantitative realm. Disciplinary research in rural sociology is, on the other hand, largely twofold, reflecting the lack of consonance between theoretical and methodological advances in the larger discipline of sociology. The theory and methodology communities in sociology are largely insulated from one another, and this isolation is to some degree reflected in rural sociology (though, in my view, far less so in rural sociology than elsewhere in sociology). Nonetheless, disciplinary research in rural sociology tends to consist of either: (1) exploration of theoretical notions from sociology or a kindred basic social science, or (2) adaptation of a quantitative-methodological innovation from sociology or elsewhere. These two categories seldom overlap substantially.

Problem-solving research activities in agricultural economics and rural sociology have tended to reflect the historic division of labor between the two disciplines and, perhaps more so, some of the ideological and institutional concomitants of this division of labor. There is a continuing tendency for problem-solving research in agricultural economics to be directed primarily to the needs of agricultural clienteles: major farm groups (e.g., commodity organizations), agribusinesses, and powerful farm policy-making groups. Rural sociology's problem-solving research has continued to be more directed to rural community-oriented clienteles. There is also a political-ideological dimension to this division of labor. Those attracted to agricultural economics have tended to be more conservative than those pursuing a career in rural sociology. Accordingly, problem-solving research in agricultural economics tends to be more oriented to the information needs of relatively powerful and privileged groups than that of rural sociology.[4] Put somewhat differently, the historic culture of rural sociology has been to place high priority on doing research relevant to the needs of underprivileged constituencies. The division of labor between agricultural economics and rural sociology has also been sustained for institutional reasons. SAES and extension administrators have tended to see agricultural economists as "agriculture people" and rural sociologists as "rural community development people." This has particularly been the case in extension. It has only been a few years since there have been rural sociology extension staff whose principal responsibility has been agricultural constituents. Whether this division of labor should be sustained or broken down is a matter to be discussed later in this chapter.

CONTRIBUTIONS OF THE RURAL SOCIAL SCIENCES TO PROBLEM SOLVING

It is quite difficult to summarize briefly and adequately the contributions of the two major rural social sciences to agriculture- and rural-related problem solving. There is simply too great a diversity among SAES rural social scientists, the clientele they serve, and the research they conduct to permit a convenient, exhaustive summary. What follows is an illustrative overview of the types of problem-solving research conducted by rural social scientists, organized roughly in terms of the institutional context of the research and information transfer:

The first category of problem-solving research is that principally conducted for *transfer within extension channels to traditional extension clientele*. This category includes research done in preparation for outlook conferences, farm management research conducted to be transferred by extension agents to farmers, marketing and production economics research to be transferred to commodity groups and agribusinesses, public policy research and education, rural community needs assessment, surveys among farm and rural residents, and research done in association with SAES "commodity teams."

The second category of problem-solving research is that intended to be *transferred directly to private groups and agribusinesses*. It should be noted that the boundary between this and the first category is fluid and sometimes problematic. That is, it has been the historic role of extension to transfer information to clientele groups—in general without remuneration to the researcher over and above base salary. Nonetheless, there has probably been a growing trend for rural social scientists (especially agricultural economists, as well as sociologists who do communication research) to aim their work directly to one or another private group through a research contract or consulting arrangement. This trend is likely accounted for by the increasingly national and multinational character of many agribusinesses and the growing importance of proprietary information. There is nothing inherently wrong with doing research of this type, but problems do inevitably arise when the social scientist doing the research has an extension appointment which involves a commitment to transfer public-domain information free of charge to clientele groups.

The third category of problem-solving research is that conducted *on behalf of "public interest groups."* The impetus for such research often is the claims or arguments made by public interest groups, typically in opposition to the interests and claims made by more powerful or dominant groups. Generally, unlike the second category of research discussed above, SAES social scientists do not receive either remuneration or significant funding for problem-solving research directed to the needs and interests of public interest groups. It is probably the case, though, that more of this type of research is being moved within the rubric of extension (i.e., the first category) as many extension establishments have come to embrace issues and groups (e.g., environmental concerns, organic or low-input farming) that historically were ignored by extension staff.

The fourth category consists of policy research done primarily for *federal, state, and local policy makers*, the results of which are typically transferred outside of extension channels. This type of problem-solving research has ebbed and flowed over the years. It is probably fair to say that this type of research has tended to be in greatest demand during periods of crisis—for example, the "Great Depression" and the current era of farm financial stress, federal fiscal crisis, and economic uncertainty. The heyday of such research arguably was that of the "Great Depression" when large teams of agricultural economists and rural sociologists moved to the U.S. Department of Agriculture and played a pivotal, though temporary role in New Deal policy making. The demise of the Farm Security Administration and Bureau of Agricultural Economics in the immediate post-New-Deal period should remind us that there is a certain political instability in this style of problem-solving research.

Policy research directed to public decision makers declined in demand and importance from the 1940s to the mid–1970s. Much of the policy research done in agricultural economics, for example, came to be commodity-oriented policy work, directed to private constituent groups. Policy research has, however, experienced something of a renaissance over the past decade due to the rise of public interest groups concerned with agricultural issues, the farm crisis, fiscal crisis, and so on. Nonetheless, many agricultural- and rural-related institutions—commodity programs, soil conservation programs, agricultural districts, and so on—have their origins in the policy/institutional-design research of rural social scientists.

The fifth category of problem-solving research is that conducted *within SAES biological or physical science "teams."* This category, to be sure, clearly overlaps with other categories (e.g., commodity teams, multidisciplinary international development research). Nonetheless, this can be considered a distinctive category of problem-solving research in that it is a relatively new focus of SAES research and can be distinguished from traditional "commodity team" research in its closer partnership among persons from several disciplines and in its stronger interdisciplinary character. This type of problem-solving research has increased in prevalence because of the growing recognition by SAES administrators and nonsocial scientists of the importance of the socioeconomic context of technological adoption and change. Research of this sort has also increased due to expansion of interest inside and outside of the land-grant system in ex ante socioeconomic impact assessment of new agricultural technologies. Useful examples of research in this category are the multidisciplinary cooperation among social, biological, and physical scientists at Washington State University in designing solutions to soil erosion problems and the collaboration between agricultural economists and animal scientists at Cornell University in projecting the socioeconomic impacts of bovine and porcine growth hormone products.

The final category of problem-solving research—*international development research*—also overlaps with previous categories (especially multidisciplinary team research and research directed at public decision makers). This category, however, deserves special mention because of its unique institutional character (in particular, its dual connections with public and private development agencies and with recipient country governments and groups).

International development research is also a problematic area of work. On one hand, it can probably be said that the land-grant universities have tended over the past decade to diminish their commitment to international development work, save for keen interest when large contracts can be signed with the U.S. Agency for International Development (USAID) for one-shot technical assistance projects. As SAES and land-grant funding has tightened, land-grant officials have had an understandable tendency to pare international development program staffing and to bolster staffing in areas that will help them appeal to state legislators and federal and industrial funding sources. Also, it has long been recognized that because of the nature of international development research—long periods of time away from campus, long gestation times in generating data, and so on—young social scientists working in this area often have difficulty in career advancement. On the other hand, there are many people who, with considerable justification, say that the land-grant system has an obligation to the rest of the world to put greater effort into international development work. The African development crisis has begun to recrystallize interest in resurrecting the land-grant commitment to development work (i.e., in terms of major staff commitments, rather than merely pursuit of large USAID grants).

THE STATE OF THE RURAL SOCIAL SCIENCES AS DISCIPLINES

Up to this point my comments have been almost entirely devoted to agricultural economics and rural sociology, the two major social science disciplines in colleges of agriculture. I will now explore the strengths and limitations of the rural social sciences as disciplines, and in so doing will examine the two major social science disciplines as well as several other disciplines. These other disciplines tend to be largely absent from colleges of agriculture and SAESs. But, to anticipate one of the points that I will make in my concluding remarks, land-grant universities should consider renewing their land-grant commitment as *universities*, not merely as colleges of agriculture and home economics. Thus, the social science disciplines other than agricultural economics and rural sociology represented on land-grant university campuses should be seen as potential contributors to the land-grant mission.

AGRICULTURAL ECONOMICS

As noted earlier, agricultural economics developed historically as farm management economics. Further, as American agriculture became increasingly specialized and as marketing and policy became recognized as being crucial to profitable production, agricultural economics rapidly became dominated by commercial agriculture-oriented personnel whose principal roles generally involved serving major commodity groups. Two decades ago, the majority of agricultural economists functioned within this framework, while perhaps up to 40 percent of SAES agricultural economists today are principally concerned with commercial agriculture and orient their work substantially toward commodity groups.

As noted earlier, agricultural economics remains very "agricultural," at least relative to rural sociology. But since the institutionalization of agricultural economics, a substantial number of other subject-matter areas—several of which are nonagricultural—have been added so that agricultural economics today can often be referred to as applied economics rather than agricultural economics. This has, by and large, been a very positive development, since it has militated against excessive specialization and has encouraged some cross-fertilization across subject-matter areas. It is almost certain, though, that the matter of whether there should be further diversification of agricultural economics programs will be a crucial issue for the future. Many observers argue that agricultural commodity specialists are at the front line in generation and transfer of knowledge to the land-grant system's important clientele group(s)—farmers—and that it would be unwise to dilute this strength. Others suggest that the nonmetropolitan economy has exhibited a progressive decline in the role of agriculture and that land-grant applied economics efforts should shift accordingly in response to the needs of new constituent groups. It should be recognized, though, that the very nature of this debate is a reflection of specialization of agricultural economics; it could be argued that the resolution of this apparent problem would be to train and hire staff who have expertise in two or more subject-matter areas so that zero-sum tradeoffs would not need to be made.

Agricultural economics has long been highly applied. Busch and Lacy (1983), in their study of research problem choices of land-grant scientists, found agricultural economics to be one of the most applied disciplines in the SAES system—substantially more so, for example, than rural sociology. Yet it is widely assumed that agricultural economics has become increasingly disciplinary (see, for example, Schuh 1986). There is an element of truth in both notions. As noted earlier, the disciplinary nature of agricultural economics has been largely manifest in its methodology, so that the character of published research in the field, particularly that which receives discipline-wide awards, has increasingly taken the form of sophisticated mathematics and analytical procedures, often with "policy implications" tacked on in conclusion. This portrait of the disciplinary aspect of agricultural economics should not be exaggerated. Agricultural economics remains a basically applied field, and most research remains oriented to real-world problems and issues. Put somewhat differently, while the vast bulk of agricultural economics research remains subject-matter or problem-solving in nature, the specific issues explored, the methods, and perspectives are often discipline-driven; the "new" or "contributory" aspect of a published article—what, in fact, makes it publishable—is increasingly not its policy implications, but rather its methodology.

This dual cast of applied basic research in agricultural economics is a two-edged sword. On one hand, this trend has had several positive consequences. Improved training in theoretical economics has put agricultural economics on a sounder empirical basis, making published research more precise and analytically stronger than was the case three or four decades earlier. This improved training and the disciplinary research that it has afforded have enabled agricultural economics to begin to mitigate one of its most important limitations—its historical overemphasis on microeconomics and neglect of macroeconomics. Indeed, agricultural economics has long been criticized for deemphasizing macroeconomics, and the nature of the contemporary agricultural economy, in which macroeconomic phenomena such as interest rates and exchange rates have been pivotal, has dramatized the importance of a macroeconomic knowledge base. To the degree that there has recently been more attention to the macroeconomics of agriculture, it is largely an outgrowth of the tendency toward more thorough training in general economic theory as well as in the economic developments of the 1970s and 1980s. It has also likely been a reflection of the trend for recent cohorts of agricultural economists to come from nonfarm backgrounds. Finally, new tools in econometrics have enabled agricultural economics researchers to make progress in quantifying, and hence rendering more precise, phenomena that formerly were not quantifiable (e.g., "endogenous policy behavior").

On the other hand, there have been some significant problems with the strong trend toward disciplinary research in agricultural economics. One, as stressed by Schuh (1986), is an increased tendency for disciplinary-oriented researchers to be primarily interested in communicating with each other, rather than with constituent groups. Intradisciplinary communication is, of course, not bad in and of itself. It becomes problematic only when it takes on a life of its own, creates increased barriers to transfer of information outside of the university, and lacks meaningful ties to subject-matter and problem-solving research.

Indeed, the major threat of an increased emphasis on disciplinary research in agricultural economics is that it will lead to focusing on trivial problems that readily lend themselves to quantification. Along with the trend toward disciplinary research in agricultural economics, there has developed a belief that, ceteris paribus, something that is quantified is inherently superior to something that is not. Unfortunately, not all important questions (from the vantage point of national policy and impacts on the dynamics of the agricultural industry and rural social structure, as well as constituent needs) can be easily quantified or involve data of sufficient quality so that methods in disciplinary favor clearly apply. Moreover, disciplinary econometric research has become increasingly removed from the cognitive plane at which most land-grant constituents operate, further increasing the threat of disciplinary research becoming irrelevant to problem solving. As Schuh (1986) has lamented, these tendencies are currently being reinforced by new incentive systems in land-grant universities. These incentive systems, which are largely driven by inter-university competition for prestige and funding and the increasingly thorough disciplinary training of new Ph.D.s, encourage young staff to do rigorous scientific analyses, sometimes of relatively trivial problems, and to publish as much of this material as possible in disciplinary journals. There currently is something of a generational conflict over this incentive system. Older cohorts of agricultural economists tend more than their younger colleagues to favor a style of research in which, first, problems are selected for their importance (on the basis of constituent needs or interests, national relevance, etc.), and then the methods are chosen in terms of the dictates of the problem at hand. Younger agricultural economists, though still a clear minority, tend to be the most likely to begin from an economic theory or method and to select problems in terms of their suitability for inquiry with preferred theoretical or methodological approach.

A further concomitant of the increased emphasis on econometrically oriented disciplinary research has been the virtual disappearance of "institutional economics." Institutional economics has been almost totally eschewed by recent cohorts of agricultural economics Ph.D.s for disciplinary and career reasons. Virtually all contemporary practitioners of institutional economics are approaching retirement. Save for Michigan State University, the University of Wisconsin, and, to a lesser extent, Cornell University, institutional economics hardly exists in the late 1980s.

The disappearance of institutional economics also has pluses and minuses. It has arguably decreased the prevalence of unsupported assertions passing as research. Yet the strength of institutional economics was its ability to focus on important questions and to deal with institutional realms—politics, power, social class, ideology, values, and so on—other than that of the market economy. Institutional economics was also more at home with macro phenomena (though generally not the issues surrounding fiscal and monetary policy and interest and exchange rates of major concern to macroeconomics) than was disciplinary neoclassical agricultural economics of a decade ago.

It should also be noted that the trend toward highly quantitative, disciplinary neoclassical agricultural economics is occurring at a time in which data availability is declining. Federal and other pubic data series are being truncated, if not terminated, due to fiscal problems. Also, with fewer farmers and the increased frequency with which they are surveyed, it is becoming more and more difficult to acquire primary data sufficient for advanced econometric techniques.

Finally, agricultural economics, like the other rural social sciences that have been institutionalized within the land-grant system, tends to be quite parochial in the sense of lacking a comparative perspective on the other advanced industrial countries. The parochial character of the rural social sciences largely derives from the tendency for SAES administrators to steer as much of the research they support as possible to issues that pertain directly to their states. As a result, only a handful of agricultural economists have a strong base of knowledge on the farm and food economies of other advanced societies. Many opportunities for problem solving and institutional design based on the experience of other countries have no doubt been eschewed.

RURAL SOCIOLOGY

In contrast to agricultural economics, rural sociology has not exhibited a demonstrable trend toward more disciplinary research over the past decade or so. As noted earlier, rural sociology has never been so insulated from its parent discipline as has agricultural economics. Also, rural sociology research staff have not had the close, intimate, longstanding relationships with client groups that have characterized agricultural economics for some time.

The principal common trend affecting agricultural economics and rural sociology has been the tightening of standards for scholarly advancement and the increased incentive to publish many papers. This multiplication of published papers in rural sociology tends to have the effect of fractionalizing knowledge and increasing the separation between theoretical reasoning and empirical data.

Despite this common trend, rural sociology as a discipline is undergoing changes that are substantially different from those of agricultural economics. Perhaps the most important is that rural sociology is currently in the process of being transformed from a peripheral to a more central research program in SAESs. For decades rural sociology was, to put it frankly, merely tolerated in SAESs. Rural sociology programs were maintained for teaching purposes and for their contributions to extension-oriented activities such as rural, community, and youth development. Perhaps with hesitation, SAES administrators have come to see the social sciences, especially rural sociology, as being crucial to many issues faced by the land-grant system.

Rural sociologists and their SAES administrators are, however, slowly feeling their way through this unexpected new partnership. Given the historic marginality of rural sociology in the SAES research enterprise, rural sociologists have not always been well prepared for their new role. Rural sociologists historically had often been critical of prevailing institutional arrangements, and it has sometimes been problematic to make the transition from critic on the periphery to policy researchers at the center. There is probably fault on both sides. To affect public policy, the rural sociological social-critic impulse must sometimes be tempered. At the same time, land-grant administrators probably tend to expect results too soon, too easily, too mechanically, and too much on their own terms.

The increased centrality of rural sociology in the land-grant system is largely the fortuitous consequence of a major transition in the discipline in the mid- to late 1970s: the establishment of the sociology of agriculture as a largely new subject-matter area. This is not to say that rural sociology lacked a research tradition in agriculture before that time. From the 1910s to the 1940s, rural sociologists had actively researched agriculture and farm organization from the vantage point of rural life and community structure. During the 1950s and 1960s rural sociological research was heavily focused on the diffusion of innovations in agriculture. Nonetheless, the emergent sociology of agriculture tradition in the 1970s can be seen as a new subject-matter area in that its emphasis was on the antecedents and consequences of farm structural change as phenomena in their own right. Its emphasis was also largely macrostructural—particularly by contrast with the diffusion of innovations tradition. The sociology of agriculture, it should be emphasized, emerged autonomously within the discipline, unprompted by SAES administrators.

The rise of the sociology of agriculture over the past 10 to 12 years is also significant in its having mirrored the lack of articulation between theoretical and methodological advances in sociology and rural sociology. As the sociology of agriculture was being codified in the mid–1970s, rural sociology, much like the larger discipline, was exhibiting a strong trend to more sophisticated methodological procedures, which tended to be applied to microsociological or demographic research issues. The "sociology of agriculture movement" was in many respects a critique of the priorities, methods, and theories that characterized rural sociology over the preceding decades (see, for example, Newby 1980). Persons actively involved in the early years of research in the sociology of agriculture frequently argued, for example, that: (1) rural sociology had overemphasized microsociological approaches to agriculture and underemphasized macrosociological or structural perspectives, (2) rural sociology was too dominated by functionalist approaches and had given too little attention to neo-Marxist theories, (3) rural sociology had tended to be biased toward researching questions that lent themselves to quantitative precision and had eschewed historical, documentary, and qualitative research methods, and (4) rural sociology had failed to take advantage of major theoretical breakthroughs in the larger discipline (see, for example, Goss 1979; Newby 1978). Accordingly, the bulk of the literature in the sociology of agriculture is structural (rather than microsociological) in orientation, and much of it is based on neo-Marxist or parallel neo-Weberian theories and on nonquantitative methodologies.[5] This literature also is arguably more theoretically sophisticated and more rooted in general sociological theory than that in rural-community development, demography and population studies, and so on.

The sociology of agriculture thus exhibits a paradox. On one hand, its general characteristics—its tendencies to structural, political economy, nonquantitative, and disciplinary theoretical approaches—would seem to make it less relevant to—perhaps even an alien presence in—colleges of agriculture. Yet, on the other hand, the sociology of agriculture is, in substantial measure, the leading edge of a more useful rural sociology in colleges of agriculture—a rural sociology that can grapple effectively with the complex economic, political, and ideological forces that now perplex and concern land-grant administrators and other public officials.

The paradox can be stated somewhat differently, by comparison with the contemporary status of agricultural economics as a discipline. Rural sociology, as typified by the sociology of agriculture, is less strong than agricultural economics in terms of quantitative precision. This is in large part due to the fact that in economics there is a close unity of theory and method due to their common rooting in advanced mathematics,[6] while in sociology the theory community tends to emphasize conceptual innovations that are most suitable for historical and qualitative inquiry.[7] Theoretical innovations in sociology often take the form of developing notions for understanding the interrelations among institutions and the complex processes through which societies develop and change. Accordingly, rural sociology is stronger than agricultural economics in its ability to understand institutional interrelations and to place problems in larger context.

Many will be tempted to conclude on the basis of this comparison that either agricultural economics or rural sociology is the superior or more useful discipline in terms of agriculture- and rural-related problem solving. But I think a more persuasive assessment would be that agricultural economics and rural sociology are *complementary* disciplines; the strengths of the one are the weaknesses of the other. In particular, agricultural economics and rural sociology reflect the divergences of ideology and perspective that are so often manifest in major social policy issues in agriculture. Both disciplines, with their differing conceptual and methodological styles, are necessary for obtaining a broad perspective on policy issues within the land-grant system.

This assessment admittedly could be made far more confidently if there were a higher incidence of collaborative work between agricultural economists and rural sociologists. Historically, such collaboration has been rare, mainly because of conceptual, methodological, and ideological differences and of the lack of encouragement by land-grant administrators. Also, given the fact that agricultural economics staffs at land-grant universities tend to outnumber rural sociologists by 4:1 or more, many agricultural economists no doubt feel little incentive to acknowledge that their poor cousins even exist. Many rural sociologists would rather work alone than be outnumbered and overwhelmed by agricultural economists.

There are, however, encouraging indications of greater collaboration between agricultural economists and rural sociologists in problem-solving research on issues of mutual interest (e.g., the Washington State University collaborative research on soil erosion and conservation referred to earlier). SAES administrators probably should have insisted on greater collaboration in the past and should see it as indispensable today.

It was noted earlier that perhaps the biggest strain in agricultural economics today is a largely generational difference of perspective about whether methodological matters should drive the selection of research topics. The principal strains in rural sociology tend to be substantially different. One such strain, which is probably most manifest in the 40 percent or so of rural sociology programs that are attached to larger departments of sociology, is the degree to which these rural sociologists should be attentive to one or the other of their dual masters: SAES officials in colleges of agriculture or sociology chairs and deans in colleges of arts and sciences. In a sense, then, there has been a longstanding struggle over how "rural" a rural sociologist should be in order to make an appropriate contribution to the SAES which provides a partial salary. Accordingly, for many rural sociology programs housed in liberal arts sociology departments there are typically stresses and strains between the arts and sciences and SAES sociologists. Arts and sciences sociologists are typically most concerned with their national visibility in the discipline, feel that their rural sociology colleagues help very little in this regard, and tend to invoke higher publication and disciplinary standards for tenure and promotion than the rural sociologists or the SAES would like. Rural sociologists in these dual programs often struggle with their arts and sciences colleagues over whether rural sociology extension is an appropriate activity for a department of sociology.

The strains between arts and sciences and SAES sociologists are obviously fewer in universities where rural sociology has a separate department or a joint department with agricultural economics. However, at universities where rural sociology is located outside of an arts and sciences sociology department, the relations between the two groups of sociologists are generally poor. Often, these rural sociology departments must operate totally separate, self-contained programs (with the duplication of effort and lack of economies that this implies) because of the fact that they have no influence on the curricula of arts and sciences sociology departments.

As suggested earlier, rural sociology, while somewhat more cosmopolitan than agricultural economics in its closer ties to its parent discipline, tends to be equally parochial in its lack of a base of comparative knowledge. Again, this lack of a comparative perspective on social institutions and problem solving derives from the tendency for SAES-funded sociology research to be focused on problems directly related to a particular state.

Finally, it should be noted that unlike agricultural economics, which has decent-sized programs at virtually all land-grant universities, rural sociology programs are very unevenly distributed across the land-grant system. About 10 land-grant universities have no rural sociologists at all. Another 15 to 20 have one to three rural sociologists, which is too few to have anything beyond a bare-bones teaching, research, and extension program. Only about a dozen land-grant universities have rural sociology programs of sufficient size to offer the Ph.D. degree and to be a major presence in their SAESs. These larger, Ph.D.-granting rural sociology programs have five or more faculty. Whereas agricultural economics departments often have 40 or more faculty, rural sociology programs with more than 10 faculty are quite rare. The largest of rural sociology programs in U.S. land-grant universities have slightly more than a dozen faculty.

NONTRADITIONAL RURAL SOCIAL SCIENCES

Five basic social science disciplines devote substantial effort to agriculture and rural societies. They are anthropology, political science, history, philosophy and ethics, and geography. Of these five, only one, history, has an established scholarly agricultural journal.

ANTHROPOLOGY

Anthropology is the first of the nontraditional rural social sciences to be considered in this paper. Of the five nontraditional rural social sciences I will discuss, anthropology has the greatest presence in SAESs at the present time. While no SAESs, to the best of my knowledge, support rural or agricultural anthropology programs, there are currently several anthropologists appointed in SAES positions (generally in rural sociology, community development, human ecology, and home economics programs) across the country. Nonetheless, it is very uncommon for anthropologists appointed in SAES positions to have any connection with their disciplinary department in a college of arts and sciences.

Anthropology as a basic discipline is older than sociology, having emerged as a discipline focused on the study of nonindustrial societies. The traditional foci of anthropology have been archeology/physical anthropology (the study of prehistorical peoples) and social/cultural anthropology (the study of contemporary preindustrial societies and tribes). Thus, there has historically been a clear division of labor between anthropology and sociology, with the former focused on prehistorical and preindustrial societies and the latter on contemporary, modern societies. It should be noted, however, that this division of labor is somewhat arbitrary and that as early as the 1930s and 1940s that were some major anthropological studies of U.S. agriculture (e.g., Goldschmidt 1947). The past one or two decades have witnessed an especially rapid diminution of this disciplinary division of labor; contemporary anthropologists have begun to devote greater attention to modern industrial and developing societies while sociologists have done an increasing amount of research, occasionally on preindustrial societies, using historical methodologies (Chibnik 1987).

Anthropology has historically been the least quantitative of all the mainline social sciences. While, for example, most sociologists or rural sociologists will at least occasionally employ quantitative methods, contemporary anthropologists do so infrequently. The tendency toward nonquantitative research is a reflection of the importance of the study of prehistorical societies in anthropology. It is also a concomitant of anthropological theories that stress the importance of "deep" (and, hence, not directly measurable) cultural phenomena and of the unity of the institutional realms of society in the complex totality referred to as "culture." Anthropological methodology typically revolves around intensive fieldwork and very close familiarity with the thought and activities of the subjects of research. Anthropologists rarely rely primarily on survey or documentary data, since such approaches would not afford the in-depth understanding of society and culture that is stressed in the discipline.

Anthropology currently plays its major role in agricultural problem solving in the area of international development (see, for example, DeWalt 1986). Anthropologists' skills have proven to be quite valuable in fieldwork-intensive, international, agricultural, technical-assistance projects. Only a small amount of this anthropological research in international development projects is done in connection with the land-grant system, however. The vast bulk is undertaken through international development agencies such as USAID, the international agricultural research centers, and so on. There have, nonetheless, been a number of anthropologists who have been hired on land-grant-administered agricultural development projects over the past decade, though few of these anthropologists have permanent appointments in an SAES.

Domestic agricultural and rural development have only recently been a significant focus in anthropology. Save for a few pioneers such as Goldschmidt (1947) and Bennett (1982) (all of whom, to my knowledge, had no direct connection with the land-grant system), very few anthropologists did work of this sort prior to the mid–1970s. The diversification of anthropology into domestic (and international) agriculture is probably, at least in part, a reflection of the tight job market in traditional academic anthropology and of the need to make anthropology more relevant to applied or problem-solving concerns. There is now a flourishing community of several dozen scholars who do agriculturally-oriented research under the rubric of the Anthropological Study Group on Agrarian Systems (which in 1986 changed its name to the Culture and Agriculture Group). Many of these anthropologists have close relationships with rural sociologists who share common interests. A good many are both members of the Rural Sociological Society and active participants in the Society's annual meetings and other activities. Indeed, there are strong commonalities between the work done by members of the Anthropology Study Group on Agrarian Systems and that done by many who work in the sociology of agriculture.

It is my observation that while the tightness of the anthropology job market has led to more attention to agriculture and other applied matters, the legitimacy of applied anthropology in the American Anthropological Association is probably no greater—and perhaps may be less—than it was a decade or two ago. That is, as the funding for anthropological fieldwork abroad through traditional sources such as the National Science Foundation has become tighter, the response of the major departments of anthropology to scarce resources has been to "purify" the discipline and make it more scholastic. This will mean that the encouraging growth of applied anthropology in areas such as international development and domestic agriculture will depend on the ability of these anthropologists to secure positions in development agencies, land-grant universities, and other nontraditional employing organizations. The reinforcement of the scholastic nature of anthropology may also make it more precarious for persons interested in applied anthropology to receive a Ph.D. from a major anthropology graduate program (though economic anthropology, the specialty area of anthropology most germane to agricultural problem solving, continues to be a recognized and viable component of the larger discipline).

Anthropology has several strengths in relation to rural- and agriculture-related problem solving. One is its more comprehensive understanding of culture and human values than is typically the case in rural sociology and the other rural social sciences. Another is the tradition in anthropology for detailed, comprehensive, multiple-method fieldwork, which provides a more thorough understanding of particular cases or situations than is usually afforded by practitioners of other social science disciplines. The work of anthropologists is often nicely complementary to that of rural sociologists, since they are often interested in a very similar phenomena but use different theories and methods. Anthropology's weaknesses are its tendency toward functionalist theorizing[8] and to downplaying phenomena such as social power and conflict. Anthropology has, in particular, been ineffective in conceptualizing the political structures and politics of advanced industrial countries. Anthropologists, because of their tendency to use nonquantitative methods, sometimes find their work being rejected by "harder" scientists, including rural sociologists and agricultural economists.

POLITICAL SCIENCE

To the best of my knowledge, there are only one or two persons currently trained as political scientists who have SAES appointments. This is, in a sense, surprising, since so many of the problems faced by SAESs and agricultural researchers today are irreducibly political in nature (see, for example, Hadwiger 1982; Browne 1987). Nonetheless, political science, much like anthropology, has almost totally remained an arts and sciences discipline even though every land-grant university has numerous political scientists among its faculty.

The absence of political scientists from SAES programs has several explanations. First, agricultural politics is a very minor area of political science, and the number of political scientists who specialize in this area is probably no more than a couple of dozen. Thus, most land-grant universities lack a political scientist whose major area of work is agricultural politics or policy. Second, given the lack of prominence of agricultural politics within the discipline, its status as an area of work and as a focus for graduate training in political science is even more precarious. Third, SAES officials probably have, until recently, been hesitant to acknowledge the political aspect of their programs by supporting the work of political scientists.

Despite the low stature of agricultural politics within the discipline and SAESs, agricultural politics is of immense relevance to rural- and agriculture-related problem solving. Given my earlier comments, no further elaboration is necessary on this point. Nonetheless, there are several political scientists including D. Hadwiger, R. Talbot, R. Hopkins, D. Puchala, W. Browne, and K. Dahlberg, who have done sufficiently sound work on agricultural and international development politics that they have been able to secure the respect of their political science colleagues and to make significant contributions to ongoing policy debates relating to agriculture and rural America.

One of the unfortunate consequences of the dominant position of agricultural economics in SAESs is that the area of agricultural policy is de facto considered to be the almost exclusive province of this discipline. Accordingly, the agricultural policy work done in the land-grant system tends toward being technical exercises which proffer policy suggestions that should be adopted by rational policy makers if there were not a highly politicized overlay of competing interests and a political structure that decisively limits policy options. But there is, like it or not, a politics of agriculture that must be understood and taken into account in agricultural policy analysis. Political scientists are in a unique position to contribute to agricultural and rural policy analysis—and hence to contribute to problem solving. Other social science disciplines have important insights to offer as well. Unfortunately, the land-grant system has elected to restrict agricultural policy research to only one discipline, and the United States and the land-grant system are poorer for it.

One of the key strengths of political science in complementing the other rural social sciences is that this discipline is substantially more oriented to comparative knowledge and insights than are the major rural social sciences. Comparative politics is one of the major areas of political science and is significantly more prominent in this discipline than are comparative sociology or comparative economics in theirs.

Twenty years ago political science was largely a nonquantitative discipline—far less quantitative than sociology, for example. Since that time political science has become far more quantitative, and today it is equal to or greater than sociology in the extent to which quantitative methods are used in papers in major disciplinary journals. Agricultural politics, however, has largely remained a nonquantitative specialty area of political science. It is unclear whether this is largely due to the subject matter or to the training that agricultural politics specialists have received.

HISTORY

There are virtually no historians appointed in SAESs, despite the fact that agricultural history is of palpable relevance to land-grant institutions and the fact that agricultural history has been in existence for many decades. For example, *Agricultural History*, the journal of the Agricultural History Society, has been published since the 1920s. This absence of agricultural history from SAES programs has likely been the case for two reasons. First, the institutionalization of the land-grant social sciences largely derived from the Country Life Commission and the agricultural extension movement of the first two decades of this century (see, for example, Danbom 1979), and there was no call for a major role for history in the SAESs, to the best of my knowledge.[9] Agricultural economics and rural sociology became established in the aftermath of the publication of the Commission report, while rural and agricultural history did not. Second, agricultural history, much like agricultural politics in political science, has tended not to be a high status area of work in the larger discipline of history. Today there are very few faculty in major, nationally respected departments of history who identify themselves as agricultural historians.[10] The bulk of contemporary agricultural historians are located in second- or third-tier universities (in terms of the reputed strength of graduate programs in history). Without the generosity of the University of California, Davis and the Economic Research Service of the U.S. Department of Agriculture, the Agricultural History Society would probably have a difficult existence. Nonetheless, because of the marginality of agricultural history in the discipline of history and in its major Ph.D.-granting departments, there are few agricultural historians in American universities, including but not limited to land-grant universities.

Agricultural history is arguably of less direct relevance to rural- and agriculture-related problem solving than the two other nontraditional disciplines discussed previously. Given the very subject matter of this discipline—especially the emphasis on historical precision and detail—historians will not often have the tools and background for solving problems of the here and now. Not only do historians have relatively little background in the specifics of contemporary agricultural problems and institutional structures, but the discipline of history tends to de-emphasize generalizing theories about the connections between historical data and larger patterns of social change. But agricultural and rural history can be said to be of demonstrable *indirect* significance in delineating the context of problem-solving research and public service in land-grant institutions. Students in colleges of agriculture today tend to receive virtually no background on the historical development of American agriculture and agricultural institutions, especially about the agricultural colleges at which they study. Land-grant administrators and scientists likewise tend to have a selective historical vision, largely confined to the positive contributions of their land-grant institution to agriculture in the state. Seldom, for example, have students, faculty, and administration become aware of the research by A. I. Marcus, R. S. Kirkendall, M. W. Rossiter, or D. B. Danbom on the conflictual and meager scientific character of the agricultural colleges and SAESs in the late nineteenth and early twentieth centuries. Seldom has the land-grant community been aware of the work of P. W. Gates on the subversion of the Homestead Act by rampant land speculation, the widespread tenancy and indebtedness that resulted, and the connections between the founding of the land-grant colleges and farm real estate speculation.

Our tendency in the land-grant system to ignore our history and to paint self-serving historical portraits innocent of actual historical data is, at a minimum, one of the alarming limitations of the land-grant undergraduate programs. The lack of a historical perspective on agriculture and agricultural research is part of a larger pattern of neglecting the liberal arts in undergraduate instruction in agriculture—a problem that only recently has begun to be addressed due to its having been prompted by catastrophic declines in college of agriculture enrollments across the country.[11]

A more historically informed land-grant milieu might also indirectly improve the scope and quality of problem-solving research in the SAESs. Historians are in a unique position to educate us all about the rapidity of change in the past as well as historical continuities that are not often recognized. For example, in the close aftermath of the centennial year of the Hatch Act it is striking that technological change and transfer have become highly politicized, much like the situation of the agricultural colleges at the time of the passage of the Hatch Act. The implicit role of historians—debunking extant historical mythology promulgated out of self interest along with placing the present in historical context—is very much needed in today's land-grant system. As technological development and transfer have become more politicized, uncertain, and subject to accountability to external groups, we seemingly alternate between celebration of imagined utopias of the past and congratulation of the ability to solve the problems of the present. Closer integration of agricultural history into the land-grant system would help us to place the present in context and to learn from the past.

PHILOSOPHY AND ETHICS

Philosophy is the epitome of the learned disciplines that the architects of the Morrill Act and the land-grant system hoped to overwhelm with practical science, pragmatism, and concern for the "common man." The vision behind the land-grant system was to create a more democratic system of higher education that would reduce the role of the aristocratic disciplines that dominated private universities during the mid-nineteenth century and to substitute practical curricula geared to the needs of the rank-and-file of rural people. While every land-grant university today has a philosophy department, the land-grant system has "succeeded" in steering the college of agriculture curriculum away from the humanities and in emphasizing matters scientific, technical, and pragmatic. We are now just realizing the costs of this narrowing of background and vision.

A decade ago there was probably not a single philosopher with any significant connection to a college of agriculture. This has changed to a small degree over the past several years, thanks largely to the role of the W. K. Kellogg Foundation in spearheading a national "Agriculture and the Liberal Arts" program[12] and to the RICOP "agricultural ethics project." Still there are probably a half dozen or fewer philosophers, broadly construed to include "ethicists" of various stripes, in colleges of agriculture today (Thompson 1984).

Unlike agricultural history or agricultural politics, there currently is no large subdisciplinary cadre in the area of "agricultural ethics" than can make an immediate contribution to the land-grant system and its problem-solving activities. Philosophy today, not unlike the situation in the mid-nineteenth century, remains a very scholastic discipline. Applied philosophy is generally not highly valued in the discipline. There are only a few substantive areas in which applied ethics is considered an appropriate disciplinary activity (e.g., biomedical and legal ethics), and agriculture is clearly not among them. With the partial exception of the University of Florida, graduate training in agricultural ethics does not exist.

Philosophy and applied ethics can make several contributions to the land-grant system and problem solving. By prompting agricultural scientists and research administrators to consider issues they face from an ethical standpoint, their vision may be broadened and the quality of their work improved. Students, faculty, and administrators could all benefit from acquaintance with the perspective of philosophy of science (particularly in terms of the critique of positivism and the limitations of positivist approaches to problem solving). It should be noted, however, that philosophy of science has been one of the most common areas of philosophical inquiry and has been available to college of agriculture undergraduates for decades, with little interest on the part of either land-grant students or faculty.

Agriculture is among the last of the major professions to welcome philosophers and ethicists into their fold. A good many schools of law, medicine, and business have staff philosophers or established linkages with ethicists. But even the more forward-looking professions with many years of experience with ethicists tend to look to philosophical input in a fairly mechanical way—one that may not be compatible with the work a philosopher would prefer to do. Professional schools, organizations, and other institutions want philosophical input so that practitioners can be given guidelines for avoiding "unethical" conduct (and so that the professional group can avoid embarrassing public scrutiny). This dichotomization of individual conduct into the ethical and unethical typically is alien to a disciplinary philosopher or ethicist who will often resist such a "cookbook" approach to matters ethical and moral.

The future of philosophy, ethics, and the other humanities in colleges of agriculture is quite unclear at this time. Through the Kellogg Foundation program, these humanities disciplines have a discernible, but tenuous footing in agriculture colleges. With the impending termination of Kellogg funding, the future of these efforts lies in the priorities of RICOP and in the response of colleges of agriculture to declining enrollments. It is probably sad but true that linkages between the humanities and agriculture are now stronger and more secure in the liberal arts colleges that have received Kellogg funding than in the land-grant institutions that have been funded. This is probably because of the absence of agricultural scientists and other professionals in liberal arts colleges and the greater latitude on the part of philosophers and ethicists to do their work on their own terms. But, unfortunately, the growth of agricultural ethics programs in liberal arts colleges will have little impact on agricultural practitioners and the research and decision making they undertake.

GEOGRAPHY

Many reject the very notion that geography is a discipline, strictly speaking. Geography is arguably more eclectic than economics, political science, sociology, anthropology, and history. In fact, geographers are often given to borrowing freely from the theoretical traditions of the other social sciences, particularly economics. Geography and its closely related fields of regional science and urban and regional planning can perhaps best be viewed as "interdisciplines."

Geography is a field of enormous diversity. Not only does its largest branch draw on several of the major social sciences and exhibit a wide range of specialty areas—regional geography, environmental geography, geography of natural hazards, geography of urbanization, and so on—but the discipline also contains a minority of physical geographers who draw just as eclectically on meteorology, geology, soil science, botany, and the like. Even in agricultural geography there is great heterogeneity. The diversity of agricultural geography can be gauged for example, by contrasting the work of Fuller (1984), Gregor (1982), and Vogeler (1982).[13]

Geography is of substantial relevance to the land-grant system. Clearly, its principal relevance would be in the area of rural development. Economic geography—especially the geography of industrial and employment location—could be highly complementary to the work of sociologists and economists who work in the rural development area. This field of geography is also a fairly large one, with most land-grant universities having one or more geographers whose work has relevance to rural development.

Agricultural geography is potentially even more directly germane to SAES programs. Research in the geography of agriculture could be highly complementary to agricultural economics and rural sociology research, especially since both of the mainline rural social sciences tend to give relatively little attention to spatial aspects of agricultural economics and social structures. Agricultural geography, however, is not a large specialty area in the discipline, and the typical land-grant university lacks a person with such expertise. Again, it would appear that the small size of the agricultural geography community is accounted for by the same reasons that have led to the modest scope of agricultural history. In particular, agricultural geography is not a high-status specialty area in the discipline, particularly by comparison with its higher status in most European countries.

THE AGRICULTURAL-RURAL RESEARCH AND INFORMATION DELIVERY SYSTEM

The agricultural-rural research and the agricultural-rural information delivery systems are currently at a crossroad, the outcome of which is quite unclear at this point. Most broadly speaking, the agricultural-rural research system finds itself cornered in the midst of a triangle of forces over which it has little leverage. These triple forces are as follows: (1) National-level institutions and organizations, primarily agribusiness firms and the executive branch of the federal government, want the land-grant system to undertake a nationally coordinated effort to pursue basic biological research, largely for generic application across the country. The results of this research into new opportunities for increased agricultural productivity are to be transferred to industry for their own benefit and to assist the U.S. effort to compete in high technology with other countries. (2) Public interest groups and other social justice and environmental critics of the land-grant system want the land-grant system to restrain the development of (actually or potentially) socially and environmentally disruptive technology and to put the needs of people above the imperative of efficiency. These groups prefer that efficiency and productivity in the traditional sense be downplayed as criteria for research problem choice and that new criteria—ecological sustainability, the needs of small and family farmers, human health and nutrition—be pursued with equal or greater vigor. (3) State-level groups and institutions, historically the major constituencies of the land-grant universities, want the land-grant system to continue to give highest priority to the needs of traditional state client groups and to be cautious about diverting land-grant resources to pursuing national agendas.

In some ways, the Cooperative Extension Service (CES), the bulwark of the land-grant system's information delivery system, faces a similar triangular configuration of forces and pressures. The federal government, particularly the Office of Management and Budget, wants the CES to serve national needs, rather than merely to coordinate a patchwork of state-oriented programs. Social justice and environmental critics of the land-grant system want to heighten the social and ecological sensitivity of CES staff and to induce the CES to expand its clientele in the direction of small farmers, organic farming, and so on. Established state-level client groups jealously guard their prerogatives against encroachment by national and social justice/environmental competitors.

In addition, the CES faces further problems—particularly its severe fiscal problems and the fact that the traditional county-agent-based extension system has begun to lose its relevance in the current milieu of agriculture. Ironically, at the same time that social justice and environmental critics of CES began to scrutinize its tendency to work most closely with large farmers, many of these large, technologically dynamic farmers were beginning to bypass the CES as their principal source of technical information. As farmers become increasingly well educated, many have technical backgrounds that rival those of county CES staff. These farmers have increasingly come to rely upon agribusiness sales representatives, private management consulting services, and direct contact with land-grant faculty as information sources. Thus, whereas the land-grant research system faces competing claims on its services and allegiance, the CES's problem is, in part, the ominous trend for some of its historically important client groups to go elsewhere for services.

These dilemmas facing the larger research and CES systems are currently being experienced unevenly across the rural social sciences. Agricultural economics, for example, has historically been, and continues to be, very closely tied to state client groups, mainly through the CES. Rural sociology, on the other hand, generally has close relationships with client groups only in its rural-community development extension and public service programs; rural-community development, however, does not have a large research base (i.e., it is heavily CES oriented) and is progressively being downplayed by the majority of land-grant universities. There is, as yet, only a small CES component in the sociology of agriculture, despite the fact that the research base in the sociology of agriculture has expanded by leaps and bounds over the past decade and is already quite substantial. Also, rural sociology, community development, the communication sciences, and perhaps other rural social sciences are among the land-grant departments that rely least on the CES for information transfer, which at times creates discomfort among extension administrators. In contrast to the SAES biological sciences, there is generally little pressure on the land-grant system from national-level institutions for the research services of the rural social sciences. Finally, the land-grant social sciences, especially rural sociology, are in some sense contributors to the pressures currently being exerted on the SAESs and CES by public interest groups (e.g., by conducting ex ante socioeconomic impact assessments of new agricultural technologies that are drawn upon as ammunition by public interest groups). Not surprisingly, many land-grant administrators are less than happy when their own staff help add to these pressures and especially when they represent an internal source of opposition to the traditional priorities of the research and extension systems.

I would, admittedly somewhat unconfidently, offer some observations on why the SAES social sciences tend to accomplish less than they could. First, my experience at several land-grant universities suggests that SAES administrators, who are primarily recruited from the biological and physical sciences, tend to not understand the social sciences very well and tend to not have a broad sense of the range of contributions that the social sciences can make. Each SAES should ideally have at least one social scientist among its research directors in order to increase the likelihood that the rural social sciences will be used most effectively. Second, the rural social sciences appear to be underused in terms of collaborative research with scientists from the nonsocial science disciplines. SAES administrators should create incentives to encourage such collaborative research, the specific composition of which would depend on the strengths of a particular SAES' social science staff.

Third, it is my observation that SAES administrators tend to have major limitations in evaluating the performance of the rural social sciences. Other than generating grants and publishing papers, the principal criterion employed in evaluating the rural social sciences tends to be the effectiveness of the linkage between research and extension. The extent of research-CES linkages is not an irrelevant criterion, but perhaps a more important gauge would be the linkages between disciplinary, subject-matter, and problem-solving research. For large social science departments, such as agricultural economics, this standard should be applied to a department as a whole. For smaller social science programs, as rural sociology tends to be, the criterion would need to be applied with reference to the SAES social science departments as a whole.

Fourth, I am persuaded by the notion that many SAES and land-grant administrators have yet to grapple on an intellectual basis with the social forces that affect their programs. Many still seem to hold hope that the increasingly politicized milieu of agricultural research of the past decade will disappear. Many yet view the symbols and personalities of the past two decades—Rachel Carson, the Pound Report, Jim Hightower, Jeremy Rifkin, organic farming—as aberrations that are destined to disappear sometime soon. It is my guess, however, that the research politics of the past two decades is here to stay. To the degree that this is the case, the rural social sciences should be integral to problem solving and institutional restructuring.

Fifth, it is surprising how little the land-grant social sciences have been employed to do research on the land-grant system. Social scientists have many skills that could be allocated effectively to researching the organization and effectiveness of research and the extension service. To date very little of this type of social science research has been done. These efforts have been largely confined to IR–6 (which has coordinated the "returns to research" activities of agricultural economists), to a small cadre of rural sociologists who work in the area of the sociology of agricultural research, and to occasional social science research in international technical assistance projects. Social science research resources should be drawn on far more aggressively in assisting in the design and evaluation of agricultural research and information delivery systems.

These preceding observations largely apply to the CES and the larger information delivery system as well. In addition, it can probably be said that CES organizations have been even less given to internal critiques and less aware of the broader social forces affecting the land-grant system than have their SAES colleagues. The CES largely functions within a state-bounded milieu, so that many extension administrators do not experience the national and international forces affecting the land-grant system in the course of their daily work.

Arguably because of the historic lack of flexibility in the CES over the past two decades, it now finds itself in a crisis. Ongoing reactions to the crisis may lead to some long overdue changes such as the expanding and diversifying CES clientele, a major revamping of the county-agent-based information delivery system, and encouraging extension faculty to conduct applied research. But there is also some threat of overreacting; for example, if the CES is transformed into a pseudo social service agency, it is not likely that it will do a high quality job or receive political recognition for its efforts. The CES stands in need of a major restructuring. But the changes that are made should be carefully selected, preferably on the basis of research which considers CES's two major roles: transferring information to client groups and building political support for the land-grant university.[14]

Two other principles should be considered in redesigning the land-grant social science research and information transfer system (as well as the research and information delivery system as a whole). First, as sketched several times in the foregoing, the land-grant system currently finds itself at the center of a number of socioeconomic forces and interests. The long-term legitimacy of the land-grant system will likely lie in assuming a posture of institutional neutrality. The land-grant system must be perceived as being *neither captured by nor hostile to any of its clientele groups:* big farmers or small farmers, "conventional" or "organic" farmers, state-level or multinational agribusinesses, public interest groups and private interests, and so on.

Second, colleges of agriculture and home economics should bear in mind that they are only part—rather than the entirety—of land-grant universities. That is, universities as a whole, rather than merely colleges of agriculture and home economics, have been assigned the land-grant mission. This means, on one hand, that agriculture and home economics colleges have no necessary monopoly on agricultural and rural matters, and on the other, that land-grant administrators often have untapped resources (including but not limited to the "nontraditional rural social sciences") elsewhere in the university upon which to draw.

Most faculty in contemporary land-grant universities—in agriculture and home economics as well as the liberal arts and professional colleges—understand the nature of the land-grant university only very little. Liberal arts and professional college faculty rarely see themselves as part of a land-grant university and its mission. Agriculture and home economics faculty see agricultural and rural matters as their exclusive province and often resent it when others claim expertise or interest in these areas. As my colleague Lawrence Busch has suggested, one of the healthiest things a land-grant university could do would be to reaffirm publicly its land-grant commitment as a university as a whole. Such a reaffirmation would not only have important public relations benefits, but may over time expand the resources that agriculture and home economics staff can call upon in problem-solving research.

SOME CONCLUDING COMMENTS ON THE STATUS AND FUTURE ROLES OF THE RURAL SOCIAL SCIENCES

In my view, the rural social sciences have made major strides over the past decade. Yet there remain several significant limitations to the social science research effort in colleges of agriculture and home economics. These problems cannot be attributed solely to either the disciplines or land-grant university administrations; each bears some responsibility, and each must be part of the solution.

From my perspective, the major limitations of the rural social science effort are as follows. First, there is a far too rigid division of labor among the rural social science programs in SAESs. For example, agricultural policy is generally the exclusive province of agricultural economists, even though several other disciplines could make major contributions to agricultural policy analysis. At the same time, agricultural economics has tended to move out of rural-community development, and on many campuses this work is largely relegated to rural sociology. With the exception of a handful of agricultural economists, anthropologists, and geographers (mainly from Canadian universities), rural sociologists tend to be the only rural social scientists interested in devoting major effort to research on farm structural change. By the same token, one of the more encouraging developments in the rural social sciences is that a number of disciplines are beginning to focus on the causes and consequences of technological change in agriculture. The increasingly multidisciplinary character of research on technology change should be a blueprint for militating against the specialization present in most other areas of rural social science research.

Second, the incentive systems in colleges of agriculture and home economics are such that scientists—be they social, biological, or physical—are given the greatest rewards for conducting disciplinary research and publishing many papers. The shift of land-grant incentive systems in this direction is not entirely unwelcome in that land-grant research historically has tended to be parochial and not as productive as it could be. But there are several possible concerns about the nature of these evolving incentive systems. One is that decisions about promotion, tenure, and rewards have de facto been increasingly transferred to professional organizations whose journal editors and well-placed scholars have tremendous influence over land-grant personnel decisions. Another concern is that disciplinary research may have little or no relevance to or implications for problem solving. Further, the structure of the incentive system may steer future cohorts of the best and brightest of graduate students away from problem-solving research.

Third, as noted earlier, there has been relatively little attention to the linkages between disciplinary, subject-matter, and problem-solving research in the rural social sciences. The biological sciences in the land-grant universities are probably well ahead of us in this regard, since the trend to basic research in SAESs has at least raised the issue of the articulation between research efforts at various points along the continuum from basic to applied.[15] Land-grant administrators, department chairs, and professional organizations have done relatively little to address this issue in the social sciences.

Fourth, rural social science research is largely uncoordinated with the "production sciences" in the land-grant system. This comment should not be construed to imply that social science research should be approached merely as an adjunct to the technical activities in other land-grant departments. Rather, the social sciences typically have little influence on the research of other departments and vice versa. It is only recently that the land-grant system has encouraged multidisciplinary team research on high-priority problems.

Finally, virtually no efforts have been made to incorporate the "nontraditional social sciences" (anthropology, political science, history, philosophy, and geography) into the land-grant social science effort.[16] It would, of course, be gratuitous to recommend a major financial commitment to the nontraditional social sciences at this time of general fiscal austerity in the land-grant system. Nonetheless, the traditional rural social sciences lack some major areas of expertise in problem solving that can most readily be provided by persons from the nontraditional disciplines.

Moreover, judicious incorporation of faculty from these nontraditional disciplines (for example, within multidisciplinary centers) would reinforce the notion that universities as a whole, not colleges of agriculture and home economics alone, have land-grant responsibilities (and opportunities).

NOTES

1. Frederick H. Buttel is a professor of Rural Sociology and faculty associate, Program on Science, Technology, and Society, Cornell University, Ithaca, New York. Dr. Buttel would like to thank David R. Lee and B. F. Stanton for their helpful comments on an earlier draft of this paper.

2. See Buttel and Busch (1988) for an expanded version of this argument. It should be stressed at the outset, however, that this "first approximation" rendering of the content of public agricultural research is *not* intended to suggest that public research consists only of productivity-increasing biological research (or that it is largely funded by federal appropriations). Obviously, the scope of public agricultural research is broader, and includes social science, home economics, nutrition, environmental, and other types of "nonproduction" research. Nonetheless, fiscal year 1986 expenditure data for agricultural research in the SAESs and USDA (Joint Council on Food and Agricultural Sciences 1987) show that fully 60 percent of public funding is accounted for by crop production and protection and animal production and protection research. An additional 21.5 percent is accounted for by research in natural resources, the lion's share of which consists of forestry production research. Thus, this first approximation is a relatively accurate portrayal of the dominant thrust of public agricultural research expenditures in the United States.

3. An anonymous reviewer has stressed that the land-grant system *never could* do this. This point has a strong element of truth, but the fact remains that the rapid differentiation of U.S. agriculture since World War II has led to a diversity of farm groups with different technical needs.

4. An anonymous reviewer has also made the useful observation that the dominance of the neoclassical paradigm has a major connection with the ideological orientations of agricultural economists. Neoclassical economics tends to begin with an assumed set of endowments, and the theory has little to say about what a socially desirable distribution of endowments would be. Accordingly, given an assumed set of endowments, analyses lead to prescriptions in which groups' interests are represented in proportion to their endowments.

5. It should be emphasized, however, that the lack of articulation between theory and method and, more specifically, the nonquantitative character of the contemporary sociology of agriculture can be exaggerated. There have, for example, been a number of examples of exploring hypotheses from neo-Marxist theory in the sociology of agriculture with quantitative data (e.g., Perry 1982). Also, the sociology of agriculture should not be seen as largely neo-Marxist and/or nonquantitative in nature. My argument merely is that neo-Marxist, political economy, and nonquantitative approaches are more common in the sociology of agriculture than in the other subject-matter areas of rural sociology.

6. It should be noted, however, that this characterization of unity of theory and method in mathematics in economics is more so the case in North America than elsewhere. In many other western countries econometrics is not nearly so dominant in theoretical economics as it is in the United States. Elsewhere, institutional and Marxist economics are far more prominent than they are here.

7. For example, it is arguably the case that Anthony Giddens (1979, 1984) is the most productive, provocative, and influential theorist in Western sociology today. Yet Giddens' theoretical work involves a conceptual vocabulary such that its empirical testing will in all likelihood remain confined to historical analysis (see, for example, Giddens' [1985] own test of his earlier [1981] ideas on capitalism and the modern state) or "interpretive" or "phenomenological" analysis. It should also be noted that U.S. sociology is substantially more quantitative—and the status and predominance of social theory as a specialty area far less—than in virtually every other advanced industrial country. Thus, the highly quantitative character of American sociology parallels the situation of its economics discipline.

8. Functionalist theories are those that explain social phenomena with reference to the "functions" they provide in meeting the "needs" of society as a whole. Functionalist theories thus may tend to be teleological (i.e., the phenomenon to be explained is simultaneously used as its own explanation) and to have a conservative bias (i.e., there is an implicit assumption that if a phenomenon exists, it must be functional in some way for the society). It should be noted, however, that over the past decade there has been a significant decline in the prevalence of functionalist theorizing in anthropology.

9. This is, in a sense, ironic, in that many of the leaders of the land-grant system at the time of the Country Life Commission were trained in the humanities.

10. By comparison, agricultural history is a highly respected specialty in departments of history in most European universities.

11. It should also be noted that, somewhat ironically, one of the major forces behind reevaluation of land-grant undergraduate curricula has been agribusiness criticism of the training of agriculture students. Agribusiness has become increasingly critical of land-grant university curricula which, in their view, place too much stress on the traditional production sciences (e.g., agronomy, horticulture) and underemphasize training in basic biology, the liberal arts, and writing.

12. Other precipitating factors leading to a larger role for philosophers in colleges of agriculture have been curriculum concerns (see note 11) and the fact that many issues now facing the land-grant system (e.g., animal rights, patenting of novel life forms) have an "ethical" component.

13. Fuller's approach is largely sociological, Gregor sees his book as being an "interpretative atlas," and Vogeler is a Marxist political economist.

14. The notion that the extension system, in addition to its educational function, can and must generate political support for land-grant universities (see, for example, McDowell 1985) is obviously controversial. An anonymous reviewer, in fact, objected to such a role being stated so explicitly in this paper. My point, however, is virtually the same as the reviewer's—that if extension is effective in bringing people's problems to the attention of land-grant researchers and in transferring information to the public, political support will follow.

15. This is not to suggest that the biological sciences have solved the problems of articulating research along the continuum from basic to applied. Rather, the articulation between basic and applied research is an issue that is more widely discussed and considered to be a more important issue in the biological agricultural sciences than in the rural social sciences.

16. The two major exceptions to this generalization are Rutgers University and the University of California, Davis, both of which have established interdisciplinary, problem-focused social science departments (Human Ecology and Applied Behavioral Sciences, respectively).

REFERENCES

Bennett, John W. 1982. *Of time and the enterprise: North American family farm management in a context of resource marginality.* Minneapolis: University of Minnesota Press.

Browne, William P. 1987. *Private interests, public policy, and American agriculture.* Lawrence: University Press of Kansas.

Busch, Lawrence, ed. 1981. *Science and agricultural development.* Montclair, N.J.: Allanheld, Osmun.

Busch, Lawrence, and William B. Lacy. 1983. *Science, agriculture, and the politics of research.* Boulder, Colo.: Westview Press.

Buttel, Frederick H., and Lawrence Busch. 1988. The public agricultural research system at the crossroads. *Agricultural History* 62:303–24.

Buttel, Frederick H., and Charles C. Geisler. 1989. The social impacts of bovine somatotropin: Emerging issues. In *Biotechnology and the new agricultural revolution.* Edited by J. Molnar and H. Kinnucan, 137–59. Boulder, Colo.: Westview Press.

Buttel, Frederick H., Martin Kenney, Jack Kloppenburg, Jr., and Douglas Smith. 1986. Industry-university relationships and the land-grant system. *Agricultural Administration* 23:147–81.

Buttel, Frederick H., Olaf F. Larson, and Gilbert W. Gillespie, Jr. 1990. *The sociology of agriculture.* Westport, Conn.: Greenwood Press.

Chibnik, Michael, ed. 1987. *Farm work and fieldwork: Agriculture in anthropological perspective.* Ithaca, N.Y.: Cornell University Press.

Cochrane, Willard W. 1979. *The development of American agriculture.* Minneapolis: University of Minnesota Press.

Danbom, David B. 1979. *The resisted revolution.* Ames: Iowa State University Press.

DeWalt, Billie R. 1986. Halfway there: Social sciences in agricultural development and the social science of agricultural development. Department of Anthropology, University of Kentucky. Unpublished manuscript.

Fuller, Anthony M. 1984. Part-time farming: The enigmas and the realities. *Research in Rural Sociology and Development* 1:187–219.

Giddens, Anthony. 1979. *Central problems in social theory.* Berkeley: University of California Press.

_____1981. *A contemporary critique of historical materialism.* London: Macmillan.

_____1984. *The constitution of society.* Berkeley: University of California Press.

_____1985. *The nation-state and violence.* Berkeley: University of California Press.

Gillespie, G. W. Jr., and Frederick H. Buttel. 1989. Farmer ambivalence toward agricultural research: An empirical examination. *Rural Sociology* 59: 382–408.

Goldschmidt, Walter. 1947. *As you sow.* Glencoe, Ill.: Free Press.

Goss, Kevin F. 1979. Consequences of the diffusion of innovations. *Rural Sociology* 44, no. 4 (Winter): 754–72.

Gregor, Howard F. 1982. *Industrialization of U.S. agriculture: An interpretive atlas.* Boulder, Colo.: Westview Press.

Hadwiger, Don F. 1982. *The politics of agricultural research.* Lincoln: University of Nebraska Press.

Joint Council on Food and Agricultural Sciences. 1987. *Fiscal year 1989 priorities for research, extension, and higher education.* Washington, D.C.: Joint Council on Food and Agricultural Sciences.

McDowell, George R. 1985. The political economy of extension program design: Institutional maintenance issues in the organization and delivery of extension programs. *American Journal of Agricultural Economics* 67, no. 4 (November): 717–25.

Newby, Howard. 1978. The rural sociology of advanced capitalist societies. In *International perspectives in rural sociology.* Edited by H. Newby, 23–30. Chichester: Wiley.

_____1980. Rural sociology: A trend report. *Current Sociology* 28, no. 1 (Spring): 1–141.

Office of Technology Assessment (OTA). 1986. *Technology, public policy, and the changing structure of American agriculture.* Washington, D.C.: OTA.

Perry, Charles S. 1982. The rationalization of U.S. farm labor: Trends between 1956 and 1979. *Rural Sociology* 47, no. 4 (Winter): 670–91.

Ruttan, Vernon W. 1982. *Agricultural research policy.* Minneapolis: University of Minnesota Press.

Schuh, G. Edward. 1986. Revitalizing land-grant universities: It's time to regain relevance. *Choices—The Magazine of Food, Farm, and Resource Issues* (2d Quarter): 6–10.

Schultz, T. W. 1977. Uneven prospects for gains from agricultural research related to economic policy. *Resource allocation and productivity in national and international agricultural research.* Edited by T. M. Arndt, et al., 578–89. Minneapolis: University of Minnesota Press.

Swanson, Louis E., ed. 1988. *Agriculture and community change in the U.S.* Boulder, Colo.: Westview Press.

Thompson, Paul. 1984. What philosophers can learn from agriculture. *Agriculture and Human Values* 1, no. 2 (Spring): 17–19.

Vogeler, Ingolf. 1982. *The myth of the family farm.* Boulder, Colo.: Westview Press.

ORTHODOXY: COMMENTS ON KIRKENDALL AND BUTTEL

Richard P. Haynes[1]

By beginning with Jefferson and focusing on the struggle between *industrializers* and *agrarianizers*, Richard Kirkendall (see Chapter 2 in this part) reinforces what I shall call the establishment version of the farm-crisis debate. This version focuses attention on the desirability of preserving the "family farm." In doing this, Kirkendall ignores other traditions which are more connected to "alternative" agriculture. Contemporary agrarianists should not lose hope, Kirkendall argues, for there is a certain resilience and natural advantage to the well-managed family farm that will ensure its survival in some quarters. But that is no consolation to agrarianists like Wendell Berry (1977). A well-managed family farm may still be highly industrialized—dependent upon inputs which are produced off-farm by means of a technology whose components can be mastered only by specialists. While the skills in using this technology can be passed on to other family members on the farm site, the externalized production costs that Berry is so concerned about may elude the grasp of this farmer. The model of the caring farmer that Berry develops finds little place in the agrarian tradition to which agrarianizers have appealed. To find that model, one must go outside of the style of agriculture imported from Europe, a style whose impact on the environment has been described by William Cronon in his book, *Changes in the Land: Indians, Colonists, and the Ecology of New England* (1983). Kirkendall mentions in passing U.S. policies designed to "reduce savagery" by taking the use of lands out of the hands of indigenous people. But if his history had started at an earlier date, and included an account of the social and environmental changes caused by the agriculture practiced by the European "settler," alternatives to the common orthodoxy shared by both agrarianizers and industrializers would be more apparent. Components of Berry's vision of agrarianism are shared today by various practitioners of "alternative" agriculture. The agricultural establishment has done little to assist this mode of farming. Recognition of its value is now being given by some researchers in international development. Even many of the proponents of "low-input" agriculture still envisage commercial control of its technologies. "Caring farmers" with detailed site-specific ecological knowledge equipped with a variety of survival strategies engaged in continuing experimental farming could provide a valuable resource for a region whose agricultural future is uncertain. If Lester Thurow's (see Chapter 4 in this part) skepticism about the likelihood of creating new major export markets to solve our abundance problems is true of all new technologies that are developed to establish new national comparative advantages, we should prepare for cutbacks in our national standard of living. Decentralization and local productive autonomy will increase in importance as a way of avoiding politically unacceptable levels of deprivation. Rural social scientists, who played such a major role in converting the rural economy to industrialization, should not suddenly become libertarians because of the positivist orthodoxy of their disciplines. Here is one agenda to explore what Kirkendall's chapter overlooks.

Buttel (see Chapter 3 of this part) acknowledges the role that philosophers might play in helping to exorcise the ghosts of Hume from the social scientists' fetters to positivism. They have already done this work, but it has failed to penetrate social-science practitioners to any depth. This is a testimony to the limitations of "multidisciplinary" research. But my skepticism is different than Buttel's regarding the acceptability of philosophers. Buttel thinks that agricultural-ethics programs will not develop in colleges of agriculture because of the resistance of agricultural scientists. I think that the constraints on the involvement of philosophers in agricultural-research issues lie more on the side of the liberal-arts colleges. Buttel acknowledges this difficulty. Philosophy, like many liberal-arts disciplines, according to Buttel, is "scholastic," i.e., addressed to the community of scholars that constitute the discipline. Given the reward structure of universities seeking increased prestige, neither subject-matter nor problem-solving research is likely to produce publications that will be acceptable to the "well-placed" scholars that "guard the gates" to the disciplinary journals. Even though the "professionalization" of academia has received justified criticism, philosophy may be one of the last disciplines to let go of its hard-won professional status, for it is a discipline that constantly finds difficulty in defining its area of expertise and in being taken seriously by other disciplines. Although philosophers who have received the type of training that is traditional in U.S. institutions since the 1950s can play an important role in cutting through some of the basic distinctions that oversimplify problems revealing alterative "paradigms" and a new range of solutions to be considered, as partners in transdisciplinary research (research that cuts through disciplinary boundaries), they must be informed of an enormous body of theory and literature. And their co-researchers must be equally informed. One especially relevant body of literature that has become transdisciplinary is "Science and Technology Studies" (STS). Only in the last decade have these studies begun to penetrate agricultural research thinking. Given the present structure of land-grant colleges, well-informed philosophers can play an important role in professional development programs for agricultural scientists, and an even more critical role in helping to restructure agricultural education. But I think that significant contributions to research will be made by philosophers at this stage primarily by raising neglected issues or identifying limiting assumptions and paradigms. It remains to be seen whether a philosopher whose main task is to challenge orthodoxy can survive without the protection of a parent discipline that understands this role. But to perform this role well, our philosopher may also have to challenge the orthodoxies of both the parent discipline that frowns on problem-solving research and the liberal-arts faculty that supports it.

THE RELEVANCE OF "SCIENCE AND TECHNOLOGY STUDIES" LITERATURE

STS is clearly relevant to a critical analysis of social science research in agriculture. A state-of-the-art report provides extensive bibliographies of material that is concerned with the "ethical and value" implications of science and technology (Durbin 1980). Some of this literature has already been applied to agricultural research (Busch and Lacy 1983), and more is relevant. Literature that falls into the areas characterized as: (1) professional ethics; (2) social responsibilities of the scientist; (3) technology, social change, and future societies; and (4) environmental ethics is clearly applicable to agricultural research. I shall briefly discuss the relevance of only the first two.

Literature in the area of professional ethics includes critical examinations of ethical problems created by the exercise of professional skills and knowledge, such as the appropriate roles and moral responsibilities of professionals, how these standards can be incorporated into practice, and whether professional codes of ethics define the limits of responsibility. This literature is germane to questions about the social responsibility of scientists who are pursuing professional careers, belong to professional associations, and claim to have their careers judged by the ideals and standards of these associations. In this regard issues about the social responsibility of scientists clearly overlap issues about the professional responsibilities of researchers. Some of the difficulties associated with assessing professional responsibilities arise out of the contexts in which many professionals work, and in the relationship between individual and collective responsibilities. Professional ethics, as a subject matter, is concerned with problems associated with determining the responsibilities of persons who occupy specific social roles. Literature concerned with the conceptual, historical, and sociological foundations of professional roles and their social status and function, as well as with general role theory in ethics, is relevant to discussions about the social responsibilities of agricultural researchers. Historical and sociological studies provide the empirical base for evaluating claims about the social function of the professions and the social stratifications of professionalized societies. Accounts of the norms by which professional groups purport to govern themselves provide valuable background for attempting to understand the social and political role of these norms and their legitimacy as codes of ethics (Kultgen 1982; Newton 1982). Studies in the sociology of science and technology also provide an important background for discussions about the social responsibilities of scientists. These studies have already been applied to an analysis of the social implications of the values of agricultural researchers (Busch and Lacy 1983). Merton's approach to understanding the institution of science in terms of its goal of attaining "certified knowledge with maximum efficiency," has been used to justify the institutional norms that make achievement of this goal possible. These same norms are used by the scientific community to police themselves (Gaston 1978). Various sociological studies of reward systems provide material for identifying areas of conflict of interest for researchers (Gaston 1978; Larson 1979; Collins 1979).

There is another area of sociological analysis that is relevant to discussions about the responsibility of scientists. In this area, competing models are given of the relationships between the projects of individual scientists, the paradigms of professional disciplines, and the total scientific enterprise. For example, the justification for the "corporatization" or "collectivization" of science on the basis of a "Baconian Model" of the scientific enterprise (Busch and Lacy 1983) is challenged by the Kuhnian and other recent philosophical analysis of the relationships that actually hold between practicing scientists. This challenge may be taken to suggest that scientists must take an increased responsibility for viewing their own work in relationship to the overall social goals for science (e.g., Dundon 1982; Perkins 1982).

Science and technology policy studies is another area of scholarship that has application to agricultural research ethics. Discussions about the criteria for selecting priorities for the allocation of research funds and about the role of the scientist and technologist for the assessment of social impacts are all significant (Crane 1980). Discussions concerning this area suggest a strong emerging connection between policy-group criteria and individual problem-choice criteria, as competition for limited resources for research increases. The use of this type of criteria suggested by Weinberg (1968) has serious implications for the use of the basic/applied distinction to insulate scientists from responsibility for impact. They bring into stronger focus problems concerned with the relationship between institutional goals and individual scientist-employee goals. Questions about individual scientist-employee responsibilities are further complicated when research decisions are made largely by administrators. This is another area that is especially relevant for agricultural research to the extent that policy, even for basic research in agriculture, emphasizes accountability rather than autonomy (Nicholson 1977). Literature on the freedom and the responsibility of the scientist in the role of advisor and advocate (Crane 1980), and in the role of public disseminator of information also has some obvious application to agricultural research ethics. This is especially true of literature in the general area of the philosophy of technology, which is concerned with criteria for evaluating the social role and effects of types of technology as well as the effect that technology has on human values and on the quality of human life.

The emerging literature and scholarly activity in this field suggest a number of topics that apply to agricultural ethics. These topics are each concerned with estimating the degree to which the agricultural scientist or technologist should be held accountable for enlarging the conception of their field of responsibilities: (1) What goals should public-sector agricultural researchers pursue, who should be the clientele and the beneficiaries, and what are the appropriate criteria for selecting research problems to help ensure that benefits and costs are appropriately distributed? (2) How should the mode of classification of research by type (e.g., basic, disciplinary, etc.) affect the autonomy or accountability of the researcher? (3) To what extent are the individual researchers, the professional disciplines, the research community in general, and the organizations to which they belong, responsible for assessing the consequences of research, for identifying research needs and for choosing research problems accordingly? (4) What should be the role of technology in modern society? What should be the respective responsibilities of the researcher and the general public in determining that role? How should conflicts be resolved? To what extent are agricultural researchers responsible for conforming their research according to well-thought-out resolutions of views about this role? (5) When doing research, what are the appropriate professional norms to follow (e.g., Merton 1973) concerning the use of evidence and hypotheses, secrecy, scholarship, value neutrality, impact distortion, skepticism, open-mindedness to innovation, etc.? How should these norms be interpreted and what priority should be given to them when they conflict with norms regarding social responsibilities? (6) What responsibilities do researchers have when functioning as political advisors or as advocates? (7) What personal values or ideals influence problem choices, methodology choices, and solution ranges? Should a researcher allow these ideals and values to function in this way? What responsibility do researchers have to examine their own values, ideals, and assumptions? (8) What responsibilities do professionals have to expand their areas of expertise? To become generalists? (9) What responsibility do researchers have to explore unconventional and alternative techniques, technologies, etc.? (10) What criteria should be used in setting research priorities, at a personal level, professional level, organizational and national level? (11) What general obligations do researchers have in serving the interests of clients? To consider adverse effects on others at risk?

NOTE

1. Richard P. Haynes is a professor of Philosophy at the University of Florida.

REFERENCES

Berry, Wendell. 1977. *The unsettling of America*. Totawa, N.J.: Sierra Club Books.

Busch, Lawrence, and William B. Lacy. 1983. *Science, agriculture, and the politics of research*. Boulder, Colo.: Westview Press.

Collins, Randal. 1979. *The credential society: An historical sociology of education and stratification*. New York: Academic Books.

Crane, Diana. 1980. Science policy studies. In *A guide to the culture of science, technology, and medicine*, edited by Paul T. Durbin, 583–668. New York: The Free Press.

Cronon, William. 1983. *Changes in the land: Indians, colonists, and the ecology of New England*. New York: Hill and Wang.

Dundon, Stanislaus. 1982. Hidden obstacles to creativity in agricultural science. In *Agriculture, change, and human values: Proceedings of a multidisciplinary conference*, edited by R. Haynes and R. Lanier, II:836–68.

Durbin, Paul T., ed. 1980. *A guide to the culture of science, technology, and medicine*. New York: The Free Press.

Gaston, Jerry. 1978. *The reward system in British and American science*. New York: Wiley Interscience.

Kultgen, John. 1982. The ideological use of professional codes. *Business and Professional Ethics Journal* 1, no. 3: 53–70.

Larson, Magali Sarfatti. 1979. *The rise of professionalism: A sociological analysis*. Davis: University of California Press.

Merton, Robert K. 1973. *The sociology of science*. Chicago: The University of Chicago Press.

Newton, Lisa. 1982. The origin of professionalism. *Business and Professional Ethics Journal* 1, no. 4: 33–43.

Nicholson, Heather Johnston. 1977. Autonomy and accountability of basic research. *Minerva* 15 (Spring): 32–61.

Perkins, John H. 1982. *Insects, experts, and the insecticide crisis: The quest for new pest management strategies*. New York: Plenum Press.

Weinberg, Alvin M. 1968. Criteria for scientific choice. In *Criteria for Scientific Development*, edited by Edward Shils, 21–33. Cambridge: MIT Press.

DISCUSSION OF CHAPTERS BY DRS. KIRKENDALL AND BUTTEL

William F. Freudenburg[1]

We have been presented with two very competent overviews of large bodies of work by people who have done their homework very well (see Chapters 2 and 3 of this part). One of the hardest things in the world is to summarize a broad area competently and fairly, but both of these chapters have managed to accomplish that task quite well. Outside of a few quibbles, I basically want to commend the authors; their chapters are full of good stuff.

This is almost the end of my "standard commentary" on the chapters themselves, although it is far from the end of what I have to say, for reasons I am about to point out.

When I was first asked to be a reviewer, I was not quite sure why I had been selected. My own background includes very little that has obvious relevance to the history or study of agriculture. For much of my career, I have studied rural industrialization, community change, social-impact assessment, and the so-called "energy boomtowns." During the last three to five years, I have been spending much of my time on nuclear waste and sociology of risk. This kind of background has only marginal relevance to agriculture, as traditionally defined; none of it would exactly be considered part of the central emphasis of this project.

Thus, my initial assumption was that I had been brought in simply to offer a fresh or outside perspective. As I thought about it further, however, I realized that it might be a useful contribution if I were to focus on, rather than avoid, the whole question of marginality. Accordingly, that is exactly what I plan to do.

To begin, marginality has always been important in community studies. The best informants in a community are often not the "core" members of the town, so to speak, but the marginal members—people who are close enough to the day-to-day interactions to be able to see what kind of town it is, and yet far enough removed that they can focus on the forest as well as the trees.

Similarly, in biophysical ecology, the most productive ecosystems are often at the margins. The middle of an ocean, for example, is essentially a desert, but there is tremendous productivity at the margins, where the ocean meets the shore. And maybe, I started thinking, the traditionally "weak" or marginal position of social sciences within colleges of agriculture should be considered a bit differently. Perhaps, in short, our traditional weakness should be seen as a source of strength today. That is the point I would like to make, and I will try to do so in three steps—first, by asking you to think about a concept; second, by giving you some of examples; and third, by noting some of the implications.

To begin by emphasizing the obvious, these are challenging times. The future, as the old saying goes, "ain't what it used to be." From farm crises to faltering institutions, the trends of the time seem to say that the continued pursuit of business as usual may soon put us all out of business. Dr. Kirkendall points out, however, that times have been challenging and changing for at least the last forty years—or seventy, or a hundred. What is remarkable about the history presented by Dr. Kirkendall, if we stop to think about it, is the extent to which our reactions have always been, within colleges of agriculture, to close our ranks, to circle the wagons, and to try to keep out those external forces that we did not like. To borrow Fred Buttel's phrase, we have tended to fall into agricultural fundamentalism.

This brings us directly to the concept I would like to emphasize; it has to do with a tradeoff between two polar tendencies. One extreme of this tradeoff is the tendency to focus, specialize, or draw the wagons tightly around the camp; at the other extreme is the tendency to hedge your bets, to diversify, or to bring in dissenting points of view.

This concept of the tradeoff between focusing and diversifying is similar to a basic notion from economists' work on investments. It is well known that there is a risk-versus-return tradeoff on investments. In general, the highest returns tend to come from the riskiest investments since riskier investments need to pay a higher rate of return to be able to attract money. What that means is that if you are highly confident in your predictions, if you are in a situation where there are likely to be no surprises, and if the institutions in which you invest do not go belly-up, then the rational thing to do is to make the "riskiest" investments you can find. If none of your investments self-destruct, then you will be the person on the block with the highest rate of return.

What happens, of course, is that surprises sometimes do show up. In those situations, you tend to get not a high rate of return, but a lecture on the wisdom of putting all of your eggs in one basket.

Similarly, in biophysical ecology, the difference between a monoculture and a diversified ecosystem is that if someone guesses right on pesticides, fertilizers, and so forth, a monoculture can get a tremendous level of productivity from a given piece of turf. In biophysical ecology, however, it is an old saying that diversity equals stability—that in the long run, the plant communities that tend to be most stable are the ones that are most diverse.

As a crude rule of thumb, scientists tend to get ahead by being focusers, rather than diversifiers. Perhaps three-fourths of the time, as a rough guess, scientists appear to get ahead more rapidly by focusing their efforts, ignoring minor problems and minority points of view. But even if that means that scientists are "rational" to narrow their field of vision "most" of the time, it still leaves us with the other fourth or so of the time—or fifth, or tenth, or whatever—where the usual approach will prove to be distinctly unwise. These are the times when we will only know afterwards that we should have hedged our bets at the outset.

Land-grant universities, I am suggesting, have tended very much toward the specialization end of the continuum. Our tendency has been to focus on increasing production, to home in on congenial specialties and perspectives, and essentially to ignore dissenting or critical voices. What I am about to argue, however, is that one of the primary reasons for having social scientists in land-grant colleges, or at least one of the potential reasons, is that we can provide a counterbalancing tendency, a tendency toward the diversification of perspectives.

This is a potentially dangerous prescription, particularly in the subset of our institutions that considers it an act of disloyalty, rather than of loyalty, to point out that the emperor is not wearing clothes. It is also a bit of an irony for it to fall to social scientists to bring alternative perspectives to the very kinds of colleges that brought the concept of hybrid vigor to general public consciousness. In fact, the whole discussion raises the question of why we do not already find a strong tendency toward diversification in land-grant colleges—and that leads directly to some examples.

The first comes from a town I visited last week—Caliente, Nevada. Those of you who have done community studies may remember a famous article by Fred Cottrell (1951) called "Death by Dieselization." The article had to do with a small town in eastern Nevada that had been a division point for coal-fired steam locomotives. When the railroad switched from coal to diesel, the trains only needed to stop half as often, and Caliente was one of the unlucky towns that was axed. What is more, Caliente had no obvious reasons for existence other than to be a railroad town. Cottrell wrote an article on Caliente's impending death, and the injustice of it all. The injustice may have been real, but having visited the town 30 years later, I am happy to tell you the rumors of Caliente's death were greatly exaggerated. It still does not have the healthiest economy, but the community is definitely still there, and it is not about to disappear; the "fact" of its impending death was obvious, but wrong.

Another example, as several of us have noted, is the current agricultural crisis. Ten years ago, any number of people were saying that farmers needed to borrow more money, to buy more land, and to plant more crops. The farmers who took that advice were not ignorant or behind the times, but award winning, progressive, and aggressive. The people offering the advice were not a handful of weirdos or critics of the system, but part of the mainstream of the land-grant system and the agricultural establishment. I remember thinking at the time that the advice and logic were obviously on target—but, it turns out, they were not.

Whenever I am told, therefore, that we need to "face the facts," I swallow a little bit harder than I used to; I also think of something geographer Bob Kates (1985) once said: "Science often fluctuates between humility and hubris." My willingness to tell someone else to "face the facts," in short, is starting to be tempered by the realization that, sometimes, what we expect to be the facts will turn out to be something else; making predictions is always hard, but predicting the future is especially so.

Another set of studies had to do with a place where, fortunately, I have never been, namely the Nazi death camps. The "obvious" guess would be that the people who were in death camps would have hated and despised their captors, but what often happened was that some prisoners started dressing like, acting like, and essentially identifying with the Nazi captors.

Years later, when the U.S. military draft was made random (i.e., on the basis of birthdays), there was an interesting study that brought together a group of draft-age men to watch the birth-date "numbers" being drawn and to fill out questionnaires. Soon after the results came out, the young men were asked how much they liked the other participants in the study—something we would normally expect to be essentially random with respect to the day of the year on which someone was born. In fact, the people whose birthdays were in the low numbers—i.e., the ones who were almost sure to get drafted—started being seen as much less popular. It is possible that their behavior changed because they were worried about getting shot, but it is also possible that there is something about a crisis that causes many of us to shun those who are in trouble, and to redouble our commitments, often, to the very system that got us into trouble in the first place. There are informal reports of the same kinds of tendencies, incidentally, in the current farm crisis, with farmers shunning, rather than supporting, their colleagues who are in the greatest difficulty—almost as if there is a concern that failure might prove to be a contagious disease, if only psychologically.

To move back to my larger concept, the "circle-the-wagons-around-the-land-grant-system" tendency may involve organizational and institutional factors, not just individual-level ones. At the researcher level, as we have already said several times, there is a tendency for promotions to emphasize an individual's contributions within a discipline. If you spend an hour on a problem-focused piece of research, odds are you are spending at least half of that hour on something that will not get you tenure or bring you promotions within your discipline. (While several of us have discussed the problem, I should probably say that those of us who really enjoy multidisciplinary, problem-focused research may get enough hybrid vigor out of that research that maybe we are still better off in the long run.)

I want to move beyond the forces that encourage specialization at the researcher level, however, and talk about what happens a few levels higher, among our upper administrators. The Peter Principle (Peter and Hull 1969) is a good-humored way to describe it: If people do a job well, they get promoted, and, if they do that job well, they get promoted again. The pattern repeats until the people get to the point where they are not doing their job well—and that is where the promotions stop. The net result, by this humorous perspective, is that people tend to get promoted out of the jobs they do well, and into the jobs they do not do well.

It gets a bit less humorous, unfortunately, when dealing with universities, because there are different "screens" through which we need to pass. The way to get tenure, in general, is to specialize—to do one thing in a way that is focused, efficient, and specialized, and to do it very, very well. People who do not pass the tenure test are no longer "available"—they are not part of the pool from which promotions are drawn to upper administrative levels. I say "unfortunately" because administrative positions call for something very different—not necessarily someone who gets through the "specialist" screen, but someone who does not get screened out because of an inability to see the bigger and broader picture. If what you need to succeed as a specialist, 75 percent of the time, is to be someone who takes a narrow view, then it may be that what you need 75 percent of the time to be a good administrator is to be a generalist—to be someone who instinctively looks for the broader view, not the narrower one.

Which brings us back to the chapters, and I hope to the whole project. I frankly am still not sure what the Social Science Agricultural Agenda Project is about, even though Glenn Johnson (personal correspondence) has been kind enough to explain it to me four or five different times. It may be, however, that one of our broader functions is to provide a counterweight to the forces of focus. We need to acknowledge the importance of what the land-grant system has traditionally done well, to be sure, but we may also need to remind our colleagues, and ourselves, not to overlook the larger picture.

The chapters are excellent, first of all, because they are examples of looking at the bigger picture. More importantly, they are successful examples of the very kinds of bigger-picture analyses that both of them advocate.

Second, they show the importance to social scientists of permeating those semipermeable membranes that separate our disciplines—of having rural sociologists talk to agricultural economists, for example, rather than throwing rocks at them, and vice versa—and also for bringing in some of the "nontraditional" social sciences (I would add psychology to the ones that Fred Buttel mentioned, and believe he would concur).

Third, and still more significantly, these chapters help show the importance of having some of the critics on the inside—not throwing rocks at the system from outside the circle of wagons, but welcomed inside as valuable contributors to the system—and for at least two reasons. One is that it is by having a variety of points of view inside the system that we can maximize the opportunity to improve the system: I would much rather be told my faults by my friends than by my enemies, in general, partly because my friends are kinder to me, but partly because I am more likely to listen to them. For this function, even if no other, we need friendly people in the system who do not share the "orthodoxy," to use Richard Haynes' term (see first discussion paper in this part). The other reason is a point made by Fred Buttel that I want to emphasize. Particularly, when times are changing and there are new and complex forces at work politically, it is vital to the long-term survival of the institution that it be seen as institutionally neutral—as neither fighting for nor against any one set of combatants in an ongoing controversy. Given that the institution itself cannot afford to take sides, perhaps the safest countermeasure to partisanship is to make sure that the critics have a legitimate role inside the system.

Fourth, I think the papers are important because they allow a discussant to expand at least one additional step. It is important for the future of all of us, I would argue, that we look at more than just "traditional agriculture," writ narrowly. Instead, we need to expand in at least two ways: First, even if we are just looking at "agriculture," perhaps the majority of what is influential in agriculture takes place not in rural areas, but in urban ones. Whether we are talking about banks, middlemen, consumers, Congress, or other influences, perhaps the majority of the forces that shape agriculture are outside of the "agriculture" that is defined by the borders of specific farms. Second, it is important to expand not just beyond rural areas in looking at agriculture, but rather to expand beyond agriculture in looking at rural areas. Even if we are simply being pragmatic, we need to ask whether we want to put all of our eggs in any one basket, let alone one that is being carried by a segment of the population that, once a majority, is now down to three percent, and is still shrinking. And, if we are responding to humanitarian or intellectual motivations, we have still more reason to look at other rural activities that do provide significant hope for rural areas. Given what we are hearing about the likely future of American agriculture, it only makes sense to ask if other activities might provide hope for rural diversification, whether through traditional rural activities, such as forestry, fishing, or even mining, or through other activities that are taking on increasing importance in rural areas today, activities such as tourism and recreation.

What happened in Caliente, to oversimplify, is that Cottrell (1951) overlooked the importance of transfer payments and the fact that people simply wanted to live in that community, the place where their friends and families were. It seemed logical to expect that people would "obey the economic facts of life" and that, if they were not going to get much in the way of income, they would leave. That expectation turned out to be wrong, however, because it ignored "the cultural facts of life." Even our emphasis on money, an anthropologist would remind us, is a culturally defined preference. What the residents of Caliente found more important than maximizing their income, was maximizing their well-being through family ties, community "roots," and so forth. That does not mean, by any sense of the imagination, that they did not care about money; they did, and they still do, maybe more intensely than your average academic, because money is a crucial and scarce commodity. Yet the real bottom line was the fact that they were not willing to give up other things they also wanted for the sake of money alone.

In short, Caliente has survived, in a sense, by hedging its bets, by diversifying, and by finding other ways to support its population. Similarly, we may find that the way for all of us to survive in the long run is by hedging our bets and by diversifying our perspectives, both as social scientists and as citizens of colleges of agriculture.

NOTE

1. William F. Freudenburg is an associate professor of Rural Sociology at the University of Wisconsin.

REFERENCES

Cottrell, W.F. 1951. Death by dieselization: A case study in the reaction to technological change. *American Sociological Review* 16:358–65.

Kates, Robert W. 1985. Excerpt from address at the National Academy of Engineering's symposium on hazards: Technology and fairness. National Research Council. *News Report* 35, no. 7: 24–25.

Peter, Laurence J., and Raymond Hull. 1969. *The Peter principle*. New York: W. Morrow.

DISCUSSION OF CHAPTERS BY DRS. KIRKENDALL AND BUTTEL

Billie R. DeWalt[1]

My sense of the strength of anthropology as a discipline is that it attempts to develop a holistic understanding of the relationship of people to the social environment and natural habitats within which they exist. While anthropologists have traditionally been weak in determining policy directions and making recommendations about what *should* be done (as Buttel points out in Chapter 3 in this part), they often are able to present a much broader and useful view of the *context* within which such decisions can be made. Taken as a set, the chapters create a carefully-drawn background within which to develop an agenda for the social sciences in agriculture. My commentary will attempt to pull together what I have learned from this book *and* present what I believe to be the lessons that we should derive from it.

First, as Kirkendall so nicely develops (see Chapter 2 in this part), the history of American agriculture has been one of increasing labor productivity and decreasing involvement of people on the farm. Although we now hear more talk about the farm crisis, Thurow (see Chapter 4 of this part) convincingly argues that the present situation is only the continuation of long-term trends. In fact, the current "crisis" is not as severe as past ones. At present, however, agriculture makes up a much smaller proportion of the gross national product (GNP) than it ever has before, farmers are a much smaller percentage of the population, and these trends are unlikely to change irrespective of what happens in terms of short-term government policy. There is still a substantial percentage of the population involved in the food system (about 20%) but most of these individuals are involved in the processing, marketing, and transportation of food. They are usually employed in large-scale, frequently multinational, agribusiness corporations.

Put bluntly, the implications for colleges of agriculture and for social scientists whose concern is domestic agriculture are quite clear: (1) There will be less of a need for agricultural research to serve farmers. Many of their technical research needs are already being served by the corporations that sell them supplies and process their products. Biotechnology is being done in corporations, and much of that occurring in public universities is not being done in colleges of agriculture. To be sure, there is still a role for public research to meet the needs of groups and individuals whose needs will not be met by the corporations. Many of these individuals will not be the traditional "family farmers" but part-time farmers, people who live in rural areas for aesthetic reasons, and people managing rural landscapes for nontraditional uses (e.g., hunting, fishing, green belts, etc.). (2) In the same way, social scientists doing research for and about farmers are also focusing on a diminishing clientele. Some researchers will be needed to look at the activities of the 17 or 18 percent of nonfarmers involved in the food industry and, as Hite points out (see Chapter 3, Section 1, Part III), for economists and others who focus on the use of natural resources. We face the prospects of a declining need for commodity and production agricultural economists.

The second thing I have learned is that this does not mean that colleges of agriculture, agricultural experiment stations, and social scientists involved in the study of agriculture are or will become obsolete. Their perspective and mandates need to become much broader. As Schuh argues (see Chapter 6 in this part and Part II, Section 2, Chapter 2), we can no longer just think about domestic agriculture without also considering the international dimension. My view is that we are in the midst of a global reorganization of agriculture. The developed countries are increasingly going to only generate those crops that can be produced using highly mechanized means (mostly grains)—and perhaps a few crops that are too highly perishable to be transported very far. Labor-intensive fruits and vegetables are probably destined to be produced in the developing countries where labor costs are much lower. The message for those individuals in the United States who are concerned with agriculture is that there is a great need for their expertise—if they are willing and able to employ it within the context of the internationalization of agriculture.

The narrowness of perspective of some of the commodity interest groups will have to be overcome. Though Brazil may compete with the United States in soybeans and Mexico may now be producing substantial amounts of sorghum, the overall level of imports in these countries has been stimulated by the modernization and development of their economies and agricultural sectors. Davan has presented an incredible paradox (see Part II, Section 1, Chapter 2). He reports that the highest priorities for research in agricultural economics are questions concerning what agricultural products foreign countries wanted from the United States and how competitive U.S. products are in world markets. Yet the lowest priority was assigned to questions of how to pursue policies that would raise the income of Third World countries. This indicates a real narrow-mindedness among the individuals interviewed in the Davan et al. study; apparently they only are concerned with selling to developed markets rather than expanding the potential base of consumers by developing new markets.

U.S. development can no longer be based on the underdevelopment of significant parts of the rest of the world. It is becoming politically and economically indefensible (and has always been on moral grounds). For this reason, international development should become the key to the future of the land-grant system. All of those involved in colleges of agriculture and experiment stations will inevitably have to attempt to convince their traditional supporters (commodity interests) to accept their involvement in the international arena. While in the short run this may be painful, my view is that long-term survival may hinge on the outcome of whether these hard decisions are made. The revitalization of the land-grant system will require visionary, entrepreneurial, and risk-taking administrators.

A third point that arises (if my first two points are accepted) is that there is a significant need for a reorientation and redirection of our educational system to allow us to more effectively participate in the newly internationalized context of agriculture. Our land-grant system contains many disciplines that are relevant to the international context, yet few agricultural scientists or even agricultural social scientists have taken advantage of these educational opportunities. International marketing and production of agricultural products will require much more in the way of cross-cultural learning. It is also important to emphasize that there is a great need for more widely trained people who focus on international dimensions of natural-resource use. Issues like desertification, deforestation, and the like include both aspects related to the natural environment as well as a significant relationship with poverty. Anthropology, geography, economy, philosophy, and the foreign languages are key elements here. Can we hope to understand our competitors and our customers if we cannot communicate with them or understand their customs and behaviors? It is especially imperative that we recognize that a simple transference of American agricultural technology is not what is needed in most developing countries. The United States was able to absorb the many people displaced from agriculture by the new technology. Developing countries, with many more hundreds of millions of people involved in the agricultural sector, simply cannot generate the needed industrial and service-sector jobs that would be needed if capital-intensive agriculture displaces the rural population.

My own viewpoint is that the agricultural social sciences have become overly specialized in their training and perspectives. This increasing specialization has diverted us from understanding many of the most important and significant questions that face world agriculture in the years ahead. How many individuals are focusing on the global reorganization of agriculture? Do we know what the effects of this will be? If we were unable to predict what occurred in our own agricultural sector, can we predict what will happen in the rest of the world? How can we prevent the vast majority of Third-World farmers from being displaced in the process of their agricultural development? What is appropriate technology for these farmers? If there is plenty of food in the world, then how do we solve the poverty problems of those who are too poor to access enough of it? We need many more synthesizers of research to answer such questions.

As many people have emphasized in this book, we need much more in the way of multidisciplinary research. It is more important to recognize, however, that in order to do more effective research in the social sciences, I think that we need many more interdisciplinary people—that is, people who are able to think beyond the strictures of their own disciplines. Just as we need to get away from the agricultural fundamentalism that makes us focus on the "family farm" and individual commodities, we also need to expand beyond disciplinary fundamentalism and chauvinism. No one discipline has all of the answers or even all of the right questions.

NOTE

1. Billie R. DeWalt is a professor and former chair of the Department of Anthropology, University of Kentucky.

GEARING UP FOR THE SOCIAL SCIENCES FOR THE TWENTY-FIRST CENTURY: COMMENTS

Leo V. Mayer[1]

It is a pleasure to have the opportunity to review the Kirkendall and Buttel chapters (Chapters 2 and 3, respectively, of this part). They contain the kind of information that is essential for establishing a goal framework. I have taken the liberty of listing one of those goals as "gearing up the social sciences for the 21st century."

From the Washington perspective, however, simplicity itself is an objective. And it has also been an objective of land-grant universities. "Making two blades of grass grow where one did before" is perhaps the best example. Unfortunately, that goal has left something to be desired from the standpoint of the social sciences in the land-grant universities. That is the other side of the simplicity coin.

One cannot read through these two chapters without gaining an increased appreciation for the impact the social sciences have had on land-grant universities and on rural America. Buttel reviews those contributions and ends by suggesting that "one of the healthiest things a land-grant university could do would be to reaffirm its land-grant commitment." If by this he means its problem-solving orientation, I can understand the recommendation. If not, he may want to explain it in more detail.

There is another broader view of the contributions that land-grant universities have made that I also like. I was reminded of it as I read the Kirkendall chapter. Kirkendall observed that the Jeffersonian ideal ". . . achieved its most spectacular victory in 1862 with the passage of the Homestead Act." That may be accurate political history but having read biographies of what I consider to be our greatest president and visited his home (Monticello) in Charlottesville, Virginia, with all its innovations for that time period, I suspect that Jefferson's goals for improving rural America were also achieved with the establishment of the land-grant colleges. The only disappointing part of that historical review was to be reminded that "the greatest push for the land-grant system came from critics of the farmers," rather than from farmers themselves.

The implications of this point are what I want to discuss. What was true in 1862 is still true today. It often takes leadership to discover where the self-interest of American agriculture lies or, to put it into more economic terms, where among the many competing ends we ought to apply our scarce resources. Left to their own devices, farmers often view the need for research and extension through microlevel glasses. The result is a heavy emphasis on state-oriented, production-oriented research.

Under certain conditions, this would not be all bad. For example, in an environment in which markets are growing fast enough, such as existed very early in this century in this country (with its enormous in-migration and rapid income growth) and again during the war periods of 1914–17 and 1941–47, a production-oriented research and extension policy can make a positive contribution itself. Unfortunately, this represents the exceptional period rather than the norm. The remainder of the time, markets have not expanded automatically to absorb all of the production that farmers with their new technology can create. This has been the record of the last half-century although, as I look at the land-grant universities today, I must say in all honesty that I do not find much indication that they have learned from the experience.

Of course, I must add one more caveat. As long as government is willing to step in and buy up all the excess product that farmers are willing to produce at the guaranteed prices government provides, there is little wonder that farmer-supported universities do not allocate more resources to increasing the understanding of marketing, especially overseas marketing.

This caveat also moves us into the area of public policy. The question now becomes how long the public will stand for a support-price storage-program policy. It is a question that has been asked numerous times over the past thirty years and it is again being asked today. I do not know the answer and, as Buttel points out, there are no political scientists in the state agricultural experiment stations to answer questions like this.

My conclusion, however, is that whether or not the public will withstand the cost of "support and store" policy, it is an ill-advised policy for the long term. American agriculture should be better served than this. The land-grant universities should reexamine their focus and assure their support base that their mandate includes not only producing commodities at the lowest cost, but also marketing them in the most effective manner possible. In the global market the agricultural industry now faces, marketing includes a broad range of social science disciplines, including those that can help us understand other cultures, their tastes and preferences, their income levels, as well as their governments' policies relative to phytosanitary restrictions, customs requirements, and other trade policies.

Obviously, selling this kind of package of new research challenges to the taxpayers of any one state will not be easy. In fact, I would argue that this is a challenge that should be borne by the federal government. What is needed is a new Hatch Act devoted to supporting our export efforts. Otherwise, we should begin to question whether it makes good sense to create all this excess capacity that must then be held out of production under one or more expensive government programs.

NOTE

1. Leo V. Mayer is associate administrator, Foreign Agricultural Service, U.S. Department of Agriculture.

CHAPTER 4

AGRICULTURAL INSTITUTIONS UNDER FIRE

Lester C. Thurow[1]

Viewed from the outside, two facts dominate post-World War II American agriculture: First, agriculture has shrunk rapidly compared to the rest of the economy and, second, critics of agriculture and its public policies have multiplied like fleas. Agricultural institutions and leadership have not been coping well with either phenomena.

THE RELATIVE DECLINE OF FARMING

From 1945 to 1986, net farm income fell from $78 billion to $33 billion in 1982 dollars, and agricultural employment fell from 8.6 million to 3.2 million (*Economic Report of the President [ERP]* 1990, 330, 403). Most of this decline occurred between 1945 and 1970 when more than 200,000 farmers per year were leaving farming (*ERP* 1990, 330). In the end, the number of workers who had left farming, 5.4 million, was much larger than the number remaining in farming, 3.2 million in 1986.

While the real farm gross national product (GNP) was expanding by $30 billion (from $54 billion to $84 billion in 1982 dollars) between 1945 and 1986, the total GNP was expanding by $2,363 billion (*ERP* 1990, 305). Farming accounted for just 1.3 percent of America's growth over this period of time and by 1986 accounted for only a little over 2 percent of the GNP. Farming once was the largest American industry; it is now one of the smallest. For a time in the 1970s, agriculture was an important element in the balance of payments but, by the mid-1980s, it had ceased to be an important net contributor to America's trade position. In 1986, agricultural exports exceeded agricultural imports by only $3 billion (*Survey of Current Business [SCB]* 1989, 36). By 1989, however, net agricultural exports were back to more than $16 billion (*SCB* 1990, 38). U.S. farm exports are quite sensitive to macroeconomic conditions (and policies) in both the United States and the world, especially developing countries.

In 1986, it took 1 million American workers to produce $34 billion worth of GNP (1982 dollars) (*ERP*1990, 296, 330). As a consequence, if one assumes that the 5.4 million reduction in the farm labor force involved people who were average in terms of their abilities, $184 billion was added to the GNP when they went to work in alternative industries—an addition to GNP far greater than that contributed by those that remained in farming. Farming's greatest contribution to the economy since World War II is not what it directly produced but the extra workers that it contributed to the urban economy. Economically, those that left farming were far more important than those that stayed.

Given these facts, it would be fair to ask whether America's agricultural institutions had helped to plan for this decline, and whether they had acted to make the transition from agriculture to alternative employment easier for millions of people. Not surprisingly, the truthful answer to this question is, of course, that the system did essentially nothing to plan for decline or to help those leaving agriculture. Political leadership avoided the issue. When such recommendations were made by some of the intellectual establishment in agriculture, they were ignored or rejected (Hathaway 1963, 378–79).

At best, it is only possible to argue that inadvertent aid was given to those leaving farming. Farm price supports kept some farmers in farming slightly longer than they otherwise would have been able and, as a consequence, the movement away from farming was spread out over a longer period of time and was perhaps less painful than it could have been if nothing had been done. Even so, 41 million Americans left farms between 1920 and 1978—a migration and an economic adjustment of stupendous size (*Historical Statistics,* 457; *Statistical Abstract,* 649). Over two decades, from 1940 to 1960, more than 1 million people per year left the farm population.

The migration was not only massive, it was complex in nature. Historically, many of those that left farming quickly, if not immediately, found jobs that provided higher levels of living, however, others, especially low-income migrants that were poorly prepared for nonfarm employment, did not (Hathaway and Perkins 1968, 185–237). A large portion of the farm operators leaving the farm over this period were retirement age; others left for better opportunities. Those forced to leave ranged from good farmers who had taken on more debt than they could sustain when the farm markets were depressed, to others who had failed because they were not good farmers or financial managers. Others were young farmers who had made no mistake other than to start farming just before a major decline in farm prices. In the South, significant numbers of farm workers were forced out of agriculture by farm policies that created incentives for farmers to eliminate sharecroppers or tenants. Other than price supports, the only public policy that facilitated this transition to other occupations was the investment in rural education made by state and local governments. Farm policies have long worked to keep people in agriculture; they have never consciously and effectively tried to help those that had to leave.

While it is true that economists argued well into the post-war period about the nature of demand-and-supply behavior in agriculture, as far back as World War II leading economists in agriculture were forecasting a continuing decline in the number of farms and farm population. They talked of the need for adjustment policies for agriculture, including programs to move land resources out of farming, assistance for farmers who were facing downward pressures on farm prices and income, and also aid for farm families who were being forced to leave (e.g., Schultz 1943, 1945; *Postwar Agricultural Policy* 1944, 50–58). Nobel Laureate T. W. Schultz characterized the effort needed to help those migrating from farming as "homesteads in reverse" (Schultz 1961). Over the years since, there have been repeated recommendations to provide "help for those leaving" (cf. Heady 1967; Bishop 1969). Nothing was ever done in the political process to act on this obvious social need.

In the past, the focus of agricultural institutions has been on those clients left in agriculture, and this attention has focused almost exclusively on expanding farm productivity and production. This was an individually rational solution to a problem (how to stay in farming) for each farmer. If one could become the most productive farmer, one could survive in agriculture. But it was collectively a nonsolution. The greater the expansion in production per farmer, the more farmers (and their families and workers) that would have to be squeezed out of farming. However, the dilemma is even more extensive. From the Civil War to the 1950s, the industrial development and improved welfare of Americans depended on increasing agricultural productivity and production to feed an expanding U.S. population and to releasing labor for the urban labor force. The benefits of improved agricultural productivity have accrued mostly to American consumers and through a lower wage bill to U.S. industry and business.

Farming confronts a situation wherein both the price and income elasticity of demand for farm products are substantially less than one. Thus, if there is any well-known truth in farming, it is that more productivity has to lead to fewer commercial farmers. Increases in productivity due to the replacement of labor with alternative factors of production (chemicals, energy, capital) will lead to a faster reduction in the number of farmers and farm workers than increases in productivity that use labor-intensive technologies, but both lead to the need for fewer commercial farms. While using labor-intensive technologies produces more farmers and farm workers than capital-intensive technologies, it also creates price pressures that lead to a lower income per farmer. Thus, there is a direct tradeoff between commercial farm numbers and relative income.

The number of commercial farmers can only stabilize if farm productivity is growing at a rate that is substantially less than the rate at which real incomes are growing in the consumer sector. With the output per hour of farm-labor input growing at five percent per year in the 1980s and real personal income growing at less than three percent per year, simple arithmetic guarantees fewer farmers (*ERP* 1990, 325, 404). With large productivity gains from biotechnology and other innovations looming on the horizon, there is also little reason to believe that any slow down in the growth of farm productivity is about to occur. Of course, if farm productivity does not grow, the comparative advantage of the U.S. farm sector in international trade will soon erode. There is no escape from this dilemma.

Socially, one can argue that the outcome has been optimal. More production led to lower prices for agricultural products and higher real urban incomes. The farmers and farm workers who left agriculture went to work in other industries, expanding production above what would have been possible without them. This is the central transformation necessary for the industrial development of an agrarian nation. Overall, the benefits are substantial.

While focusing on raising productivity may have been a rational social strategy given the desire for higher material standards of living over the last century, it would seem to carry with it, however, the social obligation to plan for the decline of agriculture and to provide some farm aid to the millions of workers who would be forced to move from farming to other careers. Those who left, plus the rural communities that lost their economic base, were forced to absorb the costs that would allow millions of others (those remaining on the farms and urban consumers) to make real income gains. Most of those that moved may have ended up with higher material standards of living than they would have had back on the farm, but they bore the human costs of leaving a farm environment and had to go through a transitional phase where they often had lower incomes. Also, in the process, much of the investment rural communities made in young people was transferred to urban centers, and the economic base of many rural communities was destroyed. Since the price-support system and other production subsidies supported the income of those staying on the farm, *the failure to aid low-income movers in this transition is the central failure of U.S. agricultural institutions and leaders.* The decline of many rural communities was, and is, unavoidable but, as critics point out, the costs of improving agricultural productivity were imposed on rural communities without serious consideration of the equity issues involved.

If an outsider looked at the farm "crisis" of the 1980s and was not allowed to look at the statistics for the 1970s, that outsider would wonder what the crying was all about. In the period from 1945 to 1970, when America was losing 5 million farm jobs, it generated 31 million nonfarm jobs, and farmers had to gain only 16 percent of those jobs if they were to work in alternative employment. From 1980 to 1986, farm employment fell by only 200,000. Over the same period, the nonfarm economy generated 10.5 million jobs. Farmers had to capture only 2 percent of these jobs to become employed in alternative employment (*ERP* 1990, 330). Whatever the job transition problems of today's unemployed farmers, in the aggregate they are minimal in comparison with the past.

The real farm GNP (1982 dollars) rose $7 billion from 1945 to 1970, rose another $3.5 billion from 1970 to 1980, and then jumped by $20 billion from 1980 to 1986 (*ERP* 1990, 305). Farm output actually grew much faster in the 1980s than it did in the earlier decades. Even in the peak years of the 1970s, output was only $4 billion higher than 1970 and only one-half billion higher than 1980. Whatever was happening in the 1980s that created a crisis is not to be found in output figures.

The feeling of crisis is, of course, produced by comparisons with the boom of the 1970s and the financial obligations that were incurred because of this boom. If one ignores the 1970s, what was happening in the 1980s was merely a continuation of a long-term trend toward shrinkage. Decline is once again occurring—but, in fact, at a much slower rate than in the past.

In the export boom of the 1970s, farm employment did not decline as it had earlier. Real net farm income (1982 dollars) more than doubled; from $34 billion in 1970 to a peak of $69 billion in 1973 (*ERP* 1990, 403). The 1970s were an exception to the rule that each decade would see a substantially smaller farm sector than the previous decade. Remember, however, that the real farm GNP grew very little in the 1970s. Incomes rose because prices were going up, not because farm output was increasing.

Realistically, given the low income and price elasticities that dominate markets for agricultural products, and a worldwide high rate of growth of agricultural productivity (both widely known facts), there was no possibility that agricultural prices could forever remain at the levels of the 1970s. When prices fall, as they inevitably do, farm incomes fall and farming returns again to a shrinking industry. This was already understood in 1945 (Schultz 1945).

The truth is that farming inevitably was, and will be, a shrinking industry (Anderson 1987). Real production will grow slowly with domestic population, and beyond that only with export expansion. Given the rapid rates of growth of total-factor productivity in the future, fewer people, less land, and fewer units of other input will be necessary than in the past. Clearly, the industry has to plan for decline and to help ease the pains of transition for those that will inevitably be forced out of farming. There is no solution to this problem within agriculture.

The good news is that the number that will now be leaving agriculture is very small in relation to the rest of the economy. The transition for this small number should be easier than it was for those who left in the past. Since part-time farmers with off-farm income and large commercial (full-time) farmers have exhibited more staying power than farmers with middle- to small-sized commercial farms, the pressure to move is apt to be the most acute on the latter group.

The current feeling of crisis has not been caused by the very small number of family farmers that have left farming since 1980; it has been generated by the false expectations of the future that were built into the career plans, the land prices, and the bank loans of the 1970s. If one is faulting agricultural institutions and leadership, one then has to ask whether they did see, or should have foreseen, the abnormal nature of the 1970s, and whether they did convey, or could have conveyed, this information to their clients so that the clients could have avoided building career plans, overpricing land, and taking bank loans on misleading beliefs about the future.

The current feeling of crisis is also created by the fact that those in agriculture psychologically understand that decline is once again upon them. But, the collapse of the boom was simply too rapid and too unforeseen, and what seemed like a "bust" was merely a return to normal. People are going to continue to leave farming and some regions are going to decline or go out of farming almost entirely. Agriculture is once again a shrinking industry. Not surprisingly, it is the nature of humans to be unwilling to confront this reality and plan for it. At the political level, farmers and many that serve them want a magic cure that will change this long-standing reality but, by now, they also should know that there is no such cure.

IT'S UN-AMERICAN TO PLAN FOR DECLINE

While the facts about agriculture's decline are clear, Americans find it virtually impossible to face this reality and plan for it no matter what the industry. Part of Japan's Ministry of International Trade and Industry is charged with planning "strategic industrial retreats." Recessionary cartels (group planning as to how an industry can collectively cope with long-run decline) are allowed by law when it becomes clear that an industry (aluminum is a current example) will inevitably decline. America has no analogous arrangement.

This happens, in part, because Americans believe that the market takes care of failure. In theory, free markets drive the most inefficient producers out of business with no need for planning. In fact, as the Japanese point out, markets drive those with the least financial staying power out of business. Those leaving an industry need not be the least efficient managers working with least efficient productive resources. This is also true in farming today; it is not the least efficient farmer that is driven out of business, but the farmer with the most debts and the least financial staying power. During the period when those with the least financial staying power are being driven out of business, it is also usually necessary for those that remain in the industry to incur losses. Those losses deprive them of the resources that they will need in the future to compete more effectively with foreign competitors.

The effects of this are now being felt in farming. American farmers have been falling behind European farmers in buying the latest technology. Europe has erected a protectionist wall around its agriculture with subsidies that help to drive its growth; Europe's subsidies are second only to Japan's. European farmers have had more money than American farmers for improving productivity. As a consequence, in many farm commodities, European farmers are rapidly closing the productivity gap that once existed. Planning a strategic retreat often results in a much stronger industry than simply letting the market rip.

It is certainly possible to charge that agricultural institutions and leadership have been unwilling to plan for decline. But, it is equally true that other sectors have not planned for decline, and that Americans do not want to plan for decline. Much of this attitude comes from the political process where the deliberate depopulation of congressional districts does not appeal to incumbent congressmen, but it partly relates to deeper psychological resistances. To forecast that decline will occur, or to plan for it, is to be a pessimist, and Americans are optimists. Pessimists are ignored, muzzled, or dismissed.

If one is willing to forecast decline and plan for it, the technical problems of how to do it are trivial. Everyone knows what must be done. Knowledge is first conveyed as to whom and what are marginal and apt to be forced out of agricultural production. This applies to people, farm commodities, and land. One accurately conveys information as to where marginal farm lands are located geographically and where real land values are most likely to fall in the future, so that the fewest mistakes will be made in current investments and plans. Government land-retirement schemes would not be spread evenly across the country, but focused on those geographic areas that should retire from agricultural production.

One raises the saleable urban skills of those who are going to be forced to leave farming, if one wants to ease the transition from farm to nonfarm employment. One provides geographic, occupational, and industrial information as to where former farmers and farm workers should move, and aid is given to help facilitate those moves.

Farm expenditures would be focused on those that leave farming rather than on those that remain. No one would pretend that the current problems are temporary and hold out the hope that, if one would just hang on by their fingertips long enough, there would be a return to the good old days of high incomes and rapidly rising land values. Farmers would be advised to declare bankruptcy rather than to struggle if their situation is really hopeless. If those farmers in trouble are actually efficient producers and have simply made one bad mistake (taken on too much debt in the 1970s), debt write-downs would be negotiated. The chronic, high-rolling gamblers among farmers would not be allowed to impose their losses on the taxpayer. (Of course, the United States has bailed out even less deserving savings and loan institutions.) Small rural towns would be told that their agricultural base was going to disappear. One would talk about nonagricultural rural revitalization only in areas where it was possible. In most areas it would not be possible, given the realities of inadequate transportation, inferior infrastructure, and generally low levels of skill among the local work force.

In the past, rural areas could compete for low-skilled American industrial operations with low wages. This was the strategy of the rural American Southeast. But, with the development of an integrated world economy, there will always be other places in the world where wages are lower. Rural communities in today's world economy can only compete in producing internationally traded products if they can generate labor forces more skilled than those found in places such as Korea, or if they have recreational and retirement potential, or if they can serve as bedroom communities close to metropolitan areas. Over the past six years, much of the decline in American manufacturing employment has, in fact, been located in rural areas because the low skill levels of their population make them the most marginal manufacturing areas in the United States.

The decline in farm numbers was routinely forecast by both the economists and demographers in the USDA and the colleges of agriculture. The problem is not what to do or what to say, but to be willing to confront reality. On one level, it is easy to castigate the agricultural establishment and its leaders for not responding to decline by developing plans as to how best cope with it; on another level, it is not. If those in the agricultural establishment had planned for decline, at best they would have been ignored; at worst, they would have been denounced or dismissed so that their pessimism could be replaced by optimism and views more congenial to the traditional American spirit.

There is just enough individual truth in the doctrine "that planning for expansion (more production) will save you" to obscure the collective reality that, in the aggregate, precisely the reverse is true: More production will lead to the need to move more, not less, people and resources to other uses.

Planning for decline also confronts another harsh reality: Those who win the production wars will remain inside the industry and be available to help public agricultural institutions in future battles for resources; those who lose the production wars will become outsiders. They may remember fondly the aid given in their transition to nonfarm activities, but they will have been dispersed across the economy, be difficult or impossible to mobilize for future political battles, and have little interest in devoting resources to those that remain in farming or its supporting activities, such as agricultural colleges or the extension service. To aid those who must leave an industry is to spend one's time and resources undercutting one's own political base. It should be, but is rarely done.

The responsibilities for the failure of agriculture to plan for decline were laid out clearly over a quarter of a century ago by Hathaway (1963):

> ...every knowledgeable policy maker in agriculture realizes that further reductions in the farm population and labor force are not only essential to even a partial solution to the disequilibrium problem, but also inevitable. However, the values relating to agriculture and the folkways of farm politics are such that it is unheard of for a national official to even admit this—let alone advocate policies to improve the resource transfers. Instead, every Secretary of Agriculture is obliged, almost as a ritual, to guarantee that under his administration all who might wish to farm will become prosperous (378).
>
> ...economists have known for ten years that the labor force in agriculture was declining and would continue to do so. Even so, it has not generally been openly discussed in colleges of agriculture because of the hostility of production-oriented colleagues. This has contributed to continuation of programs geared to another age and other needs (379).
>
> The agricultural industry in the United States has been largely dependent upon public research and education agencies to develop and disseminate information about new technology and new practices. These organizations have never developed an accompanying research and education program regarding the aggregate impact of these changes or the equilibrium level of their adoption. At present much of the new technology is developed and promoted by private businesses, and it is not in the interest of these businesses to tell farmers that they cannot expect future prices to remain as high after the new output-increasing technology is widely adopted. These companies want to sell feed, seed, fertilizer, and machinery, and while it is in their individual interest to have good research to avoid overinvesting in productive facilities that will prove unprofitable, it is not in their interest to do the same for their customers (380–81).

THE TECHNOLOGICAL FIX

Since the Manhattan Project in World War II, Americans have held the belief that there is a technological fix to every problem. If we are simply willing to put in enough money, any problem can be solved. The equivalent of the atomic bomb can be found. The man-on-the-moon project of the

1960s firmly fixed that belief in the American mind. But the belief is basically false. Every problem is researchable, but every problem is not solvable.

In agriculture, this belief is seen as the idea that the problems in agriculture are somehow caused by the fact that agricultural research has been focused on helping the big farmer and not the smaller family farmer. According to this argument, if the research had been properly focused in the first place, the problems would not have occurred and if research were now properly refocused, the problems could be eliminated.

This argument makes a basic arithmetic mistake. Some commercial family farmers must go out of business even if all research is focused on medium- and small-sized family farmers, as long as the supply of farm products is growing faster than the demand for them. As long as income and price elasticities of demand for farm products are less than one and productivity growth equals or exceeds the growth in real incomes, farm employment must decline even if all research is focused on family farmers. The result is: Family farmers drive family farmers out of business. Research and development on raising production cannot solve the problem of decline no matter how this research is directed.

One can argue inconclusively as to whether past research has, in fact, been too focused on activities that were expected to yield more gains to large farmers than to small- or medium-sized farmers since it is not clear how one measures the extent to which research money is focused on the problems of farmers with different sized farms. No researcher has ever been given the instructions, "Do whatever you want as long as it helps large farmers." Researchers work on problems such as pest control, and one would have to decide, before anything had been discovered, whether pest control is intrinsically something that would more aid large farmers than it would aid middle- or small-sized farmers.

More importantly, even if it could be shown that the agricultural research establishment had been given instructions to aid large farmers, those instructions would have been irrelevant. Research simply cannot be directed to come up with particular outcomes and there is a large economic literature that documents this result. What is called "induced technical progress," a piece of technical progress designed to use some particular input, simply does not occur (Samuelson 1965). A pest-control research project, designed with large farmers in mind, may end up producing a pest-control technique that helps small farmers much more than it helps large farmers. No workable research results have been suppressed simply because they ended up helping middle-sized farmers. Basically, the agricultural establishment has no ability to direct its research results so that these results come up with ideas that help the large farmers and not the small- to middle-sized family farmers.

The current excitement about superconductivity, for example, was started by some European scientists working for IBM, who happened upon superconductivity by accident as they were exploring new ceramic materials. Superconductivity may well revolutionize the world, but its current potential feasibility was not discovered by scientists who had been directed to work on superconductivity.

Expost, there is also no evidence that the productivity of farms that require the labor of one or two workers has gone up more slowly than that of farms large enough to require the work of many laborers. Many large corporations have retreated from their 1970s' farming investments since they could not, in fact, compete with family farms.

If one wants to fault the direction of technology, the real fault lies in other directions. By focusing on raising the production of large-volume crops, such as corn, wheat, soybeans, and cotton, many of the manmade comparative advantages that might have been created have been ignored. Cut flowers are probably the best example. Most of America's cut flowers are imported from Holland—a very high-wage country. Flowers could be grown in America, but they are not. The problem with cut flowers is not production (growing flowers), but the marketing and distribution system that is necessary to deliver flowers that are fresh to the right place at the right time. Research on production could never make cut flowers an American industry. The research would have to be focused on management and distribution systems. A successful example of this in the United States is the California almond growers that have successfully established a growing almond market in Japan through an imaginative marketing strategy.

Many other examples can be given. There is a current proposal to make a large area of East Central Montana into what is called the "Big Open." This is essentially an effort to regenerate the original Great Plains, with its teeming wildlife, into an area where an organized farm collective would allow today's very marginal farmers to make a much better living serving and guiding tourists and hunters. The proposal did not come out of the state's agricultural college, however, since it does not involve farm production. It does, however, involve turning farming into a recreation industry. It should also be said that local farmers are not enthusiastic about a proposal that essentially gives up on more production as a solution to their problems.

Similarly, urban desires for food raised without chemicals opens up a high-priced market for agricultural products. Some critics argue that agricultural colleges have been slow to explore this potential since, in this case, the food has to be raised with techniques that reduce rather than raise productivity. The colleges of agriculture have worked extensively on low-input tillage and integrated pest management, but finding and combining "profitable" low-energy technologies with market niches is not easy. The "chemical-free" food market is also not likely to be large enough to accommodate all U.S. food output. It might also be argued that these demands were responded to slowly because they cast aspersions on the technologies recommended by agricultural colleges in the past.

Creative suggestions as to manmade comparative advantages in rural areas have been infrequent in the agricultural colleges of America. This is because they are precisely colleges of agriculture and because these alternative proposals usually require a set of experts different from the plant and animal scientists who dominate the faculties of our colleges of agriculture and whose mentality is circumscribed by the belief that the ultimate aim of research is to raise productivity and thus production (Hathaway 1963, 379).

Unfortunately, the biotechnology revolution that is now upon us is apt to bias our vision even more so toward the traditional goals of increasing the production of our traditional products. It will be seen as the new miracle cure—a chance to, once again, get ahead of other countries in productivity. It will not happen. The rest of the world will keep pace with our agricultural research just as it now keeps pace with our industrial research. If biotechnology is, in fact, a big boost to productivity, then even more farmers will be forced to leave farming than would otherwise have been the case. What is needed in both biotechnology and older technologies is more imagination to create new man-made comparative advantages. The falling dollar will uncover some of our old comparative advantages, but in the modern world, comparative advantages depend more upon human ingenuity than they do on the intrinsic gifts of mother nature.

THE FOREIGN SOLUTION

Because Americans cannot eat all that American farmers can grow, it became popular in the 1970s to believe that Americans could become farmers for the rest of the world. Agricultural incomes went up and the industry stabilized because it became much more of an export industry—at the peak, 60 percent of the wheat crop, 40 percent of the soybean, rice, and cotton crops, and 25 percent of the corn crop were being exported. This upward trend was seen as permanent. It proved to be temporary. By 1986, agricultural trade surpluses had all but disappeared. While exports and the agricultural trade surplus have rebounded, it is not likely that the early 1980 trade-surplus levels will be seen again soon. Before U.S. agricultural exports expand much beyond current $40-billion levels, the economic growth of Third World nations will have to improve.

This raises a question as to whether the mid-1980s decline could have been foreseen and those exports stopped from becoming embedded in the plans of those involved with agriculture (farmers, suppliers, bankers, etc.), or whether something could have been done to prevent the actual decline in exports.

What happened in the rest of the world is clear. The "green revolution" worked, if one means by the "green revolution" not just new varieties of plants, but a new awareness of the need to give peasants a financial incentive to produce; commit major investments in equipment, such as wells and tractors; make new investments in human capital; create new institutions; and promote strong local research and development efforts. Agricultural productivity rose dramatically in many Third World countries and, for the first time in many generations, they now feed themselves.

In addition, the Third World debt crisis has led to a situation where fewer middle-income countries are reaching the stage of development where per capita income attains a level wherein meat enters the diet in substantial amounts. Humans, who consume their grain indirectly in the form of meat, use much more grain in this manner than if they ate the grain directly. (Animals can be thought of as machines that convert grain into more tasty forms but they do so at the cost of using many more grain calories than if humans ate the grain themselves.) A rapid rise in meat consumption usually makes a country into a grain importer for some period of time because the need for grain to feed animals, to satisfy meat demands, grows faster than domestic grain production. As a result, the debt crisis aborts the growth in demand for American grain.

The growth of agricultural productivity in much of the developed world and among traditional food-exporting nations has also reduced or sometimes even reversed America's traditional comparative advantages in agricultural production. In the mid-1970s, the Common Market imported 25 million tons of grain; in 1985, after years of large agricultural subsidies and protection, it exported 16 million tons of grain (*ERP* 1987, 149). To know such facts is to know that world grain prices will be under strong pressures from surpluses.

The policies that led to a high-valued dollar and high domestic-support prices for U.S. agricultural products accelerated the decline in exports, but they did not cause it, for it would have occurred without these policy "mistakes." The problem was caused by higher foreign productivity and growing export and production subsidies in industrial nations. Conversely, better policies—a lower-valued dollar, a different price-support system—may alleviate, but cannot cure the problem.

American farmers live with the myth of American agricultural supremacy. They believe that their unit costs of producing almost anything are lower than those to be found in the rest of the world. This belief in their supremacy is false. The current GATT (General Agreement on Tariff and Trade) round of negotiations is supposed to lead to free trade in agricultural production, yet how many American farmers know that free trade between Europe and the United States might result in more wheat exports from Europe and the substantial demise of the U.S. dairy industry for anything other than fluid milk? (*Agricultural Trade in Disarray* 1986, 21). When Americans demand open access for rice in Japan, how many farmers know that Thailand is the world's lowest-cost producer of rice? How many farmers know that with the same technology and capital investments, Brazilian soybean producers may dominate American producers with higher yields per acre and per person?

To know the future of American farming, one must have a realistic understanding of where Americans really do have a comparative advantage in agriculture and, more importantly, how that comparative advantage is apt to change over time as the rest of the world catches up with the United States in terms of agricultural technology and capital investments in farming and its supporting industries. Like the rest of the American economy, the American farmer now lives in a world where he is better at some things, worse at other things, but on the whole, he is average. He cannot compete based on the effortless technological superiority or higher capital investments that he had in the past. America does not have a comparative advantage in all agriculture; it only has a comparative advantage in some parts of agriculture. An understanding of where we do and do not have a real comparative advantage or where we can make a real comparative advantage should be a central concern of agricultural economists.

Foreign productivity is no longer dependent upon the export of technology or capital equipment from the United States. Institutions to provide these factors of production now exist elsewhere in the developed world, and foreign productivity growth is not dependent upon the U.S. research establishment. New techniques are now, in fact, being increasingly imported into the United States. When it comes to productivity-enhancing innovations, American farmers have much to learn from foreign practices, yet our institutions for tapping these foreign sources of expertise are limited. The solution is not to limit our existing institutions for exporting technology, but to expand our institutions for importing foreign technology and to monitor advances in foreign farm practices that might be transferred profitably to the United States.

More importantly, if the American farmer was able to become the food supplier for the world, that ability would not solve the farm problem—it would merely move the decline of agriculture from the United States to the rest of the world. Farmers here would be forced to leave farming less rapidly, but farmers elsewhere in the world would be forced to leave farming more rapidly. Globally, the decline that must occur would remain the same (Anderson 1987). Foreign farmers, who love to be farmers just as American farmers love to be farmers, would be forced to leave farming.

At this point, one can ask to what degree the agricultural establishment was, or is, ignorant of what was, or is occurring, in the rest of the world; the extent to which the agricultural establishment engaged in wishful thinking that foreign markets were permanent, or can now be recaptured; the extent to which the agricultural establishment knew, or knows, the truth; and did not, or does not, clearly convey the painful truth to its clients; and the extent to which farmers and their organizations would not, or do not, hear the truth even if it was, and is, clearly being stated. To some extent, all of the above are probably true. Ignorance, wishful thinking, the desire not to be the deliverer of bad news, an unwillingness to confront reality—all of these conditions probably contributed to the present problems.

To eliminate the current crisis and plan for the future, the American agricultural establishment has to have a clear understanding of what is happening in the rest of the world and what will happen dynamically, over time, as America's lead in technology and capital investment per farmer, or per acre, diminishes and changes. They then need to convey the truth, whatever it is, to both farmers and policy makers.

There also needs to be a fair dose of political realism. If one looks at income and price elasticities and looks at the rate of productivity growth in agriculture worldwide, farmers somewhere in the world are going to have to leave farming. Politically, the rest of the industrial world is not apt to agree that its farmers should be the ones to leave farming, even based upon hard economic evidence, unless the United States would also agree that its farmers should be the ones to leave farming if hard, economic and agricultural science analysis were to show that American farmers did not have a comparative advantage in some specific product. Would America do so if the data showed, as it seems to show, that American dairy farming is inefficient relative to that of Europe? The answer is clearly no.

With government farm programs, especially in the United States, Japan, and Europe, having disguised where their real comparative advantages actually lie, there is great uncertainty as to where the different countries have their advantages. Few countries know what parts of their farm sectors would disappear in a world with fewer trade restrictions on farm products. No one will dramatically lift trade restrictions with such uncertainties. The best that might be achieved is a very small marginal reduction in trade restrictions as a test, akin to "dipping one's toe in the water to see how cold it really is" for one's own farmers. It should be remembered that, in the 1950s, it was the U.S. Congress, not the foreign countries, that kept agricultural products from being included in the original GATT agreements that led to a freer trade for manufactured products.

The chances that the current GATT round will lead to a substantial opening up of foreign agricultural markets is slight, simply because no country wants its farmers to be the ones to go out of business and each country will seek to preserve its domestic markets for its farmers. Farmers in other countries love to be farmers as much as American farmers do and have as much political influence as American farmers, or more. To ask for the probability of success, one merely has to speculate on the probability of the United States signing an agreement leading to the demise of many, and perhaps most, of its dairy farmers. The United States does not want free trade in agriculture any more than anyone else. We want free trade where we have a comparative advantage, and the right to protect where we do not have a comparative advantage. But if we and everyone else wish to maintain such protection, there is no possibility of a movement to free trade in agriculture.

Just as importantly, it is impossible to have free trade in agricultural products internationally without having free trade in agricultural products domestically. Otherwise, there is no way to know where real comparative advantages lie. But, this means that a successful conclusion to that GATT round would essentially dictate U.S. domestic agricultural policies—there could be no domestic agricultural support system (subsidies), or they would have to be identical to those adopted in other industrialized countries.

Currently in the popular press, the opening up of foreign agricultural markets is held up as the salvation of the American farmer. It will not happen and, even if it did, it would not change the nature of the problem. Fewer feedgrain farmers might go out of business and more dairy farmers might go out of business, but it is doubtful that the shrinkage of U.S. agriculture would be noticeably affected in the aggregate with freer trade in agricultural products.

Wishful thinking and a refusal to confront reality are parts of human nature, but the question here is the extent to which that natural human characteristic should be discouraged by agriculture's intellectual establishment and the extent to which the political process will back up that "reality treatment." Intellectuals in agriculture, especially social scientists, have a special responsibility in this process.

EXPLORING ALTERNATIVE SYSTEMS

Capitalism is the doctrine with which the efficient can, should, and will drive the inefficient out of business. It is precisely this process of creative destruction that generates higher standards of living for the average American, although it can, and does, often lead to lower standards of living for specific Americans. A belief in capitalism does not stop anyone from receiving psychic income from a particular activity, such as farming, but it does say if persons love to be farmers, they must pay for that love by being willing to work for less than those that do not have such a love and are willing to work wherever their income is highest. Those who are willing to incur the monetary and human costs of moving deserve to have a higher standard of living than those that are unwilling to move. What those who choose not to move cannot do under pure capitalism, however, is to demand that those who have been willing to make the sacrifices of moving be forced to give up some of their income to provide nonmovers with parity in living standards.

This doctrine can be challenged—it relies on a set of ethical propositions that do not have to command acceptance and, in much of human history, have not commanded majority acceptance (highly successful societies, such as the Roman Empire, have not been built upon capitalistic principles)—but the doctrine of capitalism cannot be selectively challenged. If it is to be challenged for farmers, it must be challenged for everyone. There is nothing that sets farmers apart from others. In the last six years, others that love their occupations equally well as farmers (copper miners, manufacturers, etc.) have been forced to switch occupations. The decline in mining employment has been about as large as the decline in farm employment, and many more workers have been forced to leave manufacturing than were forced to leave farming (*ERP* 1990, 342, 405). Those people loved their work mates, neighborhoods, and occupations just as much as any farmer loved his.

Farm populists have long argued that agriculture is different and deserves special treatment. This agrarian fundamentalism has persisted from this nation's early days and it is shared widely beyond agriculture. Over many decades, it has successfully sustained special treatment for farmers in public policy. When examined, agricultural fundamentalism has been rejected by almost all social scientists as factually and logically indefensible (Davis 1935; Griswold 1948).

Thus, it cannot be argued that somehow farmers are treated differently in our capitalistic system; i.e., they sell in competitive markets and buy in ologopolistic markets. Others are treated similarly; anyone selling his labor is a little guy selling to a big guy. (Only 14 percent of the urban work force had a union negotiating on their behalf in 1986.)

Thus, to be defensible, the idea that a different system needs to be constructed for farmers must be buried in a more general argument that those who love their work should not be forced to endure much lower material standards of living if they express this love by not moving. Because of this general principle, whatever it is, it becomes legitimate to tax those willing to move into urban areas to support the lifestyle of those not willing to move.

Before this argument can be made, a lot of humanistic or social science work has to be done. What is there about farming that makes it different, unique, or better than other occupations? When someone says that farmers are "nearer to nature," what does that mean? Farmers are certainly not natural ecologists. Once the characteristics, whatever they are, that make farming better and/or unique are clearly outlined and enumerated, then, and only then, can we discuss the extent to which these characteristics are worth preserving and the alternative ways for doing so. I join Don Paarlberg (1980, 5–13) in doubting that such a case can honestly be made today.

To use an example, since it is easier to understand arguments not directly affecting one's own lifestyle, let us consider mining. Miners protest at being driven out of mining. Why? Let me give you my answer that is based upon growing up in a mining community. When the mines close, miners are forced to leave their communities. These are very close-knit communities given their usual geographic isolation and the shared dangers of working underground. Miners do not love their jobs, but they love their communities and do not want to be forced to leave. If feelings of community are really at the heart of the issue, one can then think of how communities might be maintained, but this would not necessarily lead to the conclusion that mining should be subsidized. In fact, there might be much better techniques for keeping these communities alive.

I suspect that, like mining, the real issue is not farming itself but the feeling of community and of having to move away from one's friends and relatives. But, I am open to other arguments. Perhaps it is no more complex than farmers have discovered that enough of the public holds agrarian-fundamentalist values to make them responsive to farmers' views. Thus, farmers have found it worthwhile to organize and complain.

What are the limits of an economic market? What things should it not be allowed to decide? These are good questions. But, they are not questions where the answers are of relevance only to farmers. If the decision is made that market forces cannot be allowed to drive farmers and others who share in the same characteristics out of business, then different systems for bringing about such a result could be explored, and the costs and benefits of each could be enumerated.

The agricultural establishment has not explored the precise uniqueness of farming or the techniques for preserving this uniqueness, but it is equally true that, if they had done so, they would have been denounced by many of their farm clients as subversive. In the 1970s, patriotic free-enterprise speeches sold as well to farmers as they sold in urban America. Thus, it is difficult to argue that the intellectual agricultural establishment did not do what it should have done.

ENVIRONMENTAL ISSUES

Critics have charged that issues of sustainability have not rated high priority in the agricultural agenda, that agriculture has been treated as if it were an extractive industry, like mining, where one expects ultimately to have to go out of the business because the natural resources will have been depleted and exhausted. Slow to respond perhaps, but, today, sustainability is high on the agenda of both the USDA and the colleges of agriculture. Preserving groundwater availability and limiting the toxic pollution of water or land is seen as urgent in most colleges of agriculture. Historically, efforts have focused on soil conservation and the proper management of irrigation projects (waterlogging or salinity), but perhaps this has not been enough. Alternatives to the current dependence upon energy-intensive forms of agriculture were slow to be explored despite the well-known uncertainties and expected variability in future energy prices. For over a century, the central goal has been production rather than sustainability (*Agriculture and the Environment* 1986).

One can argue that this blind spot is simply part of American culture and not specific to agriculture. This is certainly true. Externalities are not handled well anywhere. Witness our problems in coming to grips with acid rain. Environmental regulations are now far more stringent in other developed foreign countries than they are here and, as a consequence, their water- and air-quality improvements have been greater than ours. Stewardship of our natural resources for the benefit of future generations is little preached and even less practiced in America. Visual pollution mars almost all of our recreational areas.

In this day and age, planning for the future is not an American trait. Our steel industry cannot roll steel to the tolerances or with the lack of impurities of its foreign competitors because no steel executive has been willing to build the necessary new mills. During the time needed to construct such mills, the executive's profits and bonuses would have been hurt while helping those of his successor. A gift to the future was required, but no one was willing to make such a gift. To say that others also erred, however, is not to say that agriculture has not erred.

To correct these systematic errors requires an understanding of how our values and institutions were led to such practices. Social scientists have not led the way to better understanding. Instead, we have tended to choose up sides for an unproductive fight over environmentalism—one is either for it or against it. While I am encouraged by the growing research efforts in the colleges of agriculture that are now being focused on sustainable agriculture, I foresee a long road ahead.

The lack of interest in sustainability springs from several factors. Many American institutions look to short-term horizons. The Deutsche Bank, for example, with its controlling interest in Daimler-Benz, has a longer time horizon for Daimler-Benz than the legally required arms-length financiers who bankroll Ford Motor Company. The ease and availability of consumer credit in the United States leads to a world where instant consumer gratification is a way of life. Other nations demand larger down payments and faster repayment periods.

Problems with long time lags are not taken seriously until the bad results actually begin to occur. For example, the danger of asbestos has long been known but only recently acted upon.

Americans believe that a technical cure will always turn up. No matter how bad things may seem, there will be a technical solution that will not require changes in current practices. Someone will find a magic cure for falling groundwater tables or groundwater pollution.

Today, Americans have been led to believe that free-market behavior solves all problems. As a natural resource vanishes, its price will gradually rise and America will smoothly move to alternative resources. The discontinuities of the 1970s' oil shock are forgotten here—all of our synthetic fuel projects have been discontinued as unnecessary, while abroad such projects continue.

The adversarial nature of our institutions encourages us to argue without information. To be really useful, environmental-impact statements should be cheap and simple so that they can be used in the planning process before anyone is locked into some specific action. Instead, environmental-impact statements are complex and expensive. As a result, they are never commissioned unless someone already knows what they want to do. Essentially, they become tools of advocacy useful in legal battles rather than social and environmental-impact statements useful in community decision making.

Intelligent pest control is not practiced because it requires detailed knowledge to be effective, requires one to accept risks (the pests may get out of control) and uncertainty (too much pesticide may cause long-run environmental problems but increase the certainty of short-run production results) (*Agriculture and the Environment* 1986, 149). The technology cannot be implemented unless some values are changed and perhaps some institutions (insurance?) are altered. Work on the supporting human values and institutional structures simply has not been seen to be important by most agricultural research directors.

The problem is not better assessment of the consequences of new technologies, but being willing to build the values and institutions that can make those new technologies useful and environmentally benign in the context of the long-run sustainability of agriculture. This is a leadership role to be played in both agriculture and the larger society. As long as the colleges of agriculture limit their vision to technology and their staffing primarily to the natural sciences, they will remain part of the problem and not the solution. And, the critics of the performance of the agricultural establishment will continue to accumulate.

THE CURRENT CRISIS

As a continuation of the trends of the 1950s and 1960s, the 1980s' farming shrinkage was not objectively a farm crisis. As has already been demonstrated, the shrinkage of farming occurred at a much slower rate in the 1980s than it occurred in earlier periods of time. Farmers have left farming at a much faster pace in the past with no talk of "crisis."

The answer is found in farm wealth. Those left in farming have been made poorer. By 1986, farm real estate values (per-acre prices) had fallen, on average, more than 30 percent from peak values in 1981 and much more in some states (*ERP* 1990, 408). Because of a run-up in farm debt in the 1970s, proprietor equity has fallen more. Since the "Great Depression," market declines have not led to falling farmland values over sustained periods or reduced wealth for those left in farming. This time, those who stayed in farming have sustained significant reductions in their wealth while, in the recent past, most of the costs of shrinkage had been borne by those that left farming. Yet, at even the depressed levels in 1986, the average farmer had more net equity than the average urban person. Farm-asset values are rebounding from their 1986 low, and, after correction for inflation, farm wealth has returned to about the level of 1971 (Survey of Consumer Finances 1983, 1984, 863; *ERP* 1990, 408).

The problem is obviously the 1970s. That decade was a temporary deviation from the long-run trend. It led to unrealistic expectations and unrealistic plans that then came back to haunt those that embarked on those unrealistic plans (for a contrary view, see Tweeten 1986). Could this situation have been prevented? Without the run-up in land values, those debts would not have been taken on, and much of the current decline in farm wealth would not have occurred. The run-down in wealth would not have occurred because the earlier run-up in farm wealth would not have occurred.

There is every reason to believe that this situation could not have been prevented. Real interest rates were negative during much of the 1970s, and similar speculative bubbles occurred in oil and office-building investments. Recent declines in wealth have been just as rapid there as in farming.

It is also true that even at the height of the boom, land values could not be justified in terms of the then-current prices for crops. The current value of land had to be justified by the fact that future value of land would rise and, if anyone bothered to work out how high future crop prices would have to be to justify those expected future land values, no one would have believed they could occur. Most of the time, people simply did not want to know how much they were gambling. As an old aphorism puts it, "There is nothing like the prospect of a lot of money to fog the minds of otherwise intelligent people."

Nothing the agricultural intellectual establishment could have done would have stemmed the run-up in paper wealth. Nothing that it could have done would have stemmed the subsequent run-down in paper wealth. This does not mean, however, that it should have been quiet. Being ignored is not an excuse for not giving warning. And, some warnings were given.

CONCLUSION

Can Americans plan for decline? Those who cannot plan for decline suffer more when decline occurs than those who smooth their transitions to new activities and who are wise enough not to attempt to fight the inevitable tides of economic change. Agricultural development inevitably leads to decline and the future will be characterized by further decline. The fundamental parameters of rapid productivity growth and the low income- and price-elasticities of demand for agricultural products require planning for a decline, but, for Americans, this kind of planning is difficult in the best of times and circumstances.

America's agricultural institutions and leaders have focused almost exclusively on the insiders left in agriculture, whatever the pace of decline. Little attention and aid have been given to those who were about to become outsiders. This is not unprecedented: Labor unions worry about their current members and not their unemployed former members. How one corrects this outsider/insider bias, however, is not obvious. The insiders will be around in the future to reward those that helped them in the past. The outsiders are gone and, in the future, are unlikely to be in a position to reward those that helped them leave. Nevertheless, in this respect neither the performance of labor nor agriculture provides much to admire.

If the current farm crisis was simply that another 200,000 farmers had been forced from insider to outsider status in the past six years, there would be no farm crisis. The current farm crisis is produced by the fact that, for the first time since the "Great Depression," insiders have suffered large reductions in their wealth. These insiders remain and are searching for either a magic cure (the agricultural establishment should be forced to produce one) or a scapegoat (the agricultural establishment should be punished for not having stopped them from doing what they did in the 1970s). Returning to the old virtues—let us get production and productivity up—always feels good. While, in reality, there are no magic cures.

NOTE

1. Lester C. Thurow is dean of MIT's Sloan School of Management and a Gordon Y. Billard Professor of Economics. He states he found the following consultants were helpful, but were not to be blamed for any of the paper's arguments: Gary Comstock, Chester D. Black, Richard P. Haynes, William Lacy, and Luther Tweeten.

REFERENCES

Agriculture and the environment. 1986. Edited by Tim T. Phipps, Pierre R. Crosson, and Kent A. Price. Washington, D.C.: National Center for Food and Agricultural Policy, Resources for the Future.

Agricultural trade in disarray. 1986. New York: Council on Foreign Relations.

Anderson, Kym. 1987. On why agriculture declines with economic growth. *Agricultural Economics* 1, no. 2: 195–207.

Bishop, C. E. 1969. The need for improved mobility policy. In *Agricultural policy in an affluent society.* Edited by Vernon W. Ruttan, Arley D. Waldo, and James P. Houck, 242–54. New York: W. W. Norton.

Davis, Joseph S. 1935. Agricultural fundamentalism. In *Economics, sociology and the modern world.* Edited by Norman E. Himes, 3–22. Cambridge: Harvard University

Economic Report of the President. 1987. Washington, D.C.: Council of Economic Advisors.

_____1990. Washington, D.C.: Council of Economic Advisors.

Griswold, A. Whitney. 1948. *Farming and democracy.* New York: Harcourt, Brace.

Hathaway, Dale E. 1963. *Government and agriculture.* New York: Macmillan.

Hathaway, Dale E., and Brian E. Perkins. 1968. Occupational mobility and migration from agriculture. In *Rural poverty in the United States.* Washington, D.C.: President's National Advisory Commission on Rural Poverty.

Heady, Earl O. 1967. Help for those leaving. In *A primer on food, agriculture, and public policy, 99–121. New York: Random House.*

Historical statistics of the United States: Colonial times to 1970, Part 1. 1975. Washington, D.C.: U.S. Department of Commerce, Bureau of the Census.

Paarlberg, Don. 1980. Agriculture loses its uniqueness. In *Farms and Food Policy.* Lincoln: University of Nebraska Press.

Postwar agricultural policy. 1944. Report of the Committee on Postwar Agricultural Policy of the Association of Land-Grant Colleges and Universities.

Samuelson, Paul. 1965. A theory of induced innovation along Kennedy-Weisacker lines. The *Review of Economics and Statistics* 47 (November): 343–56. (This is the last in a long series of articles.)

Schultz, Theodore W. 1943. *Redirecting farm policy.* New York: Macmillan.

_____1945. *Agriculture in an unstable economy.* New York: McGraw-Hill.

_____1961. A policy to redistribute losses from economic progress. *Journal of Farm Economics* 43, no. 3: 554–65.

Statistical abstract of the United States, 1982–83. 1983. Washington, D.C.: U.S. Department of Commerce, Bureau of the Census.

Survey of consumer finances, 1983. 1984. *Federal Reserve Bulletin.* (December): 863.

Survey of current business. 1989. Washington, D.C.: U. S. Department of Commerce. (March).

_____1990. Washington, D.C.: U.S. Department of Commerce. (March).

Tweeten, Luther. 1986. A note on explaining farmland price changes in the seventies and eighties. *Agricultural Economics Research 38, no. 4: 25.*

DISCUSSION OF THE CHAPTER BY DR. THUROW

Gary Comstock[1]

Since I am most interested in criticisms raised against the agricultural establishment, my response focuses on Mr. Thurow's chapter. I was pleasantly surprised to learn that Mr. Thurow had agreed to give the talk called "Agricultural Institutions Under Fire." I knew of Professor Thurow's reputation as an economist, but I was not aware that he was also known as a critic of the "agricultural establishment."[2]

After reading his chapter, I am no more certain that he is a critic. His account of agricultural institutions under fire seems to show that Thurow is about as harsh a critic of agriculture as Tammy Faye Bakker is of husband Jim. Consider his argument: Agriculture has shrunk and will continue to shrink. If we really want to "confront reality . . . if we really want to know the future of American farming," we'll have to face the fact that farmers "are going to have to leave farming." But, Thurow complains, the agricultural establishment has not faced this "reality," and has not led the way in retraining corn farmers to be computer programmers. Naughty agricultural establishment.

Never mind, for now, the very unrealistic assumption here that taking farmers out of agriculture is going to solve the problems of overproduction. If the reality of the last 30 years is to be believed, the fewer the farmers the greater the problems of overproduction. (A true "political realist" might well argue, against sacred agricultural orthodoxy, that what America really needs is *more* farmers.) But I am less concerned with specific failures to confront reality in Thurow's chapter, and more concerned with the general implication of his single-minded focus.

Suppose that the only unkind word you had ever heard about the USDA, the land-grant universities, private colleges engaged in agricultural research, and agribusiness involved in the farm supply and food manufacturing industries was that they had not planned for decline. Suppose you had never heard of Jim Hightower and his book *Hard Tomatoes, Hard Times* (1973), Wendell Berry and his book *The Unsettling of America* (1977), Jack Doyle and his book *Altered Harvest* (1985) or the U.S. Catholic Bishops and their pastoral letter *Economic Justice for All* (1986). If so, you might well wonder why this conference had devoted an entire session to this topic.

Why indeed? The impression left by Mr. Thurow's criticism is that these other criticisms are out in left field and, apparently, should be left out there. I am not sure why the author chose not to bring these folk into our conversation. Perhaps he wanted to confine his remarks to matters pertaining to agricultural economics narrowly construed. Or, perhaps he does not find the critics' arguments compelling. Whatever the motivation, I think a discussion of "Agricultural Institutions Under Fire" would be unobjective were it not to acknowledge that at least five important criticisms are still being pressed against modern agriculture. They relate to (1) the environment, (2) large farms, (3) developing countries, (4) economic power, and (5) spiritual identity.

THE ENVIRONMENT: THE AGRICULTURAL ESTABLISHMENT HAS ENCOURAGED RESEARCH AND PRODUCTS THAT ARE HAZARDOUS TO THE ENVIRONMENT

In my state, the groundwater of northeastern Iowa shows alarming traces of pollutants from farm chemicals. Unacceptable amounts of nitrate-nitrogen and soluble phosphorus have been found in wells and surface water. The greatest source of these chemicals (in our state at least) is farmers using methods recommended by agricultural experts.

It is bad enough that modern agriculture is so heavily dependent on petroleum-based products, but now biotechnology firms like Calgene of California are doing research not on plants that can withstand greater weeds around them, but on plants that can withstand greater doses of herbicides. At a recent conference, Bob Goodman of Calgene was asked by Jack Doyle why his company began this research direction. His answer was remarkably candid: "The technology was do-able and a market was there." Translated, this means: "We could make big profits for our company." Meanwhile, the people, plants, fish, and animals in northeastern Iowa continue to drink the water. I am just waiting for the biotechnology entrepreneur who first sees the market potential of herbicide-resistant *people*. Think of all the problems that would solve!

One might respond that this is a problem for the hard sciences, not the social sciences. But sociologists and anthropologists could help us answer questions like: Why have the land-grant universities pushed monocultural and chemically-dependent farming methods so heavily? Why have we not stressed sustainable agriculture? Economists might help us answer these questions: How can we internalize the externalities? How can we factor into our cost/benefit analyses the long-term damage we are causing soils and plant, animal, and human life? Incidentally, I noticed that some of these questions were not only not given high priority on Clarence Davans's list (see Chapter 2 in Section 1 of Part II), they were not even on the list.

LARGE FARMS: THE AGRICULTURAL ESTABLISHMENT HAS ENCOURAGED FARM RESEARCH, PRODUCTS, AND TECHNIQUES THAT FAVOR LARGE CORPORATE FARMS

Mr. Thurow acknowledges this criticism, only to say it is "probably untrue." Rather than guessing, perhaps we need a little research to find out. My very extensive sociological survey of all the farmers I know (about seven) reveals that farmers think universities have done nothing but research for the big guys. And they think this irrespective of whether they are large corporate farmers or small parttime farmers. The only thing they disagree about is whether this research has helped them. Their answer here, as you might guess, depends on the scale of their operation.

If you do not think my farmers are "facing reality," you might consult the Superior Court judge in California who says he will soon find in favor of the small farmers who sued the University of California land-grant system for using Hatch Act funds for big farms and not for family farms. Specifically, the judge has said he will rule that the Hatch Act obligates Agricultural Experiment Stations to give "primary consideration" to the needs of "small or family farmers." The university has already offered a factual concession that it is not doing what the judge says it should be doing.

DEVELOPING COUNTRIES: THE AGRICULTURAL ESTABLISHMENT HAS BEEN MORE CONCERNED WITH THE PROFITS OF MULTINATIONAL AGRIBUSINESSES THAN WITH THE HEALTH OF THIRD WORLD COUNTRIES

The agricultural establishment has enthusiastically endorsed a particular foreign policy toward the world's developing countries: viz., the development of the private sector. It has unreflectively stressed the need to expand and diversify the export of crops of, for example, Central America. Measured by macroeconomic indicators, writes Robert G. Williams (1986), this policy has been a success. "During the decade of the Alliance for Progress, the average annual growth rate of the Central American economy approximated six percent," a very healthy economy. Macroeconomic indicators, however, are not the only ones we should use to evaluate our policies. One role for philosophers is to point this out. Measured by cultural, ethical, and theological indicators, this policy has not been an unquestioned success. The case can be made, in fact, that it was a failure of tragic proportions as social unrest, governmental repression, and communist revolution have followed hard on the heels of rapid economic growth.

Why? Perhaps the leaders of multinational chemical and pharmaceutical companies would give some insight here. Firms such as Royal/Dutch Shell, Monsanto, ITT, and Ciba-Geigy—along with the biotechnology and seed companies they have recently gobbled up—are making profits in the Third World that look like inverse curves of the suffering found there. As new markets open, these firms benefit most. They are the ones who stand to benefit most from continued adherence to the Reagan doctrine, pushing capital investment accompanied by vast military expenditures as the prescription for stability in the region. Yet we have every reason to think that this policy will only lead to continued instability for the peasants. The firms, on the other hand, can look forward to continued financial growth. Pushing export agriculture as the answer to the problems of the Third World is not our only option. And yet you would not know this from reading any of the chapters in this book.

Social scientists could be of help here, too. Economists could tell us what the major causes of the export boom were. "To what extent was export success due to favorable market conditions and unusually low costs of production in Central America?" To what extent was it "the result of favorable government policies" and exploitation of labor (Williams 1986)? Who were the real beneficiaries of the export boom? The cotton growers and cattle ranchers? The poor of Honduras? Or Dow Chemical and American Cyaniamid? Who came to own the cotton gins and beef-export houses? Mr. Thurow claims that "the Green Revolution worked." Did it work for everyone? Is there really such a thing as a free lunch in international agriculture? Critical historians and economists could help us figure out exactly for whom the Green Revolution worked.

Rural sociologists and political scientists, on the other hand, could help us understand the effects of our agricultural foreign policy on the material well-being of the peasants. "How did people use the land before it was turned into cotton fields and cattle ranches? How did each export drive influence opportunities for [the peasants] making a living? How did it affect the environment [the rain forests, the plant and animal ecosystems]? How did it affect the relations between large landowners and the rural poor" (Williams 1986)? More chemically-based export agriculture, combined with military aid, seems likely only to shore up existing regimes in Central America. "At a cost of billions of dollars and thousands of lives, the program promises to prolong the rule of the current governments of Guatemala and El Salvador. In Honduras and Costa Rica, the program will temporarily support individuals in the military and other sections of the government who will enthusiastically embrace U.S. policy" (Williams, 1986). Meanwhile, the agricultural establishment in this country treats the policy with an attitude of reverence that would put Jim and Tammy to shame.

ECONOMIC POWER: THE AGRICULTURAL ESTABLISHMENT HAS NOT OPPOSED THE INCREASING CONCENTRATION OF WEALTH AND POWER IN THE FARM SUPPLY, FARM LAND OWNERSHIP, AND FOOD MANUFACTURING SECTORS OF THE ECONOMY

There is evidence to suggest that medium-sized farmers are "caught in a competitive sector (namely, farming) sandwiched between sectors of extremely concentrated (and noncompetitive) economic power," and that high levels of concentration exist in the procurement of live cattle and the sale of boxed beef. In some sectors of the agricultural economy there seem to be noncompetitive markets, which may be leading to an unfair price squeeze for producers. (See Smith 1987 quoting Wessel 1983. On noncompetitive markets, see Marion 1986 and Comstock, 1990.) Consider the concentration of companies in the farm input sector alone (a sector, by the way, not nearly as concentrated as food manufacturing). "The four largest companies selling tractor attachments accounted for 80 percent of sales in 1977. In the same year, the top four firms selling harvesting machinery (like combines and cotton pickers) had 79 percent of sales. The eight largest companies selling nitrogen and phosphate fertilizers had 64 percent of total agricultural chemical sales. And the pesticides industry was similarly dominated by a handful of companies: four firms had 60 percent market share (in 1976)") (Wessel, 116). I am not an economist, and I do not pretend to know whether entry barriers in these sectors are high, or whether shared monopolies are always a bad thing. I suspect they often are. What I do know is that when I listen to mainstream agricultural economists I rarely hear mention of this debate. What is going on here? Is there some professional mechanism of repression at work? If an interested academic like me has to dig around in the corners of a university library in order to learn that there is a live debate about the value of agribusiness monopolies, how will the average citizen ever learn? If they ever do learn, will they trust the economists in the future as they do now? We need greater openness and honesty about these research controversies.[3]

May I suggest you also help us with the question of the increasing concentration of farmland ownership? It is true that most farmland is still being bought by neighboring farmers, but outside and foreign investors are more and more prominent in these transactions. More research, it seems to me, is needed here.

SPIRITUAL IDENTITY: THE AGRICULTURAL ESTABLISHMENT HAS ENCOURAGED ALL OF US TO THINK OF FARMING IN PURELY TECHNOLOGICAL AND ECONOMICAL TERMS, IGNORING (AT BEST) OR DENYING (AT WORST) ITS UNIQUE CULTURAL, PHILOSOPHICAL, AND SPIRITUAL QUALITIES

Consider these lines from Wendell Berry (1987) about the life of farming:

> The small family farm is one of the last places—they are getting rarer every day—where men and women, girls and boys, can answer [the] call to be an artist, to learn to give love to the work of their hands. It is one of the last places where the maker—and some farmers still do talk about "making" the crops—is responsible from start to finish for the thing made. This will perhaps be thought a spiritual value. . . In fact, from the exercise of this responsibility, this giving of love to the work of hands, the farmer, the farm, the consumer, and the nation stand to gain in the most practical ways: they gain the means of life; they gain in the goodness of food; they gain longevity and dependability of the sources of food, both natural and cultural. The proper answer to the spiritual calling [of farming] becomes, in turn, the proper fulfillment of physical need.

Berry's eloquent defense of the cultural and spiritual value of farming, along with the actual labor of farmers who love their land, makes me wonder about Thurow's claim that "there is nothing that sets farmers apart from others." To say there is unique value in farming does not deny unique value in other forms of labor. This is a mistaken inference that critics of the agrarian tradition often ask us to draw. But it does not follow from the claim that farming has unique value that other forms of labor have inferior value. If anything, getting clear about the specific virtues and vices of farm labor helps us to see more clearly the specific virtues and vices of other forms of work. It is false to say there is nothing that sets farmers apart from others. It is true nothing sets them *above* others. The agrarianizers' claim that farmers are closer to nature, animals, and the rhythms of creation is not a claim that farmers are better than others. They are just different. Instead of emphasizing this point, however, the agricultural establishment seems to be embarrassed by it, and responds by dogmatically training its young to insist that farming is a *business*. It is a business. But it is also a unique and specific way of life. Here, again, I recommend that the new agenda for social scientists emphasize the importance of making relevant discriminations such as this one, and trying to figure out how they might change our ordinary way of assessing agricultural "progress." As Fred Buttel (see Chapter 3 of Part I) correctly notes in his chapter, not everything we value is convertible into quantifiable, economic terms.

This prejudice against farming as a way of life and the attempt to think of agriculture in purely technical terms is manifest in the rhetoric of agricultural experts like Clarence Davan. I was interested, too, in Lester Thurow's confident assertion that "agriculture has been marked by decline and in the future it will be characterized by decline." Can an economist really extrapolate from past trends, boldly predicting "inevitable tides of economic change" if one is dealing with the realm Aristotle called *praxis*, i.e., the realm of human choices? Compare Willard Cochrane's assessment, quoted in footnote 21[4] of Richard Kirkendall's piece: "The current farm crisis could be relieved by two bad crop years in a row. . . Or. . . by the inception of a worldwide economic depression (a distinct possibility as of 1987). The only safe prediction is that the future of U.S. agriculture, economically speaking, is unpredictable." This seems to me a more scientific and objective claim in that, as David Hume taught us, it matches the strength of our beliefs to the relative certainty of the evidence.

I conclude by thanking Professor Thurow for his humanitarian concern. In drawing attention to the plight of the displaced farmers, he has reminded us that we are all too prone to self-interested forgetfulness, concerned only with taking care of our own needs while ignoring the needs of others. But I hope we can extend this particular criticism to other areas and take a hard look at our fundamental assumptions. As Mr. Hite's chapter (see Part III, Section 1, Chapter 3) shows, there are real problems in farm country. I hope we will not confine ourselves to disciplinary business-as-usual as we try to find solutions.

NOTES

1. Gary Comstock is in the Philosophy Department at Iowa State University.
2. The phrase "agricultural establishment" is often used in a loose and ambiguous way: I follow standard practice in what follows. I also admit that the term is often used as a euphemism for whatever it is in agriculture that one does not like. Critics of the establishment need to be more specific. Helping critics to be clearer about the charges is one way social scientists could help.
3. Cf., Parker and Connor 1979 and Marion 1986.
4. Editor's Note: Footnote 21 was not included in the final version of Richard Kirkendall's paper.

REFERENCES

Berry, Wendell. 1977. *The unsettling of America: Culture and agriculture.* New York: Avon.

_____1987. A defense of the family farm. *Is there a moral obligation to save the family farm?*Edited by Gary Comstock. Ames: Iowa State University Press.

Comstock, Gary (ed.) 1990. *Is There a Conspiracy Against Family Farmers? Agricultural Economics, Public Policy and Catholic Theology,* USF Mongraphs in Religion and Public Policy, No. 5, Department of Religious Studies, University of South Florida, Tampa, FL.

Doyle, Jack. 1985. *Altered harvest: Agriculture, genetics, and the fate of the world's food supply.* New York: Viking Penguin.

Hightower, James. 1973. *Hard tomatoes, hard times.* Cambridge, Mass.: Schenkman Publishing.

Marion, Bruce. 1986. *The organization and performance of the U. S. food system.* Lexington, Mass.: Lexington Books.

National Conference of Catholic Bishops. 1986. Economic justice for all. Pastoral letter on Catholic social teaching and the U.S. economy, presented at the U.S. Catholic Conference, Washington, D.C.

Parker, Russell C., and John M. Connor. 1979. Estimates of consumer loss due to monopoly in the U.S. food-manufacturing industries. *American Journal of Agricultural Economics* 61:629-39.

Smith, Tony. 1987. Social scientists are not neutral onlookers to agricultural policy. *Is there a moral obligation to save the family farm?* Edited by Gary Comstock. Ames: Iowa State University Press 176–86.

Wessel, James. 1983. *Trading the future: Farm exports and the concentration of economic power in our food system.* San Francisco: Institute for Food and Development Policy.

Williams, Robert G. 1986. *Export agriculture and the crisis in Central America.* Chapel Hill: University of North Carolina.

CHAPTER 5

THE ROLE OF THE SOCIAL SCIENCES IN RURAL DEVELOPMENT AND NATURAL RESOURCE MANAGEMENT

Vernon W. Ruttan[1]

INTRODUCTION

Over the last several decades social scientists have made major contributions to our understanding of the impact of advances in natural science knowledge on technical change and of the impact of technical change on economic development and on the distribution of the gains and losses associated with development. We have also significantly advanced our understanding of the sources of demand for and supply of technical change. Work carried out within the framework of the induced technical change paradigm has demonstrated that technical change can be treated as largely endogenous to the development process (Hayami and Ruttan 1971, 1985; Thirtle and Ruttan 1987).

Social scientists have made less progress in efforts to understand the contributions of advances in social science knowledge to institutional innovation or of contribution of institutional innovation to economic, political, or social change. There has, however, been a renewed interest in issues of institutional change among social scientists. Within economics a new more analytical institutional economics has emerged to supplement the older historical institutional economics. The rational choice and public choice paradigms have facilitated more effective dialogue among economists, political scientists, sociologists, psychologists, and historians. Despite these advances our knowledge of the sources of demand for and supply of institutional change remains rudimentary.

In this paper I present a framework for thinking about the role of social science knowledge in the generation of institutional change. I then discuss the role of rural social scientists in the public institutions that generate, disseminate, and evaluate technical and institutional change. I follow the lead of Commons (1950) and Knight (1952) and define institutions to include both the behavioral rules that govern patterns of relationships and action as well as decision-making units such as government bureaus, private firms, and individual families.[2]

INSTITUTIONAL REFORM AND THE DEMAND FOR SOCIAL SCIENCE KNOWLEDGE[3]

The basic concept on which the evaluation of the returns to agricultural production research rests is that the demand for knowledge is derived from the demand for technical change in commodity production. Once the output of research was clearly conceptualized as an input into the process of technical change in commodity production, processing, and distribution, this link made it possible to develop models to measure the ex poste returns to research. It then became possible to make ex ante estimates of the relative contribution of alternative uses of research resources and to attempt to begin to specify rules that research managers might follow in the allocation of research resources.

Social scientists have only begun, perhaps somewhat reluctantly, to conceptualize adequately the contribution of knowledge in the social sciences (Stigler 1982, 60).[4] The first step in an attempt to value new knowledge in economics, and in the social sciences generally, is to specify the sources of demand for that knowledge. It is clear that the demand for knowledge in economics is not derived primarily from either private or public demand for technical change in commodity production. The demand for knowledge in economics and in the other social sciences—as well as in related professions such as law, business, and social services—is derived primarily from a demand for institutional change and improvements in institutional performance.

Shifts in the demand for institutional innovation or improvements in institutional performance may arise from a wide variety of sources. The Marxian tradition has emphasized the importance of technical change as a source of demand for instructional change. North and Thomas (1970, 1973) attempted to explain the economic growth of western Europe between A.D. 900 and A.D. 1700 primarily in terms of innovation in the institutional rules that governed property rights. A major source of institutional innovation was, in their view, the rising pressure of population against increasingly scarce resource endowments. Schultz, focusing on more recent economic history, identified the rising economic value of labor during the process of economic development as the primary source of institutional innovation. North and Thomas would apparently have agreed with Schultz that "it is hard to imagine any secular economic movement that would have more profound influence in altering institutions that would the movement of wages relative to that of rents" (Schultz 1968, 1120). It also seems more apparent today than a decade ago that in nonmarket environments, or in environments where prices are severely distorted, the shadow prices that reflect the real terms of trade among factors and products (or the gap between shadow and market prices) convey information to economic and political entrepreneurs that leads to shifts in the demand for institutional innovation and performance.

Conceptualizing the demand for institutional change in this manner opens up the possibility of a more precise identification of the link between the demand for institutional change and the demand for knowledge in economics and in the social sciences generally. Advances in knowledge in the social sciences offers an opportunity to reduce the costs of institutional innovation, just as advances in knowledge in the biological sciences and agricultural technology have reduced the costs of technical innovation in agriculture. The demand by policy makers for advances in knowledge about price and market relationships is, for example, appropriately viewed as derived from the demand for improved performance on the part of market or nonmarket institutions.

What evidence can be brought to bear against the hypothesis that the demand for social science knowledge is derived from the demand for institutional innovation? Let me refer to two examples that tend at least to establish the plausibility of the hypothesis:

The first example draws on U.S. historical experience. During the last one hundred years, the United States has experienced three major waves of institutional reform. The first was the "Progressive Period" that spanned the last decade of the nineteenth century and continued until U.S. entry into World War I. The demands for reform were induced by the rapid technical and economic changes that had dramatically altered the conditions of American life since the Civil War.[5] The unifying theme that underlaid the reform proposals of the "Progressive Era" was a rejection of unregulated free-enterprise capitalism. Reforms reflecting this perspective were initiated in the areas of income distribution, labor relations, social services, financial markets, transportation, industrial organization, and resource conservation. Popular demands for "direct democracy" were translated into expansion of women's suffrage, direct election of senators, and more active participation of voters in the legislative process through the initiative, referendum, and recall. A major consequence of these reforms was to widen substantially the participation of the federal government in economic affairs and in areas previously reserved to the states.

The second major wave of institutional innovation and reform was during the "New Deal" period in the 1930s. The question of whether the New Deal reforms represented a drastic new departure in American reformism (Hofstadter 1955) or primarily the realization of reforms proposed originally during the Progressive Era (Scott 1959; Hughes 1977, 146–98) and incubated during the 1920s (Chambers 1963) has been debated by political scientists and historians. But the New Deal reforms are not too difficult to characterize. They were in defense of security of property, of work, and of income—a reshuffle of the cards that had too long been stacked against the working man, the farmer, and the small businessman (Commager and Morris 1963, xii). But the acceptance by the federal government of responsibility for maintaining economic life represented a radical break with tradition. The result was a period of six years, 1933 to 1938, that represented the most rapid period of institutional change since the Civil War (Leuchtenburg 1963, xv).

The third wave of institutional reform occurred during the Kennedy and Johnson administrations—the "New Frontier" and "Great Society" years of 1960–68. The Kennedy and Johnson administrations sought to complete the liberal agenda. They sought to eradicate racial discrimination in voting, housing, jobs, and schooling. And they sought to eliminate poverty—both African-American and Caucasian and urban and rural (Matusow 1984, 180–271). These reforms were followed in the late 1960s and early 1970s by rapid innovation in new forms of property rights in natural resources induced by a rising concern about the impact of technology on both material resources and environmental amenities (Ruttan 1971).

During each of these periods there was rapid growth in the demand for social science knowledge. The first period drew on a broad range of intellectual capacities and expertise in law, in economics, and in the newer social science disciplines—but there was relatively little theory and even less research on which to draw. During the second period economists played a much larger role in policy design. Unfortunately, lack of an adequate understanding of macroeconomic relationships and a pervasive pessimism about the prospects for growth led to a structuralist reform agenda. But the demands for institutional innovation did lead to substantial growth in the resources devoted to social science research and to strengthening the statistical services of the federal government. By the late 1930s new theory and new information were being brought to bear on institutional innovation and reform. A new class of "service intellectuals" emerged in policy roles in the federal government. During the 1960s social science research played an even larger role in program design than in the two earlier periods. This was in part because of a greatly expanded body of social science knowledge, a large social research capacity, and improvements in capacity to generate, process, and analyze social science data. Attempts were made to introduce experimental design as a stage in program development. But despite the advances in theory and method, the policy-relevant social-science knowledge on which the Kennedy and Johnson administrations were forced to draw in the design of the poverty programs of the 1960s was too weak to respond effectively to demands that were placed on it (Matusow 1984, 217–76).

IDEOLOGY AND THE DEMAND FOR SOCIAL SCIENCE KNOWLEDGE

The sources and impact of ideology have represented a blind spot in contemporary social science—especially economics—theory and research. Geertz argues that formal ideologies first emerge and begin to guide social thought and political and economic behavior at that point at which a society begins to free itself from the dominance of received traditions—"from the direct and detailed guidance of religious or philosophical canons...and from the unreflective precepts of conventional moralism..." (Geertz 1964, 64). Furthermore, it is the ability of "ideologies to render otherwise incomprehensible social situations meaningful, to so construe them as to make it possible to act purposefully within them, that accounts...for the intensity with which, once accepted, they are held" (Geertz 1964, 64).

In my work on induced institutional change I have tended to focus on the implications of economic growth and technical change on the demand for institutional change (Ruttan and Hayami 1984). I am now pursuing research on the evaluation of the United States development assistance policy. When I initiated this research I assumed that the theory of induced institutional change would provide substantial insight into the initial development and subsequent evaluation of development assistance policy. It is apparent, however, that we cannot understand the large commitment of U.S. foreign assistance since World War II, first for the rehabilitation of western Europe and east Asia, and later in the developing world, without understanding the implications of the American "exceptionalist" ideology.[6]

American exceptionalism has spawned two conflicting doctrines about the relationship of the United States to the rest of the world. One is the *liberal doctrine* that American experience represents the perfection of political and economic evolution. An extension of this view is that it is the mission of the United States to lead the world, through example and assistance, into a more democratic and prosperous future. The second is the *realist doctrine* that a virtuous America, prosperous and democratic, exists as "an island of political and economic virtue in a surrounding sea of world corruption" (Noble 1985, 13). An extension of this view is that the United States must be continuously on guard against the corrupting influence of reactionary and radical ideology. It must manage its relationships with other countries primarily in the interests of its own security. American assistance policy has shifted back and forth in its relative emphasis on these two variants of exceptionalist ideology unimpeded by significant contributions by social scientists to policy generation or evaluation.

One might argue that I have overstated the case against the contribution of social science knowledge to both foreign economic and foreign assistance policy. A critic might point to the contribution of George F. Kennan's memoranda and articles urging a policy of containment.[7] One can also point to a large body of literature on development assistance policy and impact (Krueger, Michalopoulos, and Ruttan 1988). But the commitment to economic and strategic assistance, reflects, in my judgment, deeper ideological roots.

A second example draws more broadly on comparative experience. Stop for a minute and ask, which societies tend to draw the most extensively on social science knowledge and in policy design and reform? It seems clear that societies in which the design of social institutions is strongly determined by ideology or religion exhibit a very weak demand for social science knowledge. The Union of Soviet Socialist Republics (USSR), for example, tends to draw primarily on that narrow range of economics most closely related to engineering—input/output analysis, mathematical programming, and sector modeling. In China, until very recently, much of the capacity of economics was devoted to clarifying the implications of shifts in economic ideology (Calkins 1984). Relatively little social science capacity was devoted to institutional design.

It also seems clear that the demand for social science knowledge is strongest in those societies and those historical periods in which the burdens of ideology, religion, and tradition impose relatively weak constraints on institutional design. And within any society it seems apparent that the demand for social science knowledge is strongest when the society is attempting to confront the problems of the present rather than when it is attempting to recapture romantic memories of the past or pursuing utopian visions of the future.

In the 1960s it was possible for a brief period to believe that the exhaustion of the ideologies that had dominated social thought for the previous century and a half had permanently shifted the demand for social science knowledge to the right (Bell 1960, 369–75). But this vision is somewhat more clouded when viewed from the perspective of the 1980s. It is difficult to avoid the conclusion that budget reductions, reflecting a decline in the demand for social science knowledge, have been used to reduce the accumulation of social science knowledge in order to reduce the challenge to ideology in policy design.[8]

SOCIAL SCIENCE KNOWLEDGE AND THE SUPPLY OF INSTITUTIONAL INNOVATION

If one accepts the notion that the demand for knowledge in economics, and in the social sciences generally, is derived from the demand for institutional change, it then becomes necessary to consider the sources of supply of institutional change.

The view that emerges from my own work is that advances in social science knowledge act to shift the supply of institutional change to the right. Throughout history, improvements in institutional performance have occurred primarily through the slow accumulation of successful precedent or as a byproduct of expertise and experience. Institutional change was traditionally generated through the process of trial and error much in the same manner that technical change was generated prior to the invention of the research university, the agricultural experiment station, or the industrial research laboratory. With growth in social science research capacity it is becoming increasingly possible to substitute social science knowledge and analytical skill for the more expensive process of learning by trial and error.

But, how responsive are advances in social science knowledge to demands arising out of social conflict or economic growth? Is the supply of social science knowledge for institutional innovation relatively elastic? Or is society typically faced with a situation wherein the demand for institutional innovation shifts against a relatively inelastic supply curve? Stigler has argued that the supply of knowledge in the social sciences is relatively impervious to the impact of economic events (Stigler 1965, 16–30). He also has argued the opposite position (Stigler 1982, 63–66). My own perspective is consistent with Stigler's more recent view that social scientists respond rapidly to changes in the economic and political environment. Advances in social science knowledge are becoming an increasingly effective substitute for trial and error in the design and reform of economic institutions and economic policy.

If we accept the arguments that (a) the value society places on social science research is derived primarily from its contributions to institutional change and performance and (b) advances in social science knowledge are responsive to demands generated by social and economic change, we are then forced to consider several additional questions: How much freedom does a society have in choosing the path of institutional change that it will follow? Is society as free to design new institutions as planners frequently assume? Or is institutional change so dominated by historical or evolutionary forces that rational design has relatively little role to play in the process?[9]

The response by economists to these questions can be grouped in two major intellectual traditions. One tradition can be characterized as the design tradition, the other as the evolutionary tradition.

The strategy adopted in the design literature is to attempt to distinguish between institutional mechanisms, over which the designer or planner can exercise some degree of analytical control, and institutional environments, in which changes are treated as exogenous (Hurwicz 1972a, 1972b, 1977; Reiter 1977). The research agenda is then to study the performance characteristics of different institutional mechanisms under a wide class of institutional environments.

My own work (with Hayami and Binswanger) on induced institutional innovation falls more within the evolutionary tradition. In this work we have attempted to test and examine empirically how changes in the institutional environment have been induced by long-term changes in resource endowments and changes in technology.

The history of the rural social sciences suggests a strong commitment to the design tradition. Agricultural economists have been intimately involved in the process of institutional design almost since the origin of the field. We have been involved both through our research and through personal involvement in the design and reform of land tenure, credit, and marketing institutions. And our leading practitioners have contributed to both the agricultural policy debates and the design of agricultural policies and programs. The history of our successes and failures suggests that we have been less sensitive to the constraints placed on design by changes in the economic and social environment. And we have often been insensitive to the design opportunities made possible by changes in resources and cultural endowments or by changes in technology.[10]

In a recent article I reviewed the history of the contribution of agricultural economists to the policy proposals and program design that were in the older literature referred to as the "direct payment" approach and in newer literature as "de-linking" of price and income supports (Ruttan December 1984). While considerations of space preclude repetition of the review in this paper it maybe useful to draw attention to what appears to be the lessons of more than half a century of contribution to institutional design in the field of agricultural policy.

A first lesson is that deficiencies in social science knowledge relevant to institutional design have at times imposed a substantial burden on the design of effective policy. The production control proposals advocated by Department of Agriculture economists such as Wilson, Ezekiel, and Tolley, in the 1930s reflected the pervasive deficiency in the understanding of macroeconomic relationships. In spite of advances in the understanding of the macroeconomic relationships during the 1940s, it seems apparent that the limited ability to translate that understanding into a system of demand and supply relationships, and to estimate empirically the parameters of commodity and sector models, imposed a severe burden on both the design and the acceptance of the Brannan Plan. For example, except for a few illustrative estimates for individual perishable commodity programs (for hogs, eggs, potatoes, and milk and milk products), Secretary of Agriculture Brannan was not able to present to the Congress overall cost estimates for implementing his proposals.

By the early 1960s, the theory and method for the preparation of such estimates had become fully regularized in the USDA and were consistently referred to in debates over commodity policy. It had become customary to estimate the farm price and income effects, the consumer price effects, the federal budget impact, and the income distribution impact of the farm policy alternatives that received serious administrative or legislative attention. And, I am prepared to argue that these estimates contributed to both the quality of the policy debates and to better policy than would have emerged in the absence of the advances in analytical capacity that occurred over the previous two decades.

A second major lesson that emerges from the cases examined in this paper is that short-run economic and political events can exert a major impact on the effectiveness of social science contributions to institutional design or reform. The depression of the early 1930s generated a dramatic increase in demand for social science knowledge for the design of policies and programs.

But the capacity of social scientists to respond to such opportunities with effective program design is itself dependent on the state of social science knowledge. Roosevelt's election resulted in a discrete shift to the right in the demand for institutional innovation. The USDA economists who contributed to the design of the commodity and price policies of the 1930s were clearly among the most brilliant members of the profession. However, the economic theory and economic research on which they were forced to draw for policy design was underdeveloped. The policies that were designed in the 1930s have imposed a continuing burden on professional dialogue in the field of agricultural policy and heavy social costs on both farmers and consumers.

A third inference is that the agricultural commodity programs were induced by fundamental economic forces associated with the development of the American economy in general, and the agricultural economy in particular. Before the beginning of this century, the gains in productivity in American agriculture were almost entirely a consequence of increased mechanization. The technological revolution of the nineteenth century contributed to increasing output per worker but contributed very little to growth in aggregate output (Hayami and Ruttan 1971, 138–52). The period immediately after the turn of the century was a period of technological stagnation. But by the mid–1920s a new biological technology capable of enhancing output per acre and output per unit of breeding stock was beginning to come on stream. Gains in total productivity, in output per unit of total input, made it possible to increase aggregate output more rapidly than aggregate demand thus putting downward pressure on agricultural commodity prices.

In the absence of public intervention in agricultural commodity markets, the gains from the new technology would have been transferred almost immediately from agricultural producers to consumers. In this environment it should not have been surprising that farmers would be unsatisfied with policies that protected them only from the effects of cyclical fluctuations in economic activity. Although farmers and farm leaders articulated these demands in different terms, it seems clear in retrospect that they were demanding economic policies that would dampen the transfer of productivity gains from farm products to consumers.

The role of rural social scientists—or social scientists, whether concerned with the problems of agricultural commodity markets, rural communities, or rural people—is influenced by the environment in which they work. It is both enlarged and constrained by the mission of the organization in which they are employed. In the following sections I consider the role of social science research in the agricultural college or university and in the agricultural ministry or department. In an earlier writing I have also discussed the role of the social sciences in the agricultural research institute (Ruttan 1980; 1982, 308–13).

SOCIAL SCIENCE RESEARCH IN THE COLLEGE OF AGRICULTURE

The role of the social sciences in an agricultural college or university or in the college of agriculture in a comprehensive state or national university derives directly from the mission of the college itself. The mission and responsibility of a social science department located in a university setting is much more diverse than a social science unit in an autonomous research institute. It also differs significantly from a social science department located in a college of arts and sciences. At the University of Minnesota, for example, the Department of Agricultural and Applied Economics has responsibility for teaching the undergraduate and graduate applied economics courses dealing with the agricultural economy and rural development. It is responsible for the economics research functions of the Minnesota Agricultural Experiment Station. It is also responsible for off-campus educational programs in the area of agricultural economics and rural development that are organized through the Cooperative Extension Service.

The pattern that I have described for agricultural economics is also characteristic of many rural sociology departments. There is, however, a somewhat greater tendency for rural sociology to be organized as a section in a sociology department than as an independent department. Anthropology departments usually include a relatively high proportion of staff members whose professional interests focus on rural communities. Students of agricultural history, agricultural geography, or agricultural politics are often found in colleges of liberal arts (CLA)—in departments of history, geography, and political science. An important implication of the difference in the college of agriculture's and the college of liberal arts' mission is that the social scientist located in a CLA department is likely to feel a primary commitment to a discipline rather than to the mission of the college. It is contributions to the discipline which assure professional mobility and minimize the financial and bureaucratic constraints of the college or the university.

The social scientist with an appointment in a college of agriculture is subject to many of the same constraints and incentives that are operative in a college of arts and sciences. There are, however, additional incentives and constraints which arise from the institutional (state and federal) funding of research and service (extension). Institutional funding of agricultural research has the effect of placing a high priority on research that will contribute to state economic development. Public service activities involving programmed educational efforts in the college of agriculture are typically structured to encourage a state or regional orientation of research and extension efforts. There is always, however, a tension between the incentives and reward structures that are relevant for a college of agriculture and those that are accepted as relevant for those parts of the university which have only limited state support for research and extension teaching programs.

It is also useful to contrast the role of social science research in a college of agriculture with that in a free-standing research institute. One major difference stems from the autonomy of academic departments in the university environment. It is much more costly in terms of both physical and intellectual effort to organize multidisciplinary research efforts within, for example, the University of Minnesota College of Agriculture than at the International Rice Research Institute. I do not intend to imply that such interdisciplinary efforts do not occur in a university environment. My argument is that the structure of organization and incentives that operate within the university act to discourage such collaboration. When it does occur, however, it typically takes place within a somewhat looser coordinating structure. It is often organized through a series of interrelated subprojects or other relatively independent contributions.

Even within agricultural economics, research involving group efforts tends to be informal or loosely structured rather than tightly organized. One of the more successful efforts was the series of studies of supply and demand relationships for agricultural commodities organized by the Interregional Committee on Agricultural Policy. A major product of this research effort was the definitive report by George Brandow on *Interrelations Among Demand for Farm Products and Implications for Control of Market Supply* (1961). The study provided the empirical foundations for the estimates of the program impacts of the agricultural commodity programs that were introduced in the 1960s.

A more typical example is the pattern of evolution of research method and accumulation of research results that have resulted in the accumulation of a large number of studies of rates of return to agricultural research (Ruttan 1982, 242–46). The first rate-of-return estimates for hybrid corn and sorghum were made in the mid–1950s by Zvi Griliches. This initial study was followed by estimates of the rate of return to agricultural research on a sectorwide basis in the early 1960s. The work by Griliches was continued by several of his students in the mid- and late 1960s. Willis Peterson estimated rates of return to poultry research; Robert Evenson developed new methodology for estimation of rates of return for the U.S. agricultural sector as a whole; and Barletta estimated rates of return to research on wheat and maize in Mexico. Since the early 1970s, there has been a virtual explosion of studies which have: (1) further advanced the methodology for estimating rates of return; (2) covered a number of additional commodities; and (3) extended the work on rate of return to the agricultural sector of a number of other countries (Ruttan 1982, 242–46).

In stressing the limitations that the academic environment places on the capacity to focus research effort, even when such effort is organized under the auspices of the agricultural experiment station, one should not lose sight of the factors which make a major research-oriented university a highly favorable research location as compared to a free-standing research institute, or a to a ministry of agriculture. Perhaps the most important factor in the university environment is the intense interaction that occurs between graduate students, junior faculty, and senior faculty within the framework of graduate and postdoctoral training activities. Graduate teaching forces senior researchers to continuously relate their own work to an expanding range of research issues and methodology. Graduate students and postdoctoral researchers are often more severe critics of the quality of research effort than more senior colleagues. The opportunity does exist, in spite of the constraints suggested above, for productive interaction between basic and applied research (or theoretical and empirical investigations) and across disciplines. The interaction among teaching, research, and service (or extension) does provide an opportunity for flexible career development. The result is that one rarely finds within the academic environment of a major research university the intellectual stagnation which the Pound Report identified in several of the USDA regional utilization laboratories (National Research Council 1972).

SOCIAL SCIENCE IN THE MINISTRY OF AGRICULTURE

A modern ministry of agriculture has three primary functions: (a) the conduct and coordination of agricultural research; (b) the management of agricultural development programs; and (c) the operation of the nation's agricultural commodity and food programs. As a result of these three responsibilities, the minister of agriculture, together with his support staff, is a central figure in the formulation of agricultural policy. The minister's office becomes a central focus for dialogue within the national administration, between the government and the several political constituencies with interests in agricultural development, natural resources, and commodity and food policies. In some governments these responsibilities are concentrated in a single ministry. In others they may be fragmented among, for example, a ministry of natural resources, a ministry of agriculture, and a national food board. Within the administration, important coordinating functions are often exercised by a council of economic advisors, a national planning commission, a budget office, or a ministry of finance.

The role of social science within a ministry of agriculture depends both on historical tradition and the capacity of a particular minister or his senior deputies to utilize social science knowledge. There are, however, essentially two functions involved regardless of tradition or personality. One is a *staff function*. This involves organizing the information about programs and policies that the minister needs to interact effectively at the policy level with the rest of government, with the legislature, with the several agricultural and food constituencies, and, in nations in which agricultural trade is important, with other governments. A ministry of agriculture which has inadequate staff capacity in the social sciences leaves a minister naked—with little clothing to protect himself from shifts in the political winds or social and economic currents.

Social scientists in a ministry of agriculture also have a very important *analysis and information function*. It is important that the dialogue within the government and between the government, the several constituencies, and the public be conducted in an environment within which there can be reasonable agreement about the social and economic impact of policy or program alternatives. This permits the dialogue to center on the desirability of the impact rather than to degenerate around arguments of "my facts versus your facts."[11]

Even under the most favorable circumstances the development of effective social science capacity in a ministry of agriculture is not an easy task. Maintaining a high level of capacity over time is even more difficult. In part this stems from the close link between social science analysis and the agricultural policy process. Within a ministry there is no way to avoid considerable tension between the needs of short-run analysis of current policy issues and the development of analytical capacity. Nor is it possible to obscure the political implications of the analysis that is conducted in the ministry. Information on regional or personal income distribution, or the implications of particular rural development or commodity policies, can generate political support or opposition to policies or programs to which the government (or administration) is committed. Even the refinement of a commodity model can enhance the capacity of program managers to administer a commodity program—and more effective administration may generate gains or losses for producers, middlemen, or consumers.

As a result, there are typically substantial lacunae in social science staffing. Ministries have typically been more successful in institutionalizing capacity for statistical services and economic analysis than in the other social sciences. As ministries of agriculture have expanded their concern with rural development, in addition to commodity policies and programs, lack of capacity in anthropology and sociology has often been a serious constraint on effective policy formulation and program design. In the late 1940s the USDA was forced to dismantle its emerging capacity for sociological research on community development because of congressional dissatisfaction with a series of sociological studies of the adjustment problems in racially segregated rural communities in the south (Hardin 1955). Continued congressional opposition has prevented the rebuilding of more effective social science capacity to work on problems of rural development. Even in the case of economics, the development and maintenance of analytical capacity in a number of important areas has periodically been jeopardized by controversy over the appropriate role and organization of economics in the USDA.

It seems clear that the simple expedient of reorganization cannot resolve the continuing tension in ministry or department social science research units (1) between the demand for expansion of analytical capacity; (2) responsiveness to the latent demand for social science knowledge by the social and economic constituencies that are not adequately represented in the political marketplace (such as the rural poor); and (3) the biases in demand for knowledge by politically powerful clientele. In his 1976 presidential address to the American Agricultural Economics Association, Kenneth R. Farrell, then deputy administrator of the USDA Economic Research Service, suggested that one way to overcome the parochialism of state experiment station social science research would be to establish an autonomous national food and agricultural policy research institute (Farrell 1976). He argued that the institute should be funded largely by private funds. In my judgment, however, these issues are even more difficult to resolve than suggested by Farrell. Effective demand for social science knowledge in those areas which are not now represented by effective political constituencies is dependent on changes in the structure of economic and political power.

THE DEMAND FOR SOCIAL SCIENCE KNOWLEDGE—AGAIN

There are today, few agricultural research programs in which the social science disciplines are not represented. The ability of the social sciences to "colonize" agricultural research institutions has, however, been highly uneven. Agricultural economics is the only field that is represented across the broad spectrum of agricultural research institutes, university-related agricultural experiment stations, and agricultural ministries.

What accounts for the limited development of professional capacity in the other social science disciplines in agricultural research institutions? Lester Thurow has argued, in the case of economics, that "part of the imperial success of economics is due to the fact that the profession has a client relationship with society. Economists have not been generally instrumental in shaping society's agenda, but they have been willing to work on that agenda—whatever it is (Thurow 1977, 80).

The social science research agenda, in the field of agricultural development and policy, has clearly been heavily weighted in terms of economic criteria. The other social science disciplines have been more critical than economics of the agenda that society—often represented by a legislator or a minister picked from one of the more conservative rural constituencies—has drawn up for social science research. It has been exceedingly difficult to resolve the problem of how to respond to the biased demands for social science knowledge that are channeled through existing institutions and at the same time attempt to reform the process by which the existing agenda has been established.

Don Paarlberg (1978), in a series of important papers, has argued that in the United States a new agenda in which community, environmental, and equity considerations are more heavily represented has been created. In the 1970s, international aid agencies attempted to force issues, such as integrated rural development and programs designed to meet basic needs, higher on the policy agenda in the development programs for which they provide assistance. This resulted, for a short time, in a stronger demand for social science knowledge of the type that psychologists, sociologists, political scientists, anthropologists, and historians are more able than economists to supply. A question that the social science disciplines have never answered effectively is whether they are willing to respond to this rising demand—or does past alienation from the policy process limit their capacity to respond?

I have suggested in this paper that society is able to realize the gains from investment in social science research capacity to work on problems of agricultural and rural development in terms of more rapid institutional innovation and improved institutional performance. These gains are not realized without substantial cost.

The development of a social science capacity capable of producing a continuous stream of new knowledge directed to institutional innovation and performance imposes severe stress on a number of institutions. There will be stress within the several social science disciplines over the allocation of professional resources between attempting to understand basic behavioral relationships and the utilization of social science knowledge to speed innovation and improve performance; there will be stress among the several social science communities and disciplines regarding priorities in expanding professional capacity and over the priorities of disciplinary and multidisciplinary research activities; there will be tension between the social-science- and the natural-science-based disciplines and professions over the extent to which each will be guided in its own choice of priorities or by the findings of related disciplines.

Finally, the results of the new knowledge that flows from social science research will produce tension between the political system, the broader society which it represents, and the institutions that are responsible for the conduct of social science research—research institutes, experiment stations, universities, ministries—over the value, the legitimacy, and the implications of the new knowledge that emerges from social science research.

NOTES

1. Vernon W. Ruttan is Regents Professor in the Department of Agricultural and Applied Economics and in the Department of Economics and adjunct professor in the Hubert W. Humphrey School of Public Affairs, University of Minnesota.

2. This usage is consistent with my earlier work (Binswanger and Ruttan 1978, 327–57; Ruttan and Hayami 1984), where the term "institution" is used to include that of organization. The term "institutional innovation" will be used to refer to innovations that lead to changes (a) in the behavior of a particular organization, (b) in the relationship between such organization and its environment, or (c) in the rules that govern behavior and relationships in an organization's environment. This definition is more inclusive than Veblen's (Seckler 1975, 61), but is consistent with that used by Commons (1950, 26) and Knight (1952, 51). The definition used here also encompasses the several classes of institutional entities and behavior employed by Davis and North (1971). For a criticism of the definition employed in this paper see Bromley (1988).

3. This section and the section on the supply of institutional innovation draws on earlier discussions in Ruttan (December 1984).

4. For two initial attempts see Hayami and Peterson (1972) and Norton and Schuh (1981b). See also the reviews by Norton and Schuh (1981a) and Norton and Norris (1984).

5. For a very useful review of thought regarding the "Progressive Era", see Scott (1959). For the intellectual, political, and social origins of many of the reforms of the "Progressive Era" in the earlier farmer protest movements, see Hicks (1961, Chapter 15) and Hughes (1977, 96–145).

6. The ideology of "American exceptionalism" emerged out of the encounter between Puritan theology and

the American frontier. The Puritans viewed themselves as a chosen people trapped within the bondage of the European medieval establishment. Their migration from the old England to a new England was interpreted as analogous to the exodus of Israel from Egyptian bondage to the Promised Land. The encounter with the frontier contributed to the secularization of the metaphors of Puritan theology and of freeing American political culture of its bondage to history (Hartz 1955; Packenham 1973; Noble 1985).

7. The seminal ideas that provided the rationale for the containment policy was first put forward by George F. Kennan in a "long telegram" written from the U.S. embassy in early 1946. It was rewritten as a memorandum to Navy Secretary James Forrestal in December 1946 under the title "The Soviet Way of Thought and Its Effect on Soviet Foreign Policy." It finally appeared in print under the pseudonym "X" (1947).

8. There has also been a growing lack of appreciation in government for the usefulness of a comprehensive database as part of the infrastructure of social science research. There is a tendency to evaluate expenditures data collection and interpretation narrowly in terms of utility for federal policy and program needs rather than more broadly in terms of social utility. For more thorough discussion see Bonnen (1975 and 1984).

9. This issue has been of concern since the origin of modern social science. In 1744 Giambattista Vico, whose role in the origins of political science is comparable to that of Adam Smith in economic thought, argued that it is "naive to regard political and social institutions as owing their origins to acts of rational planning... motivated either by considerations of enlightened self-interest or by respect for an abstract concept of justice..." (Gardiner 1959, 10). For a more recent expression of a similar perspective, see Hayek (1978).

10. This perspective was initially outlined in Hayami and Ruttan (1971, 59–61). See also Binswanger and Ruttan (1978), 227–357, and Ruttan and Hayami (1984). The complementarity between the design and induced innovation perspective was explored at a seminar at the University of Minnesota in February 1983 (Runge). The importance of feedback between experience and design has been emphasized by Johnston and Clark (1982).

11. When I worked as the agricultural economist on the Council of Economic Advisors in the early 1960s, for example, there was a very intensive effort made to achieve agreement between the Council, the Bureau of the Budget, and the Staff Economics group in the Department of Agriculture on the commodity production, farm income, consumer price, and the budget implications of the alternative commodity programs that were under consideration. Policy debate could then proceed without disagreement on alternative programs-impacts. This process has broken down in several recent administrations.

REFERENCES

Barletta, N. Ardito. 1970. Cost and benefits of agricultural research in Mexico. Ph.D. diss., University of Chicago.

Bell, Daniel. 1960. *The end of ideology*. Glencoe, Ill.: Free Press.

Binswanger, Hans P., and Vernon W. Ruttan. 1978. *Induced innovation: Technology, institutions and development*. Baltimore: Johns Hopkins University Press.

Bonnen, James T. 1975. Improving information in agriculture and rural life. *American Journal of Agricultural Economics* 57 (December): 753–63.

_____1984. Federal statistical coordination: A disaster or a disgrace? *Milbank Memorial Fund Quarterly* 62 (Winter): 1–41.

Brandow, G. E. 1961. *Interrelations among demands for farm products and implications for control of market supply*. Pennsylvania Agricultural Experiment Station Bulletin No. 680.

Bromley, Daniel. 1988. *Economic interests and institutions: The conceptual foundations of public policy*. Oxford: Basil Blackwell.

Calkins, Peter H. 1984. Efforts to reconcile the new policies with Marx-Leninism. Paper presented at AAEA annual meeting, 8 August, Ithaca, New York.

Chambers, Clarke A. 1963. *Seedtime of reform: American social service and social action: 1918–1933*. Minneapolis: University of Minnesota Press.

Commager, Henry Steele, and Richard B. Morris. 1963. Editor's introduction. *Franklin D. Roosevelt and the New Deal, 1932–1940*. Edited by William L. Leuchtenburg. New York: Harper & Row.

Commons, John R. 1950. *The economics of collective action*. New York: Macmillan Co.

Davis, Lance E., and Douglass C. North. 1971. *Change and American economic growth*. Cambridge: Cambridge University Press.

Evenson, Robert E. 1968. The contribution of agricultural research and extension to agricultural production. Ph.D. diss., University of Chicago.

Farrell, Kenneth R. 1976. Public policy, the public interest and agricultural economics. *American Journal of Agricultural Economics* 58 (December): 785–94.

Gardiner, Patrick, ed. 1959. *Theories of history*. Glencoe, Ill.: Free Press.

Geertz, Clifford. 1964. Ideology as a cultural system. In *Idealogy and discontent*, edited by David E. Apter. Glencoe: Free Press of Glencoe; London: Collier Macmillan.

Griliches, Zvi. 1958. Research costs and social returns: Hybrid corn and related innovations. *Journal of Political Economy* 66:419–31.

Hardin, Charles M. 1955. *Freedom in agricultural education*. Chicago: University of Chicago Press.

Hartz, Louis. 1955. *The liberal tradition in America: An interpretation of American political thought since the revolution*. New York: Harcourt Brace and World.

Hayami, Yujiro, and Willis Peterson. 1972. Social returns to public information services: Sstatistical reporting of U.S. farm commodities. *American Economic Review* 119–30.

Hayami, Yujiro, and Vernon W. Ruttan. 1971. *Agricultural development: An international perspective*. Baltimore: Johns Hopkins University Press.

_____1985. *Agricultural development: An international perspective*. Rev. ed. Baltimore: Johns Hopkins University Press.

Hayek, F. A. 1978. The errors of constructivism. In *New studies in philosophy, politics, economics and the history of ideas*, 3–34. London: Routledge and Kegan Paul.

Hicks, John D. 1961. *The populist revolt*. Lincoln: University of Nebraska Press.

Hofstadter, Richard. 1955. *The age of reform: From Bryan to F.D.R.* New York: Alfred A. Knopf.

Hughes, Jonathan R. T. 1977. *The governmental habit: Economic controls from colonial times to the present.* New York: Basic Books.

Hurwicz, Leonid. 1972a. On informationally decentralized systems. In *Decision and organization*, edited by C. B. McGuire and Ray Radnor. Amsterdam: North-Holland Publishing Co.

_____1972b. Organizational structures for joint decision making: A designer's point of view. In *Interorganizational decision making*, edited by Mathew Tuite, Roger Chisholm, and Michael Radnor. Chicago: Aldine Publishing Co.

_____1977. On the interaction between information and incentives in organizations. In *Communication and control in society*, edited by K. Krippendorf, 123–47. New York: Scientific Publishers.

Johnston, Bruce F. and William C. Clark. 1982. *Redesigning rural development: A strategic perspective.* Baltimore: Johns Hopkins University Press.

Knight, Frank H. 1952. Institutionalism and empiricism in economics. *American Economic Review* 42 (May): 45–55.

Krueger, Anne O., Constantine Michalopoulos, and Vernon W. Ruttan. 1988. *Aid and development.* Baltimore: Johns Hopkins University Press.

Leuchtenburg, William L. 1963. *Franklin D. Roosevelt and the New Deal.* Edited by Henry Steele Commager and Richard B. Morris. New York: Harper & Row.

Matusow, Allen J. 1984. *The unraveling of America: A history of liberalism in the 1960's.* New York: Harper & Row.

National Research Council. 1972. *Report of the Committee on Research Advisory to the USDA.* Pound Report. Springfield, Va.: National Technical Information Service.

Noble, Daniel W. 1985. *The end of American history.* Minneapolis: University of Minnesota Press.

North, Douglass C. 1981. *Structure and change in economic history.* New York: W. W. Norton.

North, Douglass C., and Robert Paul Thomas. 1970. An economic theory of the growth of the western world. *Economic History Review* 22:1–7.

_____1973. *The rise of the western world.* London: Cambridge University Press.

Norton, George W., and Patricia E. Norris. 1984. *Evaluating agricultural economics research.* Department of Agricultural Economics, Virginia Polytechnic Institute and State University.

Norton, George W., and G. Edward Schuh. 1981a. *Agricultural social science research evaluation.* Department of Agricultural Economics, Virginia Polytechnic Institute and State University.

_____1981b. Evaluating returns to social science research: Issues and possible methods. In *Evaluation of agricultural research*, edited by Walter L. Fishel, Arnold A. Paulsen, and W. Burt Sundquist, 246–61. *University of Minnesota Agricultural Experiment Station Misc. Pub.* No. 8 (April).

Paarlberg, Don. 1978. A new agenda for agriculture. *Policy Studies Journal* 6 (Summer): 504–6.

Packenham, Robert A. 1973. Liberal America and the Third World: *Political development ideas in foreign aid and social science.* Princeton, N.J.: Princeton University Press.

Peterson, Willis L. 1967. Return to poultry research in the United States. *Journal of Farm Economics* 49 (August): 656–69.

Reiter, Stanley. 1977. Information and performance in the (new) 2 welfare economics. *American Economic Review* 67:226–34.

Runge, Carlisle Ford. 1983. Sources of institutional innovation: An interpretive essay. Discussion paper no. 176 (June). University of Minnesota, Department of Agricultural Economics.

Ruttan, Vernon W. 1971. Technology and the environment. *American Journal of Agricultural Economics* 53:707– 17.

_____1980. The social sciences in agricultural research. Proceedings of the 1980 annual meeting, 4–7 August, University of Alberta, Edmonton. *Canadian Journal of Agricultural Economics.*

_____1982. *Agricultural research policy.* Minneapolis: University of Minnesota Press.

_____1984. Social service knowledge and institutional change. *American Journal of Agricultural Economics* (December): 549–59.

Ruttan, Vernon W., and Yujiro Hayami. 1984. Toward a theory of induced institutional innovation. *Journal of Developmental Studies* 20:203–23.

Schultz, Theodore W. 1968. Institutions and the rising economic value of men. *American Journal of Agricultural Economics* 50:1113–22.

Scott, Andrew M. 1959. The progressive era in perspective. *Journal of Politics* 21:685–701.

Seckler, David. 1975. *Thorstein Veblen and the institutionalists.* London: Macmillan & Co.

Stigler, George J. 1965. *Essays in the history of economics.* Chicago: University of Chicago Press.

_____1982. *The economist as preacher and other essays.* Chicago: University of Chicago Press.

Thirtle, Colin G., and Vernon W. Ruttan. 1987. *The role of demand and supply in the generation and diffusion of technical change.* London: Harwood Academic Publishers.

Thurow, Lester C. 1977. Economics, 1977. *Daedalus* 106 (Fall): 79–94.

"X" (George F. Kennan). 1947. The sources of Soviet conduct. *Foreign Affairs* (July): 566–82.

CHAPTER 6

SCIENCE AND TECHNOLOGY POLICY FOR THE TWENTY-FIRST CENTURY: THE UNITED STATES IN A GLOBAL ECONOMY[1]

G. Edward Schuh[2]

This nation's past investments in science and technology have contributed importantly to its economic growth, giving it one of the highest standards of living of any country in the world and contributing importantly to making it the most powerful nation on the international scene since the end of World War II. The challenge is whether we will be able to sustain our economic and political preeminence into the twenty-first century, now only little more than a decade away.

The thesis of this paper is that sustaining our position in the world will require a major recommitment to and redirection of our investments in science and technology. Part of this redirection requires that we recognize that we have rapidly become integrated into a global economy. This means, among other things, that we must shift from closed-economy economics to open-economy economics. It also means that we must view our challenges in a much broader context.

As we look to the future, the economic, political, social, and technological forces impinging upon this nation will be greatly different from those impinging upon it in the past. Significantly, the science and technology community will no longer be able to identify its tasks and missions in the context of "Fortress America"—a huge economy that until fairly recently was almost completely autonomous and independent. Instead, the various forces impinging upon this nation in the future will come in large part from external sources. An important consequence of that development is that we will need in the future to give a great deal more attention to *strategic* issues than we have in the past. These strategic issues have to do with how to sustain and strengthen this nation's economic, political, and military positions in the world. Whether we sustain our position or not will be important in determining what our standard of living will be in the future, and whether we will continue to have the freedom we as a nation value so highly.

In assessing our position in this changed economic, political, and technological environment, and in identifying new missions for our scientific and technological community, a second major change in perspective will be needed. Contrary to what many seem to believe, the issue will not be the scarcity of natural resources to sustain our economic development. Instead, the issue will be this nation's dwindling share of the world's stock of human capital as the population masses in the developing countries for the first time in history become empowered with economic growth.

The remainder of this paper is divided into three parts. The next section provides an overview of the forces at work on the U.S. economy. This will be followed by a discussion of the critical factors that will influence our economic development in the future. The third section is an agenda for research in sustaining our economic performance for the future. At the end there will be some concluding comments.

THE FORCES AT WORK ON THE U.S. ECONOMY

The major forces affecting the U.S. economy can be summarized under four headings: (1) basic developments in the international economy; (2) factor price equalization; (3) strategic developments on the international scene; and (4) developments in the domestic economy. Each of the topics is discussed in the sections which follow.

BASIC DEVELOPMENTS IN THE INTERNATIONAL ECONOMY

Perhaps the most powerful set of forces on the international scene are the technological breakthroughs in the transportation and communication sectors and the emergence of the computer revolution. The technological developments in the transportation and communication sectors have significantly lowered the real costs of transportation and communication services while at the same time broadening the market and scope for action of economic and political agents everywhere. Investments in physical infrastructure and in the means of transportation and communication will continue those processes well into the future. It is already possible to conduct market transactions almost instantly throughout a major share of the world. The scope of and ease with which these transactions can be conducted can only be expected to improve as we look to the future.

The computer revolution and the increased value it gives to data and information is, so far, limited to the developed countries and to some of the middle-income countries. As we look to the first decades of the twenty-first century, the availability of computers can be expected to have expanded dramatically. At the same time, the power of what they can do will have increased equally as dramatically.

These developments in the transportation, communication, and computer sectors are having far-reaching effects on the global social system. For one thing, they are the driving force behind many of the political developments now underway on the international scene, especially those involving the centrally planned economies. Second, they are driving the global economy to a greater reliance on markets as the means to transact economic activities. Both of these developments can be expected to continue in the future.

The second set of basic economic forces on the international scene includes those which are bringing about significant changes in the bases for comparative advantage. Developments in the transportation, communication, and computer sectors are significantly changing the basis for comparative advantage in their own right. But three additional forces are at work: (1) the spread of general education in the developing countries; (2) the expansion of investment in research and development (R&D) outside the United States; and (3) the emergence of a growing capacity for agricultural research for the food sector in the developing countries.

The spread of general education in the developing countries makes it possible for manufacturing technology to spread rapidly in the developing countries. The technology for this sector is general, not location-specific, in terms of ecological conditions. The major barrier to the spread of this technology has been the lack of a literate and skilled labor force. As general education spreads, this barrier is removed and manufacturing sectors are now seen to slip rapidly from one country to another.

The growth in investment in R&D outside the United States changes the basis for comparative advantage globally. As the United States lets its commitment to R&D decline, other countries such as Germany and Japan increase theirs. This, too, changes the basis for international comparative advantage.

Finally, there is a growing capacity to produce new production technology for the global food sector. Part of this capacity is reflected in the International Agricultural Research Centers (IARCs) that comprise the Consultative Group for International Agricultural Research. There are now 13 such international centers located strategically around the world, supported by an annual budget of over $200 million. These centers now turn out a steady stream of new production technology for tropical agriculture.

Equally as important, many developing countries are developing their capacity for agricultural research as well. Although many of these new systems now face severe budget difficulties as a consequence of the international debt crisis, they can be expected to recover as the international economy is revitalized. Agricultural research capacity in the developing countries can be expected to grow in the future.

The spread of general education in the developing countries and the emergence of a capacity to produce new production technology for the tropical food sector promises to do more than change the basis for comparative advantage on the global scene. It also provides the basis for more rapid economic growth in these countries in the not-too-distant future.

FACTOR PRICE EQUALIZATION

There is a theorem in economics which says that free trade in goods and services will lead to factor price equalization on a global scale, even though the factors of production are not mobile. This proposition means that in such a world the "prices" of the services of factors of production will converge to equality on a global scale.

Clearly, we do not have a world of free trade. Nevertheless, there is a trend towards such equalization and this development appears to have contributed importantly to the decline in real earnings in this country over the last 20 years. In effect, the decline in real wages occurred as the U.S. economy became well integrated into the global economy. Further impetus to the decline was given by the entrance into the civilian labor force of large numbers of workers over the last 20 years.

Equal earnings or wage rates do not, of course, mean equal per capita incomes across countries. Per capita incomes are determined by the prices or wages the factors of production are paid, the amount of resources individuals or families own, and the productivity of those resources. Hence, there can be wide disparities in per capita incomes among countries even though factor prices have equalized. Put somewhat differently, national economic and social policy can influence the level of per capita income in a country even though that country is well integrated into the international economy.

STRATEGIC DEVELOPMENTS ON THE INTERNATIONAL SCENE

As this nation looks to the future, its economic, political, and technological hegemony will be challenged as it has not been challenged in some time. Contrary to what many seem to believe, however, our relative stature and position in the world will have little to do with our military power. Instead, it will have almost everything to do with our economic power, as it has in the past.

The United State's share of total economic power has already declined significantly in the post-World War II period. In 1950, for example, the United States accounted for about 50 percent of global gross national product (GNP), with approximately 6 percent of the world's population. Today, it accounts for only about 30 percent of global GNP, with a somewhat smaller proportion of the world's population.

What is truly remarkable about this relative decline is that it has occurred while many, if not most, of the major and potentially important countries of the world have mismanaged their economic policies. The population of these countries accounts for a significant share of the world's total population. China, now with approximately 1 billion people, has grossly mismanaged its economy. India, rapidly approaching 1 billion in population, has pursued very inefficient economic policies. The Soviet Union has a smaller population base, but an enormous endowment of physical resources. It, too, has grossly mismanaged its resources. There also is the relatively long list of countries that are potentially important economically that have also pursued inefficient economic policies.

The list of countries that have pursued relatively efficient economic policies is fairly small, with relatively small populations. This includes Japan, Germany, and the newly industrialized countries (NICs) of southeast Asia, South Korea, Hong Kong, Taiwan, and Singapore.

The challenge this nation faces is that many of the nations of the world that so grossly mismanaged their economies in the past are no longer doing so. China was the first to undertake major economic reforms and the results in terms of economic growth have been dramatic. India has undertaken a significant reform process, and now Mr. Gorbachev is liberalizing his political system so he can eventually reform the economy.

Similar economic reforms are underway in many developing countries, driven in part by the international debt crisis. Although political difficulties abound in these countries, true reform processes are underway. If these processes continue, countries as disparate as Brazil, Indonesia, Mexico, and Nigeria have the potential to be economic powerhouses in the future.

What this nation faces, therefore, is a world in which the masses of the developing world will be empowered for the first time in history with economic growth. The Soviet Union, although less populous than some of these other countries, also has the potential to be economically strong. The issue, then, will be whether the United States will have the economic strength and know-how to defend its economic and political position. Whatever happens, the United States obviously will have to increasingly live by its wits in an increasingly competitive international economy.

A second set of strategic developments on the international scene is the shift towards economic integration. The Canada/U.S. Free Trade Agreement is an outstanding example, with the cross-border trade between these countries already being the largest between any two countries in the world. The European Economic Community is rapidly moving towards EEC-92, with the complete elimination of barriers to trade and resource mobility among these 12 nations.

If this economic integration comes to fruition, and there is every reason to believe it will, the result will be an economic powerhouse. The total population of the EEC is significantly larger than the United States and its GNP is almost as large. Moreover, the establishment of EEC-92 is politically motivated, in large part to establish a third force between the United States and the Soviet Union.

Pressures for further economic integration are growing. It has been proposed, for example, that Mexico be brought into the Canadian/U.S. agreement, or alternatively, that Japan be brought in. Others suggest that Japan create a common market in southeast Asia. And so on.

These moves towards economic integration are important in a number of respects. First, they are an important means of reducing trade barriers globally and thus are collectively a potentially important source of economic growth. Second, when political unification follows economic integration, it has the potential to change the balance of political/economic power on the international scene.

A third set of strategic developments on the international scene is the potential for unprecedented economic growth. Many of the developing countries have been experiencing economic stagnation for over a decade, and some for longer than that. Economic reforms provide the potential for rapid and sustained recovery from these economic doldrums. These reforms will be reinforced by the rapid adoption of new manufacturing technology in these countries and the availability of new production technology for tropical agriculture. These two developments can fuel rapid economic growth and if biotechnology has even one-half the potential many observers believe it to have, it could fuel an even more rapid rate of growth.

The significance of this development is that sustained and rapid growth on the international scene could generate a significant growth in the demand for agricultural output. This growth in demand will occur at a time when much of the labor in the developing countries has been prematurely pushed out of agriculture and at a time when these same countries can, and probably will, industrialize under more rational conditions than they have in the past. We can thus expect to see a fairly rapid rise in agricultural wage rates globally. This will provide the impetus for greater investments in human capital in those countries. It will also raise the floor under wage rates in this country, and thus have a potentially significant effect on the value of time.

DEVELOPMENTS IN THE DOMESTIC ECONOMY

Perhaps the most significant developments in the domestic economy are associated with demographic changes that are taking place. This nation has had a birth rate for some years now that is approximately zero-population growth rate. That has led to a significant aging of our population, with considerable potential for additional aging still before us. This aging has also led to a substantial increase in the demand for health services. Moreover, it appears that the demand for health services has a relatively high income elasticity of demand, with the result that as per capita incomes rise, there will be a continued increase in the demand for health services on top of that driven by demographic changes.

An important part of the present population growth in the United States comes from immigration. There are attempts to impose limits on that process, but in the future we may be more willing to accept these immigrants. They already provide a significant share of the labor services for agriculture. In the future, they may be needed for our manufacturing and service sectors.

Agriculture's share of the U.S. labor force continues to decline. It now accounts for less than 3 percent of the total, and 25 to 30 years from now it may well account for less than 1 percent of the total. It will have to be that small if people employed in agriculture are to have per capita incomes comparable to those in the nonfarm sector.

In a world in which population growth is modest and in which most of the supply of labor has been drained out of agriculture, the United States faces a number of other constraints to continued economic expansion. First, a significant share of the women in this country have already been drawn into the labor force. This raises the costs of producing children.

Second, there is a significant breakdown of the family in this country. Divorce and remarriage has become common, while at the same time the number of single-parent families is growing rapidly. These socioeconomic developments have significantly changed the economics of investing in human capital in the household. And it is in the household that a significant share of the investment in human capital has taken place in this country. It is popular in this country to point to the schools as the cause of the declining academic and intellectual performance of our children. We need to give at least equal weight to developments in the household where the incentives for investing in human capital are declining.

Third, as noted above, there are substantial reasons for believing that the value of time will be rising globally over the next decades. This will impose even more severe constraints on our potential population growth rates. Thus, the resource scarcity which will impose a constraint on our economic growth in the future is not likely to be our natural resource base. It promises instead to be the growing scarcity of time for the economy, with the value of that time increasing rapidly.

SUMMARY

What we can expect to see in the future is the emergence of a well-integrated global economy in which most of the rest of the world is rapidly catching up with the United States in terms of investments in physical infrastructures, general education, and production of new knowledge. This catching up will generate powerful sources of economic growth which will increase the demand for output from the U.S. economy at a rapid rate. In general, this nation—as well as others—will be responding to a global demand, not a national demand.

On the international political scene, the key to our future will be determined by our ability to sustain our economic growth at the very time that our population growth rate is leveling out and the demands from the service sector for such things as education and health care are increasing at a rapid pace. The challenge will be to foster our economic growth and augment our supply of human services in a world in which the constraint to attaining those goals is the limitations of time, not the limitations of natural resources. The challenge will be to ease that constraint of time.

THE CRITICAL FACTORS THAT WILL INFLUENCE OUR ECONOMIC GROWTH IN THE FUTURE

These factors were reviewed briefly in an earlier paper and in a context not greatly different from the present paper (Schuh 1981). For present purposes, it is necessary only to draw on a few points from that paper.

The first is to recall that T. W. Schultz, in papers published in 1947 (a and b), defined a high-level equilibrium for an economy experiencing economic growth. Basing his ideas on Becker's time allocation model and the new household economics, Schultz argued that the ultimate constraint to development is the limit that a 24-hour day puts on the development process. On the surface, this is a resource-based stagnation model in the tradition of the classicists, but Schultz stands the classical world on its head. The ultimate constraint to development in his view comes from limitations on time for the consumption of household-produced goods and services. This is a constraint within the household that does not arise from scarcity of natural resources or from rising costs in production.

Schultz's equilibrium is at a high income level, not at starvation wages as in the models of the classicists. The theory is quite rich, moreover, since by including children as consumption goods, it includes a population as well as an income equilibrium.

The problem with this perspective is that it is too limiting in the context of the challenge we envisage for the U.S. economy. We see the need for the United States to expand its supply of labor services if it is to sustain its position in the global economy, and to provide for an increase in output per "worker" over time.

Nerlove, although obviously in the Schultz tradition, provides a somewhat different perspective that is more suggestive for the dilemmas the United States faces. He argues that productivity in the household, where both production and consumption take place, can be raised on a continual basis. Because human capital is one of the main outputs of the household, further investments in human capital actually increase the efficiency with which it can be produced. Hence, there is no reason for an equilibrium level of per capita incomes or population to exist.

The limitation of the Nerlove perspective is the importance it attaches to the household as the producer of human capital. With the family undergoing a rapid transformation in U.S. society, and the economics of investing in human capital in the household undergoing significant change at the same time, the problem of investing in human capital needs to be viewed in a larger context.

There are four points that need to be stressed in considering the present challenges faced by the United States. First, the services from our population are not constrained by numbers alone. Labor services from a given population can be raised by increasing the productivity of that labor, or the productivity of time. The accumulation of physical capital is important in that context, but it is the accumulation of human capital that really matters. Human capital includes the stock of knowledge in the society, the skills—cognitive and otherwise—of the labor force, the health and nutritional status of the population, and the institutional arrangements which govern the relations among people in society.

Second, increases in the value of time set in motion forces that lead to investment in human capital. The decline in real earnings per unit of time in the United States, which has been underway for almost 20 years now, undoubtedly contributed to the decline in investment in human capital over recent decades. By the same token, if the value of time rises significantly in the future, as I expect it to, we should experience a revitalization of our investment in human capital.

Third, this shift of the economy to a more human capital-intensive configuration will have important implications for international trade. We should seek to increase our exports of goods and services that are intensive in human capital, and import those intensive in natural resources.

Fourth, unless the increased demand for human capital should revitalize the family in American society, this nation is in serious need of new institutional arrangements to assure that investments in human capital are made at a socially optimal rate. Unless this problem is solved, we may well see our standard of living decline and our position in the global economy wane.

THE RESEARCH AGENDA

The research agenda focuses on agriculture and rural America, although the implications of the above perspective goes far beyond that. Issues needing additional attention include the following:

RESEARCH DESIGNED TO UNDERSTAND WHY THIS NATION PERSISTENTLY UNDERINVESTS IN AGRICULTURAL RESEARCH

The evidence that we underinvest is provided by the high social rates of return found for almost every study that has attempted to estimate these rates of return (Ruttan 1983). Improving performance in this area is important for three reasons. First, given that food is a wage good, a decline in food prices makes possible a rise in real wages without raising nominal wages. This improves the competitive potential of the economy as a whole, while enabling real wages to rise. Second, a decline in the real price of food will lower the costs of producing children and thus shift the supply curve of population to the right. These two reasons make it clear that agriculture is important not just because it is one of the larger sectors of the economy, but because everybody consumes food.

Third, greater investments in agricultural research help raise resource productivity generally in agriculture, and thus help make this sector more competitive globally. Improved performance in this respect will help earn the foreign exchange the United States needs to sustain its position in the global economy.

RESEARCH DESIGNED TO IMPROVE THE PHYSICAL AND SOCIAL INFRASTRUCTURE OF RURAL AMERICA

Rural America has inherited a social infrastructure that was designed for another day. The system of county governments was designed to accommodate citizens so they could go from their home to the county seat and back in one day on horseback. Hardly anybody makes the trek this way anymore, but county governments still persist.

In today's world, there is a proliferation of local governmental units. Minnesota alone has some 4,000, only 92 of which are county governments. This grossly inefficient system, with its costly duplication and lack of size economies, is a luxury we can no longer afford. More importantly, these overlapping systems are still not able to deliver in an efficient way the social services needed for a modern, productive society.

The physical infrastructure in rural America is also falling into serious disarray. Research is needed to design new systems which reflect the technological breakthroughs in the transportation and communication sectors. A revitalized physical infrastructure is critical to remaining competitive on the international scene.

RESEARCH DESIGNED TO UNDERSTAND THE RAPID CHANGES IN THE INTERNATIONAL ECONOMY AND SOCIETY

This nation will increasingly need to live by its wits. To do that, it needs a greatly expanded knowledge base on the global economy and policy. It needs to better understand how comparative advantage is changing on the international scene. It needs to know how policy interventions distort that underlying comparative advantage, and why governments intervene as they do. It needs to better understand other cultures in the world, and it needs to do a better job of keeping up with technological developments in other countries.

RESEARCH DESIGNED TO UNDERSTAND WHY SOCIETY SIGNIFICANTLY UNDERINVESTS IN THE HUMAN CAPITAL OF ITS RURAL POPULATION

It is well known that society significantly underinvests in the education of its rural population, whether measured as levels of school attainment or in terms of quality of education. Health and nutrition services in rural areas are also below those in urban centers, with the result that a disproportionate share of poverty in this country is found among the rural population.

This nation can no longer afford such underinvestment in scarce human resources as it emerges into an increasingly competitive global economy. Continued wastage of these resources can only accelerate the day of our further economic and political decline on the international scene.

RESEARCH DESIGNED TO UNDERSTAND THE BREAKUP OF THE AMERICAN FAMILY

A major share of the investment in human capital in this country has traditionally taken place in the household. The breakup of the family makes such investments less and less feasible, with the result that population growth rates decline and the quality of the remaining human resources declines as well. There is probably no topic more important on our agenda than to find ways of revitalizing this source of human capital.

RESEARCH WHICH LEADS TO THE DESIGN OF NEW INSTITUTIONAL ARRANGEMENTS FOR INVESTING IN HUMAN CAPITAL

It may be that fundamental economic and social forces are driving the breakup of the American family and that its decline will continue into the future. If that is the case, new institutional arrangements are needed to assure that the investments previously made in the household are provided by alternative means. (See Schuh 1989, for additional detail.) These new institutional arrangements will need to include improved day care centers, as well as possible new configurations of schools.

CONCLUDING COMMENTS

Two counterpart themes have run through this paper: The first is the challenge the United States faces on the international scene as its economic, and ultimately its political strength, wanes. The other is the potential for a significant increase in the value of time in the future, with limitations of time being the ultimate constraint to sustaining our economic strength and, in turn, our political power.

The solution to these joint problems is to increase our investments in human capital, thus raising the productivity of time. To do that will require significant increases in social science research designed to understand the present causes of our underinvestment in human capital, and to design new institutional arrangements that will help us invest at socially optimal levels.

NOTES

1. This paper is an expansion and modification of "The Challenge of Change in Agriculture and Natural Resources: Implications for Science," presented at the Michigan Agricultural Experiment Station Centennial Symposium on "The Challenge of Change: Science in the 21st Century," the Kellogg Center, Michigan State University, East Lansing, February 25, 1988.

2. G. Edward Schuh is Dean of the Hubert H. Humphrey Institute of Public Affairs, University of Minnesota, Minneapolis.

REFERENCES

Nerlove, Marc. 1974. Household and economy: Towards a new theory of population and economic growth. *Journal of Political Economy* 82:5200-18.

Ruttan, Vernon W. 1983. *Agricultural research policy.* Minneapolis: University of Minnesota Press.

Schuh, G. Edward. 1981. Economic and international relations: A conceptual framework. *American Journal of Agricultural Economics* 63:767-78.

_____1989. Investment in human capital: Public and private responsibility. Paper presented at Beatrice Paolucci Symposium, Ecological Decision-Making for the Future: Interdependence of Public and Private Spheres, 19-21 January, at Michigan State University, East Lansing, Michigan.

Schultz, T. W., ed. 1947a. *Economics of the famlily: Marriage, family and human capital.* Chicago: University of Chicago Press.

Schultz, T. W. 1947b. The high value of human time: Population equilibrium. *Journal of Political Economy* 82:52-10.

CHAPTER 7

FROM THE PERSPECTIVE OF USERS AND AFFECTED PERSONS

Richard J. Sauer[1]

INTRODUCTION

As an administrator within the U.S. public agricultural research system, my challenge is to provide a description of how users of the system and other persons affected by it view the system. While starting from the premise that our agricultural research system has accomplished much, the primary focus of this paper will be on the following:

- Public criticisms and perceptions—a summary of criticisms, actual and perceived, from various users and affected persons.
- Some observations, as a research administrator, of other complicating factors in land-grant universities and state agricultural experiment stations.
- Challenges for the future—to which social scientists at land-grant universities must respond.
- A new agricultural agenda.

WHAT'S RIGHT ABOUT US

Over 100 years ago, land-grant universities and their state agricultural experiment stations were charged with developing new scientifically based technologies to improve the productivity of U.S. agriculture. This in turn would allow a labor force to be freed for the development of the industrial capacity of the country. The results have been impressive. These institutions can largely take credit for laying the foundation for the tremendous improvement in U.S. agricultural production, literally making two blades of grass grow where one grew before. They enabled the United States to be the world's largest food and fiber exporter, as well as being the major supplier of world food aid, literally keeping millions alive in the world today. Techniques borrowed from here have fueled the green revolution in Third World countries, staving off hunger and starvation.

When we—the agricultural science establishment—look at these accomplishments, we like what we see through the rose-colored light of success: a productive United States where less than 10 percent of the population can now process and distribute the food and fiber for the other 90-plus percent, with that 90-plus percent producing other things of value for an affluent nation. U.S. citizens are getting the greatest variety of safe and healthful food for the smallest part of disposable income anywhere in the world.

At the beginning of this decade, just seven short years ago, we saw an abundance of published reports on projections for food production and agriculture. Among them were the Final Report of the Presidential Commission on World Hunger (Presidential Commission on World Hunger 1980); the Global 2000 Report (Council on Environmental Quality and U.S. Department of State 1980); Resources, Society and the Future (Swedish Secretariat for Future Studies 1980); the World Food and Nutrition Study (National Academy of Sciences 1977); the Bonn Conference (Food and Agricultural Development Center 1980); the Brandt Commission Report (Brandt Commission 1980); the Report of the Food and Agriculture Organization of the United Nations (United Nations 1980); the proceedings of the Conservation Foundation Symposium on the Future of American Agriculture as a Strategic Resource (Batie and Healy, eds. 1980); and the Agricultural-Food Policy Review (U.S. Department of Agriculture 1981). The general tone was one of pessimism. All raised questions about the future productive capacity of U.S. agriculture, the environmental consequences, resource availability, and technological capabilities.

One hears less concern about the world food production issue. Perhaps it is masked partly by the burgeoning surpluses of food and feed grains in the United States and by transferring our technology to other countries. Developing countries have also made enormous gains in their own food-producing capability. New technologies, including the new biotechnologies, offer the potential for significant increases in productivity, assuming an adequate sustained level of public support for agricultural research and education programs.

PUBLIC CRITICISMS AND PERCEPTIONS

Despite the successes of the past, our incomparably productive agricultural system has developed cracks. The list would keep you awake at night: eroded soils; heavy silting; increased flooding; an alarming depletion of aquifers; a disturbing pervasiveness of chemicals; runoff pollution; destruction of forests; wholesale resistance to chemicals by insects and weeds; scarce water used for producing costly agricultural surpluses for which there is no market or commercial use; farm policies that favor production for production's sake; farm exports down and farmers struggling awash in their own production; and the United States may no longer be the world's economical producer of grains and oilseeds.

There is no doubt that there is a rapidly changing public perception about us in the agricultural system, our programs, and our value to society. Public attitude in general towards agricultural science has shifted from unqualified support to a questioning ambivalence toward and even fear of its consequences.

To understand that changing perception, leading to ways in which we can improve the perception, we need to hear and understand what our critics say about us. Various groups have criticized the agricultural research establishment in recent years. Consideration of these criticisms is essential in reaching objective recommendations on agricultural science policies, the introduction of new technologies, and decisions on priorities for research projects.

One group of critics are the biological and physical scientists outside the land-grant system. They suggest that agricultural science lacks a basic science foundation and is a third-rate enterprise, using too many of its resources on applied research. Not everyone agrees. Farm lenders, farmers and farm-oriented legislators argue that transferring these resources to more basic disciplinary research would lead to neglect of problem-solving research and to expansion of academic bureaucracies. Thus, we see line item earmarking in state and federal agricultural research appropriations to ensure that certain kinds of problem-solving and commodity research will be done.

There are also critics who are dissatisfied with the way technological advance sometimes restructures agriculture and society. They argue that the present economic woes in agriculture are the result of too much research, too much information, too much capability. They argue that the new technologies exacerbate the problem and, in effect, say that agriculture would be better off it were less efficient. Some go so far as to promote a return to less intensive/low input/small farm agriculture of 50 years ago.

Next consider the criticisms of humanists, social scientists and religious leaders. They maintain that the agricultural research establishment pays inadequate attention to the values involved in rural poverty, human nutrition and malnutrition, endangered species, environmental pollution, energy, water and the structure of the rural society.

Also, there are a broad group of critics called "activists." As advocates, activists often sacrifice objectivity to promote solutions that they put beyond research.

Two major groups of activists concerned with agricultural research establishment are the antiestablishment and the proestablishment activists. The antiestablishment activists include some members of religious organizations, hunger and poverty workers, environmentalists, people concerned with the preservation of nonfarm rural values, those who are worried about mistreatment of migrant and small farmers, people concerned with the so-called demise of the "family farm," those who have fears about the exhaustion of nonrenewable resources, people who promote their own political futures, and some nutritionists and other academicians promoting their disciplines or fields or, for that matter, themselves. Despite lapses in objectivity, the antiestablishment activists have often placed important problems and issues on the agenda, and we should not forget that. However, some of them have been demonstrated to be poorly informed about the technology and institutions of agriculture; others have lacked knowledge about the nature of farm people. Some see almost innumerable "conspiracies" among the agricultural research establishment, agribusinesses and large farmers to exploit small farmers, farm laborers, and consumers.

Proestablishment activists who unobjectively defend the agricultural research establishment come from the establishment itself, from agricultural businesses and various groups of agricultural fundamentalists, both inside and outside of government. Not all defenders of the establishment are unobjective. The defenders also include those who try objectively to listen to the antiestablishment activists and to provide them with objective knowledge about agricultural institutions, technologies, people and capital accumulation. Others, of course, react emotionally, in uninformed, unobjective ways, in defending the agricultural research establishment against the antiestablishment activists.

Among important issues placed on the agricultural research establishment's research agenda, in part by activists, is the need for agricultural technologies that are less exploitive of our resources and more sustainable during the decades ahead. A variety of alternatives are promoted under such descriptive attractive names as regenerative agriculture, sustainable agriculture, closed-system agriculture, and organic farming. Activists often view pesticides and fertilizers as threats to the environment of human health. This concern has promoted research on possible adverse impacts.

Though the complaints of all groups are sometimes in conflict, they are all primarily ethical in the sense that they assert that the agricultural research establishment has made and is making wrong decisions, often on the basis of incorrect values, on agricultural science policies and research priorities, goals, and objectives. Do their criticisms have validity? I suggest they do, without making a judgment as to what extent. For too long our scientists and research administrators have assumed that all externalities of their research would be positive. That only good would accrue from newly introduced technological change, such as a new pesticide or harvesting machine. That is not the case, and it never was, but for too long we have blindly moved ahead with that assumption. It can no longer be. Society will demand that we ask all the questions about potential impact, negative as well as positive, while we are conducting research and perhaps before the technology is ever introduced into commercial use.

Society should insist and, in fact, is insisting that agricultural research be concerned with the effects of agricultural technology upon the health and safety of agricultural producers, with the nutrition and health of consumers, with the impacts of agricultural practices on the aesthetic and productive qualities of natural and modified environments, and with the quality of life in rural communities.

There is a substantial element of validity in each of the other criticisms I have mentioned as well. The agricultural research system has been less than adequately responsive to the needs of many elements of its potential constituency. The agricultural research establishment has at times devoted excessive resources to applied research that has little application—or application for only a limited clientele. The appropriate allocation of responsibility for research between the public and private sector is an issue that must be continuously reexamined in response to institutional, scientific, and technological change. Each of the criticisms, although perhaps excessive and sometimes not well informed, has generated response and the beginning of reform in the agricultural research establishment.

In addition to the criticisms of agricultural research from outside of the establishment, there has been a rising level of criticisms of agricultural research and of the productivity growth generated by research by the traditional agricultural research clientele—by those who have traditionally benefitted from agricultural research or by their representatives. During 1980–85 a global recession and the rising value of the dollar combined to dampen the demand for U.S. agricultural commodities abroad. High interest rates, associated first with inflation and later with massive federal borrowing, imposed severe financial burdens on farmers and their suppliers. These combined to enforce the decline in farm commodity prices, severe deflation in land values, and a financial crisis for many farmers. Confronted by the buildup of commodity stocks, the federal government engaged in increasingly expensive programs designed to slow the growth in agricultural production.

These difficulties have prompted some critics to suggest a moratorium on agricultural research and technology development. They say the present economic woes in agriculture are the result of too much research, too much information, and too much capability. They feel that we should slow down our research until society has had a chance to catch up and assimilate the gains we have made. They suggest a moratorium would result in slower economic growth in agricultural production and permit domestic and international markets to absorb surplus production capacity at no real cost to consumers or producers.

While the agricultural research establishment is being criticized for generating too much new technology, there are also critics who maintain that both the agricultural research establishment and the state cooperative extension service system are too slow, too conservative, and too unresponsive. We are too slow in releasing the results of research to benefit farmers. We are too conservative, testing the same production systems and technologies over and over, and do not take enough risk with radical new alternatives. We lack responsiveness to changing needs. We are dinosaurs, having outlived our usefulness and unable to adapt fast enough to a changing world.

In addition, we no longer have a monopoly on the technology development and the marketing of information. The private sector has developed an increased interest in agricultural technology, especially through the new biotechnologies and the use of computers. Farmers can seek reliable advice on production, marketing, and financing from other sources. This has caused us no small degree of concern. We even find our own employees wondering whether we have a future. This has affected our recruitment of high-quality staff and our securing of additional resources to continue to serve the public well.

What do we do about all of these criticisms? If they are not valid, do we simply ignore them? I do not think we can afford to ignore them, even if they are unfounded. However, I do find some amount of validity in most of these criticisms. That should bring us even greater concern.

SOME COMPLICATING FACTORS

I am not a social scientist who has studied agriculture and knows agricultural science and education from that perspective. Rather, I am an agricultural research and education administrator with experience at three land-grant universities. I have interacted with numerous clientele, legislators, other public officials and a broad range of people both within the academic community and throughout the agricultural community, during one of the most stressful times in midwest agriculture. Based on these experiences I would like to discuss several complicating factors.

AGRICULTURE'S COMPLEXITY

The word *agriculture* conveys different meanings to different people, from a farmer on a tractor plowing his fields to frenzied traders on the floor of the Chicago Board of Trade. Others might think of agriculture in terms of foreign trade, crop research, heavy equipment industries, herds of cattle grazing, aisles of groceries in a supermarket, or a rural community. We all have different images of agriculture. Although each of us sees a part of the picture, few see the whole picture. Comprehending the connections and relationships among the many disparate elements of American agriculture is exceedingly difficult. Thus, we often are not even able to start from the same point in initiating a dialogue with one other person let alone reach agreement on the ideal structure of rural America of the future.

LACK OF COMPREHENSIVE AGRICULTURAL POLICY

Likewise, no single law exists that defines an agricultural policy. Congress periodically adopts omnibus farm bills but these bills, by themselves, have never constituted a complete, self-contained "agricultural policy." Frequently, Congress, the courts, foreign governments, and agribusinesses make decisions that have extensive ramifications on the farm economy. Commodity price supports, for example, have reduced the competitiveness of American crops on international markets that public investments in increased productivity have been trying to achieve. Fiscal, monetary, and credit policies have run counter to programs to save the family farm and encourage rural economic development.

In recent years, the state of agriculture has been in an upheaval due to a changing economy, fluctuating policies, technological developments, and new consumer habits. Farming has always been risky. Historically, much of our government's policy has been aimed at stabilizing agriculture, insulating private landowners from the consequences of change. Public policies, however, have failed to maintain the status quo and protect farmers from risk; some policies have even exacerbated the problems. It is no wonder that current discussions of farm policy are fraught with frustration, anger, and confusion.

AGRICULTURAL RESEARCH IS UNDERFUNDED

Annual rates of return on public investments in agricultural research are high, often 30 to 50 percent or more. This suggests that agricultural research and development is substantially underfunded by standard investment criteria. Yet today we face the counter argument that the world's markets are awash with the products of excess agricultural capacity because of research. This is pure hogwash. This excess capacity was caused by bad investment decisions by farmers based on excessively optimistic expectations, induced in part by subsidies and foolish national policies.

A related issue is that from the local (state) perspective public investment in agricultural research and development looks adequate. A large part of the benefits of research funded by one state spills over into other states. An excellent example is the recent spillover of wild rice production technology from Minnesota to California. Such losses of state-level benefits inhibit state investments in agricultural science. The spillover argues for a greater federal investment, and yet in real terms growth in such federal funding essentially stopped 20 years ago. Without compensating federal funding, the states, acting alone and rationally, will never achieve an optimum level of national investment in agricultural research.

INTERDISCIPLINARY TEAM SCIENCE

We still unduly organize, fund, and practice science, especially basic science, in this country around a nineteenth-century tradition of an individual scientists in his or her laboratory surrounded by a few laboratory technicians or graduate assistants. However, not all technology arises out of basic disciplinary research. Further, many of today's problems in science, including agricultural science, can be solved only by a team of scientists from several disciplines—each contributing a unique expertise toward the solution of the problem, at least in a multidisciplinary fashion if not in a systems approach.

While the numbers of interdisciplinary centers and multiuniversity consortia have grown, and linkages between university and industry R&D are more common, the efforts are still inadequate. The majority of state agricultural experiment station research is still organized by disciplinary or subject-matter projects with a single principal investigator. Most regional research projects are not interdisciplinary; even those that are generally lack an adequate level of funding to really tackle the task at hand.

A major problem is that universities have not found ways to recognize and reward this work appropriately. Tenure and promotion come largely through success in the disciplines. Land-grant universities should take greater responsibility to support and reward those who make the necessary academic investment and risk to work on interdisciplinary teams.

LAND-GRANT UNIVERSITIES AS PREDICTORS OF CHANGE

With the severe problems in agriculture in recent years, one of the most often heard criticisms of state agricultural experiment stations is that we failed to predict the changes and to warn the farmers. My own experience is that many of our faculty, including several prominent agricultural economists and rural sociologists, did predict the financial problems and warned farmers not to expand, not to purchase land at inflated prices, not to incur more debt. However, relatively few farmers listened and now, after some have lost their farms, they are looking for someone else to blame.

Recently our Department of Agricultural and Applied Economics released a publication which contains the principal conclusions that now is a good time to enter farming. It points out that the opportunities for beginning or reentering farmers to succeed in the agricultural industry have improved significantly in the last few years, especially if a crop-share rental arrangement is utilized rather than the ownership option of land acquisition. However, I have received criticism from both farmers and legislators for the release of this study. Of course, these critics include those who have lost their farms and feel victimized, especially if someone else will now acquire and farm their land for a lower cost and make a profit. We should expect worthwhile information to bring some criticism, and the criticism should not deter us from continuing such efforts.

LAND-GRANT UNIVERSITIES AS CHANGE AGENTS

While land-grant universities have predicted change with some success, particularly on the financial side of agriculture, we have been much less successful in leading the way for major change in agricultural production systems. Our biological and physical scientists have been slow to redirect research to alternative crops, reduced or low-input systems, nonchemical pest control, or other major changes that might improve profitability and/or sustainability of our agricultural systems.

Our social scientists have also been hesitant to depart radically from their studies and analyses of the traditional production systems. Their research should be providing some of the economic and social rationale for giving alternative approaches to food production a legitimate test. On the contrary, in defense of the social scientists, we have not organized our SAES research projects with sufficient interdisciplinary linkages between the social and biological/physical scientists, nor have we allocated adequate resources to our social scientists.

LAND-GRANT UNIVERSITIES AND AGRICULTURAL POLICY DEVELOPMENT

It has become increasingly obvious that the United States needs the development of sane, constructive, complementary agricultural, natural resources, and rural development policies. The new configuration of the international economy, the problems in rural America, and the increasing numbers of critics throughout society heighten this need. These policies must be based on our science and technology knowledge and data bases, using the skilled professionals in our land-grant universities and other public and private institutions. All too often, however, our agricultural, natural resource, and rural development policies have been formulated by amateurs and politicians in response to the intense pressures from and vested interests of many special-interest groups. Land-grant universities have the people resources to provide informed recommendations and analyses of the potential impacts of draft legislation. These resources, heretofore, have been largely underutilized.

CHALLENGES FOR SOCIAL SCIENTISTS

Land-grant universities have a mandate to lead their state's and this nation's efforts in higher education and research in agriculture and in turn chart a course for the future of U.S. agriculture and rural communities—a mandate we have had for 100 years—but the mandate has changed. We must now determine how we can constructively lead while agriculture is undergoing considerable stress and change. Several challenges lie ahead, and social scientists must play a key, if not pivotal, role in a successful response to them.

AGRICULTURE AND THE ENVIRONMENT

We know surprisingly little about the long-term impacts of agricultural practices and land use on the environment. The questions must be addressed in terms of ethics and values as well as in terms of technical impact. As more is known about agriculture's impact on the quality of the environment, fundamental policy changes should emerge. Agricultural and natural resource policies in the future will not be formulated so much by examining the impact of resource quality, quantity, and price on farm income and production; rather, policies will be formulated by examining the impact of farm practices on resource quality and quantity and on our quality of life.

There will be more interest in farming systems that reduce chemical usage, use less energy, and reduce soil erosion. Some farmers may return to more rotations. More farmers will need and want to adopt integrated pest management practices that substitute biological control and crop monitoring for traditional pesticide use, which will lower costs for the farmer and improve the aquatic and wildlife environment. Much research—biological, economic, and sociological—remains to be done to make this future a reality.

PUBLIC OPINION AND AGRICULTURE

Public opinion about agriculture and its use of resources is changing. At one time most Americans either lived on a farm or were only one generation removed from a farm. They saw a link between the farmer's welfare and the nation's welfare. They saw the farmer as the steward of the environment, and they had faith that science and technology would bring social benefits. As citizens have become further removed from farming enterprises, farmers are losing their special place in society. Increasingly, they are finding their traditional programs and practices questioned, and these same questions are being directed to the agricultural scientists who developed the current technologies.

While these changing views can be threatening to the agricultural community, they can also be challenging. This is the time for farmers and those with interests in agricultural policies to search for compromises with the environmental community and to forge alliances that are sensitive to both agriculture's unique constraints and the public goals of an improved environment. Land-grant university scientists can play the lead role in forging the changes.

ECONOMIC DEVELOPMENT AND RURAL COMMUNITIES

It is clear that governments and educational institutions must promote economic diversity in rural areas that are suffering as a consequence of their heavy dependence on agriculture. Rural economic development may be the most effective and realistic way to help many of these communities. Among other things, the availability of off-farm jobs in rural areas may make it possible for existing farms to stabilize their incomes and for more Americans to be involved in agriculture via part-time operations.

Land-grant universities have the knowledge base to assist rural entrepreneurs and thus stimulate economic development and job creation. Cooperative extension services should provide the leadership; to do so they will have to break out of their traditional molds and draw upon people resources within the university with whom their programs have not been strongly linked in the past—such as faculty in law, management, and high technology.

A NEW AGRICULTURAL RESEARCH AGENDA

The new agricultural research agenda that is emerging is beginning to look at productivity in terms other than yield-per-acre or yield-per-animal. Lower operating costs, the preservation of natural resources, and sustained yield have become as important as simple yield. Biotechnology can be a powerful tool, but if the goal is poorly defined, inefficiency may result. We have to learn that we must first ask, "Where do we want to go?" before we ask, "How do we get there?"

The agenda of issues in agriculture today strongly suggests that more social science and humanities knowledge is needed. This is due to growing needs of the modification of old institutions or development of new institutions, the adaption and transfer of technologies, for the resolution of numerous ethical problems as well as the sustained input of ethics into research, decision making and priority setting, and in the creation of new human capital. The mix of relevant disciplines varies with the problems addressed. Implementing the right mix is imperative to future public support for agricultural research. The growing complexity of the agricultural industry, and thus the chance of error, as well as the fact that science is increasingly expected to minimize deleterious impacts on society, means that we may not ignore current criticisms and expect continued and adequate public funding. The need for social science and humanistic research on agriculture and rural life is growing.

However, the mix of disciplines in most state agricultural experiment stations, due to tenure and relatively little turnover during the past decade, is generally appropriate to serve a pre-1980s agriculture. That is, the faculty are dominated by scientists in the hard (biological and physical) sciences with a production/maximum yield orientation.

In most SAESs, the social sciences became institutionalized at a later stage and generally did not receive an adequate allocation of resources. There were many reasons for this, including the domination of the production departments, the fact that most station directors came from a biological or physical science discipline, and that there was the misperception that it costs much less to support a social scientist than it does to support a biological or physical scientist.

Today many SAESs have static or even declining resources. Thus, increased support of social science research will have to come from internal reallocation. Do station directors recognize this need? And if they do, do they have the courage to reallocate? I have some reservations.

CONCLUSIONS

The problems of the future in agriculture and rural America cannot be solved by the research programs of the past. Major changes in the research agenda and priorities, the organization and funding of research projects, and in the mix of scientists will be necessary.

Research must be driven by a new set of concerns and priorities, including sustainability, environmental quality, human health, consumer desires, and what is best for rural communities. We must confront many criticisms of an ethical nature. Societal values will be incorporated into research decision making and technology development and transfer. Productivity will still be a priority, but profitability coupled with resource efficiency and conservation will be the focus.

The mix of disciplines and relative research investments in state agricultural experiment stations will change. Social scientists will play a more pivotal role in developing the research agenda and helping us answer the question "Where do we want to go?"

Land-grant universities and their state agricultural experiment stations face major challenges. By reorganizing the challenges and making the changes necessary to successfully address them, these institutions can play a key leadership role in determine what U.S. agriculture and rural communities become in the twenty-first century. But they must be willing to make major, even radical, changes in the way they do business and must have adequate resources to back their convictions.

NOTE

1. Richard J. Sauer is the former vice president for Agriculture, Forestry, and Home Economics, and director of the Agricultural Experiment Station, University of Minnesota, St. Paul. Currently, Dr. Sauer is president and chief executive officer of the National 4-H Council.

REFERENCES CITED IN THIS CHAPTER

Batie, Sandra S., and Robert G. H. Healy, eds. 1980. *The future of American agriculture as a strategic resource.* Conservation Foundation, Washington, D.C.

Brandt Commission. 1980. *North-south, program for survival.* Cambridge: Massachusetts Institute of Technology Press.

Council on Environmental Quality and U.S. Department of State. 1980. The global 2000 report to the President. Washington, D.C.

Food and Agricultural Development Center, German Foundation for International Development. 1980. Agricultural production: Research and development strategies for the 1980s. Bonn, West Germany.

Food and Agriculture Organization, United Nations. 1979. Agriculture toward 2000. Rome, Italy.

National Academy of Sciences. 1977. The potential contributions of research. World Food and Nutrition Study Report of the Steering Committee, National Research Council, Washington, D.C.

Presidential Commission on World Hunger. 1980. Final report. The White House, Washington, D.C.

Swedish Secretariat for Future Studies. 1980. Resources, society and the future. Stockholm, Sweden.

U.S. Department of Agriculture. 1981. Agricultural-food policy review: Perspectives for the 1980s. Washington, D.C.

REFERENCES DRAWN ON OR RELEVANT FOR CONTENT OF THIS CHAPTER

Batie, Sandra S. 1985. Environmental constraints: The new limits. *Issues in Science and Technology* (Fall): 134-43.

Benson, Fred, and Michael Boehlje. 1986. Starting or reentering farming: Is the timing right? Ag. and Applied Economics Staff Paper No. P86-14, April, University of Minnesota, St. St. Paul, Minn.

Bonnen, James T. 1986. A century of science in agriculture: What have we learned? Agricultural Economics Staff Paper No. 86-79, Michigan State University, East Lansing, Michigan.

Brown, George E., Jr. 1985. A view from Congress. *Issues in Science and Technology* (Fall): 147-48.

Buttel, Frederick H. 1985. The land-grant system: A sociological perspective on value conflicts and ethical issues. *Agriculture and Human Values* 2(z):78-95.

Cook, Kenneth A., and Susan E. Sechler. 1985. Agricultural policy: Paying for our past mistakes. *Issues in Science and Technology* (Fall): 97-110.

Evenson, Robert E., Paul E. Waggoner, and Vernon W. Ruttan. 1979. Economic benefits from research: An example from agriculture. *Science* 205:1101-7.

Havlicek, Joseph, Jr., and Fred C. White. 1983. Interregional transfer of agricultural research results: The case for the northeast. *Journal of the Northeastern Agricultural Economics Council* 12 (Fall): 19-30.

Johnson, Glenn L. 1985. Agricultural surpluses—Research on agricultural technologies, institutions, people and capital growth. In *Crop productivity: Research imperatives revisited*, edited by M. Gibbs and C. Carlson. East Lansing, Mich.: Michigan State University, Michigan Agricultural Experiment Station.

_____1990. Ethical dilemmas posed by recent and prospective developments with respect to agricultural research. Presented at the annual meeting of AAAS, May, Detroit, Mich. Published in *Agriculture and Human Ethics,* Vol 7, 1990.

Meeks, Gordon, Jr. 1986. The state of agriculture: Some observations. National Conference of State Legislatures, August, Denver, Colorado.

Oehmke, James F. 1985. Persistent underinvestment in public agricultural research. Agricultural Economics Staff Paper No. 85-101, Michigan State University, East Lansing, Michigan.

Ruttan, Vernon W. 1982. *Agricultural research policy.* Minneapolis: University of Minnesota Press.

Sauer, Richard J. 1986a. *Agriculture and Human Values* Confronting the changing perceptions of agricultural research and extension. Presented at "Changing Strategies for a New Era," a national conference for experiment station and extension service administrators and communicators, 22 April, Minneapolis, Minnesota.

_____1986b. Agriculture: Current state, future prospects—An educator's perspective. Presented at National Agricultural Forum: The Health of the Land and Its People, 30 October, Washington, D.C.

Schuh, G. Edward. 1986a. Impact of national and international economic policies on U.S. agriculture. Proceedings of the 35th annual meeting of the Agricultural Research Institute, 8-10 October, Washington, D.C.

_____1986b. Revitalizing the land-grant university. *Choices*. 2d quarter.

CHAPTER 8

ABRIDGED WORK GROUP REPORTS FROM SSAAP'S PHASE I SPRING HILL CONFERENCE

June 9–11, 1988

INTRODUCTION

Several of the papers incorporated into Chapters 2 through 7 were available to the participants at the Spring Hill Conference. Also available were previous agenda- and priority-setting exercises for agriculture, rural nonfarm resources, rural nonfarm people, rural communities, and the like. The Spring Hill conference papers and the generally available priority- and agenda-setting exercises were used by four work groups to develop the general road map for SSAAP's subsequent agenda-setting exercises. *One* work group considered farmers, agribusinesses, and consumers; a *second,* natural and rural community resources and the environment and their uses; a *third,* international affairs; and a *fourth,* administrative and funding strategies. The reports of these work groups were major influences in structuring subsequent SSAAP activities. Therefore, abridged versions of the work group reports are presented in this chapter along with the membership rosters of the work groups.

WORK GROUP 1 ON FARMERS, AGRIBUSINESS, AND CONSUMERS

PERSONNEL IN WORK GROUP

Leader: Frederick Buttel, Department of Rural Sociology, Cornell University
Rapporteur: John E. Lee, Economic Research Service, U.S. Department of Agriculture
Members: William Cromarty, Clarence Davan Jr., Kenneth Farrell, Richard Haynes, Erwin Johnson, Carol Kramer, Bruce Marion, Paul Rosenblatt, Burt Sundquist, Kenneth Tefertiller

ABRIDGED AND EDITED REPORT

Under the leadership of Fred Buttel, this group had a lively, wide-ranging debate on the scope and content of its assigned area; the relative emphasis that should be put on problem-solving (PS) versus subject-matter (SM) and disciplinary (DISC) subareas; the appropriate balance between more aggregate or macro issues versus micro issues; and the need to provide help to individuals and families.

The subareas chosen for further development tended to reflect problem areas and subject-matter concerns. Nevertheless, there were strong views expressed that the social science agenda for the years ahead should not ignore the urgent need to improve the capacity of the basic disciplines to assist in PS and SM research, education, and other work. Capacity-enhancing needs include improvements in theory and methodology, applied disciplinary work in interdisciplinary and multidisciplinary contexts, enhancement of databases and improvements in educational techniques.

Concern was expressed that the social sciences not lose sight of their ultimate responsibility to help individuals and families. Even when the problem area to be addressed is of a broad policy nature, it was agreed that it is important to give careful consideration to the distributive aspects (income, age, race, rural/urban, regional, etc.) of the problem.

There was considerable discussion of the issue of information. The discussion resulted in two subareas for future priorities: information and information technology as research and education resources, and information as a product for constituent use. Most of the subareas presented below need work and pertain to a broad range of social sciences. No attempt was made to spell out the challenges for individual social science disciplines in each of the subareas. Important subareas within which it was thought agendas should be set by SSAAP are identified in the paragraphs that follow.

Competitiveness of U.S. Agriculture in Global Markets

This urgent topic has important implications not only for trade and the aggregate economics of U.S. agriculture, but also for the adjustments that regions and rural communities have to face and the well-being of farm and rural people. This is a broad and complex subarea that includes work for most rural social sciences. Work includes study of where U.S. agriculture shakes out in the world market; determination of the forces affecting U.S. comparative advantages; analysis of how to enhance competitiveness; appraisals of competitive prospects by commodities and products; and examination of the implied adjustment pressures for producers of specific commodities, resource use, rural people and communities, agribusinesses, and infrastructure.

Agricultural and Food Policy in a Global Economy

This topic includes analysis of the origins and consequences of present and alternative farm commodity, food, resource, and trade policies, including the redistributive aspects of these policies. It requires studies useful to formulating policies to achieve societal values while minimizing undesirable consequences. It also includes analysis of regulations that affect food supply and cost, demand, and trade.

Performance of and Consequences for the Food and Fiber System

Performance relates to achievement of a broad array of more ultimate and instrumental values, including: efficiency of resource use, distributive equity, equality, environmental enhancement, system-wide resiliency and innovativeness, consistency with other national policy objectives, and assurance of safe, high-quality food at reasonable cost to consumers. This subarea includes the evaluation of current performance, status, and alternative approaches for improvement. Performance is to be measured against other than purely monetary criteria. Input from most of the social sciences is required, including those major parts of economics that are concerned with the maximization of nonmonetary values.

Structure of Agriculture and Agribusiness

Structure is so important for the food and fiber system that it must receive major attention. This includes understanding the existing and emerging structure, organization and control of the entire agricultural sector, the consequences and for whom. It includes understanding what drives structure and structural change, and how those driving forces and resulting structures can be changed to improve system performance. This topic also consists of resource ownership and control, tenure, access to resource services, and rural communities.

Science and Technology Policy, Technology Assessment, and Productivity

This subarea includes: (1) understanding what drives technological development and change; (2) determination of the monetary and other social consequences of present, emerging and prospective technologies (including information technologies); (3) description of the linkages of technology and productivity changes to U.S. competitiveness; and (4) ascertainment of the implications of changes now taking place in the organization, location, and control of production, marketing and consumption, in terms of how winners and losers place pressures on institutions.

Food Consumption: Demand, Socio-Cultural Influences, and Nutrition and Health Consequences

This includes understanding food consumption patterns, habits, and preferences. Food quality, safety, and human nutrition are also involved. Also important are the determination of monetary, cultural, and other factors that affect food consumption and demand, and dynamics; as well as food/health relationships and regulatory assessments with their linkages back to food demand.

Effective Information/Knowledge Delivery and Utilization

This topic includes the education and enhancement of all constituent groups' abilities to determine their information needs, acquire information, and process it to make decisions more consistent with their enlightened self-interests. It includes public policy education and new, innovative information/intelligence delivery systems in addition to improved traditional systems. Research to better understand information use and decision-making processes may be required. This topic includes providing information/understanding to those who set the rules that govern performance as well as to those who are the actual performers (farmers, businesses, households, etc.). The topic also includes more effective identification of information users and their needs.

Information Systems, Improved Databases, and Information Property Rights

This subarea includes improved statistics on agriculture, the food and fiber system, and farm and rural households; design and use of modern information systems; understanding the impacts of modern information systems on rural institutions; and property rights in information and software.

Agriculture, Natural Resources, and the Environment

This includes the development of farming systems, technology, policies, and the institutions that assure the protection and conservation of land and water resources, and environmental quality for health and safety, and a higher quality of life. It includes water quality, water use, soil erosion, land use, protection of open space, air quality, and wildlife preservation as examples. Natural-resource preservation includes the preservation of genetic diversity, wildlife species, and the spatial openness and integrity of farmland.

Quality of Farm and Rural Family Life

This subarea focuses on rural households and their needs. The topic includes, at the aggregate level, more basic data on what is happening to farm and nonfarm families, including data on stress, satisfaction, time expenditures, access to social services, social indicators, etc. For individuals and families, needs include family counseling and adjustment assistance (sometimes financial, but more often educational).

RECOMMENDATIONS FOR THE SECOND SSAAP CONFERENCE FROM WORK GROUP 1

The group felt that it was important that each broad area have an "area coordinator" at the second SSAAP conference to: keep progress going for all the subareas; assure comprehensive coverage while minimizing overlap; assure development of adequate materials; and assure adequate communication among all of the scientists involved prior to, and during, the second conference. Those present also debated alternative ways to group the subject matter into broad areas and concluded that the present four areas were as good as any they could suggest. The area descriptions might be elaborated to point out that "Farmers, Agribusiness and Consumers" is a sectoral approach, while "Natural and Rural Community Resources and the Environment and Their Uses" deals primarily with the spatial and territorial dimensions of our overall problem universe. It was agreed that international issues probably deserved special attention but would require close coordination of the sectoral and spatial groups to assure proper integration of agendas for work on domestic and global economic/social/political systems and to avoid duplication. Such concerns indicated the importance of having strong area coordinators.

Finally, while the group did not spend much time on the question of whether additional "think" papers should be commissioned, the following suggestions were offered as possibilities:

- Science and technology policy and assessment
- Information
- Competitiveness of regions and nations as an area of research and education
- Human ecology

WORK GROUP 2 ON NATURAL AND RURAL COMMUNITY RESOURCES AND THE ENVIRONMENT AND THEIR USES

PERSONNEL IN WORK GROUP

Leader: Larry Libby, Department of Food and Resource Economics, University of Florida

Rapporteur: James Bonnen, Department of Agricultural Economics, Michigan State University

Members: William Browne, William Freudenburg, Thomas Hady, James Hite, C.RI1C. Kaltenbach, Glenn Nelson, Barbara Osgood, Russell Perkinson, Tim Phipps, Alan Randall, Neill Schaller, T. T. Williams, Gene Wunderlich

ABRIDGED AND EDITED REPORT

Eight subareas for the general area were developed. These are described below. The work group initially developed a list of 48 individual subjects and problems. These were then consolidated into eight subareas of relative homogeneity. The scope and complexity of the various subareas differ greatly. No effort was made to assign relative priorities to the eight subareas.

Subarea 1: Conservation and Use of Land and Water Resources

Land use, preservation, and development decisions: origins of attitudes toward rural land use (zoning, development, property rights); effectiveness of voluntary versus regulatory land-use policies; unanticipated effects of both voluntary and regulatory land-use policies; roles of market and nonmarket forces; and planning and decision-making processes.

Soil conservation: voluntary versus regulatory policies; marketing strategies for conservation; attitude/behavior linkages and the role of stewardship; nonmonetary and monetary impacts of offsite erosion; behavior and attitudes regarding conservation tillage (e.g., toward use of pesticides); and the roles of market and nonmarket forces.

Water quality and quantity: definition of the resource; nonmonetary and monetary impacts of changes in water quality and use; evolving institutions, shaping the pattern of water use; and roles of market and nonmarket forces.

Subarea 2: Development Strategies for Rural Communities and Areas

Development and local resources: human capital formation; manufacturing; amenities, tourists, retirees; rural entrepreneurialship; disadvantaged groups; transfer payments; and rural labor markets.

Relationships among local, area, national, and global economies: regional impacts of fiscal and monetary policies; financial deregulation; changes in health programs; income assistance and related programs; and urban versus rural.

Local government administration and infrastructure: rural tax base and local government; adjusting to a declining base; new rural elites; volunteerism; local environmental management; and civic participation.

Subarea 3: Valuation of Natural Resource Systems

Role of and validity of benefit/cost analysis in public decisions on natural-resource use: benefit/cost as a conceptual paradigm for choice, organization of information, extension of logical positivism; benefit/cost as technique, rules for use (its role in incremental policy processes in the sometimes nonrational world of government decision making); ethical implications of using benefit/cost in public choice (better-measured impacts get priority).

Technical measurement questions: nonmarket valuation of natural systems; and hedonic pricing, contingent valuation, inferential techniques.

Risk that technical "progress" may permanently destroy natural systems: biodiversity; coevolution; optimum demand.

Subarea 4: Institutional Design and Analysis

Alternative means for organizing response to conflicts, alternative rules for information generation and presentation, various incentives to affect public and private behavior.

Subarea 5: Natural Resource Commodities

This subarea involves traditional questions about the production, management, and marketing of saleable, offsite commodities from natural-resource systems. In this area, questions are raised about behavior and tradeoffs for extractive, saleable commodities, and other resources such as wildlife habitat and such natural amenities as clean air in rural areas: or, in the case of forestry, forest products, scenery and timber on public and private lands; or coal stripped land in the case of mining.

Subarea 6: Resource Information Systems: Design, Development, Management, and Evaluation

Resource information is a basis for decisions on land and water use, environmental protection, taxation, ownership, and transfer. The need for timely, accurate, and consistent information is increasing. The technical capacity to generate data is also increasing as are the problems of consistency, quality, distribution of cost, access, and control. Information technology is affecting persons, communities, institutions, and jurisdictions. Social scientists working with engineers, lawyers, systems analysts, and officials, can assess impacts and recommend solutions to problems of design, management, and policy. In the longer run, social scientists can foster multidisciplinary relations and create subdisciplines to conduct research, develop curricula, and extend knowledge to users, commercial enterprises, and governments. Research may include investigation of the effects of resource information systems on local governmental decisions, social structures, distribution of benefits and costs, privacy, welfare of specific groups, location of rural industry, and structure of local and state government. Computerized land database will impact local government decision processes (political science). There are concerns about how resource databases enhance community cohesiveness, change status of individuals by separating them into groups or castes (sociology). Questions include: Is it possible to identify demand and supply functions for information (economics); can we identify a benefit/cost relationship for specific information products (economics); privacy (political science, sociology, psychology); and market information (sociology, economics)?

Subarea 7: Structuring Effective Research

It is important to link other actors into agricultural research—the 1890 land-grant colleges, the non-land-grant universities, private-sector industrial research to achieve a user-oriented delivery system capable of organizing effective social science research and then finance, coordinate, and evaluate its DISC, SM, and PS components.

Subarea 8: Risk and Regulatory Policy

Risk assessment and criteria; regulatory rule making; and regulatory policy.

WORK GROUP 3 ON INTERNATIONAL AFFAIRS

PERSONNEL IN WORK GROUP

Leader: Jimmye Hillman, Department of Agricultural Economics, University of Arizona
Rapporteur: G. E. Rossmiller, National Center for Food and Agricultural Policy, Resources for the Future
Members: Tom Carroll, Billie DeWalt, Gary Hansen, Don Paarlberg, Margaret Sarles, Bernard Stanton, Paul Thompson

ABRIDGED AND EDITED REPORT

Discussion of the scope and perspective necessary to establish the broad categories of research needed in the international arena led to dropping the word "development" from the title of this discussion group. The title thus went from international development and affairs to simply international affairs. It was felt that the original title placed undue emphasis on the development aspects of international activity relative to the other important dimensions, including trade and international finance. A second issue related to the need for addressing not only the research dimension but also the teaching or curriculum dimension and the extension or public affairs dimension of international affairs to develop a broad and balanced approach. The main reason this became important was the view that international is no longer, if it ever was, a separate and distinct area that can be juxtaposed against teaching, research, and extension programs. During the 1970s, an irreversible internationalization of agriculture took place. The U.S. agricultural sector came to rely heavily on the international market for a significant portion of its income. Moreover, rural communities throughout both the capital and goods markets in which they participate have become part of an integrated open economy. This subjects them to forces exerted by events and policy shifts at national and global political economy levels.

Social science research, teaching, and extension programs throughout the land-grant university system must adapt to this new and continuing reality. The international political and economic dimensions and linkages need to be accounted for and included as integral parts of the research agenda, the curriculum, and the extension program, particularly the public-policy education dimension of the extension program.

This imperative has significant implications for the organizational structure in land-grant universities, especially for colleges of agriculture. The question must be raised as to the present and future adequacy of the solution taken in the past of appending an international program to stand in forced parallel to the traditional research, teaching, and extension components of agricultural colleges in the land-grant university system.

Given the impossibility of separating the domestic and international dimensions of problems and issues, particularly in the policy area, and given the large proportion of foreign graduate students in many social science programs, particularly agricultural economics, the international dimension must be integrated into all aspects of a university's program when and where appropriate.

This suggests that the international dimension is more important than is indicated by an international-program dimension in the college of agriculture paralleling the research, teaching, and extension functions. This is not to say that the international-program function should be done away with entirely. Rather, it should be redefined along with the integration of the international dimension into the ongoing programs. The redefinition of the role of international programs should include facilitating the spread of the international component within the other programs and to provide a catalytic role in helping to incorporate course work and other experiences in the curriculum that develops a cultural and substantive sensitivity to a changing international environment within which U.S. agriculture performs and of which U.S. rural communities are a part.

The group considering the international-affairs research agenda, therefore, recommends that those participants concerned with administrative and funding strategies in the second phase of the SSAAP work specifically address the issue of integration of the international component into the research, teaching, and extension programs of the land-grant universities, with particular emphasis on the college of agriculture.

International affairs includes two major headings: "The Political Economy of Agricultural Trade" and "Development Processes and Economic Assistance." A third heading, "Multilevel Food and Agricultural Data Systems," highlights the fact that data and information deficiencies are severe enough in the international-affairs arena that special consideration needs to be given to their improvement as a specific and separable topic.

The first-level subheadings under the three major headings indicate the subareas of emphasis that, in the view of the international-affairs discussion group, represent the most pressing set of issues. The second subheading indicates more specific efforts of importance.

The Political Economy of Agricultural Trade

Competitiveness and comparative advantage: factors affecting the global supply and demand for agricultural commodities, including the international market: production, supply, and excess-supply elasticities; demand and excess-demand elasticities; price-transmission elasticities; domestic agricultural and trade policies; institution-parastatal, state trading; technology; and elasticity of trade with respect to growth.

Incidence, Causes, and Impacts of Trade Protection and Trade Liberalization

Political factors (flexibilities, rigidities, social objectives); measurement and monitoring instruments; welfare gains and losses; mechanisms; negotiation strategies and packages.

Macroeconomic and International Finance Linkages

Monetary and fiscal policies; exchange rates; international capital flows and debt; international institutions—role, rules, and adequacy—GATT (trade), IMF (finance), IBRD (development).

Development Processes and Economic Assistance

Agriculture under alternative political philosophies: The geo-politics of economic assistance; international and cross-cultural social-accounting methodologies and philosophies.

Plant and animal genetic resources and protection: intellectual property rights (patent rights); development of alternative crops; multinational ethics and involvement in international agricultural development; protection, regulation, productivity, and human health.

People, resources, environment, and development: labor/land ratios; resources management (fragile lands, water, desertification, tropical forests, pastoralism); land-use patterns (causes and consequences); labor mobility and migration; food, nutrition, and health (adequacy and regulation); rural (urban links)—employment, resource use, population, family planning, and rural development; nutrition, health, productivity, agricultural production; energy sources and uses.

Social impacts of food aid and technology transfer: impacts of economic assistance, including, in agriculture, economic development and growth; self-sufficiency, food security, self-reliance; and benefits and costs of food aid.

Institutions: farmer organizations; research/education/extension links and organization; diffusion and innovation of technology; international organizations; land-tenure patterns.

Multilevel Food and Agricultural Data Systems: data needs; measurement statistics, concepts, and techniques.

WORK GROUP 4 ON ADMINISTRATIVE AND FUNDING STRATEGIES

PERSONNEL IN WORK GROUP

Leader: Gerald Klonglan, Department of Sociology and Anthropology, Iowa State University
Rapporteur: Glenn Johnson, Department of Agricultural Economics, Michigan State University
Members: Eric Chetwynd, Sue Coates, Larry Connor, Richard Kirkendall, Harry Kunkel, William Lacy, James Nielson, Daniel Padberg, Richard Sauer, Barbara Stowe

ABRIDGED AND EDITED REPORT

It was also recognized that the general subject of administrative and funding strategies would increase in relative importance as SSAAP proceeded through its first to second and third stages, the last of which will focus on administrators and funders of agricultural research. Much of the research needed on the administration of the rural and basic social sciences vis-à-vis agricultural and rural communities and people is related to administrative and funding strategies.

Each of the following major topics was concluded to be an important separate topic for the second SSAAP conference—important subtopics are also indicated. The group recognized, of course, that as the second conference is designed and implemented, the Executive Committee and Advisory Board will have to consolidate, coordinate, eliminate and, in some instances, even add sections to those suggested.

Alternative models for organizing rural social science efforts at university, experiment station, center, governmental agency and institute levels: It is important to identify and describe the various organizational arrangements that could be used. Explicit rationales for alternative administrative structures to facilitate discipline, problem-solving and subject-matter research by rural and basic social sciences for agriculture and rural societies.

- There are currently many different possible organizational structures for rural social sciences in the colleges of agriculture. These include separate departments of agricultural economics and rural sociology, combined departments of agricultural economics and rural sociology, combined agricultural economics and economics departments (and similarly combined rural sociology and sociology departments), as well as other combinations. The future academic homes of rural social scientists need thorough research analysis. Should the separate rural social science departments be merged with their basic disciplinary department (agricultural economics to economics, rural sociology to sociology, etc.)? Should all rural social scientists be in one (expanded) department to include agricultural economists, rural sociologists, political scientists, agricultural historians, rural geographers, socio-cultural anthropologists, etc. Assessments are needed of the advantages and disadvantages of alternative administrative structures in carrying out future teaching, research, and extension functions.

- Should social scientists in colleges of agriculture be structurally related with social scientists in colleges of human ecology/home economics? Should social science programs in agriculture/home economics be merged? Should new colleges with new names be created for rural social scientists? How should rural social scientists relate to social scientists in business schools? Many business schools are focusing on some of the same problems as agricultural economists and rural sociologists. Are there separate domains or duplication?

- What organizational structures are needed to integrate rural social with technical agricultural science faculty? Should centers and institutes play a more prominent role in fostering multidisciplinary research teams? Should station directors exercise more control over research projects to attain multidisciplinary research?

- Should agricultural experiment stations become parts of university-wide research units no longer administered as if primarily in agricultural and home economics colleges?

- To what extent should there be new interstate programs involving the rural social scientists? If downsizing occurs, do we need more multistate or regional centers of expertise? What should the criteria be for establishing new multistate centers or institutes? What divisions of labor strategies are most workable and need to be given priority attention?

Managing Public/Private Research Linkages for Rural Social Scientists: The ramifications of increased linkages between universities and private companies, especially as they relate to biotechnology and other technical fields, need to be assessed for social scientists. Are there opportunities for rural social scientists to participate on interdisciplinary teams that are joint public/private ventures? Are potential social/economic/legal problems so important as to warrant increased involvement of social scientists in future activities?

Obtaining Administrative Capacity and Flexibility: Universities are faced with many new challenges, but have little if any flexibility in budgets to initiate new program thrusts. Universities are considering many different ways of initiating new programs. It is important that rural social scientists investigate the ramifications of several university-wide policy options for the rural social sciences. These include:

- Changing the tenure appointment base of faculty from 12 months to 9 months.

- Hiring a certain portion of faculty on term contracts to work on a specific problem or subject matter. (Perhaps tenure, in its current sense, should be eliminated, especially given the scheduled elimination of retirement-age limits for faculty?)

- Encouraging the development of research entrepreneurs to establish special programs either inside or outside the university using "soft money" resources.

- Encouraging faculty to do more special interest consulting.

- Creation of endowed chairs. How many such chairs will there be for rural social scientists? Will these chairs be for DISC, SM, and PS purposes?

Evaluation and Recognition for Problem-Solving and Subject-Matter Excellence: Special administrative problems are associated with evaluating and awarding PS and SM work by social scientists. What constitutes excellence for social scientists in doing these kinds of work is controversial. The group was concerned with the need to widen participation of social scientists in PS and SM efforts and of doing this in such a way as to promote career development while maintaining the freedom so essential for effective research, teaching, extension, advising, consulting, administering, and entrepreneuring. Obtaining promotion and tenure for faculty who do primarily multidisciplinary PS or SM research or work in extension is difficult at many universities. Yet many rural social scientists do PS and SM work. Efforts are needed to clearly articulate the role of SM and PS functions in universities. When SM and PS activities are truly an explicit mission of a university as they now are in land-grant colleges of agriculture, faculty evaluations for promotion and tenure should recognize excellence in carrying out these functions. This includes work in both domestic and international settings.

- The range of social science participation in agricultural colleges should be widened.

- There is a need for increased participation from agricultural historians, political scientists, anthropologists, human ecologists, geographers, philosophers, and others. This generates a number of key issues: Can we persuade top-of-the-line personnel from the basic social science disciplines to participate with the rural social sciences in doing PS and SM work? Can we demonstrate to university administrators (as well as state and federal funding sources) that these fields have something useful to offer agriculture, rural societies, and rural people? Can these individuals be guaranteed that they can function according to academic standards to do PS and SM, as well as DISC, work free from vested-interest pressures? Can they be guaranteed access to records they need to see to study key issues such as those on the relationships between colleges of agriculture and their clientele groups? (The historian or anthropologist must be able to report what they find, even if it may be somewhat embarrassing to an administrative group.)

Strategies for the Development of Human Capital for the Rural Social Sciences: We should ascertain the needs for rural scientists at the beginning of the twenty-first century and communicate this need to relevant constituencies, priority setters and funders.

Restructuring of graduate education in rural social sciences is needed, given the increasing need for multidisciplinary teams to focus on the complex problems of the agricultural and rural societies of today. Rural social science graduate programs should be reviewed for adequacy and appropriateness. Consideration should be given to the required breadth of social science training, perhaps even to requiring different rural social scientists to include the other rural and other basic social sciences and philosophy in their programs of study. Similar requirements should be considered for students in the basic social science disciplines expecting to apply their expertise in agriculture in relation to the rural social sciences. Given the likelihood of significant general technological, institutional, and human capacity advances in society, there will be increased demand-impact assessment of new technologies, institutional changes, and human capital development by rural social scientists. Graduate educators need to question how well present Master's and Ph.D. programs prepare rural and basic social scientists to be effective members of multidisciplinary teams of biological, physical, and social scientists addressing rural and agricultural problems. Reciprocally, biological and physical science graduate-program administrators need to incorporate rural and basic social science knowledge and perspectives in their graduate programs. Special attention needs to be given to the types of rural and basic social science graduate education different universities will provide in the future. There may be need for greater division of labor among graduate schools in the future. Some may be needed to educate primarily disciplinary-oriented social scientists, whereas others may need to emphasize multidisciplinary PS and SM efforts. Regional, state, and national assessments are probably needed to determine whether or not all present Ph.D. rural and basic social science programs are needed. Perhaps some departments should obtain excellence in broad applied-research, teaching, and service programs, while others should stress more narrow disciplinary excellence. An effort to establish a new division of labor based on the different kinds of excellence needed for PS, SM, and disciplinary work may actually improve the overall quality of higher education compared to the present situation where schools try to strive for disciplinary excellence.

Restructuring Rural Social Science Mixes in Colleges of Agriculture Undergraduate Programs: Undergraduate education in colleges of agriculture is undergoing review at most universities due to declining enrollments, occupational changes, institutional changes, the internationalization of agriculture, changing technological changes, and other factors. The role of the social sciences in undergraduate agricultural degrees should be reconsidered. Should a broader-based "liberal arts" education be provided instead of narrower, more technical degrees? Should the master's degree become the accepted specialization degree in technical arenas? Should colleges of agriculture hire philosophers, geographers, political scientists, agricultural historians, anthropologists, and others to broaden their undergraduate understanding of agriculture and rural life as we prepare to enter the twenty-first century? Staffing innovations now being experimented with in some universities should be evaluated for consideration by other schools.

Building Political Power Bases for the Rural Social Sciences: There is a need for the rural social sciences to build more effective power bases at state and national levels for bachelor, graduate, professional master's, leadership-training, public-service, extension, and other programs: Historically, the rural social scientists have not had the natural constituencies that animal and plant scientists have had with commodity and other farm organizations. However, agricultural economists did successfully develop clientele groups among farm record keepers, cooperative organizations, commodity (dairy, cotton, tobacco, horticulture, etc.) groups, governmental (federal, state, local, international) officials, farm credit (public, private and parastatal) agencies, and land-grant administrators. More recently, rural sociologists have been successful in developing clientele relationships with land-grant extension service and experiment-station administrative groups. Internationally, agricultural economists and, to a lesser extent, rural sociologists and anthropologists have been successful in developing meaningful clientele relationships. By meaningful clientele relationships, we mean those with constituencies who understand the role that rural social sciences can play in solving the problems of agriculture, rural America, and the world. At least some members of meaningful constituencies should understand the concepts, models, and methods of rural social scientists.

Most of the contemporary problems of agriculture and rural areas have major political, social, geographic, and economic dimensions and will, therefore, be solved in part by utilizing the knowledge bases of the different rural social scientists. Too often we hear that the solution of a problem is to be found in a "technological fix," e.g., a biotechnical, electronic, chemical, or mechanical innovation. Such new technologies alone typically fail to solve problems as most problems have important social dimensions that must be addressed before they can be solved.

Rural social scientists need to identify specific new constituencies and build special linkages with them. There are many possible individuals and organizations that could help speak on behalf of the rural and basic social sciences. These include our former undergraduate students who have taken our classes or majored in our fields and who are now in key positions. Similarly, graduates of our professional master's programs are often in key business, government, and education positions. Participants in our many special short courses (on leadership, finance, marketing, policy, etc.) at state and local levels have benefitted from our research and knowledge base and should be supportive of our programs. Also there are many public-service groups that have utilized our work extensively. These include the National Governors Association, Council on State Governments, National Conference of State Legislatures, National Industry-State Agricultural Research Committee, Council of State Policy and Planning agencies, National Association of State Development Agencies, National Association of Counties, and the National Association of Towns and Townships.

Rural social scientists also need to take a more active role in state and national legislative processes to better understand how these processes work and to provide timely information to both authorizing and appropriations committees about rural social science needs.

Funding Strategies: It was felt that special groups at the second conference should address the following topics having to do with the funding of rural social science and agriculturally related basic social science efforts.

- Attention should be given to *federal funding* strategies and levels for problem-solving, subject-matter, and disciplinary research in the ERS, CSRS, and the CSES. In this connection, consideration should be given to the roles of ESCOP, ECOP, NASULGC, AASCARR, the Joint Council, Congressional offices and their staffs as well as COSSA.

- Attention should be given to the *special support, facilities, and services needs* for social science research in the universities and agricultural experiment stations. The support, services, and facilities needed in the social sciences are substantially different from those of the biological and physical agricultural sciences. Unfortunately, the majority of agricultural experiment station directors are not experienced in using or providing support, facilities, and services for the social sciences.

- The problems associated with *state funding* of the rural social sciences and agriculturally related research of the basic social sciences should be specifically addressed. Increasingly, agricultural research and extension support comes from state governments. Such support is often most easily earned and attained by addressing specific problems of specific interest to state legislators and governors.

- *Private sector funding* of social science research relevant for agriculture. Though the social sciences do not receive substantial support from the private sector, there are opportunities in this area that should be explored at the second SSAAP conference.

CHAPTER 9

SSAAP'S HOUSTON WORKSHOP/CONFERENCE AND THE STRUCTURE OF THIS BOOK

The purpose of this chapter is to explain the structure of the remainder of this book. How that structure was determined substantially by the organization of the SSAAP conference held at Houston, March 13–18, 1988, is explained in the first part of this chapter. The second part of this chapter deals with the organization of the remainder of the book.

THE ORGANIZATION OF SSAAP'S HOUSTON WORKSHOP/CONFERENCE

The conference was opened with John Lee, administrator, Economic Research Service, U.S. Department of Agriculture, as chairperson. James Bonnen, professor of Agricultural Economics at Michigan State University, made a plenary presentation entitled "The Rural Challenge for the Social Sciences." The conference was then organized into seven areas, one of which was informal. The area titles and the names of the work-group leaders indicate the breadth and depth of participation in the SSAAP exercise. Three of the areas were substantive. The first substantive area dealt with "Farming, Agribusiness, and Consumers" under the leadership of James Hildreth, director, Farm Foundation. The second substantive area was "Community and Natural Resources" under the joint leadership of William Heffernan, professor of Rural Sociology, University of Missouri, and Allan Schmid, professor of Agricultural Economics, Michigan State University. The third substantive area was "LDC Rural Development" under the leadership of Bruce Johnston, professor, Food Research Institute, Stanford University. There were four crosscutting areas. They are called crosscutting areas because they are of interest in all three of the substantive areas discussed above. The first crosscutting area dealt with "Disciplinary Social Science Research" under the joint leadership of Peggy Barlett, professor of Anthropology, Emory University, and Bonnie McCay, professor of Human Ecology and Social Science, Cook College, Rutgers University. The next crosscutting area was "Administration, Funding, and Strategies" under the leadership of Larry Connor, professor of Agricultural Economics, Michigan State University. A third crosscutting area was entitled "Public Choice and Private Decision Making, including Agroethics" under the leadership of Joseph Havlicek, chair, Agricultural Economics and Rural Sociology, Ohio State University. The fourth crosscutting area was informal and it dealt with databases. James Bonnen, who has done extensive advisory and other research and work on agricultural databases, was in charge of this crosscutting area.

WORK GROUPS AND THEIR LEADERSHIP UNDER EACH OF THE MAIN AREAS OUTLINED ABOVE

Initially there were seven work groups in the "Farming, Agribusiness, and Consumers" area under the leadership of James Hildreth, director, Farm Foundation. The seven work groups were:

1. National Policies and International Trade and Monetary/Fiscal Programs and Domestic Price, Production Stabilization and Production Expansion Programs—David Blandford, professor of Agricultural Economics, Cornell University.
2. Structural Change and Performance in Rural Communities, Farming, Agribusiness and with Regard to Consumers, Disadvantaged Farm and Nonfarm Rural Groups, Farms, and Agribusiness in Crisis—Lyle P. Schertz, Economic Research Service, USDA.
3. Social Science Aspects of Forces that Influence U.S. Agricultural Productivity and/or Promote the Development of U.S. Agriculture—Frederick H. Buttel, professor of Rural Sociology, Cornell University.
4. Homes, Family Life, Food and Nutrition—Sue Coates, chair, Consumer Resources and Technology, Western Michigan University.
5. Farm and Agribusiness Management—Steve Sonka, professor of Agricultural Economics, University of Illinois.
6. Macrolevel Data and Analysis Systems of Agriculture, Food, and Rural Societies—Leroy J. Hushak, professor

of Agricultural Economics, The Ohio State University.

7. Farm, Agribusiness, and Consumer Dimensions of Public Choice an Private Decision Making including Agroethics—Bobby Eddleman, resident director, Texas A&M University Research and Extension Center.

The "Natural and Community Resources" area was divided into two subareas. The first, *Natural Resources*, under the leadership of A. Allan Schmid, Michigan State University, had four work groups.

1. Conservation, Use, Development, Disinvestment, and Investment in Land, Water, and Other Natural Resources—Barbara T. Osgood, Economics and Social Science Division, Soil Conservation Service, USDA.
2. Evaluation, Assessment, and Utilization of Environmental Resources and Characteristics—James C. Hite, professor of Agricultural Economics and Rural Sociology, Clemson University.
3. Natural Resource Commodities—Larry Libby, chair, Food and Resource Economics, University of Florida.
4. Waste, Environmental Pollutants, Food Chain Contaminants—Internalization, Regulation, and Risk Analysis—William M. Park, professor of Agricultural Economics, University of Tennessee.

The second subarea was Community Resources led by William Heffernan with four subgroups as follows:

1. Change and Development of Rural Communities and Areas—Ronald C. Wimberly, professor of Sociology and Anthropology, North Carolina State University.
2. Disadvantaged Farm and Nonfarm Rural Groups Including Minorities—T. T. Williams, director, Human Resource Development Center, Tuskegee University.
3. Design, Evaluation, Assessment, Analysis, and Utilization of State and Local Rural Institutions, Programs, and Policies, and the Community Services they Create—Paul Lasley, professor of Sociology and Anthropology, Iowa State University.
4. Local Government Revenues, Expenditures, and Effectiveness of Operations—Donald Lacy, extension specialist, Community Resource Development, Virginia Polytechnic Institute and State University.

The general area of Natural and Community Resources also had two work groups that dealt with both natural and community resources. The two work groups under this category follow:

1. Public Choice and Private Decisions in the Use of Natural and Community Resources—Tom Ruehr, professor of Soil Science, California Polytechnic State University.
2. Macrolevel Data, Social and Economic Accounting and Analysis Systems for Natural and Community Resource Decisions—David L. Brown, associate director, Agricultural Experiment Station, Cornell University.

The area "Rural Development of LDCs" was under the leadership of Bruce Johnston. It had nine work groups with titles and leadership as follows:

1. Trade and Monetary/Fiscal Policies Including Regional Common Market Proposals and Their Impact on LDCs—Paul Farris, professor of Agricultural Economics, Purdue University.
2. Development Processes and Assistance to LDCs—Kenneth Shapiro, director, International Agricultural Programs, University of Wisconsin.
3. Farm and Agribusiness Management in LDCs—James O'Connor, private consultant.
4. LDC Data Systems, Social Accounts, and Sector and Subsector Analysis—Jacques Kozub, Economic Development Institute, World Bank.
5. LDC Planning, Consultative, and Advisory Functions of Rural Social Scientists and Social Science Disciplinarians—Price Gittinger, private consultant.
6. Potential for a Rural Social Science Collaborative Research Support Project—Hugh L. Popenoe, director of International Programs, University of Florida.
7. LDC Markets: Conduct, Structure, and Performance in Input as Well as Product Markets—Paul L. Farris, professor of Agricultural Economics, Purdue University.
8. LDC Food Security and Income Distribution—John M. Staatz, professor of Agricultural Economics, Michigan State University.
9. International Dimensions of Public Choice and Private Decision Making Including Agroethics—Paul Thompson, professor of Philosophy, Texas A&M University.

There were no work groups within the four crosscutting areas; instead, the leaders in these areas handled each area as a unit. However, the agroethics and database areas had subsections and work groups in each of the three substantive areas that fed information into the deliberations by members of these areas.

PLENARY PRESENTATIONS AT SSAAP'S HOUSTON CONFERENCE

In addition to Bonnen's plenary presentation, "The Rural Challenge for the Social Sciences," on the first day, there was a plenary luncheon panel chaired by Gerald Klonglan, chair of the Department of Sociology and Anthropology, Iowa State University. The panel included Barbara Stowe, dean of Human Ecology, Kansas State University; Wayne Swegle, director of Public Affairs and Communication, Winrock International; Richard Stuby, sociologist, Cooperative State Research, U.S. Department of Agriculture; and Jim Hildreth, agricultural economist and director, Farm Foundation. The panel summarized recent priority-setting efforts in the rural social sciences. At another plenary session, Johnny Ford, mayor of the City of Tuskegee, Alabama, presented his views about the possible contributions of the rural social sciences to the resolution of issues involving African-American minorities and international relationships.

At still another plenary session, Dan Bromley, professor of Agricultural Economics at the University of Wisconsin, presented a paper entitled "Economic Institutions and the Development Problem: History and Prognosis." Special note is made of this paper. While not well digested by the participants at the conference, Bromley's paper has had an important, exciting impact on SSAAP's editorial group since SSAAP's Houston conference. The result is that the transaction-cost approach to public choice has materially influenced every one of the remaining nine sections and Part V of this book, in ways that are indicated in the portion of this chapter that explains the organization of the remainder of this book. At still another plenary session, Edward McClennen, Department of Philosophy at George Washington University, presented a paper entitled "Utility, Utilitarianism, and Public Policy."

At a plenary luncheon session, C. West Churchman, from the Center for Research in Management at the University of California, was assigned the task of discussing "Public Choice and Private Decision Theories Relevant for Farmers, Homemakers, and Agribusinessmen—Status, Potential Uses, and Needed Advances." His written paper was entitled "Decision Making: Private or Public."

At the end of the workshop there were plenary sessions involving area and work group reports. The conference was terminated with meetings of the SSAAP Executive Committee with area coordinators or their representatives.

COMMISSIONED PAPERS

SSAAP had special funds to commission certain kinds of papers for its second conference. The outline below indicates three sources of the funds, the purposes, and the papers that were commissioned.

Under a National Science Foundations (NSF) Grant

Six papers were funded under this proposal to provide background papers for the work groups of SSAAP's Houston conference that were most concerned with the work of basic social science disciplinarians vis-a-vis agriculture. The names of the authors and the titles of the six papers follow:

- Churchman, C. West. "On Agricultural Decision Making: Private or Public."
- DeWalt, Billie R. "Anthropology, Evolution, and Agriculture."
- Flora, Cornelia Butler. "Studies of Households Reviewed in Relation to Farm and Home, Balanced Farming, Farming Systems and Farm Management Programs and Studies in the College of Agriculture."
- Fox, Karl A. "Progress and Advances Needed in Social Indicator Research of Potential Value in Researching Rural Issues and Problems."
- Haney, Wava G. "Theoretical Advances Arising from Studies of the Role of Women in Farming and Their Usefulness for the Study of Agribusiness."
- McClennen, Edward F. "Utility, Utilitarianism, and Public Policy."

Under a U.S. Agency for International Development (AID) Grant

Twelve background papers on the work of basic and rural social sciences in relation to international rural development were commissioned:

- Adams, Dale W. "On-farm Capital Formation and Rural Financial Markets: Research Issues."
- Bromley, Daniel W. "Economic Institutions and the Development Problem: History and Prognosis."
- Fortmann, Louise P., Daniel C. Mountjoy, and Bruce F. Johnston. "People, Processes, and Products: Potential Contribution of the Social Sciences to the Preservation and Enhancement of Natural Resources in Third World Countries."
- Hoben, Allan. "Improving the Administration of the Social Sciences in International Donor Agencies."
- Huffman, Wallace E. "Contributions of Social Sciences to Augmentation of Human Capital for General Economic Growth."
- Josling, Timothy E. "The Relationship Between International Rural Development and International Trade and Finance."
- Lipton, Michael. "Social Science Roles in Meeting the Needs of International Donors for the Assessment of Agricultural Technologies."
- Reynolds, Clark W. "Agricultural Sector Analysis and Rural Development: Social Science Research Priorities."
- Ruttan, Vernon W. "The Role of the Social Sciences in the Generation, Dissemination, and Evaluation of Institutional Change."
- Staatz, John M. "Designing Social Science Research to Inform Agricultural Market Reforms and Structural Adjustments in Developing Countries."
- Thompson, Paul. "Potential Social Science Contributions to the Resolution of Conflicts Between U.S. Commodity Groups and AID with Respect to Technical Assistance for Foreign Agriculture."
- Weber, Michael T. and Thomas S. Jayne. "Food Security and Its Relationship to Technology, Institutions, Policies, and Human Capital."

Aspen Institute (Ford Foundation)

After the Woodlands conference, it became clear that social science work with disadvantaged farm and nonfarm rural groups was not adequately covered. Consequently, Ford Foundation/Aspen Institute funds, previously available to SSAAP to pay attendance costs for persons concerned with disadvantaged farm and nonfarm rural groups, were made available for special meetings and to commission needed papers. The following meetings were held or participated in by SSAAP with respect to disadvantaged groups:

- PAWC at Tuskegee University, December 4–6, 1988
- Meeting with Hispanics, Scottsdale, Ariz., December 27–28, 1988

The following additional papers were commissioned in order to strengthen those parts of the book dealing with disadvantaged farm and nonfarm groups and needed research on the administration of the rural social sciences:

- Christy, Ralph. "The African American, Farming and Rural Society."
- Forbes, Jack. "Rural Farm and Nonfarm Native Americans in the U.S."
- Beegle, Allan. "Poverty Among Caucasians in Nonmetro America."
- Rochin, Refugio. "Disadvantaged Rural Farm and Nonfarm Rural People in General."

- Stevens, Robert. "Increasing Health in Rural America—Research Issues during a Transitional Period."
- Mulford, Charles L., Gerald E. Klonglan, and Ge Xiao Jia. "A Systems Approach for Understanding Research on the Organization and Administration of the Agricultural Scientific Enterprise."

PHASE III SSAAP MEETINGS AFTER ITS HOUSTON CONFERENCE

Phase III conferences, seminars, and meetings in which SSAAP participated prior to publication of this book include:

- A 1st Latin American and Caribbean Conference on Economic Policy, Technology, and Rural Development, Mexico City, October 26–28, 1988
- AID, Washington, D.C., December 13, 1988
- INTSORMIL, Phoenix, Ariz., January 2, 1989
- ECOP, New Orleans, La., February 21, 1989
- RICOP, Arlington, Va., March 1, 1989
- ICCA Administrators, Costa Rica, March 12–16, 1989
- North Central Chairs of Agricultural Economics, April 3, 1989
- Joint Council, April 13, 1989
- ESCOP, May 1, 1989
- Seminars for Agricultural Economists and Administrators at Karl Marx University, Budapest, September 5–6, 1989
- Seminar for Agricultural Economists and Administrators at the University of Warsaw, September 7, 1989
- Seminar for Agricultural Economists and Administrators at the University of Helsinki, September 14, 1989
- ICOP, at Annual Meeting of NASULGC, November 18, 1989
- Seminar for Agricultural Economists and Administrators at the University of Delaware, May 14, 1990
- Report to Charles Hess, Assistant Secretary for Science and Education, USDA, May 15, 1990
- Seminar for Economic Research Service, USDA, May 21, 1990
- Report to North Central Experiment Station Directors, Lead, S.Dak., July 11, 1990
- Symposium for the American and Canadian Agricultural Economics Associations, Vancouver, British Columbia, Canada, August 6, 1990

Other Phase III meetings will be held after publication of this book, its separate executive summary, and related public relations material.

THE ORGANIZATION OF THE REMAINDER OF THIS BOOK

While the content of this book is closely related to the organization of SSAAP's Houston meetings, its organization differs substantially from that of the conference. For one thing, there is Part I that includes this chapter. Part I provides background on SSAAP and introduces the book. The major divergences between the organization of this book and the Houston conference grew out of what was learned at Houston and out of what has been learned since in appraising and summarizing those conferences. Some areas of the work of rural and basic social scientists were underemphasized at Houston while others were poorly organized and covered.

This book has five parts including its introductory Part I. Part II deals with the rather traditional domestic and international work of rural social scientists and basic social science disciplinarians concerned with agriculture and rural societies. Thus, it has two sections, *one* on domestic agriculture (farming, including homes, agribusiness, and consumption) leaving to Part III the domestic rural development work involving institutional change mainly at community, local, and state governmental levels; technical advance; human development; and growth and enhancement of natural and manmade biological and physical resources, and a *second* section on international rural development. Each of these two sections of Part II contains an introductory chapter that summarizes what was generally available before the Houston conference or has become available since then. Each section also contains chapters presenting the papers delivered at either the Spring Hill or Houston SSAAP conferences, as well as a few other selected papers from the "phantom literature." Relevant materials published in readily available sources are cited and, in some cases, summarized but not reproduced in this book. Each of the two sections of Part II presents abridged versions of work-group reports from the Houston conference, as well as agendas and conclusions reached after Houston. Summaries of these chapters also appear in the last chapter of this book (Part V, Chapter 9) and in the executive summary that is published separately from this book.

Part III of this book contains four sections, one each for the four driving forces in agricultural and rural development, namely: (1) institutional improvements, (2) human development, (3) enhancement and growth in natural resources and manmade capital, and (4) technological advance. Again, each of these sections contains an introductory chapter, chapters from SSAAP's effort and unpublished and/or phantom literature, and a final chapter of abridged work-group reports from Houston, additional agenda items developed since Houston, and conclusions. Again, these final chapters become part of the overall summary chapter of this book and the executive summary.

Rural and basic social science thought, with respect to the four driving forces considered in Part III, has developed differently in sociology, anthropology, history, political science, and economics. Consequently, there is a long introduction to the whole of Part III that precedes the four separate sections. This introduction to Part III provides background with respect to sociological, anthropological, political science, and philosophic thought concerning the four driving forces. In this review, care is taken to relate these developments to institutional economics, a la Veblen and John R. Commons; land economics; the public choice/transaction cost approach to the analysis of institutional change; and the "induced" institutional and technological change and the closely related theories of human capital formation. This long introduction to Part III is necessary in order to interrelate the various contributions of the rural and basic social science disciplines to our understanding of the four driving forces for agricultural and rural development. In describing Part II earlier, it was noted that Part II's section on domestic agriculture does not deal adequately with human development, natural-resource enhancement and capital growth, technological advance, and important aspects of institutional changes. Thus, the agendas developed in Part III provide this coverage for the international as well as domestic work of rural and basic social sciences.

Part IV deals with crosscutting agendas for the rural and basic social sciences. It contains three sections. Section 1 deals with databases. It is made up, in part, of crosscutting "database" contributions from the Houston work groups corresponding more or less to the two sections of Part II and the four sections of Part III. Section 2 of Part IV deals with the potential contributions of the basic social science disciplines to work considered in the two sections of Part II and Sections 1, 2, 3, and 4 of Part III. Section 3 deals with agroethics, a crosscutting concern that was considered at Houston in dealing with the two sections of Part II and Sections 1, 2, 3, and 4 of Part III.

Administration and funding are considered in Part V. In the last chapter of Part V, results from SSAAP's Houston Conference are presented: *first*, administrative and funding strategies and research agendas about the administration and funding of rural and basic social science work on rural societies and agriculture. *Second*, the results of the work by SSAAP's editorial group after the Houston conference are presented covering, again, administrative and funding strategies and research agendas about administration and funding. The stress is on *administrative and funding strategies* and the needed *research* on administration and funding to enable the rural and basic social sciences to play appropriate, legitimate, and constructive roles vis-a-vis farming (including homes), agribusinesses, consumers, and rural societies. *Third*, attention is given to the need for a long-term counterpart of SSAAP.

As indicated above, a summary chapter for the entire book is included in Part V that is virtually identical to a separately printed Executive Summary.

INDEX TO PREFACE AND PART I

D

E

G

H

I

M

N

T

U

V

W

Z

Part II

Introduction to Domestic Farm, Agribusiness, and Consumer Work and All International Agricultural Development Work

Part II of this book contains two sections. The first section deals with social science work done for domestic farms, agribusinesses, and consumers. It includes work done on price, trade, and macro policies that are important for them. The second section deals with international rural development. At the Houston conference, there was a somewhat parallel substantive area, labeled "natural, human, and community resources," that emphasized domestic work while giving lesser attention to international work on the topic. After the Houston conference, the work on natural, human, and community resources was expanded to deal with the four driving forces for development: (1) technical advances; (2) human development; (3) institution, policy, and program improvements; and (4) enhancement and conservation of natural- and manmade-resource bases. Thus, while all of these forces are logical components of the domestic and international work considered in Part II, they are given separate, specific, and more detailed consideration in Part III.

CHAPTER 1

INTRODUCTION TO SECTION ON DOMESTIC AGRICULTURE

A major substantive area for which social science agricultural agendas were developed at SSAAP's Houston meeting is domestic agriculture—farms (including homes), agribusinesses, and consumers. This is, perhaps, the area in which rural social scientists have worked the longest. Traditionally, domestic agriculture included farm management, production economics, home economics, family sociology, input markets, product markets, cooperatives, private agribusinesses, human nutrition, food consumption, conservation, as well as price-support policies, production controls, subsidies, food stamps, agricultural credit, labor, food and drug protection, and the like. Current related versions of these traditional areas of work include farming systems, food safety, environmental protection, family financial management, food-chain contamination, water quality, stress management, integrated decision-support systems, regenerative or sustainable agriculture—and the list goes on.

Participants of SSAAP's Houston conference had access to and were more or less familiar with several reviews and assessments of social science accomplishments and needs with respect to these areas. Some of these assessments are summarized in the next section. These summaries, along with Chapters 2 through 6 of this section, and the cross references to other parts and sections of this book (listed at the end of this chapter), describe the background against which SSAAP participants developed their domestic agricultural agenda items at Houston for farmers, farm households, agribusinesses, and consumers.

CONTRIBUTING ASSESSMENTS

Periodic reviews and evaluations are necessary functions for public institutions. Although major crises have historically been the triggering mechanisms, routine monitoring, evaluation, and needs assessment are increasingly routine for the disciplines, professions, and institutions serving U.S. agriculture. The Joint Council on Food and Agricultural Sciences was established by Congress in 1977 to encourage and coordinate research, extension, and higher education in food and agricultural sciences throughout the United States (Joint Council 1984). Assessments by the Joint Council, its committees, and cooperating organizations and professional associations have contributed to SSAAP's work. Some of these are briefly reviewed below as they relate to domestic farms (and homes), agribusinesses, and consumers.

NEEDS ASSESSMENTS FOR TECHNICAL ADVANCES

Production techniques and methods are important for farm and agribusiness productivity and consumer welfare. Several assessments and priority-setting exercises for the technical agricultural sciences were reviewed in Chapter 1 of Part I. These are listed here but not reviewed again. Included in Chapter 1 of Part I were reviews of:

- *World Food and Nutrition Study* (WFNS): *The Potential Contributions of Research,* published by the National Academy of Sciences, 1977.
- *Overcoming World Hunger: The Challenge Ahead*, generated by the Presidential Commission on World Hunger, 1980.
- *Crop Productivity—Research Imperatives,* edited by A. W. A. Brown et al., 1975.
- *Animal Agriculture—Research to Meet Human Needs in the 21st Century,* edited by Wilson G. Pond et al., 1980.
- *Crop Productivity—Research Imperatives Revisited,* edited by Martin Gibbs and Carla Carlson, published in 1986.

Other technical reviews and assessments not considered in Chapter 1 of Part I are summarized in the paragraphs that follow.

January 1984—Needs Assessment for the Food and Agricultural Sciences, A Report to the Congress from the Secretary of Agriculture: Conducted under the auspices of the Joint Council on Food and Agricultural Sciences, this assessment was published in two parts: a summary and a reference document. It dealt with long-term needs for food, fiber and forest products and the supporting roles of research, extension programs, and higher education. It emphasized support of the technical and economic bases for agricultural and rural development and provided a good description of the linkages between farm families, rural communities, and commercial agriculture. It recognized agriculture and rural America to be an integrated, natural-resource-based, socioeconomic system. However, in its prioritizing of problems, the report did not foresee the severe stress that would be placed on farmers, rural families, agribusinesses, and communities by the then imminent financial crisis and that this crisis would, in turn, reduce the short-term value of technical advances relative to the values of human development and institutional improvements.

The *Five-Year Plan for the Food and Agricultural Sciences: A Report to the Secretary of Agriculture* (Joint Council on Food and Agricultural Sciences 1988) was the second biennial updating of the first such "five-year plan" published in 1984 as part of the Joint Council's national effort to coordinate research, extension, and higher education activities in the food and agricultural sciences throughout the United States as called for by Public Law 97-98. This update complemented the Council's long-term (20 years) needs assessment of the food, fiber, and forestry products sectors, published in 1984. After an introductory invitational paper on the overall theme of "the food and agricultural science and education system prepares for the 21st century," the report briefly summarized seven critical societal concerns for the agricultural sciences to address over the 1988-1993 period: (1) restoring a competitive and profitable agriculture; (2) revitalizing rural America; (3) maintaining water quality; (4) enhancing the future through biotechnology; (5) advancing knowledge and scientific expertise in agriculture; (6) understanding food, diet, and health relationships; and (7) managing germ plasm and maintaining genetic diversity. Detailed goals and objectives for addressing these concerns were summarized under 12 program areas: (1) developing and maintaining professional expertise in agriculture; (2) water, soil, and air; (3) range, forest, and wildlife; (4) cropping systems; (5) animal production systems; (6) processing, marketing, and distribution; (7) human nutrition; (8) agriculture and resource policy; (9) families and consumers; (10) youth; (11) community and rural development; and (12) international science and education. Although the five-year plan report recognized the need for social science efforts, the main emphasis remained on support for the generation of technical advances.

Agricultural Technology Until 2030: Prospects, Priorities, and Policies by Johnson and Wittwer (1984), while recognizing the importance of technology and natural resources, also explicitly recognized institutions and people as driving forces behind agriculture and rural development. The report complemented and used earlier assessments of technical needs and used agricultural projections to indicate levels of productive capacity that needed to be developed for U.S. agriculture through the year 2030, even if not actually used. The general conclusion was that it would be nationally advantageous to strive for a 60 percent increase in production capacity by 2010 and a 100 percent increase by 2030. Such increases would require an annual average growth rate in capacity of 2 percent per year. Attention was given to the need for improved institutions, policies, and human skills, and in resource enhancement to remove those constraints on future contributions of technical research to development. In addition to the standard kind of public investments to improve production techniques and enhance natural resources to provide for a 40 to 50 percent increase in crop yields by 2010 and 65 to 80 percent increase by 2030, the report stressed policy and institutional changes that would also be needed to increase the intensity with which land is farmed and to increase the quality of life for both rural and urban people. The problem-solving, subject-matter, and disciplinary research necessary to create the needed capacity were translated into budgets, skilled personnel requirements, and needed improvements in administration and coordination. While projecting the need for continued support for technical advance and resource growth, the report showed a need for balanced support for human and institutional development as well.

Though technical change is of obvious importance for farms, homes, agribusinesses, and consumers, this section still needs to review and summarize the assessments available to those at Houston who sought to establish agendas for farm management including farm-level resource sustainability, home management, agribusiness management, nutrition, and consumption and policy. These are addressed in the subsections that follow.

FARM MANAGEMENT (INCLUDING FARM-LEVEL RESOURCE SUSTAINABILITY)

In the American Agricultural Economics Association's (AAEA) literature review volumes entitled *A Survey of Agricultural Economics Literature*, Volume I, *Traditional Fields of Agricultural Economics, 1940s to 1972*, contains an informative contribution by Harold R. Jensen (1981) on "Farm Management and Production Economics." Another contribution, "Agricultural Production Function Studies," by Roger Woodworth (1977), is found in Volume II of the AAEA volumes, *Quantitative Methods in Agricultural Economics 1940s to 1970s*. The bittersweet relationship between farm management and production economics has been praised, deplored, and appraised in an early article by Johnson (1957) and in two reviews (Johnson 1963, 1987) of Earl O. Heady's landmark book entitled *Economics of Agricultural Production and Resource Use*.

Long before the Houston conference (1988), there had been the so-called Interstate Managerial Study (IMS) of managerial processes of Midwestern farmers (Johnson et al. 1961). Also, there were innumerable, increasingly sophisticated, linear programming research and extension programs, computerized farm accounting systems, integrated decision-support systems (IDSS), simulation models, etc. Further, the expected utility hypothesis provided a regrettably uniform framework for an almost endless number of farm management risk assessment and credit studies. In the same period, experimental and survey data were generated by farm management research for use in describing farming systems, in fitting enterprise and farm-level production functions, and for establishing unit requirements for linear programs.

Another Revolution in U.S. Farming? (Schertz et al., eds. 1979) was supported by the economics side of the Economics and Statistics Service (earlier and now the

Economic Research Service) of the U.S. Department of Agriculture. This report provided SSAAP's Houston participants with a detailed review of the major aspects of the structural adjustments that were underway in U.S. agriculture and rural America during the late 1970s, a period closely following the short-lived food shortages of the early 1970s. This report did not anticipate the financial crisis looming on the horizon for farming, despite an informative chapter on agricultural finance which noted a growing dependence on debt. Neither the *World Food Study* summarized in Part I, Chapter 1, nor this report fully recognized the propensity toward overproduction in U.S. agriculture due to the chronic overcommitment of resources to farm production and the asset fixity or the increasing dependence of the economic viability of U.S. agriculture on subsidies and macroeconomic and international forces.

The extension service's *Regaining Farm Profitably in America: A Cooperative Extension System Response* (Bolen and Lucas 1984) provided the first national ex post financial-crisis assessment of U.S. agriculture. It reported that poor weather, high interest rates, declining agricultural exports, and other factors had caused real net farm income to reach very low levels. As net farm income dropped in the early 1980s, agricultural assets also fell in value causing severe cash-flow and debt-management difficulty for heavily leveraged farmers and ranchers, a financial crisis for U.S. agribusinesses and consequent adverse pressures on many communities in rural America. The extension-service assessment projected two to five years of continued stress, excess production capacity, relatively high interest rates, severe cash-flow problems for some farmers, slow demand growth, and relatively stable or possibly declining asset values. The report addressed conventional farm management problems with emphasis on improved extension performance in the area of financial management. It did not deal with rural family needs.

Before SSAAP's Houston meeting, a conference was held at Iowa State University for historians, activists, ethicists, sociologists, theologians, economists, politicians, and farmers. The question for the conference was *Is There a Moral Obligation to Save the Family Farm?* (Comstock 1988). Both large and small, subsistence as well as commercial farms were considered. This conference stressed ethical and social science dimensions of the agricultural crisis. The conference proceedings were edited by an Iowa State University professor of religious studies, Gary Comstock. Though published after SSAAP's Houston meeting, the conference's review of cultural, ethical, and social-equity dimensions of the farm crisis of the 1980s did affect agendas developed by SSAAP participants at Houston. The Iowa conference helped reconceptualize the family farm in the context of the agricultural crisis and sampled the viewpoints of historians, sociologists, activists, theologians, economists, politicians, ex-farmers, surviving farmers, and corporate farmers. It speeded reconceptualization by asking some of the right questions about people and our failures to treat nonmonetary values in farm management and policy analyses. It also challenged rural and basic social scientists to provide better approaches for analyzing public choices for agriculture, and revealed the need for both value-free and value knowledge sufficiently rigorous to serve the public and private decision makers.

A conference on *Determinants of Farm Size and Structure* (Robison 1988) was sponsored by the North Central Regional Committee NC-181, January 16-19, 1988, in San Antonio, just prior to SSAAP's Houston meeting. Luther Tweeten presented a useful discussion of the linkages between world trade, exchange rates, and comparative advantage, and the implications of these linkages for farm size and structure in *U.S. Agriculture*. There was also a useful article by Steve Sonka (who also participated in SSAAP's Houston conference) that demonstrated the productivity of the less theoretical, farm management methods of the pre-World War II period.

Risk management is an important aspect of farm management. It includes both (1) ensuring (controlling probabilities of both favorable and unfavorable events) and (2) insuring against unfavorable events and taking chances to attain favorable events using, in either case, both formal contractual agreements with third parties and informal arrangements. In addition to ensuring, insuring, and chance taking, there are two other important aspects of management—learning about the probabilities of future events and the joys and fears of risk taking. It was pointed out, in a paper on technological innovations at the AAEA's 1985 conference on "Agriculture and Rural Areas Approaching the 21st Century: Challenge for Agricultural Economics," (Hildreth et al., eds. 1988) that the widely used current distinction between risk preferrers and risk averters among managers is based on their utility functions rather than their enjoyment or fear of uncertain situations. With respect to learning about probability distributions, conceptualizations of the optimal amounts of learning for managers were developed in the IMS discussed above. These concepts were considered again at San Antonio. A number of attendees at the San Antonio meeting also attended SSAAP's Houston meeting. At San Antonio, the past and present statuses of farm management inquiry were reviewed. Technology, theory, classification, and measurement; the conduct, structure and performance approach; families, farming, and the impacts of community organizations; agricultural policy and farm programs; world trade, exchange rates, and international comparative advantage; and financial stress were considered. Blame for the reduced ability of farm management workers to serve farmers was placed on a disciplinary preoccupation with static production economics (Johnson 1988; Just and Rausser 1990). A need was noted for farm management analysts to return to systematic, multidisciplinary empirical studies of the managerial processes based on increased contact with the real-world managerial activities of farmers. Also, the need was stressed for multidisciplinary attention to problem definition, learning, and problem solving for: academic farm management (research, teaching, and extension); and farm management consulting, advising; and farm entrepreneurship. The importance of values—nonmonetary as well as monetary—in farm management was noted. Finally, attention was devoted to improvements in policies and programs that can result from providing better multidisciplinary, microlevel (grass roots) knowledge about needs for public policy and program modifications. A historical perspective was provided with reviews of pre-World War II farm management, the post-World War II domination of farm management by production economists, the post-World War II studies of the managerial processes of farmers, the resistance of farm management extension workers to the constraining dominance of static production economics in academic farm management, and earlier noncomputerized scenario analyses in farm management. Attention was also given to more modern systems analyses, integrated deci sion-support systems (IDSSs), expert systems, and the need to screen theoretical developments across the rural and basic social sciences for innovations that can be used to improve farm management concepts and analyses. The work of Williamson (1985) on firm-level institutions of capitalism was cited.

Research and Agricultural Marketing: A Paper Prepared for the Experiment Station Committee on Organization and Policy (Babb et al.), published in 1985 and sponsored by ESCOP, provided background information about farm-input and product-marketing chains for farm management as well as for agribusiness management. Farmers have to manage for themselves the consequences of what goes on behind their back gates as well as beyond their front gates in the form of improved processing and marketing techniques, institutional changes in markets, changes in the people in control of domestic and international markets, and changes in policies, regulations, and market intervention.

Prior to SSAAP, Davan Associates conducted a survey of researchable questions in agricultural economics. That survey focused heavily on marketing and agribusiness as being relatively more important than the production of primary farm products. As such, it provided valuable background for farm management workers concerned with marketing problems. Davan's paper, published as Chapter 2 of this section, was available at the Houston conference.

Agriculture and Rural Areas Approaching the 21st Century (Hildreth et al. 1988) was based on a conference sponsored by the American Agricultural Economics Association of the same title except for an added subtitle *Challenges for Agricultural Economics*. A useful chapter in this book was written by King and Sonka. It considered managerial problems of farm and agribusiness firms—the stress was on instability and change, risk management, and organizational problems with implications for research, extension, and resident instruction being developed.

Farmers have a basic concern about environmental pollution, groundwater contamination, and the safety of the food chain. Stewardship is important to a high proportion of farmers. More recently, they have been joined in these concerns by environmentalists, nutritionists, and less scholarly activists. Participants of SSAAP's Houston conference had, as background, many papers on such issues presented at a University of Florida conference on "Agriculture, Change, and Human Values," October 18-21, 1982. Also available were articles published in the journal *Agriculture and Human Values*. Publications of the Rodale Press should also be mentioned, as well as a 1984 conference on sustainable agriculture (Edens et al. 1985). The Limited Input Sustainable Agriculture (LISA) program of the USDA and the Soil Conservation Service (SCS) cross-compliance requirement that all farms must develop and adopt soil-conserving plans to receive price support and other benefits makes attention to environmental pollution and degradation essential parts of farm management agendas.

Alternative Agriculture (Board of Agriculture 1989). This very recent study, based on 11 case studies of the practices and performance of alternative farming systems in the United States, maintains that farming practices offering alternatives to the heavy use of chemical fertilizers, pesticides, and erosion-prone tillage practices are economical, and that they can maintain crop yields, conserve soil, maintain water quality, and lower operating costs. The phrase "alternative agriculture" is one of about a dozen that have come into use as labels for agricultural systems that share such basic goals as reduced use of purchased inputs, especially toxic or nonrenewable inputs; less damage to the environment; better protection of water, soil, and wildlife; and complementarity between agriculture and viable rural communities (Lockeretz 1989; Batie 1990). One assumption of the "alternative," "sustainable," or "regenerative" agricultural movement is that farmers have been maximizing output rather than profit, and have used inorganic fertilizers and other agricultural chemicals beyond levels that equate their marginal products with their marginal factor costs—this would, of course, be contrary to years of farm management teaching and extensive joint agronomic/economic research (Woodworth 1977). While the case studies presented in *Alternative Agriculture* are impressive, they are anecdotal. The output-maximizing as opposed to the profit-maximizing assumption has not been empirically substantiated across any broad type of farming system. Nonetheless, the sustainable-agriculture movement does recognize important basic social science concerns about farm management—the need for social scientists to go beyond short-run, static microeconomics of agriculture to a broad-based concern with the socio/economic/technical systems of rural America. *Alternative Agriculture* provides direct linkages between agriculture and the environment, which is also a major concern of Part III, Section 3, of this volume, "Resource Enhancement and Growth in Capital Bases."

Since the Houston conference, the USDA has published its 1989 yearbook of agriculture entitled *Farm Management: How to Achieve Your Farm Business Goals*. In that book, almost ninety authors reflect much of the general body of farm management thought used commonly at the time of SSAAP's Houston conference. Papers are grouped under eight headings: (1) farm managers, (2) strategic management, (3) tools of farm managers, (4) resources, (5) the environment, (6) information, (7) management services, and (8) the future. Consistent with the title, the book does not consider the interdependency of farm business and home management, and does not address the management of small, part-time, and limited-resource farms except in a four-page chapter entitled "Management Needs of Small-Scale Agriculture" in which small-scale farms are defined as those producing less than $40,000 of sales annually.

The transaction-cost approach of Williamson (1985) and others can be extended as suggested below and in Part III of this book. Extended it becomes consistent with: early farm management planning techniques (Bradford and Johnson 1953), the case-study approach of the Harvard School of Business Administration, the general, systems simulation analysis (*European Review of Agricultural Economics*, Vol. 3, No. 2/3, 1976), the more recent project by the National Agriculture and Natural Resources Curriculum Project on "Systems Approaches to Food and Agricultural Problems" (Wilson et al. 1990), and the recent Fox/Miles (1987) book on systems economics. Williamson's transaction-cost work is regarded as part of the "public choice" literature even if Williamson addresses private sector, corporate "institutions of capitalism." Use of the adjective "public" in the term "public choice" is somewhat unfortunate because the approach really deals with "multiperson" choices that, of course, are important in the private as well as in the public sector, as Williamson clearly recognizes. With respect to farm management, a high proportion of the choices are multiperson, involving husband, wife, mature children, partners, and creditors and other business contracts, in inputs and product markets. In Part III of this book, the section on ethics, private decisions, and public choice that considers the general need to extend the public choice/transaction cost (PC/TC) approach in several ways is noted and agendas for making such extensions are presented. This need is also relevant for home management and for farm and home management combined as will be noted in the next section on home management.

HOME MANAGEMENT

Though the interdependency of the firm and household parts of a family farm seem too obvious to be noted here, this interdependency is not always recognized in agricultural research, extension, and resident instruction programs involving farm business and home management. The home aspect of family farms has often been left to the home economists who, in turn, have left business management mainly to farm management specialists in the departments of agricultural economics, with little interaction between the two. Prior to World War II, one or two farm management specialists estimated the monetary value of a farm wife in the business/home-farm complex and came out with large figures to the gratification of farm women and home economists, even if the computations were somewhat degrading of women. There is a current related study by Nils Westermark (1986) from Finland.

After World War II, two management books appeared, one on home economics and one on farm management. Both books approached management in similar ways although their authors were never in contact prior to the publication of their books. *Management for Modern Families* by Gross and Crandall (1954) viewed home managerial processes in a manner similar to that in *Farm Management Analysis* by Bradford and Johnson (1953). Bradford and Johnson viewed the home and business ends of farming to be so intimately interrelated as to make it impossible to separate them in dynamic farm management analyses of the type they developed in their book and of the type found in the Gross/Crandall book.

It was in the post-World War II period that Albert Hagan, at the University of Missouri, took the lead in developing Missouri's Balanced Farming Extension Program. The program was balanced in the sense that it gave appropriate attention to both the farm and home components of a family farm and, in doing so, drew heavily on the work of extension home economists and researchers at the University of Missouri and elsewhere. The Missouri program influenced the Bradford/Johnson effort and was consistent with, even if it did not influence, the Gross/Crandall book. The success of the program in Missouri led to the initiation of a farm and home development program by the University of Kentucky's extension service. The Kentucky and Missouri extension programs were subsequently incorporated into a national agricultural extension program under the title of "Farm and Home Development." The title of the national extension program, like that of the Kentucky program, made explicit the contributions of farm wives, the home, and home economists to farming.

The national farm and home development program tended to succeed best in states with smaller farms where there was less opportunity for extension workers to specialize in the business problems of farming versus the home management problems of farming. In the main corn-belt states, home economist extension workers and farm management extension workers could more easily go their separate ways than they could on smaller, more subsistence, limited-resource farms of the mid-South where the interdependencies of business and home expenditures and investments were almost always too tight to be ignored. A subsequent subsection of this chapter addresses small farms; the transformation of home economics into human ecology is further considered in Parts III and IV of this book.

In the years before and just after World War II, home economists gave major attention to such multidisciplinary subjects as nutrition, home management, marriage and the family, clothing, and the like. Such multidisciplinary subject-matter research by home economists served the extension home economists well as they carried out useful activities and projects to serve homemakers, family members, and, indeed, farmer/husbands on both large and small farms.

It seems fair and accurate to assert that an identity crisis developed for home economists in the 1960s and 1970s. Cooking, homemaking, family, child rearing, and clothing appeared mundane and not very satisfying academically. Some home economists sought a new identity and found it in what they called "human ecology" which, while extremely multidisciplinary, seemed to some to be more academic. The transformation of home economics into human ecology is dealt with in Chapter 6 of this section by Bubolz and Sontag. Interestingly enough, extension workers in home economics have a tendency to continue to call themselves "home economists" rather than "human ecologists." Farm women and their husbands know what cooking, homemaking, marriage and the family, and clothing are all about—they are less sure about human ecology. As background for the SSAAP Houston meeting, it is important to note the National Extension Initiative on Building Human Capital conducted from 1986 to 1988 under the leadership of Patrick J. Borich, Director of Extension, University of Minnesota, and V. Milton Boyce, Assistant Deputy Administrator, 4H. Home economists and human ecologists played an important role in this initiative, as did extension educators and 4H Club administrators. In human ecology research, there has been a deepened, more academic interest in human development. This work by human ecologists in the area of human development is given additional consideration in Part III, Section 2, on human development. Currently, human ecologists and extension home economists are interested in such topics as aging, health care, AIDS, crisis and stress management, environmental pollution, gender equality, substance abuse, food safety and food-chain contamination, child development, spouse and child abuse, off-farm work, and rural latch-key children. Family financial management has always been important in home economics and continues to be in human ecology. In 1988 and in 1989, the assembly of the American Home Economics Association (AHEA) passed resolutions pertaining to gender issues, the balance between work and family, homelessness, minority leadership in the AHEA and home economics, support for the U.N. International Year of the Family, support for the 1991

White House Conference on Aging, youth at risk, world hunger, child abuse and neglect, the development of education for global understanding, and care giving for the elderly. In 1988, the Association passed resolutions on AIDS and on library and archival improvements to benefit home economics.

Meeting in January of 1986, the North Central Regions NCA 5 developed a list of priorities that reaffirmed those developed in January and revised in February of 1985. Those priorities involved research on family economic stability and financial security; family, food consumption; nutrition and health; family energy and environmental resource utilization; family constraints and social environment; and family and high technology.

While the above summary is far from complete with respect to the information available to the participants at SSAAP's Houston conference, it does indicate something about that part of the work of home economists and human ecologists most relevant for establishing SSAAP's agendas for farming (including homes) in the United States. The last paragraph in the subsection above on farm management deals with multiperson choices in an interrelated view of home and farm management—as such, it is at least as relevant for this subsection on home management as it is for farm management.

THE SPECIAL CASE OF SMALL FARMS

For some time, farms of the United States have been bimodalizing as to size. The relative number of larger and smaller farms has increased while the relative number of middle-sized farms has decreased. Though the large farms include nonfamily operations that depend upon capital markets for financing and compete in local labor markets for their help, they also include large family farms that supply most of their own labor. Some of the large family farms are leveraged while others are not. Large farms, whether they are family farms or not, tend to get into difficulty because of the more or less continual price squeeze on agriculture that makes it difficult to pay competitive wage rates for their hired labor while competing in national credit markets for capital. Exceptions to this generalization occur when large, nonfamily farms have special monopolistic or monopsonistic positions in the markets. Some large farms, for instance, are in a position to take advantage of disadvantaged laborers while others receive public subsidies for inputs such as water. A few have found special niches in product markets, sometimes with the assistance of governmental price-support programs and import restrictions. In this portion of this chapter, the concern is with the increasing number of small farms, not with the medium and larger farms that were considered in the previous two subsections that dealt with farm and home management.

The small farms of the United States include full-time subsistence farms without access to off-farm employment opportunities for either husband or wife. Even when characterized by underemployment, some such farms do not enjoy off-farm employment because either no work is available or the husband and wife are unable to take advantage of off-farm employment opportunities because they are physically or in other ways unqualified.

A large proportion of the small farms of the United States became part-time farms because there was access to off-farm employment. Some of these small farms were originally large enough to provide full-time employment at a then satisfactory level of living for a farm family; however, as living standards increased for the U.S. population in general, the families on these farms found it necessary to supplement their farm income with nonfarm employment in order to "keep up with the Joneses" on larger commercial farms and in nonfarm employment. Though agrarian romanticists deplore this development, it must be realized that it is off-farm employment that keeps these people from becoming part of a disadvantaged rural peasantry, not unlike those other disadvantaged families now on inadequate-resource farms without access to off-farm employment either because such opportunities are nonexistent or because they are not qualified to work off the farm. These groups are considered further in Part III, Section 2, of this book.

Another group of small farms are not really farms at all; instead, they are rural residences for hobby and/or recreational farmers. It must be stressed that both part-time farmers on inadequate-resource farms and persons living in rural residences constitute important potential clientele groups needing the services of rural and basic social scientists. This is as true of the hobby and recreational farmers as it is of the farmers selling farm products with or without off-farm work. (See Part III, Section 1.)

Among the many references, conferences, and assessments available to participants at SSAAP's Houston conference was a report of a Kansas State University symposium on small farms, the Comstock book (1988) considered earlier in the subsection on farm management, and the Dahlberg book entitled *New Directions for Agriculture and Agricultural Research: Neglected Dimensions and Emerging Alternatives* (1986). In addition, many participants at the SSAAP conference were aware of and influenced by the writings of such persons as Wendell Berry and the research and other activities of such organizations as the Aspen Institute, the Center for Rural Affairs in Nebraska coheaded by Marty Strange, and "The Land Institute" headed by Wes Jackson in Salina, Kansas. Most participants were also aware of positions about small family farms taken by the National Farmers Organization and the Grange, as well by as such relatively new organizations as "Prairiefire Rural Action," the "North American Farm Alliance," and the "Iowa Farm Unity Coalition." The Comstock book contains chapters presenting the points of view of the last groups.

The Kansas State University "Symposium on Small Farms in a Changing World" (Sheppard 1982) dealt with Third World as well as U.S. small farms. The emphasis was on farming-systems research (FSR) viewed as a way whereby social scientists investigate the technical biological and physical science needs of small farms. Though home consumption of new varieties calls for attention to family needs in FSR studies, firm/household interactions such as those considered in the Missouri Balanced Farming Program are not given much attention despite the tight firm/household interrelations on limited-resource farms. In another arena, the farm firm/household interrelationship, long familiar to farm management and home economics personnel, is being "rediscovered" more and more often by development economists abroad and by general economists worldwide. Two, and sometimes a few more, equation models have been developed and used to analyze firm/household interrelationships but, of course, without the realism, for instance, of the work done earlier at Missouri and Kentucky on balanced farming and on farm and home development.

AGRIBUSINESSES

Paralleling the large increase in U.S. agricultural productivity there has been a phenomenal structural transformation of the farm input supply and product marketing, processing, and distribution infrastructure of the United States. From individual farmers supplying a high proportion of their own inputs and the dominance of "mom and pop" grocery stores that persisted almost to World War II, the inputs and other parts of the food and fiber system both beyond the farm front gate and behind its back gate have changed into highly industrialized sectors often monopsonized or monopolized by a few dominating firms. There is general agreement that several successive waves of mergers over the last several decades contributed to world-renowned efficiency in the supplying of farm inputs and, especially, in the marketing, processing, and distribution of food and fiber via greater geographic distribution, horizontal acquisitions to broadened product lines as well as vertical acquisitions to reduce costs; however, some analysts now question whether such efficiency claims can be made for the consequences of the merger mania that developed among agribusinesses in the 1980s (Marion 1986).

Inputs: The Economic Research Service (ERS) of the U.S. Department of Agriculture is updating a 1968 study on *Seven Farm Input Industries.* This report analyzes the 20-year trends in the use of fertilizer, pesticides, energy, livestock feed, credit, farm machinery, and hired labor. Trends in input use are related to agriculture output and productivity as well as to concerns about farm financial risks, the environment, and food safety. Because of the role of manmade capital in enhancing the development and use of natural resources and environmental concerns, the report also serves as the basis for Part III, Section 3, Chapter 3, covering natural resources, farm inputs, and the environment.

At SSAAP's Houston conference, inadequate attention was given to agendas pertaining to agricultural credit markets and their utilization. Consequently, Peter Barry, University of Illinois, and John Brake, Cornell University, were asked to draw on work of NC 161 (Financial Markets for Agriculture) to develop social science agendas for this area. They produced the agenda items on agricultural finance that are identified with their names and NC 161 in Chapter 7 of this section. They also produced the background statement that is published here verbatim.

> Financial markets and institutions have played a vital role in the capitalization and modernization of farm businesses, financing the production and marketing of agricultural commodities, providing important risk bearing services, and making available other financial services to farmers. The major credit suppliers include the Cooperative Farm Credit System, commercial banks, the Farmers Home Administration, life insurance companies, merchants and dealers, state credit programs, and individuals. These credit suppliers represent a diverse set of financing sources for farmers that differ in their degree of specialization in farm lending, legal and regulatory environment, degree of government affiliation, and source of funds. Moreover, they provide financing to an agricultural industry that presents unique risks to the cost and availability of credit. Farm businesses typically are capital intensive, have low liquidity, are subject to variable prices and production as well as seasonality, and have limited diversification.
>
> Agricultural lenders were severely tested by the events of the 1970s and 1980s. Farm debt grew rapidly during the favorable financial times of the 1970s only to encounter significant changes in financial markets and in agriculture during the 1980s. Financial deregulation increased competition among financial institutions, lessened the insulation of farm credit from national and international markets, and, along with a shift away from interest rate targeting in monetary policy, contributed to higher and more volatile interest rates. Commercial banks are experiencing structural changes such as formation of bank holding companies, removal of geographic barriers to lending, interstate banking, expansion of services, and the emergence of regional and national lending markets. Financial stress in agriculture during the 1980s was especially difficult for the specialized farm lenders—the Farm Credit System and the Farmers Home Administration. The Farm Credit System has begun a financial recovery through significant downsizing of operations, organizational restructuring, and utilization of federal financial assistance. Farm lending from federal and state credit programs continued at relatively high levels, with significant deterioration in the credit quality of loan portfolios. A substantial shift toward guaranteed versus direct lending by FMHA represents a movement toward privatization of public credit services for agriculture. The new Federal Farm Mortgage Corporation, established to create a secondary market for farm real estate loans, holds the potential to significantly change the nature of long-term lending in agriculture, although the ultimate impact is subject to considerable uncertainty. Within agriculture, continued improvements are needed in farmer skills in financial management, risk assessment, and credit worthiness. Also needed is the development of financial accounting systems with greater depth, uniformity, and use.

Products: A useful place to begin an appraisal of almost any significant area of agricultural economics research and analysis is the AAEA *A Survey of Agricultural Economics Literature*. Volume I of the survey contains a section on "The Analysis of Productive Efficiency in Agricultural Marketing: Models, Methods, and Progress," by Ben C. French (1977). French describes and evaluates the contributions of many studies of production efficiency of agricultural markets and the improvement of marketing operations. Severe conceptual difficulties attend the commonly made distinction between economic and technical efficiency (Johnson 1988, 95–98). These deficiencies are not always fully recognized in marketing research (Kilmer and Armbruster 1987).

In 1985, ESCOP published a report on research and agricultural marketing that reviewed critical agricultural marketing issues and recommended agricultural marketing research for the following decade. The report concluded that the productivity and efficiency of the American food and fiber system beyond the farm gate could be greatly improved by a research program that would develop new technologies, evaluate the feasibility of alternative systems, develop strategies for industry adoption of low-cost options, and analyze alternative public policies to promote productivity and efficiency. New areas of agricultural marketing research were seen to be: international marketing; information and coordination mechanisms; policies, regulation, and market intervention; consumer behavior; improved marketing strategies; and research methodology. Considerable attention was also directed at recommending improvements in institutions to foster innovative and effective marketing and related food and fiber system research (Babb et al. 1985). Other than the recommendation for international marketing research, this assessment expressed no significant concern for other marketing dimensions of the agricultural adjustment problem, such as difficulties in maintaining marketing and consumer services for agricultural products and inputs in rural communities.

The report of Regional Research Project 117 (NC 117), coordinated and edited by Bruce Marion (1986), followed in the tradition of the earlier *Food From Farmer to Consumer: Report of the National Commission on Food Marketing* (Brandow 1966). For their respective time periods, both of these reports did an excellent job of recording the structural changes taking place in the food and fiber system beyond the farm gate and provided useful insights into the performance of the food system. The NC 117 report entitled *The Organization and Performance of the U.S. Food System* (Marion 1986) summarized ten major policy issues relating to the farm sector crisis, the decline in the ability of the United States to compete in world markets, the massive number and size of mergers and takeovers, deregulation and overdependence on "market" solutions, labor market turmoil, and the huge and growing national debt.

Marketing, like farm management, had, and has, its more applied analysts and extension types. For instance, Clarence Davan Jr. has focused sharply on practical marketing problems and subjects relevant for farmers and agribusinessmen. His then current analysis was available to participants at SSAAP's Houston conference, and Chapter 2 of this section was distributed there.

As was noted above for farm management, the academic phase of agricultural marketing had been going through a series of reorientations prior to SSAAP's Houston conference. In marketing, interest had shifted from commodities to a conduct, structure, and performance or an industrial organization approach. This was followed by some attention to transaction-cost approach a la Oliver Williamson's *The Economic Institutions of Capitalism* (1985). The movement away from commodities to structural and institutional analysis was viewed by some (probably including Davan) as a move away from emphasis on the marketing problems of farmers and agribusinesses towards more academic interests of a subject-matter and disciplinary nature. Farmers, extension farm management specialists, and agribusinessmen found the results of the industrial organization approach less relevant to their problems. Some of the more academic farm management analysts probably did not detect the change as they, too, had become more academic and less practical as they concentrated on production economics, the expected utility hypothesis, and ways of making do with secondary data to the neglect of experimental, survey, and farm accounting data.

Williamson's work on the economic institutions of capitalism has attracted some attention in academic agricultural marketing circles though less than in resource-development circles (see Part III of this volume: Introduction and Chapter 1 of Section 1). Shaffer (1987), Staatz (1989), and Ollila (1989) have used the approach in studying cooperatives. There appear to be many unexploited opportunities to apply this approach as it now exists and can easily be extended to address agricultural marketing problems. Multiple-person, private-sector choices about institutional arrangements are commonplace in agribusiness—mergers, cooperatives, partnerships, buy-outs, the new Farmer Mac, Chapter 11 bankruptcies, etc.

FOOD CONSUMPTION AND NUTRITION

Periodically, world food assessments proclaim that only starvation can balance food needs with supplies; despite such pronouncements, world food problems are manageable. World population passed the inflection point from increasing at an increasing rate to increasing at a decreasing rate over two decades ago. Several developing countries have now gained "middle-income" status and are importing and paying for needed food and feed grains to meet increasing demands for livestock commodities, while simultaneously developing their own agricultural sectors. More and more developed countries are approaching zero-population growth, while continuing agricultural productivity growth permits many consumers around the world to spend a smaller share of their incomes on an increasingly bountiful food supply.

But serious food and nutrition problems remain, not all of which were considered in developing SSAAP's Houston agendas. Chapter 7 in this section needs more agenda items on nutrition and food than were developed at Houston. Population is growing faster than food production in many African countries. The economics of many such countries are stagnant, with burdensome international debt, overvalued currencies, civil wars, and other serious impediments to progress. Although the "Green Revolution" and general development have led to remarkable progress in countries of the Asian and Pacific region, the sheer sizes of populations there means that hundreds of thousands of poor people are at risk for malnutrition and hunger due to inadequate food supplies and incomes. Poverty and landlessness in Latin American countries are caused by lack of income-producing resources and, in turn, continue to deprive many rural people of access to income-producing resources. The centrally planned economies of eastern Europe and Asia, long suffering from a lack of individual opportunity and motivation, bureaucratic inefficiencies, and stagnant economies, are experiencing social unrest even as their governments strive to bring about economic, political, and social reforms.

Proceedings of the Western Hemisphere Nutrition Congresses held in Chicago in 1965 and in San Juan, Puerto Rico, in 1968, and the XI International Nutrition Conference (Congresso Internacional de Nutricao) held in 1978 in Rio de Janeiro, Brazil, are major sources of multidisciplinary knowledge about nutrition.

A World Food Conference was held in Rome in 1974. Shortly after that conference, the National Academy of Sciences assessed world hunger problems and offered recommendations on how the United States' research and development capabilities could be applied to meeting the world food challenges. An interim report was published in November 1975 with the final report, *World Food and Nutrition Study* (WFNS): *The Potential Contributions of Research* being published in June 1977. Because this effort was summarized in Part I, Chapter 1, of this volume, we only note here the reports of Study Team 6 ("Food Availability to Consumers" in Volume III) and Study Team 9 ("Nutrition" in Volume IV) of the study's four-volume set of reports (NAS 1977). The WFNS initiated a decade of assessments prior to SSAAP. Conducted just following a period of world food shortfall and the World Food Conference, it concluded that increases in demand for U.S. food production from domestic sources, other high-income countries, and developing countries presented a challenge and opportunity to fund an impressive array of technical agricultural research programs to help meet the world food challenge. It also recommended increased efforts to help countries, that so desire, cope with population problems and attention to institution, policy, and infrastructural problems.

Even in such developed and affluent countries as the United States, burdensome public debt, military expenditures, and balance-of-payment problems reduce the ability of low-income people to avoid hunger and malnutrition, poverty, and homelessness.

In the United States, current food consumption issues relate to improving the nutritional status of the poor and food safety. Fourteen percent of the U.S. population was living below the poverty standard in 1982 and this percentage increased significantly during the 1980s (Shaffer and Stallman 1983). Shaffer and Stallman interrelated issues concerning the objectives of federal food and nutrition programs: supporting farm incomes, eliminating hunger, and improving nutritional status. With the reemergence of agricultural surpluses came a shift of concern to (1) people without the income to convert nutritional needs into enough effective demand to cover the costs of food production by farmers, many of whom worldwide are also too poor to satisfy their own nutritional needs, and (2) those endangered nutritionally by their own inadequate knowledge and food-chain contamination beyond their control. More specific concerns about food safety involve: (1) obtaining more protection from food hazards, (2) information about food-safety hazards, (3) education and training on safe food handling and choice, (4) who should provide food-safety protection and information, and (5) who should pay additional costs according to an assessment of Burbee and Kramer (1985).

Public choices are still needed to control and regulate food-chain contamination, food and dietary knowledge, packaging, labeling, container recycling, and the like. The public choice/transaction cost approach discussed above has potential useful applications in this connection.

POLICIES AFFECTING FARM PEOPLE, AGRIBUSINESSES, AND CONSUMERS

The importance of agriculture, food, and related industries; inherent instability of agriculture; and the relatively disadvantaged position of farmers and consumers in food and fiber markets have long been cited to justify government intervention in U.S. agriculture as well as in the agricultures of most countries (Knutson 1988).

U.S. agricultural and food policies generally relate to: (1) farm production, (2) agricultural marketing, (3) food and nutrition, (4) natural resources, (5) input—credit, land, and labor, and (6) international trade and development (Knutson 1988). Research and extension programs on agricultural technology are so important that technical agricultural science policy is given separate consideration in Section 4 of Part III. For similar reasons, rural human-resource-development policy, resource conservation and enhancement policies, and general institutional-change policies also have their own separate sections in Part III. These dimensions of U.S. food and agricultural policy cover the four driving forces around which much of SSAAP's work has been structured.

Clearly, when the basic farm programs were established in the 1930s under the influence of the farm "bloc," farm interests were put before consumer interests. But, these government interventions have had initially unforeseen, very favorable impacts on consumers. Farm price supports, subsidies, technical advances, and resource development have increased economic stability, promoted growth in production, decreased long-run average costs, influenced economics of size, promoted the industrialization of agriculture, and exerted downward pressure on real farm product prices. The end results included bountiful, low-cost food and fiber supplies, both for U.S. consumers and to augment U.S. aid and development efforts abroad; a drastic decline in farm population; and a shifting of public concern to food safety, nutrition, environmental quality, and competing urban and industrial demands for natural resources. The shift in relative political strength from farm to urban interests is evident even in the titles of successive food and agricultural legislation from the Agricultural Adjustment Act of 1933 to the Agricultural and Food Act of 1981 to the Food Security Act of 1985 (Flinchbaugh and Edelman 1984). In the debate about the 1990 farm bill, the emphasis is on farm-support "flexibility" and such environmental issues as soil erosion, pollution control, flood control, improvement of wildlife habitat, water quality, conservation, and sustainability. Other issues concern food quality, nutrition, product labeling, safety, hunger and, increasingly, the high cost of these programs to taxpayers (Sorenson 1990).

Assessments of U.S. food and agricultural programs and policies have been numerous and almost continuous. The Economic Research Service (ERS), always a participant in agricultural policy analyses and dialogue, maintains (in addition to other policy-related publications such as the *Agricultural Outlook*) an *Agricultural Information Bulletin 500 Series* pertaining to current debates on farm policy. This report is a follow-up to the Food Security Act of 1985. Also, ERS periodically issues the *Agricultural Food Policy Review*. Here, the subtitles signal some shift away from commodity program emphasis.

University agricultural economics departments and organizations have helped conceptualize and analyze policy issues through research, teaching, and publication of agricultural policy books. Iowa State University's Center for Agriculture and Rural Development (CARD) has a long, productive history of contributing to policy analyses and dialogues. The departments of agricultural economics in the land-grant universities of North Carolina, Oklahoma, and Missouri all have nationally oriented policy efforts. A recent productive and unique effort of cooperative university and federal government work is the Michigan State University/Federal Extension Service-sponsored project entitled "The Farm and Food System in Transition: Emerging Policy Issues." This project produced 58 policy briefs or reports, numbered in an "FS" series, that addressed current and emerging issues concerning farmers, agribusinesses, and consumers under the authorship of leading agricultural economists across the country in universities, government, and private industry. The objective of this project was to develop an extension education program to improve understanding of the food system and the emerging policy issues (Shaffer 1987; Sorenson, Shaffer, and Libby 1981). University economists also cooperate continuously with ERS and testify before federal congressional and state legislative committees concerning policy issues. Resources for the Future (RFF), too, is an important existing influence. Its National Center for Food and Agricultural

Policy, supported in part "at arms's length" by the ERS, had started its policy work and was beginning to influence policy thought before SSAAP's Houston meeting. Of current note is the National Center's annual policy review (Kramer, ed. 1989). Also to be noted are the Farm Foundation's National Public Policy Conferences. These conferences are held to improve the policy education efforts of extension workers responsible for policy programs. Improved extension public-policy programs should help citizens make more intelligent and responsible decisions when faced with solving local and national problems. The 39th Conference, held in September 1989, in New Orleans, Louisiana, emphasized the shifting agricultural policy agenda and addressed such issues as the global environment for the U.S. economy in the 1990s, family policy, rural-development policy, public-policy education, and water quality.

There are marked similarities between the farm crisis of the 1980s and that of the 1920s. Land prices fell sharply in both periods. Excess productive capacity exerted downward pressure on prices in periods following governmental exhortations to expand production. Leveraged farmers went bankrupt in both periods, particularly if they were so large that they were dependent on both (1) labor hired at going wage rates and (2) money borrowed at going interest rates. One big difference between the two periods was the existence of much greater price supports and subsidies in the 1980s than in the 1920s—in fact, these programs are often blamed for the crisis of the 1980s by those without enough knowledge of history to know that the absence of such programs did not save leveraged farmers in the 1920s and that the price support, production-control programs were developed to mitigate conditions such as those that developed in the 1920s and have reappeared repeatedly since then to become particularly pronounced in the 1980s. Clearly, the programs developed in the 1930s, as modified since then, have not been successful in controlling overproduction however much they have helped farmers and rural communities in times of crisis. It is questionable whether the recurrent farm crises can be either blamed on the price support, production control, and subsidy programs or cured by their elimination. This is not to argue that these programs have not aggravated overproduction, in many instances, at considerable cost to taxpayers; instead, it is to argue that considerable research is needed on new and better programs and policies by rural social scientists. We badly need programs that will reduce the overproduction tendencies of our market-controlled (still largely family-run) feed grain, food grain, fiber, feeder cattle, and dairy subsectors without substantially increasing our food costs and at much lower costs to our taxpayers than they now pay.

In the 1920s and 1930s, policy analysts paid attention to total, average, and marginal returns. Returns then were often but far from uniformly low enough on all three counts to justify the price-support production stabilization, "conservation," and other programs developed in the 1930-1965 period to assist farmers.

At, and since, the onset of the recent farm crisis, economists and agricultural economists have tended to concentrate on average farm and nonfarm incomes of farmers. Few studies have concentrated on return at the margin for labor, capital investments, and land even in studying leveraged farmers in crisis. Two ethics are involved, the one that accepts equality in total income as a social goal and the other that accepts equal returns at the margin as a goal recognizing that total incomes will vary with resources owned, as well as marginal returns, and that farmers with total incomes twice the national average may or may not be receiving "justice" at the margin. In recent years, agricultural economists, for reasons not quite consistent with the stress economists usually place on margin returns, have placed greater emphasis on total (net) incomes (Kalbacker and Brooks 1990). Leveraged farmers with investments yielding lower marginal returns than the interest rates they pay have a considerable concern with returns at the margin. Noneconomists have often been more sensitive than economists (Comstock 1988).

Large numbers of disadvantaged farm and nonfarm rural African-Americans, Hispanics, Native Americans, and Caucasians receive low incomes as a result of owning few income-producing rights and privileges that are employed or sold at low marginal returns. These groups are considered in Part III, Section 2.

Of particular importance in recent years has been the International Trade Consortium sponsored by ERS and the land-grant universities. It draws together policy analysts with expertise in international agricultural trade and macro agricultural affairs including the impacts of domestic and international monetary/fiscal operations and policies. Personnel from the trade consortium have participated in SSAAP's conferences and are members of its executive committee.

In a sense, agricultural programs and policies are like rust-resistant varieties of wheat—they soon "run out" and need replacement as entrepreneurs, consumers, and political forces learn to circumvent, modify, and exploit them. This similarity is often missed by biological scientists serving as agricultural administrators who sometimes denigrate policy and institutional research because policies and institutions don't "stay fixed;" they should recognize, instead, that it is precisely for this reason that policy, program, and institution work needs continuous support in the agricultural establishment.

Establishing and maintaining productive dialogue among social scientists from different disciplines and with public and private decision makers is necessary if the rural social sciences are to be effective. The above partially summarizes efforts to provide social science dialogue with public and private decision makers relative to agricultural and rural policy issues. Perhaps the most recent innovative and successful publication effort to maintain nontechnical, ongoing dialogue among social scientists and public and private decision makers concerning farmer, agribusiness, and consumer issues is the AAEA-sponsored *Choices* magazine. *Choices* provides a forum for economists, philosophers, politicians, and other social scientists from a broad spectrum of institutions and positions to present their ideas to a national audience.

Insofar as methods and techniques for analyzing traditional price control, price support, production control, and subsidy policies are concerned, we are now in a period of substantial institutional change. This suggests the wisdom of reviewing herein the history of the analyses of such policies in the United States. We start the review by noting that in the 1930s such institutionalists as O. C. Stine, working with Howard Tolley and Secretary of Agriculture Wallace, placed great emphasis on combining qualitative-historical with more quantitative-statistical analyses of policy changes in a rather broad institutional framework that supplemented historical understanding of the social and political forces demanding changes in agricultural institutions with careful statistical work. It was in the early 1930s that our agricultural databases for such policy analyses were developed and molded into a coherent picture of the agricultural sector. These databases were used to develop what would now be called "scenario" or "uncomputerized, general, systems-science" analyses. These were often done iteratively and interactively between analysts in the U.S. Department of Agriculture and the agricultural colleges, on one hand, and members of the farm bloc in Congress or administrative officials, on the other. In the earliest years of this relationship, mainly graphic correlation analyses were carried out under the leadership of persons such as Louis Bean. Later, Mordecai Ezekial introduced mathematical correlation techniques.

During and just after World War II, the method of simultaneous equations began to be used by econometricians to estimate parameters of so-called "structural" equations from estimates of the parameters of reduced forms of structural equations. In the post-World War II years, econometric agricultural policy analyses concentrated more and more on economics and on particular parts of economics and the agricultural sector. As this took place, interest in maintaining a coherent database lessened. Further, as problems changed with time, the inadequately maintained databases became increasingly obsolete (Bonnen 1977).

In the late 1960s and early 1970s, some overseas policy analysts moved beyond the paper-and-pencil scenario analyses of the types used earlier in analyzing the U.S. policy problems of the 1930s to computerized analyses that became known in some circles as the "general, systems simulation analyses" (Manetsch et al. 1971; Rossmiller et al. 1972, 1978; and Csaki 1985). These general, systems simulation analyses were multidisciplinary and modeled the consequences of changes in social, political, technical, and institutional variables while placing less emphasis on maximizing concepts from neoclassical economic theory. Unfortunately, these analyses followed a period in which very large econometric models had been focused narrowly and unrealistically on neoclassical economic phenomena to the exclusion of social, political, and other relevant variables and had, therefore, lost approval and favor among both analysts and public decision makers. These more general, systems simulation analyses were confused with the large-scale, very specialized econometric models and were appraised adversely as similar to them even though they were fundamentally broader and more general in ways that tended to overcome the shortcomings of the large-scale, econometric models.

It is instructional to examine the history of a U.S. agricultural-sector systems-simulation model developed in part by the International Institute of Applied Systems Analysis (IIASA) in Laxenburg, Austria. IIASA took the lead in developing a world food and agriculture model as part of its Food and Agricultural Project (FAP). Its FAP model included a submodel of the U.S. agricultural sector that is relevant here. Those working on the U.S. agricultural-sector model attempted to develop the models at three levels: (1) a simple, specialized, economic model to link via a neoclassical world-trade model with similar country models for about 80 percent of the world's food production, (2) a detailed holistic model of the U.S. agricultural sector, and (3) a model of intermediate complexity. Though this work was supported by what is now the Economic Research Service (ERS) of USDA, it did not prove possible to incorporate the numerous existing USDA models into the detailed model. Instead, a USDA/IIASA model of some intermediate-level complexity was developed to become another of the USDA's uncoordinated partial models of the U.S. agricultural sector. Though the model was unduly specialized on economics, it lacked the specificity and the probabilistically estimated parameters of more econometric models. Consequently, it was adversely appraised by econometricians and economists as having insufficient disciplinary rigor and as well by general, systems-science simulators as well, who felt it lacked sufficient multidisciplinary holism to be realistic, and for both reasons has experienced little acceptability among decision makers and choosers. The model was moved from the USDA to the Center for Agriculture and Rural Development (CARD) at Iowa State University.

Meanwhile, there has been something of a rebirth of the institutionalism that had guided the widely accepted policy analyses of the 1930s. In marketing and in policy analyses, the industrial-organization (conduct, structure,and performance) approach was used to understand the consequences of institutional changes growing, in turn, out of changes in social, political, military, and technical variables. Then came the PC/TC approach to public-policy analysis under the leadership of persons such as Buchanan and Tullock; Williamson; and North. At Houston, Bromley's paper, commissioned by SSAAP and published as Chapter 5 in Section 1 of Part III, puts the PC/TC approach at the center of policy analyses involving institutional change and made the case for a PC/TC approach to the analyses of institutional changes affecting agricultural development and, for that matter, price supports, production controls, subsidies, etc.

Earlier, it was noted that the similarities between the crisis of the 1920s (that developed prior to the institution of present-day price supports, production controls, and subsidies) and that of the 1980s (that developed in the presence of such market interferences) tell us two things: (1) that such crises develop without governmental interference in markets, and (2) elimination of market interferences will not necessarily eliminate them. In Part III to follow, it will be (1) seen that market adjustments tend to be ex ante Pareto optimal, but not necessarily ex post Pareto optimal, (2) stressed that a Pareto optimal cannot be regarded as either inferior or superior (from joint equality/efficiency) standpoints to the Pareto optimal organization corresponding to an alternative institutional structure in the absence of, (3) interpersonally valid knowledge of intrinsic as opposed to monetary and nonmonetary extrinsic (exchange) values. These arguments have profound implications for those who believe that "letting the market do it alone" will solve the crisis of farm overproduction and increase welfare and efficiency. These implications need to be addressed in policy research for commercial agriculture, as well as in connection with the changes in our research, human development, resource development, and institutional policies, organizations, and programs that are considered in Part III of this book. There are similar concerns with respect to the roles of markets in international rural development, the subject of Section 2 of this Part. When these implications are addressed, serious deficiencies in our basic social science disciplines are revealed that are considered in Part IV, Section 2, on the basic social science disciplines. Samuels and Schmid (1981) have edited a book on *Law and Economics: An Institutional Perspective* that has useful conceptual insights vis-a-vis the regulation (often in non-Pareto optimal ways) of markets.

In this volume, Larry Busch's chapter (Part III, Section 1, Chapter 2) takes a systems approach very similar to that followed by the general, systems-science analysts who went beyond large-scale, specialized, econometric models to develop much less specialized models involving a broader range of social, political, and technical variables. These models worked when used iteratively and interactively with decision makers and affected persons to "sort things out" well enough for the decision makers and affected persons to see the goodnesses and/or badnesses of the consequences of proposed institutional changes (as well as the nonconsequential goodness or badness of the changes themselves) not only through time (as stressed by Busch) but also in space and in various other dimensions involving income distribution, gender equality, nutritional status, etc. (Mitroff and Turoff 1973) The agendas presented in Chapter 7 of this section will call for explorations of extended versions of the PC/TC approach to policy analyses involving iterative/interaction between analysts, policy makers, and affected persons that take into account social, political, and technical variables and knowledge of both nonmonetary and monetary variables.

Of particular importance is the on-going study of price support, production control, trade, monetary (fiscal), and related institutions of the federal government. The 1989 Athens meeting of the International Economics Association devoted one day to agricultural economics and, more specifically, to public choice. Papers to be published in the proceedings include presentations by Gordon Tullock and Jimmye Hillman; Monika Hartmann, Wilhelm Henrichsmeyer, and Peter Schmitz; Konrad Hagedorn; and Peter Soderbaum. Among other topics, these papers addressed problems of price support, production control, and subsidy institutions in the Common Market, the United States, and the developed world in general, using a PC/TC approach. With the exception of Soderbaum, most authors stressed the evils of "rent collection" on the part of farmers with little attention to the constructive reasons for establishing these institutions, some of which had (originally, at least) more constructive purposes and benefits than the establishment of rent-collection opportunities for farmers.

In this book, Section 3 of Part IV on ethics, private decision making, and public choice considers this approach in a general way. Chapter 1 (Part IV, Section 3) considers the approach in a manner more specialized on the content of this section. Parallel presentations are to be found in other substantive sections of this book.

SETTING SOCIAL SCIENCE AGENDAS FOR FARMS (INCLUDING HOMES), AGRIBUSINESSES, AND CONSUMERS

In this section and beyond this survey chapter, the complex and difficult task of reviewing and summarizing the contributions of SSAAP with respect to farm businesses and homes, agribusinesses, and consumers is approached by first presenting several papers that help us understand the social-science-related problems of agriculture and rural America. Thus, in Chapter 2, Clarence F. Davan Jr. reviews the potential payoffs from identifying and prioritizing researchable questions with respect to marketing and agribusiness. In Chapter 3, Cornelia Butler Flora reviews studies of households in relation to farm and home, balanced farming, farming systems, and farm management programs. Wava G. Haney summarizes theoretical advances that are arising from studies of women and farming in Chapter 4. In Chapter 5, Margaret M. Bubolz and M. Suzanne Sontag provide a discourse on the integrative evolution of home economics toward multidisciplinary human ecology. Timothy E. Josling conceptualizes the relationship between rural development and international trade and fiscal affairs in Chapter 6. Work group agenda reports from the SSAAP Phase II Workshop are presented in Chapter 7 which also includes conclusions and more agendas developed by SSAAP's editorial group since the Houston meeting.

CROSS REFERENCES IN THIS BOOK

PART I: INTRODUCTION

Ch. 2 A History of American Agriculture From Jefferson to Revolution to Crisis, Richard S. Kirkendall

PART II: DOMESTIC FARM, AGRIBUSINESS, AND CONSUMER WORK, AND ALL INTERNATIONAL AGRICULTURAL DEVELOPMENT WORK

Sec. 2 Ch. 2 International Affairs and Economic Development, G. Edward Schuh

Ch. 7 Institutional Reform: Accomplishments and Unmet Needs in China, Newly industrialized Countries of Asia, the Soviet Union, and Eastern Europe and the Developed Countries, Glenn L. Johnson

Ch. 8 On-Farm Capital Formation and Rural Financial Markets in Low Income Countries: Research Issues, Dale W. Adams

PART III: THE FOUR DRIVING FORCES FOR DEVELOPMENT

Introduction to Part III

Sec. 1 Ch. 1 Introduction to Section on Institutional Improvements

Ch. 4 Economic Institutions and the Development Problem: History and Prognosis, Daniel W. Bromley

Ch. 5 Irony, Tragedy, and Temporality in Agricultural Systems or How Values and Systems are Related, Lawrence Busch

Sec. 2 Ch. 3 Education and Tomorrow's Workforce: A National Agenda, Clifton R. Wharton Jr.

Sec. 3 Ch. 6 Abstract—Sustainable Development: Challenges to the Profession of Agricultural Economics, Sandra S. Batie

PART IV: THREE CROSSCUTTING CONCERNS

REFERENCES

American Home Economics Association. 1989. Assembly passes resolutions. *AHEA Action* (July/August).

Babb, E. M., et al. 1985. *Research and agricultural marketing: A paper prepared for the Experiment Station Committee on Organization and Policy*. Gainesville: University of Florida, Institute of Food and Agricultural Sciences, Editorial Department.

Batie, Sandra. 1990. Sustainable development: Challenge to the profession of agricultural economics. *American Journal of Agricultural Economics* 71:1083-1101.

Board of Agriculture, National Research Council. 1989. *Alternative agriculture*. Washington, D.C.: National Academy Press.

Bolen, Kenneth R., and Leo E. Lucas. 1984. Regaining farm profitability in America: A cooperative extension system response. Prepared for the Extension Committee on Organization and Policy. Lincoln: University of Nebraska, Institute of Agriculture and Natural Resources, Dept. of Agricultural Communications.

Bonnen, James T. 1977. Assessment of the current agricultural data base: An information system approach. In *A survey of agricultural economics literature*. Vol. 2, *Quantitative methods in agricultural economics, 1940s to 1970s*, 386-407. St. Paul: University of Minnesota Press.

Bradford, Lawrence A., and Glenn L. Johnson. 1953. *Farm management analyses*. New York: Wiley and Sons, Inc.

Brandow, George E. 1966. *Food from farmer to consumer: Report of the* National Commission on Food Marketing. Washington, D.C.: Government Printing Office. (George E. Brandow is executive director of the National Commission on Food Marketing.)

Brown, A. W. A., et al. 1975. *Crop productivity—Research imperatives*. East Lansing: Michigan State University, Michigan Agricultural Experiment Station. Yellow Springs, Colo.: Charles F. Kettering Foundation.

Buchanan, James M., and Gordon Tullock. 1962. *The calculus of consent: Logical foundations of constitutional democracy*. Ann Arbor: University of Michigan Press.

Burbee, Clark, and Carol S. Kramer. 1985. Food safety issues for the eighties: Their implications for agriculture. The farm and food system in transition: Emerging policy issues. Federal Extension Service report FS 36.

Comstock, Gary. 1988. *Is there a moral obligation to save the family farm?* Ames: Iowa State University Press.

Csaki, Csaba. 1985. *Simulation and systems analysis in agriculture*. Amsterdam: Akademiai Kiado and Elsevier Science Publishers.

Dahlberg, Kenneth A., ed. 1986. *New directions for agriculture and agricultural research: Neglected dimensions and emerging alternatives*. Totowa, N.J.: Rowman & Littlefield.

Economic Research Service, U.S. Dept. of Agriculture. 1985. *Agricultural food policy review: Commodity program perspectives*. Washington, D.C.

_____1989. *Agricultural food policy review: U.S. agricultural policies in a changing world*. Washington, D.C.

_____n.d. *Seven farm input industries*. Washington, D.C.

Edens, Thomas, et al. 1985. *Sustainable agriculture and integrated farming systems*. East Lansing: Michigan State University Press.

XI Congresso Internacional de Nutricao. 1978. Proceedings of meeting held 27 August-1 September, 1978, Rio De Janeiro, Brazil.

Flinchbaugh, B. L., and Mark A. Edelman. 1984. The changing politics of the farm and food system. The farm and food system in transition: Emerging policy issues. Federal Extension Service report FS 26.

French, Ben C. 1977. The analysis of productive efficiency in agricultural marketing: Models, methods, and progress. In *A survey of agricultural economics literature*. Vol. 1, *Traditional fields of agricultural economics, 1940s to 1970s*. Edited by Lee R. Martin, 93-206. St. Paul: The North Central Publishing Co.

Fox, Karl A., and Don G. Miles. 1987. Systems economics: Concepts, models, and perspectives. Ames: Iowa State University Press.

Gibbs, M., and C. Carlson, eds. 1985. Crop productivity-research imperatives revisited. Report of an international conference held at Boyne Highlands Inn, 13-18 October, 1985, and Airlie House, 11-13 December, 1985.

Gross, Irma H., and Elizabeth Walbert Crandall. 1954. *Management for modern families*. New York: Appleton-Century-Crofts, Inc.

Hagedorn, Konrad. Forthcoming. Public choice and agricultural policy. In *International Economic Association Congress Proceedings, 9th World Congress*. Athens, Greece: The Athens School of Economics and Business, Economic Research Center.

Hartmann, Monika, Wilhelm Henrichsmeyer, and Peter Michael Schmitz. Forthcoming. Political economy of the common agricultural policy in the European community. In *International Economic Association Congress Proceedings, 9th World Congress*. Athens, Greece: The Athens School of Economics and Business, Economic Research Center.

Hildreth, R. J., et al. 1988. *Agriculture and rural areas approaching the 21st century: Challenge for agricultural economics*. Ames: Iowa State University Press.

Jensen, Harold R. 1981. Farm management and production economics. In *A survey of agricultural economics literature*. Vol. 1, *Traditional fields of agricultural economics 1940s to 1972*. Edited by Lee R. Martin, 3-89. Minneapolis: University of Minnesota Press.

Johnson, Glenn L. 1957. Agricultural economics, production economics and the field of farm management. *Journal of Farm Economics] 38, no. 2: 441-50.*

_____*1963. Stress on production economics. Australian Journal of Agricultural Economics* 7, no. 1: 12-26.

______1987. A second perspective on Earl O. Heady's economics of agricultural production and resource use. *American Journal of Agricultural Economics* 69, no. 3: 707-11.

______1988. Technological innovations with implications for agricultural economics. In *Agriculture and rural areas approaching the 21st century: Challenges for agricultural economics*. Edited by R. J. Hildreth et al., 82-108. Ames: Iowa State University Press.

Johnson, Glenn L., et al. 1961. *A study of managerial processes of midwestern farmers*. Ames: The Iowa State University Press.

Johnson, Glenn L, and Sylvan H. Wittwer. 1984. Agricultural technology until 2030: Prospects, priorities, and policies. Special report 12. East Lansing: Michigan State University, Agricultural Experiment Station.

Joint Council on Food and Agricultural Sciences. 1984. *Summary: Needs assessment for the food and agricultural sciences, a report to the Congress from the Secretary of Agriculture*. Washington, D.C.: U.S. Dept. of Agriculture.

______1988. *Five-year plan for the food and agricultural sciences: A report to the Secretary of Agriculture*. Washington, D.C.: U.S. Dept. of Agriculture.

Just, Richard E., and Gordon C. Rausser. Forthcoming. An assessment of the agricultural economics profession. *American Journal of Agricultural Economics* 71 (December).

Kalbacker, Judith Z., and Nora L. Brooks. 1990. Farmers are part of the American mainstream. *Choices* (1st Quarter).

Kilmer, Richard L., and Walter J. Armbruster, eds. 1987. *Economic efficiency and agricultural food marketing*. Ames: Iowa State University Press for the Farm Foundation and the Institute of Food and Agricultural Sciences of the University of Florida.

Knutson, Ronald. 1988. Technological innovations with implications for agricultural economics: A discussion. In *Agriculture and rural areas approaching the 21st century: Challenges for agricultural economics*. Edited by R. J. Hildreth, 115-20. Ames: Iowa State University Press.

Kramer, Carol S., ed. 1989. The political economy of U.S. agriculture: Challenges for the 1990s. Annual policy review 1989, National Center for Food and Agricultural Policy, Resources for the Future, Washington, D.C.

Lockeretz, William. 1989. Defining a sustainable future: Basic issues in agriculture. *Northwest Report* (December): 1-15. (Reprinted in Part III, Section 3, Chapter 5, of this book.)

Manetsch, Thomas J., et al. 1971. *A generalized simulation approach to agricultural sector analysis: With special reference to Nigeria*. East Lansing: Michigan State University.

Marion, Bruce W., and NC 117 Committee. 1986. *The organization and performance of the U.S. food system*. Lexington, Mass.: Lexington Books, D.C. Heath and Co.

McClennen, Edward F. 1983. Rational choice and public policy: A critical survey. *Social Theory and Practice* 92, no. 3: 335-79.

Mitroff, I. I., and M. Turoff. 1973. Whys behind the hows: Effective applications of the many forecasting methods requires a grasp of their underlying philosophies. *IEEE Spectrum* (March): 62-71.

National Academy of Sciences. 1977. *World food and nutrition study: The potential contributions of research*. Washington D.C.: National Research Council, Commission on International Relations.

North, Douglass. 1984. Government and the cost of exchange in history. *Journal of Economic History* 44.

Ollila, Petri. 1989. Coordination of supply and demand in the dairy marketing system—With special emphasis on the potential role of farmer cooperatives as coordinating institutions. *Journal of Agricultural Science in Finland* 61, no. 3: 135-317.

Pond, Wilson G., et al. 1980. *Animal agriculture: Research to meet human needs in the 21st century*. Boulder, Colo.: Westview Press.

Proceedings: Western Hemisphere Nutrition Congress—1965. 1966. Chicago: American Medical Association.

Robison, Lindon J., ed. 1988. Determinants of Farm Size and Structure. Proceedings of the program sponsored by the NC-181 Committee on Determinants of Farm Size and Structure in North Central Areas of the United States. Journal article no. 12899. East Lansing: Michigan Agricultural Experiment Station.

Rossmiller, George E., et al. 1972. *Korean agricultural sector analysis and recommended development strategies, 1971-1985*. East Lansing: Michigan State University, Dept. of Agricultural Economics.

Rossmiller, George E., et al., eds. 1978. *Agricultural sector planning: A general system simulation approach*. East Lansing: Michigan State University, Dept. of Agricultural Economics.

Samuels, Warren J., and A. Allan Schmid, eds. 1981. *Law and economics: An institutional perspective*. Boston: Martinus Nijhoff Publishing.

Schertz, Lyle P., et al. 1979. *Another revolution in U.S. farming?* Agricultural economic report no. 441. Washington, D.C.: U.S. Dept. of Agriculture, Economics and Statistics Service.

Shaffer, James D. 1987. Thinking about farmers' cooperatives, contracts, and economic coordination. In *Cooperative theory: New approaches*. ACS report no. 18 (July). Washington, D.C.: U.S. Dept. of Agriculture.

Shaffer, James D., and Judith I. Stallman. 1983. Domestic food and nutrition programs: Sorting out the policy issues. The farm and food system in transition: Emerging policy issues. Federal Extension Service report FS 13.

Sheppard, Wendy J., ed. 1982. *Proceedings of Kansas State University's 1981 farming systems research symposium: Small farms in a changing world: Prospects for the eighties*. Manhattan: Kansas State University, International Agriculture Programs.

Soderbaum, Peter. Forthcoming. Environmental and agricultural issues: What is the alternative to public choice theory? In *International Economic Association Congress Proceedings, 9th World Congress*. Athens, Greece: The Athens School of Economics and Business, Economic Research Center.

Sonka, Steven T. 1988. Factors we observe on successful midwest farms today. Determinants of Farm Size and Structure. Proceedings of the program sponsored by the NC-181 Committee on Determinants of Farm Size and Structure in North Central Areas of the United States. Journal article no. 12899. East Lansing: Michigan Agricultural Experiment Station.

Sorenson, V. 1990. Shaping the farm bill. *Michigan Farmer* 1(January).

Sorenson, V., J. Shaffer, and L. Libby. 1981. Working paper no. 1: The farm and food system in transition: Emerging policy issues. Agricultural Economics staff paper no. 81-88. East Lansing: Michigan State University, Dept. of Agricultural Economics.

Staatz, John M. 1989. *Farmer cooperative theory: Recent developments*. ACS report no. 84 (June). U.S. Dept. of Agriculture.

Tullock, Gordon, and Jimmye Hillman. Forthcoming. Public choice and agriculture: An American example. In *International Economic Association Congress Proceedings, 9th World Congress*. Athens, Greece: The Athens School of Economics and Business, Economic Research Center.

Tweeten, Luther. 1988. World trade, exchange rates, and comparative advantage: Farm size and structure implications. Determinants of farm size and structure. Proceedings of the program sponsored by the NC-181 Committee on Determinants of Farm Size and Structure in North Central Areas of the United States. Journal article no. 12899. East Lansing: Michigan Agricultural Experiment Station.

United States Department of Agriculture. 1989. Farm management: How to achieve your farm business goals. In yearbook. Washington, D.C.: Government Printing Office.

Westermark, Nils. 1986. Gender partnership: A postulate for socioeconomically viable family farms. *ACTA Agriculturae Scandinavica* 36, no. 4: 429-34.

Wilson, Kathleen, et al. 1990. *Systems approaches for improvement in agriculture and resource management*. Edited by E. B. Morren Jr. New York: Macmillan.

Williamson, Oliver. 1985. *The economic institutions of capitalism*. New York: Free Press.

Woodworth, Roger. 1977. Agricultural production function studies. In *A survey of agricultural economics literature*. Vol. 2, *Quantitative methods in agricultural economics, 1940s to 1970s*, Edited by Lee R. Martin. Minneapolis: University of Minnesota Press.

CHAPTER 2

IDENTIFICATION AND PRIORITIZATION OF RESEARCHABLE QUESTIONS IN AGRICULTURAL ECONOMICS: WHERE ARE THE POTENTIAL PAYOFFS?

Clarence F. Davan, Jr.[1]

INTRODUCTION

Declining farm commodity prices, sharply rising interest rates, world overproduction of agricultural commodities, depressed world economy, increasing world competition for the same agricultural markets, changing consumer diets, and U.S. agriculture becoming more export dependent during the early and mid-1980s dealt severe financial blows to many U.S. farmers and agribusinesses.

The project reported herein sought to identify the major problems facing agriculture, to identify and prioritize the major agricultural economic researchable questions to solve these problems, and to identify the users of the research results from these major researchable questions.

SITUATION

Global supply/demand balance for agriculture is the most important component of the agricultural economic environment. The long-run trend since the late 1800s has been for lower farm prices, except during World War II and the early 1970s. The major theme in the 1950s and 1960s was *"Feed the World"*—we will never have enough food to feed all the people in the world. This was also evident during this period by our own farm policies which encouraged agricultural production. In the 1970s, it was predicted that this lower price trend would reverse and we would see continually higher prices for agricultural commodities. The report "The Global 2000 Report to the President," concluded: "After decades of generally falling prices, the real price of food is projected to increase 95 percent over the 1970–2000 period" (Barney 1982, 17). This price prediction, like many others, was wrong. The theme of "The Agricultural Golden Years Are Before Us" portrayed during this period had a tremendous influence on our agricultural problems.

Production of total grain in the United States increased about 30 percent between 1980 and 1985. During this same period, domestic demand increased only 16 percent. The major driving force for change in farm commodity prices is the level of export demand. In 1980, approximately 30 percent of U.S. farm production was exported; this dropped to 20 percent in 1985. Exports grew from $7 billion in 1970 to $41 billion in 1980, but declined to $29 billion in 1985. The United States had 60 percent (119 million metric tons) of the total world coarse grain exports in 1980. This dropped to 94 million metric tons in 1986, thus giving the United States only 37 percent of the total world coarse grain export (Newman et al. 1987, 15, 25, 29).

The United States farm debt soared from $141 billion in 1979 to over $212 billion in the mid–1980s. We have gone from a labor-intensive to a capital-intensive agriculture. During the same period, farm assets, primarily land, dropped in value about $100 billion, creating a big imbalance in the farmer's debt-equity ratio. This coupled with world overproduction, a depressed world economy, greater competition by foreign producers, and changing diets to create the present situation: (1) low commodity prices, (2) the highest number of farm and bank failures since the 1930 depression, and (3) accelerated adjustments in the size, location, and number of agribusiness firms.

The United States and foreign agricultural environment is changing so rapidly that it has become unclear where the experiment stations' agricultural economics research programs should focus their efforts. There has been a significant decline in funding support for agricultural economics from CSRS-administered sources. In 1978, 12.8 percent of CSRS-administered funds were allocated to experiment station economics research programs. By 1983, only five years later, this relative share had declined to 8.2 percent (Christensen and Robinson 1985, 1251–55).

METHODS

The methods used in this study to identify and prioritize researchable questions in agricultural economics are similar to those used by agribusinesses. Data and information were obtained from many expert sources from the area being investigated. This leads to timely recommendations. A steering committee included agricultural experts from:

farm suppliers, banking, farming, cooperatives, international, commodities, congressional committees, American Agricultural Economics Association, the World Bank, experiment stations, extension service, Farm Foundation, consumers, food processing, National Governor's Association, retail food, restaurants, the National Academy of Sciences, and the Economics Research Service/USDA.

The work was conducted in five phases. The literature sources (1982–1986) dealing with research priorities, specifically in agricultural economics, were reviewed. These books, reports, and articles were written by agricultural experts in the industry, academic institutions, and government.

A questionnaire was designed to identify: (1) the major problems in agriculture (domestic and international), (2) the researchable questions in agricultural economics, and (3) the users of the results from the agricultural economics research to be conducted.

Over 550 persons were surveyed from the Chicago Board of Trade, CSRS Steering Committee, U.S. Export Development Council, AAEA Executive Council, agricultural economics department heads, Extension Committee on Organization and Policy (ECOP), International Trade Council, Economic Research Service, agricultural finance, farmers, fertilizer and seed wholesalers, Experiment Station Committee on Organization and Policy (ESCOP), Extension Subcommittee on Natural Resources, elevator operators, consumers, and agricultural commodity brokers.

The problems in agriculture and the related researchable questions in agricultural economics identified in the survey, were prioritized. The researchable questions identified in the survey were compared to the problems identified in the literature review. Also, the researchable questions identified in the survey were compared to the agricultural economics research being conducted in 1985 to determine research opportunities.

Finally, this study identified the major users of the research results from researchable questions to be answered by agricultural economics research.

IDENTIFICATION AND PRIORITIZATION OF MAJOR AGRICULTURAL PROBLEMS

The Joint Council on Food and Agricultural Sciences, a congressionally mandated group representing the participants of agricultural research, extension, and teaching in government, universities, and the private sector, set the following national agricultural priorities (Joint Council, FY 87 *Priorities*): (1) increase agricultural profitability through management; (2) improve water quality and management; (3) expand biotechnology efforts on plants, animals, and microbes; (4) develop necessary scientific and professional human capital; and (5) improve human nutrition and understanding of diet/health relationships.

Though all the priorities set by the Joint Council warrant economic research, there was a lack of prioritized researchable questions for agricultural economics provided by this study. Following are major agricultural problems as prioritized in this study on a scale of 1–10, 10 being highest:

1. Foreign countries are increasingly competitive with U.S. farmers. 10
2. U.S. producers and agribusinessmen have inadequate international marketing skills and knowledge. 10
3. U.S. and foreign import/export policies discourage free trade. 10
4. Transfer of new U.S. technologies abroad without regard to long-run consequences. 10
5. Overproduction is encouraged by U.S. and foreign farm policies. 10
6. Unknown agricultural consequences of U.S. macroeconomic policies. 9
7. Production orientation of U.S. farmers—neglect of marketing and financing. 8
8. Research, teaching, extension, and research activities of universities and government have not changed to meet agricultural challenges. 7
9. Diet changes are occurring in the United States and abroad with unknown impacts on future demand for commodities. 7
10. The increased export dependency of U.S. agriculture is increasing market instability. 6
11. U.S. agricultural programs are sending wrong signals to producers. 6
12. Deteriorating infrastructure, income, and employment opportunities in rural communities are increasing input and product marketing costs. 6
13. Farm income is unduly dependent on government programs. 5
14. Research not directed to specific users (audiences). 5
15. Lack of alternatives for chronically unprofitable crops and livestock. 5
16. More non-food and industrial uses are needed for farm products. 5
17. Poor soil and water conservation practices increase long-run costs. 4
18. Over-valued agricultural assets. 4
19. Too many resources committed to agricultural production. 3
20. Third World debt reduces U.S. agricultural exports. 3
21. Consumer indifference to farmer's problems. 2

During the survey, members of each group prioritized their problems. Table 1 presents priorities for each major agricultural problem area for each group of agriculturalists surveyed according to the data collected from them.

The data study showed that farm suppliers, including bankers, found the major problem areas (finance problems and loss of international markets) to be those that restrict operating income of farmers. These major problem areas were also stressed by farmers as those that limit their operating capital and net returns. Consumer evaluations were related to plentiful food and fiber at reasonable prices, employment, income, and quality of life. Academic and government personnel stressed essentially the same problem areas. Collectively, they ranked international trade (loss of markets, lack of comparative advantage, and poor trade policies) as our biggest problem area, followed closely by agricultural marketing (at the farm level), agricultural finance, agribusiness management, agricultural policy (U.S. farm policy), and agricultural prices and incomes. Of lesser importance were: farm production (efficiency), overproduction, community resources, consumer economics, and economic theory.

IDENTIFICATION AND PRIORITIZATION OF RESEARCHABLE AGRICULTURAL ECONOMIC QUESTIONS

The researchable agricultural economic questions identified in this study are from 19 separate surveys, including

TABLE 1: PRIORITIZATION OF MAJOR AGRICULTURAL PROBLEM AREAS BY VARIOUS AGRICULTURAL DISCIPLINES[1]

AGRICULTURAL DISCIPLINE	Problem Areas										
	FARM PROD.	AGRIC. MKT.	AGRI-BUS. MGT.	PRICE/ INCOME	AGRIC. POLICY	INT'L. TRADE	AGRIC. FINANCE	NAT'L. RES.	COM. RES.	CONS. ECON.	ECON. THEORY
Farm Suppliers	4	7	6	8	5	9	10	2	1	3	0
Banking/Finance	4	8	6	7	5	10	9	1	3	2	0
Farmers	2	10	7	6	5	8	9	3	4	1	0
Farm Retailers	5	9	7	4	6	10	8	1	2	3	0
Consumers	6	5	4	1	3	7	2	8	9	10	0
Academics	4	9	8	5	6	10	7	3	2	1	0
Government	3	9	8	5	7	10	6	4	2	1	0
TOTAL	**28**	**57**	**46**	**36**	**37**	**64**	**51**	**22**	**23**	**21**	**0**
Rank[2]	7	2	4	6	5	1	3	9	8	10	11

[1] Prioritization on a scale of 0-10, 10 being the highest
[2] One (1) being the highest

TABLE 2: EMPHASIS OVER TIME FOR AGRICULTURAL ECONOMIC RESEARCH (*REPRESENTS EMPHASIS—SEE NOTE)[1]

RESEARCH AREAS	Time Periods				
	1945–55	1956–69	1970–81	1982-PRESENT	NEXT 5 YEARS[2]
Production and operations management control	***	*****	**	*	*
Financial analysis	*	****	***	**	*****
Organizational structure	***	*****	***	*	*
Marketing management	***	****	***	**	****
Human resource planning and development	*	***	***	**	***
Business performance evaluation	**	***	**	**	****
Management information systems	*	*	**	***	*****
Ownership and control	*	*	*****	**	**

*Emphasis is assessed on a scale of 1–5 when 1 star shows very little research activity and five stars represents an extensive research effort.

[1]Litzenberg, K. K. and Schneider, V. E., "A Review of Past Agribusiness Management Research," paper presented at AAEA annual meetings July 30, 1986, Reno, Nevada.

[2]Results of agribusiness participants in AAEA July 30, 1986, workshop (55 university, 12 business and government, and 3 unclassified).

approximately 550 people, plus over 50 persons individually surveyed. They represent most segments in the total agricultural system.

Information in Table 2 from the 1986 American Agricultural Economic Association meetings, indicates that emphases over the next five years (1987–1992) for agricultural economics research should be in financial management, management information systems, marketing management, and business performance evaluations.

As indicated in Table 3, the 1982–1986 literature review of this study for 15 different agricultural groups indicated that future agricultural economics research should be concentrated in the following major areas (in order of priority): (1) international agricultural trade and development, (2) agricultural management, marketing, and finance, and (3) agricultural price, income, and policy analysis. The categories in Table 3 without x's, denote that the literature reviewed did not consider these areas for research in agricultural economics.

Following are the researchable questions in agricultural economics identified from the study (the researchable questions are prioritized in three groups—on a scale of 1–10, 10 being highest. The researchable agricultural economic questions are listed according to priority within each group:

GROUP 1. PRIORITY SCALE FROM 8–10 (HIGHEST PRIORITY GROUP):

1. What processed farm products do other countries want from the United States?
2. How competitive are the United States' agricultural and processed products in the world?
3. What are the United States' comparative advantages in world agriculture?
4. How to improve quality of agricultural commodities and products.
5. How can the United States better merchandise in international markets?

TABLE 3: RECOMMENDED AREAS FOR AGRICULTURE ECONOMIC RESEARCH[1]

RESEARCHABLE QUESTIONS BY CATEGORIES	Source													
	AAEA	JC	OTA	ESCOP	RFF	CSRS	WB	UN	NASA	LILP	NRC	FAS	ERS	AMS
Farm Market & Production Economics:														
None listed														
Agricultural Marketing:														
–How should farmers participate in prepricing	X		X				X	X			X	X		
–Post-harvest losses	X	X						X	X					X
Agribusiness Management:														
–Minimize fluctuating farm inc.	X		X			X		X						
–Useful data for farmers, etc.	X	X	X	X		X		X		X				X
–Programs to produce profit	X	X				X		X		X				
–Management, financial, marketing capabilities in agriculture	X	X	X			X		X		X				
–New management services		X	X		X			X		X				X
Agricultural Price, Income and Policy Analysis:														
–Impact economic policies on trade	X	X		X	X		X	X		X		X		
–U.S. international trade policy	X	X		X	X	X	X	X				X	X	
–Future agriculture input marketing system	X			X	X	X		X		X			X	
–Future agriculture with *no* farm progress	X	X			X			X		X				
–Role of federal government in agriculture	X	X	X	X	X	X		X		X	X			
–Inst. & org. changes in agriculture	X	X	X	X	X	X		X		X	X			
–Assess implications restrict trade	X	X		X	X	X	X	X		X		X	X	

(Continued)

TABLE 3: RECOMMENDED AREAS FOR AGRICULTURE ECONOMIC RESEARCH (Continued)

International Agriculture Trade and Development:														
–Train agriculture to sell					X	X				X		X		
–U.S. production cost competitiveness	X	X		X		X	X	X				X	X	
–Role U.S. agriculture next 50 years	X	X		X	X	X	X	X		X		X	X	
–Strategy to improve exports	X	X		X	X		X	X		X		X	X	
–Future International markets		X		X	X	X	X					X		
–U.S. agricultural products—barter		X		X	X	X	X							
–Analyze monetary linkages														
–Tradeoffs U.S. agriculture & international trade		X		X	X							X	X	
–Competitiveness of U.S. agriculture in 2000–2050	X	X		X	X			X		X				
–Transfer U.S. agricultural technology					X					X		X		
–How foreign controls transfer technology				X					X					
Agricultural Finance:														
–Steps to attract capital to agriculture	X	X	X		X	X				X				
–Restructure farm debt	X		X		X			X		X				
–Finance & survival guidelines	X		X			X				X			X	
Natural Resources: None listed														
Community Resources: None listed														
Human Resource Economics: None listed														
Consumer Economics: None listed														
Economic Theory: None listed														
Research Methods: None listed														

[1] 1982–86 Literature review from 15 different agricultural disciplines.

6. How should the United States restructure its policies and become more competitive internationally?
7. Can we cut production costs to make the United States more competitive?
8. Impacts of U.S. policies on agricultural trade.
9. Impact of other countries' policies on U.S. agricultural exports.
10. Appropriate 50-year role for U.S. agriculture in world markets.
11. How competitive should U.S. agriculture be in world markets in the years 2000, 2025 and 2050?
12. What would U.S. agriculture be like and how competitive would it be in the world market without support programs over five years? In ten years?
13. How should the United States transfer and receive new agricultural technologies internationally and at what price—overall impact of such transfers?
14. The national and international economic feasibility and overall effect of new major technologies (biotechnology included).
15. The economic and political consequences for the United States of *not* being competitive in world biotechnology and computer research.
16. Twenty-five year prospects for foreign agriculture.
17. Sources of timely factual information and data on foreign countries for U.S. agribusiness and policy maker decisions.
18. Effects of macro policy on agriculture and agribusiness profitability.
19. Linkages between U.S. macro policies and international trade.
20. How should we train farmers in marketing and financial management?
21. Ways to solve financial difficulties in U.S. agriculture.
22. How should agriculture be financed in the future?
23. Data and information needs of farmers.
24. What are and will be the sources of equity for farmers?
25. Training agricultural students to manage the changing agribusiness and farming environment.

GROUP 2. PRIORITY SCALE FROM 5–7:

1. Needed restructuring in the agricultural research, education, and extension programs of universities and government agencies (USDA).
2. Major factors affecting U.S. and international food demands.
3. What are the consumption patterns for food eaten away from home?
4. Likely changes in U.S. and international food and fiber demands in 2000, 2025 and 2050.
5. How to develop public and private multidisciplinary agricultural research.
6. Effect of eliminating U.S. farm subsidies on farm income (by farm size and enterprise) in the short and long run.
7. Using farm and agribusiness resources that cannot compete in world agricultural markets.
8. Policy alternatives for moving resources within and out of or into agriculture.
9. Impacts of structural changes in the agricultural input, food processing, and grain trade industries.
10. Consequences of subsidies for agricultural land, labor, and capital.
11. Probabilities of worldwide commodity crop disasters.
12. What type of farm and rural structure does society want and how much is society willing to pay—who pays and who decides who pays?
13. Impacts of rural development on farm employment and incomes.
14. How can employment opportunities be increased in rural areas?
15. Alternative policies for improving human capital in rural areas.
16. Policies and programs to facilitate adjustments in rural areas.
17. Can vertical and horizontal integration improve competitiveness?
18. Financial feasibility of alternative agricultural production systems.
19. What are the non-agricultural uses of farm land?
20. What are the profitability potentials for new agricultural products and new markets, including non-food markets?
21. What is the future of agricultural co-ops?

GROUP 3. PRIORITY SCALE = 4 AND BELOW:

1. Effects of higher energy costs on farms, markets and agribusinesses.
2. How can we better manage groundwater contamination by agriculture?
3. How do U.S. development programs such as PL480 affect international market products?
4. How to raise income in the Third World countries.
5. What new policies are necessary to raise Third-World incomes?

CURRENT AGRICULTURAL ECONOMIC RESEARCH PATTERNS

This section compares agricultural economics research currently (1985) being conducted with recommendations from this study to show agricultural economics administrators and researchers their opportunities. It will also aid in putting together joint research studies on a regional, national, or an international basis.

AERIS is the acronym for Agricultural Economics Research Information System. AERIS is being designed to complement the existing Current Research Information System (CRIS) by satisfying additional information needs primarily of administrators of agricultural economics research programs.

Who is developing AERIS? AERIS is being developed by agricultural economists in the Cooperative State Research Service, USDA. The AERIS project has been conducted as part of this study.

When will AERIS be available? AERIS has been developed by administrative regions with the progression being from the 12-state North Central Region followed by the Northeast, the South, and the West Regions.

By 1988, AERIS permitted comparisons of what was being researched in 1985 in agricultural economics in all administrative regions with the prioritized researchable question identified in this study.

Research funds for the North Central SAES totaled $315 million in FY 1985, of which agricultural economics

TABLE 4: RESEARCH FUNDS FOR NORTH CENTRAL SAES AND AGRICULTURAL ECONOMICS DEPARTMENTS, FY 1985

STATE	SAES DOLLARS (000)	Agricultural Economics Departments		
		DOLLARS (000)	SHARE OF SAES (%)	RESEARCH PROJECTS (NUMBER)
Illinois	23,598	2,162	9.2	31
Indiana	32,950	1,891	5.7	29
Iowa	27,980	1,787	6.4	35
Kansas	27,596	650	2.3	16
Michigan	29,416	1,716	5.8	22
Minnesota	33,741	1,373	4.1	34
Missouri	20,078	2,000	10.0	23
Nebraska	30,472	785	2.6	12
North Dakota	18,399	1,369	7.4	24
Ohio	24,234	1,310	5.4	22
South Dakota	7,661	369	4.8	8
Wisconsin	38,849	1,383	3.6	27
REGION TOTAL	**315,334**	**16,795**	**5.3 (Avg.)**	**283**

Source: CRIS

departments received approximately $17 million or 5.3 percent of the total SAES Research Funds (Table 4). This $17 million was spread over 283 agricultural economics research projects. It amounts to about $60,000 per project.

The use of approximately $21 million of research funds by the North Central SAES traditional and nontraditional departments for economic research in fiscal year 1985, varied from $49,000 in economic theory to about $4 million each in (1) agricultural price, income, and policy analysis, (2) natural resources, and (3) agricultural marketing. Over 63 percent of the research funds were concentrated in those three areas plus farm management.

The North Central Region only spent about 34 percent of its research funds on the top four areas ranked in this study: (1) international trade, (2) agricultural marketing, (3) agricultural finance, and (4) agribusiness.

International trade research, ranked number one in this study, received less than 7 percent of the North Central research funds in fiscal year 1985. International trade ranked 6th in the allocation of research funds, in the North Central Region. Agribusiness and agricultural finance research, which ranked in the top four of the CSRS economic study, received less than 10 percent of the North Central research funds in 1985 and ranked 11th, compared to ranking 4th in the CSRS economic study (Tables 5 and 6).

Ongoing 1985 research by agricultural economics departments in the North Central Region, shown in Table 6, indicated that most emphasis, over 87 percent of the research funds, in agricultural economics research is concentrated in the following research areas: (1) agricultural marketing, (2) agricultural price, income, and policy, (3) agricultural finance, and (4) farm management.

The above comparisons indicate emphasis on adjustments in the North Central Region's 1985 research agendas should be undertaken to focus agricultural economics research on higher 1987 priority research areas, especially international trade, as indicated by this CSRS economic study.

USERS OF AGRICULTURAL ECONOMICS RESEARCH RESULTS

The survey results provided primarily from agricultural economics administrators and researchers indicated that identifying the ultimate user of their research results was badly neglected in determining agricultural economics research undertaken. There was agreement among the groups surveyed that it is of the utmost importance to review the needs of various agricultural groups to determine the researchable questions that would provide the information necessary for them to make timely decisions.

The survey revealed some major problem areas in the development of an agricultural economics research agenda, which are (not in order of priority):

1. The rewards system does not encourage multidisciplinary and interdepartmental research relevant to the solution of many researchable problems.
2. Promotion and tenure is based upon writing for the professional economics journals that favor theoretical and empirical articles of a disciplinary nature with relevance for current problems.
3. Identification of the ultimate users of the research results is seldom considered in developing research and extension programs and strategies.
4. The researchers seldom communicate their findings to the ultimate users via SAES bulletins, extension articles, radio or TV appearances, or directly to the user.
5. International trade and market development research has not been a primary concern of researchers.

TABLE 5: USE OF FUNDS BY NORTH CENTRAL SAES TRADITIONAL AND NONTRADITIONAL DEPARTMENTS FOR ECONOMIC RESEARCH, FY 1985[1]

RESEARCH AREA	Use of Funds			
	DOLLARS (000)	PERCENT OF TOTAL (%)	RANK	RANK IN CSRS STUDY[3]
Farm Management	2,023	9.5	4	7
Agricultural Marketing	3,719	17.5	3	2
Agribusiness	470	2.2	11	4
Ag. Price, Income, Policy	3,928	18.5	1	5 and 6[4]
International Trade	1,420	6.7	6	1
Agricultural Finance	1,580	7.4	5	3
Natural Resources	3,855	18.2	2	9
Community Development	1,266	6.0	7	8[5]
Human Resources Dev.	70	0.3	12	
Consumer Economics	986	4.6	9	10
Economic Theory	49	0.2	13	11[5]
Research Methods	1,057	5.0	8	
Other	809	3.8	10	—
TOTAL	**21,232**	**100**	—	—

[1]Source: CRIS, 2630 economic subclasses.
[2]Ranked according to the percentage spent on the research area.
[3]Refer to Table 1, page 9, of this CSRS/USDA study.
[4]Agricultural prices and income ranked 5th, and agricultural policy ranked 6th (these were separated in the CSRS/USDA study).
[5]Considered one research area in the CSRS/USDA study.

TABLE 6: REGIONAL RESEARCH OF TRADITIONAL DEPARTMENTS FOR NORTH CENTRAL SAES, FY 1985[1]

RESEARCH AREA	Use of Funds			
		TOTAL FUNDS (%)	RANKED[2]	RANK IN CSRS STUDY[3]
Farm Management	330	6.8	4	7
Agricultural Marketing	2,101	43.0	1	2
Agribusiness	0	0	—	4
Ag. Price, Income and Policy Analysis	964	19.8	2	5 and 6[4]
International Trade	257	5.3	5	1
Agricultural Finance	874	17.9	3	3
Natural Resources	63	1.3	9	9
Community Development	0	0	—	8[5]
Human Resources Development	0	0	—	
Consumer Economics	85	1.7	7	10
Economic Theory	0	0	—	11[5]
Research Methods	138	2.8	6	
Other	71	1.4	8	—
TOTAL	**4,883**	**100**	—	—

[1]Source: CSRS, 2630 economic subclasses.
[2]Ranked according to the percentage spent on the research area.
[3]Refer to Table 1, page 9, of this CSRS/USDA study.
[4]Agricultural prices and income ranked 5th, and agricultural policy ranked 6th (these were separated in the CSRS/USDA study).
[5]Considered one research area in the CSRS/USDA study.

6. Much agricultural economics research has become specialized and disciplinary with limited applicability.
7. Most agricultural economics research is oriented to economics to the exclusion of consideration of major changes in the other areas important for agriculture.
8. Communication networking among agricultural departments and groups is poor to nonexistent.
9. Production and farm management research has not considered marketing, finance, and consumer economics.

The groups surveyed indicated that for future agricultural economics research to have maximum value to its users, the users must be made an integral part of the research planning process. For example:

1. U.S. agriculture has increased its dependence on the international market; therefore, government policy makers and agribusinesses trading internationally, need information and data on the competitiveness of U.S. commodities in the world market to make fair and equitable trade decisions. These groups also need to understand the effects on them of trade policies of other countries.
2. Agricultural input industries should be able to foresee periods of major economic changes well in advance of their expected occurrence based on accurate forecasting.
3. Farmers are in desperate need of clear, concise, and usable research results on alternative marketing techniques, alternative financial approaches, organizational alternatives, and alternatives to present government programs to ensure survival and profitability.
4. Consumers need to be educated about needs for and the impacts of government policy and subsidy programs for agriculture.

This survey identified the major users of the agricultural economics research results to be: (1) national, regional, state, and local policy makers, (2) governmental agencies advising policy makers, (3) lobbyists, (4) agribusiness and related groups, (5) farmers, (6) agricultural consultants, (7) farm organizations and commodity groups, (8) extension service, (9) university administrators, (10) consumers, (11) news media, and (12) researchers including economists.

Most of the groups surveyed expressed the opinion that improved processes are needed for defining, pursuing, and disseminating research results, data, and information at strategic times on key issues affecting agriculture. There was complete agreement from participants in the survey, that if results from agricultural economics research were not communicated to the ultimate users in an understandable and timely manner, there is little need to conduct the research. Also, it was agreed by those surveyed it was a responsibility of researchers to communicate the results of their research to all principal user groups.

TIME, COSTS, AND RETURNS TO CONDUCT RESEARCH ON THE AGRICULTURAL ECONOMICS RESEARCHABLE QUESTIONS

The net value of research can be measured by comparing the value received from the research with the expenditures and the investments needed to conduct the research. The value of research depends on the results being timely for prudent, profitable, and socially advantageous decision making.

This section provides the estimated money value to the agricultural system of the probable results of research on the researchable questions identified and prioritized in this study. These estimates were made by agricultural economics researchers. It was understood by those making the estimates that the results could not be exact and that much judgment had to go into the estimates. The analysts were to: (1) make estimates for only one cycle of the research, (2) use 1987 dollars, (3) regard the research questions identified as researchable, (4) determine if research results will have an impact, and (5) make estimates they could justify and live with as if their promotions depended on them. It is realized that finding solutions to some researchable questions listed would require several research cycles. The researchers were to determine how long it would take and how much it would cost to obtain results of benefit to the agricultural system.

Summarizing, the benefit/cost estimates indicate that it would require approximately $12 million over two years to conduct research on all the research areas identified in the study (Table 7). This $12 million investment (expenditure) on research is estimated to return a direct benefit of $195.5 million. If the research were not conducted, it is estimated that there would be a gross loss to agriculture of $91 million. Therefore, there is an estimated swing factor for conducting the research of $286.5 million or a 24-fold increase over the investment in research on the questions identified in this study. When the research areas were listed in the order of importance according to these estimates, international trade ranked number one and was estimated to need $4.2 million, or about one-third of the total research dollars. This investment would produce about a 19-fold increase while it would provide a 27-fold increase over *not conducting* the research. All research areas in Table 7 show large returns. The leverages are high enough to warrant research in all areas.

This $12 million investment is not regarded as a one-shot investment or expenditure. Instead, it is thought that more dollars will have to be spent on a continuing basis to ensure continuing returns because of dynamic changes and emergence of new problems.

CONCLUSIONS AND RECOMMENDATIONS

The U.S. total agricultural system is and will continue to be faced with many critical problems. Agriculture (including agribusinesses broadly defined) is the largest U.S. industry and is a key component for a viable U.S. economy and our overall competitiveness in the world markets.

Several important conclusions regarding future agricultural economics research are drawn from this study:

1. Today's realities indicate that agricultural economics research cannot be justified only by saving consumers dollars, or minimally lowering the per-unit cost of production. Justification also depends on increasing profitability and competitiveness in the world markets.
2. Agricultural economists have contributed significantly to the understanding and operations of the

TABLE 7: ESTIMATED TIME, COSTS, AND RETURNS TO CONDUCT RESEARCH ON THE AGRICULTURAL ECONOMIC RESEARCHABLE QUESTIONS IDENTIFIED IN THIS STUDY[1]

	Estimates To Conduct The Research			
RESEARCH AREA[2]	TIME (YEARS)	COSTS (MILLION DOLLARS)	RETURNS (MILLION DOLLARS)	ESTIMATED COST TO AGRICULTURE IF RESEARCH NOT CONDUCTED[3] (MILLION DOLLARS)
International Trade	1–4	4.2	78	34.5
Ag. Marketing	2	1.45	26	13.5
Ag. Finance	1–2	1.1	19.5	9.0
Ag. Business Mgt.	1–2	1.4	24	14.0
Ag. Policy	1–2	1.8	28	12.5
Price and Income Analysis	1–2	.5	7	3.0
Farm Production	2	.2	2	.5
Community Resources	1–2	.5	3.5	1.0
Natural Resources	1–2	.3	2.5	1.0
Consumer	2	.5	5	2.0
TOTAL	—	**11.95**	**195.5**	**91.0**

[1]This table is derived from estimates on the 51 researchable agricultural economic questions identified in this study.
[2]Each research area is ranked in the order of importance according to the findings in this study.
[3]This estimate is a gross loss to the agricultural system if *no research* is conducted on the researchable questions identified.

agricultural system. Tomorrow's needs for knowledge to support timely decision making should determine agricultural research projects and priorities.

3. The October 19,1987, stock market fall indicates how much influence the world economic factors have on the U.S. agricultural economics researchers must research the total world economic and trade system.
4. Agriculture in the United States is becoming more export dependent and, hence, subject to increasing market instability.
5. The United States has lost the cutting edge in international agricultural commodity and product competitiveness and marketing skills. Future agricultural economics research should be directed toward achieving cutting-edge competitiveness.
6. As consumption patterns (diets) are changing, more research emphasis is needed on both domestic and foreign consumer preferences for agricultural commodities and products.
7. U.S. farmers have been educated and continually taught to be production oriented. As indicated in the survey, the U.S. farmers consider marketing, finance, and agricultural business management to be the most important areas that will produce farm profitability in the future. Agricultural economics research should concentrate more effort in these areas and communicate the research results directly to the farmers.
8. Farmers have few profitable alternative uses for land.
9. Farm management research should include marketing and finance at the farm level for maximum profitability—"Total Agricultural Systems Management Research."
10. Agricultural economics research should be user oriented and the research results communicated to the ultimate user.
11. Continual restructuring of agricultural research, teaching, extension services, and research communications programs at universities and government agencies is needed to cope with foreign and domestic changes.
12. Rural communities have deteriorating infrastructures, incomes, and employment opportunities which increases input and marketing costs to agriculture.
13. Consumers of agricultural products are indifferent to agricultural problems so long as they have access to plenty of cheap, high-quality food.

Following are recommendations for the development and administering of a special program to obtain funds and conduct research on the agricultural economics researchable questions identified in this study:

1. Use the information from this study to develop a program to obtain $12 million funding over two years to conduct research on the agricultural economics researchable questions identified.
2. All agricultural economics research identified in this study needs to be funded through the special grants program on a competitive basis.
3. Have the economists in the Natural Resources, Food and Social Science/CSRS develop guidelines for communicating, administering, and monitoring this special program.
4. Have the researchers conducting the research report results on a timely basis, answering the following questions:

   a. What has been learned to date,

b. how can the results be applied to real problems,
c. who are the users of the research results,
d. are they on schedule and budget, and
e. how are they going to communicate the final results of their research on a timely basis to the ultimate user?

Many questions arose from the various agricultural groups that were surveyed. These questions are listed in no order of priority:

1. Who should set research agendas?
2. Who are the major users of agricultural economics research results?
3. Who can get the attention of politicians and policy makers?
4. How should researchers be evaluated for promotion?
5. How should research results be communicated to the ultimate user?
6. How should more interdisciplinary (interdepartmental) research be created?
7. How should networking between agricultural disciplines and departments be enhanced?
8. What influences politicians to vote the way they do for various agricultural legislation?

Agricultural economists should take a leadership role in influencing the future changes that will take place in the U.S. agricultural system by accepting the challenges identified and prioritized in this study.

The challenge to each agricultural economics researcher is to utilize his or her expertise to research the questions identified and prioritized in this study on the basis of clear, concise proposals directed toward specific users so as to garner both societal support and adequate funding and, then, to conduct and communicate the research so that timely decisions can be made by the users of the research results.

Results from researching the prioritized agricultural economics questions identified in this study will positively influence the future competitiveness and profitability of U.S. agriculture in this rapidly changing world; therefore, everyone in the agricultural system will be a winner.

NOTE

1. Clarence F. Davan, Jr., is president of Davan Consulting International, Englewood, Colorado, and was the facilitator for the CSRS/USDA research project to "Identify and Prioritize Researchable Questions in Agricultural Economics." Roland R. Robinson and Clark R. Burbee, Principal Agricultural Economists, CSRS/USDA, conducted the research on AERIS/CRIS for this study; also, acknowledgments to each of them for input and recommendations throughout the research study.

REFERENCES

Barney, G. O. 1982. *The global 2000 report to the President.* New York: Penguin Books.

Christensen, R. L., and R. R. Robinson. 1985. Federal funding of SAES economics research: Trends and possible strategies for improving support. *American Journal of Agricultural Economics* 67:1251–55.

Joint Council on Food and Agriculture. 1986. FY 1987 priorities for research, extension and higher education: A report to the Secretary of Agriculture.

Newman, M., T. Fulton, and L. Glaser. 1987. Comparison of agriculture in the United States and the European community. (June) Economic Research Service, USDA.

OTHER REFERENCES USED BUT NOT SPECIFICALLY CITED

Agricultural Marketing Service, USDA. 1986. Foreign agricultural trade of the United States.

American Agricultural Economics Association. 1985. Agricultural and rural areas approaching the 21st century: Challenges for agricultural economics. Conference papers from the Agricultural Economic Association annual meeting, Ames, Iowa. Book forthcoming.

Andrews, M. S., and G. C. Rausser. 1986. Some political economy aspects of macroeconomic linkages with agriculture. *American Journal of Agricultural Economics* 68, no.2: 413–17.

Babb, E. M., et al. 1985. Research and agricultural marketing. Prepared for Experiment Station Committee on Organization and Policy.

Benbrook, C. M. 1985. Funding agricultural economics research: Discussion. *American Journal of Agricultural Economics* 67:1262–63.

Blume, S. S. 1980. A managerial view of research. *Science* (4 January):48–49.

Bonnen, J. T. 1986. The institutional structure associated with agricultural science: What have we learned? Paper presented at the Agricultural Science Policy Workshop, May.

Brake, J. R., and M. D. Boehlje. 1985. Solutions (or resolutions) of financial stress problems for the private and public sectors. Paper presented at the American Agricultural Economics Association annual meeting, August, Ames, Iowa.

Busch, L., and W. B. Lacy. 1983. *Science, agriculture and the politics of research.* Boulder, Colo.: Westview Press.

Castle, Emery N. 1970. Priorities in agricultural economics for the 1970's. *American Journal of Agricultural Economics* 52:831–40.

Chapman, R. 1986. Technology transfer activities in the U.S. Department of Agriculture. Research project for NASA technology transfer.

Cochrane, W. W. 1985. The need to rethink agricultural policy in general and perform some radical surgery on commodity programs, in particular. *American Journal of Agricultural Economics* 67:1002–9.

Crowder, R. T. 1986. A private sector view of public agricultural marketing research. Paper given at the American Agricultural Economics Association meetings, August, Reno, Nev.

Dahlberg, K. A., et al. 1985. *New directions for agriculture and agricultural research.* Totawa, N.J.: Rowan and Allenheld.

Davan, Clarence F., Jr. 1970. Graduate training needs for agricultural economists in the business world—As viewed by: Academicians, businessmen, and private consultants. Research findings presented in a paper to the Western Agricultural Economics Association meeting, Tucson, Ariz.

_____1979. Strategic operating plan. Great Western Sugar Company.

_____1980. Management reorganization and strategic planning. Solar Energy Research Institute, Golden, Colo.

_____1983. Reorganization of Inspector General for the U.S. Navy. Proprietary study done for Navy Inspector General.

_____1984. Colorado agricultural marketing program. Commissioner of Agriculture, Colorado Department of Agriculture.

Davan, Clarence F., Jr., et al. Forthcoming. Agriculture during the next century. 1985 Symposium. Book to be published by Lincoln Institute of Land Policy.

Davan, Clarence F., Jr., J. Gilmore, et al. 1983. Senior corporate management reorganization and communications. Proprietary study done for Mountain Bell Telephone Company, Denver, Colo.

Donald, J. 1986. World and agricultural outlook. Agricultural Outlook Conference, U.S. Department of Agriculture.

Farrell, K. R. 1986. Need changes in agriculture marketing institutions, resources for the future. Panel remarks at Farm Policy/Technology Symposium, University of California.

Farris, P. L. 1986. Priorities for research and education programs, in agricultural marketing. Paper presented at the AAEA meetings, Reno, Nev.

Food and Agricultural Organization of the United Nations. 1984. Food Outlook No. 3. April 1985, Rome, Italy.

Gardner, B. 1983. Domestic policy options for future of U.S. agriculture. Department of Agriculture and Resources Economics, University of Maryland.

General Accounting Office. 1986. Farm finance: Farm debt, government payments, and options to relieve financial stress. RCED–86–126BR. (March)

Hajda, J. 1983. Agricultural trade relations: Facing the future. Prepared for Curry Foundation Agricultural Policy Project.

Hoch, Irving. 1984. Retooling the mainstream. *American Journal of Agricultural Economics* 66:791–97.

Hughes, D. W., et al. 1982. Financing the farm sector in the 1980s: Aggregate needs and the roles of public and private institutions. ERS Staff Report No. AGES 820128. (February) Washington, D.C.: National Economic Division, ERS, U.S. Department of Agriculture.

Johnson, D. G., K. Memmi, and P. Lardinois. 1985. *Agricultural Policy and Trade*. New York: New York University Press.

Johnson, D. G., et al. 1984. Research and agricultural trade. Paper prepared for the Experiment Station Committee on Organization and Policy.

Johnson, G. L., and S. H. Wittwer. 1984. Agricultural technology until 2030: Prospects, priorities and policies. Special report 12. Michigan State University.

Johnston, W. E. 1985. The alternative funding of agricultural economics research: The experience of the past decade and challenge to the profession. *American Journal of Agricultural Economics* 67:1256–61.

Joint Council on Food and Agricultural Science. 1986. Five-year plan for the food and agricultural science: A report to the Secretary of Agriculture.

Jolly, D. 1986. The situation and outlook for U.S. agriculture: The next ten years. *The Cooperative Accountant* (Fall): 38–54.

Jordan, John P. 1985. Aeconomicus agriculture: Who shall lead us? *American Journal of Agricultural Economics* 67:1247–50.

Judson, H. F. 1980. *Search for solutions*. New York: Holt, Rinehart & Winston.

Lipman-Blumen, J., and S. Schram. 1984. The paradox of success: The impact on priority setting in agricultural research and extension. USDA, Science and Education, Office of Assistant Secretary of Agriculture.

Litzenberg, K. K., and V. E. Schnieder. 1986. A review of past agribusiness management research. Paper presented at AAEA annual meetings.

McCalla, A. F. 1986. Embargoes, surplus disposal, and U.S. agriculture: A summary. USDA Economic Research Service, Agriculture Information Bulletin No. 503, November.

Mintzberg, H. 1979. *The structuring of organizations: A synthesis of the research*. Englewood Cliffs, N.J.: Prentice-Hall.

Naisbitt, John. 1982. *Megatrends*. New York: Warner Books.

National Agricultural Research and Extension Users Advisory Board. 1986. Appraisal of the proposed 1987 budget for food and agricultural science. Report to the President and Congress.

O'Brien, P. 1983. World market trends: Implications for U.S. agricultural policy. Research study prepared for Curry Foundation.

Office of Technology Assessment. 1985. Congress of the United States, technology, public policy, and the changing structure of American agriculture.

Padberg, D. I. 1987. Presidential address. American Association of Agricultural Economists, Michigan State University, East Lansing, Mich.

Pasour, E. C., Jr. 1984. The free market answer to U.S. farm problems. No. 339. Washington, D.C.: The Heritage Foundation.

Peters, T. J., and R. H. Waterman, Jr. 1982. *In search of excellence*. New York: Harper & Row.

President's Commission on Industrial Competitiveness. 1985. Global competition—The new reality 1.

Price, K. A. 1985. The dilemmas of choice. The National Center for Food and Agricultural Policy, Annual Policy Review, Resources for the Future.

Quinn, J. B. 1981. Formulating strategy one step at a time. *Journal of Business Strategy* (Winter).

Rausser, G. C. 1987. Toward agricultural policy reform. Economic report of the President. U.S. Council of Economic Advisers. 147–178.

Rausser, G. C., and E. Hochman. 1979. *Dynamic agricultural systems: Economic prediction and control*. New York: North Holland Press.

Robinson, Bob H. 1986. Meeting the EC agricultural trade challenge: Economic situation and outlook. Presentation to FAS/USDA Counselor/Attache Conference, December, Brussels.

Schnittker, J. 1983. Prospects for integrating the trade strategies of agricultural exporting nations. Prepared for Curry Foundation Agricultural Policy Project.

Schuh, G. E. 1984. United States agriculture in the world economy. *Journal of Agribusiness* 2 (February): 27–34.

_____1985. Trade and macroeconomic dimensions of agricultural policies. World Bank.

Schultz, T. W. 1964. Changing relevance of agricultural economics. *Journal of Farm Economics* 46:1004–14.

Smith, M. 1987. Increased role for U.S. farm export programs. A1B–515. Economic Research Service, USDA.

Tweeten, L. 1982. Prospective changes in U.S. agricultural structure. Edited by D.Gale Johnson. *Food and agricultural policy for the 1980s*, 113–46. Washington,D.C.: American Institute.

U.S. Department of Agriculture. 1986. *Agricultural Statistics 1986*. Washington, D.C.: U.S. Government Printing Office.

Wallace, L. Tim. 1987. *Agriculture's futures: American food system*. New York: Springer-Verlog.

CHAPTER 3

STUDIES OF HOUSEHOLDS REVIEWED IN RELATION TO FARM AND HOME, BALANCED FARMING, FARMING SYSTEMS, AND FARM MANAGEMENT PROGRAMS AND STUDIES IN THE COLLEGES OF AGRICULTURE

Cornelia Butler Flora[1]

INTRODUCTION

Within U.S. colleges of agriculture, farm management is currently the dominant paradigm linking the technical knowledge derived by researchers to farm families. As it is now practiced, farm management is both a field of research and an extension-service tool. Farm-management research calculates the economically optimal application of agronomic and animal technology in a way to maximize market yields. The goal is to make money in the farm business by manipulating, as efficiently as possible, all the variables under the farm manager's control (Kadlec 1985). While early work in farm and home and balanced farming included calculation of long-term sustainability, perhaps because agronomists were the early innovators in developing farm management as a separate specialty, current farm-management texts stress calculation of yearly profits and equity accumulation (net worth) and give only lip-service to questions of resource deterioration. Farm management has now become the exclusive purview of agricultural economists.

Farm management included the implicit assumption that a major goal of the farm family (assumed to be equivalent with the goal of the male "farmer") was to maximize net worth. Capital expansion, including the acquisition of land and implying an ever-decreasing number of farmers, was a major means to that goal. A rapid survey of farm-management textbooks over time suggests that only since around 1982 was "cash flow" included as a goal. Both of these goals, net worth and cash flow, as indicated by the measures used, have had a very short-term horizon, since they followed the basic business principles of other U.S. enterprises—accounting procedures that may, in part, account for the problems U.S. industry is now having in world competition.

Farm management assumes a market orientation and commercial agriculture. While farm-and-home and balanced-farming assumed a family farm, with noncapitalist relations of production since the farm family neither bought nor sold labor, farm management assumed a movement toward a capitalist agriculture, with hired labor and farm machinery replacing the physical labor of the farm manager. All three approaches were innovative in moving beyond yield-per-acre by including economic costs, but each took technology development as a given. While in the 1950s, balanced-farming and farm-and-home focused on the need for flexibility in the organization of multiple-farm enterprises under conditions of market uncertainty and long- and short-term planning opportunities, current practice seems much less concerned about variability in household vulnerability and how that differential vulnerability might influence farm-management recommendations.

Farming systems as an approach was initially established in developing countries, including those of less-than-optimal conditions of production (Norman 1971; Collinson 1982; Bradfield 1967; Hildebrand 1979). Not only were at least part of the farms involved producing a substantial portion of their output for domestic use, but harsh climatic conditions and unreliable rainfall, especially in Africa, meant that the "appropriate" technology was not necessarily on the shelf for the farm-management expert to work into the regression equations. As a result, farming-system research focused not only on what farmers (and later farm households) should do to maximize their goals, which were gradually expanded from narrow economic and agronomic indicators, but what production scientists should undertake in the way of research (Conway 1987). Farming-systems research attempted to make the household a part of the research team, not only through on-farm trials but in setting research agendas (Caldwell and Lightfoot 1987). As such, researchers were forced to think beyond the farm to the producer, and to realize that, in a great many farming situations, the relevant unit was not the male farmer, but the household, and that members of the household might have different goals. A farming-systems approach led researchers to realize that farming objectives may vary for different commodities in different parts of the farm and that the objectives of different individuals within the farm household may vary (Okigbo 1986).

Given that the generalized goal of all these approaches is to increase the well-being of farmers and that farmers are located in households that are also production units, what can social science studies of households contribute to understanding farmer behavior and explaining the relations between policy, technology, and rural welfare? Do such studies have a contribution to make to studies and programs in U.S. colleges of agriculture today?

HOUSEHOLDS IN AGRICULTURE

Much of the work on agricultural households has been done in developing countries. While that limits exact comparability of study results to what might be found in agriculture in the core countries, such studies do introduce a number of important components that could be integrated into studies and programs in U.S. colleges of agriculture. This paper attempts to use that literature to suggest ways in which current programs could be strengthened.

Although there is extensive anthropological literature on the definition of the household (Guyer 1981, 1986; Harris 1984; White 1980; Yanagisako 1979), this paper will focus on the strengths of using the household (instead of the contemporary U.S. term, the family) as a tool for research and applied programs. One important insight from the household-definition literature is that what constitutes the household can vary considerably depending on definition; i.e., do we mean a unit of consumption, a unit of production, a unit of investment, or a group united by a variety of kin-based obligations and rights. Further, households change radically over time. Just as households in developing countries can vary depending on the definition used (Jones 1986; Peters 1986), so can households in the United States. If we define the unit inappropriately, we are likely to come up with results that cloud, rather than clarify, the phenomenon we are examining. For example, we may be using an entirely inappropriate definition of household when we look at farm survival if we do not use a household based on shared risk and shared investment. Many of the older farmers that are in serious financial difficulty became exposed financially by underwriting their children's expansion or entry into farming. If we define the household as the nuclear family, we miss key elements of family-farm survival.

WHEN IS THE HOUSEHOLD A RELEVANT UNIT?

The household can be an appropriate unit of analysis in agriculture where there is a market economy, but before the farming enterprise becomes totally capitalistic with the separation of the factors of production and the presence of hired management and labor. Studies in various parts of the world (Collins 1986; Guyer 1981; Kahn 1978) suggest that the household becomes the relevant social unit for production and survival only when a group becomes integrated into wage and commodity markets. Prior to this integration, mutual interdependence among many members of the community, reinforced by rituals, shared labor, land, and agricultural inputs, makes the household much less important as a unit of analysis or for initiating change. When there are not linkages to larger markets through the sale of labor or products, particularly when resources are scarce, networks of non-household productive relations provide access to the resources for subsistence agriculture, including the deployment of labor (Collins 1986, 654). Such extra-household interchanges compensate for small farm size and cyclical labor shortages. In contrast, in situations where all labor is hired, the household's primary function becomes that of reproducing and sustaining the labor force.

The household is production-relevant and internally consistent only in certain historical and economic circumstances. Studies and programs in the colleges of agriculture should look beyond the household to community and larger kin- and friendship-based networks, as well as within the household, to determine under which circumstances individuals act collectively, separately, or in opposition.

EXTRAHOUSEHOLD CONSIDERATIONS

Studies of the household also point to the importance of exchange relationships for survival, and make clear that exchange relationships involve complex interdependencies that go far beyond the limits of the household. As a result of extrahousehold interdependence, individual members may make decisions based on gender-based affinial ties. These obligations may appear economically irrational at a single point in time, but taken over the life cycle, serve as a source of labor and capital for production and domestic needs. Indeed, for farm families in the United States, it might mean that farm/nonfarm exchange relationships that are both kin- and affinity-based may be more important for farm survival in times of crisis than any particular management decision on the farm.

HOW DO WE KNOW ABOUT HOUSEHOLDS?

Studies of households in developing countries point out the limitations of existing data-gathering techniques for understanding what goes into agriculture. Most of the current techniques for measuring labor-force participation were designed in response to high unemployment, based on the assumption that each individual had one (and only one) source of income, generally from wage labor. Such data-gathering techniques, and the reliance on such data common in our colleges of agriculture, have as their basic premise that each person has one simple formal link to the economy and receives direct payment for that activity. Such statistics distort the intrahousehold contributions to agricultural production, as well as disguise multiple survival strategies within households. Studies of households comparing findings based on careful household and within-household measurement from official data sources question the accepted methods for gathering data on rural-labor-force participation (Beneria 1982; Buvinic 1982; Rossini 1983; Deere 1983; Santu 1979; Hoffman and Sciara 1979; Dixon 1982).

APPROACHES TO THE HOUSEHOLD IN AGRICULTURE

A major theoretical issue addressed in the new household studies is how a noncapitalist form of production (either peasant production or the family farm) manages to maintain itself in an economy dominated by capitalist relations of production (Long 1984). Both modernization and Marxist theorists have predicted the demise of such petty capitalist production forms as represented by family-farm operations. Much of the research on the agricultural household documents the ways precapitalist relations of production coexist with capitalist relations of production. Configurations within the household are key to the survival of family farms in such situations, providing unpaid labor, subsistence production, and capital through off-farm work (Schumann 1985; Kervin 1984). Understanding the balance between multiple income strategies within the household helps explicate differential labor availability as well as differential solutions to labor and capital constraints.

Household studies have addressed the contradiction of the maintenance of family farms from two perspectives. One perspective assumes that there will be an increasing differentiation of the rural population between land owners and workers. These studies view the growing number of household members seeking off-farm work as the beginning of a transition to full proletarian status. The development of other household-diversification strategies, such as diversified crop production and crafts, are a part of this transition process (Archetti 1978; Archetti and Stolen 1975; Cliffe 1977). Indeed, this Leninist view might well characterize the approach taken by many U.S. colleges of agriculture in their research and programs, as they tend to dismiss small and part-time farmers as outside the domain of their mandate, which has become defined as producing food and fiber as cheaply and in the largest quantities possible. Smaller farmers are thus viewed as "in transition out of" agriculture. This view is reinforced by the major agricultural organizations, particularly commodity groups, which tend to be dominated by large growers for whom the household serves an ideological function when arguing to save the family farm (Flora 1981). Much research in agricultural economics buys into the "decomposition" argument by stressing the need for farmers to get bigger or to get out of farming.

The other approach stresses the intensive use of nonwage-household and extrahousehold labor by farm households that make them competitive in an economy dominated by large capitalist firms (Friedmann 1980). Most household studies follow this approach, looking at resource use within the household and the types of cognitive orientation and economic rationality that facilitate and motivate households to remain in farming despite getting the majority of income elsewhere and the tendency, noted by Chayanov (1966), to exploit their own labor. Values-and-meaning structures are, therefore, much more important in these types of household studies. U.S. colleges of agriculture in both their research and programs would do well not to assume that all actors in a given rural situation share the same meaning for similar actions or events, and to investigate more fully how the values of scientists and extensionists may differ from those of different kinds of households and different members within those households.

INTRAHOUSEHOLD ISSUES

DECISION MAKING AND POWER

Most traditional studies within colleges of agriculture have viewed the household in a relatively undifferentiated fashion, ignoring issues of gender and age. When rural women were considered at all, researchers and practitioners viewed them as either totally and unquestionably subordinate to men, who were the logical representatives of familial interests, or as clever, behind-the-scenes manipulators. The presence of elderly and young people seemed a temporary phenomenon, as brief guests, until financial independence could be attained. In the United States, studies of decision making within the household, building on the urban-based studies of Blood and Wolfe, began to look at production decisions, as well as the urban-biased focus on consumer and labor-force decisions (Wilkening and Morrison 1963; Wilkening 1958, 1981; Burchinal and Bauder 1965; Wilkening and Bharadwaj 1967, 1968). The focus was almost entirely on the husband and wife, although a few studies looked at the interaction of generation and gender (Salamon and Keim 1979; Rogers and Salamon 1983; Salamon and Lockhart 1983). Awareness of the importance of multiple household members as decision makers had little impact on the structuring of either production-oriented extension or farm-management research and practice. Decision making was not tied to control of resources (beyond Blood and Wolfe's [1960] use of differential education and income within the family as indicators of differential power). It was only when a growing number of rural households were without men that the intrahousehold access to and use of the factors of production were addressed (Buvinic and Youssef 1978; Chaney 1983; Abbott 1976; Ehlers 1987). Programs and research in U.S. colleges of agriculture could benefit from attention to the implication of different household structures for not only who performs specific productive labor, but who makes the decisions concerning that labor and who controls the profits of that labor.

The new scholarship on agricultural households questioned old concepts of homogeneous rural family structures and unified, family-centered production processes. Stolke, among others, questioned the notion that the family is a "collectivity of reciprocal interests, a pooling of efforts for the benefit of all members" (Stolke 1984, 265). There are many productive relationships that divide, rather than unify, family members (Collins 1986). Indeed, an intensive household study by Phillips suggests that households should be viewed as arenas of struggle among generations, between genders, etc., rather than as a harmonious, finely tuned machine working for the collective good.

CHANGES IN HOUSEHOLDS AND THE STRUCTURE OF AGRICULTURE

Research looking within the household makes clear that power relations within the household have changed as the rural economy has changed (Aranda Baeza 1982; Babb 1976; Hewitt de Alcantara 1979; Roldan 1982; Rubbo 1975; Wilkening 1981). Colleges of agriculture need to give more attention to the interaction of household dynamics with the larger economic structure in order to make programs and research fit the emerging needs and potentials of households in rural areas. Further, studies and programs in colleges of agriculture need to look beyond who does what work (division of labor) to who controls the fruits of that labor (division of resources). As economic relations change, so does the willingness of wives, sons, and daughters to unquestioningly hand over either their labor or their earnings. Colleges of agriculture need to begin to address the implications of growing vertical integration in agriculture, the increase in contract growing, the movement of management decisions off the farm, and the degree to which all these effect and are effected by different types of households and intrahousehold relations.

The impact of shifts in the structure of agriculture on household dynamics has been well documented by household studies. These studies suggest that it is not the labor performed by each household member that is critical, but the labor relations under which they are performed that influence whether members of the household accept patriarchal authority or resent patriarchal privilege. Stolke 1984, in looking at households over time in Sao Paolo coffee production, demonstrates how share-cropping was much more acceptable to women than was wage labor, although women did the same work in both kinds of labor relationships. It is important whether or not an agricultural enterprise is defined as a family enterprise. In the latter case, the family may make the consumption sacrifices necessary to remain in farming. While family incorporations may mean little as to who owns the land, an examination of family corporations may reveal that they are written contracts among male relatives that, in essence, exclude women from their previous decision-making roles.

THE IMPORTANCE OF RELATIONS OF PRODUCTION

Studies that link the relationship of production to household structure emphasize the importance of petty commodity production, where the farm family neither buys nor sells labor, as motivation for the entire household, both on and off the farm, to provide capital and labor for the enterprise. Studies in U.S. colleges of agriculture would do well to look beyond land ownership to other mechanisms of integrating the farm household into a capitalist mode of production. Studies of the poultry industry and its impact on households, suggested by Heffernan 1984, would be a good place to start in removing simplistic opposition to corporation farming as the populist weapon in the struggle to "save the family farm." If relations of production are separated from the dominant mode of production when the farm household is examined, the variety of ways capitalist firms extract surplus value from agriculture could better be analyzed, as well as the benefits and costs of maintaining such relationships for the farm household.

Much of the anthropological research on households has examined how changes in the relations of production affect gender and generational relations. Such research shifted focus away from the individual or family as units of production to the intrahousehold division of labor, responsibilities, and resources (Poates et al. 1987).

THE HOUSEHOLD AS A SOURCE OF LABOR

The work of Chayanov 1986, on the Russian peasant alerted researchers interested in labor availability to the importance of household life cycle to farm-management decisions in developing countries, focusing on which family members provided what labor under what conditions (Garrett and Espinosa 1986; Bouquet 1982; Friedmann 1980; Arriagada and Noordam 1982; Deere 1977, 1978, 1983; Deere and Leon 1981). Work in the United States has suggested that family farmers plan their farming operations in light of the labor available at different stages in the household life cycle (Vidich and Bensmen 1968; Salamon and O'Reilly 1979). Tienda 1980, looking at the household in Peru, suggests a reverse causality—that households expand through a variety of fictive kin arrangements when labor needs are high, and expell members when opportunities of generating household-linked income decline.

THE HOUSEHOLD AS A TOOL IN DEFINING AGRICULTURAL RESEARCH

Studies including intrahousehold considerations help explain agricultural strategies that maximize income, minimize risk, and maximize return to labor (Tripp 1982; Maxwell 1986). A farming-systems approach, which requires interaction among social scientists and production scientists, when coupled with an awareness of intrahousehold issues, provides a powerful tool for both commodity-specific research and the development of alternatives that meet the specific needs of different types of farmers with different resources available. U.S. colleges of agriculture, up to this time, have used agricultural economics to help design field trials in order to determine the optimum level of inputs to achieve the highest monetary output per acre. The household literature, particularly that related to farming systems, suggests that involving other social scientists could alert production scientists to key issues in breeding, cultural practices, and crop mixes that might increase the utility of their research for a wide variety of farm families (Poates et al. 1987; Flora 1981, 1987; Feldstein forthcoming).

An interdisciplinary approach, utilizing intrahousehold considerations that might be adopted by U.S. colleges of agriculture to better research and extend knowledge to improve agricultural welfare, involves analyzing constraints, types of household with different resources to overcome constraints, and working with appropriate members of a household to test technologies which are compatible with their resources to overcome those constraints.

THE IMPORTANCE OF SEPARATE ENTERPRISES WITHIN THE HOUSEHOLD

Identification of gender-based management roles in animal and crop production maximizes research efficiency as well as facilitates extension effectiveness (Fernandez and Salvatierra 1986). Changes in the scale of animal production, in particular shifts in relations within the household, reduces women's traditional dominance in animal production (and the household's flexibility to adjust to shifting commodity markets), and increases the dependence of the household on a single source of cash income, without the resulting subsistence savings (Hecht 1985). The inequalities that result from assuming that males within the household are responsible for all production decisions are documented in the United States as well (Fink 1986). The increased inequality within the household related to production of a single export crop is reinforced by household studies focusing on agricultural crops (Rubbo 1975).

Studies of households document how economic specialization, especially export agriculture, changes the traditional divisions of labor within the household (Aranda and Gomez 1970; Deere and Leon 1981). These shifts have also been suggested by household studies in the United States. Much of farm management, despite the increased use of the gender-neutral term "farmer" instead of "the farmer, he," does not systematically analyze the differential inputs within the household by gender and age. Gender- and age-specific inputs and expectations have enormous implications for farm survival and farming strategy employed. For example, Salamon has shown how households of different ethnic backgrounds choose different farming strategies, resulting in different farming systems and different divisions of labor within the household—even in the same agro-ecological area of Illinois (Salamon and Davis-Brown 1986).

RURAL DEVELOPMENT AND THE HOUSEHOLD

Household studies in developing countries have examined the impact of off-farm work. Household studies in Mexico (Young 1978) and Chile (Campana and Lagos) demonstrate the disadvantages to the household when such work is seasonal and piece work. In contrast, Blumberg 1985 found in Guatemala that the whole agricultural household welfare was more positively influenced by female off-farm work than by male off-farm work when the wages were high and working conditions stable. Colleges of agriculture need to systematically look at the interplay between on-farm and off-farm work of different family members under different conditions of employment. Household research to date suggests that the nature of off-farm employment sought by various members of the families throughout the year is crucial in determining the success of changes in farming systems and in predicting the impact of different kinds of economic development on rural communities.

WHAT CHANGES COULD HOUSEHOLD STUDIES BRING?

Most programs in U.S. colleges of agriculture have taken an implicitly Leninist stand, assuming the ultimate transformation of family farms into capitalist units of production, where land, labor, management, and capital all come from different sources. As a result, households have been relegated to reproducing and caring for the ever-decreasing labor force required by production agriculture. Household studies have been equated with what women do. The farm crisis has given new appreciation of the household as a buffer between the male farmer and the larger society, but that buffer tends to be defined as emotional rather than economic. For example, the family has been seen as helpful in helping a male farmer make the "choice," described in farm-management texts as early as the 1950s, to leave farming. For these researchers, teachers, and extensionists in colleges of agriculture, the disappearing middle is proof of the ultimate demise of family farming as petty commodity production. The move will be toward more substitution of capital for labor, including household labor. More specialized—and less specialized—labor will increasingly be hired to replace household labor, including custom planting, integrated pest management (IPM), and harvesting, as well as management services, which tend to disguise the sharp shift in the relations of production from small businesses to the dependence on selling of labor for survival. The household is a given in this scheme. Efficiency, marketing, and other management techniques are assumed to be either irrelevant to the household or to be implemented by the household working as a team. Small farms from which most household members work off-farm will be viewed as disguised proletarianization, with the identity as wage worker taking precedence over the identity as farmer (Mintz 1974; Rosenberry 1978).

Researchers that adopt a framework that confronts both neo-classical economics and traditional Marxist theory are much more likely to look within the household and see many more options for households in the face of modern economic challenges. Such research can help widen the options for rural households by stressing the relationship of farm and off-farm work, not that one substitutes for another. Such an approach means substantially different policy directions as well. Agricultural production research would be redesigned to take into account not only the currently organized pressure groups, but the needs and strengths of various types of households and configurations within households. Policy at the national level would be shifted from an agricultural policy to a rural-development policy, recognizing the historical ubiquity of diversified household strategies.

NOTE

1. Cornelia Butler Flora is a professor of Sociology at Virginia Polytechnic Institute and State University, Blacksburg, Virginia.

REFERENCES

Abbott, Susan. 1976. Full-time farmers and week-end wives: An analysis of altering conjugal roles. *Journal of Marriage and the Family* 38, no.1 (February): 165-74.

Aranda Baeza, Ximena. 1982. El diptico campesina-salariada agricola. In *Las trabajadoras del agro*. Edited by Magdalena Leon de Leal, 161-178. Bogota: ACEP.

Aranda Baeza, Ximena, and Sergio Gomez. 1979. *Las transformaciónes en un area de minifundio y la participación de la mujer: Valle Putaendo 1960-1980*. Santiago de Chile: Facultad de Ciencias Sociales.

Archetti, E. P. 1978. Una vision general de los estudios sobre el campesinado. *Estudios Rurales Latinoamericanos* 1, no. 1: 7-33.

Archetti, E. P., and K. A. Stolen. 1975. *Explotación familiar y accumulación de capital en el campo Argentino*. Buenos Aires: Siglo XII.

Arriagada, Irma, and Johanna Noordam. 1982. Las mujeres rurales latinoamericanas y la division del trabajo. In *Las Trabajadores del Agro*. Edited by Magdalena Leon de Leal, 39-54. Bogota: ACEP.

Babb, Florence. 1976. The development of sexual inequality in Vicos, Peru. Special series no. 83. Council on International Studies, State University of New York at Buffalo.

Beneria, Lourdes. 1982. Accounting for women's work. In *Women and development: The sexual division of labor in rural societies*. Edited by Lourdes Beneria, 119-48. New York: Praeger.

Blood, Robert O., and Donald M. Wolfe. 1960. *Husbands and wives: The dynamics of married living*. Glencoe: The Free Press.

Blumberg, Rae Lesser. 1985. A walk on the "WID" side: Summary of field research on women in development in the Dominican Republic and Guatemala. (June) Washington, D.C.: USAID, LA and PPCI/CDIE.

Bouquet, Mary. 1982. Production and reproduction of family farms in south western England. *Sociologia Ruralis* 22, no. 3/4: 227-44.

Bradfield, R. 1967. Multiple cropping in the tropical rice belt of Asia. IRRI paper no. 6, Los Banos, Philippines.

Burchinal, Lee G., and Ward W. Bauder. 1965. Decision-making and role patterns among Iowa farm and non-farm families. *Journal of Marriage and the Family* 27, no. 3 (August): 527-28.

Buvinic, Mayra. 1982. La productora invisible en el agro centroamericano: Un estudieo de caso en Honduras. In *Las trabajadoras del agro*. Edited by Magdalena Leon de Leal, 103-14. Bogota, Colombia: ACEP.

Buvinic, Mayra, and Nadia Youssef. 1978. *Women-headed households: The ignored factor in development planning*. International Center for Research on Women, Washington, D.C.

Caldwell, John S., and Clive Lightfoot. 1987. A network for methods of farmer-led systems experimentation. *Farming Systems Support Project Newsletter* 5, no. 4 (Fourth Quarter): 18-24.

Campana, Pilar, and Maria Soledad Lagos. . . . Y las mujeres tambien trabajan. Serie resultados de investigacion no. 10. Grupo de Investigacines Agrarias, Academia de Humanismo Cristiano, Santiago de Chile.

Chaney, Elsa M. 1983. Scenarios of hunger in the Caribbean: Migration, decline of smallholder agriculture, and the feminization of farming. Women in International Development working paper no. 18. East Lansing: Michigan State University.

Chayanov, A. V. 1966. *On the theory of peasant economy*. Homewood, Ill.: Irwin Press.

Cliffe, L. 1977. Rural class formation in East Africa. *Journal of Peasant Studies* 4, no. 2: 195-224.

Collins, Jane L. 1986. The household and relations of production in southern Peru. *Contemporary Studies in Society and History* 28, no. 4 (October): 651-71.

Collinson, Michael. 1982. Farming systems research in eastern Africa: The experience of CIMMYT and some national agricultural research services, 1976-81. International Development paper no. 3. East Lansing: Michigan State University.

Conway, Gordon R. 1987. Helping poor farmers: A review of foundation activities in farming systems and agroecosystems research and development. Report prepared for the Mid-Decade Review of the Ford Foundation's Programs on Agriculture and Natural Resources, January. New York: Ford Foundation.

Deere, Carmen Diana. 1977. Changing social relations of production and Peruvian peasant women's work. *Latin American Perspectives* 4, no. 1/2 (Spring): 48-69.

_____1978. The differentiation of the peasantry and family structure: A Peruvian case study. *Journal of Family History* 3, no. 4: 422-38.

_____1983. The allocation of familial labor and the formation of peasant household income in the Peruvian Sierra. In *Women and poverty in the Third World*. Edited by Mayra Buvinic, Margaret A. Lycette, and William Paul McGreevey, 104-29. Baltimore: Johns Hopkins University Press.

Deere, Carmen Diana, and Magdalena Leon. 1981. Peasant production, proletarianization, and sexual division of labor in the Andes. *Signs* 7, no. 2 (Autumn): 338-60.

Dixon, Ruth B. 1982. Women in agriculture: Counting the labour force in developing countries. *Population and Development Review* 8, no. 3: 539-66.

Ehlers, Tracy Bachrach. 1987. The matrifocal farm. In *Farmwork and fieldwork: American agriculture in anthropological perspective*. Edited by Michael Chibnik, 145-63. Ithaca, N.Y.: Cornell University Press.

Feldstein, Hilary, and Susan V. Poats. 1990. Conceptual framework for gender analysis in farming systems research and extension. *In working together: Gender analysis in agriculture*. Vol. 1: 7–37. Edited by H. Feldstein and S. Poats. New York: Kumarian Press.

Fernandez, Maria F., and Hugo Salvatierra. 1986. The effect of gender-related production management on the design and implementation of participatory technology validation. In *Farming systems research and extension: Food and feed*. Kansas State University Farming Systems publication series, no. 12. Edited by Cornelia Butler Flora and Martha Tomecek, 739-51.

Fink, Deborah. 1986. *Open country, Iowa: Rural women, tradition and change*. Albany: State University of New York Press.

Flora, Cornelia Butler. 1981. Farm women, farming systems, and agricultural structure: Suggestions for scholarship. *The Rural Sociologist* 1, no. 6 (November): 383-86.

_____1987. Intra-household dynamics in farming systems research: The basis of whole farm monitoring of farming systems research and extension. *The Rural Sociologist* 7, no. 3 (May): 201-9.

Friedmann, Harriet. 1980. Household production and the national economy: Concepts for the analysis of agrarian formations. *Journal of Peasant Studies* 7, no. 2: 158-84.

Garret, Patricia, and Patricio Espinosa. 1986. Phases of farming systems research: The relevance of gender in Ecuadorian sites. Paper presented at the Gender Issue in Farming Systems Research and Extension conference, February, University of Florida.

Guyer, Jane I. 1981. Households and community studies in African studies. *African Studies Review* 24, no. 2/3: 87-138.

_____1986. Intra-household processes and farming systems research: Perspectives from anthropology. In *Understanding Africa's rural households and farming systems*. Edited by Joyce Lewinger Moock, 92-104. Boulder, Colo.: Westview Press.

Harris, Olivia. 1984. Households as natural units. In *Of marriage and the market*. Edited by Kate Young, Carol Wolkowitz, and Roslyn McCullagh, 136-55. London: Routledge and Kegan Paul.

Hecht, Susanna. 1985. Women and the Latin American livestock sector. In *Women as food producers in developing countries*. Edited by Janie Mouson and Marion Kalb, 51-70. Los Angeles: UCLA African Studies Center.

Heffernan, William D. 1984. Constraints in the U.S. poultry industry. *Rural Sociology and Development* 1 (JAI Press): 237-60.

Hewitt de Alcantara, Cynthia. 1979. La modernizaciǒn y los cambios en las condiciones de la vida de la mujer rural. Santiago, Chile: CEPAL, July.

Hildebrand, Peter E. 1979. Generating small farm technology: An Integrated multidisciplinary system. Presented at the 12th West Indian Agricultural Economics conference, Caribbean Agro-Economics Society, Antigua, West Indies.

Hoffman, Helga, and Angel J. Sciara. 1979. *Diagnostico de las estadisticas y bibliografía sobre el empleo rural en Centroamerica y Panama*. Santiago, Chile: International Labor Organization.

Jones, Christine W. 1986. Intra-household bargaining in response to the introduction of new crops: A case study from North Cameroon. In *Understanding Africa's rural households and farming systems*. Edited by Joyce Lewinger Moock, 105-23. Boulder, Colo.: Westview Press.

Kadlec, John E. 1985. *Farm management: Decisions, operation, control*. Englewood Cliffs, N.J.: Prentice-Hall.

Kahn, Joel. 1978. Marxist anthropology and peasant economics: A study of the social structure of underdevelopment. In *The new economic anthropology*. Edited by John Clammer, 110-37. New York: St. Martin's Press.

Kervin, Carol. 1984. The impact of wage labor and migration on livestock and crop production in African farming systems. In *Animals in farming systems*. Edited by Cornelia Butler Flora. Manhattan: Kansas State University.

Lenin, V. I. 1977. *The development of capitalism in Russia*. Moscow: Progress Publishers.

Long, Norman, ed. 1984. *Family and work in rural societies*. New York: Tavistock Publications.

Maxwell, Simon. 1986. Farming systems research: Hitting a moving target. *World Development* no. 14 (January): 65-77.

Mintz, Sidney W. 1974. The rural proletariat and the problem of rural proletarian consciousness. *Journal of Peasant Studies* 1, no. 3: 291-325.

Norman, David. 1971. Initiating change in traditional agriculture. *Agricultural Economics Bulletin for Africa* 13, no. 1 (June): 31-52.

Okigbo, Bede. 1986. Forward to *Understanding Africa's rural households and farming systems*. Edited by Joyce Lewinger Moock, ix-xii. Boulder, Colo.: Westview Press.

Peters, Pauline E. 1986. Household management in Botswana: Cattle, crops and wage labor. In *Understanding Africa's rural households and farming systems*. Edited by Joyce Lewinger Moock, 133-54. Boulder, Colo.: Westview Press.

Phillips, Lynne. 1986. Gender dynamics and rural household strategies. CERLAC, York University, Downsview, Ontario.

Poates, Susan, Marianne Schmink, and Anita Spring. 1987. *Gender issues in farming systems research and extension*. Boulder, Colo.: Westview Press.

Reinhardt, Nola, and Peggy Barlett. 1987. Family farm competitiveness in United States agriculture: A conceptual framework. Presented at the Rural Sociological Society, August, Madison, Wisconsin.

Rogers, Susan Carol, and Sonya Salamon. 1983. Inheritance and social organization among family farmers. *American Ethnologist* 10, no. 3: 529-50.

Roldan, Martha. 1982. Subordinaci6n generica y proletarizacion rural: Un estudio de caso en el Noroeste de Mexico. In *Las trabajadoras del agro*. Bogota: ACEP.

Rosenberry, W. 1978. Peasants as proletarians. *Critique of Anthropology* 3, no. 11: 3-18.

Rossini, Rosa Ester. 1983. Women as labor force in agriculture: The case of Sao Paulo, Brazil. *Revista Geografica* 97, no. 1 (January-June): 91-95.

Rubbo, Anna. 1975. The spread of capitalism in rural Colombia: Effects on poor women. In *Toward an anthropology of women*. Edited by Rayna R. Reiter, 333-57. New York: Monthly Review Press.

Salamon, Sonya. 1980. Ethnic differences in farm family land transfers. *Rural Sociology* 45, no. 2: 290-308.

_____1985. Ethnic communities and the structure of agriculture. *Rural Sociology* 50, no. 3: 323-40.

_____1987. Persistence among inevitably declining middle-range farmers. Paper presented at the Rural Sociological Society, August, Madison, Wisconsin.

Salamon, Sonya, and Karen Davis-Brown. 1986. Middle-range farmers persisting through the agricultural crisis. *Rural Sociology* 51, no. 4: 503-12.

Salamon, Sonya, and Ann M. Keim. 1979. Land ownership and women's power in a Midwestern farming community. *Journal of Marriage and the Family* 41, no. 1, 109-19.

Salamon, Sonya, and Vicki J. Lockhart. 1980. Land ownership and the position of elderly in farm families. *Human Organization* 39, no. 4, 324-31.

Salamon, Sonya, and Shirley M. O'Reilly. 1979. Family land and developmental cycles among Illinois farmers. *Rural Sociology* 44, no. 3: 525-42.

Santu, Ruth. 1979. Formas de organizacion agraria, migraciones estacionales y trabajo feminino. *Revista Paraguaya de Sociologia* 16, no. 46: 49-62.

Schumann, Debra. 1985. Family labor resources and household economic strategy in a Mexican ejido. *Research in Economic Anthropology* 7 (JAI Press): 277-87.

Stolke, Verena. 1984. The exploitation of family morality: Labor systems and family structure on Sao Paulo coffee plantations, 1850-1979. In *Kinship ideology and practice in Latin America*. Edited by Raymond T. Smith, 264-96. Chapel Hill: University of North Carolina Press.

Tienda, Marta. 1980. Age and economic dependency in Peru: A family life-cycle analysis. *Journal of Marriage and the Family* 42, no. 4: 639-52.

Tripp, Robert. 1982. Including dietary concerns in on-farm research: An example from Imbabura, Ecuador. CIMMYT Economics working paper no. 82/2.

Vidich, Arthur, and Joseph Bensman. 1968. *Small town in mass society*. Princeton, N.J.: Princeton University Press.

White, Benjamin. 1980. Rural household studies in anthropological perspective. In *Rural households in Asia*. Edited by Binswanger, et al. Singapore: Singapore University Press.

Wilkening, Eugene A. 1958. Joint decision-making in farm families as a function of status and role. *American Sociological Review* 3, no. 2 (April): 187-92.

_____1981. Farm families and family farming. In *The family in rural society*. Edited by R. T. Coward and W. M. Smith, 27-37. Boulder, Colo.: Westview Press.

Wilkening, Eugene A., and Lakshimi Bharadmaj. 1967. Dimensions of aspirations, work roles, and decision-making among husbands and wives in Wisconsin. *Journal of Marriage and the Family* 29, no. 4 (November): 703-11.

_____1968. Aspirations and task involvement as related to decision-making among farm husbands and wives. *Rural Sociology* 33, no. 2 (March): 30-45.

Wilkening, Eugene A., and Denton E. Morrison. 1962. A comparison of husband and wife responses concerning who makes farm and home decisions. *Marriage and Family Living* 25, no. 4 (July): 349-51.

Yanagisako, Silvia Junko. 1979. Family and household: The analysis of domestic groups. *Annual Review of Anthropology* 8:161-205.

Young, Kate. 1978. Changing economic roles of women in two rural Mexican communities. *Sociologia Ruralis* 18, no. 2/3: 197-216.

CHAPTER 4

THEORETICAL ADVANCES ARISING FROM STUDIES OF WOMEN AND FARMING

Wava G. Haney[1]

INTRODUCTION

The central thesis of this paper is that feminist scholarship has helped us to better understand U.S. agriculture. First, it has made visible women's contributions to agricultural production, agricultural politics, and rural community development. Second, by moving beyond the bounds of an urban-based model of feminist theory, theoretical work on the lives of farm women has given us a more complete understanding of the divisions of labor on farms, within farm households, and in farm communities. The implication of these insights is to focus agricultural research on the household and the farm—rather than the farmer—as the units of analysis.

Third, the marriage of feminist theory and macrosocial theory (on macrosocial theory, see Buttel 1987) is generating critical assessments of the impact of economics policy, type of commodity, agricultural technology, and transformations in the structure of agriculture on gender relations in agricultural firms and rural communities. Fourth, the multicultural and multidisciplinary nature of feminist study of farm women has drawn attention to the multiple ways women relate to agricultural production. Fifth, these theoretical tools offer a rich framework for cross-cultural comparison of women's relationships to agriculture.

To address the relationship between feminist scholarship and U.S. agriculture, the paper is divided into two sections: (1) a review of some of our early understandings of farming and farm communities and women's role within them and (2) a discussion of the challenges to some traditional theoretical assumptions that have guided most of the previous empirical work on gender relations in agriculture.

Historical scholarship on farm women like that of other social science disciplines is in its infancy. Yet, the few historical studies of the lives of U.S. farm women are helping us develop a more accurate picture of women's roles in subsistence production, in early family-centered commercial agriculture, and in earlier forms of "larger-than-family" commercial agriculture (e.g., plantation agriculture and sharecropping). The first national survey of contemporary farm women's work, together with select statewide and local data, confirm women's involvement in U.S. agriculture today. Although most of these studies are region- and commodity-specific, they begin to expose fallacies of prior assumptions and to raise new research questions. Even at this stage, however, when historical analysis is linked to studies of contemporary farm women, we see a continuity in women's roles and in their contributions (Haney and Knowles 1988).

WOMEN'S ROLES IN FARMING

LAND

In the eighteenth and nineteenth centuries, with rare exceptions, U.S. women involved in agricultural production controlled neither the land they worked nor much of their own labor. Yet, there was a clear sexual division of labor in U.S. agriculture. As Jensen (1984, 1) wrote, "[Women] worked on land legally owned by their fathers, husbands or sons and participated in a patriarchal system where land was passed down from father to son." When women married, they lost their civil rights to own property in their own name. Since most farm women married, only when there were no male heirs did widows or daughters inherit land and sometimes the control of its use and disposal; the female heirs often found it necessary to have male relatives manage the land.

Even as legal barriers to women's direct ownership of land fell, social custom effectively prevented women from acquiring land except through inheritance. In 1978, men owned about 85 percent of the U.S. farmland (Waters and Geisler 1982). Since ownership of land often served as the gate-keeping characteristics for public and private credit and other agricultural services, women were left out of the capitalization of U.S. agriculture.

But women who inherit land, or who otherwise acquire land, do not necessarily exercise control over it. Land owned by women is often controlled by male family members (Salamon and Keim 1979; Salamon and Davis-Brown

1988), family corporations, or banking institutions (Waters and Geisler 1982). Much of the farmland owned by women is held as a joint tenant. Of the women surveyed in the first national study of contemporary farm women, about 45 percent of the married farm women owned the farm jointly with their husbands (Rosenfeld 1985). Moreover, until 1982, federal inheritance-tax laws discriminated against women, rather than being blind to the gender of the surviving joint tenant of agricultural property.

LABOR ON THE FARM

A sexual division of labor characterized production in the diversified subsistence economies of the Northern colonies and the frontier (Sachs 1984). Men cleared the land, grew field crops, and raised large livestock. Women grew vegetables, tended small livestock, processed food, made cloth and clothing; they also plowed, planted, and harvested field crops, and managed labor when male labor was unavailable. Growing numbers of women began to process agricultural products for sale and to market surplus vegetables and animal products (Jensen 1986). By the late nineteenth century, however, industrialization began to displace women's domestic production to factories, thus undercutting women's ability to earn cash by sale of either surplus farm products or processed foods.

Meanwhile, Sachs argues, the switch in the nineteenth century to market-oriented production in agriculture perpetuated the dominance of men's labor in the fields and increased its economic value. At the same time, the emergence of a domestic ideology supported by science, the church, and the state reinforced household work, including gardening for family consumption, as women's proper roles. In reality, however, often only wealthier farmers could restrict their women's work to the home and family (for a discussion of this point for Western frontier women, see Jeffrey 1979; Jameson 1987). Farm men faced with labor shortages and recurring cost-price squeeze in agriculture often needed women's labor on the farm and in earning cash. Thus, farm women—wives and daughters—worked as family laborers in the fields and barns under the direction of their husband or father (Myres 1982; Harris 1987) and for wages in the fields, factories, and homes of others (Harris 1987). These farm women's wages were often used for land and capital purchases, but seldom for the purchase of domestic technology to relieve the drudgery of women's housework (Flora and Stitz 1984).

Jones (1985) and Sachs (1985) show that plantation agriculture of the South also depended on women's labor. In fact, Sachs argues that historically, Southern women, Black and White, have been more active in agriculture than women in other parts of the country. White women of the plantation managed the domestic realm, overseeing food production—processing, purchasing and distribution—and the estate's domestic labor force. Most Black slave women on cotton plantations worked in the fields throughout the crop cycle. They were also responsible for child care and domestic activities. In the crop-lien system that succeeded plantation agriculture, the tenant contracts bound both Black and White women's as well as men's labor. Women worked in all phases of production along with their domestic duties (Jones 1988).

Several studies have looked at the kind of farm work contemporary farm women do. Wilkening and his students pioneered in showing the sexual division of labor on Wisconsin farms and the multidimensionality of farm women's work (Wilkening and Bharadwaj 1967). Wilkening found that Wisconsin farm women were more likely to do barn chores than field work and most likely to keep farm records. Women's farm work varied by commodity group (dairy farm women were the most involved in all tasks) and by level of farm debt (women's farm work increased as farm debt increased). Despite slight declines in barn and field work, farm women's overall involvement in farm tasks was greater in 1978 than 1961 because of their role in record keeping. Except for the largest of the farms (10 percent), he found that the time farm women spent keeping records increased as farm size and farm indebtedness increased (Wilkening 1981).

Rosenfeld (1985) reported that few farm women surveyed in the national sample indicated they did no farm work. Rather, most farm women did a range of farm tasks. Both the amount and scope of women's farm work were heavily dependent on the need for their labor. Women on livestock farms were more active in farm work than those on farms that specialized in crops. Similarly, smaller farms demanded more of women in terms of both the amount of farm work and the variety of farm tasks. Thus, women's farm work was more specialized in ancillary services on large commercial farms with hired management and those that produced mostly crops, while women on specialty or small, limited-resource farms frequently assumed major responsibility for field work and farm management. Women who had legal control over the land farmed and those whose husbands were employed off the farm were likely to attend to most aspects of farm production. On the other hand, farm women employed off the farm were somewhat less likely to engage in farm chores. When both work off the farm, the division of labor on the farm was reportedly more equally distributed.

MANAGEMENT AND DECISION MAKING

About one-half of the married farm women in this national sample saw themselves as partners in the daily operations and management of the farm, and 60 percent said they felt capable of running the farm without their husbands (Rosenfeld 1985). As with labor, whether women made or were displaced from making farm production decisions depended on the presence of men. Thus, Rosenfeld found that women engaged in a wide range of farm activities participated in a greater proportion of production decisions. More specifically, women on larger farms, on crop farms, and on farms that hired labor were less involved in farm decisions.

Wilkening's earlier work in Wisconsin suggested that joint decision making was more likely to occur among middle-income farm families than among those reporting either low or high income. But overall, he found that women were more involved in farm-resource decisions (e.g., land and equipment purchases, assumption of farm debt) than in farm-operation decisions (Wilkening and Bharadwaj 1967).

Married farm women not only feel they can operate farms without their husbands (Rosenfeld 1985), some do. Rosenfeld and Tiggs (1988) classified farm operations by the absence of men's labor and compared these married and unmarried independent farm women with other farm women and then with farm men, using the same classification scheme. They reported that regardless of marital status, independent farm women got lower economic returns from their farms than did other farm operators. Married, independent farm women and married farm women who were not independent farmers reported about the same average family income which was higher than that of unmarried, independent farm women. Despite their low economic return and a need for many of them to work off the farm to supplement their farm income, unmarried, independent farm women reported they are very satisfied with farming. They were more satisfied with farming than other farm women. In contrast, although unmarried, independent farm men reported farm earnings nearly as low as independent farm women; married, independent farm men reported the highest farm earnings and the highest levels of satisfaction with farming.

WORK OFF THE FARM

A variety of statewide studies show that about 40 percent of married farm women are employed off the farm (Fassinger and Schwarzweller 1980; Salant 1983; Bokemeier et al. 1983; Moore 1984). In the national study, 36 percent of the farm women surveyed and about one-half of the farm men were employed off the farm in 1980–1981 (Rosenfeld 1985). In one-fourth of the families, both men and women reported off-farm employment.

Whether farm women work off the farm or not was conditioned by farm and family characteristics, but the kinds of jobs farm women held off the farm were mainly affected by their personal characteristics. Farm women were less likely than farm men to work full time, but they are more likely to hold professional jobs. Farm women earned about 40 percent of what farm men earned, reflecting both the total hours worked as well as the wage differentials between men and women. Even though farm women earned less, their earnings made important contributions to family income, especially among the lower-income farm families (Rosenfeld 1985). Salant (1983) found that women's off-farm income contributed cash to the farm operation to maintain its solvency. An analysis by McCarthy et al. (1988) of early and mid–1980 data led them to conclude that declining net farm income and financial stress explained part of the off-farm employment of married farm women.

The combined farm and off-farm labor pattern of farm men and farm women suggested by the national study is that men stay primarily in farming when farming pays. When farming does not pay, men go off the farm for employment and women substitute their labor for their husband's (Rosenfeld 1985). In sum, off-farm employment patterns give farm families increased flexibility in the on-farm division of labor.

WOMEN'S ROLES IN FARM COMMUNITIES

Women's farm production and processing work overlapped their family work. Farm women devoted a large amount of time to the reproduction of the farm family, including caring for other members and maintaining the farm household (Jeffrey 1979; Myres 1982). Farm households tended to be large and it was women's work to care for household members too young and too old to meet their own needs, as well as tend to members when they were ill. In addition, women's household labor provided for the daily needs of able-bodied adult members of the household. This enabled men to spend more time outside the household buying and selling in the market town, and developing and managing the institutions of the community.

Although excluded from the formal political process by law and then custom, women have been credited with "building the base" of many rural neighborhoods and communities (Neth 1988). Through church and family activities, women built and tended kinship and neighborhood networks that provided for the welfare of community members, created a sense of mutuality, and defined the social meaning, purpose, and identity in rural communities (Myres 1982). The formalization of these networks led to women's organizations that were instrumental in tending to the general welfare of the community and its members.

Boom-and-bust cycles of market-oriented agriculture did spur farm women to defy rural political traditions during the late nineteenth century and the early twentieth century. The records of agrarian and third-party protest movements, farm organizations, and early survey efforts by rural social scientists show farm women's involvement in efforts to change macroeconomic policies (Jones 1984; Starr 1984; Wagner 1984, 1988) and the direction of agricultural education and research (Knowles, 1988). Women's participation in agrarian movements and farm organizations was legitimized because women were very skillful in popularizing the economic plight of farm families through poems, songs, and stories, and because money issues were seen in moral terms and women were assumed to be morally superior.

The National Farmers' Alliance—as well as the Populist Party to which many Alliance members belonged—integrated entire families into the organization (Wagner 1988)). Perhaps as much as one-fourth of the Alliance membership were women (Jones 1984). Women's work on the farm and their knowledge of farming, especially farm finances, were important reasons that women were active in the substantive issues of both groups. One national female leader said that women got involved in the Party not for reasons of relaxation or social honor—her assessment of a major motivational factor for men—but because of their concern about the economic salvation of their home and family. They spoke and wrote extensively urging the unity of women and men against a common set of enemies that eroded farm income: rail rates, bank interest, and cost-price squeeze (Wagner 1988).

For a short period in the late 1800s, women had the right to participate as individual delegates and it was not uncommon for them to be elected to state conventions, though only occasionally to statewide office. Women also devoted many hours of voluntary labor to the operation of the Alliance, sometimes rearranging family space to accommodate those political operations. However, as the Party became more concerned about winning national elections, tending the organization and political decision making became men's business.

Some successive farm organizations, such as the National Farmers' Union and the Non-Partisan League, did integrate men and women into one organization and grant membership rights to all (Starr 1984). However, women's contributions to these organizations tended to be through their traditional roles of education and social activities (Neth 1988). Despite their exclusion from formal leadership positions at the state and national levels, women were welcomed in the local units and were quite active in organizational affairs. Therefore, Neth argues, these organizations rested on a firm base that integrated men and women. Women built this social base: they kept people informed and created social occasions where issues could be discussed and debated, and people could talk out their problems and grievances. They also instilled the value of community and some knowledge and skills about how to achieve it.

Writing about the first two decades of the twentieth century, Knowles (1988) argues that a second wave of agrarian protest split along two lines: a movement by large prosperous farmers to make agriculture more scientific and more businesslike and a movement by rural people, including many farm women, concerned about the overall quality of rural life. Knowles' study of responses to early surveys sponsored by state and federal agricultural programs and of letters from farm women to extension personnel indicates that rural women were advancing the idea of a relationship between the welfare of the family and that of the farm. These women advocated programs for farm women that would enable women to contribute to their families' welfare by advancing their knowledge of agriculture, business, sanitation, and nutrition (Knowles 1984; Elbert 1988).

The national survey of farm women shows that rural women continued to be involved in voluntary organizations and political bodies (Rosenfeld 1985). Most farm men and women belonged to at least one farm or community organization. More farm women than men belonged to community organizations, but more men than women belonged to commodity associations and agricultural cooperatives. Women and men were most likely to belong to a general farm organization; few women belonged to a women's auxiliary of any farm or commodity organization or to farm women's organizations. While women and men were equally as likely to attend extension activities, men mostly took part in agricultural-related activities while women mostly attended programs related to home and family.

More indicative of farm women's role in policy making was their involvement in advising, planning, and governing councils. Here again, Rosenfeld found that farm women participate relatively often on extension committees and boards, but not on those addressing agricultural issues. Also, women did not hold many elected or appointed positions on local governing bodies, such as school or hospital boards.

Gender differences in levels of participation in community organizations and advisory boards cannot be explained by farm women's multiple roles. Neither school-age children nor politically active husbands inhibited farm women's participation in either community organizations or boards. Farm women who did a range of farm tasks and those who lived on larger farms participated more extensively in their communities. Indeed, farm women with off-farm employment were more likely to be those few women appointed or elected to governing bodies.

Less than 10 percent of the farm women responding to the national survey had served on policy-making bodies, but over one-third said they would be willing to do so. Thus, it is perhaps not surprising that, coincident with the second wave of feminism, there has been growth in farm women's participation in farm organizations, from the grassroots to the national levels, and a continuity in their concerns about family welfare and farm economics. Still, there are few women on decision-making boards of traditional farm organizations and agricultural policy-making bodies. Gender-based obstacles like stereotypes of women's work and their leadership abilities, ideas about "women's place," and feelings of being patronized continue to limit women's effective involvement in the political arena and account, in part, for farm women founding new organizations. In addition, gender-neutral obstacles, such as entrenched farm leadership and top-down decision making, limit farm women's impact on agricultural policy (Miller and Neth 1988).

THEORETICAL CONTRIBUTIONS AND IMPLICATIONS

Studies of the relationship of women to agriculture cited in the previous sections, together with a growing number of studies generated by the farm crises of the 1980s, challenge assumptions of functional analysis that guided earlier works which rendered women's contribution to agriculture invisible. Parsonian functionalism assumed that families had a highly differentiated and specialized gender-based role structure in which men were responsible for task activities and women were responsible for nurturing and supportive activities. Consequently, even though agriculture was characterized as family farming, to the extent that researchers were concerned with women's farm activities they assumed that the activities were shaped by family and personal characteristics. Therefore, they hypothesized variation in women's involvement in farm economics by family composition, stage of the family cycle, and educational level; the sample population was farm wives.

However, by the 1970s, Third-World-agriculture, women-and-development, and sociology-of-agriculture literature began to influence the study of the role of women in U.S. agriculture. This research emphasized the structure of agriculture and gender relations within particular structures. At the same time, feminist scholarship drew attention to the separation of work and family, and the ideology of women's domesticity to underpin that separation. Collectively, these forces have lead to four areas of theoretical advancement: (1) consideration given to men's and women's relations to the factors of production—land, labor, capital, and management—and reproduction (Flora 1981); (2) attention to the unity of labor and ownership within the farm household (Friedmann 1981); (3) specification of men's and women's roles in relation to the organization and scale of agriculture (Sachs 1984), as well as in relation to larger social and economic forces like markets and policies (Flora 1988); and (4) consideration of the role of domestic ideology in circumscribing women's roles in agricultural production and agricultural policy development (Sachs 1984) and men's roles in family and household matters.

Examining relationships to factors of production by gender gives a better description of who is involved in U.S. agriculture and how they are involved. Two important lines of work have emerged as a result. One is the development of several typologies which show the heterogeneity of "farm women" and "farm families." For example, Pearson (1979) developed a four-part scheme including independent agricultural producers, agricultural partners, farm helpers, and farm homemakers.

A second line of research is more difficult to access as strictly a consequence. But, attention to the multicultural composition of farm women and how ethnicity may vary with relationship to productive factors seems to have been fostered by this structural and gender approach to agriculture. This approach also renews attention to social-class differentiation in U.S. agriculture. Consequently, historical and sociological studies are beginning to sort out class, race, and gender issues (cf. Jones 1985; Rosenfeld and Tiggs 1988).

Finally, this theoretical approach permits us not only to consider whether there is differential accessibility by gender but it also helps us to look at common assumptions about differential farm productivity, profitably, and viability by gender (Rosenfeld and Tiggs 1988; Salamon and Davis-Brown 1988). Rosenfeld and Tiggs found that farm productivity varies among men by marital status. Thus, the assumed importance of men's farm productivity to the farm income of couples seems to underestimate women's contributions to farm productivity.

Consideration of the unity of labor and ownership within the farm household brought new attention to the household as the unit of analysis (Flora 1981) and to the multidimensionality and nesting of women's roles in a family-farm labor system (Haney 1983). Research has concentrated in this area as scholars show the impact of farm women's on-farm labor on family-farm survival and farm-family well-being, as well as their economic contributions via earnings from off-farm employment. Again, typologies have been developed to identify composite pictures of the on-farm and off-farm work of farm men and women (Buttel and Gillespie 1984). One of the important implications of this research for agriculture is the flexibility and persistence of family-farm agriculture.

Attention to the relationship of the organization and scale of agriculture, and variation in gender roles and relations helps us to more accurately understand who moves in and out or persists in agriculture, under what conditions, and it enables us to do so cross-culturally. Sachs (1984) predicts that large-scale agriculture displaces large numbers of farm families and farm workers, fosters reliance on off-farm employment, and reduces control over production decisions. She sees the impact upon women as unduly severe because these trends are coupled with a domestic ideology that emphasizes women's domestic work and devalues their farm work and management. It points to the need to consider how the social value attached to women's work, normative prescriptions, and economic conditions affect women's allocation of their labor.

Deere and Leon (1987) followed this approach in comparing women's roles in Colombian agriculture over time, across types of structures, and by commodity. They found that large-scale production was associated with agricultural wage labor. More recently, Flora (1988) used historical and cross-cultural examples to illustrate the role product, capital, and labor markets, together with economic policies, play to limit women's agricultural options.

Taken together, the earlier and the more recent theoretical formulations help us to understand certain individual and structural factors that shape agriculturalists and agricultural families. They give us a more detailed understanding of the complexity of agricultural production and how it persists and changes. It is enough to challenge some old assumptions. Yet, there is an urgent need for more information on the historical and contemporary contributions of women, and the impact of women on policies and policies on women.

Although theoretical advances clarify many questions about women and agriculture, research needs to look both backward and forward to explore the acceptability of these theoretical arguments for farm women of various social classes, and racial and cultural backgrounds. At the same time, more theoretical attention needs to be directed at the way farm women shape the structure and politics of agriculture and rural areas.

NOTE

1. Professor Haney is with the land Tenure Center, University of Wisconsin.

REFERENCES

Bokemeier, Janet L., Carolyn Sachs, and Verna Keith. 1983. Labor force participation of metropolitan, nonmetropolitan and farm women: A comparative study. *Rural Sociology* 48 (Winter): 519–39.

Buttel, Frederick H. 1987. Social science institutions, knowledge, and tools to address problems and issues. (See Part I, Chapter 3, of this volume.)

Buttel, Frederick H., and Gilbert W. Gillespie, Jr. 1984. The sexual division of farm household labor: An exploratory study of the structure of on-farm and off-farm labor allocation among farm men and women. *Rural Sociology* 49:183–209.

Deere, Carmen Diane, and Magdalena Leon. 1987. *Rural women and state policy: Feminist perspectives on Latin American agricultural development.* Boulder, Colo.: Westview Press.

Elbert, Sarah. 1988. Women and farming: Changing roles, changing structures. In *Women and farming: Changing roles, changing structures.* Edited by Wava G. Haney and Jane B. Knowles, 245–64. Boulder, Colo.: Westview Press.

Fassinger, Polly A., and Harry Schwarzweller. 1980. Exploring women's work roles on family farms: A Michigan case study. Paper presented at the Rural Sociological Society Meeting, Ithaca, N.Y.

Flora, Cornelia Butler. 1981. Farm women, farming systems and agricultural structure: Suggestions for scholarship. *The Rural Sociologist* 1 (November): 383–86.

_____1988. Public policy and women in agricultural production: A comparative and historical analysis. In *Women: Changing roles, changing structure.* Edited by Wava G. Haney and Jane B. Knowles, 265–80. Boulder, Colo.: Westview Press.

Flora, Cornelia Butler, and John M. Stitz. 1984. Land tenure, patriarchy, and the family farm: Changes and continuities in dryland agriculture in western Kansas. Paper presented at the American Farm Women in Historical Perspective Conference, Las Cruces, N.M.

Friedmann, Harriet. 1981. The family farm in advanced capitalism: Outline of a theory of simple commodity production in agriculture. Paper presented at the annual meeting of the American Sociological Association, Toronto, Canada.

Haney, Wava G. 1983. Farm family and the role of women. In *Technology and Social Change in Rural Areas.* Edited by Gene Summers, 179–93. Boulder, Colo.: Westview Press.

Haney, Wava G., and Jane B. Knowles, eds. 1988. *Women and farming: Changing roles changing structures*. Boulder, Colo.: Westview Press.

Harris, Katherine. 1987. Homesteading in northeastern Colorado, 1873–1920: Sex roles and women's experience. In *The women's West*. Edited by Susan Armitage and Elizabeth Jameson, 165–78. Norman: University of Oklahoma Press.

Jameson, Elizabeth, 1987. Women as workers, women as civilizers: True womanhood in the American west. In *The women's West*. Edited by Susan Armitage and Elizabeth Jameson, 145–64. Norman: University of Oklahoma Press.

Jeffrey, Julie Roy. 1979. *Frontier women: The trans-Mississippi West, 1840–1880*. New York: Hill and Wang.

Jensen, Joan. 1984. Women in agricultural production: Introduction. Department of History, New Mexico State University. Photocopy.

_____1986. *Loosening the bonds: Mid-Atlantic farm women, 1750–1850*. New Haven, Conn.: Yale University Press.

Jones, Jacqueline. 1985. *Labor of love, labor of sorrow: Black women, work and the family from slavery to the present*. New York: Basic Books.

_____1988. Tore up and a movin': Perspectives on the field and family work of black and poor white women in the rural South, 1865–1940. In *Women and farming: Changing roles, changing structures*. Edited by Wava G. Haney and Jane B. Knowles, 15–34. Boulder, Colo.: Westview Press.

Jones, Lu Ann. 1984. The pursuing phantom of debt: The diary of Nannie Haskins Williams. Paper presented at the American Farm Women in Historical Perspective Conference, Las Cruces, N.M.

Knowles, Jane B. 1984. Origins of the cooperative extension service: The gender gap. Paper presented at the American Farm Women in Historical Perspective Conference, Las Cruces, N.M.

_____1988. It's our turn now: Rural American women speak out, 1900–1920. In *Women and farming: Changing roles, changing structures*. Edited by Wava G. Haney and Jane B. Knowles, 303–18. Boulder, Colo.: Westview Press.

McCarthy, Mary, Priscilla Salant, and William E. Saupe. 1988. Off-farm labor allocation by married farm women: Research review and new evidence from Wisconsin. In *Women in farming: Changing roles, changing structures*. Edited by Wava G. Haney and Jane B. Knowles, 135–51. Boulder, Colo.: Westview Press.

Miller, Lorna Clancy, and Mary Neth. 1988. Farm women in the political arena. *Women and farming: Changing roles, changing structures*. Edited by Wava G. Haney and Jane B. Knowles, 357–80. Boulder, Colo.: Westview Press.

Moore, Keith M. 1984. The household labor allocation of farm-based families in Wisconsin. Ph.D. diss., University of Wisconsin, Madison.

Myres, Sandra L. 1982. *Westering women and the frontier experience, 1800–1915*. Albuquerque: University of New Mexico Press.

Neth, Mary. 1988. Building the base: Farm women, the rural community, and farm organizations in the Midwest, 1900–1940. In *Women and farming: Changing roles, changing structures*. Edited by Wava G. Haney and Jane B. Knowles, 339–55. Boulder, Colo.: Westview Press.

Pearson, Jessica. 1979. Note on female farmers. *Rural Sociology* 44 (February): 189–200.

Rosenfeld, Rachel Ann. 1985. *Farm women: Work, farm and family in the U.S.* Chapel Hill: University of North Carolina Press.

Rosenfeld, Rachel Ann, and Leann M. Tiggs. 1988. Marital status and independent farming: The importance of family labor flexibility to farm outcomes. In *Women and Farming: Changing roles, changing structures*. Edited by Wava G. Haney and Jane B. Knowles, 171–92. Boulder, Colo.: Westview Press.

Sachs, Carolyn. 1984. *The invisible farmers: Women in agricultural production*. Totowa, N.J.: Rowman & Allanheld.

_____1985. Women's work in the U.S.: Variations by region. *Agriculture and Human Values* 2, no. 1: 31–39.

Salamon, Sonya, and Karen Davis-Brown. 1988. Farm continuity and female land inheritance: A family dilemma. In *Women and farming: Changing roles, changing structures*. Edited by Wava G. Haney and Jane B. Knowles, 195–210. Boulder, Colo.: Westview Press.

Salamon, Sonya, and Ann Mackey Keim. 1979. Land ownership and women's power in a Midwestern farming community. *Journal of Marriage and Family* 41, no. 1: 109–19.

Salant, Priscilla. 1983. Farm women: Contributions to farm and family. Mississippi State University AERR 140. Washington, D.C.: Economic Research Service.

Starr, Karen. 1984. Farm women in the nonpartisan league. Paper presented at the American Farm Women in Historical Perspective Conference, Las Cruces, N.M.

Wagner, Mary Jo. 1988. Helping papa and mamma sing the people's songs: Children in the Populist Party. In *Women and Farming: Changing roles, changing structures*. Edited by Wava G. Haney and Jane B. Knowles, 319–37. Boulder, Colo.: Westview Press.

_____1984. A question of party allegiance: The political ideology of women Populists. Paper presented at the American Farm Women in Historical Perspective Conference, Las Cruces, N.M.

Waters, William, and Charles Geisler. 1982. The changing structure of female ownership of agricultural land in the United States, 1946–1978. Paper presented at the Annual Meeting of the Rural Sociological Society, San Francisco, Calif.

Wilkening, Eugene A. 1981. Farm husbands and wives in Wisconsin: Work roles, decision-making and satisfaction, 1962–1978. R3147.1. Madison: University of Wisconsin.

Wilkening, Eugene A., and Lakshmi Bharadwaj. 1967. Dimensions of aspirations, work roles and decision-making of farm husbands and wives in Wisconsin. *Journal of Marriage and the Family* 29 (November): 703–11.

CHAPTER 5

INTEGRATION IN HOME ECONOMICS AND HUMAN ECOLOGY[1]

Margaret M. Bubolz and M. Suzanne Sontag[2]

The purpose of this paper is to stimulate discourse in the field about integration in home economics as it is evolving toward human ecology, and to serve as a basis for further discussion and action to move the field to a level of integration encompassing both diversity and unity. It is not the intent of this paper to provide a blueprint for integration but to present some underlying assumptions, meanings, and issues. A series of models building toward integration are presented. The paper is based on analysis and synthesis of assumptions, concepts, philosophical perspectives, and review of historical traditions in the field.

INTRODUCTION

Human ecology has had a diverse history, emerging from the study of ecology in the natural sciences and developing as a perspective for analysis and problem solving in several social sciences (Micklin and Choldin, eds. 1984, 51–90). One of the earliest fields to adopt a human ecological perspective was home economics. An account of this development is reported in Robert Clarke's (1973, 113–20) biography of Ellen Swallow, the first woman admitted to and to receive a degree from the Massachusetts Institute of Technology (in chemistry), the first woman MIT faculty member, the first woman faculty member of any science school, and the woman who was primarily responsible for founding the field of home ecology. In 1908, Swallow's "home ecology" was officially named "home economics."

Home economics grew out of a concern, in the latter part of the 19th century, to strengthen families and households, and out of the growing interest in applying principles of science to the home environment. Since its inception, a human ecological perspective has been implicit in home economics. The early founders of the field, constrained by biologists to refrain from labelling the field "ecology," did emphasize the interest of the profession in the study of individuals as members of families in interaction with their environment. Brown (1985), in her study of the historical and philosophical heritage of home economics, has stated that "the central concern has been rather consistently with the *family* or *home,* with the *individual* as a person whose life is influenced by the family, and with the *society* which affects and is affected by both." This statement extends the concern of the field to the reciprocal relationship between the family and society. Whereas this statement does not emphasize the total environment, it does not exclude it; historically, human-environment interactions have been of central concern to the field (Creekmore 1968). Enhancement of the well-being of families and improvement of the conditions of their existence has been a dominant value orientation of the field since its origins (Brown 1985).

During the 1960s, the concept of human ecology reemerged as a unifying philosophical perspective for home economics. Many home economics units in public and private educational institutions throughout the United States have incorporated a human ecological perspective, and a growing number have changed their name to human ecology. Examples include the Colleges of Human Ecology at Cornell University, Michigan State University, University of Maryland, University of Tennessee, and Kansas State University, and the Departments of Human Ecology at Mercyhurst College (Pennsylvania) and Marygrove College (Michigan).

Recently, integration of the concepts, theories, education, and practice in the several disciplines within home economics has surfaced as a critical need and issue in order to address effectively the practical problems of families. Given the history, present status, and anticipated future development, we focus in this paper on integration within home economics as it continues to evolve as a unified field into human ecology. It is recognized that human ecology is a very broad, comprehensive perspective that can incorporate the relationships of humans to all of their environments from the micro to the macro level. The conception of human ecology as it is evolving from home economics is a necessary part of this holistic perspective. To avoid redundancy, we will hereafter refer only to human ecology. Some of the ideas may be particular only to human ecology as it is evolving from home economics, but many of them have application to human ecology in its totality.

In this paper we do not argue that integration is needed in human ecology. Commitment to integration is assumed as a basic premise. The purpose of this paper is to stimulate discourse in the field about integration and to serve as a basis for further discussion and action to move the field to a higher level of integration encompassing both diversity and unity. It is not the intent of this paper to provide a blueprint for integration, but rather to present what we see as underlying assumptions, meanings, and issues. A series of models building toward integration within human ecology will be presented. The paper is based on an analysis and synthesis of assumptions, concepts, philosophical perspectives, and a review of historical traditions in the field.

UNDERLYING ASSUMPTIONS ABOUT HUMAN ECOLOGY

There is a basic unity underlying the field of human ecology. This unity is based on both the nature of the field and on its mission. Human ecology can be considered as both an interdisciplinary field and a profession. As an interdisciplinary field it is a branch of knowledge and learning, as an academic field it discovers new theoretical knowledge through research. However, it is not a single discipline but integrates conceptual frameworks, theoretical formulations, and methodologies used in other disciplines into new and distinct paradigms.

There is no inherent contradiction between considering human ecology as both an interdisciplinary field of study and a profession (East 1980, 3–5; 1978). Problems that arise in professional practice are interdisciplinary in nature and require integration of knowledge within an interdisciplinary field. The co-existence of the interdisciplinary field and the profession ensures the generation of the knowledge base required for solution of practical problems.

From the interdisciplinary standpoint, human ecology can be defined as the study of humans as social, physical, biological beings in interaction with each other and their physical, socio-cultural, aesthetic, and biological environments, and with the material and human resources of these environments. The uniqueness of human ecology lies in its focus on viewing humans and their near environments as integrated wholes, mutually influencing each other.

The professional dimension of human ecology flows from its mission orientation. A profession is concerned with the application of knowledge in the service of some component of society, toward a valued social end or "good."

The mission of human ecology incorporates the mission of home economics as defined by Brown and Paolucci (1978, 23):

> The mission of home economics is to enable families, both as individual units and generally as a social institution, to build and maintain systems of action which lead (1) to maturing in individual self-formation and (2) to enlightened, cooperative participation in the critique and formulation of social goals and means for accomplishing them.

The mission of human ecology extends the above mission to incorporate the global interdependence of individuals, families, and communities with the resources of natural, constructed, and behavioral environments for the purpose of wise decision making and use of resources essential to human development and the quality of life and the environment. Human ecology views the family as a major source of nurturance and renewal of its members, helping prepare them for productivity for self and society. Human ecology views the near environment as a source of essential resources and as the setting for human behavior and development.

As a profession, human ecology seeks to create and maintain an optimum balance between people and their environments. The core of human ecology is the human ecosystem: the reciprocal relations of individuals and families with their near environments. An ecological model provides a philosophical and conceptual basis for integration as both an interdisciplinary field and a profession. Integration in human ecology flows from these assumptions about its nature and mission. Before examining assumptions underlying integration in human ecology, we will first explore the meaning of integration.

THE MEANING OF INTEGRATION

The verb "to integrate" is derived from the Latin verb "integrare" which means to make whole. Several dictionaries define integration as (a) a process of making into a whole by bringing all parts together, (b) a combination and coordination of separate and diverse elements or units into a more complex and harmonious whole, and (c) a unification and mutual adjustment of diverse groups or elements into a relatively coordinated and harmonious whole.

One may also trace the meaning of integration as the concept has been used in mathematics, sociology, psychology, and nutrition. Central concepts that are common to many definitions and uses of the term "integration" are wholeness, harmonious coordination, unification or unity, sum total of, and functional relationship. Elements are summed or coordinated and unified into a gestalt through functional relationships. The whole is greater than the sum of its parts.

When viewing phenomena as integrative in nature, one could focus on the hierarchical organization of subunits within the whole and as they function in their environment. In short, a systems approach is a preferred method of analysis and synthesis.

In an expository paper on *Integration of Knowledge in Human Ecology*, Jungen (1985, 25) stated that one strategy for integration is the selection of central problems or themes around which members of the field must be able to build up an overview of the related disciplinary aspects of knowledge, handle summarized knowledge, develop constructive thinking and an ability to synthesize into a "new object for analysis." At Gothenburg University, Jungen and other faculty members attempted to develop an integrated human ecology around the central theme of humans' use of natural resources. Jungen states that:

> The unifying idea of system ecology was necessary but not sufficient to integrate the broad interdisciplinary field of knowledge. The interdisciplinary work can be characterized as an oscillation between a search for the elements of knowledge, that is working bottom-up, and the integration of these with the help of ideas from system ecology, system theory and physics, that is working top-down.

As used in this paper, integration means that we view phenomena holistically as a complex system of interdependent parts, bounded through coordinated interaction and functional relationships.

ASSUMPTIONS UNDERLYING INTEGRATION IN HUMAN ECOLOGY

In order for integration to take place, there must be something to integrate and a purpose around which to integrate. Integration in human ecology can function in a variety of ways and in differing levels and degrees. Before developing a conceptual model for integration, we found it necessary to make explicit underlying assumptions about integration in human ecology. The following are proposed in regard to this. Integration can take place:

- *On a theoretical and conceptual level of knowledge generation.* For example, theories which can help explain and understand behavior, development, and adaptation in the human ecosystem must draw upon concepts and findings from several disciplines. Theories which explain humans' use of clothing or food can be drawn from several disciplines and be integrated into a new theory. Theories specific to the structure and functioning of the human ecosystem may also be developed within the field itself, drawing on the tenets of systems ecology.
- *On an organizational level in the structure of a unit* in a college, business, or other organization in which professionals from varying specializations or disciplinary orientations are brought together toward a common focus.
- *On a programmatic level* in the development and operationalization of academic majors, courses, research, and public service programs.
- *On the level of professional practice* in which knowledge about various components of the structure and behavior of the human ecosystem are brought to bear in the solution of practical problems of individuals and families.
- *On an interpersonal level* in which individuals interact and communicate and come to have shared norms, goals, and beliefs.
- *On an intrapersonal level* in which inner consistency in one's thought and action becomes more possible and conflicts and contradictions are resolved.

In order for integration to take place on the theoretical, organizational, professional, and programmatic levels, some degree of inter- and intrapersonal integration is necessary. Within each of these kinds of levels of integration there can be degrees of integration. Different forms of integration may be required because of the different presuppositions and methodologies in the disciplines integrated in human ecology.

An integrated philosophical perspective in human ecology does not mean that there should not be specialization on the basis of component parts or by professional functions. Specialized, in-depth knowledge of components of the ecosystem is required in order to understand the functioning of the parts in relation to the whole. A division of labor is essential in any enterprise; this is true for human ecology. No one person can acquire the level of knowledge about each part that is required to accomplish the mission. This means that within the profession of human ecology there should be subprofessions. This does not, however, preclude subscription to a common goal or mission.

A MODEL FOR INTEGRATION IN HUMAN ECOLOGY

The component parts of the interdisciplinary field and profession of human ecology constitute a metasystem that

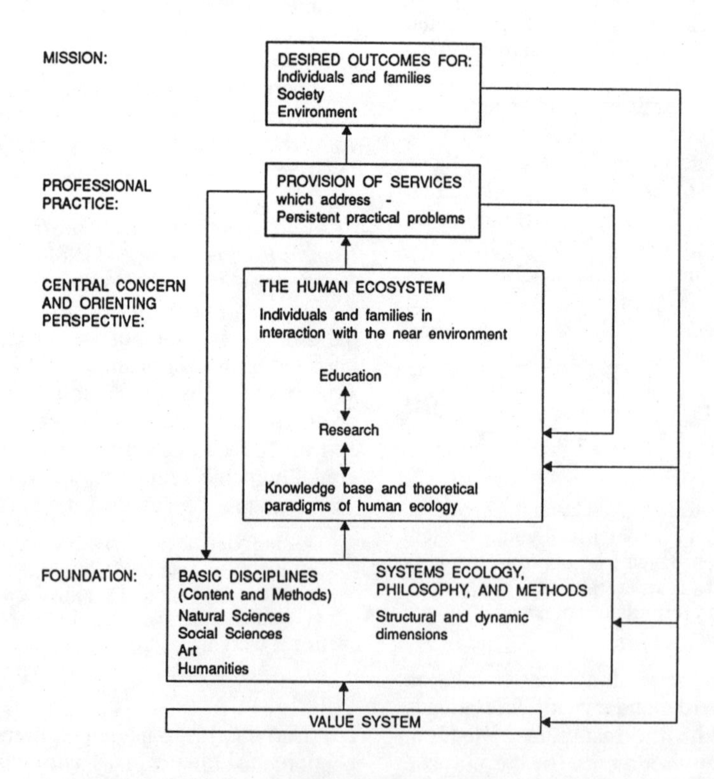

Figure 1. The metasystem of human ecology

enables one to see the relationship of the knowledge base to the professional practice and realization of mission (Figure 1). At its present state of evolution, knowledge in human ecology is rooted in a multidisciplinary base coupled with systems ecology, philosophy, and methodology. Underlying this disciplinary foundation is a system of values which implicitly or explicitly influences our knowledge, our mission, and our action. Values according to Tengstrom (1985) help to answer three critical questions in an area of study: (a) What is worth knowing? (b) Why is it worth knowing? and (c) How is it possible to know more?

The central concern and orienting perspective of the human ecosystem provide a basis for answering the first question. The structure and dynamic functioning of individuals and families in interaction with their near environment constitutes a major theoretical paradigm for knowledge in human ecology. The second question is addressed by the persistent, practical problems of individuals and families toward which the mission is directed. Knowledge in the field grows through research and professional practice, both of which help to answer the third question. Decisions about education of professionals in human ecology require answers to all three questions.

The human ecology metasystem must be viewed and work as a coordinated whole in order for effective integration to take place. Only by realizing the interrelationships among values, knowledge, education, and practice can the mission be achieved.

Kilsdonk (1983, 36–7) made the following assumptions about human ecology as it is evolving through home economics:

1. An ecological systems framework facilitates the understanding of the interrelatedness of systems.
2. The near or immediate environment of an organism is a valid delimitation of the broad concept of human ecology.
3. The home is considered a significant social and physical environment affecting human development.
4. The development of a human being is affected by and affects not only the immediate situation or system of which it is a part but all systems that directly or indirectly relate to it.
5. There is a valid need for developing an understanding of and for continued research in the interrelationships between humans and the larger environment as it emanates from the interplay of humans and their near environment.
6. The traditional subject matter areas associated with home economics (food, clothing, shelter, family, and human development) are bodies of knowledge fundamental to analyzing the effectiveness of societal systems developed to support the human existence.
7. The delimitation of human ecology to the immediate or near home and living environment does not exclude the consideration of broad-based, complex societal problems (that is, population growth, energy resources, pollution, food supply, resource distribution, etc.).

Figure 2 provides a more detailed model of a human ecosystem and identifies dimensions of individual and family systems and their environments. It is presented as an input-throughput-output model focusing on the transformation of matter-energy and information input from the environment within the unit system of study. With this perspective, one can assess the adequacy of the near environment for meeting individual and family values and goals.

By studying the transformation of input in the unit system and resultant output, one can assess the use of environmental resources and the consequences or outcomes for the unit, for society, and for the environment.

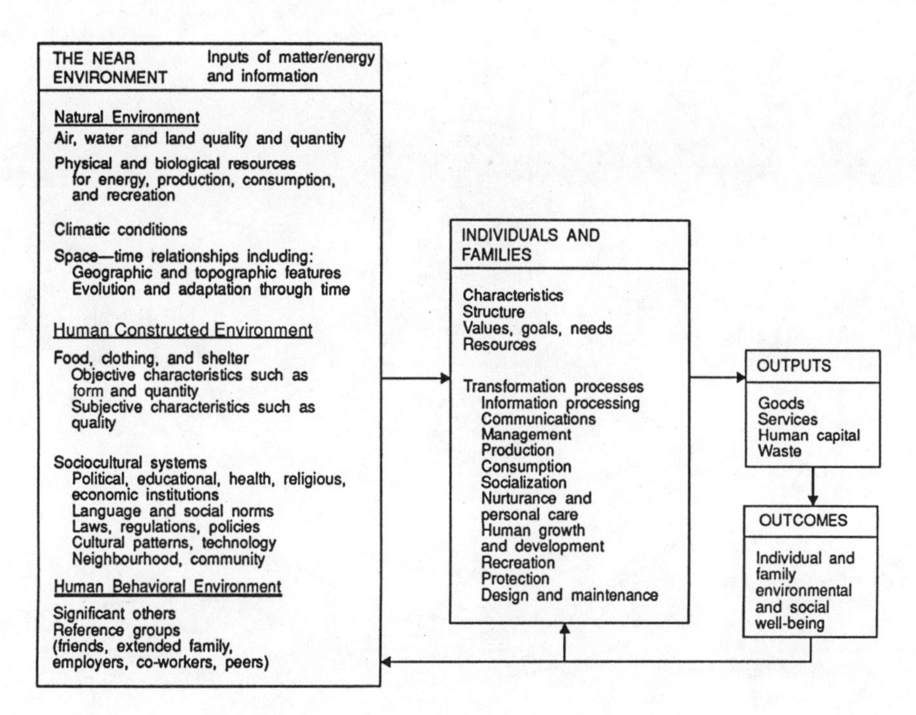

Figure 2. A human ecosystem

Individuals and families are embedded in three conceptually distinct but interrelated environments; the natural, human constructed, and human behavioral environments (Bubolz, Eicher, and Sontag 1979). These environments provide the context or setting in which individual and family activity takes place. Individuals may attach special meanings to various environmental components, and the meaning of each environmental component may differ within and across families. Environmental meanings structure human conduct with respect to each other and to the environment. Environmental meaning affects the selection of input resources and the manner of transformation.

Brown and Paolucci (1978) proposed that persistent practical problems should provide the basis for knowledge and practice in home economics. Persistent practical problems of individuals, families, and the environment derive from the structure and functioning of the human ecosystem. To identify such problems, one must examine human-environment interactions and relationships. An ecological perspective, as distinguished from a social systems perspective, must address the interactions between humans and all of their environments as these influence each other. Kilsdonk (1983, 24) has identified several complex problems of psychological health and safety, communication linkages, and the development of human potential. Although she states that the quality of the human condition is the ultimate objective, these problems "...must be viewed in the context of the dynamics of human life with a realization of the interdependency of human behavior and subsequent environment conditions."

The ecological model also provides the basis for delineation of core competencies, values, and concepts which we propose undergird the discipline and profession. By "core" we mean that all professionals in human ecology share these in common. We do not mean to imply that these necessarily require a set of "core courses" common to everyone. Certain concepts must be understood by all professionals in the field in order for them to utilize an ecological perspective in fulfillment of their contribution to the mission of human ecology. Core values, likewise, provide a common justification and motivation for action. We further believe that a core set of competencies is also necessary for the mission to be achieved. These core values, concepts, and competencies make it possible for integration to take place in education, research, or practice.

Figure 3 provides a skeleton framework for viewing the relationship between the central concern with problems of the human ecosystem and these core elements. The inner circle represents the human ecosystem of individuals and families in interaction with their near environment. Encircling this are the core values, concepts, and competencies which all subfields and all professionals should possess. Surrounding the core are various subfields or professions encompassed in the total field of human ecology. These represent traditional areas in home economics such as dietetics, interior design, child development, as well as new and emerging professions which carry out specialized functions in relation to the whole. In addition to core concepts and competencies, the various subprofessions or subfields have unique concepts and skills. For example, family policy analysis might be one of these subfields and would require in-depth understanding of public policy models and strategies and ways to determine policy impacts.

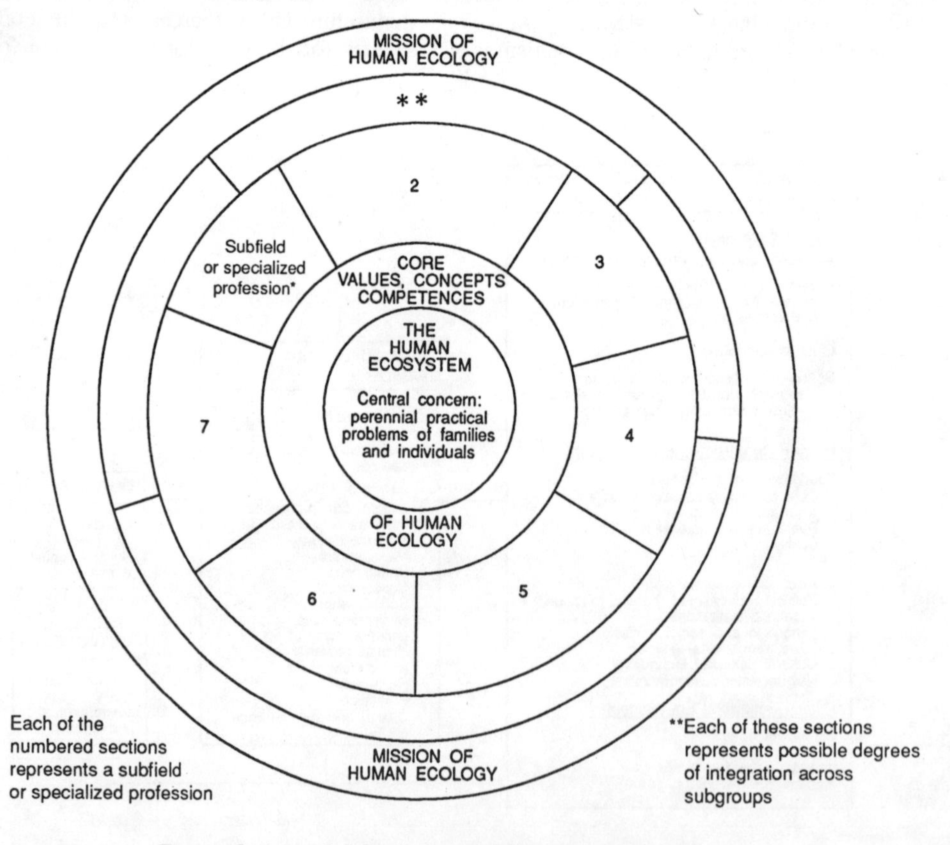

Figure 3. A model for integration in human ecology

It is emphasized that while integration can take place within each subfield, it also takes place across subfields and the total field. The overlapping segments in the next ring illustrate various degrees and permutations of integration that could occur across fields. Other patterns would, of course, be possible. For instance, the policy analyst would need to work closely with a nutritionist in order to work on policy related to hunger and feeding programs; a human development specialist would bring needed understanding of human growth and development. This example indicates that integration could take place at the level of research, education, and professional service around a significant practical problem. Surrounding the whole is the mission of human ecology which integrates the separate parts into a unified whole.

We have taken the position that human ecology has a core of concepts, competencies, and values. Some of these are shared with other disciplinary fields and professions which are also concerned with human well-being. The uniqueness of human ecology may lie not so much in individual concepts, competencies, and values, but in their interrelationships and integration in the generation and use of knowledge in service toward the mission.

In the following, we have identified what we see as some of the concepts, competencies, and values of the field and profession. We emphasize that this is a beginning list and that further discourse is required.

CORE CONCEPTS, COMPETENCIES, AND VALUES

A beginning list of core concepts includes:

GENERAL SYSTEM CONCEPTS

For example, input, throughput, output, feedback, homeostasis, morphogenesis, boundaries, interfaces, entropy, open and closed systems.

ECOSYSTEM CONCEPTS

1. Environment concepts. For example, food, clothing, shelter, form, use, design, aesthetic qualities, meaning, adequacy, resources, matter, energy, information, sociohistoric-cultural patterns, reference groups, significant others.
2. Individual/family concepts. For example, human development, human needs, family functions and structure, values, goals, transformation processes, family roles and transitions, individual life transitions, resources, decision making.
3. Interaction concepts. For example, interdependence, functional relationship, perception and response, adaptation, communication, stress, conflict, information processing, management, space-time relationships.
4. Outcome concepts. For example, quality of life, environmental quality, self-formation, social goals.

A beginning list of interrelated core competencies includes:

1. Ability to seek out and synthesize information, to see relationships among phenomena.
2. Skill in practical reasoning about what is to be done, including moral reasoning and value reasoning, i.e., ability to take value and moral judgments into account when deciding what is to be done.
3. Problem solving and decision making, including problem recognition and definition, determination of goals and alternatives, consideration of consequences, taking action, and evaluation of results.
4. Resource assessment, identification and acquisition skills.
5. Ability to communicate effectively and determine meaning in symbolic interaction.
6. Identification and clarification of values.

Some attention will need to be given to the level and complexity at which these competencies are taught and learned.

A beginning list of core values which underlie the interdisciplinary field and profession of human ecology and around which knowledge and practice can be integrated includes the following:

1. Equity and justice in social relations and in access to opportunity for optimum human development and access to resources.
2. Respect and caring for the survival, worth, and dignity of all humans.
3. Respect for the conservation and preservation of the environment, i.e., an ecological ethic.
4. Coexistence of humans in harmony with nature.
5. Adequacy of the environment for meeting human needs.
6. Work as a means to fulfillment, social and economic productivity and support.
7. Aesthetic values, e.g., beauty of environments.
8. Autonomy and independence of action and determination.
9. Cooperation in securing the common good.
10. Excellence and quality in human endeavor.
11. Health and well-being.
12. Knowledge and learning.
13. Personal and social values of trustworthiness, honesty, integrity, courage.
14. Peace at the personal, familial, and societal levels.

These values are interrelated and might be summarized in concern for, as Kenneth Boulding (1985) puts it, "human betterment."

ISSUES FOR FURTHER CONSIDERATION

As stated in the introduction, our purpose was not to provide a blueprint for integration, but instead to present a position paper and propose a conceptual model as a basis for discourse, decision, and action. Further exploration of a number of issues that we have raised is needed. These are listed below.

1. Is there agreement that human ecology is both an interdisciplinary field and a profession?
2. Is the human ecological framework the most fruitful conceptual framework for the field?
3. What levels, degrees, and forms of integration are possible and desirable in human ecology? What role does the specialist play in integration?
4. How should education in systems ecology, philosophy, and methods be acquired?
5. How should the core concepts, values, and competencies be acquired?

6. What is the relation of existing subfields to those needed in the future?
7. What kind of organizational and administrative structures and resources are needed for integration in human ecology?

FURTHER WORK NEEDED

Those in the field who are concerned with the future development of human ecology will need to continue to develop strategies to achieve integration at the organizational, programmatic, and professional practice levels. Further delineation of core concepts, values, and competencies and persistent practical problems is needed. Progress needs to continue toward building integrated theory and conducting integrative research in human ecology.

ACKNOWLEDGMENTS

The authors gratefully acknowledge the suggestions of faculty and students in the College of Human Ecology at Michigan State University. Ann Kilsdonk, Marygrove College, Detroit, Michigan, and Margaret Boschetti, Kansas State University, Manhattan, Kansas, reviewed the paper and provided insightful comments.

NOTES

1. Reprinted with appreciation and the kind permission of the *Journal of Consumer Studies and Home Economics*, 12 (1988): 1–14.

2. Margaret M. Bubolz is a professor of Family and Child Ecology, Michigan State University; and M. Suzanne Sontag is a professor of Human Environment and Design, Michigan State University.

REFERENCES

American Home Economics Assoc. 1967. *Concepts and generalizations: Their place in high school home economics curriculum development*. Washington, D.C.: American Home Economics Assoc.

AHEA. 1974–5. *Home economics—New directions II*. Washington, D.C.: American Home Economics Assoc.

Bailey, L., ed. 1985. Focus on accreditation and specializations in home economics. In *AHEA Agency Member Unit Newsletter* (Autumn). Washington, D.C.

Baugher, S. L., et al. 1985. Exploring strategies for enhancement of integration in home economics. In *Proceedings of the 1985 Chicago meeting*. St. Paul: University of Minnesota.

Belck, N. 1985. Delivering home economics information to families in developing nations: Building on the extension model. *Journal of Home Economics* 77:46–48.

Boulding, K. 1985. *Human betterment*. Beverly Hills: Sage Publications.

Brown, M. M. 1980. *What is home economics education?* Minneapolis: Minnesota Research and Development Center for Vocational Education.

———1985. *Philosophical studies of home economics in the United States: Our practical-intellectual heritage* 1:3–421. East Lansing: Michigan State University.

Brown, M., and B. Paolucci. 1978. *Home economics: A definition*. Washington, D.C.: American Home Economics Assoc.

Bubolz, M. M. 1984. Home economics and a family discipline: Relationships and implications. In *Report from the National Council on Family Relations*. St. Paul, Minn.

Bubolz, M. M., J. B. Eicher, and M. S. Sontag. 1979. The human ecosystem: A model. *Journal of Home Economics* 71:28–31.

Clarke, Robert. 1973. *Ellen Swallow: The woman who founded ecology*. Chicago: Follett Publishing Company.

Creekmore, A. M. 1968. The concept basic to home economics. *Journal of Home Economics* 60:93–102.

East, M., and J. Thomson. 1984. *Definitive themes in home economics and their impact on families: 1909–1984*. Washington, D.C.: American Home Economics Assoc.

East, N. 1978. Home Economics: A profession? A discipline? In *Proceedings of the conference on current concerns in home economics education*. Urbana-Champaign: University of Illinois.

———1980. *Home economics: Past, present and future*. Boston: Allyn and Bacon, Inc.

Hawthorne, B. E. 1983. Echoes of the past—Voices of the future. *Journal of Home Economics* 75:36–45.

Hill, R. 1983. Family studies and home economics: Towards a theoretical orientation. Paper presented at dedicatory services for the new home economics building, University of British Columbia, Vancouver.

Home economics seminar: A progress report. 1961. Washington, D.C.: American Home Economics Assoc.

Horn, M. J. 1981. Home economics: A recitation of definition. *Journal of Home Economics* 73:19–23.

Horn, M. J., and M. East. 1982. Hindsight and foresight: Basis for choice. *Journal of Home Economics* 74:10–17.

Hultgren, F. 1983. The past is prologue. *Journal of Home Economics* 75:21–23.

Jungen, B. 1985. Integration of knowledge in human ecology. *Humanekologiska Skrifter* no. 5: 25. Göteborg, Sweden: Institution für Fredsforskning och Humanekologi, Göteborgs Universitet.

Kilsdonk, A. G. 1983. Human ecology: Meaning and usage. Human Ecology monograph series no. 102. East Lansing: Michigan State University, College of Human Ecology.

Lee, J. A., and P. L. Dressel. 1963. *Liberal education in home economics*. New York: Columbia University, Teachers College.

Malmberg, T. 1985. Human ecology as part of other sciences and as discipline of its own—Some general and historical aspects. Paper presented at the Conference for the Society for Human Ecology, College Park, Md..

McFarland, K. N. 1985. *Home economics: A federation of career-oriented specializations*. St. Paul: University of Minnesota.

McGrath, E. J. 1965. The changing mission of home economics. *Journal of Home Economics* 60:85–92.

Micklin, M., and H. M. Choldin, eds. 1984. *Sociological human ecology: Contemporary issues and applications*. Boulder, Colo.: Westview Press.

Natl. Council on Family Relations (NCFR) Task Force on the Development of the Family Discipline. 1985. What is family science? Paper presented at the annual meeting of the NCFR, Dallas, Tex.

Paolucci, B. 1980. Evolution of human ecology. *Human Ecology Forum* 10:17–21.

Paolucci, B., O. A. Hall, and N. Axinn. 1977. *Family decision making: An ecosystem approach*. New York: John Wiley & Sons Inc.

Pedersen, E. L. 1984. The ecological alternative: An option for the future. *Clothing and Textiles Research Journal* 2:22–24.

Preiser, W. F. E. 1983. The habitability framework: A conceptual approach towards linking human behavior and physical environment. *Design Studies* 4:84–91.

Report of the Committee on the Future of Home Economics. 1968. East Lansing: Michigan State University.

Schoenrock, C. J. 1984. Home economics: A philosophy of integration. Paper presented at the annual meeting of the American Home Economics Association, Anaheim, Calif.

Tengstrom, E. 1985. Human ecology: A new discipline? *Humanekologiska Skrifter* no. 4. Göteborg, Sweden: Institution für Fredsforskning och Humanekologi, Göteborgs Universitet.

Vincenti, V. 1983. Antecedents of reformism. *Journal of Home Economics* 75:26–31.

Weddle, K. G. 1985. *The integrated undergraduate core curriculum in home economics*. Knoxville: The University of Tennessee.

CHAPTER 6

THE RELATIONSHIP BETWEEN INTERNATIONAL RURAL DEVELOPMENT AND INTERNATIONAL TRADE AND FINANCE

Timothy E. Josling[1]

INTRODUCTION

Not too long ago, it would have been necessary to begin a paper with this title by emphasizing the importance of international trade and financial developments on rural life. Such an introduction now seems superfluous. The case has been made extensively in recent years by writers on agricultural policy issues, and it would have been apparent to the casual observer even if the profession had chosen to ignore the matter. Among the papers given at the Social Science Agricultural Agenda Project's (SSAAP's) Phase I Workshop was an extensive treatment of the topic by Schuh (Part II, Section 2, Chapter 2) under the heading of "International Affairs and Economic Development," and similar themes were echoed by Hillman (1987) in his paper "Social Sciences in a Global Context." Schuh, in particular, has been influential in broadening the discussion of agricultural development and agricultural policy to include trade and the macroeconomic environment.

Just as it is not necessary to repeat the case for broadening the agenda, it is not sufficient to stop with a description of the ways in which trade and macroeconomic events impinge upon agriculture. The case has been accepted; the task is now to devise policies that are appropriate in the current environment, realistic in terms of their objectives, and acceptable to those most affected by their implementation. The social sciences clearly have a role to play in analyzing the situation, informing the participants of their conclusions, and exposing misleading arguments. This is a substantial agenda. In this paper, I confine my arguments to the economic dimension of the subject and, hence, focus on the agenda for the agricultural economics profession.

The paper begins with a description of why the linkages between trade, monetary, and agricultural conditions are more important and apparent now than in the past. Changes in the structures of both the domestic economy and the global economy play a role in this. The linkages themselves are discussed in two parts. The first part deals with agriculture's links with the nonfarm sector, and the second part with interagricultural links through commodity-market trade. After a brief look at the likely continuation of trends toward greater market integration, the issue of policy response is addressed. The paper ends with some tentative ideas on research priorities.

STRUCTURAL CHANGES IN AGRICULTURE AND THE WORLD ECONOMY

The world economy has been in a state of flux for the past 15 years. Commodity prices have boomed and gone bust (twice, in the case of sugar); oil prices have jumped on two occasions, causing major economic disruptions in most countries; inflation soared in the 1970s and has been brought in check by expensive policy adjustments in the 1980s; the dollar has fallen, risen, and fallen again; many countries have become heavy debtors to the world's capital markets, including some that had previously supplied capital; and trade markets have wavered between protectionist retrenchments and rapid growth. In such an uncertain world, much of the traditional economic analysis seemed to be misleading and the conventional prescriptions appeared unhelpful. Policies that had performed well in the past suddenly became an embarrassment. New policies had to be fashioned to deal with the new reality. This period presented a significant challenge to economists as well as to policy makers.

Compared with the stability and steady growth of the 18 years following the Korean War, the volatility since the early 1970s is remarkable. What is more significant is that it coincided with another development, the growing interdependence of national economies through "global" markets for goods and financial instruments. The two developments are not unconnected. For example, the emergence of an offshore capital market, the Euro-dollar market, greatly facilitated the tremendous increase in the borrowing of the 1970s and early 1980s, that, in turn, led to the present debt burden of many developing (and some developed) countries. Those markets recycled funds generated by oil price increases. The adjustment problems arising from price shocks were dissipated more widely as a result of this integrated capital market, and the market itself became more global in order to accommodate the shocks.

The development of global markets has had three main components: the expansion of trade, the integration of capital markets, and the liberalization of exchange rates. Manufactured trade in the world has expanded at a faster rate than the gross national produce (GNP) over most of the period since 1960. For many types of trade, tariff barriers around the major industrial markets are either zero or too low to act as a major impediment. Nontariff measures abound, but have not been able to halt this process. Developing countries—in particular those in Asia—have participated actively in this expansion. For developing market economies as a whole (a category used by international organizations to refer to all developing countries except the Asian centrally planned economies), manufacturing exports are now more important than primary (non-oil) commodities (Josling 1987). Asian market economies have led this trend, followed more slowly by Latin America. African countries have not participated in this trade expansion in manufactured goods, a fact that is itself a major cause of the severe economic problems in that region.

The internationalization of capital markets, both private- and public-sector borrowing and lending, has radically altered the global economy. It has been estimated that outstanding credits in the Euro-currency market reached $1.7 trillion by the early 1980s (Schuh 1984). This financial market has swamped the market for foreign exchange—traditionally needed for financing trade balances—that now has to handle enormous flows of funds among the major economies in the course of a year. One implication of this is that fiscal policy, the management of the government's budget balance, has a new significance. Once fiscal policy was mainly an internal problem; how the government balanced its books had an impact on the domestic economy but was of little interest abroad except insofar as it influenced growth rates. Now the budget deficits of the major countries are the subject of international discussion. National debt is as likely to be held by foreigners as by domestic individuals and institutions.

The third leg of the somewhat-rickety global stool is the liberalization of the foreign-exchange markets themselves. Set loose in the 1970s from the Bretton Woods constraints, exchange rates have floated—more or less cleanly—ever since. Responding as much to interest-rate differentials as to trade balances, exchange rates of the major industrial countries have been on a roller coaster. Developing countries often set their own currencies to that of one of the major countries and, hence, get taken along on the ride. Exchange-rate fluctuations, in many cases, are more important than trade barriers in determining the profitability of imports and exports. Such volatility can mask, for several years, the underlying trends in productivity and competitiveness that are supposed to determine trade flows.

In parallel with the rapid development of global markets, another development has been taking place within national economies. This process is also one of integration and interdependence. In the developing world, the transformation of agriculture from a traditional and largely self-contained sector to a participant in the larger process of exchange, either through markets or through planning decisions, has been progressing apace. All except a handful of countries, many of them in Africa, have now undergone this transformation process. Farmers provide increasingly for a market outside their own villages and regions. In turn, they purchase both productive input and consumer goods from other sectors. This market-oriented agriculture, rather than subsistence farming, is now the norm. Governments have created this environment by providing incentives, capital goods, and education; they have also relied on it to feed a growing urban population. This process has been encouraged by the newfound confidence of policy makers and economists in the ability of agriculture to provide an engine of growth.

In the older economies, an equally remarkable change has taken place, although it has been less heralded. In the mature economies, the integration of the agricultural sector with the rest of the economy has also been proceeding rapidly. Indeed, in many cases this process has reached the stage where it is no longer clear where to draw the boundaries of the agricultural sector. The proportion of the labor force in agriculture has continued to fall. In many countries, this proportion is less than the unemployment rate. Even those that remain "in agriculture" earn, in many cases, the greater share of their income from nonfarm sources. Part-time farming has become a way of life in a number of industrial countries, rather than an aberration of the urban fringe. The transporting, processing, and retailing of food is usually a larger employer of labor than farming.

The large majority of full-time farms that remain in this new agricultural sector are capital-intensive, technically sophisticated, medium-sized businesses. They pay the going wage for (nonfamily) labor, compete for capital with other businesses, and earn roughly comparable rates of return on managerial skills and equity capital. Where such management is allied to land ownership, considerable risks are involved, many of them related to the course of government policy. But the business of farming is increasingly viewed as but one of a number of competing uses for land and rural labor. In such economies, the transformation of traditional agriculture is essentially complete.

IMPLICATION OF INCREASED LINKAGES BETWEEN AGRICULTURE AND THE NONFARM SECTOR

The development of global goods and capital markets implies that events in one economy spill over into others—for good or ill. The transformation of agriculture to a market-based sector means that these influences will be felt by farmers and rural families, as well as by governments and city-based industries. The result of the combination of these trends is to pose a number of problems for both developing and developed countries' agriculture—as well as offering some new possibilities that come along with interdependence. Many of the problems arise through non-agricultural impacts on the level and stability of input and output prices. Domestic macroeconomic policy will also influence these prices and those for labor and capital. If the goods are tradeable, then exchange-rate variations will also potentially influence their price. Although these influences can be positive as well as negative, it is the adverse impacts that naturally demand more attention. A brief description of the linkage may be helpful.

Exchange-rate influences are perhaps the most pervasive and least understood links between monetary and trade developments and agriculture. The exchange rate acts as the pivot between internal economy and the external world.

Imbalances occur when this pivot is out of place. A controlled economy can sublimate exchange-rate imbalances within the trade and financial mechanisms of the state. In such circumstances, the impact of exchange rate on the domestic economy is indirect and obscure. In a closed economy, the exchange rate plays a shadowy role; it exists as a concept without any practical significance. In a colonial economy, where no independent currency exists and no autonomous monetary policy is possible, exchange rates are mere accounting conventions. But, in an independent, mixed, open economy the role of the exchange rate is crucial. As more countries opt for autonomy in economic affairs and openness in commercial relations, the exchange rate gains in importance.

The exchange rate directs the price ratio between traded goods and nontraded goods and services. Governments rarely leave such price levels entirely to the marketplace; not only the exchange rate itself but also the domestic price levels are often controlled. As with any controlled price, the secret is to choose the right level; problems rapidly build up if this price is set at an unsustainable level. Two situations are common in developing countries that illustrate the influence of inappropriate exchange rates. The first situation is where the government, in order to keep down living costs in urban areas, allows the currency to be overvalued. Reserves of foreign exchange are used, along with overseas borrowing, to pay for increased levels of imports. All domestic production of tradeable goods is, in effect, taxed. If agriculture is in a "traditional" phase, producing for a local market with little purchased input, it may be relatively unaffected by such a currency policy. In the market-oriented phase, by contrast, the overvalued currency will depress output prices of both export commodities and those that compete with imports. A number of estimates have now been made of the extent of this implicit tax on tradeable agriculture, and the results indicate that the magnitude may be very considerable (Kreuger, Schiff, and Valdes 1988).

The second situation of the exchange-rate impact on agriculture arises where the currency appreciates in value (against the major trading currencies) because of a sharp rise in export earnings. This has become known as "Dutch disease," after the impact on the Netherlands of the development of North Sea oil and gas deposits. It has been diagnosed in Indonesia, Nigeria, Venezuela, and other developing countries with oil reserves. Governments often handle favorable developments as badly as unfavorable events. A flood of foreign exchange from a boost in export earnings from one sector can cause severe disruption in other sectors. The exchange rate leads the way. Tradeable-goods prices fall, cutting the cost of food imports and the profitability of exports. Labor leaves agriculture for the towns and the jobs created by the boom. Investment in farming is curtailed and policies to stimulate rural development are undermined by the country's good fortune. In this case, in contrast to the government-inspired overvaluation, there is a legitimate economic reason for the pressure on agriculture through the exchange rate. If the new inflow of foreign exchange is stable and long-lasting, and the proceeds used wisely, then the pressure on agriculture signals the direction of long-term resource deployment; if the inflow is temporary and funds are squandered on consumption or invested unwisely, then the disruption of the rest of the economy could have very severe consequences for living standards.

The exchange rate is not the only link between trade and monetary conditions, on the one hand, and developments in a market-oriented agricultural sector, on the other. Several other "macroprices" are important. Inflation rates influence the cost of purchased input, and the government's reaction to inflation is often to peg those prices that it controls. Inflation should cause a depreciation of the exchange rate (insofar as it outpaces inflation in trading partners), that would increase the price of agricultural (tradeable) goods. But this gives the government the additional opportunity to "fight inflation" by keeping the currency overvalued.

As agriculture develops more market linkages, it becomes more susceptible to this inflationary squeeze. Interest rates are also heavily controlled by governments in an attempt to influence investment. Low official interest rates imply a capital-rationing process, that often works to the disadvantage of agricultural sectors, and to the development of high-cost informal credit systems in rural areas. In this respect, greater integration of agriculture with the nonfarm economy may reduce some of the disadvantages suffered by the sector in attracting and investing capital.

Macroeconomic conditions also impact on agriculture through the level and growth of income. This linkage is also likely to increase over time. The process of development leads to a growing domestic market for agricultural produce to be filled by imports or home production. Economic growth stimulates agricultural development in the middle-income nations, just as agricultural progress has been proved to initiate general development in the lower-income countries. Where consumption growth is halted, for instance by the need to generate a trade surplus to meet debt obligations, agriculture slows down. By contrast, in the mature industrial economies, the influences of growth on agricultural demand tends to decline as the share of income spent on foodstuffs becomes low.

Other factors influence the agricultural sector to an increasing extent with the growing market orientation. One such factor is the level of protection on nonagricultural imports. Such protection has three effects on agriculture: it raises the prices of imported inputs for the farming and processing sector; it lowers the purchasing power of incomes from agriculture; and it causes an appreciation of the exchange rate that acts as a tax on tradeable goods, as explained above. Restriction of the availability of foreign exchange is often used in conjunction with tariffs and import quotas, and has similar effects. Available foreign exchange in such a system often goes to more "modern" sectors of the economy. The acceptance of agriculture and food processing as legitimate growth sectors can minimize this effect, as can a move towards the removal of trade barriers in developing countries.

The combination of overvalued currencies, scarce foreign exchange, anti-inflationary price controls, and capital rationing has often put agriculture at a severe disadvantage. Sector-specific policies often aimed at the improvement of marketing have usually not been enough to offset these macroeconomic impacts. The increased market orientation of agriculture has highlighted these issues. Governments are taking steps to ameliorate the negative and emphasize the positive linkages. Much of their success lies in their own hands; an important part is influenced by conditions in the world agricultural markets. These, too, have undergone dramatic changes of the past 15 years.

IMPLICATION OF INCREASED LINKAGES AMONG AGRICULTURAL SECTORS IN THE WORLD ECONOMY

As countries develop, they typically make more use of international markets, to both export and import. This seems to be true of agricultural trade as well as other types of goods. Imports of agricultural products now exceed exports for developing countries as a whole, but several countries have had success in developing agricultural export markets. This expanded use of trade brings with it significant new problems for governments. Among the most important of these is the level and stability of world prices for agricultural products. This price level is itself a function of government policy decisions in the major trading countries. The high level of integration of domestic agriculture in the economy of industrial countries coupled with the phenomenon of global markets has turned once parochial issues of farm support into major international political and economic concerns.

This linkage of sectors and policies through world markets can be illustrated with a few examples. The cereals market situation has perhaps the most relevance for the majority of developing countries as well as being a key commodity in industrial country policy. Cereal trade expanded rapidly in the 1970s as a result of the process of growth and development, stimulated, in particular, by years of harvest failures in certain importing countries. Government programs encouraged an expansion of investment in cereal production, and financial institutions stepped in with the necessary capital. Land prices soared as farmers, convinced that the future was assured, sought to expand their holdings. Trade volumes peaked in 1982 when world markets were hit by recession, debt problems, and increased production in importing regions. Output continued to climb in the face of slack demand, leading to depressed prices, expensive bail-out measures, and high levels of stocks. The struggle for market shares led to further disregard for GATT (General Agreement on Tariff and Trade) rules on export subsidies. The twin processes of domestic and international agricultural policy reform now underway is the direct result of the disarray in cereals and related markets.

Disharmony can spread rapidly between sectors and into other commercial areas. The case of cassava pellets from Thailand is a well-known example. In order to protect wheat producers, the European Community (EC) increased the levies on corn in the early 1970s. This led German and Dutch feed compounders to substitute a mixture of soybean meal and cassava for the grain in animal rations. The Community negotiated a series of "voluntary" export quotas in 1982 with the major suppliers, of which Thailand was the largest. By this time, compounders had already begun to turn to corn gluten as the source of starch to balance the high-protein oilseed meal. A ready supply was available from the corn wet-milling industry as a by-product of the production of ethanol. Attempts by the EC to limit these imports provoked a heated reaction from the United States.

Arousing even stronger U.S. opposition have been attempts by the EC to tax vegetable oils within the Community in order to preserve the market for butter, and prevent the further deterioration in the market for olive oil. The simmering trade war between the United States and the EC nearly boiled over on the issue of Spanish accession to the Community that threatened a reduction in U.S. grain sales into southern Europe. Japanese agricultural policies arouse almost as much hostility in the United States as do EC policies. Even United States-Canadian relations have been put to the test on occasion, as when the Canadian courts found enough evidence of "dumping" to justify putting a countervailing duty on corn imports from the United States.

The world markets for dairy and sugar are perhaps those where the influence of domestic farm-support policies are the most pervasive—with rice and beef close behind. With few exceptions, producers of these products face the artificial prices of government programs rather than the much lower world price. The market is made by the willingness of governments to pay export subsidies to remove their surplus stocks and output, and by the unwillingness of all but a few importers to open up the door to these surpluses.

POLICY ISSUES ARISING FROM THE LINKAGES

This uncertain trade environment poses particular problems for developing countries. The "new" agricultural policies, that emphasize producer incentives and a market orientation, come face-to-face with those of the industrial countries. Export possibilities are severely constrained by both the surplus production from exporting developed countries and by the protective policies of devalued importers. However, the prospects for change in national policies seem, at present, to be better than for many years, though such developments are still not by any means assured. Countries are finding the combination of the budget cost at home and the displeasure of trading partners abroad is making the notion of reform politically acceptable. The Uruguay round of GATT trade negotiations includes agriculture as a centerpiece, as governments attempt to coordinate their policy changes.

The changes fall under two headings: the *decoupling* of domestic income support from price incentives, and the *recoupling* of domestic prices with world prices. Decoupling is necessary to allow countries that have pressing political or economic reasons to transfer income to particular groups of producers, to fulfill these obligations without imposing a cost on trading partners. Such notions face an uphill struggle. They typically involve bringing farm program costs out into the open and placing the burden on the taxpayer. They also imply selective assistance to farmers, with the implication that such rights to income support have to be argued on merit whenever policies are under scrutiny. The politics of such decoupled policies is so different from that of the commodity-based price support schemes that the transition will not be smooth.

The case for recoupling with international markets is equally compelling. Countries will, no doubt, continue to manage domestic agricultural markets to some degree even if income support is removed as a major objective. If their domestic price levels can keep in touch with those on international markets, this market management will be made easier and less costly. A policy of limited stabilization, through storage schemes, is often consistent with domestic and trade objectives. A fixed domestic price unrelated to movements abroad is both costly domestically, and disruptive to world markets.

This twin goal might have seemed merely a pipe dream a few years ago. It was, however, the main thrust of the agricultural component of the Punta del Este agreement that launched the Uruguay round of GATT negotiations. It has since been supported by declarations from the Economic Summit and the OECD (Organization for Economic Cooperation and Development). In 1987, both the EC and the United States, along with the Cairns Group, tabled suggestions for negotiations on agriculture in the Uruguay round that laid out precisely such objectives and the means of achieving them. Though neither the U.S. administration nor the EC Commission have entirely sold their proposals to their own domestic interests, the ideas have formed the basis for negotiations with the GATT.

Developing countries have an interest in the outcome of this process in at least two respects. First, any negotiated agreement on domestic price policies will alter, possibly dramatically, the world market for temperate-zone agricultural products. Prices will tend to be higher and probably more stable if the agreement binds and reduces support levels. If there is no agreement, the chances are that the world market for many of these products will move towards one of managed trade, with agreed trade shares for the major exporters, and managed prices, to protect national budgets. In such an environment, developing countries will have less opportunity to emerge as exporters and lose much of their freedom as importers.

Second, international discussions on global monetary arrangements will also have major impacts on developing countries. The largest industrial countries are exploring ways to implement the increased coordination of macroeconomic policies that will help to stabilize financial and foreign-exchange markets. If these coordination policies work, then the tasks of developing countries will be made easier. Without an increase in stability, the percent commitment to liberal trade and flexible exchange rates may evaporate. Under these conditions, developing countries may find themselves having to form closer alliances with individual industrial countries as a way of preserving at least some of the gains from trade.

RESEARCH PRIORITIES

The research agenda suggested by the arguments in this paper is both broad and deep. At the level of disciplinary research, it is clear that we do not know enough about the behavior of complex political/economic systems, whether it be the international monetary system or the agricultural trade arena. Fundamental issues need to be resolved before one can confidently point to ways in which governments can improve the stability of these systems. One such issue is that of the relationship between stability and interdependence. One would expect the establishment of global markets to impart stability to a system, when compared with separate regional or national markets. Shocks would be more widely dissipated. It is not clear that this has happened in either agriculture or the general economic sphere. Is this an illusion, or does government behavior change in the presence of a global market, to take advantage of new opportunities for "exporting" instability? How does one measure the externalities inherent in such antisocial government policies? Can one "internalize" these externalities so as to prevent "misuse" of world markets? Or is instability just the price one pays for the income-enhancing effects of specialization and the benefits from global access to capital? Economists working in the area of international trade and monetary theory can contribute to our understanding of the new global markets and of the implications of greater economic intimacy among countries. Policy-coordination issues bring into play the areas of systems analysis and decision theory.

In terms of subject-matter research, there are a number of emerging issues with respect to the role of government policy in an open and unstable environment. Economists preach the virtues of exploiting comparative advantage; in practice, that concept is not easy to pin down. It assumes a recognizable world price level to use as a yardstick and a reasonable idea as to domestic costs. Forecasts of world market prices, for a long enough period into the future to allow for investment decisions to bear fruit, require projections of exchange-rate movements and national policies, as well as the more traditional supply and demand trends. Such calculations are difficult, even when basic information is available.

One line of research might focus on the set of problems facing governments when trade and monetary conditions change rapidly. What constitutes a "safe" trade policy for agriculture? How much risk is involved in pursuing an "open" policy for agriculture? Risk analysis in project appraisal is, of course, well established; risk analysis in trade and agricultural policy is less common. Models that include both domestic monetary variables and foreign-trade conditions would be needed, and these, in turn, should be linked (formally or in an ad hoc way) with broader models of the macroeconomic environment and of world agricultural trade. Simulations of outcomes, under certain sets of macroeconomic and trade conditions, would lay the groundwork for agricultural policy choices in the new environment.

Such policy simulation exercises presuppose a body of information on the quantitative impact of current and past macroeconomic and trade policies. A major study conducted by the World Bank on the political economy of agricultural policies in developing countries will fill in some of the gaps in our knowledge. This study covered some 20 countries and involved the calculation of income and output effects of agricultural policies over the past quarter-century—including the unintentional impacts of exchange-rate disequilibria and commercial policy. Some preliminary results are given in a paper by Kreuger (1988).

These policies studies tend to focus on the impact of government actions on national commodity markets. Another approach takes as the object of enquiry a farming system, or other microeconomic unit, and examines the effect of policies at that level. Private and social costs of input, factors, and output are analyzed to give private and social profits. Conclusions are then drawn about the impact of various policies, including macroeconomic factors, on farm profits. Clearly, there is some cost to the extra detail; putting together the information from enough "representative" systems to be able to answer aggregate questions is costly and time consuming. But as a complement to the market-level studies, these analyses are proving to be of considerable value. USAID and the World Bank, together with some of the international agricultural research centers, are pursuing this line of investigation (Pearson, Josling, and Falcon 1986). At some stage, there will be a research payoff to combining elements of farm-level and sector-level research in a policy model, just as there have been interesting attempts to combine agricultural-sector analyses with broader computable general equilibrium models (Heytens 1987).

These models and types of analyses are aimed at improving decision making in developing countries, although there is no reason why similar approaches should not be taken to changes in developed-country policy. In that area, the research priorities are somewhat different. Policy makers need assistance in two areas in particular. The first is the question of the trade impacts of national policies. In this regard, the major study by the OECD, that carefully measured the subsidy equivalent of national policies and evaluated their trade impact, paved the way for the proposed policy changes (OECD 1987). Other studies, such as those by Tyers and Anderson, USDA and IIASA, have added greatly to our knowledge on international transmission of policy effects (Tyers and Anderson 1988; Parikh et al. 1988). The task is now to refine these analytical studies to be able to answer the queries of policy makers on such basic issues as whether U.S. cereal programs (including target prices and set-asides) actually increase or decrease production. Similarly, the output effect of Canadian stabilization policies is also a matter of dispute. Framing rules for controlling the negative impacts of domestic policies would be easier if we knew more about the link between income support and commodity output.

The second agenda item is the need to develop domestic policy alternatives consistent with better trading rules. It is easier to talk about decoupled policies than to define them. Are "pure" transfer and stabilization policies possible? If not, how does one measure the degree of decoupling? Might decoupling involve more rather than less government intervention if output effects are to be eliminated? Are there other ways of negating or internalizing the external effects of national policies?

As the GATT round proceeds, these issues will be of interest to both developed and developing countries. The focus of the negotiations will be on framing rules within which domestic policy can operate. This will be possible only if countries can develop alternative policies to meet domestic objectives. Developing countries have a clear interest in the improvement of the performance of world agricultural markets, but they also will be affected by the trade rules in other ways. As actual or potential GATT members, developing countries will be under pressure to revise their own policies in the light of an agreed-upon set of trading rules, unless blanket exceptions are granted. In the longer run, the outcome of the GATT round may have as profound an impact on rural development as on the more obvious issue of industrial-country trade conflicts.

NOTE

1. Timothy E. Josling is with the Food Research Institute, Stanford University.

REFERENCES

Heytens, Paul. 1987. *Egyptian agricultural policy in a general equilibrium framework: Surviving the short run.* Ph.D. diss., Stanford University.

Hillman, Jimmye S. 1987. Social sciences in a global context. In *Proceedings of Phase I Workshop, SSAAP.* Compiled by Neill Schaller.

Josling, Timothy E. 1987. The changing role of developing countries in international trade. In *Poverty, development and food.* Edited by Edward Clay and John Shaw. London: Macmillan.

Kreuger, Anne. 1988. Some preliminary findings from the World Bank's project on the political economy of agricultural pricing. Invited papers 1 and 20. International Conference of Agricultural Economists, Buenos Aires.

Kreuger, Anne, Maurice Schiff, and Alberto Valdes. 1988. Impact of sector-specific and general economic policies towards agriculture. *World Bank Economic Review* (September).

Organization for Economic Cooperation & Development. 1987. *National policies and agricultural trade.* Paris: OECD.

Parikh, Kirit S., et al. 1988. *Towards free trade in agriculture.* Laxenberg, Austria: International Institute for Applied Systems Analysis.

Pearson, Scott, Tim Josling, and Walter Falcon. 1986. *Food self-reliance and food self-sufficiency: Evaluating the policy options.* Washington, D.C.: Aurora Associates.

Schuh, G. Edward. 1984. Future directions for food and agricultural trade policy. *American Journal of Agricultural Economics* 66.

Tyers, Rodney, and Kym Anderson. 1988. Liberalizing OECD agricultural in the Uruguay round: Effects on trade and welfare. *Journal of Agricultural Economics* 30, no. 2.

CHAPTER 7

FARM (INCLUDING HOME), AGRIBUSINESS, AND CONSUMERS: AGENDAS AND CONCLUSIONS

Farmers and their wives and children, agribusiness people, and consumers are of core concern for rural social sciences. Along with the institutions with which they are affiliated and their natural- and manmade-resource bases, they make up the domestic U.S. food and fiber complex. The U.S. population is provided with a bountiful and low-cost food supply and, as an integral part of world agriculture, the United States is increasingly one of the most important suppliers of food and fiber. The agricultural sciences—physical, biological, and social—along with their associated research, teaching, and extension-service activities, have played a crucial role in these phenomenal developments, and they have even more important roles to play in the future.

Although the world food situation is manageable, serious problems remain for farmers and their families, agribusiness people, and consumers that require rural and basic social science as well as physical agricultural science input. Even in such a developed, affluent country as the United States, burdensome public debt, military expenditures, and balance-of-payment problems have reduced the ability of low-income people to meet their nutritional needs. Our farmers must deal on a first-hand basis with the fragility of our natural resource base and the vulnerability of our food chain. These three groups—farmers and their families, agribusinesses, and consumers—face problems with our expensive price support, production control, subsidy, and trade policies and institutions that require research, and educational and regulatory attention.

The appraisals of various dimensions of food and agriculture relating to farmers, farm families, agribusiness people, and consumers; the commissioned papers presented in previous chapters; and the deliberations of the large interdisciplinary group of agricultural and general social scientists that attended the two national SSAAP conferences have led to the agendas presented here. These focus mainly on the needs of farmers and their families, agribusiness people, and consumers, with attention to policies and institutions that affect these groups. Additional social science agendas for agricultural technical advance, human capital formation, other institutional changes, and the enhancement of natural and manmade resources are found in the four sections of Part III that deal with the four driving forces for farm and rural improvement.

As explained in Part I, at the SSAAP Phase I Spring Hill Conference, work groups were organized around SSAAP's major areas of concern. In turn, reports of those work groups determined in major part the structure of SSAAP's Phase II conference. The Phase I work group report presented in Part I concerning farm, agribusiness, and consumers respecified the areas of concern with respect to these participants in the food and fiber system as: (1) globalization of agriculture; (2) structural change in rural America; (3) farm and agribusiness management; and (4) homes, families, food and nutrition. Consequently, work groups were established at the SSAAP Phase II Houston Conference for each of these areas of concern. Reports of participants in these work groups are summarized below. Two other work groups at the Houston conference dealt with the farmer, agribusiness, and consumer aspects of two crosscutting areas: (1) databases for agriculture that support the work of rural social sciences; and (2) ethics in food, agriculture, and public policy. While portions of this chapter present specific crosscutting agendas with respect to databases and ethics for farmers and their families, agribusinesses, and consumers, more general aspects of these two crosscutting areas of concern are summarized in Part IV, Sections 1 and 3.

The remainder of this chapter consists of (1) work-group agenda reports from SSAAP's Houston conference, and (2) additional agendas and conclusions developed by SSAAP's editorial group since the Houston conference, as that group has tried to fill gaps and reconcile the inconsistencies revealed by difficulties experienced with the organization of the Houston conference.

ABRIDGED WORK GROUP REPORTS FROM SSAAP'S HOUSTON CONFERENCE

At Houston, there were eight work groups within the area labeled "Farming, Agribusinesses, and Consumers" that were coordinated by James Hildreth, Director, Farm Foundation. It was understood that farming included farm households and that price support, subsidy, production control, international trade, and monetary policies relevant for commercial agriculture were to be included. The abridged work group reports follow.

WORK GROUP ON U.S. AGRICULTURAL POLICIES, NATIONAL ECONOMIC POLICIES, AND INTERNATIONAL TRADE

Leader: David Blandford, Professor, Department of Agricultural Economics, Cornell University

Invited members (some of whom may not have participated) Harry Baumes, Bob Bohall, Tom Hady, William Hudson, Mel Lerohl, and Kelly White.

The environment facing agriculture has changed dramatically during the last two decades. Agricultural markets have become increasingly global and interdependent. The sector has become more integrated into both the domestic and the international economies. These developments have increased the sensitivity of the U.S. agricultural sector to changes in the global economy and to global macroeconomic policies.

The rural social sciences should work to:

- Increase public understanding of the globalization of agricultural markets, international comparative advantage and competitiveness in farm products, and the economic and social implications of such market integration for United States agriculture.
- Raise public awareness and knowledge of the ways in which agricultural and trade policies are formed and implemented in the United States and foreign countries.
- Identify implications of global income growth and the macroeconomic policies of nations around the world for U.S. agriculture and rural areas.
- Upgrade the ability of social science extension educators and other professionals to analyze and teach U.S. farmers and nonfarmers about the globalization of agriculture—this should be done through international collaborative research, teaching, language training, data development, and improved communication among social scientists.
- Improve the public's and the policy makers' understanding of the current and prospective changes in the structure of America's food and fiber system; the influence of such changes on the distribution and ownership of wealth, and opportunities for farm and rural nonfarm people; and the implications of these changes for food marketing, agribusinesses, and consumers.
- Help policy makers by identifying alternative commodities and activities with potential to enhance the well-being of rural people who can no longer depend solely on their usual agricultural products for their incomes.
- Increase knowledge and understanding of the likely comparative advantages of states and regions by examining geographic shifts in agricultural production, processing, and consumption due to new methods of producing farm products and marketing services; changes in the availability and costs of irrigation water and other production inputs; and changes in international trade, public policies, lifestyles, and income levels.
- Assess the impacts of structural changes in agribusiness industries on farmers' access to input and product markets, the effectiveness of competition at various levels in the food system, and their implications for market performance, as well as policies to alleviate undesired outcomes.
- Assist policy makers and the agricultural industry by increasing knowledge and facts on how consumers decide what food products to buy, how nutrition information influences those decisions, and how food corporation executives and supermarket managers decide what to offer for sale.
- Raise understanding of policy makers, regulators, and the agricultural industry of how price and cost changes are transmitted up and down the food system.
- Determine ways in which consumers, producers, and marketing firms evaluate, adjust to, and manage risks that affect them—such as food-borne disease and quality risks facing consumers, changes in farm programs affecting farmers, and volatile price risks confronting marketing firms.

WORK GROUP ON STRUCTURAL CHANGE IN RURAL AMERICA

Leader: Lyle Schertz, Agricultural Economist, ERS, USDA.

Invited members (some of whom may not have participated) James C. Barron, Ralph Christy, Mark Drabenstott, James Houck, Lester V. Manderscheid, Bruce Marion, Les Meyers, David Mulkey, Harry K. Schwarzweller, Jerry Skees, and Dale Stansbury.

Fundamental structural changes are occurring throughout the food and fiber system that impact agricultural producers, providers of farm input, processors and handlers, and consumers. The magnitude of the required adjustments is increased by the deregulation of financial, communication, and transportation industries; shifts towards a service-based economy; the agricultural financial crisis; farm production capacity greater than demand; technical change; and changing consumer demands for food products. At the same time, structural changes within food processing and delivery systems pose questions regarding market performance, food quality, and the health and safety of food products. The complexity of these structural changes requires multidisciplinary endeavors to understand their causes and effects. The following research, extension, and teaching agendas were identified by the work group. The rural social sciences should:

- Improve our understanding of the structure of the nonfarm rural economy to help develop superior, more comprehensive and better-integrated information systems and better estimates of the effects of economic, social, political, and governmental forces on the welfare of farm and nonfarm rural people, the delivery of rural community services, and the generation and utilization of the capabilities of rural people.

- Develop an improved understanding of, and anticipate how, social, political, economic, and governmental forces are changing the structures of farming, the food marketing system, rural communities, and consumption.
- Examine the geographic shifts that are occurring and anticipate future geographic shifts in agricultural production and processing as a result of technical advances (especially biogenetic advances) and changes in consumer preferences, supply and cost of key inputs (e.g., water), international trade, and public policies and programs.
- Assess the impact of structural change in agribusiness industries on the farmers' access to input and product markets, the effectiveness of competition at various levels in the food system, and the effects on market performance and evaluate private and public alternatives to deal with market access and/or competition issues.

WORK GROUP ON PRODUCTIVITY AND DEVELOPMENT OF U.S. AGRICULTURE

Leader: Fred Buttel, Professor, Department of Rural Sociology, Cornell University.

Invited members (some of whom may not have participated) Kenneth Dahlberg, Michael J. Phillips, Hope Shand, and D. Michael Warren.

Rural social scientists need to:

- Increase their capacity to identify, assess, and evaluate the potential implications that changes in climate, energy supplies, resource prices, policies, and biological trends (such as the loss of genetic and biological diversity) have on rural people and the productivity of American agriculture.
- Identify and evaluate the origins, processes, adoptions, and impacts of technical advances in the food system. For this task and for the recommendation listed immediately above, efforts are needed that would involve multidisciplinary teams of agricultural, biological, physical science, agro-ecosystem, agro-forestry, and, of course, social science scholars. Extension and resident instruction professionals should teach the implications of these changes to appropriate clientele groups, students, and future social and technical agricultural scientists.
- Help policy makers and the administrators of research and educational institutions to increase their knowledge and understanding of the social, political, and economic forces driving agricultural research and educational institutions, and help assess the capabilities of research, extension, and teaching institutions to adapt to change and respond to the needs of their diverse constituencies. (Also see Part V on needed research on social science administration and funding.)
- Investigate and design institutions for controlling the tendencies for market-controlled agricultural sectors and subsectors to outproduce effective demand, at prices that do not permit full recovery of expenditures and investments by individual farmers and society as a whole.
- Increase the available facts and understanding of "alternative farming systems" that have the potential to be economically, socially, and environmentally sustainable at broadly optimal levels, taking into account nonmarket adverse and beneficial impacts on human and animal health and natural resources, and help to identify policies and educational programs necessary to support such systems. (In this connection, see Part III, Section 3, for additional agenda items on resource enhancement and growth in capital bases.)
- Assist the public decision makers to make better assessments of the sources of growth (or decline) in American agricultural productivity and output, and of the consequences of changes in the nonfarm food system. (Also see the four sections of Part III that deal with the four driving forces.)
- Raise the public understanding of the international dimensions of transfer of production methods that change productivity and promote agricultural development, including knowledge of global agricultural research, and the relationships *between* the transfer of genetic resource and technical advances among nations, *and* the implications for the comparative advantage and international competitiveness of U.S. agriculture. (Also see Part III, Section 2.)

WORK GROUP ON FARM AND AGRIBUSINESS MANAGEMENT

Leader: Steven Sonka, Professor, Department of Agricultural Economics, University of Illinois, Urbana.

Invited members (some of whom may not have participated) Bernie Erven, Cornelia Butler Flora, Art Fogerty, Christina Gladwin, Erwin H. Johnson, Eugene Jones, Robert King, Kerry Litzenberg, Ridgely Mumin, Wesley Musser, Claudia Parliament, Randy Westgren, and Robert Zabawa.

Rural social scientists should:

- Assist farm firm and household decision makers by analyzing and interpreting the impacts on these groups of changes in the business and social environments, technology, and labor and capital markets.
- Assess the technical, institutional, and marketing-information needs of farm, agribusiness, and household managers, and then develop and test effective prototype information systems to meet those needs.
- Help improve the conditions of the self-employed in farm and rural nonfarm households by increasing the understanding of the linkages between the firm and household aspects of selfemployed households, and how those linkages influence household production and family well-being, as well as farm production.
- Increase understanding of the changes in goals, values, and skills of the different types of farm and home

managers, and help develop improved teaching and extension programs that include educational targeting, consulting, new electronic techniques, and continuing education through agricultural, home-economics, and business schools.

- Assess the effectiveness of present teaching and extension programs in reaching older and part-time farmers and homemakers.
- Evaluate the similarities and differences among decision-making processes, rules, and strategies that are used by farm firms, households, agribusinesses, and rural nonfarm firms, and then develop improved support tools and methods of analysis to strengthen and extend the capabilities of the relevant managers for analysis, planning, and control.
- Enhance management skills by instituting additional on-campus instruction and off-campus extension programs that place expanded emphasis on the managerial skills and procedures in producing farm products; managing households, home consumption, and families; marketing; handling financial risks; and dealing with people.

WORK GROUP ON HOMES, FAMILIES, FOOD, AND NUTRITION

Leader: Sue S. Coates, Chair, Department of Consumer Resources and Technology, Western Michigan University.

Invited members (some of whom may not have participated) Howard Barnes, Robert P. Boger, W. Keith Bryant, Karen E. Craig, Diane K. Flynn, Robert Griffore, Jeanne Hafstrom, John Murray, Mary Ann Paynter, Judy Powell, Jean D. Skinner, and Eileen van Ravenswaay.

Rural social scientists should:

- Identify, assess, and improve the educational, counseling, and other strategies families can use to manage institutional, technical, human, and resource changes as employment and incomes change the level and incidence of rural poverty, reduce the relative importance of farm income in rural households, influence substance abuse, increase outmigration of the young, increase marital disruptions, affect teenage pregnancy, and create family stress.
- Assess the changes needed in the public and private support systems for the families in rural America including education, food entitlements, retraining, health, nutrition education, child care, elderly care, rural transportation, employment service, and family planning.
- Assist those who design and administer the educational programs and family support systems by identifying and measuring the determinants of consumer behavior and demand with respect not only to food, nutrition, and clothing, but also to public and private family-support services.
- Increase the understanding of household decision processes, information management, risk bearing, and preference development as they relate to farming, family finances, and nonfarm employment.
- Improve food-safety knowledge and education.

Crosscutting Areas of Concern

As indicated in the introduction, two work groups at the SSAAP Houston conference dealt with the farmer, agribusiness, and consumer aspects of two crosscutting areas of concern: (1) data and analysis systems for agriculture, and (2) ethics in food, agriculture, and public policy. Though SSAAP had a third crosscutting interest in the roles of the basic social science disciplines, there was no work group for that interest in the domestic farming, agribusiness, and consumer area.

WORK GROUP ON DATABASES FOR FARMING, AGRIBUSINESS, AND CONSUMERS

Leader: Leroy Hushak, Professor, Department of Agricultural Economics and Rural Sociology, Ohio State University.

Invited members (some of whom may not have participated) Richard Allen, Deb Brown, Dean T. Chen, and Charles Paulter.

The rural and basic social sciences should support efforts to:

- Improve the databases on rural America by including more data on the employment patterns, skills, and capabilities of rural people and on the rural market structures.
- Increase the knowledge of the food industry beyond the farm front gate and of the input industries behind the farm back gate by developing the databases on such subjects as state/regional comparative advantage; concentration ratios; food safety and quality; inputs such as pesticides, fertilizers, and toxic substances (for use in addressing problems of ground and surface water contamination); worker safety; biological impacts; and the like.
- Improve farm, home, and family-management recordkeeping and accounting services either inside or outside the land-grant system, as deemed appropriate on a state-by-state basis. Additional attention should be devoted to the advantages of coordinating the generation and use of microdata from these systems at the national level.
- Develop a comprehensive, integrated information system that is focused on the rural nonfarm economy in order to support work that is related to better understanding the economics of part- and full-time farm people and their communities. This should include state- and nationwide rural household surveys to provide needed information on household employment, income, and other characteristics.

WORK GROUP ON ETHICS IN PUBLIC CHOICE AND PRIVATE DECISION MAKING

Leader: Bobby R. Eddleman, Director, Texas A&M University Agricultural Research and Extension Center.

Members: James Bonnen, Joseph Havlicek, Richard Haynes, Jean Kinsey, Harry Kunkel, and Loren Tauer.

The following are major ethical issues confronted by farmers, agribusinesses, and consumers that require research by rural social scientists and subsequent extension, resident instruction, advising, consulting, administrative, and entrepreneurial efforts.

- For farming and agribusiness, some important ethical issues include:
  - Animal wastes
  - Animal welfare
  - Food processing wastes
  - Farm workers health and safety
  - Sedimentary runoffs
  - Regenerative and low-input agriculture
  - Groundwater contamination
  - Agribusiness practices
  - Market concentration, structural change, and antitrust policy
  - Gender inequities and inequalities
  - The redistributive impacts of farm commodity and other agricultural programs and policies
  - Private-sector funding of public-sector research
  - Release of technically advanced inanimate input
  - Research, release, and patenting of biologically engineered plants, animals, and biologicals
- For consumers, some important ethical issues and problems include:
  - Alteration of food characteristics as they affect food quality and standards
  - Sale or donation abroad of agricultural inputs and food of lower quality and safety than is legally permitted in the United States
  - Food safety and food-chain contamination
  - Water quality
  - Influences on human health of various food and fiber products, and their production processes
  - Human nutrition and nutritional advice
  - Rural health care
  - Poverty and hunger—both domestically and in LDCs
  - Product liability for defective or misrepresented, processed agricultural products sold to domestic and foreign consumers
  - Advertising

ADDITIONAL AGENDA ITEMS AND CONCLUSIONS

After SSAAP's Houston meeting, its editorial group interrelated the Houston agendas, checked them for completeness of coverage and selected additional materials for summarization and, in some cases, for publication herein.

A result of these activities was the development of additional agenda items for this chapter under the subheadings of farm management, home management, small farms, marketing and agribusiness, resource sustainability, and policies and programs. Agenda items developed by SSAAP's editorial group are specifically identified in the summary chapters (such as this one) for each of the last ten of the eleven sections in this book; however, the agendas developed at Houston and by SSAAP's editorial group since the Houston meeting are blended into the executive summary that is published separately.

FARM MANAGEMENT

For this subarea, rural social scientists should:

- Reestablish a multidisciplinary approach to farm management in academia that includes sociology and anthropology and relates integrally to human ecology as well as to technology and economics.
- Focus on expanding the multidisciplinary understanding of managerial processes for family-operated, full- and part-time farms, and for larger-than-family-operated farms.
- Do more subject-matter research, but concentrate (as extension workers, advisors, and consultants) on helping farmers solve specific problems.
- Encourage social scientists with interests in farm management to attempt to integrate their views of managerial processes with the views of home-managerial processes held by home-management specialists and human ecologists.
- Expand sociological and psychological studies of the managerial activities of farm entrepreneurs, homemakers, and family members.
- Extend the farming-systems research approach to include the home end of farming and the nonmonetary costs and returns important for both the business and home aspects of farms.
- Address more adequately the management problems of small and part-time farms.
- Develop farm-business databases that are better coordinated with home-management databases and develop them across states to support farm management, agribusiness, and policy analyses.
- Consider the use of the transaction-cost approach to better research and analyze multiperson choices in farm firm/household units with respect to such within-farm institutional changes as the establishment and dissolution of partnerships, gender relationships, wills, long-term contracts, estate-management plans, disinheritances, marriages, divorces, arrangements to care for the elderly, long-term health-care contracts, and the like. The role of flow transactions costs vis-a-vis information, negotiation, and enforcement costs should be related to the stock costs of establishing and dismantling such institutional arrangements and their associated organizations, facilities, equipment, and human skills. Also, attention should be given to understanding and measuring the nonmonetary and monetary values of such institutions.
- Investigate the nonmonetary values important in dynamic, imperfectly known and understood environments for farm and home managerial interactions.
- Extend present, integrated decision-support systems to handle firm/household interrelationships and relevant nonmonetary values.

HOME MANAGEMENT

For this subarea, rural social scientists should:

- Use the multidisciplinarity of human ecology in direct attacks on problems and subjects important in the management of farm and other rural homes and families.
- Focus on expanding the multidisciplinary understanding of home- and family-management processes important in family-operated full- and part-time farms and nonfarm homes.
- Integrate human ecology views of home and family managerial processes with corresponding views of the processes of managing the business end of farming. In this connection, attention should be given to attaining the effective use of the large capital investments, expenditures, and human efforts devoted to within-home production. It is important to properly manage the substantial production of goods and services that takes place in farms and rural homes including, particularly, the education, training, and motivation of children.
- Encourage human ecologists and home-management specialists to help extend farming-systems research to include the home aspects of farming.
- Coordinate home with farm business databases.
- Incorporate a transaction-cost approach to multiperson choices involving changes in such farm firm/household institutional arrangements as partnerships, gender rights, marriages, divorces, adoptions, wills, estate-management plans, and agreements with children and aging persons. Both flow and stock costs of establishing and dissolving such institutional arrangements are important. (See Part III, Section 1, for additional agenda items with respect to multiperson/public choice/transaction cost approach to institutional change.)

AGRICULTURAL MARKETS AND AGRIBUSINESS

Rural social scientists should:

- Focus, in academia, more sharply on the practical marketing problems and subjects of farmers and agribusinesses. Researchers should address multidisciplinary marketing subjects at farm, agribusiness, sectoral, national, and international levels while extension workers, advisors, consultants, governmental administrators, entrepreneurs, and private-sector employees should emphasize assistance with problem solving.
- Address more basic efforts to understand the managerial processes of agribusinesses, including cooperatives. More specifically, there appear to be important opportunities to develop:
  - Multidisciplinary conceptualization of the managerial processes, and
  - To extend the transaction-cost approach to the analysis of multiperson choices concerning institutional changes in agribusinesses and marketing pertaining to mergers, takeovers, leveraged buy-outs, establishment of cooperatives, lobbying of government for program and policy changes, and the like. As was noted above for farm and home management, stock, as well as flow establishment and dismantlement costs are involved. Such costs include information, negotiation and enforcement costs. Relevant returns, as well as costs, are both monetary and nonmonetary. (See Part IV, Section 1, Chapter 3, Social Science Agendas for Databases and Information Systems, for items with respect to use of a multiperson/public choice/transaction cost approach to institutional change.)

As discussed in Chapter 1, the agricultural financial crisis of the 1980s caused many heavily leveraged farmers and agribusinesses to go out of business and placed severe pressure on the public and private financial institutions serving rural America. Because agricultural finance did not receive adequate attention at the Houston SSAAP conference, the supplemental agenda for this important area of agricultural finance is rather substantial. It was contributed by Peter Barry of the University of Illinois and John Brake of Cornell University. It drew on materials formulated in the winter of 1990 by the North Central Regional Project NC 161 on financial markets for agriculture:

- Evaluate the social costs of state and federal credit programs for agriculture, including the levels of credit, scope of lending programs, degrees and forms of subsidies, eligible borrowers, the distribution of credit among borrowers, and the effects on the structure and performance of the agricultural sector.
- Analyze the impacts of the regulatory environment on the competitive position of major farm-lending institutions and on the cost and availability of credit for agricultural borrowers.
- Evaluate the efficiency of financial intermediation among agricultural and rural lenders, including the relationships of operating, funding, and risk-bearing costs to the size and scope of lending operations.
- Analyze the potential impacts of the Farm Credit System's restructuring and recovery on the cost and availability of credit and other financial services for agricultural borrowers and their cooperatives, as they relate to the structure and performance of the agricultural sector.
- Assess the impacts of the changes in the legal structure of banking and the modification of geographic barriers to lending on the cost and availability of credit to agriculture.
- Assess the availability of secondary markets for farm real estate loans, governmental guaranteed loans, and other types of farm loans on the competitive position of agricultural lenders, the sources of lending, interest-rate risks in agriculture, and the performance of financial markets for agriculture.
- Formulate and evaluate the mechanisms for channeling outside equity capital into the agricultural sector in a fashion that preserves managerial freedom, maintains asset control by farmers, and relieves cash-flow pressures associated with the financing of farm land and other fixed assets.
- Identify and estimate the impacts of domestic and international monetary and fiscal policies on agricultural commodity prices and on the cost and availability of

credit for farmers; focus the implications for financial performance of farm businesses and structural change in the agricultural sector.

- Provide training to further develop farmers' skills in financial management, risk management, and financial accounting as a basis for better farm management and for improving credit worthiness in the agricultural sector.
- Create more uniform and valid financial standards for evaluating the performance of farm businesses.
- Analyze financing implications and risks from new and restrictive environmental policies and regulations that, among other results, increase lender liability from on-farm environmental and human hazards.
- Continue research to evaluate the impacts of changes in the structure and capital requirements of farming on: entry into farming, controlling farm capital in a changed environment, multiparty operating arrangements, debt structure, tax management, and estate transfer.

FOOD CONSUMPTION AND NUTRITION

Rural and basic social scientists recognize the mutual interests of farmers and agribusinesses, on one hand, and consumers, on the other, in an effective food system that delivers safe, adequate supplies of pleasing food of high nutritional quality to consumers at low cost. The following items concerning food should be high on rural and basic social science agendas.

- Research on the implications for consumers, farmers, and agribusinesses of technical changes in crop and livestock production, food processing, nutrition, and nutrition-related medicine. Also important are more transitory food and nutrition viewpoints. Both more and less transitory changes affect farmers and consumers, sometimes adversely and sometimes favorably. The ability of social scientists to analyze behavioral responses to such changes is essential in determining the demand consequences of such changes and whether those consequences create problems or open up opportunities.
- Identification of the opportunities for farmers and agribusinesses to produce new, or modify old, goods and services, including the estimation of the extent of market demand and the price and income elasticities of those demands.
- Accomplishment of the research agenda noted above would enable social scientists to add to their agendas significant improvements in resident and extension food, nutrition, health, farm-management, and policy educational programs.
- Research, advising, and consulting on the establishment of governmental regulation of food advertising, labeling, recalls, pure food and drug approval or disapproval, health and dietary claims, and the like.
- Research the food needs of the disadvantaged and assess the domestic U.S. food-entitlement programs to make them more effective, not only in meeting the short-term needs of the hungry and malnourished but in serving those needs so as to create, when possible and practical, independent earning power of recipients for use in buying food in the market rather than the long-term dependency on welfare agencies and workers.
- To use and extend the public choice/transaction cost approach to the analyses of institutional change when researching, educating, addressing, consulting, and administering changes in:
  - Food-regulation institutional programs and organizations.
  - Food-entitlement institutional programs and organizations.

POLICIES AND PROGRAMS

The concern here is with price support, subsidy, trade, monetary fiscal, market development, food stamp, and similar policies and programs important for farmers, agribusinesses, and consumers. The rural and basic social sciences should:

- Help carry out the multidisciplinary research and related activities with respect to the policies and programs indicated above and of concern to farmers, their families, agribusinesses, and consumers. Partnerships are needed involving political scientists, sociologists, economists, and historians (both rural and basic), as well as biological and physical agricultural scientists. The ethical dimensions of such work make it crucial that ethicists be involved.
- Avoid undue emphasis on any one discipline, such as economics, sociology, or political science, in doing research and related work on policies and programs.
- Develop policy and program analyses that:
  - Cover the relevant different disciplinary dimensions of the domain of a policy or program problem or subject.
  - Consider the values essential for defining and solving the problem or set of problems of concern.
  - Include iterative, interactive processes with the decision makers or choosers involved, as well as with affected people; iterative interactions are important sources of value and value-free knowledge for decision makers and choosers to use in reaching prescriptions to solve policy and program problems.
  - Avoid maximization and the use of maximizing behavioral assumptions until iterative, interactive processes reveal that they are appropriate.
  - Deal with the possibility of changing distributions of power—market, political, social, gender, policies, racial, military, religious, moral, and the power of knowledge itself—as parts of needed changes and reforms in the institutions (rules, organizational facilities, and staffs) that control our farm, agribusiness, and consumer policies and programs.
  - Study the stock and flow, monetary and nonmonetary costs of dismantling and establishing the different manifestations of our farm, agribusiness, and consumer policies, programs, organizations, and facilities.
  - Ascertain the values, nonmonetary as well as monetary, of our existing institutions for comparison with

transaction costs in making decisions to add to, replace, and/or dismantle the institutions that control and carry out our policies and programs. In this connection, see Part IV, Section 3, on ethics, decision making, and public choice.

- Cooperate among themselves in developing ways of incorporating more qualitative variables of social, political, and economic consequence in policy and program analyses.
- Strive for holistic multidisciplinary conceptualizations of large parts of the food and fiber system by striving to integrate present "piles" of specialized component analyses into larger, more complete analyses and models but, in doing so, avoid creation of large-scale, unduly specialized models of questionable relevancy.
- Develop databases for policy analyses that:
  - Include the social, political, anthropological, and technical variables needed for holistic systems analyses of subject-matter and problem-solving domains relevant for policies and programs of concern to farmers and their families, agribusinesses, and consumers.
  - Include descriptive knowledge about monetary and nonmonetary values including, in the latter, knowledge about relatively more intrinsic as well as exchange or extrinsic values. It is important that such knowledge include flow and stock-transaction costs and returns for institutional changes expressed as changed rules, organizations and facilities, equipment, and staffs.

CHAPTER 1

INTRODUCTION TO THE SECTION ON INTERNATIONAL RURAL DEVELOPMENT

This section on international rural development will first review knowledge generally available to the SSAAP participants at Houston. The social science agenda for international rural development that evolved at the Houston conference is presented in Chapter 11. In addition, the SSAAP editorial group has reviewed information that has become available since the Houston conference, as a basis for determining additional agenda items for social scientists in international rural development. In addition to the papers presented at Houston (Chapters 2 through 9), the sources utilized include the findings and recommendations of several important conferences and commissions and published literature on rural poverty and development in the Third World. A short synopsis of the Houston papers is also presented in Chapter 1.

Over the past twenty years, substantial changes have occurred in the world food situation and in the level of development in many developing countries. These events are reasons for greater optimism that people in most developing countries can achieve a more adequate diet and enjoy a higher standard of living. Countries with vast populations, like India and China, have become capable of feeding themselves and some newly industrialized countries, especially in Asia, demonstrate real economic growth and the potentials for development.

At the same time, much remains to be done. Pervasive problems of poverty, inadequate and unstable food supplies, and poor or nonexistent health services still demand major attention in many developing countries. Except for a few sub-Saharan countries that have made and maintained progress in development, Africa is in a crisis situation. Population growth continues to exceed food production, a problem exacerbated by two major famines in the past two decades. A weak institutional structure for education and research, lack of physical and human capital, and minimal health facilities combine to create massive problems that result in human misery and despair. While India and other Asian countries have made impressive gains in food production, major distribution problems persist. More than 65 percent of the 340 million people in the world who suffer from acute malnutrition and poverty live in Asia. Economic stagnation, hyperinflation, rural poverty, and urban slums characterize much of Latin America.

Two additional problems that must be addressed by the developed and developing nations include the Third World debt crisis, and deterioration of our global environment. These more recent concerns impinge directly on rural-development issues and they need to be addressed by social scientists. Globalization of the economies and the well-being of all nations require a much broader approach to development than has been taken up to now. This is evident from the conferences, study papers, and political concerns expressed by various country leaders.

REVIEW OF WORLD FOOD SITUATION

The 1974 World Food Conference in Rome—133 nations representing most of the world—was a landmark meeting to discuss ways of coping with world hunger and malnutrition, problems that had reached crisis proportions in many poor countries in the early 1970s. Bad weather, a sharp decline in world food production for 1972 and 1973, and an unexpected and major grain purchase by the Soviet Union greatly depleted grain stocks in the exporting countries and caused prices to skyrocket. The Arab oil embargo of 1973 created huge oil shortages and increased oil prices that, in turn, contributed to a sharp rise in the price of fertilizers and pesticides that are derived from petroleum. Many developing countries that desperately needed food could neither produce it themselves nor afford to buy it. In response to this crisis, delegates to the World Food Conference adopted a strategy embodied in 22 resolutions that was supposed to eliminate hunger and malnutrition within a decade. A World Food Council was created to coordinate and implement some 174 proposals for action that were embodied in the 22 resolutions.

Concurrently, President Ford commissioned the National Academy of Sciences to assess the world food and nutrition problem and to "make specific recommendations on how the research and development capabilities of the

United States could best be applied to meeting this major challenge." A broad comprehensive study was undertaken by fourteen teams of experts whose findings are incorporated in the *World Food and Nutrition Study, The Potential Contributions of Research* (National Academy of Sciences 1977). Major conclusions were that "given the political will here and abroad it should be possible by the end of this century to eliminate most of the hunger and malnutrition now associated with mass poverty." This called for a doubling of food production in the developing countries, that would be accomplished principally through the development and application of technology. Success would depend on increasing the supply of the right kinds of foods where they were needed, reducing poverty, stabilizing food supplies, and decreasing population growth.

The 22 selected priority-research areas comprised four categories: food production, nutrition, food marketing, and policies and organizations. Approximately seven of the 22 research areas required social science input: policies affecting nutrition, farm production systems, and market expansion; national food policy and organization; trade policy; food reserves; and information systems. Incentives and opportunities for increased food production and better distribution to consumers are critically affected by government policies and organizations. The study concluded that science and technology alone are unable to improve the world food and nutrition situation, and that research on social and economic policy is essential. "The size and difficulty of the research needed on policies and organizations require a large increase in current social science research capabilities, both in the United States and the developing countries." Unfortunately, only a minuscule fraction of the recommended research budgets was allotted to areas involving social science.

In 1978, President Carter appointed a Presidential Commission on World Hunger. The mandate was to identify the causes of domestic and international hunger and malnutrition, assess past and present national policies and programs that affect hunger and malnutrition, review existing studies and research on hunger, and recommend to the President and Congress specific actions to create a coherent national food and hunger policy. The final report, issued in March 1980, emphasized that world hunger is "as much a political, economic, and social challenge as it is a scientific, technical or logistic one," (Presidential Commission on World Hunger 1980, 1). It further declared the major hunger problem is "chronic undernutrition that affects as many as 800 million people who live in poverty," and suggested that solutions must be based on reducing poverty, unemployment, disease, and the high rate of population growth.

Most of the poor in many developing countries live in rural areas where they are landless or command too few resources to make a decent living. Land and other resources are often of low quality resulting in both low yields and total production. Lack of training, capital, and technology are partial explanations. Environmental degradation leads to a downward spiral in level of living for many. Price policies to keep food prices low in urban areas often discriminate against farmers. More resources and investment are needed in rural areas, as well as a better distribution of resources to generate more income and employment opportunities in rural areas. Better marketing institutions, including transportation and communication infrastructure, are often critical limitations. Some of these problems are not unlike those in the United States, but are much more severe.

Most developing countries cannot solve their problems with their own resources. They need the financial help and the expertise of developed countries such as the United States. It was stressed that both the developed and developing countries should make the security of food supplies and the elimination of poverty a major policy objective. Four goals were established: more equitable economic growth in the less developed countries (LDCs); redistribution of existing wealth; production of enough food, especially in the developing countries themselves; and a world food-security system that would include the maintenance of adequate grain stocks for distribution in times of shortage. U. S. policies toward developing countries must also change by increasing trade, making adequate and more appropriate investments, and by developing a global food-security system.

Five years after the World Food Conference, a *Report to the Congress* (Comptroller General of the United States 1980) concluded that while there had been some progress toward alleviating hunger and malnutrition, a great deal remained to be done. Substantial amounts of money and resources had been expended for food production and agricultural development in the LDCs, but increases in production fell short of the modest goals set at Rome. "Attitudes of complacency and lack of political will are evident, calls to reduce military expenditures have not been successful, continued population growth has worsened the balance between food supplies and population, and efforts to include women in food and development projects have been minimal." Food-production assistance rose from $2.7 billion in 1973 to $4 billion in 1977, substantially short of the estimated $8.3 billion needed to increase food production to a goal of 4 percent annually. Food production had increased only 1.2 percent in the most needy countries by 1976. At the same time, it was concluded that available funds tended to exceed suitable development projects!

The World Food Council was not particularly effective in its efforts to coordinate the resolutions of the World Food Conference because their power was limited to persuasion and they lacked control over any funds available for development. By 1980, the problems of hunger and malnutrition, which had generated so much concern, had solicited some additional investment in development assistance and some increase in food production. But, the crisis that generated the World Food Conference was past and the political will to take the kind of actions needed to reach goals set for the year 2000 was lacking. This was as true in the United States as it was in most of the rest of the world.

By 1985, the world food situation had continued to improve. In the United States alone some 60 million acres of land had been returned to production. Western Europe had become a major exporter and impressive gains in food production had been made in many developing countries through "Green Revolution" technology and more appropriate government policies. The oil crisis was in abeyance and the Malthusian fears of the mid–1970s had been replaced by new concerns of a greatly changed international monetary system; a major Third World debt problem; globalization of the world economy, including trade and exchange-rate issues for both developed and developing countries; increased concern for the environment; and an emerging emphasis on protection of natural resources and sustainable agriculture. The long-term decline in the world price of cereals had resumed and the prospects for a growing abundance (except in sub-Saharan Africa), through the end of the century, were much stronger than for scarcity. These developments have been reflected in policy discussions and conferences to better define the changing issues and priorities for research and development, and an increasing role for the social sciences is evident.

AFRICAN RURAL DEVELOPMENT PRIORITIES

Carl Eicher and Doyle Baker (1982) made an exhaustive literature review on the rural economies of sub-Saharan Africa as part of a worldwide survey for the American Agricultural Economics Association. This study was completed in 1982 and has recently been updated, although the bulk of the materials cover 1960–82. The review includes the work of economic historians covering the pre-Colonial and Colonial development period, a brief overview of the literature by technical scientists on farming and livestock systems, research on the rural nonfarm economy, as well as the principal research findings of political scientists, anthropologists, sociologists, and geographers. The principal goals were to identify the major theoretical and policy debates, the empirical findings on rural development in Africa, and to set a research agenda for the 1980s and 1990s.

Major conclusions of the review are that agrarian stagnation has been the major problem in Africa since independence, and that the economic crisis is mainly an agrarian crisis. Many of the 45 sub-Saharan countries are behind Asia and Latin American in scientific and human development, as well as in political and institutional maturity. Universities and national agricultural and extension systems are generally weak and poorly developed. Africa can be characterized by extreme diversity: a huge land mass, over 1,000 ethnic and tribal groups, over two-thirds of the population employed in agriculture, a predominance of small-holder production, a vast range of farming systems, rudimentary input delivery systems, and a low level of purchased input. Africa has the highest population growth rate in the world and food production increased at only half the population growth rate between 1970–84. Over 80 percent of the food-production increase in this period came from an expansion in planted area, but declining availability of productive land means that further production increases must come increasingly from improved technology and expanded capital investment. Better technology is either not available or not used for a variety of economic, social, and political reasons. It is estimated that employment in agriculture over the next 30–40 years will only decline from 68 to 58 percent of the total, while the size of the agricultural labor force will triple. Greater inequalities and a landless labor class are emerging.

It is against this background that Eicher and Baker established their research priorities on how to raise rural productivity and rural incomes across the board in sub-Saharan Africa. Significant attention should be given to the interactions between the transformation of the agricultural and industrial sectors, population growth and development of human capability, and sustainable African institutions. This will require the combined attention of a broad range of technical and social scientists. Many countries lack the political stability and commitment to come to grips with poverty, malnutrition, and access to food. Institutional innovations are essential for agrarian change. The authors state "the study of institutions has moved to center stage in both industrial countries and the Third World, including Africa" (1982, 304).

Other priority topics include the macroeconomics of food and agricultural policy; rural poverty and growing inequality; economics of producing food, livestock, and export commodities; irrigation potential; food-marketing systems; and alternatives to nonsustainable food consumption patterns. Food-security policy options need to be determined at family and national levels, and in response to drought and famine. The problems of African rural development are deep-seated and complex. The balanced implementation of the four basic forces for development outlined in SSAAP's analysis are essential to reach solutions.

Since 1984, in response to the critical state of agriculture in most African countries, a major long-term, cross-country comparative study called "Managing Agricultural Development in Africa" (MADIA) has been underway in the World Bank under the direction of Uma Lele (1989). The importance of agriculture for total economic growth is increasingly recognized, but systematic, data-based analysis has not been conducted on African agricultural problems, including their implications for government policies and donor agencies. The Bank study has included the active collaboration of six African governments and seven other donors. Eleven of 14 discussion papers had been published by March 15, 1990, and five additional volumes will be available in book form by mid–1991. The findings of the MADIA study were discussed at a symposium of senior African and donor policy makers in June 1989.

The studies were conducted in Kenya, Tanzania, and Malawi in East Africa, and in Nigeria, Cameroon, and Senegal in West Africa. Important comparative insights were gained on the relationship between domestic macroeconomic and agricultural policy and agricultural performance, donor roles and effectiveness in the development of agriculture, and the politics of agricultural policy.

Conclusions reached "emphasize the fundamental importance of a sound macroeconomic environment for ensuring the broad-based development of agriculture and, at the same time, stress the need for achieving several difficult balances: among macroeconomic, sectoral, and location-specific factors that determine the growth of agricultural output; between the development of food and export crops; and between the immediate impact and long-run development of human and institutional capital. The papers also highlight the complementarity of, and the need to maintain a balance between, the private and public sectors; and further the need to recognize that both price and non-price incentives are critical to achieving sustainable growth in output" (Lele 1989). The findings generally support the conclusions and research priorities outlined by Eicher and Baker in their literature review.

REVIEW OF ASIAN RURAL DEVELOPMENT

John Mellor and Mohinder Mudahar (forthcoming) have reviewed the literature on the "evolution in thought about the role of agriculture in economic development (in Asia) and the processes by which agriculture develops." Most of these references were generally available to SSAAP participants at Houston. Modern thought about economic development was formed in the 1930s and 1940s and emphasized industrialization and the important role of capital in development. Surplus labor from agriculture was expected to facilitate capital formation in nonagricultural sectors. Agriculture and labor were given only a passive role in the development process. These theories were initially applied and later modified in the Asian experience from the 1960s through the 1980s. This is the period included in Mellor's and Mudahar's review of the literature.

In 1961, Johnston and Mellor emphasized the importance of increasing agricultural production in order to supply wage goods for the support of labor transfers to industry and to provide industrial capital through foreign trade. It was also stated that rising rural incomes would increase the demand for industrial goods and stimulate the growth of the nonagricultural sector. However, the prevailing thought in the 1960s was that resources should be concentrated in capital-goods industries and not in consumer goods, including agriculture. This strategy "culminated in highly sophisticated, multisectoral, mathematical growth models based solely on capital." The policy prescriptions were very similar to the import-substitution industrialization policies that prevailed in Latin America during the same period.

By the late 1960s, it was increasingly apparent that growth from capital investment alone was slow and the benefits too narrowly distributed. Alternative strategies were explored in the 1970s including implementation of supplemental programs to alleviate poverty directly. The basic-human-needs approach had a broad following in the West, but gained little support from most leaders of Asian countries who felt the benefits would be quickly eliminated by high population growth. Of even greater significance, neither the politically powerful urban consumers nor the large-volume farmers would be helped. Development of agriculture and its linkages with other sectors was gaining attention.

In the late 1970s and in the 1980s, emphasis turned to agricultural production as the way to raise agricultural incomes through "Green Revolution" processes and in expanding the linkages and multiplier effects with other sectors of the economy. As the process continued, increased emphasis was given to rural infrastructure investment as a basis for more rapid agricultural growth and in meeting the food needs of massive populations. The evolution of thought about how to develop agriculture moved from the prevailing belief in the 1950s that farmers were ignorant, inefficient, and exploited, to the view in the 1960s that farmers were rational economic decision makers who were constrained by their environment and lack of incentives to increase output (Schultz 1964). As a result, agricultural development programs were redesigned to provide water, fertilizers, pesticides, and credit, but agricultural production did not increase significantly until the limitations of technology were recognized. Subsequently,emphasis was given to the development of new technology, particularly new high-yielding varieties and associated input, in a package approach.

Progress from new technologies has tended to be more rapid in those regions where investment in physical infrastructure and supporting services of extension, credit, input distribution, and marketing systems were most developed. Problems of implementation have received greater attention as knowledge of how to develop agriculture has grown. There is also increasing concern with other issues, such as the emerging patterns of income distribution, the determinants of the effective demand for agricultural output, and more effective allocation of resources to agricultural research, as well as the attempt to understand the development processes that broaden participation in economic growth. Even though countries such as India have achieved a positive overall balance between cereal production and consumption, millions still subsist at less-than-poverty levels. Small farmers and the landless have been the least able to participate and to benefit from the institutions essential for agricultural growth and development. How can they be included in the process? Nutrition intervention programs and their effectiveness also need further study. These are all important agenda items for social science research.

The work of Mellor and Mudahar includes a vast literature on agricultural and economic development in Asia. Their approach has been to integrate the principal theories, policies, and results to give an integrated view of the accumulated knowledge about agricultural development over the past thirty years and some of the principal agenda problems that still need attention. Much has been learned from the Asian experience that has relevance for other developing regions. Technology, institutions, and human-resource development have been emphasized as key movers in the successes that have been achieved. Massive populations and limited land resources characterize the major countries in the region, but they have been able to achieve near self-sufficiency in food production. Increasingly, more pragmatic market-oriented approaches are producing the best results.

A brief outline of the topics covered by Mellor and Mudahar includes:

- A brief description of the characteristics and importance of agriculture in Asian countries and its role in the dominant theories of economic growth.
- The processes by which agricultural modernization has occurred, with particular attention given to technology generation and transfer, and domestic market development.
- Issues of income distribution and welfare in the context of agricultural growth.
- Examination of the linkages through which agriculture stimulates growth in other sectors including its multiplier effects.
- The importance of trade and foreign aid in economic growth, including resource transfer and generation of income and employment.
- Issues of implementation and assessment of agricultural development policies, programs, and projects.

This extensive review of literature demonstrates that a great deal of research has been done on Asian development and much has been learned about the role of agriculture in development and the processes by which it is achieved. Empirical studies providing knowledge of the economic relationships involved have grown even faster. Most of the more recent work has been done by Asian scholars and it reflects the concern of the countries themselves to improve their development policies. There has been a rapid growth in trained researchers and institutional capacity to conduct research and train new professionals. The authors concluded that more studies on the same topics are needed in countries where they have not been done and where different conditions prevail. Four areas are identified that are inadequately conceptualized and lack empirical documentation. These areas include:

- The linkages through which a dynamic agriculture multiplies its effects on other sectors of the economy and on total economic growth. Also, what role does technology, physical infrastructure, and education play in these processes? The role and development of local government is a particularly important issue.
- Multidisciplinary studies of the processes by which policy measures can be implemented quickly and efficiently. Comparative analysis of development projects is needed.
- Relationships between improved income, food intake, nutrition, and human well-being including health. Economists, nutritionists, and public health practitioners need to work together to understand and to find solutions to nutrition and health problems.
- Interactions among Third World countries as they accelerate rates of economic growth, and the relations of developing countries with the developed, industrialized countries. Little is known about the effect the accelerated growth of highly populated developing countries will have on the aggregate demand for food and international trade, on the aid and the food-security relationships, and on the ways they interact with development strategy, political participation, and political systems. Many issues exist in the areas of trade and comparative advantage as markets become more accessible.

REVIEW OF AGRICULTURAL DEVELOPMENT IN LATIN AMERICA

Edward Schuh and Antonio Brandâo (forthcoming) have recently completed a review of the agricultural development literature on Latin America. This work is comparable to the review completed for Asia and Africa and is intended for publication as a part of Volume IV, *A Survey of Agricultural Economics Literature on LDC Rural Development,* that is sponsored by the American Agricultural Economics Association. Because Schuh participated in the SSAAP conference and has written two chapters included in this volume, the analysis that follows was generally available to SSAAP participants. Schuh and Brandâo's literature review relates advances in development thought to empirical research and development policy in Latin America. Development theory and policy have been closely linked and help explain the current status of agricultural development and the policy issues that remain.

The survey focuses on English language and Brazilian literature. Brazil's experience has been used to illustrate some of the development issues prevalent in Latin America since the 1950s. While the authors do not claim their review is exhaustive, the historical context and concepts of dependency theory, import substitution, industrialization, structuralism, and monetarism have been well developed to enhance our understanding of agriculture's role (or lack thereof) in development efforts and policy in Latin America. Other theories of agricultural development, including the Hayami and Ruttan induced-innovation model, Schultz's urban industrial-impact model, Schuh's eclectic interpretation of Brazil's agricultural modernization, and Paiva's model of technological dualism in Brazil, are also used to explain development in the region.

While most Latin countries have democratic constitutions similar to the United States, military interventions and extended periods of authoritarian governments have caused great political instability over the years. Colonialist dependence continued after independence through continued export of raw materials and import of manufactured goods. Latin America did not benefit from the industrial revolution between 1820 and 1910. While income levels in the United States and Latin America were essentially equal in the early 1800s, by 1970 U.S. per capita income was 18 times greater, and the gap has continued to widen.

In the twentieth century, a population explosion and massive rural/urban migration has been underway in Latin America. Labor unions and socialist parties of the left were established and grew in influence. Universities became the centers of open political activity and of demands for reform in many countries. The United States government has given minimum attention to Latin American problems and development except in times of crisis, such as that involving Cuba and Nicaragua and the severe debt problems of the 1980s.

Economically and demographically, great diversity exists in country size, level of development, per capita incomes, and rural/urban composition of the population. In 1985, agriculture contributed less than 30 percent of the gross domestic product (GDP) for all Latin American countries, and substantially less than that in most. At the same time, considerably more of the total labor force was found in agriculture, an indication of low labor productivity. Rural incomes are, on average, only half the level of urban incomes. There has been a significant decline in the agricultural labor force in the 1970s and 1980s through rapid rural/urban migration. Most countries have large urban concentrations of population.

Agriculture has not been a dynamic development force in Latin America. Per capita production of food has risen at about the same rate as population growth in the period from 1973–83. Agriculture remains a largely natural-resource-based industry in most of the region. Technological change will have to be the major source of growth in the future. Food consumption has increased at an annual rate of 2.8 percent over the past two decades, that is approximately the same as population growth. Nutrition levels have probably not deteriorated, but many people still suffer from malnutrition, with the rural population being the most disadvantaged.

Most countries in Latin America neglected or discriminated against their agricultural sectors in the post-World War II period up to the late 1970s. The experience of the 1930s and World War II provided fertile ground for the ideology of Argentine economist Raul Prebisch and his followers. Import substitution, through industrialization, was promoted as the means to achieve economic growth and development. The terms of trade were considered to be declining against primary products and agriculture was considered an impediment to development. Industrialization was promoted through high tariffs and quotas on imports, overvalued currencies, and export taxes on primary products. Governments intervened extensively in their economies, substituting government planning for open market forces. National economies were increasingly isolated from international trade and price relationships.

In addition to unfavorable price and production incentives, agriculture also suffered from a significant underinvestment in human capital in terms of low research capacity to produce new technology, lack of modern institutional infrastructure, inadequate nutrition and health, and limited education and training of rural people. Government subsidies focused mainly on urban workers and consumers.

The international debt crisis and the severe world economic recession of the early 1980s had a severe impact on Latin America. This reinforced the changing attitude of many countries to give more attention to agriculture in order to promote economic growth. Attempts were made to shift the domestic terms of trade in favor of agriculture, through stabilization and adjustment policies. More exports were needed to service the international debt. Significant attempts were also made to strengthen agricultural research in the region and to rely more on market forces to allocate resources. Agriculture responded in the 1980s, but more action is needed to establish policies that promote greater economic efficiency and provide incentives to increase productivity.

Schuh and Brandâo outline several policies to promote agricultural development including: price or incentive policies, factor market policies, investments in human capital, and investments in physical infrastructure. The appropriate role of government and open markets is still a critical issue in many Latin American countries and deserves more pragmatic analysis.

Trade and exchange-rate policies have shifted the domestic terms of trade against agriculture. Protection of domestic industries against imports also has undesirable impacts. Protected infant industries tend to become more inefficient over time, and generate large economic rents for privileged groups with the economic and political power to maintain protection. Monetary stability should have a higher priority than government support of commodity prices. Lack of government intervention in commodity markets creates more incentive for the private sector to carry stocks to even out price fluctuations. Establishment of futures markets can also help.

Latin American governments have intervened heavily in agricultural factor markets, including land, labor, and credit (capital). Factor prices are often far different from their shadow prices or scarcity values. Minimum-wage laws, payroll taxes, and labor unions backed by government have pushed wage rates above market-clearing levels in many countries and creates unemployment. Given the longer-term need to transfer labor out of agriculture as development proceeds, more emphasis is needed on broad-based formal schooling, training programs, and labor-market information systems.

When land reform is needed or has occurred, it should be accompanied with appropriate price policy, new production technology, training of new owner/managers, and adequate credit. Both economic and political transaction costs must be taken into account. Credit policies should strive to develop true financial intermediaries as part of broader capital market policy. Government's role should be to provide stable monetary conditions, adequate information systems, and the institutional framework needed for capital markets to function efficiently.

Schuh and Brandâo put investments in human capital on the priority list for Latin American countries. The need to invest more in agricultural research capacity exists in all countries. An effective research system needs institutional arrangements that articulate an appropriate balance between applied, strategic, and basic research; reflect society's problems to researchers; and rewards them to work in the system and invest in their own training and development. Funding of the whole system should be at a level needed to produce new technology at a socially optimum rate and the researchers themselves need to be trained to international standards.

An effective extension service is important to complement the research system. It should serve as a means to disseminate new knowledge and to identify rural-sector problems to feed back to researchers. The level of training and compensation for extension workers, as well as the resources they have to work with, are critical variables affecting the performance of extension.

Significant underinvestment exists in formal education and technical or vocational training of rural people. Greatest deficiencies are found at the primary and secondary levels. More attention should be given to the high opportunity costs of going to school. The potential of internationally or country-provided food aid to help alleviate these costs through targeted feeding programs needs further research. The extent to which some countries should provide training at higher education levels is less clear.

Nutrition and health is the most basic area of human-capital development. Without adequate nutrition, other forms of human capital will not be able to make their full contribution to economic development in a physical-input sense or in terms of cognitive or operational skills. There are too many malnourished people in the region to be helped by economic development alone in the foreseeable future. Multidisciplinary research is needed on targeted feeding programs and other means to meet this important need. There is also significant disparity between rural and urban health services and rural people are poorly served.

Institutional-design issues are paramount in expediting the reforms in policies and programs outlined in the preceding paragraphs. Financial resources are necessary, but equally important are improved institutional structures that recognize changing economic and social conditions, including the rising value of time as development proceeds. Schuh and Brandâo stress the importance of "adequate research capacity in the social sciences...in order to evaluate economic policies, to design new economic policies, to design and redesign new institutional arrangements, and to provide information to decision makers, both public and private. The 'technology' output of the social sciences is, among other things, new institutional arrangements. Most countries in the region significantly underinvest in the design and implementation of new institutional arrangements."

Rural physical infrastructure has also been neglected in Latin America. This includes roads, railroads, rural electrification, telephone service, port facilities, etc. Modern agriculture cannot develop without these services.

They also facilitate regional and rural industrial development including the relocation of human resources out of agriculture.

Crosscutting-policy issues identified by Schuh and Brandâo include the mobilization of resources out of agriculture to improve income distribution, declines in the external terms of trade, and population policy. Better means of transferring resources out of agriculture are needed than the discriminatory measures of the past. Land taxes would appear to be especially ideal but are very difficult to implement politically. Transformations of the credit system into true financial intermediaries is another means to use market forces to transfer resources from agriculture.

Skewed income distribution in the region is a serious and pervasive problem. Investment in the human capital of the disadvantaged would improve income distribution and promote economic growth if more favorable economic policies were pursued. Import substitution industrialization has exacerbated income distribution problems in the region. It is felt that more outward-oriented policies would broaden employment and income-earning possibilities in most Latin American countries. New production technology, especially for food crops, should improve income distribution by making cheaper food available to low-income consumers. Reforms in fiscal policy in all sectors are key elements in improving income distribution.

Most Latin American countries are faced with chronic and persistent declines in the external terms of trade that threaten their balance of payments and their ability to service their foreign debt. Both declines and increases can cause serious adjustment problems in their domestic economies. More research is needed on the relationships between balance of payments, sector productivity, and national welfare. Currency devaluation is a classic response to an adverse shift in the external terms of trade but it does not address the problem of changes in national welfare. International commodity agreements, as advocated by Prebisch and his followers, are frequently prescribed as a solution but they have many problems, as illustrated by past performance. Provision of better market-information services to all market participants would be of real value, especially to small nations.

Population policy has a major impact on the agricultural sector, but it is seldom considered as a specific part of agricultural development programs. Schuh and Brandâo state that family-planning knowledge and technology should be made available to all members of society, including rural families. Rising per capita income changes the alternatives that families have, leading them to substitute quality of children for quantity of children. The problem is that economic growth alone is too slow to affect population growth rates. Government needs to intervene by supporting education and training, and improving nutrition and health programs. The demand for more children tends to decline as the mortality rates decline. Nutrition and health programs should be parts of a larger program for population and family planning. Government policy should focus on accelerating the rate of social investment in human capital as a means of reducing population growth rates.

National economic policy has to be the first priority of national governments, but international institutional arrangements and institutions are in serious disarray. Institutions such as the Food and Agriculture Organization (FAO) and other organizations under the United Nations, the World Bank, the International Monetary Fund (IMF), and General Agreement on Tariffs and Trade (GATT) were created after World War II to deal with a wide range of international monetary, trade, and development needs. Unfortunately, many of these arrangements have broken down as a result of changing economic conditions. The world's economic interdependence and integration resulting from rapid technological developments in transportation, communication, and computerization sectors has outmoded many institutions and they need to be updated and modernized.

Arrangements that lead to greater monetary stability and freer trade are high on Schuh's list of priorities. This will facilitate a more equitable distribution of the world's income and reduce the great disequilibrium in global agriculture. Reduction of the high protection of agriculture in Japan, the United States, and the European economic community (EEC) is considered a good place to start. Social scientists need to address these issues, that will also require the political will of the government leaders to take the necessary actions.

INSTITUTIONS, TECHNOLOGY, AND POLICIES FOR RURAL DEVELOPMENT

The work by Hayami and Ruttan has added a great deal to the theory and understanding of agricultural development processes. Their initial work in 1971, *Agricultural Development: An International Perspective,* introduced the concept of induced technical change as an endogenous factor in the explanation of changes in national agricultural productivity over time. Hayami and Ruttan have helped shape the development policies of international donor agencies and the developing countries, particularly in the area of investment in national and international agricultural research systems. In 1985, they produced an updated and substantially expanded book that extended their theory of induced innovation to include the process of institutional change. Additional topics include an examination of the interrelationships between the role of land development and technical change; the relations between growth and equity in the process of agricultural development; and the efforts of national governments and donor agencies to implement land-reform programs, credit-institutions development, and integrated rural development.

The importance of institutions and their organizational structures and linkages in agricultural development research has been elaborated by William Foote Whyte (1975). Behavioral scientists need an organizational framework to facilitate the diagnosis of problems and understand the existing (or needed) vertical relationships within each organization, as well as the horizontal and diagonal relationships linking the various units that make up the total organizational system of agricultural development. Information flows and relations between organizations should be studied in the following structural frameworks, including organizational behavior and interorganizational relations in research and extension, socioeconomic organizations of agricultural activities, social structure and distribution of power in rural areas, and structural implications of social and technical innovations in rural areas. The myth of the passive peasant must be abandoned by researchers and agricultural development planners to examine the socioeconomic conditions that cause farmers to accept or reject change. A new strategy for rural development research is to look at the social system in terms of technology, work flow, division of labor, structure of work activities, and system of economic and noneconomic rewards and penalties.

In 1989, the *Journal of Agriculture and Human Values* devoted the entire Winter/Spring issue to "The Crisis in European Agriculture." An earlier issue (Fall 1986) of this interdisciplinary journal looked at the farm crisis in the United States and raised the question of its being a simple adjustment or a structural defect. Institutions, policy and structural adjustments, technology, and investments in human and physical capital are identified as key factors in the development process. Changes in European agriculture are similar to those taking place in the United States. The favored position of farmers is being eroded by budgetary reality in the EEC, and there is a need to deal with environmental issues that are increasingly in conflict with production agriculture. The decentralization of nonfarm production activities from traditional industrial areas in Europe to rural regions, through subcontracting or horizontal integration of smaller farms and the less formal organization of the labor force, are part of the political, economic, and structural processes underway. How to deal with a dual structure of many small farms and a few large ones, the disparity and difficulty of adjustment among countries in the EEC as trade and other economic integration continue within the community, and the pressure from the fiscal crisis to change current agricultural policies are major issues calling for interdisciplinary analysis and solution.

In August 1985, the American Agricultural Economics Association, on the occasion of its 75th anniversary, held an important conference at Ames, Iowa, on "Agriculture and Rural Areas Approaching the Twenty-First Century: Challenges for Agricultural Economics." The purpose was to set a broadly based agenda for the agricultural economics profession in order to meet the needs and problems likely to be faced by farmers and rural communities into the next century. While the major focus was on the United States, it was recognized that major changes are occurring in both this country and world agriculture. Globalization of agriculture and environmental issues are of increasing concern and in need of greater understanding and policy analysis. The role of institutions, human capital, and technology were emphasized because the challenges facing rural areas today are much broader than those facing production agriculture alone.

New technology, including the emerging biotechnology revolution, has major implications for both DCs and LDCs in comparative advantage, trade, and the structure of agricultural production itself. Mellor categorized the issues in world agriculture under the headings of international trade in food, alleviation of poverty, and human-capital development, and stressed the importance of these interrelationships in achieving viable development in LDCs (Mellor 1988). Johnson (1988) emphasized the importance of understanding the relationships between technology, institutions, human capacity (capital), and physical capital as the driving forces in agricultural development. These topics are focal points in the SSAAP agenda and recommendations. They are equally relevant for both developed and developing countries.

In the area of agricultural technology, international donor agencies, including USAID, have invested many resources in establishing the 13 International Agricultural Research Centers (IARCs) and in strengthening national agricultural research systems in developing countries. The IARCs have made major contributions to world food production in many poorer countries through the development of high-yielding varieties of wheat and rice that have been adapted by national scientists for local use. Many more benefits can be cited from improvement in genetic materials and production practices for other crops as well. The international research network is well established and receives continuing support from many donors. A significant but lesser contributor is the Collaborative Research Support Program (CRSP) that established joint research programs principally between the U.S. land-grant universities and LDC institutions, but also involves the IARCs and USDA. Eight CRSPs were formed between 1978 and 1985 to do collaborative multidisciplinary research on defined-priority food and nutrition problems. The program has involved 40 U.S. land- and sea-grant institutions and 66 host-country institutions in 30 countries. Each CRSP involves a direct relationship between U.S. and LDC agencies, universities, and professionals, and is funded on a five-year renewable basis. Most have been considered quite successful in meeting their objectives.

The role and contributions of social scientists in the IARCs and CRSPs have not been universally accepted or understood. Economists have well-established roles in most IARCs and work in collaboration with production scientists. There has been less acceptance and involvement of sociologists and anthropologists. More of the CRSPs have utilized the latter two disciplines in designing, targeting, and in implementing project activities. A recent book edited by Constance McCorkle (1989) with the title *The Social Sciences in International Agricultural Research—Lessons from the CRSP* examines the contributions and problems of sociologists and anthropologists in five of the CRSPs but inexplicably omits contributions of economics and agricultural economics. The general conclusion is that these social scientists have stimulated a more holistic approach to problems with emphasis on who benefits and by how much. Greater contact has been established between biological scientists and farmers. It is unfortunate that the contributions of economists were not included in this analysis.

Another major conference that coincided with the SSAAP conference in Houston was the 1988 World Food Congress held in Des Moines, Iowa. It's theme was "Hunger in the Midst of Plenty: A World Policy Dilemma" and the proceedings were published in February 1990 (Helmuth and Johnson, eds.). World leaders from private industry, government, and academia participated with the goal of promoting cooperation and coordination of worldwide economic and agricultural policies through the exchange of ideas and information. Principal topics covered included: food and the agricultural policies of major countries; moral and ethical issues of hunger and malnutrition; world hunger, malnutrition, and food production and distribution systems; and policy options for improving the functioning of the world food production and distribution system.

The major driving forces that impact on rural development policies and structural change, including the role of social science analysis, are further elaborated in Chapters 2 through 10 of this section. A brief synopsis of each of these chapters is included at the end of this chapter. It should also be noted that all of Part III is devoted to the four driving forces for development.

PRIORITIES FOR U.S. DEVELOPMENT ASSISTANCE

In 1988, a national project was organized to examine U.S. involvement in international development in order to advise the government on more effective policies of economic cooperation with the Third World in the 1990s. This project was the most extensive of its kind and included 11 cooperating institutions, more than 100 papers, and more than 800 individuals from around the world. Winrock International Institute for Agricultural Development (January 1989) hosted the first of a series of fifteen symposia in February 1988 on "The Future of U.S. Development Assistance; Food, Hunger, and Agricultural Issues." Wayne Swegle reported informally on this symposium at Houston. Topics in following sessions included the environment, population growth, science and technology, health, education and training, urbanization, the changing nature of poverty, and more.

Participants in the Winrock Conference were asked to address the major questions of whether Third World countries can grow and equitably distribute the food they need over the next decade, what the international-development community should and could do to help in both production and distribution, and what role the United States should play in these activities. In addition to development leaders, farmer representatives and the news media were invited to participate. Support from the latter two groups is the key to public understanding and support for development assistance.

There was general agreement that accelerated development in the LDCs is both desirable and achievable, that the right kinds of development assistance are essential, and that agricultural and broad-based, employment-led growth is the best model for most developing countries. Evidence from the past forty years indicates that the United States has a comparative advantage in training people and in institution development (universities and national research systems). Some of the ideas elaborated included:

- Integrating food aid with technical and economic assistance.
- Making agricultural resource systems sustainable.
- Synchronizing U.S. food and agricultural policy with our foreign policy.
- Recognizing the costs of restructuring and creating institutions and policies.
- Having substance guide process, not the other way around.
- Increasing continuity and decreasing faddism.
- Creating mechanisms to stay with countries as they succeed in development.
- Making women full partners in development.
- Exploring debt/equity swaps.
- Making more studies of the assistance efforts in specific countries and increasing the dissemination of results.
- Measuring health and other factors in evaluating progress.
- Differentiating between emergency food assistance (famine/disaster) and food aid as a development tool.

Recommendations from the series of fifteen symposia were extensively reviewed in a national conference held at Michigan State University in May 1988 and were later published as a major reference for ongoing discussions about U.S. international-development policies in the 1990s (Smuckler et al. 1988). Participants in the MSU conference had also participated in SSAAP's Houston conference. The consensus reached was that the "United States has much to gain from a global system that promotes broadly based growth, an effective attack on poverty and an end to degradation of the world's environment." A great interdependence exists among all nations. The United States has a national interest in helping solve the Third World debt crisis. It has a political interest in LDCs in the terms of national security to promote democracy and the rule of law, and to solve the contemporary problems that affect our daily lives: drugs, AIDS, and terrorism. Global environmental pollution affects all people. Development cooperation requires broad participation from government, private sector, and NGOs. Programs must be developed jointly with LDCs and must reflect a commitment to cooperation for development.

It was concluded that special attention needed to be given to three increasingly urgent problems that transcend traditional development concerns. These include the Third World debt crisis that threatens the basic growth potential of many Latin American and African countries and the credibility of the international financial system; severe problems of environmental degradation, poverty, and institutional deterioration in Africa; and global environmental concerns that require massive cooperative efforts.

In the future, when LDC needs and U.S. capabilities are well matched, U.S. programs of development cooperation should focus on four substantive areas. These areas include: (1) improved health systems and population planning; (2) more sustainable agricultural systems, including increased food supplies and forests; (3) protection and development of natural resources through new environmental programs and facilitating policies; and (4) development of sound urban development policies. Both (2) and (3) above are among the direct concerns of SSAAP. U.S. capabilities to address these substantive areas are particularly strong for human-resource development, science and technology, and institutional development; they are the major driving forces for rural development identified by SSAAP.

Another part of the national project (to study and advise on U.S. policies of economic cooperation) was the commissioning of a book on this topic by noted authorities from government, universities, and international development agencies (Berg and Gordon, eds. 1989). This book addresses three broad themes: the international context in which development activities will occur in the 1990s; U.S. interests in the Third World, and the capacities of public and private U.S. universities to participate in international development; and the issues involved in the organization and implementation of U.S. policies and programs for international development cooperation. The essence of these papers reinforces the need for U.S. action in the substantive areas identified above. Dramatic changes have occurred (and are occurring) in the economic, political, and natural-resource environments of countries around the world that require new rationales, priorities, and approaches to meet the challenge of increasing interdependence in the 1990s and into the next century.

An official policy statement of USAID, issued in 1989, outlines the goals, directions, and priority areas of investment for the agency's food and agriculture programs, and includes recommended steps for implementation and achievement. Program goals for the 1990s are "to increase the income of the poor majority, and expand the availability and consumption of food, while maintaining and enhancing the natural resource base" (USAID 1989). As rural poor comprise a majority of the population in many LDCs, it is important to expand their agricultural production and real income. Increased farm output stimulates agribusiness and leads to other industrial and nonindustrial growth, creating more jobs and income in rural areas. Increased food availability enhances the nutrition and the health required for increased human productivity. Maintaining and enhancing the natural-resources base is essential for sustained food production and income. Investment in agriculture and rural development will continue to receive major agency attention and investments in the 1990s.

Food self-reliance is emphasized in contrast to food self-sufficiency as a means for LDCs to achieve food security. Food aid is also considered as a potential contributor to income and human-capital growth especially in countries at initial low levels of development. It can also relieve pressure on fragile natural resources while technology, institutions, and policies are developed to increase agricultural production without resource degradation. This approach recognizes the potential benefits of expanded trade with the countries we help, as well as improved national security and conservation of the environment. Enlightened self-interest must be recognized along with humanitarian motives.

Development assistance should be tailored to the special needs of the individual developing country including its stage of development, potential for economic growth, political commitment to growth with equity, etc. Expanded production and the availability of basic food crops will continue to be the agency's focus in many poorer countries. "In countries that have advanced and as others advance in income, agency programs will move toward animal agriculture, aquaculture, and horticulture; food processing, packaging, and distribution; consumption and nutrition enhancement; agricultural business; private sector research and technology initiative; and international trade" (USAID, ii). The agency is committed to invest talent and money in meeting the goals and directions outlined above through strengthening country policies, institutions, technology, and the private sector.

A recently published book by Nicholas Eberstadt (1988) provides some provocative views on the purpose of U.S. foreign aid, many of which coincide with ideas expressed at the Winrock conference. The major purpose of U.S. development assistance should be to increase American political power throughout the world and to support the post-war, liberal-economic order the United States helped to create and is committed to maintain. It is asserted that the United States can achieve the greatest security under a world order that accepts, as legitimate, the free international flow of information, trade, technology, and capital. The strategic goal dictated by United States moral and humanitarian concerns is to use American power to promote a system that offers all nations and peoples opportunities to participate in broad-based material improvement. All U.S. foreign aid, Eberstadt argues, should be based on the foregoing principles.

Development aid should encourage self-sustaining economic growth, but Eberstadt asserts that too much of past U.S. aid has been spent on social programs that merely perpetuate the existing LDC governments' inefficiency and the vested interests of the ruling classes. It is not the volume of concessional aid that sets the limit on economic growth in LDCs, but rather their own policies, administrative competence, and willingness to take advantage of economic opportunities in international markets. He asserts that AID policy makers have paid too little attention to the policy environment in LDCs or the resulting incentives and disincentives. Many social programs "fund unproductive public consumption" rather than create human capital. Development-assistance projects that do not promote self-sustaining economic growth and increasing government competence should be revised or eliminated. Some of Eberstadt's recommendations include: put AID back into the State Department, review U.S. contributions to U.N. development activities, cut back soft lending for development, reform PL 480, encourage statistical competence in LDCs, increase technical assistance through U.S. universities, expand competitive funding in support of technical innovations in LDCs, develop moveable "policy hospitals" for rulers and decision makers in LDCs to dispense information on the economic and social consequences of alternative policies, and help governments make markets work.

Luther Tweeten (1989) states that the economic destiny of developing countries depends more on their internal policy decisions than on external forces. What he terms as the economic degradation process (EDP) cannot be attributed to external factors, such as declining international terms of trade, transnational corporations, dependency, and colonialism, but rather to poor economic-performance results from internal factors, including culture, a late start in development and, especially, domestic macroeconomic policies. These are manifested in persistent deficits, debt accumulation, inflation, overvalued currency, and foreign-exchange shortage.

A more unorthodox view of foreign aid and development somewhat similar to Tweeten's is expressed by P. T. Bauer (1981) who contends that in even the poorest countries, economic growth is possible without foreign assistance. What is needed is a certain amount of thought and enterprise among people with the appropriate social mores to sustain them, and a firm but limited government that permits market forces to operate. Egalitarianism is challenged as an appropriate goal. Also, in Bauer's view, the conventional rationalizations for foreign aid are found to be weak. He contends that the powerful political proponents of foreign aid in the Western countries may benefit more from it than the intended recipients. The linkage between the "special drawing rights" of the International Monetary Fund and the aid process contain the potential for world inflation through politicization of the IMF.

TRANSACTION COSTS AND MULTIDISCIPLINARY SIMULATIONS IN THE HISTORY OF THOUGHT AND RESEARCH ON INTERNATIONAL RURAL DEVELOPMENT

Bromley's paper (Part IV, Section 1, Chapter 5, entitled "Economic Institutions and the Development Problem: History and Prognosis") profoundly affected the work done by SSAAP's editorial group after the Houston conference, by greatly increasing the editorial group's interest in the public choice/transaction cost approach to the study of institutional change. A recent paper by Rausser entitled "A New Paradigm for Policy Reform and Development" (1990) is also relevant.

Chapter 1 of the previous section (Part IV, Section 1) on domestic agriculture stresses the historical consistency among the scenario policy analyses of the 1920s, farm-management-planning procedures, general systems simulations, and such holistic multidisciplinary analyses as described by Busch (Part III, Section 1, Chapter 5) and Bubolz and Sontag (Part II, Section 1, Chapter 5). This review does not need to be repeated here; instead, we need to review the corresponding parts of the history of thought and the work on international rural development that were not sufficiently covered in the works reviewed above by Eicher and Baker, Schuh and Brandão, and Mellor and Mudahar.

A book, *Systems Economics: Concepts, Models, and Multidisciplinary Perspectives* (1987), edited by contributing editors Fox and Miles, views systems models in a broad multidisciplinary way that differs markedly from large-scale econometric simulation models that contain time dimensions in a manner highly specialized on economics. What is described in the Fox/Miles book is generally similar to the less formally described systems analysis of Busch and the Bubolz/Sontag views of human ecology. Chapter 5 of the Fox/Miles book relates multidisciplinary modeling to traditional farm management and policy analysis, and, more importantly for this section on international rural development, to the use of general systems-simulation models in Nigeria and South Korea. Particular attention is also paid (pp. 100–105) to problems of evaluating such models versus the large-scale econometric models that have fallen in repute (Johnson et al. 1969; Johnson et al. 1971; Lee et al. 1982; Thorbecke and Hall 1982). Further, stress is placed on the importance of iterative interactions among analysts, decision makers, and affected persons in what may be described as a multidisciplinary socio-politico-administrative process. It was also stressed that the size of the models, their degree of formalization, and whether or not they are computerized are less important than holism, multidisciplinarity, iterative interaction, and focus on the domain of a problem or a well-defined set of problems. This is, of course, consistent with the Busch and Bubolz/Sontag chapters mentioned above.

ORGANIZATION OF THIS SECTION

The chapters that follow provided background and analysis for the agenda-setting exercise at Houston. They focus on structural change and globalization of the world's agriculture, four driving forces for development, and the policy prescriptions for accelerated rural development in the developing countries. A brief description of the contents of Chapters 2 through 10 is presented in the following paragraphs. Chapter 11 includes the social science agendas, vis-a-vis international rural development, that were developed at Houston and later supplemented by the SSAAP editorial staff.

Schuh's chapter entitled "International Affairs and Economic Development" (Part II, Section 2, Chapter 2) elaborates the significance of the rapid emergence of a global food and agriculture system for agricultural development in both developed and developing countries, as well as the critical, but still poorly understood, impact of macroeconomic policies. Schuh elaborates what is currently known about the processes of agricultural and economic development, stresses the need for further work toward a general theory of development, and presents a list of strategic issues that require social science research.

Chapter 3 by Michael Lipton explores the roles of social scientists in agricultural technology assessment. Donors and recipient countries generally agree that the goals of development are to maximize some agreed-upon combination of increased growth, reduced poverty, and environmental stability. The agenda for social scientists is to help identify "What technology works where and most effectively in a given country." He stresses the importance of the knowledge of time sequences, cross sections, and case studies to better understand the processes and causal sequences underlying technology creation-and-adoption successes that can be achieved in a manner consistent with Section 4 of Part 3 on the use of a public choice/transactions approach to technical advance. Finally, he stresses that social scientists need to advise what type of technology is most likely to produce favorable outcomes (more successful or faster) with respect to growth, poverty alleviation, and environment. Assessments, he argues, will be more useful if social scientists explore the interests, perceptions, and power of groups that influence agricultural research, and take these into account when making recommendations.

John Staatz focuses Chapter 4 on structural adjustment and market reform in the developing countries. A case is made for needed social science research in assessing the appropriate roles and performance of the state and private sectors in planning and price formation, as well as the most effective institutions to handle input and output marketing. Today's dramatic changes in the political and economic structures of many nations are being caused by disillusion with central planning in general, state production-and-marketing policies, institutions, and the economic austerity of many socialized developing countries, together with a more interrelated and open world economy. The need has never been greater for a better understanding of the private-/public-sector roles in market development and the creation or modification of institutions to facilitate agricultural development. Staatz outlines research needs. A need for multidisciplinary problem-oriented research is stressed.

Chapter 5 by Paul Thompson on the Bumpers Amendment deals with issues concerning the legitimacy of U.S. development assistance in helping foreign producers increase their production of commodities in direct competition with U.S. farmers, and the need for further research to document how international agricultural development impacts U.S. agriculture. He also raises questions about how a trade-based theory of national interest and geopolitics relates to agriculture and development.

Food security, with special reference to Africa, is the topic examined by Michael Weber and Thomas Jayne in Chapter 6. They highlight the chronic and transitory dimensions of food security, the available supplies and effective demands, and the aggregation problems to be considered at country or regional levels. The prime movers or determinants of food security include technology, institutions, policies, resources, and human capital. These dimensions and their interrelationships are illustrated with examples from research on food security in several African countries. Food and hunger problems are examined by identifying the vulnerable groups, how they relate to food and labor markets, the factors that impede their ability to grow more food or raise cash incomes, and how they adjust to natural crises and changes in policies, institutions, and technology. Only by understanding the constraints can strategies be designed to alleviate food insecurity. These interrelated knowledge gaps are outlined, including how to operationalize food security research and policy analysis, the appropriate balance between short- and long-run food security strategies, and how to determine the dynamic interaction among the prime movers and their disaggregated effects on incentives and welfare. Nine priority issues for research attention are outlined.

Chapter 7 by Glenn L. Johnson is a reprint of a 1988 paper. He explores the critical role that institutional reform was playing in the fall of 1988 in the socialist bloc, Western Europe, North America, and in the Western Pacific Rim. He uses the "transaction cost/institutional approach" to analyze institutional reforms, changes in agricultural institutions. The paper summarizes and interprets some 50 papers presented at the Symposium on Rural Development Strategies jointly conducted by the International Association of Agricultural Economists (IAAE), Chinese Society of Agricultural Economics (CSAE), and the Chinese Association of Agricultural Science Societies (CAASS) in October 1987 (Longworth 1989). Countries presented as cases included the socialist economies of China, Eastern Europe, and the Soviet Union; the NICs including Japan, Taiwan, and South Korea; India; and the developed Western countries. The "transaction cost approach to institutional change" was initially developed by Buchanan and Tullock, O. E. Williamson, Douglass North, William Baumol, and Allen Buchanan. This analytical approach has considerable merit from a multidisciplinary standpoint in that it explicitly includes institutional transaction costs and allows for irrationality, ideological commitments, and opportunistic use of power in forming and disbanding governmental institutions.

On-farm capital formation and rural financial markets (RFM) in developing countries are explored by Dale Adams in Chapter 8. As natural-resource enhancement and growth in physical capital is one of the four driving forces for rural development, more knowledge is needed on the institutions and processes by which increased productivity and capital formation occur at the farm level. Adams feels that farm capital formation in the aggregate is poorly understood and very difficult to analyze. Instead of attempting to measure or document its contribution to development, researchers might better focus on policies and other means to accelerate investment in particular forms of capital. Types of capital needed are highly time-and-place specific; mechanization, conservation practices, livestock expansion, and modern farming practices are potential areas for investigation. The efficiency of rural financial markets has a highly important impact on on-farm capital formation. Adams outlines five priority areas for research: loan transaction costs, differential access to loans and deposits among farmers, loan recovery, the relation of deposit mobilization to performance of RFMs, and the relations of informal financial arrangements to the design of better formal financial systems.

The focus of Clark Reynolds' analysis in Chapter 9 is on the "need for applied multidisciplinary problem-solving research on the linkages between agriculture and the rest of the economy, and the transition process between rural and urban development." A strong case is made for the need to expand nonagricultural production and employment opportunities in rural households, villages, small towns, and regional centers (the rural-transitional sector) because of the inability of major urban centers to productively incorporate the massive rural/urban migration to major cities that has occurred in many developing countries. The type of agricultural-sector modeling proposed calls for a more comprehensive and less formal framework than most previous rural-development work using this approach. Detailed microlevel economic, social, and technological studies of farm households and related agricultural and nonagricultural production units, as well as rural industry and service activities at the local and regional level would be utilized. The analytical framework would include both agricultural and "rural-transitional" sectors. Twelve research approaches are outlined that draw on the analyses developed in the chapter and from discussions at the Houston SSAAP conference.

In Chapter 10, Joe Kunsman responds on behalf of RICOP to the challenge of SSAAP's agendas for resident instruction in land-grant universities. Three major issues raised by SSAAP are targeted including globalization of agriculture and world economies, structural change in American agriculture, and the question of teaching disciplinary skills versus problem-solving education. There is no doubt for Kunsman that these are critical issues, and unless major changes are made in the structure and content of resident instruction, including increased social science emphasis, the land-grant universities will continue to fail in meeting the challenge.

CROSS REFERENCES IN THIS BOOK

PART I: INTRODUCTION

Ch. 5 The Role of the Social Sciences in Rural Development and Natural Resource Management, Vernon W. Ruttan

Ch. 6 Science and Technology Policy for the 21st Century: The United States in a Global Economy, G. Edward Schuh

PART II: DOMESTIC AND INTERNATIONAL FARM AND RURAL DEVELOPMENT

Sec. 1 Ch. 1 Introduction to Section on Domestic Agriculture

Ch. 6 The Relationship Between International Rural Development and International Trade and Finance, Timothy Josling

REFERENCES

Bauer, P. T. 1981. *Equality, the Third World and economic delusion.* Cambridge: Harvard University Press.

Baumol, William. 1986. Williamson's "The economic institutions of capitalism." *Rand Journal of Economics* 17, no. 2: 279-86.

Berg, Robert J., and David F. Gordon, eds. 1989. *Cooperation for international development: The United States and the Third World in the 1990s.* Boulder, Colo.: Lynne Rienner Publishers, Inc.

Buchanan, Allen. 1985. *Ethics, efficiency and the market.* Totowa, N.J.: Rowan and Allenheld.

Buchanan, James M., and Gordon Tullock. 1962. *The calculus of consent: Logical foundations of constitutional democracy.* Ann Arbor: University of Michigan Press.

Comptroller General of the United States. 1980. Report to the Congress. United States General Accounting Office, ID-80-12, 11 January.

The crisis in European agriculture. 1989. *Agriculture and Human Values* 6, nos. 1 & 2.

Eberstadt, Nicholas. 1988. *Foreign aid and American purpose.* Washington, D.C.: American Enterprise Institute for Public Policy Research.

Eicher, C. K., and D. C. Baker. 1982. Research on agricultural development in sub-Saharan Africa: A critical survey. International development papers, no. 1. East Lansing: Michigan State University, Department of Agricultural Economics.

Fox, Karl, and Don G. Miles, eds. 1987. *Systems economics: Concepts, models and multidisciplinary perspectives.* Ames: Iowa State University Press.

Hayami, Yujiro, and Vernon W. Ruttan. 1985. *Agricultural development: An international perspective.* Revised and expanded version. Baltimore: Johns Hopkins University Press.

Helmuth, John W., and Stanley R. Johnson, eds. 1990. *1988 World Food Conference proceedings.* Vol. 1, *Policy addresses*, & Vol. 2, *Issue papers*. Ames: Iowa State University Press.

Johnson, Glenn L. 1988. Technological innovations with implications for agricultural economics. *Agriculture and rural areas approaching the 21st century: Challenges for agricultural economics.* Edited by R. J. Hildreth, Kathryn L. Lipton, Kenneth C. Clayton, and Carl C. O'Connor, 82-108. Ames: Iowa State University Press.

Johnson, Glenn L., et al. 1969. Strategies and recommendations for Nigerian rural development, 1969/1985. Consortium for the Study of Nigerian Rural Development, July. East Lansing: Michigan State University, Department of Agricultural Economics.

Johnson, Glenn L., et al. 1971. *A generalized simulation approach to agricultural sector analysis with special reference to Nigeria.* East Lansing: Michigan State University, Department of Agricultural Economics.

Johnston, B. F., and J. W. Mellor. 1961. The role of agriculture in economic development. *American Economic Review* 51: 566-93.

Lee, Jeung-Han, et al. 1982. Structure and application of the Korean agricultural sector model. In *Agricultural sector analysis in Asia.* Edited by Max R. Langham and Ralph H. Ketzlaff. New York: Agricultural Development Council.

Lele, Uma. 1989. Agricultural growth, domestic policies, the external environment, and assistance to Africa—Lessons of a quarter century. MADIA discussion paper 1. Washington, D.C.: The World Bank.

Longworth, John W., ed. 1989. *China's rural development miracle with international comparisons.* Brisbane, Queensland, Australia: University of Queensland Press.

McCorkle, Constance M., ed. 1989. *The social sciences in international agricultural research—Lessons from the CRSPs.* Boulder, Colo.: Lynne Rienner Publishers, Inc.

Mellor, John W. 1988. Issues in world agriculture. In *Agriculture in rural areas approaching the twenty-first century.* Edited by R. J. Hildreth, Kathryn L. Lipton, Kenneth C. Clayton, and Carl C. O'Connor. Ames: Iowa State University Press.

Mellor, John W., and M. S. Mudahar. Forthcoming. Agriculture in economic development: Theories, findings and challenges in an Asian context. In *A survey of agricultural economics literature.* Vol. 4. Minneapolis: University of Minnesota Press for the American Agricultural Economics Assoc.

National Academy of Sciences. 1977. *World food and nutrition study: The potential contributions of research.* Washington, D.C.: National Research Council, Commission on International Relations.

North, Douglass. 1981. *Structure and change in economic history.* New York: W. W. Norton.

Presidential Commission on World Hunger. 1980. *Overcoming world hunger: The challenge ahead.* Abridged version.

Rausser, Gordon G. 1990. A new paradigm for policy reform and economic development. *American Journal of Agricultural Economics* 72, no. 3: 821-26.

Schuh, G. Edward, and Antonio Brandâo. Forthcoming. The theory, empirical evidence, and debates on agricultural development issues in Latin America: A selective survey. In *A survey of agricultural economics literature.* Vol. 4. Minneapolis: University of Minnesota for the American Agricultural Economics Assoc.

Schultz, Theodore. 1964. *Transforming traditional agriculture.* New Haven, Conn.: Yale University Press.

Smuckler, Ralph H., Robert J. Berg, and David F. Gordon. 1988. *New challenges new opportunities: U.S. cooperation for international growth and development in the 1990s.* East Lansing: Michigan State University, Center for Advanced Study of International Development.

Thorbecke, E., and L. Hall, eds. 1982. Agricultural sector analysis and models in developing countries. FAO economic and social development paper 5. Rome: Food and Agricultural Organization.

Tweeten, Luther. 1989. The economic degradation process. Fellows address at AAEA annual meetings, 30 July– 2 August. *American Journal of Agricultural Economics* 71, no. 5 (proceedings issue).

U.S. Agency for International Development (USAID). 1989. Food and agriculture goals, directions, and operations for the 1990s. 30 March. Washington, D.C.: Government Printing Office.

Whyte, William Foote. 1975. *Organizing for agricultural development human aspects in the utilization of science and technology.* New Brunswick, N.J.: Rutgers University, Transaction Books.

Williamson, O. E. 1985. *The economic institutions of capitalism.* New York: The Free Press.

Winrock International Institute for Agricultural Development. 1989. The Future of U.S. Development Assistance: Food, hunger and agricultural issues. Development Education Series. (January).

CHAPTER 2

INTERNATIONAL AFFAIRS AND ECONOMIC DEVELOPMENT

G. Edward Schuh[1]

INTRODUCTION

Agricultural economists have made important contributions to the understanding of agricultural and economic development. They have made far fewer contributions to understanding how the international agricultural economy functions, or to the role of economic (especially agricultural economic) forces in shaping international diplomatic relations and the distribution of political and economic power.

These deficiencies probably have a number of explanations. First, agricultural economists have traditionally had a microeconomic perspective, focusing on either the problems of the farm and farm people or on the narrowly defined agricultural sector. Second, international trade became significant to U.S. agriculture only in the 1970s and 1980s, and the profession has been most well developed in this country. Third, it was only in the last two decades that other, more general issues of agricultural affairs emerged on the international scene.

Today, a global perspective on agriculture suggests a number of important issues in urgent need of additional knowledge and research. Agricultural and economic development are both continuing challenges to policy makers, with very uneven rates of development characterizing the global economy. Economic policies are highly distorted, creating significant inefficiencies in the use of the world's agricultural resources. Global income is distributed very unequally, and international institutional arrangements provide for neither equity nor efficient use of agricultural resources. Global and transboundary problems, such as ozone depletion, the "greenhouse" or warming effect, acid rain, and deforestation, have emerged on the international scene, and there is a growing concern about the sustainability of agricultural output. Disagreements over these issues, about their causes, and about how to deal with them has set the stage for potentially serious international conflicts.

These problems and the research agenda that they imply are discussed in three stages: First, the setting for later analysis is provided by a discussion of the changing context of international agriculture. This is followed by a general discussion of international affairs in this changing setting. The third part is a more narrowly focused discussion of agricultural development. The paper closes with some concluding comments.

THE CHANGING CONTEXT OF INTERNATIONAL AGRICULTURE

The international economy underwent enormous change during the post-World War II period. At the beginning of that period, the system could best be characterized as a system of fairly autonomous national economies linked together with relatively small amounts of international trade. International capital markets were debilitated or nonexistent, and the international community had agreed to a system of fixed exchange rates to link the value of national currencies. For most countries, closed-economy economics could be used as a guide for economic policy.

Five significant changes in the "structure" of this economy have emerged over time; each is of substantial significance to global agriculture. Each of these changes, which are to a greater or lesser extent driven by technological breakthroughs in the communication and transportation sectors and by the computer revolution, are briefly characterized in the paragraphs that follow. This is followed by a discussion of the implications of the changes, and then the research agenda that they imply.

One important change in the structure of the international economy has been the persistent growth in trade relative to global gross national produce (GNP). There have been only five years that have been exceptions to this general tendency, and these have been years associated with serious economic recessions. This growth in trade, which accelerated in the 1970s due to the rapid expansion of the global economy and a surge of liquidity created by the increase in petroleum prices starting in 1973, caused most national economies to become more open to forces from the international economy.

A second significant change in international economy was the emergence of a well-integrated international capital market. Impetus to this market came when commercial banks in Europe discovered in the mid-1960s that they could lend the dollars they had on deposit and make a profit. Soon labeled the "Eurodollar Market," this market grew rapidly and soon emerged into what was called a "Eurocurrency Market" as the banks learned they as well could lend other currencies they had on deposit.

Major growth in this market came in 1973 with the OPEC-induced increase in petroleum prices. Because petroleum is priced and transacted in U.S. dollars, the world was soon flooded with what were called petrodollars. There was great concern among some observers that unless these petrodollars were recycled, the international economy would collapse. Thus, commercial banks were urged to recycle them, and they did—to a fault. The result is today's international debt problem.

In today's world, this international capital market is as important (if not more important) a link among national economies as is international commodity trade. In 1984, for example, total international financial flows were on the order of $42 trillion, while total international trade amounted to only $2 trillion. Of equal importance are the links that these capital markets created among national macroeconomic policies, a point to which we will return below.

A third major change in the structure of the international economy was the shift from the Bretton Woods fixed-exchange-rate system to what can be best described as a system of bloc-floating exchange rates. In this system, the values of the major currencies float relative to each other, but the values of a number of lesser currencies are fixed to them. The result is a system that, on the surface, appears to have a great deal of fixity but, in practice, has a great deal of implicit flexibility.

A fourth change in the international economy was the emergence of a great deal of monetary instability starting about 1968. This increased instability is not well understood but, as we will see below, it is of great significance to international agriculture, especially in light of the other changes that have been outlined above. The instability has two important components: The first is the short-term instability that increases transaction costs for international transactions. The second component is the long swings in currency relationships which have characterized this period, and which have important trade consequences. The dollar, for example, experienced a six-year fall from 1973 to 1979, then a six-year rise until 1985, and then another sustained decline until late 1988 when the U.S. Federal Reserve began pursuing a tighter monetary policy in an attempt to dampen the emerging signs of inflation in the U.S. economy.

The fifth and final change in the international economy, which is of significance to agriculture, is the apparent shift of comparative advantage in the global economy. This shift seems to be rooted in two fundamental developments. The first is the growing capacity for agricultural research in the countries of the tropical south. Part of this capacity is in a system of some thirteen strategically located International Agricultural Research Centers (IARCs) funded by the international community. Each center has its own research capability, but the system also works to strengthen research capacity in the developing countries. In addition to this capacity, many developing countries are belatedly developing their own capacity for agricultural research. The result is, for the first time in modern history, a capability to produce new production technology for food crops in tropical regions.

The second development affecting international comparative advantage is the growth in general education in the developing countries. This growth in general education makes it possible for highly transferable production technology in the manufacturing sector to shift from one country to another. Such shifts have been taking place quite rapidly in labor-intensive sectors, and have contributed importantly to the emergency of the so-called newly industrialized countries.

These developments are changing comparative advantage on the international scene at a rapid pace. Newly industrializing, developing countries are emerging as major exporters of manufactured products and importers of agricultural commodities. At the other extreme, developed countries such as the United States have become increasingly competitive in commodity markets, while losing their edge in some manufacturing sectors. This process is more complicated than these two polar examples suggest, however: as an example, Brazil has become an important exporter of some manufactured products and, at the same time, has garnered a significant share of the soybean exports and has come to dominate exports of frozen orange juice.

Turning now to the implications of these changes in the structure of the international economy, there are a number worth singling out. First, the growth in trade relative to global GNP plus the vast expansion of international capital markets implies national economies that are far more open than they were at any time in the past. This means that open-economy economics now has to serve as the framework for understanding international agriculture and as a guide for agricultural policy. It also means that national economies are increasingly beyond the reach of national economic policies. This, alone, has been a major source of frustration to policy makers and citizens alike as they see policies that were designed in the past for closed economies lose their effectiveness in the more open economies.

This increased openness also implies a bifurcation of policy making and implementation. Some part of policy shifts upward to the international level and becomes imbedded in the codes, rules, and disciplines of the General Agreement on Tariffs and Trade (GATT), the International Monetary Fund, and the United Nations' environmental agency. Another part of policy making and implementation shifts downward to the state and local levels. In the process, the character of the policy changes as it shifts away from its previous focus on commodity markets to deal, instead, with factor markets, resource use, and locally adapted income policy. These shifts probably lead to more efficient resource use since policies can be tailored more closely to local resource endowments. However, they may lead to a decline in the attainment of equity goals if geographic variations in income reflect differences in resource endowment.

Other important implications are associated with the emergence of the international capital market and the shift to flexible exchange rates. Prior to these developments, agriculture was almost totally exempt from the effects of changes in monetary and fiscal policies. In the presence of these developments, however, agriculture—as a tradeable sector—shares in the burden of adjustment to changes in these policies. Changes in monetary policy, for example, instead of being totally reflected in changes in interest rates, now induce international flows of capital. These, in turn, influence exchange rates, and these influence how competitive the tradeable sectors are in foreign markets.

Thus, agriculture—as a tradeable sector—shifts from almost complete isolation from monetary and fiscal policy to being one of the sectors that has to bear the burden of the adjustment to changes in these policies. This has rendered agriculture a great deal more instability than it had in the past. The problem is complicated by the bloc-floating nature of the system, since large adjustments may be imposed implicitly on the tradeable sectors of countries that peg the value of their currencies to the value of currencies that float. This explains, in part, why a country such as Brazil did so well in the 1970s and so poorly in the 1980s. In the 1970s, Brazil benefited from the fall in the value of the dollar, while in the 1980s it suffered the consequences of the large rise in the value of the dollar.

The combination of well-integrated international capital markets and flexible exchange rates also establishes a strong linkage between financial and commodity markets. In fact, today, one can hardly understand commodity markets without understanding developments in international financial markets. Moreover, in understanding these linkages between financial markets and commodity markets, it isn't just domestic monetary and fiscal policies that matter. The policies in other countries are important as well, since they help determine the size of intercountry differentials in interest rates and, hence, the size of the induced flows of capital.

In this kind of world, there are also important linkages among the conditions of financial markets, exchange rates, and domestic-commodity programs, especially if the domestic-commodity programs involve rigid price-support levels. In the first half of the 1980s, for example, the large rise in the value of the dollar eventually caused market prices in the United States to settle on support levels. As the value of the dollar continued to rise, U.S. commodities were increasingly priced out of international markets as stimulus was given to the producers in other countries to increase their supplies. This was a classic case of shooting oneself in the foot.

A related problem is the implication of the large and sustained swings in the value of national currencies. Such large swings tend to mask underlying comparative advantage while, at the same time, imposing large adjustments on the tradeable sectors and generating protectionist pressures. For example, U.S. agriculture was not as inherently competitive as it seemed to be in the 1970s when the dollar was falling, nor was it as inherently lacking in competitiveness as it seemed to be in the first half of the 1980s when the dollar was strong and rising. Moreover, the first half of the 1980s witnessed the strongest pressures for protection in the United States since those that were experienced in the post-World War II period.

The misleading signals produced by long swings in exchange rates, especially when they are driven by conditions in international capital markets, are of special significance when biological cycles (tree crops and livestock) and gestation periods (livestock) are long. An important consequence is that resource commitments are almost always wrong in an ex post sense. This leads to a significant loss in resource efficiency over time.

The research agenda implied by the above issues should include the following:

1. The design of domestic agricultural policies and programs that are consistent with changes in the international economy. This should include some means of dealing with the unstable prices created by monetary instability and the large adjustments implied by the large and sustained swings in the values of national currencies. Some means of decoupling income-support measures for agriculture from domestic agricultural prices also needs to be found.
2. International financial markets and foreign exchange markets are still poorly understood. Improved knowledge of these markets is needed if: sound economic policies are to be designed, outlook work is to be based on sound fundamentals, and private economic agents are to have a sound basis for decision making.
3. The linkages among financial markets, foreign exchange markets, and commodity markets are still poorly understood. The models needed to understand these various linkages are inherently complex. The political dimensions of the international financial markets and foreign exchange markets are also poorly understood.
4. The linkages among the policies in different countries are now very important in understanding the trade flows, the domestic terms of trade within national economies, and the prices of agricultural commodities. Very little research on these linkages has been done. More research is also needed to understand the political forces that drive trade interventions and influence the rural and urban biases in food and agricultural policies.
5. The instability in financial and foreign exchange markets needs to be better understood. Sound institutional arrangements that transmit the risk and uncertainty inherent in these markets cannot be designed unless the sources of the instability are better understood.
6. More research is needed to understand why governments do what they do. The government sector is large in all economies. It is not possible to understand the economy as a whole without understanding why governments intervene in the way they do.
7. Agricultural policies and development strategies are needed for a world of large and sustained swings in the value of national currencies. More effective adjustment policies are also needed.
8. Research is needed to better understand the international shifts in comparative advantage and the economic forces driving these shifts. Projections of these shifts into the future are needed if policy makers are to have a sound basis for economic policy.

INTERNATIONAL AFFAIRS

For the purposes of the present paper, international affairs are defined as those issues that cross national borders and involve the relationships among countries, either bilaterally or multilaterally. Given the rapid integration of the international economy, these issues are becoming increasingly important and receive more and more attention from policy makers.

One such issue is the problem of famines that occur periodically in some countries and dominate our television screens. The magnitude of such famines and their frequency are not nearly what they used to be. The reason for this is that the growth in international trade of food and agricultural commodities has given the world a true global system of food and agriculture. Consequently, shortfalls in one part of the world are offset by "surpluses" in other parts, with the imbalances evened out by the means of trade.

The emergence of this system is a significant accomplishment and a consequence of general economic development in the international scene. The system has evolved so well, in fact, that there have been no major famines in the post-World War II period except in those countries where the governments have hidden the problem from the international community for political reasons, or advised this community of a problem after it was too late to deal with the logistic problems of getting food to the disadvantaged people. The African famines of recent years have been of this nature.

The solution to this problem is to find the means to prevent governments from committing crimes against their own people. This is an aspect of international government that the world still needs to address. If the international trading system is not able to deal with localized shortfalls in production, however, the World Food Programme is an international agency that has the means to address such localized problems if it knows about them in time. The difficulty lies in finding ways to identify these problems earlier, and of finding means to deal with the political issues involved.

Widespread and chronic malnutrition on the global scene is a related problem. Unfortunately, the problem is not as well understood as it ought to be. Governments strive for food self-sufficiency or propose to carry large stocks to offset production shortfalls as the means to deal with malnutrition and potential famines. In point of fact, neither problem is typically associated with a supply problem, nor can they be dealt with by these means except at a very high cost. Both problems, the political cases cited above excepted, are a consequence of inadequate income for acquiring the needed food. Thus, chronic malnutrition is basically a poverty problem and not a production problem.[2]

In cases of generalized malnutrition, such as is found in India and parts of northeastern Brazil, the solution to the problem will be found only in economic development. More generally, but even in these cases, the solution rests with targeted feeding programs that get the food to those most in need by the means of income transfers either in kind or in the form of cash. The state of knowledge and the global availability of food is such that malnutrition and hunger could be wiped from the face of the earth. What is lacking is the political initiative and the will to bring it about.

A second issue of international affairs in agriculture is the large distortions of the use of the world's agricultural resources. Because of the policies practiced by national governments, a large part of the world's agricultural output is produced in the wrong places. Developed countries tend to protect their agriculture and deal with the chronic income problems of that sector with policies that set domestic agricultural prices above international border price levels. On the other hand, developing countries discriminate against their agriculture by the means of overvalued currencies, explicit export taxes, quantitative limitations on exports, and marketing boards or other parastatals—all of which contribute to shifting the domestic terms of trade against agriculture. The consequence is that too much of the world's agricultural output is produced in the high-cost, developed countries and too little is produced in the low-cost, developing countries.

This configuration of national agricultural policies, which is implemented in a large part by the means of trade and exchange-rate policies, sacrifices a great deal of agricultural output. It also sacrifices a great deal of national income on the international scene. The world could afford to expend a great deal to eliminate these distortions.

The ninth round of multilateral trade negotiations in the post-World War II period is currently underway in Geneva. For the first time in this period, agricultural issues are high on the agenda. Unfortunately, these negotiations are focusing almost exclusively on problems of access and on the use of export subsidies. The widespread use of distortions in exchange rates as barriers to trade and the discriminatory policies used by the developing countries against their agriculture are being almost totally ignored. This is to ignore most of what is important and it leads one to believe that the chances for successful negotiations are almost nil (Schuh, 1988).

A related issue is the export-subsidy war currently being waged between the United States and the European community. In addition to threatening a more general trade war between these two important economic blocs, this "war" imposes large economic costs on the developing countries. By causing international prices to be lower than they would otherwise be, they reduce foreign-exchange earnings on the parts of competing developing-country exporters while, at the same time, imposing large adjustment costs on the agriculture of importing countries. These costs are real, despite the fact that export subsidies are income transfers to importing countries.

The emergence of global environmental problems is another important issue of international affairs. Many of these problems are within national boundaries and need to be resolved primarily by the means of national policies. There are significant problems that are global or transboundary in nature, however, and they require international cooperation. These include the growing concern about global warming or the "greenhouse" effect, the ozone problem, the problem of acid rain, and deforestation.

The high rates of interest in developing countries give a short-term bias to the economic activities in these countries. Thus, they exploit their soil resources and create problems of erosion and they chop down their forests for short-term gain, ignoring the longer-term effects on the climate for both themselves and other countries. In other cases, the absence of property rights leads to overgrazing and the loss of vegetation that holds soil in place.

Many of these issues are problems of the international community. The opportunities for international collaboration are great; moreover, in some cases, the need for such cooperation is rapidly becoming an imperative. The means to bring about this collaboration and cooperation need to be found.

Significant attempts at economic integration are another issue of international affairs. The recently concluded Canada/United States Free Trade Agreement is an important example. Although this agreement did little to liberalize agricultural trade between the two countries, more general liberalization is significant. EED-92, which proposes to eliminate all barriers to trade and resource mobility in the European community by the year 1992, is another such initiative. Other suggestions for further economic integration are circulating on the international scene, including proposals for the integration of Mexico and/or Japan into the Canada/United States agreement, or the possibility of Japan creating its own Southeast Asia trading bloc.

These exercises in integration can bring about a great deal of trade liberalization in their own right. A key issue, however, is whether, in the process of establishing the integration, protectionist barriers are created against the rest of the world. If they are, the net effect may well be negative. On the other hand, these various efforts at integration have the potential to further trade liberalization. The United States and Canada, for example, could well extend an open invitation to other countries to join their agreement as long as they were willing to abide by the same rules. Such an initiative may have far more potential for general trade liberalization than multilateral negotiations.

The need for reform of the international monetary system is another issue that should be high on the international-affairs agenda. This monetary system is now of critical importance to the global agricultural system. Monetary disturbances and large swings in exchange rates are major sources of shocks to global agriculture.

At least two things are needed to improve this system (Schuh 1986). The first is the need for an international central bank to provide for the stable growth in liquidity for the global economy. This would relieve the U.S. Federal Reserve from its present role of being central banker for the world, which it is playing rather badly, and enable it to manage the U.S. economy more effectively. The second reform needed is for the world to shift to generalized floating-exchange rates. Current suggestions to return to something along the lines of the Bretton Woods fixed-exchange-rate system are misguided. The magnitude of international financial flows makes that an unrealistic proposal. Generalized floating, on the other hand, will lead to more stability in exchange rates since the effects of shocks and disturbances to the system will be spread more widely.

The need to strengthen the global system for agriculture research is another important international-affairs issue. Significant progress was made in the late 1960s and in the 1970s in building an effective international system, with rapid increases in support from the international community. As noted above, there are now thirteen strategically located centers (IARCs) in this system, with an annual budget of slightly over $200 million. Unfortunately, this system has now lost a great deal of its momentum. Donor support is leveling off and new initiatives to expand the system are resisted.[3]

Production and distribution of new production technology are keys to agricultural modernization in the developing countries, as we will see below. Moreover, research is needed as the basis for addressing the rapidly emerging environmental problems on the international scene. Expanding and improving the existing system should have high priority.

Finally, there is the issue of the strategic role of agriculture in the international distribution of economic and political power. Most developing countries turned away from agriculture as the means to strengthen their economies in the post-World War II period. Yet, the developed countries tend to have a strong agricultural sector, even though the experience of Japan should caution against agricultural fundamentalist instincts.

The importance of agriculture has little relation, over the longer term, to the number or share of the people employed in that sector. Its importance derives from the fact that everybody consumes food. Equally as important, the contribution that agriculture can make to general economic growth and development depends importantly on the ability to raise productivity in the sector. These are issues to be addressed in the next section.

Some strategic issues needing research in the area of international affairs are as follows:

1. High priority should be given to research that helps to eliminate the massive disequilibrium in world agriculture. Such research should try to understand why governments distort their economies in the way they do, and also lead to the design of institutional means to bring about economic adjustments.
2. Little is known in a systematic way about international capital markets and their interactions and linkages with commodity markets. Improved knowledge is needed if national policy makers are to design policies for dealing with the instability that comes from these markets, and to design international institutional arrangements to make these markets work more efficiently.
3. Research that leads to improvements in the international monetary system also has a high payoff. The present system, based as it is on the remnants of an old system and ad hoc arrangements as periodic problems arise, may be the worst of all possible worlds. A key issue is to devise the means to gain the support of international commercial banks for reform of the general system. Research that diagnoses current problems and designs new institutional arrangements should have high priority.
4. Research designed to help eliminate malnutrition and hunger from the global scene should also have high priority. The means to do this is at hand, but the institutional arrangements and the political will are not yet present. Improved nutrition is an important form of human capital. It is thus an important means of raising productivity on the international scene. This is an issue of investment and economic growth; it is not an equity issue except in the sense that it provides economic growth so that the poor and disadvantaged share in it.
5. A great deal more research is needed to better understand global environmental issues. For example, there is still a great deal of disagreement over whether the greenhouse effect is real or not. Similarly, it is not known whether cutting down tropical forests reduces the supply of oxygen, as some people believe. In cases such as the greenhouse effect, the long lags of the projected effects suggest that the measures to deal with the problem should not await convincing evidence that the effects are detrimental. Research that leads to the design of institutional arrangements that deal with these problems should also have high priority.
6. Rapid growth in the world's population contributes importantly to the emergence of environmental problems. Many countries can still be classified as Malthusian, with strong links between agricultural development, the

availability of food supplies, and population growth. The economic incentives for rapid population growth need to be better understood. Institutions providing the means of contraception and thus enabling families to control their number of children need to be improved.

7. Improved knowledge is also needed on the role of agriculture as a source of economic growth and the basis of political power, both nationally and on the international scene (Schuh 1981). This knowledge provides the basis for improving policy, and for bringing about institutional change.

AGRICULTURAL AND ECONOMIC DEVELOPMENT

Agricultural economists have probably contributed as much to understanding the processes of economic development as have any other class of economists.[4] Growth models have been produced in abundance by general economists, but these models have little policy content of any significance and have limited value in understanding what actually takes place as an economy develops. Similarly, political scientists have given little attention to understanding the forces that drive agricultural development, and social scientists in general have neglected the important problem of designing new institutional arrangements for an ever-changing economy and society.

Unfortunately, we do not yet have a theory of economic development, or even of agricultural development. What we have is a general consensus that the production and distribution of new production technology is a cheap source of income streams and thus must be the engine of economic growth at early stages of political and economic development. When most of the resources in an economy are in agriculture, as they are in the case of low-income countries, then the process of technological change must start in that sector.

Both elements of this proposition are primarily empirical in nature, however; they are not elements that come as theoretical propositions. A recent paper by Bob Lucas (1985) casts the problem in the context of searching for high-payoff information. This may yet give us a general theory of economic development.

A general theory of development would explain why and how particular nations grow and develop, in both their political and economic dimensions. It would also explain how and why the economies of other nations stagnate and fail to develop or, at best, grow at very slow rates. In this respect, it is noteworthy that development theories that emerge from developed countries tend to put the emphasis on the positive side, while those from the developing or low-income countries tend to concentrate on explaining stagnation or slow rates of growth.

Another dichotomy in these theories is that those from developed countries tend to be based on closed-economy models and ignore, or give little emphasis to, international trade issues, while those from the developing countries are rooted firmly in the international system. Generally described as dependency theories, these paradigms usually posit that the developed countries get that way by exploiting their underdeveloped brethren. The central mechanism by which this exploitation is supposed to take place is through changes in the external terms of trade, which are hypothesized to shift from the low-income countries to the favor of the developed countries. An important, but very questionable, implicit assumption in this perspective is that the total economic pie is fixed and, thus, one country can grow only at the expense of others.

Four sets of empirical data have largely discredited these theories. First, during the 1970s, the developing countries (the periphery) in the aggregate grew at a faster rate than the developed countries (the center). This was contrary to one of the main predictions of the theory. Second, countries that pursued import-substituting and inward-looking industrialization as the engine of development, an important policy prescription of the theory, generally obtained disappointing results. Third, countries that did the reverse by pursuing outward-looking and export-driven development policies have done unusually well. And fourth, the upper-income, industrialized countries of the west have rapidly become the major exporters of agricultural commodities, important importers of manufactured products, and importers of agricultural commodities. This is contrary to the main empirical assumption of the theories.

Economic development has produced significant political and economic forces in the international economy during the last 10 to 15 years and has significantly changed the relations among national economies. Central to this process has been the emergence of the newly industrialized countries (NICs), seven nations that have pulled themselves up by their bootstraps in a short period of time. These countries include Taiwan, Hong Kong, Singapore, and South Korea in Asia, and Argentina, Brazil, and Mexico in Latin America. Labor-intensive manufacturing sectors slipped rapidly from Japan to these countries as the level of general education in these countries rose. A new set of NICs is emerging on the international scene and includes countries such as India, China, and the Philippines. Because of the rapid growth in these economies, the consequences to the international economy will indeed be great.

Similar development experiences, on the agricultural side, are taking place among the developing countries, with new production technology as the driving force. The combined effects are, as noted above, shifting comparative advantage on the international scene in a dramatic fashion, and they can be expected to change it even more rapidly in the future.

An important feature of economic development is what can, perhaps, be best described as the one iron law of economics. This is the tendency for agriculture's share of employment to decline as economic development proceeds. This tendency and the conditions that give rise to it were first noted by John S. Mills. T. W. Schultz later popularized the notion and, in the 1950s, Colin Clark documented the trend. Later, Bruce Johnston (1970) pulled the evidence together again.

This "law" is important because it creates a serious adjustment problem for agriculture that is rooted in the forces of economic development. In response to those economic forces, labor tends to migrate from agricultural to nonagricultural employment fairly early in the development process. At first, this is reflected in lower growth rates in agricultural employment than in nonagricultural employment, with the result that agriculture's share of employment tends to decline even though total agricultural employment continues to increase. Later in the development process, agricultural employment declines absolutely. Moreover, this process continues until late in the development process, as evidenced by the fact that agricultural employment in a highly developed economy, such as the United States, is still declining.

The significance of this tendency is that it creates a chronic income problem in agriculture, and trade and other adjustment problems are on top of it. Paradoxically, those who argue that agriculture should be the employer of last resort don't seem to realize what a serious income problem they create in recommending such policies.

The closest thing we have to a theory of agricultural development is a theory of human capital formation. An important part of this general theory is a theory of technical change and a theory of institutional innovation, as articulated by Hayami and Ruttan (1985). The starting point for this latter theory is the empirical proposition that investments in research that produce new innovations for agriculture tend to have high social rates of return. This is the same as saying that such investments are a cheap source of growth, or a cheap source of income streams.

The theory of induced innovations implies that these innovations will be focused on an efficient growth process in the sense that they will tend to ease the constraint implied by the most inelastic factor supply. As this process continues, it produces an agricultural "surplus" in the Nicholls (1963) sense, and this surplus can be used for the development of the rest of the economy. In addition to this product surplus, which can be used both to feed the nonfarm sector as well as for exports to earn foreign exchange, the process of technical change releases resources to the nonfarm sector, usually in the form of capital and labor.

As this process continues, backward and forward linkages emerge. The industrial sector becomes a source of input, such as fertilizer and mechanical instruments, for the further modernization of agriculture. And, as agriculture becomes more commercialized, the need for processing and marketing services arises. Labor leaves agriculture in response to economic forces, agricultural output grows, but the sector makes up a relatively small part of the economy as the development process goes forward. These processes continue as development proceeds. Agriculture can be a source of growth until fairly late in development processes.

Investments in improved nutrition and education complement the investments in producing new technology. Additional forms of human capital, nutrition, training, and education combine with technical advances to generally raise resource productivity in agriculture.

Success in agricultural development is creating a number of important problems on the international scene. For example, the success of the miracle rices has caused many countries in Asia to become self-sufficient in rice. This problem is widely referred to as the need for diversification. A common view is that the diversification will take place at the farm level, with individual producers shifting out of rice and into oilseeds, fruits, vegetables, and livestock products. However, a major component of the diversification process, which is inherently an adjustment problem, will probably involve adjustment of resources out of agriculture, especially labor. Moreover, a great deal of the diversification process will involve regional specialization, with the diversification taking place on a global scale. This specialization will involve the introduction of and/or an expansion in the production of maize and other feed grains, oilseed crops, fruits and vegetables, and livestock.

An important feature of this whole process will probably be a significant growth in international trade. Much of that trade may involve within-region flows, but much of it may also take place with countries outside the region. Thus, this regional development has important global implications.

Another important issue is the impact that agricultural and economic development have on the distribution of income. This has been an important controversy in recent years in many developing countries. Superficial studies in countries such as Brazil and Colombia have suggested that the relative distribution of incomes has become more unequal as these countries experienced rapid economic development. More careful analyses, however, suggest this is not the case, and that the broad masses of the poor tend to benefit significantly from economic growth.

A number of issues are important in understanding the income-distribution consequences of agricultural development. First, most developing countries are characterized by massive low-level productivity, with the bulk of the low productivity concentrated in agriculture (where most of the poverty is concentrated as well). The key to reducing this poverty is to produce and distribute new production technology, and to invest in human capital, including formal schooling, improved nutrition, and improved health. The issue is, in large part, one of reducing or eliminating absolute poverty. This can be done, in general, only by raising resource productivity; trying to raise the income of the masses by confiscating the income and assets from the wealthy would have little impact on the poor since there aren't enough assets or income to go around.

Another issue is that, under these conditions, doing something about poverty does not necessarily need to be at the expense of faster economic growth. To the contrary, if poverty-alleviation measures focus on productivity-enhancing investments in human capital, the distribution of income can be improved at the same time the rate of economic development is improved. Within the agricultural sector, however, the distribution of income will be influenced by land tenure arrangements and the distribution of property rights.

Finally, there is the problem of responding to the concern of farmers in developed countries that the development of agriculture in low-income countries poses a threat to their markets. There are circumstances in which such development activities can reduce markets for producers in these countries. In general, however, the relationship goes the other way. Future markets for developed-country agricultural commodities are likely to be in the developing countries. The key to realizing these markets is for there to be sustained increases in per capita income in those economies. The key to that will be modernization of the agricultural sector.

Brazil's experience illustrates this point very well. Its agricultural output expanded at a rate of 5 percent per year from 1960 through 1981. This was the highest rate of agricultural growth in the world, and significantly above the population growth rate. Yet imports of agricultural commodities grew at an annual rate of 15 percent a year, in physical terms, in this same period and, in value terms, at an annual rate of 25 percent per year. What U.S. farmers fail to recognize is that there is a demand effect as well as a supply effect when there is agricultural development. The demand effect may well outweigh the supply effect.

The research agenda, which emerges from this discussion of development issues, includes the following:

1. Basic research is needed to develop a more complete theory of agricultural development. What we have now is ad hoc and based on empirical propositions.
2. The mechanisms by which agricultural development is propagated needs to be better understood.
3. A great deal of work is needed on intersectoral labor markets. The speed with which labor is adjusted out of agriculture often plays an important role in determining how rapidly the development process proceeds. It also has a great deal to do with how equitably the benefits of agricultural development are distributed.
4. An important barrier to more rapid adjustment of agricultural labor is the fact that intersectoral labor adjustment often involves geographic migration of labor. Research is needed to determine how other economic activities can more efficiently be taken to the suppliers of agricultural labor. More effective decentralization of economic activities makes it possible to avoid the negative externalities associated with outmigration from rural areas.
5. A particular topic of considerable importance is what the new biotechnology will do to comparative advantage on the international scene. Will this technology be easily transferrable, or will it help give producers in the developed countries a competitive edge in the future? Of equal importance is the need to understand the severity of the adjustment problem in developing countries that will result from the diffusion of this technology.
6. Improved knowledge on the international agricultural system is needed if we are to understand how successful agricultural development in one point of the world is to effect other regions.
7. Research is needed to clarify the extent to which development of agriculture in low-income countries benefits or harms agricultural producers in the developed countries.

CONCLUDING COMMENTS

A global food and agriculture system has emerged on the international scene. At the same time, changes in the structure of the international economy have established strong linkages between financial markets and agriculture, and thus increased the importance of macroeconomic policy to the food and agriculture sector. This increased interdependence and expanded linkages with the rest of the economy create serious gaps in our knowledge about the food and agriculture sector.

Similarly, the global economy now finds itself in a period of sluggish growth, but the potential for widespread economic development is quite great. Once the global economy recovers from its present slump, these development processes will be unleashed and the forces for change will indeed be great. We should be anticipating these changes and designing strategies for the future. This will further increase the demand for knowledge on the international agricultural system.

NOTES

1. The first draft of this chapter was written while the author was director of Agricultural and Rural Development, the World Bank, Washington, D.C. The views expressed herein are the author's alone and in no way should be construed as official views of the World Bank. The current position of the author is Dean, Humphrey Institute of Public Affairs, University of Minnesota, Minneapolis. The author benefitted from comments on the earlier version of the paper by Glenn Johnson and two anonymous reviewers.

2. For a more ample discussion of these issues, see A. K. Sen (1981). For a policy perspective, see S. Reutlinger and J. van H. Pelekaan (1986).

3. For a discussion of what a global agricultural research syste m might consist of, see Ruttan (1983).

4. Surveys of the literature on agricultural development in Africa, Asia, and Latin America, written by Carl Eicher, John Mellor, and G. Edward Schuh, respectively, can be found in Volume IV of the American Agricultural Economics Association's Survey of the Postwar Literature in Agricultural Economics, forthcoming

REFERENCES

Hayami, Yujiro, and Vernon W. Ruttan. 1985. *Agricultural development: An international perspective.* 2d ed. Baltimore: The Johns Hopkins Press.

Johnston, Bruce. 1970. Agriculture and structural transformation in developing countries: A survey of research. *Journal of Economic Literature* 8:369–404.

Lucas, Bob, Jr. 1985. On the mechanics of economic development. Prepared for the Marshall Lectures, May, Cambridge University. Photocopy.

Nicholls, William H. 1963. An agricultural "surplus" as a factor in economic development. *Journal of Political Economy* 71:1–29.

Reutlinger, S., and J. van H. Pelekaan. 1986. *Poverty and hunger: Issues and options for food security in developing countries.* Washington, D.C.: World Bank.

Ruttan, Vernon W. 1983. Reforming the global agricultural research support system. In *Issues in Third World development.* Edited by Kenneth C. Nobe and Rajan K. Sampath, 405–18. Boulder, Colo.: Westview Press.

Schuh, G. Edward. 1981. Economics and international relations: A conceptual framework. *American Journal of Agricultural Economics* 63:767–78.

______1986. *The United States and the developing countries: An economic perspective.* Washington, D.C.: National Planning Assoc.

______1988. Exchange rates and their role in agricultural trade issues. In *World agricultural trade: Building a consensus.* Edited by William M. Miner and Dale E. Hathaway, 193–210. Halifax, Nova Scotia: Institute for Research on Public Policy. Washington, D.C.: International Food Policy Research Institute.

Sen, A. K. 1981. *Poverty and famine: An essay on entitlement and deprivation.* Oxford: Clarendon Press.

CHAPTER 3

SOCIAL SCIENCE ROLES IN MEETING THE NEEDS OF INTERNATIONAL DONORS FOR THE ASSESSMENT OF AGRICULTURAL TECHNOLOGIES

Michael Lipton[1]

I. INTRODUCTION

A title this long, set by others, tempts an author to an orgy of definitions. To some extent, I shall resist. However, three obvious and correct concerns of SSAAP—with "agroethics," the logic of social science, and the interest groups mediating between social science findings and policies—do require some effort to define terms.

1. *Social Science* includes not only economics, but also (at least) anthropology-cum-sociology, geography, demography, and politics. The perspective of this paper is largely economic. However, agricultural technology assessment—ex ante and ex post—requires an increasing ratio of the last four social science components to economics. There is, of course, a lot of theory and a good deal of statistical macrotesting around the noneconomic social sciences of technical change, and a good deal of modeling and testing of diffusion and innovation in the Everett Rogers tradition (very usefully reviewed, along with much economics material, in Thirtle and Ruttan [1987]). However, specific microstudies of institutions of interaction affecting technology generation or change—research labs, villages, extension services—are rare.

A few sociologists (notably, Rudolph and Rudolph 1967) and anthropologists (Richards 1985) have explored the role of societal factors such as religion, lineage, or community in affecting the extent of indigenous technical change, the speed of technology diffusion, or the impact of both on social structure and farm practice. Similarly, geographers—challenged, perhaps, by such economists as Pingali, Bigot, and Binswanger (1987)—occasionally try to explain why, given the economic and political variables, some spatial (agroclimatic, population-density linked, infrastructural [Wanmali 1985], etc.) characteristics appear to accelerate while others retard technical change. A handful of demographers has begun to measure the effects of alternative project technologies upon the fertility transition (Schutjer and Stokes 1984; Stoeckel and Jain 1986; Basu, Roy, and Nikhil 1979). Even fewer political scientists have explored the impact of alternative structures of authority upon the performance of technology-linked institutions (e.g., Leonard [1977] on extension in Kenya).

Economists usually find that such work is more useful than their own work in the branches of other people's subjects that they themselves have partly colonized (political economy, etc.; cf. Ruttan [1988] on economic versus classical anthropology), just as broad-range history of past agricultural change is usually more useful than cliometric reconstructions. Partly, this is a matter of taste; probably, however, economists can usefully participate in interdisciplinary work on "technology assessment" only when there exists a lot more ground-floor, descriptive microwork on the *operations* of social, political, spatial, and demographic *institutions* affecting technical change—not simply on the *statistical links* to such change of *variables* studied by these disciplines. The thin list of references cited above partially exposes my ignorance but, perhaps, it also suggests that attempts to explain technology outcomes in terms of political economy, economic anthropology, etc., may need a stronger ground floor (of empirical studies even more than of theoretical microfoundations) in politics, anthropology, etc.[2]

2. *Needs of international donors* present intriguing problems of definition. There are three distinct "aid purviews" involved:

a. All donors (not only those with agricultural projects, but also those giving program- or policy-supportive aid) need some "assessment" of where agricultural technology is going—of how its changes are likely to affect the gross national product (GNP), income distribution, and balance of trade of recipients, and also factor-mixes, and product prices via extra output, for major commodities.[3]
b. A (smaller) group of donors, supporting the appraisal or design stages of agricultural projects that have major technical options, needs assessment of likely technical progress, during project construction and use, that could change the relative efficiency of the alternative technologies.
c. A different subset of donors, aiding national or international agricultural research, needs to assess the likely

rate of progress on, and effects of progress with, research options (e.g., upland versus delta rice; conventional versus biotechnology-based plant breeding), and the likely impact of the donors' aid on these alternative rates and effects.

However, different donors have (or perceive)—with respect to their needs for assessment under a, b, or c above—different goals, different amounts of cash with which to meet them, and different domestic constraints upon turning knowledge into aid allocations. This last point is perhaps the least discussed. But if 90 to 95 percent of U.S. bilateral aid is preassigned by Congress, then United States Agency for International Development's (USAID) scope for making use of "technology assessment" is limited; for, to a large extent, the country-mix of aid determines the medium-term impact of technologies generated or diffused as a result of aid. Similarly, if the United Kingdom is undergoing severe pressure to use aid in support of exports, UKODA (United Kingdom Overseas Development Administration) can make little use of any success of social science in assessing agricultural technologies; social scientists' demonstration that British tractor aid displaced labor in Sri Lanka without raising output (cf. Farrington and Abeyratne 1982) demonstrated their intellectual freedom, but did little to reduce the success of lobbyists in diverting aid to subsidize otherwise unprofitable labor-displacing exports. There is nothing wrong with *overtly* using aid as a servant of domestic self-interest, but doing so while asking researchers to examine only "optimal" use of aid, or choice of technique, confuses the audience and wastes the skills of the researchers.

However, it is probably useful to limit needs of international donors to those needs related to the success of agriculture-linked projects and programs—a, b, and c above—in meeting a few goals generally agreed to be "good" for LDCs' (less-developed countries') populations. All donor and recipient governments and agencies prefer (subject to a huge, often hidden ceteris paribus) that aid should reduce poverty, accelerate economic growth, and prevent environmental degradation;[4] most donors, indeed, assert that these are the main goals of aid (though this is probably true, most of the time, for only some multilateral aid agencies and nongovernmental organizations (NGOs). This paper, therefore, concentrates mainly on the roles of social science in assessing agricultural technology to help donors, with recipients, reach these three goals.

3. The brief for this paper specified *agricultural* technologies. However, the effects of agricultural technology—on efficient growth, poverty, and sustainability—depend partly on the linkages between agriculture and other sectors and, therefore, on technical change in those sectors, whether or not it is induced by the agricultural technologies being assessed. For example, some characteristics of some new rice or corn varieties increase the relative cost of some methods of post-harvest processing; these methods tend to be rather more expensive, but also much more employment-generating per ton, than other methods more appropriate for new varieties (Greeley 1986). Hence, it is often useful to assess changes in agricultural technology alongside concomitant change in technologies of nonfarm production (and perhaps of consumption) affecting rural people.

4. What are donors' needs for *the assessment of technology* on the farm for its effects upon growth, poverty, and sustainability in recipient LDCs? If we are concerned with a, b, or c (detailed above), it is useful to approach this question via the language of the project cycle (Baum 1979).

A project's cycle comprises its identification, design, appraisal, approval, implementation, and monitoring-cum-evaluation. "Assessment" of alternatives (including termination) should enter at each stage, but is usually confined largely to appraisal and evaluation. "Technology assessment"—ex ante at appraisal, ex post at evaluation—involves comparisons of the effects (on growth, poverty, and sustainability) of the set of techniques, introduced as a result of project hardware or incentives, with the effects of alternative sets. The alternatives may involve different new technologies (alternative project designs or incentives) or continuation with the old farm methods (no project).

Often gains and losses from alternatives are summarized in benefit-cost analysis (BCA), which provides alternative benefit/cost ratios, or else internal rates of return. These summary "scores" per dollar spent include, in principle, all gains (net of all losses) to the nation attributable to a project: not only net national-product gains and (via income-distribution weights) net poverty gains or losses, but even desiderata not readily aligned with economic welfare gains, e.g., increased choice. In practice, most BCA pre-appraisals or post-evaluations confine themselves to net effects on total income within the project area.

Two difficulties are created by project-cycle approaches for technology assessment. First, confinement of assessment (whether for preappraisal or postevaluation) to the project area is especially inappropriate; successful new methods spread beyond it, displace older methods, and affect growth, poverty, and choice elsewhere. Second, "agricultural technology assessment" cannot be disassociated from the crop-mix, the facilities (e.g., roads and irrigation) supplied, and the effects of extra food production on consumers' prices; all have substantial implications beyond the project area. Even the borders of the project country may be unsuitable limits on technology assessment; the introduction of clonal teas into Sri Lanka probably benefitted that country despite price effects, but the net effect on LDCs has almost certainly been negative.[5]

II.

What happens if we extend the project-cycle approach to the assessment of technology *generation*—of donors' alternatives in type "c" activities (detailed in I above)? The last example shows that some of the problems of formal cost-benefit analysis loom especially large. Most of the remaining problems concern uncertainty.

The choice of a crop, region, or method to be favored in research will usually have a payoff—if at all—5 to 15 years after research begins. Relative factor and product prices will then be different; how different is hard to predict, but probably labor will be more plentiful (and labor-using research outcomes more desirable) than when the research choice was made. The location of poverty will be different, also not very predictable, but there is a fairly strong chance that a bigger proportion of the poor will be urban, or rural but near-landless. The environmental priorities will also be different.

There are at least two other uncertainties. "The big one" concerns the date (if any) and the extent of success in producing research outcomes, profitable for farm adoption, along each alternative research line (region, crop, etc.). To predict major conceptual breakthroughs in science would be to make "then" become "now" and, hence, invalidate the prediction (Popper 1968). In applied farm technology, some prediction is feasible, though I know of no systematic assessment of accuracy of past predictions, let alone of predictive methods; such an assessment is clearly a priority "social science role." A less daunting uncertainty concerns the rate and intensity of adoption of any profitable innovation that eventually comes out of research.

None of these problems in using BCA is special to projects seeking to generate new technology. They are, however, more serious for such projects. The gestation period of such projects is unusually long (and itself uncertain). Also, the date of success of any line of research is inherently harder to predict—and likelier to be "never"—than the date of completion, or even of social profitability, of a dam or a factory.

But, such problems are not the result of applying BCA to a project choice. They face appraisal, however informal, whether it be of the best way to design a dam or the best new technology to research. Placing a few numbers on the probability and value of outcomes—not "formal, structured models [but] informal, subjective intuition supported by some relatively simple systematic aids" (Scobie 1984, 4)—allows us (1) to compare the "subjective intuition" of persons with authority (to spend on, or to plan the use of, resources for agricultural technology generation or diffusion) with the intuitions of others, or with relevant evidence; (2) to test the sensitivity of the claim that the proposed research is best, both to different perceptions of the numbers ex ante or realization ex post, and to different relative valuations of goals, e.g., growth and poverty reduction.

Suppose that an aid donor wishes to allocate bilateral aid of $x among 36 possible areas for research into new agricultural technologies: for example, upland or lowland; amply rain-fed, drought-prone, or irrigated; concentrated on a major exported cash crop or on rice for domestic consumption; and based on agronomic practices, conventional plant breeding, or tissue culture (2 x 3 x 2 x 3 = 36). The simplest situation features:

(a) Discontinuity of investment, i.e., a given outlay on each route that will "buy" success by a known date—less outlay means failure, more means neither faster nor greater successes; following the date of "success," a reliably predictable adoption path;
(b) Known impacts on GNP, poverty, and environmental sustainability in the success-affected area (e.g., from conventional plant breeding for drought-prone, upland rice farmers);
(c) No cross-effects (via price, research, or otherwise) through which success in one area, or its diffusion to farmers, increases or decreases the prospects for success, or GNP, environmental sustainability, or poverty elsewhere;
(d) And no interaction between the degree of success in any research line and the price of the commodity produced by it.

In this case, the recipe is simple. Establish an *Indicator,* reflecting an agreed weighting between extra GNP, poverty reduction, and environmental sustainability. Spend the "given outlay" first on the amount of research needed to ensure "success" in the area (e.g., tissue culture of the lowland, irrigated, export crop) where success and adoption will produce the largest positive outcome on the "indicator" per research dollar spent. If any such dollars remain, "buy" the research needed to secure success in the area producing the second-largest outcome, and so on. Stop "buying" research when the positive impact on the "indicator," from buying success in the next area, would fall below the impact obtainable from spending the cash on activities other than technology development.

Of course, this certainty-equivalent model of assessing priorities in technology development is hopelessly crude. However, its crudities draw attention usefully (and fairly obviously) to the needed refinements. Also—notably in suggesting that research into many possible lines of technology development possesses, over a definable range only, economies of scale so dramatic as to imply near-discontinuity[6]—the model is in some ways nearer to reality than the probability approach suggested elsewhere (e.g., Scobie 1984; Lipton 1985, 40–41). However, the probability approach compels attention to crucial uncertainties affecting research, diffusion, and impact. It also pinpoints where political pressures could enter. And it suggests how its own recipe, "maximize expected net gain," might fail as a method of allocating funds for technology development under uncertainty.

The recipe would proceed roughly as follows: When confronted with two claims on resources for technology development, meet the claim with greater expected value. For each claim, expected value depends on three things. The first is research "success"—its likelihood, probable speed, and probable extent. The second is the new technique's area spread, viz. its logistic diffusion path, given "success." The third is the change in the "indicator," given diffusion. In a sense, the tendency to confine technology assessment to a calculation of a single "rate of return to research" misleadingly runs all three together (just as it misleadingly runs together the various, possibly separable, stages of the research process).

Can the claims on research resources be better judged by thus separately establishing expected values[7] for "success," diffusion, and impact? As for predicting the "success" of research, despite Popper's objection (1968) that if we could accurately predict future discoveries we could make them now, plausible Delphi-type procedures exist for consulting researchers and their peers and thereby estimating the likely degree and timing of research "success" (Scobie 1984); social scientists need to test whether, in fact, scientists correctly predict (or tend to overstate or understate) the expected time and extent of research successes.

Sufficient evidence on innovation diffusion exists to make some estimate of a new technique's likely diffusion speeds and patterns, given the effect on output, prices, and inputs. However (although M. Cernea [personal communication, 1981] has shown that postevaluations of World Bank agricultural projects tend to show good returns to the extent that preappraisals had carefully reviewed probable technology diffusion), few rural projects, especially from European donors, are properly preappraised to assess likely rates of diffusion. The proportion of *research* projects so preappraised must be very small.

As for the impact of diffusion on the "indicator," the standard approach is to estimate extra producers' income by looking at factor employment levels and returns implied by production functions before and after the new technique.

Where the adopting country or area is not a pure price-taker—e.g., if it supplies or demands a large part of world trade in the affected product; or if it restricts net imports—or if the impact of the technique on output is very large or covers many countries, benefits to consumers must also be considered.

It is, of course, possible to refine this model, but it already outruns available data. (Crucially, *past* attempts to predict new technology developments—e.g., in respect to their timing, extent, and effects in shifting production functions—must be assessed, so that *current* predictions can be evaluated, and set against known facts about existing technologies.) The first necessary step is surely not to over-refine this simplistic, "three-probability" normative model of technology and research choice, but to try and assess how it performs ex post in "retrodicting" the development and impact of major recent new technologies, and to try it out ex ante for some new technologies currently being researched.

The implied agenda for social science is first to find out *what works where*, as follows. First, establish what *sorts* of new agricultural technology have been relatively rapidly researched, diffused, and effective in altering GNP, poverty, and environmental sustainability in LDCs. Second, by establishing time sequences and exploring cross-sections, as well as by case studies, understand the processes and causal sequences underlying success and failure. Finally, advise what sort of agricultural technology developments are likely to bring more favorable outcomes—to show better benefit/cost ratios, i.e., to be more successful or faster—in respect to growth, poverty alleviation, and environment. The best type of new technology to seek will vary with the *set* of local circumstances (notably agro-ecology; current and historical agricultural policy, research organizations and resources, extension, etc.; and socio-economic variables such as income distribution). At present, many of the building blocks for such an approach are in place,[8] but the house remains to be built.

Technology assessment will be more useful if social scientists explore the interests, perceptions, and power of groups seeking to influence agricultural research—producers versus consumers, town versus country, dairy versus crop interests, scientists versus politicians, etc.[9] Agricultural research choices, and hence technology developments, are to some extent "protected" by apparent obscurity; they are left to experts. But each expert, at the same time sincere and self-serving, tends to advocate more research along the lines that he or she has learned, practiced and taught. Especially if these lines appear to show past success, this tends to perpetuate them; why leap into the unknown? At some point, however, economies of scale, in further researching the known, must give way to diminishing returns, but the pressure of established experts and the prestige of their past success frequently lead to over-emphasis on developing technologies for (say) securely irrigated rice, as against cassava, yams, upland rice, or millet.

It is not only the *output-mix* where technology development has been distorted by the justifiably high prestige of past success, and hence by the reputation, power, and interests of the successful scientists. The neglected, unfashionable *topics* about which farmers complain—rats, birds, weeds—remain neglected and unfashionable, as long as other forms of research remain both "successful" and intellectually challenging. We need, at least, to suspect such "success." In some respects, e.g., pest management (via pesticides, or even via breeding for varietal resistance), this procedure resembles the success of a doctor in treating an iatrogenic disease. This can further camouflage diminishing returns to traditional areas of research priority, which often remain the current lead areas of active research publication, patronage, and employment.

Thirtle and Ruttan (1987) carefully explore the evidence about the extent of supply-induced, as against demand-induced, research findings—responding to the pulls, respectively, of scientific discovery and producers' (or consumers') economic pressures. Cutting across this important distinction, and much less investigated by social scientists (important exceptions are Grabowski [1981] and de Janvry [1977]), is the distinction between technology developments induced by the structure of power, by economic resources (existing market supplies and demands), or by the capacity of locally usable scientific knowledge to improve the value of the "indicator." Many discussions of technology assessment appear to consider only one of these three pressures on the supply of, and demand for, technology. At most, two are allowed for: the alleged wickedness of market outcomes is set against the virtues of scientific judgment, or vice versa; or the desirability of technologies to improve the "indicator" is set against the alleged effects of economic rents created by state actions (or against the alleged negative externalities across markets) that engender technologies that worsen the "indicator."

This is unfortunate because international agricultural research institutions create major prospects to obtain "'indicator'-improving" technology outcomes, if the market-based and power-based pressures are understood (and allowed for) in research planning. *National* agricultural research in LDCs, at worst, is exposed to both market-based and power-based pressures to provide it with minimal, or irregular, domestic resources—and to concentrate those resources on export crops. In better circumstances (e.g., in India, China, Kenya, or Mexico) national agricultural research, while properly financed and organized, is under great pressure to conform to three requirements. First is the political requirement to obtain cash-crop and food surpluses for urban uses. Second is the economic pressure to concentrate research on bigger farms in well-watered surplus areas and, hence, on people who gain rural power by meeting increasing proportions of such urban needs. Third is the thrust within the scientific establishments to continue research and publications along the paradigms currently confirmed by each discipline. International agricultural research has better prospects of reducing or offsetting such pressures.

III.

I now briefly review some issues affecting the social science role, in donor-oriented agricultural technology assessment, for each of the three components of the "indicator" (efficient growth, poverty reduction, environmental sustainability)—still assuming we are confining "donors' needs" to their shared interest with LDC people in raising the value of the "indicator." For each component, I examine the three areas a, b, and c (detailed in section I above) respectively—assessment of: the effects of changing future technical change on existing aid programs and projects, technology choice in project design, and choices in projects for research, i.e., for technology development—but with heavy emphasis on the project cycle (detailed in section I above). In the closing section (IV), I review a few overarching issues, for social science roles in technology assessment, raised by the evidence on aid-effectiveness (Cassen and Associates 1986; Lipton 1987a, 1987b; Lipton and Toye 1990).

Suppose that maximizing efficient[10] growth were the only valued component of the "indicator." Standard BCA might then seem to suffice, but two problems remain. First, effects outside the project area are very hard to capture. If the project is big, a computable general equilibrium (CGE) model may be needed, but there is a choice of models, yielding different results. Second, planners or voters may wish to sacrifice some "efficiency" for extra growth—i.e., to boost research (or technology choices) leading to faster growth via more investment, even at modest returns.

However, if efficient growth is the only aim of research, then technology assessment is *relatively* simple. Such an aim would not rule out all considerations of poverty or sustainability. Poverty considerations are directly addressed through technology choices tending to raise the demand for labor relative to capital and land; price policy in most LDCs tends to undervalue the land factor, so that the use of accounting prices in BCA choices (instead of "distorted" market prices) automatically tends to favor higher employment among laborers and smaller farmers with relatively low costs of labor search and supervision. Indirectly, a growth-oriented technology policy can help the poor by creating resources for redistribution, at less cost in social and political tension than if a less growth-oriented technology policy had left the government unable to help the poor except by reducing the *absolute* incomes of the rich.

However, to put it mildly, such trickle-down arguments are in practice often defeasible. If private incentives are to match those that guide public resource allocations (and the economic consequences of nonmatching are normally, at best, very odd) direct benefits to the poor (from BCA decisions favoring "more-than-market" levels of employment intensity) via extra employment must be set against the fact that real wage/interest and wage/land-rent ratios must tend to fall in the marketplace, not only in accounting prices measured according to the BCA manuals.

The upshot is probably that technology choices seeking "only" rapid, prolonged, efficient, widespread agricultural growth—if, and only if, they succeed—always, *eventually,* trickle down to the quite poor. Experience suggests that such success is rare.[11] Hence, specific complements to, or parts of, growth-orientated farm-technology programs are normally required, if poverty issues are to be handled properly.

This is not to blame technology for politics, nor to saddle it with the main responsibility for poverty reduction. However, social scientists owe aid donors an assessment of the likely poverty impact of major technical change. As with the growth impact, this usually cannot be established by looking at the effects in just one region of adoption. There are cross-regional effects (Lipton with Longhurst 1989, Chapter 3). Modern cereal varieties have usually *helped* the poor, not only in lead areas like the Punjab or Sonora (where they have induced yield growth sufficient to offset the cost/price squeeze), but also in areas with widespread adoption of crops, such as groundnuts and some fodder crops, abandoned by the lead areas (to switch into modern wheats and rices) and thereby made scarcer and costlier. Modern cereals have *harmed* poor farmers, and probably their employees, in near-stagnant, nonadopting regions—and perhaps in several African *nations*—via price effects, but these have helped the urban poor in such areas. As for regions specializing in crops initially little affected by modern cereal varieties, the initial (price) effect on poor growers and employees is harmful, but as the research methods have been applied to crops earlier neglected, this effect can be reversed, e.g., with hybrid sorghum in Karnataka and probably Zimbabwe.

As for the national-level effect of modern staple varieties on the poor as *consumers*—the predominant effects in urban and rural non-food-producing regions—they may have been overstated. Many poor countries, in respect to cereals, function in the long run as small, open economies, where the pattern of extra domestic output, at best, brings down consumers' prices slightly (by reducing transport costs) and may somewhat reduce price fluctuations.[12] Moreover, even if consumer prices do fall, the supply of unskilled (poor) labor is (1) growing with population, (2) often migrant, and (3) probably, in the medium term, highly real-wage-elastic; hence, lower food prices, even if achieved, need not mean higher real income for the laboring, rural non-food-growing poor or the urban poor.

Regional issues loom largest in technology selection and projection for poverty reduction. Should research favor neglected regions with the poorest *producers and laborers* (regions that usually have the least internal inequality), or lead regions where research appears likeliest to increase the surplus for the poorest *consumers*? The latter research must at some point hit diminishing returns; it is naturally favored by the self-confirming effects discussed in II above. And, gains for consumers and laborers, as we have seen, can well be frustrated if medium-term labor supply is wage-elastic.

However, it does not follow that, for example, biotechnology (BT) and/or rice research needs to be redirected to meet the needs of upland rice farmers. Perhaps technology can best help such farmers by opening alternatives to rice crops, to other crops, or even to agriculture or upland residence. Technology development, with its segregated crop-research institutions, is not ideally organized to handle such options in poverty alleviation. They *are* considered together in good farming-systems analysis, but this microinformation seldom impinges on research allocation, say, for upland areas between the IRRI (International Rice Research Institute) and ICRISAT (International Crop Research Institute for the Semi-Arid Tropics; or (in India) as between the All-India Rice and Millet Research Programs, or between research for Eastern and Southern India.

Of course, the choices among regions (or nations)—whether in respect of total research resources to be allocated to each, or of different research emphases, e.g., crop mixes or labor intensities, suitable to different regions—are not the only poverty-related issues for technology policy, or for social science analyses seeking to improve it. They are, however, the main such issues. The very poor are heavily concentrated by region within, for example, India or the Sudan, and by country within Africa or South Asia. Interregional movements of labor and capital—in default of special policies towards them—tend to increase disparities (as savings and skilled persons seek economies of agglomeration) at least as often as to decrease them. Extreme poverty (by impeding risk-taking, knowledge acquisition, and capacity to save) often locks its victims into "technologically backward" places or agro-ecologies. These "regionally immobile poor" are especially exposed to sudden declines, due to drought or price changes, in their already low incomes.

It is thus vital to disentangle the correlates and, if possible, the causes of poverty in the technologically retarded regions, so as to identify what sorts of technical change might best relieve it. Poor people who depend mainly on farm assets, nonfarm assets, casual or steady labor income, or remittances, are likely to benefit from different sorts of technical progress. So are poor people with big and small families; or those whose poverty is associated with a steady, low level of welfare, as against those who make periodic gains that are repeatedly eroded by downward shocks; or those able to respond to incentives and opportunities, as against those so underfed and unhealthy that more food and better health are preconditions for substantial economic response.

The point is that these different correlates of poverty are highly area-specific. A simple inventory seeking to define the poor, rather than to count them, is as necessary for a poverty-oriented selection among technologies for an agricultural region, as is a similar inventory of the region's agroclimatic conditions. Both inventories also suggest—and limit—options for new technology development.

Although the rural poor are heavily concentrated by region, the literature of technology choice, and of its role in combating poverty, concentrates heavily on the distribution of gains within a region—usually, even more narrowly, on the effect of major technical change on "small farmers" within advanced agricultural areas. Some unjustified innovations, such as subsidized combines or weedicides, undoubtedly help big farmers much more than small farmers. So does research (not absent even from international crop-research institutes) seeking to make such labor-displacing techniques relatively more attractive. The main losers are not small farmers, but the laborers that such innovations "unemploy." Laborers now are a growing majority of the rural poor in much of Asia, and increasingly in parts of Africa as land becomes scarcer. Also, agricultural boom regions are not the poverty heartlands, even for laborers. The evidence shows that the most dramatic agricultural innovations of the past quarter-century—improved cereal varieties—eventually become as widespread on "small" farms as on large, but only in appropriate areas.

Hence, the extension of research gains to some less affected, but poverty-prone, agricultural areas is central to antipoverty thrusts in technology selection and development. (However, for other such areas—where it can be shown that such gains are unlikely to show adequate "indicator" returns and, at the same time, raise real income-per-person—nonfarm, or migration-orientated, solutions must be sought instead.)

The poor in many "backward" regions are still largely dependent on operating small farms for income. Also, they still have a high income elasticity of demand for staples. Hence, two limitations on the antipoverty impact of technology development, experienced in some "lead regions," are probably less important with a thrust towards "backward regions." These limitations are (a) that in the more internally unequal lead regions where the poor mostly depend on labor income, technical change can harm the poor by displacing labor even if total factor productivity rises sharply; and (b) that even where such technical change increases food supply, there is often no substantial increase in hungry people's capacity to buy food. If the poor retain their operated land, they can to a great extent both (a) select the labor-intensity that suits them, and (b) consume the extra food that they grow. Only on a simplistic short-term (and fungibility-neglecting) view is such a strategy in conflict with specialization and exchange.

However, care is needed lest technology strategies for "backward" areas increase the inequalities—at first, usually slight—in access to land there; or limit to the well-off access on good terms to irrigation, credit, or transport. Also, the output-mix of research is important because of (1) the price effects on poor producers of higher rice and wheat yields in other areas, (2) risks of soil mining and monocultures to poorer farmers with lower capacity to afford fertilizers, and (3) above all, dominance of coarse grains, roots, and tubers in the consumption bundles of the poorest people in "backward" agricultural regions—still including most of sub-Saharan Africa—for reasons of agro-ecology on the supply side, income elasticity on the demand side, and risk aversion on both sides.

The issues of generating "suitably" labor-intensive research outputs, and of ensuring that success in expanding food supply is not frustrated in its poverty impact by failures in poor people's effective demand, loom much larger in countries and regions where technical change has substantially improved agricultural performance over a longish period, and where, partly as a result, land and controlled water are both scarce and unequal, and labor plentiful. These two issues for antipoverty technology choice—labor-intensity and demand adequacy—are closely linked in these lead areas, because highly real-wage-elastic, medium-term labor *supply* prevents rises in labor *demand,* even if induced by technical progress, from durably and substantially raising real-wage-rates of farm labor (even if food prices fall). Hence, extra welfare for the laboring poor depends mainly on nonfarm labor income, and/or on extra duration of available farm work, especially in slack seasons.

This seasonal balance is the first sense in which technical change in lead areas needs to be "suitably" labor-intensive if it is to be effectively pro-poor. The second is to raise labor skills (and, hence, marginal labor product) alongside labor demand—not only by educating the work force formally,[13] but also, perhaps, by selecting technologies that create learning-by-doing, e.g., in improved drainage management or fertilizer placement. The third is that on-farm technical change will do more for the poor if it raises demand for nonfarm labor.[14]

Such "refinements" aside, the declining "crude" employment effects even of biochemical progress in agriculture are worrying. In the early years of modern semidwarf cereal varieties, the employment elasticity of yield growth in South and East Asia was about 0.4; for diverse reasons, it appears now to be only around 0.1–0.2 (Jayasuriya and Shand 1986). Meanwhile, growing proportions of the rural poor in Asia and, increasingly, Africa depend on labor for most of their income, rather than on land; yet the thrust of poverty-orientated agricultural research is towards "small farmers" first, towards price reduction and stability for townspeople second, and towards labor incomes third, or not at all. Most agricultural growth due to new technology is much less employment-generating than the modern cereal varieties have been: most farm machinery displaces labor (see, for example, Binswanger 1978); and the great concentration of cost-cutting agricultural research in Western economies (with high wage/rent ratios), plus the transmissibility of such research results to LDCs, imparts a labor-saving bias to LDC agricultural growth paths also.

If the South Asian experience—a genuine, if patchy, "green revolution;" with as yet little, and in some countries no, fall in the incidence (or average severity) of poverty—is to be improved upon, these "regional" and "labor" issues need to be tackled. *This is not to saddle technology development and choice with sole or main responsibility for solving them*—only to insist that BCA of technology choices takes account of these effects. But the poor also depend, in the longer term, on another result of technical change. What can social science do to help donors (and, more importantly, recipients) to select among agricultural techniques, either to apply or to research, in respect to their impact on the environmental sustainability of livelihoods (ESL) in LDCs—on reasonable assumptions about the pace at which industrialization, etc., might reduce poor people's dependence upon rural land and water resources?

Four main tasks of identification suggest themselves. First, the role of the rate of interest (time preference) needs to be clarified, and not used crudely as a pretext for dismissing environmental concerns in project selection or research planning. Such use corresponds closely to the claim that technology selection via efficient growth-oriented BCA—directly and via labor pricing, indirectly via creation of resources to redistribute—suffices to deal with poverty issues. Second, the concept of "carrying capacity" needs to be clarified and not used crudely as a pretext to select only those projects or research paths that elevate environmental concerns above considerations of medium-term poverty and growth. These are mainly, though not wholly, tasks for economists. The third and fourth tasks fall mainly on other social scientists. Third is the analysis of demographic effects from major technology options. Fourth is the clarification of what forms of institutional arrangements or alterations—in different physical and social environments, but especially in circumstances of rapid rural population growth and/or technical change—are more (or less) likely to induce the adoption or development of farming, grazing, and watering methods that maintain or improve ESL, or that lower the costs (especially to poor people) of doing so.

(1) *Time preference.* Economists sometimes claim that "the" pattern of market rates of interest on loans of varying maturities, if it is "undistorted," adequately "reflects" the tradeoff of "the community" between "welfare" now, next year, and later years, even into the "distant" future. (Each word in quotation marks, of course, signals major problems.) If that claim were even roughly correct—and if the approximate effects of alternative actions on the environment and, hence, on later income streams were known to all actual and potential agents—it would follow that standard benefit/cost analysis, by discounting future net-income streams at the proper rate, would select the technology T (whether for implementation or for research development) that "optimally depleted," or enhanced, environmental resources. The tradeoff between T_1 and T_2—where T_1 preserves resources at the cost of slow short-term growth, but T_2 depletes resources (and, hence, slows or reverses growth eventually) but achieves fast short-term growth—could appear to be "optimally" made by such a selection process. Environmental sustainability is handled by considering the effects of a technology on the value of income streams many years hence; standard BCA, discounting at the social rate of time preference, will reject any project or research proposal leading to the adoption of a technology for which this value is sufficiently negative.

Apart from the familiar problems with this scheme (externalities, incomplete or separated capital markets, etc.) and the deeper problem that the observed rate of time preference between income now and later depends on the level *and distribution* of income now but not later, there is an empirical difficulty that almost destroys the usefulness of the above approach. It is fact that, in very poor communities, apparent or market-reflected rates of time preference are so high as to rule out projects, or technologies, seeking to preserve long-run ESLs at any significant short-run cost—yet such "ruling out" violently contradicts both the revealed preference and the statements of most people in these societies. Suppose a technology exists, or can be inexpensively researched, that enables a rural area to use its water supplies so that, at zero capital cost or operating cost, net income-per-person doubles for 30 years, and then falls to zero. Almost any reasonable BCA, based on observation of time preference as indicated by the high real rural interest rates in most LDCs, would advise going ahead with this technology. But, suppose also that there exist neither opportunities for emigration nor prospects to save or reinvest the extra income at good returns—i.e., that it is high-risk consumption borrowings, not good investment prospects, that fuel high interest rates—then the project would lead to disaster after 30 years.

Small farmers, even very poor ones, select techniques in a much more rational way, as regards ESLs, than by considering only local interest rates, as if they reflected both time preference and the true long-term return on capital available to each farmer. For example, small owner-farmers[15] usually avoid "soil mining" rotations and other practices, and state their concern to pass on land in good condition to children. As another example, there is strong evidence that rural couples' family-size norms depend partly on their perception of their need for security in old age; yet, for a poor couple aged 30, the rates of interest at which consumer credit is available are much too high to "justify" an extra child on the grounds of any plausible contribution by it to the expected values of the couple's income 20 (let alone 30) years hence.

There seems to be a sense in which even very poor rural people—both in what they say and in what they do in the market place—reveal a preference for family survival, implying a long rate of interest far below the short rate. It is useless for economists to stress that the long run is a sequence of short runs; the complex and integrated capital markets needed to transfer short into long credit contracts (and vice versa) are not perceived as accessible to rural "ordinary people." Their common sense—and surely ours?—rejects the view that high real short rates imply the worthlessness of life 30 or 50 years from now. ESLs count, even if the real short rate is 25 (or 250) percent.

However, social science—social psychology as well as economics—owes technology decision makers a better theory of interest rates and, hence, of socially optimal capital assignments, than is now available. In the United Kingdom, a treasury real interest rate of four to five percent correctly reflects market signals *now*. Yet, such a rate rules out the planting of trees by the Forestry Commission, except for quick-yielding but low-value conifers. Can this be a sensible way to determine the appearance of Britain's countryside *later*, even when greater prosperity shall have (presumably) lowered real rates of time preference? In planning food-technology development for LDCs, the issues are much more vital (literally); but the source of conceptual confusion is the same.

(2) *Carrying capacity.* If "revealed preference via market interest rates" is a chop-logic social science stick with which to beat ESLs, then "carrying capacity" is a static natural science given with which to deify them. Given the management and the technology, it is possible to define limits of stress upon a resource that will permit it to regenerate fast enough to avoid depletion. For example, we can define the number of livestock units per acre, above which—given the management of land, water, and beasts—that number is bound to fall over time. This is then used as an argument to rule out levels of activity, forms of land use, and types of technical change that cause land to be operated in excess of "carrying capacity."

In a sense, in technology planning, this is the opposite error to the unquestioning acceptance of interest rates. There is nothing necessarily wrong about exceeding the carrying capacity of a piece of land, if *either* the costs of restoring that capacity later are shown to be worth paying in order to obtain the extra income meanwhile *or* that the extra income is partly used to provide new livelihoods for those displaced when the land goes out of production.

Concepts of carrying capacity are useful, but as parts of dynamic economics, not as static "givens." It is surely desirable that, for example, yield-increasing research in crop production should be scanned for the sources of that extra yield: higher inputs, greater conversion efficiency of inputs into dry matter, better partitioning of that dry matter (e.g., between grain and stalk), or more rapid extraction of soil nutrients? The last source is doubtful unless either land is plentiful, or the inputs will be restored and the land rehabilitated (e.g., by rotation or mixing). The widespread enthusiasm for "low-input, high-output agriculture" can readily conceal, not greater conversion efficiency of the crop cover, but soil mining and loss of carrying capacity. If so, we need to ensure that the short-term rise in incomes suffices to offset long-term consumption of land "capital"—*and* that it is used to create sufficient ESLs in other activities or places.

(3) *Population effects.* For major innovations, it may be important to estimate the effects on fertility and mortality. If innovations raise the demand for labor, especially labor that can be done by children or adolescents, family-size norms *increase.* Innovations that raise income-per-person from very low levels are associated with increases in several variables, notably female health and perhaps education, that cause fertility *first to increase, then to decrease* as the variables surpass a threshold level. Since it is plainly necessary, if technology is to combat poverty effectively, to shift the focus from asset holders (even small ones) to labor intensity, there is the danger of delaying fertility decline by encouraging large families among the poorest. Thus, in selecting a technique to apply or to research, the goal of environmental stability and the goal of poverty alleviation may conflict.

This is an almost unresearched area (exceptions are Basu et al. 1979; Schutjer and Stokes 1984; and Stoeckel and Jain 1986), but two implications for technology policy suggest themselves. First, complementary measures to improve female health, completed primary or subsequent education, and *off-farm* employment—or choices of technologies likely to improve them—increase the chances that new technology will speed the fertility transition. Second, and less welcome to most development economists, effective antipoverty policy—on technology options or more generally—in very poor countries may be compatible with rapid fertility transition only if heavily concentrated on certain poor groups or areas; the cost of reconciling poverty alleviation with fertility reduction may be to abandon regional, or other, equity among the very poor. With resources scarce, if they are spread across many very poor people and places, they may well achieve only small rises in income; these will induce improvements in health, etc., that—alongside better prospects for young workers—will increase fertility. If rapid technical progress and income increases bring *substantial* gains in female health and education (and in prospects for couples to substitute quality for quantity in their children) fertility declines can be expected.

These hasty and speculative remarks—owing an obvious debt to the findings of Paul Schultz, Easterlin, and others—are intended mainly to show that population effects of technology options need careful review if ESLs are an objective. Direct evidence on such effects is very scanty. Yet, major agro-technology decisions, notably on the development of new seed varieties, were taken by international organizations, scholars, and foundations on a very crude—and now quite outdated—neo-Malthusian prospectus: grow the extra cereals to feed people while they learn to plan their families! A major "social science role" is now to insert, into agricultural research planning, an awareness of the findings of modern demographic work from before and during the World Fertility Survey.

4. Finally, what forms of *social organization* are conducive to responses to technical change that improve "indicator" values? This has two main aspects. First, some communities respond faster than others to similar innovations—or are "better" at generating indigenous technical change—and/or produce better impacts on growth, poverty, and sustainability from given responses. Second, some communities are better at handling the process of decline as old technologies are pressured by growing populations and by "transition of trust" from traditional to modern authorities; this involves both Boserup-style "technology shifts" and the management of common property resources.

IV

I have tried to give a sense of some major issues in the assessment of agricultural technology and research options, writing "as if" donors could make these choices entirely with a view to improving "indicator" values in LDCs. Maintaining this fiction for a moment, what sort of choices are likely to be addressed by donors?

1. The aid-effectiveness literature, reviewed in Cassen (1986) and Lipton (1987a, 1987b), reveals a few areas of clear and persistent success and failure. Livestock projects, and irrigation projects in most of sub-Saharan Africa, show consistently weak results in many aid agencies. Rural credit support (though there are real measurement problems) reveals generally good returns economically, but poor returns to financial intermediary institutions. Certain crops and agro-ecologies show persistently better returns to agricultural research than others. Agricultural research as a whole shows excellent returns (on a wide range of estimation methods) outside Africa, but—despite high outlays—low returns in Africa. Should technology development, in each of these cases, "fill gaps" or "back winners"? (It should be noted that the World Bank's *Annual Reviews of Project Performance Audits* repeatedly identify, as a main cause of the 10–15 percent of agricultural funding that leads to failed projects, a lack of clear and profitable technology.)

2. How should the biggest single unknown now affecting rural futures—third-generation biotechnology—be assessed and developed for LDCs? Crops grown by poor small-holders in tropical areas, especially monocots and, above all, cereals, are in several respects medium-term Cinderellas of BT research. Yet, this very fact implies shifts, in the relative profitability of different products and areas and farm sizes, that are of the greatest importance for poor people and ESLs, even in LDCs. Also, BT appears least likely to greatly improve photosynthetic efficiency, as compared to likely improvements in disease resistance or nutrient efficiency; this has to increase the long-run comparative advantages, in crop growing, of places with less severe constraints on plants' capacity to use sunshine all year.

One could give many more examples, but the main point is that attempts to measure—however crudely—the "three probabilities" (research success; diffusion; impact on GNP, poverty, and ESLs) provide a useful way to assess options in these and similar areas.

NOTES

1. Michael Lipton is with the Institute of Developmental Studies, Brighton, England.

2. A few striking exceptions appear in Part Two of Ruskin et al. (1985) but most of these papers are concerned with the common property *economics* of ground-floor institutions managing *given* (or decaying) technologies—not with the anthropology, politics, etc., of managing technical progress.

3. These changes are not always continuous and smooth; when a clan adapts some new technologies, such as "Neolithic" settlement, its structure of power and income distribution usually changes drastically (Lipton with Longhurst 1989).

4. (i) The last goal is presumably defined in net degradation; it is not demanded that a microenvironment never deteriorates, but that a region's sustainable environmental resources per person (subject to the scope for trade, and for migration) should not deteriorate. (ii) Enlargement of the range of individual choices is another widely agreed goal, but the impact of public-sector technology options upon that goal is very obscure.

5. Price elasticity of demand for black tea—almost all grown in LDCs—is about –0.3. So when clonal tea doubles yield in a tea area, as is quite common, prices (unit revenues) to *all* LDCs fall by about 3.3 x the rise in total output. Of course, marginal grower-farmers then reassign some tea land to other crops; but this is a long and costly process, especially if other tree crops replace the tea. Even then (and more so otherwise), revenue per acre will usually be well below the level that had been earned by growing seed tea, before clonal varieties arrived.

6. Suppose a developing country were considering the development, for water buffalo, of a milk stimulant analogous to bovine somatotropin. Even if enough capable researchers were available, the cost of the biotechnology development involved would probably mean a zero return for most small countries acting alone. A substantial return to a very large outlay could probably also be predicted, as could a near-zero return to further rises in outlay.

7. Risk-averse researchers, research directors, and resource allocators might want to know the *distribution* of outcome around the mean, not just the *expected* value. In particular, in LDCs with politically weak or fragile agricultural research systems, there is a case for some research with very high probability of *some* clear success, diffusion, and impact, even if other research options, taken together, promise higher *expected* values of effects on the "indicator" per dollar spent.

8. The most outstandingly useful "building blocks" include the work in Evenson and Kislev (1976), Hayami and Ruttan (1971, 1985), Pingali et al. (1987), and in a different tradition Leonard (1977). Helpful summaries include Pinstrup-Andersen (1982).

9. Of course, not all of these games are always constant-sum, or fully noncooperative.

10. This word implies that revealed market preferences, notably between income and effort, affect policy; growth is not maximized "at all costs," e.g., by driving marginal returns to effort well below the marginal disutility of the effort.

11. Apparent cases usually experienced substantial equalizing land reform before the growth-centered policies began to reduce poverty (e.g., Taiwan and South Korea, 1953–70), or were set in a context of poverty-oriented public action outside agriculture (e.g., Sri Lanka, 1964–71; Indian Punjab, 1966–85).

12. This is also the effect if extra domestic output is offset, as regards availability, by reduced net imports, whether due to public policy (rice in Colombia) or to the fact that effective extra demand is not substantially generated by extra income for groups with high income-elasticity of demand for food staples, viz. the poor (India).

13. This *alone* may well induce "qualification escalation" among the poor, without enough extra income to offset the costs of education (including opportunity cost and interest). Even genuine skill acquisition increases poor people's income only if demand for such skills is expanded (usually by technical progress in farming) at a rate not too much slower than supply, given the elasticities of the family of demand curves.

14. However, I dissent from the position (implicit in Hazell and Roell [1983]) that most such linkages are, or should be, localized and/or based on consumer demand from technology-enriched farmers.

15. Even sharecroppers and other tenants often take the long view, knowing that they otherwise risk nonrenewal of their tenancy contracts.

REFERENCES

Basu, D., R. Roy, and P. Nikhil. 1978. *Impact of agricultural development on demographic behaviour*. New Delhi: Abhinav Publications.

Baum, Warren C. 1978. The World Bank project cycle. *Finance and Development* 15, no. 4 (December): 10–17.

Binswanger, H. 1978. *The economics of tractors in South Asia*. New York: Agricultural Development Council.

Cassen, Robert, and Associates. 1986. *Does aid work?: Report to an intergovernmental task force*. New York: Oxford University Press.

de Janvry, A. 1977. Inducement of technological and institutional innovations: An interpretative framework. In *Resource allocation and productivity*. Edited by T. M. Arndt, D. Dalrymple, and V. Ruttan. Minneapolis: University of Minnesota.

Evenson, R., and Y. Kislev. 1976. *Agricultural research and productivity*. New Haven, Conn.: Yale University Press.

Farrington, J., and F. Abeyratne. 1982. Farm power and water use in the dry zone of Sri Lanka. Devel. study no. 22., University of Reading, Reading, U.K.

Grabowski, R. 1981. The implications of an induced innovation model. *Economic Development and Cultural Change* 30, no. 1.

Greeley, M. 1986. Food technology and employment: The farm-level post-harvest system in developing countries. *Journal of Agricultural Economics* 37, no. 3.

Hayami, Y., and V. Ruttan. [1971] 1985. *Agricultural development: An international perspective*. Baltimore: Johns Hopkins University Press.

Hazell, P., and A. Roell. 1983. Rural growth linkages. Research report no. 40. Washington, D.C.: International Food Policy Research Institute.

Jayasuriya, S., and R. Shand. 1986. Technical change and labor absorption in Asian agriculture. *World Development* 14, no. 3.

Leonard, D. 1977. *Reaching the peasant farmer: Organization theory and practice in Kenya*. Chicago: University of Chicago Press.

Lipton, M. 1985. The place of agricultural research in the development of sub-Saharan Africa. Discussion paper 202. Brighton, U.K.: Institute of Development Studies.

_____1987a. Improving the impact of aid for rural development. Discussion paper 233. Brighton, U.K.: Institute of Development Studies.

_____1987b. Improving agricultural aid impact on low-income countries. Discussion paper 234. Brighton, U.K.: Institute of Development Studies.

Lipton, M., with R. Longhurst. 1989. *New seeds and poor people*. Baltimore: Johns Hopkins University Press.

Lipton, M., and J. Toye. 1988. *Aid-effectiveness: India*. London: Methuen.

Pingali, P., Y. Bigot, and H. Binswanger. 1987. *Agricultural mechanization and the evaluation of farming systems in sub-Saharan Africa*. Baltimore: Johns Hopkins University Press.

Pinstrup-Andersen, P. 1982. *Agricultural research and technology in economic development: The impact of agricultural research and modern technology on food production, economic growth, and income distribution in developing countries*. New York: Longman.

Popper, K. 1968. *The logic of scientific discovery*. 2d ed. London: Hutchinson.

Richards, P. 1985. *Indigenous agricultural revolution*. London: Hutchinson.

Rudolph, L., and S. Rudolph. 1967. *The modernity of tradition*. Chicago: University of Chicago Press.

Ruskin, F., et al. 1985. *Common property resource management*. Washington, D.C.: National Academy of Sciences.

Ruttan, V. 1988. Anthropology and economic development. *Economic development and cultural change*. 36:3 (S247–90).

Schutjer, W., and C. Stokes. 1984. *Rural development and human fertility*. New York: Macmillan.

Scobie, G. 1984. Investment in agricultural research: Some economic principles. Mexico City: CIMMYT.

Stoeckel, J., and A. Jain. 1986. *Fertility in Asia: Assessing the impact of development projects*. New York: St. Martin's Press.

Thirtle, C., and V. Ruttan. 1987. *The role of demand and supply in the generation and diffusion of technical change*. London: Harwood Academic Publishers.

Wanmali, S. 1985. Rural household use of services. Research report no. 48. Washington, D.C.: International Food Policy Research Institute.

CHAPTER 4

DESIGNING SOCIAL SCIENCE RESEARCH TO INFORM AGRICULTURAL MARKET REFORMS AND STRUCTURAL ADJUSTMENTS IN DEVELOPING COUNTRIES

John M. Staatz[1]

INTRODUCTION

Much of the debate during the 1980s and early 1990s about development policies in low- and middle-income countries has focused on defining appropriate roles for the state and the private sector in the economy. Often phrased in terms of "structural adjustment," this debate has involved four issues: the role of planning in the economy, the importance of prices as a constraint on production, the rules governing price formation (e.g., the wisdom of using border prices as a guide for setting domestic prices), and the design of appropriate institutions to handle input and output marketing. Among social scientists, economists have been the most deeply enmeshed in this controversy, although political scientists and sociologists have also been involved (e.g., Bates 1981). To the extent that the debate has involved Westerners, it has focused most strongly on sub-Saharan Africa, where many the of the arguments are reminiscent of debates that took place in South Asia, particularly India, twenty years earlier.[2]

The resurgence of concern about the balance between public- and private-sector responsibilities is due to several factors. Many policy makers have become disillusioned with economic planning in general and price controls and state marketing agencies in particular as a result of their poor performance during the 1960s and 1970s. In addition, economic austerity in many developing countries has made continuing subsidization of state marketing enterprises more problematic. This is particularly true given the greater openness of the world economy, which makes it increasingly costly for countries to maintain domestic prices that are out of line with international prices (Schuh 1987). There are also concerns that unfavorable market conditions may have discouraged adoption of new technology, as well as ideological shifts among some of the major donors towards a more promarket orientation.

Consequently, beginning around 1980, many countries began giving greater emphasis to the market in guiding resource allocation in their economies. Within Africa, Senegal, Mali, Somalia, Madagascar, and Zaire have liberalized the marketing of major staple foods as part of structural adjustment programs and, in the process, have drastically restructured parastatal agencies (Berg 1987a). Zambia followed a similar path until May 1987, when, following food riots, President Kuanda renounced the IMF-sponsored structural adjustment program. He returned the country to its prior system of administered pricing, arguing that if the country was to be forced into poverty, at least it would do so under its own policies rather than those of the IMF. Zimbabwe, in contrast, has followed a different path since independence, *extending* the activities of the state grain marketing board to communal areas previously unserved by this state agency.

This widespread experimentation with market restructuring offers both a challenge and an opportunity for social scientists. The *challenge* lies in designing research that can provide an empirical and analytical basis for the reforms so policies can be built upon more than just theory and ideology. Without such a basis, the risk is high that when reforms have unintended consequences (as they inevitably do) policy makers will conclude that the programs are complete failures and go back to the policies which prompted the reforms in the first place. The *opportunity* for social scientists lies in using these reforms as a quasi-experimental design (Campbell and Stanley 1963) to learn more, both empirically and theoretically, about the process and impact of changing the relationship between the state and the market in economic organization.

This paper elaborates on the challenge and opportunity, particularly as they apply to economists. The rest of this section discusses the conceptual approach adopted here to viewing the relationship between the state and the market. The "Research Challenges" section then elaborates on the challenges facing social science in general and applied economics in particular in designing research to provide an analytical and empirical basis for these reforms. The "Implications for the Organization of Social Science Research" section discusses the implications of these challenges for how social scientists organize themselves to carry out this type of work. The paper draws most of its empirical examples from sub-Saharan Africa because Africa has been the focus of many of the recent reforms and because, over the past three years, I have been involved, along with colleagues at Michigan State University and at several African institutions, in studying the interactions between changes in institutions, policies, and technology on food-system performance in a number of African countries.[3]

CONCEPTUAL APPROACH

In discussing the role of the state in "market interventions," analysts sometimes seem to forget that there are no markets in which the state does not intervene. Without state action to define rules of property, legal tender, norms of acceptable behavior, and the like, the market would not exist (Shaffer 1979, Bromley n.d.). If regulation means "to control, to direct, to govern directly and indirectly" (Shaffer 1979, 722), then the market is simply one of many forms of regulation, with market outcomes reflecting prior political decisions regarding distribution of rights and resources. Consequently, social scientists should not get caught up in ideological debates about the virtues or shortcomings of "state intervention in markets," but concentrate on what social science can contribute to understanding how, in different country circumstances, responsibilities for various economic activities can be more productively allocated among individual entities and the state. The task is ultimately one of institutional design.

Saying that state involvement is ubiquitous does not mean that all forms of state involvement are equally desirable. For example, during the past three decades many developing countries have attempted to rely exclusively on state action to determine the prices and quantities of goods in the economy. Such an approach has heavy costs, and several factors, including the process of economic growth itself, have made this approach even less tenable in recent years. Economic growth involves a transformation from small-scale household-level production to a more specialized, interdependent economy (Reynolds 1983; Johnston and Kilby 1975). In farming, this is reflected in the shifting of input production and output processing and distribution off the farm to specialized entities. One consequence of the growing interdependence of the economy is a phenomenal growth in the number of people, in both urban and rural areas, who depend on the market for their food.[4] At the same time, sustained growth in productivity in the food system requires the introduction of new technologies, which places increased demands on the market system to deliver new inputs effectively and help create an environment that encourages their use. The difficulty of organizing the distribution of goods and services purely by a system of command increases exponentially as the number of people and the complexity and affluence of the economy grow.[5]

In addition to the process of structural transformation itself, since the early 1970s several fundamental shifts have occurred in the international economy that have made many previous market policies more problematic. The move to floating exchange rates, the integration of financial and commodity markets, and the increased integration across commodity markets, both domestically and internationally, have resulted in a much more open, dynamic and unstable environment for agricultural markets (Schuh 1987; White 1988). Policies aimed at influencing domestic agricultural markets can no longer be made in isolation from the rest of the domestic or international economy. One consequence is that it has become increasingly costly for governments to maintain price structures that are divergent from world prices. Yet, in order to insulate their domestic economies from the increased volatility, many high-income countries have attempted to do just that. Consequently, they have shifted the burden of adjustment to supply and demand shocks onto international markets. The weak financial position of most developing countries precludes them from adopting such a strategy, so they have been forced to try to cope with this volatility. This poses problems both for the day-to-day management of state marketing enterprises and price stabilization schemes and for the planning of long-term investments. A major challenge for these countries is to use their scarce government resources to help develop mechanisms to deal with this risk rather than devoting those resources entirely to tasks that can be handled by the private sector.

RESEARCH CHALLENGES

Governments launch market reforms and structural adjustments for many reasons but, inevitably, some of the consequences of the reforms are unforeseen and unintended. The objective of ex ante policy analysis is to anticipate the effects of proposed policy changes under alternative scenarios and thereby help policy makers achieve their objectives while minimizing unintended consequences. The policy analyst seeks to identify and quantify the impacts of the reforms on levels of production, prices, incomes, and consumption; to identify who gains and who loses; to predict responses of various groups in society to the reforms; to assess intersectoral effects; and to analyze how each of these varies under a broad range of possible conditions (White 1987, 1). Carrying out such analyses requires an understanding of how the economy in general works, as well as the sectors that are subject to the reforms and knowledge of the political-economic process of policy reform (White 1988, 10). Yet, in many developing countries, particularly in Africa, agricultural market reforms often proceed with very little empirical or theoretical information to guide them. In these countries, the challenges to social scientists, particularly economists, in helping build the empirical and analytical foundations for such reforms lie at four levels.

EMPIRICAL TESTING OF THE BASIC ASSUMPTIONS UNDERLYING CURRENT OR PROPOSED REFORMS

All market reforms are based implicitly or explicitly on a model of how the economy operates. The models arise from theory, conventional wisdom, and ideology. Often policies derived from them are imposed with little testing of the underlying assumptions. Testing these assumptions, however, through analyses of past, current, and proposed reforms, is critical to the design of effective policy. Consider the argument that the maintenance of low official consumer and producer prices for agricultural products acts as a major constraint to economic growth and governments should, therefore, abandon such prices in favor of import and export parity prices. (This is the basic argument presented in chapters 4 and 5 of the World Bank's *World Development Report 1986*.) Implicit in the hypothesis that abandoning official prices will lead to faster economic growth are several subhypotheses, each subject to empirical testing:[6]

1. *Changes in official pricing policy taken at the ministerial level actually get translated into new policies at the rural market level.* Evidence from Senegal (Newman, Sow, and Ndoye 1987), Mali (Dérnbéle, Dioné, and Staatz 1986), and Madagascar (Berg 1987b) indicates that in the initial stages of a market reform, government officials in the field often misinterpret ministerial decrees. In Senegal, for example, local officials interpreted a declared *floor* price as a *ceiling* price and fined traders who tried to buy at prices above that level. Berg (1987b) reports how parastatals and others favored by previous marketing policies in Madagascar have attempted to create cartels to avoid facing the loss of rents that would result from implementation of the announced policy of paddy market liberalization.
2. *Official prices matter.* If a small proportion of total production enters the market and little of that moves at official prices due to the existence of a parallel market, then changes in official prices are unlikely to have much effect on total production although they may dramatically affect the relative volumes handled by the official and the parallel markets. In Mali, for example, during the 21 years of official state monopoly over the grain trade (1960–81), only about 15 percent of coarse grain production ever entered the market and, of this, the parastatal's share varied between 20 percent and 40 percent (Humphreys 1986, 5). Hence, only 3 to 6 percent of total production moved at official prices. It is unlikely in such a situation that changes in the official producer prices will have much short-run impact on production.
3. *The new prices change farm-level incentives enough to induce farmers to modify their behavior in the desired direction.* Two issues are important here: to what extent do farmers make their production decisions on a commercial basis, and are the changes in price levels large enough to change the relative profitability of different enterprises? To the extent that farmers base their production decisions, particularly for staple crops, on criteria other than profit maximization, the effect of increased farm-gate prices on production will be dampened. Risk is a particularly important consideration here. In semiarid areas where markets are poorly integrated (e.g., in much of Africa), farmers' tendency to give priority to food crop cultivation over cash crops seems to reflect not so much the relative monetary returns to growing different crops as the riskiness of putting one's sustenance at the mercy of unreliable grain markets. Furthermore, even if farmers do make their decisions primarily on a commercial basis, shifting to world parity prices may not change the relative profitability of different enterprises enough to induce the sought-for change in output mix.
4. *Farmers have capacity to respond significantly to the price changes*, i.e., farmers have additional resources, new technology, or both, that can be drawn into production. Although a few cross-country studies of supply response (e.g., Peterson) have argued that the long-run price elasticity of supply for agricultural commodities is high, such studies attribute most cross-country differences in production to price, ignoring the highly complementary effects of technical and institutional factors on farmers' ability to respond to higher prices (Johnson 1988; Krishna 1984).[7] Country-specific studies report much lower supply responses; Scandizzo and Bruce's (1980, 72–74) survey of supply elasticity estimates for major staples in 103 developing countries found that 62 percent of the long-run elasticities were less than 0.5 and 27 percent were negative. The supply elasticity for aggregate agricultural production is even lower, as the individual-crop elasticities reflect farmers' ability to shift their crop mix in response to changes in relative prices (Krishna 1984). In many countries, institutional rigidities, such as poorly functioning input and product markets, and lack of improved technology, severely limit farmers' ability to respond to higher prices, particularly in the short run.
5. *Increased production, if it is forthcoming, can be effectively marketed.* This assumption is critical to sustaining higher farm prices and, hence, incentives to produce.
6. *The increase in agricultural production induced by higher prices leads to faster overall economic growth.* This assumes strong linkages between agriculture and the rest of the economy and that an agricultural surplus, if it is generated by higher prices, can be effectively mobilized and productively reinvested, either in agriculture or in other sectors of the economy. This may be problematic due to barriers to the intersectoral transfer of resources (poorly functioning fiscal and financial systems, fixed consumer food prices, etc.) and to barriers to productive investment of those resources (corruption, lack of effective investment planning, and the like).

Similar sets of subhypotheses could be elaborated for theories of how devaluation will stimulate agricultural growth, how changing the relative prices of domestically produced and imported cereals will change consumption patterns, how private traders will respond to changing the rules regarding who may legally participate in the trade, and so on. Obviously, the degree to which each subhypothesis holds true will differ by country and by groups of farmers and consumers within each country. Testing these subhypotheses requires more comparative studies of both successful and unsuccessful policy reforms to identify which variables were critical in limiting or facilitating the response of food-system participants to the changes in the incentive structure engendered by the reforms.

MEASURING THE INCIDENCE OF MARKET ADJUSTMENTS AND REFORMS

One of the greatest political barriers to market reforms and structural adjustments is concern about the distribution of costs and benefits of these actions on different groups of the population. Although theory offers a guide to understanding who will be helped and hurt by changes in food prices (Mellor 1978), policy makers often lack basic data on consumption patterns, degree of market involvement of farmers, access to state marketing institutions, subsidized input distribution, and the like to make informed judgments about the incidence of these reforms. Such information is crucial, however, for any sort of targeting of interventions and for evaluating the tradeoffs among alternative policies. Lacking such information, discussion has often rested at a theoretical level, with some arguing that reforms help all but a small group of rent seekers, and others arguing for the need for "adjustment with a human face" (United Nations 1987).

The importance of such information for guiding policy can be illustrated with examples from Mali and Rwanda. In 1985–86, both countries attempted to raise farm-level prices for major staples (coarse grains in Mali and beans in Rwanda) through purchases by state grain boards in order to increase production incentives and rural incomes. Because both countries are characterized by smallholder agriculture, the policy makers assumed that the farming population was fairly homogeneous, with the majority of farmers being net sellers of staples who would benefit from higher prices.[8] Subsequent research showed these assumptions to be wrong. In Mali's two major surplus zones for coarse grains, only 48 percent of farmers were net sellers of these cereals, while 39 percent were net buyers, even though 1985–86 was a year of record production. Furthermore, 20 percent of the farmers accounted for 78 percent of total sales. These were the better-equipped farmers, living in higher rainfall areas, who were also the most involved in cotton production and other aspects of the commercial economy. The situation in Rwanda was even more striking, with only 22 percent of farmers being net sellers of beans, while 73 percent were net buyers. Furthermore, 7 percent of farms accounted for 81 percent of total net sales. Weber et al. report similar results for smallholders in Zimbabwe, Senegal, and Somalia. Obviously, discussions of price policy in these countries take on a different light in view of these findings.

Similar types of information are needed on the incidence of consumer and producer subsidies that are the target of policy reforms.[9] Basic knowledge of the incidence of anticipated and ongoing reforms is essential for anticipating barriers to changing current policies, assessing the cost effectiveness of alternative policies, preparing to deal with some of their adverse consequences, and helping to build coalitions to support reform. The incidence of price policy also affects the degree to which price policy can be effective in shifting production and consumption patterns. To the extent it affects mainly those who do not have capacity to respond due to technological, income, or institutional barriers, aggregate price response will be limited.[10]

RESEARCH ON THE DESIGN OF IMPROVED INSTITUTIONS

Applied economics research can make critical contributions to the design of institutions to: (a) deal effectively with the changing environment discussed in the "Introduction" section and (b) foster the transformation of the economy from one based on small-scale production to a science-based, integrated system with a broad distribution of benefits. In designing such research, it is important to avoid assuming that the sole institutional constraint to good performance of the food system is "excessive government involvement" in the market. Good private-sector performance requires substantial government action in providing the public goods necessary for a market to operate (standardized weights and measures, market information, and so on). Given the extremely constrained budgets of many low-income countries, one of the challenges is to help design low-cost means of providing these services.

Another trap to avoid is the belief that atomistic competition is always the best market structure for fostering technological change in the economy. For the handling of certain types of goods or services, particularly perishables and inputs that embody more sophisticated technologies, larger, more vertically integrated systems may be preferable. For example, in much of the Sahel, the most effective agricultural input supply system is that run by the cotton parastatals that are affiliated with the French transnational cotton corporation CFDT (Lele and van de Walle 1988). In analyzing the design of appropriate institutions, the use of transaction cost economics (TCE) may be a particularly useful tool (Williamson 1985; Johnson 1988). This school of analysis focuses on the design of institutions as a function of the nature of the transactions they are intended to mediate. TCE pays particular attention to problems posed by relying solely on the spot market when asset-specific investments are being made in the context of uncertainty and opportunistic behavior by market agents. This is exactly the situation faced by most countries undergoing a structural transformation of their economies.

Below is a short list of some of the types of social science research needed to help design better marketing institutions:

1. *Improved methods of input delivery*. The productivity of certain types of agricultural inputs like fertilizer is not immediately apparent to the purchaser through visual inspection, and the scope for opportunism (e.g., through adulteration) is large. Many of these inputs also require a complement of technical information on their proper use. Research is needed on the efficacy of alternative methods of delivering such inputs, considering, for example, the use of franchising tied with private provision of extension advice, provision through transnationals (e.g., via contract farming), and distribution through farmer cooperatives.
2. *Factors leading to good performance by farmer cooperatives*. Many of the recent reforms call for an increased role and autonomy for farmer cooperatives in the marketing of agricultural outputs and inputs. The performance of cooperatives in most developing countries has been dismal, in part because they have often been directed from outside, serving as little more than local agents of the state. Not enough work has been done on what factors contribute to successful cooperatives in LDCs and to which tasks they can contribute the most.
3. *Risk management tools*. The traditional risk management tools of farmers in developing countries have been diversification and holding of stocks, while those of state enterprises have been holding stocks and borrowing (accumulation of arrears). Both have high opportunity costs. For example, diversification limits the gains from specialization. As the market environment has become more risky, there is a need to develop mechanisms to deal with that risk. For example, what is the scope for marketing boards and farmer cooperatives to manage risk through the use of international futures and options markets, passing on the benefits to farmers and consumers?

4. *Improved methods for targeting subsidies*. Although there is a large discussion in the literature about the need to target subsidies, considerable work remains to be done on how this can be accomplished effectively.
5. *Improved rules for using world prices*. Most structural adjustment programs call for countries to price their tradeable goods at import and export parity prices. While in theory the world price represents the opportunity cost of a small country's resources, given the volatility of certain international markets such as those for rice and sugar, it is not always clear what the relevant world price is. Countries that allow transmission of every fluctuation of the world price into their domestic economies may send very confused signals to producers trying to plan long-term investments. Timmer, Falcon, and Pearson call for medium-run (one-to-two-year) stabilization of the domestic price for staples around the long-term trend in the world price, but this leaves unaddressed the problems of determining what the long-term trend is and the operational difficulties poor countries face in running even in short-term price-stabilization programs. Economists need to help develop workable rules for tying domestic prices to world prices while still maintaining a stable enough set of expectations within the country to encourage warranted investment in the food system.

Many of the ideas for improved institutional designs need to come from observation of what has and has not worked elsewhere. (For an example of this type of approach, see Abbott 1987.) This requires improvements in our techniques of comparative institutional analysis. Economists and other social scientists need to pay particular attention to designing cross-country studies in a manner that controls for enough variables to allow valid inferences to be made. Particular attention should be paid to success stories. Social scientists studying "the poorest of the poor" sometimes spend all their time studying failures of development, which leads to few insights into how to design successful institutions.

IMPROVING THE THEORY OF MARKETS AND STATES IN THE DEVELOPMENT PROCESS

A fourth and longer-term challenge to economists and other social scientists is to develop an improved theoretical understanding of the relationships between market changes and economic development. Economists have been rightly criticized for analyzing the issue of market reforms and development too narrowly. Economic analyses of market reforms often focus primarily on short-run static efficiency gains rather than on the fundamental challenge of growth—how to produce economic disequilibria and productively use the rents generated by them. Despite the admonition from Timmer, Falcon, and Pearson (1983) that food policy analysts need to consider the full range of constraints facing policy makers, economists have also often underrated the political and social barriers to rapid shifts in economic policies. Here, particularly, increased collaboration between political scientists and economists on the process of market reform would be extremely useful. For example, if economists' ex ante analyses of the likely incidence of policy reforms could be combined with political scientists' work on interest group dynamics, it might prove possible to redesign reforms in a way that would make them more politically acceptable while still being effective.

More generally, there is a need for a more integrated social science understanding of the interactions between institutional, technological, and policy changes. As Schuh points out, currently we have partial theories, such as the induced innovation work of Hayami and Ruttan. While that theory stresses the interdependence of technical and institutional change, it sees both as being driven primarily by the market. But the market itself reflects prior institutional decisions regarding the distribution of rights and resources in society, so to say that the market forces can lead to the evolution of "efficient" institutions seems circular, as the prices used to judge "efficiency" themselves reflect a prior institutional arrangement.

In developing improved theories of the relationships between markets and development, social scientists need to balance induction with deduction. Applied rural social scientists have a long tradition of empiricism, while theorists, particularly in economics, have relied primarily on deduction. In studying many of the areas of policy reform, we are hypothesizing about the behavior of individuals within large economic entities, such as parastatals, or about the behavior of the large entities themselves, behavior for which economics has only poorly developed theories (Timmer 1986, 12–16). It is, therefore, prudent to let empiricism help guide the development of realistic behavioral assumptions.

IMPLICATIONS FOR THE ORGANIZATION OF SOCIAL SCIENCE RESEARCH

Building the empirical and analytical foundation for market reforms involves mainly what Johnson (1986, 12–13) has termed "subject matter research"—multidisciplinary research on a subject of interest to a *set* of decision makers facing a *set* of problems. Subject-matter research provides information that is broadly useful in helping address practical problems facing policy makers, but it is seldom sufficient *by itself* to solve the specific problems they face. Rather, it provides basic understanding about the structure and behavior of that part of the social system (e.g., the food system) with which policy makers are most immediately concerned. Such subject-matter research needs to be complemented with "problem-solving research"—timely, multidisciplinary analysis that draws on the body of knowledge created by subject-matter researchers and complements it with additional information to help solve specific problems.

Decision makers involved in agricultural market reforms and structural adjustments in developing countries often view social scientists skeptically, in part because social science is seldom well organized to carry out the type of subject-matter and problem-solving research outlined above. Social science tends to be disciplinary while problems are multidisciplinary, and social science research in developing countries often is not structured in a way that provides timely, policy-relevant results to policy makers in an easily understandable manner (Weber et al. 1988).

Several authors have treated the problems of organizing multidisciplinary, problem-oriented research (see, for example, Johnson 1986), so only a few summary points are made here. The problems lie at three levels. First, in an age of disciplinary specialization when renaissance people are increasingly rare, there is a danger of multidisciplinary research going in one of two directions. It may become a series of separate disciplinary studies carried out in parallel, with little integration. Or, it may descend to the lowest common denominator of understanding among the team, ending up being mediocre analysis from the standpoint of each discipline involved. A second barrier to multidisciplinary work are the obstacles to coordinating such research across institutions organized on disciplinary lines (Johnson 1986, Chapters 13–14). Third, in such institutions, there may be few professional rewards for such work.

Much of the needed research discussed above is not amenable to study through two-week consultancies. Research on testing the underlying assumptions of the reforms, investigating their incidence, and designing improved institutions requires long-term research and, hence, strengthening of social science research capacity within developing countries. This raises several issues.

The first issue is whether there is demand in the country for such research. Where there is little tradition of such work, researchers may initially have to devote considerable attention to "selling" their results, i.e., demonstrating the relevance of the research for policy and thereby building the effective demand for such work. Including staff from the policy agencies in research design and implementation is a particularly effective way of doing this. In our research in Africa, we found short working papers, coupled with seminars, to be effective means of diffusing research results to policy makers and building their interest in the research program. This is, in many ways, similar to policy extension work carried out by land-grant universities in the United States.

Even if policy makers in poor countries are convinced of the usefulness of applied social science research as an input into policy design, they may be unable to afford its recurrent costs. Without improved market policies, many poor countries are likely to continue to experience poor economic performance. Yet, as long as these countries remain so poor, they will be unable to retain their best-trained social scientists on local salaries and, hence, draw on these professionals to help design improved policies. Donors may have to "bite the bullet" and support some limited recurrent costs of policy-analysis units to help get out of this vicious cycle. Innovative models are needed that perhaps involve greater use of locally run consulting firms within the country to help design and analyze policy reforms.

The location of social science research units is another challenge. Such units need strong enough links with policy makers to make their results felt, yet enough insulation from the political process to be able to do objective research. In many countries, social science research is carried out largely in universities, which often have very poor links to policy makers. Planning units do some research, but often in isolation from their academic colleagues. Fostering professional associations, where social scientists from different organizations can exchange views on an unofficial basis, may be an important means of strengthening the links between policy making and research. In order to help facilitate comparative institutional analysis, donors should also consider increased financing for national and international research networks that allow policy researchers in developing countries to meet and exchange experiences with their counterparts from neighboring countries.

The fourth challenge is to design the research in a way that facilitates rapid analysis and feedback of findings to decision makers. Elaborate reports presented after two years of analysis are often of little immediate value to policy makers, as the issues they analyze are frequently out of date. Providing timely analysis and feedback requires very careful attention to research design and data processing. Researchers have to be highly selective in determining which variables to observe because it is easy to fall into the trap of collecting too much data, which prevents timely analysis. The availability of microcomputers facilitates timely analysis, but only if research objectives are clear and huge data sets are avoided.

This type of applied research and extension described above involves a lot of nitty-gritty work including basic description of how the market system works, who has access to subsidies, and so on. Often, it is not the stuff of journal articles. To encourage academics to participate in such work, administrators of academic units may need to consider "market reforms" in the incentives facing social scientists.

NOTES

1. John M. Staatz is an associate professor in the Department of Agricultural Economics, Michigan State University. Dr. Staatz is grateful to Stephan Goetz, Thomas Jayne, Robert Stevens, T. Kelly White, and an anonymous reviewer, who provided helpful comments on earlier drafts of this paper.

2. The most significant debate, in terms of the number of people affected, has been in China. This debate, however, has been primarily among the Chinese themselves. There have been other important debates outside of Africa, such as those leading to the liberalization of fertilizer marketing in Bangladesh (Berg 1987a), of agricultural product and input markets in Ecuador, and to general economic restructuring in Turkey.

3. This research has been financed through the "Food Security in Africa Cooperative Agreement" between US-AID and the Department of Agricultural Economics, Michigan State University.

4. Between 1970 and 2000, the urban population of developing countries is forecast to grow by 1.5 billion, or 250 percent (Mittendorf n.d.). In addition, many rural residents, even in Africa, are dependent on the market for much of their food (Weber et al. 1988).

5. For a good treatment of the difficulties posed by increasing affluence for attempts to direct an economy primarily by central planning, see Balassa (1976).

6. See Lipton (1987, 201–2), for a similar list.

7. Defenders of such studies may argue, following Hayami and Ruttan (1985), that new technologies and institutions evolve in response to prices and, hence, are part of the long-run supply response. For a critique, see Krishna (1984).

8. While analysts recognize the adverse impact that higher food prices have on low-income consumers, most continue to assume that in Africa, in contrast to Latin America and South Asia, the vast majority of rural residents are net sellers of food and, hence, would be helped by higher food prices. For example, in discussing the adverse effects of higher prices on consumers, Lipton (1987, 206) states that "it is not a serious risk in most of sub-Saharan Africa, as long as most poor people can farm some land."

9. Research spearheaded by scholars at Ohio State University, for example, shows that a high proportion of the benefits of subsidized credit is often captured by elites (Adams, Graham, and Von Pischke 1984).

10. In Mali, for example, the main technological innovation currently available for increasing coarse grain production is the use of animal traction. Yet the farmers most benefitted by the price support had already obtained this technology, while the semiequipped and nonequipped farmers, most of whom were net sellers of food, were hurt by the price policy (Dione and Staatz 1987).

REFERENCES

Abbott, John C. 1987. *Agricultural marketing enterprises for the developing world.* New York: Cambridge University Press.

Adams, Dale W, Douglas H. Graham, and J.D. Von Pischke, eds. 1984. *Undermining rural development with cheap credit.* Boulder, Colo.: Westview Press.

Balassa, Bela. 1976. Proposals for economic planning in Portugal. *Economica* 43 (May): 117–24.

Bates, Robert H. 1981. *Markets and states in tropical Africa: The political basis of agricultural policies.* Berkeley and Los Angeles: University of California Press.

Berg, Elliot. 1987a. Obstacles to liberalizing agricultural markets in developing countries. In *Agricultural marketing strategy and pricing policy: A World Bank symposium.* Edited by Dieter Elz, 22–27. Washington: World Bank.

_____1987b. *Report on the economic reform program in Madagascar.* Report prepared for USAID/Madagascar. Alexandria, Va.: Elliot Berg Associates.

Bromley, Daniel W. n.d. Markets and agricultural development: The promise and the challenge. Draft report to USAID, Bureau for Science and Technology, Madison, Wisc.

Campbell, Donald, and Julian Stanley. 1963. *Experimental and quasi-experimental designs for research.* Chicago: R. McNally.

Dembélé, N. Nango, Josué Dioné, and John Staatz. 1986. Description et analyse de la structure du marché des céréales (mil, maïs, sorgho) au Mali. Bamako, Mali: Ministére de l'Agriculture, Institut d'Economie Rurale, Secretariat Technique de la CESA, MSU-CESA Projet Sécurité Alimentaire, Document de Travail 86–04, September.

Dioné, Josué, and John Staatz. 1987. Market liberalization and food security in Mali. Agricultural Economics staff paper no. 87–73, Michigan State University, East Lansing.

Hayami, Yujiro, and Vernon W. Ruttan. 1985. *Agricultural development: An international perspective.* Rev. and expanded edition. Baltimore: Johns Hopkins University Press.

Humphreys, Charles P. 1986. *Cereals policy reform in the Sahel—Mali.* Report to CILSS/Club du Sahel. Alexandria, Va.: Elliot Berg Associates.

Johnson, Glenn L. 1986. *Research methodology for economists: Philosophy and practice.* New York: Macmillan.

_____1988. *The urgency of institutional changes for LDC, NIC, and DC agricultures.* Paper presented at the "Symposium on Future U.S. Development Assistance," 17–19 February, Winrock International Conference Center, Morrilton, Ark. East Lansing: Michigan State University, Department of Agricultural Economics.

Johnston, Bruce F., and Peter Kilby. 1975. *Agriculture and structural transformation: Economic strategies in late-developing countries.* New York: Oxford University Press.

Krishna, Raj. 1984. Price and technology policies. In *Agricultural development in the Third World.* Edited by Carl K. Eicher and John M. Staatz, 168–75. Baltimore: Johns Hopkins University Press.

Lele, Uma J., and Nicolas van de Walle. 1988. Cotton in Africa: An analysis of differences in performance in the MADIA countries. Draft paper. Washington: World Bank.

Lipton, Michael. 1987. Limits of price policy for agriculture: Which way for the World Bank? *Development Policy Review* 5:197–215.

Mellor, John W. 1978. Food price policy and income distribution in low-income countries. *Economic Development and Cultural Change* 21, no. 1: 1–26.

Mittendorf, Hans. n.d. The challenge of organizing city food marketing systems in developing countries. *Zeitschrift für Ausländische Landwirtschaft* 17(4):323–41.

Newman, Mark D., P. Alasane Sow, and Ousseynou Ndoye. 1987. Regulatory uncertainty and grain market performance in Senegal. In *Agriculture and economic instability.* Edited by Margot Bellamy and Bruce Greenshields, 11–15. Brookfield, Vt.: Gower.

Peterson, W.L. n.d. International farm Prices and the social cost of cheap food policies. *American Journal of Agricultural Economics* 61, no. 1: 12–21.

Reynolds, Lloyd G. 1983. The spread of economic growth to the Third World: 1850–1980. *Journal of Economic Literature* 21, no. 3 (September): 941–80.

Scandizzo, Pasquale L., and Colin Bruce. 1980. Methodologies for measuring agricultural price intervention effects. World Bank staff working paper no. 394, June.

Schuh, G. Edward. 1987. International development and affairs. In *Proceedings of Phase I Workshop.* Compiled by Neill Schaller, 179–98. Social Science Agricultural Agenda Project, 9–11 June, Spring Hill Conference Center, Minneapolis, Minn. Washington, D.C.: U.S. Dept. of Agriculture, Economic Research Service, Resources and Technology Division.

Shaffer, James D. 1979. Observations on the political economics of regulations. *American Journal of Agricultural Economics* 61, no. 2 (November): 721–31.

Timmer, C. Peter. 1986. Private decisions and public policy: The price dilemma in food systems of developing countries. MSU International Development paper no. 7. East Lansing: Michigan State University, Department of Agricultural Economics.

Timmer, C. Peter, Walter P. Falcon, and Scott R. Pearson. 1983. *Food policy analysis.* Baltimore: Johns Hopkins University Press for the World Bank.

United Nations, World Food Council. 1987. The global state of hunger and malnutrition and the impact of economic adjustment on food and hunger problems. Report by the Secretariat, no. WFC/1987/2, 8 April, Rome.

Weber, Michael T., John M. Staatz, John S. Holtzman, Eric W. Crawford, and Richard H. Bernsten. 1988. Informing food security decisions in Africa: Empirical analysis and policy dialogue. *American Journal of Agricultural Economics* 70, no. 5 (December).

White, T. Kelly. 1987. The policy analysis process. Paper presented to the Conference on Agricultural Policy Reform, 18–20 July, Cairo, Egypt. Washington, D.C.: USDA, ERS. Mimeographed.

_____1988. Agriculture and trade policy issues—The economic and policy setting and implications for ERS research. Paper presented to the ERS planning retreat, 5–8 April. Washington, D.C.: USDA, ERS. Mimeographed.

Williamson, Oliver E. 1985. *The economic institutions of capitalism.* New York: The Free Press.

World Bank. 1986.

World Development Report, 1986. New York: Oxford University Press.

CHAPTER 5

THE BUMPERS AMENDMENT: AID AND TRADE ISSUES FOR U.S. AGRICULTURE

Paul B. Thompson[1]

INTRODUCTION

In November 1985, Senator Dale Bumpers first offered an amendment (No. 1129) intended to prohibit the availability of funds for foreign-aid activities that would assist the export of agricultural commodities that compete with U.S. exports. Now commonly referred to as the "Bumpers Amendment," it became law in May 1986 (U.S. Senate 1986a, 56). In Bumper's words, the act is to "prevent American tax dollars from being used to help foreign countries who [sic] are trying to take our export markets," (U.S. Senate 1986b). Under this law, the U.S. Agency for International Development (USAID) is required to suspend research and implementation projects that could enable poor foreign farmers to increase commercial production of commodities (such as meat, maize, or wheat) that are exported from the United States, and also of commodities (such as palm oil) that, while not produced for export in the United States, may substitute for U.S. commodities.

This paper undertakes a philosophical analysis of the cases for and against the Bumpers Amendment. The first section is an analysis of arguments made by Senator Bumpers' constituents in the U.S. farm community that led him to propose the law in the first place. These arguments must be understood as making philosophical claims about the role of U.S. government in international development, rather than simply as claims expressing the private interests of American farmers. The second section is a brief review of economic analyses intended to show that, contrary to popular belief, development assistance is in the interests of U.S. farm producers. The argument of the third section demonstrates why the pro-development-assistance claims of the second section fail to adequately enjoin the anti-development-assistance claims of the first. The final section offers a sketch of a more effective argument in favor of aggressive U.S. policy to develop the agriculture of Third World nations.

PUBLIC RESEARCH FOR FOREIGN COMPETITIVENESS: THE MORAL ISSUE

The Bumpers Amendment reflects a longstanding sentiment among U.S. food and fiber commodity growers. Domestic producers, who have come to rely heavily on foreign markets for agricultural commodities, have often cast doubt upon the wisdom of USAID programs to increase agricultural productivity in Third World countries (Scobie 1979; Dalrymple 1980). This concern grew into a groundswell of public support for a Bumpers-type law after an August 1, 1985, mailing to members of the American Soybean Association (ASA), the soybean producers' trade association, pegged U.S. public support for international farm production research at $341,137,588. The ASA mailing stated that USAID's support of agricultural research in developing countries harmed the United States' already-weakened foreign trade in agricultural commodities, and, hence, the incomes of agricultural producers.[2] USAID questions the accuracy of ASA reports, concluding that ASA could have arrived at their figure only by including amounts intended to be expended over a period of several years and by failing to distinguish accounts dedicated to health and nutrition projects from those dedicated to agriculture. Although fairness to USAID demands accuracy in reporting programs, the argument made by USAID's critics does not depend on the technical accuracy of ASA figures. This argument can be broken down into two distinct themes. The first is an *interest argument* asserting that U.S. foreign agricultural assistance programs are in conflict with the interests of U.S. farmers. The second theme is a *philosophical argument* that the use of public funds to aid foreign producers at the expense of U.S. citizens overreaches USAID budgetary authority. Both of these themes were represented simultaneously in most statements of the criticism, although some individuals undoubtedly gave little thought to anything beyond their own interests. The argument cannot be interpreted as *merely* an interest argument, however, as the following analysis shows.

THE INTEREST ARGUMENT

It is entirely appropriate that U.S. citizens should express their opinions (both in print and through personal communication) to lawmakers and government officials regarding the impact of government actions and programs upon their personal or commercial interests, and it is not only reasonable but necessary for government officials in a democracy to take these expressions of their constituents' individual interests under consideration in the formation of public policy. Public policy is, in many instances, an attempt to balance competing interests of individuals against one another. The principle that assures everyone of the right to have their own interests considered as this balance is struck is fundamental to democracy in a republic. This very picture of the policy process, however, entails that sometimes governments will inevitably act in ways that are *not* in the interest of some individuals, since it presumes that there will be occasions on which the competition among individual interests is irreconcilable.

There is, therefore, no *general* correlation between policies that conflict with individual interests and those that are illegitimate in the sense that they violate principles of ethics and justice. A claim asserting that the policy is unjust (or otherwise morally unacceptable) implies that the policy violates one or more of the moral standards that govern the use of state power. The simple claim that a given policy conflicts with individual interests does not do this, since there may be other interests at stake. These other interests might be regarded by everyone as at least equal to, if not more important than, those interests that are thwarted.

The basic distinction between a simple interest argument and an ethical argument can be illustrated by contrasting the case at hand, use of public funds to support research for foreign producers, with the more common case in which public funds are spent for research on commodities that compete with one another (either on a commodity-by-commodity or region-by-region basis) within the domestic agricultural economy. Sugar, for example, is produced from beets in some areas of the United States and from cane in other areas. A sugar beet producer can claim, with some accuracy, that government funds for research and extension activities in sugar cane help the producers of these products and, thus, harm any competitive advantages that a beet producer might otherwise enjoy. The beet producer might demand to be compensated (through funds expended for research and extension on sugar beets, for example) when such actions are taken. None of this, however, could be construed as a moral claim that government acts illegitimately when it helps cane producers in the Southeast, but rightly and with justice when it helps beet producers in the Great Northwest. Such a claim is so patently ridiculous that even the most ardently partisan supporter of the beet industry could utter it only in jest.

THE PHILOSOPHICAL ARGUMENT

The corresponding claim (that the government acts rightly and with justice when it helps U.S. producers, but wrongly and illegitimately when it helps foreign commercial growers of the same products) needs to be (and is) made with all seriousness. Producers who criticize USAID express an interest argument, to be sure, for they claim that helping foreign growers is contrary to the interests of American farmers; but they also make a moral claim that is philosophically distinct. While the Colorado beet grower who criticizes cane programs in Louisiana is somewhat placated by a policy that provides commensurate support for beets, the Illinois soybean grower would not be at all satisfied to learn that the government spends far more to support development of the Illinois soybean industry than it does to support the soybean industry of Brazil or Argentina. Such a response misses the point.

The point that it misses is one that is absolutely fundamental to social and political philosophy, generally, and is clearest in social contract theories of the state. Since Hobbes (1651), social contract theories have founded the establishment of government upon an argument claiming that individuals unbound by obligations and constraints of government have, would, or (rationally) should abandon some of the personal liberties that they enjoy in that freedom in exchange for certain guarantees and benefits that can be secured only by enforceable schemes of mutual cooperation. The philosophical basis for the Bumpers Amendment sentiment can be found in either of two implicit themes of social contract argument. First, it is the standard assumption of contract theory that benefits accrue primarily to contracting parties. Second, although the state's responsibility to protect individuals from foreign threats is ambiguous with regard to economic interests, it cannot plausibly be understood to permit state intervention on behalf of foreign competitors, unless significant state interests are at stake.

With regard to the first point, it almost goes without saying that the greater part of any plausibility that follows from social contract arguments in political theory comes from their analogy to standard sorts of personal contracts in which parties consent to be bound by terms and conditions. The presumption is that parties so agree because they perceive a mutual benefit in making the contract. There may be, to be sure, cases where parties contract for services that will benefit others indirectly, as when the services I contract from a house painter so beautifies my neighborhood that others benefit aesthetically (or even in increased property values). There may also be cases in which others benefit directly as a result of altruistic intentions, as when I contract with the same house painter for services to be rendered to a local charity. These exceptions might be cogent for the point under review if Third World agricultural development were an indirect benefit, or if it were altruistically desired by the parties being required to sacrifice in its behalf. The mere fact that arguments for a Bumpers-type law were made indicates that neither of these aforementioned conditions were met. The model of mutual benefit to contracting parties demands that any altruistic motives be explicitly and voluntarily expressed by the parties.

Second, among the most basic of these arguments is one that assures parties to the contract that the newly created state power will secure their person and property against any foreign threat. This guarantee can be interpreted to entail, at a minimum, that state power may not be actively used to place them at a competitive disadvantage to foreigners.[3] It is, in fact, somewhat reasonable to expect that state power will be used collectively to gain advantage over noncitizens; although many versions of contract theory would not support this stronger claim. It is not, therefore, unambiguously clear that the state's duty to protect citizen interests extends into the economic realm. It does seem clear that this duty would entail neutrality, at a minimum; and neutrality would, on the face of it, at least, be all that is required to support the pro-Bumpers philosophical argument. That is not to say, however, that government might not favor a foreign competitor if some vital national interest were at stake. If, for example, national security demands that the mineral production of some foreign state remain or become economically viable (in order, perhaps, to secure a continuing source of supply), one might encounter situations where government initiatives to support this foreign industry would be justified, even if they harmed (in some nonfundamental way) U.S. producers. As such, there is a general type of argument, stressing national interest, that might be raised against the Bumpers-type form of reasoning. Such an argument will, in fact, be proposed in the final section, but first it is important to review some of the arguments that have thus far been proposed to counter the kind of argument raised by ASA and its friends against development assistance.

INTERNATIONAL AGRICULTURAL ASSISTANCE AND THE INTERESTS OF U.S. AGRICULTURE

Contrary to the central claim of the ASA criticism of USAID, economic theory, as well as the empirical evidence, would suggest that foreign assistance intended to develop Third World agriculture creates an expansion of international markets for commodities exported by the U.S. farm community. The theoretical foundations for this view are argued by Mellor, de Janvry and Sadoulet (1986), Houck (1986), and Rossmiller and Tutwiler (1987). Empirical support has been demonstrated in analyses by Bachman and Paulino (1979); Kellogg, Kodl, and Garcia (1986); and Christiansen (1987). These works are, for the most part, offered as straightforward economic results, not as philosophical arguments. Nevertheless, they form the foundation for a counter argument made to explicitly counter pro-Bumpers claims in general, and ASA claims in particular. In the following discussion, this sophisticated economic argument will be represented by two simplified versions of it that have appeared in the popular press. These popular versions would be strengthened in some of their theoretical and empirical claims by full documentation, but neither theoretical nor empirical claims will be questioned in the analysis that follows. As such, the popular versions have an advantage over more technically adequate arguments, both in their intuitive appeal and in their clear and intended applicability to the political environment created by the ASA literature and by the Bumpers Amendment itself.

It is this popular version of the sophisticated argument that I shall refer to as the *True Interests Argument*. It is offered to accomplish two related goals: (1) it is intended to demonstrate that a hidden premise of the ASA criticism of agricultural development assistance is false; and (2) it is intended to erode support for the viewpoint advocated by ASA among the U.S. farm community. After an initial review of the "true interests argument" itself, it will be useful to evaluate the relevance of each of these goals to the two versions of the pro-Bumpers arguments as they have been discussed above.

THE TRUE INTERESTS OF U.S. AGRICULTURE

The "true interests argument" assumes (quite reasonably) that future increases in demand for basic farm commodities will come primarily from the people of the developing world. The people of the Third World have yet to become large-scale consumers of imported commodities. As they gain purchasing power, they promise to expand markets for food and fiber both because of their sheer numbers, and because, as they become more wealthy, they can be expected to make dietary shifts toward meat consumption that will increase per capita consumption of agricultural commodities. Impressive demand growth will not come from a developed world where population and diets have stabilized. Increasing demand from potential Third World customers awaits only economic growth in those societies that would allow them to command commodities in world markets.

But how to achieve economic growth in the developing world? Writing in *The Wall Street Journal*, Randall B. Purcell (1987) answers:

> Contrary to conventional wisdom, the best way to achieve this is through the development of local agriculture in the developing countries themselves. Because most Third World workers are employed in agriculture, the development of this sector achieves a more even distribution of income than does the development of other sectors. And in the early and middle stages of economic development, as people have more money, the first thing they spend it on is increasing and diversifying their consumption of food.

Theories of economic development from the 1950s recognized the importance of industrialization in general economic growth, and for this reason stressed the formation of manufacturing capabilities in developing countries. This "conventional wisdom" referred to by Purcell has been significantly revised as development economists have improved their understanding of agriculture. Investment in capital-intensive manufacturing industries created severe political problems in many developing economies. Wealth tended to accrue to relatively small elites, while industrial workers (and the urban poor lured to cities by false expectations of industrial growth) expended a high percentage of their incomes upon basic necessities. Agricultural sectors still organized for plantation production of commodities for export (and subsistence production of commodities for personal use) were unable to meet the food needs of the new urban proletariate. Government attempts to supply urban food needs through imports (sometimes of PL480 donations) depressed markets for endogenously produced food and exacerbated problems in foreign exchange (Todaro 1985).

It has been suggested that some of these problems might be avoided by revising the assumption that agriculture is relatively unimportant for general economic development. A carefully chosen investment in agriculture should, as Purcell (1987) notes, spread capital (and, hence, return on capital) across many more people in the developing economy than does a single large investment in industrial manufacturing. The multiplier effect of increasing incomes throughout the economy is greater when more incomes are increased, even if by relatively smaller amounts. Furthermore, increases in rural incomes are less likely to be expended on imported luxury items, thus easing pressures on foreign exchange. Finally, the increased production of food and improved efficiency of farming should release labor for industrialization (thus creating demand for purchased food) at the same time that it increases the supply of basic foods available on commercial markets. Agricultural development does not replace industrial development under such a scenario, but it is seen as of coequal importance in contributing to overall economic growth (Mellor and Johnston 1984).

In short, agricultural development in the Third World is important for U.S. exports of agricultural commodities because it is a prerequisite for general economic growth, and economic growth in the Third World is, in turn, the best hope for expanding demand of U.S. exports. This argument from economic theory has been advanced as a direct response to the critics of foreign agricultural assistance by G. Edward Schuh (1986), director of agriculture for the World Bank. Schuh writes:

> It is important to understand where the true interests of U.S. agriculture lie and especially where future U.S. markets are likely to be.... These markets are likely to grow most rapidly in the developing countries including China)...[but] only if their economies expand and their living standards rise.... Increasing productivity and incomes in agriculture is thus the key to raising per capita incomes in the economy as a whole. Those higher incomes are the source of a strong demand for agricultural imports.

IS THE PRO-BUMPERS ARGUMENT TRUE?

If the True Interests Argument is sound, it provides an important counterweight to one feature of the criticism directed at USAID. The critical arguments share an assumption that agricultural assistance programs are contrary to the trade interests of American farmers. This assumption is called into question by the closer analysis of the relation between aid and trade given in the "true interests argument." If the claim is false that development assistance harms the competitiveness of U.S. farmers, why take ASA claims seriously, or enact a Bumpers-type law? Two points need to be discussed in response to this question.

First, although the "true interests argument" is quite persuasive when U.S. agriculture is considered in the aggregate and in the long run, it neglects short-run consequences that may, indeed, be negative for some sectors of the U.S. farm economy. It was noted by de Janvry and Sadoulet (1986) that effects upon U.S. export markets may even be negative in the short run. Paarlberg (1986) notes that although increased agricultural productivity has led to an increase in agricultural imports for some often-cited developing countries, counter examples abound as well. Peterson (1986) points out that arguments citing aggregated results for the entire U.S. farm economy are unlikely to be persuasive to producers of individual commodities, some of whom face stiff competition from growers in climatically well-suited developing country contexts. It is not appropriate to review the accuracy of "true interests argument" claims in light of such skepticism, but it is worth noting that the key substantive assumptions of the ASA claims cannot be dismissed out of hand.

Second, the short-run/long-run discrepancy noted by these critics is of particular importance given the political context in which the ASA argument was made. If it is philosophically wrong to directly assist the competitors of U.S. producers, the mere fact that this will lead to long-term benefits to U.S. producers does not make it right. The producers who are (temporarily) harmed today may be different individuals than the producers who are benefitted tomorrow. Given the high rate of farm failures occurring during the years preceding the Bumpers debates in 1985 and 1986, individual farmers would appear to have prima facie justification for rejecting arguments in which individual farm failures would be concealed by aggregate growth in U.S. agriculture.

In conclusion, although the "true interests argument" casts considerable doubt upon the essential claims of the pro-Bumpers case, it is not decisive. Its highly aggregated nature leaves plenty of room for skeptics in the farm community to doubt that foreign agricultural development will benefit them. U.S. agriculture as a whole may benefit, but in an era of rapidly evolving farm structure, many individuals may question whether they (or their heirs) would be involved in U.S. agriculture long enough to reap the rewards.

SHOULD THE PRO-BUMPERS CASE BE MADE?

The previous discussion indicates that many individual producers may still feel strongly motivated to press the central claim of the ASA mailings in letters and petitions to congressional leaders. It should also be noted that, even if the factual claims to the "true interests argument" are correct, they have far more relevance to the interest version of a pro-Bumpers position than to the more sophisticated (and more persuasive) philosophical claim. It is certainly true that, once convinced that foreign aid serves his interest, a U.S. farmer will have little personal interest in opposing it through a Bumpers-type law. As a philosophical claim, however, the case is different. If it is wrong for government to help foreign competitors, the mere fact that there are indirect benefits for U.S. citizens does not make it right. Indeed, there would almost always be some domestic beneficiaries to *any* case of helping foreign competitors. The injunction against this sort of activity is stated on principle and is not mitigated by the fact that some people who thought they might be hurt are, in fact, helped. The plausibility of the pro-Bumpers case depends upon two very basic assumptions of social contract theory. An argument overturning that principled philosophical case must attack it either at the level of the founding principles, or by showing that some overriding social good is more important for this case. Simply showing that the people who offered the argument may have harmed themselves by having done so counts for nothing; as a philosophical argument, it did not matter who made the argument, but only its logical force. This point will become clearer in the following section.

WHY THE TRUE INTERESTS ARGUMENT FAILS TO ADDRESS THE PHILOSOPHICAL CASE

In this section, the distinction between the interest argument and philosophical argument for a Bumpers-type law is discussed a second time in the context of a familiar philosophical distinction between presumptive and discretionary goods. The main point, addressed in the second section below, is to show that the main philosophical claims behind ASA criticisms of USAID involve presumptive goods, while the True Interests Argument presumes that the issue is merely a dispute over discretionary goods. This distinction points the way for the conclusion of this analysis, an argument sketch for a strong case for development assistance.

PRESUMPTIVE AND DISCRETIONARY GOODS

The dual nature of the U.S. farm community's case against international agricultural development can be clarified by noting a standard distinction between presumptive and discretionary goods in social and political philosophy.[4] It is generally recognized that the benefits citizens enjoy from government services are of two kinds. Discretionary goods are benefits that may be enjoyed and desired by a majority of citizens (or even unanimously), and which are provided solely because they are desired and supported by a majority of citizens. If tastes or opinions change, the government would not only be justified in discontinuing its support of discretionary goods, but would be mandated by public opinion to do so. Among the frequent examples of discretionary goods are parks, roads, museums, and public art projects. Presumptive goods, on the other hand, are benefits, services, or guarantees that necessarily must be provided for just continuance of the state. If a government fails to provide presumptive goods, it not only weakens itself, it calls its legitimacy into question. National defense and protection of basic rights to life and liberty are among the standard examples of presumptive goods.

The line between a discretionary and a presumptive good is neither unambiguous nor noncontroversial. While some of the paradigm examples cited above may seem clearly discretionary or presumptive, many government actions might be described by their advocates as securing presumptive goods, and decried by their critics as providing only discretionary (and, indeed, unwanted) goods. The classic debate has been over welfare benefits. Liberals have seen the redistribution of wealth to secure minimums of welfare and opportunity to all citizens as a presumptive good, one required both to stabilize society and to guarantee human rights required for the legitimation of government (Nagel 1977; Levin 1981). Conservatives and libertarians have disputed the presumptive character of welfare benefits, arguing that the state is founded instead upon minimal protection of security, liberty, and property claims of individuals, and that active state welfare programs would be justified only to the extent that individuals support them through voluntary contributions (Nozick 1974). As such, the conservative view not only makes welfare benefits discretionary, in founding them on the willingness of citizens to contribute, but also finds the unilateral use of tax dollars to support welfare programs to be a coercive violation of property rights (and, hence, a governmental failure to provide a presumptive good) (Klosko 1987).

Although the details of this classic disagreement over discretionary and presumptive goods are not directly relevant to the issue at hand, it is important to see why the philosophical debate turns upon whether welfare benefits are presumptive goods. Although government may provide many discretionary goods to its citizens who want and support them, when the provision of a discretionary good conflicts with government's ability to secure presumptive goods, it is the presumptive goods that must prevail. Presumptive goods "trump" discretionary goods because they are essential to the just foundations of the state. They prevail without regard to the preferences or opinions of the majority, and, indeed, provide the philosophical basis for protection of minorities against the tyranny of a majority view. This is not to say that presumptive goods are always finally decisive in determining policy, since two or more presumptive goods may not be mutually satisfiable, too. In such a case, one is forced back to fundamental philosophical goals in the establishment and legitimation of the state in any attempt to set priorities or fashion a compromise.

PRESUMPTIVE GOODS AND THE TRUE INTERESTS ARGUMENT

The distinction between presumptive and discretionary goods sheds light on the "true interests argument." Advocates of this view address the U.S. farm community with evidence intended to show that their initial presumption of conflict between their trade interests and USAID's development assistance policies is false. In fact, the "true interests argument" states, U.S. farmers should join in support of these policies; it is in their commercial interests to do so. In making this type of claim, the "true interests argument" treats USAID development goals as if they were an attempt to secure discretionary goods, goods that are justified simply because Americans want them and are willing to support them. The attempt to build political support for these goals implies that they are appropriate actions for USAID only to the extent that they are endorsed by American citizens in the political process.

The philosophical argument against agricultural development aid, however, claimed that these policies were in conflict with presumptive goods. The philosophical argument against AID depends upon seeing USAID's actions as beyond the scope of governmental activities sanctioned by the implicit terms of a social contract, at a minimum, and as most probably in conflict with the presumed purposes of state power. As such, the mere fact that the farm community might be shifted from the column of those opposing a discretionary good to those supporting it carries little philosophical weight. The number of people supporting the discretionary good against the presumptive one is irrelevant; the claim to violate a presumptive good "trumps" all discretionary arguments.

TOWARD A REHABILITATION OF USAID'S INTERNATIONAL DEVELOPMENT GOALS

The distinction between presumptive and discretionary goods also indicates the strategy that a philosophically adequate response to USAID's critics must take. Such an argument must not place much importance upon discretionary benefits that USAID's policies might return to members of the U.S. public. Such benefits will never override the presumptive character of the ASA argument. Instead, a reply to the philosophical version of the ASA argument must demonstrate that USAID's efforts at international agricultural development itself attempts to secure presumptive goods, goods that the U.S. government is, as a matter of justice or national interest, required to pursue.

It is not possible to present a full account of how such a claim might be established here. However, the purpose of this paper is, in part, to indicate areas in which further research is needed so the incompleteness of the argument can be regarded as a virtue rather than a deficiency. In this vein, the concluding remarks that follow are intended as a sketch of how such an argument might go, although it is acknowledged that there are important gaps in the account that is given here. In addition to this sketch, I shall point out several topics that are in particular need of multidisciplinary research for any resolution to the general issues raised by discussion of the Bumpers Amendment.

INTERNATIONAL AGRICULTURAL DEVELOPMENT AID AS A PRESUMPTIVE GOOD: AN ARGUMENT SKETCH

The "true interests argument" has two deficiencies that have been noted above. First, an empirical deficiency is found in its highly aggregated and time-dependent portrayal of benefits to U.S. agriculture. Critics of the argument question whether particular individuals could reasonably be expected to receive any of the benefits alleged to flow from development assistance, at least within the time frame in which such benefits would be of the most value to them. The second deficiency of the "true interests argument" is that in portraying the outcomes of USAID's developing programs in terms of discretionary goods to benefit U.S. producers, the argument fails to address the fundamental philosophical objection, namely that these programs aim to supply competitive benefits to foreign nationals. These two deficiencies notwithstanding, the "true interests argument" makes a convincing case for the thesis that foreign agricultural assistance is beneficial to national interests, and to the U.S. economy as a whole. If this aspect of the "true interests argument" is emphasized, rather than its appeal to individual farm producers, it might be restructured in a way that would allow it to form the basis for showing how these development activities help the government secure a presumptive good, rather than a discretionary one.

In a recent book, *The Rise of the Trading State*, political scientist Richard Rosecrance (1986) argues that the balance of geo-political power and prestige has shifted in the last century (and particularly in the last 25 years) from those nations with dominant military strength to those nations with the most cultivated and extensive networks of trade. Rosecrance's thesis, in part, is that national interest cannot be defined exclusively or even primarily in terms of armed might and military alliances. Increasingly, it is the ability of a nation to enter mutually beneficial trade relations with other countries that determines the parameters of national interest (Rosecrance 1986). If Rosecrance is right, then healthy, nondomineering trade relations cultivated with developing countries through helping in the growth of their agricultural sector may play a greater role in U.S. national interest over the long run than does the more celebrated and discussed supply of arms and military support. If national interest hangs, in an important way, upon these economic and cultural relations, there is good reason to think that it is a presumptive good being sought by these development goals, rather than a discretionary one.

The argument as presented thus far is hypothetical. An adequate presentation of it would require far more analysis of the adequacy of Rosecrance's thesis, its broader implications, and the links that might be made between aid, trade, and an enlightened view of national interest. Even if the empirical and conceptual links could be established, one would still need to show that the presumptive goods secured by aid were philosophically more fundamental than the presumptive constraint upon aiding foreign nationals. Nevertheless, these tasks seem achievable, and once completed, might provide a firmer philosophical foundation for international development activities, generally, and not just in agriculture. The research needed to round out this perspective is considerable, and it is therefore important to turn, in closing, to some of the priority needs.

RESEARCH NEEDS

In identifying areas for more research, it may be useful to start with some of the most obvious needs for data collection and analysis. The empirical claims of the "true interests argument" are a case in point. There is a need for more data and more empirical analysis to determine the scope and validity of the claim that international agricultural development helps U.S. agriculture. This research should address not only the broad aggregate relationships mentioned in the popular arguments given by Schuh (1986) and Purcell (1987), but should also involve country-by-country and commodity-by-commodity study of impact upon three groups of affected parties: developing-country producers (including the rural community), developing-country consumers, and U.S. producers. In light of the long-term goals of linking the "true interests argument" with a broader view of national interest, empirical research on development should also be sensitive to a broad view of the political aims and effects of trade.

There is also a fairly obvious need for research on the central thesis proposed in Rosecrance's book and, in particular, with regard to how a trade-based theory of national interest and geo-politics has implications for agriculture and development. This is a fairly open-ended research need with applications in many disciplines, most assuredly including economics, political science, and philosophy. Even apart from Rosecrance's thesis, there is a clear need for both speculative and empirical research on the cords that bind trade, development, poverty, and political power.

More specifically, on the level of political philosophy, there is a general need for research on the philosophical foundations of development policy. The argument presented here would place the emphasis upon the concepts of presumptive and discretionary goods and where a nation's development assistance policy would fall with respect to this distinction. A popular view may be to see international aid as a form of charity, something that a wealthy and developed nation should do, but not essential to the fundamental aims of the state. Such a view would seem to place USAID policy within the category of discretionary goods, but if the argument sketched above has any force, that categorization needs to be rethought. The concepts of discretionary and presumptive goods must themselves be analyzed more carefully, and must be more carefully integrated into economic development theory where, to my knowledge, they have not been widely applied.

In connection with philosophical research, it should be noted that other philosophers have seen promise in a strategy other than the one outlined above. If development assistance is to be defined as a presumptive good, it must involve either justice or national interest. The strategy chosen above stresses national interest, but perhaps the goals of development assistance are demanded by justice. Although there are reasons to be skeptical of this strategy, it has been pursued in books by Peter Brown and Henry Shue (1977) and James W. Nickel (1987), papers by Charles Beitz (1975), Thomas Nagel (1977), and William Aiken (1977), as well as in popular books such as *Food First* and *Ill Fares the Land*. It is not appropriate to initiate a critical discussion of this literature here, but it is important to note that philosophical research demands an environment of healthy criticism and debate among opposing points of view. As such, it is important to continue this research stream to determine where it leads and to encourage debate over the philosophical goals of the development process.

NOTES

1. Paul B. Thompson holds a joint appointment in the Departments of Agricultural Economics and Philosophy, Texas A & M University, College Station, Texas.

2. For confirmation, see John Baize, "Farmers Must Fight for World Market Share," *Pennsylvania Farmer*, September 14, 1985, page 48. Baize is an ASA executive based in Washington, D.C.; also, "World Bank Loans Stir Ire of U.S. Farm Groups," *The New York Times*, June 5, 1987.

3. It is worth noting that this second point would quite probably be endorsed even by those political philosophers who, following Hume (1986) or Burke (1982), see little cogency to a social contract argument. This view might be (over)simplified as holding that, although the use of state power is not justified by consent, as the social contract theorist would have it, the state is nevertheless useful, and its existence helps the law-abiding citizens prosper and flourish. The limits on state power could be derived more from tradition or common practice than from the terms of an implied contract. Although it is always somewhat speculative to assert how a traditionalist might argue, it is plausible to think that the state's traditional duty to protect its citizens in the international arena would preclude exactly the sort of actions that the Bumpers Amendment constrains.

4. A distinction between discretionary or presumptive goods (or duties) is implicit in traditional theorists such as Locke (1690), who recognized in Chapters IX and XI of the *Second Treatise* that government has both ends and self-generated requirements that are prerequisites to the existence of a just state, but also notes in Chapter XIV that governments may provide services (for the public good) that are not required by the duties of justice. The distinction (but not the terminology) has become standard in political theory at least since John Rawls (1971) based much of his argument in *A Theory of Justice* on the distribution of what he called *primary goods* (e.g., presumptive goods).

REFERENCES

Aiken, William. 1977. The right to be saved from starvation. In *World hunger and moral obligation.* Edited by William Aiken and Hugh LaFollette. Englewood Cliffs, N.J.: Prentice-Hall.

Bachman, K. L., and L. A. Paulino. 1979. *Rapid food production growth in selected developing countries.* Washington, D.C.: International Food Policy Research Institute.

Baize, John. 1985. Farmers must fight for world market share. *Pennsylvania Farmer* (14 September): 48.

Beitz, Charles R. 1975. Justice and international relations. *Philosophy and Public Affairs* 4.

Brown, Peter, and Henry Shue. 1977. *Food policy.* New York: The Free Press.

Burke, Edmund. 1982. Excerpts. *The Conservative Reader.* Edited by Russell Kirk, 1–48. New York: Penguin Books.

Christiansen, Robert E. 1987. The impact of economic development on agricultural trade patterns. ERS staff report no. AGES861118. Washington, D.C.: U.S. Dept. of Agriculture, Economic Research Service.

Dalrymple, Dana G. 1980. The demand for agricultural research: A Columbian illustration: Comment. *American Journal of Agricultural Economics* 62:594–96.

de Janvry, Alain, and Elizabeth Sadoulet. 1986. The conditions for harmony between Third World agricultural development and U.S. farm exports. *American Journal of Agricultural Economics* 68:1340–46.

Hobbes, Thomas. [1651] 1950. *Leviathan.* Edited by C. B. MacPherson. New York: Penguin Books.

Houck, James P. 1986. A note on the link between agricultural development and agricultural imports. Staff paper 86–26. Department of Agricultural and Applied Economics, University of Minnesota.

Hume, David. 1986. Of the original contract. In *Readings in social and political philosophy.* Edited by Robert M. Stewart, 32–41. New York: Oxford University Press.

Kellogg, Earl, Richard Kodl, and Philip Garcia. 1986. The effects of agricultural growth on agricultural imports in developing countries. *American Journal of Agricultural Economics* 68:1347–52.

Klosko, George. 1987. Political obligation and consent. *Philosophy and Public Affairs* 16, no. 3.

Levin, Michael E. 1981. Equality of opportunity. *The Philosophical Quarterly* 31:110–25.

Locke, John. [1690] 1980. *Second treatise of government.* Edited by C. B. Macpherson. Indianapolis: Hackett Publishing Co.

Mellor, John W., and Bruce F. Johnston. 1984. The world food equation. *Journal of Economic Literature* 22, no. 2: 531–74.

Nagel, Thomas. 1977. Poverty and food: Why charity is not enough. In *Food policy.* Edited by Peter Brown and Henry Shue, 54–62. New York: The Free Press.

The New York Times. 1987. World Bank loans stir ire of U.S. farm groups. (5 June): A9.

Nickel, James W. 1987. *Making sense of human rights.* Berkeley: University of California Press.

Nozick, Robert. 1974. *Anarchy, state and utopia.* New York: Basic Books.

Paarlberg, Robert L. 1986. Farm development in poor countries: The disputed consequences for U.S. farm trade. American Journal of Agricultural Economics 68:1353–57.

Peterson, E. Wesley F. 1986. Third World development and trade: Discussion. *American Journal of Agricultural Economics* 68:1360–61.

Purcell, Randell B. 1987. Develop their agriculture to save ours. *The Wall Street Journal* (23January).

Rawls, John. 1971. *A theory of justice.* Cambridge: The Belknap Press of Harvard University Press.

Rosecrance, Richard. 1986. *The rise of the trading state.* New York: Basic Books.

Rossmiller, G. E., and M. Ann Tutwiler. 1987. Agricultural trade and development: broadening the horizon. In *United States agricultural exports and Third World development,* 265–93. Boulder: Lynn Reiner for the Curry Foundation.

Schuh, G. Edward. 1986. Some healthy competition for U.S. farmers. *Washington Post* (4 September): A17.

Scobie, Grant M. 1979. The demand for agricultural research: A Columbian illustration. *American Journal of Agricultural Economics* 61:540–45.

Shue, Henry. 1980. *Basic rights.* Princeton: Princeton University Press.

Todaro, Michael P. 1985. Ethics, values, and economic development. In *Ethics and international relations.* Edited by Kenneth W. Thompson, 75–97. New Brunswick, N.J.: Transaction Books.

U.S. Senate. 1986a. Report 99–301, Urgent Supplemental Appropriations Bill 1986. (15 May). Washington, D.C.: Government Printing Office.

U.S. Senate. 1986b. Congressional Record—Senate. (6 June) S7028. Washington, D.C.: Government Printing Office.

CHAPTER 6

FOOD SECURITY AND ITS RELATIONSHIP TO TECHNOLOGY, INSTITUTIONS, POLICIES, AND HUMAN CAPITAL

Michael T. Weber and Thomas S. Jayne[1]

INTRODUCTION

Food insecurity has plagued the world for centuries. Yet not until the time of the 1974 World Food Conference, when poor world harvests and rapidly growing demand evoked the specter of mass starvation, did the concept of food security gain prominence among researchers and policy makers. Shaped by international events at the time, food security was largely defined in terms of promoting food production and national and international food reserves. Fifteen years later, the current food situation is characterized by ample world supplies, depressed prices, chronic overproduction in North America and the European community, and relatively high carry-over stocks in selected developing nations, yet the number of hungry people in the world is estimated to have grown by over ten percent since the early 1970s (World Food Council 1987a).

The paradox of abundant world food supplies and increased hunger throughout the world has required a rethinking of the concept of food security. The objective of this paper is to discuss the dimensions of food security and their relationship to key aspects of technology, institutions, policies, and human capital. We conclude with a priority research agenda to inform and guide food security policy implementation, with special reference to Africa.

Notwithstanding hunger and poverty problems in almost all nations of the world, this paper focuses on food security in sub-Saharan Africa for two principal reasons: First, food insecurity in Africa appears particularly intractable; this is the only continent where the undernourished as a percentage of total population has not fallen since 1970 (World Food Council, 1987a). Second, along with colleagues at Michigan State University and various African institutions, we have spent the past four years conducting food security research, and will use selected empirical results as illustrations.

DEFINITION AND DIMENSIONS OF FOOD SECURITY

The starting point for research on food security is agreeing on its definition (Eicher 1986). Since 1974, its essential elements have evolved into: *availability of food* and *ability to acquire it* (Siamwalla and Valdes 1980; World Bank 1986; Eicher and Staatz 1985). We define food security as a situation in which all individuals in a population possess the resources to assure *access* to enough food for an active and healthy life.

This definition highlights three critical dimensions: (1) supply/demand, (2) time, and (3) level of aggregation.

SUPPLY/DEMAND

Food security is a matter of effective demand as well as available supply. It has become increasingly apparent that the world's chronically undernourished lack the resources to either grow enough food for themselves or generate sufficient income to purchase it. Hence, food security has a supply/demand dimension:

Supply: assuring that the food system provides a supply of food (through local production, stocks, trade, and/or aid) accessible to, and sufficient to meet the nutritional needs of, the total population.

Demand: assuring all elements of the population the purchasing power (from farm and nonfarm income, subsidized prices, etc.) and access to a nutritionally adequate diet.

Sufficiency of supply should be defined not only with respect to the volume of food, but also with respect to its cost. The fact that in some countries supply of certain crops has expanded only at great cost to the national budget or to consumers emphasizes the need to develop an appropriate mix of production, stock, and trade policies to meet food security objectives.

Moreover, attention must focus not only on the aggregate supply of food but also on who has the resources to produce it. For example, price and macro policies designed to increase the aggregate supply of food may have limited effects on food security if additional output comes from a narrow segment of well-equipped farmers. Higher food prices may actually exacerbate food insecurity for a large segment of rural farm families who are net purchasers of food and who lack the productive resources or access to inputs to expand production. The incidence of supply expansion may be as important as the rate of supply expansion.

The demand dimension of food security relates to Sen's (1981) concept of "entitlement," or the ability of households to transform their productive resources into food or the income to obtain it. This quickly broadens the scope of analysis beyond the agricultural sector, since a large proportion of household income, even in rural areas, may come from nonfarm sources.[2] Where incomes are inadequate, transfers to vulnerable groups may be important; if targeted effectively, they raise the real income of the poor, and thus their entitlement to food.

The supply and demand dimensions of food security are both critically affected by the organization and behavior of the marketing system, which influences the transactions of buying and selling, prices paid and received, and, hence, the availability and consumption of grain.

FOOD SECURITY ALSO HAS AN IMPORTANT TEMPORAL DIMENSION

Chronic: Ability to increase and sustain food supplies and effective demand over the long run.

Transitory: Ability to sustain adequate food consumption during temporary food production and/or income shortfalls.

Chronic food insecurity in most African countries largely reflects the low productivity of the food system. Low labor and land productivity affect both the supply dimension, through depressed food availability, and the demand dimension, through low surplus marketings and cash incomes that are insufficient to stimulate demand for farm and nonfarm goods and services. Lacking the demand stimulus to exert upward pressure on prices, production incentives and economic growth may be caught in a low-level equilibrium trap in which neither incomes nor productivity can increase (Mellor 1984). In this context, food security requires disequilibrium induced by changes in institutions, technology, and knowledge to raise resource productivity and incomes on a broad-based level. These factors determine the extent to which the poor can transform their resources into food through production or income-earning activities.

Because the poor typically spend over half of their disposable income on food, fluctuations in food prices greatly affect their real incomes and consumption. For low-income countries dependent on food imports, vulnerable groups' access to food is jeopardized by international food price swings and shortfalls in foreign exchange earnings, as well as domestic production shortfalls (Huddleston et al. 1984). Although food and income transfers will continue to be used to fulfill emergency needs, an important task for food security policy is to develop financially viable mechanisms that alleviate short-run supply shortfalls without losing sight of the chronic determinants of transitory food insecurity. For example, transitory food insecurity may be the manifestation not only of short-run shocks per se, but of long-standing policies and institutions that work against broad-based income generation, dampen long-run investment and growth in the food system, and, therefore, weaken the ability of an economy to cope with transitory disturbances.

LEVEL OF AGGREGATION

Food adequacy on a national or intraregional level may mask serious food insecurity on the household level. Food insecurity is usually associated with particular groups: food-deficit farmers with too little land, given their present technology, to produce enough food, cash crops, or other income to support the family; underemployed, low-wage rural and urban laborers; rural small-scale entrepreneurs facing declining demand for their goods when agricultural incomes drop due to poor harvests; agro-pastoralists living in marginally productive areas. Because wealthier segments of a society tend to adjust their consumption relatively little in response to short-run production shortfalls, the burden of adjustment to a crisis falls largely on the poor.[3] Even with national economic growth, selected groups may be unable to participate in the expansion around them. Large segments of the rural population in marginal sectors (e.g., dryland millet producers) may be unable to shift their resources into growth sectors with specific capital, knowledge, or climatic requirements. For these reasons, food security research must be addressed at both the household and national levels.

Food insecurity can also differ greatly within households. Targeted interventions such as maternal and baby clinics often cannot reach malnourished children too old to qualify for support. The work of nutritionists and health planners indicates the importance of food security research on the intrahousehold level.

Defining the hunger problem in terms of food security stresses three important dimensions: time, level of aggregation, and supply/demand. Unfortunately, food security has often been equated with food self-sufficiency or agricultural development, which does little to clarify its meaning. Many countries have expressed their goal of food self-sufficiency. But what does food self-sufficiency mean when a country is exporting food while millions of its inhabitants are malnourished due to lack of effective demand? The case of Zimbabwe, Zambia, and a number of other African countries illustrates that food self-sufficiency can be associated with a low level of food security.

Important mechanisms to alleviate temporal and supply/demand dimensions of food insecurity are illustrated in Figure 1. The viability of these mechanisms are, in turn, fundamentally influenced by critical "prime movers:" technology, institutions, policies, and human capital. In the following section, we discuss the links between these prime movers and the various dimensions of food security.

PRIME MOVERS OF FOOD SECURITY AND THEIR INTERRELATIONSHIPS

Since the majority of the poor in Africa are engaged in subsistence food production, a direct means to enhance

CHRONIC SUPPLY DIMENSIONS	CHRONIC DEMAND DIMENSIONS
Problem: Persistent shortfall in supplies from production, stocks, or imports to meet consumption requirements.	**Problem: Persistent inability to produce and/or purchase or otherwise gain access to required food needs.**
Mechanisms to Alleviate: — Stabilize political institutions — Capable education system to develop trained administrators, business managers, farmers, and scientists — Productive agricultural research and extension institutions—improved technology development, adoption, and diffusion — Adequate physical infrastructure — Better organized input and product marketing systems — Stockholding and trade management capability	**Mechanisms to Alleviate:** — Land tenure system—improved access to land — Strong and growing rural and urban small-scale industry/ employment opportunities — Improved rural/urban trade linkages — Foreign exchange earnings to finance food imports — Reliable access to input and product markets
TRANSITORY SUPPLY DIMENSIONS **Problem: Inability to sustain adequate food supplies to meet consumption needs due to shortfalls in production, imports, or stocks.**	**TRANSITORY DEMAND DIMENSIONS** **Problem: Inability to sustain adequate purchasing power or entitlement during temporary shortfalls in real cash income.**
Mechanisms to Alleviate: — Food price stabilization capacity through stock and trade management — Emergency food distribution system — Early warning monitoring system	**Mechanisms to Alleviate:** — Food price stabilization capacity through stock and trade management — Emergency income transfer mechanisms — Diversify and stabilize household income — Diversify and stabilize foreign exchange earnings

Figure 1. Dimensions and Related Mechanisms to Alleviate Food Insecurity

their real incomes and food access is to increase the productivity of their staple food production (Eicher and Staatz 1985). While the importance of productivity-increasing technology has been universally stressed, the origin of productivity is often poorly understood. Bonnen (1982, 1) observes that "increased agricultural productivity is commonly explained solely in terms of technological change. Technology, in turn, is often seen as the exclusive product of research and development. Both notions are erroneous." A new maize variety—an ostensible product of technology—has many things embodied within it: prior human capital investments, institutions, past policies, and basic research. In a dynamic, evolving system, these prime movers "interact in a continuing process of innovation in one factor followed by the managed adaptation of the other factors to find a new, more efficient equilibrium of resource use" (Bonnen 1982, 4). In short, technology is a product of prior institutional organization and human development, just as these are products of technology.

The relationship between the adoption of on-shelf technology, institutions, and policies is also strong. The rate of return to investments in new technology depends not only on input/output response rates but also on the prices and transaction costs of obtaining and selling inputs and commodities. Hence, concomitant improvements in marketing institutions and policies are generally required to stimulate use of otherwise viable technology. Conversely, evidence is beginning to emerge that a conducive policy environment, while necessary, is not sufficient to greatly stimulate food security in Africa.[4] How a change in price or macroeconomic policy affects the food security of vulnerable groups depends on their access to additional inputs, the reliability of product markets, available technology, the price effects of market-wide resource reallocations, and the returns to other employment activities. The gap between expectation and actual results of several current experiments with market liberalization in Africa reflects a lack of knowledge regarding the effects of broad macroeconomic policy changes on the micro behavior of various groups, especially the most food insecure.

As the world become progressively economically interdependent, food availability and effective demand in developing areas are increasingly influenced by foreign economic policies (Schuh, see Part II, Section 2, Chapter 2, this book). Many industrialized countries insulate their own domestic farm economies from price instability via price supports, effectively venting instability into world markets. This subjects countries still open to world market forces to even greater price volatility, encouraging them to pursue internal stabilization and self-sufficiency as well. Hence, price instability and domestic self-interest combine to create a "tragedy of the commons" social trap, in whichthe world market becomes more thin and unstable as more countries insulate themselves. But because of the high treasury costs of stabilization/self-sufficiency policies, developing nations are less able to uphold them. Food security policy is increasingly dependent on research clarifying the effects of developed-country macroeconomic, trade, and commodity policies on prices, income growth, and stability in LDCs (lesser-developed countries). In the long run, human capital investments may be the most important determinant of food security. One need not search far to find examples of this in the United States.[5] Unfortunately, Africa's stock of trained administrators, technicians, and entrepreneurs required to innovate out of low-level equilibria is alarmingly low. Many national research services do not have the scientific capacity to screen or borrow technology from neighboring countries or the world scientific community. The stock of human capital in scientific fields in Africa in 1980 was about one-fourth the relative scientific strength of Asia in 1970 (Shapiro 1985). Because of limited incentives and rewards for returning to many local agencies, a vicious cycle can result in which the more training professionals obtain, the higher the probability that they will be bid away by foreign institutions. The institutional challenge is to create an environment that gives incentives to simultaneously train and retain a critical mass of local technical and administrative capacity. Unfortunately, investments in human capital, as with technology and institutional development, have mainly long-term payoffs and will require a substantial gestation period (Eicher 1985, 82–101).

EXAMPLES OF PRIME MOVERS AND THEIR INTERRELATIONSHIPS IN AFFECTING FOOD SECURITY

In this section, we draw on selected results of research conducted with various African institutions under USAID-supported Bilateral Projects and a "Food Security in Africa" Cooperative Agreement at Michigan State University.

ZIMBABWE

Poverty and malnutrition appear endemic among Zimbabwe's rural areas (World Bank 1983). Prior to independence in 1980, smallholder farming in Zimbabwe was generally characterized by low productivity and slow growth: production of maize, smallholders' principal farm enterprise, was stagnant. By 1985, smallholder maize production had more than tripled, yields had roughly doubled, contributions to national production had risen above 50 percent, and maize sales had increased to over one-third of total market transactions (Rohrbach 1988, 256).

Is this a food security success story, and if so, why? Rohrbach (1988) attributes the causes of maize output expansion to five interrelated factors (p. 258). First, the ending of the independence war allowed smallholders to both replant abandoned holdings and to establish new ones. Second, the research and extension service had developed commercial maize hybrids that would work under smallholder conditions. Third, both public- and private-sector marketing system improvements converted the potential of proven technologies into the reality of rapid growth in smallholder seed and fertilizer purchases, and output sales. Fourth, a modest but reasonably effective production credit program resulted in 10 percent of smallholders receiving credit by 1985. Fifth, maize prices were sharply increased in 1980 and 1981.

What are the effects of these production increases on household food security in Zimbabwe? Successes on the national level have masked considerable subnational disparities. The top 10 percent of smallholders, largely concentrated in the nation's high-potential (rainfall) regions, are estimated to account for over 50 percent of all smallholder production and 75 percent of market sales (Rohrbach 1988, 268). Overall, the majority of smallholders who live in the semiarid areas and face frequent or constant production shortfalls have benefitted least, if any.[6] Improved technology appropriate for crops in low-rainfall regions is basically not available (Rohrbach 1988, 275). Preliminary research in two other semiarid smallholder areas suggests that 59 percent of the farm households surveyed could not produce enough food for their own needs in a good rainfall year (Chopak 1988). The figure rose to 79 percent in the previous drought year. These sober statistics highlight the importance of alternative income sources to gain access to needed food. Twenty to forty percent of most households' estimated total income (including the value of farm perquisites) comes from sources other than crop production, such as livestock, remittance, and other nonfarm activities. While this income is absolutely essential to the food security of poorer households, it is frequently not adequate (especially in drought years) and the government must mount costly food aid programs to address transitory food insecurity, as it did in 1987.

MALI

Dione and colleagues (1987) carefully examined the effect of climate, institutional support for cash crops, and level of ownership/use of animal traction equipment on food security. They find that for households that are semi-equipped or nonequipped with animal traction, their own grain production is rarely enough to assure adequate food access. Income-generating activities from cash crops, livestock, artisanal activities, small trade, nonfarm wages, and remittances were also important sources of entitlement used to purchase supplemental grain needs. Their findings likewise reveal the critical relationship between entitlements, food crops, and cash crops. The households that produce cotton are more likely to have animal traction, have access to credit and technical inputs, use these inputs, and, as a result, produce more cereals (both in total and on a per capita basis.) for own consumption and sale (Dione and Staatz 1987, 9).

Other results indicate how two important macro policies have affected household food security in unanticipated ways. First, the government raised support prices for coarse grains to create an incentive to expand output. The assumptions were that farmers make their cereal production decisions primarily based on commercial considerations; that if prices increased, farmers had the capacity and willingness to expand production; and, more fundamentally, that all farmers were net sellers of grain and, hence, raising prices would raise rural incomes. Empirical findings question all of these assumptions. Only 48 percent of the farms studied were selling any coarse grains at all, and 25 percent of the whole sample was selling over 80 percent of grain sold. This fact alone tends to concentrate the benefits of price increases, not to mention the adverse effects of inducing higher market prices for the 30–40 percent of rural households who must purchase some of their cereal consumption needs (Dione and Staatz 1987, 9). And it was mostly the well-equipped farmers in the cotton-producing areas that had the capacity, the technology, and the inputs available to respond to the high prices.

Even more disruptive of household food security is the government head tax policy (a fixed amount per adults of 18–60 years). In both 1986 and 1987, the head tax accounted for 90 percent of all direct rural taxes, and total taxes paid by farmers amounted to 13 to 20 percent of the total value of coarse grain production, depending on the producing area. Farm households that sell cotton or have other sources of cash income have little difficulty paying these taxes, even though they are collected during grain harvest season. Farmers who are able, prefer storing grain until later in the season when prices rise. In contrast, in zones where cash-crop production opportunities are low, most farmers are forced to sell grain to pay taxes even if they have no real surplus, and must use any alternative source of income to buy back grain throughout the year for their own consumption. The real food deficit of these households is compounded by an additional deficit imposed by taxes (Dione 1989, 3). Even more disruptive to long-run food security is the effect of this tax on disinvestment in traction equipment and draught animals, thereby reducing the productive capacity of the household. In the non-cotton-growing zone studied, 65 percent of the equipped and semiequipped farmers have experienced disinvestment, and the majority identify the head tax as a major cause (Dione n.d., 3). This case clearly illustrates the importance of interaction between policy and technology in influencing food security.

RWANDA

Rwanda has the distinction of being the most densely populated country in Africa and one of the highest per capita consumers of dry beans. Since grazing area is shrinking, beans have become an increasingly important source of protein for the rural population. In 1986, the government attempted to expand production incentives by raising prices significantly above market levels in Rwanda and bordering countries of Zaire, Uganda, and Tanzania. Loveridge (1988), with researchers in the Ministry of Agriculture, found that informal imports from these neighboring countries make up an unanticipated 60 percent of the total volume of beans in the national market. If actually implemented, the relatively high floor price would benefit mostly foreign producers, as well as the 11 percent of Rwandan farmers who produce 92 percent of marketed surplus. At the same time, the higher floor price would have also raised consumer prices in rural as well as urban markets and hurt the 72 percent of rural households that were found to be net bean buyers (SESA/MSU 1987). Especially affected would have been the 30 percent of rural households purchasing about one-half of their available supply. And, these households indicate that land area, soil fertility, and fertilizer access (given existing technology) are their main constraints to expanding output, rather than low prices.

The Rwanda results reiterate the importance of cash crops and other forms of entitlement, along with own food crop production, to food security. Households purchasing the most beans report being almost three times more dependent on coffee and tea income to finance food and other household purchases than are the farms selling the most beans. Balanced increases in productivity of food and high-value cash crops are critical, especially for the most land-poor and food-deficit households in Rwanda.

In summary, these example countries illustrate that food and hunger problems, viewed in terms of food security, focus on identifying the vulnerable groups, how they relate to food and labor markets, what factors impede their ability to grow more food or raise cash incomes, and how they adjust to natural crises and changes in policies, institutions, and technology. Without this knowledge, there can be little ability to understand the constraints to food security, or to design strategies to achieve it.

RESEARCH AGENDA

The most general lesson learned since the 1974 World Food Conference is that food security generally includes, but must go beyond, the technical question of increasing per capita food availability. As stressed by current definitions of food security, the major objective is increased food access. Yet, this does not elicit a clear plan of remedial action. Three interrelated knowledge gaps are discussed below: (1) how to operationalize food security research and policy analysis, (2) the appropriate balance between short-run and long-run food security strategies, and (3) the dynamic interactions among the prime movers and their disaggregated effects on incentives and welfare. In the context of sub-Saharan Africa, research on these issues should be pursued on a national basis within a regional framework (e.g., Sahel, Eastern Africa, Southern Africa) thus accounting for significant resource and structural differences (Eicher 1986).

OPERATIONALIZING FOOD SECURITY

To be meaningful, the concept of food security must be operationalized in such a way that it informs and guides policy. Multidisciplinary social science research is needed to develop an appropriate set of measurable indicators of food security. Such a list would provide operational benchmarks to evaluate the effects of changes in technology, institutions, policies, and human capital on the various dimensions of food security. A set of appropriate indicators would also provide a more explicit and systematic guide for policy analysis. Inevitably, the list will be modified as our understanding, objectives, and resources change. An imperfect set of indicators might include households' per capita income, grain availability, and measures of nutritional status among various groups and regions. Unfortunately, these indicators are neither quickly measurable nor obtainable at low cost.

BALANCING SHORT-RUN AND LONG-RUN OBJECTIVES

Multiple dimensions imply competing objectives. Over emphasis on remedies to transitory food insecurity (e.g., short-run food supply stabilization, relief, and welfare programs) may have a high opportunity cost if they divert attention and resources from measures to overcome chronic impediments to food security. For example, much research on grain stock and trade management has focused on short-run supply stabilization to alleviate temporary production shortfalls, even while large segments of the population are continually food insecure, even in good harvest years. Much less research has been devoted to how such policies may be designed to promote investment and growth over the long run to stimulate production and market access to food in ways that improve rural and urban households' ability to withstand transitory production and income fluctuations. On the other hand, interventions with complementary effects on short-run and long-run food security are stressed by Reutlinger (1984).

Hence, research is needed on the appropriate allocation of resources to address chronic and transitory problems. Ultimately, the issue is one of political choice: to what extent is society willing to forego future benefits to alleviate malnutrition now. But, effective food security research can inform the policy choice by specifying the tradeoffs and complementarities, and stressing the sober fact that good food security policy, in a world of scarce resources, means choosing not to do a wide range of tactically attractive things.

Greater attention to institutional design may facilitate the development of cost-effective food aid and income-targeting mechanisms with complementary effects on long-run food security. An important research task is to design feasible short-run measures that sustain health and human capital development, reduce urban migration, and attack the underlying causes of food insecurity as well as its symptoms.

DYNAMIC INTERACTIONS AMONG THE PRIME MOVERS

Food security—its level and incidence—is determined by the functioning of a complex, interrelated system of food, input, employment, and international markets. Many of the behavioral relationships, the dynamic interaction effects, and technical input/output coefficients are poorly understood (Johnston and Clark 1982). Food security policy making requires better knowledge of the type, magnitude, and incidence of change resulting from these dynamic interactions between the prime movers. A starting point for the systematic accumulation of knowledge about the role of the prime movers could be a "cataloging system" within which past and current development experiences can be conceived, analyzed, and compared (Johnston and Clark 1982). Such a catalog of comparative case studies, similar to recent work by Morris and Adelman (1986), would facilitate understanding of how different configurations of the prime movers might interact, given particular resource bases and relations to the international economy, to produce different effects on food security. While realizing that knowledge is ephemeral, policy analysts could draw from this inventory to make appropriate comparisons between their development problems and what has been effective in the past.

The payoffs to such a cataloging system, however, are dependent on concomitant advances in deductive research. Knowing what data to collect for the catalog system, what indicators to examine, requires a model, implicit or explicit, of how an economy works. Theory informs research and policy; past experience improves theory. Work on induced technical and institutional innovation, while still in its early stages, is moving toward defining relationships between variables that ultimately may improve our understanding of the dynamic interactions between the prime movers and food security.

A beginning list of priority issues to be addressed in this process of accumulating systematic knowledge includes:

1. Microlevel research that clarifies knowledge about vulnerable groups: who are they; what do they consume; what factors constrain their ability to transform their resources into food, income, nutrition, and health; and how do they adjust to natural crises and changes in technology, institutions, and policies?
2. What food *and* cash-crop technology components are needed in Africa, and what does this imply for technological, institutional, and human capital development? While creating new bio- and agronomic technology per se is in the realm of technical sciences, social science research is critically needed to identify (a) the characteristics that viable technology must possess to be compatible with farmers' resources, risk attitudes, food security, and other goals, and (b) institutional and policy changes needed to facilitate the adoption of otherwise viable technology.
3. How do rural industry and farm sectors interact? How can coordinated investments in human capital, institutions, and technology best exploit multiplier effects between these sectors, thereby stimulating effective demand in rural and urban areas?
4. Current experimentation with market liberalization in Africa reveals that simply dismantling inefficient parastatals will not assure the development of a vibrant private trading sector. In many cases, neither markets nor government coordination perform very well. The existence of market failure does not mean that a bureaucratic solution exists, nor does bureaucratic failure mean that private sector offers a better alternative. Social science research must identify key constraints in the private system so that when the political coalition for reform is achieved, appropriate public programs and policies can be implemented that are capable of promoting desired private-sector performance.
5. Many countries in Africa have announced goals of domestic food self-sufficiency, although cost implications to consumers (especially the food-insecure) and national budgets are significant, if not prohibitive. Research is needed on the micro and macro implications of pursuing food self-sufficiency versus self-reliance strategies that balance the costs and risks of obtaining food from domestic *and* international sources.
6. What are the effects of border pricing strategies on rural incentives and incomes in a second-best world of artificially low and unstable international food prices due to policies of major grain exporters? Are there alternative institutional mechanisms and policies that can mitigate dislocations and food insecurity caused by market instability without incurring severe budget losses? To inform price policy adjustments, disaggregated information is needed on how specific macro policies and institutional changes affect the micro decisions and welfare of various groups, especially the food-insecure.[7]
7. What is the role of food aid and/or insurance mechanisms to address transitory food insecurity, especially under fragmented market conditions or where private traders hold a significant share of total grain stocks?
8. Improved strategies are needed to develop greater human capital in Africa, especially management, research, and policy analysis capacity. While governments are often motivated by short-run interests, training and research investments have mainly long-run payoffs. What is needed to raise both supply and effective demand for research and policy analysis capabilities?
9. What role does population growth play in the food security equation in Africa? Why is there so little debate in Africa today on population and family planning, let

alone on generating political support for measures to reduce the average number of children from seven to five per family (Eicher 1985, 82–101)?

NOTES

1. Michael T. Weber is a professor of Agricultural Economics at Michigan State University. Thomas S. Jayne is a visiting assistant professor of Agricultural Economics at Michigan State University.

2. A survey of employment data in Africa, Asia, and South America indicates that rural nonfarm activities provide primary or secondary employment for 30–50 percent of the rural labor force in developing nations (Chuta and Liedholm 1984). Nonfarm employment appears to account for over 20 percent of total cash income of rural households. The importance of nonfarm employment in achieving food security is even more obvious in urban areas.

3. For example, a recent study by Shapouri, Dommen, and Rosen (1986) indicates that "if the upper 30 percent of the population were able to avoid adjusting consumption during a food emergency, a shortfall of only 5 percent aggregate would translate into a 20 percent decline in already low availability in the lower 30 percent of the income distribution" (Christensen 1987, 71). A similar analysis of Indian data by Mellor concludes that "it is clear. . . that it is essentially impossible to protect the poor from the major income effect of a short crop by market measures" (1978, 149). See also World Bank (1986).

4. The empirical record on food grain supply response in Africa and Asia reveals the multivaried constraints on food production and marketing systems in developing countries. Scandizzo and Bruce (1980) report that of 103 studies in developing countries, 71 percent had short-run estimates below +0.5. In the long run, 62 percent were below +0.5.

5. For instance, the contributions of farm management to improved allocative and technical efficiency in production (Bonnen 1982; see also Griliches 1988; Evenson 1981).

6. Evidence suggests, however, that consumption among most poorer maize households has likely not declined, which could easily have been the case without the aggregate gains in maize production and market sales (Rohrbach 1988).

7. A recent comparative analysis of the impacts of structural adjustment on food security in developing countries reports that "relative income distribution has become more skewed and that, in some cases, the highest-income groups have gained in both absolute and relative terms, while considerable losses have occurred among the poor" (World Food Council 1987b, 1). However, it is not altogether clear whether these trends reflect lagged results of the economic recessions that led to adjustment, or to the adjustments themselves.

REFERENCES

Bonnen, J. T. 1982. Technology, human capital and institutions: Three factors in search of an agricultural research strategy. Paper prepared for the 1982 binational conference on U.S./Mexico Agriculture and Rural Development, Cocoyoc, Mexico.

Chopak, C. 1988. Family income sources and food security. *Household and national food security in southern Africa*. Edited by G. Mudimu and R. Bernsten. Proceedings of the 4th annual conference on Food Security Research in Southern Africa, 31 October–3 November, 1988. University of Zimbabwe/Michigan State University Food Security Research in Southern Africa Project, Department of Agricultural Economics and Extension, Harare, Zimbabwe.

Christensen, C. 1987. Food security in sub-Saharan Africa. In *Pursuing food security: Strategies and obstacles in Africa, Asia, Latin America, and the Middle East*. Edited by W. L. Hollist and F. L. Tullis. Boulder, Colo.: Reinner Publishers.

Chuta, E., and C. Liedholm. 1984. Rural small-scale industry: Empirical evidence and policy issues. In *Agricultural development in the Third World*. Edited by C. K. Eicher and J. M. Staatz. Baltimore: Johns Hopkins University Press.

Dioné, Josué. 1989. Informing food security policy in Mali: Interactions between technology, institutions and market reforms. Ph.D. diss., Michigan State University.

Dioné, Josué, and John M. Staatz. 1987. Market liberalization and food security in Mali. Paper presented at the 3d annual conference on Food Security in South Africa, Harare, Zimbabwe.

Eicher, Carl K. 1985. Famine prevention in Africa: The long view. East Lansing: Michigan State University, Department of Agricultural Economics.

_____1986. Food security research in sub-Saharan Africa. Keynote address presented at the OAU/STRC/SAFGRAD International Drought symposium, Nairobi, Kenya.

Eicher, C. K., and John M. Staatz. 1985. Food security policy in sub-Saharan Africa. Paper presented for 19th Conference of the International Association of Agricultural Economists, Malaga, Spain.

Evenson, R. E. 1981. Benefits and obstacles in developing appropriate agricultural technologies. *Annals of the American Academy of Political and Social Science* 458:54–67.

Griliches, Zvi. 1958. Research costs and social returns: Hybrid corn and related innovations. Journal of Political Economy 66.

Huddleston, Barbara, D. Gale Johnson, Shlomo Reutlinger, and Alberto Valdes. 1984. *International finance for food security*. Baltimore: Johns Hopkins University Press for the World Bank.

Johnston, B. F., and W. C. Clark. 1982. *Redesigning rural development, a strategic perspective*. Baltimore: Johns Hopkins University Press.

Johnston, B. F., and P. Kilby. 1975. *Agriculture and structural transformation: Economic strategies in late-developing countries*. London: Oxford University Press.

Loveridge, Scott. 1988. Users of farm and market survey date to inform food security policy in Rwanda. Ph.D. diss., Michigan State University.

Mellor, J. W. 1976. *The economics of growth*. Ithaca, N.Y.: Cornell University Press.

_____1978. Food price policy and income distribution in low income countries. *Economic Development and Cultural Change* 27, no. 1: 1–26.

_____1984. The world food equation: Interrelations among development, employment, and food consumption. *Journal of Economic Literature* 22, no. 2: 53–74.

Morris, C. T., and I. Adelman. 1986. Economic development and institutional change in the 19th Century.

California Agricultural Experiment Station working paper no. 434. Gianni Foundation.

Reutlinger, Shlomo. 1984. Project food aid and equitable growth: Income-transfer efficiency first! *World Development* 12, no. 9: 901–11.

Rohrbach, David D. 1988. The growth of maize production in Zimbabwe: Causes and implications for food security. Ph.D. diss., Michigan State University.

Scandizzo, P., and C. Bruce. 1980. Methodologies for measuring agricultural price intervention effects. World Bank staff working paper no. 394. Washington, D.C.

Sen, A. K. 1981. *Poverty and famines: An essay on entitlement and deprivation.* Oxford: Clarendon Press.

SESA/MSU Research Team. 1987. Observations on price support and research program for beans in Rwanda. East Lansing: Michigan State University.

Shapiro, K. 1985. Strengthening agricultural research and educational institutions in Africa: Using the lessons of the past to develop a strategy for the future. In *Strategies for African development.* Edited by R. Berg and J. Whitaker. Berkeley and Los Angeles: University of California Press.

Shapouri, S., A. Dommen, and S. Rosen. 1986. Food aid and the African food crisis. Foreign agricultural economic report no. 221. Washington, D.C.: U.S. Department of Agriculture.

Siamwalla, A., and A. Valdes. 1980. Food security in developing countries. *Food Policy* 5, no. 4: 258–72.

World Bank. 1983. *Zimbabwe population, health and nutrition sector review.* Washington, D.C.: World Bank; Population, Health and Nutrition Dept.

_____1986. *Poverty and hunger: Issues and options for food security in developing countries.* Washington, D.C.: World Bank.

World Food Council. 1987a. *The global state of hunger and malnutrition and the impact of economic adjustment.* Rome: FAO.

_____1987b. *Consultation on the impact of economic adjustment on people's food security and nutritional levels in developing countries.* Rome: FAO.

CHAPTER 7

INSTITUTIONAL REFORM: ACCOMPLISHMENTS AND UNMET NEEDS IN CHINA, NEWLY INDUSTRIALIZED COUNTRIES OF ASIA, THE SOVIET UNION AND EASTERN EUROPE AND THE DEVELOPED COUNTRIES[1]

Glenn L. Johnson[2]

My assignment is to summarize and interpret the papers presented at the Symposium on Rural Development Strategies conducted jointly by the International Association of Agricultural Economists (IAAE), the Chinese Society of Agricultural Economics (CSAE), and the Chinese Association of Agricultural Science Societies (CAASS) held near Beijing from October 26 to 30, 1987. In carrying out my assignment, I intend to interpret these papers in terms of my own extended version of the "transaction cost/institutional" analysis used increasingly by economists and economic historians. This will be advantageous because the Beijing symposium concentrated largely on the institutional changes that have been so large and important with respect to Chinese agriculture since the mid-1930s and, particularly, since the demise of the "Gang of Four." Future institutional changes for the agriculture of socialist China will be substantially interrelated with changes in the agricultural institutions and investment structures of the newly industrialized countries (NICs) and areas (NIAs) of Asia and of the developed countries (DCs). These countries and areas now face the task of changing their own agricultural institutions in order to adjust to the trade and income crises now affecting world agriculture.

For world agriculture as a whole, understanding the institutional changes that have taken place and are now being considered requires us to go considerably beyond the market adjustments analysis of many economists. Persons such as Frank Knight, Kenneth Boulding, James Buchanan, William Baumol, and a number of others, have granted or readily grant this even when markets are redefined broadly to include the political markets of concern to induced institutional analysts. This can be done by using the transaction cost/institutional interpretation of institutional change as expounded by O. E. Williamson in his *The Economic Institutions of Capitalism* (1985) and Douglass C. North in his *Structure and Change in Economic History* (1981). In carrying out my assignment, I will accept Baumol's position (1986) that there is no inherent conflict between the institutional analyses of many neoclassicists and those of the transaction cost/institution analysts. The absence of conflict, however, does not mean that the two are the same and that neoclassicists commonly include transaction costs in or always exclude them from their analysis. The common but far from unusual exclusion of transaction costs from analysis of investments and disinvestments in productive assets as well as from analysis of institutions and change has disastrous and almost irrational consequences for realistic policy analysis (Chambers and Vasavada, 1983; Hoover, 1973; M. Johnson and Pasour, 1981; Edwards, 1985). Baumol's constructive view is that the transaction cost/institutionalist analyses adds to or goes beyond common neoclassical interpretations without destroying or replacing them. It should also be noted that those who developed the transaction cost/institutional approach regard their work as incomplete, with many drawbacks and in need of further development. Nonetheless, the transaction cost/institutional analysis is easily extended to help clarify our understanding of changes and rigidities in agricultural institutions of socialist China, the newly industrialized countries (NICs), and newly industrialized areas (NIAs) of Asia and of the developed countries (DCs) of the world.

This paper has three major parts. The *first* reports on papers presented at the Beijing symposium that I deem particularly important for understanding the institutional reforms of agriculture that have taken place in all of China, including Taiwan, as well as the changes and rigidities in the agricultural institutions of the Asiatic NICs and NIAs, the DCs of the west, and the socialist countries of Eastern Europe including the Soviet Union. The *second* part will deal with an extended version of the transaction cost/institutional analysis as it applies to agriculture. The *third* part will use the extended transaction cost/institutional approach presented in the second part to reach tentative conclusions and to speculate about unmet needs for institutional reforms for the agricultures of China, the NICs and NIAs of Asia, the Soviet Union, the socialist countries of Eastern Europe, and the developed western countries.

THE PAPERS PRESENTED AT THE BEIJING SYMPOSIUM

The joint IAAE/CSAE symposium held near Beijing was entitled "An International Symposium on Rural Development Strategies." The major emphasis of the fifty or more papers presented there was on institutional change. Technical change was a rather minor subject at the symposium. Some attention was paid to the fourth "driving force for agricultural development," the generation, accumulation and use of physical and biological agricultural capital. Even less attention was paid to human capital formation as an "engine of growth."

For my subject, the most important Chinese paper was that by Minister Runsheng Du, Research Center for Rural Development under the State Council, Professor, and President of the Chinese Society of Agricultural Economics. His paper "Advancing Administrative Reform" (1987) was elaborated on further in his remarks at a banquet held for symposium participants. Du stressed the importance of breaking up the dual structure of a modern urban industry and traditional agriculture that had developed in socialist China by 1978. He attributed this unfortunate development to the people's communes and the "unified purchase price system." He views current reforms as important ways of breaking down the barriers between urban and rural areas and of promoting the shift of rural manpower to secondary and tertiary industry as a way of promoting urbanization. The reforms did away with the communes as organizational units for farm production, raised farm product prices, introduced the contract responsibility system that linked individual incomes from labor and publicly owned farmland to output, and gave farmers more decision-making power. At the same time, more income is left in local governmental hands. This helps local units establish local industry and employment opportunities for surplus farm labor to permit farmers to "change their jobs, without moving." Du stressed that this raises the opportunity cost of rural labor and necessitates subcontracting of land among individuals to increase farm sizes to permit the total earnings of farmers to keep up with the rising incomes of nonfarmers. He stressed that while the state should provide some of the new capital required by agriculture, reforms should be such as to motivate "the greater part of the investment by farmers." He recognized the implications of income demand elasticities for the need to reform China's marketing and processing institutions as consumption patterns will shift in response to higher incomes to include more nongrain products.

Among several other papers considering reforms for Chinese agriculture was one by Wen Lu, Vice President and Secretary General of the Chinese Society of Agricultural Economists and Research Fellow (1987). An opening address delivered by Vice Premier Jiyun Tian (1987) also dealt with institutional reforms. Throughout the symposium, reforms important for the agricultural and entire economy of socialist China were considered in formal papers and in informal discussions during coffee breaks and at meal times when we ate together for four days in groups of eight to ten people. Some of these informal discussions are reflected in this paper.

The long-term significance of the reforms discussed at Beijing was underscored by actions taken at the 13th meeting of the Central Committee of the Communist Party of China (CPC) while we were meeting. Zheng Zhao was elected General Secretary along with the other four members of the standing committee of the CPC's Political Bureau with the endorsement of Xiao Ping Deng. Zheng Zhao reaffirmed the Party's commitment to a continuation and extension of the reforms taking place in socialist China including those affecting its agriculture. Though the CPC was portrayed as monolithically supporting the agreed upon direction, many observers claimed to be aware of tensions between conservative and "liberal" factions within the CPC. Nonetheless, the CPC did commit socialist China to a continuation and extension of the kinds of reform discussed by Runsheng Du, Wen Lu, Jiyun Tian and many others. It was an exciting time to be in Beijing at an International Symposium on Rural Development Strategies.

The agricultural institutions of socialist China have been extraordinarily flexible (one could say unstable) since the late 1940s. Land tenure has been restructured three times. Even greater institutional changes were made outside of agriculture. The power of the CPC to make the changes it wants has been clearly demonstrated. What is less clear is why so many institutional arrangements have been made. Some of the changes have been beyond the rationality of common "induced institutional changes" analyses of market adjustments in broadly defined markets. Imperfect knowledge of agriculture on the parts of military revolutionaries and Marxist ideologues and ideology, itself, played important roles. Such factors provide us with some understanding of why the costs of establishing and dismantling so many institutions were paid. The transaction cost/institutional approach is useful in explaining such institutional changes and, in other instances, rigidities. More common induced institutional change analyses that neglect transaction costs and imperfect knowledge have little capacity to explain institutional mistakes and institutional rigidities.

An important paper by Hsi-Huang Chen from Taiwan was entitled "Strategies of Agricultural Development in Taiwan"[3] (1987). Taiwan's rural agricultural development policies became roughly similar to the present reform policies of socialist China much earlier and without incurring the establishment and dismantling costs of so many institutional mistakes. Taiwan's land reform started in 1949 and was completed in 1952. After the land reform, land ownership has remained in widely dispersed private hands with the government reserving unto itself substantial rights in the control of land. Ownership of land on the mainland remains with the state with substantial "property" rights now being acquired by private persons, families, and agencies. In a sense, public and private ownership are blended in both areas of China. Fortunately, neither Taiwan nor the farmers in Taiwan were subjected to the institutional instability experienced on the mainland and, hence, to the public costs of establishing and dismantling institutions and to the private costs of investing and disinvesting in durable factors of production. Traumatic nonmonetary costs as well as property losses were experienced on the mainland when the government took ownership of the land it had previously redistributed to peasants from feudal landlords so as to reconcentrate its ownership and control of land in the hands of government. More costs were incurred in establishing the institutions and programs of the "great leap forward" and the cultural revolution that are now so widely regretted by the CPC and its leadership.

With the demise of the "Gang of Four," the mainland provinces of China were again submitted to transaction costs as control over the use of land was shifted away from the state farms and communes to individual households in order to obtain the advantages of the "household responsibility system." By contrast, Taiwanese farmers began reaping the benefits of policies rather similar to those of the mainland's present reforms near the completion of their land reform in 1952; thus, Taiwanese agriculture has benefitted from favorable institutional structures for almost forty years, rather than only about ten years on the mainland, without the high public and private costs of establishing and of subsequently dismantling so many mistaken institutions. With respect to labor utilization and mechanization, Chen (1987) reported that Taiwanese farmers were permitted and were quick to use the large amount of labor then available to increase multicropping and *exploit foreign markets* for such labor-intensive crops as mushrooms and asparagus. Labor-saving technology was introduced in Taiwan in the late 1960s as farm labor surpluses began to dwindle with successful development of the nonfarm sectors. Agriculture in Taiwan was also well served with innovative public institutions. China, including Taiwan, has made substantial progress in establishing rural industries to absorb excess rural labor. Taiwan is a relatively small area in which decentralization of industry was both easier to accomplish and less important to do than in the mainland provinces. In doing this, Taiwan had the advantage of being able to orient its economy to the outside world for industrial products much earlier in time than the mainland provinces. It was not until after the "Gang of Four" that the mainland provinces could begin to orient their local rural industries to the outside world.

In the relatively short period since the end of the cultural revolution, institutional arrangements on the mainland have been such that a large part of actual governmental revenues and of the potential "rent" of land to the state as landlord has been left with local governmental units and agencies (*Economist*, 1987, 3–22). These income flows have often been used to finance local industries to provide local employment for rural laborers. In the *Economist* article, it is pointed out that important questions exist about whether these local industrial investments are being properly located and whether they will fit the patterns of comparative advantage likely to emerge for socialist China in the years ahead. Despite such doubts, the mainland provinces are preventing a great deal of questionable off-farm migration to urban centers. There remains the question of how great the dismantling (transaction) costs may turn out to be if many of the local industrial investments now being sunk in rural areas have to be dismantled or written off in the future. There also remain questions about how much some of these investments will have to be devalued in line with lower-than-anticipated earnings even when dismantlement or abandonment can be avoided.

At the Beijing symposium, there were several useful papers about non-Chinese countries including some from Asiatic NICs. Dong Hi Kim's South Korean paper had a strong institutionalist slant being entitled "Optimizing the Roles of Government in Modernizing Agriculture: The Korean Experiences" (1987). The devastation the Korean war imposed upon the Korean economy was more complete than those imposed on Chinese agriculture by the Japanese and Chinese civil wars. Further, peace came to South Korea somewhat later than to Taiwan and the mainland provinces of China. Like Taiwan, South Korea carried out its land reform early, starting in 1949 and completing it in 1950. Early in the post-Korean war period, the emphasis of the Republic of Korea's government was on the development of the nonfarm industrial economy to the neglect of its agriculture. In doing this, South Korea, of course, was not following Soviet policy; instead, it was following the similar earlier orthodoxy of western development economists of the period. Later, as western development opinion on this matter changed, the South Korean government, like the government of socialist China, shifted additional emphasis to agriculture without diminishing its efforts to develop industry. Despite wars and an initial false start, South Korean agriculture has made great progress.

South Korea has paid less attention than socialist China to decentralization of industry to absorb rural labor in local communities. South Korea is larger than Taiwan and decentralizing her industry to absorb rural labor was more important than in Taiwan but less important than for China's mainland provinces. Because little effort was made to distribute industry widely in rural areas, South Korea has suffered from large-scale, off-farm migration to industrial centers. Seoul has now grown to over 10 million persons. Like Taiwan, South Korea has consistently been an export-oriented economy and has benefitted from this policy, its benefits coming somewhat later in time than those for Taiwan.

Taiwan and South Korea have institutions and programs in place that subsidize and protect their agricultures. Their establishment and maintenance costs were originally and are still partially justified in terms of food security. Agricultural production is being maintained at higher levels than would be forthcoming at domestic price levels synchronized with prices in international markets. If the subsidies and import protection arrangements were to be eliminated, total dismantlement costs would certainly include destruction of some of the present values of sunken public and private investments in agricultural production, farm service facilities, and the like. Such transaction costs help explain why institutional and program structures are relatively rigid in South Korea and Taiwan.

A very interesting, insightful paper at the Beijing symposium was that by Vijay Vyas entitled "India's Rural Development Strategies—Lessons in Agricultural Growth and Poverty Alleviation" (1987). Vyas tells the story of India's attempt to modernize and improve its very large, predominantly agricultural, internally oriented economy. As India has not been export oriented, it has not benefitted as much as Taiwan, South Korea, and Japan from external markets for its farm and industrial products. Nor has India been particularly concerned with distributing its industrial investments widely into rural communities to absorb excess rural labor. India's industries have not developed as rapidly as those of South Korea and Taiwan. On the agricultural side, India has been moderately successful in generating its own and obtaining new agricultural technologies abroad and in carrying out the modest institutional reforms that have made it agriculture productive and profitable enough in later years to enable it to alleviate its overall food shortages. Poverty and hunger alleviation have been less successful than in South Korea and Taiwan and much less successful than for the mainland provinces of China (Vyas 1983, 52–62; Johnson 1983, 592–608).

Development of Japan's modern agricultural sector got started far earlier than in China (including Taiwan) and South Korea, both of which suffered from Japanese military actions and exploitation prior to and during World War II. Japan also had a substantial head start on India. At this symposium, Tsuchiya (1987) concentrated largely on Japanese mechanization and how the government, manufacturers, and farmers responded to the wage increases that went along with successful development efforts. Successively, the Japanese went from animal draft power to power tillers to mechanized transplanters and harvesters for rice.

Since independence and the partition of Pakistan from India (Collins and Lapierre 1975), India has not paid high establishment costs for institutional reforms in its agriculture and fortunately has not been faced with the necessity of incurring heavy dismantlement costs for agricultural institutions mistakenly put in place.

Renfeng Li, of the Institute of Soviet and East European Studies, Chinese Academy of Social Sciences, presented a very interesting paper entitled "Problems of Rural Reform in the Soviet Union and Eastern Europe" (1987). Li's paper concentrates on Eastern Europe and the early dominant role Soviet agricultural development thought has played in organizing agricultural production in Eastern socialist Europe as well as in the Soviet Union itself. Li's paper recounts the accomplishments of the Soviet approach to agricultural planning and development and the extension of that approach to the countries and areas that became part of the Soviet's sphere of influence after World War II. The main defects of the earlier Soviet approach were summed up by Li as those of (1) implementing socialist planned management in an "absolute" way using standard planning indexes to create a plan with the "effect of law" for implementation by all production organizations, (2) ignoring the "active role of commodity production" as if the Marx/Engels assumption that commodity production had disappeared were true when, in fact, it is not, and (3) disregard of benefits for farmers and the need for a certain amount of equality in the distribution of income between farmers and nonfarmers in order to motivate farmers, farm laborers, and the managers of agricultural production enterprises.

Li indicates that the USSR and Eastern Europe started reforming their agricultural systems away from the original Soviet approach in the mid-1950s. These reforms reduced the compulsory use of planning indices and granted more power to local decision makers particularly at enterprise levels, reduced use of compulsory selling systems and raised purchase prices for farm products, reorganized machinery and tractor stations and enterprises for producing farm inputs, and partially shook off rural collectivization in favor of rural cooperatives. Li points to Hungary as having made dramatic achievements. In Poland and Yugoslavia, Li is concerned with the fragmentation of land holdings occurring as the result of the inheritance of privately owned land. He indicated that despite the progress in the USSR and eastern socialized countries, their agricultures still remain the "weak point in their economies." Li sees major continuing problems that slow the progress of reforms: (1) how to make rural enterprises truly independent commodity producers; (2) how to enable farmers to be "true owners" of land and active producers; (3) how to bring the initiative of rural managers into full play and how to supervise them; (4) how to coordinate rewards for working with the results of working; and, (5) how to utilize sideline occupations. He does not consider institutional dismantlement costs and sunken production investments as possible explanations of the slow pace of reform in agricultural institutions of Eastern Europe and the Soviet Union.

At a broader level, Li expressed his belief that the reforms currently being made in total economic management systems of socialist countries originated with rural reforms. He also states that the trend toward "political and economic" reforms in the USSR and east European socialist countries has become "irresistible" and that rural reform is now in ascendancy. We must note, however, that rural reforms in the Soviet Union and the eastern European socialist countries are encountering considerable resistance. It is this resistance that keeps their agricultures the weak points in their economies. "Irresistible" reforms seem to be more resisted in socialist eastern Europe (Hungary partially excepted) than they were in post-cultural-revolution, socialist China. This should not be surprising. Under the cultural revolution, socialist China's agricultural institutions failed so miserably that the CPC itself found it was worthwhile to incur the costs of dismantling many of the rural institutions it had earlier established. Those in charge of the more successful state farms and communes did have vested interests (benefits they received from their positions in such institutions) but these paled in view of the overall poor performance of state farms and communes during the general instability of the Red Guard period.

In most of socialist Europe, agricultural reform appears to have been resisted more than in China since 1979 not only by communist parties but by those who benefit from the existing systems. In Eastern Europe, agricultural systems have been moderately stable and passably workable for a long while. People have found niches in the systems wherein they collect benefits. Even urban consumers benefit from low food prices if not from high quality, diversity, and quantity. Further, powerful party members and military leaders are conservative and fear changes that may deprive them of benefits. In Poland, both agricultural and nonagricultural reforms have been staunchly resisted by the party and government—in Hungary reform came a little easier. Reform of agricultural institutions does not come easily in socialist Eastern Europe.

It seems appropriate to follow Li's more general paper about the agricultures of East European socialist countries with discussion of the well-written, carefully considered paper about Hungary by Csaba Csaki (1987), Rector of Karl Marx University of Economics, Budapest, Hungary. As one reads this paper, one grasps the adaptive conservatism of Hungarian agricultural planners as they made their agricultural reforms. Hungary did not abandon its state and cooperative farms. It did, however, become more flexible and adaptive with respect to them. Hungary's reforms transferred much decision-making power and operational control from Budapest to the managers of state and cooperative farms. Further, farm product prices and rewards for work and accomplishments were increased and placed under increased local control. Some land is owned by cooperatives and some by their members. Though the Hungarian government continues to place heavy reliance on large-scale productive units operated as state farms or cooperatives, Csaki (1987) reports that there are one-half million plots and small farms under cultivation. He does not attribute the diversity of Hungary's agricultural production organizations to the superiority of small-scale farming. Instead, he notes that the large-scale state and cooperative enterprises produce most of the grain, sugar beets, sunflowers, and green forages. On the other hand, smallholder operations are important for vegetables, fruit, and wine. Livestock production is distributed among both large- and small-scale units with the small-scale producers being relatively more important for pork, eggs, and rabbit meat. Even the large-scale farms of Hungary are regarded as dependent on technical assistance. They are served by Technically Organized Production Systems (TOPS). In turn, the large farms help the smaller ones. Csaki (1987) reports that Hungary is developing a large number of intermediate organizational structures including a wide variety of "joint" ventures. Some of the joint ventures are cooperative and others are legally and economically independent enterprises. Joint ventures provide construction, food processing, marketing, and other services for the agricultural sector.

Hungarian agriculture is more outwardly oriented than that of most socialist states, somewhat resembling in this respect South Korea and Taiwan. A very high proportion of Hungarian land is cultivatable. Hungary has virtually no other renewable natural resource to use in earning foreign exchange. Therefore, it is important that it use land wisely to earn foreign exchange from both within and outside socialist countries. Csaki (1987) characterizes Hungary's agricultural reforms as: (1) based on "voluntary gradualness" on the part of all decision-making units, (2) granting much independence from central control to local decision-making units, (3) recognizing a national financial interest in the productivity of agriculture, (4) stressing socialist democracy, and (5) requiring substantial state support for Hungarian agriculture. Hungarian policy makers rely on Hungary's agricultural and food industry to meet all of the increasing demands of its citizens for the products its agricultural system can produce; regard socialist, large-scale enterprises to be the basis for increases in production and the fundamental pillars of the Hungarian agricultural system; rely heavily on agriculture in achieving the socio-economic and financial possibilities of the country; regard small-scale agriculture as an integral part of Hungarian agriculture; stress the nonagricultural and service activities of its agricultural enterprises; encourage a multiplicity of diverse enterprise types within agriculture; and, lastly, rely heavily on the independence of enterprise managers pursuing their unit's financial material interest to replace earlier more centralized management procedures.

V. R. Boyev, Director of All Union Scientific Research, Institute of Agricultural Economics, presented a paper entitled "The Strategy of Development of Agro Industrial Complexes in the USSR" (1987). Boyev's brief written paper contains little in the way of specific references to reforms in Soviet agriculture. In his final paragraph, he notes the need to "suit. . . the corresponding indicators in individual regions, zones, and enterprises." This implies that managerial forms and production organizations must be flexible. "The general task," he indicates, "in agricultural development and development of agro-industrial complexes is to concentrate production in places with the most favorable and natural economic conditions and to carry out a socio-economic policy which can be regarded as fundamental principles for development of agro-industrial complexes." In his ad hoc public remarks at the Beijing symposium, Boyev placed much greater emphasis on the reforms he described as now being put in effect for Soviet agriculture. He indicated that these reforms are so significant and important that Chinese agricultural planners should be able to benefit substantially from studying them. In private conversations, Boyev placed even greater reliance on the importance of current Soviet agricultural reforms and, particularly, on the importance of successfully carrying out Gorbachev's view of how to manage the Soviet economy in general and its agricultural sector in particular.

Reforming Soviet agricultural institutions is understandably slow. The Soviet system has been in place for decades and the party and the government it controls have vested interests in it. The individuals who manage present Soviet agricultural institutions also have vested interests. Further, there are extensive sunken investments in physical capital specialized on the needs of the present institutional structure of Soviet agriculture—state farm facilities and the like. Consequently, institutional reforms for Soviet agriculture involve more dismantling costs than they did in socialist China and Hungary. Reforms are likely to be marginal, gradual, and much less extensive than in China and probably less so than the conservative gradual reforms of Hungary.

Particularly interesting was a verbal presentation by Raanan Weitz of materials published elsewhere (1972, updated). In one of the previously published papers entitled "An Institutional Framework for Rural Development: A Multiple-Level Integrated Planning Approach" (undated), Weitz traced out the history of the Israeli experiences with the kibbutz', the "collective moshaves," the moshave communities, and private enterprises in both farming and the farm service industry. There were obvious parallels between the Israeli experience and those of China (including Taiwan), South Korea, and of the Eastern Bloc socialist countries. Israel created a complex, diverse, multiple-level set of agricultural production organizations not unlike those that have developed in Hungary and now tend to be developing in the People's Republic of China. Many of Israel's original production organizations resembled those developed in Taiwan and South Korea. Each of Israel's many diverse institutional forms of production agriculture was put in place at a cost. No single arrangement has performed so poorly that Israel has been willing to incur the costs of completely dismantling and eliminating it. Consequently, the different institutional arrangements have persisted.

Insofar as the developed countries of the world are concerned, Bergmann/Petit (1987) covered continental developments in Western Europe. George Peters gave special attention to the British Isles (1987). It would have been helpful had the history of the Japanese development been presented at the symposium to facilitate comparisons between the Japanese and Chinese experiences. Also, there were no papers devoted to the history of agricultural development in North America, Oceania, South America, or Africa. Fortunately, Japanese and North American histories and the current farm crises of the developed world are well enough known (Johnston 1969; Ohkawa and Rosovsky 1964; Cochrane 1979; Kirkendall 1987; Schultz 1945; Benedict 1953, 1955; Benedict and Stine 1956) for me to take them into account in this paper without specific papers from the Beijing symposium. I need to do this because problems with the agricultural institutions of the DCs are important determinants of the needed future institutional changes in the NICs and LDCs.

The Bergmann/Petit (1987) post-World War II account of West European agricultural development experience is interesting and informative. In this period, important institutional improvements were made in Western Europe to promote and create new technologies for agriculture, to serve agriculture better with credit facilities, and to provide production services in effective manners. The immediate post-World War II concern of Europeans was for food self-sufficiency during periods of international conflict. This concern prompted and supported the creation and continuation of institutionalized subsidies and import restrictions that tipped the terms of exchange farther in favor of agriculture than did corresponding North American institutional arrangements but not as far as those in Japan. Many of these institutional arrangements were protectionist. Further subsidies and import restraints were taken to higher levels than required for food security needs. European agriculture has now accumulated large governmentally held stocks of farm products. As such stocks developed, Europe also created institutional arrangements for subsidizing exports. Europe in effect became a dumper of surpluses not needed for food security as well as protectionist to attain food security. The costs of establishing these institutions were large. In addition, the recurrent costs of running and maintaining them are now so large that demands for their elimination are arising with increasing frequency from European consumers, taxpayers, and political leaders. Nonetheless, it would be very expensive for Europe to dismantle these institutions and programs now. Included in the dismantlement costs would be not only the dismantling costs of institutions and programs themselves but reductions in the values of the public and private agricultural investments made in the expectation that the subsidies, price supports, and import protection would continue. Further, the futures of politicians in common market countries and, indeed, the political future of the common market itself depend in part on how these costs would be distributed. The EEC's mistaken agricultural institutions are not easily or cheaply dismantled and institutional change is likely to be slow.

There were no general papers at the Beijing symposium concerning the agricultural histories of North American and Oceanic countries. These countries, like the West European countries, have developed successful scientific, educational, credit, and other service support institutions and policies for their agricultures. North America has been an agricultural exporting area since its initial development; hence, fears about food security have not prompted the development of subsidies and import restrictions to promote self-sufficiency and food security. North American agricultural economies have tended for decades (with or without price supports and subsidies) to outproduce effective demand with disastrous consequences for farmers with leveraged fixed costs (Johnson 1984, 1985). The price support, production control, marketing, and subsidy institutions of the grain exporting North American countries were set up originally to control and manage this tendency to overproduce (Benedict and Stine 1956; Schultz 1945; D. Gale Johnson 1947; Cochrane 1947, 1958, 1979; G. Johnson 1958; Johnson and Quance 1972). We previously noted that irrationality, ideology, and power have played roles in establishing and maintaining the agricultural institutions of the socialist countries, Japan, and Western Europe. They have also played roles in determining the institutional structures of North American agriculture. This is in accord with the Williamson (1985)/North (1987) transaction cost/institutionalist analysis. In North America, family farm ideology or agricultural fundamentalism have been important. Also, free enterprise capitalistic ideology has played an important role in the pronouncements of the American Farm Bureau. Even economic analysts have unconsciously and perhaps even consciously been ideological and irrational. Such ideological tendencies may be unintentional as when transaction costs, errors due to imperfect knowledge, and opportunism are left out of analyses that consequently reveal no market failures requiring institutions to manage transaction costs. Such unrealistic analyses are then sometimes used irrationally to oppose market interventions and to support sole reliance on market adjustments even when transaction costs are important (Chambers and Vasavada 1983; Hoover 1973; M. Johnson and Pasour 1981; Edwards, 1985). However this may be, production and export subsidies, etc., have been raised to unduly high levels in North America that do little to help manage transaction costs. With price supports and subsidies, North American farmers appear, on the basis of empirical estimates of average and marginal earnings of their resources, to overinvest in capital and overpriced land relative to the subsidies and price supports. This conclusion is also generally supported by the current farm crises and numerous studies of farm financial stress. In North America, the costs of maintaining price support and subsidy institutions and programs are high and generally resented by taxpayers without solving the problem of low average and marginal earnings. Large public and private overinvestments have been erroneously made (sunk) that are not fully recoverable by either farmers or society. Contemplated institutional changes threaten these values. Thus, North American institutions and programs have been tenacious and durable precisely because the political and economic dismantlement costs of these institutions and investments are now high. Those costs, particularly the political ones, may be falling to the point where it will be judged advantageous to dismantle some of these institutions and sacrifice some resource values instead of continuing to pay the cost of maintaining and operating these institutions.

THE TRANSACTION COST/INSTITUTIONAL ANALYSIS OF THE FIRM AND INTERPRETATION OF AGRICULTURAL HISTORY

The institutional developments described and considered at the Beijing IAAE/CSAE Symposium on Rural Development are fascinating and crucially important. And, they cry out for interpretation and understanding to permit us to see better—to predict, if we dare—and improve the future. General economists and economic historians are now making some progress on what can be described as a "transaction cost approach to institutional change." In the previous part of this paper that approach helped us interpret and understand the many institutional reforms discussed at Beijing. In this part of this paper that approach is examined and applied in more detail—at times the applications are speculative in order to try to envision the potential of the approach in researching past changes and predicting future changes in agricultural institutions.

Important names in the development of the transaction cost/institution approach include those of O. E. Williamson (1985), Douglass North (1981), William Baumol (1986), and Allen Buchanan (1985). Williamson and Baumol work as economists, North as an economic historian, and Buchanan as an economic philosopher. My own acquaintance with this literature is too recent and meager for me to be entirely confident of having mastered it and not neglecting important contributors. I also note that writers in this area describe their work as being in its infancy and that they are continually culling, extending, and otherwise modifying their approach. Baumol feels that Williamson unduly differentiates the approach from a neoclassical, market adjustment approach to broadly conceived markets that would include the induced institutional change hypothesis of Ruttan (1971, 73–116) and others. I tend to agree with Baumol.

In his *The Economic Institutions of Capitalism*, O. E. Williamson (1985) examines how firms act and create institutional arrangements to obtain the benefits of progress while minimizing the costs of errors arising from imperfect knowledge and transaction costs. Transaction costs, being costs, are worth summarizing. In addition, transaction costs place firms in danger of making costly mistakes in the presence of asset specificity (I would use the term "asset fixity" [G. Johnson 1958; Edwards 1959; Johnson and Quance 1972]), imperfect knowledge, and exploiters waiting for an opportunity to take advantage of mistakes. In the absence of these conditions, the market mechanism is viewed by Williamson (1985) as capable of adequately governing the economic activities of society. In their presence, it is necessary for firms to develop institutions to help control transaction costs and their impacts.

Williamson (1985) views transaction costs mainly from the standpoint of management as the governance unit of a business or corporation. He asserts, in general agreement with Knight (1941), that without transaction costs, imperfect knowledge, and consequent errors, the firm is nothing more than a production function. In his analysis, transaction costs become important when a firm is using specialized assets in which investments can be mistakenly sunk (because of imperfect knowledge) under circumstances that offer others an opportunity to take advantage of the mistake at the expense of the firm or those within the firm making the mistake.

The transaction costs involved when a firm acquires and/or disposes of specialized assets establish a differential between what I call elsewhere (Johnson 1958; Edwards 1959; Johnson and Quance 1972) the replacement or *acquisition* cost and the *salvage value* of an asset. It should be noted and emphasized that in market-controlled economies, competitive farm firms invest in highly specialized and durable assets in unstable, almost unknowable, changing environments including a competitive market that opportunistically takes advantage of the investment mistakes of farm managers. It is also noted that the managers of socialist agricultural production units and systems, like their counterparts in privately managed agricultural sectors, encounter transaction costs in using specialized agricultural inputs in which they too sink large investments, often erroneously, as their knowledge is also imperfect under circumstances that give others in their bureaucracies an opportunity to take advantage of their mistakes. Williamson's (1985) analysis helps explain why imperfectly informed firms (and socialized farm production units) create institutions within and among themselves to alleviate the adverse effects of the transaction costs they encounter in organizing production to acquire the gains made possible by better technologies and other improvements. However, the process does not stop at the firm level. Producing units also organize themselves institutionally relative to government and, indeed, try to induce governments to make institutional changes advantageous to them (the firms).

There are also transaction costs involved in changing the internal institutional structure of a production unit. In the presence of such costs, institutions, too, often become fixed (specific); incorrect, because of errors originating in imperfect knowledge; and opportunistically exploitable. The Williamson analysis implies that managers of socialized agricultural units in seeking the gains of agricultural development will also have reasons to devise institutions to control (1) transaction costs (assembly or installation) and dismantling costs, and (2) the adverse consequences of making mistakes in creating institutions. This implication is certainly applicable to the history of institutional arrangements for socialist China's agriculture.

Douglass C. North stresses the cost of changing institutions in interpreting history in his 1981 book entitled *Structure and Change in Economic History*. A rather concise summary of his argument is to be found in his 1984 *Journal of Economic History* entitled "Government and the Cost of Exchange in History." A more recent North article (1987) is entitled "Institutions, Transaction Costs and Economic Growth"—perhaps the following summary and interpretation of pages 255–56 will be helpful. North points out there that the Walrasian models of economists typically ignore transaction costs and institutions other than those of a perfect market. He argues that the extensive use of Walrasian models by economic historians in the years before 1984 led them to neglect the institutions society developed to handle transaction costs. These institutional changes, in turn, affect related property rights. Thus, he argues that economic historians must develop the requisite theory for a transaction cost/institutional approach to history that goes beyond neoclassical economics. Whether North's appraisal applies to all neoclassical market adjustment analyses is not particularly relevant here as it certainly applies to many of them. As I have pointed out long ago and elsewhere, many neoclassical economic analyses ignore acquisition cost/salvage price differentials determined by transaction costs, imperfect knowledge, investment mistakes and consequent asset fixity, changes in length of run, irreversibilities in supply and input demand functions, opportunity costs, non-Pareto-optimal[4] losses on sunken costs, and the like (Johnson and Quance 1972; Johnson 1958).

Like this paper, North (1981, 1984, 1987) is concerned with public institutions. He argues that four variables must be taken into account in understanding the changes in institutions needed to handle better the transaction costs involved in attaining gains from development. The four variables are: *first*, the cost of measuring the goods and services exchanged and the performance of persons and agencies; *second*, the nature of the exchange process, that is whether it is personal or impersonal; the *third* is enforcement of agreements in order to avoid cheating, opportunism, and shirking; and the *fourth* includes ideological attitudes and irrationality. North's list is related to Williamson's in that it includes asset specificity, imperfect knowledge, and opportunism and to my own much earlier stress on acquisition/salvage value differentials and imperfect knowledge.

Institutions to control transaction costs are put in place at a cost and, in turn, can generally be dismantled only at a cost. Some institutions are *formal*,such as a production control program of a government; others are *informal*, such as customary arrangements governing marriage in a society.

I must point out here that in this paper I go beyond both Williamson (1985) and North (1981, 1984, 1987) in order to have a transaction cost analysis capable of interpreting all of the phenomena touched on by the Beijing symposium papers. Those papers dealt with or implied concerns with formal as well as informal institutions and with the relationships of such institutions to the assets used in agricultural production and marketing. Society incurs transaction costs in both establishing and de-establishing institutions in much the same way firms encounter transaction costs when investing and disinvesting in lumpy durable factors of production. Both kinds of transaction costs are encountered in the pursuit of agricultural development. For the remainder of this paper, I shall refer to the costs of establishing and dismantling both formal and informal institutions as *institutional transaction costs* and to the costs of putting durable productive assets in place and of dismantling them as *production transaction costs*. Still further transaction costs may be monetary as well as nonmonetary in nature whether for formal or informal institutions, the same being true for the transaction costs involved when establishing and dismantling productive assets. Moveover, returns and benefits from both institutions and productive assets may be either monetary or nonmonetary. As many of the nonmonetary values arise in technical social, political, and military contexts far more than economics is required to perceive, understand, and measure transaction costs and returns to institutional arrangements.

At this point in the discussion, some neoclassical economists may argue that all that is required to explain changes and rigidities in agricultural institutions and production plants is to broaden the concept of markets to include political process so that the induced institutional-change hypothesis can be used to explain institutional changes. North would object, however, as such explanations leave out institutional transaction costs and the roles that irrationality, ideological commitments, and opportunistic use of political, military, and other kinds of power play in forming governmental institutions (North 1981). He argues that "political systems have an inherent tendency to produce" institutions involving "inefficient property rights or decline" (North 1981, 422). His conclusion is particularly appropriate for the oft-mistaken agricultural institutions of socialist China, the Soviet Union, and Eastern Europe (Csaki 1987; Boyev 1987; Li 1987). It also applies to the many mistaken price support, subsidy, and import protection agricultural institutions of Japan, Western Europe, and North America. Further, it should be observed that neoclassical, market-oriented agricultural economists commonly analyze and even advocate institutional changes without taking into account non-Pareto-optimal gains and losses in the values of investments sunk in producer durables and storables. North certainly makes a valid point when he calls attention to how dangerous it is to disregard transaction costs, imperfect knowledge, irrationality, and ideology and power.

Institutional transaction costs when both high and low have been important for the agricultural decision makers of mainland China and the Asiatic NICs. High institutional transaction costs (including those of a civil war) were paid in mainland China to change land tenure institutions and redistribute the ownership of land from feudal landlords to peasants. Transaction costs short of war were also incurred in reforming the land tenure institutions of Taiwan, South Korea, and, earlier, Japan. Further, substantial institutional transaction costs were incurred in dismantling the original land reform of socialist China so as to reconcentrate land ownership in the hands of the state under the control of the CPC. Subsequently, in the late 1970s, both institutional and production transaction costs were incurred in dismantling a substantial part of the state farms and communes as formal institutions in order to pass control, if not ownership, of land back to individuals and families under the less formal "responsibility system." Investments in agriculture and their earnings appear to have been low during the cultural revolution. This suggests that such dismantling and disposal of production durables as was done at the end of the cultural revolution did not involve much loss of productive value.

In post-1978 socialist China, in the Soviet Union, and in the Eastern European socialized countries, agricultural reforms have been and are being sought to alleviate difficulties related to North's four variables (1981, 1984, 1987): performance measurement, exchange processes, enforcement of agreements, and ideologies and irrationality.

The institutional changes discussed in the previous part of this paper have often been non-Pareto-optimal. Also, transaction costs and imperfect knowledge combine to impose non-Pareto losses on production units, laborers, and the owners of rights and privileges and to confer gains on others. In terms of Pareto-optimality such losses represent "market failures" that motivate the creation of public institutions to avoid such losses. These losses are, of course, both private and social (Johnson 1985, 1987b). The losses imposed on some are partially offset by gains conferred on others. Interpersonally valid measures of welfare or value are required to judge superiority or inferiority of such Pareto non-optimal adjustments. Historically, socialist decision makers have seldom questioned the interpersonal validity of their knowledge of values and welfare; hence, they have been unimpeded by Pareto-optimality questions in deciding to implement coercive reforms and revolutions. In the western nonsocialist democracies, politicians and decision makers do not worry much about Pareto-optimality either, but they do have to be concerned about the voting power of those damaged by coercive non-Pareto-optimal changes. Analysts using models devoid of transaction costs and assuming perfect knowledge never encounter non-Pareto-optimal market failures in their analysis; consequently, they often advocate courses of action that politicians being keenly aware of real-world market failures are too wise to follow! In any event, non-Pareto-optimal institutional changes influencing agriculture are commonly made and rejected by the governments of western nonsocialist as well as socialist states.

At the Beijing symposium there was often widespread agreement among participants that non-Pareto-optimal changes in institutions represented improvements. Cooter and Rappoport (1984) have argued that Pareto optimalists (and ordinalists) have gone too far. Elsewhere, I have concurred (Johnson 1986) and have presented arguments to support the conclusion that in some cases, at least, Pareto non-optimal changes in institutions can be judged to be superior or inferior to the unaltered situation. By contrast, both general and agricultural economists have argued that, strictly within Pareto-optimality institutional reforms that damage some to benefit others cannot be judged to be superior or inferior to what is replaced. Particularly, it is argued with what appears to be irrefutable logic that we cannot oppose institutional reforms or, for that matter, Pareto-nonoptimal market failures on either welfare or efficiency grounds merely because they are not Pareto better. The neoclassical, Pareto-optimal market adjustment point of view produces an analysis virtually without applicability in the real world of transaction costs, imperfect knowns, mistakes that lead to costs being sunk in specific assets or institutions and consequent not Pareto optimal changes. Even "second best" choices and market failures may be superior to a Pareto-optimal "first best." Boulding (1981), Buchanan (1985), North (1981), Williamson (1985), Shaffer (1987) and Kilmer and Armbruster (1987, 301–15), among others, have stressed the limitation of Pareto-optimal measures of welfare and efficiency. The widespread agreement in Beijing that many of the non-Pareto-optimal changes being made in the agricultural institutions of socialist countries are advantageous suggests the possibility of a broader approach to welfare and efficiency than permitted by Pareto-optimality. One such approach is the one I have used earlier in doing policy analyses in Nigeria (Johnson et al. 1969), Korea (Rossmiller et al. 1972), and the United States (Johnson and Quance 1972, Ch. 4). (Also see Johnson 1986, 1987a).

I turn now to South Korea, Japan, and Taiwan as Asiatic NICs or NIAs where "A" stands for area instead of country. Their institutions have long been as favorable or more favorable for agricultural production than the reformed institutions now being sought and attained in the socialist countries. South Korea has now found that its land reform fragmented ownership so much that farmers do not have units large enough to produce incomes comparable to those now being received by industrial workers. Thus, South Korea, like socialist China is now encountering the institutional transaction costs involved in partially dismantling its earlier land reform. Japan and Taiwan are also encountering dismantling costs in changing their land tenure institutions. As socialist China succeeds in creating higher paying off-farm employment opportunities, it is adjusting the size of its farm operating units by subcontracting at the expense of further institutional transaction costs, some of which are ideological and political in nature. All three have attained more food security and higher degrees of self-sufficiency by subsidizing their agricultures and/or granting them import protection. I have argued and presented empirical work elsewhere (Johnson 1958; Johnson and Quance 1972) that asset specificity and imperfect knowledge of continuous change (technical, institutional and human) create problems for farm entrepreneurs involving the transaction costs that make up the differences between acquisition costs and salvage values of assets. These problems should be expected to materialize, but with and without subsidies, price supports, and import protection. Though Williamson is not very explicit about it, sunken costs become problems only when they are in overcommitted resources whose earnings do not cover the transaction costs involved in acquisition. Nor is he explicit about user costs—part of the economics of extracting service flows from fixed durables (Keynes 1936; Lewis 1949; Baquet 1978, 95–122; Robison and Abkin 1981). Such services earn opportunity costs or shadow prices insufficient to cover the original stock acquisition price sunk in the asset. The uses of the services of sunken assets are governed by *current* shadow or opportunity cost and, sometimes, salvage values (or off-farm opportunity costs); however, capital loss, cash flow, leverage, and bankruptcy problems are created by their *historical acquisition* costs for those using fixed or sunken assets. It is easy to demonstrate both theoretically and empirically (Edwards 1959; Johnson and Quance 1972, appendix) that random mistakes made as a result of imperfect knowledge in investing in assets with transaction costs for acquisition and disposal generate a tendency to outproduce effective demand even in the absence of price supports and input subsidies. With supports and subsidies, it is again easy to demonstrate (both theoretically and empirically) that entrepreneurs tend to overvalue land, overinvest, and overproduce the effective demand inherent in the price supports and subsidies. Whether or not Taiwan, South Korea, Japan, and western DCs are importers, self-sufficient, or exporters of agricultural products, they are all overinvested in productive agricultural assets relative to the effective demand they face within their subsidized and protected systems.

The heavy subsidies and assistance given to South Korean and Taiwanese agriculture by their respective agricultural institutions are less extensive and less expensive than is the case for Japan. Japan's agriculture is more heavily subsidized and protected than the agriculture of any other developed countries (USDA 1987). Japan is followed by the EEC countries in the list of countries that subsidize and protect their agricultures. In North America, subsidies and protectionism for farm products are not as high as in Western Europe but are high enough to increase surpluses and government costs to levels unacceptable to U.S. taxpayers. Apparently, nearly comparable subsidies and protection for Canadian farmers are less obvious to Canadian taxpayers and consumers, in part, because such costs are paid from provincial as well as federal treasuries. One cannot examine the institutions of these countries without acknowledging the realism of North's concern about irrationality and mistaken institutions. Agricultural products of Oceania are probably less subsidized and protected than those for any developed country (USDA 1987).

In general, the agricultures of the developed western nonsocialist countries now have institutions for subsidizing and protecting agriculture that were put in place at substantial institutional transaction costs. To be included in the costs of establishing these institutions are the costs associated with increases in the value of farmland (Lowenberg-DeBoer 1986; Boyne 1964), and of production allotments and increased investments in other assets. If and when such institutions are dismantled in response to taxpayer and consumer dissatisfaction, high institutional transaction costs will be incurred again. These costs will include the destruction of property values based on the price support, production control, fiscal, and import protection institutions now in place. But this is not the end of the matter as foreign exchange control and related institutions that protect nonfarm producers and laborers are also in place. Some of the most troublesome arrangements involve deficit financing and regulation of foreign exchange rates. Deficit financing and exchange controls inflate prices, distort price relationships, and redistribute property values in LDCs, NICs, and NIAs as well as in the DCs.

The United States plays a difficult, troublesome role in trade and international finance because it is a major country whose monetary unit denominates most international transactions. Deficit financing by the United States affords many opportunities for both other countries and the United States to engage in what North (1981, 36) and Williamson (1985, 31–32) refer to as malevolent "opportunism." For several decades, European countries, Japan, some of the Asiatic NICs, and the petroleum-exporting countries have built up productive capacity, reduced indebtedness, and/or built their dollar revenues from United States reconstruction assistance, military expenditures in Europe and Asia, war expenditures, and, more recently, by running trade deficits against the United States. They made their dollar reserves good, first, by cashing them in against U.S. gold reserves (until those become inadequate for that purpose); second, by purchasing securities, stocks, and real property; and, third, by loaning the dollar claims to the U.S. Treasury to cover U.S. fiscal deficits. The United States is now the world's largest debtor nation. While it is true that the holders of Euro-petro- and Asiatic dollars suffered losses from depreciation of the U.S. dollar in a number of rather dramatic instances and that the United States (including its consumers) has opportunistically taken advantage of such losses, it is also true that the two U.S. deficits (fiscaland trade), reconstruction assistance, military expenditures, developmental assistance including concessional loans and sales, and, in some instances the general schedule of preferences (GSP) have permitted Japan, Korea, Taiwan, and Western Europe to "prime their economic pumps" with trade surpluses almost since World War II in such a way as to promote their growth and prosperity. The United States did (or permitted) this in order to help rebuild Western Europe and Japan and to help create the present economies of South Korea and Taiwan to strengthen the free world. In addition, there has been an almost conscious collusion between those in the United States who wanted to use fiscal deficits to fund the domestic, international, and military programs of the United States and those in Japan and Western Europe who wanted to run trade surpluses with the United States to expand their own economies.

Whether or not the above analyses of the historical roles of the U.S. fiscal and trade deficits are accurate, it appears that the decades-long era of U.S. fiscal deficits and unfavorable trade balances is going to have to end. When it does, there will be major transaction costs for the NICs, NIAs, and DCs that have become dependent on benefits from the two U.S. deficits. The recent stock market disaster and the current plunge in the value of the U.S. dollar attest to the major transaction costs that may be ahead as the West European DCs, Japan, and the Asiatic NICs and NIAs face the necessary adjustments in their fixed investments and institutions.

Socialist China and India are both large LDCs. They also share a history of being internally rather than export oriented. Socialist China now seems to be moving to more of an export orientation. If the above view of the possible impacts of eliminating the U.S. fiscal and trade deficit has any validity, the United States is not likely to be willing and able to run trade deficits large enough to bestow on socialist China benefits comparable to those bestowed on Western Europe, Japan, Taiwan, and South Korea since World War II. The same would also apply to India were it to become export oriented like Japan, Taiwan, and South Korea. Socialist China, India, and, indeed, Japan, Western Europe, Taiwan, and South Korea should consider producing for their own markets while preparing for more balanced trade with the United States. It is likely true that Japan, Western Europe, Taiwan, and South Korea are substantially overinvested in export-specific assets (automobile factories, steel mills, shipyards, and the like) targeted on the U.S. market. These investments may have to be revalued downward and allocated on an opportunity-cost or shadow-price basis in the future in ways that will impose significant capital losses on their owners.

Generally the agricultures of the LDCs of Africa, South America, and the Middle East suffer at least as much from institutional constraints as from lack of technology. They are also severely constrained by lack of human capital. Further, this lack and inadequate (sometimes corrupt) institutions tend to foreclose the self generation and use of much biological and physical capital. The same is true for the effective use of the borrowed capital and capital grants. Some LDCs (Tanzania, Cuba, Angola, and Nicaragua) have followed the earlier Soviet institutional pattern with even less success than the Eastern European socialist countries. Cuba paid high transaction costs to establish her socialist institutions. Such costs were lower in Tanzania (which avoided war) than in Cuba, Angola, and Nicaragua. Tanzania, like China after the Red Guard period, now appears to be paying only moderate dismantlement costs in shifting away from some of its least appropriate (and least productive) institutional arrangements. In the rest of Latin America and Africa a difficult quest is on for new institutional arrangements. Unlike Taiwan, South Korea, Western Europe, and Japan after World War II, some of these countries lack the human capital required to devise and effectively update their agricultural institutions. Further, even if they have the human capital, they are unlikely to be the beneficiaries of the large-scale U.S. reconstruction, developmental, and, even, military expenditures that helped those countries reconstruct and build. Still further, Latin American and African countries face a United States that is already absorbing more imports than it is paying for. The United States cannot and the historical records of Japan and Western Europe indicate that they are unlikely to open their markets to prime the pumps of Latin American and African LDCs. Like India and China, these LDCs are likely to have to follow the slower route of tailoring their institutions, industries, and agriculture to fill their own domestic needs while competing in a subsidized restricted world for limited export opportunities. But that is not the end of the matter—Japan, Western Europe, and the Asian NICs are likely to be adversely impacted and in turmoil because of institutional changes (agricultural and other) forced on or taken by the United States. This turmoil is likely to affect LDC agricultural sectors more adversely than it does those of Japan, Europe, and the Asian NICs.

CONCLUSIONS AND SPECULATIONS ABOUT UNMET NEEDS FOR REFORMS IN AGRICULTURAL INSTITUTIONS

A. From the above, the following conclusions can be reached:

1. Transaction costs are important for agriculture. Such costs have two dimensions:
   - they involve both institutions (both formal and informal) and productive investments; thus both *institutional* and *production* transaction costs are important.
   - Some transaction costs are *establishment costs* for institutions and production facilities; others are *dismantling costs* of institutions and production facilities.
2. For production facilities, establishment costs plus dismantling costs account for the commonly observed differences between *acquisition costs* and *salvage values of assets*.
3. In the presence of transaction costs and imperfect knowledge, mistakes are made with respect to both investments and institutional changes. These mistakes result in fixed investments and rigid institutions because of dismantlement costs for both investments and institutions. The "economics" of investments and disinvestments and of institutional change is trivial and/or unrealistic if transaction costs, imperfect knowledge, errors, irrationality, and ideology were ignored or assumed nonexistent. Conversely, the economics of investment, disinvestment, and institutional change are complex but realistic if these considerations are taken into account. The Beijing papers encountered the rich complexity of reality and the extension of the North/Williamson transaction cost/institution analysis presented herein helps us somewhat in understanding what has, is, and, even, will happen to agricultural institutions around the world. The same can be said for the corresponding analysis of investments in durable factors of agricultural production; Williamson's analysis is closely related to earlier asset fixity and investment/disinvestment analyses of agriculture.
4. Institutional changes and closely related investments and disinvestments in agricultural durables made subject to imperfect knowledge leads to overproduction of effective demand, non-Pareto optimal losses and attempts to preserve the remaining earning power of sunken assets and the incomes derivable from mistaken institutions.
5. Losses (monetary and otherwise) from mistaken investments and institutions are Pareto non-optimal as are some of the direct, immediate consequences of institutional changes.
6. At the Beijing symposium, Pareto non-optimal institutional changes were often generally accepted as welfare enhancing. This implies at least some limited ability to measure and/or appraise welfare and values in an interpersonally valid, objective manner. Cooter and Rappoport (1984) and Johnson (1986) have mobilized arguments about the possibility of such measurements and appraisals.

B. Somewhat speculative interpretations of historical, current, and prospective changes and reforms in agricultural institutions include:

1. It appears that socialist China was able to make rapid major institutional reforms for its agriculture after the late 1970s because
   - the "institutional" transaction costs involved in dismantling old and establishing new institutions were low,
   - its previous institutions had created few valuable production assets and vested interests whose values will be destroyed by institutional change, and
   - the anticipated returns from institutional reforms were high.

   As socialist China's reforms succeed, its institutions will probably become more stable (rigid) as dismantlement costs for institutions will rise and gains from further reforms will decrease.
2. Institutions similar to those now being established by socialist China were also established earlier in Japan, South Korea, and in the Province of Taiwan at low transaction (both institutional and production) costs and high returns.
3. In Eastern Europe and the Soviet Union, it appears that reformation of agricultural institutions has been slower and will remain slower than in socialist China since the late 1970s because
   - *institutional* transaction (dismantlement) costs are higher than in socialist China,
   - related *production* transaction costs are also higher than in socialist China,
   - while the returns from institutional reforms are no higher and may even be lower than they have been in socialist China since the late 1970s.
4. For the Asiatic NICs, Taiwan, and Japan, it appears that reforms of present agricultural institutions will be slow and difficult because
   - institutional transaction costs would be moderately high both for dismantling present institutions and for establishing new ones in their places,
   - production transaction costs would be very high if present subsidy and trade protection institutions were dismantled, and
   - the returns would be only moderate and at least partially offset by the value of the food security that would be lost.
5. Reform of Europe's agricultural institutions should also be expected to be slow and difficult because
   - institutional transaction costs would be very high if present price support, subsidy, and import protection institutions were dismantled,
   - production transaction costs would be very high if trade protection, subsidy, and price support institutions were dismantled,
   - while anticipated returns are only moderately high, such returns would be partially offset by the value of the food security that would be lost.

6. In North America, it can be reasoned that agricultural institutions may become quite flexible because
   - transaction costs of dismantling present institutions, many of which are political, are falling as taxpayer discontent grows and the political power of farmers decreases,
   - production transaction costs for eliminating subsidies and price supports would be very high for the small proportion of the U.S. population dependent on farming and the servicing of farming for their incomes,
   - while anticipated returns appear moderately high and are not reduced by concerns about lost food security.
7. For the world, the future of agricultural institutions is made uncertain by the fiscal and trade uncertainties associated with the U.S. fiscal and trade deficits.
   - For the United States the picture is far from favorable. Depreciation of the dollar reduces the real value of the U.S. debt, and decreases the real prices of our exports while increasing the prices of imports, both of which are denominated in dollars. According to unrealistic trade theories that ignore transaction costs, imperfect knowledge and sunken costs, our production, exports, and imports should quickly come into balance as the value of the dollar falls and subsidy and support programs are eliminated. The trading partners of the United States, however, have major sunken investments in relatively new production plants. These plants will drop their prices and stay in production as long as their shadow prices or "within-country opportunity costs in use" are high enough to make it unprofitable to liquidate them. The same will be true for U.S. agriculture. Even if earnings on these assets fall with declines in the value of the U.S. dollar, foreign production and exports to the United States will not be quickly reduced—nor will U.S. production of farm products be reduced very much,
   - It is reasonable to expect that the United States is likely to be forced by the high costs of her two deficits to make institutional changes to reduce them,
   - If the United States were to eliminate farm subsidies and price supports, the transaction cost analysis (and earlier asset fixity analysis) indicates that overcommitment and overinvestments would continue to maintain
     - supplies and income problems for U.S. farmers and
     - large exportable surpluses of U.S. farm products.

     This implies a continued search for institutions for U.S. agriculture to stabilize production and prices and protect U.S. agriculture from "market failures" (Johnson and Quance 1972; Johnson 1984, 1985).
   - If the above happens, Japan and Western Europe cannot continue to count on the pump-priming effects of trade surpluses with the United States.
   - If the United States settles her two deficits, Taiwan and South Korea, because they are small, may be able to continue to keep their pumps primed for a while at modest levels by running trade deficits with the United States.
   - However, large developing countries, such as socialist China and India, should be cautious about depending on increased trade surpluses with the United States to attain economic growth comparable with that attained by Japan, Western Europe, Taiwan, and South Korea since World War II.
   - The LDCs of South America and Africa should not count on trade surpluses with the United States to boost their development.

NOTES

1. Reprinted with editing including the anglicization of the order of Asian names, from the Proceedings of *Conference on Directions and Strategies of Agricultural Development in the Asia-Pacific Region*, Vol. I, The Institute of Economics, Academic Sinica, Taipei, Taiwan, Republic of China, January 5–7, 1988, pages 9–43.

2. Glenn L. Johnson is a professor emeritus of the Department of Agricultural Economics, Michigan State University. He gratefully acknowledges helpful suggestions and criticism from Harold Riley, Allan Schmid, James Shaffer, and Vernon Sorenson. Responsibility for the interpretations of Oliver Williamson's and Douglass North's work in this paper, however, remains solely with the author.

3. Though Professor Chen was unable to come to Beijing to present his paper, it was presented at the conference.

4. Non-Pareto-optimal refers to a change where at least one person must be hurt in order to benefit one or more others.

REFERENCES

Baquet, Alan E. 1978. An economic theory of investment and disinvestment. Proceedings: Workshop on capital investment decisions. WS–77–18. East Lansing: Michigan State University, Dept. of Agricultural Economics, sponsored by Electric Power Research Institute.

Baumol, William J. 1986. The Economic institutions of capitalism. *Rand Journal of Economics* 17, no. 2: 279–86.

Benedict, Murray R. 1953. *Farm policies of the United States 1790–1950.* New York: The Twentieth Century Fund.

_____1955. *Can we solve the farm problem?* New York: The Twentieth Century Fund.

Benedict, M. R., and O. C. Stine. 1956. *The agricultural commodity programs.* New York: The Twentieth Century Fund.

Boulding, Kenneth. 1981. *Evolutionary economics.* Beverly Hills: Sage Publications, Inc.

Boyne, David H. 1964. Changes in the real wealth position of farm operators. Technical Bulletin 294. East Lansing: Michigan State University, Agricultural Experiment Station.

Buchanan, Allen. 1985. *Ethics, efficiency, and the market.* Totowa, N.J.: Rowman and Allanheld.

Chambers, Robert G., and Utpal Vasavada. 1983. Testing asset fixity for U.S. agriculture. *American Journal of Agricultural Economics* 50, no. 3: 606–20.

China's economy: The biggest developer of all. 1987. *The Economist* (August 1).

Cochrane, Willard W. 1947. Farm price gyrations—Aggregative hypothesis. *Journal of Farm Economics* 49, no. 2: 383–408.

_____1958. *Farm prices, myth and reality.* Minneapolis: University of Minnesota Press.

_____1979. *The development of American agriculture.* Minneapolis: University of Minnesota Press.

Collins, Larry, and Dominique Lapierre. 1975. *Freedom at midnight.* New Delhi, India: Vikas Publishing House Pvt. Ltd.

Cooter, R., and P. Rappoport. 1984. Were the Ordinalists wrong about welfare economics? *Journal of Economic Literature* 22, no. 2: 507–30.

Edwards, Clark. 1959. Resource fixity and farm organization. *Journal of Farm Economics* 41, no. 4: 747–59.

_____1985. Testing asset fixity for agriculture. American *Journal of Agricultural Economics* 67, no. 1: 136–37.

Hoover, Dale M. 1973. Review of *The Overproduction Trap* by G. L. Johnson and C. L. Quance. *American Journal of Agricultural Economics* 55, no. 2: 354–55.

Johnson, D. Gale. 1947. *Forward prices for agriculture.* Chicago: University of Chicago Press.

Johnson, Glenn L. 1958. Supply functions—Some facts and notions. In *Agricultural adjustment problems in a growing economy.* Edited by E. O. Heady et al., 74–93. Ames: Iowa State College Press.

_____1983. Synoptic view. *Growth and equity in agricultural development.* Proceedings of Eighteenth International Conference of Agricultural Economists held at Jakarta, Indonesia. Hampshire, England: Gower Publishing Company Ltd.

_____1984. Toward the twenty-first century: U.S. agriculture in an unstable world economy: Discussion. *American Journal of Agricultural Economics* 66, no. 5: 597–98.

_____1985. Agricultural surpluses—Research on agricultural technologies, institutions, people and capital growth. In *Crop productivity-research imperatives revisited.* Edited by M. Gibbs and C. Carlson. East Lansing: Michigan State University, Agricultural Experiment Station.

_____1986. *Research methodology for economists.* New York: Macmillan.

_____1987a. Holistic modeling of multidisciplinary subject matter and problem domains. In *Systems Economics.* Edited by K. A. Fox and D. G. Miles, 85–109. Ames: Iowa State University Press.

_____1987b. Roles for social scientists in agricultural policy. In *Is there a moral obligation to save the family farm?* Edited by Gary Comstock. Ames: Iowa State University Press.

Johnson, Glenn L., et al. 1969. Strategies and recommendations for Nigerian rural development, 1969/1985, CSNRD #33. East Lansing: Michigan State University, Dept. of Agricultural Economics.

Johnson, Glenn L., and C. Leroy Quance, eds. 1972. *The overproduction trap in U.S. agriculture.* Baltimore: Johns Hopkins University Press.

Johnson, Marc A., and E. C. Pasour, Jr. 1981. An opportunity cost view of fixed asset theory and the overproduction trap. In *American Journal of Agricultural Economics* 63, no. 1: 1–7.

Johnston, B. F. 1969. The Japanese "model" of agricultural development: Its relevance to developing nations. In *Agriculture and economic growth: Japan's experience.* Edited by K. Ohkawa et al. Tokyo: University of Tokyo Press.

Keynes, J. M. 1936. *The general theory of employment, interest and money.* New York: Harcourt, Brace.

Kilmer, R. L., and W. J. Armbruster. 1987. Economic efficiency and future research. *Economic efficiency in agricultural and food marketing.* Ames: Iowa State University Press.

Kirkendall, Richard S. 1987. The situation, problems, and issues—Today and tomorrow. Paper presented at Social Science Agricultural Agenda Project (SSAAP) Phase I Workshop, 8–12 June, Minneapolis, Minnesota.

Knight, Frank H. 1941. *Risk, uncertainty and profit.* Oxford: Oxford University Press.

Lewis, W. A. 1949. *Overhead costs.* London: Allen and Unwin.

Lowenberg-DeBoer, James. 1986. *The microeconomic roots of the farm crisis.* New York: Praeger.

North, Douglass C. 1981. *Structure and change in economic history.* New York: W. W. Norton & Co.

_____1984. Government and the cost of exchange in history. *Journal of Economic History* (June): 255–64.

_____1987. Institutions, transaction costs and economic growth. *Economic Inquiry* 25, no. 3: 419–28.

Ohkawa, Kazushi, and Henry Rosovsky. 1964. The role of agriculture in modern Japanese economic development. In *Agriculture in economic development.* Edited by C. Eicher and L. Witt. New York: McGraw-Hill.

Robison, Lindon J., and Michael H. Abkin. 1981. Theoretical and practical models for investment and disinvestment decision making under uncertainty in the energy supply industry. AER no. 390. East Lansing: Michigan State University, Dept. of Agricultural Economics.

Rossmiller, G.E., et al. 1972. *Korean agricultural sector analysis and recommended development strategies, 1971–1985.* East Lansing: Michigan State University, Dept. of Agricultural Economics.

Ruttan, Vernon W. 1971. Toward a theory of technical and institutional change. *Agricultural development: An international perspective.* Baltimore: Johns Hopkins University Press.

Schultz, T. W. 1945. *Agriculture in an unstable economy.* New York: McGraw-Hill.

Shaffer, James. 1987. Does the concept of economic efficiency meet the standards for truth in labeling when used as a norm in policy analysis? In *Economic efficiency in agricultural and food marketing.* Edited by R. L. Kilmer and W. J. Armbruster. Ames: Iowa State University Press.

U.S. Dept. of Agriculture. 1987. Government intervention in agriculture: Measurement, evaluation, and implications for trade negotiations. Economic Research Service, FAER–229. (April).

Vyas, V. S. 1983. Growth and equity in Asian agriculture: A synoptic view. *Growth and equity in agricultural development.* Proceedings of Eighteenth International Conference of Agricultural Economists held at Jakarta, Indonesia. Hampshire, England: Gower Publishing Company Ltd.

Weitz, Raanan. 1972. Social planning in rural regional development: The Israeli experience. *International Social Development Review* 4:57–72.

_____n.d. An institutional framework for rural development—A multilevel integrated planning approach. Settlement Study Centre (SSC), Centro de Estudios Regionales Urbano-Rurales (CERUR), Rehovot, Israel.

Williamson, Oliver E. 1985. *The economic institutions of capitalism.* New York: Free Press.

PAPERS CITED FROM *CHINA'S RURAL DEVELOPMENT MIRACLE: WITH INTERNATIONAL COMPARISONS*

Papers presented at an international symposium held at Beijing, China, October 25–29, 1987. International Association of Agricultural Economists in association with Australian International Development Assistance Bureau and published by University of Queensland Press.

Bergmann, Denis and Michel Petit. Modernization of agriculture in Western Europe after World War II: A result of luck, circumstances or government policies?

Boyev, V. R. The strategy for development of agro-industrial complexes in the U.S.S.R.

Chen, Hsi-huang. Strategies of agricultural development in Taiwan.

Csaki, Csaba. Agriculture and industry in the Hungarian economic development: Hungarian agricultural policy in the 1980s.

Du, Runsheng. Advancing amidst reform—Welcoming speech.

Kim, Dong Hi. Optimizing the role of government in modernizing agriculture: The Korean experience.

Peters, George H. Food and agriculture in Britain—Capitalism or control?

Renfeng, Li. Problems of rural reform in the Soviet Union and Eastern Europe.

Tian, Jiyun. Opening address.

Tsuchiya, Keizo. The role and significance of mechanization in the agricultural development of Japan.

Vyas, Vijay S. India's rural development strategies—Lessons in agricultural growth and poverty alleviation.

Weitz, Raanan. Social planning in rural regional development: The Israeli experience.

Wen, Lu. Developing strategy in rural China.

CHAPTER 8

ON-FARM CAPITAL FORMATION AND RURAL FINANCIAL MARKETS: RESEARCH ISSUES

Dale W Adams[1]

INTRODUCTION

For the past thirty years, the pace of agricultural growth in many low-income countries (LICs) has been remarkable. While a few nations continue to have trouble feeding all their citizens when disaster strikes and some people lack access to sufficient calories, there are now fewer production dilemmas and more problems of inequitable distributions of purchasing power. Social scientists have contributed to this success by helping policy makers understand the importance of product and input prices, new production technology, education, and infrastructure in agricultural growth.

Nevertheless, several important contributors to rural development, namely on-farm capital formation and rural financial markets, are still poorly understood. This is largely due to the difficulties of documenting their contributions to development. While highly visible government investments in agriculture are important, especially in relatively high-income countries, progress in agriculture has often depended on capital formation that occurs outside the spotlight, done in small increments by individuals or by small groups of farmers. Likewise, rural financial intermediation is difficult to document because it is usually diffused and fragmented, includes a large number of participants, and involves procedures that are misunderstood.

In the following discussion, I outline research priorities on the topics of on-farm capital formation and rural financial markets. Before doing this, I clarify my use of the terms "capital" and "rural financial markets," briefly describe the intersection between these markets and on-farm capital formation, and present terse summaries of recent research on these topics.

DEFINITIONS

There are few areas in economics that involve more ambiguities than capital, largely because of the elastic definitions employed. On occasion, the term "capital" is applied to things as disparate as money, a category of productive inputs, education and experience, and social relationships. In the following discussion, I restrict my use of the term to inputs that are not entirely expended in one production period and are manmade, or grow only under husbandry. Examples include the terraced rice paddies and associated irrigation systems in many parts of Asia that were constructed with huge investments of human labor. Similar capital creation can be seen in Belize or Peru where colonists are attacking jungles with axes and fire to prepare land for crops or livestock. The extensive cattle herds of the Masai in East Africa, water buffalo in Thailand, tea plantations in Sri Lanka, coca fields in Bolivia, fruit orchards in Chile, olive groves in Jordan, cocoa trees in Ghana, coconut plantations in Jamaica, rubber plantations in Malaysia, and coffee groves in Costa Rica are other examples of farm capital, mostly created by sweat-equity.

The ancient and modern irrigation systems along the Nile remind us that this capital formation has occurred for thousands of years. The hoes used by farmers in Niger, the machetes wielded by Colombian farmers, the chain saws employed by Ecuadorian colonists, and cactus fences planted by Mexican farmers illustrate that capital may come in small and, sometimes, unglamorous forms.

I also employ a narrow definition when discussing rural financial markets (RFMs). I use this term to denote transactions in rural areas that involve loans or deposits, done at least partly with financial instruments. While my main concern is with how formal or informal intermediaries help to facilitate finance, I am also interested in how individuals or small groups mobilize funds and make loans to each other without intermediaries.

I make a careful distinction between manmade capital and financial instruments (generalized claims on resources). In the sense I use these terms, only capital contributes directly to production. Funds or financial instruments, in turn, do not enter production directly, but may be used to purchase capital or noncapital inputs, held as assets, or converted into other assets or consumption goods. It is important to note that capital may play dual roles in a farm household; not only are these items gradually used up in production, but until they are worn out, they are also assets. It is only in this latter sense of being an asset that financial instruments and capital items are similar.

Another way of distinguishing between capital and financial instruments is by the transaction costs involved in converting them into something else. Typically, changing financial instruments into other forms involves few costs—low transaction costs are the major reason for the invention of money. In contrast, the transaction costs of converting capital items into other forms are typically relatively large. Also, the divergence between salvage value of most capital items and their use value deters decisions to convert capital items into other goods or services.

INTERSECTIONS

There are major overlaps between on-farm capital formation and RFMs. Loans allow farmers to purchase large capital items sooner than they could have done if they had to save sufficient funds to make the purchases. Also, firms that can borrow to cover part of the operating costs may realize higher incomes that, in turn, facilitate on-farm capital formation more rapidly than if loans were unavailable. Deposit services may also enhance capital formation by providing households with places to store savings increments until the firm has enough money to purchase a large capital item. Further, the ability to borrow may allow firms to undertake larger and riskier on-farm investments than operators would deem prudent in the absence of credit reserved (Baker 1968).

On a more aggregate scale, efficient financial markets facilitate capital formation in rural areas through helping to allocate resources more efficiently; surplus operators who expect low marginal rates of returns to investments in their operations can make deposits with financial intermediaries who, in turn, can lend these funds to individuals who expect high returns from further investments, but have too little cash to act on these opportunities. The more efficient allocation that results increases incomes of both saver and borrower and, thus, enhances their abilities and incentives to make further investments.

While financial markets play a significant role in on-farm capital formation where farmers buy and sell a large part of their inputs and products, it is important to remember that self-finance often dominates on-farm capital formation. This is especially true when RFMs are rudimentary and where these markets are severely repressed. It is too often forgotten that humans have made immense investments in irrigation systems, in clearing of land, in livestock, in terracing, in buildings, and in equipment without the assistance of formal financial systems and government credit programs.

Before leaving this topic, it is useful to briefly critique a spurious intersection between farm and RFMs—the claim that a low interest rate on formal loans induces farmers to substitute capital (machinery) for labor. While often mentioned in development literature as the main adverse effect of cheap agricultural loans, on careful analysis this appears not to be the case for two reasons:

First, most farmers in LICs operate in fragmented financial markets that have real interest rates on loans ranging from highly negative to highly positive. There is no a priori reason to conclude that one of these interest rates—the concessionary rate charged on a formal loan—dictates the subjective discount rate applied by the borrower to the future stream of benefits expected from an investment in machinery. (If this were true, it would imply that high interest rates cause farmers to substitute labor for capital.) Even if there were a one-to-one relationship between an interest rate on a loan and a borrower's subjective discount rate, what discount would an individual use who has two loans, one with a low interest rate and another with a high rate? One answer is that, in fragmented financial markets especially, interest rates on individual loans have no direct tie to a borrower's subjective discount rate.

Second, financial instruments are highly fungible (interchangeable); a borrowed unit of currency is identical to one owned by the borrower. Further, almost all farmers in LICs have multiple sources and uses of liquidity. Thus, one should not conclude that marginal changes in use of borrowed liquidity are highly correlated with the justification given for the loan. Most borrowers have the option of exercising financial substitution, even if the intent of the loan is to buy machinery. Part of this substitution may involve hiring more labor. Given this, it is not clear why a change in the price of one source of liquidity—the interest rate on a formal loan—would alter the relative desirability of two possible uses of liquidity; for example, purchasing machinery compared to hiring more labor. Interest rates have no direct effect on the marginal returns expected from labor or capital and, therefore, have little or no direct effect on factor-use proportions by borrowers.

If concessionary interest rates on formal loans affect factor-use proportions, it is more likely an indirect relationship. That is, low interest rates induce lenders to concentrate loans in the hands of borrowers who have the most secure collateral and those who impose the lowest transaction costs on the intermediary (Gonzales-Vega 1984). If these preferred borrowers happen to use a higher ratio of capital to labor than do those potential borrowers rationed from the market by the low interest rates, then the overall ratio of capital to labor will increase.

RESEARCH ON CAPITAL FORMATION

Farm capital is difficult to analyze for at least five reasons. First, complications are encountered because capital items are heterogeneous and difficult to value. This causes serious aggregation problems. What value does the researcher assign to a capital item that can only be sold for less than its acquisition price, but is worth more for production purposes than its salvage value? Second, some capital items, such as housing and vehicles, are used for both production and consumption. Third, some capital formation occurs in qualitative changes. How does a researcher measure and evaluate changes in soil productivity enhanced through drainage, fertility improvements, weed-control programs, or removal of stones? How should changes in human capital be measured when they occur largely through experience gained from trial and error? Fourth, when is a capital item held by the farm operator because it is a desirable asset rather than because of its direct contributions to production? And fifth, how can the researcher keep the costs of collecting data within reasonable bounds when farmers are often reticent, or unable, to reveal a complete inventory of their capital and assets, and when study of capital formation is best done with costly time-series information or panel data?

These problems have dissuaded most researchers, in both high-income countries as well as low-income countries, from doing comprehensive studies of this topic. Exceptions to this are extensive farm surveys carried out by Brazilian and U.S. academics during the early 1970s in southern Brazil (Adams et al. 1975), a handful of case studies by anthropologists (e.g., Firth and Yamey 1964), and interesting work by agricultural economists in Japan (e.g., Izumida 1987).

It has been more common for researchers to do partial analyses of single types of farm capital, such as machinery, irrigation systems, human capital, livestock, perennial crops, buildings, and land-quality changes. Also, it has been more common for researchers to do cross-sectional studies and treat capital generation as an event, rather than to collect time-series or panel data that would allow analysis of the process of capital formation. Because of the lack of data, researchers have often been forced to study the contribution of capital and technological change by looking at unexplained residuals.

RESEARCH AGENDA ON CAPITAL FORMATION

While the makeup of farm-level capital, how it evolves over time, and the contributions it makes to overall development are interesting intellectual questions, answering these questions exceeds the patience and resources available to most researchers, especially in LICs. Researchers will be forced to continue to limit their analyses in this area to partial studies that are most interesting to policy makers. If it is important to demonstrate that substantial amounts of on-farm capital formation occur, and to show that it makes an important contribution to development, representative case studies may be more realistic research tools than are large surveys. While not satisfying intellectually, those who are interested in the overall process of on-farm capital formation must accept this process as largely taking place in a black box.

Instead of attempting to measure on-farm capital formation or to document its contribution to development, researchers will be forced to focus on how to speed investments in particular capital items and assess whether it is desirable to do so. This will include documenting the impact of important economic policies on these investments. The bulk of the research, therefore, will be on some particular capital form and on particular conditions or policies that affect these investments by farmers.

The capital forms that receive priority in a given country will be highly time-and-place specific. For example, in the late 1960s and early 1970s, tubewell irrigation in many parts of the southern Asia was an important part of capital formation and merited substantial research. In contrast, in the late 1980s, the Peoples' Republic of China was making major decisions on farm mechanization, considerations that could have benefitted from systematic analysis. Still other countries, such as Haiti, many nations in Africa, and Nepal, need to encourage more on-farm investments to slow the ravages of erosion; research might provide assistance in making these decisions.

Because of the possibilities of labor substitution as well as complementarities, farm machinery will likely be a high-priority research item in many LICs. It is also clear the improvement and extension of irrigation systems will be necessary to sustain growth in agricultural output in many countries. Likewise, investments in conservation practices will be necessary in almost all LICs if our generation is to pass on land and water resources that sustain rather than hobble development. Many farmers will also need to expand their livestock herds, plant more tree crops, and learn modern farming practices if those who people the twenty-first century are to be fed and clothed better than those of the twentieth century.

It is easier to identify the conditions and policies that merit research priority when it comes to stimulating on-farm capital formation. On a broad scale, it is largely the ability and willingness of farmers to make farm investments that determine the pace of farm-level capital formation. Ability to invest is strongly influenced by farmers' income, ability to borrow funds or resources, and education and experience. The willingness to invest, in turn, is largely conditioned by the returns farmers expect from additional investments in on-farm capital. Expected prices of products and inputs, yield expectations, risk considerations, and subjective discount rates applied to the expected benefits from the investments are additional considerations. Insecure land title and tenure can also have a major impact on the willingness of farm operators to make investments. Where this is a problem, it merits special research attention.

As suggested earlier, RFMs facilitate on-farm capital formation and, in many countries, credit projects are the major instrument used by governments and donors to stimulate investments in machinery, tree crops, livestock, irrigation, conservation, buildings, and even education. Credit projects are frequently accompanied by sizeable subsidies through concessionary interest rates, capital grants, toleration of loan defaults, and free training. Recent research has shown that many of these projects have not worked as intended, that formal RFMs are not efficient, and that they are distributing their services and subsidies inequitably. It has become increasingly clear that RFMs can only bolster development in general, and on-farm capital formation in particular, if they operate more efficiently and equitably, a subject to which I now turn.

RESEARCH ON RFMS

RFMs in low-income countries have increasingly drawn the attention of researchers, especially since the late 1960s. Even prior to that, a few substantial studies were done on the structure of rural credit markets, especially in Asia. Increased RFM research resulted from: (1) large government- and donor-sponsored farm credit programs initiated during the 1960s and 1970s, (2) attempts to create new farm credit organizations, and (3) efforts to substitute formal loans for informal borrowing. In some countries, farm loans became the main tool for promoting rural development. These programs were usually targeted at accelerating the use of modern technology and increasing on-farm capital formation. Much of the research associated with these efforts was either in the form of credit-impact studies aimed at documenting borrowers' benefits from expanded loan use, or studies to uncover exploitation by informal lenders.

By the early 1970s, it became clear that many of these credit programs had serious problems and that much of the research done was of limited use in forming solutions. This was documented in a worldwide review of small farmer credit programs conducted by the Agency for International Development (AID) during 1972–73 (Donald 1976), and reinforced by an FAO-sponsored conference in Rome on agricultural credit in 1975. Major problems included extensive loan defaults, concentration of concessionary-priced loans in the hands of borrowers who were relatively well off, few rural people with access to formal financial services, credit programs that were not self-sustaining, few deposits mobilized in rural areas, and growing doubts about how effective loans were in stimulating investments and output.

Because financial markets are interwoven, it is important that a research matrix reflect the most important aspects of these markets, of which there are at least three: The *first* dimension is made up of the three layers of participants in RFMs: individual borrowers and savers, financial intermediaries, and policy makers. The *second* dimension divides financial activities into those carried out by formal intermediaries (regulated) and those conducted in informal markets (unregulated). The *third* dimension further subdivides the above into loan and deposit issues.

This matrix recognizes the intimate relationship between policy, intermediary behavior, and financial services. Likewise, it acknowledges that formal and informal finance are entwined, and that deposits and loans are often mirror images of each other. The matrix also encourages researchers to view RFMs as linked parts rather than as a series of independent credit projects. It further highlights the importance of considering deposit mobilization along with lending.

Placing previous research into this matrix allows identification of gaps in analysis. For example, prior to 1970, most RFM research focused on the borrower/saver dimension, with some analysis on intermediaries, but largely ignored deposits. During the 1970s, more research emphasis was given to the policy-making dimension and to deposits. In the 1980s, informal finance and research on intermediary behavior and performance received much more attention, along with study of the performance of the overall system.

RFM problems and policies in many LICs are surprisingly similar. This results in a relatively small number of research issues that are of interest to a large number of policy makers as well as researchers. Five candidates for this list are: (1) Documenting the *transaction costs* involved in RFMs and their distribution among the participants in these markets (this includes studying how new financial technologies and changes in policies affect these costs); (2) explaining why some rural people have *access* to formal loans and deposits while others do not; (3) understanding what causes formal *loan recovery* problems; (4) studying how *deposit mobilization* affects the performance of RFMs, and (5) analyzing the financial services provided by various forms of *informal finance* in order to design more desirable formal financial systems. A few additional comments on each of these topics may show why they are likely to be of interest to both policy makers and researchers.

Transaction costs show the amount of financial friction in RFMs and are, perhaps, the best measure of the overall efficiency of a financial system. Studying the allocation of these costs among participants also provides insights into how financial services are rationed. Currently, some students of RFMs are arguing that major reductions in these costs will be necessary before formal financial markets can service, on a sustained basis, many of the rural people who now do not have access to formal loans or deposit accounts. Systematic study of transaction costs can give policy makers and managers of financial institutions useful insights into the costs of their programs and projects and, at the same time, allow researchers to gain fundamental insights into the operations of RFMs. Transaction costs for a doctor of financial systems are analogous to the blood pressure taken by a physician as a measure of a person's health. Each measure tells a lot about the general health of a patient, be it a person or an RFM.

The proportion of rural individuals and firms who can borrow from, or deposit surpluses in, a formal institution is an excellent proxy for the extent to which RFMs assist in allocating resources efficiently. A repressed or underdeveloped financial system reaches only a few of the individuals who can productively use formal loans. A severely repressed financial system does a particularly poor job of connecting surplus households and firms to a system that facilitates resource reallocation. Increasing the number of rural people, especially the poor, who have access to formal loans is a primary policy objective in many LICs. Clarifying why financial markets are slow to embrace new customers in rural areas provides fundamental insights into how these markets operate and also has important short-run policy implications.

Defaults on agricultural loans made from government or donor funds are a major concern of policy makers in a number of LICs. Chronic defaults drain government budgets and also undermine the ability to sustain government-sponsored credit programs. In a fundamental sense, loan recovery reflects the quality of the relationships between borrowers and lenders. Chronic recovery problems indicate that there is an inability on the part of the lender to verify credit worthiness, that politics are heavily involved, or that borrowers find their relationships with lenders unsatisfactory and decide to seek a "divorce" through the expediency of default. Even worse, defaults destroy one of the most important products of financial intermediation: sustained working relationships between borrowers and intermediaries.

During the past few years, an increasing number of governments have been unable to sustain previous levels of funding for agricultural credit programs. This problem has been reinforced by the declining willingness of donors to provide loans for government credit efforts. This has forced some government institutions to place more emphasis on mobilizing deposits in rural areas. At the same time, a few researchers have been arguing that RFMs would operate more efficiently and equitably if their deposit-to-loan ratios were increased substantially. This ratio shows the extent to which RFMs are self-funded, or conversely, the extent to which they are dependent on outside funds. Outside funds may impose substantial costs on RFMs, open them to political intrusions, and seduce them into ignoring deposits. RFMs that have high loan-to-deposit ratios appear to perform better with respect to transaction costs, loan recovery, and proportion of rural population serviced than do those systems with low ratios.

As suggested earlier, policy makers have traditionally been interested in informal finance only in a perverse way of seeking its demise, particularly in South Asia. Recent research, however, is suggesting that some forms of informal finance in rural areas provide financial services efficiently. Also, some rural people, especially the poor, find that informal financial services are more valuable to them than are government-sponsored programs. The popularity of informal finance in rural areas and high rates of loan recovery in these systems are signs of this. Analysis of informal finance can provide valuable information on the types of financial services that many people are demanding, along with insights into arrangements and technologies that people informally develop to keep the costs of providing these services low.

CONCLUSION

Farm-level capital formation and rural financial markets in LICs are some of the most difficult research topics that social scientists treat. Both processes occur over wide geographic areas, include a large number of participants, and involve activities that are costly and tedious to substantiate. These research problems are exacerbated by fuzzy thinking about what capital is and what financial markets do. While these two sets of activities do intersect, they are vastly different processes and ought to be treated as such by researchers.

It will be extremely difficult to document the overall contribution of farm-level capital formation to development. In addition, few policy makers are willing to pay for this type of research. Those who are interested in this process must gain insights into it through case studies and through analyses of those types of capital that policy makers are attempting to promote.

Opportunities for doing useful research on RFMs are more promising. Additional analysis should focus on understanding why RFMs operate inefficiently and also limit their services to such a small part of the population. Because politics is often involved in credit programs, those doing RFM research must be sensitive to the risks and opportunities this entails.

NOTE

1. Dale W Adams is with the Agricultural Finance Program, Department of Agricultural Economics and Rural Sociology, The Ohio State University.

REFERENCES

Adams, Dale W, et al. 1975. Farm growth in Brazil. Final report of a study prepared for the Agency for International Development by the Department of Agricultural Economics and Rural Sociology, The Ohio State University, Columbus.

Baker, C. B. 1968. Credit in the production organization of the firm. *American Journal of Agricultural Economics* 50:50720.

Donald, Gordon. 1976. *Credit for small farmers in developing countries*. Boulder, Colo.: Westview Press.

Firth, Raymond, and B. S. Yamey, eds. 1964. *Capital, savings in peasant societies*. Chicago: Aldine Publishing Co.

Gonzales-Vega, Claudio. 1984. Cheap agricultural credit: Redistribution in reverse. In *Undermining rural development with cheap credit*. Edited by Dale W Adams, Douglas H. Graham, and J. D. von Pischke, 12032. Boulder, Colo.: Westview Press.

Izumida, Yoichi. 1987. Present state of money flow in rural Japan. Paper presented at a seminar on agricultural credit sponsored by the Asian Productivity Organization, 110 December, Tokyo, Japan.

CHAPTER 9

AGRICULTURAL-SECTOR ANALYSIS AND RURAL DEVELOPMENT: SOCIAL SCIENCE RESEARCH PRIORITIES

Clark W. Reynolds[1]

INTRODUCTION

The purpose of agricultural-sector models has been "to capture the most important structural and behavioral relationships within agriculture and between agriculture and the rest of the economy, on the one hand, and to be potentially useful to the policy maker as a planning tool to help select and formulate a sector program on the other hand" (Thorbecke 1973). The primary focus of this paper is on the need for applied, multidisciplinary problem-solving research emphasizing linkages between agriculture and the rest of the economy and the transition process between rural and urban development. Such research is particularly well suited to the objectives of the Social Science Agricultural Agenda Project and is essential if agricultural modeling is to be effectively accommodated within the broader scope of development analysis and policy making.

Those involved in rural development analysis must increasingly deal with the problem of pervasive underemployment and low income that results from improvements in production and productivity in the agricultural sector, given high rates of rural population growth and the limitations to labor-absorptive capacity in the modern industrial sector. The result is the rapid growth of what have been termed in this chapter the *rural and urban transitional sectors*. Because of high labor intensity, low capital requirements, and flexibility, it is necessary that employment opportunities fall between direct agricultural production and modern manufacturing services in the major urban centers if production and productivity gains are to be diffused among a growing work force, only a falling share of which can be sustained in agriculture per se. This paper focuses on the potential from nonagricultural production in rural households, villages, small towns, and regional centers (the rural transitional sector), given the tendency toward overcrowding and underemployment in major urban areas.

Although increased attention is now being paid to the urban informal sector, development analysis still tends to ignore the potential for employment and productivity growth in the rural nonagricultural sector. This is an area for which those familiar with social science agricultural research are ideally qualified, since such activities have direct functional, institutional, regional, and social linkages to the agricultural sector. Their study calls for a more comprehensive and less formal framework for rural-development analysis than that of most agricultural-sector modeling to date, a method that might be termed a cross-disciplinary social systems approach to rural development.[2]

Such an approach would draw upon detailed microlevel economic, social, and technological studies of farm households and related production units, both agricultural and nonagricultural, as well as rural industry and service activities at the local and regional level. Studies would be made in terms of dynamic optimization, technology adoption, budget analysis, on- and off-farm labor allocation including migration, and investment in physical, financial, and human capital. The research on rural development accordingly would be extended to cover links between farm-household behavior and the evolution of nonagricultural activities in the rural sector, including villages, small towns, and regional centers. Along with a better understanding of the rural development process, the research would provide policy-relevant information on the tradeoffs between diversified rural development and the present trend toward the concentration of production and employment in major metropolitan areas, as well as approaches to the goals of income and employment generation without having to resort to the "escape valve" of external migration.[3]

Initial work in the area of multidisciplinary, problem-solving sectoral modeling was begun by Glenn L. Johnson at Michigan State University. Johnson's experience as director of the Consortium for the Study of Nigerian Rural Development (CSNRD) led to the design of a computerized systems simulation model for Nigeria, based on three years of field research to learn "the crucial components to be modeled" (Johnson 1987). A multidisciplinary mixture of techniques and approaches was used to arrive at a model intended to explicitly link decision-making behavior to predicted outcomes, with the goal of increasing the usefulness of sector models to policy makers. As a result of this experience (which was also applied to the Korean case), Johnson has formulated general guidelines for what are termed "holistic models of problem-solving (PS) and subject-matter (SM) domains" (1987). These represent attempts to model the structural dynamics of society in specific problem-solving or subject-matter contexts and might well be applicable to the analysis of links between agriculture and the "transitional" sectors as discussed below.[4]

In addition to such modeling, there is the need for complementary work on the microanalysis of rural decision-making units, including the path-determined process of adaptation of individual, household, and rural-enterprise behavior to changing conditions in the social, political, economic, and technological environment. Given the growing degree of international economic interdependence, in which income and productivity levels in developing regions are likely to have an increasing impact on conditions in advanced industrial areas, such research on the relations between agriculture, the rural-transitional sector, and urban development take on major importance for both donor and recipient countries.

THE PROBLEM OF THE RURAL SECTOR AND UNDEREMPLOYMENT IN LATE-DEVELOPING COUNTRIES

Considerable progress has been made in increasing agricultural production and productivity in most developing areas. Miracles have been accomplished from new seed/fertilizer technologies applied to tropical agriculture, permitting windfall gains in the yields of a number of basic food groups. Yet in much of the developing world, malnutrition is widespread and growing. Schuh characterizes the international agricultural economy today as being "in a massive disequilibrium" (see Schuh, Chapter 2 of this section). A similar "disequilibrium" situation exists within most of the major developing countries, including Brazil, India, Indonesia, Mexico, and Nigeria (and large parts of tropical Africa). As a consequence, for many, the issue today is distribution more than production. How can agricultural-productivity growth and increased and improved goods consumption be diffused among nations, regions, and social groups to serve the joint goals of allocative efficiency and equity? The resolution of such issues is a domestic and international problem that goes well beyond the agricultural sector per se and can only be addressed by taking a broader approach to rural development and the rural/urban transition.

The issue of food distribution has given rise to moral philosophical approaches that stress the social implications of basic human needs. Such approaches focus on the reallocation of income and purchasing power in response to alleged "entitlements" to insure adequate levels of welfare to all social groups.[5] A direct short-term approach to the problem of entitlements is through policy-induced transfers. An indirect but more permanent approach is to create the means for disadvantaged groups to increase their income and purchasing power through new opportunities for productive employment.

In the area of food policy, traditional distributional schemes have tended to utilize price ceilings and broad-based state distribution and food-aid programs. These are costly measures that have been shown to work against agricultural development in countries of application by depressing farm-gate prices while subsidizing consumption, often without consideration of need. Alternative direct-transfer schemes have been devised to permit a more selective targeting of food subsidies, through the selective provision of food stamps and related measures, aimed at those groups that are most nutritionally at risk. Such programs are designed to reduce the cost of food subsidies with fewer distortions of agricultural prices and a more equitable allocation of the benefits. The programs are of considerable value, particularly where targeting is most cost effective, such as in urban slum areas, although there is a danger that the costs may become excessive in the case of the rural poor (Timmer, Falcon, and Pearson 1983).

However, even the most efficient food-distribution schemes deal, at best, with relief of symptoms of poverty rather than its root causes. Low incomes are a function of low labor productivity and the associated lack of diversified remunerative employment. Persistent and growing urban poverty in late-developing countries traces back to a lack of diversified development in the rural sector and at the regional level. This in turn stems from a failure of rural-development policy to address the problem of rural underemployment outside of agricultural production.

Notwithstanding impressive gains in agricultural production and productivity in developing countries, and the need to further diffuse such gains in regions where productivity remains low, the problem of rural underemployment has grown beyond the dimensions of traditional agricultural-development strategies. Even where distortions in factor prices have been eliminated, along with barriers to the pursuit of dynamic comparative advantage in agricultural production, agriculture alone is proving incapable of absorbing increases in the rural labor force in much of the developing world. There is an inadequate diversification of nonagricultural investment in rural areas and adjacent towns, largely as a result of insufficient infrastructure and overconcentration of industrial and service development in the major metropolitan areas.

Since agricultural growth alone is proving incapable of meeting the employment needs of the rural population, there exists a burgeoning number of rural underemployed forced to supply labor services for wages at (or temporarily below) subsistence levels. The absence of productive opportunities in the rural areas leads to excessive rural-to-urban and international migration, serving to dampen real wage increases in the receiving regions regardless of its productivity growth. In some cases, the modernization and commercialization of peasant agriculture may even exacerbate the problem by displacing peasant cultivators through the consolidation of small holdings, dividing families, and forcing them into a rural proletariat. This is not to condemn the commercialization process, which clearly generates additional rental streams that may be saved and reinvested in further employment creation, but describes its effect in terms of social dislocation, income instability, and the uncertainty of job search for peasant producers who previously cultivated their "own" plots through rental or sharecropping. The effect is to exacerbate the problem of underemployment stemming from labor abundance in rural areas.[6]

The integrated rural-development approach, which has been given considerable attention in recent years, has the advantage of focusing not only on agriculture but on programs of technical assistance, basic infrastructure, rural education, health care, and nutrition. However, there has been insufficient focus on the problems of rural underemployment and the development of diverse employment opportunities on farms and adjacent villages and towns. Hence, such programs fail to deal with the dynamic of a burgeoning rural population that (even because of such programs) learns to expect improvements in income and welfare along with ever-higher levels of education and improved employment opportunities for future generations. Moreover, integrated rural-development programs have their own limitations since they tend to draw scarce human resources and financial capital from urban centers to support programs that cannot be sustained once those inputs are removed.

LESSONS FROM THE AGRICULTURAL-DEVELOPMENT EXPERIENCE

Some of the earliest efforts to place the agricultural sector in the context of general-development theory made use of basic two-sector models, rural and urban, in which the principal link was through labor flows from agriculture to industry.[7] Raul Prebisch and the Economic Commission for Latin America argued that agricultural-productivity growth would release labor to the urban sector, along with increased food production, making possible strategies of import-substituting industrial development (to be paid for, implicitly, by distortions in the urban/rural terms of trade). In these models there was little discussion of the process of labor transition from agriculture to urban employment, or concern about the possibility of increased underemployment and lagging real wages arising from rural labor forces exceeding urban demand.[8]

Analysis of the history of Japanese agricultural development shows how that country was able to promote significant increases in both rural education and regional industrial growth, drawing labor into nonagricultural employment. Increased levels of productivity and real wages were achieved without the degree of dislocation and excess urbanization that now characterizes many of the late-deve loping countries. This was possible, in part, because of the relatively low rate of population growth in Japan (about one percent per annum) during its "demographic transition," when the farm labor force began to decline in absolute terms.[9]

The U.S. experience relied much more on migration of labor to major metropolitan centers as we see from the synoptic "A History of American Agriculture from Jefferson to Revolution to Crisis" prepared for the first SSAAP meeting by Richard Kirkendall (see Part I, Chapter 2, of this book). The impressive growth of agricultural production and productivity in the United States, along with increased rural wages and farm incomes, was associated with new income streams (to use Schuh's terminology) brought about by labor-displacing technology appropriate for large-scale cultivation on highly productive land with adequate rainfall or irrigation. Ultimately most of the U.S. agricultural work force relocated in urban areas, where growth was sufficiently rapid to permit significant increases in real wages. This pattern of massive rural-to-urban migration is not an option for many late-developing countries, at least in the short to medium run (Olmstead 1986).

Only a few years ago, the movement of labor from rural to urban sectors, which was associated with increased agri cultural-productivity growth, was regarded relatively automatic and mutually beneficial. It is now clearly a problem that afflicts not only Latin America and the Caribbean but much of Africa and Asia as well. In the case of Mexico, Ian Scott (1982) sees an example of very unbalanced regional development leading to excessive growth of the central cities that is characteristic of Latin America. The cost of overurbanization is registered in terms of environmental pollution, congestion, problems of governability, rising public infrastructure and maintenance outlays, increasing underemployment, and social unrest. These costs are associated with growth opportunities foregone in peripheral regions. The problem is not only of internal agglomeration economies gained and externalities ignored in the market process but of public-policy failure. He calls for government decisions to counteract the tendency for capital to be invested in the core areas where there is less uncertainty, greater access to markets and centers of power, and more amenities for investors, managers, and professionals. "Greater decentralization, devolution, and participation" is needed from core to "periphery" of developing countries such as Mexico (Scott 1982).

Sen has shown that India's impressive growth in agricultural production and productivity in response to new seed varieties, fertilizer, and irrigation has not led to a comparable diffusion of productive employment in the rural sector. This has led to an underemployment crisis and important components of the Indian-subcontinent population are unable to purchase the food that the country produces; the result is the export of surpluses side by side with poverty and malnutrition (Sen 1975). While some have been tempted to attack the "Green Revolution" for such disparities between productivity growth and productive employment, such arguments reflect a latter-day Luddite confusion between cause and effect. The problem was not that new technologies were bad because their incidence was uneven by region, type of agriculture, and income class, but there was a failure to develop other complementary labor-absorbing technologies in transitional sectors that might have provided new job opportunities for those unable to reap the direct benefits of agricultural technology.

Must late-developing countries wait for the pull of industrial growth in major cities in order to experience significant increases in wages and per capita incomes through rural-to-urban migration? Will rural populations tend to dry up in LDCs as they have in advanced industrial countries? Professor Schuh, citing John S. Mills, T. W. Schultz, and B. F. Johnston, refers to the "one iron law of economics" in which the agricultural share of employment declines as development proceeds. "This 'law' is important because it creates a serious adjustment problem for agriculture that is rooted in the forces of economic development." Given an income elasticity of demand for food that is less than that for nonagricultural goods and services, there is a tendency for labor to shift out of agriculture as per capita incomes rise, and this is exacerbated by the tendency of the natural population growth rate in rural areas to exceed that in urban centers, at the same time technical change in agriculture tends to reduce the demand for labor (see Schuh, Chapter 2 of this section). In the future, rural-sector analysis must deal with ways in which this iron law may be moderated so as to avoid the establishment of a low-level equilibrium trap of labor in major urban centers by providing diverse employment opportunities in rural areas and surrounding towns.

Agricultural-policy analysis will increasingly be challenged to find ways to further the diffusion of sectoral productivity gains through the rest of the economy, and analytical modeling will require more attention to nonagricultural linkages at the household and regional levels. The rural/urban transition, which was once regarded as a normal by-product of increased agricultural productivity and industrialization, has given rise to new complexities in recent years, owing to the lagged effect of the demographic explosion on the supply of labor emanating from the rural sector and the relatively limited absorptive capacity of industrial development as it has proceeded in most LDCs. Education alone and conventional definitions of integrated rural development are insufficient to deal with the economics of the transitional sector.

As Johnston, Kilby, and Tomich report in a forthcoming comparison of the earlier Taiwan and more recent Mexican experiences, "With the share of total labor force in agriculture down to 37 percent in 1980 (in Mexico), expansion of employment opportunities in the nonfarm sector, *both rural and urban* (emphasis mine), is of even greater importance than the absorption of labor into productive employment in the agricultural sector" (Johnston et al. forthcoming). The authors make the point that late-developing countries such as Mexico face more complex problems of labor absorption than did the "success-story" countries of Japan, Korea, and Taiwan. A recent book by M. S. Grindle (1987) makes a similar point, that agricultural production is no longer viable as the "engine of growth" for rural Mexico, though it was successful in Japan, Taiwan, and the Indian Punjab. Instead, she sees a *diversified rural employment strategy* (emphasis mine) as the key to rural development in Mexico. Without off-farm opportunities, the rural population will continue in increasing numbers to seek income through temporary and permanent national and international migration (Grindle 1987).

My own work on shift-share analysis of total-factor productivity growth in Mexico shows that the shift of labor from agriculture to the major urban centers is associated with a sharp deceleration and even decline in output per worker in greater Mexico City, a decline that is concentrated in the tertiary sector and particularly low-productivity services (which have absorbed most of the employment growth in the last two decades). Whereas a significant component of national productivity growth in earlier years was associated with shifts of labor from rural to urban activities, it is now evident that this movement is exerting a deterring effect on growth that has only been exacerbated by the post-1982 debt crisis. It is clear that regional productivity-enhancing policies that slow the rate of movement to the major cities are essential to Mexico's future development (Reynolds and Alejo 1986).

Finally, an ingenious and persuasive model has been developed by de Janvry and Sadoulet to illustrate that "a 'broad-based' pattern of rural development, as opposed to agricultural development with concentrated landownership and hired laborers under conditions of surplus labor, will support a larger long-run aggregate demand creation and import demand for coarse grains and feedstuffs."[10] Their paper focuses on the consequences for increased industrial growth and productivity (and demand for feed grain imports) from an increase in cereal production. The strategy would aim at increasing employment, wages, and productivity in the agricultural sector by favoring a more unimodal land-tenure system and labor-intensive cultivation methods. It would be useful to extend such an analysis beyond agriculture per se to include the impact of technical change in food production on increased employment and income, and final demand in the nonfarm rural sector (small-scale industry) on employment and income, and final demand.

LINKS BETWEEN AGRICULTURE AND THE RURAL AND URBAN TRANSITIONAL SECTORS

Given the goals of increasing real wages, alleviating poverty, and expanding the national market, it has been argued that development strategies must shift their focus increasingly to the "transitional sectors" that lie between agriculture and large-scale industry. These sectors are termed "transitional" since they provide employment for labor released from agricultural production and for labor unable to find adequate employment in the urban formal sector due to lagged demographic growth. The first and most important of these sectors from the viewpoint of a broader approach to rural development is the rural-transitional sector.

The rural-transitional sector includes nonagricultural economic activities of farm households, off-farm employment, and production in adjoining cities and towns. While such activities are not necessarily part of the food system per se, they are likely to have both demand and supply linkages to agriculture. Dennis Anderson deals with "rural nonfarm activities" (his equivalent to our "rural-transitional sector") as based primarily on linkages to agricultural activities and the supply of nonfood goods and services to the rural population. However, it can be shown that the rural enterprises are increasingly involved in the production of goods for urban and export markets (as in the cases of Taiwan, India, Iran, Mexico, and even the rural areas of northern Italy). Anderson's World Bank publication shows a breakdown of nonfarm rural employment in LDCs as follows: manufacturing (textiles, food processing, wood and furniture, metal and machinery) 20–30 percent, services 20–35 percent, commerce 15–30 percent, construction, transport. He argues that:

> Rural nonfarm activities are, thus, an essential element in the process of economic development and structural change from rural-agricultural to urban-industrial economies;
>
> Nonfarm activities lie on, or between, the boundaries of the usual rural/urban and agricultural/nonagricultural categories. These classifications inevitably involve a degree of arbitrariness in imposing a single dividing line on what is, in fact, a continuous spectrum of situations; and
>
> The prospects for a decent income for the landless and near landless will continue increasingly to become a function of earnings opportunities in nonfarm labor markets, both rural and urban.[11]

Anderson reviews the economic rationale for rural nonfarm enterprises as follows:

1. High labor intensity (410 times higher for small firms);
2. High price elasticity of product demand;
3. Competitive wage rates (low wages for unskilled rural labor in exchange for "vocational training" in the informal sector, often leading to entry into the formal sector);

4. High capital productivity;
5. Reduction of urban industrial concentration with corresponding high municipal costs, pollution, congestion;
6. Positive consequences for intersectoral income distribution.

Anderson calls upon government to play a pivotal role in providing the preconditions for rural nonfarm industrial long-term growth and development. These preconditions include the need to:

1. Remove special tariffs and subsidies that favor large industries and the importation of capital-intensive inputs;
2. Provide adequate social and economic infrastructure to rural areas: roads, electricity, water, storage, schools, health clinics (labor-intensive public works also serve as an important source of employment);
3. Facilitate needed commercial services, in cooperation with the private sector: supply and stock raw materials, support warehousing of local output, market and display goods in new markets, diffuse production innovations.

Anderson claims that nonfarm, small-scale enterprises in the "informal sector" tend to suffer more from the exclusion from government services than they benefit from the avoidance of taxes and regulations. He argues that small rural enterprises cannot compete with larger firms in the formal sector unless they are provided with equal access to credit, marketing outlets, and managerial and other skills, which helps to explain their current underdeveloped status. Along with most authors, he points out that the demand for rural industrial goods and services depends primarily on a growing agricultural sector. There has been found to be a high elasticity of demand for nonfood goods and services with respect to changes in rural incomes and agricultural output.

Chuta and Liedholm have done extensive research on the relative importance of nonfarm rural employment and income in developing countries (Chuta and Liedholm 1984). They have found that "rural industries and other rural nonfarm activities appear to provide a source of primary or secondary employment for 3050 percent of the rural labor force in developing countries." Most of these enterprises are very small scale, with less than five employees. Analysis of empirical data indicates that small-scale rural enterprises are more labor intensive and yield a higher return on capital than larger-scale urban industries. Their demand comes from three sources: local final demand; urban and international final demand; and forward and backward linkages to agriculture.

As in the case of Anderson, Chuta and Liedholm call upon government to assist in the promotion of rural nonfarm enterprises, to obtain substantial social and economic benefits, and to forestall greater rural-to-urban migration. They suggest the following policies:

1. Access to credit for the "informal sector," which usually must resort to more costly credit from moneylenders and suppliers;
2. Diversified credit-delivery system to meet the needs of very small-scale enterprises, using the support of official, private, and nongovernmental organizations (NGOs) and private voluntary organizations;
3. Technical and management assistance to improve product design, quality, and cost effectiveness;
4. Reliable provision of raw materials;
5. Market studies to determine existing and future demand of products suitable for rural enterprises; and
6. Agricultural research, extension, and infrastructure to increase production and thereby increase the demand for rural industrial goods and services.

The other locus of transitional employment for labor supplied by the rural sector is the *urban transitional (or urban informal) sector*. This sector is distinguished from the rural-transitional sector by requiring a major relocation of rural labor, customarily a movement to one of the major metropolitan centers. Earnings differentials between the urban formal and rural sectors attract rural-to-urban migrants. Gravity models of labor-market diffusion, together with queuing and segmentation theories, suggest that institutional barriers to entry into the formal sector permit these differentials to remain, leading to employment of the bulk of rural-to-urban migrants in low-level services and other informal sector activities. The hypothesis here is that increased support for employment-generating policies in the rural-transitional sector would offer greater prospects for the diffusion of productivity gains, domestic-market expansion, and labor absorption than has been appreciated by policy makers to date. The alternative to such policies is the continued flooding of the urban transitional sector, associated with "overcrowding" and the profusion of an underclass in the major metropolitan areas of the Third World.

Conventional two-sector models of rural and urban development tend to ignore the role that transitional sectors may play in the spread of productivity growth throughout the labor market. If permitted to develop, and if provided with adequate infrastructure and access to capital and intermediate goods, the rural-transitional sector may provide a demand pull, speeding the growth of real wages and the widening of the domestic market. However, lacking these conditions, it may simply act as a sponge for underemployed labor, diffusing the productivity gains from other sectors over a widening share of the work force, depressing the domestic terms of trade for informal sector activities, and perpetuating the impoverished conditions of the underclass.

When one reviews the experience of the advanced industrial countries, it is apparent that the dynamic role of these transitional sectors was critically important to the capture and transmission of rural rents into further productivity gains and the extension of national markets. Many of today's major production centers, including Sao Paulo, Chicago, and Kansas City, evolved from commercial outposts that formed part of the rural-transitional sector. Their development was spurred by improvements in transportation, communication, and infrastructure, as well as innovations in agricultural and animal-husbandry technology, and the opening of adjacent regions to cash-crop production for national and foreign markets.

There are regional centers throughout the developing world that have already begun to reveal their growth potential by providing inputs to the surrounding rural communities, engaging in food processing, and acting as entrepots for crop production for shipment to major urban markets or abroad. Gustavo Verduzco provides an excellent case study of the recent development of the city of Zamora in the Bajio of Mexico, in relation to the agricultural development of the surrounding valley. In particular, it was the "Green Revolution" of the 1960s and 1970s, combined with investment in complementary infrastructure (roads, irrigation, flood control), that made year-round cultivation of labor-intensive crops (such as strawberries) possible, greatly increasing the demand for farm labor, overall farm income, and nonfarm goods and services. He points out the key links between Zamora's growth and agricultural processing that "increasingly benefit the peasant members...the focus is on a crop that can be processed and marketed worldwide...a highly desirable form of rural development" (1984).

Zamora became the distribution center of agricultural inputs and the consumer market for goods produced locally, nationally, and abroad. Migrants came from poorer regions of nearby states to take farm jobs, while the sons and daughters of local farmers looked for small business opportunities in the town. Still, employment opportunities in Zamora have not been sufficiently large or lucrative enough to stave off migration from the region to the United States. In part, this is due to the limitation of Zamora as a commercial center for goods produced elsewhere, as well as the lack of local industry. The unequal distribution of good land and the concentration of agro-industry in the hands of the elite, which has limited the spread of benefits from agricultural expansion, also explain the continued high incidence of out-migration. Nevertheless, the case of Zamora indicates the potential for growth based on agriculturally linked rural-transitional-sector activities, as well as the need for more explicit attention by policy makers, even in the most promising circumstances, if nonagricultural production is to expand in the direction of urban and international markets (Verduzco 1984).

A review of the literature on rural industrialization by David Runsten deals with cases of successful export production (Runsten 1988). He contrasts the experience of Europe and Asia with that of Latin America where such industries are far more closely linked to agricultural and raw-material processing than to innovative production of goods for urban and export markets in competition with larger-scale urban industries. Runsten reviewed five successful case studies of employment creation in rural areas and adjacent towns in Latin America: (1) shoe production in Leon, Mexico, (2) frozen-vegetable processing linked with peasant production in Guatemala, (3) small ejido-initiated agro-industrial projects in Bajio, Mexico, (4) a wool-processing cooperative in Uruguay, and (4) a cacao producing, marketing, and processing cooperative in Bolivia.

The case study in highland Guatemala, in particular, demonstrates the effectiveness of linking agricultural production with new opportunities for nonfarm employment, thereby increasing the incomes of poor peasants and landless workers. The results show that peasants with little land but with abundant labor, sufficient water, credit, and technical assistance are very efficient producers of high-value vegetable crops; indeed, they are considerably more efficient than inexperienced and higher-cost large producers. Multinational firms contract with these small-scale suppliers, through the auspices of peasant marketing cooperatives, to obtain produce for their processing plants in adjacent towns.

Runsten compared this example with the typical situation in the Mexican Bajio region where multinational food-processing firms contract with large private farms for their produce, exacerbating income-distribution inequities in the region. He argues that the government could play an important role in providing incentives for firms to contract with ejidos that use relatively more labor-intensive cultivation methods, in order to provide more farm jobs and income, and, consequently, greater demand for nonfarm goods and services. Incentives would include access roads, small irrigation projects, appropriate agricultural research, technical assistance, cooperative formation, and access to credit.

The case study of El Ceibo, Bolivia, is another example of employment creation through agricultural production/processing/export linkages. El Ceibo is a "bottom-up cooperative where forward linkages (fermenting, drying, transporting, warehousing, and chocolate processing) increasingly benefit the peasant members...the focus is on a crop that can be processed and marketed worldwide...a highly desirable form of rural development." However, examples such as these do not yet address the potential for successful nonagricultural export production at the local level.

In his analysis, Runsten refers to the celebrated example of small-town industry in northern Italy to illustrate the industrial process of "flexible specialization" (as popularized in Piore and Sabel, *The Second Industrial Divide*.) In the Northern Italy case, "small- and medium-sized firms specializing in different manufacturing processes...combine to produce final products according to the shifts in demand." This strategy combines simple technology with relatively low-cost skilled labor (local "native" skills plus apprenticeships), often using raw materials from the surrounding rural areas.

He points out that Europe and Asia have been more successful at promoting small-scale, decentralized industrialization than Latin America, where traditionally a large-scale, mass-production-based approach to industrial policy is pursued. In order to tackle the impending employment crisis, he argues that Latin American countries must reverse that tradition and promote employment creation in rural areas and adjacent towns through a combined strategy of agricultural development and small-scale, rural industrialization. However, in Northern Italy, the failure of the flexible-specialization experience to spread to the less developed regions, such as the Mezzogiorno, and the apparent dependence of successful small-scale production on ready access to large-scale industrial, marketing, and financial outlets, indicates some of the limitations of "flexible specialization." Notwithstanding the enormous differences in the conditions of the educational, social, and political institutions, and the economic environment, there is ample scope for the study of such experiences, as well as those of the East African NICs, for purposes of comparison, contrast, and at least partial applicability to rural-industrialization policy in the Americas (Runsten 1988).

NEED FOR A BROADER RURAL-DEVELOPMENT-MODELING FRAMEWORK

An analytical framework capable of dealing with the employment- and income-generating effects of alternative rural-development strategies would include both the agricultural and rural-transitional sectors, and would show how complementary activities in each might lead to a broader social distribution of productivity gains throughout the economy. This augmented rural-sector model would fit more effectively into a national development framework in which the urban economy is also disaggregated into its formal and transitional components.

In Latin America, there has been growing interest in the role of the urban informal sector. Some see this sector as productivity enhancing in its own right (De Soto 1986), permitting economic growth in areas repressed in the formal sector by government and business barriers. Others see the informal sector as a pool of underemployed labor subject to exploitation and as a latent political-pressure group that is not co-opted by the state and that can be mobilized to apply political pressures for regime changes. Whichever approach is taken, there is little question that the urban economy, formal or informal, is unable to absorb sufficient rural labor at rising real wages in many late-developing countries. If growth is to take place with a reasonable balance in income shares by regions, social groups, occupations, and educational levels, the rural-transitional sector will require major attention in conjunction with growth of agricultural production and productivity.

The evidence of many countries indicates that there is no guarantee that improvements in agricultural production and productivity will increase real wages for the mass of the rural population if the supply of labor is sufficiently elastic. Indeed, where land tenure is skewed toward concentration, productivity gains may increase the rent-to-wage ratio with an adverse impact on the factor share of wages.[12] And if demand for agricultural production is inelastic, falling rural/urban terms of trade may depress the rural wage level, despite increases in marginal physical product. Moreover, when the rural work force exceeds the resource base available for subsistence cultivation, labor will be "pushed" into the cities, depressing wages in the urban informal sector and increasing the elasticity of supply of low-skilled labor throughout the economy. In short, just as a developing agricultural economy may release a "surplus" of resource rents for diversified development, it may also release a parallel "surplus" of low-wage labor that will swell the urban underclass and increase pressures for emigration. Hence, the rural-development problem to which sector analysis must direct its efforts in the coming years is to find ways to productively employ the labor that is released by increased productivity in agriculture.[13] Notwithstanding the experience of advanced industrial countries, if sufficient attention is paid to transitional-sector development and to conditions of small-holder agriculture, *there may be a mitigation of the consequences of an "iron law of rural development"* for some late-developing countries, even though the share of agricultural production and employment for most economies is bound to decline during the development process.

Abundant low-wage labor acts as a limiting factor on the achievement of balanced growth in productivity and income throughout the economy of such countries. To the extent that international immigration provides an outlet, such labor offers a dimension to the international-labor-market adjustment that is quite different from the typical "brain drain." In the case of the brain drain, skilled labor takes its human capital from LDCs to industrial countries, in pursuit of higher wages, complementary benefits, creative opportunities, and other amenities. In the case of unskilled labor, however, the LDC with an elastic supply of rural labor (and a growing urban underclass) is forced to export people instead of goods and services, since the productivity of their labor services is greater abroad than at home. Labor productivity-enhancing policies in the sending regions (including the rural sector), combined with increased openness to trade, could enable the export of embodied labor services in the form of tradeables, permitting the productivity gains to be retained within the exporting country along with a rising level of domestic real wages, aggregate demand, and the opportunity for economies of scale.

But there is no guarantee that this will happen. W. A. Lewis (1977) shows that for long periods at the end of the nineteenth and the beginning of the twentieth century, much of the world's tropical agricultural regions failed to exhibit significant gains in real wages, despite commercial agricultural-productivity growth per unit of land and labor. The rents from such gains remained concentrated in the hands of landowners, processors, and intermediaries. It was not necessary to impose the institution of slavery or monopsony on labor markets for such results to occur, provided that population growth (and labor supply) remained sufficiently elastic. He claims that the offer price of labor (and real wages) in the tropical regions might have increased had there been a parallel transformation of productivity in "domestic foodstuffs." There are important lessons for today's developing countries from history, since history demonstrates that agricultural-productivity growth is a necessary but not a sufficient condition for increased rural wages. If access to land and other inputs are uneven due to questions of tenancy, land tenure, or capital availability, or if the incidence of technology is uneven, or if the population growth rate is sufficiently high, rural wages may remain depressed despite significant gains in agricultural productivity. That is why Lewis attributes the growth of dualism in the nineteenth-century labor markets to asymmetrical technological progress.[14]

SUMMARY AND SUGGESTIONS FOR SOCIAL SCIENCE RESEARCH ON DIVERSIFIED RURAL DEVELOPMENT

This paper has argued that there has been inadequate analysis of peasant agriculture in terms of linkages with employment, productivity, and income-enhancing activities that would favor a diffusion and diversification of development to lagging subsectors, regions, and social groups. It has been said that the global food and agricultural problem is not one of production but distribution; but redistributional schemes do not necessarily come to grips with the problem of incorporation of rural society into the development process, nor do they address the issue of diversification of on-farm and off-farm employment in rural areas. We know that population will move out of low-income regions, but at a significant economic and social cost. Sometimes that cost includes externalities from "brain drain" of human capital (and the outflow of financial capital) that could have been applied productively at home with appropriate incentives.

What research approaches make sense if one accepts the above objectives? The following are a number of suggestions drawn from the references to this paper, from my own research and reflections, and discussions at the SSAAP conference:

1. Engage in microanalysis of farm-household decision making with regard to production and labor allocation under a range of assumptions about agricultural

production and productivity growth, education, demographics, and alternative-employment options, to estimate the future supply of "redundant farm labor."

2. Simulate the impact of a given increase in land productivity on the demand for nonfarm goods and services. Create a model of diversified rural development to explore forward, backward, and final-demand linkages between the rural farm and nonfarm sectors, both "formal" and "informal." (See de Janvry and Sadoulet 1986.)
3. Study existing case studies of rural and semi-rural "growth centers" (such as done by Runsten and Verduzco) in terms of the institutional, technological, political, social, and economic factors working for or against the growth and development of the center concerned.
4. Determine both theoretically and empirically the essential preconditions for successful labor-intensive rural industrialization, such as location, basic infrastructure, markets, tax incentives, supply of raw materials, credit, human capital, appropriate technologies, favorable prices, and others. Study successful examples of rural and semirural industrialization in Europe and Asia (Italy, Japan, Taiwan, Korea) to identify these preconditions. (Related to 3 above.)
5. Study the income-distribution impact of agricultural development and linked rural industrialization under different systems of land tenure — unimodal and bimodal. Can nonfarm employment promotion substitute for land reform as a policy to favor the rural poor? Is land reform necessary to ensure that the gains from rural farm and nonfarm development are spread among the poor? (See Lipton and Longhurst 1985.)
6. Related to 5, research is needed on the employment effects of the "Green Revolution" under different systems of land tenure (labor-using or labor-displacing?). Work is also needed on the impact of the "Green Revolution" on nonfarm working time and income — does it increase or decrease? Does diversified rural development help to increase the wage share of rising net farm income? Both theoretical and empirical research on these questions are needed.
7. Research the appropriate role for government and policy environment for stimulating employment creation in the nonfarm rural sector. How can government motivate private firms, entrepreneurs, producer cooperatives, NGOs to invest in rural enterprises? What incentives and guarantees are necessary? (Training human capital, reducing taxation and regulation, providing infrastructure, trading services and credit, etc.) What are the costs and benefits of drawing "informal" enterprises into the "formal" sector?
8. Provide case studies on the economic efficiency of rural nonfarm enterprises at different scales of operation: (a) returns to capital and labor; (b) labor intensity; (c) capital outlay per new worker; and (d) marketing and other transaction costs. Follow this analysis with the identification of the kinds of industrial activities that would be suitable for small- and medium-scale rural enterprises. (See Anderson 1978a and 1978b.)
9. Research the different ownership/management scenarios for rural industries and their relative impact on economic efficiency and income distribution: multinational corporations (MNCs), national entrepreneurs, parastatals, family businesses, and cooperatives.
10. Study the role of international trade and protectionism on the potential export markets for goods produced in the nonfarm rural sector. Are these markets accessible to rural enterprises? How can direct channels be established? What is the proper role for intermediaries?
11. Study the appropriate industrial processes for small-scale rural enterprises that take advantage of local skills and raw materials, and the low opportunity cost of labor. What lessons might be applicable from "flexible specialization?" (See Piore and Sabel 1984, Runsten 1988.) Research appropriate industrial technologies for rural nonfarm activities.
12. Since the interest is in the potential of rural nonfarm activities, generation of demand for dead-end jobs that pay subsistence wages (perpetuating "functional dualism") is unsatisfactory. Research is needed on existing and potential labor-market conditions in the rural nonfarm sector, and on the roles education, vocational training, apprenticeships, and other opportunities could play in moving labor into the formal job market.

Most of the elements that fall under the rubric "rural-transitional sector" have been dealt with in social science research at one time or another. But the emphasis here is on much more comprehensive and widespread development of such microanalysis within a broader economic, social, and historical framework, to more effectively capture the interactive process of rural and urban development, with attention to regional, sectorial, and social-structure variations, as well as national and international interdependencies. We have seen that "holistic" modeling of the agricultural sector has been done on an experimental basis for a few countries, such as Nigeria and South Korea. Some pioneer work has been done on the incidence of policies by sector, region, and income group. But much remains to be done in terms of both basic research and policy analysis before the process of rural/urban transition is to be effectively treated.

Ideally, social science research would attempt to identify examples of "successful" rural-development strategies and apply lessons from such experiences to other regions, subject to changing conditions of trade, investment, technology transfer, and migration. The interaction of economic, social, political, and technological dimensions would be explicitly examined. The object would be to take the analysis of rural development out of a "black box" in order to isolate those elements (whether they be economic, social, political, technological, behavioral, or institutional) that account for the "successes" or "failures" that have occurred.

The ultimate goal is knowledge of systemic behavior, but the applicability is in terms of the design of appropriate rural-development strategies. One wishes to build on foundations of research to date. The work should draw on a range of disciplines and conceptual models in a syncretistic manner. Judgment and field experience of the analysts involved would facilitate both the selection of cases to study and the methodological priorities. The approach taken would be designed to permit links between the broader dimensions of sector analysis in the context of changing economic and social systems, applied microeconomic analysis of production, and price behavior, savings, investment, and income determination.

The use of formal models (linear programming, input/output, computable equilibrium, and the application of social accounting matrices to such models), valuable as it is, should be subordinate and complementary to identification of the larger and more complex issues to be addressed, rather than vice versa. The use of sector analysis as a vehicle for state-of-the-art model building is certainly worthwhile, but it is not the basic objective of rural-development analysis, that is to identify the specific conditions necessary for successful incorporation of rural society into the development process in a sustainable manner. There should always be an attempt to draw policy implications from the analysis and to assure its wider applicability. In the process, the approach of "positive economics" as the application of logic and empiricism to the understanding of rural development is fundamental. The results should be presented in such a way as to permit those whose interests are the most directly affected to make the social choices from the alternative strategies and approaches.

NOTES

1. Clark W. Reynolds is a professor of Economics at the Food Research Institute and the director of the Americas Program at Stanford University. Dr. Reynolds acknowledges the valuable research assistance of Robin Marsh, Ph.D. candidate at the Food Research Institute, as well as constructive comments by colleagues, editors, and reviewers of the manuscript.

2. Stanley R. Johnson (1986, 1985); Johnson and Rausser (1977); and Thorbeck (1973) review past experience with agricultural-sector models, primarily in industrialized countries, focusing on innovations in modeling techniques. The applications of such models for solving contemporary LDC rural-development problems is at present limited, though in certain countries they have proved useful for simulating farm-level response to macrolevel policies. More relevant analyses that do address agricul ture-based linkages, in terms of farm inputs, marketing, and food distribution in the United States and abroad, are associated with the work of NC-117 and Michigan State University. U.S.-related work appears in: Marion and the NC-117 Committee (1986) and Marion (1976). For the Michigan State approach to the study of agricultural sector interactions in LDCs, see Johnson (1987). (The approach has been applied to major projects in Nigeria and South Korea.) Anderson (1978), Chuta and Liedholm (1984), and others have done pioneer research on LDC nonfarm rural employment, as discussed in a later section of this paper.

3. Some references dealing with broader, more multidisciplinary (and less formal) agricultural-sector models that begin to consider transitional processes discussed in this paper include: Rossmiller, ed. (1978); *European Review of Agricultural Economics*, vol. 32/3 (1976); and Fox and Miles, eds. (1987).

4. Glenn L. Johnson (1987). In this chapter, Johnson defines "holistic" models as: multidisciplinary; with institutional, technological, and behavioral components; stressing the importance of interaction between decision makers (who determine what is to be maximized) and model builders; iterative; normative in intent; and taking into consideration "power distributions" in the formulation of decision rules, in order to arrive at more realistic results.

5. See, for example, Sen (1981) and Rawls (1971).

6. This process may be observed throughout Central America as increased commercialization of agricultural land for export crop production has raised its rental costs to levels beyond the reach of peasant households. As a result, the growth of agricultural production, productivity, and exports took place alongside the impoverishment of the landless peasantry. See Reynolds (1978a, 1978b).

7. The classical models of W. Arthur Lewis (1954) and Fei and Ranis (1966), both of which assume an "institutionally determined" wage rate in the rural sector and zero marginal productivity of labor, and the neoclassical framework of Jorgenson (1961) where wage rates are determined in an intersector labor market and the elasticity of agricultural output with respect to labor is a function of new technology.

8. The ILO also sponsored major studies of urban underemployment for Colombia (Dudley Seers) and the Philippines (Gustav Ranis), that stressed the need to remove distortions in relative factor prices by raising the price of capital and lowering the price of labor in order to increase the demand for labor (by raising the optimal labor-capital ratio). However, such efforts tended to stay within the conventional rural-urban dichotomy rather than deal with what are termed in this paper "transitional sectors."

9. Johnston (1969).

10. de Janvry and Sadoulet (1986). This paper shows that the balance-of-payments relief provided by a shift toward food-grain production and feed-grain imports, while significant, is limited. With a 15 percent increase in land productivity of food grains over a ten-year period, there is a time lag before the associated increase in demand for food and feed grains (from income growth) will catch up with the previous growth of local production. At the end of that period, import demand will recover pretechnical change levels and will continue to rise thereafter. The time lag shortens to the extent that the strategy increases mass income and consumption, due to broad-based employment and income distribution effects, as in the cases of Taiwan, Malaysia, Korea, and Thailand. This is all the more reason for such an approach to be accompanied by policies favoring the parallel growth of rural transitional sector production and productivity in tradeables.

11. Anderson (1978a). Also Anderson (1978b). This paper addresses the problem of "small-scale enterprises" (SSEs) in a form consistent with our definition of rural- and urban-"transitional" sectors by dividing them into three groups: "formal" sector small manufacturing firms, "formal"-sector small commercial and service enterprises; and "informal"-sector artisanry, trading, transportation, household, and rural-town cottage industries. It is the third or "informal" group of SSEs that is burdened by unfavorable macroeconomic policies, despite their great potential for the alleviation of rural poverty, especially for the landless and near-landless.

12. Lipton and Longhurst (1985). This paper demonstrates how the technological innovations associated with the "Green Revolution" could have adverse distributive effects. By enabling year-round cropping, such technologies, combined with irrigation, increase the demand for farm labor per acre, so that "landless labor would, on balance, be worse off without modern varieties." However, despite an increase in employment and the total wage bill, the factor share of wages will tend to fall as the rent/wage ratio increases, with land values rising faster than wages in land-scarce, labor-abundant rural economies. This tendency is greatest where there is a high long-run elasticity of supply of unskilled rural labor keeping wages low. When

labor begins to be scarce, pushing wages up, there is a tendency to substitute labor-displacing inputs such as tractors, threshers, herbicides, and mechanized irrigation, reducing the overall positive impact on labor demand. Hence, the benefits of increased net farm output from "Green Revolution" technologies tend to be distributed principally among landowners, input suppliers, and consumers rather than hired laborers. Those countries which promote broad-based, diversified rural development will reap the greatest benefits from Green Revolution technologies in terms of the rural poor. In such countries, land tenure is dominated by small family farms with sufficient resources to adopt Green Revolution technologies; the opportunity cost of farm labor is bid up by rural, nonfarm employment; and the rate of growth of rural population is decreasing. In "unimodal" societies, mechanization results from decisions by farm households to "voluntarily take their own welfare as leisure instead of labor income." In "bimodal" societies, the decision to mechanize is one of pure labor displacement.

13. In his classic article, Owen (1966) deals with the production-and-expenditure "squeeze" on agriculture during the process of development that tends to result in the transfer of surplus income to the nonfarm sector; income that is captured for capital accumulation, industrialization, and consumerism. In the meantime, competitive pressure on agriculture to lower the costs of food and fiber to the nonfarm sector leads to labor-saving innovations and the decline of demand for farm labor. What to do with the "redundant farm labor" is the question addressed by Owen, which is also central to the theme of the present chapter. It is particularly relevant for LDCs with high population-growth rates. "Redundant farm labor, especially in the context of a family farming system, tends to take the form of involuntary underemployment.... Unlike corporate industrial enterprise, agriculture, and especially a family farming system, does not have the organic will or the social influence to plough its redundant workers into the streets, and thereby either compelling the innovation of more adequate complementary national development programs or laying claim to publicly supported unemployment compensation for the human resources concerned."

Owen emphasizes the risk of letting the farm sector absorb all of the social-welfare cost of maintaining its redundant labor supply. Such a burden may well stifle farm-sector growth, and "overall development eventually will also be seriously impeded." He argues that it is up to the government to assist the farm sector to support its redundant labor and forestall rural-to-urban migration until there is sufficient employment capacity in the nonfarm sector to absorb such labor. In his paper, Owen advises promotion of rural industries, public works, and educational and vocational training in the family-farm sector as part of an overall-balanced development strategy. It is evident from discussion at the SSAAP conference that rural extension work in the United States is increasingly involved in the support of such nonagricultural activities. However, there is growing need today to expand such efforts in the case of developing countries by drawing on the experience of social science research and extension work in the advanced industrial countries.

14. Lewis (1977). One might add, as an explanation for income and productivity differentials between countries, the effect of a historically constrained pattern of international migration, where migration flows tended to be restricted to north-south or south-south patterns. The same conditions may hold within countries, as argued by Gavin Wright (1986) to explain growing wage differentials between the North and South of the United States after the Civil War, and which help to account for rising income gaps between the United States and Mexico in recent years (author's work in progress). Promotion of the transitional sector, in order to provide productive employment opportunities, offers scope for the narrowing of income differentials where migration and constraints persist.

REFERENCES

Anderson, Dennis. 1978a. Rural enterprise and nonfarm employment. The World Bank.

———1978b. Employment and development of small enterprises. The World Bank sector policy paper, February.

Chuta, Enyinna, and Carl Liedholm. 1984. Rural small-scale industry: Empirical evidence and policy issues. In *Agricultural development in the Third World*. Edited by Carl K. Eicher and John M. Staatz. Baltimore: Johns Hopkins University Press.

de Janvry, A., and E. Sadoulet. 1986. The conditions for harmony between Third World agricultural development and United States farm exports. Presented at the annual meeting of the American Agricultural Economics Association, 2930 July, Department of Agriculture and Natural Resources, University of California, Berkeley.

De Soto, H. 1986. *El otro sendero: La revolución informal*. Editorial El Barranco.

Eicher, Carl K., and John M. Staatz, eds. 1978. *Agricultural development in the Third World*. Baltimore: Johns Hopkins University Press.

European Review of Agricultural Economics. Vol. 32/3. The Hague, Netherlands: Mouton Press.

Fei and Ranis. 1966. Agrarianism, dualism and economic development. In *The theory and design of economic development*. Edited by Irma Adelman and Eric Thorbecke. Baltimore: Johns Hopkins University Press.

Fox, Karl A., and D. G. Miles, eds. 1987. *Systems economics: Concepts, models, and multidisciplinary perspectives*. Ames: Iowa State University Press.

Grindle, M. S. 1987. *Searching for rural development: Labor migration and employment in Mexico*. Cambridge: Harvard Institute for International Development.

Johnson, Glenn L. 1987. Holistic modeling of multidisciplinary subject matter and problem domains. Chapter 5 in *Systems economics: Concepts, models, and multidisciplinary perspectives*. Edited by Karl A. Fox and Don G. Miles. Ames: Iowa State University Press.

Johnson, Stanley R. 1986. Future challenges for modeling in agricultural economics. *American Journal of Agricultural Economics* 68, no. 2.

———1985. A critique of existing models for policy analysis. In *Agricultural models for policy analysis*. Edited by A. A. Hassan and H. B. Huff. Agriculture Canada.

Johnson, Stanley R. and Gordon C. Rausser. 1977. Systems analysis and simulation: A survey of applications in agricultural and resource economics. In *A survey of agricultural economics literature*. Vol. 2, *Quantitative methods in agricultural economics, 1940s to 1970s*. Edited by Lee R. Martin, 157301. Minneapolis: University of Minnesota Press.

Johnston, B. F. 1970. The Japanese "model" of agricultural development: Its relevance to developing nations. In *Agriculture and economic growth: Japan's experiences*. Edited by Kazushi Ohkawa, Bruce F. Johnston, and Hiromitsu Kaneda. Princeton: Princeton University Press.

Johnston, B. F., Peter Kilby, and Tom Tomich. Forthcoming. Sequences of choices and consequences: Taiwan and Mexico.

Jorgenson, Dale W. 1961. The development of dual economy. *Economic Journal* 67, no. 268.

Lewis, W. Arthur. 1954. Economic development with unlimited supplies of labor. *The Manchester School of Economic and Social Studies* 22.

_____1977. *The evolution of the international economic order*. Princeton: Princeton University Press.

Lipton, Michael, and Richard Longhurst. 1985. Modern varieties, international agricultural research, and the poor. CGIAR study paper no. 2. The World Bank.

Marion, Bruce W. 1976. Vertical coordination and exchange arrangements: Concepts and hypotheses. In *Coordination and exchange in agricultural subsectors*. North Central-117 monograph 2. Madison: University of Wisconsin Press.

Marion, Bruce W., and the North Central-117 Committee. 1986. *The organization and performance of the U.S. food system*. Lexington: D. C. Heath and Co.

Olmstead, Alan, ed. 1986. *Agricultural History* 60, no. 1. (See articles by Roger Ranson, Gary Liebecap, and Warren Whatley.)

Owen, W. F. 1966. The development squeeze on agriculture. *American Economic Review* 61, no. 1 (March).

Piore, Michael J., and Charles F. Sabel. 1984. *The second industrial divide: Possibilities for prosperity*. New York: Basic Books.

Rawls, John. 1971. *A theory of justice*. Cambridge: Harvard University Press.

Reynolds, C. W. 1978a. Employment problems of export economics in a common market: The case of Central America. In *Economic integration in Central America*. Edited by W. R. Cline and W. Delgada. Washington, D.C.: Brookings Institution.

_____1978b. Fissures in the volcano: Central American economic prospects. In *Latin America and the world economy: A changing international order*. Edited by J. Grunwald. Beverly Hills, Calif.: Sage Publications.

Reynolds, C. W., and F. J. Alejo. 1986. Effects of intersectoral labor shifts on productivity growth in Mexico: Implications for the United States. Paper presented to the International Economics Association World Congress, 3 December, New Delhi. Photocopy.

Rossmiller, G. E., ed. 1978. *Agricultural sector planning*. East Lansing: Michigan State University, Department of Agricultural Economics.

Runsten, David. 1988. Linkage effects, nonagricultural activities, and employment creation. In *Rural development in Latin America: An evaluation and a proposal*. Edited by de Janvry, Marsh, Sadoulet, and Zabin. Costa Rica: IICA, Monograph.

Scott, Ian. 1981. *Poverty and famine: An essay on entitlement and deprivation*. Oxford: Clarendon Press.

_____1982. *Urban and spatial development in Mexico*. Baltimore and London: Johns Hopkins University Press for The World Bank.

Sen, A. K. 1975. *Employment, technology, and development*. Study prepared for the ILO. Oxford: Clarendon Press.

Thorbecke, Eric. 1973. Sector analysis and models of agriculture in developing countries. *Food Research Institute Studies* 12, no. 1.

Timmer, C. P., W. P. Falcon, and S. P. Pearson. 1983. *Food policy analysis*. Baltimore: Johns Hopkins University Press for The World Bank.

Verduzco, Gustavo. 1984. Una ciudad agricola: Trayectoria de la agricultura Zamorana. El Colegio de Mexico. Photocopy.

Wright, Gavin. 1986. *Old south new south*. New York: Basic Books.

CHAPTER 10

THE RELEVANCE OF SSAAP'S AGENDAS FOR RESIDENT INSTRUCTION: A RICOP RESPONSE[1]

Joseph E. Kunsman[2]

Glenn Johnson, as spokesman for the Social Science Agricultural Agenda Project (SSAAP), has raised almost all of the important issues facing resident instruction in the agricultural system. Three issues stand out for further comment: first, the concept of globalization; second, the inevitable structural change in American agriculture and the policy that attends it; and, third, the critical differences between disciplinary skills and problem-solving education. I would like to reiterate the importance of these three key issues as examples of our educational dilemma and end with what I hope are several relevant observations regarding the project and the present potential of our education system.

First, *globalization*. This is an important example of the educational problems we face in agriculture. All America loves the "Lone Ranger and the Silver Bullet" syndrome: just one quick shot and the problem is solved. J. R. R. Tolkein's *Lord of the Rings* trilogy is popular because the Orks were all bad and the Hobbits were all good. After all, when was the last time you met a nasty Hobbit? Real life is not like that. Do not be deceived. We cannot educate our students to the real meaning of globalization by the way of one three-credit course, Mondays/Wednesdays/Fridays, at 11:00. The true consequences of globalization are so complex we may presently be inadequately structured to properly deal with the issue.

It is important to realize "globalized undergraduates" means students understanding other cultures, languages, societies, myths, economics, politics, histories, and geographies. From the perspective of a land-grant academic with 23 years of undergraduate teaching experience, let me suggest this type of comprehensive educational experience, in most cases, is simply beyond our present academic ability. I believe this project report suggests the same. If we truly desire globalized students, the cost will be high.

Allow me to share a personal aside with you at this point. I believe it illustrates the size of the problem we face. If suddenly I became "Czar of Education," I would immediately require all of our undergraduates to read the popular and very insightful volume *The Rise and Fall of the Great Powers* by Paul M. Kennedy. It traces the development and decline of all the great world powers from 1500 to the present. The last two chapters make the point. The world has gone from a two-power globe to one dominated by five vibrant empires. The final chapter is very sobering—for student and teacher alike. The author chronicles the strengths and weaknesses, potentials and problems of all five powers. The final section is titled "The United States—The Problem of Number One in Relative Decline." Kennedy's point is not that we will decline and disappear, but that we are and will continue to be in decline to one of five rather than being one of one as we were in the 1950s. This is where true globalization of our students must begin. Sadly, I know of no undergraduates in my college who have read this book. Come to think of it, I do not know of any faculty who have read it either.

Glenn Johnson and his project report gently call into question the structure and policy of colleges of agriculture as they relate to the undergraduate educational experience such as globalization, and rightfully so.

Next, *structural change* in American agriculture. Water quality, soil productivity, and animal health are critical American issues. Make no mistake. But too often these issues force the penultimate questions of the well being of our rural society to some nether land. Note this particular project addresses the forces that increase rural production and welfare—resident instruction presently does not.

If you read Allen Bloom's much cussed and discussed book, *The Closing of the American Mind*, you probably noticed an important point made, almost in passing, that addresses our dilemma. Appearing early in the book was Bloom's observation that as a professor at the University of Chicago he was privileged to have the opportunity to teach the future leaders of our nation. His students go on to leadership positions in American commerce, industry, and government. They are the ones who set policy and initiate change in our nation's social and economic structure.

If Bloom's observation of the source of our leadership is true—and to a degree it is—it is because we have abrogated our responsibility to provide leadership-quality education. The Social Science Agricultural Agenda Project suggests that, and I quote, "These social science agricultural issues...are so important that increased attention must be devoted to their administration and funding."

The bottom line is obvious. If we do not deal with these agricultural problems, someone else will. In the twentieth century, everyone and every issue has an advocacy group. Social structural decisions involving agriculture will be made by our colleges of agriculture graduates or Bloom's University of Chicago graduates. Hopefully by both. But presently, it appears we are the victims of our own bad education.

This leads to what I feel is the critical point made by SSAAP: *disciplinary skills* and *problem-solving education* are both critically important—but, one we do well and the other hardly at all.

Recently someone aptly said there is no problem called chemistry, or animal science, or water quality. The problems are social, political, economic, and even mythological, involving water, animals, or chemicals. Here the Joint Council/USDA itself serves as the best example of our educational deficiencies. Consider water quality, animal diseases, or food additives and this group is clear, concise, and correct. Consider emerging social problems calling for solutions relevant to agriculture and the Joint Council's analytical skills turn indecisive. By raising the important issues facing resident instruction, this project seems to have brought to the table the question of the very future of land-grant institutions in regard to education in agriculture.

We all know one thing for sure: the future is not going to be more of the same. Yet it appears sometimes that all we can do is recite the land-grant litany as if it is holy writ. Of course, the land-grant system has nothing to apologize for. Of course, it is eminently successful. We of all people are very aware of its prodigious accomplishments. Yet that part of our cult that deals with providing a practical arts/liberal arts education for our children has been largely an unfulfilled promise. Subject-matter training and real-world problem solving were meant to be the inheritance of our graduates. This report suggests accurately that it is not.

In summary, I pose three questions and my own personal answers: (1) Can we globalize our students utilizing our present linkage with arts and sciences and humanities colleges as the report calls for? Probably not. (2) Can we prepare our students for the inevitable structural changes taking place in rural America using our present traditional academic departmental structure? Certainly not. (3) Can weprovide problem-solving education along with our traditional disciplinary training utilizing our traditionally trained college of agriculture faculty? Absolutely not.

There is no doubt that this report accurately chronicles the major issues facing our resident instruction programs. Social science agendas can contribute. However, benign neglect by the rest of us will assure failure. Project Interact, mentioned earlier in this discussion, is a multidimensional attempt to overcome the results of our present academic neglect. RICOP cannot solve the problem alone; the inertia caused by our disinterest is too great. Maybe a national project such as "Interact," instigated by RICOP, funded by the Higher Education Office, and with participation by the Council on Administrative Heads in Agriculture (CAHA), the Extension Committee on Organization and Policy (ECOP), the Experiment Station Committee on Organization and Policy (ESCOP), and the American Association of State Colleges of Agriculture and Renewable Resources (AASCARR), can stimulate meaningful changes in our undergraduate programs. I dearly hope so. As an interested American, I would dislike being number five in a group of five.

NOTES

1. Oral presentation to the Joint Council/USDA, April 13, 1989, Rosslyn Westpark Hotel, Washington, D.C.

2. Joseph E. Kunsman, Associate Dean of Resident Instruction, College of Agriculture, University of Wyoming, is the Resident Instruction Committee on Organization and Policy (RICOP) member to the Joint Council/USDA.

REFERENCES

Bloom, Allen David. 1987. *The closing of the American mind: How higher education has failed democracy and impoverished the souls of today's students*. New York: Simon and Schuster.

Kennedy, Paul M. 1987. *The rise and fall of the great powers: Economic change and military conflict from 1500 to 2000*. New York: Random House.

CHAPTER 11

INTERNATIONAL RURAL DEVELOPMENT: AGENDAS AND CONCLUSIONS

This chapter has two parts. The first and larger part presents a summary of the agendas pertaining to international rural development that were developed at Houston. The second part contains agenda items developed and conclusions reached by SSAAP's editorial group as a consequence of its review of the literature produced as a follow-up to the Houston conference.

ABRIDGED WORK GROUP REPORTS FROM SSAAP'S HOUSTON CONFERENCE

Rural development of less developed countries (LDCs) was one of the three substantive areas that received major attention at the SSAAP conference in Houston. Bruce Johnston served as the overall leader of the group that was addressing this area; the group was further subdivided into six work groups. The first four topics were major areas of substance for LDC development. Topics five and six were important crosscutting areas with specific agendas for international development. The topic of item seven addressed a specific issue and a recommendation was made. A list of the topics and chairpersons follows:

1. Macroeconomic and trade policies, and their impacts on agriculture and development in LDCs—George E. Rossmiller
2. Development processes and assistance to LDCs—Kenneth Shapiro
3. Farm and agribusiness management in LDCs—James O'Connor
4. Marketing and food security in developing countries—Paul Farris and John Staatz
5. International dimensions of public choice and private decision making, including agroethics—Paul Thompson
6. Databases for LDC development—Editorial Group
7. Potential for a rural social-science CRSP—Hugh Popenoe

The first five topics above continue as the focus of the agendas for needed work in international rural development. Databases for international study were considered by a separate work group at Houston, but no recommendations were made. The editorial group has developed agenda items that are to be found in the second part of this chapter. The four driving forces needed to increase rural productivity—including technological advances, institutions and policy improvements, human development, and the enhancement and the conservation of natural and manmade resources—were not treated as separate topics at Houston. These areas are now covered in Part III.

OVERALL SUMMARY—BRUCE JOHNSTON

The growing interdependence of the world economy is associated with the enormous contrasts in income and welfare between the industrialized countries like the United States and Japan, compared to the low-income agrarian economies where a rapidly growing population continues to depend mainly on agriculture for employment and livelihood. Those international contrasts are often matched by sharp contrasts within the developing countries. The welfares of the developed countries and the LDCs are increasingly interdependent due to closer trade, communication, social, monetary, fiscal, and political linkages. Social science research is needed to assure that LDC development and U.S. welfare advance together.

Development results from improvements not just in technologies, but also in institutions and policies, human capabilities, and natural and manmade resources. Rural social scientists can contribute to improvements in each of these as researchers and teachers, and as advisors, consultants, administrators, and staff persons working directly on multidisciplinary development *problems*. Other work is needed on such multidisciplinary *subjects* as regenerative agriculture, agricultural credit, the ramification of changes in trade policies, human capital formation, pricing policies, and the like. A third kind of work is specialized on a single *discipline* relevant for development, such as anthropology, statistics, philosophy, history, sociology, or economics. The rural social sciences (RSSs) and basic social science disciplines (BSSDs) have significant contributions to make to all three kinds of work.

Most LDCs need to increase agricultural production as an engine of growth, as well as a source of food. Generally, growth and development require completion of incomplete demographic transitions and transformations of agrarian economies. Population pressure and poverty intensify soil and water degradation thereby jeopardizing sustainable agriculture. Lack of human capital and deficiencies in institutions and organizations inhibit the development of production programs and marketing systems. Labor supplies grow so rapidly that, even with labor-intensive agriculture, additional nonfarm jobs are needed. Rural towns and small urban centers are important sources of jobs. A dynamic rural nonfarm sector reinforces and stimulates growth in the farm sector and vice versa. Failure to expand job opportunities for growing labor forces, including relatively more women, reduces real wages and increases poverty and hunger. Failure to make progress in these areas leads to growing hardship, migration to higher-income countries, and social tensions that pose major problems for the United States and other developed countries, as well as LDCs.

U.S. educational institutions, consultants, and technical-assistance personnel need to help develop the human capital and institutional competence required for effective research, policy analysis, and policy making in LDCs. Promoting rural-development policies in LDCs requires the different U.S. rural social sciences to provide technical consultation and assistance. This requires expertise about the region involved as well. It is also important that technical-assistance personnel from one country coordinate their efforts with those from multilateral and other bilateral programs. This is a two-way street. The United States and its social scientists gain much knowledge and understanding of the world and of U.S. problems. These efforts should involve reciprocity and collaboration between the U.S. and LDC social scientists.

WORK GROUP ON MACROECONOMIC AND TRADE POLICIES

Leader: George E. Rossmiller

Invited members (some of whom may not have participated) Alain de Janvry, Joachim G. Elterich, Cornelia Butler Flora, Timothy Josling, David Orden, and C. Parr Rosson

The increasing world interdependence of national economics gives rise to conflict and tensions among countries. Much of the international conflict and tension regarding trade and monetary flows result from flawed agricultural policies and programs. It is in the interest of all nations and economic sectors to find lasting solutions to the common problems of maintaining economic growth, correcting international imbalances, assuring monetary stability, and accelerating the balanced development of poor nations. We must find a remedy. A systems perspective and an understanding of trade and macroeconomic linkages are required if the rural social sciences and agriculturalists, in general, are to address the issues and help in the solution of the complex rural-development problems of LDCs that arise from these flawed national policies and programs.

Rural social scientists need to:

- Assess the impacts of macroeconomic, trade, and agricultural policies of the developed countries on growth and development in less developed countries and on the formulation of their own policies in these areas.
- Describe and analyze the dynamics of the evolution of macroeconomic, trade, and agricultural policies in less developed countries as they impact on relative prices, rates of return, resource use, and the pattern and character of rural and urban development. Important topics include the historical setting, interest groups, and institutions that determine these policies; a basis for disentangling the policy nexus; and the impacts that emerge from the interface among policies.
- Examine the social investments and institutions that contribute to growth and progress in less developed countries. Knowledge about the role of government in a given country and the relationship between the public and private sector is essential for better decision making on instruments and alternatives available for agricultural development.
- Trace the effects of the policies of less developed countries on developed countries. Important issues are: trade opportunities; opportunities for borrowing and lending, and related issues of debt management; intercountry movements of labor and capital; and shifting patterns of competitiveness and the role of each country in the world economy.

While the main focus of the work outlined above is on macroeconomic variables, impacts on microeconomic units are implied and linkages to other specialized areas in the overall SSAAP work plan are apparent.

WORK GROUP ON DEVELOPMENT PROCESSES AND ASSISTANCE TO LDCS

Leader: Kenneth H. Shapiro

Invited members (some of whom may not have participated) Daniel W. Bromley, John Bruce, J. Lin Compton, Billie R. DeWalt, Price Gittinger, Wava Haney, Fred Hitzhusen, Alan Hoben, Wallace Huffman, Gene Mathia, Wayne Swegle, and Manfred Thullen

Major advances in social science knowledge are needed to speed development processes in the LDCs through encouraging the U.S. and LDC private sectors, revitalizing LDC public sectors, educating for development, sustaining LDC environments, improving LDC institutions and policies, and encouraging the growth and accumulation of wealth. Technological advances, institutional and policy improvements, human development and enhancement, conservation and augmentation of natural and manmade capital are the four driving forces for rural development. Further, SSAAP regards these forces to be individually necessary but insufficient components of the time-consuming, dynamic, multidimensional, and complex processes of agricultural growth and rural development.

The rural social sciences should:

- Conduct research into the appropriate division of responsibilities between public and private sectors in individual countries, at particular stages of their development. This research should focus on the complementary public- and private-sector actions necessary to increase the productivity of LDC economies.
  - Encourage LDC private sectors through research on alternative institutional frameworks for stimulating and sustaining effective private sectors.

- Revitalize public sectors in LDCs with research, advice, consultation, and the education of their rural social scientists, to improve their performance in the public organizations of developing countries.

- Analyze and help develop institutional reforms. Critical limitations on the development of LDCs (especially in Africa) are imbalances, gaps, and deficiencies in their institutions. Work is urgently needed on institutions for:
  - Policy development and implementation.
  - Research and extension functions, public and private, that constitute the backbone of the system of technology and institutional change.
  - Regulation, such as weights and measures and other market standards.
  - Agricultural data.

- Increase the productivity of LDC educational institutions and systems, particularly those in Africa, with research, advice, consultation, and administrative help. USAID should significantly increase its support of the rural social sciences in LDC universities, especially those in Africa. The United States already has considerable, successful experience and a probable comparative advantage in strengthening the rural social sciences in LDC universities and research units.

- Research the economic, social, cultural, and political incentives and sanctions that affect LDC natural resources and environments. USAID should establish a sustainable agriculture Collaborative Research Support Program (CRSP). This CRSP is needed because of important interactions of farmers with their natural environment. The rural social sciences should play a major role in the CRSP rather than having the mere-token representation that is typical for most existing CRSPs. Researching sustainable agriculture demands interdisciplinary research encompassing the social as well as the biophysical agricultural sciences.

WORK GROUP ON FARM AND AGRIBUSINESS MANAGEMENT IN LDCS

Leader: James O'Connor

Invited members (some of whom may not have participated) Duane Acker, Dale W. Adams, Brady Deaton, Richard Harwood, Marilyn Prehm, and Simon Williams

The household, the farm, and the nonfarm rural firm are the key institutions through which rural-based human development evolves. A strategy for such development depends on the joint participation of households, farms, and off-farm businesses to effectively link a community's needs for adequate health, effective demand, and increased employment, in a way that emphasizes agricultural growth. The strategy for multidisciplinary social science research and educational programs includes applied social science research to accelerate the application of knowledge into practice, research to develop refined methodologies based on feedback from field experience, and educational and training programs that include: resident instruction, extension, public policy, and training for private-and public-sector decision makers.

In this area rural social scientists should work to:

- Increase the capacity of LDCs to do multidisciplinary subject-matter research, extension, advising, and consulting on the management of farms (including households), input and product agribusinesses, and nonfarm rural businesses.
  - LDC research capability needs to deal with the trade-offs between greater productivity and the environmental quality and sustainability of agriculture and biological diversity in fragile rural ecosystems. This should be done in cooperation with both biological and physical agricultural scientists and basic social scientists.

- Establish through research and utilization of existing knowledge the improved institutions, policies, technologies, human capacity, and natural and manmade resources that are required for prosperous farms, farm households, agribusinesses, and nonfarm rural businesses. This should be done by rural social scientists working in cooperation with biological and physical scientists, as researchers, extension advisors, teachers, consultants, technical-assistance experts, and administrators of indigenous programs and external grant and loan programs.

- Coordinate (with innovative use of USAID and USDA funds for CRSPs and competitive grants) U.S. and LDC disciplinary studies of decision making and managerial processes to improve farm, home, agribusinesses, and nonfarm rural business management.

- Establish and maintain undergraduate and graduate courses with sufficient multidisciplinary content vis-a-vis farm production and home technology, farm and rural people, agricultural institutions, and farm resources to qualify foreign and U.S. students for work abroad with managers of farms (including households), agribusinesses, and nonfarm rural businesses.

JOINT WORKING GROUP ON MARKETING AND FOOD SECURITY IN DEVELOPING COUNTRIES

Leaders: Paul Farris and John Staatz

Invited members (some of whom may not have participated) Michael Lipton, Thomas Mehen, Howard Steele, and Michael Weber

Food and fiber systems in developing countries are under tremendous stress due to the changing production technologies, the organization of marketing, and the growing demand resulting from rapid population growth, urbanization, and, in some cases, rising incomes. Many people in LDCs also continue to face chronic or short-term hunger. In many countries, shrinking government budgets and disillusionment with the performance of existing marketing institutions and policies have led to their widespread restructuring, often based on very scanty knowledge. There is, therefore, an urgent need to use social science knowledge to improve the organization of food systems to increase real income per person equitably in a manner consistent with broadly distributed rights. A major task in doing this is ascertaining effective and complementary roles for public and private participants in the overall operation of the system.

If properly designed, research, human-capital development, and extension in the areas of marketing and food security can be joint products. Collaborative, applied research by social scientists from low- and high-income countries expands basic knowledge on the functioning of the food system and on the factors affecting individuals' access to it, strengthens local capacity to carry out such research over the long term, and provides critical information to policy makers. Rural social scientists should help:

- Strengthen LDC social science capacity to conduct multidisciplinary problem-solving and subject-matter research, extension, and teaching to improve input and output marketing and reduce problems of food insecurity.
- Conduct studies of LDC market systems to inform the process of improving the organization and performance of LDC markets.
- Conduct studies of alternative approaches to providing market facilitating services, such as market information and grades and standards.
- Identify and describe LDC groups vulnerable to food insecurity.
- Identify constraints to overcoming poverty and chronic food insecurity in LDCs.
- Design alternative strategies to address transitory food insecurity in LDCs.
- Study the political economy of marketing-policy changes.
- Develop improved theories and techniques for resolving critical issues and solving important problems in LDC marketing processes, institutions, and policies.
- Conduct firm-level LDC studies to improve the operation and productivity of firms.

WORK GROUP ON INTERNATIONAL DIMENSIONS OF PUBLIC CHOICE AND PRIVATE DECISION MAKING INCLUDING AGROETHICS

Leader: Paul Thompson

Invited members (some of whom may not have participated) Fred Boadu, David Crocker, and Jerome Segal

This topic includes research, teaching, and extension activities focused on ethics, philosophy, and the ethical or philosophical components of international rural-development issues that are addressed throughout this chapter. The agendas that follow are concerned with the goals that underlie and guide development activities; the way the public and private actors derive the capacity or mandate to act in pursuit of goals; and the ways that research and teaching in this area can help establish links in the comprehensive vision of political economy and among disciplines.

Rural social scientists should help:

- Clarify the rural development goals of LDCs by sponsoring multidisciplinary social science/biophysical/humanistic research on the ethical aspects of improving human welfare in LDCs. This includes multidisciplinary policy research on equity, equality, and meeting human needs as part of rural LDC development. Philosophers, theologians, and others with formal training in value theory should work closely with social and biological scientists and others having extensive international experience in agriculture, agribusiness, and rural societies.
- Improve public understanding of the basis for developed-country assistance to LDCs. Sponsor research, conferences, and workshops that bring philosophical reasoning and the experiences of international workers and recipients of developmental assistance to bear on the ethical dimensions of the mutual and conflicting interests of agriculture in developed and developing countries.
- Strengthen undergraduate education in the United States by introducing into core undergraduate courses modules dealing with the moral, historical, and philosophical aspects of developed-country/LDC relationships, and the global interdependence of farm, rural, and urban societies.
- Examine philosophical bases for assigning priority to sustainable agricultural and total systems in LDC contexts by sponsoring collaborative research projects that involve persons with expertise in ethics and value theory, as one component, and those with experience with production systems, economic phenomena, and political and social systems, as a second component.
- Support new efforts to link rural social scientists and disciplinary economists, sociologists, historians, geographers, anthropologists, and philosophers into networks of administrators, researchers, teachers, advisors, and consultants working on LDC issues involving political and economic ideologies, and the theories of trade, development, and monetary/fiscal operations.

DATABASES FOR LDC DEVELOPMENT

In many LDCs today, even conventional databases are seriously deficient and need support. Strengthening those databases demands priority attention, but concurrent attention needs to be given also to the enlargement of databases. The responsibilities of the rural social sciences with respect to the rural development of LDCs goes well beyond the need for conventional, comprehensive, and reliable sets of agricultural statistics. The structural transformation that has begun will eventually require a much broader range of data than now exists in less developed and even in many developed countries. Larger, more effective databases are required to conduct vitally needed rural social science research for addressing rural development problems and issues, and to support policy decisions.

Data systems and bases are needed at three levels to permit research on: (a) farm and rural nonfarm-income-generating capacity, (b) movement of people into nonagricultural activities, and (c) transactions between farmers and rural nonfarmers, as well as with national and international entities. Work required by rural social scientists includes assisting in the establishment of databases on:

- Rural households as basic units of social and economic transformation; recipients of farm and nonfarm employment opportunities and income; a source of labor for the rest of the economy, as well as farming; major owners of resources for crop and livestock production; and as the locus of transactions with the rest of the economy. Farm- and family-record projects are especially important.

- Communities as geographically and sociologically defined units that provide the broad framework for the rural economy, institutional arrangements governing the use of its physical and human resources, and technical and social services.

- National accounts and international transactions, including social accounts, employment, income and expenditures (including their distribution), capital and other input, output, productivity, intersectoral linkages, and related data. Important approaches include sample surveys, census figures, and household-budget studies that capture the relationship between changes in the performance of agriculture and related nonfarm production and employment activities, and the investment in physical and human capital required to address national- and international-development objectives.

- Prices, exchange rates, wages, interest rates, and quasirents by sector of production and, in specific cases, by region; measures of dynamic comparative advantage and domestic-resource cost in time series and cross-sectional form.

- Medium- and long-term structural transformations, welfare indicators, and measures of poverty.

WORK GROUP ON THE POTENTIAL FOR A RURAL SOCIAL SCIENCE COLLABORATIVE RESEARCH SUPPORT PROJECT (CRSP)

Leader: Hugh Popenoe

Invited members (some of whom may not have participated) Archibald O. Haller, Peter Hildebrand, Earl D. Kellogg, Rosalie Noren, Joseph P. O'Reilly, and John Stovall

After due deliberation, this work group decided it would not be appropriate to establish a separate social science CRSP. As an alternative, the desirability of a multidisciplinary resource-sustainability CRSP was discussed and proposed by the Group on Development Processes and Assistance to LDCs. Partnerships would be established between social scientists in the United States and abroad, and between social and biological/physical scientists in the United States and similar groups abroad. Social scientists would help:

- Design new policies and institutional arrangements to:
  - Internalize costs of environmental degradation now being imposed on others by degraders, polluters, and contaminators.
  - Encourage the conservation (often by enhancement) of both natural and manmade resources.

- Evaluate and design new technologies to conserve and enhance natural resources and to reduce the use of the natural resources used to create manmade resources.

- Develop human skills needed to conserve and enhance natural resources.

AGENDA ITEMS AND CONCLUSIONS FROM THE EDITORIAL GROUP AFTER SSAAP'S HOUSTON CONFERENCE

At Houston, Bromley's chapter on "Economic Institutions and the Development Problem: History and Prognosis" (Part III, Section 1, Chapter 4) initiated a series of developments in the thinking of SSAAP's editorial group. These developments are considered in detail in Part III as they pertain to the institutions that generate institutional change itself, promote human-capital formation, create technical advance, and enhance natural and manmade resources. Also considered in Part III are expansions in the public choice/transaction cost (PC/TC) approach to the analysis of institutional change. Chapter 7 (Part II, Section 2) by Johnson, Chapter 5 (Part III, Section 1) by Busch, and Chapter 5 (Part II, Section 1) by Bubolz and Sontag explicitly or implicitly extend the PC/TC approach to institutional change. In turn, Chapter 3 (Part IV, Section 3) deals explicitly with the ethical aspects of the extended version of the PC/TC approach presented in this book, while Section 2 of Part IV deals with contributions needed from the basic social-science disciplines in order to apply the extended PC/TC approach. The agenda items and/or conclusions that follow grow out of the thinking SSAAP's editorial group did after the Houston meeting regarding these developments.

With respect to their research, advising, outreach, consulting, institutional, administrative, and entrepreneurial work pertinent to farming, rural societies, and consumers, the rural and basic social sciences should:

- Include an extended PC/TC approach to the analysis of development issues and the resolution of development problems at agricultural sector, subsector, policy, program, and project levels.

- Recognize that an extended PC/TC approach:
  - Is holistic (as contrasted to reductionistic) with the combination of social, biological, and physical sciences, being determined by the domain of the subject (alternatively issue) or problem being addressed.
  - Often requires enough philosophic eclecticism to address the value and ethical dimensions of the subject or problem under investigation.
  - May involve either noncomputerized or computerized analyses of a size and complexity determined by:
    - The domain of the issue or problem at hand, and
    - The detail in which it is advantageous to investigate the issue or problem.
  - Is multidisciplinarity in a manner that goes beyond the disciplinary constraints of more specialized economic, econometric, sociological, anthropological, political science, and geographic approaches.
  - Benefits from iterative interaction between analysts, decision makers, and those affected in a socio-politico-economic process involving:
    - Irrationality,
    - Nonoptimal behavior, and
    - In only some instances, optimization and optimal behavior.
  - Requires predictions of individual and group behavior for use in estimating the consequences of institutional changes.
  - Requires that optima be definable and estimable to a degree, at least, if existing proposed and past institutional changes can be evaluated.

- Treat institutions in three manifestations as:
  - Rules of the game,
  - Organizations, and
  - As properties, facilities, and staffs.
- Perceive of and estimate transactions costs (in both monetary and nonmonetary terms):
  - Flow costs (information negotiation and enforcement),
  - Stock costs (establishment and dismantlement), and
  - For all three manifestations of institutional change.
- Perceive of and estimate both monetary and nonmonetary returns to institutions (in all three manifestations) as both flows and stocks.
- Recognize that the essentiality but insufficiency of any of the four driving forces for progress makes it difficult to estimate returns to any one of them, including institutional change but that returns may sometimes have to be estimated for packages of the four.
- Use transaction costs and institutional returns to determine when institutions can be advantageously augmented, modified, reduced, dismantled, or regarded as fixed.
- Study quasi-rents in fixed institutions, recognizing that quasi-rents or opportunity costs for fixed institutions are negative with respect to establishment costs and positive with respect to dismantlement costs, and that optimal use of fixed institutions involves simultaneous minimizing of negative quasi-rents and maximizing of positive quasi-rents.
- Recognize that perhaps most institutional changes are made initially for constructive rather than exploitive purposes.
  - This often makes "rent collecting" respectable and socially desirable
  - although less respectable, exploitive rent collecting can be expected to develop in niches within constructive fixed institutions.
- Refer to the last chapters of Sections 1, 2, 3, and 4 of Part III for specific agendas designed to assist in the analyses of agricultural institutional changes (whether domestic or abroad) to improve:
  - Agricultural technologies (experiment stations, ministry-of-agriculture research agencies, private research units, international research institutes, and the like.
  - Institutions (decision rules, policies, organizations, programs).
  - Human beings (public and private universities, schools, families, religious organizations, and other).
  - Natural- and manmade-resource bases (conservation services; environmental protection agencies; public and private farm-credit agencies; transportation organizations; private, parastatal, and public agribusinesses; irrigation, drainage, and flood-protection organizations; and the like.

INDEX TO PART II

B

G

H

L

M

N

O

P

Q

R

S

W

Z

Part III

Part III

The Four Driving Forces for Development: Institutional Change, Human Development, Natural Resource Enhancement and Growth In Manmade Capital, and Technical Advance

At the Spring Hill conference of SSAAP, community and natural resources were considered together. In the discussions there, it soon became apparent that appropriate research-agendas for natural resources work diverge substantially from those for community resources but that the two are related. These different agendas grow out of the differing contributions of rural and basic social scientists (primarily sociologists, economists, political scientists, historians, geographers, and anthropologists) to studies of communities, institutions, and human development, both domestically and abroad. As a result of the discussions at Spring Hill, the community and natural resources area was subdivided into two subareas for the Houston conference: (1) natural resources and (2) community and human resources. This arrangement led to a neglect by SSAAP of human development and technical change that was corrected with additional papers and work concerning disadvantaged African-American, Hispanic-American, Caucasian-American, and Native American rural residents, both farm and nonfarm. Also, additional attention has been given to the generation and utilization of technical advance.

As a result of these shortcomings of the Houston Conference and of remedial work since then, this part now contains four major sections: (1) institutional (policy, program, and organizational) improvements, (2) human development, (3) natural resource enhancement and growth of manmade resource (capital) bases, and (4) technical advance. Although seldom identified in a one-two-three-four manner, these four driving forces have been considered repeatedly in the history of rural and basic social science thought. Readers not familiar with this four-fold categorization of driving forces are referred back to Chapter 1, Part I, for a more detailed taxonomic discussion of them.

INSTITUTIONAL CHANGE

Institutional change has been a major concern of sociologists, anthropologists, political scientists, and economists almost from the inception of these disciplines. In all of them, empirical work has been done concerning the generation and utilization of new institutional arrangements. Reflection on experience indicates that institutional change manifests itself in three ways: (1) as "the rules of the game" that determine, among other things, who owns what rights and privileges relative to others with respect to property, legal status, voting, and the like; (2) as policies, programs, and organizations, such as the American Farm Bureau Federation or an agricultural experiment station in a land-grant university; and (3) as physical plants, equipment, and staff (such as those of the International Institute of Tropical Agriculture in Ibadan, Nigeria).

This three-fold nature of institutions creates semantic difficulties when considering the four driving forces; each force is the subject of a section in this part. These difficulties require that we clarify our use of "institutions" and "institutional change" when we use them in this book. In Section 1 of this part, these two words or phrases are used more or less as they are used by lay "intellectuals" and professionals—to stand more for organizations, policies, programs, and even physical plants and staffs, than for "rules of the game." This introduction and Section 3 of Part IV place greater emphasis on institutions as "rules of the game," thus the word "institution" and the phrase "institutional change" are used in this introduction and in Section 3 of Part IV in a more abstract way than in Section 1 of this part on "Institutional Change."

A further explanatory difficulty about institutional change arises that SSAAP's experience indicates should be noted here. In the first chapter of Part I, the *necessary but individual insufficiency* of each of the four driving forces for rural progress and development was noted. Without human capacity, advances in the other three forces generate little improvement. Similarly, without natural and manmade resources, improvements in the other three forces result in little progress. The same is true for natural and manmade resources. Of course, institutional improvements without adequate human and other manmade capital, natural sources, or technologies avail us little. Nonetheless, in this part, much attention is given to the crucial roles played by institutions in generating technical change, improving people, enhancing natural resources, and in generating manmade resources or capital. Thus, in the four sections of this part that deal with the four driving forces, substantial attention is given to agendas for institutional change mainly in public or private organizations, policies, programs, including facilities and staff irrespective of which driving force is being considered. Section 1 focuses on changes in institutions as organizations, programs, policies, facilities, staffs, and the like not covered in the sections on the other three driving forces or in the two sections of Part II dealing with domestic and international development—namely, changes in community organizations, local government, state government, etc. Section 2 (on human development) considers the institutions that help develop people or, in economic jargon, "human capital." Section 3, on natural resource enhancement and growth of manmade resources (capital), treats "resource" institutions. Technological change, also generated by public and private organizations and their staffs and facilities, is too important to be omitted from Section 4.

Besides treatments in the four sections of this part, institutional change is also treated at several other points in this book: (1) in Part II, in the two sections on domestic and foreign rural development, and (2) in this introduction and Chapter 1 of the crosscutting section, Section 3 of Part IV, on "ethics, private and public decision making and choosing." Institutions and institutional change are treated more abstractly and generally in these areas than elsewhere in this book.

A BRIEF HISTORY OF RURAL AND BASIC SOCIAL SCIENCE THOUGHT CONCERNING INSTITUTIONAL CHANGE

In this introduction to Part III, important individuals are named but their works are not cited. Specific citations are to be found in the first chapters of each section of this part. Also, Chapter 1 (Part IV, Section 3) cites several important works.

Following earlier work of the German historical school, a school of economics referred to as "institutional economics" was developed at the University of Wisconsin. John R. Commons was instrumental in its establishment, with Thorstein Veblen serving as a precursor. This school was concerned with the "rules of the games" and organizations controlling society including its production, exchange, and utilization (both public and private) activities. The institutional economics of Wisconsin added collective action to neoclassical economics and can be characterized as multidisciplinary with major attention to law, political science, philosophy, and sociology. Wisconsinian institutional economics is linked to the rural social sciences, particularly agricultural economics, via the works of such land economists as Ely, Penn, Parsons, Wehrwein, Hobson, Salter, Timmons, and Long.

Later, the public choice/transaction cost (PC/TC) analysis of institutional change grew out of thinking led by the Chicago-trained Nobel Laureate economist James Buchanan, the legalist Gordon Tullock, and the works of Frank Knight, Ronald L. Coase, George Stigler, and Richard Posner. Essentially the public choice approach expanded the narrowly conceived markets of neoclassical economics to include some social and political activities. The introduction of transaction costs (largely information, negotiation, and enforcement costs as flows), measured in both monetary and nonmonetary terms, made it possible to consider the economics of making institutional changes on a relatively broad, but still rather economic, basis. Nonetheless, the public choice/transaction cost approach is sometimes referred to as the "new" political economy. Oliver Williamson, a business administration economist; Douglass North, a historian; Mancur Olson; and Nobel Laureate Herbert Simon use the public choice/transaction cost approach for understanding institutional change in their important contributions to business administration, history, and development. Williamson builds on the transaction focus of Commons and the organizational theory of Simon. Chapter 1 (Part III, Section 1) and Chapter 1 (Part IV, Section 3) provide more detail on the transaction cost approach to the analysis of institutional change than is found in this brief introductory review. Readers are advised to consult those chapters.

Though some analysts (such as Daniel Bromley whose important SSAAP paper is published as Chapter 4 [Part III, Section 1]) limit the concept of institutions to "rules of the game," the SSAAP editorial group has elected to include, *first*, policies, programs, and organizations along with, *second*, their properties, facilities, and staffs in a taxonomy of three different manifestations or institutional forms. This is done despite Bromley's warning that doing so will confuse "meaningful analyses of the role of institutions in defining transaction costs." SSAAP's editorial group runs this risk because (1) policies, programs, and organizations, along with their properties, facilities, and staffs have establishment and dismantlement costs (as stocks) that together have transaction costs that are often highly interdependent with those for "rules of the game" (Johnson [Part II, Section 2, Chapter 7]) and (2) policies, programs, and organizations with their properties, staffs, facilities, and the like are included in both lay and several dictionary meanings of the word "institution," although, admittedly, the sociological definition does appear in large authoritative dictionaries.

A narrower branch of thinking that is somewhat related to the public choice/transaction cost approach to institutional change was also developed from thought originating at the University of Chicago with leadership from T. W. Schultz, also a Nobel Laureate. This branch is concerned with "induced" changes in institutions (also in technology and human beings). Induced institutional change is more narrowly focused on the *economics* of institutional change than the transaction cost approach to public choices. Although some "induced-change analysts," such as Vernon Ruttan, recognize that sociological, political, anthropological, and behavioral variables influence changes in institutions (including those that create human capabilities, improve natural and manmade resources, and further technical advance), such variables are not provided specific theoretical pegs in either formulation on which one can model their effects in the processes of institutional change (Buttel [Part I, Chapter 3] and DeWalt [Part IV, Section 2, Chapter 4]).

In a multidisciplinary exercise such as SSAAP, it must be stressed that the public choice/transaction cost approach to institutional change seems unduly focused on economics even if it defines economizing and markets over a broader range of political and social variables than the induced institutional change approach. SSAAP's editorial group has concluded that the other social sciences cannot be logically or operationally regarded as subsidiaries of economics in institutional analyses. The attractive alternative to such disciplinary imperialism by economists is multidisciplinary team work in investigating multidisciplinary domains of problems and subjects involving the four driving forces. Neither the public choice/transaction (PC/TC) cost approach nor the induced-change approach has had the multidisciplinary breadth of the earlier institutional economics approach growing out of the works of Veblen and Commons. This narrowness creates difficulties in analyzing institutional changes needed for natural resource enhancement and capital growth, technical change, and human development.

There are some other difficulties involved that are worth mentioning here. It is significant to note that the public choice/transaction cost approach to institutional change is now most widely used in the rural social sciences for analyzing natural resource institutions, agricultural price supports, farm lobbies, and production stabilization programs, but has been little used with respect to other rural institutions. This, in turn, means that the section in this part on institutional change draws heavily on the public choice/transaction cost approach despite the absence of this approach in the community viability initiatives of the Experiment Station Committee on Organization and Policy (ESCOP) and the community development initiatives of the Extension Committee on Organization and Policy (ECOP).

The induced change and public choice/transaction cost approaches to institutional change discussed above presume rather specialized economizing or maximizing behavior in markets broadly enough defined to cover a considerable range of political, organizational, and some, social variables. Rural sociologists, political scientists, anthropologists, historians, and philosophers have become-concerned with the agricultural institutions that influence the four driving forces in manners that broaden the list of relevant variables to include values (nonmonetary as well as monetary), ideology, self-limits to opportunism, learning, and often emphasize that markets are embedded in social systems requiring explicit attention to conflict and the use of power.

Among the processes of concern in the making of public choices among institutional alternatives are those of political and social legitimation; validation and verification of descriptive knowledge (a form of legitimation) of both the value and value-free characteristics of conditions, situations, things, and acts; evolution of structures, systems, and institutions; holism; adaptation; and the like. For several years, systems analysts have been helping provide broad, multidisciplinary conceptualizations of the domains of practical problems and subjects. As a result, their work holds great promise for helping to operationalize the use of the PC/TC approach. Domains studied by systems scientists are often simultaneously more holistic, but less stable, than those of concern in the basic academic disciplines.

In Part III, these difficulties are examined and attempts are made to develop rather specific agendas for handling them in the contexts of the four driving forces. More general statements and agendas concerning the role of the PC/TC approach can be found in Chapter 1 of this section; Section 3 of Part IV, on Ethics, Private Decision Making, and Public Choice; and, to a lesser extent, in Section 2 of Part IV where agendas for the basic social sciences are developed.

CHAPTER 1

INTRODUCTION TO SECTION ON INSTITUTIONAL IMPROVEMENTS

Beyond the domestic and international policy and institutional (see Sections 1 and 2 of Part II) agendas considered at the Houston conference is a much broader range of very important institutional agendas for the social sciences. This section gives attention to the policies, programs, facilities, and staffs of local government, state government, and national organizations, leaving consideration of traditional federal price, income, trade, and international development institutions to the two sections in Part II, and the institutions dealing with human development, resources, and technology to the other three sections of this part. However, this chapter, along with the introduction to this part and Chapter 1 (Part IV, Section 3), deals with institutional change in a broader conceptual manner than implied by its narrower substantive content.

To expand its knowledge base with respect to institutional change and reform after the Houston conference, the SSAAP editorial group devoted considerable effort to agendas for institutional improvements and reforms. This effort involved surveying what rural social scientists have learned about the processes of improving, reforming, and building institutions. Fortunately, papers commissioned for the Houston conference and the earlier Spring Hill workshop laid much groundwork for this effort even though the Houston conference was poorly structured for bringing out the full range of agenda items.

This broader review of institutional change is made here although this section concentrates on the limited range of institutional changes described above. Four subheadings are used in the review. This chapter: *first* reviews the widespread interest society has in the limited set of more or less local institutional and policy reforms important for farms, farm communities, and rural development, *second* treats applied disciplinary subject-matter and problem-solving work on institutional and policy changes and reforms, *third* focuses on the theories and concepts used by rural social scientists and basic social science disciplinarians in analyzing institutional (including policy) changes, and *fourth* explains the roles of the remaining chapters of this section and some of the important cross references within this book.

A REVIEW OF SOCIETAL INTERESTS IN THE REFORM AND MODIFICATION OF FARM AND RURAL DEVELOPMENT INSTITUTIONS

Local agricultural and rural community institutions and policies are currently under close scrutiny both within and outside of farming and rural communities. This scrutiny is taking place in the land-grant and non-land-grant universities of the United States, as well as in other institutions, such as the USDA, the Agency for International Development (AID), the United Nations and the FAO, and various professional organizations concerned with foreign and domestic work that addresses farm and rural development problems.

In 1982, Don Dillman and Daryl Hobbs edited *Rural Society in the U.S.: Issues for the 1980s*, a report that undoubtedly influenced the agendas developed by SSAAP at Houston.

In 1986, rural sociologists identified three national priority research areas for 1986–87 (Klonglan 1986) that are important for rural community institutions:

1. Consequences of technological and economic changes in vital rural industries (particularly agriculture, forestry, and mining).
2. Improved methods of predicting the social effects of proposed developments in rural areas.
3. Strategies for enabling people in rural areas to enhance their well being through increased access to resources of the larger society.

The Experiment Station Committee on Organization and Policy (ESCOP) has proposed a research effort on community viability. This initiative originated largely with rural sociologists. With leadership from Gene Sommers, a rural sociologist, ESCOP has also published a report entitled *Social Science Research Serving Rural America* (Miron 1989).

The Extension Committee on Organization and Policy (ECOP) also has an initiative entitled *Revitalizing Rural America* (Cooperative Extension System 1986). Again, this initiative originated in substantial part with rural sociologists although other rural social scientists and basic social science disciplines were also involved.

The work of anthropologists that is relevant for this section includes research on peasant communities, rural areas of developed countries, and tribal societies. Studies of agricultural systems, ecological impacts of food production, women in agriculture, and diet are common aspects of these efforts. In recent years, these studies have come to address larger regional, national, and international institutional issues. Studies of family structure, social class, power relations, legitimization, powerlessness, alienation, participation, religion, and ethnicity contribute to a better understanding of agrarian institutions and the full cultural contexts in which they operate. Studies of cultural limitations on adoption of technical changes have been particularly useful. Anthropology stresses the holism of culture, that is, the ways in which all values and behavior patterns are interrelated and interdependent. Medical anthropology, for example, incorporates both cultural and biological perspectives to contribute to research on rural health, health-care delivery, and occupational health risks of farmers, farm laborers, and rural residents.

Much, but not all by any means, of the extensive work of agricultural economists on needed institutional changes and reforms has focused on domestic and foreign price support, subsidy and trade, and other programs and policies. This work is considered in the various chapters of the two sections of Part II of this book that deal respectively with (1) U.S. farming (including farm homes), agribusinesses, and consumers, and (2) international rural development.

The wide range of policy and institutional issues addressed by agricultural economists is attested to by USDA's *Structure Issues of American Agriculture* (U.S. Dept. of Agriculture 1979) that addressed structural issues of American agriculture and *Rural Economic Development in the 1980s* (U.S. Dept. of Agriculture 1987) that contains contributions from both agricultural economists and rural sociologists, and, among many others, the USDA book entitled *Another Revolution in U.S. Farming?* edited by Lyle Schertz et al. (1979). Many more works could be cited at state and regional as well as the national level.

Charles Hardin (1946), a political scientist, made a significant contribution to our understanding of the relationships of agrarian political organizations to national agricultural policies and to the Bureau of Agricultural Economics. This is an important piece of sociological and political science research on agricultural institutions at the national level before and after World War II. So too is William Block's (1960) study of the separation of the Farm Bureau from the extension service in Illinois. Despite this, it is only in recent years that political science has acknowledged the potential for public policy studies as an emerging subfield and, again, mainly at the national level. Don Hadwiger and Ross Talbot's (1965) and Hadwiger's (1982) works are pioneer forays of policy studies in agriculture. It is instructive to note that, even now, the subfield is most frequently linked with public administration. Moreover, the only two public policy areas where political scientists have sought specific identities are also related subfields. International relations gives rise to foreign policy experts while subnational government brings us urban, but not rural, political scientists. As public policy scholars, political scientists hasten to note their potential roles in such efforts.

Desire among political scientists to stake out agricultural institutional change as a field of endeavor has been discouraged by their own tendency to view it as one that cuts across several subfields of political science. John Hansen's (1987a, 1987b, 1989) work on the development of an agricultural policy network and William Browne's (1976 with Wiggins, 1983, 1988) several publications on interest groups in this policy domain are two important exceptions. But, for a political scientist to identify herself or himself as an "agricultural" political scientist would raise the disciplinary question, "What kind of agriculture—domestic, comparative, or international?" To satisfactorily answer that question for other political scientists requires both subfield and methodological responses that would paradoxically raise skepticism among other types of agricultural social scientists who are justifiably suspicious of someone satisfied with only knowing a very little bit about an encompassing subject.

That does not mean that important work touching on problems of rural institutions has not been done. Mancur Olson (1985), an economist operating on organizational turf, studied the behavior of people in American farmer organizations and developed a theory of voluntary organizations among large groups of those with small interests versus small groups of those with large interests. Robert Salisbury (1984) and associates (1987, 1990) have done important theoretical work on interest-group behavior dealing with agricultural organizations and comparing them with those in other policy domains.

Historians have contributed important institutional work as well. Three pieces deserve attention for the development and change lessons they teach. Gladys Baker (1939) drew on the institutional role of Extension through the county agent. Richard Kirkendall (1982) examined the work of social scientists in the Roosevelt administration. Murray Benedict's (1942, 1953) analyses of the evolution of institutional rules within agriculture remains seminal.

Pertaining to the need for institutional change and reform, the USDA published *Another Revolution in U.S. Farming?* (Lyle Schertz et al. 1979) and *Rural Economic Development in the 1980s* (U.S. Dept. of Agriculture 1987), which firmly indicated its concern with rural institutions. Joseph Molnar (1986) edited *Agricultural Change: Consequences for Southern Farms and Rural Communities*. The report on *Structure Issues of American Agriculture* (U.S. Dept. of Agriculture 1979) is also instructive. In June 1989, the Rural Revitalization Task Force delivered a report to the Secretary of Agriculture entitled *A Hard Look at USDA's Rural Development Programs*.

Many state agricultural experiment stations, extension services, and colleges of agriculture have or have had community and rural development projects. The same is true of the federal and state governments.

The U. S. Agency for International Development (AID) has administered a series of community and rural development programs and policies that have been ably summarized by Lane Holdcroft (1984) in a report for AID entitled "The Rise and Fall of Community Development, 1950–65: A Critical Assessment." Many of the community and rural development projects and programs have been very applied and more holistic than induced institutional change and current public choice/transaction cost analyses. Rural social scientists have played important roles in designing, establishing, and administering these programs. A large body of "institution building" literature has accumulated, part of which is summarized in *Institution Building: A Source Book* by Melvin Blase (1971). A number of agricultural extension services now have programs or projects for assisting local governments in managing their finances and in analyzing their tax and expenditure programs.

The three arms of the land-grant system—research, resident instruction, and extension—engage in self-examining institutional studies and exercises (of varying quality) designed to improve their service to agriculture and rural communities. The same is true of various natural resource institutions, including, but not limited to, the Soil Conservation Service and various administrative units in state governments.

PROBLEM-SOLVING (PS), SUBJECT-MATTER (SM), AND APPLIED DISCIPLINARY (DISC) WORK OF RURAL AND BASIC SOCIAL SCIENTISTS ON INSTITUTIONS

Because SSAAP is concerned with all functions that rural social scientists and basic social science disciplinarians play with respect to farms, agribusinesses, consumers, and rural societies, its interests in institutional change and reform go beyond research (whether disciplinary or subject-matter and problem-solving) to extension or outreach, resident instruction, advising, consulting, entrepreneurship, and administration. The areas of societal interest in institutional changes that are considered in this section focus on institutional change vis-a-vis state and local government, community and local nongovernmental organizations, social groups, families, and the like. The kinds of work of interest here include problem-solving (PS), subject-matter (SM), and disciplinary (DISC), as defined in the first chapter of Part I. Although PS, SM, and applied DISC work are stressed in this section, it is important to note that the PS and applied DISC work experiences of rural and applied social scientists are important for developing the disciplinary theories, measurements, and techniques of the basic social sciences. Such practical experiences help in appraising and improving the basic disciplinary conceptualizations that guide anthropologists, sociologists, economists, historians, and political scientists in their work on institutional changes and reforms of agriculture and rural societies. Reciprocally, the basic social science disciplines serve the PS and SM work of the rural social sciences with theories, techniques, and fundamental disciplinary measurements applicable to institutional change. For instance, academicians, such as political scientist Don Hadwiger, have been able to use their theories to guide problem-solving research on problems linking their own land-grant universities to state industries and development. Section 2 of Part IV of this book presents agendas to improve the basic social science disciplines. The next section of this chapter considers the status of some conceptualizations and theories about institutional change that are prevalent in the rural and basic social sciences. Many of these conceptualizations and theories are still so primitive (even if quite useful) as to suggest substantial opportunities for worthwhile disciplinary improvements.

THEORIES AND CONCEPTUALIZATIONS OF INSTITUTIONAL CHANGE

Since their beginnings, the social sciences have theorized and attempted to conceptualize the processes of institutional change. In economics, Adam Smith's work set the stage for a massive institutional change towards freer markets in the British Empire as well as elsewhere. John Maynard Keynes' work also had major worldwide impact. Billie DeWalt's chapter (Part IV, Section 2, Chapter 4) surveys the development of anthropological theories and conceptions of the process of institutional change. With the major exception of human ecologists, anthropologists have tended to be more holistic than other social scientists and have considered a very wide range of variables in explaining and conceptualizing institutional change. Rural sociologists have also had a fundamental interest in institutional change as indicated by Frederick Buttel's summary presented in Chapter 3 of Part I. Political scientists and historians have also been interested in conceptualizing institutional change. In this book, Richard Kirkendall (Part I, Chapter 2) indicates something about the work of historians in explaining institutional change with particular reference to agricultural institutions.

More recently, economic theories of "induced" institutional change (Ruttan 1978) have been developed (Part I, Chapter 5). In neoclassical economics and, particularly, in Pareto-optimal neoclassical economics, institutional change tends to be relegated to the "givens"—that is, existing institutions are taken as "givens" rather than being treated as endogenous variables. The resultant narrow kind of economics has virtually no explanatory value with respect to institutional change and reform. However, before John Hicks, neoclassical economics was broader and more productive. In his final years, John Hicks attempted to rebroaden neoclassical economics (Klamer 1979). Fortunately, neoclassical theory is now being slightly rebroadened by persons such as Vernon Ruttan and Yujiro Hayami (1984) who have expanded the concept of markets to include the optimizing tradeoffs made in political and administrative processes. This permitted them to develop a theory of "induced" institutional change that "explains" institutional change as occurring when it is advantageous for a society or a political body to change its institutions. This modest and far from new extension of the concept of markets has produced significant empirical results. Hayami's (1989) Elmhirst Memorial Lecture at the meeting of the International Association of Agricultural Economists (IAAE), in Argentina, related markets to communities. Theories of induced institutional change are now widely used and recognized as significant.

The public choice/transaction cost approach to institutional change that is now being developed is broader than the theory of induced institutional change (Schuh 1981). (See the introduction to this part.) It seems important to comment on that theory here because it has already been analytically linked to many of the concerns and variables addressed by the individual social science disciplines. It has, in consequence, brought forward multidisciplinary thought for problem-solving use (Bonnen and Browne 1989). Public choice theory gives significant attention to transaction costs, a concept that makes it possible to consider a relatively broader kind of economic inquiry in examining institutional change and, more importantly, to go much beyond economics.

Public choice theory has its roots in institutional economics as a departure from (some would prefer "an addition to") neoclassical theory. A school of economics that we now refer to as institutional economics developed at the University of Wisconsin. Thorstein Veblen and John R. Commons were instrumental in its establishment. The Wisconsin school was concerned with the "rules of the game" and organizations that control utilization of all resources including, particularly, natural resources. The institutional economics of Wisconsin can now be characterized as multidisciplinary with significant attention to law, political science theories, and sociology, as well as economics (Schmid 1989). The subfield of land economics grew up within agricultural economics largely at the University of Wisconsin as the handiwork of such institutionalists as R. T. Ely, B. H. Hibbard, George Wehrwein, and L. C. Gray.

Land economics eventually waned in agricultural economics, perhaps because it had departed so much in practice from neoclassical economics. Disciplinary agricultural economics with its neoclassical focus went into ascendancy following World War I (Johnson forthcoming). As land economics waned, such agricultural economists as John Timmons, Ranier Schickele, John Brewster, Phil Raup, Marion Clawson, S. V. Ciriacy-Wantrup, Erven Long, and Raleigh Barlowe, in part with leadership from Kenneth Parsons, tried to maintain a rather broad, multidisciplinary institutionalist analysis. Later this defensive effort was more or less abandoned by such persons as Maurice Kelso, Emery Castle, Alan Randall, Allan Schmid, Richard Noorgard, and Daniel Bromley as they consciously developed public choice theories using many sources.

Led by the Nobel Laureate economist James Buchanan and the legalist Gordon Tullock (1962), public choice theory applied neoclassical principles of individual rationality and maximization to the expanded (but still rather narrow) concept of markets to include social, political, and organizational activities. The introduction of transaction costs (largely information negotiation and enforcement costs *as flows*) in both monetary and nonmonetary terms added extra capacity to explain changes in and functions of institutional arrangements. Thus, a relatively broad kind of economics was linked to some political science and sociological thought to focus on the dynamics of institutional change.

In this connection, the reader should consult Daniel Bromley and Lawrence Busch's chapters of this part and Bromley's chapter entitled "Resource and Environmental Economics" in *Agriculture and Rural Areas Approaching the Twenty-first Century* (1988). Also in the same book, the reader is well advised to read Paul Barkley's chapter entitled "Institutions, Institutionalism, and Agricultural Economics." Other significant contributions are those of Emery Castle et al. (1981) in Volume 3 (*Economics of Welfare, Rural Development, and Natural Resources in Agriculture, 1940s to 1970s*) of the American Agricultural Economics Association's volumes that survey the post-World War II agricultural economics literature. These references more or less summarize the present status of public choice theory as related to resource institutions. Although the stress is on resource institutions in this literature, the theory is applicable to all kinds of institutional change including those considered in this section. In the literature of disciplinary economics, important references on public choice beyond the works of James Buchanan and Gordon Tullock include Kenneth Arrow (1951, 1971). For work on the use of transaction costs in business administration, see business economist Oliver Williamson's book entitled *The Economic Institutions of Capitalism* (1985); in history, see works by historian Douglass North (1987); in economics, see Mancur Olson's *The Logic of Collective Action* (1965) and *The Rise and Decline of Nations* (1982) on economic development over time; and, in political science, see the work of Terry Moe (1984) on economics of organizations. Other more eclectic institutional contributions have been made by Kenneth Boulding, Robert Heilbroner, Lester Thurow, Albert Hirschman, J. K. Galbraith, and Michael Polanyi.

Political scientists as well as economists have been instrumental in developing theories of public choice. Robert Bates' (1981) work on political-economic linkages in the development of agriculture in tropical Africa sets a model for inquiry. Kenneth Shepsle (1978, 1979); Shepsle and Barry Weingast (1981, 1987a, 1987b); Terry Moe (1989); Vincent Ostrom (1987); and Vincent Ostrom, Robert Bish, and Elinor Ostrom (1988), among others, have done work of lasting consequence in applying public choice theories to the legislative and administrative institutions. Earlier, William Riker (1962), on coalitions, and Duncan Black (1958), on committees and elections, revised disciplinary thought to allow this work to be done.

Exchange theories, first applied by sociologists such as Peter Blau (1964), have been developed to explain (1) the reasons for membership in voluntary associations as well as (2) policy-making linkages of these interests to public officials (Salisbury 1969; Hayes 1981). William Browne (forthcoming) has carried this work forward by examining the limiting effects of transaction costs on both interest-group demands and their impact on public policy.

SOME NEEDED DEVELOPMENTS OF THE PUBLIC CHOICE/TRANSACTION COST APPROACH

As indicated in the introduction to this part, institutional change manifests itself in three ways: (1) as changes in "the rules of the game," (2) as changes in organizations such as the Commodity Credit Corporation or the Farm Credit Administration or, for that matter, the Illinois Agricultural Experiment Station, and (3) as changes in the properties, facilities, equipment, and staffs belonging to organizations as institutions. Some public choice/transaction cost (PC/TC) analysts limit their interest in institutional change to changes in the "rules of the game," the works of Daniel Bromley (1988, 1989) being a case in point. However, analyses of the current agricultural reforms now taking place in the eastern socialist countries (Johnson, 1988) and of the development of colleges of agriculture in Nigeria (Johnson and Okigbo 1989) indicate that the three manifestations of institutional change are so interdependent that understanding changes in the "rules of the game" requires attention to transaction costs for organizations as well as for their property, facilities, staffs, and equipment. When these interrelationships are recognized, transaction costs begin to be viewed as the difference between establishment costs, on one hand, and dismantlement costs, on the other. This generates an interest in stock as well as *flow* transaction costs. Stock establishment costs can be advantageously incurred in establishing some durable institutions while stock disinvestment costs can be advantageously incurred in dismantling some existing institutions. To date, in the public choice/transaction cost literature, transaction costs are treated mainly as the *flow* costs of information, negotiation, and enforcement. However, Oliver Williamson (1985, 52–56) makes it clear that without investment in specialized assets that are durable and fixed for some period of time, transaction costs tend to involve minor losses since they arise from decision errors that are easily corrected. Three flow costs—for information, negotiation, and enforcemennt—necessarily enter into the computation of stock establishmennt and dismantlement costs. The public choice/transaction cost typology can be further extended to deal with the costs of operating institutions (in either of their three manifestations) and, of course, costs can be viewed as totals and averages (fixed, variable, and all), as well as marginal—seven in all. These speculations indicate that transaction cost theory is as yet still developing and is in need of further expansion and refinement.

In his survey of induced institutional change (IIC) literature, published in this volume as Chapter 5 of Part I, Vernon Ruttan touches on public choice/transaction cost theories but does not envision IIC theories as a special case of public choice/transaction cost theories. He stops short of considering establishment costs, returns to, and dismantlement costs for creating, modifying, and dismantling institutions in their three interdependent manifestations, i.e., as "rules of the game," as organizations, and as properties, facilities, and staffs of organizations.

Public choice analysts have long placed major emphasis on the vested interests of persons in position to collect "rents" within any set of institutions. The collection of rents is typically viewed as an immoral activity to be deplored and eliminated if possible (Tullock and Hillman 1989; Hartmann, Henrichsmeyer, and Schmitz forthcoming; Hagedorn forthcoming). There is sometimes even an implication that institutions are created largely to enable privileged individuals to collect morally unjustified rents. As Gordon Rausser (1982) pointed out in analyzing "political economic seeking transfers" (PESTs), it is undoubtedly true that some groups and persons seek institutional changes to establish and collect real income streams or rents whose value exceeds what is spent in order to get into a rent-collection position. However, as he also points out, there are important exceptions to this somewhat limited view of rent collection. These grow out of institutional and organizational changes *made for constructive purposes*. He refers to constructive changes as PERTs (political economic resource transactions). Institutions as organizations are often established to produce and distribute valued services such as new technical advances for agriculture, price stability, the education of farmers and rural residents, stable food supplies, the provision of credit services, resource conservation, environmental protection, food self-sufficiency in case of war, and the like. It is also clear that vested interests in rent collection can create PESTs or, at least, political economic-preserving activities (PEPAs) in PERT institutions. For instance, civil servants, farmers, experiment station administrators, rural residents, agribusinessmen, professors, and many others now have vested interests in the rents they collect in institutions set up with PERTs to accomplish essential constructive research, education, environmental and food chain protection, and stability objectives. Social science research is needed on the PEPAs that often emerge after a PERT is established.

When changing "the rules of the game," establishing organizations for constructive purposes, and when organizations acquire property, facilities, equipment, and staffs for such purposes, the new "rules of the game," organizations, and property and associated resources sometimes fail to generate enough value (often including values that are nonmonetary in nature) to cover their establishment costs (also often nonmonetary in nature). Although crucial difficulties attend attempts to measure the social costs and returns of "Pareto non-optimal" changes in institutions, society is often "stuck with" "fixed" rules of the game, organizations, and/or physical organizational facilities and staff not worth their establishment costs but nonetheless too valuable in attaining constructive objectives to justify dismantlement. Such fixed institutions and institutional resources can be viewed as producing negative returns or quasi-rents relative to their replacement or establishment costs. It is to the advantage of society to employ "fixed" institutions, organizations and properties to minimize negative "quasi rents" or negative returns on establishment or organization costs. This can be done by maximizing what can be secured from them using the opportunity cost or, in the case of specialized assets, shadow price principle. The interesting point not generally recognized in public choice/transaction cost analysis is that minimizing losses on fixed institutions and institutional resources involves maximizing the *positive* quasi rents that are the differences between what such institutions and resources are worth in use and what could be netted for them if they are dismantled. A moment's reflection will indicate that there is little derogatory or immoral about maximizing and collecting positive quasi rents so defined. This is mentioned here to indicate something about the present undeveloped status of public choice and transaction cost theories and conceptualizations and, hence, the need for further basic research on institutional change in the disciplinary social sciences (see Part IV, Section 2).

James Shaffer (1987), John Staatz (1987, 1989), and, more recently, Petri Ollila (1989) have investigated the usefulness of the transaction cost approach in modernizing the theory of cooperatives as an institutional form important in agriculture. They find the transaction cost approach to have potential for improving more traditional theories of cooperatives. Their work is not unlike the "transactional theory" developed by Raymond Bauer, Ithiel de Sola Pool, and Lewis Dexter (1963) and then enhanced by another political scientist, Michael Hayes (1981). They found that interest-group "services" to the policy-making needs of legislators improved the performance capabilities of Congress.

A shortcoming of public choice/transaction cost theory, as developed to date, involves undue specialization on economics. The public choice/transaction cost approach is sometimes viewed as the "new political economy" perhaps because it expands the concept of a market beyond that of "induced institutional change" theory to include much more detail with respect to political and social processes, costs, and returns (Schuh 1981). However, even the PC/TC approach is rather narrow when compared with (1) the holistic work of anthropologists and sociologists on institutional change, (2) the work of many practicing rural social scientists who design, consult about, advise concerning, and administer institutional changes, such as George McDowell, Ronald Faas, Philip Favero, Arley Waldo, and Theodore Alter, (3) what is done in human ecology, and (4) the very useful qualitative descriptive analyses by some less quantitative students of agricultural policy. Those in these groups commonly deal with a wider range of variables than considered by public choice analyses to date that have tended to be rather narrow economic analyses of markets conceived broadly enough to include optimizing behavior in political and social processes.

PUBLIC CHOICE/TRANSACTION COSTS IN RELATION TO SYSTEMS ANALYSIS

Some general systems science analysts who conceive their work to be holistic and multidisciplinary, in iterative/interaction with decision makers and concerned people, have built systems simulation models that have involved broader ranges of variables and processes than are covered in current PC/TC analyses. The survey of systems simulation work by Stanley Johnson and Gordon Rausser (1977) in Volume 2 of the American Agricultural Economics Association's survey of agricultural economics literature does not deal with these general systems simulation models; instead, their survey is largely confined to econometric models that "simulate" or operate through time without more explicit modeling of the wider range of technical, political, social, and demographic and anthropological variables. Uses for and the nature of general systems simulation approach (GSSA) models were discussed by Glenn Johnson and M. Petit (1976) in "Agricultural Change and Economic Method" appearing in a special issue of *European Review of Agricultural Economics*. Such models are conceived to be general with respect to use, techniques, disciplines, guiding philosophies, types of data, and behavioral assumptions, vis-a-vis maximization and other behavioral activities such as learning. This gives them the necessary flexibility to include the wide range of variables considered by anthropologists, technical agriculturalists, political scientists, statisticians, and others using the public choice/transaction cost, game theory, and other techniques. In application, the approach is an iterative process requiring close participatory interaction among analysts, designers, implementers, and administrators, as well as with those affected both adversely and favorably by institutional changes and reforms. Participatory iterative interactions are viewed as sources of descriptive value and value-free knowledge both of which are necessary for defining problems and choosing among possible prescriptions to solve them. It should be noted that although computers reduce computing cost, it is not necessary that such models be computerized. Fundamentally, similar models have been used ever since humankind began to envision the future consequences of alternative courses of action. They were, long before the GSSA was formally described, and are commonly used in farm management, the administrative and legislative circles of government, and business administration. (See Part II, Section 1.)

AGROETHICS AND PUBLIC CHOICE

Logical positivism as a philosophy of science has had its impact on the rural and basic social sciences. That impact tends to place research on value questions and on prescriptions to solve problems beyond the objective sciences (Batie 1989). Research designed to assess past and proposed institutional changes would be severely limited by logical positivism, as would work on the design and administration of rural institutions. The line of work that includes early Wisconsin institutional economics, land economics, and the current public choice analysis of rural institutions has deep roots in pragmatism, a philosophy that admits the possibility of objective research on prescriptions especially, and, to a limited extent, on values.

At SSAAP's Houston conference, there was a work group that addressed questions of public choice and ethics vis-a-vis community, human, and natural resources; the agendas developed by that work group have been divided and expanded to cover the four sections of this part.

REMAINING CHAPTERS OF THIS SECTION AND IMPORTANT CROSS REFERENCES

The remainder of this section consists of four chapters presenting papers either commissioned for the Houston SSAAP conference or taken from the "phantom literature" not generally available to most social scientists and a chapter by Lawrence Busch. Cross references are presented at the end of this chapter to other chapters in this book that are particularly relevant for this section on institutions. A final chapter in this section *first* abstracts the Houston work group reports on agendas for community institutions and *then* presents more general institutional agendas and conclusions about institutions that were developed by SSAAP's editorial group after the Houston conference.

Chapter 5 by Lawrence Busch, entitled "Irony, Tragedy, and Temporality in Agricultural Systems or How Values and Systems are Related," presents a sociological view of the importance of a systems approach to institutional change. Related to the Lawrence Busch paper is the relevant paper by Margaret M. Bubolz and M. Suzanne Sontag entitled "Integration in Home Economics and Human Ecology" from the *Journal of Consumer Studies and Home Economics*, that is reprinted in this book (Part II, Section 1, Chapter 5).

The papers presented as Chapters 2 through 4, include one by Paul Barkley (Chapter 2) on social science issues in agriculture and rural communities, another by James Hite (Chapter 3) that assesses the capabilities of the social sciences with respect to natural as well as rural community resources and the environment, and a commissioned paper by Daniel Bromley (Chapter 4) that considers institutions and development. Another commissioned paper, by Billie R. DeWalt on anthropology, evolution, and agriculture, appears as Chapter 4 of Part IV, Section 2. All of these papers contribute to our ability to work with change in farm and rural institutions. However, the Lawrence Busch, Margaret Bubolz/M. Susan Sontag, and Louis Swanson papers, plus the commissioned papers, should not be expected to support adequately the agendas developed at Houston or, for that matter, the conclusions reached and agendas developed by the SSAAP editorial group since then. In the case of this section on institutional change, work group participants and the SSAAP editorial group were able to draw on papers by Richard Kirkendall, Frederick Buttel, Lester Thurow, Vernon Ruttan, and G. Edward Schuh, all presented as chapters in Part I. These chapters deal with the history of American agriculture; social science institutions, common knowledge, and tools; American institutions and arrangements under fire; the role of the social sciences in rural development and natural resource management; and science and technology policy for the 21st century. Another somewhat different but relevant chapter in Part I is by Richard Sauer. It looks at the social sciences from the perspective of users and affected persons. Also relevant for this section is the chapter on households by Cornelia Butler Flora (Part II, Section 1, Chapter 3). Wava Haney's paper (Part II, Section 1, Chapter 4) on theoretical advances from studies of women in farming is germane, as is Timothy Josling's paper (Part II, Section 1, Chapter 6) on the relationship between international rural development and international trade and finance. Section 2 of Part II on international rural development also contains chapters relevant to this section on institutional change. These include G. Edward Schuh's paper (Part II, Section 2, Chapter 2) on international affairs and development, John Staatz' paper (Part II, Section 2, Chapter 4) on the design of social science research to inform agricultural market reforms and structural adjustments and papers by Paul Thompson (Part II, Section 2, Chapter 5) on the Bumpers amendment and Michael Weber and Thomas Jayne (Part II, Section 2, Chapter 6) on food security. Another paper on institutional reforms in the agricultural policies of various countries by Glenn Johnson (Part II, Section 2, Chapter 7) is illustrative. The paper by Dale Adams (Part II, Section 2, Chapter 8) on on-farm capital formation and rural financial markets (institutions) is also relevant. Section 3 of Part IV contains an overall crosscutting treatment of ethics, private decisions, and public choices that has a more complete, general, and abstract treatment of the public choice/transaction approach as it related to ethics.

This section on institutions concludes with Chapter 7 that presents the community and related institutional agendas developed at Houston and agendas and conclusions reached by SSAAP's editorial group after Houston.

CROSS REFERENCES IN THIS BOOK

PART I: INTRODUCTION

Ch. 2 A History of American Agriculture from Jefferson to Revolution to Crisis, Richard S. Kirkendall

Ch. 3 Social Science Institutions, Knowledge, and Tools to Address Problems and Issues, Frederick H. Buttel

Ch. 4 Agricultural Institutions Under Fire, Lester C. Thurow

Ch. 5 The Role of the Social Sciences in Rural Development and Natural Resource Management, Vernon W. Ruttan

Ch. 6 Science and Technology Policy for the 21st Century: The United States in a Global Economy, G. Edward Schuh

Ch. 7 From the Perspective of Users and Affected Persons, Richard J. Sauer

PART II: DOMESTIC AND INTERNATIONAL FARM AND RURAL DEVELOPMENT

Sec. 1 Ch. 3 Studies of Households Reviewed in Relation to Farm and Home, Balanced Farming, Farming Systems, and Farm Management Programs and Studies in the College of Agriculture, Cornelia Flora Butler

Ch. 5 Integration in Home Economics and Human Ecology, Margaret M. Bubolz and M. Suzanne Sontag

Sec. 2 Ch. 2 International Affairs and Economic Development, G. Edward Schuh

Ch. 4 Designing Social Science Research to Inform Agricultural Market Reforms and Structural Adjustments in Developing Countries, John M. Staatz

Ch. 5 The Bumpers Amendment: AID and Trade Issues for U.S. Agriculture, Paul B. Thompson

Ch. 6 Food Security and Its Relationship to Technology, Institutions, Policies, and Human Capital, Michael T. Weber and Thomas S. Jayne

REFERENCES

Arrow, Kenneth J. 1951. *Social choice and individual values.* New Haven: Yale University Press.

——1971. *Essays in the theory of risk-bearing.* Chicago: Markham Publishing Co.

Baker, Gladys L. 1939. *The county agent.* Chicago: University of Chicago Press.

Barkley, Paul W. 1988. Institutions, institutionalism, and agricultural economics. In *Agriculture and rural areas approaching the twenty-first century: Challenges for agricultural economics.* Edited by R. J. Hildreth, 313–35. Ames: Iowa State University Press.

Bates, Robert H. 1981. *Markets and states in tropical Africa: The political basis of agricultural policies.* Berkeley: University of California Press.

Batie, Sandra. 1989. Sustainable development: Challenges to the profession of agricultural economics. *Proceedings of the AAEA summer meeting 1989.* Presidential address at the American Agricultural Economics Association summer meeting, 30 July–1 August 1989, Baton Rouge, La.

Bauer, Raymond A., Ithiel de Sola Pool, and Lewis Anthony Dexter. 1963. *American business and public policy; the politics of foreign trade.* New York: Atherton Press.

Benedict, Murray R. 1942. Agriculture as a commercial industry comparable to other branches of the economy. *Journal of Farm Economics* 24:476–96.

——1953. Farm policies of the United States, 1790–1950. New York: Twentieth Century Fund.

Black, Duncan. 1958. *The theory of committees and elections.* Cambridge, England: Cambridge University Press.

Blase, Melvin G. 1971. *Institution building: A source book.* Final report, contract no. AID/csd–3392. Bloomington: Indiana University, MUCIA Program of Advanced Study.

Blau, Peter M. 1964. *Exchange and power in social life.* New York: J. Wiley and Sons.

Block, William J. 1960. *The separation of the Farm Bureau and the Extension Service.* Urbana: University of Illinois Press.

Bonnen, James T., and William P. Browne. 1989. Why is agricultural policy so difficult to reform? In *The political economy of U.S. agriculture: Challenges for the 1990s*. Edited by Carol S. Kramer, 7–33. Washington, D.C.: National Center for Food and Agricultural Policy, Resources for the Future.

Bromley, Daniel W. 1988. Resource and environmental economics: Knowledge, discipline, and problems. In *Agriculture and rural areas approaching the twenty-first century: Challenges for agricultural economics*. Edited by R. J. Hildreth et al., 208–30. Ames: Iowa State University Press.

_____1989. *Economic interests and institutions: The conceptual foundations of public policy*. New York: Basil Blackwell.

Browne, William P. 1983. Mobilizing and activating group demands: The American agriculture movement. *Social Science Quarterly* 64:19–34.

_____1988. *Private interests, public policy, and American agriculture*. Lawrence: University Press of Kansas.

_____1990. Organized interests and their issue niches: A search for pluralism in a policy domain. *Journal of Politics* 52:477–509.

_____Forthcoming. Issue niches and the limits of interest group influence. In *Interest group politics*. 3d ed. Edited by Allen J. Cigler and Burdette A. Loomis. Washington, D.C.: Congressional Quarterly Press.

Browne, William P., and Charles W. Wiggins. 1976. Resolutions and priorities: Lobbying by the general farm organizations. *Policy Studies Journal* 6:493–99.

Buchanan, James M., and Gordon Tullock. 1962. *The calculus of consent, logical foundations of constitutional democracy*. Ann Arbor: University of Michigan Press.

Castle, Emery N., et al. 1981. Natural resource economics, 1946–75. In *A survey of agricultural economics literature*. Vol. 3, *Economics of welfare, rural development, and natural resources in agriculture, 1940s to 1970s*. Edited by Lee R. Martin, 393–5. Minneapolis: University of Minnesota Press for the American Agricultural Economics Association.

Cooperative Extension System. 1986. *Revitalizing rural America: A Cooperative Extension System response*. Madison, Wisc.: University of Wisconsin, Division of Cooperative Extension, for the Extension Committee on Organizations and Policy.

Dillman, Don A., and Daryl J. Hobbs, eds. 1982. *Rural society in the U.S.: Issues for the 1980s*. Boulder, Colo.: Westview Press.

Hadwiger, Don F. 1982. *The politics of agricultural research*. Lincoln: University of Nebraska Press.

Hadwiger, Don F., and Ross B. Talbot. 1965. *Pressures and protests; the Kennedy farm and the wheat referendum of 1963, a case study*. San Francisco: Chandler Publishing Co.

Hagedorn, Konrad. Forthcoming. Public choice and agricultural policy. In *Proceedings of the 9th World Congress of the International Economic Association* (28 August–1 September 1989, Athens, Greece).

Hansen, John Mark. 1987a. Choosing sides: The development of an agriculture policy network in Congress, 1919–1932. *Studies in American political development* 2:183–229.

_____1987b. The ever-decreasing grandstand: Constraint and change in an agricultural policy network, 1948–1980. Paper presented at the annual meeting of the American Political Science Association, Chicago, Ill.

_____1989. Taking charge: The reassertion of political authority in the United States Department of Agriculture, 1935–1948. Paper presented at the annual meeting of the Organization of American Historians, St. Louis, Mo.

Hardin, Charles M. 1946. The bureau of agricultural economics under fire: A study in valuation conflicts. *Journal of Farm Economics* 28:635–68.

Hartmann, Monika, Wilhelm Henrichsmeyer, and Peter Michael Schmitz. Forthcoming. Political economy of the common agricultural policy in the European community. In *Proceedings of the 9th World Congress of the International Economic Association* (28 August–1 September, Athens, Greece).

Hayami, Yujiro. 1989. Community, market and state. (Elmhirst Memorial Lecture) In *Agriculture and governments in an interdependent world: Proceedings of the twentieth international conference of agricultural economists, held at Buenos Aires, Argentina, 24th–31st August 1988*. Edited by Allen Maunder and Alberto Valdes, 3–14. Aldershot, England: Dartmouth.

Hayes, Michael T. 1981. *Lobbyists and legislators: A theory of political markets*. New Brunswick, N.J.: Rutgers University Press.

Holdcroft, Lane. 1984. The rise and fall of community development, 1950–65: A critical assessment. In *Agricultural development in the Third World*. Edited by Carl K. Eicher and John M. Staatz. Baltimore: The Johns Hopkins University Press.

Johnson, Glenn L. 1988. The urgency of institutional changes for LDC, NIC, and DC agricultures. Paper presented at the Symposium on Future U.S. Development Assistance, 17–19 February 1988, Winrock International Center, Petit-John Mountain, Ark. East Lansing: Michigan State University, Dept. of Agricultural Economics.

_____Forthcoming. Philosophic foundations of agricultural economics thought from World War II to the mid-seventies. In *A survey of agricultural economics literature*. Vol. 4, *Agriculture in economic development*. Edited by Lee R. Martin. Minneapolis: University of Minnesota Press for the American Agricultural Economics Association.

Johnson, Glenn L., and M. Petit. 1976. Summary and conclusions of: Agricultural change and economic method. *European Review of Agricultural Economics* 3, no. 2/3: 31–43.

Johnson, Glenn L., and Bede N. Okigbo. 1989. Institution-building lessons from USAID's agricultural development projects in Nigeria. *Journal of Agricultural Economics* 71:1211–18.

Johnson, Stanley R., and Gordon C. Rausser. 1977. Systems analysis and simulation: A survey of applications in agricultural and resource economics. In *A survey of agricultural economics literature*. Vol. 2, *Quantitative methods in agricultural economics, 1940s to 1970s*. Edited by Lee R. Martin, 157–301. Minneapolis: University of Minnesota Press for the American Agricultural Economics Association.

Kirkendall, Richard S. 1982. *Social scientists and farm politics in the age of Roosevelt*. Ames: Iowa State University Press.

Klamer, Argo. 1989. An accountant among economists: Conversations with Sir John R. Hicks. *Journal of Economic Perspectives* 3, no. 4: 167–80.

Klonglan, Gerald E. 1986. National priorities for rural sociology research. *The Rural Sociologist* 6, no. 6 (November): 501–6.

Miron, Mary, ed. 1989. Social science research serving rural America. Madison: Wisconsin Agricultural Experiment Station.

Moe, Terry M. 1984. The new economics of organization. *American Journal of Political Science* 28:739–77.

——1989. The politics of bureaucratic structure. In *Can the government govern?* Edited by John E. Chubb and Paul E. Peterson, 267–329. Washington, D.C.: Brookings Institution.

Molnar, Joseph J., ed. 1986. *Agricultural change: Consequences for southern farms and rural communities.* Boulder, Colo.: Westview Press.

North, Douglass. 1987. Institutions, transaction costs and economic growth. *Economic Inquiry* 25:419–28.

Ollila, Petri. 1989. Coordination of supply and demand in the dairy marketing system: With special emphasis on the potential role of farmer cooperatives as coordinating institutions. *Journal of Agricultural Science in Finland* 61, no. 3.: 135–317.

Olson, Mancur, Jr. 1965. *The logic of collective action; public goods and the theory of groups.* Cambridge: Harvard University Press.

——1982. *The rise and decline of nations: Economic growth, stagflation, and social rigidities.* New Haven: Yale University Press.

——1986. The exploitation and subsidization of agriculture in developing and developed countries. In *Agriculture in a turbulent world economy: Proceedings of the Nineteenth International Conference of Agricultural Economists, held at Malaga, Spain, 26 August–4 September 1985.* Edited by Allen Maunder and Ulf Renborg, 49–59. Brookfield, Vt.: Gower.

Ostrom, Vincent. 1987. *The political theory of a compound republic.* Lincoln: University of Nebraska Press.

Ostrom, Vincent, Robert Bish, and Elinor Ostrom. [1980] 1988. *Local government in the U.S.* San Francisco: Institute for Contemporary Studies.

Rausser, Gordon C. 1982. Political economic markets: PERTS and PESTS in food and agriculture. *American Journal of Agricultural Economics* 64, no. 5 (December): 821–33.

Riker, William H. 1962. *The theory of political coalitions.* New Haven: Yale University Press.

Rural Revitalization Task Force. 1989. A hard look at USDA's rural development programs: The report of the Rural Revitalization Task Force to the Secretary of Agriculture. (June30) Photocopy.

Ruttan, Vernon. 1978. Induced institutional change. In *Induced innovation: Technology, institutions, and development.* Edited by Hans Binswanger et al. Baltimore: The Johns Hopkins University Press.

Ruttan, Vernon W., and Yujiro Hayami. 1984. Toward a theory of institutional innovation. *The Journal of Development Studies* 20, no. 4: 203–23.

Salisbury, Robert H. 1969. An exchange theory of interest groups. *Midwest Journal of Political Science* 13:1–32.

——1984. Interest representation: The dominance of institutions. *American Political Science Review* 78:64–76.

Salisbury, Robert H., et al. 1987. Who works with whom? Interest group alliances and opposition. *American Political Science Review* 81:1217–34.

——1990. Inner circles or hollow cores? Elite networks in national policy systems. *Journal of Politics* 52:356–90.

Schertz, Lyle P., et al. 1979. *Another revolution in U.S. farming?* U.S. Dept. of Agriculture, Economics and Statistics Service, Agricultural Economics Report 411.

Schmid, A. Allan. 1989. Law and economics: An institutional perspective. In *Law and Economics.* Edited by Nicholas Mercuro, 57–85. Boston/Dordrecht/London: Kluwer Academic Publishers.

Schuh, G. Edward. 1981. Economics and international relations: A conceptual framework. *Journal of Agricultural Economics* 63:767–78.

Shaffer, James D. 1987. Thinking about farmers' cooperatives, contracts, and economic coordination. In *Cooperative theory: New approaches.* U.S. Dept. of Ag, ACS Report Number 18 (July).

Shepsle, Kenneth A. 1978. *The giant jigsaw puzzle: Democratic committee assignments in the modern House.* Chicago: University of Chicago Press.

——1979. Institutional arrangements and equilibrium in multi-dimensional voting models. *American Journal of Political Science* 23.

Shepsle, Kenneth A., and Barry R. Weingast. 1981. Structure-induced equilibrium and legislative choice. *Public Choice* 37:503–19.

——1987a. The institutional foundations of committee power. *American Political Science Review* 81:85–104.

——1987b. Why are congressional committees powerful? *American Political Science Review* 81:935–45.

Staatz, John M. 1987. Farmers' incentives to take collective action via cooperatives: A transaction cost approach. In *Cooperative theory: New approaches.* U.S. Dept. of Agriculture, Agricultural Cooperative Service Report Number 18.

——1989. *Farmer cooperative theory: Recent developments.* U.S. Dept. of Agriculture, Agricultural Cooperative Service Report Number 84 (June).

Tullock, Gordon, and Jimmye Hillman. 1989. Public choice and agriculture: An American example. In *International Economic Association Congress Proceedings, 9th World Congress.* Vol. 3. Athens, Greece: Economic Research Center, The Athens School of Economics and Business.

U.S. Dept. of Agriculture. 1979. *Structure issues of American agriculture.* Agricultural Economics Report 438. Washington, D.C.: USDA, Economics, Statistics, and Cooperative Service.

——1987. *Rural economic development in the 1980s: Preparing for the future.* Economic Research Staff Report No. AGES870724. Washington, D.C.: USDA, Agriculture and Rural Economy Division, Economic Research Service, July.

Williamson, Oliver E. 1985. *The economic institutions of capitalism: Firms, markets, relational contracting.* New York: Free Press.

CHAPTER 2

SOCIAL SCIENCE ISSUES IN AGRICULTURE AND RURAL COMMUNITIES[1]

Paul W. Barkley[2]

INTRODUCTION

The social sciences are the scientific disciplines that deal with human behavior. This simplified definition is enough to make it clear that social scientists have a major role in studying and analyzing the problems of agriculture and rural communities. Agriculture and rural living are both social activities. This is more than a casual reflection. Agriculture and rural life are conducted following a variety of social and cultural forces that have been present over the centuries, as well as recent forces that have been imposed from external authority. It is precisely the business of social scientists to inquire how these forces affect the organization and performance of not only agriculture, but also the local environments in which it is conducted.

This observation provides little focus for the important research issues that should occupy social scientists as the twentieth century comes to a close. Operational focus for the problems requires both a narrowing and a broadening of the topics (problems) to make them fit with the ordinary language of social science and so they can be made into issues that might strike either a harmonic or a discordant note in the minds of the scientists who must deal with them: harmonic to cultivate some feeling of consistency or convergence in the pursuit of science; discordant to foster the inquisitiveness and creative tension that is prerequisite to generating fruitful research agendas regarding how the agricultural (rural) world is organized; how the non-agricultural world impinges upon it; and how agriculture impinges upon the outside world.

In the present context, a number of problems are characterized as broad social forces that are at work in the nation and the world. Where possible, these forces are changed into issues that social scientists who work in agriculture might find important as they develop their research agendas.

Almost all critical issues have a time dimension. The credit crisis in agriculture provides an arresting example. In 1982 and 1983, a number of social scientists devoted attention to it. Now, six years later, it is a problem, but not a critical issue in agriculture or in rural communities. At the opposite extreme, U.S. agriculture has been plagued by overproduction and redundant resources in nearly every year for six decades—a time period ten times as long as the contemporary problem with credit. A large number of social scientists study a number of aspects of the overproduction problem, but the problem is so persistent that it is seldom thought to be of crisis proportions. In fact, it is: it is an enduring crisis that has refused to yield to policy or program, so it has been relegated to a secondary role in social science research. Other themes are more glamorous. The point is that problems have different time spans or critical lives. The individual social scientist must learn to identify the likely time span of the problems that one will be examining.[3]

The remainder of this paper develops seven major issues that will have an immense impact on what social scientists do as they continue to deal with the problems of agricultural and rural communities over the closing years of this century. These issues include: (1) the internationalization of agriculture, (2) domestic agricultural policy, (3) the structure of agriculture, (4) the "down-sizing" of agricultural firms, (5) the creation of human capital, (6) changing rural demographics, and (7) environmental quality. Each of these includes some circularity in that agriculture both affects and is affected by certain attributes of them. Some of the circularities will be mentioned.

THE INTERNATIONALIZATION OF AGRICULTURE

Agriculture has always been an international industry. Trade in agricultural products was prominent among the ancient civilizations that bordered the Mediterranean. More recently, the great empires of Europe were designed to internationalize farming by procuring agricultural and other extractive products from the underdeveloped parts of the world. In contemporary times, the Marshall Plan and, later, the Food for Peace Program (Public Law 480) represent different kinds of internationalization, but kinds in which one people's food depends on another people's productive endeavors.

The world now appears to be moving into a period in which relative prices of agricultural commodities (which may or may not be set in a freely operating market) will increasingly determine the patterns of international trade in those commodities. The problem is that, except for some isolated cases of famine, all agricultural countries, regardless of stage of development or form of government, seem to be attempting to increase their international sales of farm products. The United States will have to be particularly careful in establishing its international role. It, as much as Argentina, depends on income from the sale of farm commodities for balance-of-payments reasons. However, by entering the world market on equal or on the slightly favorable terms afforded by export subsidies, United States trading could restrict the trading done by some very fragile nations. It is not at all clear that stability in international markets will occur as long as the United States is dispensing technical aid to Third World nations when trying to negotiate with them or with other buyers who might become either trading partners or trading rivals.[4] This is a critical issue that ultimately can affect world prices, volumes of goods exchanged, efficiency in production, and incomes (and subsequently, diets) in both developed and developing nations.[5]

The problem is even broader. Internationalization in today's terms has integrated world economic activity as never before. Federal officials in all three branches of government are concerned. Governors in farm states are watching international trade. States are setting up international trading agencies to find export markets for their products. Country bankers, who just months ago were content to watch the activity of the Mercantile Exchange and the Chicago Board of Trade, are now watching international money markets; not necessarily with the idea of investing in Yen or Deutschemarks, but to gain some insights about the relative performance of other economies and to judge how that will affect economic activity in their own areas. Social scientists in the land-grant system should afford these public and private officials all possible help during this time of significant change in world agriculture and the ordering of worldwide economic activity.

DOMESTIC AGRICULTURAL POLICY

There have always been domestic policies that affect U.S. agriculture. The phrase "domestic agricultural policy" generally summons thoughts of the vast and complex array of price and production controls that began with the Agricultural Adjustment Act of 1933.[6] The contemporary debate over agricultural policy has intensified because of the potential and real changes in general economic policy and economic performance that have occurred since the passage of the Food Security Act of 1985. The contemporary version of the policy debate will remain prominent for two major reasons: (1) the Conservation Reserve Program and (2) decoupling or making payments that are independent of production and land use to farmers.

The present Conservation Reserve Program seeks to remove 45 million acres of highly erodible land from crop production by 1990. Eligible land will be identified and idled in exchange for an annual rental payment made by the government. Contracts between individual farmers and the government come in response to bids made by the farmers. Most contracts are for ten years, and the government uses a cost-sharing scheme to help participating farmers establish permanent protective cover on the land (Glaser 1986). At this time, nearly 25 million acres have been signed into the program, and the average annual rental payment per acre is hovering around $50, nationwide.

This drastic change in land use (up to 25 percent of a county's land can be idled) is likely to have effects similar to those caused by the original Soil Bank Programs of the mid–1950s and the PIK program of 1983. Farm incomes in areas of high participation will remain high, but the local supply and processing firms that are linked to agriculture will be seriously affected by a reduction in business volume. Perhaps more importantly, most of the land removed from agricultural production through the second half of the 1980s will be free to come back into production in the second half of the 1990s. Both events, the taking and the giving back, are likely to cause instability in those parts of the nation where participation is particularly high.[7] Unless the temporary program is converted into a permanent one, agriculture and rural communities should prepare for a period of policy-engendered instability that will last for a number of years.

This period of time and this rural issue will provide many questions for a number of social scientists who are presently at work in the nation's experiment stations: sociologists, economists, political scientists, lawyers, and the handful of others. These scientists will be troubled by questions relating to who will idle the land (although this question is already half answered), what effects the program will have on the nonland resources in agriculture, what effects idling the land will have on agriculture's support industries, and, perhaps most importantly, under what conditions and in what way will the land come back into production.

The effects of decoupling are more difficult to discuss. The mechanics of decoupling are quite simple, as are the potential budget savings and the production efficiencies that come with lump-sum payments rather than payments that are based on land use and output. The questions arise with respect to how the decoupled program entitlements will be capitalized into the value of land, what arrangements will be made for the transfer of entitlements, and the ranges within which Congress or its designated agency can change the value of an entitlement. All of these factors ultimately bear on the value of farm resources, and in states that have both assessment limits and limits on tax levies the problem is transferred immediately to the local public sector that undoubtedly will suffer reduced income from property taxes. Decoupling carries a broad distribution of effects.

How urgent is this research issue? Very urgent, because farmers' responses to decoupling are generally unknown. While farmers almost always make public statements in favor of decoupling ("or getting the government out of farming"), it is not clear that this is what they actually desire.[8] Switching from production- or resource-related programs to direct-income maintenance programs and eventually to no program will surely change the distribution of income in the industry and could even modify the way in which resources are held and controlled. The collection of very high-quality primary data from a very wide geographic area will be required before the myriad questions that surround decoupling can be addressed in any but a superficial manner.

THE STRUCTURE OF AGRICULTURE

The Carter administration called attention to issues that surround the structure of agriculture. In the early efforts, the definitions of structure were not at all clear, but it seemed to have something to do with farm size and the ownership and control of farm resources—especially land. The decade that has passed since the Carter administration's interest has brought many changes in the organization of farming, the ownership of farm resources, and the sources of income for farm families.

The run-up of land prices in the 1970s, coupled with the general, society-wide decline of the insular family, broke the traditional pattern of intergenerational transfers of agricultural land. No longer was it assumed mandatory or morally correct for one sibling to remain on the farm and buy out the interests of the other siblings who had gone on to other professions. The lawyer brother in Chicago and the physical therapist sister in Des Moines began to retain ownership of their inheritances. More than this, their inculcated acquisitiveness was an invitation to them to rent out their land, not necessarily to the sibling who had remained in agriculture, but to the highest bidder or the bidder who would follow their instructions on how to use the land. This issue—a variant of the traditional absentee-owner problem—poses critical issues related to the family farm,[9] the size and geographic dispersion of the farming unit, and the rules under which farming can be conducted.

Gathering the resources for farming is more difficult now than it was in the years immediately after the closing of the frontier. At that time, the "family farm" defined the geographic as well as the economic limits of a farming enterprise, and institutional forms surrounding the disposal of the public domain governed the size of the owner-operated portion of many farm operations. Now, with the ownership of agricultural land resources becoming increasingly dispersed, the farm operator or manager may find that collecting a sufficient number of land parcels for efficient farming is one of the most onerous and time-consuming tasks.

If the land has to be rented or leased, there are no guarantees to the stability of the unit. The one-year lease provides little incentive for investment in the land and the use of superior farming techniques. Circumstances are little improved under two- or three-year arrangements. Under short-term circumstances, producers will find it difficult to match land inventories with livestock enterprises and machinery inventories. The entire effect has a possible destabilizing influence on the industry—one that could be felt through processors and on to consumers.

The problem becomes more severe when the environmental awareness of land owners is taken into account. Some owners may insist that tenants use a chemical-free method of farming; others may want a strict rotation to be followed; and still others may specify that the land is to be operated in such a way as to maximize short-term returns. It may be nearly impossible for a farm operator who has to depend on land owned by others to find a collection of land resources that is compatible with one's interests and capabilities.

Clearly, this issue that impinges on (if it does not actually define) structure is a long-term issue. Despite major studies in 1948 and 1977, the nation still does not know who owns its agricultural land. It knows even less well who controls its land resources. As the above problem becomes more widespread, it will become increasingly important to know who is in control so the policy can be directed at the appropriate decision makers.

The entire land-ownership problem has another dimension that increases the severity of the issues listed above. The problem is related to the performance of the macroeconomy. Inflationary and deflationary periods are both thought to be good times to hold land; it has almost always been a solid investment that maintains value during the downturns and allows speculative gains during a rising market. This common notion insures that nonfarm investors will continue to be attracted to agricultural land. If they succeed, it will become increasingly difficult for farm operators to exercise complete control over the land bases that they are farming. The problems envisioned by the Carter administration may have been long in coming, but their importance has not been diminished by the passage of time.

DOWNSIZING OF AGRICULTURE

Some observers divide the development of economic and social activity in the United States's rural areas into three stages (Dillman 1988). The first stage, which lasted until perhaps 1920, was a period of self-direction during which rural communities could control their own destinies or at least control the internal organization of local functions. The second stage, lasting from the 1940s until the 1980s, is defined as the era of mass society when external influences changed and homogenized the way things were done: a rural area in Indiana would behave in much the same fashion as a rural area in California. Each would, however, take orders from external authority and be dependent on the economic swings occurring outside its own boundaries. The emphasis was on size and efficiency in production units.

The era of mass society is purported to have been replaced somewhat recently by a time of great dependence on information: the information era. One of the characteristics of the information era is the potential downsizing of productive entities to enable them to be more responsive to market needs. This process has reached into agriculture and has brought with it a specialized vocabulary of its own. Producers search for "market niches" where very specialized products can be sold to very specialized clienteles. Farmers formerly grew cucumbers. Now they grow cucumbers of a particular size, mix them with special spices, bottle them, and sell them as pickles to very select customers.

There are several problems with very small and highly specialized producing firms. The first and obvious one is that they do not lend themselves to examination using the research techniques ordinarily employed in the social sciences. They are more amenable to the research techniques used by business schools that emphasize the case study approach to investigation. More important is the problem that they portend with respect to the organization and control of agriculture. Agriculture is becoming an industry of the small and the large. The new firms in the industry are small by comparison to the family farms and corporate farms that produce the bulk of U.S. agricultural commodities. Many are operated by families that earn more income from nonfarm than from farm sources.[10] The issue here is that farming or food production may be becoming a second source of income for the producers. If so, farming may become a parttime job and stability in the food supply may be threatened; in a crisis it may be more profitable for the family to abandon its farming activities than to give up its nonfarm job(s).

This issue does not appear to be serious in January of 1988. It does, however, carry the potential of becoming serious over the next few years. It is disquieting to think of a nation of parttime farmers who are quite capable of giving up food production at any time. Surely this is a social science problem that deserves immediate attention. It has farm and off-farm dimensions, but its appeal comes from the fact that it impinges on the food supply and it also reaches into the kinds of tradeoffs that families will have to make as farming becomes increasingly competitive and the off-farm income of farm families continues to rise.

THE CREATION OF HUMAN CAPITAL

Some of the earliest advocates of rural development—Liberty Hyde Bailey, G. F. Warren, Theodore Roosevelt, and Charles Galpin, among others—were convinced that rural places were good places to live. These observers were not seduced into thinking that being a good place to live also meant that rural places could create human capital as rapidly as nonrural areas. Much of their collective writing on rural area development and rural policy concentrated on the notion that the rural regions were falling behind urban America in education and health care. In the period since these scientists and leaders were active, much has been done in attempts to close the gap between rural and urban areas as these areas produce different forms of human capital.

In spite of some major efforts, the gap appears to be widening. Many rural areas appear to be falling behind in their production of education and health. Rural areas are attempting to develop. Whether they can or not remains a critical issue. One factor that may prevent them from developing is the lack of a labor force that possesses high-tech, information-age skills. The way to obtain these skills is through investment in education. Investments in primary and secondary education are not new topics for social scientists who specialize in agriculture and rural communities. To be sure, there will continue to be problems of school finance and the quality of education, but these problems are not new. While finance and quality remain, they will be joined by the problems of postsecondary education, retraining, and lifelong learning. The job retraining and on-the-job training experiences of the 1970s do not provide a happy precedent for the training and retraining of adults. Regardless of the success or failure of earlier efforts, the job has to be done if rural areas are to put together a labor force that is capable of functioning in the high-tech, information era. Innovation and adaptation—two themes frequently studied by social scientists—will have to be used in the production of human capital.

Producing and maintaining human capital is a persistent and multifaceted problem. The fact that it was observed and described by a number of scholars and policy makers early in the century attests to its venerability. But its *persistence* is more troublesome than its venerability. A rural area has no hope of developing in today's information era if it does not have an information-era labor force, but incurring the great public cost required to produce this kind of labor force provides no assurance that either the modern, information-era jobs will appear or that the newly trained and highly skilled labor force will remain in place. This is not a new phenomenon, but it is one that social scientists have been reluctant to address in recent years. This is somewhat surprising given the reasonably well-known connections between education, migration, and the welfare of local populations.

CHANGING DEMOGRAPHICS

Since about 1920, most rural areas in the United States have experienced almost continual change in the size and composition of the local population. Farm technologies, rural institutions, and market forces have mitigated in favor of outmigration and usually the young, active members of the population are the ones who have left. This has left towns and communities with excess capacity and has brought a waste of infrastructural resources. Although described by a variety of terms, this waste has again become an issue in rural areas.

The brief but widely acknowledged "population turnaround" of the 1970s brought temporary relief. Some observers look for another turnaround to secure the future of rural areas, but a repeat of the 1970s experience is unlikely. Numerous studies from several parts of the nation sought to document and explain the population turnaround (Barkley and Rogers 1986). A frequent question centered on who was moving and why they were making the move. In all but a few studies, the most prominent reason for moving to a rural area was to find a job, and the most common description for the migrant was "former resident." The people who moved in were the same people who had moved out in an earlier period. People, like salmon and the birds at Capistrano, seem to want to come home!

If this is true, then it is highly unlikely that a similar turnaround will replenish the population of rural areas in the future. The supply of people born and raised in rural areas is diminishing each year. The consequences are not casual. Efforts will continue to be made to prompt people to move to rural areas. If these efforts are successful, the people who move will have to be new to rural living and will likely require more time to adjust to their new environs. More than this, the current residents of the area may have to be trained to accept a population that is ill-prepared to deal with rurality. This has already become an issue in suburban and ex-urban regions. It may become an issue in those rural areas that are successful in their efforts to recruit new populations. If so, public resources may have to be used to help the old and the new populations make the adjustment. Adjustment in this case is in terms of human behavior, so it automatically becomes part of the domain of the social sciences.

ENVIRONMENTAL QUALITY

No list of social science issues would be complete without some mention of environmental quality. Agriculture is hard on the environment. This would be true even in the absence of the moldboard plow, chemical fertilizers, and highly toxic pesticides. The introduction of animal agriculture in New England in the seventeenth century, for example, despoiled the landscape and resulted in soil erosion that filled many of the area's natural harbors with silt. The problem was so severe that Boston eventually had to extend its wharves by as much as 1,000 feet so that ocean-going vessels could utilize the port.

The erosion problem remains and has become a national issue. It has been joined by a host of other problems under the name "non-point source pollution." This category of pollution is perhaps the most insidious of all types of pollution. It is now manifesting itself in water quality, and recent interest in water quality has shown that agriculture will be identified as one culpable party—perhaps the most culpable party. Because of its enormity and ubiquity, the issue cannot be ignored.

This issue—water quality as specific; environmental degradation as more general—carries with it an odd counterpoint among the electorate and the interested citizenry. For nearly six decades, the nation's leadership and citizenry have indulged agriculture by seeking to build institutions designed to increase opportunity and enhance farm incomes. There is already strong evidence that production agriculture will not be so kindly treated in matters related to the environment. The public will pay taxes to support farm prices, but it will not allow agriculture to trifle with the quality of groundwater or the depth of the topsoil. Moreover, the public seems unwilling to pay large sums to either clean up existing environmental problems or to compensate farmers whose incomes are reduced as a result of mandates to reduce the incidence of agricultural-related chemicals in the environment. The mood is to ban the offending chemicals and to pass laws preventing the use of agricultural practices that may be or may become a threat to some aspect of the environment.

Environmental issues are of such recent origin that finding satisfactory resolutions to them will require much inventive attention. Institutions will have to be designed to establish what farmers can and cannot do with the factor inputs or production practices that carry negative environmental externalities. Although social science researchers have always worked on institutions, laws, conventions, and restrictions, the current problem is immense enough to require the attention of expert scientists over many years. More than this, the issue has as many tentacles into the physical and biological sciences as it does into the social sciences. Success in finding acceptable resolutions to environmental problems will require a team effort.

DISCUSSION

No paper of this length can describe adequately the social science issues that are related to agriculture and rural areas in the United States. The list of real and potential problems is too long and too complex. Notably absent from the present list is the entire series of questions that surround the relationship between agriculture and biotechnology. Also missing are the problems of hunger, consumerism, the family farm, political stability, rural poverty, food safety, economic growth, policy processes, social safety nets, and the validity of neo-Malthusianism. Each of these topics has a huge social—and, hence, social science—component, so it should find a place on the agendas of the social scientists who are interested in agricultural and rural areas.

The themes that have been elaborated or mentioned here can all be subsumed under the general headings of policy, population, and pollution. All elements of this triad have both cause-and-effect interactions with the stability of the nation's rural areas. This is a serious problem that has escaped systematic examination since T. W. Schultz (1945) was writing on this theme in the 1940s and 1950s. This theme must be visited again, and it is both a logical and a necessary task for social scientists working in the land-grant system in the closing years of the twentieth century.

NOTES

1. This paper was delivered at "A Workshop on Social Science Research in the Agricultural Experiment Stations," January 25–27, 1988, Arlington, Virginia.
2. Paul W. Barkley is a professor of Agricultural Economics at Washington State University. This paper was written while Dr. Barkley was on leave with the Resources and Technology Division, Economic Research Service, U.S. Department of Agriculture.
3. The problem is more insidious than just finding the correct time frame for the critical issue. Some scientists are quite capable of spending a lifetime on one kind of problem. Others become impatient and look for new problems or challenges at frequent intervals. The fact that there are "three-month scientists" and "lifetime scientists" should in no way castigate the performance of either group. It should, however, underscore the need for scientists and their administrators to understand how essential it is to match people with problems.
4. To be sure, the United States is not alone in the vicious game of providing technical assistance to a food-poor nation and then complaining bitterly when the technical aid is so successful that the recipient nation becomes a trading rival. It is moot as to whether this is an economic, moral, or ethical issue. Regardless, it is a high-order social issue.
5. The problem is much more severe than characterized here. Instability in the international exchange of farm commodities can ultimately have an effect on such things as the activities of the Commodity Credit Corporation, the public debt, and the structure of domestic agriculture. The intensity of this problem was recognized in the early 1980s when it became a driving force in the Uruguay round of the GATT negotiations.
6. Although the modern era of agricultural policy began in the 1930s, there were acreage allotments and price support programs of a sort in colonial Virginia in the first decade after settlement. Similarly, the Farmers' Alliance of the 1870s proposed price controls, production controls, and storage programs that were remarkably similar to those in place today (Taylor 1953). Policy seems to be an eternal issue for social scientists.
7. At this time, it appears that the grain-producing regions of the central and northern plains will have the highest participation rates, with scattered small areas of high participation elsewhere in the country.

8. The only hard evidence of farmers' real dispositions about the proper role for government remains the 1963 wheat referendum in which farmers chose a low price-support program that carried no explicit penalty for over-planting over a program that was highly restrictive but included high price supports (Tweeten 1979). It is not clear that the same choice would be made today. Moreover, the "most likely choice" may have changed a number of times as the economic fortunes of agriculture have shifted during the past decade.

9. The fragmentation of farmland ownership has been slowed somewhat through the use of the institution of "undivided interests" in landed property. An undivided interest means that several parties hold part ownership, but the exact part of the land parcel that is owned by each member of the group of owners is not specifically identifiable or separable from the remainder of the land.

10. As early as 1982, nearly half of all farmers in the United States reported their major occupation as something other than farming and approximately 60 percent of all farm families earned more from off-farm sources than from the farm.

REFERENCES

Barkley, Paul W., and Denise M. Rogers. 1986. More new people in old towns: It may not indicate financial health. *Choices* (4th quarter).

Dillman, Don A. 1988. The social environment of agriculture and rural areas. In *Agriculture and rural areas approaching the twenty-first century*. Edited by R. J. Hildreth et al. Ames: Iowa State University Press.

Glaser, Lawrence K. 1986. Provisions of the Food Security Act of 1985. Agriculture Information Bulletin 498. U.S. Dept. of Agriculture, Economic Research Service, April.

Schultz, T. W. 1945. *Agriculture in an unstable economy*. New York: McGraw-Hill.

Taylor, Carl C. 1953. *The farmers' movement, 1620–1920*. New York: American Book Co.

Tweeten, Luther G. 1979. *Foundations of farm policy*. 2d ed. Lincoln: University of Nebraska Press.

CHAPTER 3

RURAL PEOPLE, RESOURCES, AND COMMUNITIES: AN ASSESSMENT OF THE CAPABILITIES OF THE SOCIAL SCIENCES IN AGRICULTURE

James C. Hite[1]

INTRODUCTION

The task to be accomplished by this paper is daunting. It is to assess the capabilities of the social sciences to address in meaningful, practical ways the problems of rural America. Deliberately excluding the production and marketing of farm products, the subject matter embraces rural people, their health, education, family lives, and civil participation; rural communities and their institutions; the economic geography of rural regions; and natural resource management and conservation.

So broad is the scope of the subject matter that it is probably impossible to do it justice. This paper can only survey the field, painting the scene with broad strokes that suggest, but do not depict all, the subtle and important details.

The paper is divided into three major parts. The first part focuses upon the nature of the manifest problems facing rural America at a time of historic change in agriculture and in the economic structure of rural regions. The second part focuses upon the epistemological assets and liabilities of the social sciences for addressing these problems. The final part examines problems within the community of social science scholars, both within the land-grant university system and beyond, that bear upon addressing the very real and serious adjustment problems rural America must confront.

RURAL AMERICA IN CHANGE

RURAL REGIONS IN A POST-MODERN WORLD

Rural America is undergoing profound economic change in the late twentieth century. As Kirkendall (Part I, Chapter 2) notes, the exact meaning of this change with regard to farm families and the location and organization of agricultural production is open to question. So, too, is the meaning of this change for the rural nonfarm population. Yet there is good reason to believe that a combination of political, social, and technological developments are now in place that are as significant in their implications for rural America as the great historical transformation that accompanied other quantum changes in the dominant mode of production (e.g., as during the Industrial Revolution).

Agricultural Technology

The first of these factors is the technological change in agricultural production, particularly that associated with computers and with biotechnology. The recent efforts by the Office of Technology Assessment to examine emerging technologies in agriculture suggest that technologies expected to come into use early in the next century will (1) greatly reduce the land required to produce those agricultural products that can be absorbed by the market at prices equal to, or greater than, production costs, (2) accentuate the trend toward larger farm production units, and (3) shift agricultural production toward those areas able to make effective use of computer-driven irrigation systems.

The implications of these changes are perhaps most troublesome to areas at the extensive margin of present agricultural production, primarily the South, where large amounts of land now used for farming could become redundant. There are also troublesome implications for the Midwest, however, where the modest-sized, family-owned-and-operated farms will be under increasing competitive pressure from large farming operations in the irrigated areas of the Southwest that are better positioned to take advantage of new sophisticated technology, particularly if federal policy persists in subsidizing provision of irrigation water to Southwestern agriculture.

Geopolitical Change

The second factor underlying change is geopolitical. The breakdown of colonialism after World War II produced many more independent agents in the buying and selling of goods and services in world markets. American sponsorship of a world economic order, centered on (more-or-less) free trade, expanded the markets in which American farmers and rural communities participated. Yet it also expanded the potential competition for American producers of both agricultural and manufactured products. American and European programs of technical assistance to developing nations expanded the capabilities of many countries to meet their own agricultural needs from domestic production and to become exporters of agricultural commodities and manufactured goods. A global economy has emerged as a result (Drucker 1986; Deaton and Weber 1985).

No longer is it sufficient that a region possess comparative advantage within the U.S. market. To achieve economic prosperity a region must be able to compete successfully in the new global economy—i.e., it must have comparative advantage in world markets.

While American agriculture, particularly the grain-oriented agriculture of the Midwest, appeared to have worldwide comparative advantage into the 1970s, it is no longer clear that the United States occupies such a favorable position. New production centers in the Southern Hemisphere are favored by lower land costs and cheaper labor. Moreover, the technology that gave the United States, and the Midwest, comparative advantage in agriculture through the 1970s is developing along lines that are unlikely to reinforce the position of family farms in the country's rural heartland.

Although the prospects for the rural Midwest are ambiguous, they are much less so with regard to the economic base of the South and other rural areas where manufacturing has replaced agriculture as the dominant sector. Long suffering from an excess of labor relative to capital in agriculture, the South was successful in programs of rural industrialization during the third quarter of the century. The work of agricultural social scientists was highly significant in achieving that success. The strategy was based primarily upon selling low-cost labor to manufacturers by attracting branch plants of U.S. firms expanding to fill niches in the markets for manufactured goods left empty by the wartime destruction of industrial capacity in Western Europe and Japan. The South (and some other rural regions) built a new, nonfarm economy by working the end of the product cycle.

Success in pursuing such a strategy was due to exploiting a set of historical conditions that were, by their very nature, transitive. Industrial capacity in Europe and Japan was bound, sooner or later, to be restored and produce competition for American manufacturers. Moreover, advances in the technology of transportation and communications were to make manufacturing production feasible in many labor-surplus parts of the world. Even though there remains (and likely will remain) important advantages to locating manufacturing within the American market, those advantages are often not great enough to offset the labor cost savings to be achieved by locating activities at the end of the product cycle in developing countries. Domestic U.S. manufacturers are having a difficult time competing with offshore operations in labor-intensive production. Since low-cost labor is one of the principal attractions for rural industrialization, there is good reason to doubt whether manufacturing remains a viable alternative as part of the economic base of many rural communities (Rosenfeld, Bergman, and Rubin 1985).

The reason for doubt is that there does not seem to be much opportunity for rural regions to compete for economic activity higher on the product cycle, or in the service sectors. Jane Jacobs (1969, 1984), Niles Hansen (1979), and a number of geographers have made convincing arguments that urban centers have inherent advantages in the early stages of the product cycle, and in the provision of those sophisticated services requiring professional competence. The emergence of new manufacturing techniques such as "just-in-time" inventory management only reinforce the economies of agglomeration available in urban locations. Indeed, the reasoning put forth by Jacobs, Hansen, and others leads to the conclusion that all rural regions are simply part of the economic hinterland of some primal city to which those regions are tributary. The role of these rural areas in a modern market economy is tied inextricably to the fate of the economy of that primal city.

Shifts in the locus of the primal city, sometimes (but not always) associated with change in the mode of production, have meant, according to some analyses, great spurts of growth and prosperity for heretofore backwater regions and communities, and dramatic declines in the status of once-prosperous communities. Whether the fate is boom or bust, both people and community institutions can be traumatized. Hence, shifts in the comparative advantage of rural regions associated with changes in agricultural technology and the emergence of a global economy imply major social adjustments for much of rural America. Public policies may be capable of making the adjustment less chaotic and painful for individuals and communities, but it is probably neither possible nor desirable that such policies can make the adjustments unnecessary.

Changing Policy Environment

The third change may be simply a result of the first two and not exogenous to history. Yet in seemingly simultaneous occurrence, the environment in which public policy is formulated in the United States is undergoing change. Our attention to cycles in the policy arena has been summoned in a recent book by historian Arthur Schlesinger (1986). The New Deal era, which corresponded to one phase of a cycle, gave way to what some predict is a new era of conservatism in political, social, and economic behavior.

Webber and Wildavsky (1986, 25) provide a conceptual model that allows for explanation of not only shifts in the political environment as a generic phenomenon, but also the shift toward the individualist, libertarian axis that could be hypothesized as now being evident in the United States. If that hypothesis is true, fundamental assumptions about how people conduct themselves relative to government must be altered. While it is not necessary to abandon rent-seeking activities, the rationale stated openly for public policies must be reformulated to speak to the commonly held precepts (what Garry Wills [1978] called the "common sense") of the body politic.

The ramifications of such changes in the policy environment for rural people, resources, and communities requires more careful thought than is possible here. Yet they possibly include such insignificant structural shifts in the social welfare function as to include reduction in the value placed on rural life as part of the nation's cultural heritage, a growing attitude of laissez-faire toward lagging regions, a reduction in the value placed on public, as opposed, to private wealth, and stronger local autonomy for natural resource management and use. Even marginal shifts in these directions would likely have major implications for rural America.

RURAL NATURAL RESOURCES

Concerns about regional land use and the natural environment are the link between regional development and problems of natural resource management and use. It is entirely possible that whatever comparative advantage rural areas possess in the next century will be related, in some way, to what they will have that urban areas do not have—relatively large expanses of open space and quasi-natural environmental amenities.

The state of the environment and the management of the society's natural resource endowment are subjects that do not require a rural focus. The urban environment and urban land use, for example, are subjects that receive considerable attention in their own right. Moreover, the use of natural resources as input into production processes is of concern to the general economy independent of the implications for rural people, communities, and regions.

Yet the greatest mass of our land is, and will remain, rural in setting; most of the nation's forest, wildlife, and water resources are, and will continue to be, located in rural areas, and the extraction of mineral resources often is associated with a rural environment. The rural environment (or, to be more accurate, rural environments) is, and will continue to be, perceived as an important part of our collective national wealth. Rural America, therefore, has important interests in the management and use of natural resources.

For the lay public and for social scientists, the 1970s were a time of unparalleled interest in resource and environmental issues. Public policy initiatives have succeeded in dealing with the most obvious and pressing of these issues. While some social scientists (particularly economists) remain less than satisfied with the content of important policies, some air and surface water pollution has been reduced, tougher steps have been taken to deal with environmental problems associated with mining, and machinery has been established to deal with groundwater contamination and control release into the environment of toxic substances. Yet it appears that a consensus on the general direction of public policy has been established and the remaining problems, while by no means insignificant, are primarily ones of detail and implementation.

There is also a whole range of resource management issues especially important to rural America. Among these issues, those associated with federal management of public lands and multipurpose development of water resources loom especially large. Long-established policies regarding federal leasing of mineral and grazing lands, harvesting of timber from the national forests, and provision of irrigation water have numerous sharp critics within both the academic community and residents of communities directly affected by federal management programs. The critics sit on both the right (e.g., Baden [1987]) and on the left (e.g., Reisner [1986]) sides of the political aisle. Western dissatisfaction has become so intense as to create a quasi-movement known as the Sagebrush Rebellion. Yet despite efforts by both the Carter and the Reagan administrations (in the case of water projects and of public lands management, respectively) to institute policy reforms, much of rural America remains a colony with its most valuable natural resources controlled by the central government in Washington.

These resources remain controlled by Washington because a substantial part of the population, particularly urbanites and Easterners, tend to see the public domain as a great "national park" reserved for the benefit and enjoyment of the whole country. That is not the view of rural residents, particularly in the West, who tend to see the resources of the public domain as part of their local resource endowment for developmental use to enhance their own utility. This fundamental difference in viewpoints shows no signs of converging, and as long as it persists, issues in resource management will remain. Demography, as much as anything else, is likely to determine which viewpoint dictates public policy because population will determine how Congress and the Electoral College will be apportioned.

Demography changes, in turn, are a function of land use in rural areas (as, conversely, rural land use is a function of demography). Demographic trends suggest that even in rural communities the divergence in viewpoints over management of natural resources will intensify. With an aging population in the country—a population that need not have jobs within commuting distance of the residence—rural areas may become populated by a disproportionately large number of the elderly seeking to live the end of their lives in places with attractive environmental amenities. Substantial population growth in some rural areas could be associated with an influx of retirees (Serow and Charity 1987), and, at the margin, this influx will improve the political position of rural areas in national councils. Yet, if these elderly are drawn to rural communities by environmental amenities, they may be less than sympathetic to the concerns of the natives desiring greater latitude in logging, mining, grazing, etc. So the demographic trends, as they are now evident, are not favorable to a political resolution of issues over control of natural resources in favor of greater local autonomy, especially if that autonomy would result in increased developmental use of those resources for private economic gain.

Two topics that may endanger new national policy are pricing policies regarding irrigation water from federal projects and soil conservation. The former is much too complicated to be treated here even in a cursory way except to note the growing acceptance among intellectuals of a more market-oriented approach to Western water (Anderson 1983). Such an approach, should it be adopted, would have profound implications for the agricultural geography of the country and perhaps restore whatever comparative advantage Midwestern agriculture may be losing. The general direction of federal policy toward soil conservation is perhaps suggested in the Sodbuster and Swampbuster provisions of the 1985 farm law, particularly its focus upon cross-compliance—i.e., conformity with certain land-use restrictions in order to qualify for farm income and price support payments (Reilly 1987). In both cases, the policy trend is influenced not so much by grassroots concerns of people in rural areas as by the interests and concerns of urban governments and urban-based conservation groups.

As already noted, the aging population in the country may provide a new economic base for some rural communities, particularly those in proximity to medium-sized centers of urban services in areas with desirable climate and other environmental amenities. The Ozarks, the Carolina mountains and foothills, the coastal counties from the Chesapeake Bay to the Rio Grande, some parts of the desert Southwest, and certain areas of the Pacific Northwest seem destined to become meccas for retirees. Yet if the elderly move to rural areas for environmental amenities, the redevelopment of those rural areas may require that these amenities be guarded and enhanced. Such agriculture as remains will need to be compatible with the desired environmental amenities, whether that agriculture is centered around parttime or commercial farms. Similarly, other types of economic activities will need to be subordinated to the protection of these amenities. Public policy aimed at protecting these amenities, be it coastal management, land-use control, farmland preservation, or something else, is likely to emerge primarily at the state level and to be viewed as tactical measures in support of the overall state development strategy.

RURAL HUMAN RESOURCES AND COMMUNITY INSTITUTIONS

Compared to urban centers, the transferable human capital held in rural America, even on a per capita basis, is relatively low. Rural Americans are less well educated, on average, than their city cousins; in part because: (1) on a per-pupil basis, education in rural areas is more expensive than in an urban setting and, (2) with few exceptions, rural areas have fewer resources to finance education than do urban areas (Gilford, Nelson, and Ingram 1981, 100; see also *The People Left Behind* [President's National Advisory Commission on Rural Poverty] 1967, 41–57). The economic distress in agricultural areas of the 1980s appears to be undermining the ability of many communities to support public education at adequate levels (Hite and Ulbrich 1986). This implies not only that the opportunities for adjustment to new economic and social conditions have been more limited for rural than urban people, but also that during a time when the adjustments are likely to be more challenging than before, the limitations on opportunities are becoming more severe.

Backwater areas typically contain a population with relatively large numbers of older and younger persons. The working-age population migrates to other locations for jobs, but the elderly, and often the children, are left behind. Not all rural areas are destined to be backwater areas, yet the possibility must be seriously entertained that more areas will be in the future than are now. Such a situation will exacerbate the human capital problem in rural America, posing serious difficulties for funding schools for children and providing medical and related care for the elderly. Even those communities that are successful in selling environmental amenities to relatively affluent retirees could encounter fiscal problems because of the political microclimate likely to arise when retirees become a significant fraction of the population.

It is generally known that older people vote in greater proportion to their number than other groups. They are also less likely to support taxes for public education, the benefits of which to them are not clear. Yet investment in human capital through improved public education may be a necessary strategy for many rural areas to both (1) improve the abilities of their young people to migrate and find rewarding jobs in other areas with growing economies, and (2) improve the competitive position of rural communities in attracting investment that provides jobs at the top end of the product cycle. Without such investments in human capital, many rural areas will have even more diminished prospects for a viable economic base in the second quarter of the twenty-first century than they face presently, and the outlook will become increasingly bleak with each successive generation.

Moreover, success in attracting retirees could produce other serious fiscal difficulties for rural regions. Even the relatively affluent retiree is potentially a burden on the state Medicaid budget. Prolonged stays in nursing homes can exhaust the assets of moderately well-to-do persons. While Medicaid is funded with both federal and state dollars, states with disproportionately large populations of older persons could be placed under very difficult fiscal pressures. Rural regions would seem to have a particularly strong interest in solving the puzzle of financing long-term and catastrophic medical care.

There is a positive side, however, to the possible influx of retirees into some rural communities. Retirees represent a valuable supply of human capital to their new communities that may help to offset the loss in human resources associated with outmigration of the more ambitious, able, and aggressive members of the working-age population. Retirees represent a potential pool of community service volunteers who have both time and experience to contribute to civic activities. If they are not blocked from participation in community life by sociological barriers erected by the indigenous population, these retirees can provide leadership in helping rural communities adapt and change. Sokolow (1986) notes, however, that considerable empirical research is needed to determine the extent to which small rural governments can substitute volunteers for professional or other paid staff. Similarly, Sokolow suggests that friction can result when the agendas and ambitions of activist volunteers clash with those of local officials and professional civil servants.

Finally, the subject of rural human resources cannot be examined without some attention to the continued presence in rural communities of relatively large numbers of Native Americans, African-Americans, and other ethnic minorities that remain on, or beyond, the edge of the mainstream culture. More than twenty years ago, the President's National Advisory Commission on Rural Poverty (1967) noted the special difficulties of these rural Americans. The stripping away of government-sanctioned racial segregation has produced some gains for minorities, but has produced material benefits for relatively few persons. If the well-being of minorities has improved in the past twenty years, the improvement has been marginal.

Minority rural Americans face all the same problems that beset most rural Americans, but because of their special history and different cultural roots, the problems are compounded. Yet the one problem that minorities face, in a much bleaker reality than other rural Americans, is poverty. If minority groups have been able to achieve only marginal material progress during a time when rural America generally achieved significant economic gains, it seems likely that they will especially be adversely affected during the years ahead when the economic success stories in rural America may be rare. That is not to suggest that public policies can address effectively the problems of minority groups in rural America, particularly when those minority groups are treated as passive targets of policy. Some contemporary opinion that doubts the possibility of success has been given serious reception (Gilder 1981; Murray 1984). Even so, these problems demand good-faith efforts to be understood as integral to the tasks that social scientists in agriculture must address. Even if democratically organized, an individualistic, laissez-faire society in a bad temper has the potential of satisfying at least one of Hobbes' conditions for a state of nature—that of being nasty.

EPISTEMOLOGICAL CAPABILITIES OF THE SOCIAL SCIENCES' FRAMEWORK FOR ASSESSMENT

Johnson (1985) provides a useful guide for classifying the information that is gained from such a reconnaissance. He divides the activities of the social sciences into three categories: (1) disciplinary activities—those aimed at advancing the discipline, particularly its theory, without much explicit concern for relevance to pragmatic problems; (2) subject-matter activities—almost always multidisciplinary and focused upon such generic matters as community development, regional growth, public administration, or natural resource policy; and (3) problem-solving activities—also usually multidisciplinary, and directed at finding answers to pragmatic questions arising out of perceptions of objective reality.

Given the human, community, and resource problems sketched above, the prime concern in this part of the paper is with capabilities in the third category of activities. Yet problem-solving capabilities often must rest upon subject-matter and disciplinary assets that also require attention in this reconnaissance. The reconnaissance involves an examination of theory and methods, data resources, and problem-solving capabilities.

THEORY AND METHODS

Theories are the way we explain facts in evidence and the basis for hypothesizing about facts not in evidence. In the absence of theory, we are unable to explain and organize, to separate the relevant facts from the almost infinite numbers of facts that might be ascertained. In the social sciences, the development and testing of both theories and methods is largely the work of disciplinary and subject-matter activities.

There are only bits and pieces of theory for explaining and organizing facts about regional change and adjustment in rural America. Although there are some candidate general theories in the work of Marx, in the urban-centered concepts advanced by Jane Jacobs (1969, 1984), and in modifications of Schumpertian development theory emerging in the work of Vernon (1986) and Markusen (1985), none are yet capable of generating hypotheses suitable for rigorous testing in ways that satisfy the requirements of logical positivism. At best, these potential general theories provide little more than a basis for speculation about the regional change and community development.

The result is that many of the social scientists working on regional subject matter are, epistemologically, instrumental phenomenalists. They have made extensive use of location theory, particularly the work of von Thunen, Weber, Losch, and Christaller, and the spatial equilibrium models of Samuelson. Greenhut and his students have made progress in integrating location theory into neoclassical microeconomics. The production models of Leontief (and the derivative input-output models) have been widely adapted for use by regional analysts. There are at least a half-dozen regional-growth theories, ranging from export-base models that can be grafted onto a Leontiefian system to the cumulative causation theories of Kaldor and Myrdal (Deaton and Weber 1985). In each case, however, these theories have been used primarily as the basis for developing tools or defining a perspective to examine particular segments of regional phenomena.

Perhaps more than in most other subject-matter activities, social scientists working on regional concerns have been able to develop some useful, institutionalized ways of working together across disciplinary boundaries. Much of the credit for that accomplishment goes to regional science. Regional science was the brainchild of Walter Isard (1969) who hoped that it would develop its own unique theory and set of methods independent of other social sciences—i.e., become an independent discipline. That has not happened (Miernyk 1982). Still, a useful multidisciplinary forum has been institutionalized.

Even though institutionalized regional science has been dominated by economists, it has attracted some gifted geographers (particularly in Europe) and a scattering of scholars from sociology, demography, political science, and even engineering (especially systems engineering). Still, large parts of the social sciences dealing with regional and rural problems have remained outside regional science, most notably rural sociology. The result is that much of the work in rural sociology has remained distant, isolated, and misunderstood by regional scientists, particularly by the economists (Hite 1985).

A series of recent papers—Randall (1986); Lynne and Milon (1984); Phipps, Crosson, and Price (1986)—have explored, with insight and subtlety, the various strains of theory in natural resource economics. (See also Batie 1984, Bromley 1985, and Lynne and Milon 1984.) Randall suggests, unlike regional science with its poverty of comprehensive theory, resource and environmental economics has great theoretical riches. Those theoretical strains, sometimes intertwined but perhaps never fused, include the reductionism of neoclassical microeconomics (which, in turn, can be subclassified into at least two component parts), the holistic methodology of the institutionalist claiming legitimacy in the pragmatism of William James and John Dewey and the individualism of the quasi-Austrian school of so-called "new resource economists." Given the policy process in the United States, Randall makes a strong case that this great diversity of viewpoints in natural resource economics is an asset of considerable value.

Having spun off a number of theoretical nuances of note in the past twenty years, particularly in the area of welfare theory, natural resource economics appears to command greater intellectual respect within the mainstream of the economics discipline than does regional economics. Moreover, resource economists have paid greater attention to the policy process than many other social scientists (with the probable exception of some political scientists like Lindblom) (Nelson 1987; Randall 1985).

The most serious epistemological liability of the natural resources subject area is lack of vigorous, ongoing dialogue across disciplinary boundaries, particularly across those boundaries separating the economic from noneconomic social sciences (Newby 1986). The institutionalists have built some bridges to legal scholars and political scientists, but, with few notable exceptions, they have ignored geographers, anthropologists, historians, and even rural sociologists. Among those notable exceptions is the synthesis regarding common-access resources fashioned by Ciriacy-Wantrup (1975). Although they have sometimes offered brilliantly provocative insights, the new resource economists have seemed particularly insular in constructing analytical paradigms and, consequently, stand in jeopardy of not exploring the subtle nuances of the individualist philosophical approach and uncovering insights for understanding how political environments change.

Given the nature of the resource problems likely to face rural America, particularly the critical issues concerning Western water policy that could shape the future American agriculture, the absence of an ongoing dialogue between the various strains of resource economics and the other social sciences risks the formulation of policy without needed and attainable information. The fault lies not in any failures of individual professionals but in the failure of institutions to evolve. If that institutional failure is not addressed and remedied, the credibility of the "agricultural" social sciences could be seriously compromised.

DATA RESOURCES

All of the subject-matter areas of concern to this paper—regional science, community development, natural resource and environmental management and use, human resources—are plagued by inadequacies in institutionalized data series. Those inadequacies are well documented in a 1981 National Research Council (NRC) Study, *Rural American in Passage: Statistics for Policy* (Gilford, Nelson, and Ingram 1981). This study also recommends some quite basic steps that should be taken regarding development and classification of needed statistical series. Some of the recommendations—for example, establishment of state statistical service centers—have been carried out in some states, but others, such as the mid-decade census, seem further from realization today than when the study first appeared.

One point emphasized in the NRC study that merits extra attention here is the need for small-area data. Recognizing that the costs of obtaining reliable data for small areas limit the possibilities of breadth in both the data series and the regularity of collection, the NRC study recommends standardization of existing reporting systems with county coding and establishment of benchmarks through the mid-decade census, to allow use of new statistical procedures for estimating intercensual small-area parameters.

The data resources problems have many implications for analysis. One such implication is a tendency for social science analysis of change in rural areas to lag behind the realities of that change, with potentially serious impacts on the formulation of relevant, effective public policy. Hite and Ulbrich (1986), for example, were seriously hampered by lags in reporting data for nonmetropolitan jurisdictions when trying to make an assessment of how the financial crisis in agriculture in the 1980s was affecting the fiscal health of rural governments. Similarly, researchers using input-output models produced by the Bureau of Economic Analysis of the U.S. Department of Commerce are forced to work with matrices containing coefficients based on technology and price relations that are at least five years out-of-date. In periods of rapid change and social flux, the lags mean (metaphorically) that policy makers shoot at a target moving faster than the speed of light.

Some of these data problems cannot be remedied at any reasonable cost. Since it is very difficult to show the marginal benefits of a data series, determination of the optimal stock of data is a matter of subjective judgment in a great many cases. An argument might even be made, following the logic offered by Nelson (1987),that policy decisions seldom turn on social science analysis and so it makes little practical difference to policy whether reliable, timely, and appropriate data are available. Even if one concedes some validity in such logic, social scientists would renounce the continued search for knowledge if they allow cynicism about policy formulation to influence design of rational, cost-effective schemes for improvements in data resources.

One promising new avenue for enhancing data resources is through remote sensing. Urban planners have made effective use of aerial photography for almost half a century. Except for geographers, however, few other social scientists have explored the possibilities of obtaining certain useful data from remote sensing. The advances in remote sensing technology associated with the space programs make the potential for its uses as a tool of social science worth attention. Combined with computer cartography and other new technology-aided analytical tools, remote sensing might allow social scientists in all the relevant subject-matter areas to achieve significant breakthroughs in insight and predictive capabilities concerning land use, human ecology, and spatial development patterns.

PROBLEM-SOLVING CAPABILITIES

Given the difference in the mix of assets and liabilities of the two major subject areas, e.g., regional science (including community development) and natural resources management and use, the two specialties have quite different current problem-solving capabilities.

Regional development/community development specialists can answer numerous well-defined empirical questions of a specific nature. Lags in data, however, often mean that the ability to do so is confined to questions about what "has been." The capacity for understanding "what is" occurring contemporarily, or to predict what is likely to occur, is, arguably, pseudo-scientific, requiring assumptions about facts not in evidence. Such assumptions are tenable as pragmatic expediencies only if there is a well-tested theory with which they are consistent. The theoretical deficiencies of regional analysis place very severe constraints on the defensible use of such assumptions. Particularly troublesome is the capacity of regional specialists to make predictions about the outcomes of alternative macro (or even some micro) policies that are likely to provoke structural change.

In some sense, however, regional specialists have greater problem-solving capabilities than students of macroeconomic policy. To the extent that many large American businesses as well as many governmental agencies are willing to subscribe to macroeconomic forecasting services, laying out impressive sums to pay for these services knowing that imprecision and errors are inherent in the forecast, there is a suggestion that the problem-solving capabilities of regional specialists have more than trivial social value. Regional specialists can measure regional impacts of various sorts within a comparative statics framework, and they can make these measurements with ever-improving levels of precision. To ask that they break out of the comparative statics framework, however, would be to ask for more than the present state of the sciences will support.

Resource specialists have a greater range of competence in problem solving. While making use of the impact-measuring capabilities of regional specialists, resource specialists can also determine, with reasonable errors, the market-realized benefits and costs associated with alternative resource policies. In a growing number of cases, they can also identify the gainers and losers, affixing reasonable approximations to the market value of the gains and losses experienced by various segments of the population. The capability to estimate non-market-realized benefits and costs through contingency valuation or other indirect means is still embryonic, but improving. Greater collaboration among economists, sociologists, and psychologists would seem to offer a relatively high probability of payoff for improvements in contingency valuation.

The other notable gain in competence by resource specialists, of recent years, has been through application of public choice paradigms to prediction of behavior in policy formulation and in regulatory administration (Niskannen 1971; Runge 1984; and papers by Downing and Yandle in Lynne and Milon 1984). These developments open exciting possibilities of inserting feedback loops into various models of natural resource public administration, perhaps along lines suggested by systems research. The result would be a capability to predict the dynamic consequences of alternative policies and programs. But that capability is still to be realized.

THE COMMUNITY OF SOCIAL SCIENCE SCHOLARS

NUMBER OF SCHOLARS

There will probably always be too few hands for the tasks to be done. Yet one of the biggest liabilities of the social sciences in addressing the problem of rural people, resources, and places is too few scholars.

This generalization applies to all the social science disciplines considered here. Even though the American Agricultural Economics Association numbers more than 2,000 economists among its members, a great many are involved in study of commodity-oriented problems in production, management, and marketing. Perhaps no more than one out of ten agricultural economists works regularly on problems of rural regional and community development, rural human resources, or natural resource management.

The total number of rural sociologists in the country is no greater than about 1,000. While perhaps a large majority of rural sociologists have professional interests that transcend production agriculture, there are few concentrations of rural sociologists in any agency or university, many administrators apparently being content with tokenism in employment of rural sociologists. Lacy and Busch (in Dillman and Hobbs 1982, 410) report in 1982 that twenty-five land-grant institutions employ three or fewer active members of the Rural Sociology Society. The lack of critical mass in many institutions is a problem, especially in collaborative research.

The only other professional social scientists (if they may be so classified) employed by more than a few agricultural institutions are lawyers. Increasingly, agricultural economics departments within the land-grant universities have been adding agricultural lawyers to their faculties. Yet many of these lawyers focus their work on the problems of farm and agribusiness firms rather than on rural communities and natural resource management. Perhaps fewer than a dozen are employed regularly in roles directly related to the substantive concerns of this paper.

Geography is the social science that, perhaps, might best serve as a catalyst for multidisciplinary subject-matter work directed at rural people, resources, and places. In the past half-century, geography has moved well beyond the descriptive discipline that it is often thought to be, and scholars working at the cutting edge of theoretical and quantitative geography make use of analytical tools equal to the most sophisticated employed in the other social sciences. Although no hard data are available on the subject, casual observation indicates that professional geographers are rarer in the land-grant agricultural colleges than bikinis in Antarctica. Indeed, more than a few land-grant universities have no organized academic geography departments that might provide scholars who could collaborate with agricultural economists and rural sociologists. A plentiful supply of well-trained professional geographers is available, especially if the European scholars are accounted for, and the addition of geographers to the faculties of agricultural colleges could substantially increase the capabilities of those colleges for understanding the problems of rural America.

The U.S. Department of Agriculture (USDA) does employ a broader mix of social scientists than do most land-grant agricultural colleges. USDA has long supported a small but influential program in agricultural history, and utilizes a sprinkling of demographers, geographers, and other social scientists on its staff. But, the bulk of the professional social science staff in USDA, as in the land-grant colleges, is accounted for by economists oriented toward commodity problems. Similarly, the programs in agriculture and (what used to be known as) home economics at non-land-grant universities seldom contain social scientists other than economists and sociologists, few of whom are free to devote substantial energy and time to anything other than the traditional core concerns in farm management, agribusiness, and home economics.

There is a substantial number of social scientists with competencies and interests in problems of rural regions, communities, resources, and people outside the institutions usually identified with agriculture. These institutions include colleges of liberal arts and business administration, and even engineering. Academic departments of urban and regional planning also involve themselves in problems of rural communities and people. In addition, there are small cadres of scholars in such privately funded research institutes as Resources for the Future (RFF) and similar "think tanks." Taken as a whole, the contributions to rural studies of these scholars employed outside of the traditional agricultural institutions probably equal that of the "in-house" scholars of the agricultural establishment.

On balance, it may be fair to say that if all agricultural economists are considered, the total number of social scientists available to work on problems of rural communities, human resources, and resource management is adequate to the need. The problem is that the composition of this body of scholars is not well suited to meeting the needs of rural America. Too many economists are employed in studying production agriculture and agribusiness in comparison to the relative size of the agricultural sector in the American economy, and too few are employed in dealing with the problems of nonfarm rural America, given the relative importance of the nonfarm population.

RECRUITMENT AND TRAINING OF REPLACEMENTS

In some respects, the numbers problem regarding social scientists in agriculture will intensify by the end of the present century.

The long-term capabilities of the social sciences to deal with the problems of rural America depend upon recruiting and training talented young people who will enter the various relevant professions. Currently, the recruitment and training of regional economists gives reason for concern.

Interest in regional economic development in the United States appears to move in cycles; that interest peaked during the New Deal years of the 1930s and again during the Great Society years of the 1960s. Since about 1970, interest has been on the wane. Young scholars, with a practical eye on their futures, are apt to move with the cycles. The result is that few graduate students in economics or agricultural economics are now choosing regional economics and related subjects as an area of concentration. Since a relatively large cadre of scholars was trained in this specialty in the 1960s, there remains a core of experienced professionals who are still active scholars. These 1960-vintage regional economists will be retiring in the 1990s, however, and if they are not replaced, there will be serious manpower limitations upon addressing the substantive problems discussed in this paper.

There is less evidence of a problem in natural resource economics. The great interest in natural resource and environmental policy in the 1970s brought an influx of talented young scholars from a variety of disciplines into this subject area. Fewer and fewer graduate students are opting to specialize in resource economics today. Even so, institutions seeking candidates to fill openings for natural resource economists generally find themselves in a buyers' market, suggesting no shortage of relatively well-qualified scholars. The job market in this specialty may tighten in the 1990s. Still, given the relatively large number of scholars of the 1970s vintage who will not begin to retire in large numbers until early in the next century, no manpower crisis appears imminent in the natural resource subject area.

It is not as easy (as least for me) to assess the situation regarding recruitment and training of rural sociologists and other noneconomic social scientists. Two institutions—Cornell and University of Wisconsin—train at the graduate level two-thirds of all the rural sociologists in the country (Lacy and Busch in Dillman and Hobbs 1982, 409). Given the relatively small number of positions traditionally open for rural sociologists, it appears that there has not been room for many institutions to obtain sufficient students to offer high-quality programs. Should there be a significant increase in the demand for rural sociologists, however, it is likely that most of the recruiting of trained scholars would be forced to concentrate on graduate programs in general sociology.

Similarly, all other noneconomic social scientists will have to be recruited from graduate programs outside the colleges of agriculture. Going to these programs, however, does not indicate any serious problem. There are some very good graduate programs in geography in the United States and many others in Europe. High-quality graduate training in anthropology and political science is available at more than a score of American universities.

INSTITUTIONAL ENVIRONMENT

The institutional environment in which the social sciences of concern here operate also is a factor in assessing their capabilities. The general range of these institutions—land-grant systems, USDA and other government agencies, non-land-grant academic programs in agriculture and home economics, and private research institutes and foundations—were observed in the section above. An encyclopedic treatment of this environment is not practical in this paper; hence, only the most salient features can be examined.

The first of these features is the relationship between the social sciences and so-called "hard sciences," particularly within land-grant colleges of agriculture. In the land-grant environment, the social scientists tend to occupy a position relative to other scientists not greatly different in form from that occupied by rural sociologists in departments dominated by agricultural economists. They are given all formal acknowledgement and treated with personal respect, but as practitioners of inscrutable disciplines of embarrassing imprecision, they are not quite members of the scientific club.

Social scientists do almost nothing that gives rise to increased physical productivity in agriculture. Increasing physical productivity is the mission with which the land-grant colleges of agriculture have been most successful, and so the social sciences may seem to some to be tangentially relevant to what colleges of agriculture are all about. The fact that social scientists are prone to question the validity of increasing the physical productivity of agriculture only exacerbates the difficulties of their position.

The situation is even more acute for social scientists working on community development, regional growth, resource use and management, etc., work that has policy as its primary focus. While it is relatively easy for "hard" agricultural scientists to concede the need to find markets for the increased physical output (which may imply management studies), it is much more difficult for many to grasp the significance of policy. Thus, the legitimacy of studying commodity futures markets, or the economics of pest control, or irrigation, or even of farm real estate markets (generally the kind of studies undertaken by production and marketing economists) has now been accepted, even if the work is sometimes considered less than scientific. But, studies of community development and natural resource policy seem to lack legitimacy because, in addition to carrying all the other baggage of the social sciences, they treat subject matter that itself is only superficially understood by many non-social scientists.

Nowhere in the land-grant institutions is the denial of legitimacy more evident than in extension programs. Even an exhaustive study of extension programs might not provide the basis for a definitive assessment of their effectiveness. Yet casual observation suggests that: (1) most states have credible programs in farm management, marketing management, financial management, etc.; (2) most states have only nominal and floundering programs in community development; and (3) most states have no programs worthy to name in resource development and policy. True, some states have succeeded in developing both of the last types of programs, but these states are the exception rather than the rule.

While the problem of legitimacy of the subject matter no doubt contributes to the failures of extension to develop effective community development and resource policy programs, the poor match between the programs and the traditional extension clientele ought not to be overlooked. In many cases, the decision makers who can use, and sometimes request, the problem-solving assistance of community development and resource policy specialists do not normally have a relationship with the county extension offices. These decision makers are government officials at the municipal, county, and state levels; professionals in planning, development, and resource conservation agencies; and leaders in citizen participation organizations who are not accustomed to seeking information from the county agent.

Yet the demand for the services of social scientists working on nonfarm rural problems is substantial and growing. In many cases, those making such demands are willing and able to pay for the services at (at least) marginal cost. The demand, however, is for very applied analysis of very specific problems. In most states, it is not sufficiently strong in most states to support overhead costs related to the depreciation of intellectual capital and, as a result, those researchers who have been forced to augment meager experiment station budgets by scurrying after many small research contracts are using up their intellectual capital without any replacement. On the positive side, however, the scurrying for nickels and dimes in contracts by some experiment station rural development researchers has kept lines of communication open with users of the research product.

On the whole, social scientists in colleges of agriculture within land-grant universities have advantages over their colleagues in other academic environments because the experiment stations provide a funding base for their work. So long as the scholar's salary is covered by experiment station "hard" money, the researcher has some flexibility to work on problems that are still not perceived generally by client groups. The degree of flexibility varies from experiment station to experiment station, but it means the researcher does not have to worry unduly about making sure there is enough grant and contract money to pay his or her salary for research time next year. Only social scientists who are outside the experiment stations and who depend upon grants and contracts to purchase release time for research can fully appreciate that advantage.

SUMMARY AND CONCLUSION

The charge for this paper was to assess the capabilities of the social sciences in agriculture for dealing with a changing set of problems in rural regions and communities, in the rural population, and in the management and use of natural resources. In three major sections, the changing situation in rural America was interpreted, the epistemological capabilities of the relevant social science subject-matter areas were critically evaluated, and the salient features of the affected community of social science scholars were described.

Any such task becomes, in the end, an assessment from the unique and limited perspective of the person with the assignment. It is useful mostly to the extent that it provokes and stimulates others in making their own assessment. Others making such an assessment may adopt very different premises. Some, while accepting the premises implicit in this paper, will come to different conclusions. Still others will come to much the same conclusions, but with different nuances. All that is not only to be expected, it is to be wished.

The conclusion of this assessment is that the social sciences in agriculture, using existing working relationships with disciplinary and subject-matter groups outside the traditional agricultural institutions, are not in a position to prescribe scientific remedies for the problems of rural America. Few social scientists of reputation even claim to understand what is going on in rural America well enough to make predictions about what policies would work. Even the most confident libertarian social scientist will make predictions only in terms of general trends that could be expected with libertarian policies. Yet the social sciences in agriculture have demonstrated capabilities for providing useful information. Even when these sciences cannot produce answers, they can often reformulate the questions so that a rational plan for securing answers can be implemented. That capability is worth a great deal to society, and there is evidence in many states that there is a willingness to pay for such capacity.

Aware of the effective demand for their services, in-house scholars working in regional/community development and resource management are generally more confident of the futures of the subject-matter areas than they are of the future of the colleges of agriculture as institutions. The concern is that the traditional obsession of agricultural colleges with increased physical productivity will blind administration to the needs of nonfarm rural people in the hard times ahead.

NOTE

1. James C. Hite is an alumni professor of Agricultural Economics and Rural Sociology, Clemson University. Dr. Hite acknowledges the useful comments of Sandra Batie, E. C. Pasour Jr., Alan Randall, and Alvin D. Sokolow on an earlier draft and states that all errors of fact, lapses of logic, or faults of judgment remain the fault of the author.

REFERENCES

Anderson, Terry L., ed. 1983. *Water rights, scarce resource allocation, bureaucracy, and the environment*. San Francisco: Pacific Institute for Public Policy.

Baden, John. 1987. Rape of the American West. *Policy Review*, no. 39 (Winter): 36–41.

Batie, Sandra. 1984. Alternative views of property rights: Implications for agricultural use of natural resources. *American Journal of Agricultural Economics* 66, no. 5 (December): 814–18.

Bromley, Daniel W. 1985. Resource and environmental economics: Knowledge, discipline, and problems. In Agriculture and rural areas approaching the twenty-first century: Challenges for agricultural economics. American Agricultural Economics Association Annual Meeting, 7–9 August, Ames, Iowa.

Ciriacy-Wantrup, S. V. 1975. "Common property" as a concept in natural resources policy. *Natural Resources Journal* 15:13–27.

Deaton, Brady J., and Bruce A. Weber. 1985. Economics of rural areas. In Agriculture and rural areas approaching the twenty-first century: Challenge for agricultural economics. American Agricultural Economics Association Annual Meeting, 7–9 August, Ames, Iowa.

Dillman, Don A., and Daryl J. Hobbs, eds. 1982. *Rural society in the U.S., issues for the 1980s*. Boulder: Westview Press.

Drucker, Peter F. 1986. The changed world economy. *Foreign Affairs* 64, no. 4 (Spring): 768–91.

Gilder, George. 1981. *Wealth and poverty*. New York: Basic Books.

Gilford, Dorothy M., Glenn L. Nelson, and Linda Ingram, eds. 1981. *Rural America in passage: Statistics for policy*. Washington, D.C.: National Academy Press.

Hansen, Niles. 1979. The new international division of labor and manufacturing decentralization in the United States. *Review of Regional Studies* 9, no. 1: 1–11.

Hite, James C. 1985. The southern contribution to regional science. *Review of Regional Studies* 15, no. 3 (Fall): 1–11.

Hite, James C., and Holley H. Ulbrich. 1986. Fiscal stress in rural America: Some straws in the wind. *American Journal of Agricultural Economics* 68, no. 5 (December).

Isard, Walter. 1969. *General theory—Social, political, economic, and regional*. Cambridge: The Massachusetts Institute of Technology Press.

Jacobs, Jane. 1969. *The economy of cities. New York: Random House.*

_____*1984. Cities and the wealth of nations*. New York: Random House.

Johnson, Glenn L. 1985. Technological innovation with implications for agricultural economics. In Agriculture and rural areas approaching the twenty-first century: Challenges for agricultural economics. American Agricultural Economics Association Annual Meeting, 7–9 August, Ames, Iowa.

Lynne, Gary D., and J. Walter Milon, eds. 1984. The political economy of natural resource and environmental use. Proceedings of a Regional Symposium, October, Southern Rural Development Center, Mississippi State University. SNERC N, 10, SRDC Series No. 79.

Markusen, Ann Roell. 1985. *Profit cycles, oligopoly, and regional development*. Cambridge: The Massachusetts Institute of Technology Press.

Miernyk, William H. 1982. Regional economics to regional science: Evolution or odyssey? *Review of Regional Studies* 12, no. 2 (Spring): 1–8.

Murray, Charles. 1984. *Losing ground: American social policy, 1950–1980*. New York: Basic Books.

Nelson, Robert H. 1987. The economics profession and the making of public policy. *Journal of Economic Literature* 25, no. 2 (March): 49–91.

Newby, Howard. 1982. Rural sociology and its relevance to the agricultural economists: A review. *Journal of Agricultural Economics* 33 (May): 124–66.

Niskannen, William A., Jr. 1971. *Bureaucracy and representative government*. Chicago: Aldine.

Phipps, Tim L., Pierre R. Crosson, and Kent A. Price, eds. 1986. *Agriculture and the environment*. Washington, D.C.: Resources for the Future.

President's National Advisory Commission on Rural Poverty. 1967. *The people left behind*. Washington, D.C.: Government Printing Office.

Randall, Alan. 1985. Methodology, ideology, and the economics of policy: Why resource economists disagree. *American Journal of Agricultural Economics* 67, no. 5: 1022–29.

Reilly, William. 1987. Agriculture and conservation: A new alliance. *Journal of Soil and Water Conservation* 42, no. 1 (January/February): 14–17.

Reisner, Marc. 1986. *Cadillac desert, the American West and its disappearing water*. New York: Viking.

Rosenfeld, Stuart A., Edward M. Bergman, and Sarah Rubin. 1985. *After the factories, changing employment patterns in the South*. Research Triangle Park, N.C.: Southern Growth Policies Board.

Runge, C. Ford. 1984. Emerging property rights issues in resource economics. *American Journal of Agricultural Economics* 66, no. 5 (December).

Schlesinger, Arthur M. 1986. *The cycles of American history*. New York: Houghton Mifflin.

Serow, William J., and Douglas A. Charity. 1987. Modelling elderly migration in the United States: A comparison on micro and macro oriented approaches. Southern Regional Science Association Annual Meeting, 26–28 March, Atlanta, Georgia.

Sokolow, Alvin D. 1986. The meaning of "small" in small government: Research questions for rural public administration. American Society of Public Administration Annual Meeting, 13–16 April, Anaheim, California.

Vernon, Raymond. 1986. International investment and international trade in the product cycle. *Quarterly Journal of Economics* 80, no. 2: 190–207.

Webber, Carolyn, and Aaron Wildavsky. 1986. *A history of taxation and expenditures in the western world*. New York: Simon and Schuster.

Wills, Garry. 1978. *Inventing America, Jefferson's declaration of independence*. New York: Doubleday.

DISCUSSION OF CHAPTER 3 BY JAMES C. HITE

Don Paarlberg[1]

I pick up on a point made by Professor Hite:

> ...there is good reason to believe that a combination of political, social, and technological developments are now in place that are as significant in their implications for rural America as the great historical transformation that accompanied other quantum changes in the dominant mode of production (e.g., as during the Industrial Revolution).

Rural America is partway through a profound transition; on this all four papers[2] agree. Is it possible, as Professor Hite suggests, to improve our understanding of this change by examining its predecessor, the industrial revolution? I believe it is, and shall attempt to do so, finding in this undertaking a theme that is, to some degree, common to the papers under review.

The industrial revolution began about two centuries ago with the advent of the steam engine, and continues with today's robots and other forms of high technology. Mechanical power made possible the replacement of cottage industry by the factory system.

The initial change occurred in the technological area, where inhibitions to change were minimal. The technological changes disrupted conventional ways of thinking and doing, and imposed great adjustment pains. In England the Luddites wrecked the printing presses, and in France the factory workers sabotaged the system by tossing their wooden shoes into the machinery.

Institutions, public and private, that were set up to serve cottage industry, came under stress. The then existing economic theory, which had assumed atomistic competition, was challenged by the advent of concentrated economic power. Utopian socialism came into being and Karl Marx developed his theory of dialectical materialism. Government sought to meet adjustment problems with the dole.

There was little understanding of the fundamental forces at work. Charges and countercharges were hurled back and forth. Financiers, factory owners, economic theorists, and politicians came under fire. There were avid supporters of the old order; ancient rhetoric was voiced in the support of cottage industry even amid the clatter of the new industrialized order.

Meanwhile, the standard of living gradually rose as the improved efficiency worked its way through the economy. But, there remained some residue of the old system—islands of cottage industry that somehow survived the change.

How does the agricultural revolution compare with its predecessor, the industrial revolution? The transformation of rural America began somewhat later than did the industrial revolution; the delay is not easily explained. A commonly accepted date is the middle of the nineteenth century. The great names of this period are Liebig, Pasteur, McCormick, and Mendel. The great institutions are the land-grant colleges and the U.S. Department of Agriculture. When the revolution began, half the American population lived on farms; the proportion is now a little over 2 percent and falling. During the height of the transformation, more than 30 million people left farms; it was the greatest migration in history. The treasured institution, the family farm, came under stress.

There was limited understanding as to the cause of the transformation. Named villains included Wall Street, agribusiness, and the politicians. Prices fell, reflecting the new abundance; the competitive market was judged adversely; government stepped in to regulate prices and production. Contrary signals were called—the land-grant colleges were working to increase production and the Department of Agriculture was trying to reduce it.

Farmers increasingly borrowed money, rented land, and hired labor like other business people. Their wives gave up gardening and canning and began buying groceries at the supermarket like their city cousins. Agriculture, formerly considered different from the rest of the economy and worthily so, began to lose its distinctive character. Those subdisciplines set up at the land-grant colleges to serve a unique clientele—agricultural economics, agricultural statistics, agricultural sociology, agricultural history, and agricultural engineering—began to wonder about their vehicle, their destination, their payload, and their fuel supply. There were efforts, public and private, to slow down the process of change, but they were of little avail.

The technology changed first, the institutions next, and the rhetoric last. The traditional family farm, the old agrarian ethic, and the revered agricultural creed were voiced long after they had lost their meaning. The point of this is: if one listens to the rhetoric, one will be misled about what is going on. It is true that in some isolated spots the old order has continued; there are islands within the flood.

While all this was happening, our capability to produce food increased, the real cost of food declined, hunger went into retreat, and real standards of living rose for both farmers and nonfarm families. Public attention focused not on the wonderful child being born but on the pangs that accompanied birth.

Change continues. We often speak of the "agricultural adjustment" as if it were a change from some fixed base to some new level of technology and institutions at which things will again be settled. This is not so; the only constant in the picture is change itself.

Before the transformation began, technology, institutions, and rhetoric were rooted in the same soil. They were mutually supportive and controversy was limited. But once we embraced the new technology, they lost their compatibility. Institutional lag and the rhetoric, with its retrograde character, failed to keep pace with technology. As long as technology advances, institutions and rhetoric will never catch up. Intellectually, politically, and philosophically, we shall continue to be in stress.

What can we learn about an agriculture in transition by examining the experience of the industrial revolution? At the risk of oversimplification, I offer these four points, which appear to me to be acceptable to the papers under review:

1. The agricultural transformation is underway and it is irreversible.
2. Agriculture's uniqueness is being eroded and, with it, the disciplines and institutions that assumed continuing uniqueness.
3. It is possible by wise public policy to reduce the adjustment pains of those caught in the change process.
4. Yet, it would be unwise to presume that we could, by advance planning, chart the precise course for the juggernaut that has been set in motion.

We can thank ourselves daily that the individual judgments of the persons most concerned were used in large measure, both in the industrial revolution and thus far in the agricultural revolution, in deciding what was best. Suppose the government had undertaken to decide which cottage industries should survive and which factories should be favored. Could government have decided, better than the 30 million people who left farms, what they should do and where they should live?

This conference, intent upon "enhancing the quality and effectiveness of research," "developing a strategic agenda," and "clarifying the different roles of the social sciences" is an excellent undertaking. But, let us recognize the transitory nature of the institutions, the fallibility of social planners, and the wrong signals of rhetoric. Let us remember the resourcefulness of individual persons, and leave ample room for their decision making in whatever comes from our conference.

NOTES

1. Don Paarlberg is a professor emeritus, Purdue University.

2. See the following chapters in this book: Part II, Section 1, Chapter 2, "Identification and Prioritization of Researchable Questions in Agricultural Economics: Where are the Potential Payoffs?" by Clarence F. Davan Jr.; Part III, Section 1, Chapter 2, "Social Science Issues in Agriculture and Rural Communities," by Paul W. Barkley; Part II, Section 2, Chapter 2, "International Affairs and Economic Development," by G. Edward Schuh; and Part I, Chapter 4, "Agricultural Institutions Under Fire," by Lester C. Thurow.

CHAPTER 4

ECONOMIC INSTITUTIONS AND THE DEVELOPMENT PROBLEM: HISTORY AND PROGNOSIS

Daniel W. Bromley[1]

I have been asked to present a perspective on agricultural history and the changing structural dimension of agriculture in both the industrialized countries and in the agrarian societies that are, euphemistically, called "less developed." More specifically, I was asked to explore the strengths and weaknesses of the transaction cost/institutional economics interpretation of these matters. I will approach the assignment by offering my particular view of institutions and transaction costs to explain observed socio-economic phenomena in the industrialized and agrarian nations. Space limitations preclude a meaningful discussion of the strengths and weaknesses of the approach I will propose, so I leave that to the reader. My presumption is that the perspective being offered can be helpful in suggesting important modifications in the way that social scientists address questions of economic and social change.

I will first describe, very briefly, the concepts of *institutions* and *transaction costs*. I will then describe what I regard to be the policy crisis in agriculture in both the industrialized and the agrarian nations of the world. I will close with some implications for social scientists who may wish to play an important role in research and public policy in these two arenas.

INSTITUTIONS AND TRANSACTION COSTS

Institutions represent the constellation of rights and duties that determine domains of choice for individual members of society. These institutions may be regarded as *conventions* or they may be regarded as *entitlements* (Bromley 1989). Sociologists are interested in institutions as they define roles and status. Economists are interested in institutions as they define property rights, contract, the "market," and nonmarket exchange. Note that institutions are the rules by which organizations function and interrelate; institutions are *not* properly regarded as those organizations.[2]

The properly orthodox economist seems to show very little curiosity about institutions, nor about the formation of individual tastes and preferences, regarding both as exogenous factors to be pondered by the political scientist and the psychologist, respectively. With those tastes and preferences given, most economists are much more interested in predicting individual and aggregate behavior under the behavior assumption of utility maximization. My perspective, on the other hand, is to argue that there are two levels of tastes and preferences of importance to the social scientists. The first level will pertain to the institutional arrangements that define choice domains, while the second level will pertain to tastes and preferences for actions selected from within those prespecified choice domains. Individuals have preferences over choices to be made at both levels. An interest in institutions would suggest that the social scientist ought to study both levels of preferences and choices.[3] I will later argue that the political-economic context of agriculture is better understood as a product of this two-part process of preference revelation.

Institutions, as the working rules of going concerns (families, firms, nations), define what is a cost, and to whom. If the institutional arrangements are permissive of widespread pesticide use then those who experience detrimental effects arising from the use of pesticides are made to suffer these costs in silence. If those adversely affected by pesticides wish to seek redress or a change in the rules then they must bear the bulk of the costs of accomplishing that change. The victims are forced by the legal environment (the institutional arrangements) to bear the unwanted costs of their situation, or to undertake the expensive process of institutional change. The party imposing the unwanted costs will be able to continue until the adversely affected party has been able to mobilize sufficient political support to bring about a change in the institutions. Hence, institutions indicate who must bear the costs of existing economic activity, and they indicate who must bear the transaction costs of changing those very institutional arrangements (Bromley 1989; Schmid 1987).

By transaction costs I mean the costs of obtaining information about a particular economic situation. Additionally, transaction costs include the actual cost of negotiating a particular exchange. Finally, transaction costs include the costs of enforcing the terms of an exchange once it has been consummated. Transaction costs can pertain to the normal exchange that might occur between two individuals, or they can pertain to the necessary costs of changing the existing institutional arrangements.

It will be useful to consider three domains of individual behavior that ought to interest the social scientist concerned with economizing activity. Call these the *domain of reproduction*, the *domain of production*, and the *domain of exchange*. I will illustrate the way in which these three domains are interconnected in the life of the individual farmer. More importantly, I will show that it is the institutional arrangements that provide the connective tissue and, therefore, it is to institutions and their derivative transaction costs that the social scientist must look for an understanding of individual behavior. One cannot understand family size or composition, productive activities, or exchange activities, let alone the interrelations among them, without understanding the institutions. An understanding of agricultural history and a prognosis for the future are equally dependent upon a comprehension of the concept of institutions.

To repeat, institutions determine the choice environment within which individuals and groups make daily decisions regarding their behavior. The basic activity of the family is to reproduce itself—this is the *domain of reproduction*. It is equally important to produce the necessities for survival—this is the *domain of production*. Finally, there is the opportunity for exchange with other social units (individuals, families, clans)—this is the *domain of exchange*. The institutional arrangements in a society influence behavior within each of these domains, and also define the sanctions and incentives that transmit signals among domains so that outcomes in the domain of exchange influence behavior and outcomes in the domain of production, and ultimately in the domain of reproduction.

POLICY CRISIS IN AGRICULTURE

The intent of the Social Science Agricultural Agenda Project (SSAAP) is to enhance the quality and effectiveness of research and related activities in the rural social sciences and in their related basic social science disciplines. The success of this effort will hinge on how clearly we define the basic problem in the agricultural sectors of both the industrial and agrarian nations of the world. I suggest that the policy crisis in agriculture in both the industrialized nations and the agrarian nations can be understood with the aid of concepts pertaining to institutions and to transaction costs.

The policy crisis in many agrarian countries is that increases in food production are barely able to keep pace with (and often fall behind) the rate of population growth. The policy crisis in the industrial world is the well-known overproduction trap driven by scandalous outlays of tax revenues for price supports, export subsidies, and surplus storage. The trite thing to say is that these crises are *political* in nature—a singularly unhelpful diagnosis. But, as we move beyond this simplistic charge to understand the political context in which economic policy is formulated then it would seem possible for the social scientist to make an important contribution to the understanding of these policy crises, and to make meaningful suggestions for reform.[4]

THE AGRICULTURAL POLICY CRISIS IN THE INDUSTRIAL NATIONS

For the past half century, the concern in the industrial nations has been to seek institutional means to insulate the producer from income swings arising from the natural variability of agriculture—all in the name of preserving something known, metaphorically, as the family farm. In the United States, the myth and romanticism associated with rurality—from wistful reminiscences about rural America being the font of democracy to the myth that life is less stressful in rural areas—have precipitated the development of institutional arrangements that now encrust agricultural policy, and that stand in the way of the necessary institutional change to escape the overproduction trap. The situation is not very different in Japan and Western Europe. Agriculture in the industrial world is the latest, and possibly the most expensive, of the "entitlement programs."

While it is the political power of the agricultural interests that partially explains the robustness of these entitlement programs, it is the full constellation of institutional arrangements (pertaining to both agriculture as well as nonagriculture) that make correction difficult. The proportion of farmers in the industrialized countries is far too small to explain the staying power of such expensive institutional arrangements. Rather, their stability is found in the fact that they are part of a far wider constellation of institutional arrangements that reflects broad social preferences regarding economic life in general. The citizenry will become animated only when government program costs, or food prices, escalate beyond some "reasonable norm" (Cochrane 1984). The complex and interrelated institutional arrangements of the modern state, reflecting politically expressed tastes and preferences, seem to prevent an abrupt solution to the overproduction trap. Agricultural policy reflects, in a general way, social preferences regarding rural life. This preference has certainly been explicitly discussed in Western Europe and in Japan; it is somewhat more implicit in the United States.

Note that it is the institutional arrangements in the agricultural sector that help to explain observed patterns of exchange, production, and reproduction. The overwhelming constant in the agricultural policy of industrialized countries is distorted price signals for both output and for inputs (Bowers and Cheshire 1983; Schultz 1978). These distortions created a production plan in agriculture that encouraged monoculture, the substitution of purchase inputs for produced inputs, and the substitution of capital for family (and other) labor. The exploitation of the scale economies that flow from this mode of production means that producing units get larger and larger. These production tendencies show in the domain of reproduction in terms of farm family size that, lately, is not materially different from that of urban households. In the domain of production, increased specialization has led to the much-lamented "commoditization of agricultural policy" (Cochrane 1984). This evolution of narrow and powerful farm commodity groups has increased the degree of fragmentation among agricultural interests in the industrialized world and, coupled with the acquiescence of the general public, has made a reform of agricultural policy somewhat difficult.

Institutions in the domain of exchange influence enterprise choice in the domain of production, and this then gives rise to a convergence of economic interests and the derivative collective behavior that reflects back to influence the domain of exchange (where agricultural policy works directly).

THE AGRICULTURAL POLICY CRISIS IN THE AGRARIAN NATIONS

Whereas the industrial nations are caught in an overproduction trap, the agrarian nations are, for the most part, caught in an underproduction trap. In these countries, many being newly independent in the past thirty years, we have an explicit state presence in agriculture and the accompanying absence of the institutional foundations of exchange. This heavy presence of government is a natural reaction to the excesses of powerful landlords and patrons during precolonial (and even during colonial) rule. Upon independence, the first mandate of the new rulers was to protect the small producer from the arbitrary and capricious actions of the economically powerful. We now have a system in which the small producer is at the mercy of the arbitrary and capricious actions of bureaucrats.

One should not be thought overly ideological to observe that agricultural production is, for the most part, inversely related to the extent to which the state plays an explicit role in agriculture. In the agrarian nations we see the state as an explicit economic actor in agriculture, providing inputs directly to farmers, buying output, providing credit, and even providing tractors. Yet, against this backdrop of explicit economic activity on the part of the government, the institutional arrangements that might otherwise encourage increased production are missing (Bromley 1986). In the absence of the state as omnipotent planner and rationalizer, these missing institutional arrangements would provide an alternative mechanism for risk spreading beyond the family and circle (network) of acquaintances, and they would stimulate the sort of exchange activity that would draw individual farmers out of their current self-sufficiency. These institutional arrangements would permit a greater degree of risk spreading in the domain of exchange, thus permitting greater specialization in the domain of production. With production more specialized, the farmer would have an easier time mastering the required management processes of a more restricted enterprise set and it is reasonable to suppose that production would increase. Obviously, the danger is that, just as in the industrialized nations, these narrow commodity-oriented producers would eventually obtain untoward economic and political power and soon distort agricultural policy. Persistent famine and starvation, however, seem a rather steep price to pay for the avoidance of this eventuality.

It is common in the agrarian nations to find that the domain of exchange is not well developed. The legal foundations of the economy were never fully established following independence but were, rather, thought unnecessary given the active role to be played by state enterprises and state tinkering. This explicit and often overbearing role for the state has not allowed alternative institutional arrangements to evolve. In consequence, there are limited opportunities for farmers to engage in transactions across time and space. Most exchange occurs within the family or a limited network of friends and acquaintances. Occasionally there will be transactions with traders, but these are over a limited domain of goods. The meager opportunity for exchange then influences the domain of production by encouraging the family to produce a variety of commodities. This imperative to diversify arises for two reasons, one related to risk, the other related to the desire for a more complete consumption set on the part of the family.

When a farmer cannot rely on a wide array of institutional mechanisms (including the market) to offer some degree of risk spreading, then enterprise choice will, of necessity, need to provide that function. By undertaking several types of productive activities, preferably those with uncorrelated distributions of stochastic variation, the farmer can hedge against weather variability, disease, or other unforeseen events. If drought kills the millet, at least he will have goundnuts, cassava, and livestock. If he is lucky, he can get a good price for some of these products and purchase the necessary millet. The greater degree of enterprise diversification will also mean that there is an increased need for family labor to assist in management of the varied production enterprise. The implications for the domain of reproduction are obvious.

On the consumption side, if the farmer has limited access to exchange opportunities to acquire the variety of products that the family needs (or desires), it will be necessary to produce that variety internally to the decision unit (the family). The enterprise mix will, of necessity, be more heterogeneous to meet this consumption imperative as a result of the absence of greater opportunity in the domain of exchange. Transaction costs explain the prevalence of exchange within the family-network arena, and the absence of exchange in the larger market economy. That is, the essence of exchange within the family and the network is that of low information, contracting, and enforcement costs. Members of the family or of the network have fairly reliable information about the products they might exchange, they are familiar with one another and, hence, negotiation is both straightforward and nonstrategic, and there is great confidence that once a deal is struck it will not be contravened by one of the parties to the exchange.

On the other hand, if a farmer is to enter into exchange with a stranger, then information may be unreliable, contracting can be protracted and uncertain, and enforcement is a potential problem. It is the higher transaction costs for exchange beyond the comfortable domain of the family or the network that tend to stifle transactions there, and, hence, we observe, not surprisingly, an enhanced reliance upon the more restricted domain of the family and the network of acquaintances. While the family and the network are reasonable domains across which farmers can spread risk, the scope for risk spreading is limited. This forces a more diversified production plan than if there were greater scope for market exchange. Institutional arrangements, which determine the nature and magnitude of transaction costs, provide the explanation to the patterns of reproduction, production, and exchange in the agrarian economy (Bromley and Chavas 1989).

Of equal importance, it is the existence of high transaction costs that explains the absence of well-developed market systems in the agrarian state. If transaction costs are high for the farmer, they are also high for those who would seek to establish themselves as market intermediaries—a necessary part of any well-functioning market. An aspiring grain merchant or input supplier will face the same impediments that the farmer faces. Information is costly, negotiations, because they are not routine or standardized, are protracted, and enforcement, because there is a poorly developed concept of contract law and administrative procedures, is haphazard (Bromley 1986). The absence of the institutional foundations of exchange create high transaction costs for all parties.

THE CHALLENGE TO THE SOCIAL SCIENCES

While there is a policy crisis in agriculture in both the agrarian and the industrialized nations, I suggest that there is an equally serious crisis in the agricultural social sciences, of which I am most comfortable addressing the problem within economics. Indeed, the policy crisis may be partly attributable to the virtual absence of politically acceptable policy alternatives emanating from the research of economists. Economists, by training and disposition, are reasonably dedicated to the idea that markets are best when they are the least manipulated by extramarket forces. Since the worldwide depressions of the 1930s, the citizens of the market-oriented countries have made it abundantly clear to their political leaders that while the upside of markets can be exhilarating indeed, they wish to have nothing to do with the downside. Economists have been consistently slow to comprehend this fact. Indeed, many economists spend a good bit of their time puzzling over the fact that politicians seem more intent on pandering to the wishes of their constituents than paying obeisance to the gospel according to Adam Smith; a behavior that is attributed to the inscrutability of those elected to serve in a democracy.

One can speculate on the state of our science and its policy advice if more economists would spend an equal amount of time helping to develop a system that was both efficient and politically acceptable, rather than advocating a system that the citizenry has resoundingly declared it does not desire.[5] While the citizenry pays frequent homage to the virtues of markets—and this may be the source of confusion to economists—this celebratory cant is just that. The average citizen knows full well that unrestrained markets can be ruthless; prices might go up, wages might go down, and people might be put out of work. Most economists, insulated in the secure halls of the academy, find it rather easy to suggest the kind of market discipline that we have fought so hard to escape. What is said to be wonderful for the goose is a source of considerable terror for the gander.

This market faith among economists shows up in several ways when attention is turned to the rural sector. When the food problems of the agrarian nations are being discussed, the answer is predictable; get government out of the market so that free enterprise can flourish. This is called "getting prices right." In the industrialized nations most economists will offer the same advice. Agricultural economists, more in the thrall of their employment in colleges of agriculture, are usually a little more circumspect. But even there, the search is to get government out of agriculture in a way that will not overly jeopardize the "family farm." Consequently, policy analysis consists of tinkering around the margins, suggesting supply control, buy-out schemes, and other forms of bribes and subsidies that will slow down the embarrassing abundance of food and fiber.

The belief in getting government out of agriculture in the agrarian nations, and in reducing its prevalence in the industrialized nations, is strong in spite of little analytical understanding for the institutional environment of agriculture in either the agrarian nations or the industrialized nations. For the most part, the development debate concerning the food production problems of the poorest countries, especially those in sub-Saharan Africa, has focused on either the technical fix or the facile nostrum of getting government out of the way so that the entrepreneurial skills of the farmer can take over. To cast the problem thusly is to miss the sociocultural context of agriculture in the poorest countries, and it is to believe that markets and their associated institutional arrangements, including those that allow markets to operate in the first place, simply spring from thin air. Modern inputs cannot spread their benefits to a wide spectrum of farmers in the absence of an institutional structure that facilitates a wide market for those inputs, that indicates who shall reap the benefit stream from those inputs, that establishes functioning credit markets, and that generally creates the conditions for a market-related, as opposed to a family-related, agriculture. Likewise, the recent interest in "getting prices right" by limiting the role of government confuses the implicit and the explicit roles of government in agriculture.[6]

Government's role in agriculture in most of the poorer countries is an explicit one; the government is an active economic agent for both the input and the output side. But to reduce or eliminate this explicit role, without at the same time replacing it with an implicit role, is to leave the individual farmer at sea. By an implicit role for the state, I mean that government must establish the legal foundations for exchange—institutions—such that independent farmers, often separated by great distances, will have the opportunity to enter into the market (or marketlike) transactions on the input side as well as on the output side. This is not to say that the small farmer in Africa should necessarily be subjected to the very market forces that have been so convincingly rejected in the industrialized countries. But, it is my maintained hypothesis that food production in the agrarian nations is low precisely because farmers are locked into a system of excessive dependence on family and a small coterie of acquaintances for the bulk of economic exchange. This means that the domain over which risks might be spread is extremely restricted.[7]

In the industrialized countries there is growing concern among both economists and the general public that the expensive and counterproductive agricultural policies must be exorcised from the policy arena. The discussion is usually cast as one of keeping the current system or of resorting to "free market" conditions. The national treasuries cannot long afford the status quo, and there is scant political support for the free market alternative. The realistic alternative is to suggest modifications around the edges of the existing structure, and this economists have done. But, there seems to be far less serious interest among economists to study the industrialized nations' agricultural sector in the broader socioeconomic milieu. The focus seems to remain, for the most part, on tinkering with different support programs to ameliorate the strong production incentives that they create.

I suggest that a closer look at the institutional arrangements and the transaction costs of the status quo, and some sweeping alternatives, would reveal policy options that have not, as yet, been recognized. Why is there so little agricultural policy analysis that attempts to analyze the political economy of agriculture? The answer, I believe, is that most policy research, like most political action, is focused on particular commodities. The policy analysts will likely protest that the various commodity programs are now so complex that it is all they can do to study them individually. And, that may be so, given the current focus of policy research which is largely confined to computer simulations of "what if?" scenarios. Social scientists in the agricultural colleges, with a few exceptions of sociologists concerned with the social implications of biotechnology, are singularly incurious concerning the institutional context of agricultural policy.

The concern has been recently expressed that the 1985 Farm Bill, regarded as a policy disaster by most economists, was adopted in spite of an unprecedented amount of agricultural policy modeling and advice. Yet the critic might comment that the computer runs cannot provide a substitute for a careful understanding of the political context of emerging policy. In the agrarian economies, I see little evidence that economists understand the institutional basis of a functioning and vibrant economy. The plant breeders search for miracle seeds while the economists preach faith in free markets.

The challenge to the agricultural social sciences is to move beyond faith and simulation models. It will be necessary to see the economy as a set of ordered relations (institutional arrangements) that define choice domains for individuals. Classical economists were interested in aggregates of income, how it was distributed, and the general welfare of the society. The ascendance of neoclassical economics was accompanied by the felt need to purge economics of an ability to comment on social well-being. It was Lionel Robbins (1935) who, playing on the scientific aspirations and insecurities of economists, advocated the position that a scientific approach required the elimination of interpersonal comparisons of utility. In his confusion, he failed to understand that to make interpersonal comparisons of utility is not to make value judgments, but rather to offer untestable propositions. Such propositions are simply true or false. A proposition that is untestable does not automatically become a value judgment (Blaug 1980).

If economists have become irrelevant to agricultural policy, and some may argue the point, it is in all probability due to the all-consuming fear of appearing unscientific, such concerns being sufficient to drive economists into a retreat from the political economy of agriculture. This retreat is reinforced by the belief, fostered by the new welfare economics, that it is possible to have policies without politics, or that controversial policy recommendations can be made without value judgments (Bromley 1989). We have allowed the illusion to persist that political decisions and difficult choices can somehow be whisked away magically by welfare economics.

Hutchison (1964) expressed concern almost three decades ago that a belief in the objective and scientific basis of policy pronouncements, and a retreat into the false security of welfare economics, would lead to public confusion and disillusion regarding the application of economics to questions of public policy. The fact that many believe this to describe the current situation may be the ultimate challenge to the agricultural social sciences.

NOTES

1. Daniel W. Bromley is Anderson-Bascom Professor in the Department of Agricultural Economics at the University of Wisconsin, Madison.

2. Some writers use the term "institution" to denote both rules as well as organizations (banks, hospitals, and universities are called institutions). This confusion stands in the way of a meaningful analysis of the role of institutions in defining transaction costs, and in explaining individual and aggregate behavior.

3. It should not be assumed that the same models that are used so successfully for the second level maximization problem are appropriate for choices at the first level. See Field (1979).

4. See Sandbrook (1985) for a thoughtful assessment of political reality and the development problem.

5. There is an efficient allocation of resources for any particular institutional setup and distribution of endowments. Welfare economics does not provide an unambiguous basis for concluding that one particular efficient allocation is to be preferred to another efficient allocation. Hence, one must be cautious in one's complaint that, if only the politicians would leave things alone, we could attain efficiency.

6. See Timmer (1986) for a discussion of how to get prices right.

7. These ideas have been worked out more thoroughly in Bromley and Chavas (1989). I am indebted to my colleague Jean-Paul Chavas for assistance in clarifying these issues.

REFERENCES

Blaug, Mark. 1980. *The methodology of economics*. Cambridge: Cambridge University Press.

Bowers, J. K., and Paul Cheshire. 1983. *Agriculture, countryside and land use*. London: Methuen.

Bromley, Daniel W. 1986. *Markets and agricultural development: The promise and the challenge*. Binghamton, N.Y.: Institute for Development Anthropology.

———1989. *Economic interests and institutions: The conceptual foundations of public policy.* Oxford: Basil Blackwell.

Bromley, Daniel W., and Jean-Paul Chavas. 1989. On risk, transactions and economic development. *Economic Development and Cultural Change* 37, no. 4: 719–36.

Cochrane, Willard. 1984. Agricultural policy in the United States—A long view. Benjamin H. Hibbard Memorial Lecture Series. Department of Agricultural Economics, Univ. of Wisconsin, Madison.

Field, Alexander James. 1979. On the explanation of rules using rational choice models. *Journal of Economic Issues* 13, no. 1: 49–72.

Hutchison, T. W. 1964. *"Positive" economics and policy objectives*. London: Allen and Unwin.

Robbins, Lionel. 1935. *An essay on the nature and significance of economic science*. London: Macmillan.

Sandbrook, Richard. 1985. *The politics of Africa's economic stagnation*. Cambridge: Cambridge University Press.

Schmid, A. Allan. 1987. *Property, power, and public choice*. New York: Praeger.

Schultz, T. W., ed. 1978. *Distortions of agricultural incentives*. Bloomington: Indiana University Press.

Timmer, C. Peter. 1986. *Getting prices right*. Ithaca: Cornell University Press.

CHAPTER 5

IRONY, TRAGEDY, AND TEMPORALITY IN AGRICULTURAL SYSTEMS OR HOW VALUES AND SYSTEMS ARE RELATED[1]

Lawrence Busch[2]

INTRODUCTION

There is clearly a move afoot worldwide today to subsume the older reductionist approaches to agriculture with a broader, multidisciplinary, ecological, and systems-oriented approach. This represents a vast improvement over the older approaches. However, while systems approaches are a significant advance, they retain certain curious features of older approaches which, I shall argue, unless eliminated, will ultimately doom them to failure. Specifically, I shall argue that systems may contain ironies and tragedies, and that they are temporally bounded. However, before so doing, I should like to make several comments about science itself.

In the most obvious sense, science is a form of literary criticism. Bacon talked about reading the Book of Nature. We can go further and argue, as some have already done, that the typical conventional article found in scientific journals always criticizes those who came before, always aligns the author with some previous tradition, and always attempts to stake new claims (Latour 1987). Moreover, these claims are made with the hope on the part of the author that readers will be convinced not only by the methodological skills and results reported in the article, but by the incorporation of those results within an established tradition. In the extreme case, an article or two can virtually revolutionize a given tradition, as Einstein once did to Newtonian physics. Yet, even in such a case, it is essential that the author at once show how the paper both fits into the established tradition and how it upsets it.

Even the contemporary proponents of the positivist tradition of science take great pains to discuss the language that science uses. It is their belief that through the careful use of language, erroneous information can be flushed out and better (if not correct) information can replace it. Indeed, Radnitzky (1973) has called this the positivist critique of ideology. Thus, even those of a positivist persuasion look at science—in a way—as a form of literary criticism.

Nevertheless, it might well be asked why it should be that literary themes—irony, tragedy, temporality, etc.—appear never to enter the realm of science. [The sole exception appears to be metaphor (e.g., Black 1966; Arnon 1968)]. I submit that there are several reasons for this: First as Knorr-Cetina (1981, 42) has remarked, "Scientific papers are not designed to promote an understanding of alternatives, but to foster the impression that what has been done is all that could be done." In short, the rhetoric of scientific literature glosses over the myriad choices that constitute science. This is done most effectively by insisting that papers be written in the passive voice. It would appear that scientific equipment simply worked by itself! In addition, the reductionist bent of much conventional science obscures the ironies, tragedies, and even the temporality of science.

Finally, the convention that prohibits the publication of papers that confirm the null hypothesis conceals the ironies and tragedies that occur in the laboratory. This is true on several levels. At the level of the published paper, the false starts, time wasted, paths to nowhere are virtually never discussed. If nothing promising is found—and promising is defined as supporting some aspect of the existing tradition—then the paper is neither written nor published. Boyle vigorously argued that all results, whether positive or negative, should be published (Shapin and Schaffer 1985), but his position was not accepted by the scientific community. The same prohibition is observed when recounting the history of science. We can read with pleasure how Barbara McClintock was vindicated (Keller 1985) after years of being taken for an obscure and even cantankerous fool. Yet, where can we read of the hundreds or even thousands of scientists—good scientists—who spent their lives following blind alleys, false hopes, or wild dreams? Where are the stories of the brilliant minds that explored Lamarckian biology? In short, the ironies and tragedies of science are concealed by the very methods used in conceptualizing it and reporting it to the rest of the world.

The recent development of the systems approach in agriculture promises to transcend the limits of reductionism and to permit us to deal with problems and situations that are much bigger and more complex. It promises to permit us to deal not only with problem solving but with situation improving (Bawden et al. 1984). Moreover, as Dillon (1976, 7) has noted:

> There are also profound methodological implications of the systems approach. As soon as we recognize that physical systems are embedded in, or interact with social systems, we recognize that science—conceived in terms of understanding phenomena for purposes of manipulation—can no longer be free from value judgments. Social systems involve not merely the interactions of physical forces but also contests of will arising from the purposiveness of behavior of animate elements in the system.

Yet perhaps even this does not go far enough. In particular, this and other systems approaches still leave a void—indeed a chasm—with respect to the answer to a simple, but very important question: A system for what?

In this paper I shall proceed by first examining briefly the nature of agricultural systems themselves. What are they? What purposes do they serve? Whose purposes do they serve? Then, I shall look at three phenomena[3] that systems thinkers, like their reductionist colleagues, seem to avoid: Temporality, Irony, and Tragedy. I shall further argue that it is through these three portals that links between systems and ethics must be forged, links without which systems thinking remains empty and trapped in the legacy of a misunderstood tradition. Moreover, given that neither you nor I, dear reader, have all the time in the world, I shall confine myself to several suggestive remarks, each subject to further refinement by others as well as myself.[4]

THE NATURE OF AGRICULTURAL SYSTEMS

In the last few decades there has been a veritable explosion of literature on the subject of agricultural systems (e.g., Dalton 1985; Lowrance, Stinner, and House 1984; Dahlberg 1980; Duckham and Masefield 1970; Spedding 1979; Wilson 1988). This literature employs the systems metaphor to do one of two things: First, it is used to make sense out of natural processes that we can observe but that we did not create. For example, one might talk of the plant nutrition system as the process whereby a plant takes up nutrients from the soil and in turn, on the death of the plant, returns nutrients to it. Here the term "system" is used entirely metaphorically. The system itself is not observed but the system metaphor is used to make sense out of what otherwise would be an overwhelming number of unintelligible facts.

The work here consists of "making sense." It consists largely of observation, but not any ordinary observation will do. It requires disciplined, theoretically informed observation that focuses on those aspects of things that are of concern to us. For example, our ancestors spent a great deal of time and energy studying the motions of the sun, planets, and stars because they theorized (apparently correctly) that cropping cycles could be optimized by such knowledge. They were similarly concerned with whether the planets had smooth or rough surfaces. However, when Galileo focused his telescope on the planets in an effort to develop better navigational calculations and discovered mountains on the moon and moons circling Jupiter, he quickly discovered that he had challenged the entire Aristotlean cosmology and the Church that rested on it (Drake 1978). Thus, the definition of metaphorical systems, such as the solar system, in little or no way changes the objects observed, though it may very well change the people doing the observing.

However, of greater import for us is the second use of systems which has its roots in metaphor but does not remain there; they are metaphors made real. These are the systems that we have ourselves created. They include, for example, virtually all the cropping cycles that have been developed over the centuries as well as the people who organize those cycles. These systems are real in the sense that they have been materially constructed by people in order to attain certain ends—ends which are, of course, human. The creation of this type of system also requires the work of "making sense." But, in addition, it requires the work of actually "making." It involved shifting from the two-field to the three-field system during the Middle Ages (White 1962). It involved shifting from horse-drawn to tractor-powered farm equipment at the turn of the century. Today, it involves shifting from local landraces to improved varieties to (perhaps) artificial seed produced through biotechnology.

Moreover, once such a transition occurs, it must be maintained, worked at, or the new system will simply fall apart. As Wilson (1988, 41) puts it, "The first consideration in understanding agriculture is to think of the farmer as constantly intervening to maintain this imposed order." Indeed, we may go so far as to argue that the simplification of technical systems in the field through the use of monocultures, pesticides, rectangular plots, and so on, demands the maintenance of ever more complex social systems outside the field.

We can go still further in noting that the creation of systems by people actually predates the use of the metaphor. Indeed, it appears that the metaphor of agricultural systems was not developed first, i.e., before the practice, but instead it developed out of observing the practice and trying to make sense out of it. Only after the metaphor was fully developed, clarified, and articulated, could one begin to design systems that were systems as such.

Systems of both types have certain very important, but often overlooked properties:

1. Their designers have clear ends in mind. To put it another way, they are designed to maximize or optimize some end or set of ends. These ends may be ultimate ends—life on the planet—or they may in turn be means for something else—turning a profit on the farm.
2. They involve conscious decisions by human beings in accordance with their (shared) wishes, desires, ambitions, compulsions, etc. In short, all agricultural systems are essentially decision systems even if those decisions are not always conceptualized as part of the systems themselves.

These two properties of agricultural systems are of the utmost importance to my theme here as they illustrate that agricultural systems are fundamentally linked to issues of ethics and values. We can even go further than that in saying that when we design or conceptualize an agricultural system, we are always standing at the interface of means and ends. Most of those who have worked to date on agricultural systems have paid a great deal of attention to means but have, for a variety of reasons, left the ends outside of their analyses. They have done this, I believe, by making the erroneous assumption that deciding which values are to be attained is a task that lies outside the competence of scientists and is in any case merely a matter of personal preference. I shall argue that both these assumptions are false and that an agricultural science worthy of the name must incorporate both ethical concerns and technical proficiency.

Consider Alisdair MacIntyre's (1984, 58) definition of a "good farmer:"

> From such factual premises as "He gets a better yield for his crop per acre than any farmer in the district," "He has the most effective programme of soil renewal yet known," and "His dairy herd wins all the first prizes at the agricultural shows," the evaluative conclusion validly follows that "He is a good farmer."

In short, MacIntyre argues that ends can be drawn from the facts. Of course, in a certain sense MacIntyre is cheating. He is well aware that the facts he has described are themselves impregnated with numerous widely held values. For example, having a better yield or a more effective program imply considerable leeway for value judgments, for choices about what is good, true, or even beautiful.

However, value judgments of this type are made constantly by farmers, scientists, and lay persons. Moreover, there is widespread agreement over these values. Indeed, without that agreement, we would find it impossible to do science or farming at all. What a systems analysis does—or ought to do—is to make the values involved in those choices conscious ones, in so far as that is possible. As we shall see, it is through ironies, tragedies, and temporality that the ethical character of systems approaches is revealed. But before focusing on that, let us first examine the nature of nature for, after all, most of the practitioners of a systems approach to agriculture claim they are talking about nature.

THE NATURE OF NATURE

It is usually the case that we Westerners distinguish between nature and culture. Indeed, it is one of the basic distinctions of our culture. Yet, this distinction, while useful in certain instances, tends to lead us astray when thinking about or designing agricultural systems. To put it as bluntly as possible, I will argue that what usually passes for nature is, in fact, culture. (One might argue the reverse of this as well, but I shall refrain, as it is of less relevance here.)

Every time that we walk or drive by a cultivated field, walk down a tree-lined street, fly over a "designated wilderness," and admire its beauty, we are extolling the virtues of culture—not nature, but culture. Each of these things exists not because of some power beyond us but because of some power within us.

In the late nineteenth century, the biologist von Uexkull developed the insight that every living thing had its *umvelt* or world. Ethologists today use this concept to describe the behavior of living organisms. In the early part of this century, Husserl (1970) and other phenomenological philosophers developed the notion of a *lebenswelt* or *lifeworld* within which human beings lived. The idea, simply put, is that each of us lives in a world which is the taken-for-granted world of daily life and which we see as "natural." Part of the world of daily life of Western (and many other) peoples is the notion that nature stands apart from as opposed to culture. Let me put it another way: Each culture constructs its own world out of the infinite variety of nature. It selects those facts,[5] those things that are valued, and claims them as nature itself. Yet, the very selection—necessary to survival itself—involves intercourse with that natural world and its transformation into something intelligible. In short, it involves the socialization of the natural world.

Consider the double work that plant breeders perform. First, they look far and wide in nature in order to find the most diverse set of "raw materials." Then, they select those materials that have the particular characteristics that they believe are useful and desirable. Deciding what to select involves the complex interplay of the science that breeders are willing and/or able to supply and the demands of more or less powerful groups of farmers, food processors, input suppliers, and others concerned with the new seed. Through negotiation, persuasion, and coercion, agreement is reached as to which characteristics shall be selected. Supply is matched to demand here, not through the market, but through the power and persuasiveness of the various parties in the negotiation process (see Busch, Lacy, Burkhardt, and Lacy 1991). These characteristics are then designed into the new plant. This entire first part of plant breeding consists of shaping plants to human desires, or remolding nature to fit our wants. Then, the variety is released and we are told that it is the best that nature had to offer! Suddenly, the creative work of the breeder is hidden and all that we see is a plant that looks (at first glance) much like other plants. It appears to be nature, pure and simple. Yet, this new nature, created by the breeder, can only be successful if coupled with a change in the behavior of persons. Thus, the genetic makeup of the plant and the social behavior of the actors in the agricultural system are (if the breeder is successful) at once changed.

The apparent paradox in all of this is that those things which we (or some particular social group or class) have appropriated, have made part of our lifeworld, is then taken to be nature itself. Thus, an agricultural system is seen as involving cows, sheep, grass, grain, tubers, insects, weeds, but often not us! Moreover, the nature that makes up that agricultural system is certainly not nature in the wild—in which only sparse populations of hunters and gatherers can survive anyway, and then only by beginning to tame it—but nature as socialized, as reorganized, as made into a material manifestation of social structure with all its inequities, contradictions, hopes, and promises (Lipton and Longhurst 1989). Thus, paradoxically, the study and improvement of agriculture tells us as much about people and society as it does about plants or animals.

Since agricultural systems are both networks of people and of things, all of the aspects of human life that are usually seen as outside the purview of technical agriculture must also enter into agricultural systems. I shall devote the remainder of this paper to three aspects of human affairs that need to be considered in designing, maintaining, and modifying systems: Temporality, Irony, and Tragedy.

TEMPORALITY

Central to all human affairs, including science, the maintenance of agricultural systems, and all other everyday activities, is temporality. Temporality affects us on at least two levels. On the level of the mundane world of everyday life, the temporality of human existence means that there is never "all the time in the world." Human life being finite, we are always under pressure to complete our life's tasks, whether they are trivial or profound. This temporality imposes itself on us in two ways: It demands that we wait for others, and it demands that we wait for things, despite our impatience with waiting (Schutz and Luckmann 1973).

The importance of this form of temporality to systems should be apparent. We never have enough time to construct the perfect system; what we develop is always a compromise between some ideal that we may have and the press of time. The obverse of this is that systems must themselves work within some definable time, as is apparent to the farmer whose fertilizer arrives too late in the growing season, as well as to the scientist whose specimens die from lack of delivery of a proper chemical medium. In fact, all of our systems are constantly in danger of falling apart, of breaking down. As a result, they must be maintained, worked at, modified.

Moreover, to make things even more complicated, the press of time demands that we establish priorities not only within a given system but across many systems. And the very act of setting priorities is itself limited by the time available. We cannot take the time to sit down and prioritize everything because we do not have enough information to do so and we don't have the time to gather that information. Time spent in the field is time not spent milking the cows. Time spent on the farm is time not spent at work in the factory. Time spent in production is time not spent in consumption or leisure. The need to attend a marriage or funeral, to rejoice in the birth of a child, to discuss the weather with our neighbor, to read a good book, or to reflect on the world, pulls us away from the operation of an agricultural system.

Temporality also imposes itself on systems in a quite different way. Simply put, we are born into a world that was here before we arrived and will be here after we die (Ricoeur 1973). Paradoxically, it is not a world of our making though we participate in making it what it is. In short, we are always born into a tradition, and even our rejection of it signifies its important power over us. These traditions are sources of values for us. They tell us what is good and what is bad, what is true and what is false, what is beautiful and what is ugly.

Science, far from standing outside tradition, is a tradition in and of itself, as is evidenced by the careful review of the literature that precedes the body of every scientific article. Thus, we cannot truly oppose tradition and modernity, only alternative traditions (Gusfield 1967).

The interpretation of traditions, the conflict of interpretations (Ricoeur 1974) constantly changes traditions even in the most "traditional" societies. Traditions are not static unless they have been abandoned, like the rites of the Aztecs. Otherwise, they are the places where discourse goes on, where changes are made, where life is lived.

Tradition plays an important and central role in agricultural systems. In the design of such systems, it is virtually impossible to make them of whole cloth; they must be fitted into existing systems, existing social relationships, existing traditions. Even wholly new types of production systems, such as those developed for the poultry industry in the last several decades, must fit into the existing market channels at some point so as to furnish the feed to the birds, to arrive at retail stores, and eventually to enter the mouths of consumers. And, as poultry scientists and farmers are now discovering, a significant segment of the public finds the break with tradition that large-scale poultry production represents to be abhorrent. The values embedded in the barnyard raising of chickens are still paramount for many consumers.

Tradition also enters into the actual practice of agricultural systems. The modern poultry farmer rapidly creates a tradition in which certain inputs are bought from certain sources, certain practices are repeated regularly, certain tasks are performed on schedule. But, at the same time, that poultry farmer does not rigidly and mindlessly adhere in a mechanical way to the tasks at hand. In fact, to do so would be economic suicide in a business as volatile as the poultry business. Instead, a good poultry farmer is always looking for new approaches that will improve his operation, that will increase the survival rate of the birds, that will make the tasks at hand easier to perform. This work, in turn, is performed within larger systems in which government policies, processing oligopolies, and marketing channels are constantly being renegotiated and altered as various groups attempt to make others yield to their desires. Nor is this limited to the high-technology of poultry farming; the same might accurately be said of the most "backward" farmer in the most remote regions of the Third World. All living traditions are both stable and changing in response to an ever-changing environment.

In short, time is the context within which all systems operate. Time imposes itself on us in a variety of ways. Agricultural systems, no matter how elegant they may appear on paper, will hardly function properly if they fail to take time into account. Moreover, they must do this not only in the obvious way of sequencing the events to take place in the system, but also by taking into account the temporality of existence and the centrality of tradition in human life.

Temporality also forces us to confront two other phenomena that characterize human existence: Irony and Tragedy. Let us consider each in turn.

IRONY

Webster's defines irony as "the incongruity between the actual result of a sequence of events and the normal or expected result" (Merriam-Webster 1987, 639). In other words, irony involves the unforeseen (and often disastrous) consequences of human endeavor.

Machiavelli (1985), long known most for his discussion of the role of the Prince, also wrote at length in that same volume on what he called "fortune." To Machiavelli, fortune or luck was an unavoidable aspect of human life. In short, even though one might make elaborate plans, supported by the best information available, it is always possible simply to have bad luck, to fail to take into account some key factor, to have the misfortune to see one's plans go awry. More recent thinkers coming from the rationalist tradition have tended to ignore or even deny the role of luck.

Yet it appears that the luck described by Machiavelli is what makes for irony. Examples of this sort of irony in agricultural systems abound. For example, Justus Liebig spent much of his career identifying the essential elements of plant nutrition. He felt that only by increasing the level of nutrients available to plants could the Malthusian calculation of geometric growth in population and arithmetic growth in food production be avoided. His work led to the development of the worldwide fertilizer industry. Yet, Liebig could never have envisioned the deleterious effects of fertilizer runoff, the single largest source of nonpoint water pollution in the United States today.

A similar argument could be made for the use of cytoplasmic male sterility (CMS) in maize. CMS was developed in order to increase maize production, yet its widespread use in breeding programs created the Southern corn leaf blight of the 1970s. Yet another example is the development of agricultural experiment stations in the latter half of the nineteenth century. Scientists and administrators of these stations were quite concerned about the plight of American farmers (e.g., Bailey 1910, 25–32; Davenport 1919). Yet, the very success of the experiment stations led to the elimination of many smaller producers who lacked the capital, education, or market access to compete in the changed agricultural economy (Busch et al. 1984; Rosenberg 1976). In short, ironies in agricultural systems are commonplace; by learning to recognize them rapidly, we may be able to design better systems in the future.[6]

TRAGEDY

As the great playwrights of the past have long known, tragedy is also a feature of human existence. It, too, is inextricably linked to temporality. What makes an event tragic is the apparent legitimacy of the several actors whose positions are contradictory in a given situation. Indeed, tragedies are often foreseen in advance and yet are impossible to avoid. Consider the competing claims of farmers and ranchers in the American West during the last century. Farmers, in order to farm, needed to enclose large areas and plant crops. Ranchers, on the other hand, required huge unfenced expanses to graze their animals. We might even go further and argue that the ethic of farming demands fixed boundaries while that of ranching demands vast, unfenced areas. Putting this in systems terms, we might say that the goals of farming systems are incompatible with those of ranching systems.

In practice, in most places and most times, the conflict between farmers and ranchers, herders, or other nomadic or seminomadic peoples has been ended by the victory of the farmers, in part due to the press of growing population and in part due to the desire of nation-states to have fixed, more easily manageable populations. Nevertheless, the tragedy remains; each side could and has made legitimate moral claims and yet the two claims are clearly incompatible.

A similar tragedy (or at least the potential for it) occurs in the Chatham River case (Sowell and Miller 1986, 5d.138–68), a scenario used to illustrate systems concepts in agriculture. In brief, the case concerns a river that flows through a city. The farmers in the area currently draw water from the river to irrigate their fields. They would like to increase their draw. Townspeople, on the other hand, wish to divert part of the flow of the river to an industrial park which will provide jobs for the unemployed in the city. Finally, environmentalists are concerned about the impact of the irrigation and industrial water use on rare and endangered species of wildlife in the river. It is clear that legitimate arguments, based on legitimate legal and moral principles and shared traditions, can be made for all three parties in the conflict. It is, of course, possible that the conflict might be resolved in other ways—by bringing water from somewhere else to the region, by creation of jobs in industries that require no water, or by some other exogenous intervention. However, the potential for tragedy is there. A system might well be designed that would produce a compromise between the three parties, but the very fact that it would be a compromise means that moral principles involved would be compromised.

Yet another example of tragedy is reported by Faki (1982). He describes the situation within the Gezira scheme, the world's largest single irrigated farming area, located between the Blue and White Niles in Sudan. The scheme was established at the turn of the century by the British in an effort to provide long staple cotton for the Lancashire mills. Today, the million-acre agricultural system still produces large quantities of cotton, but while the yields of everything else grown in the scheme have been rising, that of cotton has declined. Faki lays the situation squarely in the lap of the system itself, arguing that while cotton yields the greatest return in terms of foreign exchange, it provides the smallest return for the individual farmers; hence, it receives water last, and yields poorly. The key to Faki's argument is that, "Both the tenant farmers and the scheme management aim at an economically efficient resource use within the limitations imposed by the system" (Faki 1982, 58). The tragedy is that the system, itself, produces perverse, yet rational, behavior.

Given that we all must live within several systems at once, the potential for tragedy is always there. Sometimes, even foresight provides little or no hope of avoidance of tragedy. Nevertheless, understanding that tragedy is always possible might make it possible to design systems (at least occasionally) that avoid it. At the very least, the potential for tragedy might be the subject of deliberation in the design of improved systems.

CONCLUSIONS

It is common to the practice of plant breeding that all breeders must have certain breeding objectives. And, what is important about these objectives is that they do not emerge out of plants at all but out of the desires of people. Moreover, every breeder knows that there are numerous goals that may be desirable under certain circumstances—yield, resistance to lodging, pest resistance, fertilizer response, protein content, photosensitivity, etc. There is no way to maximize all these goals at once. A choice must be made among them, both for the practical reason that it is infeasible to breed for more than three characteristics at once, and for the technical reason that there is often an inverse correlation between goals. This choice is fundamentally an ethical choice, for it involves decisions about who shall benefit, who shall incur costs, and what the good society ought to be. And, this implies that an unethical breeder, or more likely a breeder uninformed by an image of the good society and the good person, will do a poorer job of breeding than will a breeder who understands the ethical aspects of his or her work. In making these decisions, the "good" breeder will weigh the competing and sometimes incompatible claims of diverse interests. He or she will also draw on the "facts" of the social sciences, and on the common tradition that we share, a tradition that owes more to philosophy and to religion than to science.

The same may be said for those who direct our experiment stations and who formulate agricultural policy. They, too, need to conceive of agricultural systems as involving more than merely objects to be manipulated. They need to ask who benefits from a particular system or policy. They need to project reasonable or probable deleterious consequences in designing new or improved systems or policies and ask who shall be asked to bear them and for how long. They need to recognize that science and technology are powerful ways to change the world that must be matched by responsibilities for consequences. And, perhaps most importantly, they need to understand that systems analysis can never substitute for dialogue in a democratic society (Sagoff 1988).

Those who directed our experiment stations at the turn of the century understood this and often talked about the need to revitalize rural life, to maintain there the values that were desirable even while transforming it. Today, sadly, this appears to have been forgotten. The systems approach contains within itself the potential to rediscover these values, but to do so it must include people and their shared values within its horizon. By acknowledging temporality, irony, and tragedy as the limits of systems analysis (and all human endeavors), it can begin to accomplish just that.

NOTES

1. Presidential Address to the Agriculture, Food, and Human Value Society, November 1989, Little Rock, Arkansas. Reprinted from *Agriculture and Human Values* 6, no. 4 (Fall 1989):4–11.

2. At the time of the address, Lawrence Busch was a professor in the Department of Sociology, Kentucky Agricultural Experiment Station. Dr. Busch is currently a professor in the Department of Sociology, Michigan State University. Dr. Busch would like to thank Katherine L. Clancy for her comments on a previous draft of this paper.

3. These are among many themes often ignored by systems thinkers. Others include metaphor, spatiality, and allegory.

4. Literary critics have written entire libraries on these themes and would no doubt find their treatment here sketchy at best. See, for example, Lang (1988) and Muecke (1982).

5. This is implied in the very word "fact." It is derived from the past participle of the Latin verb *facere*, meaning "to do."

6. This is not to say that those in ironic situations have no moral obligation to attempt to rectify the problems they have created. To the contrary, to the extent that such consequences arise from human actions, those persons have a clear obligation to rectify the situation. Thus, those who unknowingly pollute a steam with fertilizer runoff or create genetic vulnerability bear the responsibility both to rectify the situation once they are made aware of it and to cease actions likely to engender the same consequences in the future.

REFERENCES

Arnon, Isaac. 1968. *Organization and administration of agricultural research*. Amsterdam: Elsevier.

Bailey, Liberty Hyde. 1910. The better preparation of men for college and station work. In Proceedings of the 23rd Annual Convention of the Association of American Agricultural Colleges and Experiment Stations, Portland.

Bawden, Richard J., et al. 1984. Systems thinking and practices in the education of agriculturalists. *Agricultural Systems* 13:205–25.

Black, Max. 1966. *Models and metaphors*. Ithaca, N.Y.: Cornell University Press

Busch, Lawrence, et al. 1991. *Plants, power, and profit: Social, economic, and ethical consequences of the new plant biotechnologies*. Oxford: Basil Blackwell.

Busch, L., et al. 1984. *The relationship of public agricultural R&D to selected changes in the farm sector: A report to the National Science Foundation*. Lexington: University of Kentucky Agricultural Experiment Station.

Dahlberg, Kenneth A. 1980. *Beyond the Green Revolution*. New York: Plenum.

Dalton, G. E., ed. 1985. *Study of agricultural systems*. London: Applied Science Publishers.

Davenport, Eugene. 1919. Wanted: A national agricultural policy. Address of the President of the Association of American Agricultural Colleges and Experiment Stations. Urbana: University of Illinois.

Dillon, John L. 1976. The economics of systems research. *Agricultural Systems* 1, no. 1: 5–22.

Drake, Stillman. 1978. *Galileo at work: His scientific biography*. Chicago: University of Chicago Press.

Duckham, A. N., and G. B. Masefield. 1970. *Farming systems of the world*. London: Chatto and Windus.

Faki, Hamid. 1982. Disparities in the management of resources between farm and national levels in irrigation projects, example of the Sudan Gezira scheme. *Agricultural Administration* 9, no. 1: 47–59.

Gusfield, Joseph R. 1967. Tradition and modernity: Misplaced polarities in the study of social change. *American Journal of Sociology* 73 (January): 351–62.

Husserl, Edmond. 1970. *The crisis of the European sciences and transcendental phenomenology*. Evanston: Northwestern University Press.

Keller, Evelyn Fox. 1985. *Reflections on gender and science*. New Haven: Yale University Press.

Knorr-Cetina, Karin D. 1981. *The manufacture of knowledge*. Oxford: Pergammon Press.

Lang, Candace D. 1988. *Irony/humor: Critical paradigms*. Baltimore: Johns Hopkins University Press.

Latour, Bruno. 1987. *Science in action*. Milton Keynes, England: Open University Press.

Lipton, Michael and Richard Longhurst. 1989. *New seeds and poor people*. Baltimore: Johns Hopkins University Press.

Lowrance, Richard, Benjamin R. Stinner, and Garfield J. House, eds. 1984. *Agricultural Ecosystems*. New York: John Wiley and Sons.

Machiavelli, Niccolo. 1985. *The prince*. Translation by Harvey C. Mansfield Jr. Chicago: University of Chicago Press.

MacIntyre, Alisdair. 1984. *After virtue*. 2d ed. Notre Dame: University of Notre Dame Press.

Merriam-Webster. 1987. *Webster's ninth new collegiate dictionary*. Springfield, Mass.: Merriam-Webster, Inc.

Muecke, D. C. 1982. *Irony and the ironic*. New York: Methuen.

Radnitzky, Gerard. 1973. *Contemporary schools of metascience*. 3d ed. Chicago: Henry Regnery.

Ricoeur, Paul. 1973. Ethics and culture. *Philosophy Today* 17 (Summer): 153–65.

———1974. *The conflict of interpretations*. Evanston, Ill.: Northwestern University Press.

Rosenberg, Charles E. 1976. *No other gods*. Baltimore: Johns Hopkins University Press.

Sagoff, Mark. 1988. *The economy of the earth: Philosophy, law, and the environment*. Cambridge: Cambridge University Press.

Schutz, Alfred, and Thomas Luckmann. 1973. *The structures of the life-world*. Evanston, Ill.: Northwestern University Press.

Shapin, Steven, and Simon Schaffer. 1985. *Leviathan and the air-pump: Hobbes, Boyle, and the experimental life*. Princeton: Princeton University Press.

Sowell, Robert, and David Miller, 1986. Chatham River: A case study. In *Systems approaches to food and agricultural problems*. New Brunswick, N.J.: National Agricultural and Natural Resources Curriculum Project.

Spedding, C. R. W. 1979. *An introduction to agricultural systems*. London: Applied Science Publishers.

White, Lynn, Jr. 1962. *Medieval technology and social change*. Oxford: Clarendon Press.

Wilson, Jim. 1988. *Changing agriculture: An introduction to systems thinking*. Kenthurst, Australia: Kangaroo Press.

CHAPTER 6

THE RURAL DEVELOPMENT DILEMMA[1]

Louis E. Swanson[2]

Even while Congress considers major legislation to boost rural development, both policy makers and the public hold on to outmoded assumptions about farming and rural well-being. Real progress will remain elusive until everyone gains a clearer grasp of what truly constitutes the fabric of rural America and how each level of government can most effectively support the rural economy.

Evidence that much of rural American is once again falling behind metropolitan areas socially and economically has mounted throughout the 1980s. As the evidence has emerged, a long-overdue discussion of policy issues and options for rural development has begun, advancing now from identification of problems to questions about what has to be done. The principal stumbling blocks for a comprehensive rural development policy continue to be outmoded assumptions regarding rural America and its relationship to both farming and society. The identification of rural America's ills and development of a coherent public policy to correct them have proven to be much more difficult than anticipated.

Progress has been hampered by at least five factors: (1) an unrealistic, often romantic, view of a bucolic rural economy and society; (2) serious limitation to existing social and economic data on sparsely populated areas; (3) the treatment of rural America as a geographical entity unconnected to the larger U.S. economy and society; (4) a perception that many rural areas do not have viable political solutions; and (5) the absence of a unified rural constituency and the presence of a formidable opposition to renovated and new rural development programs.

We will examine each of these factors in turn. The development of a good public policy requires an accurate appraisal of problems and a clear understanding of program goals. Perhaps the first factor presents the most difficult hurdle, since it involves popular cultural perceptions.

FLAWED VIEWS OF RURAL AMERICA

At least two false assumptions have guided rural public policy. The first is a pervasive tendency to associate rural economies and community well-being with farming. The second is that with the possible exception of farmers, rural people are faring relatively well.

Nationally, a half century ago, farming was the dominant economic activity for many rural economies, and the family was the primary type of social organization of production. Hence, it was reasonable to assume that the well-being of family farms directly influenced the well-being of rural communities. However, the intervening fifty years have witnessed a major transformation of rural society.

During this period, America generally experienced a transition from dependence upon natural resource extraction (such as agriculture, mining, forestry, and fishing) to reliance on economic enterprises in secondary and tertiary activities, including the manufacture of nondurable goods, the provision of services, and government. In 1984, rural employment was distributed as follows: manufacturing, 40 percent; services and trade, 16.5 percent; government, 13 percent; farming, 9 percent; and mining, about 5.5 percent. Moreover, for the same year, farm families reported that more than 60 percent of their net family income came from off-farm jobs.

The 617 agriculturally dependent counties in the United States now account for less than 7 percent of the national rural population. By the late 1980s then, the old axiom that farm well-being, and by inference farm programs, determines rural well-being was no longer useful. Certainly some rural economies continue to depend on farming, but this is the exception rather than the rule.

The second popular misperception—that rural America on the whole is doing relatively well—has been empirically grounded on reports of rural population growth. Between 1973 and 1983 the populations of nonmetropolitan counties grew at a faster rate than those of metropolitan counties. Social scientists proclaimed that this demographic turnaround signified a rural renaissance. The most common explanation was that the population had a desire to live in rural areas and that this demographic anomaly was a result of these people acting on their residential preferences by migrating to rural areas. Those rural areas having recreational and retirement amenities and/or the presence of universities experienced relatively rapid growth (and continue to do so). However, most of the population growth was due to a combination of residential mobility and natural population growth. The former was simply a part of the post-World War II process of suburbanization, not migration.

The retention of population growth among nonmetropolitan counties was primarily a result of a lack of job opportunities in metropolitan areas during the 1970s, which counteracted the historical rural-to-urban migration pattern. We now know that during the 1973–83 period nonmetropolitan counties dependent upon natural resource and manufacturing industries were hard hit by loss of jobs.

The year 1973 was also significant statistically, since it was at that time that the brief six-year period (1968–73) of a narrowing of per capita income differences between metropolitan and nonmetropolitan areas ended. Since 1973, and during the period of rural population growth, per capita income differences have continued to expand.

The overly optimistic interpretation of rural well-being was important for contributing to a dismissal of concerns about the vitality and well-being of rural areas. After all, if rural populations were growing, they must be prospering. The public-policy consequence was the justification of a minimalist rural development policy in the 1980s. During the 1980s, public programs for rural areas were cut dramatically, and the U.S. Department of Agriculture (USDA) and the land-grant universities pulled back from research and extension efforts focused on community development. This withdrawal occurred simultaneously with the recession of the early 1980s; not surprisingly, the consequences were devastating for most rural economies.

It was the financial crisis in farming during the mid–1980s that, ironically, provided the need for a revised rural development policy. Since part of the problem was the assumption that farm well-being determines rural community well-being, the reintroduction of rural development in the context of a farm crisis had the effect of reaffirming this assumption.

A change in policy assumptions is a difficult process to effect. The public still appears to associate farming with rural well-being and to believe that the farm programs of the past fifty years have helped farm families. In fact, the evidence is that these programs have facilitated the decline in the number of family farms.

Despite empirical evidence to the contrary, these outmoded assumptions about farming and rural areas are still resilient. Recent Senate discussions concerning rural development have been punctuated by comments from influential senators who view the drought relief effort of 1988 as a rural development effort. And, a powerful farm organization testified before the Joint Economic Committee of Congress that an extra $40 billion in farm programs would kick-start the rural economy. The continued use of this assumption by farm groups has been called a cynical effort to maintain their lucrative farm entitlements.

LIMITED DATABASE

The second factor inhibiting the development of rural policy is an inadequate database. Professional rural social scientists repeatedly decry the inadequacy of data on rural well-being. There is a considerable knowledge gap about both the specific conditions of rural people and the effectiveness of past government programs for rural areas.

The knowledge gap about rural community life has not significantly narrowed since the classic community case studies of the 1930–50 period were conducted. It is paradoxical that during the 1980s—when federal policy was shifting toward decentralized planning and toward greater participation by state and local governments—research on the ability of local societies to act on their own behalf to promote economic development was virtually eliminated by the land-grant colleges of agriculture.

The third factor preventing a broader policy dialogue on rural development is the narrow scope in which the problem is defined. Rural interest groups, academics, and policy makers continue to treat rural development as a territorial or sectoral phenomenon. This focus has tended to preclude placement of rural economic and social problems in the context of regional, national, or even international political economies. The interconnectedness of rural issues in other arenas has thus been overlooked.

A quick examination of rural problems reveals a remarkable similarity with those of the inner cities. Both populations are being left behind in the economic expansion of the 1990s, and for many of the same reasons. Each of these geographic areas has similar problems with education and health services and, increasingly, in areas of social pathologies—particularly violent crimes and crimes against property.

LACK OF VIABLE SOLUTIONS

The fourth hurdle is that it is often assumed that rural economic problems are not the result of failure of the markets—for both capital and information—but of a clear competitive disadvantage in most markets. Coupled with this is the notion that government, especially the federal government, is part of the problem and not part of the solution. From this perspective, it is concluded that the primary way of fostering economic development is through the operation of free markets, and since such market mechanisms have not fostered the type of economic development necessary for a viable rural economic sector, and government is not able to induce such development, those areas that are left behind are simply the unfortunate byproducts of national economic adjustment. To the extent that this ideological perspective directs rural development policy, we can expect only more of the minimalist policies of the past several decades.

NO POWERFUL CONSTITUENCY

The development of a comprehensive rural development program lacks a unified constituency while facing considerable organized opposition. There are no politically powerful interest groups promoting rural development, with the notable exception of the National Rural Electric Cooperative Association. Chief among the opponents are farm organizations and agricultural commodity groups who view rural development as a threat to their agricultural entitlements. However, rural development *should* be attractive to farm organizations, given the dependence of farm families on viable off-farm economic opportunities. Since local taxes are often raised from property taxes, further deterioration of the nonfarm sector will likely lead to an increase in those local property taxes. The more hearty the local nonfarm economy, the less the local tax burden will be upon farmers.

Relatively passive opponents of rural development have been the Department of Agriculture and the land-grant universities. Their opposition has taken the form of neglect. They define their mission as primarily to assist commercial agriculture, and in so doing believe they help all rural people. In other words, most key USDA administrators and deans of colleges of agriculture still accept the myth that farming determines rural well-being.

At this time, the USDA does not have a clear mission statement on rural development. However, this view of its mission may change over the next decade as the nonfarm public's concerns over food safety issues and pollution of the environment by agricultural chemicals, as well as the plight of rural people, press upon the USDA the idea that its mission is much more than just farm production.

A possible source of support for rural development might be current concern with agricultural trade at the General Agreement on Tariffs and Trade (GATT) negotiations. It is increasingly apparent that concern for the negative consequences of reduced trade barriers for rural communities is a major obstacle to GATT agreements. It is reasonable to assume that national rural development programs that account for the possible high cost of transition to lower trade barriers will be a necessary part of any future broad-based agreement.

Rural development in the United States is possible. A wide range of public policy analysts have provided economic and social rationales for rural economic development. Each has argued that there is a role for all levels of government in the development and execution of a public policy.

COMPREHENSIVE RURAL POLICY?

For a comprehensive rural development policy to emerge, each of the five hurdles discussed above will have to be addressed. In particular, the public and Congress will have to accept that while farming and other extractive industries primarily occur in rural areas, these are no longer the industries that dominate the rural economy nationally. While no single industry dominates that economy, many rural economies are dependent upon single industries. Furthermore, the public and policy makers should learn to view rural problems (as well as those of the inner cities) as structural rather than cyclical. The current restructuring of rural economies presents opportunities as well as difficulties. These changes could severely constrain the range of options, but they will not close out all options.

A new approach to rural policy seems to be emerging. The trend is to assign rural economic development to rural communities and the states, and social policy (especially for education and health care) to the federal and state governments. Such decentralization of the locus of policy initiative can have positive results. However, the decentralization of planning is less a consequence of truly believing that local societies can direct their own economic development than a realization that the shotgun social programs of the past have been expensive and inefficient, and have often bypassed local political bases.

Many, if not most, rural communities lack the ability and the resources to foster their own economic development. This does not mean that there is not a great deal of potential for new rural economic activity. Rather, economic development will require a cooperative effort by all levels of government. Local governments must initiate a broad-based review of existing human, natural, and capital resources. This review should be done in cooperation with development professionals available from the states and the land-grant universities. Once a plan has been democratically agreed upon, it can be implemented and monitored, with the cooperation of state governments and the financial support of the federal government. Infrastructure development and maintenance should be the primary responsibility of state governments in cooperation with local governments.

While the economic development of local resources should occur at the local level, the provision of education and health care ought to be part of a national economic development policy. Neither rural America nor the inner cities have the capital and human resources to provide an adequate education or offer minimal health care. Given the considerable proportion of the U.S. population living in rural areas and the inner cities, it is detrimental to long-term economic development to neglect this generally ignored portion of the labor force.

To date, legislative activity to create a comprehensive rural development policy by renovating old policies, developing new missions for existing public institutions, and initiating new programs has fallen short. The Congress appears to be on the verge of considering a major rural development bill; but given the budget deficit and the lack of a clear strategy for an omnibus approach to rural education, employment, and health needs, it is unlikely that this initiative will immediately ameliorate the identified problems. Rural development should be seen as part of a long-term national strategy to greatly upgrade our human resources while providing employment opportunities and basic services. Unfortunately, neither Congress nor the general public appears to be willing to make such a long-term national commitment.

NOTES

1. Reprinted from *Resources*, Resources for the Future, Summer 1989, No. 96, pages 14–16.

2. Louis E. Swanson has been a resident fellow in the National Center for Food and Agricultural Policy at Resources for the Future and is associate professor of Sociology at the University of Kentucky.

CHAPTER 7

INSTITUTIONAL IMPROVEMENTS—AGENDAS AND CONCLUSIONS

In order to develop a better focus on the four driving forces (institutional change, human development, resource improvements, and technical advance), SSAAP's editorial group divided the reports of the Houston work groups on community and human resources into two parts, *one* concerned with community resources for consideration in this section and *the other* with human development for consideration in Section 2 of this part. Resources are considered in Section 3 and technical advances in Section 4. The matter is complicated because institutions are important in all four sections since there are human development, resource, and technical change institutions, as well as community institutions. Moreover, institutions were considered in both of the two sections of Part II that dealt with domestic and international rural development. With institutional changes considered substantively in so many other places, the substantive content of this chapter deals mainly with local and community institutions.

However, abstractly and conceptually this chapter and section treat institutional change in a much broader fashion. Papers commissioned for the Houston and the earlier Spring Hill workshop conferences and a number of other readily available books and papers provided the groundwork for the survey (found in Chapter 1 of this section) by the editorial group of what rural social scientists have contributed to (1) our understanding of the processes of improving and building institutions and (2) the development of a number of additional general agenda items that go much beyond the specific agenda items developed by the Houston work groups mainly for community institutions.

To help keep a clear distinction between the specific substantive community resource agendas developed by the Houston work groups and the broader, much more general and abstract agendas developed since then by SSAAP's editorial group, the remainder of this chapter is divided into two parts. The *first* reports specific substantive community resource agendas from the work groups at Houston while a *second* presents the more abstract and general agendas reached by the editorial group after the Houston conference.

ABSTRACTS OF HOUSTON WORK GROUP REPORTS RELEVANT FOR INSTITUTIONAL CHANGE, MAINLY AT LOCAL AND COMMUNITY LEVELS

One of the three substantive areas considered at Houston was community and human resources and natural resources under the joint leadership of William Heffernan, professor of Rural Sociology, University of Missouri, and Allan Schmid, professor of Agricultural Economics, Michigan State University. Heffernan was responsible for community and human resources and Schmid for natural resources. In this chapter, there are abridged versions of reports from the three work groups under William Heffernan that were concerned with community as opposed to human resources. With those abridged versions, there are portions of two work groups' reports dealing with databases and the ethics of making public choices and private decisions that pertain to communities and local institutions.

The Houston group dealing with natural, human, and community resources produced a prologue to their work group reports. Those parts of the prologue *most relevant for communities and institutional change* follow:

- Rural America is undergoing profound social, economic, and demographic changes that raise important issues of research, education and policy; the nature of the changes; the ability of communities to respond to them; the problem of underserved and underutilized populations; and the creation of sustainable rural economies.

- Currently, many communities are reeling from the effects of diminished foreign demand for products, high exchange rates, and depreciating land values. The social problems that stem from economic hardship, such as chronic depression, inadequate employment, job displacement, and lack of services and facilities often are the secondary or tertiary impacts of inconsistent public policies.

- The diversity of rural communities and the uniqueness of rural problems require specialized responses. Because of the disparity between rural and urban places, policies often perpetuate an urban bias in program design and delivery systems.
- Rural communities encompass farms of all types, rural nonfarm residents, villages, and small cities. The concept of rural community denotes a way of life and its associated beliefs and values. It is a dynamic process of social interaction and ordering that is constantly being recreated and redefined. And, it is a structural/geographic unit containing institutions, local governance and service systems, local economies, families and households, and many other components.
- Many of the traditional differences between rural and urban communities are in flux. Therefore, there is a crucial need for research to identify the unique aspects of rural life and culture that presently distinguish rural from urban.
- Ensuring and sustaining an adequate quality of life for rural people requires a commitment by the total society.

The agendas that follow present ways in which social sciences can address the broad range of issues facing communities in rural America.

WORK GROUP ON CHANGE AND DEVELOPMENT IN RURAL COMMUNITIES AND AREAS

Leader: Ronald C. Wimberly, Professor of Sociology and Anthropology, North Carolina State University

Invited members (some of whom may not have participated) Donald M. Crider, Adela de la Torre, Paul Eberts, Rebecca H. Flores, Christina Gladwin, Tom Johnson, Howard Ladewig, Kevin T. McNamara, Marvin E. Olsen, Justin R. Ormsby, Fred Schmidt, and Joseph Schmidt.

Social scientists need to:

- *Understand better the changes occurring in rural communities.* New relationships between people, land, economic activities, and social institutions are emerging in rural areas. These must be viewed broadly to see the full range of work needed from rural social scientists. In this connection, critical needs include:
- Predictions on how people will likely distribute themselves across the land and the kinds of land-use patterns they will establish;
- Descriptions of the new work patterns and enterprises that will likely develop in rural communities;
- Determination of the likely impacts of changing family roles and structures on rural communities;
- More knowledge of how sociodemographic and socioeconomic changes affect the needs of rural communities; and
- Exploration of new linkages likely to evolve between rural and urban communities, the larger society, and the world.
- *Enhance the Ability of Rural Communities to Cope with Change.* Change management can no longer be based on traditional growth models.A model that assumes or emphasizes only demographic, monetary incomes, or institutional growth will not necessarily be desirable or even plausible for rural communities. Critical needs include:
- More knowledge of desirable and sustainable land-use patterns and how rural communities can develop those patterns;
- Processes to broaden and enhance citizen involvement and leadership skills for effective community decision making;
- Knowledge of ways in which voluntary interest groups can contribute;
- Help for rural communities to benefit from urban influences and opportunities while maintaining their desirable rurality;
- Assessment of new communication and transportation methods and techniques to assist rural communities;
- Determination of critical resources (e.g., natural, human, economic, institutional) needed of rural communities; and
- Identification of effective roles of federal and state government in assisting rural communities.

WORK GROUP ON DESIGN, EVALUATION, ASSESSMENT, ANALYSIS, AND UTILIZATION OF STATE AND LOCAL INSTITUTIONS, PROGRAMS, AND POLICIES, AND THE COMMUNITY SERVICES THEY CREATE

Leader: Paul Lasley, Professor of Sociology and Anthropology, Iowa State University

Invited members (some of whom may not have participated) Phillip Baumel, Janet M. Fitchen, Roy Frederick, Juan L. Gonzales, Judith B. Heffernan, Quentin A. L. Jenkins, Gladys J. Lyles, Sharon L. Randolph, Richard Santos, Margaret Weber, Lionel Williamson, and Mary Winter.

Some rural communities are experiencing outmigration, institutional consolidation, and contraction of services and facilities that jeopardize the key institutions giving them identity. Other communities are experiencing population growth and increased demand for local services and facilities that exceed their abilities and resources. In other settings, long-term deterioration of community and human capital resources leads to a downward spiral of poverty, unemployment/underemployment, crime, and diminished health statuses. Research and educational assistance is needed to help communities sustain a decent quality of life as well as to develop. Rural social scientists can help:

- Develop processes to identify local needs for services and facilities that ensure involvement of local people, including those not usually heard.
- Enhance local generation of data and access to appropriate secondary data for local needs assessments.

- Identify and improve understanding of existing services and facilities in rural communities, both public and private, and recognize informal as well as formal systems of service delivery.
- Evaluate existing community services and facilities, assessing their adequacy and quality and analyzing their utilization patterns.
- Document existing and anticipated gaps in community services and facilities.
- Design approaches for meeting present and anticipated needs, including program strategies and procedures for overcoming barriers to those strategies.
- Determine what financial and organizational resources are needed to implement necessary programs to meet present and future needs for services and facilities.

WORK GROUP ON LOCAL GOVERNMENT, REVENUES, EXPENDITURES, AND EFFECTIVENESS OF OPERATIONS

Leader: Donald Lacy, Extension Specialist, Community Resource Development, Virginia Polytechnic Institute and State University

Invited members (some of whom may not have participated) Richard Barrows, David L. Chicoine, Ronald C. Faas, Lynn Harvey, and Jeff Luke.

Rural America needs to be served by state and local governments that have the fiscal and management capacity to provide the level and mix of public services that will adequately meet local needs. Federal, state, and local decision makers often lack relevant information or management issues to effectively, efficiently, economically, and equitably serve rural people and communities. They need:

- Models and methods for comparing cost differentials resulting from alternative institutional/structural/procedural arrangements for delivering and financing services, including such methods as consolidation, special service districts, intergovernmental contracting, privatization, joint public/private ventures, user fees, and economies of scale.
- Improved methods for analyzing the interrelationships between state and local governments in the provision of community services and the distribution of financial burdens between state and local governments.
- Improved forecasting models for local governments to use in analyzing expenditures and revenues to reduce revenue shortfalls and/or expenditure overruns.
- Better models to predict the performance of state and local revenue systems through business cycles.
- Improved models to analyze the impact of alternative tax structures or tax incidence and burdens by income classes and sectors.
- Better financial trend and impact analysis models to evaluate financial conditions.
- More effective measures of local fiscal stress.
- Improved databases relating to local communities and more effective use of communication technology to help local decision makers gain access to data.
- Knowledge of how to create sustainable rural economies. The role of agriculture in rural economies is steadily diminishing. If the economies of many rural communities and areas are to be sustainable and viable in the future, their economies must become more diverse, complex, and better linked to national and world markets. Rural social scientists can help by:
  - Determining how the unique cultural, sociodemographic, and economic attributes of rural communities respond to national industrial transformations, the changing nature of rural-urban economic ties, and the internationalization of markets.
  - Exploring the activities and products for which particular rural communities have a comparative advantage in domestic and world markets.
  - Ascertaining how rural communities can identify and implement specific strategies to adapt to changing national and world conditions and create sustainable local economies.
  - Examining the effects of alternative public policies on the sustainability of rural communities.
  - Analyzing the impacts of changes in family structures and roles on the function of local rural communities.
  - Assessing how changes occurring in rural economies will affect the life chances, standards of living, and welfare of rural people.

WORK GROUP ON PUBLIC CHOICE AND PRIVATE DECISIONS IN THE USE OF COMMUNITY RESOURCES

Leader: Tom Ruehr, Professor of Soil Science, California Polytechnic State University.

Invited members (some of whom may not have participated) Gary Comstock, M. Janice Hogan, Douglas MacLean, Robert Matthews, Alan Randall, Neill Schaller, and Robert L. Vertrees.

This work group also produced a prologue to their agenda items.

Again and again, agricultural technology, industry, research, extension, and teaching have been blind-sided by ethical concerns and objections that are unexpected, and with which we have been ill-prepared to deal. These involve labor displacement, loss of community viability, educational inadequacies, health care deficiencies, racial issues, and the rural disadvantaged to mention only selected items from a long list. Many of the rural people who are affected are not part of the traditional clientele of the agricultural establishment. The interests and values of these groups need to be studied, researched, and considered in policy formulation and the groups themselves need to gain some access to the decision process. This would benefit the groups concerned and protect the agricultural establishment and community leaders from surprises.

It is now becoming apparent that self-interest models in political science and economics offer only incomplete explanations. People act upon self interest in community political arenas, to be sure, but also on the basis of principled beliefs about the nature of the good life. Thus, decisions about changes in community institutions are motivated by social as well as self interests. Systematic research can identify broader ethical foundations of institutional choices, the ethical principles that alternative procedures promote, the potential for constructing policies that go beyond individualistic ethical positions, and the points at which ethical conflict is inevitable. Rigorous research about ethics is a duty of rural social scientists. The ethical aspects (public as well as individual) of the processes of creating and sustaining community institutions need to be taught to the agricultural extension workers, and to graduate and undergraduate students in our various institutions.

Some ethical aspects relevant for community development are listed below. These areas can be researched and the results disseminated to users and students. Experiences with attainment and loss of "goods" and the incurrence of "bads" should be used along with logic to analyze and better understand:

- Ethical aspects of choices available to the various affected parties using (or seeking to use) the same resources. The productive and detrimental consequences associated with each of the alternative choices for using a given resource need to be ethically assessed.
- Ethically improved mechanisms for conflict resolution. Extension workers need assistance in dealing with the alternatives and in evaluating the potential consequences of resource conflicts and their resolution.
- The institutions and social processes that direct human ingenuity in beneficial, more ethical ways of assessing the status quo, developing alternatives, and predicting their impacts; designing institutions and processes; monitoring the results; and improving rural communities.
- How to help people become more comfortable in dealing with the moral and ethical concerns facing rural communities by helping to develop a common language, documenting experiences with community values, and promoting dialogues concerning ethics in agricultural and rural affairs.
- Rural settlement issues were selected to elucidate the process of ethical reasoning (including the use of experience) about real-world community choices. Several questions should guide investigative and educational work in this area:
  - What obligations or claims do nonrural people have on those who choose a rural lifestyle?
  - What obligations do rural people have to urbanites?
  - What obligations do rural people have for one another?
  - More importantly, what are the basic principles and foundations for any of these claims?
  - To what extent is experience useful in answering such questions?
  - To what extent do these questions reveal problems requiring special policies? To what extent do these ethical questions result in major conflicts?
  - How can the answers to these questions be used as inputs to different models or as constraints on various processes and policies?
  - How can the answers to the above questions affect the methods to be used?

WORK GROUP ON DATABASE NEEDS FOR COMMUNITY RESOURCE DECISIONS

Leader: David Brown, Associate Director, Agricultural Experiment Station, Cornell University (originally Macrolevel Data, Social and Economic Accounting and Analysis Systems for Natural and Community Resources)

Invited members (some of whom may not have participated) Kenneth Baum, James T. Bonnen, Stephen Lilley, Steve H. Murdock, and Alton Thompson

Six important categories of data needs for rural community work were identified. The social sciences should strive to improve databases concerning:

- Local economic structures:
- Industrial restructuring (especially service sector)
  - Effects of technological change (including telecommunications on local economy
  - Effects of policy (including macroeconomic) on local economy and credit
  - Interdependence with other rural and urban economies
  - Employment patterns and labor markets
  - Business climate and rural enterprise development
  - New market niches for rural products and services (including for agricultural products)
- Populations and human capital in rural communities:
  - Income sources and distribution
  - Human capital
  - Rural and farm household composition
  - Population composition and distribution
  - Educational attainment
- Rural community and social services and physical infrastructure:
  - Transportation, education, health, safety, and waste disposal
  - Financing of public services and infrastructure
  - Physical infrastructure—roads, bridges, water/sewer, telecommunications, etc.
- Structures of food and fiber sectors in rural communities:
  - Resource and input use and competition
  - Environmental impacts of agriculture
  - Changing agricultural structure
  - Relationships of agriculture to national and global economies
  - Effects of technology (including biotechnology) on structure of agriculture, input use, and the environment

- Technical advance as it impacts rural communities:
  - Social, economic, employment, and community consequences of technological change
  - Effects of technological change on structure of food and fiber sector
- Social structures of rural communities:
  - Equality or inequality in the distribution of access to and ownership of resources and economic activities
  - Changing structure of rural households including changes in decision-making roles
  - Policy, technology, and market interdependencies between rural and urban areas
  - Patterns of interdependence among groups within rural communities
  - Institutional (including governmental) capacity to manage change and conduct public affairs
  - Community attitudes, values, beliefs, perceptions, and satisfaction

In addition to the above improvements in the database, this work group recommended that social scientists help establish a "national rural and agricultural statistical service" with responsibility to (1) develop, maintain, coordinate, and assure access to an integrated rural database including primary, secondary, and administrative data; (2) conduct all USDA surveys; and (3) coordinate rural and agricultural survey activities of other federal agencies. The rural database should include information for each of the six database headings above. This same agenda item is repeated in Sections 2, 3, and 4 of this part.

AGENDA ITEMS DEVELOPED AFTER SSAAP'S HOUSTON CONFERENCE

After the Houston conference, the papers presented there and previously at Minneapolis, generally available published material, and reports of other conferences (some of which are referenced in Chapter 1 of this section) became the basis for the much more general and abstract institutional agenda items presented below. It is stressed here that these agenda items were developed within SSAAP's editorial group rather than by work groups at the Houston conference. Social scientists need to provide a new conceptualization of both public and private institutions relevant for agriculture, rural societies, and consumers. To do this requires that they:

- Recognize that institutional change manifests itself in interdependent changes in:
  - "Rules of the game"
  - Organizations
  - Physical properties, facilities, staffs, and equipment of organizations
- Work on institutional changes (in all of the above manifestations) to examine:
  - Stock establishment costs for new institutions being considered for farming, agribusiness, rural societies, and consumers;
  - Stock dismantlement costs for farm, rural, and consumer institutions being considered for elimination or replacement;
  - Stock nonmonetary as well as monetary costs of and returns from institutions being considered for dismantlement and establishment; and
  - The incidence of such costs and returns.
- Recognize that establishment and dismantlement costs, which sum to transaction costs, include the following:
  - Information
  - Negotiation
  - Enforcement costs

  These are generally experienced as flow costs that must be converted to stock costs for valid comparisons with the stock costs of establishing and dismantling institutions.
- Distinguish between institutional changes made
  - for constructive purposes of providing services and goods, and
  - those made mainly to create income streams for noncontributing groups and individuals.
- Consider the potentially protected income (both monetary and nonmonetary) streams that may be generated in institutions originally set up for productive purposes. In this connection it is important to distinguish between
  - income streams that arise from maximizing positive quasi-rents arising from past mistakes in establishing institutions for productive constructive purposes or, what is mathematically the same thing, minimizing the negative quasi-rents (losses) of those same mistakes, and
  - income streams that do not minimize the losses of past mistakes in establishing constructive institutions but, instead, increase losses by maximizing rents collected by noncontributors.
- Distinguish between
  - operating (flow) transaction costs for a fixed or given institution in any of the three manifestations and
  - the stock costs of dismantling old and establishing new institutions, again, in any of the three manifestations.
- Anticipate that transaction costs conceptions are likely to be further developed to include:
  - Total and average variable and fixed and their sum as well as marginal costs, the lists of fixed and variable and marginal costs depending endogenously on whether it is advantageous to dismantle or establish all or parts of all of any of the three institutional manifestations considered above; and
  - Sharper distinctions between flow and stock costs and returns.
- Help determine monetary and nonmonetary worths of existing and replacement institutions.
- Recognize that it is not advantageous to change an institution worth too much in place to justify its dismantlement and not enough to justify its expansion or replacement. Thus, an important agenda item is that of conceptualizing the nature of institutional fixity and/or variability in terms of establishment and dismantlement

stock costs as they relate to the use values (again stock) of institutions in any of their three manifestations.

- Recognize that administrators, employees, and those served by fixed institutions having constructive purposes often receive quasi-rents (opportunity costs or shadow prices) and that
  - maximization of such rents figured with respect to establishment costs is
  - tantamount to minimizing losses on the past mistake(s) that cause(s) the institution to be worth less than what it cost to establish it.
- Expect to find that some institutions were established for the sole purpose of creating and collecting rents (again, opportunity costs or shadow prices). Such institutions can be regarded as "mistakes," in which case maximization of rents with respect to dismantlement costs is of questionable value to society even if privately advantageous to the rent collector.
- Expect that even institutions established for constructive purposes will have components that were established to create rent-collecting opportunities for noncontributors rather than to produce institutional services.
- Do quantitative research on the "rents collected" by administrators, employees, and clientele of our agricultural and rural institutions including rents not justifiable in terms of minimizing losses on earlier errors in organizing institutions for the constructive purposes of generating and disseminating services. This agenda item is related to what is known in the literature of agricultural economics as political economic resource transactions (PERTs), political economic seeking transfers (PESTs), and political economic preserving activities (PEPAs). High on the agenda is the need to relate these concepts more precisely to public choice/transaction cost theory.
- Recognize that public choice/transaction cost theory has potential for extending the applicability of
  - the "induced" institutional change and
  - the industrial organization approaches by
  - including the wide range of social, political, technical, and normative variables dealt with
  - in less formalized studies of institutional change and
  - by rural social scientists who advise and consult with those designing institutional changes, creating new, and administering existing agricultural institutional organizations and developing physical institutional facilities and properties and
  - by rural social scientists actually participating in the design and implementation of institutional changes and, in turn, administering new and modified institutions in all three of their manifestations.
- In extending the public choice/transaction cost approach as suggested in the above agenda items, give consideration to using general systems simulation models developed *iteratively* and *interactively* with institutional administrators and *affected persons*. Such models should be conceived as multidisciplinary, to be general enough philosophically to deal with both monetary and nonmonetary values (*performance* or *criteria* variables), to deal with alternative *structures* and *states* of institutional systems, and with premaximization and both maximization and other *behavior*, and eclectic with respect to techniques from different disciplines and philosophic orientations. In many instances, noncomputerized but iterative and interactive scenario analyses will likely be adequate. In other instances, computerized, general, systems-simulation models built and run interactively and iteratively with concerned persons will be needed.
- Encourage basic social scientists to extend and further develop the theories, measurements, and techniques of their respective disciplines in ways that improve the ability of multidisciplinary teams dong iterative/interactive, problem-solving and/or subject-matter modeling to deal better with social, political, power, psychological, demographic, structural, and related variables.
- Avoid neglect of problem-solving and subject-matter research in developing public choice/transaction cost analyses. Development can be expected to come faster and more effectively with fewer dead ends and omissions if "real world" problematic institutional changes are modeled and analyzed. Specific real-world institutional agendas and problems are found in:
  - The first part of this chapter that is concerned mainly with agendas about rural community and local institutions;
  - Chapter 10, Section 2 of this part that deals with the institutions that serve and develop human beings;
  - Chapter 7, Section 3 of this part that is concerned with the resource institutions that deal with the generation, use, conservation, regulation, and enhancement or growth of manmade and natural resources; and
  - Chapter 2, Section 4 of this part that treats the institutions that generate and disseminate new production methods and techniques.

CROSS REFERENCES TO REPORTS OF OTHER WORK GROUPS WITH AGENDA ITEMS ON INSTITUTIONAL CHANGE

In addition to the other sections of Part III that deal with the other three driving forces, agendas pertaining to institutional changes are prominent in other chapters of this book:

- Part II, Section 1 on *farmers, agribusinesses, and consumers*, Chapter 7—Institutional change agendas were touched on by the work groups dealing with "National Policies and International Trade and Monetary/Fiscal Programs and Policies, Production Stabilization and Production Expansion Programs" under the leadership of David Blandford, Professor of Agricultural Economics, Cornell University.
- Part II, Section 2 on *rural development of LDCs*, Chapter 11 has institutional change agenda items. See, for instance, the report from the work group on "Trade and Monetary/Fiscal Including Regional Common Market

Proposals and Their Impacts on LDCs" under the leadership of G. E. Rossmiller, Director, National Center for Food and Agricultural Policy, Resources for the Future.

- Part IV, Section 1, Chapter 2 of this book deals with *database institutions* for farms, households, agribusinesses, consumers, and rural societies done under the leadership of James T. Bonnen.

- Part IV, Section 2, Chapter 5 on *basic social science disciplines*, under the joint leadership of Peggy Barlett, Professor of Anthropology at Emory University, and Bonnie McCay, Professor of Human Ecology at Rutgers University, has agenda items that will contribute to social science work on institutional change and reform.

- Part IV, Section 3, Chapter 3 of this book deals with the *ethics of private decisions and public choices* done under the leadership of Joseph Havlicek and Paul Thompson.

- Part V, Chapter 8 is on the work group report on *needed research on social science administration and funding vis-a-via farming and rural development*, under the leadership of Larry J. Connor, Department of Agricultural Economics, Michigan State University, and Gerald E. Klonglan, Department of Sociology and Anthropology, Iowa State University, presents institutional change strategies for the rural and basic social sciences.

CHAPTER 1

INTRODUCTION TO SECTION ON HUMAN DEVELOPMENT

Human development is a major and critical problem for the entire United States, and it is particularly so for disadvantaged groups many of which reside in rural areas. Questions are raised about the effectiveness of our general educational system. We are alarmed at the effect of drugs (including alcohol) on our youth. We are concerned about health, nutrition, long-term health care, and catastrophic health costs. We are dismayed by lack of student motivation, teenage pregnancy, adult drug addiction, and alienation. We shudder at the prospect of a future labor force with a high proportion of its workers born of disadvantaged parents and inadequately educated and trained for a modern, high-tech society. While many of these difficulties are found in all income classes and ethnic groups, they are also related to the poverty of disadvantaged rural groups.

This chapter considers first how human development was addressed by SSAAP at Spring Hill and Houston. It then reviews the general background information on human development that was available to SSAAP participants from the literature and priority exercises that took place before and during SSAAP, but outside of SSAAP. This chapter then addresses the challenge posed for the agricultural establishment by disadvantaged farm and nonfarm rural groups and their children. Lastly, the chapter turns back to the introduction to this part (III) and its first section to supply background for examining the contributions the social sciences can make to the improvement of the institutions that further human development in our rural areas, with particular attention to disadvantaged groups.

HOW HUMAN DEVELOPMENT WAS ADDRESSED BY SSAAP AT SPRING HILL AND AT HOUSTON

Initially, SSAAP neglected human development! At SSAAP's first conference (Spring Hill), attention was given to community and natural resources, but human development was not on the formal program although it was considered in a number of instances (see Part I, Chapter 8). Perhaps human development was neglected because it was taken for granted that the agricultural establishment (AE) and the universities within that establishment devote adequate effort to rural human development via resident instruction, extension, 4-H Clubs, Future Farmers of America (FFA), and other efforts, such as leader development programs. After the Spring Hill conference, however, human development was added to a substantive area considered at the Houston conference under the rubric of "Natural, *Human*, and Community Resources." Wallace Huffman (1988) was also commissioned to develop a background paper on human development for the Houston conference. His paper is published as Chapter 2 of this section. It deals with human development in relation to farm and rural communities in the United States and in less and more developed countries abroad. At the Houston conference, the participation of African-Americans from the 1862 and 1890 land-grant institutions led to considerable emphasis on disadvantaged farm and nonfarm rural African-Americans. While Hispanics participated in the Houston conference, inadequate attention was given on that occasion to the human development problems of disadvantaged rural Hispanics.

After the Houston conference, part of SSAAP's editorial group participated in the Professional Agricultural Workers Conference held at Tuskegee University in the Fall of 1988 where additional emphasis was placed on disadvantaged rural African-Americans. As a consequence of looking at human development and other problems of rural African-Americans, the SSAAP editorial group realized how badly SSAAP's Houston conference had neglected the role of the social sciences vis-a-vis human development and other problems of the disadvantaged farm and nonfarm rural groups. A subsequent SSAAP meeting was held in Phoenix in early 1989 where a group of Hispanic scholars and SSAAP representatives addressed the problems of disadvantaged rural Hispanics. In turn, the greater understanding of Hispanic problems that grew out of the Phoenix meeting made the SSAAP editorial group aware of the need for SSAAP to devote additional attention to the problems of Native Americans and poor rural Caucasians, as well as African-Americans and Hispanics.

In the resultant stock taking in reference to what SSAAP had up to then done about human development agendas, it became clear that the agendas developed at Houston under the rubric of "Natural, Human, and Community Resources" needed to be expanded and broken down according to the four driving forces, as they are discussed in the introduction to Part III of this book. This section, Section 2 of Part III, is designed to remedy the shortcomings of the SSAAP's Houston conference with respect to one driving force— human development—with emphasis on its relationship to the poverty of disadvantaged rural groups. Additional papers were commissioned on disadvantaged rural African-Americans, Hispanics, Native Americans, and Caucasians. These deal with the human development issues and problems—education, poverty, discrimination, health, motivation, and the like—of these ethnic groups. An additional special paper was commissioned on health. The paper on African-Americans is by Ralph D. Christy of Louisiana State University; the one on Hispanics is by Refugio I. Rochin and Adela de la Torre of the University of California; the one on Native Americans is by Jack D. Forbes of the University of California; and the one on Caucasians is by J. Allan Beegle of Michigan State University. Because the paper on Native Americans does not deal with the large Eskimo population of Alaska, attention to these Native Americans is still inadequate. Permission was obtained to publish a paper by Clifton R. Wharton Jr. on the disadvantaged people of the United States. Robert D. Stevens of Michigan State University wrote a special paper for SSAAP on the health-care problems of rural Americans, including both the advantaged and disadvantaged, as well as the young and the aged.

A report entitled "Social Science Research Serving Rural America," published for the Experiment Station Committee on Organization and Policy (ESCOP), has a section stressing the impact of education on economic development, services for adolescents, families, families in crisis, disabled children, and the elderly. This report, produced under the leadership of Gene F. Sommers and the editorship of Mary Miron (1989), indicates the many different kinds of efforts that are needed from the research and education institutions of the AE if they are to play their appropriate roles in meeting the human development needs of our disadvantaged rural farm and nonfarm groups, and help generate the skilled people whose productivity will be important for the United States in the decades ahead.

Perhaps the most dramatic indication of the importance of developing more fully our disadvantaged human resources in the United States is Wharton's estimate that minorities and immigrants will provide 60 percent of the entrants to the U.S. labor force by the year 2000, while the proportion of Caucasian male entrants (many of whom will also be disadvantaged and from broken homes) will fall from its present 47 percent to 15 percent. Clearly, we must increase our investments in the children of disadvantaged people, including the large number from rural areas. The agricultural establishment needs to go beyond resident instruction, leadership training, and extension programs for commercial farmers, and the vocational agriculture teaching and youth (4-H and FFA) programs for the youth of commercial farm families. The educational institutions of the agricultural establishment now neglect disadvantaged rural groups across the board—in their research, youth, extension, and resident instruction programs. This neglect can only increase with the current attempts to privatize and switch to user fees for the services of our public agricultural establishment.

BACKGROUND ON HUMAN DEVELOPMENT FROM OUTSIDE OF SSAAP

Long before SSAAP came into existence, rural and basic social scientists were doing sound work on human development. Some worked on educational processes and the organization and operation of educational institutions. Attention was given to both traditional academic education and to more specialized, practical, professional education in fields such as agriculture, business administration, medicine, pharmacy, law, and vocations. In economics, theories of induced human capital formation developed under the leadership of Nobel Laureate T. W. Schultz at the University of Chicago (1971). This line of work tended to deal with education in general with little specific attention to disadvantaged groups, rural or urban. The human capital formation ideas from Chicago stimulated rural social science research on the effectiveness and productivity of institutions for resident instruction, extension and, to a lesser extent, vocational instruction and the 4-H and FFA programs. Moreover, there were other efforts to appraise the status of disadvantaged groups including, particularly, the efforts of the U.S. President's National Advisory Commission on Rural Poverty (1968) that inevitably considered the interrelationship between poverty and education of the disadvantaged.

Among the background documents available to SSAAP participants at Houston was the report entitled *Human Resources Research, 1887–1987: Proceedings*, edited by Ruth Deacon and Wallace Huffman (1986). Also important were chapters by Don Dillman (1988) and Wallace Huffman (1988) in the book entitled *Agriculture and Rural Areas Approaching the 21st Century* (1988) that contained papers presented at an American Agricultural Economics Association conference, August 1985, in Ames, Iowa. In an earlier 1979 report, *Structure Issues of American Agriculture*, is an instructive chapter by David L. Brown entitled "Farm Structure and the Rural Community." In July 1988, the Population Reference Bureau drew together material and data, much of which had been available to SSAAP's Houston participants, in a report entitled *The Rise of Poverty in Rural America* by William P. O'Hare (1988). Other important references are to be found in the reference lists for Chapters 2 through 8 of this section.

THE CHALLENGE FOR THE AGRICULTURAL ESTABLISHMENT

Human development of both advantaged and disadvantaged groups is important for agriculture and rural societies. Female and male agricultural and rural leaders, scientists, administrators, technicians, social workers, health-care professionals, educators, and extension workers from both advantaged farm and nonfarm groups will continue to be needed. By and large, the formation of such human capital takes place rather effectively among advantaged farm and rural groups. The greatest difficulties face the members of disadvantaged farm groups; families and individuals in these groups lack the resources necessary to invest in education and skills for either themselves or their children. Further, public educational institutions for such groups are often inadequate structurally and financially to make public investments in the disadvantaged to offset their private inability to invest. Perhaps an even greater constraint on human capital investment in disadvantaged farm and nonfarm rural youth is the deterioration of the family and the social facilities of poverty-stricken communities. Traditionally, much human capital formation took place in the family, but family structures are deteriorating, especially among the disadvantaged, and the lack of family resources among the disadvantaged limits investments. Wharton's paper (Chapter 3 of this section) reports that between now and the year 2000, one-third of the labor entrants will be from single-parent homes—these are often poor homes that have been shattered by divorce, drug abuse, and other social ills. The picture is clear—the challenge ahead, with respect to human capital formation in farm and rural areas, is both redistributive and institutional. This is a major challenge for the AE as well as society, and within the AE for its rural and basic social scientists. How do we get more resources to invest in the children of disadvantaged rural farm and nonfarm people? And, how do we improve our rural human development institutions—schools, churches, 4-H Clubs, FFAs, scouts, and, especially, families—to function better in creating human capital among disadvantaged rural groups? More generally, how do disadvantaged rural people acquire income-producing resources, including (but not limited to) human capital, to use to generate more income so that they will not be disadvantaged? So viewed, the problem is one of investment and redistribution—not one of subsistence relief.

THE PUBLIC (MULTIPERSON) CHOICE/ TRANSACTION COST APPROACH TO HUMAN CAPITAL GENERATING INSTITUTIONS

Part III's introduction and Chapter 1 (Part III, Section 1) survey the present status and anticipated extensions of the public choice/transaction cost (PC/TC) approach to the study of institutional change. In turn, more specific potential uses of this approach are considered in other sections and chapters of Part III—Section 3, Chapter 1, on changes in resource institutions, and Section 4, Chapter 1, on technical change institutions.

In the case of technical change, rural sociologists developed the diffusion approach in studying adoption rates for which there does not seem to be a sociological equivalent pertaining to education. However, sociologists, educational psychologists, philosophers, educational researchers, and others have considered the social, psychological, familial, peer group, nutritional, ethnic, health, and other variables that motivate, demotivate and, in other ways, influence the capacity of those being educated and trained.

Then, too, the U. S. educational systems had been repeatedly studied, analyzed, criticized, assessed, and appraised by national, state, and local commissions, committees, and groups. Few of these appraisals have concentrated on rural people, although rural areas have not been entirely neglected (Deacon and Huffman 1986, Huffman 1988). Different disadvantaged rural groups have received varying attention; some studies are summarized in this section's chapters on African-Americans, Hispanics, Native Americans, and disadvantaged rural Caucasians.

There have been concerns in the agricultural establishment about inadequate numbers of biological and physical scientists and engineers being trained for both the agricultural and general research establishments. Schertz et al. (1976), Connor (1989), Fienup and Riley (1980, 1981, 632–44), and Johnson (1983) have addressed needs for agricultural economists with graduate learning.

Though "equal opportunity" slogans are prevalent in the AE, focus has not been on disadvantaged rural groups as sources of scientists. While women have been increasing their roles in baccalaureate and postgraduate work in the agricultural, physical, biological, and social sciences, the AE still underinvests in women. Moreover, the AE has not focused enough on making human capital investments in the rural disadvantaged as a way of providing them with the means with which to produce more income.

Though engineers and physical and biological scientists are required by the AE, farming, rural communities, and food systems, we need to go beyond an unbalanced emphasis on technology to a balanced emphasis on education and training, improvement of institutions and policies, and to the enhancement of both natural and manmade resources, as well as on improving technology. Also, as Erick Bloch (1990) has stressed, we need to develop our human resources in a way that does not deprive our society of the potential human contribution of presently disadvantaged groups (including females from both the advantaged and the disadvantaged groups). However, we must also go beyond the technocracy in Bloch's *Science* article (1990) entitled "Education and Human Resources at the National Science Foundation," that neglects the human resources needed to improve institutions, policies, natural and manmade resources, and our human resources. In the same issue of *Science*, the authors of another article (Palca and Marshal 1990, 848) even rejoiced that the social science budget "stayed level or declined" in the National Science Foundation, while they stressed human development with a technocratic emphasis on biological and physical social science and engineering!

The ground-breaking work of T. W. Schultz (1961) of the University of Chicago on human capital formation focused on how private costs and prospective income gains influence individual and familial decisions concerning educational investments. Despite the complementarities between human capacity, technology, institutions, and natural and manmade resources, it is clear that returns to "reasonable" combinations of the four typically make both public and private investments in education highly advantageous. The Chicago group has placed considerable emphasis on the importance of public educational investments in women and other disadvantaged groups, but has not stressed the redistributive nature of such investments, stressing instead that it "pays" the public to invest in its disadvantaged.

Educational institutions, both public and private, are important. Changes in existing institutions are needed, and some new institutions may also be required depending on how existing institutions can be modified and reformed. Both the 1862 and the 1890 land-grant institutions are candidates for reforms to serve rural African-Americans better. Hispanics do not have the educational equivalent of the 1890 land-grant institutions although an increasing number of community colleges are being established in Hispanic communities. The same is true for Native Americans. Neither group is well served by the 1862 land grants. Disadvantaged rural Caucasians are also constrained from using "their" institutions (the 1862 land-grants) by increasing entrance requirements that are difficult to meet with rural K–12 educations, increasing tuition costs, reduced acceptability and feasibility of living in off-campus poverty while "working one's way through," and lack of scholarships for the disadvantaged. Clearly, our educational institutions require modifications, even extensive reform, to serve the rural disadvantaged.

The educational institutions serving agriculture are in need of social science research that goes beyond a rather individualistic human capital approach to a PC/TC approach. Further, the PC/TC approach needs to be expanded to cover stock, as well as flow costs and returns, that are involved in modifying, reforming, replacing and, possibly, establishing new "rules of the game," organizations, campuses, staffs, and facilities for education. To do this we must get by the chauvinisms that separate the disciplines and the subdisciplines within the disciplines. Many problems and issues must be addressed, without disciplinary loyalties, across numerous disciplines.

Whether public or private, the changes needed to help the disadvantaged acquire ownership of income-producing rights and privileges are often redistributional within and between generations. Nonmonetary values are probably more important than monetary values. Serious intellectual discussions and thought have long questioned the very existence of an interpersonally valid common denominator to use in optimizing redistributive modifications and reforms in our institutions. Also, one needs only to think of the prejudice, alienation, drug abuse, and teacher disillusionment to question the use of any optimization model for predicting educational investment behavior and designing changes in educational institutions. Moreover, complicated social, psychological, political variables and rent seeking are involved in socio-administrative, politico-economic processes requiring iterative exploration and learning among interacting participants. The kind of interactive/iterative systems analyses that appear useful in analyzing redistributive reforms are discussed in the first chapter of Part III, Section 1, and are illustrated by Busch (Part III, Section 1, Chapter 5) and Bubolz and Sontag (Part II, Section 1, Chapter 5). There is a need for systems analyses that go beyond an expanded PC/TC analysis (which is, essentially, a form of specialized economic analysis) to become truly multidisciplinary, iterative/interactive (participatory) systems analyses.

INTERDEPENDENCIES BETWEEN HUMAN DEVELOPMENT AND THE OTHER THREE DRIVING FORCES IN ASSISTING DISADVANTAGED RURAL GROUPS

None of the four driving forces, however essential, is individually sufficient for assisting a disadvantaged group—and, that includes human development. Further, each driving force can also become limiting if overemphasized to the neglect of the others. Skilled workers without natural resources and, for that matter, without physical and biological manmade capital and advanced technology produce little more income than unskilled workers. Poor institutions and policies and a lack of infrastructure can also can negate skills. Thus, while this section stresses the importance of investing in the skills and capabilities of numbers of disadvantaged rural groups, it must be remembered that in order to provide full benefit to the disadvantaged and, through them, to society, educational programs require concomitant increases in the ownership of other income-producing rights and privileges including physical property and financial assets; improved institutions, organizations and infrastructure; and technology to employ the advanced skills. While disadvantaged groups can benefit from many improvements in the four driving forces that do not harm others, it is *often* necessary to consider interventions and reforms that will damage some persons in order to benefit the rural disadvantaged. But, not all such changes are equally acceptable or, conversely, objectionable. The challenge for the AE and its rural social sciences is to find *appropriate* interventions and reforms to help the disadvantaged rural groups and, in this way, help the rest of society.

THE CHALLENGE FOR THE RURAL AND BASIC SOCIAL SCIENCES

Rural social scientists serve as consultants, advisors, governmental administrators, and entrepreneurs, as well as researchers and professors. Thus, in their less academic capacities, rural social scientists have the obligation to solve problems, assist in problem solving by contributing to prescriptive conclusions and, in some instances, acting and then taking responsibility for those acts.

Solving the human development and poverty problems of disadvantaged rural farm and nonfarm people requires choices or decisions and actions that are often redistributive in nature. As McCloskey (1990) and Johnson (1986a ,1986b, forthcoming) indicate, such actions require going *beyond* reductionist, logically positivist research and teaching, and Pareto optimality *to* the objective pursuit and use of interpersonally valid knowledge of cardinally measured values (Cooter and Rappoport, 1984). The role and use (by decision makers) of iterative/interactive systems and scenario analyses were discussed above under the rubric, "The Challenge for the Agricultural Establishment." Here the challenge is for rural social scientists as advisors, consultants, administrators and entrepreneurs. But the rural social science challenge does not end with "action people," because such people (1) must be educated by rural and basic social science educators to do such work and (2) need the support of multidisciplinary problem solving and subject-matter research, including research on values and prescriptions. (Boulding 1981, 153; Knight 1936, 1951, 9–10; McCloskey 1990; Johnson 1986a, 1986b)

CROSS REFERENCES IN THIS BOOK

PART I: INTRODUCTION

Ch. 5 The Role of the Social Sciences in Rural Development and Natural Resource Management, Vernon W. Ruttan

Ch. 6 Science and Technology Policy for the 21st Century: The U.S. in a Global Economy, G. Edward Schuh

REFERENCES

Bloch, Erick. 1990. Education and human resources at the National Science Foundation. *Science* 249 (24 August): 839–40.

Boulding, Kenneth. 1981. *Evolutionary Economics*. Beverly Hills: Sage Publications.

Brown, David L. 1979. Farm structure and the rural community. In *Structure issues of American agriculture*. Washington, D.C.: U.S. Government Printing Office, for U.S. Dept. of Agriculture.

Connor, Larry. 1989. Land-grant undergraduate ag programs: They need revitalization. *Choices* (1st quarter): 12–16.

Cooter, Robert and Peter Rappoport. 1984. Were the ordinalists wrong about welfare economics? *The Journal of Economic Literature* 22, no. 2: 507–30.

Deacon, Ruth, and Wallace Huffman, eds. 1986. *Human resources research, 1887–1987: Proceedings*. Ames: Iowa State University, College of Home Economics.

Dillman, Don A. 1988. The social environment of agriculture and rural areas. In *Agriculture and rural areas approaching the 21st century: Challenges for agricultural economics*. Edited by R. J. Hildreth, Kathryn L. Lipton, Kenneth C. Clayton, and Carl C. O'Connor, 61–81. Ames: Iowa State University Press.

Fienup, Darrell F., and Harold M. Riley. 1980. *Training agricultural economists for work in international development*. New York: Agricultural Development Council.

_____1981. Training agricultural economists to serve the needs of a changing world. In *Rural change—The challenge for agricultural economists*. Proceedings of Seventeenth International Conference of Agricultural Economists. London: Gower Publishing Co.

Huffman, Wallace E. 1988. Human capital for agriculture. In *Agriculture and rural areas approaching the 21st century: Challenges for agricultural economics*. Edited by R. J. Hildreth, Kathryn L. Lipton, Kenneth C. Clayton, and Carl C. O'Connor, 499–516. Ames: Iowa State University Press.

Johnson, Glenn L. 1983. The relevance of U.S. graduate curricula in agricultural economics for the training of foreign students. *American Journal of Agricultural Economics* 65, no. 5 (December): 1142–48.

_____1986a. *Research methodology for economists*. New York: MacMillan.

_____1986b. Economics and ethics. *The Centennial Review* 30, no. 1: 57–68.

_____Forthcoming. Normative dimensions of production economics. In *Essays in honor of Karl A. Fox*. Amsterdam: Elsevier Science Publishers.

Knight, Frank. 1936. Chaps. 56, 57, 58 in *The ethics of competition*. New York: Harper and Bros.

_____[1933] 1951. *The economic organization*. New York: August M. Kelley Inc.

McCloskey, Donald. 1990. Agon and ag. ec.: Styles of persuasion in agricultural economics. *American Journal of Agricultural Economics* 72, no. 5: 1124–30.

Miron, Mary, ed. 1989. *Social science research serving rural America*. Madison: Wisconsin Agricultural Experiment Station, for the Experiment Station Committee on Organization and Policy.

O'Hare, William P. 1988. *The rise of poverty in rural America*. Washington, DC: Population Reference Bureau, Inc.

Palca, Joseph, and Eliot Marshal. 1990. Bloch leaves NSF in midstream. *Science* 249 (August 24): 848–85.

Patenkin, Don. 1962. Frank Knight as teacher. *The American Economic Review* 663, no. 5: 798.

Schertz, L. P., A. R. Stevenson, and A. M. Weisblat. 1976. *International training in agricultural economic development*. New York: Agricultural Development Council.

Schultz, T. W. 1961. Investment in human capital. *American Economic Review* 51:1–17. American Economic Association Presidential Address. (Reprinted at least 20 times and translated into Slovak, Spanish, Portuguese, Hungarian, Italian, French, and Japanese.)

———1971. *Investment in human capital: The role of education and research*. New York: The Free Press. (Translated into Portuguese.)

U.S. President's National Advisory Commission on Rural Poverty. 1968. *Rural poverty in the United States*. Washington, D.C.

CHAPTER 2

HUMAN CAPITAL FOR FUTURE ECONOMIC GROWTH

Wallace E. Huffman[1]

INTRODUCTION

Human capital is created by investments in human beings. It is a form of capital because it is the source of future cash income or of future nonmonetary satisfaction, or both, to someone. The investments in human capital include the following: schooling and higher education, post-school training and learning, preschool learning activities, human migration, creating improved health, acquiring useful information, and children (additions to the population). See Schultz (1972, 4–5). Human capital is largely an economic concept and does not include many of the attributes that are included in human resources.

A country's economic growth rate is the rate of sustainable increase in its ability to produce goods and services per capita (Kuznets 1971). T. W. Schultz (1961a, 1961b) and E. F. Denison (1962, 1967) were the first to attribute a significant role to human capital in the growth process. They showed that education contributed directly to growth of national income by improving the skills and productive capacities of the labor force. Later studies have confirmed these contributions and have shown that human capital has effects that go beyond the labor market.

The objective of this paper is to focus on human capital for future economic growth of poor and rich countries. The emphasis is primarily on the agricultural sector. The next two sections of the paper develop two broad themes for poor countries and rich countries, respectively. Many relationships are suggested, but more evidence is needed for most of them. The final section presents a fairly long list of researchable topics.

HUMAN CAPITAL FOR POOR COUNTRIES

If poor countries succeed in going from a relative static to a more dynamic technical environment, this will cause increased demand for formal schooling and reduce the importance of accumulated experience. Also, further increases in life expectancy are anticipated to continue and to increase the demand for all forms of non-health-related human capital. These changes are viewed within the framework of agricultural household models.

Agricultural household models combine the agricultural production, consumption, and labor supply decisions of households into a single conceptual framework. These models are quite versatile because they can be formulated for households that function in different economic environments. These models, however, refer primarily to the behavior of agricultural households where part of the agricultural output is sold and part is used for their own consumption, and where the household purchases some of the farm inputs (fertilizer, chemicals, labor, etc.) and provides some of the other resources (family labor, land, etc.) (Singh et al. 1986, Chapters 1 and 2). The models can be easily modified for labor supplied to units outside the household; for example, work for pay on another farm or nonfarm work. Government policy and environmental variables will affect the production, consumption, and labor supply decisions of these households and can be easily incorporated.

LESS EXPERIENCE AND MORE EDUCATION

In a static environment, accumulated experience of individuals seems to be a better investment than schooling. When a steady stream of new technologies become available, formal schooling has an advantage over experience. Information accumulated through experience in farming or working in the household does not depreciate when technology is unchanging. Its accumulation seems to be facilitated by an extended-family type of household structure.

Given cultural norms and role expectations for boys and girls, the peasant family faces economic incentives for boys to start working on the family farm and girls to start working in the household at a young age and for them to continue this work as they become older (Becker 1981, Chapter 2; Rosenzweig and Schultz 1982). Boys obtain valuable on-the-job knowledge of the idiosyncratic nature of the family's heterogenous land. Furthermore, they are willing, on average, to work for a wage that is much lower (could be zero) than the wage rate acceptable to nonfamily hired labor because of future benefits they expect to receive from the accumulated experience on the family's farm (and because of lower transactions costs). Girls learn valuable skills associated with caring for and raising children, preserving food, making clothing and handicrafts, and managing a household (Bryant 1986; Nichols 1986).

When technology is static and nonagricultural employment is unlikely, the expected return to formal schooling of boys (and girls) is low. Thus, children from peasant families in a static environment are expected to complete few years of formal schooling (Rosenzweig and Evenson 1977), and the boys are expected to attend irregularly because of fluctuations in demand for farm labor due to its seasonal nature. Work experience is the valuable form of human capital in a static environment.

Male relatives are more likely to be retained in extended families than female relatives because of differences in the amount of family-specific capital they possess. Where women have no property rights and working in the market is socially frowned upon, boys are more likely than girls to be retained in the (extended) family when they become adults. The boys have, on average, more family-specific human capital (land) than the girls. The male's family can best take advantage of their stock of accumulated family land-specific knowledge by keeping him in the extended family. Thus, women from other families are brought into these extended families to be wives.

Among brothers, the oldest is in a unique position for having accumulated the largest stock of farm-specific human capital at any point in time. Thus, if there are insufficient resources to employ all sons in the family business, the younger ones will be encouraged by the family to pursue nonagricultural interests. The opportunity cost of going to school will be lower for them than for the oldest son, and the return from formal schooling is expected to be higher. Thus, in this type of environment, younger sons are expected to obtain more years of formal schooling, on average, than the oldest son.

Elderly males have a unique perspective because of their large accumulated stock of farm-specific human capital. The usefulness of this extensive information and kinship ties seem to be major reasons why elderly males are retained in extended agricultural families in poor countries (Rosenzweig and Wolpin 1985).

In a poor country, the family can be expected to be the primary source of insurance against random events, and the insurance role is best served by having large families. This is accomplished by having a large number of children and an extended-family structure. This is so that the extended family has a uniform supply of labor over time and that the parents have a diverse portfolio of earning streams in old age.

When technology is dynamic or a steady stream of new technologies are becoming available, formal schooling has an advantage over on-the-job experience. Most new agricultural technologies are geo-climatic or land-specific, and changing technology causes rapid depreciation in land-specific human capital. Being able to make abstract decisions on the goodness or badness of agricultural technology is now valuable. Thus, dynamic agricultural technologies are expected to reduce the expected payoff to farm-specific human capital (i.e., reduce the opportunity cost of schooling of male youth), reduce the differential between wages acceptable to nonfamily hired labor and family labor (i.e., makes hired labor economically more attractive), increase the expected return to formal schooling, and reduce the productivity of the elderly. Schooling levels of farm youth are expected to rise, on average, even when they expect to work a lifetime in agriculture (Rosenzweig and Evenson 1977).

When the technology of household production changes (Bryant 1986), the future value of on-the-job training in the household is also reduced. Formal schooling of girls now becomes relatively more attractive from the family's perspective. One reason is the reduced long-term value of household on-the-job experience, and the other is that additional schooling of the girls may increase the success of their marriages, given that incentives exist for males to obtain more schooling than in a static economic environment. See Becker (1981, 108–11) for evidence on rising schooling levels in several countries.

Rapid technical change also seems to reduce the net advantage of an extended family structure. First, elderly males are less valuable for their extensive information, and they tend to be too conservative in making necessary changes. Second, male youths will acquire less farm-specific on-the-job experience. The changing technology eliminates the long-run returns to this form of human capital. Thus, the frequency of nuclear families and the likelihood that nonfamily members will be hired to do part of the farm work and will pay more for a family's land than family members increases.

A weakening of the family structure may lead to an increased role of the state in financing human capital investment. The economic incentives are for the investments in human capital to occur early in the lives of the children, which occurs in the mid-life of most parents. These investments in children may drain most of the family's resources. If the parents do not expect to benefit much from these investments in the human capital of their children, they may let the state do the investing. Furthermore, when children do not feel a moral obligation to assist their parents in old age, and the parents do not have a moral obligation to invest in their children's human capital, the state is frequently called upon to raise revenues to pay for the schooling of children and to provide for the income maintenance and medical expenses of the elderly.

IMPROVED HEALTH AND OTHER HUMAN CAPITAL INVESTMENTS

Significant increases in the life spans of people in poor countries have occurred during the past thirty years (Ram and Schultz 1979; Schultz 1984) and are expected in the future. The changes are unmistakably linked to the production of good health in households and have many implications for human capital investments in nonhealth forms (Fuchs 1979). With an increase in length of life, an individual has more days for work and leisure in a lifetime.

Several effects of good health can be seen in an agricultural household model. First, good health (services) enters the household welfare or utility function; i.e., better health status leads directly to a higher level of welfare or satisfaction. Good health is most likely produced by inputs of food, market health, work time, health environment or endowment, and schooling. Good health can be expected to increase the efficiency of farm (and household) production, the effective units of labor services available per day, and the number of days available for work or leisure over the lifetime (Pitt and Rosenzweig 1986).

This model of good health has a number of implications. First, if hired and family labor are perfect substitutes (but need not be at a ratio of one to one) in farm production, poor family health does not change total farm labor input but there is less family labor and more hired labor on the farm. Farm output, farm profit, and farm inputs (excluding hired labor) are left unchanged. Household full income is, however, reduced by poor health; for example, there are fewer available days for work and leisure per year, the efficiency of available family human time is reduced, and the efficiency of other inputs may be reduced. Second, if hired and family labor are not perfect substitutes in farm production, as seems likely to be the case because of different skills (family members are expected to have more allocative or adaptive skills and land-specific information) and incentives, then better health will affect farm input and output decisions and the level of farm profit. It will increase the quantity demanded of family labor (measured in constant efficiency units) and increase the quantity supplied of farm output and farm profit. The effects on hired farm labor and other farm inputs are uncertain. Third, a change in the price of food—one input into the production of health—has several own- and cross-price effects that taken together are, in general, indeterminant in direction. A rise in the price of food (or one food group) could either increase or reduce health status. Fourth, in developing countries, the quality of drinking water or other factors determining health "environments" are key inputs in producing good health. Other things being equal, an improvement in water quality will directly increase households' welfare by improving health and raise real full-incomes because of production efficiency effects and increased number of days available for work and leisure.

The expected length of life is one key variable for determining the expected returns to investments in nonhealth forms for human capital that are relatively durable (Becker 1975; Psacharopulos and Woodhall 1985, Chapter 3). In particular, if the expected length of life is only 45 years, large amounts of formal schooling will be a bad investment. However, it may be a worthwhile social investment for a large share of the population to complete four to five years of formal schooling. When the expected length of life and the days available for work or leisure increase, the benefits to investments in formal schooling seem likely to increase and, other things being equal, social-optimal schooling-completion levels increase. Thus, improved health status and increasing expected length of life are undoubtedly factors in the rising schooling-completion levels that are associated with economic growth and development (Becker 1981, Chapter 5). The two factors taken together—longer life and more schooling—can be expected to be major factors driving the increase in the real value of human time and real income per capita worldwide (Schultz 1977).

Schooling undoubtedly enhances the efficiency of household production, including the efficient production of good health. Females' schooling seems to be much more important for the production of good health than males' schooling because women, on average, spend a much larger share of their time in household production activities that affect the health status of other family members. For example, in developing countries, infant death rates are lower and babies' weights at two years of age are, on average, higher when mothers have more schooling, other things being equal (Psacharopulos and Woodhall 1985, Chapter 10). The nutrition status of adults also seems to be related to the education of the wife or adult female in the household. See Swan (1986) for a review of nutrition research and its implications for the production of health. Schooling also seems to be important for understanding the implications of hazardous-to-personal-health activities on the production of good health (smoking cigarettes, using drugs, exposure to harmful agricultural chemicals and air pollution, using poor transportation facilities [such as open or enclosed trucks]).

Advances in medical technology have changed the inputs and their prices for treating morbidity and mortality (diarrhea, small pox, measles), diseases associated with aging, and injuries arising from various types of accidents, and have altered the basic biology of human cells. The effects of these changes on health status and increased life-length expectancy are still to be measured.

HUMAN CAPITAL FOR RICH COUNTRIES

In the developed countries, the share of the labor force employed in agriculture is small and declining, and agriculture is technically dynamic. In these countries, higher-quality education for rural people and the organization of science to produce new technology are two important human capital issues for the future.

HIGHER-QUALITY EDUCATION

The relative importance of agriculture is expected to continue to decline in the future and the technology for agricultural production is expected to advance rapidly. To be able to function efficiently in these conditions, people need high-quality education and adaptive ability. Good schooling becomes relatively more valuable than vocational education and accumulated experience. This is not an environment where narrow technical schooling can be expected to be a good investment over the lifetime. The reason is that this vocational-technical training, including farming experience, is useful for enhancing human skills for a very narrow set of activities or conditions. When conditions, including technology, change, these skills can be expected to have a much higher rate of depreciation than schooling focused upon science, math, and communication skills.

Adaptive ability—the ability to adapt efficiently to an environment that has been altered in a specific way—is a valuable asset in this type of environment (Huffman 1985). Two aspects of adaptive ability seem to be important: market- and production-related adaptive skills. Market-related adaptive ability refers to ability to adapt to unanticipated changes in input and output prices. If these changes are truly unknowable, then various types of "insurance" become a means of dealing with this type of uncertainty. When agricultural technology, especially biological, is location-specific, production-related adaptive skills refer to the ability to deal with changing agricultural technology.

Adaptive ability seems to be related to schooling of decision makers and information when the potential exists for replacing existing technology with new technology (Wozniak 1984; Rahm and Huffman 1984; Mercier 1988). Historically, the public extension service has been an important source of information about technologies for farm households. However, as schooling-completion levels of economic agents rise, the extension information that is most useful to farmers changes. One of the challenges to public extension worldwide is to be flexible and insightful enough to supply information that is valuable to decision makers (Huffman 1978, 1985). This seems to imply combining extension work with an applied research program.

In the United States, a large share of the rural school districts are too small to provide high-quality education at a low cost. These districts need assistance in reorganizing their districts so that high-quality basic education could be provided at a relatively low cost. This includes applied research on the costs of education in different-sized school districts and on developing organization skills for implementing reorganization plans.

Human resource adjustments to restructuring of rural industries and between the rural and urban sectors (Singelmann 1978) could be assisted by existing public institutions. The extension service, community colleges, and the land-grant universities could cooperate in performing local labor market analyses and providing testing and career counseling of rural adults. Both individuals and firms need information on likely local labor market conditions in the near future. This would be an aid to good decision making by individuals and prospective or expanding firms. When local labor market conditions are poor, individuals could make better decisions on whether to leave an area. For prospective firms, the local labor market information would reduce their cost of evaluating a new location. When local workers are available but they do not possess the necessary training, the local community colleges could provide the training, even if they needed to restructure their curriculum.

ADVANCING SCIENCE

The organization of science (Busch and Lacy 1983) and the training and allocation of scientists are important for future economic growth.

Science and agricultural invention can be viewed as having four important levels (Huffman and Evenson 1987, Chapter 6): general science, pretechnology science, technology invention, and technology screening and subinvention. Pretechnology science is research directed specifically toward producing discoveries that enable and assist technology invention. Pretechnology science is an intermediate product that is not generally patentable. Furthermore, pretechnology sciences link general sciences and applied agricultural sciences together in a way that speeds the incorporation of general science into the applied areas.

The evidence for linkages across sciences comes from an examination of cross-journal reference citation patterns (Huffman and Evenson 1987, Chapter 6). Journal articles in the pretechnology science fields (genetics, entomology, plant and animal physiology, environmental sciences, botany, zoology) have a relatively high frequency of citation upstream to articles published in journals of general science fields (chemistry-biochemistry, biology-molecular biology, microbiology) and to articles published downstream in journals of the applied agricultural sciences (agronomy, soils, animal science, horticulture, food science and technology). An untested belief exists that a relatively balanced set of scientific activities has the largest impacts on agricultural productivity, but more evidence is needed.

Several studies have shown that U.S. agricultural productivity is positively related to public agricultural research expenditures. The studies include Griliches (1964) and Evenson (1980). In excess of 75 percent of the state agricultural experiment station research expenditures during 1967 to 1984 were on basic or applied biological science research. Social science research accounted for less than 9 percent of the total (Huffman and Evenson 1987). Thus, the results from these productivity studies are most likely dominated by biological research.

Social science research seems less likely to be a major source of sustainable growth—at least for agriculture—than the biological sciences. Social science research is, however, important for helping to exploit the full potential of biological advances. Economics research can help identify efficient resource combinations, sociology and economics can help speed up the adoption process for superior new technologies, and sociology and political science can examine the efficiency of social and political organizations. The social sciences in general can help in understanding the social costs and benefits of change. Thus, the social sciences seem to complement the biological sciences in the growth process.

The training of new scientists or of graduate students in the sciences is an important part of the research activities carried on by universities. Although scientific papers leave the impression that research is a very methodical and orderly process, the creative activity of discovery of new knowledge is primarily an art rather than a science (Ladd 1987; Zellner 1984). When this is the situation, apprenticeships, on-the-job training, or learning-by-doing are means of teaching. The university institution for this activity is the research assistantship. Graduate students learn about the art and science of research as they work with or for one or a small group of faculty members. Because they are learning skills that have long-run usefulness in doing research, they are willing to work for a wage that is lower than their opportunity cost in the market. Research assistantships have been an institution developed by faculty who have agricultural experiment station appointments to jointly complete research projects and to train graduate students or new scientists (Huffman and Evenson 1987, Chapter 5).

Because of the complementariness of agricultural research with graduate education, a large share of the high-quality graduate education programs in the agricultural sciences are located in the developed countries. A successful research and graduate education program in a field seems to require at least a modest-sized faculty (10 to 25) and reasonably strong departments in complementary fields—pretechnology and perhaps general science fields. Thus, universities in developed countries have a significant comparative advantage over those in developing countries for providing most of the graduate training. In fact, more than 28 percent of the doctorates awarded by U.S. institutions in the applied agricultural sciences since 1960 have been to individuals who are not U.S. citizens or permanent residents (Huffman 1986a, 223; National Research Council 1988, 67). Some of these Ph.D. recipients stay in the United States or go to other developed countries to work, but more than half of them return to developing countries.

The on-going rapid advances in molecular biology associated with biotechnical advances raise new issues about the allocation of scientists between the public and private sectors and between developed and developing countries. With the advances in science that are associated with biotechnology, the distance between general science, applied science, and invention has been compressed. Some of the advances in knowledge from research in general science led directly to patentable forms of biological materials that are marketable (Bull, Holt, and Lilly 1982; National Research Council 1984, 1988). In essence, the skills of general scientists, which traditionally have not been employed in research that has direct usefulness in the market, became extremely valuable in the private sector. The result has been a shift of some general science research and scientists trained in the general sciences out of the public- and into private-sector research. From the perspective of socially optimal resource allocation, this move may be in the right direction but it is unrealistic to believe that the private sector faces the right incentives in general to produce socially optimal quantities of general and pretechnology science. The primary reason is the public good aspects—the spillovers or positive external effects—of much of general and pretechnology science.

Developing countries might find it socially optimal to borrow general and pretechnology sciences from the rest of the world and to engage in only applied agricultural science research (Hayami and Ruttan 1985, Chapter 9; Evenson 1977). For this activity to be successful, the insights and imagination of at least a small staff of excellent scientists are required. The international centers (e.g., International Rice Research Institute) are institutions that are designed to perform agricultural research on problems in developing regions at a scale and with a quality of staff that may be reasonably efficient and effective. A world labor market exists for outstanding scientific talent, and this means that developing countries and international centers must pay some attention to world competition when they consider salaries and working conditions that will attract or retain good scientists (Huffman 1986b).

RESEARCHABLE TOPICS

The topics are organized into three groups: one primarily for developing countries, one primarily for developed countries, and another for both.

FOR DEVELOPING COUNTRIES

- Examine the wage rates paid to boys of farm families relative to the wages paid to hired labor to see if the difference decreases as the agricultural sector becomes technically more dynamic. A move toward equality is evidence of a reduced role of farm-specific human capital in agriculture.
- For agricultural societies that are in transition from large to small family sizes, examine the frequency that oldest sons go into farming as an occupation and younger sons obtain more formal schooling and choose nonfarm occupations.
- Examine the differences in the value of older males as decision makers to agricultural households in static versus technically dynamic agriculture. A decrease in the importance of accumulated experience relative to schooling is expected to reduce the economic contribution of older males.
- Examine the relationship between the number of children per farm household and the average child quality and relate them to the dynamics of agricultural technology, market opportunities, and government-provided social programs.
- Examine the effects of the pace of technical change on the tendency toward extended versus nuclear families.

FOR DEVELOPING AND DEVELOPED COUNTRIES

- Examine the relative importance to girls of good on-the-job household training and schooling and relate them to the pace of change in technology of household production and to labor market opportunities for women.
- Examine the effects of nutrition, schooling, and the environment (water and air quality) on the number of work days, work intensity, and length of life of individuals.
- Test for the effects of health status of farm operators on supply of farm outputs and demand for farm inputs (excluding farm labor) when hired farm labor is available. No effect of health status would imply that operators and hired labor are perfect substitutes. This is unlikely.
- Test for the effects of increased life expectancy on the average amount of schooling obtained by young men and women.

FOR DEVELOPED COUNTRIES

- For long-term, high-growth environments, test whether quality general education is more important for a long-term perspective than vocational-oriented training.
- Test for the contribution of formal schooling, experience, extension, and a well-balanced family background to the adaptive ability of decision makers.
- Investigate the types of extension activities that have the highest social rate of return in environments having dynamic technology and high schooling levels for farmers.
- Investigate the efficient organization of educational services for rural children and adults. Examine substitution possibilities between traditional and new technology for learning/teaching.
- Examine rural labor markets for the effects of occupational/industrial restructuring of jobs and other changes on labor demand for men and women.
- Examine the contributions of social science research to economic growth.
- Examine the effects of mixing scientific activities (general sciences, pretechnology sciences, applied sciences) on the rate of developing new agricultural technology and on agricultural productivity.
- Examine the relationship between public and private research for affecting agricultural productivity. To what extent are they substitutes versus complements?

- Investigate alternative institutional arrangements for the successful sharing of biotechnical scientists between the public and private sectors.
- Examine the effects of graduate program size on the quantity and average cost of graduate student training.
- Identify the productivity of U.S.-trained, foreign graduate students and examine sources of differences in productivity that are due to ability, undergraduate training, and graduate training.
- Show how the successful borrowing of agricultural sciences internationally is related to the quality and quantity of agricultural scientists working in developing countries and to the advances in science of developed countries in similar geo-climatic regions.

NOTE

1. Wallace E. Huffman is a professor of Economics at Iowa State University. Helpful comments were obtained from T. W. Schultz, P. Orazen, Helen Jensen, Glenn L. Johnson, Todd Sandler, and two reviewers. Journal Paper of the Iowa Agriculture and Home Economics Experiment Station, Project No. 2738.

REFERENCES

Becker, Gary S. 1975. *Human capital*. 2d ed. New York: Columbia University Press for National Bureau of Economic Research.

_____1981. *A treatise on the family*. Cambridge: Harvard University Press.

Bryant, W. Keith. 1986. Technical change and the family: An initial foray. In *Human resources research, 1887–1987*. Edited by Ruth E. Deacon and W. E. Huffman, 117–26. Ames: Iowa State University, College of Home Economics.

Bull, Alan T., G. Holt, and M. D. Lilly. 1982. *Biotechnology: International trends and perspectives*. Paris: Organization for Economic Cooperation and Development.

Busch, Lawrence, and W. B. Lacy. 1983. *Science, agriculture, and the politics of research*. Boulder, Colo.: Westview Press.

Denison, E. F. 1962. *The sources of economic growth in the United States and the alternatives before us*. New York: Committee for Economic Development.

_____1967. *Why growth rates differ: Postwar experience in nine Western countries*. Washington, D.C.: Brookings Institution.

Evenson, Robert E. 1977. Cycles in research productivity in sugarcane, wheat and rice. In *Resource allocation and productivity in national and international agricultural research*. Edited by T. M. Arndt, D. G. Dalrymple, and Vernon W. Ruttan, 209–36. Minneapolis: University of Minnesota Press.

_____1980. A century of agricultural research and productivity change—Research, invention, extension and productivity change in U.S. agriculture: An historical decomposition analysis. In *Research and extension productivity in agriculture*. Edited by A. A. Araji. Moscow: University of Idaho.

Fuchs, Victor R. 1979. The economics of health in a post-industrial society. *The Public Interest* 56:3–20.

Griliches, Zvi. 1964. Research expenditures, education, and the aggregate production function. *American Economic Review* 54 (September): 961–75.

Hayami, Y., and Vernon W. Ruttan. 1985. *Agricultural development: An international perspective*. Baltimore: The Johns Hopkins University Press.

Huffman, Wallace E. 1978. Assessing returns to agricultural extension. *American Journal of Agricultural Economics* 60 (December): 969–75.

_____1985. Human capital, adaptive ability, and the distributional implications of agricultural policy. *American Journal of Agricultural Economics* 67 (May): 429–34.

_____1986a. The supply of new agricultural scientists by U.S. land grant universities: 1920–1979. In *The agricultural scientific enterprise: A system in transition*. Edited by Lawrence Busch and W. B. Lacy. Boulder, Colo.: Westview Press.

_____1986b. Changes in human capital, technology, and institutions: Implications for research and policy. In *Agriculture in a turbulent world economy*. Edited by Ulf Renborg and Allen Maunder, 769–75. Aldershot Hunts, England; Crookfield, Vt.: Gower Ltd.

Huffman, Wallace E., and R. E. Evenson. 1987. The development of U.S. agricultural research and education: An economic perspective. Parts I-III. Iowa State University, Department of Economics, Staff Papers Nos. 168, 169A, 170A.

Kuznets, S. 1971. *Economic growth of nations*. Cambridge: The Belknap Press of Harvard University Press.

Ladd, George W. 1987. *Imagination in research: An economist's view*. Ames: Iowa State University Press.

Mercier, Stephanie. 1988. An econometric examination of the adoption and use of microcomputers by Iowa farmers. Ph.D. diss., Iowa State University.

National Research Council Board on Agriculture. 1984. *Genetic engineering of plants: Agricultural research opportunities and policy concerns*. Washington, D.C.: National Academy Press.

_____1988. *Educating the next generation of agricultural scientists*. Washington, D.C.: National Academy Press.

Nichols, Sharon. 1986. Human resources and household time allocation. In *Human resources research, 1887–1987*. Edited by Ruth E. Deacon and W. E. Huffman, 173–86. Ames: Iowa State University, College of Home Economics.

Pitt, Mark, and M. Rosenzweig. 1986. Agricultural prices, food consumption, and health and productivity of Indonesian farmers. In *Agricultural household models: Extensions, applications and policy*. Edited by I. Singh, L. Squire, and J. Strauss, 116–52. Baltimore: The Johns Hopkins University Press.

Pollak, Robert A. 1985. A transaction cost approach to families and households. *Journal of Economic Literature* 23 (June): 581–608.

Price, Derek J. 1986. *Little science, big science—And beyond*. New York: Columbia University Press.

Psacharopulos, G., and M. Woodhall. 1985. *Education for development: An analysis of investment choices*. New York: Oxford University Press.

Rahm, M. R., and W. E. Huffman. 1984. Adoption of reduced tillage. *American Journal of Agricultural Economics* 66 (November): 405–13.

Ram, Rati, and T. W. Schultz. 1979. Life span, health, savings and productivity. *Economic Development and Cultural Change* 27 (April): 399–422.

Rosenzweig, Mark, and R. E. Evenson. 1977. Fertility, schooling and the economic contribution of children in rural India: An econometric analysis. *Econometrica* 45 (July): 1065–79.

Rosenzweig, Mark, and T. P. Schultz. 1982. Market opportunities, genetic endowments, and intrafamily resource distribution: Child survival in rural India. *American Economic Review* 70 (September): 803–15.

Rosenzweig, Mark, and K. Wolpin. 1985. Specific experience, household structure and intergeneration transfers: Farm family land and labor arrangements in developing countries. *Quarterly Journal of Economics* 100:961–88.

Schultz, T. W. 1961a. Education and economic growth. In *Social forces influencing American education*. Edited by N. B. Henry. Chicago: National Society for the Study of Education and The University of Chicago Press.

_____1961b. Investments in human capital. *American Economic Review* 51:1–17.

_____1972. *Human capital: Policy issues and research opportunities*. Fiftieth Anniversary Colloquium VI of National Bureau of Economic Research, distributed by Columbia University Press.

_____1977. The economic value of human time over time. *Lectures in agricultural economics*, U.S. Dept. of Agriculture, Washington, D.C., June.

_____1984. The changing economy and the family. Department of Human Capital Paper no. 84. Chicago: University of Chicago.

Singelmann, Joachim. 1978. *From agriculture to services: The transformation of industrial employment*. Beverly Hills: Sage Publications.

Singh, I., L. Squire, and J. Strauss. 1986. *Agricultural household models: Extensions, applications, and policy*. Baltimore: The Johns Hopkins University Press.

Swan, Patricia. 1986. A history of nutrition research in the United States with emphasis on agricultural experiment stations. *Human resources*, 27–42.

Wozniak, Gregory. 1984. The adoption of interrelated innovations: A human capital approach. *Review of Economic Statistics* 66 (February): 70–79.

Zellner, Arnold. 1984. Philosophy and objectives of econometrics. In *Basic issues in econometrics*. Chicago: The University of Chicago Press.

CHAPTER 3

EDUCATION AND TOMORROW'S WORK FORCE: A NATIONAL AGENDA[1]

Clifton R. Wharton, Jr.[2]

Today, I want to address issues that go beyond agricultural economics. Yet, they are of urgent importance to you as scholars, as minorities, and as American citizens. Without being too dramatic, I can say that what I want to talk about is the sheer economic survival for the nation as a whole.

The United States stands on the verge of a revolution. And like most, this revolution is a mix of promise and peril.

Simply put, in the next decade, Blacks and Hispanics are going to reshape the American work force. From now until the year 2000, new minority and immigrant entrants to the labor market will outnumber new White entrants by three to two. And, by the turn of the century or shortly afterward, one in every three U.S. residents will be non-White.

There is no mystery or conspiracy here. The reason is clear for anyone to see in the nation's vital statistics. For some time, the White birthrate has been falling, to a point where it is now below the zero-population-growth level. The Black birthrate is down too, but not by nearly as much. Because of this and immigration, the Black and Hispanic fraction of the population is growing.

The nation's school systems reflect the transformation. Already, our 25 largest city school systems have a majority of non-White students. In New York City for example, the public schools are 79 percent non-White. In California, minorities are the majority in elementary schools statewide.

The trend is set for the foreseeable future. By the year 2000, what we see today in the schools will have become increasingly apparent in the adult work force, as today's minority youth move into the nation's labor market in the years just ahead.

From now until the end of the twentieth century, an estimated 25 million people will be needed for the U.S. labor force. Native White males, who now constitute 47 percent of the labor force, will provide only 15 percent of all entrants to the labor force by the year 2000. Minorities and immigrants will provide about 60 percent.

Well, what's wrong with that? Doesn't it mean the country may finally be moving toward real equal employment opportunity?

On the surface, the answer would appear to be yes. The coming decades *can* be a time of tremendous opportunity for Blacks and minorities. And everyone in this room can and should commit themselves to helping make sure it happens.

But, serious obstacles and major pitfalls may block the way.

The problem isn't that minorities will be a growing presence in the work force. The problem, rather, is: Will they be able to do the kind of jobs the United States needs most?

The economy's greatest demand—and, therefore, the strongest job market—will be for highly educated, highly skilled workers. Yet, because the next generation of American workers will include so many minorities, it will inevitably include a disproportionate number of poor people, high school dropouts, even functionally illiterate men and women.

Between now and 2000, nearly one out of three of the new work force entrants will come from single-parent homes. One out of five will have grown up in families below the poverty line. And, according to the Children's Defense Fund, poor youths are almost three times more likely to drop out of high school than their peers who are not poor.

So, when we look at today's poorest Blacks and Hispanics, particularly at the so-called underclass in our major cities, we must ask ourselves some questions:

- Do these children's early lives lay any groundwork at all for jobs that put an ever-higher premium on technical know-how?

- How will these children develop the necessary skills, habits, and attitudes to take advantage of the changing labor market?

- How can drug- and crime-ridden schools help disadvantaged children develop the skills and ambition to beat out the competition from abroad?

- And, if we can't somehow do a better job of preparing these children as the future workers of America, what will be our competitive prospects for the future?

AGING AND PRODUCTIVITY

Complicating the picture even more is the aging of the population.

In 1985, 28.5 million people were elderly (65 or over). By 2000, that number will increase to 34.9 million; by 2010, it will be 39.2 million. Looking further out to 2030, when all the baby boomers will have reached age 65, the number will have soared to 64.6 million.

In 1950, 17 people were at work for every retired person. By 1992, that will have dropped to roughly 3 active workers for every retired person. And, by 2015 or a little later, we could be looking at only 1½ workers per retiree.

In the early years of the next millennium, we are anticipating one of the tightest labor markets in recent history. To sustain the economic growth the nation has experienced for decades—to address the glaring economic inequities that continue to mar American society—or simply to remain competitive in an expanding global economy—we will need even greater productivity increases than the United States has seen over the last half century.

The burden of achieving these increases will fall to a work force that will certainly be fewer in relation to those it supports. Unless we do something soon, tomorrow's work force will also be poorer, less skilled, and with a much higher fraction of young Blacks and Hispanics from disadvantaged backgrounds. The result could be lower standards of living and less rewarding lives for an entire generation.

For over two years now, I have served as cochairman of a task force of the Business-Higher Education Forum. I have been working with many other university leaders and corporate executives to develop a comprehensive picture of the coming impact of Black and Hispanic Americans in the U.S. population and work force.

From our work, I am convinced we need a new national agenda for change. To work, the agenda must reflect experience and insights from virtually everyone—from public officials and private citizens; from government, business, and nonprofit institutions; and, particularly, from scholars and professionals such as yourselves.

With that in mind, I will touch on nine areas that I believe are central to the kind of national agenda we need if we are not to lose another generation of minority youngsters.

AREA ONE: HIGH SCHOOL GRADUATION RATES

Since 1900 or so, the U.S. high school graduation rate climbed from one in ten to seven in ten. But, as you know, not all groups do equally well.

In 1985, about half of all Black 15- to 24-year-olds had graduated, and about 40 percent of Hispanics. In each case, women ran slightly ahead of men. Again, that compares to around 72 percent of all White 15- to 24-year-olds.

Black graduation rates have recently been rising overall. But, dropout rates remain appallingly high in many areas, particularly inner-city school systems. Hispanic graduation seems to be dropping—from 36 percent of high school graduates in 1976 to 27 percent in 1985.

Elementary and high school preparation is the bedrock, the foundation, for later achievement. Students from kindergarten to 12th grade must learn the foundation skills—basic literacy, mathematics, and reasoning. Without such a foundation, there can be no progress in addressing the problems posed to our work force by the changing demographics and beyond the basics.

AREA TWO: TEENAGE FULL EMPLOYMENT

Teenage unemployment is a crippling problem for Blacks and Hispanics.

Especially in the cities, the shortage of after school, weekend, and summer jobs has become central in sustaining the poverty cycle of the so-called underclass. Joblessness prevents young Blacks and Hispanics from contributing to their family income and setting aside money for other purposes, such as future schooling.

At TIAA-CREF, where I am chairman, we have a number of programs to attack the problem. Our High School Cooperative Education Program offers part-time employment during the school year and full-time summer employment to high school students, most of them minorities. Our participation in the Summer Jobs for Youth Program provides high school and college students with summer employment. In addition, disadvantaged youths participating in the program have a chance to obtain full-time employment.

The point is that idle teenagers may come to see the underground economy, welfare dependency, and petty and serious crime as their only real choices. After school and summer jobs help teenagers contribute to family support and build good work habits, and provide on-the-job skills training that may carry on into later life. And, linking future job opportunities with staying in and graduating from high school is a promising way to reduce the dropout rate for Blacks and Hispanics.

AREAS THREE AND FOUR: COLLEGE ATTENDANCE AND GRADUATION RATES

From the 1960s into the early 1970s, Blacks steadily closed the college attendance gap between them and the White majority.

Black attendance started to slide in 1977, when about half of all Black high school grads were signing up for some form of post-secondary study. We hit a low point in 1982, when only 36 percent of recent Black graduates headed for campuses. By 1985, Black attendance was back up to 42 percent, but still below the 50 percent figure of the late 1970s. As for Hispanics, their figures are well below White and Black figures for comparable age groups.

Once in college, staying there can be even tougher. Blacks are only half as likely as Whites to finish college. Up to half of Black students leave college as freshmen or sophomores; the hemorrhaging continues afterward at a somewhat slower rate.

With the changes taking place, America's colleges, universities, and professional schools have a responsibility to strengthen their efforts to increase minority recruitment, retention, and graduation. This is where America's future professionals, leaders, and role models will be shaped. We must demand more cooperation between these institutions and K–12 educators to improve training and preparation of minority students. When minority students do arrive, colleges must create an academic atmosphere that nurtures them and encourages them to succeed.[3]

AREA FIVE: GRADUATE/PROFESSIONAL STUDIES

In 1987, Blacks earned 904 research doctorates, 26.5 percent fewer than ten years before. Hispanics received only 709 Ph.Ds.

Although Blacks were about 12 percent of the U.S. population in 1987, they received only about 3.5 percent of the doctorates granted to U.S. citizens in that year. Hispanic citizens, 8 percent of the U.S. population in 1987, received about 3 percent of the doctorates from our research universities.

Not only do minorities lag behind in graduate studies, but their areas of specialization run counter to workplace demand as well.

Of the 904 doctorates earned by Blacks in 1987, about 413 are in education, 35 are in the physical sciences, 25 are in engineering, and two in computer science. The shortage of Blacks and Hispanics entering the key areas of the future work force will only serve to further restrict their entry into the top positions in business and industry, government, and civic affairs.

I would like to make one more point. I mentioned before that colleges and universities need to nurture minority students. Identifying and encouraging students capable of graduate work need to be part of the nurturing process as early as possible. That means immediately upon college matriculation, if not before. 1890 institutions are particularly well equipped to play a key role in this area.

AREA SIX: FACULTY REPRESENTATION

As part of the higher-education initiatives I have touched on, we must not overlook the importance of faculty representation.

More than two-thirds of all Black college students (and an even larger fraction of Hispanics) now attend predominantly White institutions. In most cases, what this has meant up to now has too often been having a few minority instructors to conduct ethnic studies programs or to act as highly visible "role models." This is not a problem of the 1890s, but those of you who have studied or taught at predominantly White campuses know what I mean.

This was never enough. Today it is intolerable.

Until Blacks and Hispanics are a representative part of the broader academic community, is it not naive to expect more Black and Hispanic success in undergraduate and graduate education? How otherwise can we hope for greater representation in the country's scientific, technical, professional, and managerial work force?

AREA SEVEN: PRIVATE AND VOLUNTARY ORGANIZATIONS' INVOLVEMENT

Because of governmental budgeting restrictions, we see today a constant battle going on to protect programs designed to increase minority advances and achievements. Broad, new, public initiatives meet ever stiffer resistance among taxpayers and voters.

The country's vast network of private and voluntary institutions must share the burden in ensuring continued progress on all fronts. Initiatives such as job training, scholarship and student assistance programs, talent searches, and internships need to be strengthened, not reduced. And, many organizations that have such programs need to expand them.

AREA EIGHT: CORPORATE LEADERSHIP

With few exceptions, our corporations have been less than successful in bringing Blacks and Hispanics into executive and policy-making roles.

There are, of course, many firms with strong affirmative action records for entry-level and middle management. Even there, however, top Black and Hispanic administrators are usually in short supply.

At my own company—TIAA-CREF—46 percent of the staff is made up of minorities; nearly one-third is Black. But, our goals don't focus on numbers alone. We are trying to bring minority leaders into highly visible, influential roles. And, we firmly believe that, if we as a company are to succeed in the future, we will have to succeed in this aspect of minority employment.

Today, perhaps as never before, the long-range needs and interests of our nation's Black and Hispanic minority are fundamentally at one with the needs of the society-at-large. Any company that eschews Black and Hispanic leadership will be at increasing risk in a society where one-third of the consumers and workers will soon be non-White, and where up to two-thirds of all new workers will be Black or Hispanic.

AREA NINE: MINORITY LEADERSHIP

Gradually—but certainly increasingly—minorities are occupying positions of influence and leadership in government, business, and academia. All of you here today are proof of that.

Leadership brings with it the added responsibility of setting an example. It is a responsibility none of us can ignore. You and your peers around the country must help motivate and inspire the many still trapped in poverty and hopelessness.

With leaders like yourselves, we increase daily our visible presence and effectiveness. We add to our resources; we spread the message. Ultimately, we add significantly to our prospects and power.

CONCLUSION

I said when I began that this was an issue of sheer economic survival for the nation as a whole.

For us in the Black community, the situation translates broadly into two possible scenarios.

The first could be catastrophic. It would be disastrous not only for Blacks, but also for Hispanics and the country as a whole. In this scenario, the nation is caught unprepared by the coming revolution in the work force. Government and corporate efforts to respond remain isolated and inadequate—in effect, placing band-aids over gaping wounds. As the wounds go untreated, infection sets in, and the patient slowly deteriorates until there is no hope.

In real life, those wounds take the form of desperate family lives, crumbling school systems, soaring dropout rates, unemployment, crime, and drug addiction. The infections are endemic hopelessness and hate, despair and desolation. And, for many, all hope truly is lost.

The United States must realize that as disastrous as it sounds, this could be the terrifying reality in the years ahead.

But there is another scenario, one of promise, hope, and true opportunity.

It does not take a great deal of imagination to realize that if minorities will account for most of the growth in the work force, they will have a great opportunity to move ahead. For the first time, economic and demographic changes have created the absolute necessity to bring Blacks, Hispanics, and other minorities into the mainstream of the U.S. work force. And, in our second scenario, they are brought in, along with the skills to rise successfully to the productivity challenges ahead.

What will take a great deal of imagination is developing the strategies to make the second scenario a reality. Indeed, I would argue that we need a full-scale blueprint for investing in the future—a comprehensive, national policy on minorities and the work force.

Once and for all, the country must awake to the realization that Blacks, Hispanics, and other minorities are not now and certainly will not be in the future a burden to be lifted, but rather a great source for social and economic strength.

In an international economy that is increasingly interdependent, on a planet where the majority of the population is non-White, it is also an issue of simple realism. The question is not whether the United States *should* come to grips with the challenge. Rather, the question is whether we can do so in time to avert a precipitous decline of our national fortunes both at home and abroad.

To bring that realization about, we need a new policy—a new agenda—a new plan. And, it will have to be broader, more sweeping—a more courageous plan than any we have seen so far.

Quite simply, the full participation of Blacks and minorities is vital to our success as a world leader and a prosperous, caring nation.

In the next quarter century, minorities will be the most dynamic part of the U.S. work force. At the same time, the market for trained manpower will become increasingly competitive.

Because of these converging trends, the United States has both an urgent need and a once-in-a-lifetime opportunity.

For the first time, the dictates of the national self-interest have become identical to those of national conscience. We *have* to bring Blacks and Hispanics fully into the work force. And because we have to, for the first time we may actually be *able* to.

It is not merely that a great deal is at stake.

What we honor in the American past is at stake.

What we cherish in the American present is at stake.

What we hope for in the American future is at stake.

For a society built on the ideals of freedom, equality, and full participation, *everything* is at stake. And the time to act is now.

NOTES

1. This paper was presented to a July 30, 1989, preconference symposium organized by the AAEA Committee on the Status and Opportunity for Blacks in Agricultural Economics at the summer 1989 meetings of the American Agricultural Economics Association in Baton Rouge, Louisiana. The proceedings of that symposium, entitled *A Century of Service: The 1890 Land Grant Colleges and Universities*, edited by Ralph Christy and Lionel Williams, were published with copyright © by Transaction Publishers, of Rutgers University. This paper is reprinted here with permission of the author and the original publisher, and may be freely used with due credit to the author and the initial publisher.

2. Clifton R. Wharton, Jr., is Chairman and Chief Executive Officer of the Teachers Insurance and Annuity Association and College Retirement Equities Fund (TIAA-CREF). Dr. Wharton is also an agricultural economist and former president of Michigan State University.

3. The predominantly White campuses have much to learn in this area from the traditionally Black campuses, such as the 1890s.

CHAPTER 4

DISADVANTAGED RURAL FARM AND NONFARM PEOPLE IN GENERAL

Refugio I. Rochin[1]

OUR MAJOR CONCERN

We doubt that the readers of this chapter will include any of the people we are concerned about—the *rural disadvantaged, underrepresented, homeless, marginal, disenfranchised, powerless, and persistent poor.* The very fact that we talk about them suggests, quite frankly, that we are not in a position to talk for them because of our own employment in academia, located in a few ivory towers of this world.

The rural disadvantaged by all definitions and descriptions are the least likely to receive a complimentary copy of this tome. Some would neither understand the English nor be literate enough to comprehend these token statements. Others would not be reached by Cooperative Extension of the land-grant system and some would not care. They will never know what is being said about them or of the social science agenda that is being proposed for the future.

Unfortunately, the situation of the rural disadvantaged continues to be serious and largely unattended. Considering all of the persons who live in rural America, our best judgment is that up to 30 percent might be disadvantaged, amounting to at least 20 million Americans. The poverty population alone is about 20 percent of rural Americans (Ross and Morrissey 1987), but that count leaves out many persons who are destitute, are without general public support, have relatively few amenities, and live in substandard housing or have no housing at all.

"Disadvantaged" is more than a euphemism for the poor. By definition, "disadvantaged" implies unfavorable circumstances and conditions; injury to interest, reputation, credit and profit; and influences that are detrimental, harmful, and damaging. Every social and ethnic group is subject to disadvantages, but there are always certain groups that suffer more than others (Jensen and Tienda 1989).

Specifically, the rural disadvantaged include: female-headed households with children; Caucasians "left behind"; traditionally low-income minorities (Native Americans, African-Americans, and Hispanic-Americans); new immigrant groups, such as refugees from war-torn Vietnam and Central America; the Caucasian elderly on Social Security; and numerous people fleeing urban impoverishment to find lower-cost shelters in rural communities. What characterizes most of these rural disadvantaged is their relative isolation from large urban centers and the absence of targeted assistance or information that is usually found more readily available in metropolitan areas.

It used to be common to find rural communities promoting many self-help activities and local types of support for the disadvantaged. But today, this kind of rural relief is waning. Instead, many rural communities find themselves in jeopardy of surviving as competitive towns or townships with viable businesses and services. Because of numerous transformations in the economy, hundreds of thousands of rural communities no longer serve integrative functions to protect the disadvantaged. Except for the young enrolled in school, today's rural disadvantaged are seldom part of programs for "community development" or the focus of local training and business opportunities.

THE THESIS FOR THIS CHAPTER

The main purpose of this chapter is to provide a broad overview of some of the issues confronting the disadvantaged, the principal concepts used to study these issues, and the social science agenda needed to address their situation. Included in this coverage are several assumptions and theories about why people are disadvantaged. This chapter is intended to be read along with the other chapters in this book that deal specifically with various racial and ethnic groups in rural America, as well as their disadvantaged segments. Moreover, this chapter is a companion to others in this section on human development.

Although the disadvantaged need education and human capital formation in general, it is the thesis of this chapter that many of the disadvantaged face unique problems as "minorities," problems that are not removed by education and training. While investments in education may affect the supply or quality of workers from disadvantaged groups, such investments ignore the demand side of the disadvantaged. In other words, regardless of the human development programs designed to raise their incomes, many of the rural disadvantaged are still left to cope with the persistent problems associated with minority status and being treated unfairly or inequitably in today's society.

It is not news that the disadvantaged do not reap the benefits of investments in human capital formation (see Frost and Hawkes 1970). Although billions of dollars have been spent to provide compulsory education, schooling is still a problem for disadvantaged Americans. As Annie Stein (1971, 447) poignantly illustrated the problem:

> The average child in 85 percent of the Black and Puerto Rican schools [in New York City] is functionally illiterate after eight years of schooling in the richest city in the world. This is a massive accomplishment. It took the effort of 63,000 teachers, thousands more administrators, scholars and social scientists, and the expenditures of billions of dollars to achieve.... Perhaps an even greater achievement of the schools has been their ability to place the responsibility for this extraordinary record of failure upon the children themselves, their families, and their communities.

A good question asked by Stein: "How is it possible to fail the disadvantaged after eight years of trying in elementary school?" As Stein (1971, 448) suggests: "Merely to recognize the existence of these realities is only to begin to understand. One must go on to examine how it is that these realities have persisted through almost two decades of legal, dramatic, and forceful attempts to change them."

As in New York City, many of the rural disadvantaged, especially migrant youth, suffer inequities in education. Today, after years of studies, we will find the problems of education deprivation that were first encountered in the 1930s. Why is education failing to help the disadvantaged in rural America?

Thomas D. Hall (1984) purports that a reason for such gross neglect is "core ethnocentrism" that affects all of the processes of economic and social change in America. According to Hall, core ethnocentrism occurs when the dominant (usually majority) members of society (defined by class and racial differences) behave as though people on the fringe or periphery of society (i.e., the minority) and all things in it or associated with it are of little importance to the core. In schooling, for example, core ethnocentrism exists when the textbooks and teachings focus exclusively on the European experience, with little added on the importance of the minority populations of the periphery. In the rural social sciences, core ethnocentrism is evident by the general lack of research on the disadvantaged.

"Core ethnocentrism" should not be taken lightly. A problem with "core ethnocentrism" may be reflected in the token efforts to understand the complex relationships between the cores and their peripheries. Such an inadequate response may be, in turn, responsible for the serious distortions in strategies for rural development. By not knowing enough about disadvantaged population groups, more harm can result in the long run.

How might we distinguish between periphery and core populations? According to Arnold Rose (1951, 5):

> A group is a minority group [of the periphery] if it is the object of prejudice and discrimination from the dominant groups [the core], and if the members think of themselves as a minority. It is not a minority because its members have a distinctive racial or nationality background, or because its members adopt a certain religion or language, although minority status is attached to at least one of these four characteristics.

It is further argued in this chapter that the study of the periphery and the minority disadvantaged is vital for understanding their interactions with the core, for the periphery is where much interaction takes place. It is only in the periphery that questions may be examined about how and to what extent the disadvantaged are used by the core. This is not to say that such "use" does not have important consequences for the core. It does. But as suggested here, core treatment of the disadvantaged actually occurs in the periphery. And from that perspective, knowledge of the disadvantaged tells us much about our society as a whole.

BRIEF PERSPECTIVES ON HUMAN DEVELOPMENT

Any study of the disadvantaged must include a comment on "human development" because society places great emphasis on human development to combat social ills and to equalize employment opportunities (Strober 1990). Why the emphasis on human capital formation to help the disadvantaged? What are the implications? Basically, the answers are posed in economic terms. Let us examine the following logic for a moment: Assuming that the economically active population is one-half of the total population and knowing that the other half is engaged in either a dependent role or in household activities and the maintenance of the family life, it may be safely stated that about half of the national income is spent on the reproduction of, caring for, educational formation of, and maintenance of the work force. How long is this amount tied up? Considering the period strictly needed for child rearing and schooling, the formative period lasts from 14 to 25 years. In the United States, the time span devoted to rearing and schooling has been steadily increasing and, moreover, an increasing share of the work force receives a relatively longer schooling at high schools, colleges, and universities. With the abolition of child labor and the introduction of compulsory education, the amount of national income tied up in human development is significantly large. Moreover, the value tied up in the work force has been and is still constantly growing, with respect to both its absolute magnitude and in relation to the stock fixed in the market economy.

Now, if the potential accumulated in the work force is a necessary component of the driving forces of society, then, evidently, this will determine the ultimate degree and rate of growth of the rest of society. With a more skilled, educated work force, the productivity of labor should increase and, hence, so would the output and wealth of the nation.

The flip side to this logic is the perception that unproductive, disadvantaged Americans depend on state welfare. Also, a society that neglects its disadvantaged also deprives itself of the potential productivity of these members. As such, the disadvantaged are perceived to pose a double cost to society when we are denied their productive potential and have an added social burden to support.

Is the problem of the disadvantaged a combined problem of a high social cost and unproductive workers? Recent research has shown that the issues of the disadvantaged are more multifaceted and complex. Many of them want to work but cannot find employment and most are not persistent wards of the state or dependents of welfare. Ross and Morrissey's (1987) study indicates that many of the rural poor are blue-collar workers thrown into temporary poverty because of some disruption in their lives. Axinn and Stern (1988) also find that the disadvantaged are not welfare dependent. For the most part, they are idle members of the periphery who are largely ignored by the core and its institutions. According to Axinn and Stern (1988, 170):

> ...it is important to remember that compared to other advanced societies, the United States still spends relatively little on social welfare, even after the expansion in the 1970s. Indeed, by 1984 the United States was spending a smaller proportion of its gross national product on social welfare than in any year since the early 1970s. The evidence from international comparisons supports the view that the United States certainly can afford an expanded welfare state.

It is evident from most research that the working poor and displaced are disproportionately African-American, Hispanic-American, Native American, and female-headed households, though the largest absolute number of this group is Caucasian. But, it is not always made clear that their problems touch all workers (and taxpayers), whatever their race, gender, or family structure. Although the issues of interdependence between the periphery and core have yet to push onto the current political and social agenda, they will not go away. The issues of the rural disadvantaged affect the general well being of the nation in the fullest sense of that term. If the nation is unable to understand the basic needs of the disadvantaged, or to make use of their potential as human resources, the nation will be less fulfilled than it could be.

How do we develop a fuller understanding of the rural disadvantaged and the periphery? What methods and means of research are available in the rural social sciences?

STUDIES OF THE DISADVANTAGED AND HUMAN DEVELOPMENT

There are two distinct foci of interest in the study of the periphery and the disadvantaged, and each of these subdivides the field in different ways.

1. The first focus of the periphery concentrates on demographics, education, and training, and the different patterns of relationships that develop when people of different classes, genders, racial and/or cultural backgrounds come into contact with each other. The interest here is in the numeric representation and presence of different groups and also the social, economic, political organization, and cultural products. Processes of educational attainment, competition, conflict, affirmative action, diversity, accommodation, pluralism, and assimilation are described and analyzed, as are characteristic institutions of women and minorities (such as ethnic studies and women's associations or publications). The studies are almost exclusively descriptive and usually within an analytical context or theme, e.g., diversifying academe, improving "participation," "social classes," etc.
2. The other focus of social science study takes a social-problem approach and concentrates on the existence of exclusion, segregation, powerlessness, discrimination, and the processes of income and earnings generation, the attitudes and effects of prejudice and avarice, and the consequences for these on both minority- and majority-group human development.

The social-problem approach usually requires a comparative analysis of the advantaged and disadvantaged in our society and statistical tests of significant differences between populations. It postulates hypothesis, uses computerized models, and tests the validity or "contribution" of various parameters. In short, this category of research is usually called "applied social science research."

APPROPRIATE SOCIAL SCIENCE THEMES

The above suggests the need for more applied studies of the disadvantaged that address three common themes: (1) discrimination, (2) poverty and inequality, and (3) powerlessness and limited control. Although these three phenomena usually affect the disadvantaged and are interrelated, they can be handled as three separate areas for research in the social sciences. In the following, we give attention to the ways rural social scientists might define and address issues of discrimination, poverty and inequality, and powerlessness of the rural disadvantaged and hence, focus on the periphery.

Discrimination is commonly defined as the unfavorable treatment faced by women, minorities, and others that has no relation to individual capacities or merits or to the concrete behavior of the individuals or groups. There can be advantageous discrimination, at times, such as the chivalrous treatment of women or the aged. But the disadvantaged usually face negative treatment everywhere, especially when dominant peoples resort to various devices for the economic, political, and social restructuring of the racial and ethnic groups over whom they have set themselves. The result of negative discrimination is succinctly explained by Brewton Berry (1958, 433) who wrote:

> One of the functions of these [negative] discriminations is to isolate the dominant and subordinate groups and to limit contact and communication between them. Isolation and segregation, accordingly, help to preserve the status quo, impede the process of assimilation, and, in fact, serves to dull the appetite for higher status on the part of the underprivileged group. What is more important is the fact that discriminatory policies make it difficult for the oppressed group to acquire the knowledge, skills, and tools with which to improve their status.

Discriminatory actions go beyond segregation and isolation. They may be seen also as the parallel of "prejudice," acts growing out of unfavorable attitudes toward a group or its individual members. Discrimination can be interpreted also as the opposite of "privilege," a benefit or right enjoyed by a particular person or class of persons and not shared with or available to the generality of persons.

The concept of discrimination as the overt manifestation of segregation, prejudice, and/or the opposite of privilege has a valuable role in the social sciences. Interest in its existence has usually centered on groups that are either numerical minorities (such as African-Americans, Native Americans, Hispanics, untouchables in India, or women in professional careers) or political, social, or economic minorities (such as blacks in South Africa, women in most countries, or immigrant refugees).

In the past, the study of discrimination was generally seen by social scientists as "exploitation" of minorities by majorities. In addition, psychologists looked at prejudice in discrimination as a negative attitude that violated some important norms or values nominally accepted in the society. Over the last twenty years, economists have come to study discrimination with an approach that is based not as much on exploitation of attitude as it is on considerations of earnings based on productive skills or abilities. As a somewhat loose statement of economic discrimination, Gary S. Becker (1968, 208) says, "...economic discrimination can be said to occur against members of a group whenever their earnings fall short of the amount 'warranted by their abilities.'"

On the other hand, by Becker's interpretation, discrimination would not exist if all persons maximized money incomes and if all markets were competitive. Accordingly, to have economic discrimination, Becker (1968, 208) reasoned that:

> ...discrimination in competitive markets is said to occur because some participants have tastes for discrimination, more loosely called 'prejudice.' Because of these tastes they are willing to forfeit money, income, or other resources in order to avoid employing, working with, or buying from members of a particular group. Indeed, the intensity of their prejudice is measured by how much they are willing to forfeit.

It is not so important anymore to prove that discrimination exists. It does. Instead, rural social scientists are challenged to root out its causes by means of research and through the elimination of ignorance. The real challenge is to bring forth knowledge that will stimulate general feelings for *acculturation* (in the case of minorities), *pluralism* (in the case of all disadvantaged), and *equality of opportunity* (across all beings).

Poverty and inequality are old themes (Coulter 1989). Before the modern world, they were usually considered the inevitable reality of human existence. Egalitarian movements tended to take a religious posture with regard to unequal differences between men, and frequently concluded that the solution to problems of poverty and inequality was not to be found in the city of man, but in the city of God. But in the twentieth century, it was assumed that the primary framework of social action was the nation-state, i.e., the remedy to inequality and poverty would lie with public intervention and programs paid for by taxation and income transfer from the "haves" to the "have nots."

It has always been the case that some people have more than others. And in the modern world, inequality is a phenomenon about which most men, women, and groups are conscious. Concerns about inequalities are almost never left unquestioned. Surely, it is evident in the universities and in the expressions of intellectuals that inequities (i.e., unjustified adverse conditions) and unequal allocation of privileges and resources should be the focus of most social endeavors.

What has not changed in the twentieth century are the existence of poverty and inequalities and the felt need to discuss them intellectually. What has changed is the current belief that inequalities are not predestined or inevitable. Now we are challenged to believe that inequality may somehow diminish. This new way of thinking is at the base of the "war on poverty," the laws for equal employment opportunity, affirmative action, and other socio-economic decisions of the nation-state.

The most critical societal question of equality is: How unequal—or how equal—should be the incomes of different families in an economy? To address this issue, social scientists have examined different possible standards for judging income inequality: (1) the standard of the marketplace, (2) the standard of full equality, and (3) the standard of equality of opportunity.

Using the standard of the marketplace, economists have shown that income generated in a pure market economy is necessarily unequal according to different skills, levels of education and training of workers, and the demand for workers of various productive talents. On the other hand, by using the standard of full equality, social scientists would contend that the ideal of full equality can be realized only through complete equality of income and/or purchasing power. Still to contend with is the question of whether we aim for full equality in terms of each family, each person, or each worker. Since families can differ in size, full family equality would mean lower income per capita for individuals in larger families. Karl Marx defined the third standard of equality of opportunity in terms of the statement: From each according to his ability, to each according to his need.

However, defining equality in Marx's sense ignores many realities of the labor market. Workers' needs and abilities are not easily matched at the right time and place with the demand for workers. The skills required to run a large corporation are far different from those required to wash dishes, but many more dishwashers are needed than corporate managers. Many people may claim to have the ability to manage a large corporation, but many of these claimants will never attain their aspirations and will end up washing dishes due to limited employment opportunities.

Thus far, we have dealt with equality in philosophical terms, asking about the possible standards for judging income inequality and the degree to which it can be accepted by society. In the real world, government is called upon to intervene in society to insure that everyone has a fair chance for equality of opportunity, but not to insure that everyone comes out equal. Laws that require procedures for affirmative action and equal opportunity for employment are examples of efforts to move in the direction of equality. These laws call into question the issues of meritocracy and the degree to which people and differences should be viewed as merited or awarded, another topic that should be considered in the social sciences.

For most social scientists, "equality of opportunity" is too weak a policy for addressing the disadvantaged. They would like to see some other standard, such as some relative standard of living, as the measure for determining how unequal—or how equal—family incomes should be. In an attempt to determine some level of inequality, social scientists have developed the "poverty line" or "threshold of poverty."

The social scientists' concern with poverty is particularly acute in stratified societies, in which the upper and lower strata have direct contact with each other. The poverty concept is usually some measure of a lower strata, based upon situations where economically unequal groups coexist spatially. The result is "poverty" as a relative concept as opposed to an absolute concept of fulfilling basic needs.

Yet, beginning in 1963, economists in the federal government devised an absolute standard of poverty. Basically, poverty was defined as the condition of having too little money to fulfill basic needs as society defined those needs. The measurement began by estimating the cost of sufficient food to meet minimum nutritional requirements. After observing that poor families typically spent one-third of their incomes on food, the government researchers defined the poverty line as three times the income required to buy the minimum food budget.

"Relative" and "absolute" measures of poverty are imprecise concepts for addressing issues of the rural disadvantaged. Yet the issues of rural poverty and income inequality are among the most perplexing in America. Measures to redistribute income have fallen short of alleviating poverty and in closing the gaps between the lowest and highest strata of society. Although frustrating for most social scientists, there is no simple way to view and analyze issues of poverty and inequality in the United States. Perhaps, through a greater understanding of the periphery, the core will breach the gap between minority and majority populations.

Power and/or control, in a most general sense, denote the ability (exercised or not) to produce a certain occurrence on the influence exerted by someone or a group over the conduct of others in intended ways. Power is sometimes used to mean "political power" that, in turn, may denote aspects of rights, authority, influence, coercion, and sometimes credibility or legitimacy. Each of these aspects connotes something inherited, earned, and/or taken by a right to use force or to be obeyed. Powerlessness is the absence of power and, hence, the absence of authority, legitimacy, etc.

"Power" covers a very broad category of human relations and interests from the social sciences. Considerable effort has gone into ways for classifying these relations in society, especially between minorities and other groups. The great variety and heterogeneity of these relations may, in fact, make it impossible, or even fruitless, to develop general theories of power intended to cover all terms.

In practice, social scientists usually confine their attention to particular aspects of power. However, there is no agreement on the common characteristics of most terms and concepts. What can be accomplished is usually a conceptual framework of study that takes into account dimensions of the following:

- *Magnitude*—"amounts of power," numbers of eligible voters.
- *Distribution*—control of certain representatives of congressional seats; geographic concentrations and affiliations by area.
- *Scope*—degree of specialized interest, advocacy or focus; level of agreement and commitment to use.
- *Domain*—Who has control or influence over whom and how numerous are they? What is the degree of autonomy and/or interdependence?
- *Strength*—patterns and ownership of resources; influence in the marketplace.

In short, "power" and control are worthy topics for addressing the rural disadvantaged. The subject matter is wide open for more and continued research by social scientists.

SUMMARY AND ACTION AGENDAS

This chapter is intended to increase the attention given to issues of the rural disadvantaged and social periphery. For the past few decades, the United States has devoted considerable attention to human development without due consideration to the disadvantaged of the periphery. Also, a variety of policies and programs have been pursued to address issues of discrimination, poverty and inequality, and powerlessness of disadvantaged groups. The limited successes of these efforts and the many changes occurring in rural America call into question the adequacy of our concepts, theories, and studies for public policies and programs. More importantly, we are probably at a stage where we are no longer certain that human development is a driving force. Educational standards are rising in the United States, yet the United States is losing its competitive edge in manufacturing, retail goods, and items demanded by our consumers. Simultaneously, issues of minorities and women, homeless, and the poor are on the rise. In short, advances in human development and education broadly defined are not ameliorating serious social problems affecting minority groups. By emphasizing the importance of research within peripheral regions, this paper provides a look at some of the appropriate issues of the day that include: issues of discrimination, poverty and inequality, and power and control.

For the rural social sciences to be relevant for rural America, they must include increased attention to the following:

ISSUES OF DISCRIMINATION

It should be noted that quantitative evidence on the extent of economic discrimination of the rural disadvantaged, in particular that facing women and minorities, is surprisingly limited. Most of what is available is based upon studies of residential concentrations and employment patterns of groups in urban and nonagricultural settings. Yet, elements of market prejudice and segregation can be found in rural communities; they might even be increasing. The growing numbers of ethnic enclaves in rural towns, the high proportions of minorities as migrant and seasonal farm workers, and the absence of women and minorities as owner/operators of farms, confirm elements of economic discrimination.

Likewise, there are several nonmarket aspects of discrimination that should be explored. The political appointments of boards and commissions and directors of educational institutions reflect practices that exclude women and minorities. Representatives of the disadvantaged are conspicuous by their absence in appointed bodies. Why is this so?

For the Social Science Agricultural Agenda Project (SSAAP), considerably more study of institutional arrangements is required in order to know more about the factors that determine the exclusion of minorities and women from contributing more effectively to rural America.

ISSUES OF POVERTY AND INEQUALITY

The SSAAP must continue to address the rural disadvantaged in terms of their poverty and inequality of opportunity. Research is needed to adequately define and measure their predicament and levels of need. Welfare and income redistribution may be a partial prescription for the rural disadvantaged facing learning or physical disabilities. For the majority of the rural disadvantaged, research on the correlates and causes of persistent inequality may lead to measures that will solve their problems.

Studies are also needed of working poor, children in poor families, the elderly, and others of rural America. Moreover, we have not been very successful in explaining inequality of education, occupational status, income, and employment opportunities (Coulter 1989).

Of the studies that exist, the association between one variable of inequality and another is usually quite weak, which means that equalizing one thing is unlikely to have much effect on the degree of inequality in other areas. We must, therefore, learn if attempts to produce equality by more direct interventions would be more effective, or whether the status quo is essentially unalterable. Simply establishing public responsibility for inequalities is not sufficient to change it, but it can be a vital beginning.

ISSUES OF POWERLESSNESS

The SSAAP should develop approaches to gaining an understanding of the complex social phenomena regarding power and powerlessness of rural disadvantaged. At the very least, there should be attempts to analyze the way certain aspects of power affect human and social relations. There must be attempts to clarify central concepts of power, i.e., specify particular subsets that are most interesting for social analysis, develop methods of measurement, and undertake empirical investigations of concrete political phenomena. At least, attempts are needed to arrive at a better understanding of the more concrete phenomena of the political powerlessness of the rural disadvantaged, their absence from legislature or commissions, their underrepresentation on governing boards or institutions, and their separation or exclusion from the core. Power sharing and control are fundamental requisites for human and rural development.

OTHER AGENDAS ON THE DISADVANTAGED

In the following chapters, we focus on particular groups and ask how "human development" studies have addressed their lives. Each paper refers to the studies of a targeted group, the foci of past research, and the current thinking. Where appropriate, each will make a critical assessment of the relevant concepts, evidence, and facts. Moreover, relevant issues of discrimination, poverty and inequality, and powerlessness will be raised. Each author will contribute his or her list of major agenda items for future social science research.

NOTE

1. Refugio I. Rochin is a professor of Agricultural Economics and Director of Chicano Studies at the University of California, Davis.

REFERENCES

Axinn, June, and Mark J. Stern. 1988. *Dependency and poverty: Old problems in a new world.* Lexington, Mass.: Lexington Books.

Becker, Gary S. 1968. Economic discrimination. In *International encyclopedia of the social sciences.* Vol. 4. New York: Macmillan Co. and The Free Press.

Berry, Brewton. 1958. *Race and ethnic relations.* Boston: Houghton Mifflin Co.

Coulter, Philip B. 1989. *Measuring inequality: A methodological handbook.* Boulder, Colo.: Westview Press.

Frost, Joe L., and Glenn R. Hawkes, eds. 1970. *The disadvantaged child: Issues and innovations.* Boston: Houghton Mifflin Co.

Hall, Thomas D. 1984. Historical sociology of the periphery: A peripheral enterprise. Paper read in April at the Midwest Sociological Society, Chicago.

Jensen, Leif, and Marta Tienda. 1989. Nonmetropolitan minority families in the United States: Trends in racial and ethnic economic stratification, 1959–1986. *Rural Sociology* 54, no. 4 (Winter): 509–32.

Rose, Arnold M. 1951. *Race, prejudice and discrimination.* New York: Knopf.

Ross, Peggy J., and Elizabeth S. Morrissey. 1987. Two types of rural poor need different kinds of help. *Rural Development Perspectives* (USDA) (October): 7–10.

Stein, Annie. 1971. Strategies for failure. In *Educating the disadvantaged.* Edited by R. C. Doll and M. Hawkins, 447–85. New York: AMS Press.

Strober, Myra H. 1990. Human capital theory: Implications for HR managers. *Industrial Relations* 29, no. 2 (Spring): 214–39.

CHAPTER 5

POVERTY AMONG CAUCASIANS IN NONMETRO AMERICA

J. Allan Beegle[1]

This chapter examines the incidence and special circumstances contributing to poverty among Caucasian persons living in nonmetropolitan areas.[2] While poverty has never been a stranger to the people of rural America, public attention has largely eluded them in favor of the poor minority groups living in urban as well as rural environments. The frequent failure to recognize the problem of rural poverty among Caucasians was succinctly stated by Bird and McCoy (1967, iii) more than twenty years ago.

> White Americans in rural areas are a major and persistent poverty problem in the Nation... Special problems of these whites in poverty reflect their relative anonymity, lack of organization, and lack of a common identity. Although concentrated in parts of Appalachia, the Ozarks, and the South, they are for the most part a scattered population located in many small hamlets, farming villages, and open country, including affluent farming areas.

Harrington's book *The Other America* (1962) did much to elevate the level of public and private consciousness concerning the plight of poor people in this country. He argued that the poor are poor due to forces beyond their control—being born to the wrong parents, in the wrong section of the country, in the wrong occupation. Thus, he viewed the poor as having been enmeshed in a cycle of poverty from which there was little chance of escape. Those caught in this cycle, he argued, developed customs, habits, and a particular life style—a culture of poverty.

In many ways, the work of Oscar Lewis (1959, 1966) coincided with that of Harrington in depicting the realities of life among the poor and in amplifying the meaning and consequences of a culture of poverty. Both Lewis and Harrington succeeded in gaining national awareness and concern for the problems of poverty.

The so-called war on poverty, a part of President Johnson's Great Society Program, was initiated with the passage of the Economic Opportunity Act of 1964. This Act established or expanded various programs designed to provide the poor with a "safety net of basic income, medical care, food and shelter, or—as with job training and educational programs—to offer an escape from poverty" (O'Hare 1989, 10).

As part of the war on poverty, a presidential commission report, *The People Left Behind* (U.S. President's National Advisory Commission on Rural Poverty 1967), focused on the problems of poverty in nonmetropolitan areas. Among the salient findings of this commission were: (1) that rural poverty is widespread and so acute as to constitute a national disgrace; (2) that rural poverty is found in pockets, often in isolated remote areas, and, therefore, is relatively invisible; (3) that governmental assistance programs are tailored to the urban poor and are ill adapted to the rural environment; and (4) that rural people imbued with an extra measure of independence (and for other reasons) are reluctant to seek help from others, let alone government programs.

Despite the public perception that poverty is more or less confined to Blacks[3] in urban ghettos, the poverty rate is actually considerably higher in nonmetro areas than in metro areas. The poverty rate among Blacks in our central cities, of course, generally exceeds that of Caucasians, except in a few isolated instances. The magnitude of the problem of poverty among rural Caucasians is suggested by the fact that about two-thirds of all counties are nonmetropolitan and that more than one-fifth of the nation's population resides in these counties. According to Hoppe and Bellamy (1989), 71 percent of the poor in nonmetro areas are Caucasian, while a much smaller share (54 percent) of the poor in central cities are Caucasian.

This chapter addresses first the incidence of rural poverty. The number of poor as well as rates for Caucasians and non-Caucasians living in both nonmetro and metro areas will be examined. Attention will be given to regional variations in the incidence of poverty. The rural context in which poverty occurs is then explored. The restricted economic base, unemployment and underemployment, and the rural-urban income gap are examined, followed by infrastructure deficiencies, family composition, and culture of the rural Caucasian underclass. Finally, the issue of selective out-migration from rural areas is considered.

THE INCIDENCE AND TRENDS IN RURAL CAUCASIAN POVERTY

According to official estimates for 1987, 32.5 million persons (more than one in eight) in the United States were regarded as living in poverty.[4] More than nine million persons residing in nonmetropolitan areas, or 28 percent of the nonmetropolitan population, were classed as poor. In the total population of the country, 10.5 percent of Caucasians and 33.1 percent of Blacks were living in poverty.

Overall trends in the numbers and rates of poverty in the United States are shown in Figure 1. This graph depicts the trend in the total number and rate of poverty, and trends in the number of Caucasians in metro and nonmetro areas in poverty from 1970 to 1987. The graph shows a period of moderate ups and downs in the early and mid–1970s, and a sustained rise in poverty beginning in 1979, followed by a decline after 1983. There was a peak number of poor persons in 1983 at which time over 35 million persons, or 15.2 percent of the total population, were below the poverty line. The low point on the graph is 1973 when slightly over 23 million persons, or 11.1 percent of all Americans, were in poverty. Both the peak and low points of poverty were true of the total population as well as nonmetro and metro Caucasians.

A rise in poverty began in 1978 and reached a peak slightly earlier than the so-called farm crisis. The total number of poor as well as both metro and nonmetro poor Caucasians declined markedly by 1987. The total number of poor in the United States declined by more than 2.5 million persons between 1983 and 1987. All of this decline took place among Caucasians, with the exception of 150,000 persons.

Slightly less than 21.5 million Caucasian persons were considered to be living in poverty in the United States in 1987. Somewhat less than one-third (30.4 percent) resided in nonmetropolitan areas. The remainder of poor Caucasians resided in metro areas, a slightly larger number inside central cities than outside central cities.

The poverty rate for nonmetro Caucasians (13.7 percent) exceeded that for metro Caucasians (9.6 percent) in 1987. The poverty rate for Blacks in both residence areas, however, greatly exceeded that for Caucasians. The 1987 rates for Blacks in nonmetro and metro areas were 44.1 and 30.7 percent, respectively. The trend in the numbers and rates of poverty among Caucasians is shown in Table 1. Overall, the number and rate of poverty among Caucasians reached a peak in 1982 and 1983. After 1985, the number and rate of Caucasian poverty declined.

Between 1970 and 1987, the number of poor Caucasian persons living in nonmetro areas ranged between a high of 10,204,000 in 1983 and a low of 5,508,000 in 1987. The number of nonmetro Caucasians in poverty fluctuated modestly in the 1970s but rose markedly in the early 1980s, then declined to a low point in 1987. The poverty rate among nonmetro Caucasian rose from a low of 11.2 in the 1970s to 15.6 in 1985, and then declined but remained relatively high in the last year for which data are available (13.7 in 1987).

As shown in Table 1, poor Caucasians living in nonmetropolitan areas of the United States comprise a large proportion of all poor Caucasians. In 1970, the nonmetro poor comprised over 48 percent of the total Caucasian population in poverty. That proportion remained well over 40 percent through 1983. It fell to slightly more than 30 percent in 1987. Except for the last year for which data are

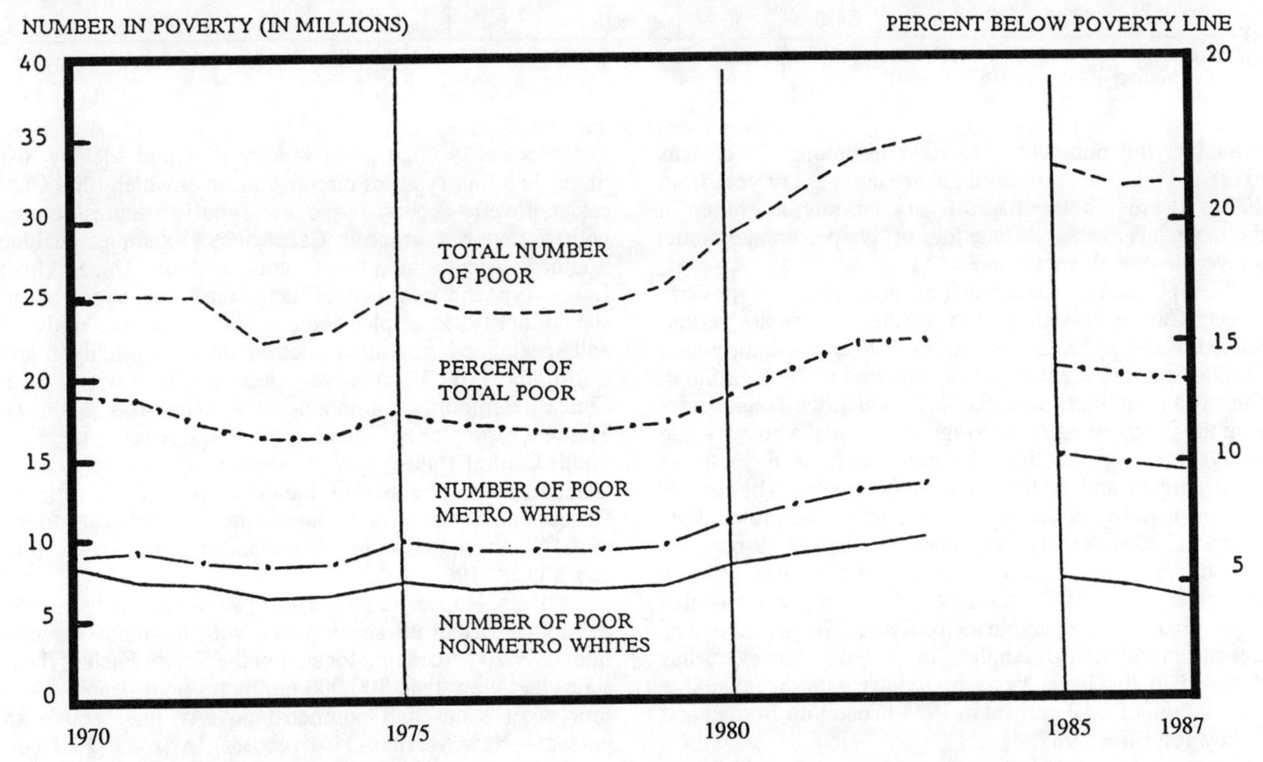

Source: Current Population Reports.

Figure 1. Total number and percent in poverty and number of caucasians in nonmetro and metro areas of poverty, 1970-87.

TABLE 1: NUMBER AND PERCENTAGE OF CAUCASIANS IN POVERTY, BY NONMETRO AND METRO RESIDENCE, 1970–87. (IN THOUSANDS)

Year	Total		Nonmetro Areas		Total		Metro Areas Inside Central Cities		Outside Cities	
	No.	%	No.	%	No.	%	No.	%	No.	%
1987	21,409	10.5	6,508	13.7	14,901	9.6	7,526	13.8	7,376	7.3
1986	22,183	11.0	7,136	15.1	15,048	9.7	7,537	14.0	7,511	7.4
1985	22,860	11.4	7,445	15.6	15,415	10.1	8,105	14.9	7,310	7.4
1984	N.A.	N.A.	N.A.	N.A.	N.A.	N.A.	N.A.	N.A.	N.A.	N.A.
1983	23,974	12.1	10,204	15.4	13,770	10.5	6,661	14.1	7,110	8.4
1982	23,517	12.0	9,955	15.1	13,563	10.4	6,757	14.5	6,806	8.1
1981	21,553	11.1	9,393	14.3	12,160	9.4	5,761	12.7	6,400	7.7
1980	19,699	10.2	8,494	12.9	11,205	8.8	5,449	12.1	5,755	7.0
1979	17,214	9.0	7,388	11.3	9,926	7.8	4,883	10.7	5,044	6.2
1978	16,259	8.7	7,036	11.2	9,222	7.5	4,590	10.2	4,632	5.9
1977	16,416	8.9	7,151	11.2	9,265	7.6	4,762	10.7	4,503	5.9
1976	16,713	9.1	7,054	11.4	9,659	7.9	5,068	11.3	4,591	5.9
1975	17,770	9.7	7,757	12.6	10,014	8.2	4,874	10.8	5,139	6.7
1974	15,736	8.6	6,984	11.5	8,752	7.2	4,290	9.4	4,462	5.9
1973	15,142	8.4	6,690	11.2	8,452	6.9	4,305	9.3	4,147	5.5
1972	16,203	9.0	7,283	12.3	8,920	7.4	4,599	9.8	4,320	5.8
1971	17,780	9.9	7,982	13.9	9,798	8.0	5,178	10.6	4,620	6.3
1970	17,484	9.9	8,460	13.2	9,024	8.0	4,775	10.8	4,249	6.1

Source: Center on Budget and Policy Priorities, 1987, *Supplementary Tables on Rural Poverty*, Washington, D.C., 1989. Based on various *Current Population Reports*, P–60.

available, the nonmetro poverty rate among Caucasians exceeded that for those inside metro areas every year from 1970 onward. The nonmetro Caucasian rate, as shown in the table, has averaged some four or five percentage points above the overall metro rate.

The problems accompanying high rates of poverty among Caucasians residing in nonmetro areas are further intensified by the high incidence of poverty among young families and those having young children in the household. Caucasian nonmetro households in which the householder is in the youngest age group (age 15–24) had a poverty rate in 1987 three times that of householders aged 35 to 44 (30.3 percent and 10.6 percent, respectively). These rates are considerably higher than comparable metro rates. Furthermore, considerably more than one-sixth (17.9 percent) of poor Caucasian families in nonmetro areas had children under 18 as part of the household. This proportion is also higher than the comparable metro figure. The percentage of Caucasian nonmetro families in poverty, however, has declined in the latest years for which data are available from a high of 20.3 percent in 1983 (Center on Budget and Policy Priorities 1987, 4).

The regional distribution pattern of poor rural Caucasians in the United States has changed little since *White Americans in Rural Poverty* was written in the 1960s (Bird and McCoy 1967). In that report, Bird and McCoy distinguished four types of circumstances in which rural Caucasian poverty occurs. These are: Type 1, a depressed area with a majority of poor Caucasians. Examples include Southern Appalachia, the Ozarks, and the Upper Great Lakes. Type 2, a relatively affluent area with a poor, Caucasian minority. Examples include the productive midwest and specialized crop areas such as those in Michigan and California. Type 3, a relatively depressed area with a poor, Caucasian minority within a poor, non-Caucasian majority. The best examples are found in the South Atlantic and East South Central states. Type 4, areas ranging from poor to affluent with a relatively balanced proportion of poor Caucasians and poor non-Caucasians. Examples are found in the South as well as in states adjacent to the South (Bird and McCoy 1967, 4–12).

Deavers, Hoppe, and Ross (n.d.) show (based upon 1980 census data) that all seven states with nonmetro poverty rates over 20 percent are located in the South. Each of these states had more than 300,000 nonmetro poor people. Only four other states had nonmetro poverty rates above 15 percent—New Mexico (19.4 percent), Arizona (19.3 percent), South Dakota (18.5 percent), and Missouri (16.4 percent). These numbers and rates, of course, encompass other minorities but include especially Blacks, Native

Americans, and Spanish-Americans. A map of nonmetro poverty presented by Deavers, Hoppe, and Ross demonstrates the wide distribution of nonmetro poverty in all states, including many with very few minorities.

In her study of nonmetro poverty, Morrissey (1985) ranked all nonmetro counties in the United States as of 1980 according to level of poverty. She then chose 100 nonmetro counties with the highest poverty rates and 100 nonmetro counties with the lowest rates. Of the 100 high poverty counties, 81 were in the Mississippi Delta, the Appalachian Mountains, and the Black Belt of Alabama. All others were located near Indian reservations and in the Rio Grande Valley in Texas and New Mexico. Except for Appalachia, these high poverty counties contain large proportions of minorities. Morrissey found that the high poverty counties in contrast to the low poverty counties were highly rural, had low population density, and decreased (or had no change) in population between 1970 and 1980.

The annual index of poverty, that is, the count based upon the poverty index at a given point in time, fails to inform us about the persistence of poverty. Obviously, there is an ongoing process that incorporates those escaping from a cycle of poverty and those moving in and out of poverty. In their analysis of data from the Panel Study of Income Dynamics,[5] Ross and Morrissey (1989, 59–73) found few differences in the extent to which poverty was persistent between nonmetro and metro groups. Overall, two-thirds of poverty in both areas was found to be temporary (nonpersistent) in the five-year period examined. Regardless of residence, the poor elderly, children, and persons in female-headed households were more prone to persistent poverty.

THE CONTEXT OF RURAL POVERTY IN THE UNITED STATES

Two perspectives as to the causes of poverty are dominant in the literature. The first attributes poverty to be a by-product of qualities possessed by the individual. These may range from lack of education and skills to mental deficiencies and attitudes toward work. Some writers argue that attitudes and values associated with a culture of poverty are transferred from one generation to another. The other perspective considers poverty to be caused by the society at large and the manner in which it is structured. The ability of society to provide equal access of opportunity to all regardless of residence or race, is viewed as an important factor in the level of poverty. Access to education and employment are seen as being closely related to the problem of poverty.

The context in which poverty emerges in nonmetro areas is not identical with that in metro areas. The pages to follow elaborate some major conditions or circumstances in nonmetro areas that contribute to poverty.

RESTRICTIVE ECONOMIC BASE

By definition, nonmetro counties contain smaller populations and have lower densities than metro areas. As a consequence, the population tends to be more homogeneous and the industrial and occupational structure are less differentiated. This condition leads to high levels of commuting by nonmetro residents in order to find appropriate employment in metropolitan areas. According to central place theory, villages, towns, cities, and central places are linked in a hierarchical fashion. Because of their size, functional differentiation, and specialized human resources, large central cities tend to dominate the countryside. Technological innovations generally take place in large centers, and information flows from these centers to smaller places and, finally, to the hinterland (Christaller 1966).

Commenting on the industrial specialization of rural America, Deavers (1989) has this to say:

> Manufacturing, agriculture, and mining are important industries in rural America. Collectively, nonmetro counties with one of these economic sectors as the dominant economic base make up about one-third of all nonmetro counties and contain nearly 40 percent of all rural people. . . All three of these county types have performed worse than the nonmetro average in terms of employment growth from 1979–88, with the mining counties by far the worst.

McGranahan (1988) also points out the concentration of rural workers in agriculture, mining, and manufacturing but also notes that rural workers are much less likely to be found in services, an area of recent expansion. Manufacturing industries in nonmetro areas tend to have few professional, technical, and managerial jobs. The specialization of nonmetro industries, McGranahan argues, "makes rural workers more vulnerable than urban workers to business cycles, foreign competition, and technological change. The vulnerability is compounded by the relative isolation of many rural communities and low education levels." (McGranahan 1988, 29)

McGranahan further contends that the vulnerability of rural people to business cycles and job instability is exacerbated by low density in rural areas and distance to employment centers. There is only a small pool of employers in most rural areas, and the problem of finding work when layoff occurs often requires a wide search and long-distance commuting to work. In addition, rural areas are disadvantaged in starting new businesses due to factors such as the lack of skills on the part of the local labor pool, access to markets, and market information (McGranahan 1988, 42–43).

UNEMPLOYMENT AND UNDEREMPLOYMENT

In view of the nature of the industrial mix found in nonmetro areas, it is not surprising that these areas are characterized by high levels of unemployment and by large fractions of working poor. As shown in Figure 2, the metro unemployment rate exceeded that of nonmetro areas from 1973 to 1979, after which the reverse is true. The excess nonmetro rate was especially marked in the years following 1984. Hoppe (1989) points out that the nonmetro economic problems of the 1980s stem from past successes of the 1960s and 1970s when nonmetro areas competed successfully with metro areas in attracting and creating new jobs in manufacturing. As a consequence, rural manufacturing employment is concentrated in low-wage industries and many rural communities are not diversified.

Deavers (1989) points out that nonmetro employment growth in the 1980s failed to keep pace with metro employment growth. Slower nonmetro than metro employment growth not only characterized the recession of the early

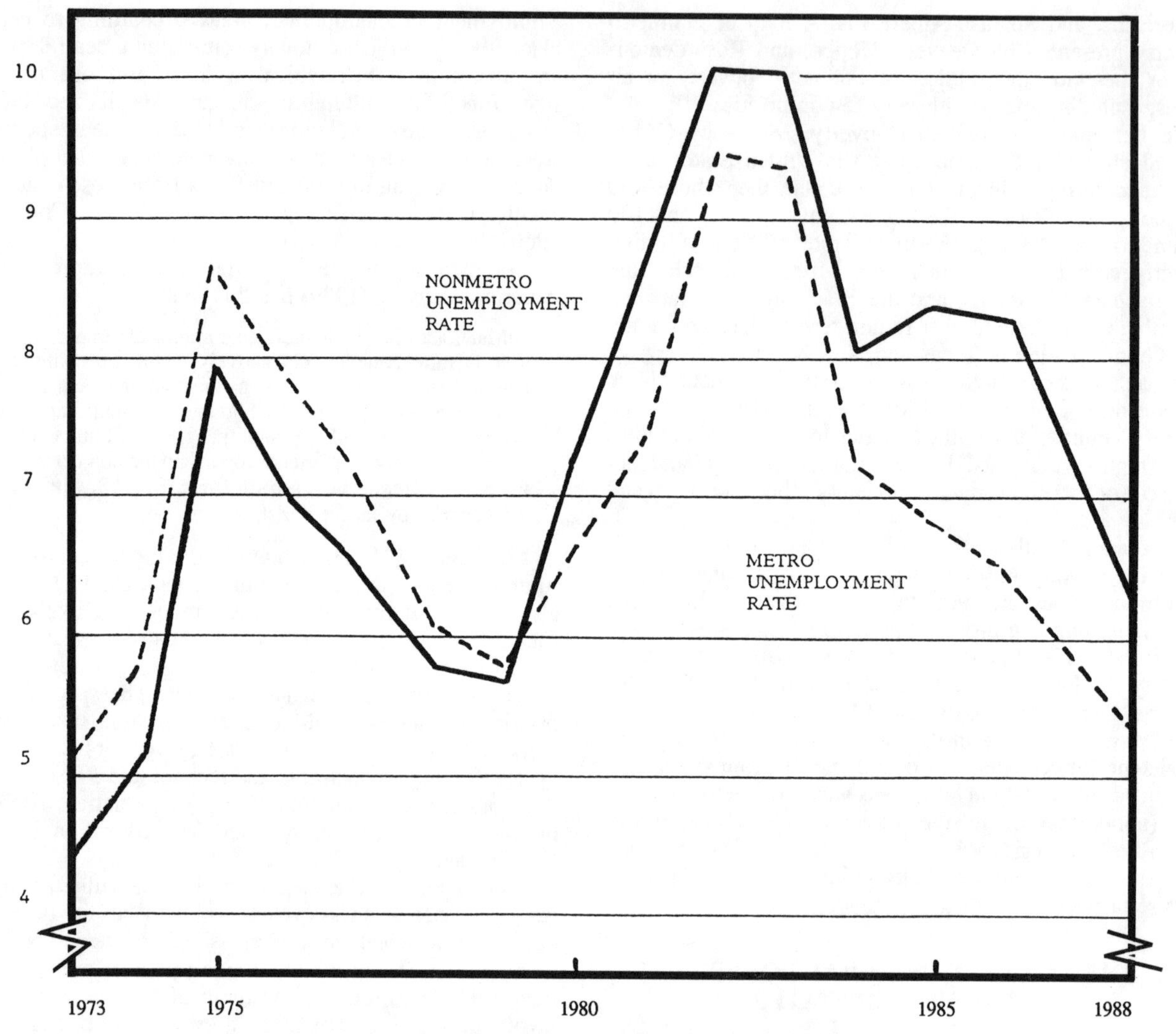

Source: Timothy S. Parker, "Nonmetro Employment, Industry and Occupation: First Quarter 1989, Current Population Survey," The Nonmetro Employment Situation, U.S. Department of Agriculture, Economic Research Service, May 19, 1989.

Figure 2. Unemployment rate for nonmetro and metro areas, 1973-88.

1980s but also characterized the recovery period. Average employment growth between 1982 and 1988 amounted to 17.3 percent in metro areas compared with only 9.0 percent in nonmetro areas. As a consequence, higher rates of nonmetro unemployment prevailed in virtually all regions and years since 1979. See Figure 2.

While nonmetro unemployment rates still exceed those of metro areas, average unemployment in nonmetro areas has declined from the recession of 1980–82 into the first half of 1989. This level, however, has not yet reached prerecession levels (Parker and Whitener 1989).

In their research, Klein and Rones (1989) found that the working poor numbered more than six million persons as of 1987, and thus represented about one-third of all persons 16 years old and over living in poverty. Although they had worked or had looked for work for at least half of the year, they still fell below the poverty level. Three in ten of the working poor live in nonmetro areas. Seventy-three percent of the working poor in nonmetro areas were Caucasian as contrasted with 87 percent in metro areas. Finally, about 10 percent of poor workers, but only 3 percent of nonpoor workers, were agricultural workers in nonmetro and metro areas, respectively.

INCOME

Historically, incomes in rural areas have lagged behind those in urban areas, even after cost-of-living adjustments have been made. The income gap has been substantial and has been increasing since the mid–1970s. In addition, as O'Hare (1988) points out, rural jobs carry fewer fringe benefits. While half of all urban workers (51 percent) had employer-sponsored pension plans, only 44 percent of rural workers had such plans.

Median income (in constant dollars) for Caucasians residing in metro and nonmetro areas is shown in Table 2. The median income for nonmetro Caucasians in the last three years has been more than $9,000 less than for metro Caucasians. In the period shown, the difference between the two residence areas has expanded. At no time has the difference in income among Caucasians in the two residential areas been less than $6,918.

TABLE 2: MEDIAN FAMILY INCOME OF CAUCASIANS IN METRO AND NONMETRO AREAS. (1987 Constant Dollars)

Year	Nonmetro Areas	Metro Areas		
		Total	Central Cities	Outside Central Cities
1987	25,736	35,117	30,669	37,136
1986	25,189	34,539	30,770	36,753
1985	24,129	33,359	29,583	35,165
1984	N.A.	N.A.	N.A.	N.A.
1983	24,824	31,882	28,211	34,100
1982	24,570	31,488	28,148	33,356
1981	24,996	32,281	28,597	33,935
1980	25,922	32,847	29,368	34,672
1979	27,481	34,571	31,145	36,511
1978	27,511	34,601	30,812	36,348

Source: Based on Bureau of the Census, "Money Income of Households, Families and Persons in the U.S." Reports for 1978–1986 and 1987.

Means-tested benefits derived from government programs do, indeed, elevate personal income and lower rates of poverty. Even when transfer payments such as cash social insurance, cash public assistance, and in-kind programs are taken into account, however, the nonmetro rate of poverty exceeds the metro rate (Hoppe and Bellamy 1989; see also Bentley 1987).

Hoppe (1987, 4) reports a study by the Federal Reserve Bank of Kansas City in which the widening gap between metro and nonmetro income is attributed to a number of factors, among them: (1) industries important to nonmetro areas have disproportionate difficulties from competition abroad, a strong dollar, and weak markets; (2) agriculture is undergoing structural changes; (3) the shift to a service-based economy has been concentrated in urban areas; and (4) due to the high degree of specialization in nonmetro areas, a decline in one type of business is less likely to be balanced by growth in another.

THE PEOPLE AND THEIR INFRASTRUCTURE

While rural and urban people have become less and less differentiated over time, some differences still persist. Many of these differences, of course, may be attributed to the environment in which they are born, live, and work. As already noted, nonmetro areas have smaller, less dense populations and a highly specialized economic base. As a consequence, local institutions and services are often less well supported in nonmetro than in metro areas. The cost of providing an adequate infrastructure and necessary services to a dispersed population is a stress on the residents of nonmetro areas. For example, it is well known that the cost of building and maintaining extensive transportation links in nonmetro areas is a major problem and that educational facilities in these areas characteristically lack the quality found in wealthier urban districts.

The problem of providing a competitive infrastructure in rural areas, particularly those remote from a large city, is intensified by the loss of population and selective out-migration. While rural areas between 1970 and 1980 experienced a revival, they grew less rapidly than urban areas after 1980. Between 1970 and 1980, the annual rate of growth in rural areas was 1.4 percent as compared with only 1.0 percent in urban areas. During the first part of the 1980s, however, the annual rate of growth in urban areas was nearly double that of rural areas. O'Hare (1988, 2) points out that rural areas during the 1970s had a net in-migration of about 350,000 each year, but during the 1980s the number leaving rural areas grew substantially. The net out-migration from rural areas between 1986 and 1987 amounted to nearly one million persons, an increase over the 630,000 out-migrants in the previous year.

O'Hare further points out that the out-migration from rural areas has been pervasive and that there has been a net movement to urban areas for every age group, racial group, males and females, all family types, and for all regions of the country. Those leaving rural areas in largest numbers have been young adults and the better educated. Almost one-third of the net loss to rural areas between 1986 and 1987 were young people aged 18 to 24, and about 27 percent of the adult migrants from rural areas had at least one year of college (U.S. Bureau of the Census 1988, Table 6).

Compared with those living in metro areas, Caucasian persons living in nonmetro areas are more likely to be living in a family unit, less likely to be living in a house-Hold headed by a female (no husband present), more likely to be a part of a family with children under 18, more likely to be elderly, and less likely to be well educated. The 1987 CPS data show that nearly one person in eight (11.9 percent) of nonmetro Caucasians was below the poverty level. The comparable figure for metro Caucasians was 8.2 percent. More than one-third (35.8 percent) of Caucasian persons living in a household headed by a female were poor as compared with 27.9 percent in metro households. Nearly 18 percent of nonmetro Caucasians in families with children under 18 were in poverty; the corresponding metro percentage was 14.0. The rate of poverty among Caucasian elderly persons in nonmetro and metro areas was 12.6 and 9.3 percent, respectively (U.S. Bureau of the Census 1988, 2).

Due to selective out-migration to the cities and the nature of the occupational mix in rural industries, the educational level in rural areas is below that of urban areas. The median number of school years completed by nonmetro Caucasians 25 years old and over was 12.5 as compared with 12.8 for metro Caucasians in 1987, and the proportion of the two residence groups completing high school was 71.3 and 79.4 percent, respectively (U.S. Bureau of the Census 1988, Table 16).[6]

While the attitudes and values of rural and urban Caucasians have merged through time, rural people probably remain somewhat more conservative, more religiously fundamental, and more attached to origins. While the first attributes can be verified by various national samples, the latter (attachment to origin) is a highly popular theme in the nonscientific, creative literature. This point is well illustrated in their oral history of Appalachia, in which Shackelford and Weinberg (1977, 319–20) report the reflections of a return migrant who had lived and worked in Cleveland.

> This doesn't have near as much to offer socially and culturally that a place like Cleveland has [where] there are all kinds of stage plays, ice follies, and athletics going on.... There's no comparison along those lines. You might say, "why would you leave a place like that to come back?" and many people don't. In my case, those things just don't hold the fascination for me that they held at one time....
>
> Maybe the things that I really set value on were the things of childhood, the things my mother said, her simple way of looking at life and some of her mottos, things that seemed to apply more in a city like this than they would in a place like Cleveland.
>
> In a small town everybody knows you, everybody speaks. [I'd] be in the garden working and I'll see a hand [wave], sometimes a white hand, sometimes a black, it doesn't matter. Same thing if I go down to the bank, I can stop and chat with the teller quite a while. This means a lot. I'll go to a Little League baseball game, well, you're sitting up there with the Mayor and he knows you. When you go to a Little League baseball game in Cleveland, I'd know a few of the parents but I wouldn't know any Mayors."

SUMMARY

Despite a widespread public perception, the problem of rural poverty in the United States is not restricted to Blacks and other minority groups. More than seven in ten of the poor living in nonmetro areas are Caucasians. Nonmetro areas of the United States comprise two-thirds of all counties and account for one-fifth of the total population. Slightly more than 6.5 million Caucasian persons living in nonmetro areas, or 30.4 percent of all poor Caucasians, fell below the poverty level in 1987. The poverty rates in that year for nonmetro and metro Caucasians were 13.7 and 9.6 percent, respectively.

The number of poor Caucasians in nonmetro areas increased sharply in the early 1980s to a peak of more than 10 million in 1983, then dropped to 6.5 million in 1987. The poverty rate among Caucasian persons living in nonmetro and inside central cities of metro areas in 1987 was nearly identical, 13.7 and 13.8 percent, respectively.

The special circumstances in nonmetro areas from which Caucasian poverty develops include a restrictive economic base, a high rate of unemployment and underemployment, a large income gap, and a less highly developed human resource base and infrastructure.

Nonmetro areas are characterized by a specialized industrial and occupational economic base consisting of manufacturing, agriculture, and mining. The nonmetro portions of the country have failed to participate in the recent expansion in service industries. Unemployment and underemployment, especially since 1980, have exacerbated rural area problems and have augmented the number of Caucasians in poverty. Because of the particular industrial mix and its workforce requirements, among other reasons, average income in nonmetro areas is sharply lower than in metro areas.

Following a period of more rapid growth in nonmetro than metro areas in the 1970s, the nonmetro portions of the country are again losing population through out-migration. These migrants are disproportionately young and better educated. Finally, the quality of educational facilities, as well as other features of the infrastructure and institutional services, are usually less highly developed in nonmetro areas.

NOTES

1. J. Allan Beegle is a professor emeritus, Department of Sociology, Michigan State University.

2. Nonmetropolitan and rural will be used interchangeably throughout this chapter. Technically, the two terms are not synonymous. In essence, a metropolitan area consists of a county with a city of 50,000 or more, or a group of counties surrounding a core county having a city of 50,000 or more, tied together economically. All other counties are nonmetropolitan. About two-thirds of all counties are classed as nonmetropolitan and contain almost one-fourth of the total population. Urban, as used by the Census Bureau, includes large cities and their densely settled suburbs as well as all places of 2,500 or more people. All other areas are considered rural.

3. Because the populations referred to in this chapter as "Black" include some persons who are other than African-Americans, this term is used instead of "African-American."

4. The official estimates of poverty in this paper are derived from the Current Population Survey (CPS) conducted annually by the U.S. Bureau of the Census. The sample consists of about 60,000 households representing the population of the United States. No CPS data on poverty were published for 1984. Poverty data for nonmetropolitan and metropolitan areas reflect revisions in the classification of counties as the population changes. Three different designations of counties are to be noted: nonmetro and metro area classifications before 1971 are based on the 1960 census; those from 1971–83 are based on the 1970 census; and those from 1985–87 are based on a revision made in 1984. Such changes create problems of strict comparability over time. Because of increasing urbanization, the changes in metro-nonmetro classifications have served to reduce the size of the nonmetro population.

A person is considered to be poor if a family's money income is below the poverty threshold for particular sizes and types of families. Hence, many thresholds are used to determine poverty status. The poverty threshold for a family of four with two children was $11,500 in 1987.

Thresholds are adjusted annually based on the Consumer Price Index. For details, see Hoppe and Bellamy (1989) and U.S. Bureau of the Census (1988a).

5. This is a national longitudinal survey of 5,000 American families conducted annually since 1968 by the Survey Research Center of the University of Michigan.

6. See also the discussion of comparative education by O'Hare (1988).

REFERENCES

Bentley, Susan. 1987. Income transfers, taxes and the poor. *Rural Development Perspectives* (February): 30–33.

Bird, Alan R., and John L. McCoy. 1967. *White Americans in rural poverty,* Agricultural Economic Report 124, U.S. Dept. of Agriculture, Economic Research Service, Washington, D.C., November.

Center on Budget and Policy Priorities. 1987. *Supplementary tables on rural poverty*. Based on *Current Population Reports*. Washington, D.C.: U.S. Bureau of the Census.

Christaller, Walter. 1966. *Central places in southern Germany*. Translated by C. W. Baskin. Englewood Cliffs, N.J.: Prentice-Hall.

Deavers, Kenneth L. 1989. Rural development in the 1990s: Data and research needs. Paper prepared for the Rural Social Science Symposium; New Directions in Data, Information Systems, and Their Uses; 28–29 July, Baton Rouge, La.

Deavers, Kenneth L., Robert A. Hoppe, and Peggy J. Ross. n.d. The rural poor: Policy issues for the 1990s.

Harrington, Michael. 1962. *The other America: Poverty in the United States*. Baltimore: Penguin.

Hoppe, Robert A. 1987. Shifting income patterns: Implications for nonmetro America. *Rural Development Perspectives* (February): 4.

_____1989. Two types of poverty, two types of policy. In *Towards rural development policy for the 1990s: Enhancing income and employment opportunities*. Joint Economic Committee. Washington, D.C.: Government Printing Office.

Hoppe, Robert A., and Donald L. Bellamy. 1989. Rural poverty: A continuing problem, Washington Statistical Society Lecture, May.

Klein, Bruce, W., and Philip L. Rones. 1989. A profile of the working poor. *Monthly Labor Review* (October):3–6.

Lewis, Oscar. 1959. *Five families: Mexican case studies in the culture of poverty*. New York: Basic Books.

_____1966. *La vida*. New York: Random House.

McGranahan, David A. 1988. Rural workers in the national economy. In *Rural economic development in the 1980s: Prospects for the future*. Edited by David L. Brown et al., Rural Development Research Report 69, U.S. Dept. of Agriculture, Agriculture and Rural Economy Division, Economic Research Service, Washington, D.C.

Morrissey, Elizabeth S. 1985. *Characteristics of poverty in nonmetro counties*, Rural Development Report 52, U.S. Dept. of Agriculture, Economic Research Service, Washington, D.C., July.

O'Hare, William P. 1988. *The rise of poverty in rural America*. Washington, D.C.: Population Reference Bureau, Inc.

_____1989. Poverty in America: Trends and new patterns. *Population Bulletin* 40 (February). Updated reprint.

Parker, Timothy S., and Leslie A. Whitener. 1989. Nonmetro employment and unemployment: Second quarter 1989 current population survey, The Nonmetro Employment Situation, U.S. Dept. of Agriculture, Economic Research Service, Washington, D.C., August.

Ross, Peggy J., and Elizabeth S. Morrissey. 1989. Rural people in poverty: Persistent versus temporary poverty. In National Rural Studies Committee, a proceedings. Second annual meeting sponsored by W. K. Kellogg Foundations, 17–18 May, Stoneville, Miss.

Shackelford, Laurel, and Bill Weinberg. 1977. *Our Appalachia*. New York: Hill and Wang.

U.S. Bureau of the Census. 1988a. Poverty in the United States: 1986. In *Current population reports*, Series P–60, No. 160, Government Printing Office, Washington, D.C., June.

_____1988b. *Current population reports: 2*, Tables 6 and 16, Government Printing Office, Washington, D.C.

U.S. President's National Advisory Commission on Rural Poverty. 1967. *The people left behind*. Washington, D.C.: Government Printing Office.

CHAPTER 6

RURAL ISSUES PERTAINING TO THE RISE OF HISPANICS IN AMERICA

Refugio I. Rochin and Adela de la Torre[1]

INTRODUCTION

This chapter provides an overview of Hispanic-Americans and identifies several agenda items germane to their rising importance in rural America. There are three parts to the chapter: The first part presents data on the demographic, social, and economic characteristics of the Hispanic population of the United States, as well as its subgroups—Mexican, Puerto Rican, Cuban, Central and South American, and "other Hispanics" (persons identifying themselves as Spanish, Spanish-American, Hispano, Latino, etc.). The second part examines issues pertaining to the history and roles of Hispanics in nonmetropolitan "rural" America. In this part, we review the often neglected contributions of Hispanics to crop and livestock production, the origins of migrant and seasonal workers, the unionization of farm labor, immigration issues, and the formation of rural settlements and communities with major populations of Hispanics. The third part provides a consensus of opinions from six Hispanic scholars who outlined a social science agenda to respond to issues concerning the well-being of Hispanics in rural America.

HISPANIC-AMERICANS

OVERVIEW

Hispanic-Americans are of many racial, national, educational, linguistic, and cultural backgrounds, and they experience widely varying levels of prosperity and success in the United States. The ancestors of some Hispanic-Americans lived in parts of the United States long before those regions became part of the nation. Today, nearly one-half of all Hispanics are foreign born.

Regardless of their diversity, Hispanics are on the rise in rural America and throughout most parts of the United States. While the populations of Caucasians and African-Americans are expected to increase gradually in the next century, Hispanic-American population is projected to increase more rapidly and become a greater share in the nation's population. As the labor-force growth of Caucasians and African-Americans continues to slow in the years ahead, the skills and productivity of Hispanic workers are likely to be an increasingly important element in determining America's future prosperity. Even now, Hispanics are the nation's largest minority after African-Americans and their numbers are important in several areas.

Low incomes and low levels of educational attainment characterize a high proportion of Hispanics. Although Hispanic poverty rates are just a little below those of African-Americans, their educational deficiencies are far more serious. For example, nearly 40 percent of Hispanic youngsters drop out of high school compared with about 17 percent of African-Americans and 14 percent of Caucasians. Like the African-American case, action by both public and private sectors is needed to break the cycle of underachievement and poverty that affects so many Hispanics.

DEMOGRAPHIC TRENDS

The nation's Hispanic population totaled 15.4 million in 1982 and 20.1 million in March 1989, a growth rate of 31 percent. This was five times the growth rate of the non-Hispanic population. In 1989, Hispanics represented 8.2 percent of the nation's population.

Hispanics originating from Mexico have constituted the largest Hispanic population subgroup and numbered 12.6 million in March 1989. Total Hispanic population is shown in Table 1. Since 1982, the Central and South American population has grown 67 percent, from 1.5 to 2.5 million. Other growth rates from 1982 were 14 percent for Puerto Ricans and 12 percent for Cubans. The groups comprising "other Hispanics" rose by 31 percent. About half of the Hispanic population growth was the result of net migration, and the other half was the result of natural increase (the number of births minus the number of deaths). At least a third of all immigrants to the United States in the 1980s came from Latin America, with up to 85 percent of the

TABLE 1: CHANGE IN THE HISPANIC ORIGIN POPULATION, BY TYPE OF ORIGIN: MARCH 1982 TO 1989*
(Numbers in thousands)

Origin	March 1989	March 1982	Percent Change 1982 to 1989
Mexican origin	12,567	9,642	30.3
Puerto Rican origin	2,328	2,051	13.5
Cuban origin	1,068	950	12.4
Central and South American origin	2,545	1,523	67.1
Other Hispanic origin	1,567	1,198	30.8
Total Hispanic Population	20,075	15,364	30.7

*Data are from the civilian noninstitutional population of the United States.Source: U.S. Bureau of the Census, *Commerce News*, CB89–158, October 12, 1989.

Hispanic immigrants coming from Mexico. A relatively high birthrate among U.S. Hispanics has contributed significantly to the high population growth rate. In 1987, the fertility rate among Hispanic women was 96 births per 1,000 women of childbearing age, compared with 83 for U.S. African-American women and 69 for Caucasian women. More than one-third (36 percent) of Hispanics are less than 18 years old, compared with about one-quarter (26 percent) of non-Hispanics. In 1987, the median age for Hispanics was 25 years, compared with 26.3 for African-American and 32.2 years for Caucasians.

In 1989, two-thirds of the Hispanic population lived in three states: 34 percent in California, 21 percent in Texas, and 10 percent in New York. Persons of Mexican origin were primarily concentrated in California and Texas, as were Cubans in Florida, Central and South Mexicans in California and New York, and Puerto Ricans in New York.

U.S. Census Bureau projections expect the Hispanic population to hit 28.7 million by the turn of the century, bringing their share of the total U.S. population to 10.7 percent in the year 2000. In contrast, recent Census Bureau projections put the increase in the African-American population at less than a percentage point from 1988 to the year 2000.

WORK FORCE PARTICIPATION

The Hispanic population explosion is already reverberating in the U.S. labor markets. From 1980 to 1987, the number of Hispanics at work jumped 43 percent, or 2.3 million, and accounted for nearly 20 percent of the nation's employment growth, compared with a growth of 15 percent for African-Americans. The greatest increase in the Hispanic workers was among those of Mexican origin, followed by "other Hispanics."

Looking ahead, the Bureau of Labor Statistics estimates Hispanics will account for about 22 percent of the labor force growth rate between 1988 and the year 2000; altogether, this is a growth of about 5.3 million Hispanic workers from 8.9 million in 1988 (Cattan 1988). The Hispanic rate of increase alone is estimated at 74 percent, and will increase their share in the total work force from 6.9 percent in 1988 to 10.2 percent in 2000. The African-American share of the labor force should rise to 12 percent in 2000; this share is up from 11 percent (13 million) in 1988. It should be noted that the labor force participation rate for Hispanics is the highest measured by the Bureau of Labor Statistics; for example, in 1988, it was 67.4 percent for Hispanics compared with 66.2 percent for Caucasians and 63.8 percent for African-Americans. The participation rate for Hispanic men was 81.9 percent in 1988.

OCCUPATIONAL PATTERNS

Occupationally, Hispanic men and women have different patterns of employment compared with non-Hispanic men and women. While nearly 50 percent of Hispanic men were employed in 1987 as "operators, fabricators, and laborers" and "in precision production, craft, and repair" occupations, only 40 percent of non-Hispanic men were employed in these areas. Hispanic men are two times more likely to be employed in "farming, forestry, and fishing" than non-Hispanic men. In 1987, 8.9 percent were thus employed, compared with 4.4 percent of non-Hispanics (Cattan 1988, 13, Table 4).

Both Hispanic and non-Hispanic women are highly concentrated in "technical, sales, and administrative support" occupations—39.9 and 45.5 percent, respectively, in 1987. However, far more non-Hispanic women are in "managerial and professional specialty" than Hispanic women—25.0 percent compared with 14.7 percent. Relatively few Hispanic and non-Hispanic women are occupationally employed in "farming, forestry, and fishing"—1.5 and 1.1 percent, respectively.

INCOME AND POVERTY

In 1979, 13.1 percent of Hispanic married-couple families were below poverty line. In 1988, the number has risen to 16 percent. Overall, 26.8 percent of Hispanic persons were poor in 1988, compared with 25.7 percent in 1979. In 1988, the comparable poverty rate for African-American persons was 32.6 percent and it was 10.4 percent for Caucasians.

Median incomes, adjusted for inflation (1987 dollars), have not improved over the 1980–1987 period for Hispanic families. In 1980, it was $20,297, and in 1987, $20,306. Over the same period, however, the median income for Caucasians (1987 dollars) increased in real terms from $30,211 in 1980 to $32,274 in 1987. In the 1980s, Hispanic families fell further behind American Caucasian families.

HISPANICS OF RURAL AMERICA

CHARACTERISTICS

Little is written about Hispanics in rural America except for their work as migrant and seasonal farm workers. As a group, approximately 1.5 million or 8 percent of all Hispanics live in rural America. Compared with Caucasians and African-Americans, Hispanics constitute a small proportion of the rural population. However, as indicated in Table 2, Hispanics residing on rural farms increased in number between 1980 and 1987, while the rural farm population of Caucasians declined by over a half million residents.

Several of the social and economic characteristics of Hispanics employed in agriculture are listed in Table 3. It is interesting to note from the first line that less than half who worked in agriculture lived in rural areas. Also, they must have had lower earnings than Hispanics living on farms and employed in agriculture, as inferred from line 4. Moreover, the incidence of poverty is extant across all Hispanic workers. Apparently, the level of schooling completed is relatively low. Judging from the data in lines 9 and 10, Hispanics in agriculture are often from abroad.

Regardless of their numbers, Hispanic-Americans have made numerous contributions to rural America. Whether as migrant and seasonal workers or as farmers, they have played prominent roles in farm production. During periods when U.S. labor markets have been tight, they have not only been welcomed but actively recruited. However, during recessions they have been perceived as a threat to unemployed American workers. At times their presence has been supported by social and cultural institutions; at other times, however, they have been treated harshly by the same or other institutions. Nowhere is institutional support or rejection stronger than in the Southwest borderlands, where over 60 percent of all Hispanics reside on farms.

HISPANIC LEGACY OF THE SOUTHWEST

The regional economy of California, Arizona, Colorado, Texas, and New Mexico has traditionally exerted a strong influence upon employment and income opportunities of Hispanics. Carey McWilliams (1969, 103) noted their legacy in these terms:

> It should never be forgotten that, with the exception of the Indians, Mexicans are the only minority in the United States

TABLE 2: RACE AND HISPANIC ORIGINS OF THE POPULATION BY URBAN-RURAL RESIDENCE: 1980–87 (Numbers in thousands)

Item	Rural		Rural Farm		Percent Change Rural Farm
	1980	1987	1980	1987	
White	54,087	58,671	5,432	4,834	−12
Black	3,899	4,143	111	123	+10
Hispanic	1,471	1,468	78	135	+54

Source: U.S. Bureau of the Census; *Rural and Farm Population, 1987.*

TABLE 3: SOCIAL AND ECONOMIC CHARACTERISTICS OF HISPANIC PERSONS EMPLOYED IN AGRICULTURE: 1980

Item	Total Employed In Agriculture	Total In Rural Areas Employed In Agriculture	Total Living On Farms and Employed In Agriculture
1) Persons 16 years and older	255,265	102,877	15,874
(2) Median age of (1)	32.6	33.5	36.0
(3) Number of (1) with income	238,985	96,653	14,956
(4) Median income of (3)	$6,651	$6,760	$7,720
(5) Mean of (3)	$7,799	$7,725	$9,584
(6) Number of (1) in poverty	67,407	30,497	3,633
(7) Percent of (1) in poverty	26.4	29.6	22.9
(8) Percent high school graduates	15.9	14.3	20.3
(9) Number of (1) with residence in 1975:			
In same House	101,052	43,779	7,935
In different house in U.S.	107,737	39,572	5,875
Abroad	43,887	17,629	2,032
(10) Percent of (1) abroad in 1975	17.2	17.1	12.8

Source: U.S. Bureau of the Census, *Characteristics of the Rural and Farm-Related Population,* Subject Reports PC 80–2–9C. The totals include farm workers and farm operators and managers.

who were annexed [in the Southwest] by conquest; the only minority, Indians again excepted, whose rights were specifically safeguarded by treaty provision.

Less than 150 years ago, the vast stretches of the Southwest belonged to Mexico and, thirty years before that time, to Spain. A system of Catholic missions first opened up the Southwest, beginning in San Diego in 1769. The missionaries were devoted to converting Indians to Catholicism, making them loyal Spanish subjects. Although there are considerable controversy and misgivings about this role of Spaniards in the Southwest, they did make numerous contributions to American farms and ranches. During the mission period, lasting to the early 1830s, the Southwest's first farms and gardens were established. The farms and gardens were patterned largely after what the missionaries had known in Spain, making needed adaptations to a raw, new land and using what the Spaniards had learned from American and Mexican Indians. The Spanish priests and early Mexican settlers introduced America's European grapes, raisins, apricots, peaches, plums, oranges, lemons, wheat, barley, olives, figs, squash, tomatoes, chili peppers, avocadoes, chocolate, and a variety of other fruits and vegetables, which today are a part of our agricultural wealth.

The Spaniards and, later, the Mexicans who took over the Southwest territory from Spain in 1822 established the system of large farm estates or ranchos. The missions were also the training grounds for the first agricultural work force in California, the mission Indians. As Indians were forced or indentured to labor on vast *ranchos* of several thousand acres each (and there were over 800 land grants recorded), they and *mestizos* (mixed Spanish-Mexican-Indian blood) developed Western techniques of large-scale ranching and agriculture. In ranching, Hispanic precursors introduced rodeos, mustang bronco busting, chaps, spurs, stampedes, barbecues, and many other ideas we think of as being typically American. In agriculture, our Hispanic forerunners introduced riparian rights and water-saving irrigation systems and technologies for the arid Southwest. The Treaty of Guadalupe Hildalgo of 1848 and the Gadsden Purchase of 1853 resulted in the United States' take-over of most of California, New Mexico, Colorado, Nevada, Arizona, and lower Utah. California was the first to become a state in 1850, due mainly to the Gold Rush and a flood of immigrants from the eastern states.

Legislative action and contrived judicial proceedings dispossessed nearly all of the 800 title holders to Mexican land grants, even though the Treaty of Guadalupe Hildalgo contained provisions to honor the former titles.

The onrush of immigrants, coupled with the completion of the transcontinental railroad in 1869 opened new areas of the Southwest, with the railroad tycoons getting the lion's share of land in California's central valley. In southern Colorado and New Mexico, however, Hispanic-Americans held on to their small plots of land. Today, Spanish titles to land continue to be disputed (Knowlton, 1985).

ORIGINS OF MIGRANT WORKERS

Much of the West's agricultural wealth that has been developed has been also due to three factors: (1) natural resources—water, climate, land; (2) management and technology; and (3) an abundant labor supply. In the last factor, the Mexican population has made a major contribution to Western agriculture.

Mexico was profoundly transformed by its 1910 revolution. The revolution caused a steady flow of Mexican migrants into the U.S. Southwest that rapidly became an important farm labor force. Mexican migrants replaced previous workers (Chinese, Japanese, Hindus, and other nationalities) that, near the turn of the century, had been recruited to meet the growing demands for agricultural labor.

Readily available in growing numbers, Mexican refugees became actively recruited and encouraged to migrate by the organized efforts of growers and agricultural associations. By the 1930s and thereafter, Mexicans were the largest single group in the fields. Their low wages and skilled, hard work have since fueled much American agricultural prosperity. As we enter the 1990s, thousands of workers from Mexico still provide millions of hours of hand labor in lettuce, cotton, fruit, and vegetable growing, primarily on some of the large farms Mexicans lost after the Treaty of Guadalupe Hidalgo.

Today, the vast majority of migrant farm workers, the most disadvantaged group of workers in the United States, are Mexican-Americans, most of whom use the lower Rio Grande Valley of Texas as a home base. The job competition of the Texas-Mexico border economy, together with the recruitment drive from Midwestern labor markets, may be seen to have supported the pattern of Texas winter residence and annual migrations of 4,000 miles northward and back. Streams of migrant workers have flowed from the valley to the upper Midwest (the Great Lakes region), to the West Coast, and some to the Eastern Seaboard regions. Many so-called "Tex-Mex" migrants have settled in states like Michigan, Wisconsin, Indiana, and Illinois, and some continue to work in the rural communities where they reside.

FARM LABOR UNIONS AND COLLECTIVE BARGAINING

The more recent story of Mexican and other Hispanic contributions to America's rural economy is not a happy one. There have been much strife and conflict in the fields, along with worker exploitation and bitterness. The earliest strikes in Californian agriculture, in the twentieth century, were organized by Mexicans: Oxnard in 1903; Wheatland in 1913; the Imperial Valley in 1928; El Monte in 1933; the San Joaquin cotton fields throughout the 1930s; and, of course, within the memory of most, the Delano grape strikes and boycotts in 1965 that lasted for ten years. In all cases, Mexican field workers struck for higher wages, better working conditions, and the right to engage in collective bargaining. However, the National Labor Relations Act purposely excluded farm labor and still does.

In 1975, as a result of the conflict between labor and management in California's fields, California legislators passed the first law recognizing farm labor organizations' rights to collective bargaining. Called the California Agricultural Labor Relations Act, most of its provisions were unprecedented in American history, for example, guaranteeing the access of unions to farms and democratic elections among workers. Since 1975, contracts have been signed between unions representing farm workers and farm employers. Today, labor conflicts continue over issues of pesticides, immigration reforms, collective bargaining, and the role of labor contractors.

Concomitantly, federal programs appear to have been of little help to most Hispanic persons, although successes may not always be realized locally; that is, recipients of education and job-skill training may find more stable and better-paying employment in other regions. Without pretending that collective bargaining is a panacea, the record in California does indicate that the traditional plight of migrant and seasonal farm workers has been eased through the organizing efforts of Cesar Chavez and the United Farm Workers Union. Now, other states must grant farm workers the unionization rights already held by California farm workers.

IMMIGRATION

California's agriculture and Mexican labor have influenced national history. In the 1940s, due to World War II and the demand for farm labor primarily in California, the United States negotiated a deal with Mexico to enable Mexican farm workers to work legally in the States. Until 1965, more than one million workers came to the United States to work in the so-called "bracero program." At the height of the program in the 1950s, about 10 percent of the U.S. farm labor force was comprised of Mexican-based migrant workers that were employed throughout the country, mostly in the Southwestern states. They accounted for 40 to 70 percent of the peak work force in crops such as lettuce, cucumbers, melons, oranges, and tomatoes. Farm labor leaders have consistently lobbied in Washington for immigrant status for Mexican farm workers. The immigration bill that passed Congress in 1986 reflects this historic past: it has provisions to reestablish a bracero-like program in the event of a labor shortage in the fields. It provides amnesty for Special Agricultural Workers (SAWs) and Replenishment Agricultural Workers (RAWs), covering up to one million Mexican workers. Today, about 75 percent of California's farm workers were born in Mexico, and most of the rest are Mexican-Americans or Chicanos.

The Special Agricultural Worker or SAW program of the Immigration Reform and Control Act (IRCA) of 1986 permitted aliens who did at least 90 days of qualifying farm work in the 12 months ending May 1, 1986, to apply for temporary resident status. After December 1, 1990, qualified SAW aliens can become Permanent Resident Aliens (PRAs), permitting them to become legal U.S. residents earlier than nonfarm illegal aliens granted amnesty under IRCA. Once the SAW aliens obtain status as PRAs, they can live in Mexico or other foreign residences and commute seasonally to the United States. The SAW program attracted 1.3 million applicants before ending on November 30, 1988; 54 percent were in California and 81 percent were Mexican. However, the elimination of fraudulent cases may result in only about 600,000 legally approved SAWs.

Since future recipients of status as PRAs may leave agriculture, IRCA provided for Replenishment Agricultural Workers (RAWs). RAW workers receive temporary U.S. residence visas provided they do at least 90 days of farm work for specially designated agricultural activities annually. After three years, a RAW can apply for a "greencard" to become a PRA.

HISPANIC FARMS AND FARMERS

Although the 1980 Census of Population identified Hispanics as a continuing force of farm workers, at the same time, it found a nearly nonexistent number of Hispanic farmers. Table 4 indicates the relative imbalance between Caucasians, African-Americans, and Hispanics, as workers and farmers. Nationally, there were 1.26 farmers per hired farm worker in 1980. The ratio was 1.87 for Caucasians, 0.17 for African-Americans, and 0.06 for Hispanics. Although Hispanics and African-Americans combined accounted for 33 percent of the farm workers in 1980, they accounted for less than 2 percent of the nation's farmers. It is very unlikely that federal legislation for farmers helps Hispanic-Americans and African-Americans in rural America.

Table 5 presents an overview of selected characteristics of Hispanic farms. In 1987, Hispanic farm land acreage was lower than in 1982 and shared by more farmers. Harvested crop land also decreased from 1.3 million acres in 1982 to 1.2 million in 1987. The overwhelming number of Hispanic farms (73 percent) are below 219 acres, about one-half of the national average. Moreover, Hispanic farmers are primarily tenants and part-owners who have rarely marketed sales above $25,000.

Table 6 shows that most Hispanic farms and land in farms are found within seven states: Arizona, California, Colorado, Florida, New Mexico, Texas, and Washington. Combined, they represent 80 percent of all Hispanic farms and 85 percent of the land area (see Table 6). In only two states do more than 50 percent of the farms have sales of

TABLE 4: FARMERS AND FARM WORKERS IN THE 1980 CENSUS OF POPULATION BY ETHNIC GROUP

Item	All Farmers		All Farm Workers		Ratio: Farmers to Workers
	Total	Percent of Total	Total	Percent of Total	
Total	1,101,060	100	874,784	100	1.26
Caucasian	1,065,022	97	568,453	65	1.87
African-American	15,814	1	92,600	11	0.17
Hispanic	11,520	1	189,263	22	0.06

TABLE 5: SELECTED CHARACTERISTICS OF FARMS OPERATED BY PERSONS OF SPANISH ORIGIN: 1987 AND 1982

Item	1987	1982
Number of Farms	17,476	16,183
Land in Farms	8,340,701	8,872,066
Harvested Acres of Cropland	1,148,619	1,226,975
Number of Farms in 1987		
Below 219 acres	12,773	
220 to 499 acres	2,006	
500 acres or more	2,697	
Total	17,476	
Number of Acres by Tenure, 1987		
Full Owner	2,745,808	
Part Owner	3,999,069	
Tenants	1,595,824	
Number of Farms by 1987 Market Value of Sales		
Less than $2,500	6,225	
$2,500 to $9,999	4,978	
$10,000 to $19,000	1,828	
$20,000 to $24,999	479	
$25,000 or more	3,966	

Source: *U.S. Census Report*, CPS 2-27, No. 61, 1988 and 1987 Census of Agriculture.

TABLE 6: FARM OPERATORS OF HISPANIC ORIGIN, 1987

Geographic Area	All Farms		Farms With Sales of $10,000 or More		
	Farms	Land In Farms	Farms	Land In Farms	% Farms With >$10,000
U.S. Total (Hispanic)	17,476	8,340,701	6,273	6,393,927	35.9
elected States					
Arizona	363	364,077	168	325,249	46.3
California	3,471	1,046,104	1,771	970,838	51.0
Colorado	710	402,040	233	281,571	32.8
Florida	624	205,542	313	193,077	50.2
New Mexico	3,013	2,540,060	649	1,727,836	21.5
Texas	5,427	2,444,808	1,421	1,751,470	26.2
Washington	325	61,016	126	56,280	38.8
Subtotal	13,934	7,063,647	4,681	5,306,321	33.6
Subtotal as % of Total	79.7	84.7	74.6	83.0	N/A

Source: *1987 Census of Agriculture*, vol. 1, part 51, "Summary and State Data," table 35, pages 414–5.

$10,000 or more, namely, California (with 51 percent) and Florida (with 50.2 percent).

In Colorado and New Mexico, Hispanic and Anglo farming has been found to differ somewhat in their cropping patterns and livestock holdings. Hispanic farmers specialize more in alfalfa and sheep whereas Anglo farmers have more potatoes and cattle (Eckert and Gutierrez, 1990).

During the 1970s, a short-lived movement took place in California to convert Chicano farm workers into owner-operators of cooperative farms, mostly for horticulture production. The efforts were successful as long as the USDA and California's systems of cooperative extension helped these farmers with technical assistance for production and marketing. By the mid–1980s, most were gone for a variety of reasons (Rochin 1988).

In the late 1970s and 1980s a number of Mexican-American farm workers became farmers through sharecropping arrangements, especially in strawberry production. The sharecropping, however, appears to have been motivated by landowners as a way to bypass several of the state's labor laws. As sharecroppers, Hispanic-Americans are treated by law as farmers and not as farm workers who can be protected by California's Agricultural Labor Relations Act and other laws covering work conditions and wage rates. With sharecroppers, landlords are protected against IRCA's sharp provisions that fine employers of undocumented alien workers. According to Wells (1984, 2–3):

> Most basically, strawberry sharecropping is a response to a changed balance of power between agricultural labor and capital. . . . In the current context, sharecropping helps landowners cope with the rising cost and uncertainty of labor. Far from hindering rational production, modern sharecropping facilitates and is recreated by capitalist accumulation.

RURAL ENCLAVE SETTLEMENTS

Although the majority of Hispanics live in heterogeneous communities within metropolitan areas, large numbers of Hispanics reside in nonmetropolitan areas and rural settlements. In California alone, over 500,000 Hispanics live in numerous small rural communities varying in size and complexity from unstructured ranchos to towns and cities. Over sixty rural settlements have been found to have a majority of Hispanic people. Most residents of these communities are of Mexican descent and most are farm workers. Recent research indicates that during peak periods in agriculture, the population of Hispanic settlements is substantially enlarged with the presence of migrant farm workers. Since annual earnings in farm employment are typically well below the poverty level, the Hispanic residents in rural settlements constitute a large proportion of rural poor.

The concern over these communities is that they become centers of rural underclasses of Hispanics, populated by an exploited and impoverished working people laboring to support the agricultural economy. These communities have relatively low tax bases and, hence, lack many of the amenities needed to provide adequate health, schooling, and safety. To date, few have been studied.

We note that the Spanish/Mexican heritage of the Southwest goes beyond a discussion of the economic development of rural America. It is a living heritage that continues to affect Hispanic cultural and social character. This heritage of farm employment and rural communities provides key agenda items for the future. It is part of what distinguishes Hispanics from other populations in the union.

RURAL HISPANIC ISSUES

Despite a variety of programs and policies aimed at migrant and seasonal farm workers, most Hispanic-Americans are relatively neglected in rural areas. Neglect has been due in part to many factors indicated above: their geographic dispersion throughout the United States, confusion as to their identity with different labels (e.g., Chicanos, Mexican-Americans, Latinos, Puerto Ricans, Cuban-Americans, Hispanics, etc.), relative absence as significant landowners and farmers, shortage of nationally recognized leaders in academic and business spheres, low income status, and limited political representation. Nonetheless, the majority of rural Hispanic-Americans can no longer be ignored or excluded from programs and policies. Hispanic-Americans are not only linked to much farm production in rural America but they are also becoming increasingly more important to rural America as demographic and political forces. In states where their numbers have grown, they have increased levels of formal political representation. Their representation includes two secretaries of the Bush administration (for the Education and Interior Departments), a congressional chair of a key agricultural committee, one governor, executives of states, and over 100 state legislators. Hispanic-Americans are also growing in terms of consumer purchasing power, and they are the majority population in many rural communities. These rapidly changing relationships offer new opportunities for Hispanic-Americans to actively participate in the future of rural America.

In an attempt to identify and prioritize from this complex set of issues, six Hispanic-American scholars met in 1989 under the auspices of the Social Science Agricultural Agenda Project (SSAAP) to specify agenda items. It should be noted that these six alone constitute nearly one-fourth of the total number of Hispanic rural social scientists with Ph.D.s and jobs at U.S. universities. The ratio of representation at the workshop was high, but the number of social scientists was extremely low compared to the work to be done on rural Hispanic problems and issues. The six included the authors of this chapter and Rogelio Saenz (Texas), Philip Garcia (Illinois), Joseph Speilberg-Benitez (Michigan), and Don Vallarejo (California). Also participating in the discussions were SSAAP leaders, Glenn L. Johnson and James T. Bonnen.

It was the consensus of the group that expanded efforts are increasingly needed at a rapid pace to improve the conditions of rural Hispanic-Americans. Increased funding, philanthropic activity, and urgent attention is essential for Hispanic community and economic development, research and policy analysis, education, social services, extension, and leadership development. Hispanic-Americans must also respond with investments in human capital formation and entrepreneurship, and become stronger in academic and business life. For the new relationships between Hispanic-Americans and others to succeed, Hispanic-Americans must develop shared policies and programs with non-Hispanics and vice versa, in both the private and public sectors of society. Enhanced awareness of differences, cultural sensitivity, and better information and research are keys to improved communication and effectiveness of efforts. So, too, is the urgent need to develop shared and augmented agendas in the rural social sciences.

AGENDAS TO IMPROVE THE STATUS OF RURAL HISPANIC-AMERICANS

Hispanic-Americans are increasing in numbers and influence, yet they are not well understood, accepted, and/or targeted as critical for rural development. They constitute a large share of the nation's poor, bear a high incidence of poverty, and work in occupations facing declining demands for workers. Their opportunities for social, economic, and geographic mobility are constrained by low job skills, limited English-language skills, education, and little money for making risky moves. Several institutions and decision makers are strategically situated for making positive contributions to the status of Hispanic-Americans. Here are suggested ways they can help.

- Land-Grant and Post-Secondary Institutions of Learning should carry out the following:
  - Apply affirmative action to increase the numbers and products of Hispanic-Americans in the rural social sciences.
  - Develop databases, information systems, and analytical methods to enhance rural social science research both for and about Hispanic-Americans.
  - Create and support multidisciplinary research projects on rural Hispanic-Americans. Appropriate topics include: income and employment, family networks and extended units, life-cycle constraints, social costs of family and community disruptions and dislocations, socially responsible technological change, labor market opportunities and occupations of the future, ethnic

enclaves, social and economic relationships and status, returns of education and training, culture, language and assimilation, entrepreneurial opportunities and challenges, and related international topics.

- Develop the capability for extending new ideas and methods to communities of Hispanic-Americans.
- Assist in the development of infrastructure for the implementation of programs and policies aimed at improving the conditions of Hispanic-Americans. Train and allocate technical assistants to work with Hispanic issues and communities. Establish a process for identifying and solving social and economic problems affecting rural Hispanics.
- Include Hispanic-Americans in the decision-making process for rural research and extension. Develop new techniques for identifying, articulating, and prioritizing social science agendas involving Hispanic-Americans.
- Develop and/or amplify programs for rural Hispanic youth and adults. Incorporate ways for addressing issues of nutrition, housing, migrancy, child care, incentives for higher education, and community leadership.
- Strengthen entrepreneurship among rural Hispanics, facilitate self-help enterprises, generate capital savings, and assist in the formation of associations or cooperatives for augmenting jobs and resource use.
- Prepare appropriate literature on the economic and social policies and laws that impinge upon the activities of rural Hispanic-Americans. Currently appropriate are new federal laws affecting the rights and responsibilities of workers and employers under the Immigration Reform and Control Act of 1986, of English language proficiency tests and requirements for registered aliens, and several new measures affecting welfare recipients and social services under welfare reform acts.

● Resident Instruction

Unlike African-Americans who have benefitted over the years from several outstanding institutions of higher education, e.g., Tuskegee University and the system of 1890 land-grant institutions, Hispanic-Americans have usually attended regular public colleges or not continued their education. The record of Hispanic admission, persistence, and completion in higher education is weak. Moreover, the educational pipeline from kindergarten through the 12th grade is known to produce just a trickle of Hispanics entering college. Within the rural social sciences, there are fewer than two dozen Hispanics with Ph.D.s teaching in land-grant departments of rural sociology or agricultural economics. They hardly cast a shadow or provide the needed base for teaching and research in the rural social sciences. Institutions of resident instruction must make firm commitments to:

- Prepare and hire by the year 2000, 100 new Hispanic-Americans in the rural social sciences of land-grant institutions.
- Offer mentorships, internships, employment opportunities, and funds to Hispanic-Americans as incentives to pursue social science Ph.D.s for employment in higher education.
- Develop effective retention programs that abet successful completion rates of Hispanics with doctoral degrees. Likewise, develop sound programs that support the research, teaching, and extension of Hispanic-Americans in the rural social sciences so that tenure can be achieved. Concomitantly, recognize the importance of research, teaching, and service in ethnic studies, and the relevance of publishing in nontraditional fields.
- Develop outreach liaisons with school systems teaching K–12 to contact, promote, and facilitate Hispanic interest in the social sciences. Field trips, student organizations, mentorships, and internships for Hispanic youth can influence their assessments about the long-run economic returns from higher education.
- Support current Hispanic rural social scientists in networking and developing sustaining programs of applied research on Hispanic-Americans. The current few cannot function effectively by themselves.

● Agencies for Advising and Consulting

Hispanic Americans own or operate just a few consulting firms that cater to public or private agencies. There are only a handful of "think tank" centers devoted to lobbying or policies on behalf of Hispanic-Americans. Noteworthy are: (1) MALDEF (Mexican-American Legal Defense and Education Fund) with offices in Texas and California, (2) the Tomas Rivera Center (a national policy institute) with offices also in Texas and California, and (3) the National Council of La Raza (a policy analysis center) with offices in Washington, D.C., and Los Angeles. All three started with philanthropic endowment funds and continue today with subscriptions, philanthropies, and corporate contracts or donations. Only occasionally do they address rural issues of Hispanics directly.

Collaboration is needed from federal, state, local, and international agencies of advising and consulting to:

- Provide social science training funds for Hispanic-Americans to work on rural issues.
- Develop skills and capabilities of Hispanic-Americans to manage and administer rural programs and to assess the impacts of public policies.
- Increase the networking across different Hispanic community organizations involved in problem solving.
- Enhance the data-generating process for use in budgeting, substantive and informative evaluations of local programs, and for human investment evaluations.
- Include Hispanic-Americans on advisory boards and commissions associated with the rural social sciences.

● Farming, Agribusiness, and Nonfarm/Rural Enterprises

Hispanic-Americans have a tremendous stake in the viability of agriculture, farm production, processing, and marketing in rural areas. The quality of life in their communities has a symbiotic relationship to the general performance of these industries. Shocks in the level of prices, production, trade, and immigration directly affect the earnings of rural Hispanic-Americans with drastic results. Few Hispanic-Americans have assets, savings, and adjustment assistance to relocate during recessions. Since most Hispanic-Americans do not own property, capital assets, or equipment, they usually rely on family or friends for loans or for cosigning notes as collateral. These financial constraints leave Hispanic families in precarious situations.

Enterprises for farming, agribusiness, and other rural businesses can contribute immensely to the well-being of rural Hispanic-Americans by:

- Considering ways to employ Hispanic-Americans in steady, long-run jobs that reduce the effects of cyclical and seasonal unemployment.
- Investing in the development of Hispanic-owned-and-operated farms and businesses, contracting for their products, and assisting in their performance.
- Including Hispanic-Americans in the rural organizations of private business, the Chambers of Commerce, Lions Clubs, Rotary Clubs, etc. By sponsoring Hispanic youth through business internships and scholarships, the private sector can influence their educational aspirations.
- Developing locally based community organizations of Hispanic-Americans like *concilios*, that provide information, forums, and social services to all Hispanics of the community.
- Cosponsoring programs for, or including, more Hispanic-Americans in agricultural leadership training. Offering a long-run solution to many problems are one- to two-year programs that coordinate with the private and public sectors to give young Hispanic men and women a chance to develop leadership skills.

● Foundations

Philanthropy is crucial for fulfilling essential needs for seed money, experimenting, consulting, forums, and networking of Hispanic-Americans. Because many new issues are emerging in tandem with the growing number of Hispanic-Americans, much effort is needed by foundations to:

- Provide funds for leveraging larger sums from private, public, and volunteer institutions. Field research and graduate student fellowships are badly needed to involve more Hispanic-Americans in the rural social sciences.
- Include more Hispanics in key decision-making positions regarding their programs and donations.
- Integrate and link diverse groups through conferences and other forms of communication to ensure Hispanic representation.
- Support self-help, grassroots initiatives of Hispanics in different regions. At the base of many Hispanic communities are many natural leaders.
- Support Hispanic networking used for building and for consolidating Hispanic groups in ways that will assist in consensus building and solidify Hispanic institutions/groups following through on initial human capital investments.
- Fund research to specify the needed database for Hispanic research. The initial inquiry would provide the database needed for policy analysis.
- Support community-organization specialists (coalition building), e.g., the Highlander Research and Educational Center (informal adult education) that spirited Rosa Parks of the civil rights movement.
- Support leadership training programs (a la the Kellogg Model), to invest in the future of Hispanic-Americans.
- Provide recognition and achievement awards to Hispanic scholars and to community leaders and contributors to the Hispanic community.
- Create rural social science societies for the advancement of Hispanic graduate training.

● Professional Societies

Hispanic-Americans are far too outnumbered and too few to create effective subcommittees or working groups within the rural social science professions. Until more are added to academic and senior government ranks, Hispanic-Americans will not be able to work alone to develop professional agendas. Professional societies must take the lead to:

- Understand, promote, and sell the ideas discussed above to enhance the visibility and participation of Hispanic-Americans within the rural social sciences.
- Provide special sessions, topics, and leadership roles at annual meetings.
- Devote journal space to articles both by and about Hispanic-Americans.
- Develop networks among Hispanic-Americans and associate these networks with non-Hispanic professionals who do research and service with Hispanics and communities.

NOTE

1. Refugio I. Rochin is a professor of Agricultural Economics and Director of Chicano Studies, University of California, Davis, and Adela de la Torre is a professor in the Health Care Administration Program, California State University, Long Beach.

REFERENCES

Cattan, Peter. 1988. The growing presence of Hispanics in the U.S. workforce. *Monthly Labor Review* 3, no. 8 (August): 9–14.

Eckert, Jerry and Paul Gutierrez. 1990. Contracts and Communalities: Hispanic and Anglo Farming in Conejos County, Colorado. Paper presented. Department of Agricultural Economics, Colorado State University, August, 1990.

Knowlton, Clark S. 1985. Land Loss as a Cause of Unrest Among Rural Spanish-American Village Populations of Northern New Mexico. *Agriculture and Human Values* II (1985): 25–39.

McWilliams, Carey. [1939] 1969. Factories in the field: The story of migratory farm labor in California. Hamden, Conn.: Archon Books.

Rochin, Refugio I. 1988. The conversion of Chicano farm workers into owner-operators of cooperative farms, 1970–1985. *Rural Sociology* 51, no. 1 (March): 97–115.

U.S. Bureau of the Census. 1989. *The Hispanic population in the United States, March 1988*, Current Population Reports, Series P–20, No. 438, Washington, D.C.

U.S. Bureau of the Census. 1989. Change in the Hispanic origin population, by type of origin: March 1982 to 1989 (table). *Commerce News* CB89–158 (12 October).

U.S. Bureau of the Census. 1988. Race and Hispanic origins of the population by urban-rural residence: 1980–1987 (table). *Rural and farm population: 1987*, Current Population Survey Series P–27, No. 61, U.S. Dept. of Agriculture, Washington, D.C.

U.S. Bureau of the Census. n.d. Farm operators of Hispanic origin, 1987 (table). *Summary and state data. 1987 census of agriculture*, vol. 1, part 51, table 35.

U.S. Bureau of the Census. n.d. Social and economic characteristics of Hispanic persons employed in agriculture:

1980 (table). *Characteristics of the rural and farm-related population*, Subject Reports PC 80–2–9C.

Wells, Miriam J. 1984. The resurgence of sharecropping: Historical anomaly or political strategy? *American Journal of Sociology* 90, no. 1: 1–29.

OTHER REFERENCES USED BUT NOT SPECIFICALLY CITED

Carlin, Thomas A., and Bernal Green. 1988. *Local farm structure and community ties*, Rural Development Research Report No. 68, U.S. Dept. of Agriculture, Economic Research Service, Washington, D.C., March.

Kawamura, Y., R. I. Rochin, D. B. Gwynn, and E. Dolber-Smith. 1989. Rural and urban poverty in California: Correlations with rurality and socioeconomic structure. *Journal of Economic and Business Studies* (June): 34–54.

Martin, Philip L., and Alan L. Olmstead. 1985. The agricultural mechanization controversy. *Science* 227:601–6.

Oliveira, Victor J., and E. Jane Cox. 1988. *The agricultural work force of 1985: A statistical profile*, Agriculture Economics Report 582, U.S. Dept. of Agriculture, Economic Research Service, Washington, D.C., March.

Rochin, Refugio I. 1989. The changing nature of American agriculture and its impact on Hispanic farm labor: Topics for research and analysis. Published Paper of the Julian Samora Research Institute, Michigan State University, E. Lansing, Michigan.

U.S. General Accounting Office. 1988. *The H–2A program: Protections for U.S. farmworkers*, GAO/PEMD–89–3, Washington, D.C., October.

CHAPTER 7

RESEARCH AREAS RELATING TO NATIVE AMERICAN RURAL HUMAN DEVELOPMENT NEEDS

Jack D. Forbes[1]

INTRODUCTION

The Native American population of the United States is rapidly growing. It is also the most rural ethnic population in the country, although many live in urban areas as well. In addition to large numbers permanently residing in rural areas, Native Americans living in urban zones frequently move back and forth between rural home bases and urban economic bases. Navajo, Papago, Kickapoo, Mixtec, Zapotec, Chinantec, and other Indian persons comprise a significant proportion of the agricultural labor stream.

The precise population figures for Native Americans are difficult to ascertain because many persons of indigenous American race (in whole or in part) are identified under other terms by the United States census, such as "Hispanic" or even "White." The 1980 census resulted in a range of figures for the "American Indians" (persons who marked "Indian [Amer.]" for the "race" question, or who marked "Other," but wrote in the name of a recognizable Native American group, or who simply wrote in a tribal designation). An early count yielded 1,418,195, while a sample and a projection yielded 1,536,997.

The 1980 ancestry question, however, saw 1,920,824 persons reporting only Indian ancestry while the "current population" count of 1979 had yielded 2,053,000 (1,957,000 to 2,149,000). Thus, we are left with a range of 1.5 to 2 million persons who identified themselves, in some way, by the use of the terms "Indian" or "Native American," or by tribal names.

However, 40 percent of the so-called "Spanish-origin" totals for 1980 identified themselves racially as "Other," that is, as non-"White" and non-"Black." This group, most of whom were of Mexican ancestry, is doubtless predominantly of Indian racial composition. (Mexican-origin persons selected "Other" in 45 percent of all cases.)

If we add together all persons of Latin American origin but probably of indigenous American race (including up to 80 percent of Mexican-Americans and eliminating those who are probably non-Indian in other groups), we arrive at a total of 7 to 8 million persons.

To further complicate matters, in addition to the above group, about 7 million persons (1980) and almost 10 million persons (1979) declared that they had some degree of Native American ancestry. Thus, we have a rather conservative total of 14 to 18 million persons with Native American ancestry. It is difficult to know what proportion of these persons primarily identify as Native Americans. Certainly large proportions of this population identify principally as Chicanos, Mexican-Americans, "White Americans," Chileans, etc., but a considerable number (especially recent immigrants from Meso-America) have strong indigenous identities, in addition to the "core" Native American group of 1.5 to 2 million persons.

Data on "American Indian"-operated farms for 1987 and 1982 indicate 7,211 farms in 1982 and 7,134 in 1987, utilizing 46,151,992 acres in 1982 and 45,674,158 acres in 1987. Significantly, the total acreage for *all* non-Caucasian and "Spanish-origin" farms was about 60 million acres and, thus, Native American farms made up the greater part of the non-Caucasian/Spanish-origin total. Much of this land, we can be sure, was not fully utilized or was grazing land since only about 630,000 to 705,000 acres were "harvested cropland." Thus, the acreages are very misleading.

Moreover, it is interesting that a high proportion of the acreage assigned by the census to "female operators" (35 to 40 million acres) in both 1982 and 1987 must have been due to Native American totals since non-Native American farms only had about 15 million acres. Thus, it would appear that about half of Native American acreage might well have been under the control of females.

In 1987, 6,325 Native American farms were on "owned land," totaling almost 43 million acres. Two thousand five hundred twenty-seven (2,527) farms were rented or leased land, totaling 2,764,504 acres. Eight hundred nine (809) Native Americans were tenants in 1987, an increase from 749 in 1982. Acreage of tenants increased sharply from 481,248 acres in 1982 to 1,061,699 acres in 1987.

But, all of these figures are apt to be very misleading due to the counting of large reservation areas as "land in farms" and to the undercounting of Native Americans away from reservation areas. There are many different kinds of Native Americans and some appear to be unrecognized as such.

To clarify the diverse research needs relating to this racial group, we must first identify and briefly describe the different kinds of Native American groups and communities. Each type of community will tend to have special needs and characteristics.

LANDLESS INDIGENOUS GROUPS

The United States has, for a century now, possessed growing numbers of landless Native Americans who, for various reasons, must live at the edge of rural towns or on "public-domain" lands or disputed lands, or in rented housing. In the past, such people have typically belonged to small tribes or communities overlooked by the Bureau of Indian Affairs (BIA) (as in California, Nevada, and parts of Arizona) or prevented from having a land base by expropriation programs of the federal government, e.g., the seizure of Indian lands. For example, large numbers of Navajo people, although tribal members, currently live on so-called public-domain land in northeastern New Mexico. This land has not been added to the Navajo Reservation because of past political opposition by New Mexican representatives in Congress.

Many Native Americans have been made landless in California and elsewhere through the operation of federal statutes such as the Termination Act and the earlier General Allotment Act that made some Indian property subject to state and local taxes and to the real-estate pressures found in the surrounding Caucasian community.

Since the 1880s, significant numbers of Yaqui people from Mexico have migrated into the United States, along with numbers of Papago people, Cocopas, Kamias, and others. Some have managed to secure reservation living sites, but others still do not own any agricultural land.

More recently, Zapotec, Mixtec, and other Mexican Indians have been entering the migrant stream in substantial numbers, many as permanent residents, with others still maintaining a home base in places such as Oaxaca or Michoacan. Since 1978, the ethnocide being carried out against Mayan groups in Guatemala and against the Pipil-Nahua in El Salvador has led to very large migrations. More than 100,000 Mayan people have been murdered since 1978 in Guatemala and 1,000,000 Indians have had to become refugees. A substantial portion have fled to Mexico and to the United States.

Many of the above migrant and refugee Indians are now living in U.S. cities, especially Los Angeles. Many others, however, are now living in rural areas, sometimes under very harsh conditions (as is the case currently in northern San Diego County).

In any case, we can distinguish the following types of rural landless Native Americans:

A. Native Americans living on or near original lands but without any formal control over a reasonable land base:
   1. Native Americans living on very small "colonies" or "rancherias" that have no agricultural capability.
   2. Terminated communities that have lost all or part of their small lands.
   3. Tribal groups living on lands claimed as "public domain" by the federal government.
   4. Communities and families renting or otherwise living in rural towns without any usable land.
   5. Formerly allotted groups whose allotments have been lost with the same result as #4 above.
   6. Native Americans whose reservation allotments are being leased by the federal government to non-Native Americans and who have no access to such lands due to lack of capital, heirship problems, etc., with the same result as #4 above.

B. Native Americans forced to migrate to new areas (as political and racial refugees or as economic refugees):
   1. "Older" groups, such as the Yaquis of the 1880s–1910s period.
   2. "Newer" groups, such as the Mayans ("legal" and undocumented).
   3. Male migrants sending money home to families in Mexico and elsewhere ("legal" and undocumented).

C. Native Americans with a land base inadequate to support population all year:
   1. Agricultural workers in the migrant stream (i.e., Kickapoos).
   2. Part-year urban workers (i.e., Iroquois high-steel workers).

RURAL FEDERALLY RECOGNIZED RESERVATION GROUPS AND TRIBAL GOVERNMENTS

There are many kinds of reservations in the United States. They vary in size, in population, in quality of lands, in natural resources, and in the degree to which the reservations's sovereignty and land base have been compromised by checkerboard patterns of non-Indian ownership of internal reservation land.

In general, we can classify reservations as follows:

A. Small reservations with few, if any, natural resources and with poor-quality land.
B. Small reservations with a slightly better quality of land.
C. Small reservations with better economic potential.
D. Medium-sized reservations as in "A" above.
E. Medium-sized reservations as in "B" above.
F. Medium-sized reservations as in "C" above.
G. Large reservations with few major natural resources and/or with mountainous, dry, or poor lands.
H. Large reservations with some valuable resources and/or with some good-quality lands.
I. Large reservations with many valuable resources and/or a quantity of good-quality lands.

Reservations can, however, also be analyzed on the basis of the degree of potential power possessed by the tribal government, since a powerful tribal government may affect the quality of economic development and the level of planning available.

A. Trust allotments, all individually held, with virtually no tribal authority (Oklahoma, parts of California and Nevada).
B. Extremely small or poorly organized reservations with no management or planning capability.
C. Medium-sized reservations with only modest governmental structures.
D. Reservations containing two or more distinct Indian nations with antagonism or rivalry between the several groups, handicapping tribal government.

E. Reservations containing large numbers of nontribal members living in checkerboard areas or on leased land, severely handicapping tribal government.
F. Medium to large reservations with well-developed governments.
G. Well-organized reservations ready to take over local government completely from the Bureau of Indian Affairs.

RURAL NON-FEDERALLY RECOGNIZED RESERVATIONS OR COMMUNITIES

In the United States, there are many rural Native American groups that are not officially recognized by the Bureau of Indian Affairs and, thus, receive no BIA assistance or supervision. From Massachusetts and Maine to South Carolina, many state-organized reservations exist, often very small but still property-tax-exempt and with powers of local self-government. There are also large numbers of unrecognized communities scattered across the eastern United States, with some similar groups in California and other parts of the Far West. Many of the these groups are attempting to secure federal recognition (a long, tedious process) while others, thus far, have not sought formal recognition or organization.

Some of these groups can best be described as essentially landless communities (see earlier section), but others possess farmland or other usable land, usually in private ownership. Some of the state-recognized reservations continue to possess tribally owned lands.

Virtually all of these groups lack any government structure capable of management or planning, except at a very informal level.

GENERAL RESEARCH NEEDS

Native American groups and governments possess a vast array of unmet research needs, largely because federal agencies, extension agencies, and land-grant universities have often ignored Native Americans because of their economic marginality and lack of political influence. Moreover, many agencies have perhaps assumed that the Interior Department and its Bureau of Indian Affairs were meeting the needs of Native Americans, an erroneous assumption indeed.

Research issues may be divided into three broad areas: (1) those dealing directly with agriculture, horticulture, forestry, ranching, and aquaculture; (2) those dealing with environmental and ecological topics; and (3) those dealing with quality-of-life topics including infrastructure of tribal governments, education, etc. In actual fact, these three areas are totally interdependent and cannot, in practice, be separated. For example, one cannot deal adequately with horticultural issues without examining ecological, economic, educational, and political factors because in Native American areas these subjects intersect. Nonetheless, for discussion purposes we can try to identify topics under each of these broad areas.

RESEARCH RELATING TO FOOD AND FIBER MANAGEMENT AND PRODUCTION ISSUES

Research in this area differs markedly from normal agricultural research, since Native Americans are usually very poor in economic terms and are either landless or possess marginal or submarginal lands. Research, therefore, must focus upon "Third World"-type conditions exacerbated by short growing seasons, aridity, erosion, lack of fertilizer, poor soil, lack of experience, and a host of other problems.

Generally speaking, research must be site specific although techniques and procedures proven in one locale may be transferable.

Research must usually be "down to earth" and practical, since successful changes will tend to be small scale and practical. For example, one area of research is to develop strains of nopal (prickly-pear cactus) capable of being introduced in high-elevation, short-growing-season areas to be used for living fences, cattle feed, human food, shade, and erosion control. It is believed that the nopal can survive on submarginal land, but many varieties will not withstand temperatures below 25 degrees Fahrenheit.

A second example relates to the study of the potential significance of the mesquite tree and its fruit in human nutrition, as well as for shade, erosion control, and animal feed. The value of the mesquite bean is well documented, but new techniques need to be developed to better utilize the product in human nutrition, to select better strains, etc.

A third example relates to the various ways in which hot-house and intensive horticulture can be introduced into Native American communities, given the lack of good land and the often inhospitable climatic conditions to which reservations are exposed.

Needless to say, it is not possible here to outline all future lines of research in this area since the latter must first be based upon very careful site-specific studies that must include the examination of social and cultural, as well as economic, factors.

RESEARCH RELATING TO ENVIRONMENTAL AND ECOLOGICAL ISSUES

Native American governments and communities are badly in need of research relating to the environment. Many groups are under pressure to open their lands to toxic-waste disposal while others face or have already experienced serious contamination and damage from coal and uranium mining and processing, and from other hazardous developments. In fact, the level of health among some Native American groups has already been adversely affected by poorly supervised uranium mining and other extractive processes. Vital reserves of underground water have also been given up, while mineral reserves have often been sold for ridiculously low prices and with woefully inadequate environmental-impact mitigation processes.

Most Native American communities need research assistance in these vital areas. The difficulty is that revenue-starved governments and high-unemployment communities often are persuaded to ignore long-term impacts for minimal short-term rewards. Thus, research must also focus on quality-of-life issues.

RESEARCH RELATING TO QUALITY-OF-LIFE ISSUES

Perhaps more than with any other ethnic group, experiment station research with Native Americans must focus upon nonproduction issues because of the vital character of infrastructural, social, and political topics as underlying factors or constraints. It can even be argued that food and fiber production problems, in spite of adverse physical conditions, will be easier to solve than the structural, cultural, and political problems. Examples of specific topic areas are as follows.

Identification and Classification of Native Americans for Purposes of Analysis

This has become an increasingly significant issue since the Bureau of Census and the federal Office of Management and Budget have made the serious mistake of inventing the artificial "Hispanic" and "Spanish-descent" categories for data collection purposes, and in limiting Indian status to only North American Indians. Literally hundreds of thousands of Indians from Mexico, Guatemala, El Salvador, and South America, not to mention the southwestern United States, may be lost statistically in an amorphous multiracial category. Because the federal government also attempts to force all persons to choose only one racial category, many persons of part-Indian descent are also lost in totals for the Caucasian and African-American populations, as well as being lost in the "Hispanic" totals. Research needs to be carried out to identify more accurately the Native American population and the various types of Native American people. Moreover, policy research should also help to unravel the steps explaining why staffs of federal bureaucracies make poor decisions in terms of classifying ethnic groups.

Education (Elementary and Secondary)

Research needs to be carried out to discover the positive and negative aspects of current schooling and why Native American youth tends to drop out or tends to be poorly prepared even after graduation. Is the curriculum still Caucasian-oriented or alienating in some way? Is it unrealistic in reservation terms? Are teachers adequately prepared? Who governs the schools? Are Indian-controlled schools more effective than non-Indian-controlled schools?

Higher Education (Indian-Controlled Colleges)

The twenty-three Indian-controlled colleges are especially significant because of their rural locations and potential for agriculturally relevant course work. The Indian-controlled colleges began operation in the 1968–71 period, but have always been only marginally funded. Studies need to be carried out that are focused on how to secure more funding for needed programs and how to add or strengthen agricultural training.

Higher Education (Non-Indian-Controlled)

Research is needed relative to public and private universities and their impact upon Native American populations, especially in relation to the land-grant missions of state university systems. Among the many researchable questions are the following: How well are Native American students recruited? What intersegmental relations exist with Indian community colleges? How well do Native American students succeed? Do "Native American studies" programs exist and receive adequate support? How well do extension service programs serve Native American communities?

Language Policy

Many Native American groups continue to speak aboriginal-American languages primarily, although individuals may often be bilingual in either English or Spanish, and some groups are losing their native language. Such nations as the Lakota, Crow, Cheyenne, Navajo, Hopi, O'odham (Papago), and Kickapoo still widely speak their American language. Similarly, many Indians from Mexico and Guatemala now in the United States speak primarily Zapotec, Mixtec, Kanjobal, Quiché, or other American languages. Tragically, our public schools, court systems, extension education programs, and social welfare agencies are often ill-prepared to deal with persons speaking aboriginal-American languages, often attempting to use Spanish or English instead. Research must be carried out to locate Indian speakers, to obtain adequate statistics, to document what is happening at the public agency level, and to discover ways to help Native Americans obtain services while maintaining their unique American-language heritage. Not only do people suffer needlessly by being an "invisible" linguistic minority, but a significant bit of America dies every time an original American dialect disappears.

The Impact of the National Park Service, U.S. Forest Service, and Other Agencies

These agencies have powerful impacts upon Native American communities since the bulk of federal land is actually recently obtained Indian land and often still contains Native American sacred areas, historic sites, village locations, food and fiber gathering areas, hunting areas, and still-viable Native American communities (such as Death Valley National Monument). National parks and forests and public-domain lands could also be vital economic resources for Native American people if Native Americans were hired as experts in history, culture, ethnobotany, and natural ecology. Unfortunately, all of these agencies tend to hire primarily non-Native Americans who possess no local expert knowledge. Research needs to be carried out relative to the Native American historical/cultural potential of all federal lands and also relative to continuing Native American religious and economic rights therein. Treaties of cession ordinarily did not refer to the cession of religious and cultural rights, and thus very real potential may exist for Native American equity remaining in most federal lands. This research will be legal in nature, but policy research is also required.

Religious and Cultural Issues

International law guarantees Native Americans their religious and cultural rights, as do treaties (i.e., the Treaty of Guadalupe Hidalgo with Mexico, 1848). Unfortunately, Native Americans have often suffered the suppression of their religions, the ghoulish scavenging of their cemeteries, the display of their bones and sacred objects in museums, their place-names replaced by alien names, and the suppressions of their cultural practices in general. Research needs to be carried out relative to the best ways to restore such rights and how to convince non-Native Americans that Native Americans are deserving of constitutional and other legal protection. This topic is related to ending the psychological oppression of Native Americans that, it is suggested, vitally affects the performance of youth in schools and other quality-of-life indicators.

Hunting, Gathering, and Fishing Rights

Research must be carried out relative to the residual hunting and fishing rights of Native Americans. In California, for example, the Native American coastal tribes may still possess valuable fishing and gathering rights between the mean high-tide line and the state boundary because no government has ever purchased their rights. Almost everywhere in the United States controversy is aroused when Native Americans seek to exercise traditional hunting and fishing rights, and yet this remains an important source of food in certain areas. Many arts and crafts, such as basketry, also depend upon traditional gathering rights.

International Boundary Crossing Privileges and Other Unique Legal Issues

Under the Jay Treaty, many Native Americans of the United States and Canada possess unique border crossing privileges. The same principle seems to apply to Mexican Kickapoo members and, potentially at least, to many other tribes whose territories were divided by international boundaries without their consent. Many Native Americans would also argue that all Native Americans possess unique border crossing rights because of being the prior sovereign in all of America before any European colonies or states were established. On more solid ground, most reservations are generally exempt from state and local taxes, including sales taxes, and this creates opportunities for economic development as well as for revenue creation by means of tribal sales taxes, tribal income taxes, tribal corporation taxes, etc. Much research needs to be carried out relative to the unique rights of indigenous people and the potential use of these rights to further economic development and to strengthen tribal government.

Closely related to this general topic is the specific issue of bingo and other forms of commercial gambling. What long-term impacts will bingo casinos have upon reservation life and culture? Will revenues contribute to a sustainable economic base or will they only be used for subsistence? What about organized crime and corruption issues, etc.?

Criminalization, Crime, and Antisocial Behavior

By the 1890s, it became illegal to be an Indian and, at the same time, to be a free human being. Native American communities were criminalized by laws that often outlawed their religion, language, dress, social organizations, ceremonies, family structure, marriage patterns, etc. Also, by taking Indian lands, Indians were made criminals if they sought to defend personal property, either real or intangible. Even the movement of reservation Indians was often restricted.

It can be argued that being criminalized creates an environment where crime as such may begin to flourish. When coupled with military defeat; poverty; the shame of being treated as inferiors, as specimens, or as objects for tourists' cameras; the loss of sacred places, of cemeteries, of land itself; we have an explosive mixture leading perhaps to deep depression, alcoholism, drug use, and suicide.

A feeling of hopelessness, a lack of pride, and psychological depression are hardly conducive to becoming a farmer or horticulturalist, especially when poverty, lack of capital, and bureaucratic obstacles are considered. In any case, these quality-of-life issues are fundamental, and research must be carried out relative to how to overcome these impediments to community development.

Land Reform and Land Return

Research needs to be implemented in relation to ways in which adequate land bases can be provided for each Native American community and family desiring such. Indian land claims to federal lands may prove the means for restoring land to many tribes. In other cases, however, we may need to find ways to facilitate the organization of new tribes under the Indian Reorganization Act (IRA). The IRA requires that all persons of one-half or more Indian ancestry be recognized by the Bureau of Indian Affairs as federally recognized Indian individuals. These individuals (Mixtecs, for example) could then pool resources, acquire some land, and form a new tribe, eventually securing reservation status. The procedures involved need to be fully researched.

Other landless Native Americans perhaps will secure land only when the United States decides to break up huge corporate holdings and to encourage family farming. Quite clearly, research needs to be carried out in this area that transcends race and ethnicity.

Tribal Governments and Quality-of-Life Issues

Tribal governments can be responsible for everything that state and local governments normally do, including running tribal school systems. This vast array of responsibilities and powers presents a tremendous opportunity and an incredible challenge. How can most tribes, that are terribly poor, possibly provide the services, planning, leadership, and protection needed? Research in this area will challenge the political economist, the political anthropologist, the public-affairs specialist, and the planner, among others. Fundamental is research relevant to a constitutional amendment or basic federal statute clearly granting the sovereign powers of tribal governments with, at the same time, the economic means to make such powers meaningful. Similar basic research must relate to the revenue issues referred to above to the best means for delivering services within specific cultural context and to alternative patterns of agricultural and economic development that are compatible with tribal values. Tribal governments will usually resent outsiders who pry into their affairs, but will often cooperate fully with researchers who are willing to carry out tasks that are seen to be both feasible and desirable, and that enhance the possibility of self-determination.

SUMMARY

Many rural sociologists, economists, agronomists, and others associated with experiment stations will be amazed at the unique problems presented by Native Americans. At first glance, it might appear that landless Native Americans in the migrant stream or those in small nonreservation communities differ little from their Caucasian, African-American, or Mexican-American rural counterparts. In fact, Native Americans are different because being Indian is a cultural statement, a statement that makes Mayan Guatemalans radically different in fundamental ways from Spanish-speaking Guatemalans, and so on. Mistakes will be made by public agencies until they realize that Native

Americans who maintain their traditional identities and languages have distinctive values and will make different choices. Even greater differences exist when we turn to deal with sovereign reservation governments that, in a sense, can be described as small Lithuanias, Estonias, and Latvias, still preserving a strong sense of their history as independent nations.

Native Americans have often been neglected by university-based researchers who possess practical skills and applied orientations. Most Native Americans have perhaps seen too many theoretical scholars who merely seek to use Native Americans as illustrations for some study to be shared with other academics. But it may well be that tribes and communities will be more receptive to other kinds of researchers, so long as they are not linked to powerful non-Native American interests that have a stake in tribal decisions.

Native American communities need objective research and planning that will empower tribal decision makers providing them with options and not attempting to make decisions for them or to implement some new form of social engineering. Within those parameters, in this writer's judgment, research is both needed and welcome.

NOTE

1. Jack D. Forbes is a professor of Native American Studies and Anthropology and Anthropologist for the Agricultural Experiment Station, University of California, Davis.

REFERENCES

American Indian Policy Review Commission. 1976. *Report on reservation and resource development and protection.* 1976. Washington, D.C.: Government Printing Office.

_____1977. The economics of Indian country. *AIPRC Final Report 1.* Washington, D.C.: Government Printing Office.

Barsh, R. L., and J. Y. Henderson. 1975. Tribal administration of natural resource development. *North Dakota Law Review 52.*

_____1980. The road: *Indian tribes and political liberty.* Berkeley: University of California Press.

Benson, M. 1976. *The Navajo nation and taxation.* Window Rock: DNA People's Legal Services.

Cahn, Edgar, ed. 1969. *Our brother's keeper.* New York: World.

Comptroller General of the United States. 1975. *Indian natural resources—Opportunities for improved management and increased productivity: Part I: Forestland, rangeland, and cropland.* Report to Committee on Interior and Insular Affairs, U.S. Senate.

Deloria, Vine, Jr. 1974. *Behind the trail of broken treaties.* New York: Dell.

Downing, Theodore E. 1985. The crisis in American Indian and non-Indian farming. *Agriculture and Human Values* 2, no. 3 (Summer): 18–24.

Downs, John. 1964. *Animal husbandry in Navajo society and culture.* Berkeley: University of California Press.

Fialka, John J. 1978. The Indians, the royalties and the BIA. *Civil Rights Digest* 10, no. 2 (Winter).

Forbes, Jack D. 1964. *The Indian in America's past.* Englewood Cliffs, N.J.: Prentice-Hall.

_____1981. *Native Americans and Nixon.* Los Angeles: UCLA American Indian Studies Center.

_____1985. *Native American higher education: The struggle for the creation of D-Q University, 1960–1971.* Davis: D-Q University Press.

_____1990. Undercounting Native Americans. *Wicazo Sa Review* 6, no. 1 (Spring): 2–26.

Hoffman, Fred, ed. 1981. *The American Indian family: Strengths and stresses.* Isleta: American Indian Social Research Development Assocation, Inc.

Hunt, R. Douglas. 1985. The first farmers in the Ohio country. *Agriculture and Human Values* 2, no. 3 (Summer): 5–13.

Jorgenson, Joseph G. 1978. A century of political economic effects on American Indian society, 1880–1980. *Journal of Ethnic Studies* 6:3.

Jorgenson, Joseph G., ed. 1978. *Native Americans and energy development.* Cambridge: Anthropology Resource Center.

Lutz, Hartmut. 1980. *D-Q University: Native American self-determination in higher education.* Davis: University of California, Tecumseh Center.

Mathieson, Peter. 1982. *In the spirit of Crazy Horse.* New York: Viking.

Nabham, Gary P. 1985. Native American crop diversity, genetic resource conservation, and the policy of neglect. *Agriculture and Human Values* 2, no. 3 (Summer): 14–18.

Natwig, Eric. 1977. *Development planning in the Navajo nation.* Window Rock: Navajo Nation, Office of Program Development.

Reno, Philip, and Billy Bahe. 1973. Navajo Indian economic planning: The Navajo Indian irrigation project. *New Mexico Business* 26, no. 11 (November): 3–12.

Snipp, C. Matthew. 1989. *American Indians: The first of this land.* New York: Russell Sage Foundation.

Stanley, Sam, ed. 1978. *American Indian economic development.* The Hague: Mouton.

Sutton, Imre. 1975. *Indian land tenure.* New York: Clearwater.

Szasz, Margaret Cornell. [1974] 1977. *Education and the American Indian.* Albuquerque: University of New Mexico Press.

Talbot, Steve. 1981. *Roots of oppression: The American Indian question.* New York: International Publishers.

Thomas, Robert K. 1966–67. Colonialism: classic and internal. *New University Thought* 4 (Winter).

U.S. Congress, Joint Economic Committee. 1969. *Toward economic development of Native American communities.* 2 vols. Washington, D.C.: Government Printing Office.

U.S. Department of Commerce, Bureau of the Census. 1973. *American Indians: 1970 census of population,* PC(2)–1F, Washington, D.C.

University of New Mexico. 1979. Economic development in American Indian reservations. University of New Mexico Development Series, no.1. Albuquerque.

Wilkinson, Charles F. 1987. *American Indians, time, and the law: Native societies in a modern constitutional democracy.* New Haven: Yale University Press.

CHAPTER 8

THE AFRICAN-AMERICAN, FARMING, AND RURAL SOCIETY

Ralph D. Christy[1]

I would make it known that the real danger does not stem from those who seek to grab their share of wealth through force, or from those who try to defend their property through violence, for both of these groups, by their affirmative acts, support the values of the system in which they live. The millions that I would fear are those who do not dream of the prizes that the nation holds forth, for it is in them, though they may not know it, that a revolution has taken place and is biding its time to translate itself into a new and strange way of life. (Richard Wright, *American Hunger*)

INTRODUCTION

The majority of African-Americans, apart from other racial and ethnic groups who came to this country, were brought primarily to serve as slave labor in the agricultural sector of the economy. Since their slave existence, the role of the African-American in the agricultural economy has been influenced by a series of institutional and technological changes that has transformed society profoundly, and has often placed this minority group in a precarious position. Slavery, as a *de jure* institution, was ended by the Emancipation Proclamation of 1863 and nearly four million African-Americans were freed. However, post-emancipation de facto slavery lessened the political, social, and economic freedoms actually attained by African-Americans. As one writer puts it, they realized that their new-found freedom gave them little more than their own clothes, a few tools, and perhaps some farm animals (Marable 1979). Increased productivity in U.S. agriculture (largely attributed to induced technological innovation) was accompanied by the exodus of many African-Americans from agriculture and rural areas as part of the so-called rural/urban population shuffle. Between 1959 and 1969, a rather dramatic shift in African-Americans who were in production agriculture occurred: the number of African-American commercial farm operators in the South declined by 84.1 percent (U.S. Commission on Civil Rights 1982).

Although these institutional and technical changes (and there are many others) were not designed to disadvantage the African-American per se, these changes occurred without the necessary policy and program mechanisms to ease the socioeconomic adjustment for the disadvantaged, many of whom were African-American. Thus, just as one institutional change—the abolishment of slavery—led to a gap in what was expected by the African-American community and what was actually received, so did another driving force—the introduction of capital-intensive technology to agriculture—provide an unfulfilled benefit to African-American farmers and sharecroppers. Both institutional and technological changes have played significant roles in the structural transformation of agriculture and rural society, but the consequences of these changes for the African-American have been little understood (or perhaps understood too late) and, up to the present, have received relatively low priority in social science research and on public policy agendas.

This chapter seeks to identify some contemporary relationships among the agricultural sector, rural society, and the economic and social statuses of the African-American. The chapter has three specific objectives: First, to examine how structural changes in agriculture influenced the role of African-American farmers over the past three decades. Second, to provide an overview of the status of rural (mostly nonfarm), economically disadvantaged African-American residents during the same period. Third, based on these findings, to identify a set of research, education, and outreach issues that should be accorded high priority by social scientists as they seek to address the contemporary social and economic conditions of rural African-Americans.

While a great deal of attention has been given to the overall question of structural change in agriculture (Penn 1979; Dorow 1984; Brewster et al. 1983), relatively little emphasis has been placed on its impact on African-American farmers. Several factors may account for the lack of information on this topic: (1) perceptions that agriculture approaches the competitive model, (2) research programs are relatively new at 1890 institutions, (3) ill-conceived and conflicting public policies, and (4) disparities in economic growth across regions in the United States. Although a major thrust of this paper will focus on the impact of the changing agricultural structure on African-American producers, the consequences of African-Americans exiting the sector have important implications for U.S. urban as well as rural areas.

The problems addressed in this paper require that social scientists, particularly agricultural economists, look beyond traditional boundaries. We must look not only beyond production agriculture to other segments of the food-marketing and distribution system, but we must also look into other sectors of the economy (rural and urban) to fully understand the impacts of the African-American exodus from agriculture on our rural and metropolitan areas. Coughenour and Christenson (1983) observe that such developments as progressive growth in industrial and service jobs in urban areas, improved transportation, the decline in family size, and undesirable central-city lifestyles served to connect rural areas to urban areas. Other researchers have verified an increased interaction between farm and nonfarm labor markets (Huffman 1977) and the associated growth in nonfarm income (Larson 1975, 1976). A myopic view is particularly dangerous when addressing the African-American problems in agriculture and rural society for a clear linkage exists between what some social scientists identify as a "permanent urban underclass" and the exodus of African-Americans from agriculture.

The paper proceeds first by describing trends of African-American participation in production agriculture over the past three decades. Second, selected characteristics of the economically disadvantaged African-American nonfarm population residing in rural America are presented. Finally, attention is devoted to developing a list of research and outreach agenda activities that are directed toward the problems of economically disadvantaged African-Americans residing in rural areas.

THE CHANGING STRUCTURE OF U.S. AGRICULTURE AND THE DECLINE OF THE AFRICAN-AMERICAN FARMER

The structure of agriculture is taken to mean how farm resources are organized and controlled. Structure includes the number and size of farms, the ownership and control of farm land, capital and labor, the arrangements for inputs and product market, and other factors that affect decision making, the control of resources, and, otherwise, the behavior of producers. Changes in the structure of agriculture raise questions about the distribution of wealth and income among farm operators, farm workers, and others who own and supply farm resources, as well as about whether new farmers can get a start in farming by any means other than inheritance. But, the structure issue has more than a direct relationship to the agricultural sector and rural communities; included is the linkage to broader problems beyond the farm gate and rural limits. Neoclassical economics provides a limited conceptual framework for explaining the exodus of firms from a market.

Several factors invalidate the competitive model assumption of free entry and exit as it relates to agriculture as an industry. Penn (1979, 17) states that "at no time in our history have people had unlimited opportunity to take up farming" due to high land prices, the lack of credit, and the cost of farm equipment. Also, the asset-fixity characteristic of agriculture has been well documented as well as the associated price and income problems (Johnson and Quance 1972; Hathaway 1964; Coffman 1970).

Economists are usually quick to apply standard economic principles to an industry that is experiencing rapid structural changes. These principles do not always explain market behavior. It is difficult to justify, in theory and in observation, the economic position that firms exiting a market somehow represent an efficient use of resources for society because the process is reflective of rational business decisions or efficient market outcomes (Shaffer 1987). This has particular implications for the African-American in production agriculture because the entry/exit assumption of the model is not likely to hold. Since entry costs are relatively high, the economically disadvantaged minority will find it difficult to enter production agriculture. Data from the U.S. Census of Agriculture indicate that African-American-owned resources in production agriculture have exited at an alarming rate. Thus, structural changes in the agricultural sector have had a disproportional negative impact on African-Americans because of the inaccessibility to capital markets, educational opportunities, and technical assistance from public and private sources.[2]

NUMBER AND SIZE OF FARMS

Table 1 represents the number of farms in the United States and in the South for selected years 1954, 1978, and 1987. The total number of farms in the United States has declined by 51 percent between 1954 and 1987. The total number of non-Caucasian farms declined by 91 percent from 481,601 in 1954 to 44,640 in 1987. Caucasian farms declined by 48 percent from 4,301,420 to 2,087,759 during the same time period. Thus, over the period of study, minority farms disappeared at almost double the rate of Caucasian farms. Moreover, in 1954, non-Caucasian farms made up 10 percent of the total farms in the United States compared to 2 percent by 1987. Conversely, Caucasian farms, which made up 90 percent of all farms in 1954, accounted for 98 percent of the total number of farms in the United States.

A similar pattern emerges if we examine the trends in farm decline in the South, a region where the majority of African-American farms exist. Non-Caucasian farms declined by 94 percent compared to a 56 percent decline for Caucasian farms between 1954 and 1987 (Table 1). Further, non-Caucasian farms in 1954 accounted for almost 20 percent of all farms but by 1987 they only accounted for 3 percent of all Southern farms.

Beale (1966) reports that the number of minority farms (mostly African-American) peaked in 1920 at 926,000 farms. The number remained about 800,000 until 1935. Since then, with the exception of the war years between 1940 and 1950, the number of minority-owned farms has declined drastically, and some would argue irreversibly.

The general trend in U.S. production agriculture is toward larger farm sizes. Between 1954 and 1987, the average farm increased in size from 256 acres to 462 acres. This increment in size represented a 43 percent growth rate. However, the growth rate in the size of minority farms was skewed by large land holding of Native Americans. In 1987, Native Americans owned 45.6 million acres (87.8 percent of land owned by minorities). Non-Caucasian farms increased in size from an average of 120.5 acres in 1954 to an average size of 681 in 1978 due largely to the

TABLE 1: NUMBER OF FARMS, LAND IN FARMS, AND AVERAGE FARM SIZE BY RACE AND REGION: 1954—87
(Figures in parentheses indicate percentages.)

Item	1954		1978		1987	
	Non-Caucasian	Caucasian	Non-Caucasian	Caucasian	Non-Caucasian	Caucasian
Number of Farms	481,601 (10.1)	4,301,420 (89.9)	79,916 (3.2)	2,398,726 (96.8)	44,640 (2.1) 22,954[1] (1.1)	2,087,759 (97.9)
LAND IN FARMS (ACRES)	58,050,255 (5.0)	1,101,993,599 (95.0)	54,463,881 (5.4)	975,230,654 (94.7)	51,974,575 (5.3) 2,636,896[1] (.003)	964,470,625 (94.7)
AVERAGE FARM SIZE (ACRES)	120	256	681	406	115[1]	462
SOUTH						
NUMBER OF FARMS	459,907 (19.9)	1,853,820 (80.1)	61,355 (6.0)	954,009 (94.0)	26,735 20,566[1] (2.4)	820,885
LAND IN FARMS (ACRES)	20,979,138 (5.4)	366,022,737 (94.6)	3,895,237 (1.2)	306,618,493	3,970,697 2,120,242[1] (.007)	280,634,246
AVERAGE FARM SIZE (ACRES)	45	197	63	321	148 103[1]	342

[1]African-American farms only.
Source: *Census of Agriculture*, U.S. Department of Commerce, Bureau of the Census (1956, 1980, 1987).

exodus of African-American farmers and the relatively large land holdings of Native Americans. African-American average farm size grew modestly from 104 acres in 1982 to 115 acres in 1987.

LAND

The decline in the number of non-Caucasian farms needs not necessarily result in a decline in the amount of land owned by minority farmers. Nevertheless, the best available data suggest that as the number of minority farms declined so did the amount of minority-owned farm land. Since 1910, the amount of land owned by minority (African-American) farmers has steadily decreased, with the exception of the period from 1940 to 1950. During that one decade, under the relatively prosperous conditions stimulated by a war economy and the immediate post-war period, both the numbers of minority farmers who owned land and the amount of land owned increased. Since that time, the gains of the 1940s have disappeared. Hall (1935) reports that the peak period for minority-owned land was in 1920 when 13,949,000 acres were controlled by African-American farm operations. By 1987, 22,954 African-American-owned farms held 2,636,896 acres of land, representing a net loss of 11.3 million acres. The amount of land owned by African-American farmers continued to be proportionately less than land owned by Caucasian farmers.

Several factors contributed to the decline of African-American-owned farmland in the United States, including credit policy, rural education, and intergenerational transfers. The problem of intergenerational transfer of property seems to be a major factor contributing to land loss by minorities in agriculture.

TENURE CHARACTERISTICS

Tenure characteristics of farmers are a primary measure of control of resources in agriculture (Table 2). In the United States, typically, non-Caucasian farmers made up a larger percent of the tenant-operated farms than did Caucasian farmers in that category. In 1954, approximately 60 percent of the non-Caucasian farms were operated by tenants as compared to 20 percent of the Caucasian farms. However, by 1987, non-Caucasian tenant farms consisted of 13 percent of all non-Caucasian farms (representing a fourfold reduction) while Caucasian tenant farms had fallen to slightly less than 12 percent. Similar trends existed in the South.[3] In 1954, 60 percent of the non-Caucasian farms were tenants and by 1987, the percentage had fallen to 15 percent. Southern Caucasian tenant farms declined from about 21 percent in 1954 to slightly over 9 percent in 1987.

While the percentage of non-Caucasian tenant farms declined between 1954 and 1987, the percentage of non-Caucasian full owners almost doubled during the time period. The percentage of Caucasian full owners remained fairly constant, relative to non-Caucasian farms, between 1954–1987. The South exhibited a fairly consistent trend with respect to full owner farms between Caucasian and non-Caucasian farms.

TABLE 2: TENURE CHARACTERISTICS OF FARMS FOR THE U.S. AND THE SOUTH (Figures in parentheses indicate percentages.)

Item	United States		South	
	Non-Caucasian	Caucasian	Non-Caucasian	Caucasian
		1954		
FULL OWNERS	139,987 (29.1)	2,604,730 (60.8)	124,257 (28.8)	1,047,275 (62.9)
PART OWNERS	54,068 (11.2)	814,112 (19.0)	48,045 (11.1)	274,255 (16.5)
TENANTS	286,897 (59.7)	862,342 (20.1)	259,202 (60.1)	343,975 (20.7)
		1987		
FULL OWNERS	28,407 (53.6)	1,238,547 (59.1)	16,240 (60.2)	524,079 (65.0)
PART OWNERS	9,996 (33.4)	609,012 (29.4)	6,577 (24.8)	207,133 (25.7)
TENANTS	6,237 (12.9)	240,200 (11.5)	3,975 (15.0)	74,897 (9.3)

Source: *Census of Agriculture,* U.S. Department of Commerce, Bureau of the Census (1956, 1987).

TABLE 3: VALUE OF PRODUCTS SOLD BY NON-CAUCASIAN AND CAUCASIAN FARM OPERATORS IN 1987 (Figures in parentheses indicate percentages.)

Item	United States 1987		United States 1982	
	Non-Caucasian	Caucasian	Non-Caucasian	Caucasian
$20,000 OR MORE	12,745 (30.8)	808,979 (38.7)	15,977 (29.4)	883,956 (39.5)
$2,500 TO $19,999	13,672 (30.6)	788,484 (37.7)	15,775 (29.0)	819,017 (36.6)
LESS THAN $2,500	17,223 (38.6)	490,296 (23.6)	22,391 (41.2)	536,327 (23.9)

Source: *Census of Agriculture,* U. S. Department of Commerce, Bureau of the Census (1987).

VALUE OF PRODUCTS BY SALE CATEGORY

Census data on the value of products sold were collected across three sales categories. Within each category, the sum of all crops, livestock, and poultry sales is included. According to recent census data (Table 3), over one-third of non-Caucasian farmers had sales less than $2,500, and just under one-third were in the $2,500 to $19,999 sales category. By contrast,Caucasian farmers are distributed across each sales category with 23 percent of the farms in the less than $2,500 bracket, 37 percent in the $2,500 to $19,999 category, and 38 percent in the greater than $20,000 category.

THE AFRICAN-AMERICAN IN A CHANGING RURAL ECONOMY

Since the end of World War II, rural America has undergone radical change as its once primary industry, agriculture, experienced remarkable gains in productivity. This economic growth was characteristic of the previous decade but, during the 1980s, rural America experienced structural change and economic dislocation. Fundamental to these economic changes is a new set of more complex problems as our economy shifts toward global markets and service-based industries, as federal support for rural communities declines, and as deregulation of financial markets places constraints on sources of private-sector funding.

The analysis of impacts of the fundamental changes occurring in rural America on the African-American must consider demographic realities. In the United States, over 90 percent of African-Americans resided in the South at the turn of the century, and despite the tremendous outflow of African-Americans from the rural South, the southern region of this country still contains more than half of the African-American population (Lichter and Heaton 1986). More importantly, Lichter and Heaton further observe that well over 90 percent of all nonmetropolitan African-Americans resided in the South. Therefore, an analysis of the social and economic well-being of the rural African-American must focus on the development of the rural South.

One of the most significant characteristics of rural America during the 1980s has been the upward trend in the poverty rate (Table 4). The 1987 Bureau of the Census data indicated that 16.9 percent of those people living in

TABLE 4: DISTRIBUTION OF POVERTY BY HOUSEHOLD TYPES, 1988
NON-METROPOLITAN AREAS

Item	All Races	Caucasian	African-American
ALL PERSONS	16.9	13.7	44.1
FAMILIES	15.1	11.9	42.4
MALES	23.4	20.7	42.2
FEMALES	32.6	29.1	69.6
FEMALE-HEADED HOUSEHOLD, NO HUSBAND PRESENT	44.8	35.8	63.0

Source: *Poverty in the United States 1987*, Current Population Reports, Consumer Income Series P–60, No. 163, U.S. Department of Commerce, Bureau of the Census, February 1989.

nonmetropolitan areas had incomes below the poverty level—up from 12.6 percent in 1970. The national poverty rate fell from 22.2 percent in 1960 to 13.5 percent in 1987. Sawhill (1988, 1082) points out that "...most of this progress occurred in the 1960s...by 1969 the rate had fallen to 12.1 percent. It remained between 11 and 13 percent for the entire decade of the 1970s, and then increased again during the early 1980s." Poverty rates are especially high among racial and ethnic minorities. For example, the poverty rate was 44.1 percent among African-Americans as compared to 13.7 percent for Caucasians in 1987. For all family categories, the poverty rates for African-Americans are three to four times higher than exist in rural America on the average.

Many segments of rural America are responsive to major sectoral shifts and macroeconomic changes that act as a tide—when the tide waters are high, they lift all boats and vice versa. However, there is growing evidence that a persistent group, the economically disadvantaged, is a visible component of our society, and this subset, for the most part, seems to be immune to aggregate social and economic forces. Wilson (1987, 8) defines the underclass as "...that heterogenous grouping of families and individuals who are outside the mainstream of the American occupational system. Included...are individuals who lack training and skills and either experience long-term underemployment...and families that experience long-term spells of poverty and/or welfare dependence." The term "underclass," as defined by Wilson (1987), also includes individuals who exhibit socially deviate behavioral patterns (values and culture) that may differ from rural people experiencing *long-term* or *persistent poverty*. To date, little is known about the complex causal links among economic conditions, family structure, and individual or group values.

Although individuals and family units may experience poverty, it is important to note that in some counties—particularly in the South[4]—poverty persists. A county with *persistent poverty* has had per capita income in the lowest quintile, i.e., the lowest 20 percent in terms of per capita incomes among counties in the United States for at least decades (Bellamy and Ghelfi 1989). These counties are characterized by having low educational levels, poor health (physical disabilities) and high portions of its population African-American. Bellamy and Ghelfi note that poor counties have lower per capita income than those counties that improved between 1979 and 1984. Understanding the characteristics of these counties may suggest policy alternatives for enhancing the socioeconomic conditions of their residents.

Policy makers at all levels are concerned with the economic health of rural America. Agricultural and rural-sector policies are beginning to change. Today agricultural policy is seen to have less of an impact on rural development goals than it did several decades ago when the terms "agriculture" and "rural" were almost synonymous. As the economic organization and public policy environment change, rural development policies must adapt to the changing economic and social conditions to encourage an economic development that will reach disadvantaged groups. Because the cause of poverty is multifaceted and not fully understood, public policy alternatives directed toward the reduction of poverty are misdirected and sometimes conflict in objectives and impacts. It is commonly recognized, though, that individuals experiencing poverty are generally less educated and exhibit unstable employment histories.

CONCLUSIONS

This paper has argued that institutional and technological changes are fundamental forces important to transforming agriculture and rural society. Understanding how these changes influence the economic well-being of rural African-Americans is a difficult task. We can assume, however, that institutional and technological changes without sufficient human capital development can disproportionately distribute the benefits of such changes. The National Academy of Sciences' Committee on the Status of Black Americans, in an attempt to document the consequences of social, economic, and political changes in the African-American community in comparison to Caucasian-Americans, concluded that gains had occurred within the African-American population (Jaynes and Williams 1989). However, relative to the mainstream, the African-American, in many respects, was falling further behind. These comparisons were drawn to emphasize a common destiny shared by all Americans. This nation must realize, as it competes in a global economy, that its future is tied to the health, education, and development of all its people.

It is widely recognized that the structure of U.S. agriculture has changed substantially over the past three decades. Traditional economic theory does not explain totally the exit of firms, particularly African-American firms, from markets. Institutional changes, as market interventions, are a major factor influencing the structure of agriculture. The impact of this structural change on African-American involvement in farming was presented. The total number of non-Caucasian farms declined 89 percent between 1954 and 1982 compared to 48 percent exit rate for Caucasian farms. With the exodus of African-American farmers, land ownership of non-Caucasians declined from an all-time high of 13.9 million acres in 1920 to 3.4 million acres in 1982. Further, the major loss of non-Caucasian farms occurred among tenants while the percentage of full owners of non-Caucasian farms increased.

The nonfarm African-American in rural areas continues, in the most recent decade, to experience high levels of poverty. By all comparisons—family or individual—poverty among rural African-Americans is three to four times the average rural poverty rate. Further, poverty has been on the rise since the late 1970s. And, in some counties of the rural South, chronic poverty has persisted for three decades.

These characteristics of rural African-American life suggest the need for a better understanding of:

- Relationships between aggregate economic conditions and the economic well-being of the poor.
- Rural/urban labor market linkages.
- Impacts of alternative human capital policies and programs (such as Headstart and Job Corps).
- Relationships among economic structure, family, and individual values.
- New theories of rural development that encompass social, economic, and political variables.
- Impacts of international trade policy on the economic and social well-being of rural African-Americans.
- How economic concentration within the U.S. food system relates to African-American participants in firm ownership and entrepreneural development.
- Influences of economic structure and public policy on poor female-headed households.
- New data and information systems needed to monitor and evaluate economic performance.

NOTES

1. Ralph D. Christy is an associate professor in the Department of Agricultural Economics and Agribusiness at Louisiana State University, Baton Rouge.

2. I am indebted to Carlton Davis for his observation that neoclassical firm theory is characterized by the "economic efficiency" criteria for judging a firm's performance. The theory implicitly ignores initial resource endowment or access to such resources of firms. As such, it ignores the maldistribution of resources stemming from institutional forces.

3. Tenant farming has considerable differences in its institutional make-up across regions in the United States. For example, tenant farmers in the South, historically, have exhibited a different (more unequitable) relationship with land owners as compared to tenant farmers in the Midwest where the relationship between tenant and land owner was more equitable. For a theoretical discussion of the implications of different tenure arrangements on resource allocation, see George Beckford (1983, 154–77).

4. More than 90 percent of the U.S. counties experiencing persistent poverty are located in the South.

REFERENCES

Beale, Calvin L. 1966. The Negro in American agriculture. In *The American Negro reference book*. Edited by John P. Davis, 170–207. Reprint. Washington, D.C.: U.S. Dept. of Agriculture.

Beckford, George L. 1983. *Persistent poverty: Underdevelopment in plantation economics of the Third World*. London: Zed Books; Totowa, N.J.: distributed in the United States by Biblio Distribution Center.

Bellamy, Donald, and Linda M. Ghelfi. 1989. Southern persistently low-income counties: Social and economic characteristics. In *Rural development issues of the nineties: Perspectives from the social sciences*. Edited by Thomas T. Williams et al. The 47th annual Professional Agricultural Workers Conference proceedings, School of Agriculture and Human Economics, G. W. Carver Agricultural Experiment Station, Tuskegee University, Tuskegee, Ala.

Brewster, David E., Wayne D. Rasmussen, and Garth Youngberg, eds. 1983. *Farms in transition: Interdisciplinary perspectives on farm structure*. Ames: Iowa State University Press.

Coffman, George W. 1970. Entry and exit barriers and incentives. *Structure issues of American agriculture*, Agricultural Economic Report 438, U.S. Dept. of Agriculture, Economic Research Service, Washington, D.C., November.

Coughenour, Milton C., and James A. Christenson. 1983. Farm structure, social class and farmers' policy perspectives. In *Farms in transition*. Edited by David E. Brewster et al. Ames: Iowa State University Press.

Dorow, Norbert A. 1984. The farm structure of the future trends and issues. *The farm and food system in transition*. FS 117. East Lansing: Michigan State University, Cooperative Extension Service.

Hall, Charles E. 1935. *Negroes in the United States: 1920–1932*. U.S. Bureau of Census. Washington, D.C.: Government Printing Office.

Hathaway, Dale E. 1964. *Problems of progress in the agricultural economy*. Glenview, Ill.: Scott, Foresman and Co.

Huffman, Wallace E. 1977. Interaction between farm and nonfarm labor markets. *American Journal of Agricultural Economics* 59.

Jaynes, Gerald D., and Robin M. Williams Jr., eds. 1989. *A common destiny: Blacks and American society*. Washington, D.C.: National Academy Press.

Johnson, Glenn L., and LeRoy Quance, eds. 1972. *The overproduction trap in U.S. Agriculture*. Baltimore: The Johns Hopkins University Press.

Larson, Donald K. 1975. Economic class as a measure of farmers' welfare. *American Journal of Agricultural Economics* 57.

_____1976. Impact of off-farm income on family farm income levels. *Agricultural Finance Review* 36.

Lichter, Daniel T., and T. M. B. Heaton. 1986. Black composition and change in the nonmetropolitan south. *Rural Sociology* 51, no. 3.

Marable, Manning. 1979. The land question in historical perspective: The economics of poverty in the blackbelt south, 1865–1920. In *The black rural landowner-endangered species*. Edited by Leo McGee and Robert Boone. Westport, Conn.: Greenwood Press.

Penn, J. B. 1979. The structure of agriculture: An overview of the issue. *Structure issues of American agriculture*, Agricultural Economic Report 438, U.S. Dept. of Agriculture, Economic Research Service, Washington, D.C., November.

Sawhill, Isabel V. 1988. Poverty in the U.S.: Why is it so persistent? *Journal of Economic Literature* 26:1073–1119.

Shaffer, James D. 1987. Does the concept of economic efficiency meet the standards for truth in labeling when used as a norm in policy analysis? In *Economic efficiency in agricultural and food marketing*. Edited by Richard L. Kilmer and Walter J. Armbruster. Ames: Iowa State University Press.

U.S. Commission on Civil Rights. 1982. *The decline of black farming in America*, Washington, D.C., February.

U.S. Department of Commerce, Bureau of the Census. 1956a. *U.S. census of agriculture 1954: Counties and state economic areas*. Vol. 1, Part 17. Washington, D.C.: Government Printing Office.

——1956b. *U.S. census of agriculture 1954: General report*. Vol. 2. Washington, D.C.: Government Printing Office.

——1980a. *1978 census of agriculture: Summary and state data*. Vol. 1, Part 51. Washington, D.C.: Government Printing Office.

——1980b. *1978 census of agriculture: State and county data*. Vol. 1, Part 10. Washington, D.C.: Government Printing Office.

——1980c. Farm population of the United States: 1979. *Current population report*, ser. P–27, no. 53, Washington, D.C.

——1989. Poverty in the United States: 1987. *Current population report*, ser. P–60, no. 163, Washington, D.C.

Wilson, Julius W. 1987. *The truly disadvantaged: The inner city, the under class, and public policy*. Chicago: University of Chicago Press.

Wright, Richard. 1977. *American Hunger*. New York: Harper & Row

CHAPTER 9

INCREASING HEALTH IN RURAL AMERICA: RESEARCH ISSUES DURING A TRANSITIONAL PERIOD

Robert D. Stevens[1]

THE NEED FOR INCREASED HEALTH LEVELS IN RURAL AREAS

With the acceleration of economic and social change in rural America as we approach the twenty-first century, the amount of investment in human capital in rural areas will increasingly influence the opportunities and constraints for one-quarter of the people in the United States. After food, clothing, and shelter have been assured, educational level and health status become the key variables in human performance. Considerable state and local decision making is focused on how to improve education (see Huffman; Part III, Section 2, Chapter 2). Less public concern is currently shown about the availability and quality of rural health services. In some rural areas, reductions are now occurring in health services. Due to the limitation of space, this paper does not include examination of research needs concerning the very serious problems of scarce psychiatric and substance abuse services in rural areas.

Inadequate rural health services impose large personal and social costs (Baker, O'Neill, and Karpt 1984, Figures 3–13). Farming is now the most dangerous industrial occupation. For the rural working poor, many of whom lack health insurance, a trip to a doctor is fraught with large economic risk to the family—a trip to be postponed for as long as possible. This delayed health care often causes a more serious health problem, with resulting lower lifetime health status. Lack of adequate access to health services and poor-quality services over the long run has a large social cost for it dooms many rural areas to stagnant growth, or decline. Such an area is unlikely to attract retirees or other rural residents, or industries that have higher socioeconomic status employees. Accessible, adequate rural health services of high quality are essential for an economically strong rural society.

What value has the United States placed on good quality health care for rural America? Over the years, humanitarian and other concerns led to the development of some health and other programs to attempt to assure that rural citizens have access to the services of a modern industrialized society. These programs included rural electrification; additional state funds for poorer school districts; the Hill-Burton Hospital Construction Act of 1946 that increased hospital availability; community health centers; Medicare health insurance for the elderly; and welfare programs, including Medicaid, that provided a safety net for the poor. These programs indicate a social agreement that all citizens should have reasonable access to basic human services. Such access has not yet been assured for health services. To achieve this, an effective rural health-service network, including urban hospitals and other urban services, is implied.

Today, the competitive model of rural health care has led, in many areas, to a confusing patchwork of different efforts to assure adequate rural health care, with many areas and many low-income people poorly served, including particularly low-income minorities. The history of U.S. public policy for rural people and economic realities suggests that the present competition model will be modified so that some more integrated, partly locally controlled, regionalization of health-service systems will emerge. Such systems would achieve greater access for all, increase the quality of rural health care, and achieve greater cost-effectiveness. Thus, in many areas, rural health services are facing a transition to new arrangements.

THE COMPLEMENTARITY OF INVESTMENTS IN HUMAN HEALTH WITH OTHER INVESTMENTS IN HUMAN PRODUCTIVITY

To remain competitive in the world economy, the United States is increasingly dependent on greater human investment. The need for greater investment in education is recognized nationally (see Huffman; Part III, Section 2, Chapter 2). The high complementarity of investments in health to educational investments is not always recognized. Two central aspects of this complementarity are the relationships between: (1) health and school performance, and (2) health and a person's productive years of labor. Good rural health care for children enables maximum participation in kindergarten-through-high-school education. Decreased days of schooling due to ill health, with attendant, often serious, problems of getting behind in school work, low grades, and the associated psychological problems resulting in increased school dropouts, reduce the potential quantity and quality of the educational investment in rural human capital and in the levels of school performance. Of equal importance is the effect of poor health care on the private and social rate-of-return on other human investments. Reduced length of life and more disability days, especially during the working years, due to poor health knowledge and inadequate access to health services, reduce the returns to society from the human investments made. And, of equal importance, they reduce the private contributions a person makes to his family. Thus, poor health-care services in rural areas undermine the returns from other private and social investments in rural people.

INCREASING DIVERSITY, INSTABILITY, AND CHANGE IN RURAL AMERICA

Rural America is increasingly being integrated into a dynamic, service-oriented, urban society. This is causing greater diversity in rural America. The diversity requires flexibility in rural health-care delivery systems. The perception of rural America as predominantly composed of an economically stable and physically healthy farming industry contrasts sharply with today's reality. Such perceptions are "...nothing more than folklore, fiction, and mythology" (Cordes 1989, 780). Knowledge of the realities of a changing rural America is essential for relevant research to increase health. One indicator of diversity is population density. Almost all of the counties with fewer than six persons per square mile (the so-called frontier counties) are west of the 98th meridian that runs north from the southern tip of Texas. (See additional research on the rural population at the Zip Code level in de la Torre, Fickenscher, and Luft [forthcoming].) Providing health services to the few people scattered over large areas of the rural West is a different challenge from providing health services in rural Michigan for example, where average population density was 163 per square mile in 1989.

The current great diversity of rural America is illuminated by research by Bender et al. (1985) that grouped rural counties according to their most important economic activity (Table 1). They report, that in 1980 only 702 of the 2,374 nonmetropolitan counties in the United States were farming-dependent (largely concentrated in the Plains portion of the North-Central Region). Farming-dependent counties were defined as having a weighted annual average of 20 percent, or more, of total labor and proprietor income from farming. Nearly as many rural counties (678), concentrated in the Southeast, were manufacturing-dependent. In these counties, manufacturing contributed 30 percent or more to total labor and proprietor income in 1979. Other groups of counties were found to be: dependent on mining (200), concentrated in Appalachia and in the West; dependent on specialized government activities (315), scattered throughout the country; persistent poverty counties (242), concentrated in the South, especially along the Mississippi Delta and in Appalachia; and federal lands counties (247), concentrated in the West. Finally, a large number of counties (515) were found to be primarily retirement destination counties, concentrated in several Northern Lake States and in the South and Southwest. The diverse economic and social climates of rural counties, as illustrated in this study, have somewhat different health-services needs.

The amount of change in rural areas since 1940 is not often appreciated. Bluestone and Daberkow (1985) pointed out that in 1940 four of ten jobs in nonmetropolitan areas were in natural resource industries (agriculture, forestry, fishing, and mining). By 1980, these industries provided less than one job in ten. "...by 1980 the service industries, manufacturing and construction had come to dominate economic activity in nonmetro areas, much as they do in metro areas" (Bluestone and Daberkow 1985, 34).

The increasing instability and vulnerability of rural counties was shown by Cordes (1989) to be due to at least three factors. One has been the accelerated flow of population first into rural counties during the "rural renaissance" of the 1970s, and then again, in the 1980s, a reverse flow leading to slower rural growth (see Beegle; Part III, Section 2, Chapter 5). The second factor is that rural areas have become industrially more like the rest of the economy. Thus, they have increasingly become more subject to the same cycles of economic activity, except that rural areas have often lagged behind the rest of the economy during a recovery. Finally, the increased linkage between the United States and the world economy has meant that the forces of international trade increasingly have an impact on rural America. In many cases, the changes in population dynamics and the breakdown of isolated rural economies have weakened an already fragile health safety net. Funding sources for health services in rural areas need to be stable to assure that during local recessions large investments in human capital are not lost. As in K–12 education, state and/or federal arrangements are needed to assure health service availability for all, especially during local economic downturns.

RURAL PEOPLE ARE IN POORER HEALTH

Good health is often associated with the rural image. The data on rural health show the opposite. Age alone is a cause for a greater proportion of persons over age 65 to live in nonmetropolitan areas in every region of the United States (Norton and McManus 1989, Table 2). Limitations of activities of daily living were found for 15.9 percent of nonmetropolitan persons, while 13.4 percent of metropolitan residents had such limitations (Norton and McManus 1989, 746). In assessing their own health status during this National Health Interview Survey, 13.3 percent of nonmetropolitan residents stated that their health was fair or poor, while only 9.4 percent of metropolitan residents considered their health condition to be fair or poor (Norton and McManus 1989, Table 70). A Robert Wood Johnson Foundation (1987) survey indicates that 14 percent of the people in nonmetropolitan counties reported that they were in fair or poor health, while in metropolitan areas only 10.9 reported this. In nonmetropolitan areas, 23.4 percent of the people had chronic or serious illnesses in contrast to 18.7 percent in metropolitan areas. Respondents in nonmetropolitan areas reported higher rates of health problems in five of the six chronic illness groupings, (Norton and McManus 1989, 751). Injury death rates are also very much higher in rural areas (Baker, O'Neill, and

TABLE 1: SELECTED CHARACTERISTICS OF DIFFERENT TYPES OF NONMETRO COUNTIES

Characteristics	Types of NonMetro County								
	Farming Dependent	Mfg. Dependent	Mining Dependent	Govern-ment	Persistent Poverty	Federal Lands	Destina-tion Retire-ment	Un-grouped	All Non-Metro Counties
Average Population, 1980	11,932	35,974	20,049	28,819	15,174	22,094	27,486	27,798	25,813
Urban population, 1980	16.4%	32.1%	29.6%	30.8%	12.7%	29.9%	25.9%	40.1%	28.6%
Population per square mile	18.3	65.9	29.2	47.2	29.9	15.4	42.4	44.1	42.0
Persons 65 and over, 1980	15.8%	12.9%	11.5%	12.3%	3.5%	11.3%	15.2%	14.4%	14.0%
Race and ethnicity									
African-American	6.4%	12.1%	2.4%	7.4%	23.3%	1.6%	7.0%	8.2%	8.4%
Hispanic surnames	4.2%	1.2%	8.4%	6.4%	2.8%	6.9%	4.6%	3.4%	3.8%
Persons 25 and over who completed high school, 1980	58.0%	54.4%	56.0%	60.8%	41.9%	68.6%	56.4%	59.1%	57.5%
Household headed by female, 1980	8.4%	11.4%	8.9%	10.8%	14.0%	8.5%	9.7%	10.4%	10.0%
Population aged 16–64 disabled but not institutionalized, 1980	9.8%	10.9%	10.8%	10.4%	14.8%	9.8%	11.9%	9.6%	10.4%
Median family income, 1980	$13,928	$16,272	$17,016	$15,257	$11,923	$16,722	$15,020	$15,442	$15,786
Transfer payments, 1979									
Per capita	$1,045	$1,022	$1,009	$1,085	$1,049	$1,030	$1,148	$1,087	$1,063
As percent of earned income	27%	24%	24%	41%	41%	25%	34%	26%	27%

Source: U.S. Department of Agriculture. *The Diverse Social and Economic Structure of Nonmetropolitan America.* Report prepared by D. Lloyd Bender, Bernal L. Green, and Thomas F. Hady et al. Rural Development Research Report No. 49, Washington, DC: GPO, September 1985. *Note:* All data are unweighted county averages.

Karpt 1984, Figures 3–13). In part, poorer health in rural areas can be explained by differing levels of access among states to Medicaid insurance (Erdman and Wolfe 1987).

LESS ACCESS TO HEALTH SERVICES IN RURAL AREAS

A critical factor in health is good access to health care (for measures of access, see Aday, Fleming, and Anderson 1984). Most studies indicate that many rural populations have limited access due to such factors as greater poverty (see Beegle; Part III, Section 2, Chapter 5), lack of health insurance, and fewer services. Fifteen percent of the nonmetropolitan population was uninsured compared to 12 percent of the metropolitan population in 1984. Also, fewer rural people were found to have private health insurance with its greater coverage (Rowland and Lyons 1989).

A regular source of care also influences a person's access to health care. Fewer rural residents reported they had a regular source of health care (Robert Wood Johnson Foundation 1987). Access is also influenced by out-of-pocket costs and opportunity costs. The higher transportation costs and associated opportunity costs of rural residents for visits to distant health services decreases access. In summary, rural people, who are older and poorer, are more likely to be: (a) without a regular source of health care, (b) without health insurance, (c) in fair or poor health, or (d) contending with a chronic or serious illness (Norton and McManus 1989, 728). In some rural areas, important minority groups have particularly poor access to health services.

The generally lower level of access to health care in rural areas is demonstrated by much empirical data. An example is the number of physician contacts per year in 1985; 5.4 within metropolitan statistical areas (MSAs), and 4.9 outside MSAs (Norton and McManus 1989, 750). The availability of health care is a particular problem for many with Medicaid insurance in rural areas. Often Medicaid reimbursement levels are so low that physicians refuse to take patients with Medicaid insurance. Thus, to find care, many poor rural people have to pay the costs of traveling longer distances to find physicians willing to accept them. Ninety-mile trips for monthly prenatal visits for women with Medicaid insurance are currently occurring in some rural areas of the Midwest. The Joint Task Force (1989) report documents the unfolding rural health crisis.

THE ROLE OF RESEARCH ON THE ECONOMICS OF RURAL HEALTH

The six roles of research that were identified for community and human resources in the Executive Summary of the Woodlands Inn Conference (Johnson and Bonnen 1988) apply directly to the problem of the low health status of rural people. To be effective, rural health research will need to contribute to: (1) understanding the changes occurring in rural communities; (2) helping rural communities manage change; (3) helping solve the problems of disadvantaged rural people; (4) improving rural communities, facilities, and services; (5) improving local governments; and (6) sustaining the viability of rural communities.

THE SOURCE OF DEMAND FOR ECONOMIC AND OTHER SOCIAL SCIENCE RESEARCH ON THE HEALTH SECTOR

Recently, the source of the demand for economic and other social science research in society has become clarified. The demand for knowledge in economics and the other social sciences is derived from the demand for improvements in the performance of social and economic systems. T. W. Schultz in 1968 pointed to the rising cost of labor as a major initiator of institutional innovation that sought to increase economic performance. As in the health field today, institutional change is commonly stimulated by the need to enable more cost-effective use of new high-cost technology, or higher-cost human capital, in such forms as physician specialties. Examples of such institutional changes are the recent arrangements that enable smaller rural hospitals to share mobile computed tomography body scanning technology. Demands for institutional change may also come from changes in voters' attitudes about society's responsibilities. The demand for some kind of health service safety net for the poor illustrates such a change. This change occurred in the 1960s with the enactment of the Federal-State Medicaid program, and is surfacing again because so many persons in the United States still do not have health insurance. Some estimates place the figure as high as 37 million persons.

Ruttan (1984) pointed out that advances in knowledge in the social sciences enable the costs of institutional innovation to be reduced, just as advances in knowledge in the biological sciences, whether in agriculture or in medicine, enable the development of more cost-effective technologies.[2] Economic and social science research discovers new, more productive institutional arrangements. It also aids decision making by evaluating the cost-effectiveness of alternative institutions and technologies. In the institutional area, it aids in designing new health policies and in arranging for improved reimbursement arrangements. Medical research, in contrast, focuses on new technologies and medications as well as the associated surgical and medical procedures.

Research in the economic and other social sciences, as in medical research, is an economic activity, that uses resources. Thus, the demand for problem-solving and subject-matter economic and social research on rural health problems depends, in general, upon the expected returns from the allocation of scarce public and private resources to this research. In periods of little economic and social change when satisfaction with health services is high, the economic and social returns from additional research are likely to be low. However, in periods of change, and when dissatisfaction with the performance and cost-effectiveness of the health-care system is high, as today, the returns to such research are likely to be high.

A FRAMEWORK FOR ANALYSIS OF FACTORS AFFECTING HEALTH STATUS

The health status of an individual depends on: (a) personal factors such as environment, lifestyle, and the effectiveness of self-care, and (b) the accessibility of health services. The level of health a person experiences is produced by both the individual through lifestyle and self-care activities and the use of needed health services. Erroneously, in the repair shop model of health prevalent today, health services are assumed to be the primary source of improved health.

Environment, Preferences, Self-Care, and Health

Increasing amounts of economic and other research on human health point to the large impact preferences and good self-care have on health status. Reducing the risks of everyday activities by regularly using a seat belt, following directions when using dangerous machinery, such as chain saws, and using a helmet while driving a motorcycle can increase health levels in a population. Healthful self-care activities including sufficient exercise, good eating habits, low levels of substance abuse, prudent alcohol use (including not more than one drink a day), and proper care of cuts and bruises can raise health levels appreciably. The central role of the family in health and rural development and the needed research in this area are presented in Part II, Section 1, Chapter 3. To be most effective, rural health programs need to incorporate a variety of educational activities and health screening to reduce adverse health behaviors and encourage improved self-care. Investment in effectively targeted programs of this nature may produce very high social returns, higher than from additional resources invested in rural health services. Research and demonstration projects are needed to estimate the social returns to investment in particular health-promotion activities in different rural settings.

Effective Use of Medical Services—Supply and Demand Factors

A supply and demand framework is used to clarify the issues facing decision makers and researchers, and to aid in identifying important variables affecting use of health services. The quantity of health services used in a rural area depends upon both the effective demand for these services and their supply cost to the consumer (Figure 1). Persons who are fully insured with a small percentage copayment for health services and have normal out-of-pocket travel and opportunity costs, use some level of health services (Q_0) with out-of-pocket and opportunity costs of C_0. This level of use depends on the demand side (represented by Curve D_1) of age, sex, education, income, the amount of health-insurance coverage, and a given level of consumer knowledge and preference regarding health services. The supply curve S_0 assumes a small percentage consumer copayment with the rest of the cost paid by third parties. It also incorporates given levels of health-care technology, trained health personnel, and a level of rural health-service investment.

Use of fewer health services in many rural areas by a significant proportion of the population is due to both reduced effective demand for visits and higher out-of-pocket and opportunity costs (unless alternative use of time has a very low value). Demand (curve D_2) is reduced by below-average income and other factors, such as lack of knowledge of the effectiveness of medical treatment, discriminatory treatment of minorities at a health service that reduces demand, or an unfriendly atmosphere in a health facility that discourage efforts to obtain these services. Reduced demand for visits decreases utilization, say to Q_1.

Still lower utilization (Q_2) is due to increased supply costs (S_c) to many consumers. The above-average consumer costs (indicated by the difference between supply

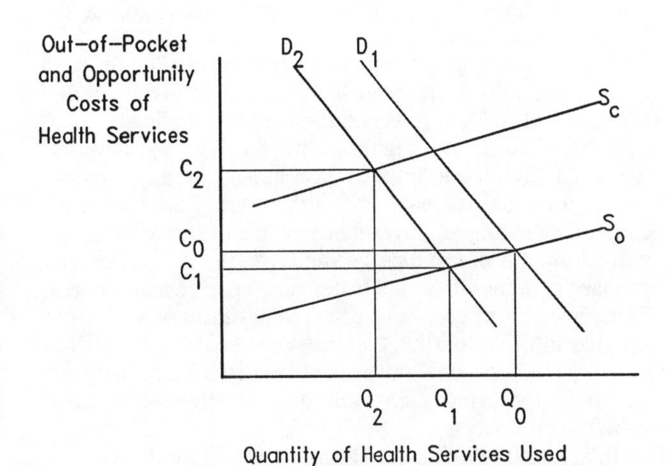

Figure 1. The effect of no insurance, and higher out-of-pocket and opportunity costs on the use of health services.

curves S_o and S_c) include: diseconomies of scale in rural health services, higher costs of certain supplies and services due to transportation costs and other factors, and the losses absorbed by health-care units for medical treatment of the uninsured who do not pay. Higher opportunity costs for health care that rural people suffer are due to longer travel distances and longer waiting times. Many rural people with Medicaid insurance incur large out-of-pocket costs in reaching physicians, due to the difficulty of finding nearby physicians who will accept them as patients. Thus, to achieve medical service utilization levels in rural areas that approach more closely those in urban areas, both increases in effective demand and a reduction in out-of-pocket and opportunity costs are required. Thus, a key policy issue affecting both the supply of and demand for health services in rural areas is the availability of affordable private health insurance and the level of public financing for health-care services for the poor.

RURAL ECONOMIC DEVELOPMENT AND THE DEMAND FOR AND SUPPLY OF RURAL HEALTH SERVICES

The general model of economic development elaborated by Hayami and Ruttan (1985) identifies four sets of variables that affect the level of performance of an economic system: resources, technology, institutions, and cultural endowments. The Social Science Agricultural Agenda Project has identified a similar set of four driving forces as affecting rural economic development: technical advance; human development (human capital); institutional, policy, and program improvement; and resource-base improvement (Part III Introduction). As applied to the health sector, these sets of variables can be more specifically identified as: (1) resources, including skilled and unskilled health manpower (human capital), health-facility buildings and equipment, etc.; (2) levels of medical knowledge and technology employed; (3) institutional arrangements, including national health policies, third-party payment arrangements, and facility rules and regulations; and (4) consumer preferences, such as values, knowledge, attitudes, and behaviors that affect the performance of the health sector and health status. Changes in any of these variables can affect the health of rural people.

Society's economic and management challenge is to achieve the highest level of health possible given limited resources. Production economics theory indicates that, when applied to the health sector, this goal is achieved when an additional unit of investment in any activity causes an equal increase in health status. This would include, for example, investment in health education, research on the economics of rural health care, improved primary care facilities, and better rural emergency services. Thus, one role of economic research in health services is to provide information that compares the health benefits obtained from additional investments in different parts of the health sector using such tools as cost-effectiveness and benefit-cost analyses.

In attempting to increase health levels in rural areas, the greatest focus of research and development has usually been on the amount of resources needed, such as the number of physicians or emergency vehicles in an area. This approach to rural health problems tends to imply that the central question for research is to determine the optimum investment in health-care resources without considering the other three sets of variables identified above. Many of the studies in the literature have taken this limited approach.

In reality, changes in one or more of the variables in the other three sets may have a much greater impact on rural health and would be more cost-effective. First, for example, changes in a rural consumer's knowledge about the effective use of certain health-care services, or in one's attitude toward medicine or medical personnel, could be a significant cause of increased use of preventive and other health-care services leading to better health status. For such a consumer, the addition of health-care resources alone might have no influence on one's health status. Second, technological advances in surgery, medicine, and the associated medical technologies—especially those that reduce costs of medical technologies for smaller physician practices and smaller hospitals—could enable increases in the health of rural persons. Specifically, new technologies from the communication revolution including the microcomputer and the fax machine have, as yet, been little exploited in rural medical practice. These technologies can increase the effectiveness of distance consultations without requiring as much patient transportation. Much more research and demonstration of how these technologies can be effectively used in rural areas is needed.

ISSUES IN INSTITUTIONAL CHANGE IN HEALTH-SERVICE DELIVERY

Improved institutional arrangements for health-care delivery are central to achieving increased health levels in rural areas. We highlight the need for research on institutional issues because these fundamental issues are often less well understood. An important general institutional question is: How can appropriate competition in the delivery of health services be achieved in less populated areas? Rural areas of the United States today have a varied mix of competing providers modified by local monopoly environments due to economies of scale and transportation costs. Current reimbursement arrangements are dominated by third-party payment arrangements (discounted at varied levels), while free public health clinics and some fee-for-service care is also provided. As they currently operate, third-party payment arrangements provide little incentive to the consumer, or the consumer's physician, to seek the most cost-effective care. Few rural people are now covered by prepaid health-care providers— HMOs, PPOs, etc. (See also Christianson 1989.) Present rules of competition bar physicians from attempting to organize a more rational cost-effective system of rural care because organized sharing opens physicians to the charge of collusion and an attempt to control the market. However, if a physician, or group of physicians, succeeds in buying out all the other providers, such a monopoly is legal! At the hospital level, current institutional arrangements provide an incentive for some larger, more financially stable urban hospitals to gain control of nearby rural hospitals to increase the flow of patients to fill the unoccupied beds of the larger, more profitable hospital and decrease services in the rural hospital. However, rural health-care monopolies in the private sector have an incentive to rationalize the use of their resources in providing health care to reduce their costs and increase profit. But, would decisions by these monopolies be in the interest of rural consumers? What institutional arrangements can provide incentives for rural monopolistic health systems to optimize the use of their resources and, at the same time, provide the highest level of health services possible for rural people?

Some institutional arrangements that have these incentives operate today. One model is the public community hospital controlled by local trustees. It has an incentive to optimize its resources for the use of its local clientele. However, other hospital users may not be represented by these boards, such as nonlocal emergency room users, significant ethnic or racial groups, or the rural poor. How can appropriate social (state and federal) interest in assuring minimum amounts and quality of hospital services in each rural area be represented? Another institutional issue concerns present state and federal regulations as applied to rural hospitals. Do they contribute to achieving the objectives of cost-effective quality care? Currently, many of the regulations that may be appropriate and cost-effective for hospitals larger than 100 beds are enforced on smaller hospitals, causing greater costs and reduced service availability in rural areas.

A second model for the provision of rural primary care that has been promoted recently is community-oriented primary care (COPC). "Community-oriented primary care is a modification of the traditional model of primary care in which a primary-care practice or program systematically identifies and addresses the health problems of a defined population" (Nutting 1987, xv). Some definition of the community is established ranging from the patients of a medical practice to a defined geographic or ethnic population. This model includes identifying the community's health problems and developing emphasis programs to ameliorate them. Nutting has assembled a range of experiences with this model in which community involvement varies. The COPC concept includes a range of institutional arrangements, some in which the physician is predominant in identifying health problems and developing programs, while in others much more community influence is present in problem identification and program decisions. The increased community orientation of primary practitioners that this model encourages should augment the cost-effectiveness of rural health care. Unsettled is the important issue of how to appropriately represent community interests in problem identification and resource allocation decisions.

A third model is the publicly operated health-care center (Bernstein, Hege, and Farran 1979). A few, mostly federally supported, community health centers now provide services in rural areas, primarily to the poor. A fourth is the public health department model. This institutional arrangement provides primary health-care services to the poor who cannot get them elsewhere. This model has never been generally viewed as a comprehensive service delivery system for all rural people in the United States. A fifth model is the prepaid health delivery system model, including the whole range of health-maintenance organizations—HMOs and preferred provider organizations (PPOs) (Christianson 1989). This health insurance and service arrangement, that relies on a monthly payment, provides an economic incentive for cost-effective health promotion measures and service delivery. But, the issue of appropriate community involvement in decisions about service and insurance-package benefits is not often addressed. Institutional models from other economic fields that might also be examined to provide the improved incentives for a rationally organized, monopolistic rural health system include cooperatives and public utilities.

The accelerating shift of health care in rural areas from individualistic, competitive, solo practices on a fee-for-service basis to larger scale, monopolistic systems with third-party payers calls for research to sort out the benefits and costs of alternative institutional arrangements for health care in the different socio-economic environments. A key focus of research should be how institutional arrangements will encourage optimization of the use of scarce health-care resources, the provision of high-quality health care that rural consumers need and desire, and equity for the poor and minorities. Such research has the prospect of providing high returns to society by finding ways to significantly increase levels of health for all people in rural areas without great increases in costs.

A RESEARCH AGENDA TO ACHIEVE BETTER HEALTH FOR PEOPLE IN RURAL AREAS

Considerable, highly varied research on rural health has been carried out in various locations over the years. Research on rural health problems has been supported by the federal-state experiment station system at least since the early 1950s (see, for example, Hoffer et al. 1950; U.S. Department of Agriculture 1974; Williams et al. 1983; Dunn and Doeksen 1980; Christianson and Faulkner 1981; Doherty et al. 1972; Stevens and Chapman 1979; Daberkow and King 1980; Doeksen et al. 1979; Department of Health and Human Services 1989). The Economic Research Service of the U. S. Department of Agriculture has contributed studies of rural health over a long period of time. Since the early 1970s, the National Center for Health Services Research (NCHSR) has supported research relevant to rural health issues. In 1986, NCHSR was mandated by congress to review rural health-care research and to develop an agenda for research. The results of this effort were published in 1989 (Hersh and Van Hook). Other rural health research has been produced from time to time by the American Medical Association (AMA) and by the American Hospital Association (AHA 1987, 1988, 1989) and its affiliate, the Hospital Research and Educational Trust. (Additional significant, more general research includes: Kane and Leuci 1988; Rosenblatt and Moscovice 1982; Hassinger 1982; Department of Health and Human Service 1989; Cordes et al. 1983; Cordes 1977.) Since 1984, the *Journal of Rural Health* has published and reviewed rural health research. A "Decade Review" of rural health research will be published and will include a paper on "Gaps in Rural Health Research." Standard works on rural health include Roemer (1976) and Hassinger (1982).

Important current funding sources for rural health research include Hatch Act funds through the federal agricultural experiment station system, as well as the Department of Health and Human Services, the Office of Rural Health Policy, and the Agency for Health Care Policy and Research (AHCPR, formerly NCHSR). The Office of Rural Health Policy has recently supported development of five rural health research centers through grant awards, in 1988, to units at the University of North Dakota; Marshfield Clinic, Wisconsin; University of North Carolina at Chapel Hill; University of Washington at Seattle; and the University of Arizona. The AHCPR currently supports rural research in three areas: (1) the effect of changes in payment systems on hospital management and performance, (2) hospital use by rural community health centers in Maine, and (3) a study of access to medical care by indigents in Nebraska (Ermann 1990, 65).

This paper takes the position that the research proposed by Hersh and VanHook (1989) in "A Rural Health Services Research Agenda" in *Health Services Research* did not sufficiently consider the Cordes (1989, 757–84) paper in that volume titled "The Changing Rural Environment and the Relationship Between Health Services and Rural Development." For example, the summary of the Hersh and VanHook (1989, 1053–64) article includes the usual set of resource-focused topics, with relatively little recognition of the large adjustments rural health is faced with today due to the rapidly changing and increasingly more differentiated rural economic and social environment pointed out by Cordes. The following agenda, therefore, relates research needs in rural health more explicitly to the issue of rapid rural social and economic change.

HOW TO ENCOURAGE HEALTHIER LIFESTYLES AND BETTER SELF-CARE

The rural health-services literature tends to focus on curative services. Health-promotion activities are seldom included; no coverage of this topic was included in "A Rural Health Services Research Agenda" (Hersh and VanHook 1989). Because specific, sharply focused health-promotion activities may provide very high returns in increased health levels at a particular time, research is needed to identify and evaluate health-promotion programs for different rural population groups. This research should estimate the returns obtained from the programs. In the future, with better cost-effectiveness information, more rational decisions about continuation and expansion of the health-promotion programs can be made.

ASSURING APPROPRIATE DEMAND FOR CURATIVE HEALTH SERVICES IN RURAL AREAS

In a rapidly-changing rural social and economic environment, assurance of effective demand for curative health services is crucial for appropriate health-service utilization. The position of the demand curve for health services is dependent upon: (1) age and sex, (2) income, (3) health insurance, and (4) preferences, or "taste" for health care. Better knowledge is needed of how different kinds of health insurance and preferences influence demand and service use.

The widely different impacts of current rural changes on health-service demand are suggested by considering the characteristics of different rural areas. Areas with increasing numbers of retirees will demand a somewhat different distribution of health services as compared with sparsely populated, low-income areas that are losing population. Rural retirees are likely to have high levels of health insurance and adequate incomes, but what local health services will they use? Will they patronize the local hospital and local physicians, or prefer, for nonemergency care, to travel considerable distances to urban areas, under the assumption that they will receive better quality care there? In sparsely populated, low-income rural areas, how adequate is health insurance coverage, and will insurance and incomes be sufficient to enable use and maintenance of adequate levels of local health-care services? What are the best approaches to assure the stable demand needed for high-quality care for highly dispersed populations?

Research on the Preferences of Rural People for Health and Health Services

In the last few decades, many factors have made rural consumers more knowledgeable about health matters and services. They include: (1) increased mixing of rural and urban people through in- and out-migration, (2) longer distance commuting to jobs, and (3) the ubiquitous presence of television. Consumers in these highly diverse, rural environments exhibit high variability in knowledge about the ability of local physicians and the effectiveness of different medical and surgical procedures in improving health. Also, increased ethnic and racial diversity in rural areas has resulted in more varied cultural preferences for health care.

Despite these increasing changes in rural areas, the empirical studies referred to above indicate overwhelmingly that rural people are in worse health and use fewer health services than urban people. Do important preference differences in rural areas cause lowered health status? Are there health-promotion services or changes in consumer knowledge about the effectiveness of curative services that could significantly increase health status? Are there important gaps in the knowledge of rural people about occupational risks and illnesses? (See, for example, Ferguson et al. 1989; Hartye and Mathis 1989; and Lubben et al. 1988). Reduced utilization of rural health-care services may be due, for example, to a lack of knowledge about the importance of early visits to physicians for certain problems or of the increase in health status possible from newer surgical and medical procedures. Rural health facilities may also be bypassed due to perceptions about the quality of care provided.

Thus, quantitative research is needed on rural consumers' preference patterns that affect the use of health services and their knowledge of the characteristics of the health services. Such research could identify important education needs related to services, aid in measuring needs and demand for local health services, and also aid local health-service personnel to understand better the health-service-preference barriers they face. Such information would also contribute to designing more effective health education and extension programs about health-service and health-care decision making.

Improved Health-Insurance Payment Arrangements and Uncompensated Care

What changes in payment arrangements for health services would increase demand by all rural people for needed services and, at the same time, encourage optimum utilization of limited rural health-care resources? Assurance of effective demand for needed health services by everyone is possible when payment for a minimum adequate amount of health services is in place for all. Currently, the working poor who are above the Medicaid poverty level and do not have health insurance are most at risk of inadequate health care.

Over the long run, the continuing national debate about how to provide health insurance for everyone will be fruitful. Until this is achieved, very useful state-level research and demonstration programs can aid in developing improved institutional arrangements that will enable national health insurance to be more cost-effective. Interim approaches to assure that health services used by rural people are reimbursed require payment arrangements and levels acceptable to rural providers. It is not socially, or privately, cost-effective for the reimbursement system to force rural people to bypass adequate local health services. Is it primarily a matter of increasing the Medicaid payment rates? Could Medicaid rates be raised through a reduction in the number of services included? Or could an alternative health-care financing system be developed that would increase both efficiency and equity?

For uncompensated care that hurts some physicians and hospitals much more than others, what payment arrangements might be made at the state level? How successful is the uncompensated hospital-care reimbursement program in Florida? Research on these issues has included Lurie, Kamberg, and Brook (1989) and Straub and Walzer (1988).

AUGMENTING THE SUPPLY OF COST-EFFECTIVE RURAL HEALTH SERVICES

In this section, we examine research questions on the supply of health services under three headings: (1) emergency and frequently used health services, including primary and continuing-care services, especially for maternal and child health and the elderly; (2) inpatient hospital care; and (3) organizational and resource-use issues, especially about arrangements for appropriate community involvement in important rural-health personnel and investment decisions.

In rural areas, health-service personnel and facilities are at a disadvantage. Rural physicians receive less income than urban physicians, partly due to considerably lower third-party payments than received by urban physicians for the same procedure. Economic theory indicates that, until rural net income and opportunity-cost considerations for health-service personnel equal those in urban areas, rural areas will continue to have shortages of health personnel, and the quality of services will be at risk. The National Health Service Corps program that sought to ameliorate this problem is being dismantled. Physicians on duty in this program will decline from 2,595 in 1988 to an estimated 800 in fiscal year 1990 (Joint Task Force 1989). For many health-service personnel, the source of most new medical knowledge, continuing medical education, and collegial relations is in urban areas. Medical specialists find it difficult to obtain enough patients in rural areas. Generalists often have difficulty arranging coverage so they can go to professional meetings and take vacations. In rural areas, alternative employment and educational and recreational opportunities (other than outdoor recreation) are much more limited. Study after study has shown that a majority of physicians, medical students, and their spouses prefer suburban and urban locations. Lower pay rates for hospital personnel, lower reimbursement rates to physicians for the same procedure, and lower net income for most health-services personnel also affect their choice of practice location. In many rural nurse-shortage areas, nurses commute to urban hospitals to obtain higher pay and fewer hours of work. The nursing problem will become worse as the total number of nurses graduating in 1992 is expected to be 10,000 fewer than in 1984 (Joint Task Force 1989). Thus, research should include study of the adjustments rural health services will have to make to face increasingly scarce and more costly personnel. The costs of obtaining and repairing specialized medical equipment is also higher in rural areas due to travel costs from the urban areas where the suppliers and trained technicians reside. Thus, to achieve high-quality, accessible health-care delivery in many rural areas, especially those that are less attractive, higher-than-average incomes may be required. Little research is now available on the opportunity costs of health-service personnel who work in rural areas, or on the costs of obtaining and maintaining medical equipment in rural areas.

With increasing specialization in health care, the old idea that the rural hospital and health-care system could provide complete care has disappeared. Hence, research on rural health services needs to be based on two criteria: (1) adequate access to essential services for emergency care and (2) how to cost-effectively provide to rural areas, through an integrated system, the right mix of primary and long-term care, from the point of view of society and the individual. This approach needs to focus on three areas of research. First, research on assuring adequate access to emergency, primary, and continuing-care services, especially for the chronically ill, in all rural areas. Second, research to answer the many questions about the location, scope, and economies of scale of different inpatient hospital services for rural areas. Many elective hospital and other health services that include highly specialized medical and surgical procedures will not be able to be locally provided.

Increased agglomeration of many rural health services is dictated by economies of scale and opportunity costs. Cost-effective use of equipment and supporting personnel, as well as transportation and patient-opportunity costs, all imply the need for rural health centers with varied configurations that provide health services at convenient locations, perhaps with satellite units operated part-time for particularly distant population groups. The maintenance of many infrequently used, competing sets of high-cost medical equipment and personnel in rural areas increases health-service costs needlessly to all payers and reduces provider and hospital income. Many rural people now regularly travel to shopping malls; local research will be needed in many areas to determine the desirability of situating medical services at malls. Some research on regionalization is available; see, for example, Berki, Luft, and Hunt (1986). But, localized, tailored research for each service area could facilitate changes and aid in reducing duplication and increasing access.

Emergency, Primary, and Continuing-Care Health Services for Rural Areas

Emergency Services. For both social and private reasons, rural residents and urban travelers in rural areas require high-performance medical-emergency systems. In the 1970s, emergency-medical-service legislation and programs at both the federal and state level sought to increase the performance of these systems. Much upgrading in equipment, training of emergency medical technicians, and improving hospital emergency services was achieved during this period, in both urban and rural areas. Better radio communications were developed, with medical control of patients established as soon as possible. Since the early 1980s, federal and state support for emergency services has been reduced. Past research includes: Georgopoulos 1986; Doeksen, Frye, and Green 1975; Navin and Stevens 1979; and U.S. Congress 1989. Current research needs include those on consolidation of small units into regional systems and alternative staffing arrangements.

Primary and Ambulatory Care Including Maternal and Child Health. Three or more physicians in primary-care practices are increasingly becoming the norm in rural as well as urban areas. Larger-size practices work better due to the increased access for collegial discussion of medical problems; the need for coverage during illnesses, professional meetings, and vacations; and economics of shared financial management. Economies of scale in the use of medical equipment and administrative personnel also lead to larger practices. Considerable research is available for use by physicians and others on the general question of the market size needed for the economic viability of general and family-practice physicians (see, for example, Bisbee 1982; Cowper and Kushman 1987). The issue of the cost-effectiveness of mid-level practitioners in rural areas is still unclear (see Moscovice and Rosenblatt 1979). The integration of community health centers into a larger rural health-care network is a continuing problem (see, for example, Wood, Hughes and Estes 1986).

A current critical need is research that can aid in assuring the availability of prenatal and perinatal health services for rural women due to the recent rapid decline in the availability of rural physicians willing to accept prenatal and obstetrical patients (McClain 1978; McCormick, Shapiro, and Starfield 1985; Mengel and Phillips 1987; Phillips and Sevens 1985). The crisis followed the very rapid increase in physician liability insurance costs in the 1980s (McManus and Newacheck 1989). Annually calculated liability insurance costs for obstetrics discriminates against rural physicians who have relatively few cases, leading to exorbitant costs per case. Nutting et al. (1987) illustrate the state of the art in primary-care quality assessment (see also DeFries and Ricketts 1989).

Long-Term and Continuing Care. In this area, two research issues stand out: the need for small-size nursing-home-type units and for cost-effective home care. What is the economic viability of the alternatives for providing quality, long-term care to the chronically ill in rural areas?

What are the health, medical, and economic issues related to operating smaller nursing-home-type care arrangements in rural areas? (Chronically ill patients have an improved life if they are near their relatives and friends.)

Home care usually contributes to higher levels of health and satisfaction for patients that do not require continual skilled care. Which arrangements in a particular area will enable high quality, cost-effective care? Do possible sources of home care include hospitals, county health departments, physicians' offices, or independent visiting-nurse services? Research tailored to local conditions is needed to enable improvements in rural long-term and home care.

Inpatient Hospital Care

Excess bed supply continues to burden both rural and urban hospitals in many areas. Increasing numbers of rural hospitals closed in the 1980s. In rural areas, economies of scale in the supply of hospital services led to local hospital monopolies. These economic conditions in a competitive environment can lead to decreased access to inpatient care in rural areas as larger hospitals, to increase their bed-occupancy rates, buy out and close smaller hospitals. Thus, consolidation of hospital systems of increasing size or regionalization of hospital resources by urban-oriented organizations may reduce inpatient services in rural areas. In the 1990s, as the costs of hospitalization grow, cost pressures will cause greater hospital specialization. Thus, networks of inpatient services that function more effectively are required for rural areas. Greater cooperation among hospitals in providing services will enable the reduction of costly duplication of services. No longer will or should the small, stand-alone, rural hospital be expected to serve most of the inpatient needs of its service area.

One important direction of change is suggested by the demonstrations of smaller, more limited inpatient facilities. These demonstrations for more sparsely populated areas are being carried out in California and Florida. They reduce local inpatient care to short time periods, limit the medical procedures that can be carried out, and have transfer arrangements with other hospitals. How would such units affect the access, cost-effectiveness, and quality of inpatient services? Such research can, in a network framework, aid decisions about bed reductions and the elimination of cost-increasing duplications of service, as the differentiation of inpatient care in rural areas proceeds. Recent useful research on rural hospitals includes: Moscovice 1988, 1989; Moscovice and Rosenblatt 1982, 1985a, 1985b; Alexander and Amburgey 1987; Weiss, Phillips, and Shuman 1986; Hogan 1988; Stevens and Chapman 1979; American Hospital Association 1987, 1988, 1989; and Glenn et al. 1988.

A current particularly critical and illustrative rural hospital issue is how to best provide prenatal and childbirth services for rural women. Recent sharp increases in physician- and hospital-liability insurance costs have greatly decreased the number of rural physicians and hospitals that provide prenatal and childbirth services, causing many women to travel considerable distances for these services—often to urban areas. Research and demonstration projects are needed on how to provide high-quality services with reasonable accessibility and cost-effectiveness in rural areas. (See McManus and Newacheck 1989; Hughes and Rosenbaum 1989; Main et al. 1989; Nesbitt, Scherger, and Tanji 1989; Gavin and Leong 1989; Bahry, Fullerton, and Lops 1989; Gordon et al. 1987; Reimer 1989; Rosenblatt 1989.)

Organizational Arrangements Affecting the Supply of Rural Health Services

Organizationally, health care in rural areas has been transformed from the era of the solo practitioner who took personal responsibility for medical care in his town. Before Medicaid, the solo practitioner subsidized care for the poor through a sliding scale of payments. Currently, the supply of health care in rural areas is organized in a highly varied manner. In most areas, no one entity has the responsibility for the health care of an identified population. The competitive approach to health care in rural areas confronts a dispersed population and economies of scale in the supply of health-care services. The result is a paradox of both high-cost redundancies and gaps in access. The wide variety of third-party reimbursement arrangements, and up to some 30 percent of the rural population without health insurance, adds to the complexity of assuring access. Currently, in many states, it is not clear where responsibility lies for assuring accessible, high-quality health care for rural people. Does the responsibility lie with the departments of public health, the legislature, or local leaders? Part of the problem lies in the area of values held about what is fair in arrangements for paying for health care.

The United States and rural people are in a transition from considering health care as simply another consumer good to accepting some level of social responsibility to assure all have access to minimum adequate health care. On the demand side, Medicare, Medicaid, and other health-insurance programs have assured effective demand for a large amount of care for more than 70 percent of the population. But, on the supply side, states and rural areas largely accept whatever the semimonopolistic rural market provides. Innovative research and evaluation of local successes are needed to identify improved organizational arrangements that will lead to a better supply of accessible high-quality health services at reasonable cost. An important dimension of this challenge is to identify ways to assure appropriate community and taxpayer representation in health-service resource-allocation decisions in these monopolistic rural environments. For an assessment of one experiment to provide improved Medicaid services to the rural poor, see Kirkman-Liff (1986). (See also "Financing of Rural Health and Medical Services" 1990; Straub and Walzer 1988.)

NOTES

1. Robert D. Stevens is a professor emeritus of Health Economics, Office of Medical Education and Research, College of Human Medicine and Department of Agricultural Economics, College of Agriculture and Natural Resources, Michigan State University. The author appreciates the comments of Adela de la Torre, Ralph D. Christy, and Andrew Hogan on an earlier draft of this chapter.

2. For more on the contributions of social science research to economic performance, see Binswanger and Ruttan (1978), Ruttan (1982, 1984), and T. W. Schultz (1968).

REFERENCES

Aday, Lu Ann, Gretchen V. Fleming, and Ronald Anderson. 1984. *Access to medical care in the U.S.: Who has it, who doesn't*. Chicago: Pluribus Press.

Alexander, J. A., and T. L. Amburgey. 1987. The dynamics of change in the American hospital industry: Transformation or selection? *Medical Care Review* 44, no. 2: 279–321.

American Hospital Association. 1987. *Environmental assessment for rural hospitals*. No. 184201. Chicago, Ill.

_____1988. *Profile of small or rural hospitals 1980–86*. No. 184203. Chicago, Ill.

_____1989. *Rural hospital closure: Management and community implications*. No. 184204. Chicago, Ill.

Bahry, V. J., J. T. Fullerton, and V. R. Lops. 1989. Provision of comprehensive perinatal services through rural outreach: A model program. *Journal of Rural Health* 5, no. 4: 387–96.

Baker, S., B. O'Neill, and R. Karpt. 1984. *The injury fact book*. Lexington: Lexington Books.

Bender, L., B. L. Green, T. F. Hady et al. 1985. *The diverse social and economic structure of non-metropolitan America*, Rural Development Report No. 49, U.S. Dept. of Agriculture, Washington, D.C.

Berki, S. C., H. S. Luft, and S. S. Hunt. 1986. Selecting categories of patients for regionalization—Implications of the relationship between volume and outcome. *Medical Care* 24, no. 2: 148–58.

Bernstein, J. D., F. P. Hege, and C. C. Farran. 1979. *Rural health centers in the United States*. The rural health center development series. Cambridge, Mass.: Ballinger Publishing Co.

Binswanger, H. P., and V. W. Ruttan. 1978. *Induced innovations: Technology, institutions and development*. Baltimore: Johns Hopkins University Press.

Bisbee, G. E., Jr. 1982. *In management of rural primary care-concepts and cases*. Chicago: The Hospital Research and Educational Trust.

Bluestone, H., and S. G. Daberkow. 1985. Employment growth in nonmetro America: Past trends and prospects to 1990. *Rural Development Perspectives* 1, no. 3: 34–37.

Christianson, J. B. 1989. Alternative delivery systems in rural areas. *Health Services Research* 23, no. 6: 848–89.

Christianson, J. B., and L. Faulkner. 1981. The contribution of rural hospitals to local economies. *Inquiry* 18 (Spring): 46–60.

Cordes, S. M. 1977. *Social science research on rural health care delivery: A compilation of recent and ongoing studies*. College Park: The Pennsylvania State University, Department of Agricultural Economics and Rural Sociology.

_____1989. The changing rural environment and relationship between health services and rural development. *Health Services Research* 23, no. 6: 757–84.

Cordes, S. M., T. W. Eiscle, M. L. Gonzalez, and R. C. Lloyd. 1983. *An annotated bibliography of rural health research, 1975–1981*. College Park: The Pennsylvania State University, Dept. of Agricultural Economics and Rural Sociology.

Cowper, P. A., and H. E. Kushman. 1987. A spatial analysis of primary health care markets in rural areas. *American Journal of Agricultural Economics* 69, no. 3: 13–625.

Daberkow, S. G., and G. A. King. 1980. *Demand and location aspects of emergency medical facilities in rural Northern California*. Research report no. 329. Berkeley: University of California, Division of Agricultural Sciences, Giannini Foundation of Agricultural Economics.

Decade review. Forthcoming. *Journal of Rural Health* 6. no. 4 (October 1990).

DeFries, G. H., and T. C. Ricketts. 1989. Primary health care in rural areas: An agenda for research. *Health Services Research* 23, no. 6: 931–1004.

de la Torre, Adela, K. Fickenscher, and H. Luft. Forthcoming. The Zip Code difference: Methods to improve identification of rural subgroups. *Agricultural Economics* 5/2.

Doeksen, G. A., J. Frye, and B. Green. 1975. *Economics of rural ambulance service in the Great Plains*. Agricultural Economics report no. 308, Oklahoma State University, Stillwater.

Doeksen, G. A., J. W. Dunn, L. Stacker, and R. Sheets. 1979. *Capital and operating costs for community clinics*. Bulletin B–742, Agricultural Experiment Station, Oklahoma State University, Stillwater.

Doherty, N., D. Halkala, W. Hanson, S. Sarkar, and G. L. Johnson. 1972. *Health care industries in the Michigan Grand Traverse and copper country regions: Case studies in community resource development*. Research report no. 177, Agricultural Experiment Station, Michigan State University, East Lansing.

Dunn, J. W., and G. A. Doeksen. 1980. A health care systems model for non-metropolitan areas. *American Journal of Agricultural Economics* 62 (February): 58–65.

Erdman, Karen, and Sidney M. Wolfe. 1987. *Poor health care for poor Americans: A ranking of state medicaid programs*. Washington, D.C.: Public Citizens Health Research Group.

Ermann, D. A. 1990. Rural health care: The future of the hospital. *Medical Care Review* 47, no. 1: 33–73.

Ferguson, K. J., G. L. Gjerde, C. Mutel, K. J. Donham, C. Hradek, K. Johansen, and J. Merchant. 1989. An educational intervention program for prevention of occupational illness in agricultural workers. *Journal of Rural Health* 5, no. 1: 33–48.

Financing of rural health and medical services. 1990. *Journal of Rural Health* 6, no. 4 (October).

Gavin, K., and D. Leong. 1989. An overview of maternal and infant health services in rural America. *Journal of Rural Health* 5, no. 4: 299–319.

Georgopoulos, B. S. 1986. *Organizational structure, problem solving, and effectiveness: A comparative study of hospital emergency services*. San Francisco: Jossey-Bass, Inc., Publishers (The Jossey-Bass Health Series).

Glenn, J. K., L. L. Hicks, A. J. Daugird, and L. W. Lawhorne. 1988. Necessary conditions for supporting a general surgeon in rural areas. *Journal of Rural Health* 4, no. 2: 85–100.

Gordon, R. J., G. McMullen, B. D. Weiss, and A. W. Nichols. 1987. The effect of malpractice liability on the delivery of rural obstetrical care. *Journal of Rural Health* 3, no. 1: 4–14.

Hartye, J. K., and N. Mathis. 1989. Delivering comprehensive health education programs for farmers in a primary care setting. *Journal of Rural Health* 5, no. 3: 193–200.

Hassinger, E. W. 1982. *Rural health organization: Social networks and regionalization*. Ames: Iowa State University Press.

Hayami, Y., and V. W. Ruttan. 1985. *Agricultural development: An international perspective*. Rev. ed. Baltimore: Johns Hopkins University Press.

Hersh, A. S., and R. T. VanHook, eds. 1989. A rural health services research agenda. *Health Services Research* 23, no. 6 (Special Issue): 725–1080.

Hicks, L. L. 1984. Social policy implications of physician shortage areas in Missouri. *American Journal of Public Health* 74, no. 12: 1315–20.

Hill, C. E. 1988. *Community health systems in the rural South: Linking people and policy*. Boulder, Colo.: Westview Press.

Hoffer, C. R., D. L. Gibson, C. P. Loomis, P. A. Miller, E. A. Schuler, and J. F. Thaden. 1950. *Health needs and health care in Michigan*. Special bulletin 365, Section of Sociology and Anthropology, Agricultural Experiment Station, Michigan State University, East Lansing.

Hogan, C. 1988. *Urban and rural hospital costs: 1981–85*. Dept. of Health and Human Services publication no. (PHS) 88–3419, Hospitals Studies Program research note 12, National Center for Health Services Research and Health Care Technology Assessment. Rockville, Md.: Public Health Service.

Hughes, D., and S. Rosenbaum. 1989. An overview of maternal and infant health services in rural America. *Journal of Rural Health* 5, no. 4: 299–319.

Johnson, G. L., and J. T. Bonnen. 1988. *Executive summary of SSAAP's Woodlands Inn conference*. Early draft, Social Science Agricultural Agenda Project meeting, 13–18 March, Houston, Tex.

Joint Task Force. 1989. Health care in rural America: The crisis unfolds. Report of National Association of Community Health Centers and the National Rural Health Association. *Journal of Public Health Policy* (Spring).

Kane, J. D. H., III, and M. S. Leuci. 1988. *Rural medical service funding: Issues and alternatives*, Publication series no. 7, U.S. Dept. of Agriculture, Rural Information Center, Washington, D.C.

Kirkman-Liff, B. L. 1986. Competition in health care and the rural poor: An assessment from Arizona's competitive medicaid experiment. *Journal of Rural Health* 2, no. 1: 23–38.

Lubben, J. E., P. G. Weiler, I. Chi, and F. DeJong. 1988. Health promotion for the rural elderly. *Journal of Rural Health 4, no. 3: 85–96.*

Lurie, N., C. Kamberg, and R. H. Brook. 1989. *How free care improved vision in the Rand health insurance experiment.* American Journal of Public Health 79:640–42.

Main, D. S., C. Tressler, N. Calonge, L. Joffe, and A. Robichaux. 1989. A subsidized rural perinatal care program in a Colorado county. *Journal of Rural Health* 5, no. 4: 397–403.

McClain, John O. 1978. A model for regional obstetric bed planning. *Health Services Research* 13, no. 4: 378–94.

McCormick, M. C., S. Shapiro, and B. H. Starfield. 1985. The regionalization of perinatal services: Summary of the evaluation of a national demonstration program. *Journal of the American Medical Association* 253 (8 February): 799–804.

McManus, M. A., and P. W. Newacheck. 1989. Rural maternal, child, and adolescent health. *Health Services Research* 23, no. 6: 805–48.

Mengel, M. B., and W. R. Phillips. 1987. The quality of obstetric care in family practice: Are family physicians as safe as obstetricians? *Journal of Family Practice* no. 2 (February 24): 159–64.

Moscovice, I. 1988. Future of rural hospitals. In *Financing rural health care*. Edited by N. Walzer and L. Straub. New York: Praeger.

———1989. Rural hospitals: A literature synthesis and health services research agenda. *Health Service Research* 23, no. 6: 891–930.

Moscovice, I., and R. Rosenblatt. 1979. The viability of mid-level practitioners in isolated rural communities. *American Journal of Public Health* 69, no. 5: 503.

Moscovice, I., and R. A. Rosenblatt. 1982. *The viability of the rural hospital: a synthesis of findings from health services research*. A report for the National Center for Health Services Research. Washington, D.C.: U.S. Dept. of Health and Human Services.

———1985a. A prognosis for the rural hospital part I: What is the role of the rural hospital? *Journal of Rural Health* 1, no. 1: 29–40.

———1985b. A prognosis for the rural hospital part II: Are rural hospitals economically viable? *Journal of Rural Health* 1, no. 2: 11–43.

Navin, R. E., and R. D. Stevens. 1979. *Estimating the cost of small scale ambulance operations*. Agricultural Economics report no. 345, Dept. of Agricultural Economics, Michigan State University, East Lansing.

Nesbitt, T. S., J. E. Scherger, and J. L. Tanji. 1989. The impact of obstetrical liability on access to perinatal care in the rural United States. *Journal of Rural Health* 5, no. 4: 321–35.

Norton, C. H., and M. A. McManus. 1989. Background tables on demographic characteristics, health status and health services utilization. *Health Services Research* 23, no. 6: 725–56.

Nutting, P. A. 1987. *Community-oriented primary care: From principle to practice*. Health Resources and Services Administration publication no. HRS-A-PE 86–1. Rockville, Md.: U.S. Dept. of Health and Human Services, Public Heal Service.

Nutting, P. A., B. R. Burckhalter, J. P. Carney, and K. M. Gallagher. 1987. *Methods of quality assessment for primary care*. Sydney, Australia: Community Systems Foundation.

Phillips, W. R., and G. S. Sevens. 1985. Obstetrics in family practice: Competence, continuity, and caring. *Journal of Family Practice* 6, no. 6 (20 June): 595–96.

Reimer, G. M. 1989. Rebuilding a rural obstetrical program: A case study. *Journal of Rural Health* 5, no. 4: 353–60.

Robert Wood Johnson Foundation. 1987. *Access to health care in the United States*. Results of a 1986 survey, no. 2. Princeton, N.J.

Roemer, M. I. 1976. *Rural health care*. St. Louis: The C. V. Mosby Co.

Rosenblatt, R. A. 1989. A lack of will: The prenatal care crisis in rural America. *Journal of Rural Health* 5, no. 4: 293–97.

Rosenblatt, R. A., and I. S. Moscovice. 1982. *Rural health care*. New York: John A. Wiley and Sons.

Rowland, D., and B. Lyons. 1989. Triple jeopardy: Rural, poor and uninsured. *Health Services Research* 23, no. 6: 975–1004.

Ruttan, Vernon W. 1984. Social science knowledge and institutional change. *American Journal of Agricultural Economics* 66:549–59.

______1982. *Agricultural research policy*. Minneapolis: University of Minnesota Press.

Schultz, T. W. 1968. Institutions and the rising economic value of man. *American Journal of Agricultural Economics* 48:1113–22.

Stevens, R. D., and J. A. Chapman. 1979. *Changes in the distribution and availability of medical services in Michigan counties and regions, 1961–1977*. East Lansing: Michigan State University, Agricultural Experiment Station.

Straub, Lavonne, and Norman Walzer, eds. 1988. *Financing rural health care*. New York: Praeger.

U.S. Congress. 1989. *Rural emergency medical services*, OTA-H-445, Office of Technology Assessment, Washington, D.C.

U.S. Dept. of Agriculture. 1974. *Assessment of Rural Health Research*, vols. 1 and 2, Office of Planning and Evaluation, Washington, D.C.

U.S. Dept. of Health and Human Services. 1989. *Rural health research compendium, 1983–1989*, Order No. PU0589-7, Office of Rural Health Policy.

Weiss, S. L., D. F. Phillips, and J. G. Shuman, eds. 1986. *Management issues for rural hospitals*. Chicago: American Hospital Publishing, Inc.

Williams, D., T. Boucher, G. Doeksen, J. Parks, and L. Stackler. 1983. *A guidebook for rural physician services: A systematic approach to planning and development*, Bulletin B-765, Agricultural Experiment Station, Division of Agriculture, Oklahoma State University, Stillwater.

Wood, J. B., R. G. Hughes, and C. L. Estes. 1986. Community health centers and the elderly: a potential new alliance. *Journal of Community Health* 11, no. 2 (Summer): 566–91.

CHAPTER 10

HUMAN DEVELOPMENT: AGENDAS AND CONCLUSIONS

For reasons explained in the introductory chapter for this section, SSAAP's Houston conference did not fully recognize the highly significant challenges posed for the agricultural establishment (AE) by (1) the human development problems and difficulties that exist in farm and rural nonfarm areas (see Part I, Chapter 6) and (2) the poverty of disadvantaged farm and nonfarm rural groups. Efforts to assist the disadvantaged need to go beyond the enhancement of human skills and capacity to include increased ownership of natural and manmade income-producing resources; policies, programs, and infrastructures that are more favorable to the disadvantaged; and improved technologies for the disadvantaged, of which technology is probably the least important. **The above two challenges present major unexploited opportunities for contributions by the agricultural establishment and rural and basic social scientists.**

To meet the human development challenge and the broader challenge of assisting disadvantaged rural farm and nonfarm groups, major agendas are required for each of the following groups:

- The agricultural establishment (AE)
- The rural social sciences (RSSs)
- The basic social science disciplines (BSSDs)

GENERAL AGENDAS FOR THE AGRICULTURAL ESTABLISHMENT (AE) TO MEET THE RURAL HUMAN DEVELOPMENT AND POVERTY ALLEVIATION CHALLENGES

These agendas are general and important for establishing favorable circumstances for rural human development and the alleviation of rural poverty. More specifically:

- The human development agendas of the agricultural extension services, 4-H clubs, and FFA should be restructured to place greater emphasis on updating the technical, institutional, resource, environmental, managerial and ethical knowledge, skills and abilities of
  - members of disadvantaged rural groups (including females)
  - without neglecting similar agendas for the rural advantaged and middle-income residents whose improved skills and knowledge are also needed, but who can finance investments in themselves and their children.
- The colleges of agriculture and the colleges of education in both the National Association of State Universities and Land Grant Colleges (NASULGC) and the National Association of State Colleges of Agriculture and Renewable Resources (NASCARR) should develop agendas to support general education (K through 12 and community colleges) that
  - focus on the needs of the rural disadvantaged (especially females)
  - does not neglect the rest of rural residents whose skills are needed and who can finance investments in themselves and their children.

RURAL SOCIAL SCIENCE (RSS) AGENDAS FOR MEETING THE CHALLENGE OF HUMAN DEVELOPMENT AND POVERTY ALLEVIATION

In order to meet the challenges posed by rural human underdevelopment and poverty among the rural disadvantaged, the rural social sciences (RSSs) should adopt the following agendas with regard to these challenge areas:

- Establish close participatory interaction with inadequately educated and trained disadvantaged rural people and their leaders, including Caucasian (the largest group), African, Hispanic, and Native American groups, in order to know their problems and the subjects and issues important for them.
- Be prepared to seek out, do, and, where necessary, initiate and lead multidisciplinary, multidepartmental

and multiagency (public as well as private sector) work on the problems and subjects to meet these challenges.

- Work in problem solving, design, analytical, descriptive, and other modes appropriate for rural social scientists as administrators, advisors, consultants, entrepreneurs, and leaders (as well as in researcher and educator roles) on the problems, issues, and subjects relevant for these challenges.
- Participate in and do iterative/interactive, general, systems science, simulation and scenario analyses of the domains of multidisciplinary challenge-area problems and subjects. Where modification and/or reforms of educational, health-care, geriatric, credit, technology-generating, resource, and other institutions are indicated, these models should utilize aspects of the public (multiple-person) choice/transaction cost approach extended as suggested in Chapter 7 (Part III, Section 1). In analyzing changes for resource institutions, Chapter 2 (Part III, Section 3) will be helpful as will Chapter 2 (Part III, Section 4) for technology-generating institutions.
- Recognize that reforms and modifications of education, resource, technology-generating, infrastructure, and policy institutions often damage some persons in order to benefit others—in economic jargon they are often beyond "Pareto-optimality" but socially desirable and needed. The simulation and/or scenario analyses recommended above should indicate who and what groups are likely to be hurt and benefitted, and how, where, when, and in what ways. Because the redistributive consequences of such reforms and changes are politically important, iterative/interactive participatory analyses are needed by choice and decision makers and affected people to indicate the political and social acceptability of alternative reform and change packages.
- At SSAAP's Houston Conference, two work groups in the community and human resources area were under the leadership of Ronald C. Wimberly, Department of Sociology and Anthropology, North Carolina State University, and Paul Lasley, Department of Sociology and Anthropology, Iowa State University. They developed a number of agenda items more or less related to human development that were collected from their reports and are presented here. These include:
  - Analyses of the changing demographic composition of rural communities and identification of needs critical for various groups.
  - Efforts to understand better the new patterns of work, enterprises, and consumption now developing in rural communities.
  - Creation of processes to broaden and enhance citizen involvement and leadership skills for effective public decision making at the community level and at broader levels where decisions affect communities.
  - Determination of critical human resources needed by rural communities to manage changes to attain their goals.
  - Improvement of the roles voluntary interest groups can play in managing change and attaining community goals.
  - Analysis of the impacts of changes in lifestyles, family structures, and roles on the functioning of local rural communities.
- Also at Houston, a special work group developed agendas with respect to disadvantaged farm and nonfarm rural groups (including minorities).

  The work group was led by T.T. Williams, Head, Human Resources Development Center, Tuskegee University.

  Invited members (some of whom may not have participated) Joyce Allen, Frank Baker, Kanand Brooks Jr., Carlton Davis, Sidney E. Evans, Gary Gordon, Delores Huerta, McKinley Mayes, Alex Moreno, Refugio I. Rochin, Peggy Ross, Ronald E. Shaffer, Doris P. Slesinger, Lacy Tilotson, and Louie H. Valenzuela.

  The work group noted that a "strong need exists to enhance our knowledge and understanding of disadvantaged rural individuals and groups (both farm and nonfarm) in order to develop policies and programs that will help them realize their potential as contributing members of society," and concluded that efforts needed from rural social scientists included:
  - Monitoring and analyzing the changing composition, causes, and impacts of rural poverty.
  - Increasing the knowledge and understanding of social scientists and the public concerning changes underway in rural nonfarm communities that result, in some instances, in financial stress, declining standards of living, and poverty, in order to help the rural residents of such communities better understand, cope with, and overcome these conditions.
  - Evaluating the effectiveness of and justification for existing federal, state, local, and voluntary programs and strategies for assisting rural disadvantaged groups.
  - Exploring ways in which youth, women, minorities, limited-resource groups, and undereducated people can more effectively participate in rural communities.
  - Exploring the feasibility of innovative concepts, models, and approaches for rural education, training, and employment-generation programs to aid the rural disadvantaged.
  - Helping to establish a "national rural and agricultural statistical service" with responsibility to (1) develop, maintain, coordinate, and assure access to an integrated rural database including primary, secondary, and administrative data, (2) conduct all USDA surveys, and (3) coordinate rural and agricultural survey activities of other federal agencies. The rural database should include information on: (a) production, market, processing, financial, and other business structures; (b) population and human resources; (c) natural resources and environmental quality; (d) community and social services and physical infrastructure; (e) technology; and (f) social structure. This same agenda item is repeated in Sections 1, 3, and 4 of this part.
- Papers commissioned by SSAAP after its Houston meetings have yielded additional, more specific agendas pertaining to the education, health, political, social, and income-producing needs of disadvantaged Caucasian, African, Hispanic, and Native American groups.
  - With respect to disadvantaged nonmetro *Caucasians* (the largest disadvantaged ethnic group in rural America), the RSSs should:

- Address the poverty of those "left behind" by out-migration in terms of care for the elderly, infrastructural services, public assistance, credit, housing, health care, etc.
- Address the problems of poverty-stricken rural youth including:
- Inadequate school systems in generally poor communities.
- Alienation and lack of motivation, substance abuse, teenage pregnancy and single-parent families, nutrition and health, and many others suggested by this list.
- Lack of credit and resources for business ventures.

- Address policy and program changes for increasing public and private investments in disadvantaged rural Caucasian people and communities, with emphasis on the creation of higher-paying, skilled-employment opportunities, including attention to needed special training and education programs.
- Investigate likely individual and aggregate monetary and nonmonetary costs and returns for subsidizing:
  - University and technical education with scholarships for merit and assistantships for work.
  - Investments in businesses owned by disadvantaged Caucasians and providing high technology employment.

- With respect to disadvantaged rural *Hispanic-Americans*, the rural social scientists should:
  - Assess the monetary and nonmonetary costs and returns for alternative ways and programs to expand federal and state support of Hispanic programs in universities and colleges, including particularly, those in community colleges.
  - Assist in the design and implementation of programs to improve health care, family life, the quality of life for the elderly, and programs to deal with substance abuse, teenage pregnancy, alienation and other social problems for Hispanic-Americans.
  - Assess monetary and nonmonetary returns for acquiring and the costs of failing to acquire command of English for Hispanic-Americans aspiring for income, social and political equality in the United States versus those satisfied with the status of unskilled laborers.
  - Assess the socio-economic status and conditions of Hispanic-American farmers and the potential for greater market and economic opportunities.
  - Assess the effectiveness of market manipulation (boycotts, strikes, hiring quotas) versus redistribution of the ownership of human, natural and manmade, physical and biological capital in raising incomes of Hispanic-Americans.
  - Redesign and implement changes in the "rules of the game," organizations, and facilities of potential benefit to Hispanic-Americans, recognizing that advising, consulting, administration, and leadership as well as research and educational efforts are required from the RSSs.

- With respect to disadvantaged rural *African-Americans*, rural social scientists and especially the increasing number of competent African-American rural social scientists should:
  - Address the poverty and related problems of those left behind in villages and on farms by the extensive rural/urban migrations since the 1930s, and assist in designing remedial efforts at local, county, state, and national levels.
  - Help design and assist in the implementation of programs to finance crucially needed improvements in the educational institutions of rural communities having large proportions of disadvantaged African-Americans in their populations.
  - Help, using a farming-systems approach, in the design of new production techniques for disadvantaged African-American farmers. This should be accompanied by the design of programs to provide more resources than owned by "limited-resource" African-American farmers because high labor earnings typically require substantial investments involving advanced, capital-intensive production techniques.
  - Direct attention to items of concern for African-Americans, such as the elderly, the young, infrastructural services, public assistance, credit, and housing.
  - Address the problems of alienation, substance abuse, teenage pregnancy and single-parent families, motivation, nutrition, health and related problems as they arise in rural African-American communities and groups.
  - Analyze the need for subsidies at all educational levels for African-Americans:
    - Vocational
    - K–12
    - Community college
    - University
  - Address the needs of the rural disadvantaged African-American for assistance in establishing nonfarm, as well as farm enterprises.

- With respect to disadvantaged rural *Native Americans*, rural social scientists should:
  - Make special efforts to recruit, train and educate, and find financial support for Native American rural social scientists.
  - Assist in the design and implementation of programs for rural Native Americans to alleviate problems dealing with health, aging, youth, substance abuse, self-identity, motivation, etc.
  - Advise, consult, and assist efforts to increase rural Native American incomes via educational and other assistance.
  - Recognize that improvement in Native American tribal and local governmental institutions will likely require participation of Native American rural social scientists working closely with their own people but also that, for some time to come, they will need
    - genuine support from, and the
    - assistance of, other rural social scientists.
  - Examine the rigidities of the present Native American institutions using a public choice/transaction cost approach (extended as suggested in Part III, Section 1, Chapter 7). Such examinations should:
    - Include attention to monetary and nonmonetary rent-collection activities (both constructive and self-serving) in niches created by "fixed" institutional rules of the game, organizations, facilities, personnel, and facilities that serve Native Americans.
    - Provide design and feasibility studies of possible changes in rules of the game, organizations, person-

nel, and facilities of Native American institutions. It is likely that valuable insights can be gained from comparative studies of the wide range of Native American institutions in the United States, as those institutions vary from the Eskimos and Indians of Alaska to the Indians of Florida, and from the Northeast to the Southwest, with respect to such things as: treaty rights, tribal authority, dependence on the Bureau of Indian Affairs, education, and the ownership of reservation lands.

- Recognize that this national report is woefully inadequate with respect to a large group of Native Americans in Alaska namely the Eskimos. Rural and basic social scientists in the United States and particularly in Alaska should develop agendas more specific to the needs of Eskimos than those presented above for Native Americans that focus on Indians to the neglect of Eskimos.

BASIC SOCIAL SCIENCE AGENDAS TO MEET THE CHALLENGES OF RURAL HUMAN DEVELOPMENT AND POVERTY ALLEVIATION

To help meet the challenges of rural human development and the rural disadvantaged, the basic social science disciplines (BSSDs) should:

- Participate actively with their RSS counterparts in multidisciplinary, multidepartmental and multiagency problem-solving and subject-matter efforts pertaining to human development and the alleviation of poverty for disadvantaged rural groups.

- On the basis of experience attainable from doing iterative/interactive scenario or general simulation analysis of the domains of multidisciplinary problems and subjects involving human development, BSSDs should strive to:
  - Provide better conceptualization of how pertinent disciplinary social, political, anthropological, psychological, geographic, historical, and economic variables can be modeled in doing scenario and systems simulation analysis of human development and poverty problems and issues in rural areas.
  - Develop improved databases for modeling the roles of social, political, anthropological, psychological, geographic, historical and economic variables in the multidisciplinary domains of subjects and problems important for underdeveloped and advantaged, as well as disadvantaged rural people.

- Increase the interpersonal validity and cardinality of our knowledge of values important in developing rural people and in reaching redistributive decisions to help disadvantaged rural groups.
  - After recognizing the tentative social nature of all human knowledge, strive for knowledge of values that is objective in the sense of having been adequately tested (logic, experience, clarity of meaning, and workability) for purposes of addressing the human-development and poverty problems of rural groups.
  - Do the above in the realization that rural and basic social scientists serve as extension workers, consultants, advisors, staff members, administrators and entrepreneurs with responsibility for deciding and acting as well as for merely doing research and resident instruction.

- Do applied disciplinary work pertinent to (even if inadequate for) the resolution of problems and issues in their full multidisciplinary, real-world complexity. The key word here is pertinent—applied disciplinary work to earn disciplinary status is not important for these rural social science agendas if it is not pertinent to the real-world problems of rural poverty and undeveloped rural people.

CHAPTER 1

INTRODUCTION TO SECTION ON RESOURCE ENHANCEMENT AND GROWTH IN CAPITAL BASES

Natural resources, such as land, water, and forests, play a major role in the continued technical, economic, and institutional development of the United States and most other countries. During the settlement of the United States, the abundance of fertile land; wide distribution of land through the Homestead Act and other governmental actions and policies; development of railroads, partially as a result of land-grant incentives; public development of locks, dams, and canal systems both for navigation and irrigation; and further enhancement of natural resources with manmade inputs developed by the land-grant colleges, private industry, the U.S. Department of Agriculture, and agricultural experiment station programs contributed immeasurably to an agricultural structure favorable to development based on a family farm and rural community complex. This structure not only provided the basis for a productive food and fiber system but also contributed immeasurably to the democratic, institutional, and human resource development of the country in general.

Within agriculture's resource base, natural and manmade resources intermingle in such a way that the traditional distinction between land and capital blurs so badly it loses its usefulness. Manmade resources combine with and enhance natural resources until, in many cases, natural resources no longer constrain production as they once did. It must not be forgotten, however, that the production of manmade resources may be constrained by natural resource limitations such as petroleum, fossil water, ores, and the ability to dispose of nuclear, biological, chemical, and physical wastes.

As recognized repeatedly in SSAAP's work, agricultural growth in the technocratic U.S. agricultural establishment has been viewed as depending heavily on technical advances, first labor-saving and land-extensive, then yield-increasing and more land-intensive. Both kinds of technology are embedded in manmade inputs such as machines, nonorganic fertilizers, pesticides, improved plant varieties, orchards, improved pastures, improved poultry- and livestock-breeding stock; biotechnology or capital structures such as buildings, terraces, and irrigation and drainage systems. Such manmade inputs have made phenomenal contributions to agricultural output. Manmade capital combines with natural resources to increase and sometimes decrease the optimum levels at which natural resources are maintained. Irrigation, drainage, terracing, and the development and use of other manmade inputs, such as chemical fertilizers, pesticides, fuel, machinery, and improved crop varieties, greatly raise land productivity to much higher levels than it had in nature. Growth in manmade capital is very much related to many of the issues concerning farmers, agribusinesses, and consumers discussed in Part II, Section 1, as well as to most of the natural resource issues discussed in the chapters of this section.

In the United States, natural resource development and enhancement permits fewer farmers to provide an increasingly abundant food supply for our growing population at a steadily decreasing cost in terms of the share of real per capita income spent on food. Agricultural productivity growth has freed labor from agriculture for industrial development and has provided foreign exchange through agricultural exports. If our food supply were produced with the technology of 1940, 1950, or even 1960, we would be paying much higher food prices, and there would be recurring and more severe food shortages worldwide. In addition, our agricultural surplus provides needed commodities for aiding other countries in times of regional and world food shortfalls.

U.S. population and income growth will continue to increase the demand for agricultural output and we have an opportunity to produce an increasing share of the world's food. According to projections by both Johnson and Wittwer (1984) and Crosson (forthcoming), the United States will likely be able to meet expected demand increases if agricultural productivity continues to increase. Even on the global level, despite the pessimistic outlook of President Carter's Global 2000 Study, our natural resources base can sustain populations in excess of most projections (Food and Agricultural Organization [FAO] 1979) for at least half a century with reasonable technological advance and investment of manmade resources.

But, there is a down side to our agricultural abundance. Problems of natural resource enhancement and growth in manmade inputs relate generally to the following issues: (1) the sustainability of natural resources in meeting the future demand for agricultural output; (2) off-farm environmental impacts of soil erosion and agricultural chemical pollutants in the nation's water, feed, and food; (3) the long-term impact of industrial pollution on the productivity of our agricultural and forestry resources via acid rain (Kneese 1984) and the greenhouse effect (Freeman 1973; Abelson 1990); (4) the role of appropriate technology via manmade inputs in providing a sustainable agriculture; (5) intergenerational and intragenerational equality and equity in the agricultural versus urban, industrial, recreational, habitat, and other nonagricultural uses of natural resources; (6) natural resource preservation and enhancement in the Third World; and (7) interdisciplinary inquiry and information system requirements for public and private decision making.

The greenhouse effect, ozone depletion, and acid rain are not well understood in either their technical or social dimensions. Nonfarm consumption and industrial pollution are believed to contribute importantly to these problems. Explorations of such issues quickly illustrate the importance of the social science dimension of attempts to devise remedial public and private action to protect our resource base to meet future agricultural and nonagricultural demands for resource services.

The sustainability of our natural resource base is a broad, poorly understood issue that is related to widespread social concern about natural resource use and enhancement and to growth in use of manmade capital. Sustainable agriculture is also central to most of the areas of concern to farmers, agribusinesses, and consumers in both the United States and in many other areas of world agriculture (Part III, Section 3, Chapter 5). Unfortunately, natural resource conservation and enhancement have been viewed mainly in one dimension—the technical. We have built large dams, irrigation canals, and drainage projects with little regard for the overall ecosystem. Improved crop varieties have led to large monocultures without adequate attention to their ability to survive major outbreaks of new diseases and the evolution of insects and diseases immune to pesticides and disease-resistant varieties. Farmers have used larger and larger doses of agricultural chemicals without adequate safeguards against potential off-farm impacts such as air and water pollutants and as contaminants of animal products, fruits, and vegetables. Larger and larger machines, higher production costs, but lower real commodity prices bring about larger and fewer farms without adequate attention to disappearing homesteads, communities, and rural infrastructure, even when the larger farms are still family farms. High-output agriculture has made farmers more dependent on unstable world commodity markets with generally declining real prices and on worldwide unstable macroeconomic, trade, and fiscal policies that are generally decided upon without adequate concern for agriculture either here or abroad.

Agriculture is basic to rural development, and the development, use, and enhancement of natural and manmade resources is one foundation for agricultural output—thus, any significant agricultural or rural development concern has a resource dimension.

Agricultural productivity growth is based on more than technical advance. The United States, for example, has enjoyed a process of rural development founded, to a very large degree, on an agricultural production complex based on a unique balance of natural resources, farm and rural community structure, manufactured inputs supply, and an institutional marketing and processing infrastructure. This effective complex has provided incentives for millions of farm families to work long hours for nominal financial rewards at the margin, reinvest their earnings in their farm businesses, and contribute to community and human resource development.

Periodic resource assessments are usually concerned with population-growth-induced demand for food, expected conversion of agricultural land to urban and industrial uses, the impacts on agriculture and the environment of emerging new technologies, and sometimes include such emerging uncertainties as the greenhouse effect. These assessments have depended, to a very large degree, on trend projections of past agricultural, rural, macroeconomic, and international structures into the future and often on naive assumptions about specific structural changes. SSAAP is based on the realization that agricultural, rural American, national, and international structures are changing so drastically and rapidly that such assessments are an inadequate basis for simulating the output and sustainability of U.S. and world agriculture. We need to better envision the use of our rural resource bases for farm and nonfarm purposes as a basis for collecting relevant and accurate data for use in estimating the parameters and coefficients of dynamic models of agriculture to analyze a rural America that is continuously undergoing structural change as it responds to market shifts and underlying changes occurring in people, institutions, techniques, and resources. This requires multidisciplinary cooperation that needs to be an integral part of a larger resources management process that includes a continuing search for efficient (appropriate) technology, human development, and improved public and private decision-making processes in agriculture and rural development, both at home and abroad. These requirements with respect to natural resources and manmade capital are treated in this section. They also receive more general treatment in Section 1 of Part III. Part IV deals specifically with three major cross-cutting SSAAP areas of concern for social science work on natural and manmade resources: databases, basic social science disciplines, and ethics. Several chapters throughout Parts I through V express SSAAP's concerns and agendas relating to the development and use of natural and manmade resources. These chapters are listed in the cross references at the end of this chapter. Chapter 8 of Part I presents an abridged report from a Spring Hill work group entitled "Natural and Rural Community Resources and the Environment and Their Uses." That report remains important background reading for this section on natural and manmade resources. We turn now to a review of academic thought about natural and manmade resources with particular attention to thinking about resource institutions.

A REVIEW OF ACADEMIC THOUGHT ABOUT NATURAL RESOURCES

Both the Introduction to and first chapter of Part III, Section 1, sketch the history of rural and basic social science thought concerning changes in various kinds of institutions. Consequently, what is needed here is only a focus on changes in resource institutions.

Since the publication of Rachel Carson's *Silent Spring* (1962), it has been increasingly clear that the technical development of U.S. agriculture cannot be guided solely by needs for cash incomes and greater volumes of agricultural products. Carson's concern about the impact of pesticides on wildlife and humans has developed into a widespread public concern involving nonmonetary as well as monetary values including the badnesses of fertilizer pollutants to ground and surface waters, soil erosion, loss of genetic diversity in plants, the impact of labor-saving technology on farm workers, the effects of large farms on the vitality of rural communities, and fewer and larger farmers (Crosson forthcoming). Such environmental and economic impacts are very much related to the equity of natural resource use, manmade inputs, natural resource inquiry, and information system issues.

Emery Castle and his colleagues (Castle et al. 1981) have traced the evolution of land, institutional, and natural resource economics from the close of World War II and earlier to the 1970s. As reported by them, some of the common threads running through the evolution of land, institutional, and natural resource economics can be summarized as follows: In addition to attention to natural resources as factors of production, there is now increased concern about natural resources as consumption goods. This, in turn, leads to concern about utility lost through consumption externalities when natural resources are used for production purposes. Thus, nonmarket as well as market valuation of natural resources have become increasingly important in thinking about resources. When various groups, while not resource owners, are deprived of some of resource "goods" or are required to tolerate resource "bads" because of externalities, they demand increasing participation in decisions and choices about resource use. Finally, resource economists, well aware of the limitations of static neoclassical economics in analyzing nonmarket resource allocation, have turned increasingly towards a public choice/transaction cost (PC/TC) approach in assessing public-choice and decision-making institutions and in considering entitlements and externalities (Castle et al. 1981, 462).

The above developments generated a methodological shift for a new generation of institutional economists, including Daniel Bromley with his emphasis on the transaction costs of changing the "rules of the game" in his new book, *Economic Interests and Institutions: The Conceptual Foundation of Public Policy*, and Allan Schmid's contributions to the theory of public choice via his *Property, Power, and Public Choice: An Inquiry into Law and Economics* (1978) and *Benefit-Cost Analysis: A Political Economy Approach to Benefit Cost Analysis* (1989).

Sandra Batie's presidential address (abstracted as Chapter 6 of this section) at the 1989 meeting of the American Agricultural Economics Association sketched the history of societal concerns with the sustainability of rural and agricultural resources. She related current sustainability concepts back to organic farming and various intellectual and activist arguments since then, including the concept that constrained economic growth occurs in two stages involving, *first*, the establishment of public-sector rules of the game concerning the use of agricultural resources and, *second*, maximization within those rules. She also explored the concept of attaining sustainable development or (resource maintenance) by minimizing use of the natural environment. In her address, she gave substantial attention to the values of such things and conditions as biosphere limits, justice, limitations on population growth, investments in human capital, nature, local renewable resources, protection of the environment and food chain from toxins and carcinogens, future generations, and life itself.

William Lockeretz, a nutritionist from Tufts University, deals with a number of sustainability values in a paper reproduced in this section as Chapter 5. He, too, is concerned with values including those to be attained by restructuring and reforming society, reforming the agricultural establishment, managing farms for sustainability, attaining input self-sufficiency, and maintaining an environment and food chain free of inorganic and harmful chemicals.

Also, at a 1984 conference on sustainable agriculture sponsored by Rodale Press, Michigan State University, and others (Edens et al. 1985), substantial emphasis was placed on the values of food self-sufficiency, stewardship for resources, communities, and family farms.

Similarly, the recent National Research Council report (1989) on alternative agriculture places heavy emphasis on values. In that report, great value is attached to groundwater free of pesticides and nitrates, the use of biological pest predators and integrated pest management, biological nitrogen fixation, nutrient recycling, resource conservation, crop rotation, soil- and water-conserving tillage, disease prevention and health maintenance, freedom from antibiotic dangers, and, lastly, genetic control of pest diseases and the use of nutrients.

Clearly, the efforts summarized above indicate that the sustainability idea has a primary concern with values. Collectively, these reports indicate the broad, somewhat confusing range of values of concern to farmers, citizens, consumers, and social groups when they think about the fate of our farm and rural resources.

VALUE DIMENSIONS

All scientists—social, biological, and physical—experience considerable difficulty in working with the value dimensions of the practical problems associated with resource use and sustainability. Descriptive, biological and physical science research on values tends to be excluded by the dominance of those disciplines by logical positivism. Logical positivism has also constrained descriptive research on values by those social scientists who "ape" the logically positivistic methods and philosophic orientations of biological and physical scientists. Because resource economists emerged out of a pragmatic tradition of Wisconsin institutionalism, their work on values was less constrained than that of social scientists more dominated by logical positivism (K. H. Parsons 1949, 1958; McCloskey 1985; Achinstein and Barker 1985; Boulding 1956, 1969). However, they do seem somewhat constrained by the cumbersome complexity of pragmatic methods (Johnson and Zerby 1973; Johnson 1986 [Chapters 6 and 9], forthcoming). These difficulties were touched on in Chapter 1 of Part I, Introduction to Part III, and are addressed in greater detail later in the crosscutting section dealing with agroethics, public choices, and private decisions (Part IV, Section 3). The abilities of social scientists and humanists are needed in addressing the value questions inherent in resource-sustainability issues and problems—even if limited, they clearly exceed those of positivistically constrained biological and physical scientists.

OPTIMAL LEVELS OF SUSTAINABILITY

It is instructive to reflect on the level at which resources should be maintained or sustained. Some resources are stocks; in which case, to use them is to destroy them. Examples include fossil water, petroleum deposits, and many ores. Other resources (although renewable) can be maintained or sustained at various levels. Some of these resources cannot be sustained at the levels at which they originally became available as, for example, the original forest resources of the United States, many of which could not be maintained at their original levels when the country was developed. We have settled for maintenance of many forest resources of the United States at different and lower levels than originally existed. In still other instances, it has proven advantageous to enhance natural resources and sustain them at far higher levels than existed in nature. For instance, much U.S. farm land is now maintained at a much higher level of productivity than in its virgin condition, largely through the use of manmade resources.

Reflection on the earlier discussion of the numerous values involved in the concept of resource sustainability, and on the different levels at which it is advantageous to maintain different kinds of resources in different circumstances, *strongly suggests that a full conceptualization of what is meant by sustainability must involve the concept of optimality.*

The optimum level of maintenance or sustainability for a resource cannot be defined as a simple market optimum determined by using static economic thoughts to equate monetary costs and returns at the margin while neglecting nonmonetary values; instead, the optima to be defined must involve nonmonetary costs and returns as well. Still further, the needed optima must depend on knowledge of intrinsic as contrasted to extrinsic or exchange values whether the latter be monetized or not and of acts as well as consequences.

It is also instructive to reflect about the geographic unit within which a resource is to be sustained at a level judged to be optimal. Sustainability advocates sometimes argue that a resource should be sustained wholly within a geographic unit as small as a farm. A moment's reflection will indicate that, if the farm is to furnish any food or feed for people and livestock in other locations, it will be necessary to replace at least the phosphate, potash, and other inorganic nutrients transported off the farm in grains, livestock, products, and fiber if the farm is to continue to provide food, feed, and fiber to those beyond its bounds. It is possible to replace a renewable input such as nitrogen on a farm at rather low levels of output with rotations involving legumes despite the movement of nitrogen off the farm in plant and animal proteins for livestock production and/or human consumption. However, for an individual farm, it is not possible to replace phosphate, potash, and other essential inorganic mineral nutrients without acquiring them from off-farm sources. One possibility, of course, would be to deal with a much larger geographic unit than a farm, such as a nation, and collect all manure from feedlots and all night soil from urban populations for return to the farms that produce the feed and food stuffs. If, as is often the case, this kind of replacement is not feasible (by which we mean advantageous or optimal in the broadest sense), sustainability or self-sufficiency is not possible for the agricultural sector, in which case inorganic and mineral nutrients have to be obtained from elsewhere in the economy, presumably fertilizer mines. Energy differs from the inorganic mineral nutrients as it, like nitrogen, is partially renewable at the individual farm level. However, a farm that produces all of its own fuel (horse feed and human food) and all of its own power units (horses, oxen, and humans) is simply not able to furnish as much livestock feed and human food to others as one that depends, in part, on fossil energy from beyond its borders. The future may possibly permit attainment of national energy self-sufficiency with nuclear fusion (as contrasted to fission), something that is not now technically possible.

Limited Input Sustainable Agriculture (LISA) advocates argue that farmers are maximizing yields rather than profits and that, as a consequence, they are wasting resources and unduly polluting our environment. While farm management workers and agricultural economists have often accused biological and physical scientists of seeking maximum yields, they have generally held that farms reduce fertilizer usage because of poor knowledge. On the other hand, economists and farm managers also argued that inputs such as fertilizer, pesticides, herbicides, and fuel will be overused if society permits farmers to avoid paying for the environmental damages caused by these inputs or if society either keeps input prices artificially low or product prices artificially high, or both. Then, too, available materials and existing technologies may promote wastage and overuse. For instance, highly soluble fertilizers may enter surface run-off waters or leech into groundwater before they can be used by plants. The same may happen to highly soluble herbicides, pesticides, and residuals with long half-lives.

OPTIMIZING USE OF MANMADE RESOURCES OR CAPITAL

Helping farmers optimize the amounts of inputs they use and the levels at which they maintain resources involves educating them about the technical aspects of using different inputs, the costs they incur, and the returns they receive, both monetary and nonmonetary. Farm management and production-economics studies have demonstrated that lease forms differ as to the degree they internalize costs and benefits of using fertilizer to rents and, in doing so, affect the optimal amounts for a renter to use. Developing educational programs about optimal input use on individual farms is difficult because (1) required technical knowledge is often very deficient and (2) knowledge of the many intrinsic values involved is imperfect in the sense of being of questionable interpersonal validity and not being readily reducible to a common denominator or even to a single complex of values to serve as a proxy for a common denominator.

Internalization of previously external costs and benefits is typically accomplished by making public choices and decisions about rules of the game and associated organizations, policies, programs, faculties, and staffs. Such choices and decisions are typically redistributive. They take away rights to dispose of contaminants and pollutants from some while conferring rights to live in and enjoy a less polluted and less contaminated environment on others. Public choices to regulate input use in redistributive ways requires reliable (1) *value-free* knowledge of how production systems, ecosystems, markets, and societies work and, (2) very importantly, descriptive *knowledge of the values* involved. The value knowledge needs to be interpersonally valid among people in the present generation as well as between present and future generations. Still further, maximization requires that there be a normative common denominator among such values. These two conditions are extremely difficult to meet. Typically, sustainability activists stand ready to promulgate strong prescriptions on the basis of knowledge that does not meet these requirements. In the practical political arenas in which regulations are established, there is typically a process involving a great deal of iterative interaction among the contending groups of people who stand to be harmed or to benefit by a proposed change. This "iterative, interactive, politico-socio-administrative-investigative" process helps establish and clarify both value-free or value knowledge with some degree of interpersonal validity. Political scientists and sociologists often refer to this process as one of "legitimization." There is a surprising similarity between the legitimization in political, social, and administrative processes and the peer-reviewed validation and verification of knowledge that takes place in scientific societies.

DIFFICULTIES WITH THE CONCEPT OF EFFICIENCY/EQUALITY TRADEOFFS

Redistributions of rights and privileges to enhance, conserve, and better use natural and manmade resources typically raise questions of equity and equality and, in turn, questions about how these relate to efficiency. Unfortunately, many social, biological, and physical scientists and laymen use the words "equity" and "equality" as synonyms (Maunder and Ohkawa 1983; Johnson 1983). Dictionaries indicate that an equitable distribution is a justified one whether equal or not, whereas equality means equal distribution whether justified or not. As resource-sustainability issues and problems involve the values attached to both justice and equality, social scientists must distinguish carefully between equity and equality. Regulations often deprive previous owners of rights and privileges in order to confer greater equality or even impose inequality on others. These observations are presented here mainly to indicate the scientific difficulties that social, biological, and physical agricultural scientists should expect to encounter in designing regulations to promote optimal resource sustainability and enhancement.

In the literature on resource use, regulation, and sustainability, we often encounter the confusing discussion of tradeoffs between productivity or efficiency, on one hand, and equality which was previously considered, on the other.

Related to the equity/equality confusion in the literature is confusion about the distinction between technical and economic efficiency. In 1933, Knight pointed out the fallacy of this distinction. In 1981, Boulding reiterated it. In 1988, Johnson wrote about the current implications of the Knight and Boulding statements regarding the fallacious distinction between technical and economic efficiency. In doing this, he drew on a Ph.D. dissertation by Barkley (1986). What appears to be technical inefficiency with respect to the "so-called" frontier production function (Farrell 1957) grows out of either (1) specification error or (2) aggregation error. Either can create apparent "inliers" to a so-called frontier production function. Sometimes it pays to correct an inlier to an apparent frontier function; in which case, the inlier point is simply inefficient. On the other hand, it may not pay to "correct" the inlier; in which case, the inlier is not inefficient, either technically or economically. The conclusion is that Knight and Boulding were correct—the distinction between technical and economic efficiency is untenable even for the frontier production function case developed by Farrell and used extensively by many general and agricultural economists since then. As Knight and Boulding implied, adjectives in front of the word "efficiency" are mainly confusing.

The confusion that arises in considering tradeoffs between efficiency and equality involves still a third difficulty. Before one can consider the equality/efficiency tradeoff rigorously, one must be clear about what it is that is being traded off and for what. When numerous goods and services are produced in a system such as a farm, farming region or sector, these goods and services must be aggregated into a measure of total output or production before we can consider tradeoffs between either output or efficiency, on one hand, and equality, on the other. Perhaps the first and simplest difficulty is that markets do not place monetary values on all of the inputs, goods, services, wastes, pollutants, and contaminants generated. This is particularly true for inputs and outputs that are not internalized. One procedure is to monetize the nonmonetized (see Fox's Chapter 3 of Part IV, Section 2). This works when the nonmonetary values are really trivial, but, when the nonmonetary values are important and the monetary ones are trivial, the need becomes one of demonetizing the monetary values. However, that is not the end of the difficulty—an even more important question arises when it is noted that exchange or extrinsic values, whether monetized or not, are affected by redistributions that increase or decrease equality. The consequence is that tradeoffs between efficiency or production (when the latter is measured using indexes of output with exchange value weights) and equality are invalidated because the meaning of efficiency or production (so measured) changes with redistributions that modify the *exchange* values. Conceptually, we need measures of intrinsic values to use as weights in constructing indexes of output (and, hence, efficiency) in order to investigate the tradeoffs between output or efficiency and equality. Some philosophers question the validity of the concept of intrinsic values. A prominent sociologist, Talcott Parsons (1957), questioned the existence of a common denominator among values while Pareto, Hicks, and Arrow have questioned the interpersonal validity and cardinality of all value knowledge in a large body of literature well known to economists, philosophers, and many other social scientists. What we seem to do, to date, is relate questionable indexes of output and efficiency based on monetary exchange values, and benefit/cost ratios to various measures of equality such as Gini ratios. When this is done in "iterative/interactive" processes, we do seem to reach at least some legitimized (alternatively verified and valid) judgments about productivity/equality tradeoffs. The process is a tedious, difficult one, at best.

The introduction to Part III and Chapter 1 of Section 1, Part III, reviewed public choice and transaction cost theory in some detail, outlined several rather heuristic extensions of that theory, and suggested how those extensions can be used. If the reader has not read those portions of this book, it is suggested that he or she do so now as the paragraphs to follow presume that they have been read. It may also help to read Part IV, Section 2, Chapter 1, dealing with the ethical aspects of public and private decisions and choices.

THE PRIMITIVE UNDEVELOPED NATURE OF PUBLIC CHOICE/TRANSACTION COST APPROACH FOR ANALYSIS OF RESOURCE ISSUES

The emphasis in this chapter is on institutional changes to enhance natural agricultural resources and to expand manmade ones. As was indicated in Part III, Section 1, Chapter 1, stock establishment and dismantlement costs for changing rules of the game, organizations, facilities, and staffs to regulate resource use are, as yet, poorly conceptualized with respect to information, negotiation, and enforcement costs as flows. Returns to resource institutions (in all three manifestations) are poorly conceptualized—again both flow and stock values are involved. These need better conceptualization for use in the design, evaluation, and choice of institutional changes to internalize costs and benefits to attain more optimal sustainment, usage, and enhancement of farm and rural resources, both natural and manmade. We need to understand more about the fixity of assets in institutions that will have growing importance in resource enhancement and recovery, as well as conservation. The difficulties discussed above with respect to the interpersonal validity of value knowledge, the need for knowledge of intrinsic as opposed to exchange values, and the possible lack of common denominators among resource values all serve to emphasize:

1. the immense task ahead for social scientists working on intergenerational and intergroup transfers of the ownership of rights and privileges vis-a-vis natural and manmade resource issues;
2. the dangers encountered by biological and physical scientists and activists who naively enter an arena that has been recognized as frought with danger for economists and policy analysts for decades;
3. the shortcomings of the basic social sciences' theories, techniques, and measurements for working on interpersonal transfers of resource rights and privileges; and, hence,
4. the need for the support of basic social science research relevant for such work on value knowledge.

In general, social scientists are not conceptually well equipped to deal adequately with the inter- and intragenerational equity and equality questions about resource generation, saving, sustainability, and use. They are, however, much less naive about these problems than biological and physical scientists. Long-run public policies and programs related to natural resource development, use, and enhancement involve the conferring of various "goods" upon certain groups, in both this and future generations, while imposing various "bads" on still others. The disparate nature of these "goods" and "bads" makes it extremely difficult to find an intrinsic common denominator among them that has intergenerational validity for use in subtracting the total of the "bads" from the total of the "goods" to obtain a net difference to maximize in choosing among alternative technical, economic, and environmental policies, programs, and projects.

A REVIEW OF ACADEMIC THOUGHT ABOUT MANMADE RESOURCES (OR CAPITAL)

For the most part, academicians treat manmade physical and biological capital separately from natural resources more or less as in classical economics' triumvirate of land, labor, and capital. This is unfortunate because we have already noted that natural and manmade capital commingle so that it is difficult to distinguish between the two. The relationship is seen to be even closer when it is realized that natural resources are used to generate manmade capital. Much of society's concern about the sustainability of natural resources arises from the use of natural resources to make the manmade capital used to enhance and sustain natural agricultural resources.

Another difficulty is that much of the academic thought about agricultural (manmade) resources deals with monetized capital flows—with the saving of income for conversion into capital, the flow of capital through financial institutions to lenders, and, hence, to farmers. This is the substance of much of the domestic literature on agricultural credit and financial institutions, the focus of international rural development literature, and the activities of international lender and grantor agencies. Non-social scientists, including biologists and environmentalists, often account for manmade resource flows in purely physical terms. Thus, we have the energy accounting of Pimental et al. (1973), and material flow studies of phosphates, potashes, and metals.

The emphasis of social science analysts on money, the monetary values of manmade capital, and loans and grants has led to a neglect of the on-farm generation and automatic saving and investment of such important manmade, farm-produced capital items as orchards, improved pastures, fences, irrigation ditches, livestock herds, and water impoundments. A very high proportion of the capital used in subsistence and commercial family farming systems is produced, saved, and generated on the farms where it is used. This aspect of manmade resources has been seriously neglected by rural social scientists working in both the developed and less developed world (Johnson 1968, 229–36; Johnson et al. 1969, 34–37). Dale Adams' chapter on "On-farm Capital Formation and Rural Financial Markets: Research Issues" (Part II, Section 2, Chapter 8) was commissioned for this book to fill this gap with respect to international rural development. No corresponding chapter was commissioned by SSAAP for domestic agriculture. These few observations with respect to an almost nonexistent literature strongly suggest that rural social scientists have much to do conceptually and empirically before they can properly relate the use of manmade resources to natural resources.

ORGANIZATION OF THIS SECTION

Many dimensions of the issues introduced in this chapter with respect to the enhancement of natural resources for both agricultural and nonagricultural uses and the environment are further explored by Crosson, Frederick, and Sedjo in Chapter 2.

To provide historical perspective on the growth in manmade capital as the primary means of enhancing the productivity of natural resources in agricultural production, Joseph Barse and John Schaub describe recent trends in agricultural inputs and relate these trends to policy and environmental concerns in Chapter 3.

Louise Fortmann, Daniel Mountjoy, and Bruce Johnston discuss the potential contribution of the social sciences to the preservation and enhancement of natural resources in

Third World countries in Chapter 4. On a global level, we cannot expect the technical successes in the United States and other developed-country agricultures to transfer directly to solving problems of agricultural stagnation in developing countries, nor can we expect such countries to forego fully the exploitation of their natural resources because the developed world is alarmed about resource conservation and environmental quality.

Challenges to agricultural economists presented by the "sustainable development" issue are outlined in Chapter 6 in an abridged synopsis of Sandra Batie's insightful 1989 presidential address to the American Association of Agricultural Economists.

The final chapter of this section (Chapter 7) contains abridged work-group reports from the SSAAP Phase III Houston Conference and additional agenda items and conclusions reached by SSAAP's editorial group since the Houston conference, these are with respect to natural resource enhancement and growth in manmade capital as a driving force in agriculture and rural development.

Crosscutting issues involving databases, the basic social science disciplines, and agro-ethics are touched upon in the above chapters, but receive more general and comprehensive treatment in Sections 1 through 3 of Part IV.

CROSS REFERENCES IN THIS BOOK

PART I: INTRODUCTION

Ch. 2 A History of American Agriculture From Jefferson to Revolution to Crisis, Richard S. Kirkendall
Ch. 3 Social Science Institutions, Knowledge, and Tools to Address Problems and Issues, Frederick H. Buttel
Ch. 5 The Role of the Social Sciences in Rural Development and Natural Resources Management, Vernon W. Ruttan
Ch. 6 Science and Technology Policy for the 21st Century: The United States in a Global Economy, G. Edward Schuh
Ch. 7 From the Perspective of Users and Affected Persons, Richard J. Sauer
Ch. 8 Abridged Work Group Reports from SSAAP's Phase I, Spring Hill Conference, June 9–11, 1988
Ch. 9 SSAAP's Houston Workshop/Conference and the Organization of This Book

PART II: DOMESTIC AND INTERNATIONAL FARM AND RURAL DEVELOPMENT

Sec. 1 Ch. 3 Studies of Households Reviewed in Relation to Farm and Home, Balanced Farming, Farming Systems, and Farm Management Programs and Studies in the College of Agriculture, Cornelia Butler Flora
Sec. 2 Ch. 7 Institutional Reform: Accomplishments and Unmet Needs in China, Newly Industrialized Countries of Asia, the Soviet Union, and Eastern Europe and the Developed Countries, Glenn L. Johnson
Ch. 8 On-Farm Capital Formation and Rural Financial Markets: Research Issues, Dale W. Adams
Ch. 9 Agricultural Sector Analysis and Rural Development: Social Science Research Priorities, Clark W. Reynolds

PART III: THE FOUR DRIVING FORCES

Introduction to Part III
Sec. 1 Ch. 2 Social Science Issues in Agriculture and Rural Communities, Paul W. Barkley
Ch. 3 Rural People, Resources, and Communities: An Assessment of the Capabilities of the Social Sciences, James C. Hite
Ch. 4 Economic Institutions and the Development Problem: History and Prognosis, Daniel W. Bromley
Ch. 5 Irony, Tragedy, and Temporality in Agricultural Systems or How Values and Systems are Related, Lawrence Busch
Sec. 4 Ch. 2 Technical Advance: Agendas and Conclusions

REFERENCES

Abelson, Philip H. 1990. Uncertainties about global warming. *Science* 247, no. 4950: 1529.

Achinstein, P., and S. F. Barker, eds. 1960. *The legacy of logical positivism.* Baltimore: Johns Hopkins University Press.

Barkley, Richard A. 1986. Efficiency and frontier production functions. Ph.D. diss., Michigan State University. Unpublished.

Batie, Sandra S. 1989. Sustainable development: Challenges to the profession of agricultural economics. Presidential address, American Agricultural Economics Association summer meeting, 30 July–2 August, Baton Rouge, La.

Boulding, K. E. 1956. *The image.* Ann Arbor: University of Michigan Press.

——1969. Economics as a moral science. *The American Economic Review* 59, no. 1: 1–12.

——1981. *Evolutionary economics.* Beverly Hills: Sage Publications.

Bromley, Daniel W. 1989. *Economic interests and institutions: The conceptual foundation of public policy.* New York: Basil Blackwell.

Carson, Rachel. 1962. *Silent spring.* Boston: Houghton-Mifflin.

Castle, Emery N., et al. 1981. Natural resource economics, 1946–75. In *A survey of agricultural economics literature: Volume 3, Economics of welfare, rural development, and natural resources in agriculture, 1940s to 1970s.* Edited by Lee R. Martin. Minneapolis: University of Minnesota Press.

Crosson, P. Forthcoming. *Management of agricultural land.* Washington, D.C.: Resources for the Future, Inc.

Edens, Thomas C., Cynthia Fridgen, and Susan L. Battenfield, eds. 1985. *Sustainable agriculture and integrated farming systems: 1984 conference proceedings.* East Lansing: Michigan State University Press.

Farrell, M. J. 1957. The measurement of productive efficiency. *Journal of Royal Statistics Society* 120:253–81.

Food and Agricultural Organization (United Nations). 1979. *Agriculture toward 2000.* Rome, Italy.

Freeman, A. Myrick, III. 1979. *The benefits of environmental improvement: Theory and practice.* Baltimore: Johns Hopkins University Press, for Resources for the Future, Inc.

Johnson, Glenn L. 1968. Agriculture: Capital. In *International encyclopedia of the social sciences.* New York: Macmillan and The Free Press.

_____1983. Synoptic view. In *Growth and equity in agricultural development.* Edited by Allen Maunder and Kazushi Ohkawa. Westmead, England: Gower Publishing Co.

_____1986. *Research methodology for economists: Philosophy and practice.* New York: Macmillan.

_____1988. Technological innovations with implications for agricultural economics. In *Agriculture and rural areas approaching the 21st century: Challenges for agricultural economics.* Edited by R. J. Hildreth et al., 82–108. Ames: Iowa State University Press.

_____Forthcoming. Philosophic foundations of agricultural economics thought from World War II to the mid-seventies. In *Survey of agricultural economics literature.* Vol. 4, *Agriculture in economic development.* Edited by Lee R. Martin. Minneapolis: University of Minnesota Press.

Johnson, Glenn L., et al. 1969. *Strategies and recommendations for Nigerian rural development, 1969/1985.* Consortium for the Study of Nigerian Rural Development (CSNRD) report no. 33. (CSNRD was headquartered in the College of International Programs, Michigan State University, East Lansing.)

Johnson, Glenn L., and Sylvan Wittwer. 1984. *Agricultural technology until 2030: Prospects, priorities and policies.* Agricultural Experiment Station special report 12, Michigan State University, East Lansing.

Johnson, Glenn L., and Lewis K. Zerby. 1973. *What economists do about values—Case studies of their answers to questions they don't dare ask.* East Lansing: Michigan State University, Department of Agricultural Economics, Center for Rural Manpower and Public Affairs.

Kneese, Allen V. 1984. *Measuring the benefits of clean air and water.* Baltimore: distributed by Johns Hopkins University Press for Resources for the Future, Inc.

Knight, Frank H. 1933. *The economic organization.* Chicago: University of Chicago Press.

Maunder, Allen, and Kazushi Ohkawa, eds. 1983. *Growth and equity in agricultural development.* Proceedings of the 18th International Conference of Agricultural Economists, Jakarta, Indonesia. Oxford, England: Gower.

McCloskey, Donald N. 1985. *The rhetoric of economics.* Madison: The University of Wisconsin Press.

National Research Council. 1989. *Alternative agriculture.* Washington, D.C.: National Academy Press.

Parsons, K. H. 1949. The logical foundations of economic research. *Journal of Farm Economics* (November): 656–86.

_____1958. The value problem in agricultural policy. In *Agricultural adjustment problems in a growing economy.* Edited by E. Heady et al. Ames: Iowa State University Press.

Parsons, Talcott. 1957. *The structure of social action.* New York: McGraw Hill.

Pimental, D., et al. 1973. Food production and the energy crisis. *Science* 182 (2 November): 443–49.

Schmid, A. Allan. 1978. *Property, power, and public choice: An inquiry into law and economics.* New York: Praeger.

_____1989. *Benefit-cost analysis: A political economy approach to benefit cost analysis.* Boulder, Colo.: Westview Press.

CHAPTER 2

NATURAL RESOURCES IN AGRICULTURE: TRENDS AND ISSUES[1]

Kenneth D. Frederick, Roger A. Sedjo, and Pierre Crosson[2]

Natural resource use and enhancement involve a range of important values. They are important in the process for producing food and fiber and a major source of the space needed to accommodate growing populations and non-agricultural economic activity. Further, they provide amenity values associated with open space and habitat for wild plants and animals of present and potential value, and are perceived by many as essential to preservation of a rural way of life that, in the Jeffersonian tradition, supports and nurtures American principles of democracy.

The natural resources of the New World must have appeared virtually limitless to the immigrants arriving from Europe 200 or more years ago. Human impacts on the resources were small then and posed little threat to their renewability. The 76 million acres in crops as of 1850 were largely carved out of what had once been part of the vast forest covering the eastern United States. But, the biggest changes were still to come as cropland acreage increased more than fourfold over the next seven decades (Fedkiw 1988). By 1920, about 384 million acres of the indigenous forest and the attendant wildlife habitat had been cleared. Elimination of the forest was so rapid that by the end of the nineteenth century there were forecasts of an impending timber famine and concerns over the loss of wildlife habitat.

Increased erosion, one consequence of the conversion of forests and grasslands to crops, became a national concern during the Dust Bowl period of the 1930s. Erosion together with the loss of cropland to urban and other uses continues to underlie doubts about the adequacy of the nation's agricultural lands to meet long-term demands for food and fiber. Whenever harvests decline and real crop prices rise, these concerns reemerge in the headlines. Recent research, however, suggests that the water-quality damages associated with cropland erosion are more important than the productivity losses.

Grassland pasture and range uses of land declined from 935 million acres in 1880 to 659 million acres in 1982 (Fedkiw 1988), a trend that has also been strongly influenced by converting lands to crops. However, much of the Western range has little, if any, cropping potential in the absence of irrigation, and supports only limited grazing on a sustainable basis. Indeed, the capacity of some of these lands to support livestock over the long term has been a matter of some concern. By the late nineteenth century, grazing on Western rangelands exceeded levels that could be supported under drought conditions. Intensification of range use early in the twentieth century led to a deterioration in the quality of large areas and reports of irreversible degradation.

Without water, land will not support crops, grazing, forests, or wildlife. Although the nation as a whole is blessed with abundant water, supplies are unevenly distributed. Recent droughts and reports of widespread contamination of supplies have commanded national attention and encouraged reports during the 1980s of an imminent national water crisis.

Many of the earlier concerns over the demise of our renewable resources have proven to be overly alarmist. Aquatic systems, forests, wildlife, ranges, and cropland have demonstrated a remarkable capacity to restore themselves either naturally or in combination with sound management once abusive and exploitative uses are reduced. Moreover, technical advances have greatly increased production with the initial natural resource base. The most notable example has been the yield gains from new agricultural methods that have overwhelmed productivity losses resulting from cropland erosion.

On the other hand, experience has shown that the long-term productive potential of our natural resources is vulnerable and renewable only within limits and under wise management. Some valuable soil and water resources have, for practical purposes, been permanently depleted or degraded. In some cases, what have been regarded as technical advances have contributed to the depletion and degradation of resource bases.

Improved scientific understanding of ecosystems as well as an increased ability to detect and monitor changes in the physical and biological world underlie some new resource concerns. Until recently, wetlands were viewed as areas to be drained so that they could be put to productive use. As we have come to understand the role of wetlands in providing wildlife habitat, controlling floods, and restoring water quality, the loss of wetlands has become a national concern. The ability to detect the presence of contaminants in water supplies has contributed to heightened concerns over water quality and increased awareness that quality can even be affected by activities making no ostensible use of the resource. Increased, but still relatively primitive, understanding of the interrelations among the biosphere, geosphere, and atmosphere have led to a host of new resource concerns including the impacts of stratospheric ozone depletion and tropospheric ozone increases on crop and forest yields, the impact of acid precipitation on forests and lakes, the overall impacts of humans on endangered species and bio-diversity, and the possibility of a global greenhouse warming.

With a population approaching one-quarter of a billion people, an annual economy of five trillion dollars, and major technological changes, the nature as well as the magnitude of the nation's resource demands have changed drastically from what they were two centuries earlier. Less emphasis is now placed on the direct economic benefits of putting the resources to productive uses; greater weight is being given to protecting free-flowing streams, wetlands, forests, wilderness, and wildlife because of their contribution to the quality of life. Resources once viewed as obstacles to economic progress until they were tamed, eliminated, or exploited are now recognized as essential to the diversity and quality of our recreational opportunities. The growth of discretionary income and leisure has contributed to a rapid growth in the demand for outdoor recreation which is now a major claimant of the nation's renewable natural resources.

THE NATURE OF NATURAL RESOURCES

Some resources are stock resources—once a barrel of petroleum is used, it is gone. Other resources are renewable. Some restoration is natural—other restoration is done by people at costs that raise the question of optimal levels of sustainability. Some resources are maintained at higher than their original levels—others at lower than their original levels. Renewability suggests a capacity for restoration after use or consumption. Natural resources have an inherent resilience; that is, they have a natural capacity to renew themselves after disruptions from natural phenomena or human use and abuse. Although these systems are typically robust, having withstood disruptions and challenges over eons, they are not indestructible. Renewal may be difficult, slow, and halting. This is more likely to be the case when the disturbance is severe and unusual, but some natural systems are more fragile than others. In the extreme, a system may be so disturbed as to preclude renewability.

Important dimensions of renewability are the time frame over which the resource will naturally be restored after a disruption; the vulnerability of the resource to deterioration, especially to the point that natural restoration is impossible or unlikely except over very long periods; and the susceptibility of the resource to restoration through management. Characterizing resources according to these dimensions is difficult because the renewability and sustainability of a given resource varies widely depending on many different factors. For instance, surface water is generally renewed more readily than groundwater, while the renewability of forests, grasslands, and croplands depends importantly on soil and water conditions.

After sunshine, water is one of the more renewable natural resources; humans have no significant impact on sunshine or the amount of water in the hydrologic system. These resources can be used and/or reused indefinitely. Even the impurities of water are substantially removed through the evaporative process.

Soil generation is a variable process with the rates of sustainability and renewability dependent upon the nature of the underlying material, vegetative covers, and other factors. Mineral soils are formed over geologic time periods as rock is gradually broken down into very small fragments through weathering or other natural processes. Yet, under favorable circumstances, soil conditions can improve from one cropping season to another through the addition of organic matter, which is formed in the soil as plant and animal residues are decomposed by microbial activity. Badly eroded soils on hilly landscapes, however, may be unable to naturally sustain the vegetation required to prevent further erosion and restore the soil base without fertilizer application and irrigation.

Forest and grassland vegetative systems have the capacity to reestablish themselves after destruction due to fire, pests, logging, or grazing. In fact, forests and grasslands are part of complex ecosystems for which destruction and restoration are parts of a continuing natural cycle. Conversion to cropland has been the principal cause of the elimination of the natural forest or grass cover in the United States. These lands have varying capacities to revert to their former status after the termination of agriculture. Vast areas in the humid East reverted naturally to forests within a few years after they were abandoned for agricultural purposes. In the arid and semiarid West, however, the fate of abandoned cropland is often problematical in the absence of some initial efforts to provide a vegetative cover to stabilize the soils. Under favorable conditions, a cover of grass may be restored within a season or two. Under less favorable conditions, wind and water erosion may further undermine the condition of abandoned range.

Wildlife populations generally renew themselves in a seemingly unending cycle, one generation being replaced by the next as long as their habitat remains undisturbed. The ability to adjust to major disruptions in habitat varies widely among species, and local extinctions have been a common result of the elimination of forests, wetlands, and other wildlife habitat over the past two centuries. In some cases, these disruptions have threatened and occasionally resulted in global species extinctions.

Renewable resources have both stock and flow characteristics. At any point in time there is a stock that exists as a result of all former net flows. Ground and surface water reservoirs and the existing forests, grasses, and wildlife populations represent resource stocks that can be consumed, managed, or left entirely to natural forces. These natural forces result in resource flows. At any point in time forces operate simultaneously to reduce and increase stocks. Evaporation reduces and precipitation increases water stocks, and even as tree mortality or soil erosion is occurring, natural processes are simultaneously generating new growth in the forest and new soil formation on the land.

Increasingly, over the past two centuries, the stocks and flows of these resources have been determined by human impacts. Resource use has sometimes depleted stocks or adversely altered the natural ability of the resources to renew themselves. On the other hand, increased understanding of the resource systems and improved management practices have tended to increase the productivity of the natural systems.

NATURAL RESOURCE MANAGEMENT

Patterns of land and other natural resource management are social constructs. They are set by the complex of institutions and policies that determine property rights in land and the incentives to which land managers and owners respond. If, as a society, we decide that existing patterns give unsatisfactory results, we can seek improvement by changing the relevant institutions and policies.

In the United States, the market, as modified by government policies, is the principal institution that drives management decisions concerning land and other natural resources. Markets for farm output, for credit, for labor, fertilizer, machinery, and other production inputs, including land itself, provide farmers the price and other information critical to these decisions. It is not surprising, therefore, that concerns about the management of land and other natural resources are usually expressed as dissatisfaction with the performance of one or more of these markets. And steps to achieve socially more desirable practices generally involve government policies designed to reshape farmers' incentives by changing the price and other information they receive from the markets perceived to be errant.

As patterns of agricultural land management differ in yield of valuable goods and services so do they differ in costs of obtaining these yields. The costs are not just the obvious ones for fertilizers, labor, machinery, land, and other inputs farmers use in production. They also include intangible and nonmonetary costs, for example, the psychic stress experienced by people displaced by the shift toward larger, more mechanized farms, and damages to water quality resulting from soil erosion. The costs of policies designed to shift patterns of land management also must be included. As other costs will differ among patterns, so will policy costs.

Sustainability of natural resources requires achieving a long-term balance between growth and loss. Systems are typically out of balance in the short run. For instance, growth tends to exceed loss in a young forest while old forests may experience stagnation and ultimately decline as a result of insects, disease, or fire. However, it is the long-term relation between growth and loss that determines sustainability.

Sustainable management implies drawing from existing stocks without seriously compromising the ability of the resource to grow and renew itself for future use. Such management involves capturing for human use the losses and mortality that would otherwise occur naturally. Sustainable management captures the normal losses that grasslands experience due to seasonal factors or fire; the timber losses that would result from insects, disease, or fire; and the water losses that would occur through evaporation or runoff to the sea.

Prudent management and investments of manmade capital can increase the products that can be extracted from a resource system on a sustainable basis far beyond any naturally occurring resource flows. In some cases, the productivity of the resource may be stimulated simply by reducing the stock. For instance, a mature forest with no net growth may become a net producer of timber after some of its existing stock is removed, thereby permitting faster growth of the remaining trees. More importantly, the knowledge and ability to manipulate resource systems gained over the past two centuries have dramatically increased the capacity to boost yields well beyond those that would occur naturally. Improved seed varieties and chemicals that increase nutrient supply and reduce natural pests enable much higher crop, forest, and range yields. Greater understanding of hydrology and investments in dams and reservoirs have increased the capacity to reliably extract water from streams.

Management can also contribute to the recovery of a resource that has been subjected to excessive use and abuse. Logged-over forests and denuded rangelands can be replanted, locally extinct wildlife can be reintroduced, and improved game management techniques can be used. Cropland fertility can be restored by introducing chemical nutrients and better managed with deep-rooted legumes, fallowing, and rotation.

The rash of resource and environmental legislation enacted over the last two decades attests to the concerns about the nation's renewable resources and the need to better understand our impacts upon them. Two of these acts require the U.S. Department of Agriculture (USDA) to undertake periodic appraisals of the nation's renewable resources and their ability to meet the long-term demands upon them. The Renewable Resources Planning Act of 1974 (RPA) requires the USDA to undertake "an analysis of the present and anticipated uses, demand for, and supply of the renewable resources of forest, range, and other associated lands. . . " every ten years (Public Law 93–378, sec 3/a). The second RPA assessment was released in October 1989 (U.S. Department of Agriculture 1989b). The Resources Conservation Act of 1977 (RCA) directs the USDA to appraise the soil, water, and related resources of the nation's nonfederal lands and their ability to respond to long-term demands (Public Law 95–192). A review draft of the second RCA appraisal was released in June 1989 (U.S. Department of Agriculture 1989a).

The RPA and RCA appraisals focus largely on the current status of and the future demands on the resources. In contrast, Resources for the Future's forthcoming volume addressing the nation's renewable resources, focuses on understanding the long-term historical trends in the condition and capability of the nation's renewable resources. It represents an extension of the historical analysis of Fedkiw's (1988) document titled *The Evolving Use and Management of the Nation's Forests, Grasslands, Croplands and Related Resources: A Technical Document Supporting the 1989 RPA Assessment.* The historical approach is based on a belief that much can be learned about the current status and likely future problems of the nation's renewable resources through a better understanding of past changes in the condition, use, and management of the resources.

LESSONS FROM THE RESOURCE STUDIES

INTERDEPENDENCE AMONG THE RESOURCES

Land and water resources tend to move into the highest value uses; urban, industrial, and commercial users have

TABLE 1: MAJOR USES OF THE LAND, UNITED STATES, 1982

Total	Acreage (In Millions)	Percent Of
CROPLAND USED FOR CROPS	331	14.6
IDLE CROPLAND	68	3.0
CROPLAND USED ONLY FOR PASTURE	65	2.9
GRASSLAND PASTURE AND RANGE	591	26.1
FOREST LAND GRAZED	155	6.8
FOREST LAND NOT GRAZED	493	26.8
RECREATION AND WILDLIFE AREAS	225	9.9
TOTAL AREA FOR RESOURCE USES	1,928	85.1
FARMSTEADS, FARM ROADS	7	0.3
TRANSPORTATION USES	26	1.2
NATIONAL DEFENSE	21	0.9
URBAN AREAS	59	2.5
OTHER[1]	226	10.0
SUBTOTAL	**337**	**14.9**
TOTAL LAND AREA	**2,265**	**100.0**

Source: **Authur B. Daugherty,** *Major Use of Land in the United States: 1987,* Economic Research Service, U.S. Department of Agriculture, Agricultural Economic Report No. 643 (Washington, D.C., Jan. 1991).

[1]Includes miscellaneous uses not inventoried, and areas of little surface use such as marshes, open swamps, bare rock areas, desert, and tundra.

almost invariably been able to bid land and water away from uses such as agriculture and forestry. Thus, expansion of the nation's cities, towns, and highways has reduced the land and water available for crops, timber, range, and wildlife over the past two centuries. The direct claims of these higher value uses on the nation's land and water resources are still relatively modest. Five percent of the nation's total land base is devoted to urban areas, roads, other built up areas, and national defense (Table 1). While public, commercial, and industrial activities account for about 58 percent of the nation's water withdrawals, they account for only about 20 percent of the consumptive use. Moreover, the consumptive use of water for these purposes is less than 2 percent of the average renewable supply in the conterminous 48 states (Solley, Merk, and Pierce 1988).

The indirect impacts of these higher value, more intensive uses, however, can be much greater than the above figures suggest. For instance, although highways occupy only a small percentage of the land, they can affect large areas by breaking up wildlife habitats or impeding efficient farming. And the environmental impacts of factories, cities, and motor vehicles are not confined to the lands and waters they use directly; these intensive uses sometimes reduce the value of the remaining resources for crops, forests, wildlife, and outdoor recreation.

Agriculture, which also is rarely a benign user of land and water, generally takes precedence over forestry and range in the use of the remaining land. Indeed, changes in the land devoted to crops have had major impacts on the status of the nation's forests, rangelands, and wildlife habitats. The impacts were particularly strong in the nineteenth and early twentieth centuries when cropland acreage increased from 76 million in 1850 to 319 million in 1900 and to a peak of 413 million in 1930, displacing forests and range in the process.

Some of the earliest impacts of agricultural settlements were on the eastern forests. Pressures to clear the lands for crops, combined with a rapidly growing demand for wood for construction materials and fuel, brought drastic changes in the vegetative cover of the lands. Wildlife that was already under pressure in many areas from hunting lost large areas of habitat. Gradually, the search for agricultural land extended to the prairies and rangelands of the West. Even where forests and grasslands were not converted to crops, the ecosystems were often seriously disturbed by the grazing of a variety of domestic animals. These disturbances also contributed to some precipitous reductions in wildlife populations.

By the early 1900s, the frontier was gone and with it much of the opportunity to expand. The prairies of the Mississippi Valley had been converted to agriculture and were no longer available for expansion. Few areas were left in the West in which to expand dryland agriculture. The former grasslands with sufficient precipitation to support crops were already in agriculture while forest lands in the West generally were not viable for cropping. Major increases in irrigated agriculture required either large-scale water projects to capture and divert stream flows or improvements in pumping technologies to tap groundwater. While substantial forest land remained in the East, most of it was poorly suited to agriculture.

Beginning in the interwar period and accelerating after World War II, technical advances for agriculture contributed to dramatic increases in crop yields that relieved pressures on the land base. The amount of land used for crops and idled cropland increased less than three percent from 1920 to 1930, about one-fifth of the rate of increase over the previous decade. Moreover, even though total agricultural output has much more than doubled, the 1930 level of 413 million acres of cropland has not been equaled since. Intensive cropping patterns, made possible by the use of agricultural chemicals, improved seed varieties, and other managerial and technological improvements made it possible to concentrate crop production on a decreasing amount of land. The higher production that accompanied the improved yields put downward pressure on crop prices, encouraging the withdrawal of marginal lands from agriculture and their return to grasslands or forest.

The expansion of irrigated agriculture also contributed to higher agricultural yields. In areas of unreliable precipitation, irrigation is essential to the profitable use of many other yield-increasing inputs such as fertilizers and pesticides. Thus, irrigation expands the land base suitable for modern agriculture and reduces the pressures on lands in the more humid regions. Irrigation's impact on the total amount of land devoted to crops is reflected in the fact that in 1982 about 32 percent of the value of the crops produced was grown on the 13 percent of the acreage that was irrigated (Day and Horner 1987). Irrigation has also altered the regional distribution of the nation's agriculture and placed heavy pressure on water resources in some of the nation's most water-scarce regions. For instance, irrigation accounts for about 80 percent of the withdrawals and 90 percent of the consumptive use of water in the 17 Western states. The expansion of irrigation in the West was not always based on economic efficiency criteria or undertaken with full consideration of the environmental implications. Generous subsidies for irrigation projects, low and often subsidized energy costs, and institutions encouraging withdrawals have encouraged the growth of irrigated agriculture at the expense of the national treasury, groundwater stocks, in-stream flows, and riparian habitat.

The shift from a land-extensive to a yield-intensive agricultural development path was generally good news for the nation's forests, rangelands, and some of its wildlife, the condition of which reached a nadir in the early 1900s. The abandonment of marginal agricultural lands was accelerated by the low level of economic activity during the 1930s. Once abandoned, these lands began to naturally regenerate into forests. As noted in a subsequent section, reforestation and restoration of these lands have also been affected by a number of government policies.

Recovery of the forest and improvements in range conditions since the 1920s have improved habitat for various forms of wildlife and, with hunting controls and species reintroduction programs, many wildlife forms have flourished in recent decades. In some instances, wildlife probably approached or exceeded precolonial levels. On the other hand, these improvements have been at least partially offset by the loss of about half the nation's wetlands that has resulted in sharp reductions in waterfowl. Moreover, the yield-increasing agricultural technologies have not been an unmixed blessing for wildlife. Agricultural chemicals employed as an integral part of these technologies often end up in water supplies with adverse effects on aquatic life. The expansion of irrigation in parts of the West have increased salinity levels of most western streams, and irrigation drainage in California's San Joaquin Valley has resulted in selenium levels in the food chain that are toxic to waterfowl.

The introduction and wide acceptance of less erosive farming practices have probably reduced the high rates of soil loss experienced during the 1930s. Although erosion is a minor threat to the productivity of the nation's croplands, sediment and agricultural chemicals carried in runoff from farmers' fields contribute to water-quality problems. In fact, the evidence suggests that the off-farm costs of sediment and chemical pollutants are much greater than the damages to soil productivity.

Demands for outdoor recreation, which might serve as a rough proxy for the overall demands for the environmental services of the nation's land and water, have had an increasingly important impact on the use of these resources. As noted below, these demands have resulted in policies that (starting with the creation of Yellowstone National Park in 1872) have removed large land areas and water supplies from any commercial development and (more recently) have restricted how land and water resources in general can legally be used.

RESOURCE USE AND TECHNICAL CHANGE

Technical changes have had varying impacts on the nation's resources. Many of the earliest developments encouraged resource use and exploitation while more recent developments have tended to be resource conserving.

Early technical advances in agriculture facilitated the clearing and preparation of land for crops and greatly increased the amount of land that could be farmed by a single worker. The single-piece cast-iron plow patented in 1797 and the wrought-iron plow with a steel cutting edge developed in 1837 were among the advances that enabled a worker to farm increasingly larger plots as the nineteenth century advanced. The gasoline-engine tractor, first developed in the 1880s and improved in succeeding decades, enabled much greater increases in labor productivity, thereby increasing the demand to clear, drain, and cultivate more land. On the other hand, the substitution of mechanical for animal power eased pressures on the land by reducing the area required for feeding farm animals.

Mechanization of earth moving and development of better concrete early in the twentieth century made it possible to build much larger water projects, and improved pumps in the 1930s facilitated the exploitation of groundwater supplies. Other innovations stimulated the demand for water and water projects. For instance, improved electricity and transmission techniques made water power much more versatile, thereby encouraging dam and reservoir construction. And, the acreage that could be practicably irrigated grew as a result of technologies such as sprinkler systems, which made it possible to irrigate very hilly terrain.

Technical changes in forestry allowed more rapid logging and transport of timber. These changes not only provided more timber, they facilitated the conversion of timberlands to agriculture. The advent of steam power and the railroad also encouraged logging and enabled previously inaccessible stands to be cleared. During the latter part of the nineteenth century, the development of new products increased the demand for wood and wood fiber. For example, wood fiber was increasingly replacing rags as the basic raw material in paper making by the end of the century.

When resource-intensive techniques were developed and adopted, the resources were not regarded, at least by the users, as being very costly. Forests and the wildlife habitat they provided were not generally regarded as scarce in the eastern United States when they were first being cleared for crops and timber. Little, if any, value was attributed to the amenity and other in-stream uses of natural stream flows when they were first being altered and diverted for irrigation.

Gradually the situation changed. Population and rural and industrial development combined with the demise of large forest, range, water, and wildlife resources to lead to a growing realization that these resources were indeed valuable. Technical developments reflected these changes: over the years, technical advances have been induced that substitute cheaper, more plentiful resources for expensive, scarce ones.

As noted above, agricultural methods and management practices began adapting to the increasing scarcity of good cropland after World War I. Use of agricultural chemicals, high-yielding crop varieties, and other yield-increasing developments enabled output per acre of arable land, which had declined from 1880 to 1920, to increase 180 percent from 1920 to 1980 (Ruttan and Hayami 1988).

Somewhat similar patterns of technical advances and changes in resource use followed for timber and water. After the unprecedented growth in the demand for wood for construction and fuel toward the end of the nineteenth century, total wood consumption declined. In the face of rising relative wood prices, improved techniques provided preferred wood substitutes for many uses and permitted more complete use of timber resources. New construction methods allowed iron, steel, and concrete to replace wood in many uses, and the growing use of fossil fuels led to a decline in the use of wood for fuel. Wood preservatives dramatically extended the useful life of wood products such as railroad ties, poles, fences, and construction, and new milling techniques provided more product from a given log. In recent years, the increased use of short-fibered woods for pulping and the development of waferboard-panel products permitted substitution of inexpensive, "low-quality" wood resources for more expensive, "high-quality" wood.

Research has contributed directly to the growth of the forest as tree planting techniques were improved, and improved trees were introduced through the planting of genetically superior seedlings. Technical innovations in fire fighting helped reduce the risk of losses due to fire and, thereby, contributed to the willingness of investors to plant trees.

It has only been within the last several decades that water has been widely viewed as scarce and that irrigators and industrial users have had to deal with rising water costs. Higher water costs have prompted large savings in the water used for industrial cooling, as firms abandon once-through cooling systems in favor of recycling. Irrigators dependent on groundwater were forced to adapt to much higher water costs as a result of the increase in energy costs in the 1970s. Those farmers who continued to irrigate successfully in the face of much higher water costs adopted a variety of water-conserving practices, including more efficient water management practices and less water-intensive crops and seed varieties.

The United States experience indicates that technical change is responsive to changes in resource scarcity as perceived by users of the resources. This experience also indicates that an individual farmer's, firm's, or consumer's perceptions of scarcity may differ greatly from that of society as a whole. These differences are particularly evident for, but are not limited to, water resources. Water has traditionally been treated as a free resource, in that users have not been charged for withdrawing water from or discharging wastes into a stream. Moreover, large subsidies have encouraged some water uses at the expense of others. The following section indicates how institutional and policy considerations have influenced the development and use of the resources.

INSTITUTIONS AND THE STATUS OF THE RESOURCES

Institutional factors including the laws, policies, programs, and administrative arrangements directed to controlling resource use have had major impacts on the changing status of the resources. The institutions themselves have evolved over time as conditions have changed. Major institutional shifts, however, have often come only after resource conditions had deteriorated to a state that attracted widespread alarm. Frequently, the institutions encouraged use, permitted abuse, and limited the incentives and opportunities for adjusting efficiently to changes in the underlying condition and availability of the resources.

The nature of the resources creates special challenges for developing institutions that provide for their efficient use. It is difficult to establish clear property rights over some resources. Rivers, streams, and groundwater resources that flow from one property to another as well as wildlife that moves over large areas, are common property resources. In the absence of property rights, they belong to no one until they are captured for use. This situation results in the problem of the "tragedy of the commons" in which a common resource is exploited excessively because it is available for the taking on a first-come, first-served basis. The inability to capture the rewards of any protective action provides individuals little incentive to manage or conserve the resource.

The depletion of American wildlife stocks during the nineteenth century is a classic example of the overexploitation of an open access, common-property resource. Wildlife was viewed as the property of the successful hunter and there was no incentive to preserve wildlife habitat. Similarly, wood for fuel and materials and grazing on the "open" range were typically available for the "taking," reflecting the lack of ownership and the inability of the government to exercise management or control, even in cases where these responsibilities had been assigned to the public sector. Water resources were also withdrawn and polluted with little concern for the impacts on downstream users.

In some cases, the unique circumstances of the American experience resulted in the creation of innovative institutions. In the East, where water was plentiful, the English system of riparian rights was adopted. In the West, however, the riparian system was soon found to be inadequate, and a system of appropriative rights developed and evolved into law.

Programs aimed at protecting and preserving important portions of our natural resource base date back to the late 1800s. The creation of Yellowstone National Park in 1872 was the first official measure to protect resources from development or exploitation. The national forest system was created in the last decade of the nineteenth century; by 1920, over 150 million acres, most of it in the West, had been placed into the system. The first serious effort to protect wildlife also dates back to this period. The last several decades have seen a number of important measures to protect the quantity and quality of the nation's land and water resources and restrict use for commercial forestry, grazing, or other activities. Laws such as the Wild and Scenic Rivers Act, the designation of wilderness and roadless areas, the Endangered Species Act, the Clean Water Act and its amendments, and a pledge by President Bush to prevent any additional net loss in wetlands reflect both the growing importance of outdoor recreation and a willingness to protect some of the remaining wildlife habitat from the pressures of future economic development.

The provision of secure private-property rights has also led to improved resource protection and management. As the open range came under secure private ownership, careful management replaced the myopic treatment given resources held in common (Anderson and Hill 1975). Similarly, private owners of croplands with secure tenure had market incentives to limit erosion losses that affect productivity. Much of the nineteenth century logging was done to both obtain the timber and convert the land for agricultural uses. However, as timber became dear and investments in tree planting became secure, private-sector tree planting came to exceed that of the public sector. Water-use efficiency has been encouraged, as rights have been made secure and transferable, permitting owners to benefit from their own conservation measures or to reallocate supplies through markets from lower to higher value uses. The private sector is also contributing to the preservation of wildlife and its habitat. In some cases, it is an inadvertent consequence of maintaining forest for timber production purposes. At other times, it is by design, like industry attempts to maintain wildlife habitat for hunting or bird watching to promote harmonious public relations (Lassiter 1980) or private-sector activities designed to provide habitat to promote fee hunting. Finally, secure land tenure allows conservation groups such as the Audubon Society to purchase and preserve lands containing unique habitat.

As noted earlier, lands have considerable capacity to return to their original condition once human interventions are eliminated or sharply curtailed. In some instances, government programs have been used to encourage the recovery of the forests and range. Although the merits of the Taylor Grazing Act of 1934 are debated, many believe it has contributed to a recovery of the public range, and that overall range conditions have improved since 1920. Reforestation and restoration of eroded lands were encouraged during the 1930s by New Deal programs established to provide employment planting trees and undertaking other erosion-control projects. Programs to prevent and control forest fires are controversial because they alter the natural cycle of the forest and the nature of the wildlife habitat it provides. But, the control of wildfires has contributed to the reestablishment of forest on abandoned croplands in the East and to continual increases in the timber stocking of U.S. forests since World War II. Controlling wildfires and animal browsing provides tree seedlings an opportunity to mature, thereby displacing brush and grasses in areas naturally suited to forest. Control of wildfire, higher real wood prices in the postwar period, taxes, and other incentives have also encouraged the private sector to emerge as a major force for forest regeneration. Consequently, tree planting has been an important mode of forest renewal in the postwar period. By the late 1980s, about 3 million acres of forest were being planted each year, over 80 percent of which was done by the private sector.

The area of timberlands reached its low point in 1920 and has increased, albeit somewhat haltingly, thereafter. Although, very recently, timberland acreage decreased, much of this decline was due to reclassifications, such as those associated with the establishment of wilderness areas. The total volume of timber has increased every year, since at least 1952 when forest inventories were initiated.

By many criteria, the nation's forests are in their best condition since the start of this century. In addition to timber values, the forests continue to provide multiple uses including recreational experiences and environmental services. The improvement in many wildlife populations is, no doubt, due partly to improved habitats provided by the renewed forests. Nevertheless, difficulties persist. The clash between timber and environmental values has intensified in recent years, with a focus on preservation of old-growth forests and concerns for threatened and endangered species and maintaining bio-diversity. Although there is potentially a considerable amount of economically available timber in the United States, conflicting demands, which have removed large areas from the timber base, threaten the future availability of timber production in some regions.

Assessments of range conditions, due in part to poorer data, are much more cautious. Nevertheless, many observers believe that the range, too, is in its best condition of the last fifty or more years. The status of wildlife is more ambiguous. Many species have made remarkable comebacks, others have partially recovered, while some waterfowl species continue to decline in number. Agricultural surpluses made possible by the large increases in crop yields have dominated farm policy concerns over the last four decades. Although erosion continued to exceed soil regeneration over large agricultural areas, these losses pose no threat to the nation's overall agricultural productivity for the foreseeable future.

The nation's water resources have undergone major changes in this century. Huge infrastructure investments have brought once unreliable rivers under control, greatly increased the quantities of water that can be reliably supplied even in drought periods, and expanded the opportunities for flat-water recreation. Moreover, water treatment technologies have virtually eliminated some of the diseases that became epidemics during the nineteenth century as a result of contaminated water supplies. The changes, however, have not all been beneficial. Increased control and use of the rivers have come at the expense of the values provided by free-flowing streams. The quality of the nation's rivers and lakes has also continued to deteriorate until about two decades ago. Since then, surface water quality has improved as a result of large reductions in the levels of the more visible conventional pollutants, such as biochemical oxygen demand, nuisance plant growth, suspended solids, and fecal coliform bacteria. But, toxics from industrial, agricultural, and municipal sources are increasingly ending up in water supplies, and these substances are now recognized to pose important health risks. The condition of some groundwater supplies continues to deteriorate as a result of mining and contamination. In many cases, the deterioration is essentially irreversible within a human life span. On balance, however, the nation has plentiful supplies of water to meet foreseeable demands as long as they are appropriately constrained by prices that reflect the costs of their use.

A clear loser over the past century has been the nation's wetlands. About half of the original wetlands in the contiguous 48 states have been drained and filled, and there is little prospect that there will be any significant return of these lands to wetlands. Furthermore, pressures to drain remaining wetlands remain. On the other hand, some of the government policies that once encouraged converting these lands into croplands have been eliminated, and a new appreciation of the value of wetlands should provide a degree of protection for these ecosystems that did not exist before.

Outdoor recreation depends in part on the availability and health of all the other resources and on society's willingness to allocate these resources for recreational as opposed to competing purposes. Many of our forests, grasslands, wildlife, and surface waters are heavily utilized in providing outdoor recreation. Legislation passed over the last two decades that is designed to restore the quality of these resources and set large land and water areas off limits for intensive development, has improved many recreational opportunities and bodes well for the future. The challenge, however, will be to meet the rising demand for outdoor recreation experiences that will accompany expected population and income increases without diminishing the quality of the experience.

NOTES

1. This chapter was compiled by the authors from a draft, "Renewable Resource Trends: An Overview," of a forthcoming book tentatively titled *The Nation's Renewable Resources: Past Trends and Future Challenges*, by Kenneth D. Frederick and Roger A. Sedjo, and from Chapter 1, "Issues in Management of Agricultural Land," in *The Long-Term Adequacy of Agricultural Land in the United States: Economic and Environmental Issues*, by Pierre Crosson; both are forthcoming from Resources for the Future, Incorporated, Washington, D.C.

2. All three authors are senior fellows at Resources for the Future, Inc., Washington, D.C.

REFERENCES

Anderson, Terry L., and P. J. Hill. 1975. The evolution of property rights. *Journal of Law and Economics* 18 (April): 163–79.

Day, John C., and Gerald L. Horner. 1987. *U.S. irrigation: Extent and importance*, Agricultural Information Bulletin no. 523, Economic Research Service, U.S. Dept. of Agriculture, Washington, D.C., September.

Fedkiw, John. 1988. *The evolving use and management of the nation's forests, grasslands, croplands and related resources: A technical document supporting the 1989 RPA assessment*, U.S. Forest Service, Washington, D.C.

Frey, H. Thomas, and Roger W. Hexem. 1985. *Major uses of land in the United States: 1982*, Agricultural Economic Report no. 535, Economic Research Service, U.S. Dept. of Agriculture, Washington, D.C., June.

Lassiter, Roy L., Jr. 1980. Access to and management of the wildlife resources on large private timberland holdings in the Southeastern United States, College of Business Monograph Series no. 1, Tennessee State University, Nashville.

Ruttan, Vernon W., and Yujiro Hayami. 1988. Induced technical change in agriculture. In *Agricultural productivity: Measurement and explanation.* Edited by Susan M. Capalbo and John M. Antle. Washington, D.C.: Resources for the Future.

Solley, Wayne B., Charles F. Merk, and Robert R. Pierce. 1988. *Estimated use of water in the United States in 1985*, U.S. Geological Survey Circular 1004, Washington, D.C.

U.S. Dept. of Agriculture. 1974. *Our land and water resources: Current and perspective supplies and uses*, Economic Research Service, Washington, D.C., May.

_____1989a. *The second RCA appraisal: Soil, water, and related resources on nonfederal land in the United States—Analysis of condition and trends*, review draft, Washington, D.C., June.

_____1989b. *RPA assessment of the forest and rangeland situation in the United States, 1989*, FRR–26, Forest Service, U.S. Dept. of Agriculture, October.

CHAPTER 3

TRENDS AND IMPLICATIONS OF AGRICULTURAL INPUT USE IN U.S. AGRICULTURE

Joseph R. Barse and John R. Schaub[1]

Emphasis on technical change as a driving force for agricultural and rural development in the United States has brought about the phenomenal transformation in U.S. agriculture discussed in Part II, Section 1, Chapter 1. Technical change has involved changes in both the quantity and quality of specific input categories over time as well as the mix of input categories. Generally, non-farm-produced capital inputs, such as machinery, energy, agricultural chemicals, and credit, have been substituted first for labor and later for land. Change in total factor productivity, measured as the change in total output divided by change in total input, is one of the best proxy indicators of technical change and is also reviewed. Impacts of trends in input use on water quality, food safety, and food prices, as well as other concerns making up the natural resource and man-made capital social science agenda in food, agriculture, and rural development conclude the chapter.

TRENDS IN AGRICULTURAL INPUTS

The mix of inputs used for agricultural production has been changing for decades (Offutt and Shoemaker 1988; Schertz et al. 1979; U.S. Dept. of Agriculture 1968). A 1968 ERS report described two major trends in input use. First, farmers began to purchase a greater portion of production inputs, relying less upon their own operations as an input source. Second, farmers substituted manufactured inputs, such as machinery, fertilizer, and pesticides, first for labor and much later for land, based on dollar values of these inputs. The use of nonpurchased inputs declined 33 percent between 1950 and 1966 while purchased input use increased 34 percent (U.S. Dept. of Agriculture 1968). The use of fertilizer, lime, and pesticides approximately tripled and labor use declined 53 percent during those years.

Those trends continued in general from 1966 to 1986, but not for the entire period and not for every item (Table 1). The share of purchased inputs (including annual "consumption" of machinery represented by depreciation) versus that of nonpurchased inputs, which stood at about 52/48 percent in 1966, was about 61/39 percent by 1986 (Table 2). The purchased input share rose gradually in the 1960s and 1970s, peaking at 63 percent in 1979, the year in which the dollar value of all inputs also peaked. Although the real value of all inputs used in agriculture has fallen dramatically from $92.6 billion in the peak year of 1979 to $76.7 billion in 1986, the share of purchased inputs has remained about steady at 61–62 percent in every year during 1980–86. Almost all of the gross change in the purchased/nonpurchased input relationship for the 1966–86 period occurred during the years 1966–79, especially in the late 1970s.

The nonpurchased (farm-origin) share of all inputs dropped from 48 to almost 38 percent during 1966–78, while purchased inputs which replaced farm-origin inputs were mainly machinery (counting depreciation), energy, feeds, fertilizers, and pesticides (Table 2). For example, pesticides, which were only one percent of inputs in 1966, tripled to over three percent by 1978.

The purchased/nonpurchased input shares did not change much after 1978. Consequently, certain purchased inputs took larger roles from 1979 on, only as other purchased inputs took smaller roles. Pesticides and borrowed funding (interest) have become relatively more important since 1979, while machinery (counting depreciation), hired labor, and energy have taken smaller shares of farmers' input dollars (Table 2).

For the entire period 1966–86, the following are key trends: rising shares of pesticides, fertilizers, and interest, the rising then falling shares of machinery and energy, and the falling then stabilized share of all nonpurchased inputs. In addition, there was a rise in constant-price value of all inputs from 1975–79, and a subsequent sharp decline in total input use through 1986.

PURCHASED INPUTS AND PRODUCTIVITY

Many purchased inputs help carry technical change to agriculture over time. Daberkow (1987) concluded, in a

TABLE 1: INPUTS USED IN AGRICULTURAL PRODUCTION, 1966-86, VALUED AT CONSTANT PRICES[1]

Year	Non-Purchased[2]	Depreciation Of Machinery[3]	Machinery Except Depreciation[4]	Hired Labor	Interest	Energy	Other Purchased[5]	Seeds: Value Added By Process[6]	Feeds: Value Added By Manufacturers[6]	Fertilizers[7]	Pesticides	Total All Inputs
	Billion dollars (1976-78)											
1966	41.0	9.2	5.3	6.2	3.5	3.7	9.3	0.9	2.2	3.4	0.9	85.5
1967	39.7	9.5	5.6	6.4	3.7	3.7	9.4	1.0	2.3	3.8	1.2	86.3
1968	39.5	9.7	5.5	5.9	3.9	3.7	9.5	0.9	2.2	4.0	1.3	86.0
1969	38.4	9.7	5.4	5.7	3.9	3.7	9.5	1.0	2.4	4.1	1.4	85.2
1970	38.1	9.7	5.2	5.4	4.0	3.7	9.8	1.1	2.4	4.2	1.5	85.0
1971	36.8	9.7	5.6	5.4	4.0	3.7	9.6	1.3	2.6	4.4	1.7	84.9
1972	36.8	9.8	5.4	5.7	4.1	3.6	9.7	1.2	2.7	4.5	2.0	85.5
1973	36.4	10.1	5.8	6.0	3.9	3.7	9.3	1.4	2.8	4.7	2.1	86.2
1974	36.0	10.5	6.1	6.5	3.8	3.9	8.6	1.4	2.6	5.0	2.0	86.3
1975	36.0	10.6	5.7	6.2	3.6	4.5	8.4	1.4	2.3	4.5	1.8	85.1
1976	35.2	10.3	5.8	6.0	3.8	5.2	9.0	1.6	2.5	5.3	1.9	86.6
1977	34.8	10.4	6.0	6.2	4.1	5.4	9.4	1.5	2.5	5.6	2.0	87.9
1978	34.6	10.8	6.4	6.5	4.3	5.7	9.4	1.5	2.9	5.2	2.9	90.0
1979	34.4	10.8	6.5	6.2	5.1	5.3	10.1	1.6	3.1	5.7	3.7	92.6
1980	34.3	10.9	5.8	6.0	5.0	5.1	9.3	1.7	3.0	5.8	3.5	90.4
1981	33.9	10.7	5.5	6.0	5.2	4.9	9.7	1.5	2.7	5.9	3.9	90.0
1982	33.0	10.4	4.8	6.0	5.3	4.8	9.4	1.4	2.8	5.3	3.6	86.7
1983	32.1	9.8	4.6	7.3	5.3	4.8	9.0	1.3	3.0	4.6	3.4	85.2
1984	31.7	9.0	4.8	5.7	5.2	4.7	9.0	1.4	2.7	5.4	3.8	83.3
1985	30.4	8.5	4.8	5.2	5.0	4.4	9.2	1.3	2.8	5.3	3.8	80.6
1986	29.8	8.0	4.4	4.6	4.7	4.1	8.9	1.2	2.7	4.8	3.5	76.7

Sources: Calculated from Evans (1987), based on data concepts explained in USDA (1986, 1987, 1988, 1989).
[1]Constant prices (1976-1978 annual average) most appropriate to individual time series (Evans). All individual input series above except nonpurchased and depreciation of machinery are classified as purchased inputs in the source data. However depreciation of machinery may also be considered a purchased input, since it represents consumption of a capital item clearly produced off-farm and purchased or leased by farmers.
[2]All nonpurchased inputs, including unpaid operator and family labor, and operator-owned real estate and other capital inputs, but excluding machinery depreciation.
[3]All depreciation on farm machinery and vehicles, excluding portions of vehicle depreciation not stemming from farm work.
[4]Includes repairs to vehicles and machinery, parts and tires, and licenses, taxes, and insurance on vehicles.
[5]Includes building repairs, grazing fees, hardware, hand tools, hired trucking, purchased livestock marketing services, real estate and personal property taxes, fire/wind/crop insurance, containers, binding materials, dairy supplies, veterinary fees, irrigation charges, telephone for farm operations, and ginning charges.
[6]Portion of purchase value represented by value added to original agricultural products by processing and transportation outside the agricultural sector.
[7]Includes limestone.

TABLE 2: PERCENTAGE COMPOSITION OF AGRICULTURAL INPUTS, 1966-86

Year	Non-Purchased[1]	Depreciation Of Machinery[2]	Machinery Except Depreciation[3]	Hired Labor	Interest	Energy	Other Purchased[4]	Seeds: Value Added By Process[5]	Feeds: Value Added By Manufacturers[5]	Fertilizers[6]	Pesticides	Total All Inputs
	Percent											
1966	48.0	10.7	6.2	7.2	4.1	4.3	10.9	1.1	2.5	4.0	1.0	100.0
1967	46.0	11.0	6.5	7.5	4.3	4.3	10.9	1.1	2.6	4.3	1.4	100.0
1968	45.9	11.3	6.4	6.9	4.5	4.3	11.0	1.1	2.5	4.6	1.5	100.0
1969	45.1	11.4	6.3	6.6	4.6	4.4	11.2	1.2	2.8	4.8	1.7	100.0
1970	44.8	11.4	6.1	6.3	4.7	4.4	11.5	1.2	2.9	4.9	1.8	100.0
1971	43.3	11.5	6.6	6.4	4.7	4.4	11.3	1.5	3.1	5.2	2.0	100.0
1972	43.1	11.4	6.3	6.6	4.8	4.3	11.3	1.4	3.2	5.2	2.3	100.0
1973	42.3	11.7	6.8	6.9	4.5	4.3	10.8	1.6	3.3	5.4	2.4	100.0
1974	41.8	12.1	7.0	7.5	4.4	4.5	9.9	1.6	3.0	5.8	2.3	100.0
1975	42.4	12.4	6.7	7.3	4.3	5.3	9.9	1.6	2.8	5.3	2.1	100.0
1976	40.6	11.9	6.7	6.9	4.4	5.9	10.4	1.8	2.9	6.2	2.2	100.0
1977	39.6	11.9	6.8	7.1	4.6	6.1	10.7	1.7	2.9	6.4	2.2	100.0
1978	38.4	11.8	7.1	7.2	4.8	6.3	10.4	1.7	3.2	5.8	3.2	100.0
1979	37.1	11.7	7.1	6.7	5.5	5.8	11.0	1.7	3.4	6.1	3.9	100.0
1980	38.0	12.0	6.4	6.6	5.6	5.7	10.3	1.8	3.3	6.4	3.9	100.0
1981	37.7	11.9	6.1	6.6	5.8	5.5	10.8	1.7	3.1	6.5	4.3	100.0
1982	38.0	12.0	5.5	6.9	6.1	5.6	10.9	1.6	3.2	6.1	4.2	100.0
1983	37.7	11.4	5.5	8.6	6.2	5.6	10.6	1.5	3.5	5.4	4.0	100.0
1984	38.1	10.8	5.8	6.8	6.2	5.6	10.8	1.7	3.2	6.5	4.5	100.0
1985	37.7	10.5	5.9	6.5	6.2	5.4	11.4	1.7	3.5	6.6	4.7	100.0
1986	38.9	10.4	5.7	6.1	6.2	5.3	11.7	1.6	3.5	6.2	4.5	100.0

Sources: Calculated from Table 1 values, based on data concepts used in Table 1.

[1]All nonpurchased inputs, including unpaid operator and family labor, and operator-owned real estate and other capital inputs, but excluding machinery depreciation.

[2]All depreciation (viewed as annual capital consumption) on farm machinery and vehicles, excluding portions of vehicle depreciation not stemming from farm work.

[3]Includes repairs to vehicles and machinery, tires, parts, and licenses, taxes, and insurance on vehicles.

[4]Includes building repairs, grazing fees, hardware, hand tools, hired trucking, purchased livestock marketing services, real estate and personal property taxes, fire/wind/crop insurance, containers, binding material, dairy supplies, irrigation charges, veterinary fees, telephone (farm operations), and ginning charges.

[5]Portion of feed or seed purchase value represented by value added to original agricultural products by processing and transportation outside the agricultural sector.

[6]Includes limestone.

recent review of agricultural input industries, that input industries are major forces in transmitting new technologies to farmers by selling them new or improved inputs. Both public-sector and private-sector research and development have created these new technologies (Schertz et al. 1979). Publicly funded extension services and private businesses are both responsible for helping create farmer demand for the improved inputs. New kinds of pesticides, improved machinery, cattle growth hormones, and new seed varieties are only a few examples of technologically changed inputs purchased by farmers in recent years.

Over time, the changed input mixture is so striking as to be clear evidence of technical change, the statistical confirmation of what we know to have been new technologies and new inputs at the farm level. Input changes continued during 1966–86, as farm use of purchased inputs increased, while use of nonpurchased inputs declined (Table 1). The use of all labor, both purchased and nonpurchased (operator and unpaid family labor), fell substantially from 1966–86. Since output rose at the same time, labor productivity rose sharply, as did the combined productivity of all farm inputs (Table 3). The productivity of cropland, as of labor and all inputs together, also rose during 1966–85 (Table 3). The record of advancing technology and rising productivity in agriculture over the past twenty years lends additional support to the widely held view among economists that, in general, technical change does lead to greater productivity (Link 1987).

The increases in the productivity of all inputs, of labor, and of land cannot be attributed solely to technical change. Agricultural output and productivity are the results of combining an entire "package" of inputs influenced by weather. A variety of economic incentives, such as government policies and programs, the general health of the economy, and export market demand, also play major roles. Nevertheless, technical change as expressed through the mixture of purchased inputs was a very important influence in boosting agricultural productivity during 1966–85. The input industries were a major source of technical change along with the extension services and the land-grant university system. However, even rising productivity cannot guarantee any given or desired level of returns to factors of production in the face of many kinds of market risks.

We now turn to brief summaries for individual input trends.

FERTILIZER

Total fertilizer use rose from 32 million tons in the mid–1960s to a peak of 54 million tons in 1981, but then dropped off to 44 million tons in the mid–1980s. Application rates per acre are now much higher than they were twenty years ago, but these rates dropped in the 1980s, perhaps because of less favorable fertilizer/crop price ratios. Greater corn acreage and more intensive nitrogen use on corn since the 1960s helped to double the total amount of nitrogen applied, making nitrogen the dominant purchased nutrient. U.S. firms increased fertilizer production capacity in response to the rising fertilizer demand, but encountered higher costs and growing world competition from foreign manufacturers. The United States can now count on being a net exporter of only phosphate, at times becoming a net importer of nitrogen, and a regular importer of potash. Foreign producers have taken advantage of their lower-cost supplies of natural gas, a nitrogen feedstock.

PESTICIDES

A very strong demand for pesticides by farmers, federal regulation, patent protection, and new pesticide technology have been major forces influencing pesticide production over the past twenty years. Pesticide sales to farmers rose from $0.9 billion in 1966 to $3.5 billion in 1986 (1977 dollars), while farmer use of pesticides rose from 353 million to 475 million pounds (active ingredients). The share of major crop acreage treated with insecticides and herbicides doubled as farmers found these chemicals to be cost-effective substitutes for some labor and machine inputs, such as tillage. U.S. pesticide output is dominated by about 28 large firms, although pesticides may be only five percent of a firm's sales. Major research and development efforts yielded many new pesticides, which have patent protection for 17 years. The rankings of industry firms by sales shifted rapidly as pesticides came on or off patent, or were canceled by the Environmental Protection Agency (EPA).

ENERGY

The food and fiber sector accounts for 10–15 percent of all U.S. energy consumption, but influences energy prices very little. Farm production uses only 3–4 percent of the U.S. energy supply. Much of the oil used in the United States has come from unstable world markets since the 1960s. Costs of energy to agriculture are much higher and energy supplies may be more vulnerable to shocks than twenty years ago. Natural gas from domestic wells is not subject to international supply disruption, but after 1974, natural gas prices increased sharply along with petroleum prices. Natural gas is a major feedstock for farm chemicals, which represent 40 percent of the energy used to produce crops. Food processors have switched from petroleum to electricity and natural gas. Farmers conserved petroleum by substituting diesel power for gasoline power and using minimum tillage. Ethanol, an alternative liquid fuel, typically produced from corn, is still a high-cost fuel relative to petroleum, and depends on government subsidies.

LIVESTOCK FEEDS

Major changes have occurred in the kinds of manufactured feeds produced in the last twenty years, as well as in the feed marketing industry, with the industry integrating vertically toward livestock farming. Feed firms are responding to demands for more supplements, superconcentrates, premixes, and pelleted feeds. Changes in the livestock sector, such as larger enterprises, fewer milk cows, and more broilers, have come from pressure to cut costs and from shifts in consumer preferences toward poultry meat and away from red meat, dairy products, and eggs. The industry has been stable with a relatively small rise in total formula feed production from 1969 to 1984, and the same market share for the top eight firms during the 1969–84 period. Yet, feed output is expanding more into the Southern Plains, Pacific States, and Lake States, while

TABLE 3: USE OF AGRICULTURAL LAND AND LABOR, AND INDICES OF OUTPUT, INPUT, AND PRODUCTIVITY, 1966-86

Year	Labor Used In Agriculture[1]	Farm Production Per Hour Of Labor[1]	Cropland Used For Crops	Crop Production Per Acre	All Agricultural Output	All Agricultural Inputs	Productivity Of All Inputs
	Billion hours	Index 1977-100					
1966	9.2	59	88	83	79	96	83
1967	8.9	64	90	86	83	98	85
1968	8.6	68	89	89	85	97	87
1969	8.2	72	88	91	85	96	88
1970	7.8	74	88	88	84	96	87
1971	7.5	85	90	96	92	97	95
1972	7.6	83	88	99	91	97	94
1973	7.5	86	93	99	93	98	95
1974	7.5	81	96	88	88	98	90
1975	7.3	90	97	96	95	97	99
1976	6.9	97	98	94	97	98	98
1977	6.9	100	100	100	100	100	100
1978	6.9	104	97	105	104	102	101
1979	6.8	113	100	113	111	105	105
1980	6.6	109	101	100	104	103	101
1981	6.6	123	102	115	118	102	116
1982	6.4	125	101	116	116	99	117
1983	6.7	99	88	100	96	97	99
1984	6.4	121	99	112	112	95	119
1985	5.9	139	98	120	118	92	128
1986	5.5	139	94	116	111	87	127

Source: U.S. Dept. of Agriculture (1988).

[1]Data series developed by ERS. Alternative series by the National Agricultural Statistics Service and the Bureau of Labor Statistics show the same general trends.

companies are improving the nutritional efficiency of their feeds and expanding on-farm animal feeding.

CREDIT

Farmers' outstanding debt (excluding operator household and crop loans from the Commodity Credit Corporation [CCC]) rose from $36 billion in 1965 to a peak of $193 billion in 1983, but has since fallen to about $143 billion in 1987. Farm debt was 16 percent of total farm assets in 1965, rising to 23 percent in 1985, and falling to 20 percent by 1987. Most debt increase took place in the late 1970s. Farmers were receiving lower returns from investment in agriculture by the 1980s and many could not service their debts. Lenders lost billions of dollars on farm loans and tightened credit standards, contributing to farmers' decisions to cut their demand for new credit. Farmers' reliance on CCC loans and advance government deficiency payments reduced their demand for short-term credit, and the drop in farmland values reduced demand for long-term credit. The Farmers Home Administration (FmHA) has been the only major lender to increase farm lending since 1983. Commercial banks increased their credit market share, although their total farm lending fell. The Farm Credit System (FCS) decreased its share and total of loans outstanding. Congress passed legislation in 1985, 1986, and 1987 to help the FCS deal with its problem farm loans.

FARM MACHINERY

Farm machinery production rose from an index value of 100 in 1967 to a peak of 146 in 1979, only to plunge to a low of 70 in 1983, barely rising to 75 by 1985. Companies manufacturing farm machinery saw inventories of unsold equipment swell alarmingly, revenues cut in half, debts rise sharply with respect to assets, and use of plant capacity fall from 80 to 35 percent. These companies suffered severe financial losses, curtailed new capital expenditures, and underwent mergers. Farm machinery exports fell in the 1980s, while imports, especially of smaller tractors, rose. The U.S. farm machinery trade balance showed a first-time-ever deficit in 1986 of almost $200 million, just five years after posting a $1.4 billion surplus. A smaller U.S. farm machinery industry which is dominated by four major firms is evolving and obtaining parts and components from both U.S. and foreign suppliers. Dealerships are becoming larger and offering more services and products to farmers.

HIRED LABOR

The total of all farm workers—farm operator, family, and hired—has dropped by more than 80 percent since 1940. At the same time, output per acre doubled, and output per worker-hour rose tenfold because of other purchased inputs. The hired work force has not fallen as fast as the total farm work force, farm operator, or family labor. Hired, domestic farm workers stabilized at 2.5–2.6 million during the 1970s and early 1980s. Hired workers were generally young, white, and male, and most worked only seasonally. There were fewer than 20,000 legally admitted foreign workers, but many more were undocumented. Foreign workers that are here illegally may account for 10–15 percent of all hired farm labor. The 1986 immigration reform legislation will influence the future of hired workers, but most will probably continue to work on large farms, including farms growing fruits, vegetables, nuts, and specialty products.

IMPLICATIONS FOR CONSUMERS AND THE ENVIRONMENT

The growth in agricultural productivity and relatively low food and fiber prices have not been realized without perceived costs on the part of society.[2]

The public has been concerned with the potential human health and environmental effects of pesticide and fertilizer use for many years. Recently, chemical residues have been discovered in ground and surface water. Also, nitrates and phosphates have been detected in surface waters and nitrates have also been identified in groundwater. These identifications highlighted water quality as a major issue and led to well-water surveys and various requests for increased appropriations to deal with the water-quality issue.

Food safety has always been a topic of concern, but it has recently received increased attention. It is likely to be an issue of national prominence for a considerable period of time. The primary focus of the food safety issue is pesticide residues on and in food.

Another concern is worker safety, particularly the safety of farm workers who are exposed to applied pesticides or who mix and apply them. Press coverage of this issue is less evident than for water quality and food safety but, nonetheless, it is an important topic with respect to pesticide use.

WATER QUALITY

Over the past several years, a number of pesticides have been discovered in groundwater. Included among those identified are the insecticide aldicarb and a number of herbicides such as alachlor, atrazine, cyanzine, and simazine. Additionally, nitrate levels in groundwater have increased. It is believed sources of these nitrates are commercial nitrogen fertilizer applied to cropland and animal manure. In addition to groundwater, some surface waters have been polluted with nitrates and phosphates. The nitrates are carried to surface water by runoff, and the phosphates are connected to soil erosion where the phosphate has adhered to soil particles.

The heightened concern over the contamination of surface and groundwater has resulted in a discussion of programs, policies, and practices that could be employed to prevent contamination. These have included banning the use of pesticides known to be leachers, changing tillage practices, imposing taxes, eliminating fall fertilizer, requiring filter strips, and adopting Integrated Pest Management (IPM) and alternative agricultural practices. Currently, research and demonstration activities are being initiated that are designed to address water quality. The interaction between natural resources, chemical inputs, and water quality is discussed in greater detail in Chapter 2.

FOOD SAFETY

The U.S. food supply is purported to be one of the safest in the world, but there is increasing consumer concern as to whether this is a correct perception. Headlines about alar on apples and the withdrawal of the Chilean fruit supply are recent examples of concerns. The National Academy of Sciences' study involving fungicide residues on fruits and vegetables is another example.

The existence of pesticide residues is a primary public food safety concern. This concern involves primarily fruits and vegetables that are produced domestically and imported. For imported products, the concern extends further because residues of pesticides that are banned in the United States could be present on or in imported produce.

As a result of food safety concerns, several bills have been introduced in Congress that propose to amend the Federal Insecticide, Fungicide and Rodenticide Act (FIFRA) and the Federal Food, Drug and Cosmetic Act (FFDCA). These bills contain features such as doing away with Delaney-clause zero-tolerance for cancer-causing residues and adopting a negligible risk concept, shortening the EPA pesticide suspension and cancellation process, adopting an imminent hazard concept, and many more. The likelihood of these bills becoming law is unknown, but a probable outcome is that various features of the proposals will be combined and passed into law.

FOOD PRICES

If measures are initiated that reduce the use of pesticides and fertilizers, there is little question that food prices will increase, and, in some cases, substantially. A possible exception to this scenario would be a large increase in food imports that would moderate or negate the rise in cost of domestically produced food. However, if a primary concern is pesticide residues on food, it is unlikely that food would be allowed to be imported without a strict and extensive residue testing and certification program. If the latter is the case, the cost of such a program would have to be covered by consumers in the form of higher food prices or by increased taxes. Either mechanism would result in decreased disposable income, reduced consumption, shifts in food consumption patterns, or a combination of all three.

The reason food prices can be expected to increase lies in price elasticity of demand for many food products. Food products, especially basic commodities, tend to be price inelastic which means that with reduced supplies, prices increase proportionately more than the percentage reduction in supply. The net result is that consumers must pay more for food, leaving less of their income for other purposes.

The increase in food prices translates into changes in farm income. Changes in farm income will be differential. Those producers depending upon the pesticide and experiencing product loss as a result of a restrictive pesticide action will be faced with lower revenue. However, those producers not dependent upon the pesticide could experience windfall gains. There is no universal outcome as far as farm income is concerned, but the consumer always faces an increase in food prices with a pesticide restrictive action, assuming the agricultural producer previously has been using the most cost-effective pest control alternative. Thus, in evaluating the implications of such actions, the consumer, or society in general, must balance the cost of such actions against the benefits perceived to be derived from the actions. The consumer price and producer income impacts of reduced dependence on agricultural chemicals is one of the main economic uncertainties facing a more widespread adoption of "alternative" or "sustainable" agriculture practices discussed in Chapters 5 and 6 (Part III, Section 3).

NOTES

1. Joseph R. Barse is a senior economist and John R. Schaub is the Chief, Agricultural Inputs and Production Systems Branch, Resources and Technology Division, Economic Research Service, U.S. Department of Agriculture. The material on fertilizer was prepared by Paul Andrilenas and Harry Vroomen; on pesticides by Theodore Eichers and Philip Szmedra; on Energy by Carlos Sisco and Mohinder Gill; on credit by Patrick Sullivan and David Freshwater; on livestock feeds by George Allen, William Lin, and Mark Ash; on farm machinery by Carlos Sisco and LeRoy Hansen; on hired labor by William Jackson Jr. and Leslie Whitener. This chapter is a synthesis of an ERS/USDA report *Seven Farm Input Industries*, AER–635, Sept. 1990.

2. The United States has low food prices compared to most other developed nations and a smaller percentage of U.S. consumer income is spent on food than is spent in other nations.

REFERENCES

Daberkow, Stan. 1987. *Agricultural input industry indicators in 1974–85: Expansion and contraction*, AIB 534, U.S. Dept. of Agriculture, Economic Research Service, Resources and Technology Division, November.

Evans, Rachel. 1987. Expansion/splice listing of purchased and nonpurchased agricultural inputs, runs D and E, U.S. Dept. of Agriculture, Economic Research Service, Resources and Technology Division. Unpublished computer tabulation.

Link, Albert N. 1987. *Technological change and productivity growth*. London: Harwood Academic Publishers.

Offutt, Susan, and Robbin Shoemaker. 1988. *Farm programs slow technology-induced decline in land's importance*, Technical Bulletin no. 1745, U.S. Dept. of Agriculture, Economic Research Service, May.

Schertz, Lyle P., et al. 1979. *Another revolution in U.S. farming?*, AER 441, U.S. Dept. of Agriculture, Economic Statistics and Cooperatives Service (ESCS), December.

U. S. Dept. of Agriculture. 1968. *Structure of six farm input industries*, ERS–357, Economic Research Service, Farm Production and Economics Div., January.

———1987a [and earlier issues]. *Agricultural Statistics.*

———1987b [and earlier issues]. *Economic indicators of the farm sector: Costs of production, 1986*, ECIFS 6–1, Economic Research Service, Agriculture and Rural Economy Div., November.

———1988a [and earlier issues*]. *Indicators of the farm sector: Farm sector review, 1986*, ECIFS 6–3, Economic Research Service, Agriculture and Rural Economy Div., January. *Earlier issues called *Farm Income and Balance Sheet Statistics.*

———1988b. *Feed situation and outlook yearbook*, FdS–305, Economic Research Service, Commodity Economics Div. February.

———1988c [and earlier issues]. *Economic indicators of the farm sector: Production and efficiency statistics,*

ECIFS 6–5, Economic Research Service, Resources and Technology Div., June.

_____1989. *Major statistical series of the U.S. Department of Agriculture*. Vol. 2, *Agricultural production and efficiency*, AH no. 671, Economic Research Service, Resources and Technology Div.

OTHER REFERENCES USED BUT NOT SPECIFICALLY CITED

Daberkow, Stan, and Katherine Reichelderfer. 1988. Low input agriculture: Trends, goals, and prospects for input use. *American Journal of Agricultural Economics* 50, no. 5: 1159–66.

Kuchler, Fred, and Harry Vroomen. 1987. Impacts of the PIK program on the farm machinery market. *Journal of Agricultural Economics Research* 39, no. 3: 2–11.

Manchester, Alden C. 1985. *Agriculture's links with U.S. and world economies*, AIB 496, U.S. Dept. of Agriculture, Economic Research Service.

CHAPTER 4

PEOPLE, PROCESSES, AND PRODUCTS: POTENTIAL CONTRIBUTION OF THE SOCIAL SCIENCES TO THE PRESERVATION AND ENHANCEMENT OF NATURAL RESOURCES IN THIRD WORLD COUNTRIES

Louise P. Fortmann, Daniel C. Mountjoy, and Bruce F. Johnston[1]

A decade ago, Walter Firey (1978) noted that the condition of a farming community and the condition of the soil are interdependent. The principle holds more generally for the condition of natural-resource-dependent communities and the state of their resources. Increasingly, development scholars and practitioners recognize that the degradation of natural resources is both a cause and a consequence of deteriorating social conditions. The litany of environmental woes is familiar—desertification, erosion, siltation, flooding, deforestation, salinization, and loss of soil fertility. The symptoms of human misery are equally familiar—famine, malnutrition, high infant mortality, short life expectancy, exhausting work days (particularly for women), high morbidity, illiteracy, fragmented families, indebtedness, landlessness, fuel-wood crisis, and violence.

In this paper we explore the question of the role of social science in addressing the intertwined issues of natural-resource preservation and management, and the elimination of rural poverty. Because of the agricultural focus of these meetings, we have limited our attention to soil, water, grazing, and trees because they are integral parts of agricultural production systems, although air, minerals, oceans, fish, and wildlife are also resources worthy of attention. Because forests serve ecological functions essential for the sustainability of downstream agricultural production and because forest and tree products are significant components of rural livelihood and production systems, social forestry is included in this discussion.

THE PROBLEM OF DEFINING PROBLEMS

Is the world going to an ecological hell in a handbasket? There is no doubt that there are several areas of the world where environmental deterioration in the forms enumerated above pose a real, and sometimes immediate, threat to present levels of production and quality of life. Many areas in sub-Saharan Africa fall into this category. Increasingly in these areas, extensive systems of production that were sustainable under lower population/land ratios are coming under stress, and the need for intensification is becoming apparent. And yet, as Thompson et al. (1986) and Blaikie (1985) have pointed out, there is by no means consensus over the cause, extent, or long-term prospects of environmental degradation. For example, while many call swidden (slash and burn) cultivation a systematic and ecologically sound form of agriculture, foresters are likely to call it devastation. Foresters, in turn, regard clearcutting as a sound forest management practice, while others call it devastation.

We do not propose to enter the lists of these debates here. Rather, we begin from the simple premise that in many places things are not as they ought to be ecologically, that the elimination of rural poverty and the sustainability of agricultural production depend on making them right, and that the protection and enhancement of natural resources depend on the elimination of rural poverty.[2]

PROBLEMS IN PAST ANALYSES AND STRATEGIES

Past approaches to the problems of natural resources, rural-production systems, and rural poverty have not always been satisfactory. In some cases, the analysis of the problem was wrong. Hence, strategies based on the analysis were ineffective. In other cases, while the analysis was reasonably correct, the strategies stemming from the analysis had unanticipated adverse consequences. An initial contribution of social science to the processes of protecting and enhancing natural resources has been the identification of the errors in these assumptions and the adverse effects of these strategies.[3]

ANALYTICAL ASSUMPTIONS

Four assumptions stand out as problems in past approaches:

1. The assumption that the issue was a production problem.
2. The assumption that the problem was overpopulation.

3. The assumption that a particular resource could be used, managed, and analyzed in isolation from other physical and community resources.
4. The assumption that environmental degradation was the result of the "tragedy of the commons."

For very good reasons, early development efforts were focused four-square on raising production. The need was clear, and the techniques for addressing the problem were known and available. Production was a reasonable place to start. Even critics of the "Green Revolution" acknowledge its successes. For example, Scott (1985), who details many adverse effects of the introduction of high-yielding varieties, especially when associated with mechanization, also notes that now no one goes hungry in the Malaysian village he studied. Nonetheless, the assumption that by increasing total production, a surplus would be generated for improving the lives of producers and for investing in their production systems has been found wanting on a number of fronts.

For one thing, increased food production is not necessarily a solution to alleviating hunger; improved *access* to the enlarged food supply is also critical (World Bank 1986). Furthermore, as discussed below, the long-run success of agricultural development in reducing rural poverty depends on the structural transformation of an overwhelmingly agrarian economy. But clearly, unless the growth of agricultural production is associated with growing domestic demand or expanded exports, the value of a product, be it cash crops, timber, or fuel wood, is likely to fall as production increases, leaving the producer in economic circumstances no better, and sometimes worse, than before increased production. This, in turn, may force the producer to practices that lead to further resource degradation (Blaikie 1985). In addition, the focus on production has often tended to lead to a skewed distribution of benefits to the elite and high-potential regions where the most significant production gains could be made (Hammer 1982; Agarwal 1986; Scott 1985). As a forester explained when asked why the benefits of a social forestry project were going to very rich farmers: "The measure of a scheme is its target. If the poor are not able to do the scheme because it is not suitable for them, then the scheme has to go to the rich so the target can be achieved." (Mahiti Team 1982)

Finally, the focus on production and a fixed idea of how it is to be achieved has sometimes masked environmental costs—erosion, flooding, and siltation (Mishra and Tripathi 1978); loss of genetic diversity (Plumwood and Routley 1982); loss of wildlife habitat and with it, food sources; and, ironically, sometimes loss of production (Callahan 1987; Weber 1982; Freeman and Resch 1985/86).[4]

"Overpopulation" has been popularly blamed for environmental degradation and rising levels of poverty. The apparent link between "overpopulation" and environmental degradation masks a more complex set of dynamic forces. In some places, including much of sub-Saharan Africa, sparse population may militate against the use of labor-intensive conservation practices and preclude the development of an adequate transportation network and other infrastructure. In other places, the effects of rising levels of population are aggravated by skewed distribution of resources. For example, in Latin America, the concentration of land in the hands of the few has forced the poor onto more fragile lands. When large landholders are, as is frequently the case, politically powerful, the "overpopulation" argument is used to prevent or avoid attention to the equity dimension of the problems (Durham 1979).

A more careful look at the "population problem" suggests that the most significant problem is not the static situation reflected in the existing population/land ratio but rather the *rate* of population growth. Under a condition of steady-but-slow population increase, rising food needs tend to lead to intensification and innovations in the farming system (Boserup 1965; Pingali, Bigot, and Binswanger 1987). The outcome of such a process reflects the quality of the natural-resource base; the availability of land, labor, and capital; the existence of markets for selling produce and for buying input; and local management skills and cultural values. Netting (1968) has documented just such a historical process of intensification among the Kofyar of highland Nigeria. In contrast, extremely rapid rates of growth can overwhelm production and management strategies as well as local institutional capacities, even where the ratio of people to land is low and skewed land distribution is not a serious problem. But the current rates of population growth in Africa, which run as high as 4 percent in Kenya, are much higher than the 1.0 to 1.5 percent rates of growth that induced technological change during earlier demographic transitions. Such rapid growth rates also exacerbate the problems of expanding employment opportunities in pace with the rapid growth of population of working age, and of increasing per capita investment in human and physical capital.

It has frequently been assumed that resources could be considered in isolation. Yet many resources are of limited value in isolation, as is the case of land or grazing without water, or water without land or grazing (Romm and Fortmann 1987). The analysis of isolated resources generally excludes local definitions and uses of natural resources and, thereby, masks adverse effects in the encompassing ecological and social systems. For example, when the focus is simply on teak, logging a tropical rainforest may appear to be a profitable and reasonable use of the resource. However, when environmental effects on the area as a whole and the loss of swiddening products are considered, the figures on the balance sheet change considerably (Dove 1983).

A corollary of this assumption is the belief that, by focusing development on one component or commodity in a system, greater advances could be achieved than by attempting to improve multiple parts of the system simultaneously.[5] In the 1960s and the early 1970s, major efforts were made to increase the productivity of rural producers using technology as the primary intervention. In the process of creating conditions conducive to the adoption of such technologies, the rest of the production system was often neglected and producers lost the ability to maintain a diversified production system, thus becoming more vulnerable to climatic and socioeconomic fluctuations. Indeed, in some cases, essential natural resources that contributed to the production system were destroyed as when extension workers urged farmers to clear trees (trees often being nitrogen fixers, as well as being sources of fuel, fodder, medicine, shade for cattle and humans, food, and wood for farm implements, house poles, and fencing) out of their agricultural fields. This approach tended to view peasants as ignorant and ineffective managers of their environment and failed to recognize the nature of local farming and resource-management systems. The work of David Brokensha et al. (1980) and Paul Richards (1985) has demonstrated to the contrary that traditional systems of farming and resource management are both complex and rational.

On the basis of some seven years of research as an ICRISAT regional economist in Burkina Faso, Matlon (1985) has been led to stress the fact that only a small percentage of cultivators are currently in a position to adopt input-intensive technologies because they face such a severe cash-income/purchasing-power constraint. Therefore, for agricultural research to be relevant to short-term objectives, it should stress innovations that require only very small cash outlays for off-farm input. He recognizes, however, that the potential increases in output and productivity that can be realized by such a strategy are quite limited so that, in the medium and longer term, research will have to develop and promote innovations such as crop varieties selected for their capacity to respond to higher levels of soil fertility and, therefore, require substantial application of chemical fertilizers. As discussed below, thinking in terms of efficient sequences of innovations to bring about transition from extensive to intensive farming systems underscores the importance of identifying feasible and profitable short-term innovations for improving soil and water management that will yield modest immediate gains in productivity, while increasing the returns to subsequent adoption of more cash-intensive technologies.

Finally, the acceptance of the premises of Hardin's (1968) theory of the "tragedy of the commons" has had serious effects on thinking about natural-resource protection. Hardin asserted that resources held in common were inevitably overexploited and degraded. This argument was based on the assumptions that common property (from which exclusion is possible) is synonymous with open-access property (from which exclusion is not possible) and that decision making is individualized and based on an economic-maximizing strategy. The assumptions of the "tragedy of the commons" have repeatedly been refuted with empirical evidence (Gilles and Jamtgaard 1981; Panel on Common Property Resource Management 1987). This is not to suggest that there are no degraded commons, only that Hardin's explanation is erroneous.

STRATEGIC SHORTFALLS

These analytical assumptions have been mirrored in the field by strategies that have had adverse effects on natural resources.

To view resources in isolation from the encompassing ecological and production systems can have the effect of promoting extractive production processes that not only deplete the supply of the particular product but also reduce the stability and productivity of the entire system (Dahlberg 1973). It also has led to exclusionary strategies of protecting natural resources. Foresters, for example, have long tried to protect forest reserves and plantations by excluding local people who often had used the forest for millennia, not only as a source of timber, food, medicine, and wildlife, but also for grazing.[6] The results have been reduced standards of living for local people and/or increased pressures sometimes followed by degradation of alternative sources of the resource. At times, violence ensued as rural people fought to regain control of their land (Guha 1985a, 1985b). The failure (or refusal) to recognize that a resource is part of a system of use may also have exclusionary effects as in the conversion of pastoralists' dry season and emergency pastures to arable agriculture by colonists and nonpastoralists.

The assumptions of the "tragedy of the commons" have led to strategies of tenurial change. One such strategy is privatization which can have both ecological and social effects that are adverse. Some resources are not easily divisible. For example, where the time and place of rainfall is unpredictable, as it is in many arid and semiarid areas, cattle producers must have the flexibility to go to where the water and grazing are. Privatizing such a resource either means locking people onto smaller units of land that may, at any given time, have none of the required resource at all, with predictable effects on both the resource base and the producer's economic well-being, or it means giving large units of the land to a few people, thereby dispossessing the rest. Another consequence of privatization may be the loss of resources located only in communal areas. For example, Brokensha and Njeru (1977) and Brokensha and Riley (1978) note that honey production plummeted ("bee trees" were generally located on the commons) and sacred groves (that serve important ecological functions) began to disappear after land privatization in Kenya. Finally, unless the existing system of land rights is very clearly understood, some groups, particularly women, are vulnerable to losing their rights in the process of privatization and registration of land (Okeyo 1980).

A second strategy arising from Hardin's thesis is governmental control of the resource. The classic case of how this strategy can go wrong is the nationalization of centuries-old village forests in Nepal that rapidly resulted in deforestation (Thompson et al. 1986). When the forests were returned to village control, village forest management resumed.

It was noted earlier that increased output of agricultural products sometimes leads to a sharp decline in prices and a reduction of producer incomes because the elasticity of demand for agricultural commodities is often less than unity. A glut of supplies leading to a sharp price decline is especially likely to occur in isolated areas where markets are thin. In addition, it is commonly alleged that small-scale farmers are exploited by middlemen. A common response to a legitimate concern with price stability, and to the dubious allegations about the monopoly power (or inefficiency) of middlemen, has been government intervention to set up a marketing board to influence or control the marketing of major food products. Especially when such marketing boards have been established with a statutory monopoly, the outcome has had very detrimental effects on farmers. Because of the inflexibility and other characteristics of a governmental agency, marketing boards tend to have high fixed and operating costs. Furthermore, there is a common tendency for marketing boards to hold down food prices, with adverse effects on producer incentives, because politicians in LDCs tend to be more responsive to city dwellers, a visible and vociferous force, than to the more numerous, but inert, farm population.

Government agencies with more limited mandates of reducing the magnitude of price fluctuations by managing a better stock are more likely to yield net benefits. However, if the "price bands," set to trigger purchases or sales by the agency, are not fixed on the basis of careful and reasonably accurate analysis of the consequences of the selected trigger prices, it is highly probable the intervention will be very costly, with the costs being much greater than the fairly modest benefits from stabilization (Newbery 1990).

The only real solution to the problems that arise because of sharp fluctuations in the agricultural sector's domestic and export prices lies in the progress of transforming a predominantly agrarian economic structure into a more diversified, more productive economy structure with a greater capacity to adapt to, and cope with, price and other economic fluctuations. Unfortunately, it is not possible to rapidly transform the structure of economies characterized by a rapidly growing working-age population of which some 50 to 80 percent still depends on agriculture for income and employment. Earlier hopes, that comprehensive planning and Soviet or Maoist approaches to a command economy or a "Great Leap Forward" might permit shortcuts, have been dashed. What has become increasingly clear is that successful development requires "a generalized process of capital accumulation," with capital broadly defined to include physical capital, human capital, and capital in the form of economically useful knowledge and an array of effective public and private institutions. Thus, the specialization that is so crucial to economic progress not only includes the specialization of economic activity, as individual firms become more specialized, but also the functional differentiation promoted by the creation of educational institutions, research institutes, and other institutions that generate and foster the technological change that leads to economy-wide increases in "total factor productivity"—that is, in output per unit of total input. (See Johnson 1969; Kuznets 1971; Johnston and Clark 1982).

THE NEED FOR SOCIAL SCIENCE

Some of the above-identified problems are the result of relying primarily on physical and biological sciences, and on scientists and practitioners from those sciences, to lead the way in designing development policies and strategies. Experience in other areas has shown that the inclusion of social science theories, questions, and methods can increase the chances for success and decrease the adverse effects of development policies and strategies. The ongoing saga of environmental troubles demonstrates the need to bring social science expertise to bear in the arena of natural-resource management as well. Social science has a role in improving the framing of questions, in providing information on social aspects of the problem, and in guiding the implementation of development policies and strategies.

The first area in which social scientists can make a considerable contribution is in a more careful framing of the problem. While not all rural poverty is resource-related, a significant portion is. Thus, a first step would be to differentiate the kinds of natural-resource-related poverty so that decision makers can respond with diverse policies and strategies to the diversity of causes. Four general causes of natural-resource-related poverty can be distinguished:

1. Lack of access to a resource because the supply of the resource is inadequate or because the distribution of control and access rights are skewed.
2. Insecure access to a resource due to natural calamities (hurricanes, volcanoes, landslides), skewed distribution of control, the operation of property laws, for example, eviction of tenants or nationalization of land, change of status within a household (e.g., when women are widowed or divorced), breakdown of or lack of accountability in civic culture, and change in the value of the resource.
3. Resource degradation due to inappropriate technology, inadequate resource base for the population, greed and inadequate regulation, skewed resource distribution, resource fragility, and natural calamity.
4. Low return or damage from a resource owned by another due to weak labor laws, or nonexistent or weakly enforced regulatory laws.

The most striking thing about this list of causes is that relatively few can be addressed with technical fixes. We are looking at questions of social relations—the distribution of resource rights, the enforceability of rights, value, equity. These are questions for social scientists. The second step in framing the questions is to break away from Western or technical definitions and to look to local definitions, in order to understand them, and to local beliefs about production and resource-management systems. Development discourse has frequently proceeded using constructs that are either too static to reflect the dynamics of rural life, or do not reflect local understandings and definitions. This leads to problems when, for example, "tree" as a social construct differs considerably from the biological construct, "tree" (Bruce and Fortmann 1987). Similarly what a professional forester defines as "worthless bush" may be considered by villagers to be a forest and an essential part of their livelihood system (Hoskins 1982). We need the local definition of natural resources and the local point of view on how are they doing—a question social scientists are particularly skilled at asking and getting answered.

The debate over land tenure has frequently been framed in terms of a dichotomy between private and common property. While we do not suggest abandoning these categories, which clearly have heuristic value, the development of policy must recognize that rural realities are often more complex than the categories. For example, in Botswana, Roe and Fortmann (1986) found that legally (under either statutory or customary law) communal water sources might be managed as if they were private, private sources might be used communally, and the pattern of use might shift with the season or with the occurrence of drought. Legal title can be less of a concern to rural people than their security of access and use (Romm and Fortmann 1987). (For an Indian example, see Moench 1988.) Because a legal title that cannot be defended is of less use than enforceable informal rights of access, it is necessary to go beyond the differences between private and common property to behavior.

A second crucial role of social scientists is to provide a systematic view of agricultural production and natural-resource management. Rather than occurring in isolation, production-and-resource management and use are organized over time and space. The utility of a single resource source may depend on the availability of the same resource at other times and in other places (fallback water points), or on the availability of complementary resources (grass and water), and on the existence of systematically organized human activity (work groups, social control of resource use, reciprocal relationships). The systematic focus of social science gives a view of natural resources that goes beyond the tree and the open well, to the systems of human and ecological interaction.

One example of this sort of social science contribution is the documentation and analysis of existing systems of agricultural production and natural-resource use and management that have provided (as in the case of agroforestry) models of alternatives to presently recommended practices. Social scientists such as Conklin (1975) and Ruthenberg (1980) have demonstrated the complexity and viability of such local systems. By identifying the units of social organization involved in managing these systems, social-science research also identifies the most appropriate points of contact for development workers. Thus, if one were introducing agroforestry to the Melaban Kantuq, one would address the longhouse apartment (Dove 1976); whereas among the Sotho, at the time Duncan (1960) did his fieldwork, the consent of the chief would have been required. Social scientists have also documented household division of labor and responsibility that is useful in helping field personnel establish contact with the right person within a household (Boserup 1970; Staudt 1975; Bryson 1989; Fortmann 1984, 1986). In the "bad old days," before social scientists (particularly female social scientists) were listened to, rural development efforts tended to proceed on the blithe assumption that only men farmed, practiced animal husbandry, used forests, or made management decisions. The results were frequently embarrassing.

A third area for social science input is the analysis of distribution, access, and security of access, issues that appeared repeatedly in our lists of causes of resource-related poverty. Security of access and control are particularly important since under what Marion Brown (personal communication) calls "The Iron Law of Subsistence," products and resources that increase in value are likely to attract the attention of more powerful claimants, leaving the original claimant trapped in the subsistence mode. We see examples of this when husbands take over their wives' crops when they assume a commercial value, when landlords evict tenants as their production becomes valuable, and when the state permits a multinational to exploit a resource in preference to local people. Questions to be asked on the general issue include:

- What constitutes security of access for what purposes?
- What conditions of access and control facilitate resource protection and enhancement of natural resources, and which encourage destructive resource use?
- Who benefits and who loses under different tenurial regimes?
- How can disadvantaged sectors of the population be provided with secure access to sufficient quantities and qualities of natural resources?

This last question requires particularly meticulous and serious attention as it is a key to the elimination of rural poverty and because many of the answers will involve changes in durable and fiercely defended institutions.

There is a growing tide of relevant social science work already under way, such as the work on common-property resource management (Panel on Common Property Resource Management 1987) and tree tenure (Raintree 1987; Fortmann and Bruce 1988).

A fourth crucial area of concern is the identification of groups-at-risk that are often socially invisible, who may be excluded from benefits, or who may be hurt by a particular development strategy. Depending on the strategy, these groups-at-risk are likely to include women (Hoskins 1982; Skar et al. 1982; Fortmann 1985), ethnic minorities (Gadgil et al. n.d.), landless (Fortmann 1985; Shiva 1986), tenants (Fortmann 1985; Scott 1985), pastoralists (Delehanty and Hoskins 1985), wage laborers (Scott 1985), and residents of less accessible areas (Chambers 1983). Identifying such groups and the risks they face is important to prevent adverse consequences for both the individuals and the natural resources that may be destroyed or degraded by human sufferers out of either necessity or revenge.

Development is a process and social scientists can be uniquely helpful in, as Norman Uphoff (1986) puts it, "getting the process right." In a similar vein, A. F. Robertson (1987, 27) has stressed "the need for patient enquiry into the *processes* of economic relations."[7] This fifth area of process needs to be considered at three levels—the bureaucracy, the community, and the individual.

Development bureaucracies in general, possibly natural-resource bureaucracies in particular, are frequently less effective than they might be because they have difficult and distant (sometimes hostile) relations with local people. This state of affairs has several roots—historical conflicts over policies of exclusion, official corruption and abuse, social distance, professional socialization that encourages the view that only the professionally educated know anything, and institutional demands for tangible results in a short time frame. Clearly, if progress is to be made, bureaucrats and local people must work together and learn from each other. Social science knowledge of bureaucracies has permitted the development of a new approach to this problem known as "bureaucratic reorientation" (Korten and Uphoff 1981; Korten 1980; Johnston and Clark 1982, Chapter 5). Briefly, this approach establishes institutionalized channels of two-way communication between bureaucrats and peasants, rewards bureaucrats for listening and adapting, and prevents them from being punished when innovations fail. The approach has had considerable success in irrigation bureaucracies in Southeast Asia.

While professionals and bureaucrats loom large in national capitals, in the heat, dust, and mud of villages most resource management is actually done by peasants. Social scientists are increasingly turning their attention to the conditions under which local organizations can facilitate or undertake resource management, and to the question of what those institutions ought to look like.[8] Much effort has been focused on the social organization of common-property resources. (See Panel on Common Property Resource Management [1987] generally, and Ostrum [1987] in particular.) A few of the questions to be answered include: How large can such a group be? How can the effects of government policy changes and takeover attempts by local or outside elites be dealt with? How can group regulations be enforced? More general work on local organizations has been done by Esman and Uphoff (1984) who consider questions such as: Under what conditions should old organizations be adapted to new tasks, or new organizations established? Under what conditions are traditional or new leaders more effective? How are leaders made accountable? What is the appropriate role for outside promoters? Such work is invaluable for those who hope to undertake their work through local organizations. Fortmann (1985) has pointed out the seasonal nature of many rural social organizations, a characteristic that is important for development workers to recognize if they are to avoid mistakes, such as writing off organizations that are simply dormant in the off-season.

Finally, at the individual level of process, it has been recognized for some time that active participation by the would-be beneficiaries in development projects is more likely to result in success than top-down methods. Social scientists have been instrumental in developing both the theory and field methods for participatory development (Cohen and Uphoff 1977; Uphoff et al. 1979; Stanley, Rick, and Zufferey 1983).

In contrast to those whose focus is on raising production by whatever means possible, the thrust of this body of work is that process may well be our most important product. For instance, the active involvement of rural people in designing and implementing strategies to address a specific problem develops their capability to address other problems. Even if a particular strategy fails (and the history of development is full of failures), the *process* of involvement will have succeeded by creating as its product an increased problem-solving capacity.

Finally, social scientists can contribute by carrying on macrolevel analysis. This might involve identifying processes and characteristics of the global political economy that have local effect. It might also involve considering whether and how it might be possible, as Thompson et al. (1986) suggest, to tinker with resource-management systems so that the quantity of power within the system is increased while its concentration is decreased. They suggest fractioning rights—separating usufructuary rights at the local level from nationally held title, for example. This is obviously an area for some imaginative social science attentions.

CONCLUSIONS

A major conclusion to be stressed is that *conservation can promote production and increased production facilitates conservation*. This potential for positive interaction needs to be stressed. Clearly, investment in resource conservation contributes to more stable production systems by lessening vulnerability to climatic variations; increasing the payoff to be realized from high-yield, fertilizer-responsive crop varieties; and enhancing the sustainability of the system. Of more immediate importance, however, is the fact that conservation will only be practiced if it yields returns in the higher productivity that can result from the preservation and enhancement of natural resources. The active participation of cultivators and local communities cannot be enlisted on the basis of long-term social and ecological benefits. Hence, conservation must be promoted as a profitable means of increasing production in the short and long term, with the latter being especially salient for cultivators who see their children as beneficiaries of the longer-term improvements.

Especially in sub-Sahara Africa, there is a critical need to identify the key ingredients of more productive and sustainable farming systems that will reduce both ecological degradation and rural poverty. A recent book by Paul Harrison (1987) describes a number of examples of "success" in devising and introducing innovations that purportedly increase both productivity and sustainability. His review of those examples was, however, cursory. The challenge for both social scientists and agricultural scientists is to regard the sort of innovations that Harrison describes as promising hypotheses that need to be evaluated more systematically to identify the agroclimatic and socioeconomic conditions in which they are likely to be successful.

Farming-systems research (FSR) offers promise as a technique for increasing the relevance of adaptive research to local farmers, provided that serious attention is given to linking FSR with on-station research and to ensuring that cost-effective techniques are used because FSR is so demanding in its requirements for trained personnel. (See Byerlee et al. 1982). A recent report by Okali and Sumberg (1986) on the work of an ILCA team evaluating a small ruminant program and alley farming in Nigeria is an interesting example. Probably the greatest need, however, is for FSR in semiarid regions to evaluate the profitability and feasibility of techniques to improve water and soil management, such as the stone lines established on the contour in Burkina Faso to slow runoff and increase infiltration (Harrison 1987, 166–70). Tied ridges are a good example of a technique that shows promise in on-station trials, but it has had little impact on local farming systems. Peter Matlon (1987) has stressed the importance of understanding the soil and other conditions that determine whether the technique is profitable, as well as the need to develop an inexpensive ox-drawn implement to reduce the labor required to establish the tied ridges.

A more general conclusion is not to marvel at the diverse roles social scientists have to play in the preservation and enhancement of natural resources, but simply to point out that it is not the role of social scientists to serve as the handmaids of technical experts, but to set the agenda for development policy and strategy. If they do not, we shall most assuredly go collectively to an ecological hell in a handbasket.

NOTES

1. Dr. Fortmann is a professor in the Department of Forestry and Resource Management, University of California–Berkeley; Mr. Mountjoy is a doctoral candidate in the Ecology Graduate Group, University of California–Davis; and Dr. Johnston is a professor emeritus, Food Research Institute, Stanford University.

2. We do not mean to suggest that rural poverty is the only cause of natural-resource degradation. Urban-biased policies and international demands on LDC agricultural and forest resources also play a major role.

3. For a particularly elegant analysis of the analytical models used by decision makers and how they can be manipulated, see Peters' (1987) study of grazing land policy in Botswana.

4. For a general discussion of the problem in forestry, see Westoby (1978).

5. We recognize both the gains that have been made with single-crop research and the difficulties of undertaking research on multiple components of a system, or even in attempting to develop an improved crop variety when plant breeders are called upon to maximize a number of attributes, e.g., yield potential, drought resistance, protein quality, storage life, etc. (see Lipton and Longhurst, Chapter 7). Nonetheless, as evidence from our own Dust Bowl has shown, the ecological dangers of monoculture and the ecological advantages of diversified production systems are also significant. Despite its difficulties, the necessity for research on systems of agricultural production and resource management is clear, perhaps especially for many of the

difficult and diverse agricultural environments in sub-Saharan Africa.

6. Exclusionary practices are often associated with colonialism, but they were utilized by European foresters and gamekeepers against their own compatriots long before the development of colonies and have continued to more recent times (Cox 1905; Linebaugh 1976; Hopkins 1985).

7. This book by Robertson (1987) presents a valuable theoretical and empirical analysis of various forms of sharecropping in Africa, stressing the dynamism of sharecrop contracts.

8. Johnston and Clark (1982, Chapter 5) note that the investment of scarce time and effort into an organization must be justified by sufficient rewards beyond those that could be realized without the organization. In some cases, benefits may accrue more efficiently through the market.

REFERENCES

Agarwal, Bina. 1986. *Cold hearths and barren slopes: The woodfuel crisis in the Third World.* London: Zed.

Blaikie, P. 1985. *The political economy of soil erosion in developing countries.* London: Longman.

Boserup, Ester. 1965. *The conditions of agricultural growth.* Chicago: Aldine Publishing Co.

_____1970. *Women's role in economic development.* London: George Allen and Unwin.

Brokensha, David, and E. H. N. Njeru. 1977. Some consequences of land adjudication in Mbere division. Working paper no. 320. Nairobi: University of Nairobi.

Brokensha, David, and Bernard Riley. 1978. Forest, foraging, fences, and fuel in a marginal area of Kenya. In *US AID Africa Bureau, firewood workshop.* Washington, D.C.: USAID.

Brokensha, David, D. M. Warner, and Oswald Werner. 1980. *Indigenous knowledge systems and development.* Washington, D.C.: University Press of America.

Bruce, John, and Louise Fortmann. 1987. Tenurial aspects of agroforestry: Research priorities. In *Land, trees and tenure.* Edited by John B. Raintree. Proceedings of an international workshop on tenure issues in agroforestry. Nairobi and Madison: ICRAF and the Land Tenure Center.

Bryson, Judy C. 1989. Women and agriculture in sub-Saharan Africa: Implications for development (an exploratory study). *Journal of Development Studies* 17, no. 3: 28–45.

Byerlee, D., L. Harrington, and D. L. Winkelmann. 1982. Farming systems research: Issues in research strategy and technology design. *American Journal of Agricultural Economics* 64, no. 5: 897–904.

Callahan, John C. 1987. International aid and the Gambian agroforestry experience: A case study of problems and lessons learned. Paper presented at Forests, Habitats and Resources: A Conference on World Environmental History, May, Duke University.

Chambers, Robert. 1983. *Rural development: Putting the last first.* London: Longman.

Cohen, John M., and Norman T. Uphoff. 1977. Rural development participation: Concepts and measures for project design, implementation, and evaluation. Monograph no. 2. Rural Development Committee, Center for International Studies, Cornell University.

Conklin, Harold. 1975. *Hanunoo agriculture: A report on an integral system of shifting cultivation in the Philippines.* Northford, Conn.: Elliot's Books.

Cox, J. Charles. 1905. *The royal forests of England.* London: Methuen & Co.

Dahlberg, K. A. 1973. *Beyond the Green Revolution: The ecology and politics of global agricultural development.* New York: Plenum Press.

Delehanty, James, and Marilyn Hoskins. 1985. Majjia Valley evaluation study-sociological report. New York: CARE. Unpublished paper.

Dove, Michael. 1976. Tree rights, tree-holding units and tree-using units among the Melaban Kantuq: The factors of scarce land, scarce labor and scarce knowledge in their evolution. Paper presented at the annual meeting of the American Association of Anthropological Association.

_____1983. Theories of swidden agriculture and the political economy of ignorance. *Agroforestry Systems* 1, no. 2: 85–99.

Duncan, Patrick. 1960. *Sotho laws and customs.* Cape Town: Oxford University Press.

Esman, Milton J., and Norman T. Uphoff. 1984. *Local organizations: Intermediaries in rural development.* Ithaca, N.Y.: Cornell University Press.

Firey, Walter. 1978. Some contributions of sociology to the study of natural resources. In *Challenges of societies in transition.* Edited by M. Barnabas, S. K. Hulbe, and P. S. Jacob. Delhi: Maximillian Co.

Fortmann, Louise. 1984. Economic status and women's participation in agriculture. *Rural Sociology* 49, no. 4.

_____1985a. Seasonal dimensions of rural social organization. *Journal of Development Studies* 21, no. 3: 377–89.

_____1985b. The tree tenure factor in agroforestry with particular reference to Africa. *Agroforestry Systems* 2:229–51.

_____1986. Women in subsistence forestry. *Journal of Forestry* 84, no. 7: 39–42.

Fortmann, Louise, and John W. Bruce, eds. 1988. *Whose trees? Proprietary dimensions of forestry.* Boulder, Colo.: Westview Press.

Freeman, Peter H., and Tim Resch. 1985/86. Large plantations of rapidly growing exotic species: Lessons from the Bandia, Senegal. *Rural Africana* 2:253–372.

Gadgil, Madhav, M. S. Hegde, and S. Narenda Prasad. N.d. *Land, trees and people.* Bangalore, India: Centre for Ecological Sciences, Indian Institute of Science.

Gilles, Jere Lee, and Keith Jamtgaard. 1981. Overgrazing in pastoral areas: The commons reconsidered. *Sociologia Ruralis* 21:129–41.

Guha, Ramachandra. 1985a. Forestry and social protest in British Kumaun, ca. 1893–1921. In *Subaltern Studies IV.* Edited by Ranayit Guha, 55–99. Delhi: Oxford University Press.

_____1985b. Scientific forestry and social change in Uttarakhand. *Economic and Political Weekly* 20 (45, 45,47): 1939–52.

Hammer, Turi. 1982. Reforestation and community development in the Sudan. DERAP publications no. 150. Bergen, Norway: The Chr. Michelsen University, Development Research and Action Programme.

Hardin, Garrett. 1968. The tragedy of the commons. *Science* 162:1243–48.

Harrison, Paul. 1987. *The greening of Africa: Breaking through in the battle for land and food.* An International Institute for Environment and Development—Earthscan study. New York and Middlesex, England: Penguin Books.

Hopkins, Harry. 1985. *The long affray: The poaching wars 1760–1914*. London: Seckler and Warburg.

Hoskins, Marilyn. 1982. Social forestry in West Africa: Myths and realities. Paper presented at the meetings of the American Association for the Advance of Science, 8 January, Washington, D.C.

Johnson, H. G. 1969. Comparative cost and commercial policy theory in a developing world economy. *The Pakistan Development Review* 4 (Spring/supplement): 1–33.

Johnston, Bruce F., and W. C. Clark. 1982. *Redesigning rural development, a strategic perspective*. Baltimore: Johns Hopkins University Press.

Korten, David C. 1980. Community organization and rural development: A learning process approach. *Public Administration Review* 40, no. 5: 480–511.

Korten, David C., and Norman T. Uphoff. 1981. Bureaucratic reorientation for participatory development. Washington, D.C.: National Association of Schools of Public Affairs and Administration.

Kuznets, Simon. 1971. *Economic growth of nations: Total output and production structure*. Cambridge, Mass.: Harvard University Press.

Linebaugh, Peter. 1976. Karl Marx, the theft of wood and working class composition: A contribution to the current debate. *Crime and Social Justice* 6:5–16.

Lipton, Michael, and Richard Longhurst. 1989. *New seeds and poor people*. London: Hutchinson.

Mahiti Team. 1982. Focusing on the real issue: Some glimpses from Dhandhuka Taluka. Paper presented at the Regional Workshop on Block Level Planning, 4–6 October, South Gujarat University, Surat, India.

Matlon, Peter J. 1985. A critical review of objectives, methods, and progress to date in sorghum and millet improvement: A case study of ICRISAT/Burkino Faso. In *Appropriate technologies for farmers in semi-arid West Africa*. Edited by H. W. Ohm and J. G. Nagy. Lafayette, Ind.: Purdue University.

_____1987. Personal communication with Bruce F. Johnston and Daniel C. Mountjoy during Matlon's study leave at the Food Research Institute, Stanford University.

Mishra, A,. and S. Tripathi. 1978. Chipko movement, Uttarakhand women's bid to save forest wealth. New Delhi: People's Action.

Moench, Marcus. 1988. "Turf" and forest management in a Garhwal village. In *Whose trees? Proprietary dimensions of forestry*. Edited by Louise Fortmann and John W. Bruce. Boulder, Colo.: Westview Press.

Netting, Robert M. 1968. *Hill farmers of Nigeria: Cultural ecology of the Kofyar of the Jos Plateau*. Seattle: University of Washington Press. (Netting and some of this graduate students at the University of Arizona have done interesting recent work updating his earlier field work.)

Newbery, David M. 1990. Commodity price stabilization. In *Public policy and economic development*. Edited by D. Lal and M. F. G. Scott. Oxford: Oxford University Press.

Okali, C., and J. E. Sumberg. 1986. Examining divergent strategies in farming systems research. *Agricultural Administration* 22, no. 4: 233–53.

Okeyo, Achola Pala. 1980. The Joluo equation. *Ceres 13, no. 3: 36–42.*

Ostrum, Elinor. 1987. *Issues of definition and theory: Some conclusions and hypotheses.* Panel on common property resource management. Proceedings of the Conference on Common Property Resource Management, 599–615. Washington, D.C.: National Academy Press.

Panel on common property resource management. 1987. Proceedings of the Conference on Common Property Resource Management. Washington, D.C.: National Academy Press.

Peters, Pauline. 1987. Embedded systems and rooted models: The grazing lands of Botswana and the 'commons' debate. In *The question of the commons*. The culture and ecology of communal resources. Edited by G. J. McCay and J. M. Acheson. Tucson: University of Arizona Press.

Pingali, Prabhu L., Yves Bigot, and Hans P. Binswanger. 1987. *Agricultural mechanization and the evolution of farming systems in sub-Saharan Africa*. Baltimore, Md.: Johns Hopkins University Press for the World Bank.

Plumwood, Val, and Richard Routley. 1982. World rainforest destruction—The social factors. *The Ecologist* 12, no. 1: 4–22.

Raintree, John B., ed. 1987. *Land, trees and tenure*. Proceedings of an international workshop on tenure issues in agroforestry. Nairobi and Madison: ICRAF and the Land Tenure Center.

Richards, Paul. 1985. *Indigenous agricultural revolution: Ecology and food production in West Africa*. Boulder, Colo.: Westview Press.

Robertson, A. F. 1987. *The dynamics of productive relationships: African share contracts in comparative perspective*. Cambridge: Cambridge University Press.

Roe, Emery, and Louise Fortmann. 1986. Common property management of water in botswana. In *Proceedings of the conference on common property resource management April 21–26, 1985*. Panel on Common Resource Management, Board of Science and Technology for International Development. Edited by the National Research Council, 161–180. Washington, D.C.: National Academy Press.

Romm, Jeff, and Louise P. Fortmann. 1987. *Progress review: Land management*. Ford Foundation.

Ruthenberg, Hans. 1980. *Farming systems in the tropics*. London: Oxford University Press.

Scott, J. C. 1985. *Weapons of the weak: Everyday forms of peasant resistance*. New Haven: Yale University Press.

Shiva, Vandana. 1986. Coming tragedy of the commons. *Economic and Political Weekly* 21, no. 15: 613–14.

Skar, S. L., N. A. Samanez, and S. G. Cotarma. 1982. Fuel availability, nutrition and women's work in highland Peru: Three case studies from contrasting Andean communities. World Employment Programme Research. WEP10/WP23. Geneva: ILO.

Stanley, J., K. Rick, and F. Zufferey. 1983. *Handbook for facilitators*. Bukana ya Baeteleditela ba Detlhopa Tsotlhe. Gaborone: Applied Research Unit, Ministry of Local Government and Lands.

Staudt, Kathleen. 1975. Women farmers and inequities in agricultural services. *Rural Africana* 29:81–94.

Thompson, Michael M., Michael M. Warburton, and T. Hatley. 1986. *Uncertainty on a Himalayan scale: An institutional theory of environmental perception and a strategic framework for the sustainable development of the Himalaya*. London: Milton Ash Editions.

Uphoff, Norman T. 1986. *Improving international irrigation management with farmer participation: Getting the process right*. Boulder, Colo.: Westview Press.

Uphoff, Norman T., John M. Cohen, and Arthur A. Goldsmith. 1979. *Feasibility and application of rural development participation: A state of the art paper*. Monograph series no. 3. Ithaca, N.Y.: Cornell University, Center for International Studies, Rural Development Committee.

Weber, Fred. 1982. Review of CILSS Forestry Sector Program analysis paper. Washington, D.C.: USAID Forestry Support Program.

Westoby, Jack. 1978. Forest industries for socio-economic development. Proceedings of the 8th World Forestry Congress, Jakarta, 5:19–27.

[The] World Bank. 1986. *Poverty and hunger: Issues and options for food security in developing countries*. Washington, D.C.: The World Bank.

CHAPTER 5

DEFINING A SUSTAINABLE FUTURE: BASIC ISSUES IN AGRICULTURE[1]

William Lockeretz[2]

During the past two decades, several agricultural problems have generated increasing concern in the United States and around the world. Notable among these are the contamination of the environment by pesticides, plant nutrients, and sediments; loss of soil and degradation of soil quality; vulnerability to shortages of nonrenewable resources, such as fossil energy; and, most recently, the low farm income resulting from depressed commodity prices in the face of high production costs. *Sustainable agriculture* is a loosely defined term for strategies to cope with these problems.

Sustainable agriculture is based on several general approaches aimed at reducing environmental contamination, conserving resources, and providing an adequate and dependable farm income:

- Diversity of crop and livestock species to enhance the farm's biological and economic stability;
- Selection of crop and livestock varieties that are well suited to the farm's soil, climate, labor supply, and other available resources;
- Preference for farm-generated resources over purchased materials, and for locally available off-farm resources, when required, over those from distant regions;
- Tightening of nutrient cycles to minimize loss of nutrients off the farm;
- Enhancement of the soil's ability to store applied nutrients for later release as needed by the crop, in contrast to immediate use at the time of application;
- Enhancement of conditions favorable to the natural control or suppression of weeds, insect pests, and pathogens; and
- Maintenance of protective cover on the soil throughout the year.

How these principles get implemented obviously varies from region to region and from farm to farm. The most important techniques include the following:

- Multiple-species cropping systems, including rotations, intercropping, and sequential or relay cropping;
- Cover crops, green manures, and living mulches;
- Rotations or mechanical cultivation to control weeds;
- Tillage implements that leave most crop residues on the surface;
- Crop varieties and livestock breeds resistant to insect pests and diseases;
- Low-density livestock housing and grazing;
- Herd size scaled to the farm's ability to produce feeds and to use livestock manure efficiently;
- Greater use of roughage in cattle and sheep rations in preference to a diet high in grains and other concentrated feeds;
- Techniques to maximize the fertilizer value of livestock manures, such as composting and proper incorporation into the soil;
- Rotations that include deep-rooted crops to tap nutrient reserves in lower soil levels;
- Use of soluble inorganic fertilizers, if at all, only at a level that the crop can use efficiently, and only to the extent that nutrient deficits cannot be met first by livestock manure and legumes; and
- Use of synthetic insecticides and herbicides, if at all, only when there is a clear threat to the crop, and only as a last resort when other methods are not adequate.

EVOLUTION AND CURRENT STATUS OF THE CONCEPT

Sustainable agriculture's principles and techniques come from many sources, some recent, some going back several decades. They clearly owe an important debt to organic farming, a term that came into use in the 1940s. Initially, organic farming emphasized recycling of farm-generated nutrient sources and discouraged bringing in nutrients in the form of livestock feeds and chemically processed fertilizers. Later, the term came to mean systems that avoid using synthetic pesticides. A related approach to farming is followed by groups with particular religious or philosophical values, such as the Biodynamic movement.

Not all sustainable agriculture ideas have come from people organized into formal groups with a comprehensive, named set of principles. Innovative farmers have always tried unconventional approaches on their own, many of which can now be included under the general term *sustainable agriculture*. Some have done so to reduce production expenses; others have been motivated by environmental concern and a strong commitment to soil conservation.

Thus, the basic content of sustainable agriculture antedates the use of the term. Only more recently, however, have these various approaches been viewed as components of a more general concept, whether labelled as sustainable agriculture or any of several related terms (as discussed later). We can now think of researchers who deal respectively with biological pest control and soil conservation, for example, as having something in common that they might not previously have explicitly recognized.

This broadening of the label from narrowly defined terms like *organic* to the more generic *sustainable* reflects the broadening of the range of people interested in the same goals because of developments since the 1970s. The depressed farm economy has caused a shift from "maximum production" to "optimal production" as a guiding principle, the latter implying that it does not make sense to increase production of a commodity that is already in surplus. This has given rise to the concept of "low-input" agriculture, a reversal of the long-standing trend towards greater production through greater use of purchased inputs.

Traditional attempts to reduce surpluses, especially acreage reductions, run into the well-known dilemma that what is best for the nation as a whole may not be best for an individual farmer. Despite national surpluses, a farmer still gains by producing more. Low-input agriculture may resolve this contradiction by reminding farmers that the appropriate measure of a system's productivity and efficiency is not how much it produces, but rather the relative value of what it produces compared to what went in to produce it. The goal is to reduce purchased inputs in ways that cut production costs by more than the reduction in gross revenues, thereby serving both the individual and the national interest. The resulting increase in net income will make low-input agriculture attractive to all farmers, not just those with particular philosophical values.

One possible barrier to its acceptance is the long-established identification of high-input levels with "top management" farming, so that those farmers who choose not to use high levels must be the ones who are incapable of managing them. The new emphasis is on clever and sophisticated reduction in inputs, based on substituting information and understanding for materials. In their 1988 article "Overview of Sustainable Agriculture," Charles Francis and James King specifically list "low-input farming means low management" among the myths that need to be set right. Whether it requires a *higher* level of management is an open question discussed below.

Often, the inputs that farmers can cut back on to save money are also environmentally damaging, hazardous to health, or derived from nonrenewable resources. Thus, the trend towards low-input agriculture can help meet other important goals that have become more prominent in recent years. We are now much more aware of the seriousness of environmental problems originating in agriculture—for example, unanticipated contamination of groundwater by pesticides. Moreover, the organized environmental movement is strong enough to persuade, or force, farmers to do something about it. Consumers' growing interest in healthful, uncontaminated foods has encouraged some farmers to reduce or eliminate toxic pesticides. The energy crisis shocked many people into realizing the potentially serious consequences of our food system's heavy dependence on fossil resources, both directly through consumption of fuel and indirectly through use of fertilizers and other purchased inputs manufactured using fossil fuels.

The need for new approaches to address these important problems is now widely recognized, and every year increasing attention is devoted to sustainable solutions. However, not only the specific details, but even the basic ideas, remain to be worked out. In part, this is because the concept of sustainable agriculture has not yet been around long enough, at least not as an explicit principle, although the general idea was certainly important for many agricultural thinkers of previous generations. Another source of difficulty is that the concept derives from many diverse sources and tries to achieve diverse goals. Consequently, the single term *sustainable agriculture* really denotes a complex, multidimensional concept. It is not surprising that so far no single view of it has gained universal acceptance.

Fundamental questions still need to be discussed, analyzed, and debated before we can know what sustainable agriculture really is about. Some of these questions may never be put to rest, given the diversity of goals and viewpoints of the people interested in them. But sometimes they are not even asked, or the answers are asserted rather than demonstrated. Until these questions are discussed explicitly, we cannot know whether we are using the same words to mean different things, whether a particular approach can simultaneously serve the several different goals we would like to achieve, or even whether there might not be intrinsic contradictions among the various goals that have been thrown together under the single umbrella term *sustainable agriculture*. Nor will we know the best economic, institutional, and political environment to allow sustainable agriculture to fulfill its potential.

FUNDAMENTAL QUESTIONS

WHAT ARE THE DIFFERENCES BETWEEN SUSTAINABLE, REGENERATIVE, ALTERNATIVE, LOW-INPUT, AND ECOLOGICAL AGRICULTURE?

In the past decade, about a dozen words have come into use as labels for agricultural systems that share basic goals: reduced use of purchased inputs, especially toxic or nonrenewable ones; less damage to the environment; and better protection of water, soil, and wildlife. In addition, the older term *organic agriculture* refers to farming methods that share these goals, but that also specifically avoid use of synthetic organic pesticides and highly soluble mineral fertilizers.

If defined according to everyday usage, these terms would have clearly differentiated meanings:

- *Sustainable* has a time dimension and implies the ability to endure indefinitely, perhaps with appropriate evolution;
- *Regenerative* implies the ability to recreate the resources that the system requires;
- *Alternative* describes something that is different from the prevailing or *conventional* situation;
- *Low-input* refers to reduced use of materials from outside; and
- *Ecological* refers to the principles and processes that govern the natural environment.

But regardless of their literal meanings, all these terms have acquired further connotations when applied to agriculture, and some have become almost like brand names. For even though they carry specific implications when used in agriculture, terms like *sustained* paradoxically have also come to be used in so many different ways by different groups that they seem in danger of losing any real meaning. By now, *sustainable* may mean little more than *good.* If you like it, it's sustainable; you can criticize something you like simply by calling it unsustainable.

In the interest of simplicity, I will use the term *sustainable agriculture* to include the concepts implied by all the other terms as well. This is not intended to suggest that sustainable actually encompasses the others, or that every system ever labelled sustainable really is. Rather, it is an expedient way of avoiding a difficult definition problem, in the spirit of a Supreme Court Justice's remark in an obscenity case: "I can't define it, but I know when I see it." Similarly, I will use the term *conventional* whenever I refer to prevailing practices, regardless of how unecological or chemical-intensive or nonsustainable they happen to be.

IS SUSTAINABLE AGRICULTURE PRIMARILY A MATTER OF REDUCING CERTAIN INPUTS, OR REDUCING INPUTS IN GENERAL, OR INSTITUTING POSITIVE PRACTICES THAT MAKE SOME INPUTS UNNECESSARY?

The common identification of low-input agriculture with sustainable agriculture raises some important questions. Organic farming, a precursor of sustainable agriculture, avoids the use of two categories of purchased inputs: synthetic pesticides and highly soluble inorganic fertilizers. The reasons for this involve soil productivity, the environment, and other biological and chemical considerations. An additional consequence is that organic farmers may have lower cash operating expenses.

More recently, the idea of eliminating certain inputs regarded as particularly objectionable has been extended to reducing purchased inputs in general, to the extent feasible. This extension has been motivated by the depressed economic conditions affecting much of American agriculture. To reduce operating expenses, some farmers have been cutting back on pesticides and fertilizers, as well as other inputs, without doing anything else differently. According to one view, by itself this qualifies as sustainable. For example, the Wisconsin Rural Development Center puts the matter simply: "Sustainable methods are those which use less commercial fertilizer, herbicide, and pesticide."

Still another view is that sustainable agricultural systems should be based on positive steps that enhance soil fertility, control pests, and perform the many other functions that in conventional systems are performed by purchased inputs. Merely doing without such inputs is not an end in itself; the goal is to develop a system in which they would not be needed anyway. This concept emphasizes nutrient cycling, natural pest controls, diversity, continuous protection of the soil by living crops or residues, and wholesome housing and rations for livestock.

In some systems, such as dryland wheat in the Great Plains without herbicide-based chemical fallowing, pesticides and fertilizers were not very important all along. Was this system sustainable? The Dust Bowl demonstrates that it wasn't. Was it the best possible system from the viewpoints of environment and resources? Certainly not. Other systems could have done more to enhance soil productivity, reduce erosion, preserve wildlife habitat, and increase economic returns, while continuing to avoid the materials considered undesirable. And this monocultural system certainly did not reflect the complex ecological structure of the shortgrass prairie it replaced.

Another interesting contradiction arises if a farm happens to be near a source of organic wastes that can substitute for purchased inorganic fertilizer. Such a farm fulfills one requirement of sustainability in that it avoids using a material that is nonrenewable and potentially damaging to the environment. (Of course, the wastes must be applied in an environmentally suitable manner, or they will create just as much of a problem.) However, it is not a low-input system; only the form of the input is changed. Therefore, it is just as vulnerable to external disruption (for example, the source of the waste may shut down) as a system dependent on inputs made from nonrenewable resources. One source of vulnerability has merely been substituted for another.

DOES SUSTAINABLE AGRICULTURE REQUIRE FUNDAMENTAL CHANGES IN EITHER THE ECONOMIC AND INSTITUTIONAL ENVIRONMENT OR FARMERS' MOTIVATIONS AND VALUES?

This question provokes widespread disagreement. Some authors confine their discussions of sustainable agriculture to agronomic, environmental, and biological factors, or to economic evaluations under prevailing conditions. They believe that the same farmers, operating the same farms, can switch production systems without a significant change in attitude or in the economic, political, and social setting in which farming occurs.

In other discussions, far-reaching socioeconomic transformations are emphasized even more than the technical differences between sustainable and conventional farming methods. These transformations include: a greatly reduced linkage between farming and the industrial economy; more direct ties between producers and consumers; greater regional food self-sufficiency; a preference for family rather than corporate farms; policies that reward resource conservation; higher employment in agriculture; equitable distribution of economic returns among different classes of farmers and between present and future generations; and the social and economic revitalization of rural communities.

The connection, if any, between such transformations and changes in specific practices can go in either direction. That is, a different socioeconomic environment could be a prerequisite for a widespread adoption of sustainable methods, or it could be a consequence of this adoption. For example, intensive use of chemical pest control is sometimes said to result from the domination of farming by agrichemical interests, who are described as exerting a strong influence on farmers' decisions and on research priorities. Therefore, this domination must be reduced before farmers will be receptive to alternatives. On the other hand, if farmers decide to switch to reduced-chemical methods because they don't like the particular agrichemicals now in use, this change will reduce the influence of the agrichemical industry. This might not be why they made the change, but some people would consider it desirable as an end in itself, apart from the undesirable properties of the pesticides farmers have given up.

Despite the diversity of views on the need for far-reaching economic and institutional change, supporters of sustainable agriculture generally agree that changes are needed to modify government policies that have inhibited adoption of sustainable methods. Whether or not intended, the effect of tax laws and acreage reduction programs has been to encourage farmers to strive for maximum yields, to invest heavily in specialized facilities, and to concentrate on a few program crops rather then more diversified rotations. If the desired changes are achieved, they would represent only an adjustment within the prevailing economic system, not a qualitative difference.

The appropriate scale of farming is an example of an important, but still open, question. Sustainable agriculture is often described as more suitable for small- to moderate-sized family farms. However, the empirical support for this view is largely lacking, and the theoretical arguments are equivocal. On one hand, the trend towards larger farms has certainly been associated historically with specialization, whereas sustainable agriculture favors diversification over specialization. Sustainable agriculture may require a greater level of management, as discussed below. If so, the farmer can give more attention to each field or each animal if the farm is not too large. On the other hand, larger farms may be in a better position to hire outside experts and to acquire the needed facilities and equipment. In any case, the first myth listed by Francis and King is that "low-input approaches are only for small farmers."

The relation between the production system and the farmer's personal values is also unclear. Some authors see little connection. Today's farmers can, if they choose, adopt sustainable methods without any rethinking of motivations, values, or philosophical considerations. Moreover, they will do so, it is argued, if the alternative is more attractive from the viewpoints of economic return or health and safety.

But, to others, the reason a farmer farms is an overriding consideration. In this view, farmers should be less concerned about short-term profits and more concerned about the well-being of future generations, the rural communities in which they live and work, the natural environment, and the resources consumed in farming. Such considerations are sometimes regarded as the distinguishing characteristic of sustainable agriculture, which lead, in turn, to specific choices of production methods that will fulfill these goals. As with the previous discussion of the political and economic environment, change can be started from either direction. If farmers can be persuaded to be more concerned about environmental values, they will adopt environmentally sounder methods. But, if they can be persuaded to adopt these methods for whatever reasons (for example, economics), the result will be a system that, in fact, protects environmental values better, even if that is not why farmers choose to use them.

A possible objection to this last point is that changes made purely for economic reasons can be transient, given the variability of economic conditions. If farmers reduce pesticide use because crop prices have been too low to justify the cost, we can confidently expect this environmentally beneficial change to be undone by the next sharp increase in crop prices, just as much good soil conservation work was undone by the exceptionally rapid price increases from 1972 to 1974. The growing interest in low-input agriculture has been closely tied to the distress in the farm economy during the mid–1980s. This may point to a key difference between low-input and sustainable approaches; even though both may have the short-term effect of reducing pesticide use, the latter does so for less ephemeral reasons than the temporary diseconomy of applying pesticides heavily when crop prices are low.

The distinction between the two is apparently eliminated by merging these two concepts under the single term *lower input/sustainable agriculture*. This term was proposed by Clive Edwards, in a 1987 *American Journal of Alternative Agriculture* article, in the hope of solving both overproduction and environmental problems. But, what happens when the problem is scarcity, not surplus? Must we give up sustainability when we need to produce more food?

Resolving such questions is difficult, but sustainable agriculture cannot ignore the economic considerations that have prompted an interest in low-input agriculture; if a system doesn't return enough income to let the farmer remain in business, it isn't sustainable. The solution may lie in the earlier discussion of whether sustainable agriculture is primarily a matter of merely doing without certain materials, or of doing positive things that make these materials unnecessary. Ideally, with appropriate rotations, crop varieties, and tillage methods, the farmer who, because of environmental reasons, doesn't want to use pesticides won't have to and won't have an economic temptation to do so, even when crop prices rise again. If it doesn't turn out that way, environmental regulations that force farmers to internalize costs of pesticide use that formerly could be ignored as external will help narrow the gap between doing good and doing well.

TO WHAT EXTENT DO THE RESOURCE-CONSERVING AND ENVIRONMENTALLY SOUNDER TECHNIQUES BEING DEVELOPED AT MAINSTREAM AGRICULTURAL INSTITUTIONS ALREADY REPRESENT SUSTAINABLE AGRICULTURE?

Two questions—whether understanding sustainable agriculture involves a fundamentally different scientific outlook, and whether its adoption requires far-reaching economic or attitudinal changes—in turn raise the question of whether existing research and teaching institutions can deal with this area adequately. Long before the term *sustainable agriculture* came into common use, techniques with similar goals were already attracting attention. Examples include integrated pest management to reduce pesticide use, improved methods for storing and applying livestock manures to maximize their fertilizer value and reduce water pollution, and reduced tillage systems to control soil erosion. More recently, many agricultural institutions have started programs specifically labelled sustainable agriculture. Such programs explicitly acknowledge the influence of the sustainable agriculture movement and indicate mainstream agriculture's interest in accommodating its ideas.

However, to some, the established research institutions are under very powerful constraints, especially those imposed by disciplinary boundaries and by researchers' need to publish frequently. The latter, in turn, may discourage long-term projects such as studies covering several cycles of many-year rotations. These constraints may make it difficult or impossible for established institutions to organize agricultural research appropriately for dealing with sustainable systems. Also, to those who believe that sustainable agriculture involves fundamentally different principles, older ways of thinking are too firmly established among the current generation of researchers to permit newer ideas to flourish. Therefore, although such people may welcome the new interest in sustainable agriculture, they do not expect that the change will be able to go far enough in the current institutional environment.

Finally, some have argued that mainstream agricultural institutions not only have not been able to grasp the essence of sustainable agriculture, but do not even want to. The flurry of recently instituted programs is said to be merely a way to create the appearance of responding to outside pressures, and perhaps also to blunt the full thrust of the movement. This view reflects the belief that advancing the cause of sustainable agriculture requires challenging some far-reaching economic, social, or political values, and that mainstream agricultural institutions are too committed to the status quo to mount such a challenge.

The relation between mainstream institutions and supporters of alternative agriculture will undoubtedly clarify itself with time. Many efforts have been made to establish better communication between them, but this development is still too new to have played itself out fully. It is too early to know whether there will always be a role for an alternative agriculture movement, even if the mainstream accepts the ideas now labelled as alternative. Perhaps it is intrinsically desirable that someone always remain on the outside to challenge the established institutions and to keep prodding them to move further than institutional inertia would otherwise permit. Perhaps, too, the next generation will look back at today's developments and wonder "Why did they call that *alternative?*"

DOES SUSTAINABLE AGRICULTURE REQUIRE A HIGHER LEVEL OF MANAGEMENT ABILITY AMONG FARMERS?

Sustainable agriculture is commonly said to require greater management than conventional practice, both in how much effort the farmer must expend and in the quality demanded. The explanation is that sustainable practices substitute knowledge and understanding for technological control of growing conditions.

Another source of greater management requirements is said to be the need for sustainable farmers to make decisions on an integrated, whole-farm basis, in contrast to the more compartmentalized approach said to be possible in conventional systems. Also, sustainable management is often depicted as the adaptation of general principles to the specific circumstances of the individual farm, whereas conventional practices are sometimes characterized as a set of prescriptions that can be applied anywhere. The sustainable agriculture literature emphasizes the need for flexibility, the idea that there is no one best method under all circumstances.

Although these arguments are persuasive, the question of comparative management requirements is still open. Certainly sustainable agriculture will require farmers to acquire different kinds of knowledge and skills, but this does not mean it is necessarily more difficult. Some proponents of sustainable agriculture may exaggerate the extent to which purchased inputs obviate the need for judgment in conventional practice and may not take due account of the many decisions that must be made even if one uses inorganic fertilizers, synthetic pesticides, and livestock antibiotics. The stereotype of "cookbook" farming may indeed apply to poorer conventional managers, but not to the more discerning ones who bring knowledge and experience to their operations despite the availability of chemical help. Also, some of the expertise required for sustainable practices can be hired—for example, professional assistance in integrated pest management.

Finally, even if sustainable agriculture imposes greater management difficulties now, this problem may be reduced after farmers have had more experience with it and after more effort has been devoted to it by established research, extension, and teaching institutions. Eventually the mystique surrounding the complexities of sustainable management may disappear, and what may now seem bewilderingly complicated very likely can be made much more fathomable. Farmers have been called upon many times in the past to take on new management challenges, and it seems plausible that with appropriate support the challenges of sustainable management can be met as well.

CONCLUSIONS

Sustainable agriculture is not so much a new idea as it is a synthesis of ideas originating from various sources, out of various motivations. Some of these ideas were a response to specific problems; others came from philosophical and religious principles or social and economic ideals. These ideas eventually attracted broader attention and support and have correspondingly been modified and refined to reflect several recent developments: severe economic pressures on farmers, increased concern over environmental problems, and a recognition of the potential disruption caused by shortages of fossil energy and other nonrenewable resources.

Although its roots are old, sustainable agriculture as an explicitly formulated concept is young compared to the time it will take to explore its ramifications and to understand fully its basic principles. Achieving this presents particular difficulties because sustainable agriculture is intended to meet several different goals, and because it has evolved from diverse origins.

Despite these complexities, several important points are already clear. First, it is widely recognized that agriculture is beset by serious problems that cannot be handled by "business as usual." Second, sustainable agriculture in a general way represents a significant and potentially beneficial future direction for agriculture. Third, specific systems embodying this general concept have already demonstrated their value. But, much more remains to be done.

Certainly, more research and development work is needed to apply sustainable agriculture concepts to specific situations and specific problems. However, additional detailed empirical studies by themselves will not fulfill the promise of sustainable agriculture. The concept is still at an immature stage and must be placed on a firmer intellectual foundation. Important conceptual questions are not being asked, let alone answered. Fundamental principles still need to be developed and refined. Too much that needs to be demonstrated is instead simply asserted, or unconsciously assumed, or removed from debate by being made a matter of definition. People with a particular view of what sustainable agriculture is all about sometimes are not willing to acknowledge that other versions may be equally legitimate.

Supporters of sustainable agriculture often claim—with considerable justification—that mainstream agricultural thinking is too reluctant to challenge basic assumptions, too dogmatic, and too quick to become immersed in technical minutiae even though fundamental questions remain unaddressed. Ironically, sustainable agriculture runs the risk of repeating these mistakes, although, fortunately, the field is still in a formative state and can take heed of previous experiences. If it does, it will generate not only new solutions to the particular problems now affecting agriculture, but also a new and better standard for thinking about agriculture in general.

NOTES

1. Reprinted with grateful appreciation from *Northwest Report,* December 1989, pages 1–13. (Adapted from an article in *The American Journal of Alternative Agriculture.*)

2. William Lockeretz is a research associate professor in the school of Nutrition at Tufts University and Technical Editor of *The American Journal of Alternative Agriculture.*

CHAPTER 6

ABSTRACT: SUSTAINABLE DEVELOPMENT: CHALLENGES TO THE PROFESSION OF AGRICULTURAL ECONOMICS[1]

Sandra S. Batie[2]

The concept of sustainable development began in the United Nations in the mid–1960s (O'Riordan and Turner 1983), and it has since gained prominence as a central feature of the United Nation's development and environmental philosophy (World Commission on Environment and Development 1987). Sustainability concepts are now increasingly incorporated into programs of the World Bank (Davis and Schirmer 1987) as well as environmental organizations such as the World Resources Institute, the World Wildlife Fund, and the Conservation Foundation (see, for example, Repetto 1987).

There is consensus among its advocates that sustainable development is a concept based on intergenerational equity—that is, the current generation must not compromise the ability of future generations to meet both their "material needs" and to enjoy a healthy environment. Within this general consensual framework, there are different interpretations. Two different general definitions encompass most interpretations; these are the constrained-economic-growth definition and the maintenance-of-the-resource definition.

The constrained-economic-growth definition perceives sustainable development as the pursuit of economic growth subject to environmental constraints. The "maximize-subject-to-constraints" criteria can be described as having two stages: first, the establishment of some contractual arrangement, incorporating ecological principles and environmental ethics to establish the "rules" applicable to the development policy. Second, within those rules the maximum economic growth is pursued (Pearce 1987). This two-stage perspective, which many economists and some environmentalists hold, leads to advocacy for discovering the "right" incentives to produce solution-oriented technologies and the "right prices" to internalize the externalities (Speth 1989).

In contrast, sustainable development as "resource maintenance" is a minimization concept that implies minimizing the use of the natural environment; this concept of development meets the "material needs" of people while protecting the environment (Tolba 1987). O'Riordan and Turner (1983) distinguish two themes in this resource maintenance view of sustainable development: one is a preservation ecocentric position that emphasizes the need for severe constraints on economic growth within a decentralized socio-economic system. The other is an extreme preservationist view, or "deep ecology" ecocentrism, that is dominated by concern with rights for nonhuman species. In agriculture, deep ecology views are frequently held by the more radical "animal rightists."

A substantial intellectual history that includes contributions from ecological sciences, ethics, and economics undergirds the concept of sustainable development. In its more extreme versions, this concept challenges a basic belief of modern industrial society (Francis 1986), that is, that economic growth is desirable. The concept also challenges the assumptions of the conventional neoclassical economics approach to policy analysis. As a result, tension exists between sustainable development concepts and those of agricultural economics, at least as the profession is usually practiced.

Sustainable development—even in its less extreme versions—resurrects the classical concept of absolute scarcity. Most sustainable development advocates believe that the possibilities for economic growth are limited both by natural resource quality and by the assimilative capacity of the environment. In addition, the advocates question conventional economic assumptions relating to the possibility of prediction, the nature of externalities, the source of values, the validity of discounting, and the concept of equilibrium.

However, the concept of sustainable development is amorphous—it is perceived differently by different people. The sustainable development theme seems to encompass everything from global warming to aboriginal cultures. This lack of precision often obstructs the drawing of implications. Nevertheless, the implications that sustainable development themes have for the discipline of agricultural economics are important, especially so since sustainable development concepts are becoming so widely debated and are gaining disciples both in the United States and abroad.

The sustainable development concept warns us as agricultural economists that if we cling too tightly to conventional neoclassical concepts, we are in danger of trivializing important global problems. We should order and examine the conceptual basis of sustainable development concepts, and explore conflicts with traditional economic approaches. We should give more attention to the interrelationships among (and evolutions of) economic and ecological systems. Furthermore, if an investment is made in a more coherent theory of sustainable development, the theory can provide a guide to research, policy, and action that may indeed lead to an improved world. Some progress is being made with respect to these issues, but there is justification for broader participation and broader reflection on the challenges posed by the sustainable development concept to our profession.

NOTES

1. Editor's Note: Sandra S. Batie's presidential address to the American Agricultural Economics Association (AAEA), July 30-August 2, 1989, is extremely relevant to this section of the book. Because it is readily available in the December 1989 issue of the *Journal of Agricultural Economics*, Professor Batie was asked to produce the brief abstract printed here. Readers are urged to also read the address in its entirety in the *Journal.*

2. Sandra S. Batie is a professor of Agricultural Economics at the Virginia Polytechnic Institute and State University, Blacksburg, Virginia.

REFERENCES

Davis, Ted J., and Isabelle A. Schirmer, eds. 1987. *Sustainability issues in agricultural development*. Washington, D.C.: World Bank.

Francis, George. 1986. Great Lakes governance and the ecosystem approach: Where next? *Alternatives* 13, no. 3 (September/October): 61–70.

O'Riordan, Timothy J., and R. K. Turner. 1983. *An annotated reader in environmental planning and management*. Oxford: Peraganon Press.

Pearce, David. 1987. Foundations of an ecological economics. *Ecological Modeling* 38:9–18.

Repetto, Robert. 1987. Managing natural resources for sustainability. In *Sustainability issues in agricultural development*. Edited by Ted J. Davis and Isabelle A. Schirmer, 167–79. Washington, D.C.: World Bank.

Speth, Gustave. 1989. A climate of apocalypse. *New Perspective Quarterly* 6, no. 1: 12–5.

Tolba, Mostafa K. 1987. *Sustainable development: Constraints and opportunities*. London: Butterworth.

World Commission on Environment and Development. 1987. *Our common future*. Oxford: Oxford University Press.

CHAPTER 7

RESOURCE ENHANCEMENT AND GROWTH IN CAPITAL BASES: AGENDAS AND CONCLUSIONS

The Houston SSAAP conference considered natural, human, and community resources with one set of work groups. Subsequent to the Houston conference, the editorial team separated natural and community resources, covering natural and manmade resources in this section of Part III and community resources in Section 1. Thus, only those Houston work group reports that relate to natural resources are covered in this chapter. These are: (1) natural resource use, development, and disinvestments; (2) assessment and utilization of natural resources; (3) natural resource commodities; (4) waste, environmental pollutants, food-chain contaminants, and natural resources; (5) public choice and private decisions with respect to natural resources; and (6) resources data. Manmade resources were badly neglected at Houston with the exception of the consideration given to capital and credit in connection with the two sections on domestic and international agriculture that are in Part II of this book. This and other neglect prompted additional work on natural resources by SSAAP's editorial group that is reported in the second main part of this chapter entitled "Developments After the Houston Conference and Conclusions."

NATURAL RESOURCE AGENDAS FROM SSAAP'S HOUSTON CONFERENCE

The natural resource agendas developed by the indicated work groups at Houston are presented under this subheading. Allan Schmid, a professor in the Department of Agricultural Economics at Michigan State University, along with William Heffernan, the chairman and a professor in the Department of Rural Sociology at the University of Missouri, was responsible for the community, human, and natural resources area. Schmid was responsible for the work groups concerned with natural resources. He developed an overall summary statement about the agendas developed by the work groups under his leadership. This statement is not reproduced in its entirety here; instead, only its more general points are presented while more specific points are in the reports of the specific groups. Schmid noted:

- The importance of such generic alternatives as educational programs, regulation of liabilities for private market transactions, and social pressures. In doing this, he called attention to the public choice/transaction cost approach stressed by Bromley at Houston and by SSAAP's editorial group since the Houston conference.
- The importance, in evaluating program alternatives, of information about behavior as it is influenced by perceptions of program incentives in ways that cause performance to differ from program intent.
- The question of what to do when interests conflict—whose preferences count?—the roles of preference aggregation, weighting selection, and even preference formation. The effect of research and decision processes on value formation versus technical measurement of preexisting value perceptions.
- The difference between conflict resolution and mediation (where the perceptions of farmers are crucial) and the use of emotive power politics.
- The difference between market choices constrained by ability to pay versus choices redistributive of the ownership of income-producing rights and privileges.
- The important ethical issues that arise in resolving conflicts within and between generations and in using benefit/cost ratios to guide public spending.
- The questions that arise in deciding how far researchers, as contrasted to teachers and extension workers, can go in "value clarification."
- The importance of trend analyses and technology assessment.
- The supply versus demand aspects of environmental and food safety.
- The importance of private management of resource commodity firms.

- The importance of spatial, physical, and social databases for natural resources.

These general points by Schmid were found to be very relevant as SSAAP's editorial group explored: (1) the ramifications of work group reports from the Houston conference, and (2) the omissions of important agenda areas in SSAAP's program before and through that conference.

WORK GROUP REPORTS FROM THE HOUSTON CONFERENCE

During the course of the Houston conference, two work groups merged with a third under the leadership of Barbara Osgood. The three groups included:

NATURAL RESOURCE USE, DEVELOPMENT, AND DISINVESTMENTS

Leader: Barbara Osgood, Economic and Social Science Division, Soil Conservation Service, USDA, Washington, D.C.

Invited members (some of whom may not have participated) Don E. Albrecht, John Carlson, I. D. Clifton, W. R. Freudenburg, and John K. Thomas

EVALUATION, ASSESSMENT, AND UTILIZATION OF NATURAL RESOURCES

Leader: James C. Hite, Alumni Professor, Department of Agricultural Economics and Rural Sociology, Clemson University, Clemson, S.C.

Invited members (some of whom may not have participated) A. J. Fellow, Mark D. Lange, John A. Miranowski, and Gene Wilken

NATURAL RESOURCE COMMODITIES

Leader: Larry Libby, Chairman and Professor, Agricultural Economics, University of Florida, Gainesville, Fla.

Invited members (some of who may not have participated) Robert Abt, James Anderson, Peter Kakela, Larry Leistritz, K. J. Roberts, and Jeff Romm

Under the general heading "toward informed choice in natural resource use," the combined work groups generated agenda items under four subheadings: (1) social and economic evaluation of natural resource policy options, (2) production and supply factors related to natural resources management and policy, (3) consumer behavior and attitudes relative to natural resources, and (4) methodological issues in the natural resources area. These agendas are presented below in an abridged form that omits the extensive lists of illustrative questions provided by the combined work groups.

Toward Informed Choice in Natural Resources

Resource users, policy makers, and managers of natural resource firms need more and better information if they are to choose among options with adequate knowledge of the likely consequences of those options. Categories of consequences include monetary and nonmonetary benefits, implementation costs, and, perhaps most importantly, *who* is affected and *how* because distributional impacts define support and opposition to policy options. The *absence* of such information leads to inappropriate and wasteful public choice. Some of the illustrative questions were converted to agenda items and are presented here.

- *Social and economic evaluation of natural resource policy options.*
  - This includes distributional and other impacts of such policies and programs as the Conservation Reserve Program, conservation compliance, and wetland preservation for individuals, firms, communities, and other organizations. Social scientists should help ascertain the:
  - Impacts of voluntary versus regulatory land-use policies.
  - Social and economic off-site impacts of natural resource management.
  - Social and economic impacts of changes in water quality and use.
  - Alternative ways of evolving better institutions to shape water use patterns.
  - Role and validity of benefit/cost analysis in public decisions on natural resource use.
  - Administrative costs of policy options.
  - Monetary and nonmonetary benefits of policy options.
  - Distribution of costs and benefits.
  - Impacts of policy interactions (for example, interactions between environmental policy and commodity policy).
  - Tradeoffs among options in real decision processes.
  - Various benefits associated with avoiding mandatory, punitive, and/or police power actions *beyond* the observed costs of implementing them.
  - Unintended interactions among various policy actions in agriculture to be avoided or mitigated—for example, incentives to increase production versus protecting wetlands or programs to increase reduced tillage versus penalties against contaminated groundwater.
- *Production and supply factors related to natural resources management and policy.*

  This includes natural resource commodities such as timber, fisheries (marine and aquaculture), minerals, wildlife, water, farmland, and coastlines. Social scientists should deal with:
  - The roles of market and nonmarket forces.
  - Natural resources as a base for rural community development.
  - Complementary mixes of outputs from natural resources.
  - Long-term supply issues.
  - Social and economic consequences of new technologies affecting natural resources.
  - Regional differences in production and marketing factors.
  - Production and marketing impacts of changes in use of agricultural and other rural land.
  - The reconciliation of market and nonmarket values in making public choices.

- *Consumer behavior and attitudes relative to natural resources.*

  This includes public responses to voluntary conservation programs, willingness to pay for natural resource preservation, and attitudes toward regulations and controls. Social scientists should be concerned about:
  - The origins of attitudes toward rural land use.
  - Planning and decision-making processes in relation to natural resources.
  - Marketing strategies for conservation.
  - Attitude-behavior linkages and the role of resource stewardship.
  - Recreation demands—current and projected.
  - The relationship between attitudes toward natural resources and behavior.
  - Improving our ability to predict behavior of consumers of resource commodities on the basis of attitudinal surveys.
  - Obtaining better understanding of decision-making processes of consumers.

- *Research methodological issues in the natural resources area.*

  Social scientists should be concerned about new paradigms, research methods and techniques, and data systems that are needed to increase the scope and effectiveness of natural resource research. Important areas for attention include:
  - Scale of data collection and intervals for data collection;
  - Integration of natural resources and social science data with theoretical concepts;
  - Formulating, testing and applying techniques for measuring nonmonetary and monetary values;
  - The role of analytical techniques in the decision-making process;
  - Appropriate risk-assessment techniques for environmental quality policies; and
  - Improving measurements of benefits and costs in evaluation analysis.

WASTE, ENVIRONMENTAL POLLUTANTS, FOOD-CHAIN CONTAMINATION, AND NATURAL RESOURCES

Leader: William M. Park, Associate Professor, Department of Agricultural Economics and Rural Sociology, University of Tennessee, Knoxville, Tenn.

Invited members (some of whom may not have participated) Sam Cordes, J. C. Headley, Peter J. Kuch, James S. Shortle, R. J. Supalla, Eileen van Ravenswaay, and David Walker

Production and consumption of food and natural resource commodities generate wastes. Some people may bear the costs of disposing of those wastes against their wishes. As a result, public policies are needed. Better policies result from a clear understanding of the problem. Social science research contributes to this understanding, to the identification of alternative policies, and to the evaluation of their consequences. Priority areas include: problems of environmental degradation, food safety, agendas for interfacing with other groups, conflicts over natural resource use, and assessment of nonmarket values.

Environmental Degradation

Farming, forestry, fishing, and mining, as well as municipal and industrial activities, can harm groundwater, surface water, aesthetic qualities, land (soil), wildlife, and air. Important agenda items for social science work include:

- Development of new institutional models for environmental protection.
- Identification and evaluation of social, monetary, nonmonetary, and technical factors influencing adoption of practices to protect surface and groundwater from contamination and to reduce other forms of environmental degradation.
- Identification and evaluation of alternative environmental protection strategies in terms of their acceptability for implementation through information and education, regulations, and incentives programs (as influenced by social perceptions of costs and benefits, effects on income distribution, legal feasibility, consistency with moral values, and macroeconomic effects on employment, competitiveness, and the like).
- Identification and analysis of social, monetary, nonmonetary, and institutional factors influencing environmental quality such as environmental policies, farm price and income programs, values and attitudes, interest group pressures, moral/ethical norms, property rights, national monetary/fiscal trade and other policies, and land-grant research orientations.

Food Safety

Opinion surveys show that consumers rate pesticide food contamination as the most significant food-safety problem. Food scientists rate bacteria and food-borne diseases as the most significant problem. Research should give priority to these two concerns.

- The causes of food-safety problems including: adverse incentives present in food production (for example, inexpensive chemical inputs that contaminate food) and food purchasing, preparation, and consumption patterns that expose food to contamination.
- The impact of policy alternatives for increasing food safety with attention to the sacrifices consumers are willing to make to attain increased food safety.
- Identification of improved criteria for making public and private food-safety choices.

Agendas for Interfacing with Other Groups

Social scientists concerned with natural resources should:

- Work with community-development specialists to exploit local natural-resource-based rural-development opportunities.
- Work with biological, physical, and production economists to estimate the marginal productivity of nutrients

and pesticides by crop and location to determine the impacts of practices and regulatory actions designed to reduce chemical use and develop low-chemical production systems.

- Help develop databases with respect to nutrient, chemical, antibiotic, and pesticide use (by crop, livestock product, and location) for assessment of pesticide, antibiotic, hormonal, herbicide, and chemical risks to health and environment.
- Work with basic social scientists and humanists to improve techniques for measuring nonmonetary benefits and costs.
- Study risk perceptions and attitudes empirically as they relate to human health and environmental degradation; this should be done cooperatively with other concerned professionals.
- Help local communities assess their fiscal capability to meet environmental standards regarding treatment of drinking water and sewage.

Conflicts Over Natural Resource Use

High cost conflicts over natural resource use are increasing. Issues of property rights often arise. The following are important items on the agenda of the rural social sciences:

- Identification of strategies to facilitate the siting of or to avoid the need for locally unwanted facilities (for example, landfills). Processes are needed to help communities deal with conflict. Research is needed to determine the appropriate roles for consensus-building, mediation, and compensation mechanisms.
- Identification of strategies to reduce conflicts between farming, other natural resource industry activities, and residential land use in rural-urban fringes, including such approaches as "right-to-farm" laws and agricultural districting.
- Identification of strategies to resolve conflicts over water rights and allocations between agricultural and other users of groundwater and surface water. The values of water in different uses and the characteristics of alternative allocation approaches (e.g., water markets versus rationing) for resolving conflicts or reallocating rights can and should be researched.
- Identification of strategies to reduce conflict resulting from multiple uses of public lands, including estimation of the distribution of benefits.
- Analysis of policies designed to influence private land use or development in terms of their impact on natural resource productivity and environmental amenities.
- Analysis of problems resulting from exploration of common-property resources to help evaluate and correct inherent incentives for overexploitation of fishery and other common-property resources.

Assessment of Nonmarket Values

Assessment of nonmarket benefits or costs in both monetary and nonmonetary terms of proposed changes in the quantity or quality of nonmarket goods related to agriculture and rural resources is needed to support policy decisions. Important agenda topics include assessing:

- The nonmarket benefits or costs of proposed changes in the agricultural land or rural resources bases (for example, wildlife values).
- The off-site costs of farming and other natural-resource-based activities. These off-site costs include reduced quantity or quality of recreational activities, negative impacts on wildlife, increased water treatment costs, and reduced flood protection, among others.
- The value of foregone agricultural productivity due to degradation of the agricultural resource base resulting from agricultural and industrial activities that may cause declining soil productivity due to erosion, groundwater depletion, pollution, acid rain deposition, the greenhouse effect, and ozone depletion.

PUBLIC CHOICE AND PRIVATE DECISIONS WITH RESPECT TO NATURAL RESOURCES

Leader: Tom Ruehr, Professor, Department of Soil Science, California Polytechnic State University, San Luis Obispo, Calif.

Invited members (some of whom may not have participated) Gary Comstock, M. Janice Hogan, Douglas MacLean, Robert Matthews, Allen Randall, Neill Schaller, Robert Vertrees, and Gene Wunderlich. James T. Bonnen and Joseph Havlicek also participated in some deliberations.

What is reported here is that portion of the public choice and private decision agendas developed for "Natural, Human, and Community Resources" that pertains mainly to natural resources. Community resource agenda items are reported in Part III, Section 1, Chapter 7. Some corresponding human development agenda items are reported in Chapter 9 of Section 2 (Part III) on human development. This group coordinated its efforts with those of the group on "Farm, Agribusiness, and Consumer Dimensions of Public Choice and Private Decision Making including Agroethics" led by Bobby Eddleman, a professor and resident director at the Corpus Christi Research and Extension Center, Texas A&M University. Although the processes of public policy formulation and private decision making about natural resources were judged important, the public choice/transaction cost approach was not given particular attention by this work group.

Social scientists should:

- Emphasize the ethics of natural resource issues in both graduate and undergraduate courses in agriculturally related programs.
- Help prepare agricultural extension workers, community leaders, and agricultural consultants to deal with ethical issues about natural resources.
- Research and debate ethical aspects in public policy formulation in relation to natural resources.
- Thoroughly study policies and programs with long histories from an ethical perspective, such as soil conservation for example. Obvious value and ethical issues

underlie this policy area that include a utilitarian ethic, an environmental or ecosystem integrity ethic that is coming to the forefront in natural resource policy debates, and a humanistic or cultural ethic that views natural resources in a spiritual sense ("Mother Earth" of the American Indians).

Resources Data (originally Macrolevel Data, Social and Economic Accounting and Analysis Systems for Natural and Community Resources)

Leader: David L. Brown, Associate Director, Agricultural Experiment Station, Cornell University

Invited members (some of whom may not have participated) Kenneth Baum, James T. Bonnen, Steven Liller, Steve H. Murdock, and Alton Thomson

Social scientists should:

- Help establish a "national rural and agricultural statistical service" with responsibility to (1) develop, maintain, coordinate, and assure access to an integrated rural database including primary, secondary, and administrative data, (2) conduct all USDA surveys, and (3) coordinate rural and agricultural survey activities of other federal agencies. The rural database should include information on: (a) production, market, processing, financial, and other business structures; (b) population and human resources; (c) natural resources and environmental quality; (d) community and social services and physical infrastructure; (e) technology; and (f) social structure. This same agenda item is repeated in Sections 1, 2, and 4 of this part.

- Help develop an integrated socioeconomic, demographic, natural resource, and environmental database with the objective of linking comparable and reliable secondary data at the county and/or other appropriate substate level. Information on individuals, households, firms, and governments should be included.

- Encourage additional and more effective intergovernmental cooperation in the collection of administrative data on social, community, natural resource, and environmental programs to enhance the geographic and subject-matter comparability and usefulness of administrative data for research, policy development, and program evaluation in relation to natural resources.

DEVELOPMENTS AFTER THE HOUSTON SSAAP CONFERENCE AND CONCLUSIONS

The work of SSAAP's editorial group since the Houston conference has made it clear that natural resource specialists are playing a ground-breaking role among rural and basic social scientists in using the public (really multiperson) choice/transaction cost approach in the study of public choices and private decisions pertaining to natural resources. SSAAP's editorial group presents the following additional agenda items for social scientists addressing natural resource problems and issues. They should:

- Continue their use of the public choice/transaction cost (PC/TC) approach.

- Recognize that the PC/TC approach is still relatively primitive and in need of further development for use in investigating natural resource issues. More specifically, social scientists concerned with natural resources should develop the PC/TC approach to:
  - Consider more explicitly than natural resource specialists have to date three aspects of institutional change—rules of the game; organizations, policies, and programs; and facilities, staffs, and physical plants. (These appear to be so closely interrelated that separate consideration of one of them without attention to the others is questionable.)
  - Distinguish better between stock and flow transaction costs.
  - Relate monetary and nonmonetary stock establishment and dismantlement costs to such flow costs as those for information, negotiation, and enforcement.
  - Consider, define, and measure flow and stock returns, both monetary and nonmonetary, to natural resource (1) rules of the game, (2) organizations, and (3) facilities, staffs, and physical plants.
  - Attempt to increase the interpersonal validity of common denominators among the various monetary and nonmonetary stock and flow costs and returns involved in changing institutions as rules of the game; organizations; and facilities, staffs, and physical plants.
  - Consider the values of acts, actions, and attitudes as well as of consequences.
  - Amplify the concept of rent collection to elucidate the roles of collecting positive quasi rents vis-a-vis dismantlement costs versus absorbing negative quasi-rents with respect to establishment costs.
  - Distinguish between resource institutions established for constructive resource-enhancement purposes and those established to create income (real and/or monetary) for rent collectors.

The editorial group has noted a characteristic absence of attention to the manmade resources that are commingled with natural resources so extensively as to make separate agendas for the two unrealistic. This omission seems to be generally characteristic of thought and work about natural resources whether done by social scientists or by biological, physical, and ecological scientists. Social scientists should take the lead in conceptualizing

- the roles played by manmade resources in enhancing, maintaining, and using natural resources, and

- the generation, saving, and use of manmade resources used in conjunction with natural resources.

CHAPTER 1

INTRODUCTION TO SECTION ON TECHNICAL ADVANCE

Technical change is, of course, one of the very important forces driving the development of farms and rural societies. In agenda- and priority-setting exercises involving agriculture, improvement in production methods ordinarily receives the primary emphasis even among social scientists developing priorities and agendas for their own work (Busch and Lacy 1986; Mellor 1966; Ruttan 1982; Peterson and Hayami 1977; Evenson 1968). The emphasis on technical change in priority- and agenda-setting exercises dominated by the biological and physical scientists had generally been so overwhelming that no separate area or work group was established for the Houston conference to deal with it. That was a mistake. Fortunately, rather appropriate attention was paid to technical change in developing SSAAP's agendas for (1) farming, agribusiness, and consumption, and (2) international rural development. In connection with international rural development, there was a special Houston work group that addressed itself to the question of whether the U.S. Agency for International Development should have a Collaborative Research Support Project (CRSP) for the rural social sciences. By and large, SSAAP participants decided that a separate rural social science CRSP was not needed; it was felt instead that the rural social sciences should play important appropriate "partnership" roles in all the CRSPs having to do with the generation, dissemination, and utilization of improved agricultural techniques.

As indicated above, SSAAP's Houston conference was not appropriately organized in relation to technical change. It was noted in the introduction to Part III that SSAAP's interest in natural and community resources broadened at and after Houston to include separate sections and agendas in this part for rural social science work with respect to technical advance, the enhancement and expansion of natural and manmade capital, human capital formation, and institutional improvements.

The public choice and transaction cost (PC/TC) approach now promises to help guide the rural social sciences to important new agenda items vis-a-vis institutional change. Inasmuch as a large proportion of the technological change for agriculture and rural communities originates in publicly supported institutions, the "new institutional economics" (Castle et al. 1981) or "new political economy of agriculture" (Schuh 1981) public choice/transaction cost (PC/TC) approach can guide and reveal important new agenda activities for social scientists concerned with the design, development, and assessment of institutions responsible for generating and disseminating technological advances for agriculture and rural communities. This promise is even stronger when the theories of public choice and private decision making are used as components of multidisciplinary, iterative/interactive systems analysis (Bubolz and Sontag, Part II, Section 1, Chapter 6; Johnson, Part II, Section 2, Chapter 7; Busch, Part III, Section 1, Chapter 2).

The remainder of this chapter will very briefly review some of the important literature on technical change in agriculture that was generally available at the time of the Houston conference. While concentrating largely on work of rural social scientists, this review will start with agenda- and priority-setting activities on the part of biological and physical agricultural scientists. After this literature review, there is a substantial section dealing with the potential contribution of the PC/TC approach and theories of private decision making to rural social science agendas for improving rural and basic social science contributions to the design, improvement, and assessment of technical change institutions and the technologies they generate.

PAST AGENDA- AND PRIORITY-SETTING EXERCISES CONCERNING TECHNICAL CHANGE DOMINATED BY BIOLOGICAL AND PHYSICAL AGRICULTURAL SCIENTISTS

After World War II, biological and physical scientists associated with the National Academy of Sciences and those who became associated with the National Science Foundation after its establishment stressed the importance of basic (as opposed to applied or subject-matter and problem-solving) research in the biological and physical sciences. Vannevar Bush's 1945 article entitled "Science:

The Endless Frontier" made the original point. By 1972, U.S. agriculture had the so-called Pound Report from the National Academy of Sciences entitled "Report of the Committee on Research Advisory to the U.S. Department of Agriculture." Neither Bush nor Glen Pound gave much attention to the rural and basic social science disciplines. Their main concern was to obtain additional support for the basic biological and physical science disciplines to undergird technical development. Combined, the Bush and Pound reports had the effect of shifting the stress in American science, both in and outside of agriculture, to the basic biological and physical science disciplines and away from multidisciplinary subject-matter and problem-solving research that typically involves the social sciences.

In 1975, a working conference sponsored by the Agricultural Research Policy Advisory Committee (ARPAC) published a report entitled *Research to Meet U.S. and World Food Needs*. Among the rural social sciences, this report dealt mainly with needed research from agricultural economists.

In 1977, the National Research Council produced the *World Food and Nutrition Study: The Potential Contributions of Research*. While the rural social sciences and basic social science disciplines were involved in the committees that generated this report, the report dealt mainly with priorities and agenda items for the biological and physical agricultural sciences. The same was true of the report of President Ford's Commission on World Hunger (1980). There have also been a number of priority- and agenda-setting exercises more specialized within agriculture. For instance, there have been two priority-setting exercises in the general area of crop (Brown et al. 1975; Gibbs and Carlson 1985) and livestock (Pond et al. 1980) productivity. For the most part, these exercises were technocratic—rural social scientists and a few basic social scientists played token roles to leave the main emphasis on the biological and physical agricultural sciences (Johnson 1977).

PAST SOCIAL SCIENCE WORK ON TECHNICAL CHANGE FOR AGRICULTURE

Technical advance for agriculture had not been neglected by the rural and basic social scientists prior to the Houston conference. This permitted the Houston SSAAP participants to draw on a substantial body of knowledge about the social science dimensions of technical advances for agriculture.

Early on, rural sociologists were instrumental in developing a "diffusion theory" of the dissemination of technical advances in agriculture that was widely used by extension administrators in administering extension programs for making information about technical advances available to farmers. This theory envisioned an S-shaped learning curve for technical advances and classified farmers as early, normal, and late adapters (Beal and Bohlen 1957; Rogers 1962). For the most part, sociological diffusion theorists paid little attention to costs and returns for adopting new production techniques and methods. The assumption seems to have been that technical advances are always advantageous to adopt.

Rural sociologists have also been concerned with the impact of technological advance on rural societies and have participated directly in studies of the sociology of agricultural research institutions that generate and disseminate new technologies for the agricultural sector. For instance, Lawrence Busch and William Lacy (1986) organized a very useful symposium, the proceedings of which were published in a book entitled *The Agricultural Scientific Enterprise: A System in Transition*. Their volume, for the most part, examines our technical agricultural research establishments as social entities. Part VIII of their book presents conclusions written by Sylvan Wittwer (1986) entitled "A Second Century Agenda for State Agricultural Experiment Stations: A View from the 21st Century." Wittwer, an agricultural biological scientist himself, concentrated more on agendas and priorities for the biological and physical agricultural sciences than for rural sociology and the other rural social sciences.

Political scientists and agricultural historians have shared a considerable interest in the politics and financial support of the public agricultural research institutions including, especially, the state agricultural experiment stations. Their studies and analyses have considered a wide range of social, political, and other variables important in the origin and day-to-day operation of the public agricultural research institutions of the United States. While some political scientists and historians have incorporated PC/TC theories in the study of history (North 1987), only a few applications have been made by political scientists and historians concerned with the agricultural research establishment (Kirkendall, Part I, Chapter 2).

There has been an increasing concern on the part of philosophers, rural social scientists, and activists about the appropriateness of roles played by the agricultural research institutions (ARE) of the agricultural establishment (AE) in generating technical advances. These and other concerns have led to a substantial number (more than ten) conferences in the last 15 years or so on the general subject of agricultural ethics. (See Part IV, Section 3, Chapter 1.) At these meetings, the operations of the publicly supported agricultural research institutions have been widely criticized and evaluated.

Agricultural economists have researched, consulted, and advised on the design, operation, resources uses, and outreach of the ARE. The concerns of Hans P. Binswanger and Vernon W. Ruttan (1978) and others have involved both domestic and international agricultural research organizations. Constance M. McCorkle (1989) has edited a book of papers about the role of the social sciences in AID's Collaborative Research Support Projects (CRSPs) other than economics and agricultural economics which she (for some unexplained reason) precludes from the social sciences.

Agricultural economists have been prominent in estimating returns to investments in agricultural research. An excellent summary of this work is to be found in Chapter 10 of Ruttan's (1982) book *Agricultural Research Policy*. More recently, summaries by regions of the world were produced by Zvi Griliches (1979) and Glenn Fox (1987). Persons such as James Oehmke (forthcoming) and Glenn L. Johnson (1988) have criticized these estimates of returns to technical agricultural research. Estimates of such returns are obtained by two methods: that of residuals and that of regression analysis. Though some of the regression analyses have been guided by the concept of a national production function for which research investments and expenditures are treated as factors of production, some have not been so guided. With or without guidance from a perceived macroproduction function, estimation difficulties are created by the high degree of complementarity that exists between technical advances, human capacity to use them, and the institutions and policies that make it advantageous to use them. The method of residuals runs a risk of ascribing the same residuals successively to technical advance, human capital formation, and institutional improvements. High correlations among the four driving forces reduces the reliability of estimates of regression coefficients for any one of them unless, of course, one or more driving forces is omitted from the analysis in which case a regression analysis adds the effect on output that would have been "explained" by the omitted force to the coefficient(s) for one or more of the included forces with which it is correlated. Recent work on returns to extension versus research by Wallace E. Huffman and Robert E. Evenson (1989) seems to have encountered such estimation difficulties—since their estimates show unexpectedly low returns to extension education (human development) and unexpectedly high returns to technical research.

George L. Brinkman (1969), doing research for the field leaders of several subprojects of the Consortium for the Study of Nigerian Rural Development (Johnson et al. 1969, 136–48), addressed the problem of reconciling proposed public investments in agricultural education, infrastructure, and productivity in Nigeria. In doing so, he was dealing with proposals simultaneously to make institutional improvements, develop human capital, advance agricultural technology, and increase access to resources. Investigators in the subprojects about which he was consulting had amassed a great deal of information about the capacities of Nigerian educational institutions and the ability of Nigeria to absorb agricultural graduates, investments in Nigeria's extension services and other rural infrastructures, as well as knowledge about the production methods and techniques then available and likely to become available in Nigeria. Brinkman abandoned the idea of trying to estimate separate payoffs for institutional and policy improvements, human capital formation, resource enhancement, and research on technical advances. What he did, instead, was to estimate expected returns to selected packages of improvements in the four driving forces for comparison with each other. Of the three packages he considered, one had been rather carefully crafted to get institutions, human capacity, technology advances, and physical resources into reasonably appropriate proportions for the conditions then existing in Nigeria. Brinkman's projected returns and costs for the three packages indicated that the balanced package was both more productive and less expensive. Apparently, the judgment that had gone into crafting the balanced package was good enough for it to promise (at least) results superior to the other two. The important point here is that the complementarity between institutional improvements, human capital formation, physical capital enhancement, and technological advance was probably so great that reliable estimates of the separate returns to the four forces could not be obtained even though it was relatively easy for Brinkman to make cost and return projections indicating the superiority of the package that had them in fairly appropriate proportions over the packages that did not. In this connection, it is important to note that Nigeria was in a "design" mode with respect to its technical research, educational, infrastructural, resource, and policy institutions. There were no long data series to use in regression analysis whether or not guided by the concept of a national agricultural production function. About all that Brinkman could do objectively was to employ the method of residuals for alternative "packages" of technical research, human development, infrastructural policies and institutions, and physical resources.

In 1985, the American Agricultural Economics Association (AAEA) held a conference in Ames, Iowa, on "Agriculture and Rural Areas Approaching the 21st Century: Challenges for Agricultural Economics." At that conference, one session was devoted to technical innovations with implications for agricultural economics. Among the agenda items for agricultural economics pertaining to technical change in Johnson's (1988) leadoff paper were:

1. Analyzing the interrelationships among technical, institutional, and human change in doing policy analyses and developmental studies
2. Assessment of technical advances and values
3. Relating assessment of technical change to private and public risk bearing and chance taking
4. The agro-ethics of technical change
5. Defining technical change
6. Studying the origin of technical change
7. Understanding the distribution and adoption of technical change
8. Analyzing technical change and efficiency
9. Conducting holistic multidisciplinary studies of technical change
10. Understanding relationships among markets, food systems research, and technical change

In commenting about the leadoff paper on the implications of technical advances for agricultural economics, Neil Harl (1988) extended the paper to deal with implications of technical changes for resource adjustment, the needs for economic adjustment, the distribution of benefits from new techniques, and the impact of new techniques in the Third World. Ronald Knutson (1988) also extended the paper by giving greater attention to the impacts of technical advances on agriculture and society as contrasted to the original paper's narrow concentration on the impacts of technical advances on agricultural economics. Knutson stressed the importance of the impacts of new techniques on the structure of rural society and the changing nature of technical physical and biological agricultural research on the administration of agricultural research and extension programs.

Agricultural economists, rural sociologists, agricultural historians, and political scientists concerned with technical change institutions for agriculture have not been as quick as resource economists in applying the PC/TC approach to analysis of resource institutions. In one sense, the "induced technical change hypothesis" (ITCH) was a "limiting case" application of a PC/TC approach to the study of technical change institutions. The ITCH approach compares the values of different kinds of anticipated research results with the costs of attaining them, probably including at least some of the costs of changing institutions in their three manifestations (rules of the game; organizations; and properties, facilities, and staffs of organizations). The ITCH approach materially improved ability to understand development of technical change institutions for agriculture and the benefits of their operations (Ruttan 1982; Peterson and Hayami 1977). However, to date, induced technical change analyses have not been specific with respect to either (1) the three different manifestations of institutional change considered herein or (2) the costs of dismantling old technical research institutions and of replacing them with new ones. In addition to suggesting useful extensions of the ITCH, the PC/TC approach tends to expand the somewhat narrow conception of social and political markets inherent in the ITCH approach. A paper by Johnson and Okigbo (1989) explores the fruitfulness of applying the PC/TC approach to the modification and creation of new agricultural research, resident instruction, and outreach institutions in Nigeria, 1962 to date. That paper somewhat parallels the applications by James Shaffer (1987), John M. Staatz (1987, 1989), and Petri Ollila (1989) of the PC/TC theory to the theory of cooperatives.

Another approach to technical change is farming systems research (FSR) (National Academy of Sciences 1974, 10–18, 145–50, 188–89; Norman 1980; Johnson 1982; Byerley et al. 1982; Harrington et al. 1989; Tripp et al. forthcoming). In the FSR approach, farms are studied as systems to determine if a new production technique or method will fit in and, perhaps more importantly, to discover what kinds of new methods and techniques are needed. The results of FSR are then communicated to outreach and research agencies to guide their work in creating new techniques and methods.

Both domestically and internationally, systems simulation approaches are sometimes used in farm management, home economics, agribusiness, farm programs, and policy analyses (Bubolz and Sontag, Part II, Section 1, Chapter 6; Busch, Part III, Section 1, Chapter 2). The approach is often holistic, multidisciplinary, iterative, and interactive with public and private decision makers and affected persons (Fox and Miles 1987). While applicable to analysis of problems involving human development, natural and manmade resources, and institutional advances, a systems approach is also useful in studying technical advances.

THE REMAINDER OF THIS SECTION

This section on technical change is unique among the sections of this book because it has only two chapters: this chapter of introduction and a chapter containing agendas and conclusions. Unlike the cases for the subjects of the other sections of Parts II through IV of this book, no agendas were developed at Houston for technical change.

CROSS REFERENCES IN THIS BOOK

PART I: INTRODUCTION TO PART I AND, IN TURN, THE BOOK

Ch. 2 A History of American Agriculture From Jefferson to Revolution to Crisis, Richard S. Kirkendall

Ch. 6 Science and Technology Policy for the 21st Century: The United States in a Global Economy, G. Edward Schuh

PART II: DOMESTIC AND INTERNATIONAL FARM AND RURAL DEVELOPMENT

Sec. 1 Ch. 5 Integration in Home Economics and Human Ecology, Margaret M. Bubolz and M. Suzanne Sontag

Sec. 2 Ch. 7 Institutional Reform: Accomplishments and Unmet Needs in China, Newly Industrialized Countries of Asia, the Soviet Union, and Eastern Europe and the Developed Countries, Glenn L. Johnson

PART III: THE FOUR DRIVING FORCES

Sec. 1 Ch. 5 Irony, Tragedy, and Temporality in Agricultural Systems or How Values and Systems are Related, Lawrence Busch

REFERENCES

Agricultural Research Policy Advisory Committee. 1975. *Research to meet U.S. and world food needs.* Vols. 1 and 2. Report of a working conference, 9–11 July, Kansas City, Mo.

Beal, George M., and Joe M. Bohlen. 1957. *The diffusion process.* Special Report no. 18, Iowa State Agricultural Experiment Station, Ames, March.

Binswanger, Hans P., and Vernon W. Ruttan, eds. 1978. *Induced innovation: Technology, institutions and development.* Baltimore and London: Johns Hopkins University Press.

Brinkman, George L. 1969. Reconciling proposed public investments in agricultural education, infrastructure and production in Nigeria, 1967–1985. Ph.D. diss., Michigan State University.

Brown, A. W. A., et al., eds. 1975. Crop productivity—Research imperatives. Proceedings of an international conference sponsored by Michigan State University and the Charles F. Kettering Foundation, 20–24 October, Boyne Highlands, Mich. East Lansing: Michigan State University Press. Yellow Springs, Ohio: Charles F. Kettering Foundation.

Busch, Lawrence, and William B. Lacy, eds. 1986. *The agricultural scientific enterprise: A system in transition.* Boulder, Colo., and London: Westview Press.

Bush, Vannevar. [1945] 1960. *Science: The endless frontier.* Washington, D.C.: National Science Foundation.

Byerley, D., L. Harrington, and D. Winkelmann. 1982. Farming systems research: Issues in research strategy and technology design. *American Journal of Agricultural Economics* 64:897–904.

Castle, Emery, et al. 1981. Natural resource economics, 1946–75. In *A survey of agricultural economics literature.* Vol. 3, *Economics of welfare, rural development, and natural resources in agriculture, 1940s–1970s.* Edited by Lee R. Martin, 393–500. Minneapolis: University of Minnesota Press.

Evenson, R. 1968. The contribution of agricultural research and extension to agricultural production. Ph.D. diss., University of Chicago.

Fox, Karl, and Don G. Miles. 1987. *Systems economics: Concepts, models and multidisciplinary perspectives.* Ames: Iowa State University Press.

Fox, Glenn. 1987. *Models of resource allocation in public agricultural research: A survey. Journal of Agricultural* Economics 38, no. 3 (September).

Gibbs, Martin, and Carla Carlson, eds. 1985. *Crop productivity—Research imperatives revisited.* A selected summary of presentations at an international conference held 13–18 October, Boyne Highlands Inn, Harbor Springs, Mich., and 11–13 December, Airlie House, Airlie, Va.

Griliches, Zvi. 1979. Issues in assessing the contribution of research and development to productivity growth. *Bell Journal of Economics* 10:90–116.

Harl, Neil. 1988. Technological innovations with implications for agricultural economics: A discussion. In *Agriculture and rural areas approaching the 21st century: Challenges for agricultural economics*. Edited by R. J. Hildreth et al., 109–15. Ames: Iowa State University.

Harrington, L. W., et al. 1989. Approaches to on-farm client oriented research: Similarities, differences and future directions. Paper presented at the International Workshop on Developments in Procedures for Farming Systems Research/On-Farm Research, Bogor, Indonesia.

Huffman, Wallace E., and Robert E. Evenson. 1989. Supply and demand functions for multiproduct U.S. cash grain farms: Biases caused by research and other policies. *American Journal of Agricultural Economics* 71:761–73.

Johnson, Glenn L. 1977. Recent U.S. research priority assessments for food and nutrition: The neglect of the social sciences. *Canadian Journal of Agricultural Economics* 25 (August): 76–89.

_____1982. Small farms in a changing world. In *Proceedings of Kansas State University's 1981 farming systems research symposium—Small farms in a changing world: Prospects for the eighties*. Paper no. 2. Edited by Wendy J. Sheppard, 7–28. Manhattan: Kansas State University.

_____1988. Technological innovations with implication for agricultural economics. In *Agriculture and rural areas approaching the 21st century: Challenges for agricultural economics*. Edited by R. J. Hildreth et al., 82–108. Ames: Iowa State University Press.

Johnson, Glenn L., and Bede Okigbo. 1989. Institution-building lessons from USAID's agricultural development projects in Nigeria. American Journal of Agricultural Economics 71, no. 5: 1211–18.

Johnson, Glenn L., et al. 1969. *Strategies and recommendations for Nigerian rural development 1969/1985*. Consortium for the Study of Nigerian Rural Development (CSNRD), Report no. 33. CSNRD was headquartered in the College of International Programs, Michigan State University. Knutson, Ronald. 1988. Technological innovations with implications for agricultural economics: A discussion. In *Agriculture and rural areas approaching the 21st century: Challenges for agricultural economics*. Edited by R. J. Hildreth et al., 115–20. Ames: Iowa State University Press.

McCorkle, Constance M. 1989. *The social sciences in international agricultural research*. Boulder, Colo., and London: Lynne Reinner Publishers.

Mellor, J. W. 1966. *The economics of agricultural development*. Ithaca, N.Y.: Cornell University Press.

National Academy of Sciences. 1974. *African agricultural research capabilities*. Washington, D.C.

National Research Council. 1977. *World food and nutrition study: The potential contributions of research*. Study on world food and nutrition, Commission on International Relations, NRC. Washington, D.C.: National Academy of Sciences.

Norman, D. W. 1980. *The farming systems approach: Relevancy for the small farmer*. Michigan State University Rural Development Paper no. 5, Dept. of Agricultural Economics, Michigan State University, East Lansing.

North, Douglass. 1987. Institutions, transactions costs and economic growth. *Economic Inquiry* 25:419–28.

Oehmke, James. Forthcoming. Optimal evaluation of research portfolios. *American Journal of Agricultural Economics*.

Ollila, Petri. 1989. Coordination of supply and demand in the dairy marketing system—With special emphasis on the potential role of farmer cooperatives as coordinating institutions. *Journal of Agricultural Science in Finland* 61, no. 3.

Peterson, Willis, and Yujiro Hayami. 1977. Technical change in agriculture. In *A survey of agricultural economics literature*. Vol. 1, *Traditional fields of agricultural economics, 1940s to 1970*. Edited by Lee R. Martin, 497–540. Minneapolis: University of Minnesota Press.

Pond, Wilson G., et al., eds. 1980. *Animal agriculture: Research to meet human needs in the 21st century*. Boulder, Colo.: Westview Press.

Pound, Glen. 1972. *Report of the Committee on Research Advisory to the U.S. Department of Agriculture*. Washington, D.C.: National Academy of Sciences.

Presidential Commission on World Hunger. 1980. *Overcoming world hunger: The challenge ahead*. Washington, D.C.: Government Printing Office.

Rogers, Everett M. 1962. *Diffusion of innovations*. New York: The Free Press of Glencoe.

Ruttan, Vernon W. 1982. *Agricultural research policy*. Minneapolis: University of Minnesota Press.

Schuh, G. Edward. 1981. Economics and international relations: A conceptual framework. *American Journal of Agricultural Economics* 63, no. 5: 767–78.

Shaffer, James. 1987. Thinking about farmers' cooperatives, contracts, and economic coordination. In *Cooperative theory: New approaches*. Agricultural Cooperative Service report no. 18, U.S. Dept. of Agriculture, July.

Staatz, John M. 1987. Farmers' incentives to take collective action via cooperatives: A transaction cost approach. In *Cooperative theory: New approaches*. Agricultural Cooperative Service report no. 18, U.S. Dept. of Agriculture, July.

_____1989. *Farmer cooperative theory: Recent developments*. Agricultural Cooperative Service report no. 84, U.S. Dept. of Agriculture, July.

Tripp, Robert, et al. Forthcoming. Farming systems research revisited. In *Agricultural development in the Third World*. 2d ed. Edited by Carl K. Eicher and John M. Staatz. Baltimore: Johns Hopkins University Press.

Wittwer, Sylvan. 1986. A second century agenda for state agricultural experiment stations: A view from the 21st century. In *The agricultural scientific enterprise: A system in transition*. Edited by Lawrence Busch and William B. Lacy. Boulder, Colo., and London: Westview Press.

CHAPTER 2

TECHNICAL ADVANCE: AGENDAS AND CONCLUSIONS

This chapter was produced by the SSAAP editorial committee largely because SSAAP's Houston conference was not organized well enough to give adequate separate, specific consideration to technical change. Conclusions and agenda items are intermingled herein.

Technical change has been and should be expected to continue to be a major force in farm and rural community improvement and/or possible degradation. Long-term population growth, domestic and worldwide, combines with a U.S. need to remain competitive in world agricultural markets to require long-term growth in the output and efficiency of U.S. agriculture. SSAAP believes that our efforts to advance agricultural technology should be maintained and made more effective. At the same time, it should be noted that the problems and difficulties arising from technical change somewhat paradoxically increase the importance of and the need for attention to institutional and policy changes and reforms, human capital formation, and efforts to preserve our environment and the security of our food chains.

The agenda items presented in the *next section* envision a growing, more productive partnership between the rural social sciences and basic social science disciplines on one hand, and the biological and physical agricultural sciences on the other. A *following section* contains agenda items to improve institutions and policies important for the generation, dissemination, and utilization of new technical advances. That section is followed by a *third* on agro-ethics and technical change and *still another* on databases; both of these pertain to handling technical change in agriculture. The final *fifth section* presents agendas for remedying deficiencies in the basic social sciences that impede problem-solving and subject-matter work of rural and basic social scientists working as partners with agricultural and physical agricultural scientists and administrators on technical advance.

PARTNERSHIPS WITH BIOLOGICAL AND PHYSICAL AGRICULTURAL SCIENCES

Rural and basic social scientists have important roles to play as partners with biological and physical agricultural scientists concerned with the generation, distribution, and utilization of improved agricultural production inputs, techniques, and methods. Important agenda items include:

- Farm management and farming systems research to help guide technical biological and physical agricultural research.
- Assessment of technical advances at
  - the farm level to determine the conditions under which technical advances can be advantageously adapted by farmers, and
  - more macrolevel studies to determine policy and program prescriptions to make advantageous technical advances attractive to farmers.
- Determination and appraisal (at national and international levels) of the distributional, social, environmental, food safety, political, nutritional, expense, income, and other effects of various technical advances as those impacts are modified by the maximizing and minimizing behavior of farmers, agribusiness people, consumers, and, for that matter, government administrators.
- The evaluation of criticisms of the agricultural establishment as a generator and disseminator of the technical advances that come from basic, biological, and physical scientists; social science and humanistic academicians; activists; and others outside of academia.
- Determination, measurement, and description of the values of goods attained (returns) and goods sacrificed and badnesses incurred (costs) important in the evaluation of technical advances. This needs to include nonmonetary as well as monetary values.

INSTITUTIONS AND POLICIES GENERATING AND DISSEMINATING TECHNICAL ADVANCES FOR AGRICULTURE

Institutions generating technical advances such as the agricultural experiment stations, the international commodity research organizations, and the many technical agricultural research institutions of developed and less developed countries are extremely important. Rural and basic social scientists have long been concerned about resource allocation to and within such institutions as well as their subsequent organization and administration. Part of the complementarity to be exploited between the social sciences on one hand and the biological and physical sciences on the other involves using the expertise of the former to understand better the processes of designing, legitimatizing, mobilizing support for, establishing, and administering such institutions. All of these processes are the concern of one or more of the rural and basic social sciences represented by SSAAP.

Individually and collectively the social sciences have made considerable progress in conceptualizing the allocation of resources to and within such technical agricultural research organizations. Progress has also been made in conceptualizing the design, creation, and administration of these institutions. Conceptualization and subsequent empirical work, however, has not been uniform and entirely consistent among the social sciences as was noted in Chapter 1 of this section. The following agenda items are important for the integration and completion of concepts across the rural and basic social sciences that pertain to the public institutions that generate and distribute new technologies.

- In order to better analyze technical change institutions, the induced technical change hypothesis (ITCH) and the earlier "technology diffusion" approaches need to be integrated into the public choice/transaction cost (PC/TC) approach to institutional change. As previously indicated in Part III, Section 1, Chapter 7, integration is needed with respect to
  - the three highly interrelated manifestations of institutional change;
  - establishment and dismantlement costs including information, negotiation, and enforcement costs; and
  - the worth of institutions.
- For agricultural research institutions, social scientists should estimate *operating costs* for fixed or existing institutions (in all three interrelated manifestations) as well as the costs of establishing, replacing, and dismantling them.
- Monetary and nonmonetary returns and the values of our technical advance institutions should be studied and estimated for use in decisions to dismantle, operate or extend existing institutions, and to establish new ones.
- Since dismantlement and establishment costs can be compared with returns on either a stock or a flow basis, both stock and flow costs are needed.
- Where technical advances are highly complementary (as they usually are) to improvements in the other three driving forces, establishment and dismantlement cost studies should take into account the costs of establishing and dismantling "appropriate packages" of institutions to create human capital, change other institutions, and accumulate natural and manmade resources to go along with the costs of generating technical advances. In turn, it is necessary to conceptualize the nature of returns to investments in such appropriate "packages." When "packages" to generate technical advances, human capital, improved institutions, and resource improvements are involved, estimates are needed of the returns from such packages rather than from their individual complementary components.
- Institutional fixity occurs when an existing technology-generating institution is worth too much to justify its dismantlement and not enough to justify its expansion or replacement. Thus, an important agenda item is that of conceptualizing the nature of institutional fixity and/or variability in terms of establishment and dismantlement costs as they relate to the use values of technology-generating institutions in any of their three manifestations.
- Because administrators and scientists in agricultural research institutions, agribusiness people, farmers, consumers, and others often find themselves in positions to collect positive "quasi-rents" in fixed technology-generating institutions, important items on the agenda of social scientists include the conceptualization of this phenomenon and identification of specific undesirable instances.
- Quantitative research is also needed on the "rents collected" by administrators, scientists, and disciplinarians within our institutions for generating technical advances for agriculture, especially those rents not justifiable in terms of minimizing losses on earlier errors in organizing such institutions for their constructive purposes of generating and disseminating new techniques and methods. This agenda item is related to what is known in the literature of agricultural economics as political economic resource transactions (PERTs), political economic seeking transfers (PESTs), and political economic preserving activities (PEPAs). If these concepts were more precisely related to PC/TC theory, they would help agriculturalists understand both the "constructive" and "exploitive" interests of those involved in efforts to maintain and change our technical agricultural research institutions.
- Among those with actual and potential vested interests in technical agricultural research establishments whose "rent collection" activities should be studied are:
  - Farmers, agribusiness people, farm homemakers, and consumers
  - Local governmental officials
  - Federal governmental and parastatal agencies (such as the Agricultural Research Service)
  - Basic disciplinarians (biological, physical, and social) and their administrators
  - Investigators engaged in multidisciplinary problem-solving and subject-matter efforts to assist agriculture, rural people and societies, and consumers
  - Administrators (research, extension, and resident instruction) in the USDA/land-grant establishment

- By way of further conceptualization, the PC/TC approach to the analysis of institutions that generate technical advances for agriculture should be made *more holistic* to include many of the sociological, political, cultural, and other variables often taken into account by less formal analyses of technology institutions done by advisors, consultants, administrators, and the like and by sociologists, anthropologists, and political scientists. A general systems simulation approach (GSSA) with flexibility and generality in relation to disciplines, philosophic orientations, techniques, behavioral assumptions and sources of knowledge done iteratively in interaction with decision makers and affected persons is needed to expand the use of the ITCH and PC/TC approaches. Such work would necessarily encompass and analyze the wide range of social, political, and other social science variables and activities involved in the generation, dissemination, and utilization of technical improvements for farming and rural societies.

- Holistic GSSA analyses of the type described above are needed to generate scenarios pertaining to the consequences in time, space, income, age, gender, and other structural dimensions of society of such technical change alternatives as:
  - Depending on publicly supported basic biological, physical, and social research in both state and private universities.
  - Depending on the private sector for the development of technically advanced inputs, production methods and techniques, and products for agriculture and consumption.
  - Depending on private promotion and advertising versus publicly supported extension programs to disseminate technical knowledge.
  - Using publicly supported research and extension personnel to generate and disseminate publicly desirable but privately unprofitable technical changes.
  - Using public agencies to:
    - Regulate private agencies to keep them from exploiting consumers and farmers in the case of privately profitable, easily monopolized or monopsonized technical advances.
    - Internalize costs of polluting the environment, contaminating food chains, and imposing other damages on others.

ETHICAL ASPECTS OF TECHNICAL ADVANCES

Ethics is evaluative of decisions and choices (public and private). This section is concerned with the ethics of decisions and choices about the generation, dissemination, and utilization of technical advances for farming and rural societies. The assessment of technical advances is obviously crucial. Choices and decisions are made better by improving the value-free and value knowledge and decision rules used in making decisions and choices. Both analytical and experiential evidence count in improving both value-free and value knowledge of the consequences of acts and of acts themselves. Rural and basic social scientists should:

- Participate (as partners) with humanists and biological and physical scientists in the assessment of technical advances for agriculture including those originating in biotechnology, ecology, chemistry, food science, physics, design engineering, plant and animal breeding, entomology, hydrology, and the like. Both ex ante and ex poste assessments are needed. Further, such assessments can and should be holistic enough to take into account how technical changes interrelate with institutional changes, human development, and the enhancement, conservation and increase of both natural and manmade resources.

- Collaborate with each other and with biological and physical scientists to improve *value-free* knowledge of the generation, dissemination, and utilization of new and prospective farm, rural and food production and processing techniques and methods including their consequences for society, people, food chains, the environment, and the like.

- Collaborate with each other and humanists to improve *value* knowledge of the generation, dissemination, and utilization of new and prospective technical changes including both the values of their *consequences* for society, people, food chains, the environment, etc., and the goodness and badness of *actions*, per se, involving technology generation. In this connection:
  - Knowledge of both monetary (prices, incomes, expenses, losses, gains) and nonmonetary values is required.
  - Knowledge of both extrinsic and more-or-less intrinsic values is needed; the extrinsic values include nonmonetary exchange values as well as such monetary exchange values as prices, incomes, expenditures, interest rates, and price-weighted indices of outputs and inputs.
  - Experiences, as well as the results of abstract analytical reasoning about the values associated with technical changes, should be recorded and analyzed as a means of acquiring descriptive knowledge of values that can be tested for
    - *correspondence* with experience, as well as
    - for *coherence* within analytical systems.
  - Seek opportunities to increase the interpersonal validity of descriptive knowledge of the "real" values associated with technical change.
  - Remember that reputable philosophers (for instance, Popper) hold that value-free descriptive knowledge is not completely provable by the test of correspondence and that others (for instance, Gödel) imply that even the analytical portion of such knowledge is not internally completely provable by coherence. Recognizing this offers hope to those concerned with the objectivity of keeping the acquisition of descriptive value knowledge "good enough for the purposes at hand" on a social science agricultural agenda. Also, the possibility of a pragmatic interdependence between the truths of value and value-free knowledge should not be neglected.

- Assist with the development of resident instruction teaching modules and extension materials addressing ethical aspects of technical advances for agriculture, rural societies and consumers.

AGENDAS VIS-A-VIS DATABASES FOR TECHNICAL AGRICULTURAL CHANGE

Social science agendas specific for databases to improve the generation, dissemination, utilization, and assessment of technical agricultural change include:

- Development of specific data and information bases on sociological, political, biological, anthropological, and administrative variables related to technical advances for agriculture. These should:
  - Be organized to assist in modeling the domains of:
    - practical, multidisciplinary problems involving agricultural technology and
    - multidisciplinary subjects useful in solving sets of problems pertaining to technology for farming, agribusinesses, consumers, and rural communities, both domestic and abroad.
  - Include data and information on the costs of establishing, extending, and dismantling institutions (public, semipublic, and private) that generate new technologies and disseminate information about them.
  - Include estimates of returns to and costs of balanced "packages" of technical advances, human improvements, improvements in institutions and policies, and improvements and increases in natural and manmade resources. The data should include both establishment and dismantlement costs. These data are needed at micro institutional and macro levels.
- Develop databases at farm, agribusiness, and household levels on private costs and returns for investing in and using new inputs, techniques, and methods. Data are needed on acquisition costs (nonmonetary as well as monetary) for durables, user costs for services generated by durables, salvage values of existing durables that might be replaced or scrapped, and on the monetary and nonmonetary earnings of one-use inputs or of services generated by durables that "carry" technical advances.
- Develop databases at governmental levels on the costs and benefits (nonmonetary and monetary) of internalizing the externalities involved in technical change for use by those making decisions about the creation and administration of regulations on the use and nonuse of new techniques, inputs, and methods for farms, agribusinesses, and consumers.
- Help establish a "national rural and agricultural statistical service" with responsibility to (1) develop, maintain, coordinate, and assure access to an integrated rural database including primary, secondary, and administrative data; (2) conduct all USDA surveys; and (3) coordinate rural and agricultural survey activities of other federal agencies. The rural database should include information on: (a) production, market, processing, financial, and other business structures; (b) population and human resources; (c) natural resources and environmental quality; (d) community and social services and physical infrastructure; (e) technology; and (f) social structure. This same agenda item is repeated for Sections 1, 2, and 3 of this part.

DISCIPLINARY AGENDAS VIS-A-VIS TECHNICAL CHANGE

Social science contributions to the generation, dissemination, utilization, and assessment of technical advances are limited by a number of shortcomings of basic social science disciplines. These, of course, are closely related to agenda items presented in Part IV, Section 2, Chapter 5, that pertain to the basic social sciences. Accordingly, the disciplinary agendas of the social sciences should include:

- Improvement of methods for increasing the interpersonal validity of data and knowledge about nonmonetary values (both negative and positive) generated by technical change.
- Better conceptualization of the interrelationships between sociological, anthropological, technical, psychological, and political variables (on the one hand) and technical advance (on the other) for use in holistic analyses of technical change.
- Better conceptualization and better measurement techniques for describing biological and physical phenomena, better science theories and improved understanding of how technically advanced biological and physical agricultural inputs interact with the environment and food chains for use in multidisciplinary assessments of the various inputs of technical agricultural advances on people and society.
- Better theories and conceptualizations relevant for PC/TC analyses of technical agricultural research institutions; more specifically, better conceptualizations are needed of establishment and dismantlement costs, different forms of institutional change, benefits and damages from rent collection in fixed institutions, and the nature of fixed agricultural research institutions.
- Better conceptualization of alternatives to macroproduction functions for studying the macroconsequences of investments in research, development, and dissemination of new agricultural techniques and methods.

INDEX TO PART III

B

C

G

H

K

L

M

N

O

P

Q

R

S

T

U

V

W

Y

Part IV

Part IV

Three Crosscutting Concerns

There are three concerns that cut across the six substantive problem-solving and subject-matter sections of Parts II and III which, it should be recalled, are: (1) domestic farming, agribusinesses, and consumption; (2) international rural development; and (3) the four sections on the four driving forces, namely, institutional improvement, human development, resource enhancement and growth in capital bases, and technological advance. The three concerns that cut across these six sections are: (1) databases; (2) the contributing basic social science disciplines that have shortcomings which need to be remedied to help the rural social sciences do more effective problem-solving and subject-matter work on farming and rural development problems, issues, and subjects; and (3) ethics and private decision making and public choice. Thus, there are three sections in this part, one for each of these crosscutting concerns.

Part IV is organized differently than the corresponding portions of SSAAP's Houston conference. At Houston, there were three formal crosscuts dealing with ethics and public choice, the basic social science disciplines, and administrative and funding research and strategies. While databases were considered at Houston in the substantive areas, there was only an informal crosscut arrangement for integrating database agendas from the substantive areas into an overall statement. Since Houston, concerns about databases have been formalized in the work of SSAAP's editorial group into a crosscutting area that deals with databases. Still further, the crosscutting area at Houston that was concerned with administrative and funding research and strategies has now been given a separate part of its own, namely, Part V. Devoting a separate part to administrative and funding research and strategies makes it a great deal easier to report what was learned after Houston in SSAAP presentations before various administrative and funding units and organizations.

CHAPTER 1

INTRODUCTION TO SECTION ON DATABASES AND INFORMATION SYSTEMS

Data are the lifeblood of the information systems serving private and public decision makers in food, agriculture, and rural development. Farmers and agribusinesses use data on crop and livestock yields, prices, costs, and returns to decide resource allocation, commodity production, marketing, day-to-day management, and investments in firm growth. Consumers use data on prices, nutrient content and other product characteristics to allocate their food and fiber budgets among alternative products. Social scientists collect and analyze a wide range of data to describe the quantity and characteristics of natural and human resources in agriculture, in rural communities, and in other rural enterprises and institutions. Data are also used to describe the flow of goods and services through the food and fiber system, to measure financial and other rewards to participants in the system, and thus to identify and analyze problems and to find solutions.

Data are required to monitor agricultural growth and development, and to identify, describe, analyze, and suggest solutions to problems facing both private and public decision makers. Once decisions are made and implemented, new data are collected and used in implementing policy, as well as to monitor and evaluate the outcomes of new, partly policy induced change. In combination with quantitative techniques, data are used to apply economic and other social theory to enrich the analytical phase of the decision-making cycle, and to make the analysis more realistic.

As national food and agricultural sectors become more interdependent, environmental and food safety concerns take on a global dimension, and as the agricultural- and rural-based developing-country economies either stagnate or fall short of development needs, the necessity for improved national and international databases increases dramatically.

Data can provide a snapshot of agriculture and rural America at different points in time and can measure change over time. If data are based on (1) the same, reasonably realistic, conceptualization of the real-world phenomena that is to be used in analyses, and (2) on operational definitions that lend themselves to practical and accurate observation and are consistent with theoretical constructs and decision or policy instruments, such data can provide a sound basis for the use of analytical methods in estimating parameters to provide a simulation of the system moving through time, as in a well-produced motion picture. If produced under different scenarios representing different managerial or policy choices, the simulations provide motion pictures of alternative futures that may be viewed and evaluated by the decision maker before they become reality. If the decision maker does not like its projected consequences, an alternative does not have to become reality.

Data and information are epistemologically identical, but data are usually viewed as the output of the collection or measurement process reflecting only limited additional processing, while information describes a decision-making input that usually involves much additional processing and combining various data sets with analysis. Because an information system is holistic, a systems approach is useful in understanding the process of transforming data into the information useful for a specific decision or set of decisions. Various types of analysis and interpretation transform data into information by putting it in a specific-problem context and giving it meaning and form for a particular decision maker or set of decision makers. Thus, an information-system approach keeps in focus the relationships between individually necessary, but only collectively sufficient, information-system functions, such as data design, collection, processing, storage, design of analytical models and modes, statistical and economic analysis, as well as other types of analysis, including the decision maker's own policy and political analysis. Primary-information-system actors include statisticians, various types of analysts, and decision makers, among whom iterative interaction is needed.

Great opportunities have arisen over the past decade for improving the information systems that provide support for decisions on rural and agricultural issues. Rapid advances in statistical theory have combined with the revolution in computer and electronic communication technologies to make possible many improvements in the collection, processing, storage, analysis, and communication of information. We have only begun to exploit these new opportunities. In our own society we need better database and information-system development. Less developed countries (LDCs), where data needs are intense and conditions for sustaining information systems are often very different and difficult, also need improved systems.

Involved in this are new educational needs. Both the rural social sciences and the basic social science disciplines need to improve the preparation of their students in mathematics, statistics, and information-system design and management.

Almost all areas of data are in need of significant improvements today (Office of Technology Assessment 1989). The database improvements needed in each substantive SSAAP area of concern were covered in the Houston conference; these subject-matter, specific database-related agenda items are presented in the database work-group reports in the final agenda chapters of each section in this book. However, it became clear at Houston that there are some global issues common to the different specific databases social scientists use. These global concerns involved issues in the development and maintenance of databases and their supporting information systems. Consequently, during the Houston conference a crosscut work group was formed by the conference organizers. This crosscut work group identified these more general concerns in the crosscutting agenda presented in the last chapter of this section.

Since the Houston conference, the SSAAP editorial group has reviewed the literature on database and information-system issues, including the important work of the American Agricultural Economics Association's (AAEA) Economic Statistics Committee (ESC), the Association of Public Data Users (APDU), the Council of Professional Associations on Federal Statistics (COPAFS), the Consortium of Social Science Associations (COSSA), the National Agricultural Statistical Service (NASS) and the Economic Research Service (ERS) of the USDA, the National Resources Inventory (USDA, SCS), The Food and Agricultural Organization of the United Nations (FAO), and other international work. From this review, the editorial group has formulated a supplemental crosscutting agenda on information systems relating to agriculture, food, and rural society.

This first chapter emphasizes the importance of data in social inquiry and decision making in domestic and international food, agriculture, and rural development; the adequacy of current databases; and our knowledge about them as revealed in the Houston SSAAP conference discussions and from a subsequent review of relevant literature on data and information-system issues. The last chapter in this section then provides a summary of the crosscutting agenda of rural information-system issues that were developed out of the efforts at the Houston conference, including the institutional investments needed to keep databases updated, relevant, and integrated with the rest of the information system serving decision makers and social scientists in food, agriculture, and rural development. This is followed by the conclusions and the agenda items that were developed from the review of the literature conducted by the SSAAP editorial committee after the SSAAP Houston conference. Agendas identifying specific data needed in support of each substantive area of concern are covered in the agendas for the five substantive areas in Parts II and III. For specific database needs for farms, agribusiness, and consumers see Part II, Section 1, Chapter 7, and for international farm and rural development see Part II, Section 2, Chapter 11. Database needs for the four prime movers are discussed in Part III: for institutional improvement see Section 1, Chapter 7; for human development see Section 2, Chapter 10; for resource enhancement see Section 3, Chapter 7; and for technical change see Section 4, Chapter 2. In addition, database implications of ethics, private decisions, and public choice can be found in Part IV, Section 3, Chapter 3. All of these are noted in the box of cross references at the end of this chapter.

REVIEW OF DATA AND INFORMATION-SYSTEM CONCERNS

Despite the importance of, and need for, greater attention to integrated national and international data for rural society, including food and agriculture, federal support for such needs declined over the 1980–88 period, when, in general, the quantity, timeliness, and accuracy of data decreased relative to expanding needs (Wallman 1988, 1989). This is especially ironic given the expanding "information-age" capabilities in which advances in statistical theory, computerization, and electronic-communications technologies have created a tremendously improved potential for collecting, processing, storing, analyzing, and disseminating relevant, accurate, and timely data. There seem to be several reasons for this decline in U.S. data quality and availability.

Over several decades since World War II, the growing burden of public and private, mandatory and voluntary collection of data has made data providers antagonistic and skeptical of the usefulness of the data collected. This resulted in the Paperwork Reduction Act of 1980, which now limits new data gathering. At the same time, new computer and electronic technologies have made it much easier to capture and match data from different sources. This has led to rising concern over the confidentiality of the microdata sets in many federal collections. In the last decade of national, political, and social discourse, our society has also been suffering from an ideological, antiempirical disease called "I have the answer, don't confuse me with the facts." All of these forces have undermined support for the basic statistical enterprise of the nation. In addition, over the same period, significant economic data has been lost through deregulation, while the Office of Management and Budget (OMB) has led an ideologically driven war for "privatization" of government information systems. Statistical-agency budgets have been cut, and it has become increasingly difficult for federal agencies to maintain adequate data-collection programs. All of this occurs despite the fact that the "public-good" nature of most basic data means that the federal government is the only entity capable of collecting most basic national data (Bonnen 1988).

Also, the very large structural adjustment and increasing interdependence that has occurred in the United States and world markets since World War II has increased the need to reassess periodically the national and global food, agriculture, and rural-societal data needs, and to review and update the information systems that serve decision makers.

We have entered the information age in which the coordination of society's functions must be built upon an information-system foundation that is consciously managed for institutional effectiveness and maximum social welfare (Dillman 1985; Parker et al. 1989). Yet, in the United States, most of our agricultural data sets have their conceptual roots in the agricultural sector of 40 to 60 years ago. The same is true of labor statistics and much rural demographic data. The concepts of rural and urban used in federal statistics involve a gross either/or distinction that is now an embarrassment in serious analysis. To the extent that rural America has changed in this half-century, these older data sets become less and less accurate because they are based on concepts, definitions, and measurements that have become increasingly obsolete and need serious revision (Office of Technology Assessment 1976).

While there are many distinguished exceptions, the agricultural economics profession in the United States has been experiencing a slow, relative drift away from its empirical tradition. The collection of original data to be used in, or to test, analytical models has declined. Secondary data not collected for the purpose is used, or axiomatic models are used, modified, reused, and conclusions drawn without recourse to data of any sort. The profession's traditional and highly successful emphasis on applied research and analysis, and as a collaborator in multidisciplinary, problem-solving efforts, has yielded ground to a growing emphasis on more disciplinary economic work. This has distorted the balance between disciplinary, subject-matter and problem-solving efforts and is most evident in the training of new Ph.D.s. Even within disciplinary activities there has been a drift toward axiomatic theory and statistical or econometric methods at the expense of actual empirical measurement. This trend appears to come from several sources. One is emulation of academic economics, where, since the 1950s, commitment to empirical data collection has declined significantly (Leontief 1971). Few agricultural economics Ph.D.s are trained in survey methods today. Another is the criteria for academic promotions, that in many institutions, places its emphasis on peer-reviewed disciplinary work published in the leading journals of the discipline. A third possible force behind the decline in academic empirical effort is the increasing economic value of time. This leads to rapidly rising costs for any labor-intensive enterprise, such as primary data collection, processing, storage, analysis, and dissemination, that are only partly offset by new information-age technologies (Bonnen 1988).

In rural sociology, the empirical tradition has not eroded. Sociology encompasses a number of competing social theories and supporting philosophic values, but no generally accepted, unifying paradigm. As a consequence, while most rural sociologists are empirical in their approach, some start from clear theoretical constructs while others have no conscious theoretical base and, consequently, drift into an ad hoc empiricism. The profession is heterodox and diverse and has maintained a broad scope of disciplinary interests, as well as subject-matter and practical-problem interests, and thus has a substantial capacity for relevance. Sociologists are committed to significant primary data collection because of their interest in opinion and attitude data, which is generally not collected by government. Despite the available detail of the decennial population census, many social-structure studies also require primary data collection. It is worth noting that the statistics and technology of survey methods are dominated today by demographers and sociologists, including rural sociologists.

Social scientists have been concerned about the rural database for a long time. Indeed, the database for the modern agricultural sector was developed over the period between 1920 and 1960 by social scientists—primarily economists, sociologists, and demographers in the old Bureau of Agricultural Economics (BAE) of the U.S. Department of Agriculture (USDA). While the database was the collective effort of many professionals in the BAE, as well as the agricultural industry plus the universities, the BAE and the Bureau of the Census presided over its development. Early BAE leaders in primary data collection included sociologists such as Rensis Likert and Angus Campbell, who developed scaling techniques and large-scale survey methods, and demographers Conrad Taeuber and Calvin Beale, who, in collaboration with the Bureau of the Census, led in the development of the rural and agricultural demographic database. Tauber moved to the Census Bureau and later became the associate director in charge of the censuses of agriculture and of population. Other BAE sociologists, led by Charles J. Galpin in the 1920s and Carl C. Taylor in the 1930s, pioneered empirical studies of rural society ranging from health, education, and land-tenure studies to the development of the field of community studies.

Other BAE primary-data collection, directed by such economists as Sherman Johnson, L. C. Gray, and geographer O. E. Baker, involved large farm-management surveys, usually by type of farm or commodity, and often in collaboration with land-grant universities. The oldest economic data, on agricultural prices, acreage, and yields, was begun in the nineteenth century by the precursor organizations to the National Agricultural Statistics Service (NASS). Leaders of this early data collection included such people as John Hyde, Willet Hayes, and Nat Murray. Later, their work was further developed and broadened by Leon Estabrook and W. F. Callander. These early data series were brought under the direction of the BAE when it was organized in 1922. H. C. Taylor, the first administrator of the BAE, firmly established the BAE empirical tradition of equal emphasis on a strong theory base for data and analysis; use of the best available, appropriate measurement techniques; and systematic, primary data collection. He was also responsible for bringing rural sociologists and other social scientists into the BAE, establishing the early tradition of a broad social science capability. BAE economist O. C. Stine and many others, including Nate Koffsky, Harry Norcross, Meyer Girschick, F. L. Thomsen, Louis Bean, Mordecai Ezekiel, Fred Waugh, O. V. Wells, Kyle Randall, and Ernest Grove, pioneered the conceptual development and data collection for secondary databases and economic indicators using such measures as farm income, input, output, supply, and disappearance tables, as well as productivity, price parity, and various other economic indexes.

The BAE was dismembered for partisan political reasons in 1953, fragmenting its functions. Later, in 1961, periodic, large-scale statistical-data collections were organized into a separate USDA statistical agency, the Statistical Reporting Service (SRS), under the leadership of

Harry Trelogan. Trelogan began the introduction of probability-based surveys and modern mathematical statistics to these oldest of USDA-data series. In the same year, 1961, the social science research functions were also organized into a separate agency, the Economic Research Service (ERS). Although the responsibility for this public database has long been the USDA's, the department's political leadership has not always recognized the importance of, or adequately supported, USDA database functions, especially those for rural community welfare and development measures.

The role of the university in rural data collection and analysis has, for a long time, been primarily focused on the collection of local problem- and subject-specific data, and the research and development of analytical modes and models, including the development of supporting bases of secondary data. This role is highly complementary to that of the federal statistical system. Examples of sustained university support of, or participation in, large databases and large-scale survey capability are few in number, and have declined over the past few decades for many of the reasons described earlier in this chapter. Even so, a revival of interest may be underway. For example, a 1989 conference, led by James Christensen and Jerry Skees, along with some of Christensen's colleagues in the sociology department at the University of Kentucky, focused on the question, "What should be the role of the public universities today in responding to rural data needs?" (*Rural People*...forthcoming). The revival of interest at the universities in large scale surveys is in part due to the cost-reducing effects and the greater flexibility of mail versus direct enumeration surveys. Now, computer-assisted telephone interviewing (CATI) techniques and associated statistical design methods are contributing to the renewed interest in rural data (Dillman 1978). Evidence for this can be seen in the growing number of university-based statistical-survey centers, most of which were created, and are now managed, by sociologists.

In quite a few states, there has also been a resurgence of state-level farm surveys by both rural sociologists and agricultural economists, some of which were cooperatively planned. Except for periodic policy surveys preceding national farm legislation, few of these efforts have been coordinated across states to provide reliable regional or national data.

Some university-based agricultural economists and rural sociologists are now working with large government databases, such as the Survey of Income and Program Participation (SIPP) and the Current Population Survey (CPS), as well as the continuing, periodic surveys of nutrition and consumption of the USDA, the food expenditure surveys of the Bureau of Labor Statistics, and the National Health and Nutrition Examination Survey of the Department of Health and Human Services. The Retirement History Survey of the Social Security Administration and the University of Michigan Panel Survey on Income Dynamics are also used by a few rural social scientists.

A starting point for any current assessment of the statistical database for food, agriculture, and rural society can be found in the 1977 AAEA-sponsored *Survey of Agricultural Economics Literature*, Volume 2, on quantitative methods in agricultural economics, that included four papers on the statistical database plus a brief review of the literature by subject matter. One paper summarizes, in some detail, the development of the agricultural economics database (Upchurch 1977) and another briefly reviews the evolution of the methods by which the National Agricultural Statistics Service (NASS) has produced agricultural estimates of crop yields, acreage, production, and prices, plus livestock statistics (Trelogan et al. 1977). A third paper provides a critical assessment of the current agricultural database (Bonnen 1977) and the fourth is an evaluation of the economic and social statistics for rural society—other than for agriculture (Bryant 1977). The list of references developed (pp. 428–64) is quite extensive and contains most of the classics that introduce statistical issues and economics of information (cf. Churchman 1971; Dunn 1974; Leontief 1971; Machlup 1962; Morgenstern 1973; Stigler 1961; Stiglitz 1985).

The AAEA Economic Statistics Committee (ESC) was established in 1969 to examine the criticisms that some agricultural data were not performing well due to faulty data collection. The first committee report, presented at the 1972 AAEA summer meetings, concluded that the primary problem underlying the statistical system was not deficiencies in data collection but growing obsolescence of the concepts on which data are based (AAEA Committee on Economic Statistics 1972). The committee's findings were elaborated on in a 1975 AAEA presidential address, placing database issues in an information-system context (Bonnen 1975).

The ESC has continued to identify and discuss problems and suggest ways to improve specific data sets. Invited-paper sessions and organized symposia were developed and sponsored by the committee at most annual summer AAEA meetings since 1972 and many useful task force reports, AAEA invited papers, and symposia have been produced. The NASS, the Census Bureau, and the ERS have played an active role in the ESC and have followed through on many of the insights and ideas produced.

An early ESC effort evaluated data on marketing margins (Brandow et al. 1976) as well as various aspects of the farm-income estimates that are a component of the national income accounts as well as an important indicator of farm welfare (Hildreth et al. 1975; Carlin and Handy 1974; Weeks, Schluter, and Southard 1974). Among the many problems identified in the farm-income accounts were a cash-accounting approach that often did not distinguish between capital investments and expenditures for current output, the increasing inappropriateness of measuring all farm income at the "farm gate" (especially in vertically integrated sectors such as poultry), the lack of clear separation of farm-operation accounts from those of the farm family, plus inadequate accounting for nonfarm income of farm operators, and lack of farm income account compatibility with the valued-added concept of the national income accounts. Over the last decade and a half, many substantial improvements have been made in the farm income estimates as a consequence of this collaboration and major internal USDA efforts (Simunek 1976; Nicol 1981). In a 1981 AAEA symposium, these and other improvements were reviewed and the remaining difficulties were identified and discussed (Gardner 1981).

A major ESC task force was formed to address problems in the measurement of agricultural productivity (Gardner et al. 1980; Christensen 1975). This effort was in collaboration with a National Academy of Sciences panel that evaluated and made recommendations for improvements in the major U.S. statistical measures of productivity.

Garkey and Chern (1986) produced the *Handbook of Agricultural Data* under the sponsorship of the ESC. The handbook is a useful compendium of information on the many varied sources of domestic agricultural data. It does not extend to information on international data. Such a handbook, of course, needs to be updated periodically to retain its usefulness.

The committee initiated a survey-based project to determine priority data needs in domestic and international agriculture, food, and rural communities in 1988 with the results discussed at a Preconference Symposium on "New Directions in Data, Information Systems, and Their Uses" at the 1989 summer AAEA meetings in Baton Rouge, Louisiana (Hushak et al. forthcoming). Workshop papers and discussions will be published in a forthcoming proceedings (Buse et al. forthcoming). In a paper prepared for the same symposium and reprinted as Chapter 2 of this section, Kenneth Deavers observed, "We spend too much time and energy debating relatively marginal changes in the content of existing data series, many of which have long since ceased to be of prime importance to an understanding of the social and economic structure of rural America and the likely future well-being of its rural citizens." Deavers was referring to the emphasis on commodity and other traditional phenomena in the farm sector as opposed to other data important to rural America, such as those relating to employment and underemployment of human resources, a point also emphasized by Lyle Schertz in summing up discussions at the 1987 AAEA ESC-sponsored symposium on "Relevance of Agricultural Economics: Obsolete Data Concepts Revisited" (AAEA/ESC 1987).

The Current Population Survey (CPS) and the Survey of Income and Program Participation (SIPP) are major sources of annual data on a broad range of economic and social characteristics of the U.S. population, including employment, unemployment, income, and poverty. Deavers suggests that the first priority in improving the availability of policy-relevant rural data should be the expansion of sample sizes for the CPS and SIPP: "Sample sizes should be large enough to support annual reporting of data on the nonmetro portion of each state." He makes a strong argument for more longitudinal data. He also endorses the recommendations of the 1979–80 National Academy of Sciences' (NAS) Panel on Statistics for Rural Development Policy for establishing measures of underemployment and cost of living for nonmetropolitan America (*Rural America*... 1981). This NAS panel report is a comprehensive assessment of rural society's statistical needs and deficiencies, both social and economic.

Many social science agenda items relate to human resources, the family, and community dimension of rural development. In fact, the absence of adequate data on many human-resource phenomena makes it difficult to gauge the magnitude of these problems and, thus, to attain public recognition and support for addressing such problems. But human resources are intimately linked to the other driving forces of natural and manmade resources, technology, and institutions. There is a pressing need for multidisciplinary efforts to clarify and conceptualize the role of human resources in agriculture and rural America, and the interactions between human resources and the other driving forces. Until this is done, it is difficult to choose a more complete set of operational definitions to serve as a basis for expanded and/or new data collection. We need a better balanced statistical picture of rural America; one that depicts the socio-economic status of rural people, the human capacities, natural resources, and institutions of rural America, as well as it does agricultural commodity prices, production, and utilization.

A related problem is that the interdependence of most rural phenomena requires analysts to integrate technical, economic, and social data within one analytical framework—a kind of rural, socio-technico-economic data system. In this connection, the ESC has addressed the potential for geographic information systems in agricultural economics (Buse et al. forthcoming; AAEA 1989). This potential should be studied further. Geo-coding could be one of the most practical ways of overlaying information on social phenomena with more traditional technical and economic data. The privately vended GIS (Geographic Information Systems) is being loaded by U.S. cities with everything from demographic and economic data to voting and tax data, and will soon constitute a major social science policy research database, but it will lack rural data or rural relevance. That, however, will not keep it from being used for policy purposes affecting rural America. The highly detailed Census Topologically Integrated Geographic Encoding and Referencing (TIGER) system, long in development, has great geo-coding potential. The 1990 Census of Population is the first Census product that is completely compatible for loading on TIGER. Earlier Census products can be put on the TIGER system but any changes in geographic boundaries between the collection date of that product and TIGER's 1990 geography create noncompatabilities in the geographic framework. Policy for updating and use of TIGER will be important user concerns. The potential of geo-coding for integrating data on small areas and for aggregation to any geography a user desires constitutes great potential power for rural analytical and decision needs, but as yet there appears to be no significant rural data-user interest. Zip Codes have been used in the past, especially by the private sector, to provide a detailed geographic frame for demographic and economic databases.

The AAEA Economic Statistics Committee is the primary liaison between the AAEA Board of Directors and the Council of Professional Associations on Federal Statistics (COPAFS) of which the AAEA is a founding member. The AAEA is also a member of the Consortium of Social Science Associations (COSSA). The Rural Sociological Society is a member of both COSSA and COPAFS. These councils are means for collectively voicing social science professional-association views at the national level. COPAFS is the primary vehicle for obtaining information on, and communicating with, federal statistical agencies. COSSA performs the same functions with respect to the major social science research-funding agencies of government and also lobbies for federal support of social science research and statistics. Both are highly respected sources of advice and information. COPAFS, for example, has been a primary consultant in helping Congress organize hearings on statistics and is frequently contacted by the media and private organizations for information on federal statistical matters.

SOME ENCOURAGING DEVELOPMENTS

Some significant improvements have occurred both because the Census Bureau, NASS, and ERS are constantly attending to issues about their databases and because of the complementary efforts of the AAEA Committee on Economic Statistics for nearly two decades. With NASS statistical design and collection help, ERS has planned and implemented a national farm costs-and-returns survey that permits major improvements in the farm financial database. This survey provides a continuing set of detailed national indicators linked to a microdata set on individual farms that has substantial potential for analysis and research on many welfare, equity, and structure issues. It is a very flexible data program that, when an adequate sample is fully funded, will represent a quantum jump in analytical power (Baum and Johnson 1986). NASS is moving toward an integrated survey system that will further expand the potential for integration of probability-based data sets and more powerful analyses. As a consequence of several years of comprehensive strategic planning, NASS is revising its organization, methods, and procedures to accommodate changes in statistical theory and in technology. They are repositioning the agency to face a changing world and to improve NASS's ability to produce relevant, high-quality statistics (Bonnen 1988). NASS and ERS are now fielding a new periodic survey on pesticide usage that, over time, will cover all crops. In prospect are new surveys on ground water and other environmental matters.

Under ERS leadership, the USDA has recently updated the documentation of its statistical series in *Major Statistical Series of the U.S. Department of Agriculture*, Agricultural Handbook No. 671 (USDA, ERS 1989). There are twelve volumes in this important series.

INTERNATIONAL AGRICULTURAL DATA

Most U.S. data on world agriculture are based on estimates by Foreign Agriculture Service (FAS) personnel stationed at U.S. embassies in host countries and on the United Nation's (UN) Food and Agriculture Organization (FAO) statistical and early-warning-system programs. FAS personnel in foreign countries often do not have adequate training, experience, or access to host government data to assemble adequate data sets, especially when such activity requires significant analysis of very limited information (Office of Technology Assessment 1976).

Given the serious deficiencies in the food and agricultural data of a developed country that has elaborate and expensive statistical programs, such as the United States, one can imagine the problems FAO encounters in collecting, processing, and analyzing data from almost every country in the world, especially when many poor, developing countries have quite inadequate government statistical programs for food and agriculture. FAO itself has suffered institutional and conceptual obsolescence in its statistical program. For example, the principal statistical development program sponsored by FAO is the decennial World Census of Agriculture Program that promotes and supports the planning and conducting of country agricultural censuses every ten years. The statistical organizations and budgets in most developing countries are inadequate to implement the type of comprehensive agricultural census traditionally recommended by FAO. Similar criticism could be leveled at other United-Nations-sponsored statistical programs.

Like most agricultural institutions in the United States and elsewhere, FAO is technical- or production-oriented and does not give very high priority to statistics. Further, because of the independent nature of UN organizations, coordination of agricultural and rural data collection across the system is difficult. Greater coordination of, and cooperation in, statistical programs across the UN system could result in much more productive efforts for its limited resources devoted to collecting, processing, and distributing statistics. FAO has made attempts to update and improve its approach to assisting developing countries in improving their agricultural and rural socio-economic data-collection capabilities. The "Programme for the 1990 World Census of Agriculture" recommends a smaller questionnaire than in previous such decennial censuses, to collect data relating only to the type and size of agricultural enterprise, and then to use the agricultural census as a list frame for an integrated program of annual sample surveys (FAO 1986a). As a follow up to the World Conference on Agrarian Reform and Rural Development in 1969, FAO drafted very useful guidelines for collecting basic data and calculating indicators of agrarian reform and rural development (Schreiner and Tweeten 1987). However, the prevailing FAO rural development philosophy of favoring equality, even at the expense of growth, prevented this useful set of guidelines from being implemented. FAO also published a statistical development manual in which it encouraged developing countries to plan and develop a food and agricultural statistical program in the context of a broader information system for food and agricultural policy (FAO 1986b).

FAO does a reasonably good job of collecting secondary data from member countries, processing it, and distributing it in various FAO statistical bulletins and yearbooks. The FAO data system was significantly improved during the mid-1980s with the development of AGROSTAT, an on-line (within FAO) time series of commodity/supply/utilization accounts, prices, and other agricultural and related data needed for any comprehensive analysis of regional or world food and agricultural issues (FAO 1987). AGROSTAT, while available, is too expensive for many non-FAO researchers and professionals to access.

CONCLUDING COMMENTS

Data are essential in developing more accurate forms of knowledge for describing subjects, defining problems, and analyzing solutions to problems. The more complex the problem or its context, the more important data and analysis become. All important knowledge needs have specific implications for databases. Data are an important part of the problem-solving capability needed by private-sector firms and by public organizations, no matter the subject matter or problem.

Data are needed at all levels of aggregation for public and private organizations. These include community-, state-, regional-, national-, and international-level data. And, they include data for individuals, firms, families, economic sectors, government units, program areas, commodities, and the like. When different subject matters or problems interact, it is necessary for the relevant data sets to be combined in ways that provide accurate, meaningful information. To do this requires standardized conceptual design, common operational definitions of needed data items, and compatible procedures for collecting, processing, validating, verifying, and using data. Thus, agreed-on statistical policies and uniform standards are needed. The parties to such an agreement range from private to public organizations, from local community to state agencies, from state to federal agencies, from federal agencies to international organizations, and from the smallest to largest country, all with varied purposes and political imperatives. The task and complexity of establishing effective statistical standards is enormous. Yet greater coordination of database design, collection, and management is essential if we are to meet the many varied, specific data needs of agriculture and rural society. Despite this, the real resources appropriated by the U.S. government to collect and disseminate social science and other databases have declined since 1980 (Wallman 1988, 1989).

In recent decades, rural and agricultural database needs have been inadequately supported, given the growing demands for such data in both public and private sectors. Indeed, we talk about the "information revolution" in agriculture and in society generally, as the new computer and electronic-communications technologies permeate human activity, expanding our potential for collecting and using data effectively in decisions but, to date, we have failed badly in financing and implementing the needed improvements.

The land-grant colleges of agriculture, state and federal government agencies, FAO, the World Bank, and other international agencies need to improve their capacity for maintaining, developing, and sustaining effective databases for agriculture and rural societies. Great opportunities have arisen over the past decade for improving the database for decisions on rural and agricultural issues. Rapid increases in statistical theory have combined with the revolution in computer and electronic-communication technologies to make possible many improvements in the collection, process, storage, analysis, and communication of information. We have only begun to exploit these new opportunities. We need database and supporting information-system improvement, not only in the United States, but in less developed countries where data needs are intense and conditions often very difficult.

CROSS REFERENCES IN THIS BOOK

PART I: INTRODUCTION

Ch. 9 SSAAP's Houston Workshop/Conference and the Structure of this Book

PART II: DOMESTIC AND INTERNATIONAL FARM AND RURAL DEVELOPMENT

Sec. 1 Ch. 7 Farm (Including Home), Agribusiness, and Consumers: Agendas and Conclusions

Sec. 2 Ch. 9 Agricultural-Sector Analysis and Rural Development: Social Science Research Priorities, Clark W. Reynolds

Ch. 11 International Rural Development: Agendas and Conclusions

PART III: THE FOUR DRIVING FORCES

Sec. 1 Ch. 3 Rural People, Resources, and Communities: An Assessment of the Capabilities of the Social Sciences in Agriculture, James C. Hite

Ch. 5 Irony, Tragedy, and Temporality in Agricultural Systems or How Values and Systems are Related, Lawrence Busch

Ch. 7 Institutional Improvements—Agendas and Conclusions

Sec. 2 Ch. 10 Human Development: Agendas and Conclusions

Sec. 3 Ch. 7 Resource Enhancement and Growth in Capital Bases: Agendas and Conclusions

Sec. 4 Ch. 2 Technical Advance: Agendas and Conclusions

PART IV: THREE CROSSCUTTING CONCERNS

Sec. 2 Ch. 3 Progress and Advances Needed in Social Indicators and Social Accounting Research of Potential Value in Researching Rural Issues and Problems, Karl A. Fox

Ch. 5 The Basic Social Science Disciplines (BSSDs): Agendas and Conclusions

Sec. 3 Ch. 1 Introduction—Ethics, Private Decision Making, and Public Choices

Ch. 3 Ethics, Private Decisions, and Public Choices: Agendas and Conclusions

REFERENCES

AAEA Economics Statistics Committee. 1972. Our obsolete data systems: New directions and opportunities. *American Journal of Agricultural Economics* 54, no. 5: 867–75.

_____1987. Relevance of agricultural economics: Obsolete data concepts revisited. Proceedings of a symposium at the AAEA annual meeting held in East Lansing, MI. Brief summary in *American Journal of Agricultural Economics* 69, no. 5: 1073.

_____1989. The potential for geographic information systems in agricultural economics. *American Journal of Agricultural Economics* 71, no. 5: 1331.

Baum, Kenneth, and James D. Johnson. 1986. Microeconomic indicators of the farm sector and policy implications. *American Journal of Agricultural Economics* 68, no. 5: 1121–29.

Bonnen, James T. 1975. Improving information on agriculture and rural life. *American Journal of Agricultural Economics* 57, no. 5: 753–63.

_____1977. Assessment of current agricultural data base: An information systems approach. In *A survey of agricultural economics literature*. Vol. 2. Edited by Lee R. Martin et al., 386–407. Minneapolis: University of Minnesota Press.

_____1988. Improving the socioeconomic data base. In *Agriculture and rural areas approaching the 21st century: Challenges for agricultural economics*. Edited by James Hildreth et al., 452–483. Ames: Iowa State University.

Brandow, G. E., et al. 1976. Review and evaluation of price spread data for foods. Report of the AAEA-ERS Task Force on the Measurement of Marketing Margins. Washington, D.C.: U.S. Department of Agriculture, Economic Research Services. Mimeo.

Bryant, W. Keith. 1977. Rural economic and social statistics. In *A survey of agricultural economics literature*. Vol. 2. Edited by Lee R. Martin et al, 408–20. Minneapolis: University of Minnesota Press.

Buse, Ruben C., and James Driscoll, eds. Forthcoming. *New directions in rural data and information systems*. Ames: Iowa State University Press.

Carlin, Thomas A., and Charles R. Handy. 1974. Concepts of the agricultural economy and economic accounting. *American Journal of Agricultural Economics* 56, no. 5: 964–75.

Christensen, Laurits R. 1975. Concepts and measurement of agricultural productivity. *American Journal of Agricultural Economics* 57, no. 5: 910–21.

Churchman, C. W. 1971. *The design of inquiring systems*. New York: Basic Books.

Deavers, Kenneth L. Forthcoming. Rural development in the 1990s: Data and research needs. In *New directions in rural data and information systems*. Edited by Ruben C. Buse and James Driscoll. Ames: Iowa State University.

Dillman, Don A. 1978. *Mail and telephone surveys: The total design method*. New York: Wiley & Sons.

_____1985. The social impacts of information technologies in rural North America. *Rural Sociology* 5:1–26.

Dunn, Edgar S., Jr. 1974. *Social information processing and statistical systems—Change and reform*. New York: John Wiley & Sons.

FAO. 1986a. *Food and agricultural statistics in the context of a national information system*. Statistical development series no. 1. Rome, Italy.

_____1986b. *Programme for the 1990 world census of agriculture*. Statistical development series no. 2. Rome, Italy.

_____1987. *AGROSTAT—Information system of food and agriculture*. Codebook. Rome, Italy.

Gardner, Bruce. 1981. Changes in the quality of agricultural statistics—Inputs, farm income, output and prices. Proceedings of the AAEA Economic Statistics Committee Symposium on Economic Statistics for Agriculture: Current directions, changes and concerns. Edited by Richard Perrin and Edward Reinsel. U.S. Department of Agriculture, Economic Research Service. Mimeo.

Gardner, Bruce, et al. 1980. Measurement of U.S. agricultural productivity. Report of the AAEA-ESCS Task Force on Productivity Measurement. Technical bulletin no. 1614. U.S. Department of Agriculture; Economics, Statistics and Cooperatives Service. Washington, D.C.

Garkey, Janet, and Wes S. Chern. 1986. *Handbook of agricultural statistical data*. Washington, D.C.: Government Printing Office, for AAEA Economic Statistics Committee.

Hildreth, R. J., et al. 1975. Report of the AAEA-ERS task force on farm income estimates. Washington, D.C.: U.S. Department of Agriculture, Economic Research Service. Mimeo.

Hushak, Leroy J., Wes S. Chern, and Luther Tweeten. Forthcoming. Priorities for data on agriculture and rural areas: A survey of the agricultural and rural social scientists. In *New directions in rural data and information systems*. Edited by Ruben C. Buse and James Driscoll. Ames: Iowa State University.

Leontief, Wassily W. 1971. Theoretical assumptions and non-observed facts. *American Economics Review* 61, no. 1: 1–7.

Machlup, F. 1962. *The production and distribution of knowledge in the United States*. Princeton: Princeton University Press.

Morgenstern, O. 1973. *On the accuracy of economic observations*. 2d ed. Princeton: Princeton University Press.

Nicol, Kenneth J. 1981. Farm sector data: Presentation and improvement. *American Journal of Agricultural Economics* 63, no. 2: 353–60.

Office of Technology Assessment, Congress of the United States. 1976. Food information systems: Summary and analysis. OTA-F-35 (August). Washington, D.C.

_____1989. Statistical needs for a changing US economy: Background paper. OTA-BP-E-58 (September). Washington, D.C.

Parker, Edwin B., et al. 1989. *Rural America in the information age: Telecommunications policy for rural development*. Lanham, Md.: University Press of America.

Rural America in passage: Statistics for policy. 1981. Edited by Dorothy M. Gilford, Glenn L. Nelson, and Linda Ingram. Panel on Statistics for Rural Development Policy, Committee on National Statistics, National Academy of Sciences. Washington, D.C.: National Academy Press.

Rural people, data, and policy: Information systems for the 21st century. Forthcoming. Edited by James Christenson, Richard Maurer, and Thomas Ilvento. Proceedings of the Conference on Rural Data Needs: The Role of the Public Universities. Boulder, Colo.: Westview Press.

Schreiner, Dean F. and Luther G. Tweeten. 1987. Socioeconomic indicators of agrarian reform and rural development. Project resources paper B–20. Report prepared for the Statistics Division, Economic and Social Policy Department, Food and Agriculture Organization of the United Nations. Stillwater: Oklahoma State University.

Simunek, R. W. 1976. National farm capital accounts. *American Journal of Agricultural Economics* 58, no. 3: 532–42.

Stigler, G. J. 1961. The economics of information. *Journal of Political Economy* 69, no. 2: 213–25.

Stiglitz, J. E. 1985. Information and economic analysis: A perspective. *Economic Journal* 95 (Supplement: Royal Economics Society Conference Papers): 21–41.

Trelogan, Harry C., et al. 1977. Technical developments in agricultural estimates methodology. In *A survey of agricultural economics literature*. Vol. 2. Edited by Lee R. Martin et al., 373–85. Minneapolis: University of Minnesota Press.

U.S. Department of Agriculture, Economic Research Service. 1989. *Major statistical series of the U.S. department of agriculture*. Agricultural handbook no. 671. Vol. 1, *Agricultural prices, expenditures, farm employment and wages*. Vol. 2, *Agricultural production and efficiency. Vol. 3, Farm income*. Vol. 4, *Agricultural marketing costs and charges*. Vol. 5, *Consumption and utilization of agricultural products*. Vol. 6, *Land values and land use*. Vol. 7, *Crop and livestock estimates*. Vol. 8, *Farmer cooperatives*. Vol. 9, *Market news*. Vol. 10, *International agricultural statistics*. Vol. 11, *The balance sheet*. Vol. 12, *Costs of production*.

U.S. Department of Agriculture, Soil Conservation Service. 1987. Basic statistics, 1982 national resources inventory. Statistical bulletin 756. Washington, D.C.

Upchurch, M. L. 1977. Developments in agricultural economics data. In *A survey of agricultural economics literature*. Vol. 2. Edited by Lee R. Martin et al., 305–72. Minneapolis: University of Minnesota Press.

Wallman, Katherine K. 1988. *Losing count: The federal statistical system*. Population trends and public policy paper no. 16. Washington, D.C.: Population Reference Bureau.

——1989. Federal statistics in the FY 1990 budget. In *AAAS report XIV: Research and development, FY 1990*. Washington, D.C.: American Association for Advancement of Science.

Weeks, Eldon E., Gerald E. Schluter, and Leland W. Southard. 1974. Monitoring the agricultural economy: Strains on the data system. *American Journal of Agricultural Economics* 56, no. 5: 976–83.

CHAPTER 2

RURAL DEVELOPMENT IN THE 1990s: DATA AND RESEARCH NEEDS[1]

Kenneth L. Deavers[2]

RURAL AMERICA: LAGGING ECONOMIC PERFORMANCE

Rural America has been undergoing significant economic adjustments throughout the 1980s. A loss of nearly 550,000 manufacturing jobs between 1979 and 1982 has left the nonmetro economy beset by continuing change. As a result, twenty years after the vaunted "rural Renaissance" began, many indicators of rural conditions show a rural America under stress.

Three aggregate indicators of nonmetro performance are particularly useful: employment, income, and migration.

EMPLOYMENT AND UNEMPLOYMENT

Since the peak of the previous economic expansion in 1979, nonmetro employment growth has generally been slower than urban growth. By 1988 metro area employment had grown by over 18 percent, while nonmetro area employment had grown by only about 8 percent. As Figures 2.1 and 2.2 show, there were higher rates of urban job growth during the recessions of 1980–82, through most of the recovery, and in nearly every region. Only in 1987–88, the most recent year for which we have data, does it appear that rural employment growth has returned to rough parity with metro areas. However, the relative improvement in that year results from a marked decline of employment growth in the metro Northeast, and only a modest improvement in nonmetro employment growth.

Because of the slow growth of rural employment, the nonmetro unemployment rate has been above the metro rate since 1979 (Figure 2.3). This is a reversal of the traditional pattern of higher urban unemployment rates. Moreover, this pattern prevailed in virtually every region in every year of the 1980s.

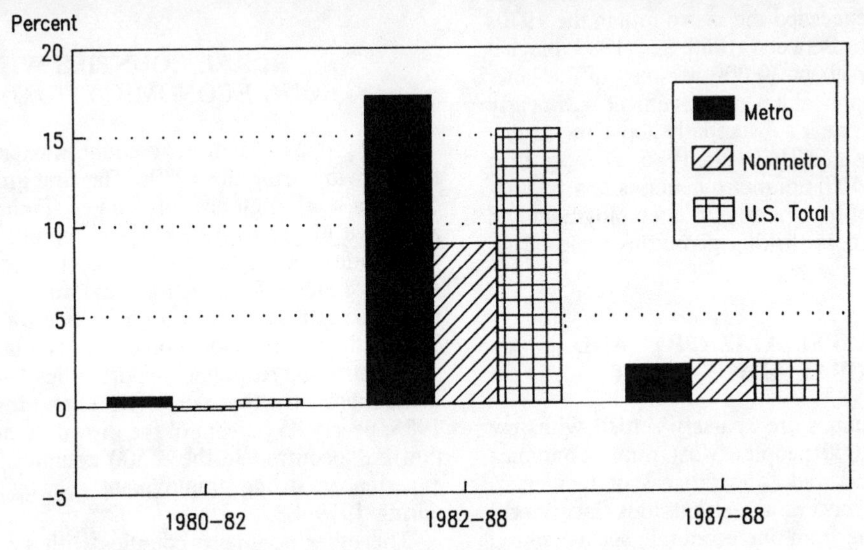

Source: Bureau of Labor Statistics.

Figure 1. Average employment growth, 1980–88.

A more troublesome fact is that the relative unemployment situation in nonmetro areas has been getting worse as the national economic recovery continues. The nonmetro unemployment rate was 107 percent of the metro rate in 1979, 118 percent in 1982, and 135 percent in 1988. Thus, while the rural unemployment rate has fallen from 11.1 percent in 1982 to 6.9 percent in 1988, the slower rate of job growth in nonmetro areas has continued to cause stress.

INCOME AND POVERTY

During the 1960s and early 1970s, there was a dramatic improvement in the relative income position of nonmetro people (Figure 2.4). That improvement continued until the energy embargo and recession of 1973. After 1973 per capita rural incomes remained at roughly 77 percent of urban incomes until the end of the 1970s. During the 1980s, there was a slow erosion of the earlier relative rural income gains. By 1987, the relative per capita income of nonmetro people was about the same as it was in 1970.

The nonmetro poverty rate, which was 13.8 percent in 1979, rose rapidly during the early 1980s recession, as did the urban poverty rate. However, contrary to previous experience and unlike the urban poverty rate, the nonmetro poverty rate has remained stubbornly high throughout the national economic recovery. The nonmetro poverty rate in 1982 was 17.8 percent. It was still nearly 17 percent in 1987 (most recent data available).

A higher share of the poor population is represented by the working poor in rural areas. This reflects, in part, the lower-skill occupational structure and higher incidence of part-time work in rural labor markets. Because so many of the rural poor work, sluggish performance in rural economies is likely to be translated directly into measured poverty in nonmetro areas.

POPULATION RETENTION

Stagnation in rural economic growth led to a resumption of rural outmigration in the 1980s. This followed a decade (the first in modern history) in which more people moved to rural areas from cities than the reverse. The nonmetro population growth rate through 1987 fell to about one-half the metro rate; it had exceeded the metro rate in the 1970s by almost 40 percent. Between 1980 and 1984 the net outmigration was only about 30,000 persons. In the latter part of the 1980s, the annual net outmovement was nearly 500,000 persons. That rate is substantially above the annual averages for the 1950s and 1960s. In 1986–87 more than 1,250 (out of about 2,400) nonmetro counties lost population. The persistence of high nonmetro unemployment and poverty rates is even more striking given this scale of net outmovement.

ECONOMIC SPECIALIZATION AND STRUCTURAL ADJUSTMENT

Most nonmetro counties are sparsely settled with few towns as large as 10,000 people. Most rural economies remain relatively specialized. The process of local economic development in most rural communities since World War II involved moving from one economic specialization to another as the dominance of natural resource-based industry receded. Many rural communities are too small to support meaningful diversification of their economic base. The decline of natural resource-based industries has resulted in greater diversity of economic activity for rural areas as a whole, but individual rural economies continue to depend upon a few major employers in a small number of closely related industries.

Economic specialization is a serious handicap for rural areas. Decline in a single sector can cause widespread dislocation which threatens the viability of an entire community; there are simply no expanding sectors available to take up the slack when decline begins. For rural areas collectively, the problem of specialization is made worse by the fact that entire regions often share a common economic specialty—farming in the Midwest, manufacturing in the South and East, mining in Appalachia.

Manufacturing, agriculture, and mining are important industries in rural America. About one-third of all nonmetro counties containing nearly 40 percent of all rural people have at least one of these economic sectors as the dominant economic base. These counties had lower employment growth than the nonmetro average from 1979 to 1988, with the counties dependent on mining performing by far the worst (Figure 2.5).

Per capita income levels vary according to type of economic base as well. Agriculturally dependent nonmetro counties have consistently had higher per capita incomes and also greater volatility in income levels (Figure 2.6). This income instability, combined with the significant asset devaluation that occurred in the farm sector in the early 1980s, contributed to the national perception of a rural/farm crisis early in the decade. But, many more people were displaced by loss of their jobs in rural manufacturing during 1980–1982. For nonmetro areas, for the first time in memory, total manufacturing employment remained below the previous (1979) peak well into the economic expansion observed in the nation as a whole.

Future job growth for nonmetro areas involves manufacturing and services, not natural resource-based industries. The employment base of the latter is likely to continue to contract. In fact, in the 1980s the service sector has accounted for all of the new employment, more than making up for declines in other kinds of employment.

RURAL COUNTIES WITH STRONG ECONOMIC PERFORMANCE

Two groups of nonmetro counties experienced substantial growth during the 1980s. The first group contains 500 counties, with high amenity values (Figure 2.7). They are attractive to growing numbers of mobile retirees moving from cities and other rural areas, to vacationers seeking various kinds of recreation, and to owner/managers of footloose industries with a preference for a rural location. Thus, they have locational assets—lakes, mountains, shorelines—recreational opportunities or climates, that make them attractive as residences and for business. Since 1983, nearly 85 percent of the growth in nonmetro population has occurred in these 500 counties. They have also experienced strong employment growth, over 26 percent during 1979–88.

The other nonmetro counties with strong employment gains during the 1980s are adjacent to metro areas. Adjacency means that at least two percent of the employed labor

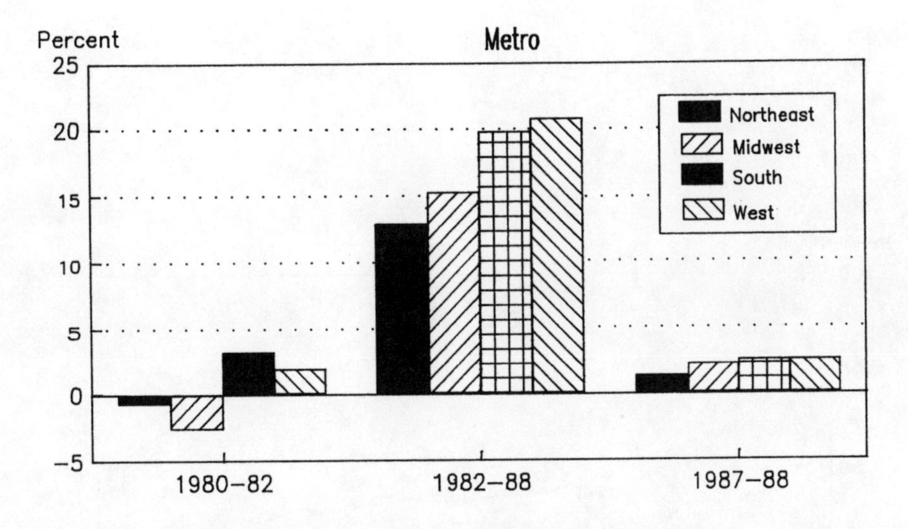

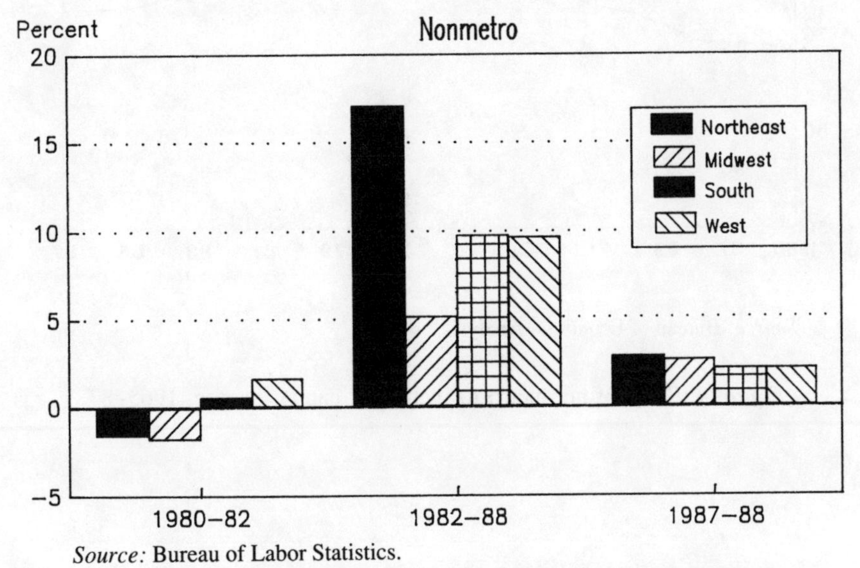

Source: Bureau of Labor Statistics.

Figure 2. Average employment growth by region, 1980–88.

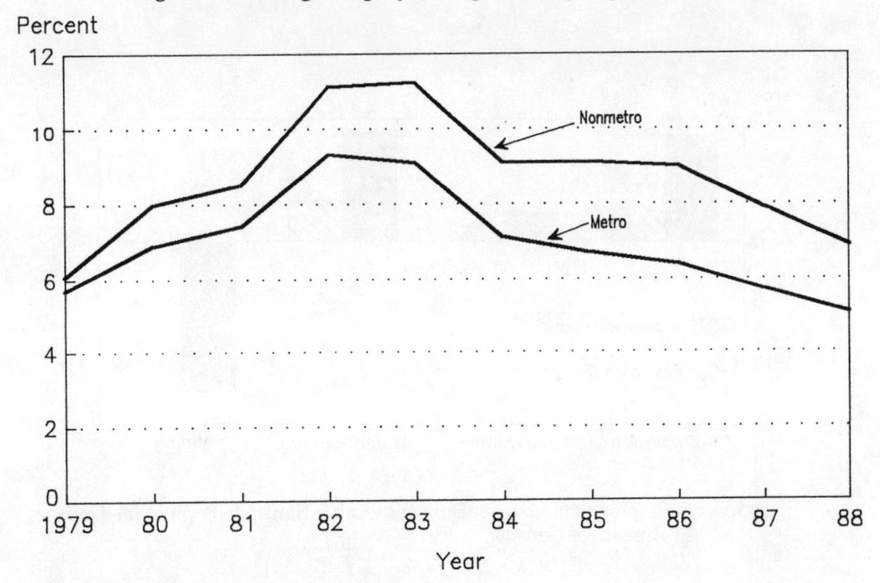

Source: Bureau of Labor Statistics.

Figure 3. Metro and nonmetro average unemployment, 1979–88.

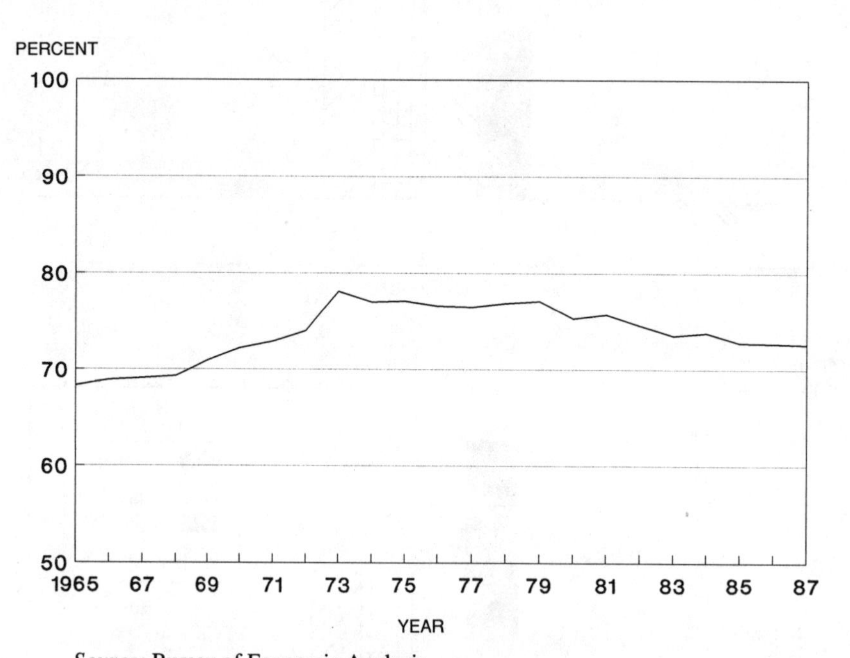

Source: Bureau of Economic Analysis.

Figure 4. Ratio of nonmetro to metro per capita income, 1965–87.

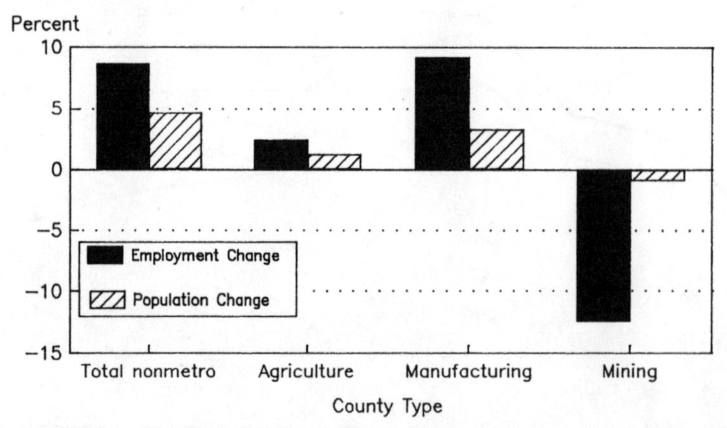

Source: Employment change, Bureau of Labor Statistics Population Change, Bureau of Census.

Figure 5. Change in employment and population by county type, 1980–88.

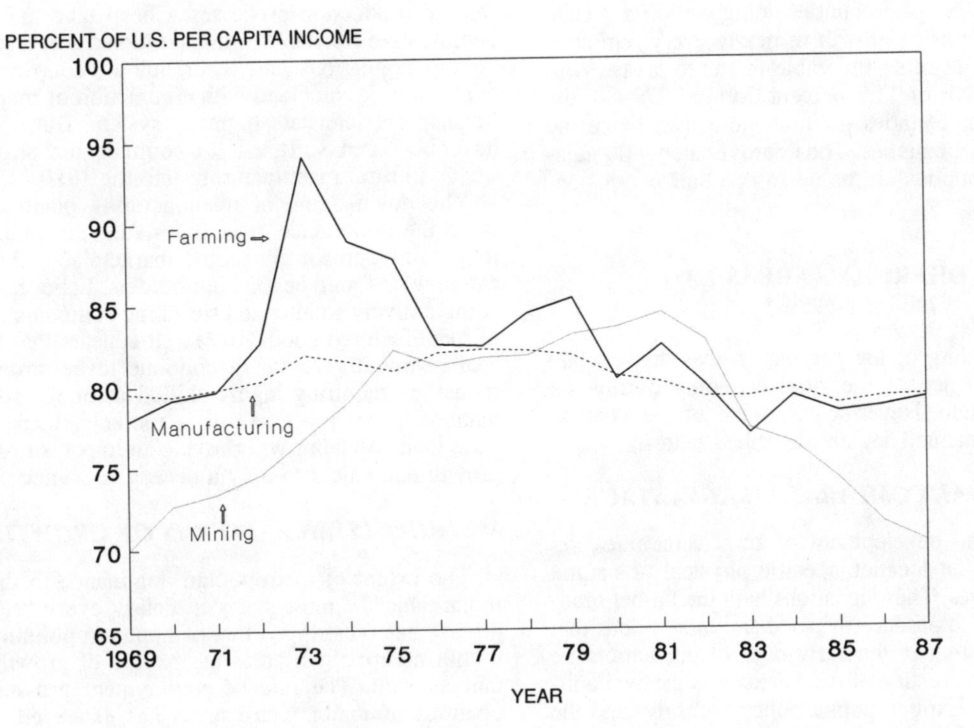

Source: Bureau of Economic Analysis.

Figure 6. Per capita income ratio: county types to U.S. (U.S. = 100).

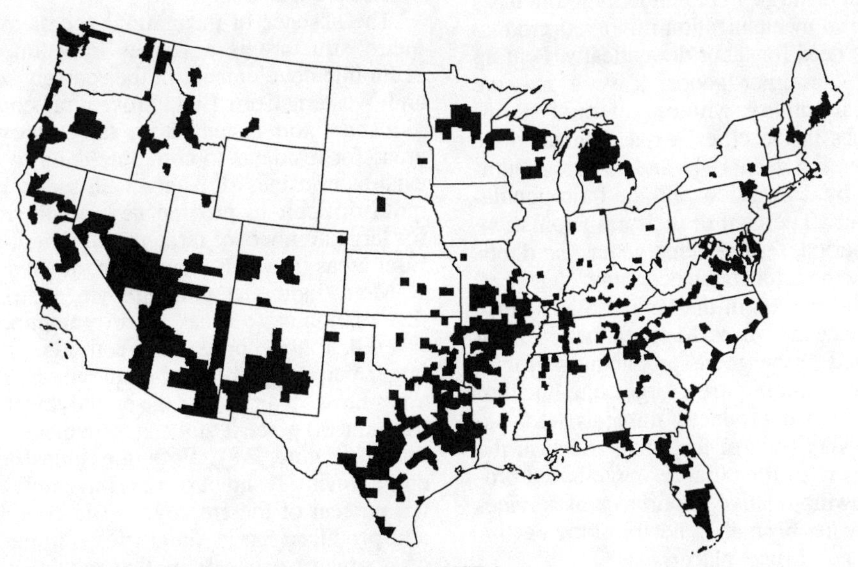

Source: Economic Research Service, USDA.

Figure 7. U.S. retirement/recreation counties.

force in a physically adjacent nonmetro county commutes to a metro area's central counties. Previous research has shown that adjacency was a significant factor in explaining rural county growth in the 1950s, 1960s, and 1970s. It is not surprising to see these counties doing well in a decade when spatial patterns of growth in nearly every region of the country have been so favorable to metro areas. With employment growth of 11.3 percent during 1979–88, the adjacent nonmetro counties grew at more than twice the rate of nonadjacent counties. The approximately 900 adjacent nonmetro counties are home to one-half of all nonmetro people.

WHY DID RURAL AREAS LAG IN THE 1980s?

Our understanding of the complex forces that explain the poor performance of the rural economy during the 1980s is incomplete. Nevertheless, some of the contributing factors are clear. They are described below.

CHANGED RURAL COMPARATIVE ADVANTAGE

Historically, the development of rural economies depended primarily on location-specific physical or natural resource advantages. These locations held the timber, minerals, and the soil to produce the food and other goods that urban people wanted. In the early days of our nation the major continuing attraction of rural areas was the availability of cheap land. Explicit public policy (subsidy) and the pressure of population growth in the cities of the East drew people to the opportunities of the frontier. Despite boom and bust cycles as timber and veins of ore played out in location after location, and recurrent periods of depression in farming, most rural citizens continued to make their living from natural resource-based activities. Even as late as 1949, farming, fishing, forestry, and mining collectively accounted for 12 percent of GNP and directly employed over 21 percent of the national work force.

After World War II, changes in technology and the composition of final demand began to undermine the basis of rural prosperity. Farm mechanization improved productivity and reduced the need for labor dramatically. Pent up wartime demand for consumer goods drove a massive expansion in industrial activity. Millions of rural (farm) people left to take jobs in the cities' expanding factories and service businesses. Between 1945 and 1980 the number of farms declined by 3.5 million, and the farm population shrank to less than 10 percent of the rural population.

During this same period, services emerged as the dominant employment growth sector in the economy. Nearly 80 percent of all new jobs created in the United States since 1950 have been in service industries. Many of these service jobs appear closely tied to the goods-producing sector of the economy, but they do not require a large component of "rural goods"—food, wood products, minerals, etc.—to produce their output. Very little of the value added in the services industries depends on natural resource-based production. Thus, the growing relative importance of services in the overall economy has been an indicator of the declining economic advantage of rural places.

The natural resource advantages of rural areas weakened, but significant expansion of goods-producing employment occurred in these areas during the 1960s and early 1970s. The rural share of manufacturing employment increased from 21 to 27 percent from 1960 to 1980. Most of the growth in rural manufacturing employment occurred in the East and South. The expansion took place mainly in routine production processes. Cheap land and labor, and comparative freedom from institutional constraints such as zoning regulations and labor unions, contributed to this expansion. It coincided with completion of major intercity links in the interstate highway system. But, these factors have not been sufficient to continue the strong growth trends in rural manufacturing into the 1980s.

The down-sizing of manufacturing plants has diminished the importance of land costs in site decisions. More importantly, in a truly global marketplace, cheaper labor can now be found beyond our borders. Labor has become a comparatively smaller and shrinking component of the cost of manufactured goods. In fact, it appears that U.S. industrial competitiveness will continue to be strong in those industries requiring highly skilled labor for sophisticated manufacturing processes. It is unlikely, then, that cheap rural land and labor will provide an impetus to future rural growth equivalent to only a decade or so ago.

METROPOLITAN PATTERNS OF GROWTH

The extent of metropolitan dominance in the 1980s is remarkable. In most states in nearly every region, metro growth has outstripped that of nonmetropolitan areas. But within metropolitan areas the pattern of growth is important as well. The rate of employment growth in fringe counties of major metro areas has exceeded the rate of growth in core counties by 11 percentage points (25.5 versus 14.5 percent). This "hollowing out" of metropolitan areas has extended the geographic reach of metropolitan economic growth, in some cases radically altering the nature of job opportunities available within daily commuting range of nearby rural residents. This metro growth pattern makes it possible for more citizens to combine a relatively "rural" residential location with urban economic opportunities and amenities. The rapid growth of metro adjacent rural counties is directly attributable to the current patterns of metro expansion.

The absence of meaningful access to a well-developed metro structure is a serious impediment to future rural economic development in the sparsely settled Great Plains and Western Corn Belt. Most rural counties in those regions are too distant from large, growing metropolitan areas for residents to commute daily to work, or to easily establish business linkages with metro markets. It will be quite difficult to provide new employment opportunities for large numbers of farmers and other rural workers in the rural areas in which they reside, or even within the region.

Metro industrial and employment structure differs from that of nonmetro areas in several important dimensions. Overall, routine production activities in rural areas are a larger percentage of total employment. For example, rural areas have 55 percent of the employment in resource industries and 30 percent of the employment in routine manufacturing (Figure 2.8). Both are industries with declining employment. Nonmetro areas have only slightly more than ten percent of the employment in complex manufacturing and producer service industries. Similarly, the proportion of nonmetro occupations that require relatively unskilled labor is twice that of metro areas, while the share of management, technical and professional jobs is less than half that of metro areas (Figure 2.9).

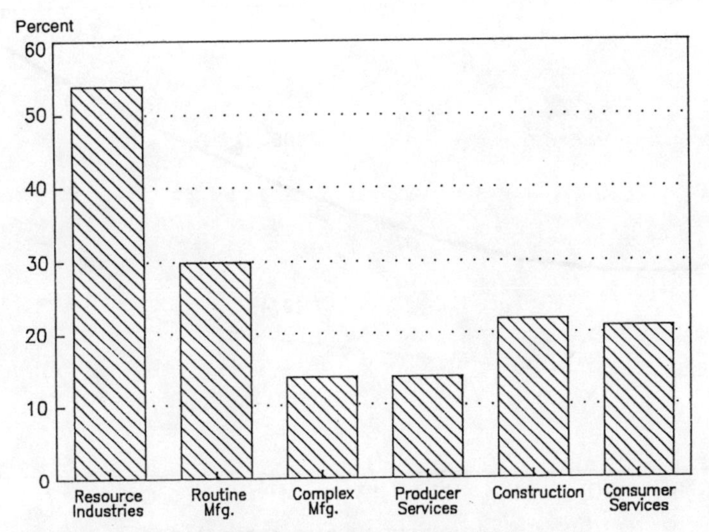

Source: Current Population Survey, March 1986.

Figure 8. Percent of industry jobs in nonmetro areas.

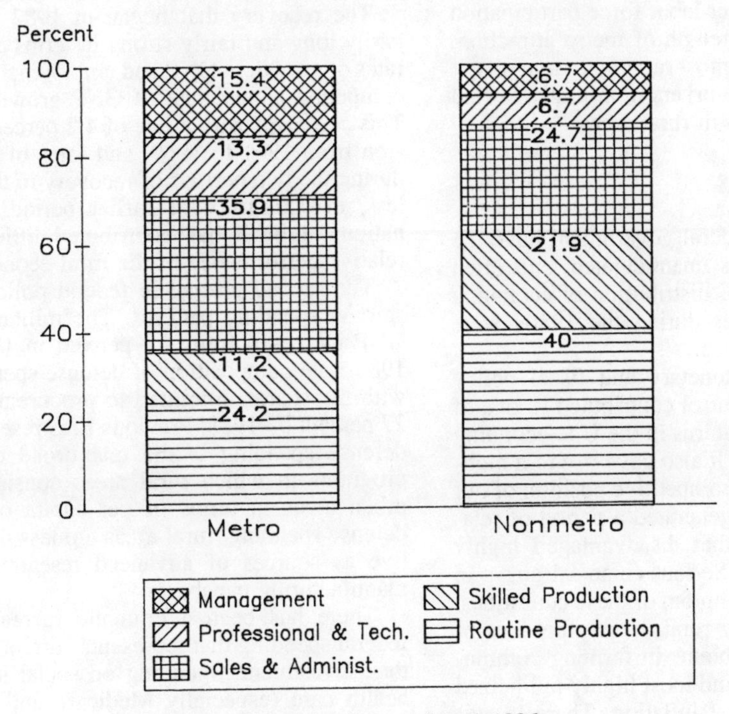

Source: Current Population Survey, March 1986.

Figure 9. Production job distribution by major sector.

These structural characteristics of rural employment are not new. But, their importance to the economic well-being of rural workers appears to have increased dramatically. Figure 2.10 shows expected relative lifetime earnings of metro and nonmetro residents by level of educational attainment. It is apparent that at every educational level there was an increase in the lifetime earnings penalty for rural employment between 1974 and 1986. In 1974 the penalty rose only slightly for rural residents as the level of education increased. In 1986, the penalty rose steeply with educational attainment, to nearly 40 percent for college graduates. It should come as no surprise, then, that rural outmigration is not only age specific but education specific. As a consequence, many of the rural citizens most important to its development are leaving rural America. Increasing the human capital endowments of rural citizens, without simultaneously increasing the opportunity to achieve higher rates of return to human capital in rural areas, seems like a dubious rural development strategy.

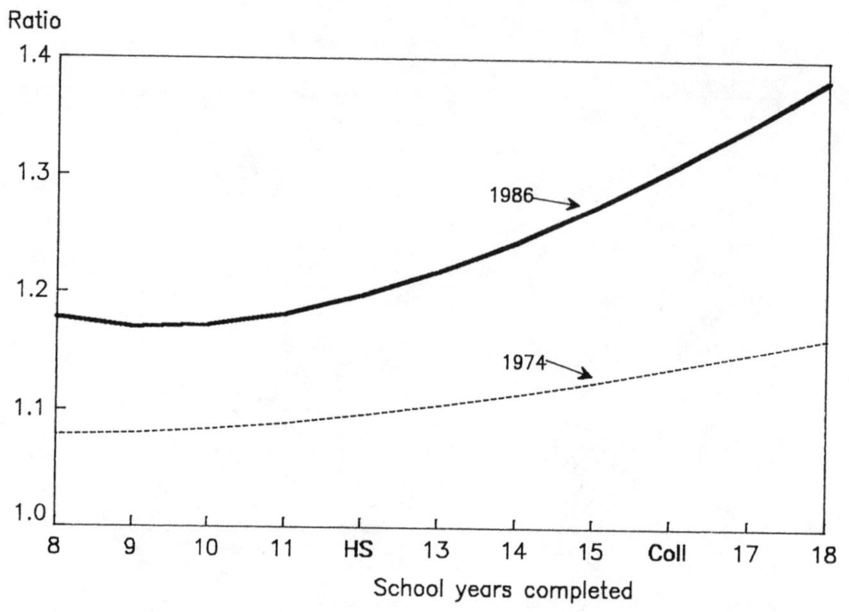

Source: Current Population Survey.

Figure 10. Ratio of metro to nonmetro estimated earnings of full-year, full-time men ages 25 to 34.

A national trend toward higher labor force participation by women contributes to the strength of metro attraction. Given the scale and structure of most rural labor markets, it is much more difficult for two workers in a family to find satisfactory career opportunities in rural areas.

FEDERAL POLICY CHOICES

Numerous policies of the federal government have the potential of unequal, sometimes unanticipated, and often unintended effects on the spatial distribution of economic opportunity. Three such policies during the 1980s were probably of particular significance.

First, the combination of monetary and fiscal policy used to bring inflation under control contributed to one of the most serious economic downturns in the U.S. economy in the post World War II period. It also gave rise to a high-valued dollar that worsened the competitive position of our traded-goods industries. It also generated a period of relatively high real interest rates that disadvantaged highly leveraged firms and industries. Serious financial stress in the farm sector was one early symptom of these conditions. Since farming remains primarily rural, largely because of its land-intensive character, problems in farming communities were the best understood and most highly publicized rural feature of the battle against inflation. There is evidence to suggest that agriculture experiences wider swings in prices and asset values as a result of sudden changes in macro economic policy than the rest of the economy, accentuating the boom and bust cycle in farming areas.

Work done by researchers in ERS suggests that the rural consequences of monetary and fiscal policy changes are broader than production agriculture. The results are ambiguous as to whether rural employment is more sensitive or less sensitive to changes in monetary and fiscal policies than is metro employment. The effects of monetary and fiscal policies appear more pronounced in the nonmetro Northeast and South, partly because of the greater importance of manufacturing in these regions.

The recovery that began in 1982 has been extraordinarily long and fairly strong in terms of compound annual rates of growth in GNP and employment. Through 1988 the compound annual rate of GNP growth was four percent. This compares with a rate of 4.2 percent during the expansion from 1961 to 1969, and rates of 4.6 and 3.4 percent during the two periods of recovery in the 1970s. Nevertheless, in contrast with earlier periods, the recent strong national growth has contributed little to improving the relative performance of the rural economy.

The second change in federal policy was a significant shift in spending patterns. The military defense share of GNP increased from 4.9 percent in 1979 to 6 percent in 1988. The composition of defense spending also changed, with the share committed to procurement rising to nearly 27 percent by 1988. Previous ERS research has shown that defense spending is the one broad category of federal programs in which rural areas consistently tend to trail urban areas in terms of per capita outlays. And within defense spending, rural areas are less likely to be competitive as sources of advanced research, engineering, and manufacturing capability.

There has been a dramatic increase in the share of federal spending that represents current consumption rather than investment. Spending on social insurance programs, health care (especially Medicare and Medicaid), etc., is increasing as a percent of total outlays. But few analysts have noted that the composition of federal spending is different between urban and rural areas, with rural areas receiving a larger share of their funds in the form of transfer payments and current consumption.

ERS documented this difference in a recent analysis for the National Governor's Association. In FY85, federal spending excluding defense per capita was $2,175 in nonmetro counties and $2,179 in metro counties. But the nonmetro total includes about $130 per capita in farm program payments, received by only a small share of rural families. The metro total includes only $19 per capita in farm payments. In contrast, per capita federal spending on community facilities and regional development was more than twice as high in metro areas: $25 compared to $10 in nonmetro. And higher education and research spending was $53 per capita in metro areas compared to $23 in nonmetro.

The pattern is even more distorted in nonmetro areas with different economic bases. Every dollar spent for farm program support in farm dependent counties costs these counties nearly a dollar in other categories of spending. These other categories often include programs that would have far more long term benefit to the community. The same is true for rural poverty counties which receive much of their federal assistance in the form of income maintenance spending. Relatively low levels of federal spending on community facilities, regional development, higher education and research, obviously make it more difficult for these counties to break out of their stagnation.

Finally, during the 1980s the federal government has made numerous changes in the regulatory environment to encourage more competitive, and therefore more efficient, operation of several previously heavily regulated industries. A price pattern and/or operating rules with large cross-subsidies that favored rural facilities or services were often a component of the regulatory structure. Removal of these cross-subsidies has reduced the competitiveness of many rural areas.

Airline deregulation is an example. There is little evidence that access to scheduled airline passenger service has declined for rural communities as a whole. But the nature of that service (timeliness, safety, convenience, and price) has changed in important ways. Other transportation deregulation has been more disruptive, with the abandonment of rail service and interstate bus service for many small rural communities. In areas like banking and telecommunications, the effects of deregulation on the competitive position of rural areas are still evolving.

In our national pursuit of economic efficiency, questions about the spatial consequences of regulatory reform have been largely ignored. Few analysts have carefully examined who wins and who loses in the process of deregulation, in large part because the rhetoric of reform was so attractive—reduced government interference in the economic decisions of businesses and individuals. This was part of a broader retreat by public policy makers from a willingness to consider seriously the distributional consequences of their actions. Yet efficiency is not the only goal of public policy.

WHY CARE ABOUT LAGGING RURAL DEVELOPMENT?

There are three basic arguments for concern about rural development policy, though they are seldom expressed in such a discrete way. The arguments rest on three distinct values: economic efficiency; equity or fairness; and a perception of broad public interest.

ECONOMIC EFFICIENCY

The economic efficiency argument contends that current rural economic underperformance is a result of "market failure." It assumes that overcoming market failure will improve the overall growth of the national economy. Within limits, public expenditures to remedy specific cases of market failure will increase competitiveness, national productivity, and thus national output, by more than their cost. In this case, more rural jobs are not achieved at the expense of urban jobs. Thus, rural policies that improve the competitiveness of rural areas by increasing efficiency are not a zero sum game.

Market failure can take many forms. One of the most obvious is the existence of externalities—a mismatch between who benefits and who pays for certain activities. The education of rural children is a good example. Much of the growth in the U. S. economy is attributable to the relatively high levels of capital embodied in the work force. We are a mobile society, adapting to changes in the spatial economic advantage of places. As a result there is a national stake in the educational attainment of all children. Thus because they migrate from one area to another, the current system of financing education at the state and local level does not serve our national interest very well. Poor rural jurisdictions (which tend to be concentrated in poor states) have limited resources to meet the educational needs of their children and the nation. They also have limited incentives to invest in the education of their children. In the Midwest and Plains, rural communities made commitments to invest in the education of their children, only to see them move away because of the unavailability of enough good local jobs. For decades the rural South has exported large numbers of poorly educated people, placing the burden of catch up on private employers, other public jurisdictions, and the migrants themselves. There is some suspicion that current problems in many central city school systems have their roots in failures of state and local educational policy many years earlier—in places far removed in space and time from where the problems now exist.

Because rural areas have few appropriate jobs for better educated workers, the best educated rural people are the most likely to move away (Figure 2.11), carrying their educational investments to other jurisdictions. At the local level, then, it may appear fruitless to invest in upgrading education since it may simply encourage people to leave.

Large scale internal migration of people and firms has been a characteristic of U.S. economic development from the very beginning. From the evidence we have, it appears that individual migration decisions are economically rational. Most people who move do better after their move than they would likely have done if they had remained where they were. But there is little analytical evidence about the public costs of migration as opposed to these purely private returns. If there is a serious divergence between the public costs and private returns, we may be abandoning existing infrastructure in rural areas that could be kept economically productive at a public cost substantially below that of constructing new infrastructure in already congested urban areas. This represents another potential dimension of market failure.

High per unit costs for services, precluding their organization and delivery in small, remote rural areas is not an example of market failure. Marshall noted that scale and extent of the market may limit specialization. A decision to subsidize some kinds of rural facilities or services because rural areas will not have such services without subsidies reflects another goal of rural policy.

The economic theory of competitive equilibrium and efficiency treats information and transactions costs as negligible. But there are many reasons to believe that may not be the case. If rural areas are disproportionately affected by

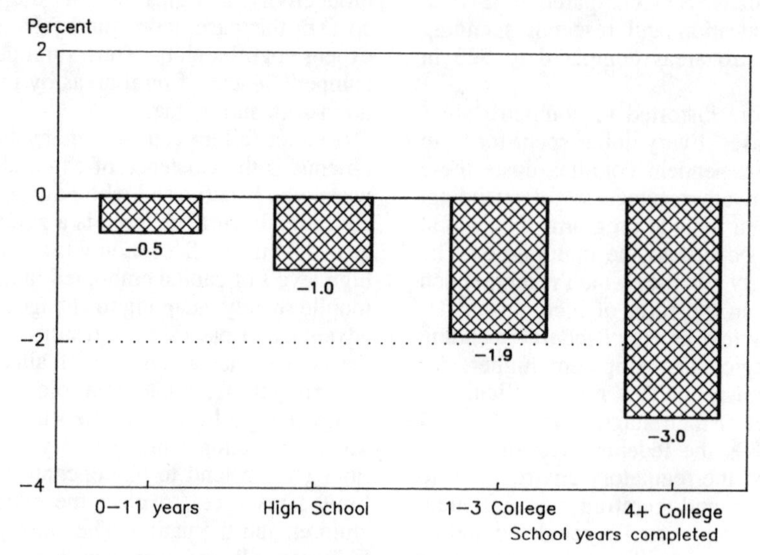

Source: Current Population Survey.

Figure 11. Net migration of nonmetro persons ages 25 to 64 out of area, 1987.

these costs, and it seems likely that they are because of the increased pace of technological and market change, then market outcomes may not result in an efficient organization of economic activity over space. If, for example, the cost of obtaining information about investment opportunities in small, remote areas and firms is very high, capital markets may systematically invest too little in potentially high return rural ventures. Such an argument may justify public efforts to reduce the overall costs of information and of small transactions, but they are not an argument for a general subsidy of rural credit.

FAIRNESS

The fairness argument states that rural people should not be expected to pay for their place of residence with a significantly lower material standard of well-being than that of urban people. The argument is particularly relevant to the disproportionately large numbers of rural poor people. The rural poor not only have low incomes but often live in poor states in local jurisdictions that are poor overall—the persistent poverty counties identified by ERS (Figure 2.12). These areas lack resources to provide the kind of public social services typically available to the urban poor.

Central place theory, perhaps the most powerful concept of regional science, suggests that in a purely market-driven economy rural territory with low population density; limited economies of scale; greater distance to markets, information, and technology; and fewer opportunities for specialization, will probably always lag behind larger urban places. Rural areas are likely to remain at a disadvantage if left to market forces alone, or to macro policies designed to achieve nationally determined employment and inflation goals.

Faced with this set of conditions, the federal government has occasionally embarked on expensive programs to address serious disparities between rural and urban incomes and standards of living. The Tennessee Valley Authority was created to aid the economic development of a defined multistate area with limited resources—an area frequently ravaged by floods and containing a very poor population. Similarly, the electrification of rural America was undertaken with massive subsidies from the taxpayers, and rural telephone systems were created with subsidies provided by all taxpayers and/or other users of the telephone system. The principal justification for these programs was fairness. There was a broad political consensus that even if the investments were not efficient in a market sense, rural (at the time, mostly farm) people should enjoy the fruits of society's advancing technology and improving well-being. There appears, however, no continuing commitment to transfers to disadvantaged areas, to what in the European context would be called the "solidarity principle." In fact, the current political definition of fairness seems to be that each jurisdiction should get back in federal spending every dollar that it pays in federal taxes.

Given adequate data, social scientists can identify, measure, and document differences between rural and urban people in income and other indices of well-being. When the political system reaches agreement on some explicit fairness objectives, social scientists can contribute analyses of the effectiveness of particular strategies in achieving those objectives. But they have no special competence to decide what is fair.

PUBLIC GOODS

The "public goods" argument recognizes a national stake in protecting certain rural resources and residential living options. It also recognizes that market price mechanisms may not be the best way of allocating the use of such resources or protecting those living options. There is a long history of such views on the preservation of prime farm land. Similar arguments are emerging for other unique rural resources—clean air and water, aesthetic and scenic settings, community structure and values, and low density settlement. The argument implies that urban people also have an interest in the spatial distribution of economic

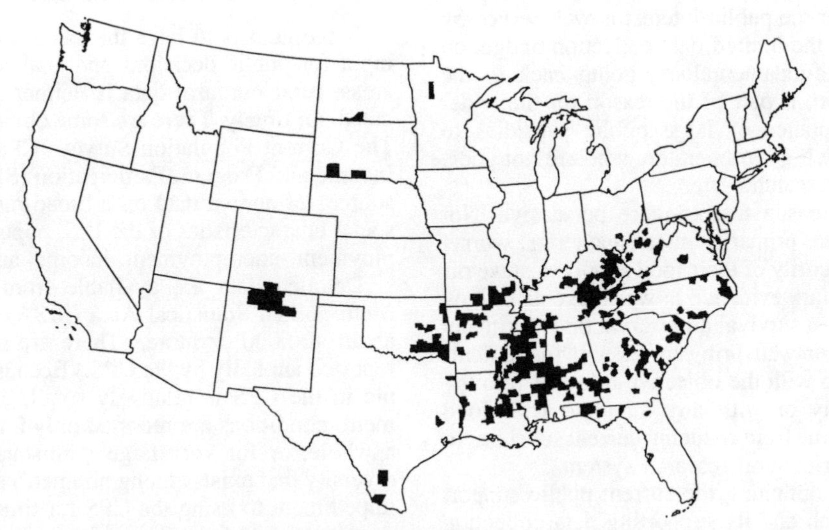

Source: Economic Research Service, USDA.

Figure 12. U.S. poverty counties.

opportunity and settlement. Urban people believe that certain kinds of rural "scenescapes" have national value and will be preserved for them to enjoy. Without explicit public policy interventions to assure their survival, they may not be.

Identifying the "public goods" aspects of rural America that should be preserved is largely a political issue, as is a decision about how much should be spent on these public goods as opposed to others. Nevertheless, social scientists can contribute to an informed debate through their analyses.

WHAT ARE THE DATA AND KNOWLEDGE GAPS?

The emphasis in answering this question is on knowledge and information to serve the process of public policy making, rather than on disciplinary priorities. That emphasis partly reflects my position in an organization whose principal clients are public officials and whose funds are provided by federal tax revenues. It also reflects my personal interest in the role of research in improving public policy.

CHANGING THE EMPHASIS IN RURAL DATA

Comments by the National Academy of Sciences committee studying rural data nearly a decade ago are still relevant. In the summary of "Rural America in Passage," the committee said:

> Its (rural America's) future is unknown. Its people are growing in numbers and diversity. A more complex economic and social fabric creates many opportunities and dangers about which decisions must be made. Many of these decisions are of immense significance not only for rural areas and rural life but for all America. Improving the data base for such decisions is imperative (National Research Council 1981, 206).

It is useful to remember that our data systems are deeply rooted in history; that history has shaped the relative emphasis given to particular kinds of data; that the availability (or unavailability) of data affects the research questions on which we work and the institutions in which we work; and that all these factors combined serve as obstacles to major changes in the data system. We spend too much time and energy debating relatively marginal changes in the content of existing data series, many of which have long since ceased to be of prime importance to an understanding of the social and economic structure of rural America and the likely future well-being of its rural citizens.

Let us suppose for the moment that we were designing a new data system to inform policy makers on current and likely future social and economic opportunities for rural citizens. What relative weight would we likely give to the collection of detailed farm sector data in that new system? What kinds of things might we consider in making such a decision? We know that the farm population peaked in 1916, that employment in farming peaked in 1907, that farm employment is now less than 10 percent of rural employment, that only about 20 percent of all rural counties continue to have an economic base dependent on farming and that only about 7 percent of the rural population lives in those counties; that poverty and deprivation of farm households is a small share of all rural poverty; and that farm poverty is not concentrated in the farming dependent counties. The overwhelming weight of such facts would suggest a very different relative emphasis than the current data system places on the collection of data on farming. In place of much of the farm data, we would almost certainly collect more information about the service sector. Services are the largest employer of rural and urban people alike. The service sector has been the only sector with overall growth in rural employment in the 1980s. No meaningful understanding of the process of urban or rural economic development is possible without an increased understanding of the service sector, but the data currently collected are inadequate to support the needed research.

Why is it so hard to change? Clearly inertia and vested interest play a role in protecting the status quo of the data system, just as they do in other public arenas. The publicly funded agricultural research system has an enormous stake in continued collection (and expansion) of farm data that provide the infrastructure supporting that system. It is questionable as to whether the public interest is well served by spending so much of the limited data collection budget on farm data. Agrarian fundamentalism, going back to the founding of the nation, is part of the reason for the widespread general acceptance of large public subsidies to farming (most of which go to operators who are not poor) and the agricultural research system.

There is another reason that is more persuasive. Not long ago, humans were primarily hunter-gatherers, worrying daily about the security of their food supply to stave off hunger. We still see stark evidence in world events of how fragile the line between survival and starvation is for many people. This is another wellspring of support for agriculture. It has little to do with the objective role that farming plays in the economy or with any threat to U.S. food security that might come from reducing current subsidies to producers and the agricultural research system.

An argument for continuing the current public support to agricultural research and its supporting data collection system cites the major role that productivity improvements in agriculture played in the rapid growth and industrialization of the U.S. economy after World War II. A USDA publication, "The Secret of Affluence," makes the point that *food* is the key to continued affluence. By inference, continued public subsidies to agricultural research are critical to the future growth and development of the U.S. economy (USDA 1976).

In recent years it would be more accurate to say that increased productivity in manufacturing has released labor for the growth of services. Farming is now a small employer in the overall economy and the number of workers released is not very important to the development of the nonfarm economy. In a modern economy there is no reason to think of farming as more fundamental than any other sector. Without transportation, communications, housing or other sectors, the economy would fail as surely as it would without agriculture. Nevertheless, when compared to agriculture, we provide little institutional support for public research in these areas.

Even though I think the evidence is persuasive for a dramatic shift in relative funding priorities for rural data, I do not believe that the current emphasis on farm sector data is likely to change soon. However, I wonder how long the general public will continue to think it is in their interest to fund a large program- and research-bureaucracy supporting an industry in which only 300,000 farmers produce almost 80 percent of the total market value of farm production. As Secretary Yeutter said recently, "I wonder how much longer you'll see barbers and dimestores and implement dealers and seedsmen and clothing stores and grocery stores supporting an agricultural regime with that kind of government involvement (covering much of the risk of changes in price, income, and weather) which they finance, when they themselves do not get that kind of risk protection."

It is useful to remember a statement attributed to President Eisenhower, who was discussing farm programs with then Secretary of Agriculture Ezra Taft Bensen. The story quotes the President as saying, "...these farm programs can't continue once the American people discover how few people are getting so much money." Of course, that was 40 years ago, and little has changed, except that fewer people now get more money.

SOME SPECIFIC DATA NEEDS

If the goal is to have the same level of information as input for public decisions and analysis in urban and rural areas, rural nonfarm data is neither sufficiently disaggregated nor timely. There are some obvious targets for action. The Current Population Survey (CPS) and the Survey of Income and Program Participation (SIPP) are the principal sources of annual data on a broad range of economic and social characteristics of the U.S. population, including employment, unemployment, income, and poverty.

Detailed data are available from the CPS for every Metropolitan Statistical Area (MSA) with a population of about 400,000 or more. (There are now some 90 MSA's reported annually by the CPS.) Because the nonmetro sample in the CPS is relatively small, detailed data on nonmetro conditions are reported only for the United States as a whole, or for very large multistate regions. Given the diversity that exists among nonmetro areas, this is a serious impediment to using the CPS for timely reporting of rural conditions and for policy relevant research. Similar problems plague the SIPP. Because the sample size is even smaller than that of the CPS, the disaggregation issue is more serious, affecting many MSA's as well as nonmetro areas.

Expansion of sample sizes for the CPS and SIPP should be the first priority for improving the availability of policy relevant rural data. Sample sizes should be large enough to support annual reporting of data on the nonmetro portion of each state. Ideally, the CPS and SIPP samples should be large enough to be reported at the county level, so that analysts could build units of analysis, like labor markets, and analyze change annually. Cost reasons alone make it infeasible. However, the annual availability of state nonmetro totals, in combination with county data from the decennial census and various local data sources, might lead to some real progress in constructing synthetic local estimates. Efforts to do this have made little headway, despite the recommendation of the National Academy Panel on Rural Data.

State level nonmetro CPS and SIPP data are indispensable to an informed rural policy attuned to the wide diversity in rural settings. They are also essential to states' having an informed basis from which to play the increasing role in rural development policy and programs that the federal government has been encouraging.

Most of our knowledge of U.S. development comes from analyses of large cross-sectional data sets like the Census of Population. But there are important insights into the processes of development that can only come from longitudinal data. Thus, improvements in longitudinal data are the next priority. An example of the value of longitudinal data is what we have learned about the poverty population from such data. The poverty population consists mainly of individuals for whom poverty is a temporary phenomenon, resulting from some reversal of personal or family fortunes. Persistent poverty is a much smaller component, more common in rural areas. The individuals who experience persistent poverty have several attributes that distinguish them from the temporary poor. Knowing that the poverty population consists of two different groups changes the context for public antipoverty policy. Without appropriate longitudinal data we might not know that.

There are important differences in the development processes across space, and these differences likely lead to very different adaptation and adjustment strategies for individuals and households and to different needs for public policy. Current longitudinal data sets (such as the Panel Study of Income Dynamics) have sample sizes too small to provide the kind of geographic detail that would allow us to learn whether that is true, and what significance it has for public policy. If we were to take the issue of longitudinal data seriously, we would also want to collect a richer set of socioeconomic variables than is currently collected in any existing longitudinal data activity.

For the past several years, ERS has been seeking support for longitudinal data on farm households, the first step toward collecting longitudinal data on a broader set of rural households. Without longitudinal data, it is difficult to understand the real economic and social significance of many year to year changes in the Farm Costs and Returns Survey of ERS/NASS. Nor can we be sure that the observed stability in some measures of financial condition in that survey are not statistical anomalies.

The report of the National Academy of Sciences remains a good starting point for a thoughtful review of critical rural data needs. Most of the data issues that it raised remain relevant, and are unresolved. Two deserve explicit mention. They are measures of underemployment and cost of living.

Those who have worked with local area data know the weakness of unemployment rates as indicators of underused human resources in poor rural areas or areas that are undergoing significant economic restructuring. As the National Academy report notes, the problems include the treatment in official unemployment statistics of discouraged and involuntary part-time workers, seasonal and self-employed workers; and the more limited coverage of rural jobs by unemployment compensation. The Academy goes on to say that "the failure of unemployment rates to measure the underuse of human resources can be costly for rural areas because government allocations to areas are increasingly tied to statistical formulas" (National Research Council 1981, 202).

Because there is no rural cost of living data, it is impossible to measure the real income gap between urban and rural people. This difficulty is important in measuring poverty. Current data indicate a higher poverty rate among rural than among urban people, but public policy continues to treat poverty as largely an urban problem. In part this is because of the widespread unsupported belief that lower rural living costs eliminate the apparent disparity in the incidence of poverty. As the Academy panel says in its report, "meaningful comparisons of the economic well-being of communities, regions, and program target groups require that wages, salaries, income, net worth, transfers, outlays, taxes, and other dollar indicators be expressed in comparable units."

RURAL RESEARCH PRIORITIES

Rural development issues are likely to climb higher on the public policy agenda during the next decade. They will be important because of the growing concern about the environment, the reemergence of public interest in distributional equity, and the continuing lag in performance of the rural economy which adversely affects rural well-being. Rural development issues will begin to supplant purely sectoral issues as policy makers seek ways to encourage rural economic activity and social development, and to preserve the institutions and infrastructure of rural life. In a more general sense, this will result from a growing understanding of how little potential there is for traditional farm programs and the farm sector as a basis for revitalizing most rural communities.

Unfortunately, the research foundation from which to build a coherent and effective rural development policy is weak. That is where I believe we need to concentrate our intellectual and data resources. Four broad areas of research deserve our attention.

ECONOMIC DISADVANTAGE AND RURALITY

It is clear that small scale, low density, economic specialization, resource base, distance, and parochialism are all problems affecting development in rural areas. Despite those disadvantages, the period from World War II to the early 1970s saw a narrowing of rural and urban income differences and a reduction in rural poverty. However, as noted earlier, it has been nearly twenty years since there was any significant improvement in the relative income position of rural people. Cost of living differences aside, we need to know whether the lack of progress means we have reached some fundamental limit in the ability of national economic growth to overcome the disadvantages inherent in rural settlement and to reduce rural poverty.

It is somewhat puzzling that the 1980s have been so unlike either the 1960s or 1970s. While there was significant rural outmigration in the 1960s, it was a period of substantial improvement in individual well-being. Work by Tom Stinson on poverty of public services shows a dramatic decline in the disadvantage of rural communities during the 1960s as well (Stinson 1968). The 1970s saw a major shift in migration patterns in favor of rural areas, and a continuation of the narrowing in the rural/urban income ratio until the oil embargo induced the early 1970s recession. Stinson's unpublished update of his earlier work for the early 1980s suggests that the decline in rural disadvantage continued. Overall, however, the 1980s has been a period of relative if not absolute rural stagnation.

We clearly need a better theoretical foundation for our understanding of spatial economic development, and for studying shifts in spatial advantage over time. Roberto Camagni, professor of economics at Bocconi University, Milan has recently proposed a first attempt to build such a model (Camagni and Capello forthcoming). He proposes to measure "regional comparative locational advantage" by comparing two aggregate indices: an index of local productivity and an index of the "general level of labor costs." He postulates the spatial relationship between these two indices for two different time periods, 1950–64 and 1965–80, as an explanation for the relative economic performance of Italian regions. In this model, development proceeds at a relatively more rapid pace in regions where the productivity index exceeds the labor cost index. A preliminary effort by Camagni to empirically estimate these indices supports the usefulness of the theory in understanding Italian regional development. What is needed is more research on the general applicability of Camagni's work. It can provide a deeper understanding of the factors that create shifts in the spatial pattern of productivity/labor cost relationships.

STRUCTURAL CHANGE, MIGRATION, AND RURAL DISADVANTAGE

Employment is declining in U.S. agriculture, natural resource, and goods producing sectors. It is a problem for rural areas, which have a disproportionate share of their employment in these sectors. Restructuring the manufacturing sector is a particular challenge for rural areas because so many rural counties have manufacturing as their principal economic base. It was the growth of rural manufacturing jobs in the 1960s and early 1970s that fueled much of the improvement in well-being, especially in the chronically poor rural South. If the future of U.S. manufacturing is in more technically sophisticated production processes, can rural areas share in that growth? Figure 2.13 shows that rural areas are virtually unchanged in their share of complex manufacturing jobs during the 1980s, while metro areas have improved their industrial job mix. That is not encouraging for rural areas. We need research that increases our understanding of the spatial implications of restructuring the U.S. manufacturing sector.

Service employment is growing nationally, but in rural areas most of the employment growth has in been in local (consumer) services, not in exportable (producer) services. What is the real potential for trade in services? Is it possible for rural areas to capture a larger share of tradable service employment as a basis for self-sustaining local growth and development? What are the factors that create locational advantage for rural places in an economy where services are the key to growth? As noted earlier, despite its growing importance, research on the service sector has lagged in part because of inadequate data. Better research and better data must go together.

A rural development theme that was popular in the 1960s is reemerging. It asserts that crowding, pollution, and high public infrastructure costs accompanying rapid metropolitan growth are symptoms of "overdevelopment," reflecting the existence of significant externalities. Slowing the rural outmigration that is fueling "too rapid" urban growth is a major justification for rural development programs. Under a full accounting of costs, such outmigration is uneconomic. At the same time, the debate about public programs has become more narrowly focused on cost-benefit analysis. If that issue continues to be a central question for advocates of rural development programs, we need a better ability to assess the implications of migration. In particular, we need a research effort aimed at measuring the benefits and costs of individual and firm migration decisions, including a full accounting of public and private costs and returns. Currently available data are not adequate for such a research effort.

PROCESS OF LOCAL DEVELOPMENT

Our current knowledge of how and why economic development occurs at the local level is weak. We have had little success in modeling the process of development over time. For example, while we can explain most of the variation in levels of development across counties at a particular point in time (typically the r^2 for such studies are in the .7 to .8 range), models attempting to explain county level rates of change in income or employment over time are much less successful. It is usual for them to exhibit r^2 in the range of .2 or less. If the model includes some measure of previous growth as an independent variable, the r^2 is often doubled. Those results should make us modest and cautious when asked to guide policy makers in the choice of local development strategies.

Camogni provides some useful insights into what may be happening. He postulates two sets of factors as explaining growth rate differentials: "objective factors" such as the supply and demand of raw materials that determine local productivity levels and which economists tend to emphasize in explaining locational advantage, and "subjective factors" such as entrepreneurial skill which sociologists and others tend to see as important determinants of local success or failure. For Camogni, "the presence of both elements is a prerequisite. . . to the birth of local firms and sustainable regional growth." He argues that the subjective elements have deep roots in the community and influence the local capability to shift resources from traditional to innovative uses.

In their current form Camogni's distinctions are not empirically operational, but his arguments are intuitively attractive. Further work to integrate the objective and subjective aspects of local development is essential to an informed understanding of local rural development. Measuring the presence and role of so-called subjective factors in development poses a serious challenge for the design of data systems. Without such measures the interpretation of causality for local development can border on tautology—there is industrial development because there is entrepreneurship (or leadership). Simply adopting a name for the unexplained residual in our regression equations is not a very useful contribution.

EFFECTS OF PUBLIC POLICY

We need better informed public policy, and I think we need more research with a specific evaluative intent. Such work is unglamorous, and so far as I can tell, largely unvalued in both the academic community and the agricultural research system but that does not diminish its importance.

An example of the need for better public policy research may help to make the point. We know that higher levels of education increase the range and quality of development opportunities at both a societal and individual level. We don't know whether local communities can devise strategies to link their efforts at educational improvement to local economic development. If they cannot, then the externalities argument for a major expansion of the federal responsibility for funding education seems overwhelming. Even if they can, the argument for assisting the poorest communities is persuasive. In either case, the role of education in local as opposed to national development may be overstated. Human capital investments as a path for local economic development may be less important than site-specific kinds of capital, or efforts to integrate rural space more effectively into the overall national and international economy through appropriate infrastructure,—e.g., telecommunications. These are difficult and complicated research questions, and public policy makers are grappling with how to choose among such programs.

Finally, we should not overestimate the role of research findings in the formulation of public policy. We all want to believe that what we do is important. Suggesting that politicians should simply implement the results of our research trivializes their role. They seem immune to that advice.

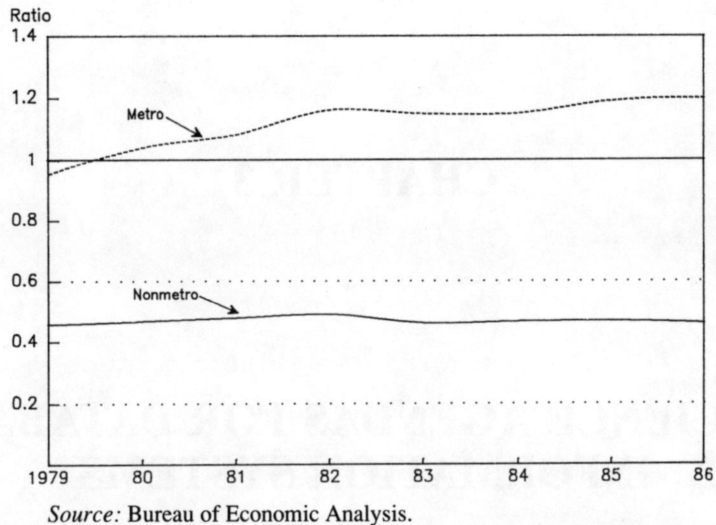

Source: Bureau of Economic Analysis.

Figure 13. Ratio of complex to routine manufacturing jobs.

NOTES

1. Reproduced with permission from Ruben C. Buse and James Driscoll, eds. Forthcoming. *New Directions in Rural Data and Information Systems.* Ames: Iowa State University Press. Edited slightly to conform to the format of this book.

2. Kenneth L. Deavers is Director of the Agricultural and Rural Economy Division, Economic Research Service, USDA, Washington, D.C. The views expressed in this paper are those of the author, not necessarily those of USDA.

REFERENCES

Camagni, Roberto, and Roberto Capello. Forthcoming. Italian success stories of local development: Theoretical conditions and practical experience. In *Success stories of local development.* Edited by Walter Stohr. United Nations University, International Project.

National Research Council, National Academy of Sciences. 1981. *Rural America in passage: Statistics for policy.* Washington, D.C.: National Academy Press.

Stinson, T. F. 1968. Drawing a poverty line for government services: An initial attempt. *American Journal of Agricultural Economics* 50:1416–20.

USDA. 1976. *The secret of affluence.* Washington, D.C.: Office of Communications. January.

CHAPTER 3

SOCIAL SCIENCE AGENDAS FOR DATABASES AND INFORMATION SYSTEMS

INTRODUCTION

Relevant, accurate, and timely data are essential for all decision making, whether by farmers, agribusiness persons, heads of households, local government officials, U.S. Department of Agriculture (USDA) decision makers, or others. Data are necessary for empirical research and analysis of any significant problem implicit in the social science agricultural agenda and to support both domestic and international food, agricultural, and rural development-policy formulation and implementation.

Despite the central role data plays in the information system and the large opportunities for improvements created by developments in statistical theory and computer technology, rural data needs have been inadequately supported in recent decades, both in the United States and internationally. Three database work groups were organized as part of the substantive areas addressed in the SSAAP Houston conference. The needs for specific data to address problems in these substantive areas of concern are discussed in Parts II and III. These work groups were:

FARMING, AGRIBUSINESS, AND CONSUMERS

Work Group on *Macrolevel Data and Analysis Systems for Agriculture, Food, and Rural Societies*

Leader: Leroy J. Hushak, Professor, Department of Agricultural Economics, Ohio State University.

Invited members (some of whom may not have participated) Richard Allen, Deb Brown, Ruben Buse, Dean T. Chen, Charles Paulter, and James Zavrel.

NATURAL AND COMMUNITY RESOURCES

Work Group on *Macrolevel, Social and Economic Accounting, and Analysis Systems for Natural and Community Resources.*

Leader: David L. Brown, Associate Director, Agricultural Experiment Station, and Professor, Rural Sociology, Cornell University.

Invited members (some of whom may not have participated) Kenneth Baum, James T. Bonnen, Wendy Cohen, Stephen Lilley, Steve H. Murdock, and Alton Thompson.

RURAL DEVELOPMENT OF LESS DEVELOPED COUNTRIES (LDC)

Work Group on *LDC Data Systems, Social Accounts, and Sector and Subsector Analysis*

Leader: Jacques Kozub, World Bank, Washington, D.C.

Invited members (some of whom may not have participated) Charles Busling, Charles K. Mann, Clark Reynolds, Earl P. Scott, Larry A. Sievers, and Alfred Thieme.

Database agendas generated by Hushak's group are found in Part II, Section 1, Chapter 7, and those of Kozub's group are found in Part II, Section 2, Chapter 11. Database agenda items from Brown's work group are distributed throughout Part III in Section 1, Chapter 1; Section 2, Chapter 10; Section 3, Chapter 7; and Section 4, Chapter 2. In the Houston conference, we found some concerns were common to all three database work groups; typically these involved national statistical policy and the shared institutional structures and information systems necessary to support effective databases. Consequently, an informal crosscut work group was organized at the Houston conference that merged the overlapping elements from the three database work groups and developed a global or crosscut agenda on rural information systems. The Houston conference organizers constituted this work group from the leaders of the substantive database work groups and appointed a crosscut leader as indicated below.

Work Group on *Crosscutting Information System Needs*

Leader: James T. Bonnen, Professor, Department of Agricultural Economics, Michigan State University.

Members: David L. Brown, Leroy J. Hushak, and Jacques Kozub.

The crosscutting social science agenda that this group developed for rural information systems is presented below. In addition, the SSAAP editorial group added to this crosscut agenda other agenda items and conclusions based on their literature review and their integration of the results of the Houston conference.

ABRIDGED CROSSCUT AGENDA FOR RURAL INFORMATION SYSTEMS FROM THE HOUSTON CONFERENCE

National and international statistical policy and institutionalized information-system capability to coordinate the development of, and access to, databases are necessary for, and cut across, the specific data needs of the substantive areas considered in the agendas of work presented in Parts II and III. These crosscutting information-system needs identified at the SSAAP conference in Houston include challenges for the U.S. government and its agencies, social scientists and their administrators, social science professional associations, and international organizations, such as the United Nations, that fund, design, or collect statistics.

- The challenge for the U.S. government is to:
  - Improve coordination of data for decisions on rural problems. At present, the responsibility for collecting, maintaining, and disseminating U.S. data on rural areas and populations is scattered throughout the federal government. Once this would have automatically been the responsibility of the Statistical Policy Division of the Office of Management and Budget (OMB), but government-wide statistical coordination and policy capability was removed from the OMB in the Carter administration. This responsibility was returned to the OMB during the Reagan administration, but drastic reduction in personnel and submersion in a regulatory unit had effectively dismantled its capability. Until adequate capacity and some believable integrity can be rebuilt, the USDA, which is the designated lead agency for rural development policy, should be the locus of responsibility for coordination and policy involving rural and agricultural data. Even with revived OMB statistical policy and coordination capability, much of the substantive work of statistical coordination would have to be decentralized to cabinet agencies, since the minimum personnel requirements for this function are too large for location in the OMB or the Executive Office of the President.
    - A single USDA agency should be given the policy authority and responsibility for coordinating the planning and implementing of all federal statistical and data-bank activities relating to food, agriculture, and rural community welfare and development. The agency so named should, under federal statistical policy and coordination authority, develop, maintain, coordinate, and assure access to an integrated, rural database including primary, secondary, and administrative data. Primary responsibility for national rural statistical policy and for the maintenance and coordination of national rural data collection and the database would reside in the designated agency. This statistical policy and coordination function might be (a) assigned to an agency established for that purpose, (b) assigned to the USDA agency responsible for implementation of "paperwork burden" reduction, or (c) assigned to the designated statistical agency for the department — depending on a number of different factors. If the latter option were chosen, this agency would plan and conduct all major USDA surveys as well as coordinate rural and agricultural survey activities of all other federal agencies.

      Much of the needed capability already exists in the National Agricultural Statistics Services (NASS) and the Economic Research Service (ERS). If the NASS, for example, were to be assigned responsibility for all rural statistics, it would have to be designated as the statistical agency for the USDA upon which all USDA operating agencies would depend for the design and conduct of all large, periodic surveys. In this role, NASS would have to maintain broad survey capabilities for households and rural economic establishments. Principal responsibilities of this agency would be to:
      - Develop integrated socioeconomic, demographic, natural resource, and environmental databases. Information on individuals, households, firms, and governments would be included as appropriate.
      - Develop a survey program with longitudinal capability for rural areas and agriculture, including rural households and economic establishments.
      - Encourage additional and more effective intergovernmental cooperation in the collection of administrative data on social, community, natural resource, and environmental programs to enhance the geographic and subject matter comparability and usefulness of other data for research, policy development, monitoring, and program evaluation. This could add substantially to the utility and benefits created by administrative data, data that are already paid for and collected.
      - Develop and publicize procedures and rules to ensure better and more rapid public access to federally collected data on food, agriculture, and rural society. Enhance and publicize procedures for the public use of microagricultural data. For example, much improved access to census data and the Farm Costs and Returns Survey would follow the development of more "user-friendly" procedures, while protecting the confidentiality commitment made to individual respondents.

Improved coordination is necessary for the effective and efficient use of existing information-system capability. It is also necessary to establish and enforce priorities on the collection of new (and elimination of old) data. Data users, including social scientists, habitually believe that more data is good and always necessary. This discredits their appeals and complaints. Data are costly economic goods that will always be rationed in some way. It is better that this be done intelligently, rather than in a random and arbitrary manner.

- Increase data systems capability. Cost effective use of federal statistics increasingly requires both mainframe and microcomputers. Three agenda items are identified:
  - Design and develop integrated, needs-based data and information systems for agricultural and rural data, stressing computer technology to integrate the use of data and analytical techniques.
  - Make U.S. government summary data on rural society and agriculture available in machine-readable form.
  - Establish a clearinghouse for U.S. rural statistics, accessible by computer, telephone, or mail.

  Work on this is already underway in the federal government (Office of Technology Assessment 1988).
- Clarify statistical policy issues. The conflicts of the last decade have confounded the purposes and rules for federal data collection. A coherent public philosophy is needed to sustain the federal statistical enterprise. Political support from users of rural data and intellectual input would help. The statistical agencies need to: Incorporate systematic social science data-user input into the purpose, design and modification of data and information systems. It is important that the rural social sciences develop improved procedures for determining the relative values of alternative kinds of data and databases. Choices must be made and priorities established. This input is now on an episodic, voluntary basis. It needs to be more systematic.

● Rural social scientists and their administrators need to:

- Work with appropriate national and international institutions to improve the quality of data in LDCs. The poor quality of statistics for many developing countries is extremely constraining even for U.S. policy purposes. The efforts of various U.S. and international agencies to promote increased quality of statistical systems should be supported following four approaches:
  - Train foreign statisticians, social scientists, and analysts.
  - Maintain or improve international statistical data-assembly programs, such as those of the International Monetary Fund (IMF), Food and Agriculture Organization (FAO), Foreign Agriculture Service (FAS), the World Bank, and the U.S. Bureau of the Census.
  - Establish or improve statistical systems in developing countries through Agency for International Development (AID)-funded projects.
  - Promote international contact of professional social scientists and statisticians of the United States and developing countries.
- Improve international statistical institutions and the information systems that support important databases. International data and information-system deficiencies are also the consequence of the limited capability of international institutions for compiling and integrating statistics from the different data systems of various countries. Even if all countries had good-quality national statistics, one would still be faced with integrating incompatible and noncomparable data from national systems. Broader use of international statistical standards is necessary. International statistical databases are maintained by a few large, mostly international, institutional users of data. These include the United Nations' Statistical Office, the FAO, and other United Nations' organizations, the World Bank, various regional international development banks, and the IMF. Various national ministries of agriculture adapt other nations' statistics to their needs, a notable example being the FAS of the USDA, which has agricultural attachés in most important agricultural producing countries. Although FAS has made much progress in improving the quality of its data, there still are many problems to overcome. Working in the proper institutional framework, rural social scientists need to:
  - Assess existing LDCs', developed countries' (DC), and international organizations' data and ongoing statistical survey and census support programs with regard to their suitability for social science research.
  - Define data needs according to policy and research objectives of end users.
  - Make greater use of microcomputers, remote sensing, and satellite-communications systems, such as ICC, BITNET, and CARINET, as means to improve data management and worldwide access.
  - Promote computer conferencing, on-line access to country databases, and better communications between individuals and institutions, especially between more and less developed and developing countries.
  - Encourage symposia and workshops to assist social scientists and policy makers in the development of collaborative programs to design data-collection and analysis systems to assist in reaching research, policy, and program objectives.

NEW AGENDA ITEMS AND CONCLUSIONS DEVELOPED SINCE THE HOUSTON CONFERENCE

If we are to get the food, agricultural, and rural-development information system in order, the first step is for the social science professions to develop a sound, positive but aggressive position of advocacy. Only a few groups in society understand or care about effective data and its uses. Secondly, as recommended at the Houston conference, the appropriate federal government policy, coordination, and statistical programs must be put into place. And, finally, the United States must provide leadership in encouraging the international community to undertake data and information-system improvements around the world, especially in developing countries.

The SSAAP editorial group has identified the following crosscut agenda items and conclusions, which supplement and extend the Houston conference agenda.

● Social science professional associations face major challenges:

- The American Agricultural Economics Association (AAEA) should continue to give the efforts of the Economic Statistics Committee (ESC) high priority and budget support as necessary. The ESC needs to extend further its cooperation with similar committees formed by other social science professional associations and with the Council of Professional

Associations on Federal Statistics (COPAFS) and the Consortium of Social Science Associations (COSSA). Broad collaboration is necessary to assure an effective social science approach to rural and agricultural data and analysis if we are to make the strongest case for an improved federal statistical policy and the institutional capacity to coordinate federal statistics. The AAEA cannot achieve its goals for statistical policy acting alone. Other rural social science associations need to establish organizational focal points for their database concerns.

- The ESC, in cooperation with the Rural Sociological Society and other professional associations, plus the Economic Research Service (ERS), National Agricultural Statistical Service (NASS), and land-grant-university social science departments, should establish an interdisciplinary task force to develop a more complete, better-integrated conceptual base for describing and analyzing the U.S. food system and rural America, to include the major macroeconomy and international linkages. Such a task force should include other social scientists with interests in agricultural and rural policy.

  Although technical and social science concepts and relationships should be covered in a fully adequate way, special emphasis should be focused on variables and relationships that link commodity and input prices, production, and utilization with the heretofore largely neglected social relationships that define the quality of life for rural people, the sustainability of rural communities, and the establishment and disestablishment of rural and agricultural institutions. For example, this should include determinants of rural employment and income patterns; educational attainment, trade skills, and capabilities of rural people; rural community services such as education, water systems, health, and transportation; and rural nonagricultural market structures, including retail consumer markets as well as agricultural input, product, and credit market facilities. A comprehensive conceptual framework should permit more effective analysis of issues such as state and regional comparative advantage, quality of rural life, food quality and safety, environmental quality, and public choice. The conceptual framework should facilitate a balanced consideration of the impact of the four driving forces of technological change, improved human capability, institutional change, and changes in natural resources.

  Necessary conceptualizations should include a verbal and graphic description of all major subsectors, institutions, variables, and causal relationships. Aggregation procedures should be included so that data are useful at the individual farm, business, and family level as well as for state, regional, and national planning and policy analysis, monitoring, and evaluation. All variables and parameters should be defined and a coding system developed to identify each such variable and parameter. This is a major research task that will not be achieved easily or quickly. The rural and basic social sciences need to get on with it.

- Based on the above conceptualization, variables should be given operational definitions that would serve as a basis for data collection and analysis. An interdisciplinary task force should be responsible for developing operational definitions (of concepts) so that the resulting measurements would provide consistent concepts, definitions, and measurements across the underlying social science theory, statistical data-collection procedures and quantitative analysis. The greater coherence and integration of concepts, data, and analysis would greatly improve the analysis and understanding upon which policy decision is based. The capacity to address relevant policy issues, choices, and their implementation, monitoring, and evaluation would be improved.

  In addition to the more traditional kinds of data, this activity should permit data collection necessary to understand better the establishment and disestablishment of both public and private institutions guiding the determination and implementation of public choice in agriculture and rural America. This will require:

  - The conceptualization and development of operational definitions describing the different types of public and private institutions relevant to agriculture and rural society. For each such type of institution, this activity should account for:
    - The relationship of human capital, manmade capital, and technology within the institution
    - The institutional life cycle
    - Establishment costs
    - Rents
    - Dismantlement costs
    - Institutional benefit/cost analyses

  It is essential that operational concepts be developed which permit collection of data on nonmonetary- as well as monetary-valued phenomena. Since data collection is costly and budgets are limited, priorities should be recommended for periodic data collection. This activity should be reviewed and updated every two or three years. All of this requires the close collaboration of rural social science professional associations and NASS, ERS, the Census Bureau, and other federal statistical and analytical agencies.

- In working with the federal government, social scientists should:
  - Apply the above conceptual framework to the operational agendas in the NASS, ERS, Bureau of the Census, Congressional Research Service (CRS), and other relevant government agencies, as a basis for reviewing federal data-collection, processing, and analysis programs in order to develop a coordinated, government-wide, ten-year statistical development program for rural policy. This program should include a reliable rural-household and economic-establishment survey capability. As each successive annual plan of work is completed, this ten-year statistical development plan should be reviewed and revised as necessary in keeping with the policy needs for different data sets.
  - In cooperation with ERS, NASS, FAS, and the CRS, establish a joint task force for designing and implementing a common food, agriculture, and rural-development data system that would provide "on line" access as well as providing for the distribution of data subsets on computer tapes, CDs, and floppy

disks. A very general and expandable data-system structure should be utilized that permits future expansion as data-collection programs are planned and implemented to collect data covering more of the nontraditional conceptual relationships, especially those relating to nonmonetary-value and institutional relationships pertaining to rural life. The data system should have a structure that allows one to use the system to combine and/or cross reference and link to analytical methods, traditional agricultural data, demographic data, manufacturing data, employment/unemployment data, public and private service-sector data, etc., by substate region. Perhaps the geographic information system (GIS) approach could be adapted to this need.

The system should be supported by a "statistical clearinghouse" including a "food, agricultural, and rural development statistical handbook" that would provide complete data-system documentation, including basic concepts, operational definitions, coding systems, data-collection and processing cycles, and the name and telephone number of a working-level state and/or federal government analyst who could answer inquiries concerning each data series. The "handbook" would be maintained "on line," updated continuously as the database itself was updated, and published in hard-copy book form perhaps every two or three years.

- Rural social scientists need to work more closely with national and international policy-analysis and statistical agencies. As the world becomes increasingly interdependent, various national ministries of agriculture share data with each other and adapt other nations' statistics to their needs. A notable example of this is the Foreign Agriculture Service (FAS) of the USDA, which has agricultural attachés in most important agricultural producing countries. U.S. agricultural attach'e reports are very useful to the Food and Agricultural Organization (FAO) of the United Nations in supplementing the FAO mail-out data surveys and national and international statistical publications collected and maintained in the FAO Statistical Branch Library. But, despite such progress and cooperation, much remains to be done. Rural social scientists need to work within the proper national and international institutional framework to:
  - Meet data needs for development and policy formulation, monitoring, and evaluation in developing countries.
  - Evaluate existing country and international data as well as ongoing statistical development and database programs. These should be evaluated with regard to their appropriateness, reliability, completeness, accessibility, and timeliness.
  - Encourage planning and implementation of long-term statistical-development programs according to priorities dictated by the policy and planning goals, objectives, and programs of developing countries.
  - Encourage the FAO and United Nations, through U.S. representation, to organize an appropriate venue within which to evaluate and conceptualize a greatly improved approach to the development and implementation of food, agricultural, and rural statistics capability in all of their member countries.

FAO's capacity to assist countries in improving their data-collection capacity is woefully lacking as is the commitment of many developing countries. The United Nations Statistical Office (UNSO) has for many years sponsored the National Household Survey Capability Program (NHSCP) in developing countries. But the NHSCP lacks a sound statistical development strategy, UN-wide coordination, and, especially, adequate funding. The World Bank has developed a Living Standards Measurement Study (LSMS) in which systems of national surveys are planned and conducted in developing countries. The LSMS is well conceptualized, utilizes some excellent field-survey techniques, and shows a lot of promise in the limited field work that has been completed. But the World Bank does not have the statistical organization or funding for the massive program needed. These agencies should pool their capacities and work together. The FAO with its proven secondary-data collection-and-processing capability, the World Bank with its well-conceptualized Living Standards Measurement Survey (LSMS), and the United Nations with its UN Statistical Office and UN Development Program (UNDP) should work in close cooperation with each other and the United States Agency for International Development (USAID), and other national donor agencies to develop, fund, and provide technical assistance for a truly integrated national-survey program for developing countries.

Even if all countries had good-quality national statistics, however, the task of assembling, processing, and distributing such data, which is often incompatible or noncomparable, would be enormous. FAO should probably remain the main world center for collecting, processing, and distributing secondary national data. FAO should continue to improve the collection of national data and its AGROSTAT storage-and-retrieval system through the further application of electronic-data media such as on-line access, floppy disks, and CDs. Charges for non-FAO access to AGROSTAT should be reduced to widen access and increase its use. FAO, the United Nations Statistical Office, and other international organizations should accelerate efforts to bring about world guidelines, standards, and definitions for food, agriculture, and rural-development statistics to make such assembly, processing, distribution, and use of international data easier and more accurate.

REFERENCES

U.S. Congress. Office of Technology Assessment. 1988. *Informing the nation: Federal information dissemination in an electronic age*. OTA-CIT–396. October.

Wallman, Katherine K. 1988. *Losing count: The federal statistical system*. Population Trends and Public Policy Paper no. 16, Population Reference Bureau, Washington, D.C.

CHAPTER 1

INTRODUCTION TO SECTION ON BASIC SOCIAL SCIENCE DISCIPLINES (BSSDs)

After a prefatory statement, this chapter considers the work of the Basic Social Science Discipline (BSSDs) and the Rural Social Sciences (RSSs) with respect to agriculture and rural societies. It then reviews literature relevant for establishing agendas for the basic social sciences to assist farmers and rural societies. Finally, the organization of the other chapters in Section 2 is explained.

In Part I, it was pointed out that decades of primary dependence on technical change as the driving force behind agricultural and rural development have placed rural societies in the United States and much of the world under severe stress. Improved resources, people, and institutions along with technical advances are all necessary but individually insufficient for farm and rural development. We have not advanced the first three as rapidly as agricultural technology. Further, the present evolving set of agricultural and rural issues and problems needing attention is such that the complementary relationships between the four driving forces require basic social science input for their resolutions. Figure 1 indicates that the rural social sciences need to join hands with the basic technical sciences, the applied technical agricultural sciences, and the basic social sciences of economics, sociology, anthropology, and political science, plus history, mathematics, statistics, and philosophy in conducting disciplinary, problem-solving (PS), and subject-matter (SM) work to create the required balanced contribution of technology, institutions, people, and resources to agricultural and rural development.

In making their practical contributions, the rural social sciences (RSSs) depend upon and are related to the basic social science disciplines (BSSDs) in much the same way that the natural and physical agricultural sciences depend on such basic disciplines as chemistry, physics, genetics, physiology, and bacteriology. SSAAP recognizes this dependence on the basic social science disciplines in this introductory chapter to this section and throughout this book.

THE WORK OF BSSDs AND RSSs WITH RESPECT TO AGRICULTURE AND RURAL SOCIETIES

We first survey the many interactions between and the potential contributions of both the rural social sciences and the basic social sciences to a partnership that is necessary among the biological, physical, and social sciences. In doing so, we will deal with: (1) the contributions of the basic social science disciplines, (2) the important complementarities between the RSSs and the BSSDs, (3) the BSSDs and ancillary disciplines important to agriculture, rural societies, and consumers, and (4) administrative and funding strategies for the BSSDs and RSSs.

BSSD CONTRIBUTIONS TO FARMING AND RURAL SOCIETIES

Work done by rural social scientists on issues and problems for agriculture and rural societies tends to be multidisciplinary problem-solving and subject-matter in nature. Subject matter and problem solving are defined as under "Scope of SSAAP Work" in Chapter 1 of Part I. Typically, PS and SM work require disciplinary excellence from a number of social sciences and, for that matter, from biological and physical science disciplines as well. This requirement for disciplinary excellence means that the rural social sciences have a constructive interest in improving the basic social science disciplines, in the teaching of the basic social science disciplines, and in promoting better utilization of disciplinary social scientists as contributors to PS and SM teams, sometimes as members and, at other times, as advisors or consultants (Johnson 1971). Basic social science disciplinarians also contribute applied disciplinary work to assist farming and rural societies. While applied disciplinary work is typically narrower and more specialized than the multidisciplinary PS and SM work of the RSSs, it often turns out to be useful to PS and SM team efforts and, for that matter, to individual decision makers.

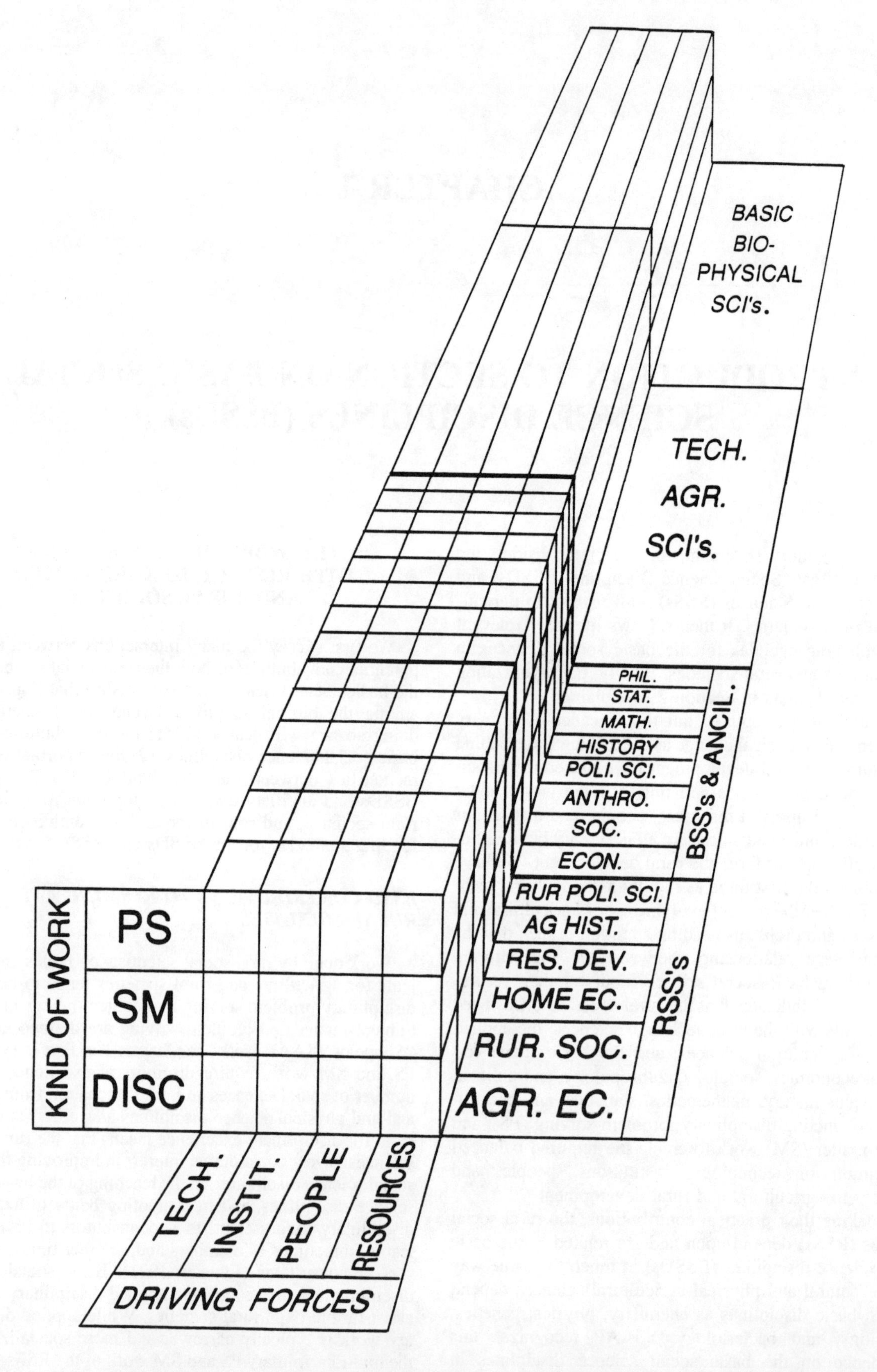

Figure 1. **Relationships** of the Agricultural and Basic Social and Biophysical Sciences **to** Problem-Solving, Subject-Matter, and Disciplinary Work on the Four Driving Forces.

IMPORTANT COMPLEMENTARITIES BETWEEN THE RSSS AND THE BSSDS

There are also important relationships between the disciplinary work and skills of the BSSDs and the multidisciplinary PS and SM work of the RSSs. These are probably more important than the somewhat similar complementarity between basic disciplinary and applied disciplinary work. The use of a basic social science discipline in a multidisciplinary PS or SM team effort often reveals important deficiencies or inadequacies in the theories, empirical techniques, and basic measurements of a that discipline. Revelation of such deficiencies and inadequacies identifies opportunities and needs for basic social science disciplinarians to improve their respective disciplines in general and to be of greater help to farming and rural societies. The complementarity, however, also runs in the other direction. Disciplinarians can make PS and SM rural social scientists aware of opportunities to improve the design and output of their multidisciplinary efforts to assist farmers and rural societies.

THE BASIC SOCIAL SCIENCE DISCIPLINES AND ANCILLARY DISCIPLINES ARE IMPORTANT FOR AGRICULTURE, RURAL SOCIETIES, AND CONSUMERS

As Frederick H. Buttel stressed in Chapter 3 of Part I, not all of the basic and rural social sciences are equally involved in agricultural, consumer, and rural affairs. Rural sociology, agricultural economics, and agricultural history are all more or less recognized university-level fields of study and all three have national associations or societies. Of these three, rural sociology and agricultural economics play the most important roles in the agricultural establishment. The existence of these rural social sciences, in turn, increases the importance for farming and rural societies of their underlying disciplines of economics, sociology, and history. Human ecology and home economics generally have vaguely defined, difficult to identify but very substantial social science components that have been and continue to be important for rural communities and farming. Home economics extension service workers play an important role in farm and rural family affairs. It has been somewhat difficult, however, for SSAAP to involve the human ecologists and home economists very deeply in its work, in part because the social science components of home economics and human ecology are not clearly identified, there being very few such departments and professional organizations that concentrate on the social science components of home economics and human ecology. They are usually well integrated, multidisciplinary subject-matter organizations.

A number of political scientists working on rural and farm issues in what might be called agro-political science have contributed to SSAAP. However, these workers are not represented by administrative units in universities or by a professional organization. Anthropologists play rather important roles in agricultural and rural affairs and have participated extensively and effectively in SSAAP conferences. SSAAP has benefitted from contributions of geographers, but has had only tenuous contacts with psychologists.

Such ancillary disciplines as philosophy, mathematics, and statistics are crucial for the RSSs and BSSDs, both of which draw heavily on them in their research and instructional orientations, theoretical structures, and empirical techniques. Some refer to mathematics as the highest form of logic; as such, it plays an important role in the formalization of theories and in structuring empirical work, particularly in econometrics. SSAAP has been concerned with philosophy, mathematics, and statistics.

ADMINISTRATION AND FUNDING FOR THE BSSDS AND RSSS

In universities, most BSSDs are housed outside colleges of agriculture, whereas the RSSs are either in colleges of agriculture or have contractual relationships with experiment stations, extension services, and resident instruction programs of agricultural colleges. Outside of universities, in other parts of the public and private sectors, somewhat similar administrative lines often separate the rural from the basic social sciences. Thus, difficulties easily arise in administering and funding joint efforts between the rural social sciences and the basic social science disciplines. In this section, attention is concentrated largely upon agendas for the basic science disciplines that are important for the rural social sciences and the farm people, agribusinesses, consumers, and rural societies they serve. Administrative and funding strategies needed to attain help for the RSSs in the agricultural establishment from the BSSDs are addressed in detail in Part V of this book, which deals with both research on and strategies for administering and funding PS, SM, and disciplinary work of the BSSDs and RSSs.

RELATED LITERATURE RELEVANT FOR ESTABLISHING AGENDAS IN THE BASIC SOCIAL SCIENCE DISCIPLINES TO ASSIST FARMERS AND RURAL SOCIETIES

The literature summarized in this section and covered more extensively by Buttel in Chapter 3 of Part 1 was generally available to participants at SSAAP's Houston conference. Literature outside this volume as well as relevant chapters in this and in other sections and parts of this volume are referenced at the end of this chapter. This literature is reviewed here more or less according to the basic social science discipline to which it pertains.

ANTHROPOLOGY

Anthropologists do a great deal of useful work relative to agriculture and rural societies. Some attempts have been made to address the contributions as well as the deficiencies and shortcomings of anthropology as a basic discipline contributing to the work of the RSSs including Chapter 4 in this section by Billie R. DeWalt.

Influential recent works in agricultural and natural resource anthropology are: Peggy Barlett's (1980) edited volume *Agricultural Decision-Making: Anthropological Contributions to Rural Development*; Robert Rhoades' (1984) *Breaking New Ground: Agricultural Anthropology*; the volume *The Question of the Commons* edited by Bonnie J. McCay and James M. Acheson (1987); and books such as *Putting People First: Sociological Variables in Rural Development*, edited by Michael Cernea (1985) of the World Bank, and *The Household Economy*, edited by Richard R. Wilk (1989). Contributors to Barlett's volume make important cross-cultural contributions to the task of better understanding the empirical nature of decision making (versus uncritical reliance on neoclassical models) and its cultural, social, and ecological contexts. Rhoades (1984) highlights many of the potentials and pitfalls of multidisciplinary work involving anthropologists, economists, agronomists, and other scientists at international research centers; his work also underscores the anthropological message about the importance of recognizing and incorporating into the design and implementation of agricultural development programs the knowledge, skills, and institutions of "client" populations. The McCay and Acheson (1987) volume of case studies on communal and common property management systems shows the influence of the new institutional economics in anthropological work on resource use and management within the context of a distinctly anthropological approach to the topic. Cernea's (1985) volume, subtitled "Sociological Variables in Rural Development," and papers by numerous anthropologists as well as sociologists, use the term "sociological" to emphasize the centrality of social organization for development policies and programs rather than to make a disciplinary claim. Wilk's (1989) book includes a range of analyses of family farm dynamics of use to academic and applied researchers.

Another influence on the thinking of participants in SSAAP was the bulletin *Culture and Agriculture*, several issues of which include discussions of the role of anthropology in relation to other BSSDs and RSSs and explicit attempts to correct for disciplinary centrism. Most anthropologists who are active in domestic and international work in agriculture and rural communities are multidisciplinary in the approaches and in the theories and methods they use, exchanging with economics, sociology, and even soil science, animal science, and agronomy. As these and other publications show, anthropologists also bring distinctive emphases on cultural variables, holistic phenomena, and long-term field research to the study of farmers, farm women and families, rural communities, and consumers. Their strength is clearly "micro" and social and cultural. Anthropologists need to improve their ability to address the nature and implications of larger-scale, even global, processes for the individuals, families, and communities they study, on the one hand, and to more clearly demonstrate the value of small-scale, long-term research to the understanding of widely shared, large-scale problems on the other.

A recent issue of *Culture and Agriculture* included an article on "Applied Methods in Agricultural Anthropology: An Interactive Approach" by Timothy J. Finan (1988) and another on "Weights and Measures Revisited: Methodological Issues in the Estimation of Agricultural Productivity" by William Loker (1988). The Loker article on the estimation of agricultural productivity does not note any of the voluminous literature in agricultural economics on the definition and measurement of productivity (French 1977; Glenn L. Johnson 1988; Gardner 1987). Perhaps this results from a greater interest in doing applied anthropology than in farm, rural-societal, and consumer problems in their full multidisciplinary real-world contexts. The adjectives "rural" in the name "rural sociology" and "agricultural" in the name "agricultural economics" and in the various titles of agricultural colleges in which these departments and home economics extension units exist and function demand multidisciplinarity from rural sociologists, agricultural economists, and extension-service home economists as they address problems of farmers, farm homemakers, rural societies, and consumers. The demand for multidisciplinarity is enforced for the rural social sciences to some extent at least by agricultural experiment-station budgets that have to be partially earned by addressing practical as opposed to disciplinary interests.

In his paper "Irony, Tragedy, and Temporality in Agricultural Systems" (see Part III, Section 1, Chapter 5), Lawrence Busch from the closely related field of sociology deals with the need to consider anthropological (cultural), sociological, political, and technical variables in analyzing and modeling agricultural systems. Dealing with such variables in studying and modeling agricultural systems requires that their roles be better formalized than they now are in the theories of anthropology and sociology. In their paper on "Integration in Home Economics and Human Ecology" (see Part II, Section 1, Chapter 5), Margaret M. Bubolz and M. Suzanne Sontag consider a wide range of BSSDs, including anthropology, that contribute to both home economics and human ecology.

ECONOMICS

Disciplinary economists devote much time and effort to improving the theory, techniques, and basic measurements of their discipline. Historically, agricultural and general economics have shared concerns about such improvements. In fact, agricultural economists took an early lead in the development of national accounts and in the development of survey methods to supplement data from the agricultural censuses in intercensual years for such accounts and for many secondary measures and indices of activity in the agricultural sector. Still further, early attempts of agricultural economists at supply and demand analysis led to some of the disciplinary breakthroughs by the University of Chicago's Henry Schultz and later in the Cowles Commission then also located at the University of Chicago. Agricultural economists contributed heavily to the attempt of economists to merge theory with experiential data in analyzing various sectors of the United States including, particularly, the agricultural sector and, in doing so, helped create the subdiscipline of econometrics. In his presidential address, Nobel Laureate Wassily Leontief (1971) from Harvard University paid particular homage to the contribution agricultural economists have made to merging economics, empirical data, and statistics into econometrics.

Many agricultural economists now seem preoccupied with applied disciplinary economics. This seems, in part, to have grown out of increased emphasis of administrators in rewarding agricultural economists on peer-reviewed disciplinary publications relative to PS and SM contributions to farming and rural societies. Schuh (1986), Johnson (1971), and Just and Rausser (1990) fear that this disciplinary emphasis may be reducing the contributions of agricultural economists to multidisciplinary PS and SM work without increasing their contributions to the discipline of economics.

Participants at SSAAP's Houston conference had a substantial number of reviews to draw on in considering agendas for economics as a basic social science. These include such earlier articles as those by Brinegar et al. (1959); the literature review volumes published by the American Agricultural Economics Association including, particularly, chapters by Harold R. Jensen (1977) on farm management and production economics, Ben C. French

(1977) on marketing, and Peterson and Hayami (1977) on technical change in agriculture, all of which are found in Volume 1 of the series of the four AAEA literature review volumes. In Volume 2 there is an important article by George C. Judge (1977) on estimating parameters of economic relations and another on optimization by Richard Day and Edward Sparling (1977). In the same volume, an article on systems analysis and simulation by Stanley R. Johnson and Gordon C. Rausser (1977) is important, but more about econometrics than about multidisciplinary systems analysis as the latter is discussed by, for instance, Lawrence Busch in Part III, Section 1, Chapter 5, of this book. In Volume 3 attention is given to human capital development by W. Keith Bryant, D. L. Bawden, and W. E. Saupe (1981) in their article on the economics of rural poverty. There is also a conceptual chapter on rural development by J. Dean Jansma, Hays B. Gamble, J. Patrick Madden, and Rex H. Warland (1981). An important chapter is the one on natural resource economics by Emery N. Castle, Maurice M. Kelso, Joe B. Stevens, and Herbert H. Stoevener (1981) that addresses conceptual and theoretical differences between institutionally oriented resource economists and neoclassical economists.

The American Agricultural Economics Association sponsored a conference on "Agriculture and Rural Areas Approaching the 21st Century" at Ames, Iowa, in the summer of 1985. A number of papers presented at that conference were useful to participants at SSAAP's Houston conference in developing agendas for the discipline of economics. These include articles by Stanley R. Johnson (1988) on quantitative techniques; Daniel W. Bromley (1988) on resource and environmental economics; Rulon D. Pope (1988) on developments in economics of importance to agricultural economics; Paul W. Barkley (1988) on institutionalism in agricultural economics; G. Edward Schuh and David Orden (1988) on macroeconomics; Glenn L. Johnson (1988) on theoretical difficulties in economics for analyzing technological innovations; and Wallace E. Huffman (1988) on human capital development for agriculture.

Mention should be made of a book entitled *Systems Economics: Concepts, Models, and Multidisciplinary Perspectives*, edited by Karl A. Fox and Don G. Miles (1987), that was at the publishers during SSAAP's Houston conference with several of its papers then in private circulation. There were chapters by Kenneth Boulding (1987) on the economy as an ecosystem; by Michael Lawlor (1987) questioning whether an economy is a closed system; and another on systems theory and mathematical economics by Roy J. Gardner (1987). Also included was an article on eco-behavior by Karl A. Fox (1987); another on the dollar values of social variables by Paul van Moeseke (1987); and still another by James R. Prescott (1987) on community dynamics.

The references mentioned above are but a small sample of the literature in agricultural economics that is concerned with needed improvements in the basic discipline of economics. Administrators and others using this book can easily expand their access to the literature on needed improvements in economics as a discipline by seeking the references at the end of the works cited above.

GEOGRAPHY

It is appropriate that geographers were represented at SSAAP's Houston meeting since geography and the related discipline of geology have done much to increase understanding of farming and rural societies. The geographer/economist O. E. Baker made a major contribution to our understanding of the spatial dimension of U.S. agriculture in the 1930s. Although not greatly influenced by geographers, there was an extensive movement to develop type-of-farming studies state by state, especially during the 1930s and 1940s. The basic data for the type-of-farming studies and for the related "typical farm" analyses for different geographic areas were developed in departments of agricultural economics working with farm-management researchers in the U.S. Department of Agriculture's Bureau of Agricultural Economics. Worldwide, geographers have also made substantial contributions to our understanding of agricultural, environmental, and related spatial dimensions of agriculture and rural societies. Currently, the advent of large-scale models dealing with environmental pollution and contamination makes it important that geographers contribute to spatial analyses of environmental pollution carried out by biological and physical agricultural scientists and the RSSs.

Karl A. Fox (1987), an economist at Iowa State University, has produced extensive conceptualizations of how rural communities servicing agriculture can be organized in space. Land and resource economists have long coordinated their work with that of geographers. The general economist Von Thunen did basic disciplinary work of interest to both geographers and economists. In the history of the RSSs many rural social scientists have played the role of amateur geographers while geographers have done applied geography in relation to farming and rural communities. Because cooperation between the RSSs and the discipline of geography has been less close than it could be, the RSSs have probably failed to inform disciplinary geographers of their needs for geographic expertise and for improvements in the basic discipline of geography. Spatial analyses are increasingly formalized and computerized by rural social scientists, often without benefit of help from disciplinary geographers who are also developing formal, computerized models.

M. Clawson and J. Knetsch (1966, 58–60) dealt with the "geography of demand" for recreational services of natural resources. Also, economists use linear-programming transportation models to analyze advantageous changes in the location of farm and rural activities. Currently, the development of public choice/transaction cost (PC/TC) analysis suggests useful, possible extensions of theories about the location of activities. Clearly, when activities are being abandoned in a region, it is important to have a theory that compares the productivity of investments in that region with their dismantlement costs. Conversely, when regional investments are expanding, it is useful to have a theory that compares the value of new investment in use with their establishment costs. When old investments are being replaced with modern ones, the values of both the old and the modern investments need to be compared with their respective dismantlement and establishment costs. This suggests that the rural social sciences would benefit substantially from an extension of geographic theory and techniques to incorporate the rapidly developing PC/TC theory into geographic theories much as Douglass North (1984) found it advantageous to use that theory in historical studies. As in history, the advances likely to occur in PC/TC theory will mean that the theory will likely be incrementally adapted and adopted by geographers.

HISTORY

History is a basic discipline that has made major contributions to the PS and SM work of the RSSs. In the depression years, O. C. Stine, trained as an institutional agricultural economist at the University of Wisconsin, established the Division of Statistical and Historical Research (S&HR) in the old Bureau of Agricultural Economics. A substantial agricultural history section developed in that division under the leadership of Everett Edwards with such then young stalwarts as Wayne Rasmussen (1988) and Gladys Baker working under him. For many years, the *Journal of Agricultural History*, now relocated at the University of California, was located in and received heavy support from the Division of S&HR. In the same division, major attention was given to the development of statistical series and the U.S. agricultural databases of great value to agricultural historians and rural sociologists. Somewhat later, under the leadership Meyer Girschick, the Division of S&HR contributed to the development of econometrics while, at the same time, taking steps to contribute and to rapidly adopt and implement the numerous econometric advances that were appearing. There is, of course, a connection between econometric analyses of time series data and history that is recognized by disciplinary historians.

In Part III of this book, considerable attention was given to theories of public choice and transaction costs. Among general historians, Douglass North (1987) has used this theory in interpreting history. This work indicates that agricultural economists and political scientists may be able to use PC/TC theory in developing historical and futuristic-scenario analyses of agriculture along the lines suggested by Larry Busch in his chapter on "Irony, Tragedy, and Temporality in Agricultural Systems or How Values and Systems Are Related" (Part III, Section 1, Chapter 5). Related to the Busch chapter is a journal article by Margaret M. Bubolz and M. Suzanne Sontag entitled "Integration in Home Economics and Human Ecology" reprinted as Chapter 5 in Section 1, Part II of this book.

HUMAN ECOLOGY

While some may question whether human ecology is itself too eclectic, holistic, and multidisciplinary to be classed as a basic discipline, it has more of a disciplinary orientation than home economics—at least it appears to be more academic. As such, it is appropriate to ask about the "discipline-like" work needed by the RSSs on human ecology theories, techniques, and basic measurements if human ecology is to be of more help to the RSSs (including the social scientists in home economics) in doing multidisciplinary PS and SM work for farm people, agribusinesses, rural societies, and consumers.

For many years, home economists had a basic interest in the theory of managerial processes of homes and institutions. Such home economists as Irma Gross and Elizabeth Crandall (1954) and others helped conceptualize managerial processes, often in collaboration with other rural social scientists. Home economists made major conceptual contributions to the creation of Missouri's "balanced farming" extension program that integrated farm business and farm household decision making. In turn, the Missouri program was followed by Kentucky's "farm and home development" extension program that was later made a national agricultural extension program. The concepts contributed by home economists to these activities were more complete in many ways and much more satisfactory for working on practical problems than the specialized farm-level, two-equation models of farm production and households used by persons such as I. J. Singh, L. Squire, J. Strauss (1986), and others working on international rural development. In the 1950s and 1960s, the linkages of the rural social sciences (including those parts of home economics that are oriented to the social sciences) with the basic social science disciplines seem to have been closer and more complementary (hence, probably more productive) than today's linkages. Today, some extension home economists retain a home economics label that continues to sell well with their clientele on farms, in agribusinesses, in rural communities, and among consumers. This maintains a valuable experiential linkage for extension home economists to these clients but, unfortunately, also tends to isolate them from the more academic human ecologists whose theories, techniques, and basic measurements generally relate to a basic home discipline (psychology, economics, sociology) they seem to regard as more fundamental than human ecology. If more closely related to extension home economists, these disciplinarians in human ecology would probably benefit from and contribute substantially to the practical multidisciplinary PS and SM work of home economists that would also reveal opportunities for them to remedy disciplinary shortcomings and deficiencies. The reader is again referred to the Bubolz/Sontag article reprinted as Chapter 5 in Section 1, Part II of this book.

PHILOSOPHY

Philosophy, including (as it perhaps does) mathematics as the highest form of logic—logic being itself a part of philosophy—is one of the most important ancillary disciplines for both the rural social sciences and the basic social sciences. Different philosophic arguments and points of view determine the various orientations of the rural social sciences to research, education, administration, extension, advising, entrepreneurship, and consulting. In short, everything done in the rural social sciences has a philosophic orientation. The rural social sciences are particularly concerned with questions involving philosophic value theory and ethics at the practical end of their work on a spectrum extending from disciplinary work to PS work.

There is a separate crosscutting section on ethics in this part of this book in which rural social science and philosophic literature pertaining to the practical PS and SM work of the RSSs and BSSDs is reviewed in considerable detail. Thus, such a review is not presented here. What is needed here, however, is some attention to the extensive philosophic literature that influences our research, teaching, and other academic activities in the rural social sciences and as well as the contributions the BSSDs can make to the RSSs.

Chapter 2 of this section, "Utility, Utilitarianism, and Public Policy," by Edward F. McClennen, a philosopher, is important for economics and the other BSSDs as well as the RSSs. Utilitarianism is fundamental to the disciplinary PS and SM work of rural social scientists and, of course, the basic discipline of economics. In recent years there has been a substantial increase in articles and books dealing with research methodology and economics. The introduction to Part III of this book reviews the more pragmatically oriented work of the "new institutionalists," particularly in resource economics but also in public policy. Generally, three broad philosophic orientations are important in the literature of economics: pragmatism, logical positivism, and various forms of normativism, one of which is the utilitarianism about which McClennen writes. Pragmatism, of course, goes back to the Greek scholars, but it appears in economics in the German historical school and in the dialectical materialism of Marxism, Wisconsinian institutionalism, and the new institutionalism based upon PC/TC theories. Positivism has had its impact on economics in the cited writings of such people as John Neville Keynes (1963), Harry Johnson (1975), and Donald McCloskey (1985), and in many uncited writings of Lionel Robbins and Milton Friedman. Volume 4 of the literature review series produced by the American Agricultural Economics Association (Martin forthcoming) contains a survey of changes in the philosophic orientations of agricultural economists from the end of World War II to 1965 with some coverage of the period between the two World Wars. This review was widely circulated prior to SSAAP's Houston meeting.

In the field of *rural sociology*, philosophic orientations have also been important. Max Weber had a major positivistic influence. Also, the pragmatic, dialectical, and materialistic orientation of Karl Marx has been important. Perhaps because of the influence of positivists, rural and basic sociologists probably spend more time researching the various monetary and nonmonetary values held by different groups of people than researching questions about what "really" has value. However, in their more practical roles as advisors and consultants, rural sociologists join other practicing rural social scientists in treating various perceptions of values as being "objectively descriptive" of the values of conditions, situations, things, and acts.

Because the rural social scientists cooperate with technical agriculturalists in PS and SM team efforts, it is relevant to recognize the importance of logical positivism among the technical agricultural scientists. Still further, even when rural social scientists are not on such teams, they are often under the administrative direction of technical agricultural scientists with logically positivistic orientations not attuned to the need to work on questions of value as values pertain to public choices and private decisions.

The field of *psychology* has also been influenced by logical positivism. Psychologists are adept at determining which individuals hold what values but, as "scientists," have tended to refrain from trying to research objectively what really has value. Perhaps it is this logically positivistic trait that makes psychology the most accepted of the basic social sciences in the National Academy of Sciences, a technocratic institution strongly dominated by biological and technical scientists who, for the most part, are heavily committed to logically positivistic orientations. On the other hand, psychiatrists and clinical psychologists who deal with problem solving and subject matter are more likely to be pragmatic and normativistic. Practicing psychiatrists prescribe and act on convictions concerning the objectivity of their knowledge about what really has value.

When rural social scientists become involved in vocational agriculture, 4-H and FFA clubs, and agricultural extension, they often encounter pragmatism as *a* philosophic orientation in the educational philosophy that undergirds so much of the methods and techniques used in colleges of education to guide both teaching and research.

Psychologists specialize in understanding the behavior of individuals and groups. Their interest goes beyond that of understanding and developing "decision rules" to deal with the learning, analysis, and responsibility bearing that are parts of the problem-solving process. Psychology also deals with abnormal behavior, an area almost entirely neglected by economists who concentrate on rational behavior. Perhaps no other basic social science has more potential than psychology to contribute to the ability of rural social scientists to deal with substance abuse, teenage pregnancy, family problems, managerial malfunctions, etc. The fact that there were no psychologists at SSAAP's Houston meeting reflects adversely on those who organized it while the resulting gap points to a need for closer associations between rural social scientists and psychologists. As the theory of induced human capital formation is broadened in the future to take transaction costs into account in more holistic, less reductionistic analyses of systems, psychologists will be needed to help model the roles of psychological variables in educational processes and human development.

POLITICAL SCIENCE

Political science does not have an agricultural component that might be labeled "agro-political science" despite the fact that a number of political scientists (including, earlier, Charles Hardin [1952] from the University of Chicago) have made important contributions to understanding the politics of agriculture. Robert Paarlberg, Donald Hadwiger, and Ross Talbot have distinguished accomplishments. Currently, William Browne (1988), from Central Michigan University, is doing agro-political science research on interest group behavior for the USDA's Economic Research Service that is proving very useful in the agricultural establishment. Some academic political scientists, like many other disciplinarians, seem more interested in applying their discipline vis-a-vis agriculture and rural communities than in addressing the shortcomings and deficiencies of their own discipline that constrain the multidisciplinary PS and SM work of the RSSs. For instance, shortcomings in political science theory make it difficult to formalize the roles of political variables in analyzing agricultural systems.

Public choice/transaction cost literature is reviewed in the introduction to Part III and in the first chapters of the four sections in that part. This approach is often referred to as the "new political economy." A good review is one by Sandmo (1990) entitled "Buchanan on Political Economy." Also, additional review material is to be found in Part III, Section 1, Chapter 1, that deals with institutional change.

SOCIOLOGY

Using National Science Foundation funds, two sociological papers were commissioned by SSAAP to address sociological issues: *one* by Wava G. Haney entitled "Theoretical Advances Arising from Studies of Women and Farming" (Part II, Section 1, Chapter 4) and *another* by Cornelia Butler Flora entitled "Studies of Households Reviewed in Relation to Farm and Home, Balanced Farming, Farming Systems, and Farm Management Programs and Studies in the College of Agriculture" (Part II, Section 1, Chapter 4). Attention is also called to Chapter 3 of Part I by Frederick H. Buttel entitled "Social Science Institutions, Knowledge, and Tools to Address Problems and Issues." In another article by Buttel (1989), "The Sociology of Agriculture: Current Conceptual Status," he examines major theoretical trends and identifies major gaps in the sociology of agriculture. His article reflects much of the thinking available at the Houston conference and at which he presented the first paper mentioned above and participated in the development of agendas. Buttel noted a trend in sociology away from deductive theories to more empirical work on the diversity of agricultural forms in time and space. He also noted that sociology is becoming more holistic both vertically and horizontally, that it is reaching its limits for "conceptualizing" the structure of U.S. agriculture, and that sociologists are paying increased attention to international food and agricultural regimes and international commodity complexes. He observed that greater attention is being given by sociologists to technical change and that there is a steady flow of innovative work on gender and households. He further noted a trend towards increased use of historical methods in rural sociology and a growing tendency to utilize periods of agrarian crises as key test cases for the evaluation of sociological propositions about agricultural change. Lastly, he noted increased attention to "spheres of circulation" in understanding the forces that affect the structure of production agriculture.

Following his attention to trends, Buttel noted five gaps in the sociology of agriculture. They include lack of sociological attention to: (1) agricultural policy; (2) credit, finance capital, and similar topics; (3) the recent farm crises and the crisis of accumulation in and the restructuring of the world economy as a whole; (4) environmental issues in agriculture; and, finally, (5) systematic comparative research in the sociology of agriculture. These gaps must be mainly with respect to the applied disciplinary interests of sociologists because these subjects have long been subjected to prolonged, intensive study by agricultural economists including many with institutionalist orientations. Agricultural policy, farm management, resource economics, marketing, credit-sector studies, systems work, farm crises, and the like have been the backbone of agricultural economics work for decades. Sociological contributions to the study of these subjects would be greatly enhanced by more formalization and systemization of sociological theory to complement the more formal theories of economics and political science particularly as those disciplines extend the PC/TC approach to the study of institutional change. As sociology succeeds in filling these gaps and forming linkages with economists and political scientists, rural social scientists can be expected to improve their service to farm people, agribusinesses, rural societies, and consumers in multidisciplinary PS and SM teams and projects. Howard Newby (1982) has reviewed the relationship between rural sociology and agricultural economics with attention to differences between the relationships that exist in Europe and America. He notes an emerging sociology of agriculture similar to that discussed by Buttel. He notes sociological attention to the relationship of landholding to social structure, including the development of vertical integration in agribusiness. He also reviews sociological work on the relationship of labor relations to community development, and on the sociology of natural resources.

Some of the original departments of rural sociology in the land-grant system started with the appointment of sociologists to deal with the sociological dimensions of farm management. Such appointees, in turn, generated rural sociology departments that were financed by experiment station, extension, and resident instruction budgets of colleges of agriculture. In time, a number of the rural sociology departments developed disciplinary orientations. Some withdrew and lost their budgetary support from colleges of agriculture to become sections or groups in general sociology departments. Currently, some sociologists interested in agriculture and rural social problems and issues are attempting to reestablish college of agriculture administrative and funding connections by committing themselves to help do PS and SM work for clientele groups in agriculture and in rural areas. Home economists, human ecologists, and agricultural economists with disciplinary predilections can learn valuable administrative and funding lessons from the experiences of rural sociologists.

After the Houston conference, members of the SSAAP editorial group devoted additional attention to public-choice theory, transaction costs, and institutional economics. At the 1989 meeting of the Food, Agriculture, and Human Values Society, Lawrence Busch, a sociologist, delivered his presidential address entitled "Irony, Tragedy, and Temporality in Agricultural Systems or How Values and Systems Are Related" (Part III, Section 1, Chapter 5). Implicitly, his paper recognizes the importance in multidisciplinary holistic systems analyses of the roles played by sociological and anthropological variables in private decisions and social choices. The Busch paper, however, is not as explicit as it might be about the lack of formal sociological theories to use in modeling and doing empirical work on how such variables influence, interact with, and also become consequences of the operation of agricultural systems.

STATISTICS

Statistics is a basic ancillary discipline for both the RSSs and the BSSDs. Although the theory of statistics is highly developed, it is still rapidly developing and being continually honed against the needs of those using statistics to analyze and interpret data. As a discipline, statistics contributes much to the quantitative techniques of the RSSs and the BSSDs. Improvements in statistical theory about choosing and decision-making processes and about estimation prove useful to students of the managerial processes of farmers, homemakers, agribusiness people, and governmental officials (Tversky and Kahneman 1981; Johnson et al. 1961). There has been a longstanding interaction between agricultural economists and leading statisticians that has both enriched the theories of economics and called the attention of statisticians and econometricians to deficiencies in statistical theories and techniques. Unfortunately, the SSAAP conferences generated little input from other RSSs and BSSDs on how the discipline of statistics could be improved to help them do better PS and SM research for farm people, agribusinesses, rural societies, and consumers.

THE ORGANIZATION OF SECTION 2

In addition to this introductory chapter, Section 2 has chapters by Edward McClennen on utilitarianism, Karl A.

Fox on social indicators, and Billie R. DeWalt on anthropology, evolution, and agriculture. The National Science Foundation provided funds to commission still other disciplinary social science chapters; these chapters and their locations in this book are listed at the end of this chapter.

At Houston, Peggy Barlett and Bonnie J. McCay served as joint coordinators of the effort to develop agendas for the basic social science disciplines in relation to the rural social sciences for farming, agribusinesses, rural societies, and consumers. Participants coordinated by McCay and Barlett were charged to develop agendas to improve the theories, techniques, and fundamental measurements of the basic social science disciplines so as to expedite RSS work to assist farmers and rural communities. This charge presumed that the basic social sciences would have shortcomings and deficiencies that would need to be remedied in order for rural social scientists to do more effective PS and SM work. Not all basic social science disciplinarians at the Houston conference reacted favorably to this presumption. Some reluctance to admit shortcomings of disciplines was experienced. On the other hand, there was a great deal of interest on the part of disciplinarians at Houston in applied disciplinary work which is, of course, rather narrow and specialized relative to the multidisciplinarity of the practical subjects and problems faced by public and private agricultural and rural community decision makers. The disciplinarians were also interested in such multidisciplinary subjects as religious studies, resource sustainability, gender inequality, and the like. The multidisciplinarity of such subjects makes it difficult for any one discipline such as economics or sociology to handle them. Even human ecologists with their avowed multidisciplinarity hold onto their connections with a parent, more "basic" discipline, such as anthropology or sociology, and display some reluctance to forget those disciplines in whole-hearted attacks on practical multidisciplinary problems and subjects. The disciplinarians gathered at Houston sometimes seemed unaware of or tended to discount the practical literature generated by rural social scientists on multidisciplinary problems, issues, and subjects. This was especially true of disciplinarians from outside the land-grant system, but was also embarrassingly true (for the RSSs) of disciplinarians from within the land-grant system. Disciplinarians sometimes display interest in initiating work in subjects on which there have been many years of ongoing RSS work of which they appear to be unaware and disinclined to investigate and recognize. Communications between rural and basic social scientists are not adequate. While basic social scientists fail to keep up with what rural social scientists do and with the disciplinary difficulties they encounter, rural social scientists also fail to keep up with progress in the basic social science disciplines.

As a result of the above, the work group agendas produced by the basic social science disciplinarians at Houston are a mixture of disciplinary work to improve the disciplines, applied disciplinary work in agriculture and rural communities, and agendas for disciplinary contributions to multidisciplinary subjects, some new and some worked on for long periods of time by rural social sciences in the agricultural establishment. This mixed nature of the disciplinary agendas developed at Houston made it advisable for the editorial group to do more than simply present verbatim in Chapter 5 of this section the BSSD agendas developed at Houston. Thus, while Chapter 5 of this section contains the clearly identified verbatim BSSD agendas developed at Houston, it also contains additional agenda items and conclusions originating with SSAAP's editorial group. The additional agenda items and conclusions reflect concerns about the inadequacies of the BSSDs for handling substantive PS and SM agendas developed at Houston.

The set of agendas from Houston also touches on administrative and funding strategies as viewed from the standpoint of the basic social sciences. The administrative and funding strategies needed to attain the second set of agendas developed after SSAAP's Houston meeting for improvements in the BSSDs to help the RSSs are to be found in Part V of this book that deals specifically with administrative and funding strategies for the rural and basic social science disciplines.

CROSS REFERENCES IN THIS BOOK

REFERENCES

Barkley, Paul W. 1988. Institutions, institutionalism, and agricultural economics. In *Agriculture and rural areas approaching the 21st century: Challenges for agricultural economics.* Edited by R. J. Hildreth et al., 313–35. Ames: Iowa State University Press.

Barlett, Peggy, ed. 1980. *Agricultural decision-making: Anthropological contributions to rural development.* New York: Academic Press.

Boulding, Kenneth. 1987. The economy as an ecosystem: Economics in the general system. In *Systems economics: Concepts, models and multidisciplinary perspectives.* Edited by Karl A. Fox and Don G. Miles, 3–18. Ames: Iowa State University Press.

Brinegar, G. K., K. L. Blackman, and H. M. Southworth. 1959. Reorientations in research in agricultural economics. *Journal of Farm Economics* 41.

Bromley, Daniel W. 1988. Resource and environmental economics: Knowledge, discipline, and problems. In *Agriculture and rural areas approaching the 21st century: Challenges for agricultural economics.* Edited by R. J. Hildreth et al., 208–30. Ames: Iowa State University Press.

Browne, William. 1988. *Private interests, public policy, and American agriculture.* Lawrence: University Press of Kansas.

Bryant, W. Keith, D. L. Bawden, and W. E. Saupe. 1981. The economics of rural poverty—A review of the post-World War II United States and Canadian literature. In *A survey of agricultural economics literature.* Vol. 3, *Economics of welfare, rural development, and natural resources in agriculture, 1940s to 1970s.* Edited by Lee R. Martin, 3–150. Minneapolis: University of Minnesota Press.

Buttel, Frederick H. 1989. The sociology of agriculture: Current conceptual status. *Rural Sociologist* (Spring).

Castle, Emery N., et al. 1981. Natural resource economics, 1946–75. In *A survey of agricultural economics literature.* Vol. 3, *Economics of welfare, rural development, and natural resources in agriculture, 1940s to 1970s.* Edited by Lee R. Martin, 393–500. Minneapolis: University of Minnesota Press.

Cernea, Michael, ed. 1985. *Putting people first: Sociological variables in rural development.* New York: Oxford University Press for the World Bank.

Clawson, M., and J. Knetsch. 1966. *Economics of outdoor recreation.* Baltimore: Johns Hopkins University Press and Resources for the Future.

Day, Richard, and Edward Sparling. 1977. Optimization models in agricultural and resource economics. In *A survey of agricultural economics literature.* Vol. 2, *Quantitative methods in agricultural economics, 1940s to 1970s.* Edited by Lee R. Martin, 93–127. Minneapolis: University of Minnesota Press.

Finan, Timothy J. 1988. Applied methods in agricultural anthropology. *Culture and Agriculture* no. 35 (Special Methods Issue/Summer): 9–13.

Fox, Karl A. 1987. The eco-behavioral view of human societies: Behavior settings, time-allocation matrices, and social system accounts. In *Systems economics: Concepts, models and multidisciplinary perspectives.* Edited by Karl A. Fox and Don G. Miles, 118–42. Ames: Iowa State University Press.

Fox, Karl A., and Don G. Miles, eds. 1987. *Systems economics: Concepts, models and multidisciplinary perspectives.* Ames: Iowa State University Press.

French, Ben C. 1977. The analysis of productive efficiency in agricultural marketing: Models, methods, and progress. In *A survey of agricultural economics literature.* Vol. 1, *Traditional fields of agricultural economics, 1940s to 1970s.* Edited by Lee R. Martin, 93–206. St. Paul: North Central Publishing Co.

Gardner, Bruce, et al. 1980. *Measurement of agricultural productivity.* Report of the American Agricultural Economics Association, ESCS Task Force on Productivity Measurement, Technical Bulletin no. 1614, U.S. Dept. of Agriculture, Washington, D.C.

Gardner, Roy J. 1987. System theory in mathematical economics. In *Systems economics: Concepts, models and multidisciplinary perspectives.* Edited by Karl A. Fox and Don G. Miles, 50–66. Ames: Iowa State University Press.

Gross, Irma, and Elizabeth Crandall. 1954. *Management for modern families.* New York: Appleton-Century Crofts, Inc.

Hardin, Charles. 1952. *The politics of agriculture.* Glencoe, Ill.: The Free Press.

Huffman, Wallace E. 1988. Human capital for agriculture. In *Agriculture and rural areas approaching the 21st century: Challenges for agricultural economics.* Edited by R. J. Hildreth et al. Ames: Iowa State University Press.

Jansma, J. Dean, et al. 1981. Rural development: A review of conceptual and empirical studies. In *A survey of agricultural economics literature.* Vol. 3, *Economics of welfare, rural development, and natural resources in agriculture, 1940s to 1970s*. Edited by Lee R. Martin, 285–362. Minneapolis: University of Minnesota Press.

Jensen, Harold R. 1977. Farm management and production economics, 1946–70. In *A survey of agricultural economics literature. Vol. 1, Traditional fields of agricultural economics, 1940s to 1970s*. Edited by Lee R. Martin, 3–89. Minneapolis: University of Minnesota Press.

Johnson, Glenn L. 1971. The quest for relevance in agricultural economics. *American Journal of Agricultural Economics* 53.

_____1988. Technological innovations with implications for agricultural economics. In *Agriculture and rural areas approaching the 21st century: Challenges for agricultural economics*. Edited by R. J. Hildreth et al., 82–108. Ames: Iowa State University Press.

Johnson, Glenn L., et al. 1961. *A study of managerial processes of midwestern farmers*. Ames: Iowa State University Press.

Johnson, Harry. 1975. *On economics and society*. Chicago: University of Chicago Press.

Johnson, Stanley R. 1988. Quantitative techniques. In *Agriculture and rural areas approaching the 21st century: Challenges for agricultural economics*. Edited by R. J. Hildreth, 177–98. Ames: Iowa State University Press.

Johnson, Stanley R., and Gordon C. Rausser. 1977. Systems analysis and simulation: A survey of applications in agricultural and resource economics. In *A survey of agricultural economics literature*. Vol. 2, *Quantitative methods in agricultural economics, 1940s to 1970s*. Edited by Lee R. Martin, 157–301. Minneapolis: University of Minnesota Press.

Judge, George C. 1977. Estimation and statistical inference in economics. In *A survey of agricultural economics literature*. Vol. 2, Quantitative methods in agricultural economics, 1940s to 1970s. Edited by Lee R. Martin, 3–56. Minneapolis: University of Minnesota Press.

Just, Richard E., and Gordon C. Rausser. 1990. An assessment of the agricultural economics profession. *American Journal of Agricultural Economics* 71 (December).

Keynes, John Neville. 1963. *The Scope and method of political economy*. 4th ed. New York: Augustus M. Kelley, Bookseller.

Lawlor, Michael. 1987. Is the economy a closed system? General equilibrium and general systems theory. In *Systems economics: Concepts, models, and multidisciplinary perspectives*. Edited by Karl A. Fox and Don G. Miles, 19–49. Ames: Iowa State University Press.

Leontief, Wassily. 1971. Theoretical assumptions and nonobserved facts. *American Economic Review* 75.

Loker, William. 1988. Weights and measures revisited: Methodological issues in the estimation of agricultural productivity. *Culture and Agriculture* no. 35 (Special Methods Issue/Summer): 9–13.

Martin, Lee R., ed. Forthcoming. *A survey of agricultural economics literature*. Vol. 4, *Agriculture in economic development*. Minneapolis: University of Minnesota.

McCay, Bonnie J., and James M. Acheson, eds. 1987. *The question of the commons*. Tucson: University of Arizona Press.

McCloskey, Donald N. 1985. *The rhetoric of economics*. Madison: The University of Wisconsin Press.

Newby, Howard. 1982. Rural sociology and its relevance to the agricultural economist. *Journal of Agricultural Economics* 33:2.

North, Douglass. 1984. Government and the cost of exchange in history. *Journal of Economic History* (June).

_____1987. Institutions, transaction costs and economic growth. *Economic Inquiry* 35.

Peterson, Willis, and Yujiro Hayami. 1977. Technical change in agriculture. In *A survey of agricultural economics literature*. Vol. 1, *Traditional fields of agricultural economics, 1940s to 1970s*. Edited by Lee R. Martin, 497–540. Minneapolis: University of Minnesota Press.

Pope, Rulon D. 1988. Developments in economics of importance to agricultural economics. In *Agriculture and rural areas approaching the 21st century: Challenges for agricultural economics*. Edited by R. J. Hildreth et al., 238–56. Ames: Iowa State University Press.

Prescott, James R. 1987. Community dynamics: Microanalytical simulation models with behavior settings as basic units. In *Systems economics: Concepts, models and multidisciplinary perspectives*. Edited by Karl A. Fox and Don G. Miles, 21–31. Ames: Iowa State University Press.

Rasmussen, Wayne. 1988. Lessons from history. In *Agriculture and rural areas approaching the 21st century: Challenges for agricultural economics*. Edited by R. J. Hildreth, 21–31. Ames: Iowa State University Press.

Rhoades, Robert. 1984. *Breaking new ground: Agricultural anthropology*. Lima, Peru: International Potato Center.

Sandmo, Agar. 1990. Buchanan on political economy. *Journal of Economic Literature* 28.

Schuh, G. Edward. 1986. Revitalizing land-grant universities. American Agricultural Economics Association *Choices* (2d Quarter): 5.

Schuh, G. Edward, and David Orden. 1988. The macroeconomics of agriculture and rural America. In *Agriculture and rural areas approaching the 21st century: Challenges for agricultural economics*. Edited by R. J. Hildreth, 347–83. Ames: Iowa State University Press.

Singh, I., L. Squire, and J. Strauss. 1986. *Agriculture household models: Extensions, applications and policy*. Baltimore: Johns Hopkins University Press.

Tversky, Amos, and D. Kahneman. 1981. The framing of decisions and the psychology of choice. *Science* 211:453–58.

van Moeseke, Paul. 1987. The dollar values of social variables: Two models of social income. In *Systems economics: Concepts, models and multidisciplinary perspectives*. Edited by Karl A. Fox and Don G. Miles, 143–57. Ames: Iowa State University Press.

Wilk, Richard R., ed. 1989. *The household economy*. Boulder, Colo.: Westview Press.

CHAPTER 2

UTILITY, UTILITARIANISM, AND PUBLIC POLICY

Edward F. McClennen[1]

INTRODUCTION

The view that the utilitarian principle is the fundamental norm for the evaluation of social, political and economic policy came into prominence in the eighteenth and nineteenth centuries—particularly in England. As formulated by Bentham, it was perceived as a needed and "objective" antidote to a variety of philosophical traditions that, it was alleged, merely served to rationalize various types of vested interests by presenting them as natural laws or eternal truths.[2]

By the third decade of the twentieth century, the utilitarian principle no longer commanded such respect. The theory of knowledge that came into vogue, as expressed in the program of the logical positivists, refused to recognize any normative principle as objectively valid. Social and ethical principles, it was argued, cannot be objectively established, since they are neither certifiable by reference to logic and meaning alone, nor are they capable of empirical confirmation. They are, then, merely the objects of emotional commitment. Utilitarianism also fell victim to increasing doubts concerning the possibility of meaningful interpersonal comparison of utility. To talk of choosing a policy that maximizes the net sum of utilities as distributed to different individuals clearly presupposes that one can compare the utilities of different persons. But, within economic theory, the trend, as expressed by Robbins (1932), was towards skepticism with regard to just such interpersonal comparisons.

In recent decades, the pendulum has begun to swing back. The theory of knowledge that has recently come into favor is not so hostile to the suggestion that there might be an objective (or rational) approach to policy evaluation and, for many, the problem of interpersonal comparisons of utility no longer appears so intractable.[3] In the last few decades, there has been a revival of interest in utilitarianism among philosophers, and a number of economists and decision theorists have offered a variety of axiomatically based constructions that yield the utilitarian principle as a theorem.[4]

In what is to follow I shall outline and critically comment on these axiomatic approaches to utilitarianism. My critical remarks focus on two issues. The first turns to an old complaint about utilitarianism, namely, that it is not sufficiently sensitive to inequalities in the distribution of goods and on the frequent reply that more equal distributions can be rationalized within the utilitarian framework by showing that they lead to a net gain in the sum total of utility. The issue here is complicated. Utilitarians can reply that representational devices can be employed, and likely stories told, to the end of insuring that a "sum-ranking" approach to social welfare rules against inequalities. The problem remains, however, that certain natural ways of measuring and evaluating inequalities are ruled out within the framework of these constructions, and the utilitarian principle that emerges is hardly more than a schematism. A second issue, considerably more straightforward, concerns the separability or independence axiom that is essential to the constructions in question. I shall argue that this condition is questionable.

In developing both of these points, I have found it useful to draw attention to the very strong parallel that exists between these recent utilitarian constructions and those that are central to modern utility theory—to the theory that individual rationality is a matter of maximizing expected utility. What one has, in effect, are variations on the same formal result. As a consequence, some of the recent objections that have been raised to the theory of expected utility can be adapted and applied to the utilitarian constructions as well.

I will end, however, on a more positive note. The criticisms I will develop leave untouched a quite different way of thinking about the utilitarian principle. It is plausible to think of it as an important but clearly subordinate principle—one that has a definite role to pay in the evaluation of at least some social policies.

SOME UTILITARIAN THEOREMS

Certain of the more recent axiomatic approaches to utilitarianism can be naturally connected with Arrow's striking theorem concerning the impossibility of a rational principle for the ordering of social alternatives. Arrow's theorem turns critically on a presupposition, implicit in the formulation of the independence of irrelevant alternative (IIA) axiom, that the preferences of individuals cannot be numerically represented in a way that makes interpersonal comparisons meaningful. With an appropriately reformulated version of IIA (as well as certain other of Arrow's axioms), and an explicit allowance for various kinds of interpersonal comparability, positive results can be obtained.[5]

The theorems in question all presuppose that the task is to find a social welfare function $W = F(\{W_i\})$ which specifies a unique social ordering R over the set X of social alternatives for any given n-tuple of real-valued "personal" welfare functions $W_i(.)$, each defined over X, for each person i in the society, where $N = \{1,\ldots,n\}$ is the set of such persons.[6] The social alternatives in question might, for example, consist of so many different ways in which income or wealth (or something else valued by persons) is distributed among different classes. (In what is to follow, I will take income as representative of a class of goods whose distribution is the object of social concern.) Correspondingly, within this context, utilitarianism can be characterized in the following manner:

Utilitarianism: For any pair of social alternatives x and y in X, $x\ R\ y$ if and only if

$$\sum_{i=1}^{n} W_i(x) \geq \sum_{i=1}^{n} W_i(y)$$

Consider, now, the following set of modified Arrovian conditions on social welfare functions:

1. Unrestricted Domain: The domain of F includes all logically possible welfare n-tuples.
2. Independence of Irrelevant Alternatives (IIA) (modified for this sort of framework): For any two welfare n-tuples $\{W_i\}$ and $\{W^*_i\}$, if for any pair x and y in X, $W_i(x) = W^*_i(x)$, and $W_i(y) = W^*_i(y)$, for all i, then $x\ R\ y$ if and only if $x\ R^*y$.
3. Strong Pareto Principle (a stronger version of Arrow's Pareto condition): For any pair x and y in X, if for all i: $W_i(x) \geqslant W_i(y)$, then $x\ R\ y$; and if, in addition, for some i: $W_i(x) > W_i(y)$, then $x\ P\ y$.
4. Anonymity (a stronger form of Arrow's Nondictatorship Condition): If $\{W^*_i\}$ is a reordering of the personal welfare n-tuple $\{W_i\}$, then $F\{W_i\} = F\{W^*_i\}$.

It is easy to show this set of conditions, together with the assumption that the W_i's are comparable with respect to unit of measurement, but not with respect to level—what is known as the cardinal unit (CU) comparability condition—entails the utilitarian rule. Alternatively, the utilitarian rule can be recovered by strengthening the comparability condition to cardinal full (CF) comparability, i.e., comparability with respect to both unit and level, and adding the following two conditions:[7]

5. Separability (With Respect to Unconcerned Individuals) (SEP): If for two welfare n-tuples $\{W_i\}$ and $\{W^*_i\}$, for all persons i in some subset of N: $W_i(x) = W^*_i(x)$ for all x in X, and for all persons j not in that subset of N: $W_j(x) = W_j(y)$ and $W^*_j(x) = W^*_j(y)$ for all x, y in X, then $R = R^*$.
6. Continuity (which serves to exclude certain lexicographical ordering rules).

As this last theorem makes clear, these results are very closely connected with the von Neumann and Morgenstern (1944) expected-utility construction.[8] Indeed, more generally yet, all of these theorems—both those pertaining to measurable utility and those pertaining to the utilitarian rule—are variations on a basic theorem in mathematics concerning the ordering of an n-dimensional vector space (see Blackwell and Girschick 1954, Section 4.3).

The constructions presented above presuppose very little regarding the nature of the Wi's except, in each case, the respects in which they are comparable. As such, they contrast sharply with an important pair of constructions due to Harsanyi (1953, 1955), which turn on the assumption that each Wi satisfies the conditions of expected-utility theory.

On the first of these—Harsanyi's axiomatic social welfare argument—utilitarianism follows from four very simple, but again allegedly plausible axioms:

1. Individual preferences satisfy the standard axioms of expected-utility theory (weak ordering, continuity, reduction, strong independence) (see, for example, Luce and Raiffa 1957, Chapter 2).
2. Social preferences satisfy the same axioms.
3. If all individuals are personally indifferent between two social options, then the social preference treats those two options indifferently.
4. The linear social welfare function implied by 1–3 is symmetric with respect to individual utilities, i.e., it treats different individuals equally.

The second of Harsanyi's constructions—the uncertainty choice argument—turns on supposing that the representative individual must choose between various social alternatives under conditions of complete uncertainty as to which position one will end up occupying. Complete uncertainty is interpreted by Harsanyi as meaning that the representative individual applies the principle of insufficient reason; i.e., one proceeds as if one is just as likely to end up being any particular person as any other. Against that background, Harsanyi is able to show that if the person's personal preferences for options satisfy the axioms of expected utility theory, then one must end up choosing so as to maximize the sum (or average) of the Wi's.[9]

THE PROBLEM OF EQUALITY

It has frequently been objected to utilitarianism that it is completely insensitive to inequalities in the interpersonal distribution of the sum of the Wi's (see, in particular, Sen 1973, 15–23). In very broad terms, the advocate of utilitarianism can reply that concern about inequality can be registered at another level, so that there is no need to give (special) weight to these concerns at the level of the evaluation of an n-tuples of individual welfare values. More specifically, a variety of plausible stories are available according to which income distributions that are more equal will be treated more favorably by the utilitarian rule.

The most frequently cited story has to do with the implications of assuming that each Wi is a strictly concave function of the income distributed to individual i, i.e., where decreasing marginal utility for income holds. This will ensure (in the presence of certain other assumptions) that redistributions of income from those who have more to those who have less will increase the sum total of welfare. If this serves to establish conditions under which utilitarianism will favor more rather than less equal distributions of income, it fails as a response to a quite distinct concern, namely, that the distribution of welfare among the members of society is also a relevant consideration. That is, on the account given, equality of income is mandated only insofar as this affects the sum total, as distinct from the distribution, of welfare.[10]

One might try to get around this objection by introducing an additional set of strictly concave transformations $W_i^* = F(W_i)$, for each i, and then defining one's utilitarian principle in terms of the maximization of the sum of the W_i^*'s. As Sen has noted, egalitarian concerns for the distribution of the original W_i's can now be accommodated (see Sen 1979, 471). W will still be an additive function of $\{W_i^*\}$, but a strictly concave function of $\{W_i\}$, and that last will ensure that a more equal dispersion among the components in $\{W_i\}$ will result in an increase in W, when the latter is defined as the sum of the W_i^*'s.

When the issue of inequality is treated in this fashion, however, with typically only a hand wave to the idea of taking concave transformations of the W_i's, one has the uneasy feeling that the point of all this is simply to "save" a sum-ranking approach to, rather than to develop a substantive principle for, the evaluation of social alternatives. In this respect, one is reminded of the legacy from D. Bernoulli: the idea that a simple sum-ranking rule for ordering gambles can be "saved" by introducing a function that transforms income amount into utility, and then aggregates with respect to these values.[11]

One can also mark here an important parallel to modern utility theory for individual decision making. The latter theory allegedly allows for any degree of risk aversion with regard to probability distributions over monetary amounts. Such risk aversion simply determines the degree of concavity of the agent's utility function for independently considered sure amounts of money. The degree of risk aversion, then, is a matter about which the individual must decide for himself: the decision theorist simply reminds the agent that once he has settled that question, a rational approach to choice presupposes application of the standard expectation rule, not to monetary amounts, but to these risk-reflecting "utilities" for money. In a similar fashion, the modern utilitarian theory leaves it up to society to decide how much attention to pay to egalitarian (dispersion) considerations. And, once this is decided, the recommendation is simply that policy should be chosen so as to maximize an additive function over the "values" that encode whatever degree of egalitarian commitment society has. Where the parallel breaks down, however, is that while it is intelligible (and perhaps even plausible) to leave it to each individual to settle for oneself how risk-averse one wants to be, it isn't clear what it means to leave it to "society" to decide how much attention is to be paid to equality.[12]

Moreover, in each case, nothing is offered by way of rationale for the summation rule approach. This is worrisome. Even if the introduction of strictly concave transformations of the original W_i's enables one to retain a simple additive rule while registering concern for the dispersion among the components of $\{W_i\}$, still additivity presupposes satisfaction of a separability or independence condition, and that condition is restrictive. In particular, it precludes registering dispersion in terms of, say, the Gini Coefficient or average deviation from the mean (i.e., in terms of non-squared or linear measures of deviation).[13]

A QUESTIONABLE AXIOMATIC PRESUPPOSITION

Regardless of how restrictive the separability condition is, it is either an explicit axiom or an implicit presupposition of each of the constructions outlined in the section "Some Utilitarian Theorems."[14] If any such construction, then, is to have more than purely formal significance (i.e., to be more than a representation theorem regarding the measurability of utility or social welfare, given that certain hypothetical conditions are satisfied), some motivation for this condition must be offered.

One possible argument, of course, would be that the condition is, as a matter of fact, satisfied by the choice behavior of nearly all, or most, decision makers. However, as the discussions to be found in Ellsberg (1961), Diamond (1967), Tversky (1975), Kahneman and Tversky (1979), Allais and Hagen (1979), McClennen (1981), Tversky and Kahneman (1981), and Machina (1981, 1982) suggest, it is doubtful that there is anything remotely like a consensus on this axiom, for either individual or social choice, even among theorists. Alternatively then, one may try to argue that the axiom is bound up with, or implied in some fashion or other, by an explicitly normative conception of rational choice; that rational agents should, insofar as they are rational, accept this as a condition governing their ordering of social or individual options.

Now it is clear that many have thought that separability (independence) is a requirement on rational choice (see, for example, Samuelson 1952; Friedman and Savage 1952; Raiffa 1961, 1970, 80–86; Marschak 1968). But, this is due, I think, to an unfortunate confusion with regard tothe way the condition is usually motivated. As it is typically presented, separability can be secured by appeal to a dominance condition. However, there is a tendency to gloss the notion of dominance in a manner that leads the casual reader to confuse a highly intuitive, simple dominance condition (dominance with respect to "sure" outcomes) with a much stronger, and by no means so intuitively secure, extended dominance condition. But, as a careful inspection of any of a number of formal constructions reveals, what is required is the extended dominance condition.

Here, for example, is how one theorist (Harsanyi 1978, 224) explicates the dominance principle as it applies to individual choice: "Other things being equal, a rational individual will not prefer a lottery yielding less desirable prizes over a lottery yielding more desirable prizes." If one understands "prizes" to be something like "sure outcomes," that is, monetary awards, or other sorts of goods, then the principle is compelling; it could be said to speak to nothing more than what it means to maximize. Unfortunately, for the theorem to go through, one needs to invoke the principle in a considerably extended form: the principle must also hold for lotteries over lotteries. And, given that much more general formulation, it is simply not at all so intuitively compelling. As Allais and Ellsberg argued decades ago, the extended (but not the simple) version is subject to a number of bothersome counter examples.[15]

Once the extended version (and with it the required separability condition) is logically distinguished from the more limited and admittedly secure version of the dominance condition, the status of separability as a rationality condition can immediately be called into question. In turn, this serves to cast doubt, for example, on both of Harsanyi's constructions (as well as the expected-utility result itself). And, once doubts of this sort have taken root, one is bound to wonder also whether separability of the social ordering is a plausible condition on a normative theory of social rationality. This means, of course, that the remaining constructions must now be questioned as well.

AN ALTERNATIVE, AND MORE POSITIVE, SUGGESTION

Despite these cautionary thoughts, I think there is a line of reasoning that can be used to show that the utilitarian principle has a place in a rational approach to social policy and, moreover, it is a line of reasoning that invokes the concept of choice under conditions of uncertainty (or risk). The argument I have in mind is one that Rawls briefly sketches in *A Theory of Justice* (1971), but it can also be seen to constitute a natural extension of an argument Buchanan and Tullock (1962) offer concerning conditions under which rational persons would be willing to agree to a majoritarian principle of voting.[16] They argue that one must expect that if social decisions can be made with less-than-unanimous consent, then policies will be implemented that work to one's disadvantage, whereas under a unanimity rule, of course, one has veto power over any policy that would disadvantage one's self. However, the decision-making costs associated with the operation of the unanimity rule are significant, as measure both in terms of the expenditure of time and other resources to reach compromise agreements that will win the support of all and in terms of opportunity costs. If these decision-making costs are sufficiently high, it will be in one's interest to support less-than-unanimity voting rules. The key argument here explicitly invokes the concept of uncertainty.

> Essential to the analysis is the presumption that the individual is uncertain as to what his own precise role will be in any one of a whole chain of later collective choices that will actually have to be made. For this reason, the individual is considered not to have a particular and distinguishable interest separate and apart from his fellows. This is not to suggest that the individual will act contrary to his own interests; however, the individual will not find it advantageous to vote for rules that may promote sectional, class, or group interests because, by presupposition, he is unable to predict the role he will be playing in the actual collective decision-making process at any particular time in the future. The individual cannot predict with any degree of certainty whether he is more likely to be in a winning or a losing coalition on any specific issue. Therefore, he will assume that occasionally he will be in one group and occasionally in the other. His own self-interest will lead him to choose rules that will maximize the utility of an individual in a series of collective decisions with his own preferences on the separate issues being more or less randomly distributed (Buchanan and Tullock 1962, 78).

Now, it is plausible that under somewhat analogous conditions individuals would agree to the use of a utilitarian calculus. Insofar as one desires to see one's own interests promoted, but is uncertain as to just what one's own specific interests will be on any given occasion, it might well find it to be advantageous to support the operation of a rule that requires the maximization of the sum of utilities (or income, or some other specific measure of value). Recognizing that the operation of such a rule will mean that on some occasions one's own interests will be sacrificed for the greater interests of others, still the expectation will be that over the long run one will be a net gainer, that one will be more often on the advantaged than on the disadvantaged side given the operation of this principle.

To the extent that any such defense of a utilitarian rule for policy decisions can be constructed, however, it would be subject to precisely the same qualifications to which Buchanan and Tullock subject the majoritarian voting principle. It is central to the argument they construct that it is rational for individuals to agree to a constitution, to the specification of different decision-making rules for different classes of policy matters. That is, it will be rational to support a simple majoritarian rule for cases in which substantial issues are not at stake, but to insist on something more approximating a rule of unanimity for cases in which the costs of an adverse decision could turn out to be prohibitively high. In that latter category, they suggest, will be policy decisions that modify or restrict the structure of individual human and property rights:

> The relevant point is that the individual will foresee that collective action in this area may possibly impose very severe costs on himself. In such cases, the individual will tend to place a high value on the attainment of his consent, and he may be quite willing to undergo substantial decision-making costs to insure that he will, in fact, be reasonably protected against confiscation (Buchanan and Tullock 1962, 73–74).

By extension, then, we may also suppose that insofar as persons would be willing to agree to the operation of a utilitarian sum-ranking rule, they would also find it prudent to restrict it to only certain types of policy issues. Roughly speaking, that some version of a utilitarian type sum-ranking rule might be selected as the appropriate rule for middle-level decision making in which one's fundamental interests or rights are not at stake in any substantial way, and where one expects a sufficiently large number of more or less similar issues to be settled by the use of the rule—issues on which one's own position is likely to be more or less randomly distributed and, hence, where one can at least expect, over the long run, that things will balance out to one's advantage (Buchanan and Tullock 1962, 73–74). On this sort of account, then, the utilitarian rule has a place, but it is not the fundamental principle in terms of which social policies are to be evaluated; in particular, it can only be applied subject to significant rights-based side-constraints.[17]

By way of bringing these speculative thoughts to a close, let me remark that the decade of the 1970s witnessed two extraordinarily articulate presentations of the case against the conception of an unlimited scope for a utilitarian principle: one set forth by Rawls (1971) and the other by Dworkin (1977). To be sure, as many have read the debate that followed the publication of Rawls' work, there is something inconclusive about the argument from behind the veil of ignorance.[18] And, again, while Dworkin's brief for a theory of rights that sets constraints on the operation of a utilitarian principle is powerfully advocated, his own argument makes, I think, altogether too much of an appeal to intuition. The line of reasoning I have pursued here, based on Rawls' own remarks and on Buchanan and Tullock's (1962) argument in *The Calculus of Consent*, offers, I think, a more secure ground for Dworkin's intuitions about the place of rights in a theory of public policy, and it also serves as a reminder that even if Rawls' argument from behind the veil of ignorance does not yield his own theory of justice, it still serves to effectively underline his objections to an unconstrained utilitarian principle.

NOTES

1. Edward F. McClennen is Regents Scholar in Moral and Social Philosophy at Bowling Green State University.

2. For an excellent treatment of this development, see Halevy (1928).

3. Usually the first development is traced back to Quine (1951). See, in particular, White (1956, Part III, especially pages 254–58, 263, and 266f) and Rawls (1951, 1971, especially Section 87).

4. The sense of this revived interest can be taken by consulting, for example, Smart and Williams (1973), Miller and Williams (1982), and Sen and Williams (1982); the last two also contain excellent bibliographies. The axiomatic constructions are outlined in the next section of this paper.

5. For a sense of how restrictive the original formulation of IIA is, Arrow's original work (1951) must be supplemented by Arrow (1977). The constructive results of particular relevance to the present discussion are due primarily to the work of Harsanyi (1953, 1955), d'Aspremont and Gevers (1977), Deschamps and Gevers (1978), Hammond (1976), and Maskin (1978). They are analyzed in a most perspicacious manner by Sen (1977).

6. Following Sen (1970, 1977), these are more properly characterized as functionals. For the sake of keeping the exposition as simple as possible, I shall pass over this important distinction. I adopt the usual conventions and let *R* stand for weak preference (strict-preference or indifference), and *P* for strict preference.

7. This last is due to Maskin (1978). See also Sen (1977, 1540–50) for a presentation of both of these and a number of other related theorems.

8. Explicit recognition of the connection is to be found in, for example, Maskin (1979) and Harsanyi (1978).

9. As suggested previously, these constructions are all connected in a formal sense with the expected-utility theorem itself. Harsanyi's uncertainty argument, of course, explicitly converts the social-choice problem into a problem of individual decision making under conditions of uncertainty. The anonymity condition employed in the first two theorems parallels the symmetry condition that Harsanyi employs in the social-choice argument, and each of these is related to the assumption in Harsanyi's uncertainty argument that one is just as likely to end up being any particular person as any other. But, all of these assumptions, in turn, amount to introducing a specific weighting system and, as such, they are related to a principle that is central to the expected-utility construction, namely, that the agent is able to assign well-defined probabilities (weights) to all conditioning events, and that these weights are relevant for the evaluation of options. Moreover, all of the constructions discussed—pertaining to social choice or to individual choice—implicitly or explicitly impose a weak ordering and a separability (i.e., independence) axiom and, in all but one case, a continuity axiom.

10. See, for example, Sen (1973, 18–19). Similar objections can be levelled against another possible story, namely, that those who are treated less equally will have a disincentive to act in a productively cooperative manner. In contrast, consider the story that the individual *Wi*'s can be taken to reflect at least some positive concern on the part of individuals for equality; that is, that each *Wi can be understood to be a function of the distribution of income to all, and not simply to the ith* person. This incorporates concern for the distributive aspects of policies as such, but it has the disadvantage of making concern for equality dependent upon a de facto direct commitment on the part of the members of society to egalitarian redistributive shifts. That is, it incorporates egalitarianism into the social welfare function by building it into the personal preferences of the members of society.

11. See Bernoulli ([1730–31] 1954). Bernoulli introduced the concept of "utility" in order to save the principle of evaluating gambles in terms of their expected monetary return from a serious counter-example. The example calls for a fair coin to be flipped until heads comes up, where the person who purchases the gamble is to receive $2*n*, *n* being the number of the trial on which heads first occurs. It is easily shown that this gamble has infinite expected monetary return and, thus, should be purchased regardless of the price at which it is offered. Bernoulli suggested that the expectation rule could be salvaged by taking expectation with respect to the "value" of each possible monetary payoff, rather than with respect to the quantity of the money involved, and by assuming diminishing marginal value for increasing amounts of money. Bernoulli's move prefigures the modern theory of expected utility, for which, once again, the fixed point is the notion that the value of any gamble is equivalent to its expected value.

12. For reasons that relate closely to the discussion in a section following called "An Alternative, and More Positive, Suggestion." it is not at all obvious that this is a matter that should be settled by democratic voting!

13. Space considerations preclude my doing justice to this rather complicated matter. Sen (1973, 33–34 [including footnotes 9, 10, 11], 39–41) is useful in this regard, but more needs to be said. That such additivity is incompatible with registering dispersion in terms of the Gini Coefficient is due to Newbery (1970). See also McClennen (1981).

14. It figures only implicitly in the first of the Arrovian constructions, but is, in fact, implied by the comparability condition CU. See d'Aspremont and Gevers (1977, 203).

15. See Allais and Hagen (1979) and Ellsberg (1961). See also McClennen (1983, Section 5; 1990, Section 4.7) for a much fuller discussion of the problem of justifying the extended version of dominance.

16. See Rawls (1971, 170–71). Rawls traces this line of reasoning back to Edgeworth (1888, 52–56).

17. Rawls concludes that "at best . . . the principle of utility has a subordinate place as a legislative standard for lesser questions of policy." It would also seem that when the principle is restricted in this way, it is better construed as a principle governing distributions of income (or other goods that are "objectively" measurable), rather than as a principle of aggregating utilities.

18. See, for example, Harsanyi's (1975) rejoinder to Rawls, and also McClennen (1981).

REFERENCES

Allais, M., and O. Hagen. 1979. *Expected utility and the Allais Paradox*. Dordrecht: Reidel.

Arrow, K. J. 1963. *Social choice and individual values*. 2d ed. New York: Wiley and Sons.

_____1977. Extended sympathy and the possibility of social choice. *American Economic Review* (supplementary issue of the proceedings): 219–25.

Bernoulli, D. [1730–31] 1954. Exposition of a new theory on the measurement of risk. Translated into English by L. Sommer from Specimen theoreiae novae de mensura sortis in *Commentaarii academiae scientiarum imperialis* 5:175–92. *Econometrica* 22:23–26.

Blackwell, D., and M. Girschick. 1954. *Theory of games and statistical decisions*. New York: Wiley and Sons.

Buchanan, J., and Gordon Tullock. 1962. *The calculus of consent*. Ann Arbor: University of Michigan Press.

d'Aspremont, C., and L. Gevers. 1977. Equity and the informational basis of collective choice. *Review of Economic Studies* 44:199–209.

Deschamps, R., and L. Gevers. 1978. Leximin and utilitarian rules: A joint characterization. *Journal of Economic Theory* 17:143–63.

Diamond, P. A. 1967. Cardinal welfare, individualistic ethics, and interpersonal comparisons of utility: A comment. *Journal of Political Economy* 75:765–66.

Dworkin, R. 1977. *Taking rights seriously*. London: Duckworth.

Edgeworth, F. Y. 1888. *Mathematical physics*. London: C. K. Paul.

Ellsberg, D. 1961. Risk, ambiguity, and the Savage axioms. *Quarterly Journal of Economics* 75:643–69.

Friedman, M., and L. J. Savage. 1952. The expected-utility hypothesis and the measurability of utility. *Journal of Political Economy* 60:463–74.

Halevy, Elie. 1928. *The growth of philosophical radicalism*. New York: Macmillan.

Hammond, P. J. 1976. Equity, Arrow's conditions and Rawls' difference principle. *Econometrica* 44:793–800.

Harsanyi, J. 1953. Cardinal utility in welfare economics and the theory of risk-taking. *Journal of Political Economy* 61:434–35.

_____1955. Cardinal welfare, individualistic ethics, and interpersonal comparisons of utility. *Journal of Political Economy* 63:309–21.

_____1975. Can the maximum principle serve as the basis for morality? A critique of John Rawls' theory. *American Political Science Review* 69:594–606.

_____1978. Bayesian decision theory and utilitarian ethics. *American Economic Review* 68:223–28.

Kahneman, D., and A. Tversky. 1979. Prospect theory: An analysis of decision under risk. *Econometrica* 47:263–91.

Luce, R. D., and H. Raiffa. 1957. *Games and decisions*. New York: Wiley and Sons.

Machina, M. 1981. "Rational" decision making versus "rational" decision modelling? *Journal of Mathematical Psychology* 24:163–75.

_____1982. "Expected utility" analysis without the independence axiom. *Econometrica* 50:277–323.

Marschak, J. 1968. Decision making: Economic aspects. In *International Encyclopedia of the Social Sciences*. Vol. 4. New York: Macmillan.

Maskin, E. 1978. A theorem on utilitarianism. *Review of Economic Studies* 45:93–96.

_____1979. Decision-making under ignorance with implications for social choice. *Theory and Decision* 2:319–37.

McClennen, E. 1981. Constitutional choice: Rawls vs. Harsanyi. In *Philosophy in economics*. Edited by J. Pitts, 93–109. Dordrecht: Reidel.

_____1983. Sure-thing doubts. In *Foundations of utility and risk theory with applications*. Edited by B. P. Stigum et al., 117–36. Dordrecht: Reidel. Also reprinted with addendum in *Decision, probability and utility: Selected readings, 1988*. Edited by P. Gardenfors and N. Sahlin, 166–82. Cambridge: Cambridge University Press.

_____1988. Dynamic choice and rationality. In *Risk, decision and rationality*. Edited by B. R. Munier, 517–36. Dordrecht: Reidel.

_____1990. *Rationality and dynamic choice: Foundational explorations*. Cambridge: Cambridge University Press.

Miller, H. B., and W. H. Williams. 1982. *The limits of utilitarianism*. Minneapolis: University of Minnesota Press.

Newbery, D. 1970. A theorem on the measurement of inequality. *Journal of Economic Theory* 2:264–66.

Quine, W. V. O. 1951. Two dogmas of empiricism. *Philosophical Review* 60.

Raiffa, H. 1961. Risk, ambiguity and Savage axioms: Comment. *Quarterly Journal of Economics* 75:690–94.

_____1970. *Decision analysis*. Reading, Mass.: Addison-Wesley.

Rawls, J. 1951. Outline of a decision procedure for ethics. *Philosophical Review* 60:177–97.

_____1971. *A theory of justice*. Cambridge: Harvard University Press.

Robbins, L. 1932. *An essay on the nature and significance of economic science*. London: Macmillan.

Samuelson, P. 1952. Probability, utility, and the independence axiom. *Econometrica* 20.

Sen, A. 1970. *Collective choice and social welfare*. San Francisco: Holden Day.

_____1973. *On economic inequality*. Oxford: Oxford University Press.

_____1977. On weights and measures: Informational constraints in social welfare analysis. *Econometrica* 45:1540–71.

_____1979. Utilitarianism and welfarism. *Journal of Philosophy* 76:463–89.

Sen, A., and B. Williams. 1982. *Utilitarianism and beyond*. Cambridge: Cambridge University Press.

Smart, J. J. C., and B. A. O. Williams. 1973. *Utilitarianism: For and against*. Cambridge: Cambridge University Press.

Tversky, A. 1975. A critique of expected utility theory: Descriptive and normative considerations. *Erkenntnis* 9:163–73.

Tversky, A., and D. Kahneman. 1981. The framing of decisions and the psychology of choice. *Science* 211:453–58.

von Neumann, J., and O. Morgenstern. 1944. *Theory of games and economic behavior*. Princeton: Princeton University Press.

White, M. 1956. *Toward reunion in philosophy*. Cambridge: Harvard University Press.

CHAPTER 3

PROGRESS MADE AND ADVANCES NEEDED IN SOCIAL INDICATORS AND SOCIAL ACCOUNTING RESEARCH OF POTENTIAL VALUE IN RESEARCHING RURAL ISSUES AND PROBLEMS

Karl A. Fox

INTRODUCTION

The "social indicators" movement in the United States was initiated in the 1960s by some outstanding social scientists. They sought a massive expansion in published data systems relevant to the analysis of social trends; the development of time-series "indicators" to measure progress, or the lack of it, towards the goals of social policies in such areas as health, education, public safety, and others; and the promotion of research on problems relating to the measurement of all aspects of "the quality of life."

While progress has been made toward all three objectives, the methodological issues have been essentially the same for rural as for urban residents and areas.

Leaders of the social indicators movement also had a fourth objective, that of developing a national system of "social accounts," analogous to the economists' national income and product accounts (NIPA) but much more inclusive. The central concept of the NIPAs is that of the "gross national product" or GNP. Together with closely related data, these accounts can summarize the state of the U.S. economy as a whole at any given time. "Social accounts" when fully developed could presumably summarize the state of the society as a whole.

Gross (1966, 271) asserted that "the maturation of social accounting concepts will take many decades" and will require "the participation of social scientists from many disciplines and the breaking down of many language barriers among them." To the best of my knowledge, few social scientists have been working toward the goal of social accounting in Gross's interdisciplinary sense.

After reviewing progress toward all four objectives, will devote the rest of this paper to the following propositions:

1. Economy and realism require that the "social accounting" methods first be developed and tested for small communities, and then for successively larger ones, in nonmetropolitan regions;
2. A promising conceptual framework for community surveys has been developed and applied to small communities by Roger Barker and his associates since the early 1950s;
3. I have shown that Barker's concepts can be linked with standard economic data systems on industries and occupations and his surveys augmented to yield aggregative estimates of time use by various age groups and other categories of community residents;
4. My work and Barker's are compatible with long-established traditions of community studies by rural sociologists and of household and family studies by home economists; and
5. Cooperation among these and other rural social scientists in developing a practical interdisciplinary social-accounting system will almost certainly deepen our understanding of the combined economic, social, psychological, cultural, and physical resources of rural communities of sizes up to and including multicounty functional economic areas. The effort will foster more interdisciplinary research and may lead to major advances in several of the basic social science disciplines. It should certainly break down language barriers among serious participants in the research and promote a common scientific vocabulary.

CONCRETE EXAMPLES OF SOCIAL INDICATORS: THE OECD LIST (1982)

The phrase "social indicators" has been used in many different ways. To focus ideas, it seems best to begin with a specific set of indicators published by the Organization for Economic Cooperation and Development (OECD) in 1982.

TABLE 1: THE OECD LIST OF SOCIAL INDICATORS

Social Concern	Indicator
Health	
Length of Life	—Life Expectancy —Perinatal Mortality Rate
Healthfulness of Life	—Short-Term Disability —Long-Term Disability
Education and Learning	
Use of Educational Facilities	—Regular Education Experience —Adult Education
Learning	—Literacy Rate
Employment and Quality of Working Life	
Availability of Employment	—Unemployment Rate —Involuntary Part-Time Work —Discouraged Workers
Quality of Working Life	—Average Working Hours —Travel Time to Work —Paid Annual Leave —Atypical Work Schedule —Distribution of Earnings —Fatal Occupational Injuries —Work Environment Nuisances
Time and Leisure	
Use of Time	—Free Time —Free Time Activities
Command Over Goods and Services	
Income	—Distribution of Income —Low Income —Material Deprivation
Wealth	—Distribution of Wealth
Physical Environment	
Housing Conditions	—Indoor Dwelling Space —Access to Outdoor Space —Basic Amenities
Accessibility to Services	—Proximity of Selected Services
Environmental Nuisances	—Exposure to Air Pollutants —Exposure to Noise
Social Environment	
Social Attachment	—Suicide Rate
Personal Safety	
Exposure to Risk	—Fatal Injuries —Serious Injuries
Perceived Threat	—Fear for Personal Safety

Source: Organization for Economic Cooperation and Development, 1982, *The OECD List of Social Indicators* (Paris: OECD).

Members of the OECD include the United States, Canada, Japan, Australia, New Zealand, and 19 countries of Western and Southern Europe. In 1970, representatives of several countries asked the OECD staff to work toward a standard set of social indicators that would be acceptable to, and implemented by, each of the member countries. The standard set proposed in 1982 is shown in Table 1.

The OECD List of Social Indicators (1982) will be highly influential during at least the next few years. The list includes 33 specific indicators grouped under eight social concerns: health, education and learning, employment and quality of working life, time and leisure, command over goods and services, physical environment, social environment, and personal safety.

These indicators are designed to measure trends in individual well-being. In most cases they are social outcomes or output (for example, "health") as distinct from actual or potential inputs (for example, hospital beds or physicians per thousand persons). The emphasis on measurable changes in the well-being of individuals is crucial, for the potential input may be underutilized and/or misdirected.

Carley (1981, 2) says that social indicators are surrogates or proxies for unmeasurable social concepts. For example, the social concern "health" in the OECD list is represented by four indicators: life expectancy, perinatal mortality rate (infant deaths at birth or shortly after), short-term disability, and long-term disability. If life expectancy increases, we say "health" has improved; we say the same if one or more of the other three indicators decrease. A great many specific diseases, hazards, and habits are reflected in these four indicators, but "health" itself remains an abstract concept. Clearly, medical scientists and public-health officials need (and have) much more detailed data than the four indicators. But the purpose of the OECD list as a whole is to provide a clear overview of progress (or the lack of it) in all eight areas of social concern. An average of four or five indicators per area may be more useful for this purpose than would a larger number.

The national average or summary indicators in Table 1 are to be supplemented by various disaggregations. The 1982 OECD report recommends that five standard disaggregations be used in presenting nearly all indicators: age, sex, household type, socioeconomic status, and community size. It suggests optional "standard" disaggregations by ethnic group and citizenship in countries where these distinctions are relevant and also by region (i.e., by geographical location within a country) according to the classifications customary in each country.

The OECD report lists other disaggregations applicable to several indicators: branch of economic activity, occupation, type of activity, working hours, level of education, tenure status (home owner versus tenant), and age of dwelling. It states that the breakdown of branch of economic activity should be based on the International Standard Industrial Classification (ISIC) codes at the two-digit level; that of occupation should follow the International Standard Classification of Occupations (ISCO) at the two-digit level, with three digits used where possible in coding occupational groups with a wide range of occupations such as managers; and that of levels of education should follow the International Standard Classification of Education (ISCED) which defines seven levels of education plus a residual category. The corresponding classifications used in the United States are closely comparable to the international codes cited.

It should be noted that 32 of the OECD indicators are objective, based on events and conditions that can be counted or measured by neutral observers. Only one indicator, "fear for personal safety," is subjective, based on the individual's own statements concerning one's feelings or attitudes. It seems appropriate for government statistical agencies to concentrate on objectively measurable phenomena.

RELATIONS OF THE OECD LIST TO VARIOUS OBJECTIVES OF THE SOCIAL-INDICATORS MOVEMENT

In the introduction, we cited four early objectives of the social-indicators movement: (1) a massive expansion of social-data systems, (2) the development of time-series indicators to measure progress (or lack of it) toward social policy goals, (3) the promotion of research on problems of measuring all aspects of "the quality of life," and (4) the development of a comprehensive system of social accounts.

The OECD list suggests that these objectives were highly complementary or mutually supportive. Annual data on most of the specific indicators over a ten-year period would measure movement toward or away from some plausible goals of social policies (Objective 2). Selection of these time series as indicators of the social performance of different nations has encouraged the expansion of social-data systems in all or most areas of concern and improvements in their timeliness, accuracy, and conformity to explicit definitions (Objective 1).

The OECD list helps to clarify some problems of measuring "the quality of life" (Objective 3). Suppose a government agency were to define an equally weighted index of the 33 indicators as "the Quality of Life (QOL) Index" and invite suggestions for improving it. Those who took the invitation at face value might suggest the inclusion of additional indicators, changes in the relative weights given to the existing indicators, and further specific modifications.

Others might reject the entire set of indicators (and, hence, the QOL index) as being too materialistic. They might argue that "the quality of life" is a subjective matter: To what extent are people "satisfied" or "happy" with the way their lives are going? The answers, they say, are to be found by interviewing, or sending questionnaires to, samples of individuals. We will comment briefly on this approach in a later section.

The OECD list also helps clarify some tasks of social accounting (Objective 4). We will defer comment until a later section.

SOME HISTORICAL COMMENTS ON THE SOCIAL-INDICATORS MOVEMENT

Space does not permit a long discussion of the social-indicators movement. It was stimulated by the dramatic change in national priorities when Kennedy succeeded Eisenhower as president in 1961. Kennedy's "New Frontier" initiatives in 1961–63 and Lyndon Johnson's "Great Society" drive of 1964–68 involved a massive expansion of programs in education, health care, social security, urban redevelopment, and community, regional, and area development—among others. The space program announced by President Kennedy in 1961 to place American astronauts on the moon within a decade implied revolutionary developments in science and technology.

Some outstanding social scientists recognized, at once, that existing data systems were totally inadequate to monitor the new programs and answer the questions their administrators were sure to face. In 1962, some of these social scientists received a grant from the National Aeronautics and Space Administration (NASA) to study the problems and difficulties of anticipating the secondary effects of the space program on American society. The foreword to their impressive and influential book *Social Indicators* (Bauer 1966) said that "our highly developed national system of economic indicators . . . needs to be supplemented by an equivalent set of indicators that will provide us with information on the state of our society in those areas not usually subject to quantitative measurement or within the professional domain of the economist" (vii-viii).

We have already cited four substantive objectives of these social scientists. For a time they also pushed an instrumental objective: the passage of a bill entitled "The Full Opportunity and Social Accounting Act of 1967" which would have established a Council of Social Advisers (CSA) and mandated an annual *Social Report of the President* to Congress. The parallel with the Council of Economic Advisers and its annual *Economic Report of the President* was intentional.

Two of the scientists, Philip Hauser and Bertram Gross, had held responsible positions in the U.S. Bureau of the Census and the Council of Economic Advisers, respectively. Evidently, they hoped that the CSA would spearhead a rapid but orderly expansion of social data systems.

The bill was not passed and no Council of Social Advisers was created. However, several agencies took actions to improve their own data systems. Sample survey techniques were improving and becoming more accessible, directly and indirectly, to such agencies. Some agencies supported research on data and social-indicator problems by university scientists and consulting firms. From about 1964, graduate students in sociology were increasingly well trained in quantitative methods, including the "path analysis" methods of Sewall Wright which emphasized the estimation of cause-and-effect relationships in systems of several or many variables. As these young sociologists moved up in universities, government agencies, and the private sector, they increased the demand for better data.

On the specific topic of social indicators, the National Science Foundation (NSF) funded, and the Social Science Research Council (SSRC) administered, a Center for the Coordination of Social Indicators Research, which was active from 1973 to 1981. Through its newsletter, and through sponsoring workshops and publishing their proceedings, this Center promoted a widespread understanding of social-measurement problems among members of several disciplines.

The idea of a "social report" to be prepared and published by government statistical agencies, and not requiring the signatures and endorsements of presidents or prime ministers, appealed to government statisticians in many countries. In the early 1970s, the governments of several countries started publishing collections of descriptive statistics under such titles as *Social Trends* (United Kingdom) or *Social Indicators* (United States). By 1981, most of the OECD countries had published at least one such report. This widespread interest in "social reporting" contributed to the development of *The OECD List of Social Indicators* (1982) already described.We will not try to summarize progress in subjective measures of "the quality of life." The journal *Social Indicators Research*, founded in 1974, publishes "research dealing with problems relating to the measurement of all aspects of the quality of life" (copyright page, June 1988). In this context, both objective and subjective indicators are regarded as measures of "the quality of life."

Subjective measures are obtained by asking people questions. The answers evidently have two components: cognitive (reasoned) and affective (felt). Questions about degree of "satisfaction" with one's life situation elicit reasoned responses involving comparisons with others and/or realistic possibilities for improvement. Answers to questions about degree of "happiness" reflect directly experienced feelings. Thus, Campbell, Converse, and Rodgers (1976, 36–37) found that older people (on the average) rated themselves lower than young ones on "happiness" but higher on "life satisfaction."

We do not know how stable these subjective measures are over time or to what extent they are responsive to changes in the levels of logically related objective indicators such as those in the OECD list.

CONTRIBUTIONS BY TERLECKYJ AND STONE, 1975

As of 1967, Gross, Hauser, and others hoped that a Council of Social Advisers (CSA) would enlist outstanding social scientists in a coordinated effort to produce a sound national system of social indicators. No CSA was established, and no coordinated effort materialized for several years. Meanwhile, "social indicators" had become a popular catch-phrase and various people sought to supply the apparent demand for them. Hence, much of the work done in the name of "social indicators" in the late 1960s and early 1970s was badly fragmented, eclectic, and atheoretical. It had little connection with the basic social sciences and most of its authors were not social scientists.

In 1974–75, some highly disciplined works appeared, written by economists who were sympathetic to the original objectives of the social-indicators movement. I will mention two of these works, Terleckyj (1975) and Stone (1975), in this section and the third, Fox (1974), in the next.

In his report *Improvements in the Quality of Life* (1975), Nestor Terleckyj selected, for the United States, 23 objective indicators like those in the OECD list; he called them "goal-output indicators." For each indicator, he estimated the maximum increase theoretically attainable by 1983—for example, an increase of 8.9 years in life expectancy. These increases were to be accomplished by specific programs that he selected in consultation with leading experts.

Terleckyj estimated the ten-year cost of achieving the maximum increases in all 23 indicators as equivalent to two-years' GNP—far more than was likely to be available for these purposes. He, therefore, specified lesser increases in the goal-output indicators (for example, 30 percent of the maximum possible increases) and estimated the least-cost combination of program levels that would achieve the reduced goals.

The important point for our purposes is that Terleckyj treated objective social indicators as output that could be produced deliberately by carefully designed programs. Each program required specified input: doctors, teachers, equipment, supplies, space rentals, new structures, educational publications, media advertising, and so on as the case might be. The programs involved coordinated activities by appropriate types of individuals, using appropriate types of supplies and equipment, in appropriate physical surroundings.

Richard Stone prepared a volume of 300 large two-column pages on behalf of the United Nations: *Towards a System of Social and Demographic Statistics* (1975). Stone had played a leading role in the development of national income and product accounts since 1939, first for the United Kingdom and later for the United Nations and the Organization for European Economic Cooperation, a predecessor of the OECD. In Stone (1971), he used accounting principles to project the movements of various age groups through the educational system and the labor force. Stone received the Nobel Prize in Economic Science in 1984.

Stone (1975, 21) presents a diagram outlining his system of social and demographic statistics; it contains 19 "boxes" or components. Eight of these are classified as *national-accounts statistics*: (1) production accounts, (2) leisure-services accounts, (3) social security and welfare-services accounts, (4) housing-capital accounts, (5) educational-services accounts, (6) employment-services accounts, (7) health-services accounts, and (8) public order and safety accounts. Nine other components (boxes) are described as *sociodemographic statistics*: (9) population size and composition, (10) social class, stratification, and mobility, (11) leisure, (12) housing conditions, (13) families and households, (14) learning activities, (15) earning activities and the inactive, (16) health, and (17) delinquency. A third category, *distribution-accounts statistics*, contains a single box, (18) distribution accounts, and the last category, *time-accounts statistics*, also contains one box, (19) time accounts.

Some boxes are connected with others by solid lines, indicating that the data in the two or more components are "integrated"; broken lines between boxes indicate that those components "are more loosely connected."

Government statisticians, as of 1975, held that Stone's complete system (call it SSDS) was too complicated to be implemented in the near future by any country. However, it sets a standard for logical consistency in data systems which ought to "add up" and encourages efforts to reduce errors and eliminate gaps in coverage.

Stone's 1975 report is a distinguished contribution towards the expansion and improvement of social data systems. However, Stone does not attempt to define specific data series as "social indicators" or measures of well-being. He does not draw on the theories of any discipline, apart from the logic of accounting.

Terleckyj (1975) also refrains from theorizing. He selects social indicators on a common-sense basis: for example, almost everyone would agree that increasing life expectancy is a good thing to do. Experts advise him that the maximum feasible increase from 1973 to 1983 would be 8.9 years (i.e., even with almost unlimited funds, medical science, people's habits, and health-care systems could not improve more than that in the next decade). Then Terleckyj and the experts spell out the technical means by which the feasible increase could be attained.

CONTRIBUTIONS BY FOX, 1974

Social Indicators and Social Theory: Elements of an Operational System is the title of a book I wrote in 1973 and published in 1974. It has a strong accounting emphasis and should perhaps have been labeled "social *accounts* and social theory," but "social indicators" was the generic name of the field and the one that would more likely reach my intended readership.

Glenn Johnson (1986, 139–48) has described my research leading up to this book and I have described it myself in Fox (1986). I had admired efforts by Boulding, Simon, and others to promote a closer integration of the social sciences, and my service on the board of directors of the Social Science Research Council (1963–67) had encouraged me to extend my own reach. Gross's (1966) scenario for the development of social-systems accounting seemed ambitious in the extreme, but I thought something like it would be necessary to bring some coherence into the badly fragmented, atheoretical, and highly eclectic field of social indicators as it stood in the early 1970s. When (in 1972–73) I found 14 months of freedom for concentrated research, I tried to make a major contribution.

In the preface, I expressed the hope "that this book will facilitate convergence toward an operational system or systems of social accounts and indicators. What is called for, I believe, is an integration of theory, methods, and data across the 'social' parts of the social and behavioral sciences..." (vii).

I did not claim to have accomplished anything of this magnitude. I *did* say that I had tried to read quite widely in the social sciences and to achieve a fairly uniform understanding of them at the level of the *International Encyclopedia of the Social Sciences* (1968). I also said that I had tried to relate concepts from several disciplines in a rough and preliminary fashion. I referred to 250 publications in my text and another 250 in an appendix, "Some comments on related literatures."

Carley (1981, 63–64) described my book as

> ...perhaps the most comprehensive attempt at a theoretically based system of social indicators to date...;
> "[The Fox-van Moeseke] total income model has a definite notion of welfare, is structured theoretically, and puts forward an accounting framework for selecting and operationalizing indicators which relate to the social model of the concept....[It] has considerable value as a paradigm for relating social indicator research to the social sciences generally. It is, in short, a necessary innovation in social indicator research.

After examining concepts from several social sciences, I suggested (Fox 1974, 20–28) "a tentative integration of concepts to measure an individual's total income." I postulated that in any given year an individual allocates time exhaustively among "behavior settings," as defined and classified by Roger Barker (1968). These settings constitute the individual's *environment* and one's allocation of time among the settings constitutes one's *life style*.

The individual chooses behavior settings because they provide various kinds of "rewards": for example, enjoyment of the activity as such; a liking for the people who participate in the setting; and/or a desire or need for "extrinsic" rewards, such as money from one's job, improved health from an exercise class, or recognition for participation in a public-service activity.

To get these rewards from participation in any given setting, one must make "contributions" to it of approximately equal value, based on one's personal resources or "behavioral capacities," such as work-related skills, other skills (social, organizational, athletic, musical, or whatever), physical health, emotional stability, personal warmth, and commitments to certain political, religious, or cultural norms (the list is not exhaustive).

Each setting is assumed to require definite amounts of specific contributions per hour that the individual spends in it; different settings require the contributions in different proportions. Money is one of the contributions in some settings. Formally, the individual faces a mathematical-programming problem, and its solution could, in principle, be used to impute money values to each of one's other contributions.

Leaving out technical details, I assume that the individual chooses the most rewarding life style available in the coming year, subject to one's limited resources and the demands made on them (per hour) by each distinct kind of behavior setting in one's accessible environment.

It follows that the value of the individual's contributions equals the value of rewards in each setting separately, and in all settings combined; the aggregate value over all settings of *either* one's contributions *or* rewards equals "total income." The economic components, income from gainful employment and income (if any) from property and transfer payments, constitute one's "personal income," a prominent category in the national income and product accounts. The difference between "total income" and "personal income" might be called "social income," also measured in dollars.

If "total income" accounts were implemented for a community, region, or nation, the corresponding economic accounts would be seamlessly embedded in them.

I hasten to say that the imputation of money values to contributions and rewards is much less urgent and important than the objective study of "behavior settings" individually, and as constituent parts of rural institutions and communities. The Fox-van Moeseke model as such occupies a small part of my 1974 book. Chapters more immediately relevant to the development of social accounts in nonmetropolitan areas include: social science concepts relevant to a system of social accounts; some other attempts to combine economic and noneconomic variables in theoretical models; time budgets, behavior settings, and total income; individuals and families; national goals accounting and policy models; social indicators and models for cities and regions; accounts and indicators for the higher-education sector; occupations and earnings; and elements of an operational system: I. individuals, families, and organizations in a small community, and II. cities and regions, and III. national and world models and data.

Roger Barker's research on behavior settings and his "behavior-setting surveys" of small communities were more important to my own thinking than the work of any other social scientist. Barker's name appears on 41 different pages of my book, while that of the social scientist next in line appears on 24 pages.

SOME CONCEPTUAL ADVANTAGES OF SOCIAL ACCOUNTS OVER SOCIAL INDICATORS

Social indicators highlight selective aspects of the performance of a society. However, the indicators lack comprehensiveness and do not reveal much about the interrelationships of the social processes reflected in different indicators.

A comparison with the economic indicators of the 1920s is relevant. They included a good many time series on production in various industries, prices of various commodities, and other phenomena. But they gave no clue as to the overall size of the economy or to the fact that the economy was a complexly interrelated system. The economic indicators gave no warning of the onset of the "Great Depression," they could not explain its course, and they were of little use in designing strategies for economic recovery.

The data situation did not improve until Simon Kuznets and others in the early 1930s drew a definitional boundary around the economy as a whole and summarized all transactions within that boundary in a set of national income and product accounts. These accounts provided a common framework for the macroeconomic theories of Keynes and others, the input-output matrices of Leontief, and the dynamic econometric models of Tinbergen. Knowledge relevant to economic policy cumulated rapidly and economic data systems were expanded and improved in a coherent manner.

Similarly, today's social indicators cannot be interpreted with confidence until we draw a definitional boundary around the society as a whole and summarize all transactions within that boundary in a set of social accounts. The boundary will have to include, in concept, the complete living time of all members of the society in any given year and (hence) all transactions among them. The development of time-use accounts is a logical first step toward comprehensive social system accounts and models.

SOME CONCEPTUAL ADVANTAGES OF BEHAVIOR SETTINGS OVER ALTERNATIVE BASIC UNITS IN TIME-USE ACCOUNTS FOR A COMMUNITY

The economic data systems relevant to describing a community are based on "establishments." An establishment is an economic unit operating at a single physical location. In essentially one-room establishments, such as jewelry stores or barbershops, the industrial classification evokes a pretty clear idea as to the activities going on inside. But a large multiroom establishment, such as a high school, may contain a bewildering array of distinctly different activities, curricular and extracurricular, in the course of a year. Moreover, high schools of different sizes may provide narrower or wider ranges of activities.

A good deal of time is spent in "nonestablishments," such as parks and playgrounds, or streets, sidewalks, and vacant lots. The largest amounts of time are spent in households. "Time spent at home" tells us next to nothing about specific activities. A reallocation of time between hospitals, high schools, and households is not specific enough to produce desired changes in, for example, the OECD social indicators.

In contrast, behavior settings (once they are understood) always involve directly observable activities with distinct boundaries in space and (on any given occasion) distinct beginnings and endings in time. Many behavior settings are literally one-room establishments in which all participants are within sight and hearing of one another. A high school mathematics class, a Sunday worship service, a club meeting, a basketball game —each qualifies as a behavior setting. Each setting has a distinct "program" which describes the roles of each kind of participant (e.g., teacher, student—minister, choir member, organist, member of the congregation). Normally, each participant understands their role in each setting: student in the math class, choir member in the worship service, player in the basketball game.

In 1963–64, Roger Barker and his associates (Barker 1968; Barker and Schoggen 1973) surveyed a small county-seat town in northeast Kansas which they code named "Midwest." They did not survey households, but confined themselves to "community" (nonhousehold) settings which were controlled by private enterprises, government agencies, schools, churches, and voluntary associations. There were 830 residents in the town itself and about the same number in the surrounding trade area.

They found 884 behavior settings occurring in the town at least once during the 12-month survey period. Settings with identical programs were grouped into categories called "genotypes." "Midwest" had only 1 bank, but it had 2 barbershops, 3 grocery stores, 4 service stations, 11 physical education classes, 42 religion classes, and 103 "business meetings!" In all, the 884 settings were classified into 198 genotypes as distinct from one another as baseball games versus basketball games versus football games—to choose some easy-to-visualize examples.

The genotypes correspond to everyday speech and to common observations on what a community offers in the way of "things to do" and "services available." Within some genotypes, the settings are age-graded and/or differentiated by sex, so the availability of "baseball games" in a community does not necessarily mean that children of all ages and both sexes have opportunities to play in them.

Barker and Schoggen (1973, 448–94) present a catalog of Midwest's 198 genotypes, with succinct descriptions of their programs and the names and distinguishing features of their individual settings—for example, Elementary Upper School (ages 11–13) Basketball Game. They found that the average "Midwest" resident entered 61 distinct behavior settings at least once during the survey—only 7 percent of the 884 available. Hence, individual residents included very different arrays of behavior settings in their "life styles" or "time-allocation vectors" (TAVs).

TIME-USE ACCOUNTS FOR A COMMUNITY

In a 1951–52 survey of "Midwest," Barker (1955) made detailed observations of the 585 community behavior settings which existed or occurred during that year and, along with many other data items, included estimates of the amount of time spent in each by town residents. He did not survey family (household) behavior settings, but he noted (Barker and Wright 1995, 84) that the common varieties were home meals, home indoors, home outdoors, home bathrooms, and home festive occasions. Barker was clearly aware that his methods could be extended to yield comprehensive estimates of time use, for on pages 97–98 he said, "During the survey year (366 days), we estimate that "Midwesterners" spent 5,130,000 hours in family settings; 1,030,658 hours in community settings; and 330,620 hours in foreign settings" (i.e., settings outside the limits of the town). The sum of these three figures amounts to 8,784 hours a year for each of the town's residents.

As to the comprehensiveness of behavior settings, Barker's colleague Gump (1971, 134) said, "People live out their lives in a sequence of environmental units; experience in these settings *is* life. If the quality of experience is good, life expands; if it is bad, life diminishes."

In terms of the 1963–64 survey, we might visualize a very large two-way table with a row for each of the 830 residents, a column for each of the 198 genotypes of community settings, columns for categories of household activities, and a column for time spent out of town. The table as a whole might be called a time-allocation matrix (TAM) and each row a time-allocation vector (TAV). The residents would be grouped into age, sex, or other categories, and an average "life style" or TAV calculated for each group.

A time-allocation matrix should be helpful in appraising a community's resources from a number of perspectives. Which subgroups of residents spend the most time out of town and in what genotypes? Are those genotypes completely lacking in this community? Do they lack settings for the relevant age, sex, or other subgroups? Or, are the settings present but of substandard quality?

A time-allocation matrix for "Midwest" and its trade area combined would be more useful for social-accounting purposes than one for the town itself. In his 1963–64 survey, Barker (1968) included estimates of the time spent in each of "Midwest"'s 884 community behavior settings by the town's residents and also by nonresidents, as summarized in Table 2. (See also Barker and Schoggen 1973). Nonresidents accounted for 52 percent of the occupancy time in settings controlled by schools and churches, and 47 percent of that in settings controlled by voluntary associations (lodges, clubs, youth organizations, and many others). Evidently the attendance and membership areas for "Midwest"'s schools, churches, and voluntary associations approximately coincided with each other and with the trade area. As customers and clients, residents and nonresidents must have been equally important, though most of the business and professional people no doubt lived in town.

Some 45 percent of the total occupancy time by nonresidents was in school-related settings. If "Midwest" lost its high school, over 20 percent of the total nonresident occupancy time would be diverted to another location; if it also lost its elementary school, another 20 or 25 percent would be diverted.

LINKING BARKER'S CONCEPTS TO THOSE OF OTHER DISCIPLINES AND TO SOCIAL INDICATORS AND ACCOUNTS

Space does not permit a discussion of Barker's complete system of concepts and measurements relating to the behavior settings of a community.

It took me a long time to work out the approximate relationship of Barker's concepts to those of other social sciences and to social indicators. The task of explaining these relationships was made easier by the publication in 1981 of two new U.S. data systems, one on stocks of physical capital (buildings, equipment, consumer's durable goods) and the other on employment cross-classified by industry and occupation, and by the appearance in 1982 of the OECD list of social indicators. I spelled out the many linkages of these three data sets to Barker's system in Fox (1983). In Fox (1984), I emphasized theoretical connections between Barkers's system and other social sciences, and in Fox (1985) I emphasized connections between Barker's measures and a proposed system of social accounts.

The titles of some chapters of my 1985 book are suggestive: the usefulness of behavior settings for classifying and describing human activities in a community, behavior settings and objective social indicators, the classification of behavior settings in social system accounts, the classification of roles in social system accounts, the classification of stocks of physical capital and consumer durables in social-system accounts, and the classification and delineation of communities and regions in social-system accounts.

Barker groups behavior settings with identical "programs" into categories he calls *genotypes*; economic data systems group establishments producing identical "products" into *industries*. In come cases, genotypes and industries are identical (for example, service stations) and each behavior setting *is* an establishment. In others, an "establishment" like Midwest High School may consist of settings from several genotypes (English classes, mathematics classes, basketball games, and so forth). Data on these genotypes are much more informative concerning behavior, skills, and experiences than are aggregative data for the school as a whole. With a moderate amount of work, data on genotypes can be reconciled with data on industries.

Barker's succinct description of each genotype's "program" identifies the occupation of each type of gainfully employed participant (for example, service-station manager, service-station assistant); these are identical with *occupations* listed in economic data systems. In "Midwest," most genotype programs involving athletics and the performing arts are implemented by amateurs whose activities are excluded from economic data systems but are extremely important to community life. Barker's programs

TABLE 2: PERSON-HOURS OF OCCUPANCY TIME IN BEHAVIOR SETTINGS, BY CLASS OF AUTHORITY SYSTEMS, MIDWEST, KANSAS, 1963–64

Class of Authority Systems	Number of Settings	Occupancy Time: Person-Hours			Percent By Town Residents
		Total	By Town Residents	By Non-Residents	
Private enterprise	132	734,183	531,555	202,628	72.4
Government	114	308,075	186,896	121,179	60.7
School	233	650,124	310,516	339,608	47.8
Church	193	69,753	33,173	36,580	47.6
Voluntary association	212	118,595	62,994	55,601	53.1
Total	884	1,880,730	1,125,134	755,596	59.8
			PERCENTAGES		
Private enterprise	14.9	39.0	47.2	26.8	—
Government	12.9	16.4	16.6	16.0	—
School	26.4	34.6	27.6	44.9	—
Church	21.8	3.7	2.9	4.8	—
Voluntary association	24.0	6.3	5.6	7.4	—
Total	100.0	100.0	100.0	100.0	—

Source: Compiled and reconstructed from various tables in Barker and Schoggen (1973).

also include the behaviors of customers, clients, patients, pupils, audience members, and spectators; these roles might be called "quasi-occupations." In short, data on roles in behavior settings can be reconciled with data on occupations.

Genotype programs also refer to, or imply, physical capital in the form of buildings or parts of buildings, machinery, equipment, and furniture, without which settings in the specified genotypes could not function. Most private enterprises keep records on such things as well as current receipts and expenditures. Churches, schools, government agencies, and voluntary associations also use physical capital; so do households in the community. Architects sometimes refer to the whole complex of buildings, streets and sidewalks, and public utilities as "the built environment." Social accounts emphasizing the input and output of behavior settings should certainly include information on the associated stocks of physical capital.

Barker's concept of *action patterns* helps to relate his system to social indicators. Barker identified 11 of these action patterns in "Midwest"'s behavior settings. He describes them as "goal-directed" or "output-oriented," representing the purposes the various settings were designed to serve. He rates each action pattern in each behavior setting on scales ranging from 0 to 9.

Barker's action patterns correspond to social concerns and cultural values. They are the microsocial equivalents of some categories used in the OECD list of social indicators and in Terleckyj's set of "goal-output indicators" (1975).

One pattern, *education*, gets high ratings in school classes devoted to academic subjects. The pattern *religion* gets high ratings in many, but not all, of the church-sponsored settings. *Government* gets high ratings in many of the government-sponsored settings, in attorneys' offices, and in high-school civics classes. *Business* rates high in private-enterprise settings conspicuously engaged in exchanging goods and services for money; "Midwest State Bank" had the highest rating of all.

Most settings sponsored by private enterprises and government agencies rate high on *professionalism*, meaning that all or most of the setting leaders, assistants, and/or performers are paid. This is true also of the school classroom settings. Most settings sponsored by churches and voluntary associations rate low on professionalism, and so do most extracurricular settings in the schools.

Recreation gets high ratings in many settings sponsored by voluntary associations, in extracurricular settings sponsored by the schools, and in bowling alleys, parks, and playgrounds. *Social contact* is present in all settings, but is particularly prominent in those sponsored by voluntary associations. Barber and beauty shops rate high on *personal appearance*; restaurants on *nutrition*, dentists' offices on *physical health*, and church weddings and funerals on *aesthetics*.

Terleckyj's "goal-output indicators" are conceptually similar to those in the OECD list. The inputs required for Terleckyj's programs, if implemented, would de facto be integrated in, or into, behavior settings; so would those required by the OECD list. We might ask ourselves whether desired changes in any of the OECD indicators could be influenced by specified changes in behavior settings of the types found in Barker's community.

SOME ADVANTAGES OF RURAL SOCIAL SCIENTISTS IN SOCIAL ACCOUNTING RESEARCH

Rural sociologists have been surveying small communities for over 70 years. Galpin published a brilliant study, *The Social Anatomy of an Agricultural Community*, in 1915. From then on, a rural community was defined as a town *and* its trade area.

The population of the town-and-trade-area community was small enough to permit a sociologist to talk with virtually all community leaders, to enter and observe most of the community's open-to-the-public settings, and to talk with many individuals about aspects of family life, visiting patterns, social stratification, and attitudes. From this perspective, Barker was simply doing a special kind of community survey. Barker and Wright (1955, 3) knew they were engaged in cross-disciplinary "colonization," but the fact that this approach sometimes led to major scientific breakthroughs emboldened them "to enter the territory of the sociologist and the anthropologist without a passport, or a guide, or even a guidebook."

I have read very little of the home economics literature, but I am confident that home economists have been making detailed observations of *household* behavior settings (under other names) for several decades. The concepts of complete time budgets for individuals and of time-allocation matrices for communities provide a framework for pilot attempts to synthesize the results of surveys already made independently by (1) rural sociologists and (2) home economists.

The residents of any actual town the size of "Midwest" make some use of genotypes found only in larger places. Barker found 198 genotypes in "Midwest" in 1963–64. In informal correspondence, Schoggen conjectured that there might be around 400 genotypes in the largest cities. My own conjecture is that there are no more than 300 in nonmetropolitan commuting fields (labor-market areas) with central cities of less than 50,000 people.

A catalog of additional genotypes and their programs in towns and small cities of successively larger sizes (up to 50,000) in agricultural regions would be useful in diagnosing the adequacy of the arrays of genotypes accessible to residents of different ages and degrees of mobility. A time-allocation matrix containing estimates of the amounts of time spent by each category of residents of a town-and-trade area in (1) specific genotypes within the local area and (2) specific genotypes outside the local area would give a clearer idea of deficiencies in the local environment and of realistic ways to remedy some of them. A time-allocation matrix for residents of the central city (of 30,000 to 50,000 people) would provide estimates of the largest arrays of genotypes regularly used by age and other groups with the fewest spatial limitations on access.

Quantitative information of this sort should facilitate the discovery and validation of opportunities to improve the spatial allocation of behavior resources (settings and genotypes) and provide shared access to existing facilities by people in different local political jurisdictions.

Disciplinary scientists in urban universities seldom concern themselves with (or know much about) nonmetropolitan areas—i.e., areas with central cities of less than 50,000 population. Given their opportunities for direct observation of samples of behavior settings, rural social scientists should be able to develop time-allocation matrices for multicounty functional economic areas (FEAs) containing as many as 250,000 people. (See Fox and Kumar 1965.) The U.S. Department of Commerce has published data for BEA Economic Areas (1977) which usually contain two or more FEAs. If justified by the needs of state governments and of nonmetropolitan residents, rural social scientists and campus colleagues could probably extend the same approach to BEA Economic Areas including as many as 2,000,000 people, without losing touch with microlevel realities.

One caveat is in order. The number of scientists who are thoroughly familiar with Barker's method of behavior-setting surveys is quite small, as is the number of economists who thoroughly understand the relationships of behavior settings to official socioeconomic and demographic data systems. Behavior-setting surveys and time-allocation matrices for communities much larger than "Midwest"'s town-and-trade area (about 1,600 people) will require sophisticated sampling techniques and innovative uses of secondary data sources. Some intensive workshops will be needed to transfer Barker's technology to interested rural social scientists and to adapt it to their needs.

CONCLUDING REMARKS: SOME BROADER IMPLICATIONS OF BEHAVIOR SETTINGS FOR THE SOCIAL SCIENCES

In my judgment, the implications of behavior settings for the social sciences are far-reaching. I believe that the behavior-setting concept may come to play as important a role in the social sciences as the cell concept does in biology. It seems to me that the interests of several disciplines converge in behavior settings. All roles are played in them; all organizations are composed of them. Felson (1979) asserts that all sociologically interesting phenomena involving direct physical contact between persons occur in behavior settings, and that they appear to be ideal units for describing and modeling social processes. Behavior settings in nonmarket organizations are empirically valid analogues of the economist's markets. Small group phenomena occur in behavior settings: they can be viewed from the standpoints of group dynamics, transactional analysis, game theory, and the theory of teams. Lewin's (1951) concept of an individual's "life space" (the things one is aware of at any given moment) remains intact as the means by which a behavior setting elicits the behavior appropriate to it.

In 1947, Barker intended to study the everyday behavior of individual children in their "natural" habitats in the town of "Midwest." He thought of this as *ecological psychology*, as opposed to experimental and clinical psychology and, to this day, Barker and his former colleagues and students are known as "ecological psychologists."

However, by 1969, Barker realized that his research on behavior settings, organizations, and communities as *environments* of human behavior had led him into a new discipline independent of psychology which he called *eco-behavioral science*. The transition in his thinking is described in Barker (1969) and Barker and Associates (1978). Eco-behavioral science has contacts with many disciplines and may provide some common ground for all of them in studies of individual behavior settings, organizations, and communities in nonmetropolitan regions.

NOTE

1. Karl A. Fox is a professor emeritus, Department of Economics, Iowa State University, Ames, Iowa.

REFERENCES

Barker, Roger G. 1968. *Ecological psychology*. Stanford: Stanford University Press.

_____1969. Wanted: An eco-behavioral science. In *Naturalistic viewpoints in psychological research*. Edited by E. P. Willems and H. L. Raush. New York: Holt, Rinehart and Winston.

Barker, Roger G., and Associates. 1978. *Habitats, environments, and human behavior*. San Francisco: Jossey-Bass.

Barker, Roger G., and Phil Schoggen. 1973. *Qualities of community life*. San Francisco: Jossey-Bass.

Barker, Roger G., and Herbert F. Wright. 1955. *Midwest and its children*. New York: Harper and Row. Reprinted 1971 by Archon Books, Hamden, Conn.

Bauer, Raymond A., ed. 1966. *Social indicators*. Cambridge: Massachusetts Institute of Technology Press.

BEA economic areas. Revised 1977. Washington, D.C.: U.S. Department of Commerce, Bureau of Economic Analysis.

Campbell, Angus, Philip E. Converse, and Willard L. Rodgers. 1976. *The quality of American life*. New York: Russell Sage Foundation.

Carley, Michael. 1981. *Social measurement and social indicators*. London: Allen and Unwin.

Felson, Marcus. 1979. How should social indicators be collected, organized, and modeled? *Contemporary Sociology* 8:40–41.

Fox, Karl A. 1974. *Social indicators and social theory: Elements of an operational system*. New York: John Wiley.

_____1983. The eco-behavioral view of human societies and its implications for systems science. *International Journal of Systems Science* 14:895–914.

_____1984. Behavior settings and eco-behavioral science. *Mathematical Social Science* 7:117–38 and 139–65.

_____1985. *Social system accounts: Linking social and economic indicators through tangible behavior settings*. Boston: Kluwer Academic Publishers and Dordrecht, Holland: D. Reidel.

_____1986. A scientific autobiography. *Journal of Behavioral Economics* 15 (Winter): 105–29.

Fox, Karl A., and T. Krishna Kumar. 1965. The functional economic area: Delineation and implications for economic analysis and policy. *Regional Science Association PAPERS* 15:57–85.

Galpin, Charles J. 1915. The social anatomy of an agricultural community. Agricultural Experiment Station Research Bulletin No. 34. Madison: University of Wisconsin.

Gross, Bertram M. 1966. The state of the nation: Social systems accounting. In *Social Indicators*. Edited by Raymond A. Bauer. Cambridge: Massachusetts Institute of Technology Press.

Gump, Paul V. 1971. The behavior setting: A promising unit for environmental designers. *Landscape Architecture* 61, no. 2: 130–34.

International encyclopedia of the social sciences. 1968. Fifteen volumes. New York: Macmillan and Free Press.

Johnson, Glenn L. 1986. *Research methodology for economists*. New York: Macmillan.

Lewin, Kurt. 1951. *Field theory in social science*. Edited by Dorwin Cartwright. New York: Harper. Reprinted 1975 by Greenwood Press, Westport, Conn.

Organization for Economic Cooperation and Development. 1982. *The OECD list of social indicators*. Paris: OECD.

Social Indicators Research (journal). 1974 through 1988. Volumes 1 through 20.

Stone, Richard. 1971. *Demographic accounting and model building*. Paris: Organization for Economic Cooperation and Development.

_____1975. Towards a system of social and demographic statistics. United Nations Document ST/ESA/STAT/SER.F/18. New York: United Nations Department of Economic and Social Affairs.

Terleckyj, Nestor E. 1975. *Improvements in the quality of life: Estimates of possibilities in the United States, 1974–1983*. Washington, D.C.: National Planning Association.

CHAPTER 4

ANTHROPOLOGY, EVOLUTION, AND AGRICULTURAL DEVELOPMENT

Billie R. DeWalt[1]

INTRODUCTION

My purpose in this chapter will be to show that anthropology and anthropological approaches can be among the most powerful tools that we have for predicting and understanding the long-term (macro) effects of agricultural development as well as for demonstrating the real-life (micro) consequences of these processes for individuals and communities. Unfortunately, anthropology's contributions are frequently minimized or misunderstood because many people outside the discipline still have some outdated stereotypes of what anthropologists do and what theoretical paradigms are prevalent. Several reviews of the very positive contribution of anthropologists to understanding agrarian systems already exist (see Netting 1974; Orlove 1980; Hill 1986) so my concern here will not be to undertake a comprehensive review of anthropological contributions. Instead, I want to show how evolutionary theory can be used to enhance anthropology's future contributions to agricultural development and to show how the agricultural development process can be improved as a result.

ANTHROPOLOGY AND AGRICULTURAL DEVELOPMENT

BACKGROUND

A popular and accurate definition of anthropology is that it is the study of *all* aspects of *all* humans at *all* times and in *all* places. What this means is that anthropology covers an immense variety of topics, with the practitioners of the discipline using a vast array of different theoretical and methodological approaches. Of the four main subfields of anthropology, linguistics is especially concerned with the study of the primary means of human symbolic communications (language) through time; physical anthropology focuses on the paleontological origins of humans and the physical and genetic characteristics of contemporary human populations; archaeology studies human remains to understand sequences of social and cultural evolution under diverse natural and cultural conditions; and sociocultural anthropology describes and analyzes the forms and styles of social life of past and present ages (see Harris 1975, 1). Within these broad subfields there are many further divisions along subdisciplinary lines (for example, psychological anthropology, agricultural anthropology, sociolinguistics), philosophical distinctions (for example, between those who emphasize the humanistic, interpretive study of meaning and those who stress scientific studies of behavior), and questions of method and theory.

Because of these differences (subfields, philosophical orientations, and theoretical persuasions), anthropology is a diverse discipline. Most anthropologists, however, are likely to share some perspectives that *are* extremely important to the study of agricultural development.

First, even though individual anthropologists are as likely as any other social scientist to be specialists in some topic or area, the training of an anthropologist usually includes at least a smattering from each of the subfields. The perspective of an anthropologist is likely to be longer-term, more comparative, and more holistic (that is, interested in the interactions and interrelationships of systems) than that of the other social science disciplinarians. In terms of development issues, this perspective can allow the anthropologist to see the broader context within which agricultural development is occurring, to perceive unforeseen linkages of agriculture with other aspects of the cultural system, and to anticipate potential negative ramifications of programs or projects.

Second, cultural relativism, the perspective that each cultural pattern is as intrinsically worthy of respect of all the rest, makes anthropologists more attuned to the "native" point of view (see Brokensha, Warren, and Werner 1980). Also, the appreciation of the anthropologist for so-called "primitive" or folk communities has meant that practitioners of the discipline have worked in some of the most isolated and logistically difficult parts of the world. While Robert Chambers' *Rural Development: Putting the Last First* (1983) persuasively argued the importance for development as a whole to focus better on the poorest and most isolated and resource-scarce communities, anthropologists have had experience in such settings for a very long time.

ANTHROPOLOGY IN AGRICULTURAL DEVELOPMENT

Within the last decade, there has been a significant increase in the number of anthropologists working directly in development agencies and in institutions directly concerned with agricultural change. In part, this resulted from the wave of legislation and initiatives in the 1970s that put more emphasis on new directions emphasizing equality, farming systems research, incorporating women into development, and a greater focus on the poorest of the poor (see DeWalt 1988a). All of these emphasized the need for greater understanding of social and cultural factors in development. Because anthropologists were the social scientists who had the language skills and the most experience in Third World settings, there was a greater demand for them in development work. At the same time, the declining academic job market resulted in many anthropologists looking for positions outside of universities (van Willigen 1986).

One result was that the number of anthropologists working in the United States Agency for International Development (USAID) quickly jumped from only one in the early 1970s to 22 by 1977 (Hoben 1980, 364). The currents that were affecting USAID were also being felt in other agricultural development settings. One of the most significant efforts was the Rockefeller Foundation's "Social Science Research Fellowship in Agricultural and Rural Development" that was created in 1974. By 1984, 33 social scientists (including 21 anthropologists) had been placed in the International Agricultural Research Centers (Rhoades 1985, 5). Two institutions—the International Maize and Wheat Improvement Center (CIMMYT) and the International Potato Center (CIP)—presently employ anthropologists as senior scientists, and anthropologists are working in several other centers as well.[2]

The role of anthropologists in these programs is essentially the same as the one that was envisioned for agricultural economics and rural sociology when they were incorporated into the land-grant institutions. As Frederick H. Buttel (see this book's Part I, Chapter 3) has written:

> The roots of the social science presence in land-grant and SAES institutions resided in problems experienced by the land-grant system in encouraging farmers to use new technology and to improve their management practices. Agricultural economics emerged as farm management economics in the first decade of this century and was oriented to assisting farmers in allocating their resources more effectively and profitably. Rural sociology largely emerged about a decade later, in the aftermath of the Country Life Commission, which recommended that the SAESs engage in social science research to assist in the transfer of technology while at the same time preserving the social and moral fabric of rural communities.[3]

This role for the social sciences is one that I have called social science *in* agriculture—that is, how social scientists contribute to the improvement of project functioning, usually by providing descriptive information that facilitates the identification, diffusion, and adoption of the new technologies created by biological scientists. Social scientists are expected to explore ways to help transfer technology, to think about ways to mitigate potential problems, and to evaluate the results of such transfers. The assumption is that the agricultural technology being generated can help to solve the problems of small farmers in developing countries.

The anthropologist in these settings serves to further the goals of the agricultural-biological scientists by acting, in effect, as a *cultural broker* between farmers and researchers. This is made most explicit in the work of Robert Rhoades and Robert Booth (1982) at the International Potato Center who have nicely illustrated the means by which "acceptable agricultural technology" can be generated. In their farmer-back-to-farmer model, social scientists should come to an understanding of the farmer's perspective and needs, then communicate these to scientists who use the findings to design better, more appropriate technology. Under ideal circumstances, the technology is tested and adapted on the farm. Anthropologists and other social scientists observe the reactions of farmers and communicate these evaluations back to the research scientists at which point the cycle can begin again.

Further examples of work in this tradition by anthropologists includes that of Robert Tripp (1984, 1985), Michael M. Cernea (1985), Timothy Frankenberger (1985), my own work (DeWalt 1983, 1985; Paul and DeWalt 1985), and many others. There is little question that, in the implementation of this model, anthropology provides an important service to both the farmer and the scientist by brokering the communication between them. Particularly in organizations like the International Potato Center, where social scientists have very effectively been incorporated into multidisciplinary teams to address technological problems, it works very well (Rhoades 1985).

The culture-broker role is only a part of what anthropology has to offer to our understanding and implementation of agricultural development. In my view, equally important and, perhaps, more important is a social science *of* agriculture: The study of the interaction of the natural environment, sociocultural patterns, market conditions, government policy, and technological systems in order to identify agricultural research and/or extension priorities; to determine appropriate institutional structures and responsibilities for research and extension; to predict economic, social, and cultural consequences of agricultural change; and to identify government, agency, and institutional policies that will facilitate development of more just and equitable social systems. Rather than performing a service-oriented role within a system in which policies have already been established, a social science of agriculture should provide an ongoing critique (emphasizing both positive and negative aspects) of research and development programs, and be a key element in the formulation of *policies* that will guide and direct research and development efforts (see DeWalt [1988b] for further development of this position). One way in which this can occur is if an evolutionary perspective is brought into the picture.

EVOLUTIONARY THEORY AND AGRICULTURAL DEVELOPMENT

EVOLUTIONARY THEORY

From my perspective, what has been missing in the practical application of anthropology to the solution of contemporary problems is an adequate theoretical and methodological grounding. Within anthropology, as with the other social sciences, there is a wide diversity in terms of theoretical perspectives. Yet there does seem to be one theoretical perspective that has proved to be of great utility in a variety of contexts. This is the theory of evolution.

The theory of evolution has historically been of substantial importance for anthropologists, especially for physical anthropologists who focus on the biological aspects of it. After Darwin formulated the idea to apply to biological forms, using the term evolution to apply to social and cultural forms became popular in the late nineteenth century attracting adherents like Morgan and Tylor in anthropology; Comte, Durkeim, and Spencer in sociology; and Marx and Engels in political economy. Evolutionary ideas fell into disfavor in all of these disciplines in the early twentieth century, probably for three major reasons. The first is that some social scientists propounded an extreme form of social Darwinism in which they argued that it was the natural order of things that the "fittest" (those groups, races, nations then in control) should survive; that is, the disadvantaged were in their conditions because they were less fit. Second, many individuals adopted the terminology of evolutionism and adapted it to apply *in an analogous sense* to culture. Third, many cultural evolutionist arguments took the form of disguised functionalism: starting from the material base of the society, the search was on for ways in which the rest of the social and cultural forms fit together to allow the society to "adapt" to its environmental setting.

Nevertheless, there is an implicit acceptance of evolutionism as a paradigm in much social and cultural research. Most anthropologists still organize much of their teaching around the type concepts of band, tribe, chiefdom, state, or those of hunters and gatherers, horticulturalists, pastoralists, peasants, and industrial society; and archaeologists have continued to find the terminology and ideas of evolutionism applicable to their research showing how prehistoric and historic cultures changed through time. Thus, the terminology of evolutionism to apply to change in sociocultural forms continues to be an important theoretical perspective in anthropology. What has not occurred is much clear thinking about how evolutionary theory can be utilized in the discussion of cultural forms.

According to Davydd Greenwood (1984), who has produced a critique of the way in which nonevolutionary ideas continue to be used in the study of human behavior, there are six basic propositions of Evolutionary Theory:

1. Variation is a ubiquitous feature of all living things. It is continuously and normally produced spontaneously.
2. Selection is the result of the interaction of specific sets of environmental conditions with variations in species of plants and animals. Selection is the force that gives rise to and alters the categories of living things.
3. The interaction between variation and selection results in adaptation or extinction. Adaptation is always relative to particular organisms and specific environments. Adaptation is never permanent.
4. All forms of life are ultimately related to each other by genealogical connections.
5. There are not nonmaterial forces at work in the evolutionary process, nor are there any "pull" factors in evolution. [Author's note: This means that evolution is not controlled (at least directly) by some Superior Being, and is not leading toward any goal, perfection, or other "end" state.]
6. There is no radical dichotomy between humans and other animals (between "culture" and "nature"), just as there are no radical dichotomies between any things in nature at all. Species are ranges of variation that intergrade into each other at the margins.[4]

Anthropology can significantly improve its theoretical and practical relevance to agriculture by further exploring the implications of these principles and improving the application of this theory to cultural phenomena. Evolutionary theory provides a macroframework within which to view human processes. It does not necessarily provide *explanations* for cultural phenomena (indeed, many people would agree that even in the biological area it is primarily useful for post hoc explanation rather than prediction) so it does not absolve us from finding other theories that can account for more micro aspects of human behavior. There are, however, some important directions that evolutionary theory provides for anthropological (and other social science) research.

ADAPTIVE STRATEGIES AND DECISION MAKING

The first three of Greenwood's principles listed above concern the importance of variation, selection, and adaptation in evolutionary theory. Microlevel anthropological research has probably dealt with these issues as well as any other social science. In order to demonstrate some of these contributions, I will adopt a conceptual apparatus used by Bennett (1976) that allows anthropologists to use evolutionary ideas in reference to agricultural development.

Variation in cultural behavior has been documented by John Bennett (1969) and by myself (DeWalt 1979) using the concept of *adaptive strategies*. Adaptive strategies are "patterns formed by the many separate adjustments that people devise in order to obtain and use resources and to solve the immediate problems confronting them" (Bennett 1969, 14). In coping with or making these adjustments, people operate under all sorts of environmental and social constraints. Understanding the parameters within which these adjustments are made can be useful in agricultural development. Several anthropologists have studied the decision-making process with regard to agriculture to discern how people formulate adaptive strategies. To give just one example, in my Mexican research I studied how small farmers adopted some specific pieces of new technology from the "technological packages" being promoted by agricultural change agents. The choices made depended on the ecological and economic circumstances of the household, the family's assessment of how they could best improve their material circumstances, and the knowledge base of the household (DeWalt 1979). The collections edited by Peggy Barlett (1980) and by Michael Chibnik (1987) contain several other similar examples (see also Barlett 1982; Eder 1982).

Another approach to decision making has been pursued by Christina Gladwin (1979, 1980) and by Hugh Gladwin and Michael Murtaugh (1980). Their approach has been to adapt psychological techniques in order to study the cognitive processes that people use to make decisions. Decision trees and mapping of the decision rules people use result from these kinds of techniques.

Both of these decision-making approaches begin from the premise that people are rational decision makers. By understanding the constraints on their decisions and by knowing their goals, it is possible to appreciate the reasons for *variability* within and among communities with regard to agriculture and other types of behavior, that is, to know why people have the adaptive strategies they do. Policy makers often make the mistake of assuming that all of the people they want to influence will respond in a homogeneous manner to adopting new technologies or new behaviors. It would be more accurate, however, to assume that there will always be considerable heterogeneity in responses of individuals even in seemingly homogeneous communities (see DeWalt 1979).

Studies of the variability of individual behavior and decision making do not assume that these adaptations are the only ones possible or that they are ones that are most positive or those that will be more successful. Indeed, by knowing something of the natural and social environment in which people live, it is incumbent on the anthropologist to attempt to make some predictions about the probability of behaviors actually being *adaptive*. Adaptation in the short term may, of course, be maladaptive in the long term, so specification about the time dimension of possible adaptive consequences is necessary. *Selection*, of course, is the process that will determine survival or extinction.

Survival and extinction in this realm rarely refer to actual life-and-death outcomes, although we can easily imagine situations in which such ultimate consequences may arise. The growing use of pesticides in the Third World, where farmers use them without taking adequate precautions, is such a case. Usually, however, survival and extinction will refer to the continuance or discontinuance of the behavior in question (for example, continue to grow maize or switch to another crop) and whether this behavior will continue to be part of an individual's adaptation. In the contemporary world, the pace of change and the range of potential solutions have meant that adaptive strategies are constantly in flux and undergoing evaluation and reevaluation. Studying decision making in such contexts is quite frustrating but, if we are to be able to implement and predict the consequences of agricultural development, we need to get a handle on such processes.

ADAPTIVE SYSTEMS

Adaptive strategies that are successful over time and that become adopted by large numbers of people within the group, having undergone what Bennett (1976, 294–95) calls adaptive selection, may be thought of as having become *adaptive systems*. The boundaries of these systems in time and space are imprecise, but conjunctions of them make up what we generally refer to as cultures. These adaptive systems can be quite variable in how they respond to different ecological and social environments, a point nicely illustrated by Bennett's (1969) study of the Hutterites, Indians, ranchers, and farmers who have evolved their own distinctive styles of coping with the Great Plains of Canada.

A considerable body of evolutionary theory in anthropology has dealt with documenting the adaptive systems of many non-Western groups. These studies have been categorized into "types" of society. One common formulation includes the stages: Band, Tribe, Chiefdom, Primitive State, and State (for example, Service). A second formulation is based much more on the material base of societies and includes the categorization: Hunters and Gatherers, Pastoralists, Horticulturalists, Peasants, and Industrial Societies. Whichever formulation is accepted, the general idea of these typologies is that the material basis of a group correlates quite well with other aspects of society; that is, we can look at these as interrelated elements or systems.

In the process of studying the different "types" of societies, classic studies of what is now known in agricultural circles as slash and burn, shifting or swidden cultivation were carried out by Harold Conklin (1957) in the Philippines, Clifford Geertz (1963) in Indonesia, Roy Rappaport (1968) in New Guinea, and P. DeSchlippe (1956) in Africa. These studies inform us about both the actual agricultural practices as well as about the social systems within which these practices exist. These studies still have contemporary relevance because they bring the issue of sustainability of agricultural systems to the forefront. Because shifting cultivation systems rely on having large amounts of land in fallow, the ratio of people to land is identified as of critical importance. Much anthropological writing has been done on how other aspects of the cultural system (for example, religion, myths, and politics) have served to maintain fallowing cycles and to keep the population from growing too rapidly (Rappaport 1968; Good 1987). Current research on sustainable agriculture has much to learn from these earlier studies. Sustainability does not just depend on identifying proper crop rotations, manuring systems, soil management, etc., but also depends on its appropriate fit within a larger cultural system. Resource sustainability cannot be divorced from political, economic, demographic, social, and ideological contexts.

Peasant studies like those of Geertz (1963) in Indonesia, Oscar Lewis (1951) and Frank Cancian (1972) in Mexico, Polly Hill (1972, 1982) in Nigeria; Allen Johnson (1971) in Brazil, and Scarlett Epstein (1962, 1973) in India have also had an important influence on our understanding of agricultural development. One of the major findings that came out of these and similar studies was that peasants were not ruled by tradition and conservatism. Theodore Schultz's (1964) important book, *Transforming Traditional Agriculture*, is based largely on the work of anthropologists and was responsible for making the larger development community aware that peasant behavior is an adaptive response to the ecological, economic, and social circumstances in which these individuals live.

There is an increasing use in anthropology of a "system perspective" that is quite compatible with agricultural research and emphasizes the interconnectedness of culture and nature (see DeWalt 1985, 1988a). Several anthropologists, for example, have become especially prominent in the area of farming-systems research (for example, Rhoades, Tripp, and Frankenberger). The systems perspective gives anthropologists what Cancian (1977, 6) identified as a "practical holism" that is important for: (1) understanding the broader context within which agricultural development occurs; (2) seeing the dangers of considering some outcomes as unintended "side effects" of development; and (3) helping to set goals for development instead of just evaluation of programs.

Walter Goldschmidt's ([1947] 1978) pioneering study in the 1940s of the effect that corporate control of agriculture had on small rural communities in California is a good example of this kind of research. Goldschmidt's conclusion that the quality of life was better in communities that still had small farms was not palatable to agribusiness concerns and their supporters in the U.S. Department of Agriculture

(USDA) and Congress. Because of this, his work was suppressed and it took intervention by a sympathetic U.S. senator to get the report published. By then, Goldschmidt had been fired from his position within the Bureau of Agricultural Economics and he has written that his work "surely contributed to" the demise of that agency (Goldschmidt [1947] 1978, 455). Perhaps because of this experience, there was little further anthropological research on North American agriculture until the 1970s (see Chibnik 1987) with the exception of Bennett's (1969, 1982) work regarding Canadian farmers.

Because adaptive systems have evolved and survived over time, the use of history has become increasingly important. Historical research on processes that lead to major changes in adaptive systems has been influenced substantially by Ester Boserup's (1965) research.[5] Boserup argued with then-conventional assumptions that agriculture came about because of some technological refinement or set of discoveries. Her interpretation was that the shift to agriculture was caused by necessity, perhaps borne of previous population increase. Her thesis is that when people deplete their environments and pass the point of diminishing returns, they change their technology to further intensify production. This hypothesis has been investigated by a number of anthropologists and nonanthropologists with somewhat mixed results (see Moran 1979, 49, for a review).

Agricultural social science has discovered anthropology as more historians, social scientists, political scientists, economists, and others adopt a more historical perspective on how agriculture and society have evolved together. In addition to Geertz (1963), Sidney Mintz's (1985) research provides a model of the utility of such research. He demonstrated how the slave trade from Africa was used to shore up the plantations in the West Indies that produced sugar, the "cheap fuel" that helped to power the industrial revolution in England. Another "commodity study" using history as a tool to show how society and agriculture coevolved to form distinctive adaptive systems is *The Rice Economies* (Bray 1986). Many of the books on "the political economy of" various regions of the world (for example, Bulmer-Thomas 1987; Bates 1983) are doing much to inform us of how adaptive systems developed. Nevertheless, there is a need for these political economic scholars to be able to link up their historical (and sometimes very abstract) studies to identify the important linkages between the microlevel and the macrolevel. These would do much to assist in the formulation of recommendations that would provide guidance to international- and national-level policy makers.

A useful model in this regard is provided by Prabhu Pingali, Yves Bigot, and Hans Binswanger (1987) who have used Boserup's thesis in their investigation of why animal traction and mechanization has failed to take hold in Africa. Their research in a large number of sites indicates that most of sub-Saharan Africa has not yet reached the point where population density has made intensification, such as that using plows or agricultural machinery, appealing to farmers. They suggest that increases in population density, or alternatively the development of market access so that farmers can profit from more intensive production, will be needed before mechanization and other more intensive techniques take hold. Thus, there are some clear policy recommendations that arise from their study.

Another example of using the historical understanding of an adaptive system as a means for introducing change comes from the work of Gerald Murray (1987) in Haiti. Responsible for designing and implementing a project that would help in the reforestation of many eroded areas of Haiti, Murray decided to look at the process as an experiment in "applied evolution." He based his plans on research that he and others had previously carried out on how the land-use system of the island had unfolded since colonial times. His previous ethnographic research had also provided him with ideas about what a successful scheme would have to be like. Knowing that the Haitian peasant was highly individualistic, he rejected community-forest schemes. Knowing that the Haitian peasant was extremely poor, he knew that reforestation would only occur if the farmers saw that it could help them to improve their own economic circumstances. He used his knowledge of cultural evolution to discard attempting to promote reforestation on the basis of conservation. He wrote that an ancient food crisis caused by rising population was not solved by conservation measures, "but rather by the shift into a domesticated mode of production" (Murray 1987, 237). The project implemented thus adopted the perspective of "domesticating" wood as a crop to be used in building houses and as a cooking fuel, and to be sold to others for those same purposes. The project achieved substantial success and is now being used as a model for reforestation efforts in other parts of the world. Murray (1987, 239) writes about the project:

> I felt as though I were observing (and had been a participant in) a reply of an ancient anthropological drama, the shift from an extractive to a domesticated mode of resource procurement. Though their sources of food energy had been domesticated millennia ago, my former village neighbors had now begun replicating this transition in the domain of wood and wood-based energy.

What the Pingali, Bigot, and Binswanger study and the Murray experience illustrate is that a historically based study of land-use patterns, along with an assumption that people are generally making good use of their resources under the constraints in which they live, can be a powerful tool for agricultural development planning. Many mistakes in agricultural development could be averted if such knowledge and assumptions were more widespread.

THE EVOLUTION OF AGRICULTURE

In some sense, the ultimate question that can be addressed by using an evolutionary perspective is the extinction and survival one that I alluded to earlier. We have little to go on here, but some of the answers to the question may be answered by beginning with the origins of agriculture. Archaeological and anthropological research within the cultural evolutionary tradition has enlightened us with a variety of interesting documentation and ideas concerning the domestication of plants and animals and, especially, the social, cultural, and demographic effects that this domestication set in motion.

V. Gordon Childe's (1951) writings on the changes wrought during the Neolithic period are probably the most well known. We forget that agriculture has been the basis of human sustenance for only a minuscule portion of our existence. Yet agriculture, which seems to have been independently discovered in Asia, Europe, the New World, and possibly Africa, enabled the human population to begin its meteoric rise and to cause a multitude of changes in our social and cultural lives. Although there is some evidence that the transition to the Neolithic period was initially accompanied by a fairly general decline in dietary quality (see M. Cohen 1987), the more long-range implications included the rapid expansion of the human population. The world population that was five million people about 6000 B.C. (Franke and Franke 1975, 157) now numbers a thousand times that figure.

Archaeologists have documented the effects of the Neolithic revolution in different parts of the world. The settling of nomadic people in villages, and then larger agglomerations, led to the increasing division of labor in society, increasing social stratification, writing and sophisticated numerical systems, monumental architecture, and a myriad of other changes. Agricultural scientists like David Pimental and Marcia Pimental (1979) and Jack Harlan (1975) have adopted a similar evolutionary perspective to write engaging, widely used texts such as *Food, Energy and Society* and *Crops and Man*, respectively. We should remember that, in evolutionary time, the number of years that has elapsed since the domestication of plants and animals is very short. For example, a recent article by Leonard A. Cohen (1987) on diet and cancer suggested that we are, in essence, confronting modern diets with Stone Age physiology.

The agriculturally based societies of the Neolithic period undoubtedly were advantaged when compared with hunters and gatherers. It soon became apparent that societies with more intensive agriculture had an advantage over those that depended on swidden techniques. Societies based on intensive agriculture expanded in terms of population. Those that developed means of social control to organize these larger populations were able to expand, conquer, and absorb their less fortunate neighbors.

If the Neolithic revolution caused a multitude of changes, the urban industrial revolution has increased the rate and the effects of change. Until the nineteenth century, the vast majority of the world's population was rural and still engaged in the production of primary commodities. By the end of the twentieth century this pattern will have changed significantly. There will be several billion more people on earth, most will live in cities rather than in rural areas, and few will be engaged in the production of food. Agricultural technology has made these changes possible. Few researchers, however, are attempting to look at what the potential social and cultural effects of this massive change in production patterns and population distribution will be. We see portions of these huge changes every day as we seek to cope with the massive migration of the Third World people to urban areas, to deal with the massive unemployment and underemployment problem in Third World countries, and to attempt to equalize the massive surpluses of grains existing in developed countries with the malnutrition of millions in the developing world.

One of the few people who is examining contemporary society within an evolutionary context and attempting to predict the evolutionary consequences of the trends now occurring is Richard N. Adams. Adams sees humans using increasing concentrations of energy, power, and regulation to try to gain greater control over nature. Unfortunately, as humans have succeeded in gaining greater control over nature, they are creating new elements of what Adams (1985) calls the "macroframework." Hierarchy and market-exchange systems (two of the primary mechanisms humans have evolved to gain greater control) thus join nonhuman natural selection as the macroframework to which humans must adapt. The result is that: "For the individual, the shift of controls from an uncontrollable nature to an uncontrollable hierarchy and market does not make things necessarily better. Things lodged in a macroframework are, by definition, beyond immediate control" (Adams 1985, 65). This results in a greater need for regulation and control; in industrial society, about 15–20 percent of the total population is devoted to the control or regulatory function but even so, regulation is not very effective. Human societies are thus caught in an increasingly disordered state caused by the vicious spiral of creating more and more controls that are themselves uncontrollable.

Seen in this light, biotechnology is just one more attempt by humans to try to gain control over nature. Yet, because of its nature, confining biotechnology to useful, productive purposes will probably require greater social controls. And, although the technology has great potential for addressing the needs of resource-poor farmers, it is likely that its effects will be directed first and foremost to the needs of those who will be most able to afford to purchase the technology. The already-developed societies will have control over biotechnology, but social control and the problems of underemployment, migration to cities, and increasing inequality are likely to be exacerbated. Yet little provision is being made for policy to deal with such effects, although the ultimate effects of continuing agricultural mechanization and biotechnology are likely to be more profound than were the changes wrought by the Neolithic period.

The scope of issues that needs to be considered in looking at agricultural development should include an "archaeology of the future." This perspective would use evolutionary ideas and concepts to attempt to identify the short- and long-term consequences of the changes in adaptive strategies and adaptive systems that are being promoted under the rubric of development. Evolutionary theory does not contain any moral prescriptions for interpreting or guiding policy with regard to continuing agricultural change such as that of biotechnology. As Greenwood (1984) has persuasively argued, those who seek to derive moral lessons from evolutionary theory are using it only as a cloak to cover their own ideological positions. While the human manipulation of the cellular and genetic structure of plants and animals will undoubtedly have biological and cultural consequences, many of these consequences will be determined by conflicts and debates within and among human societies and groups, not by some ultimate purposiveness existing in natural systems.[6]

CONCLUSIONS

Anthropology has already contributed substantially to understanding agricultural development processes, but these contributions will be even greater in the next decade or so. Agricultural anthropology as a subdiscipline is only in its infancy.

I believe that because of the Rockefeller Foundation Social Science Research Fellowship in Agricultural and Rural Development there will soon be a burgeoning of the subdiscipline of agricultural anthropology. Many of the 21 anthropologists who received fellowships to work in the international centers between 1974 and 1984 now are in teaching and research positions in U.S. universities and are passing on the skills and the experiences they have gained. A small unit has been formed within the American Anthropological Association called Culture and Agriculture, which publishes a newsletter of the same name. Although there is not yet a formal program in agricultural anthropology (to my knowledge) at any university, the departments of anthropology at the University of Kentucky, the University of Florida, and the University of Arizona have several individuals with substantial experience in international agricultural development. I suspect that it will not be long before more formal training programs are established.

No one social science discipline has a monopoly on any body of knowledge or techniques that are the sole key to understanding agricultural development issues. The complex problems in this domain require complex solutions that can only be approached through multidisciplinary cooperation. This includes the humanities; philosophers and other humanists can address issues of ethics and values in agriculture. Anthropology should contribute microlevel studies that investigate why individuals and households choose the adaptive strategies they do, documentation of the reasons why adaptive systems have evolved, and commentary on such macrolevel questions as the ultimate evolutionary consequences of these adaptive systems (see DeWalt and Pelto 1985). With an increasing number of members of the discipline receiving better training in agricultural anthropology *and* in agricultural disciplines (agricultural economics, agronomy, animal sciences), the evolutionary perspective of anthropology can be useful in broadening and sharpening the range of issues that are considered in agricultural development circles and should help to increase the appropriateness and the success of these efforts.

NOTES

1. Billie R. DeWalt is a professor and the chair of the Department of Anthropology at the University of Kentucky. Dr. DeWalt also holds joint appointments as Professor of Rural Sociology and in the Patterson School of Diplomacy. He acknowledges the helpful comments of William Y. Adams, Peggy Barlett, Kathleen DeWalt, Allan Hoben, Della McMillan, Gene Wunderlich, and an anonymous reviewer on earlier versions of this chapter.

2. Several recent books from international agencies and centers documenting the role that social sciences can play in the agricultural research and development process have prominently featured the work of anthropologists. These include: International Rice Research Institute (1982); Matlon et al. 1984; Rhoades 1985; and Cernea 1985.

3. A concern with preserving the social and moral fabric of rural communities—the cultural system in anthropological jargon—is one of the main elements that has earned sociologists and especially anthropologists a reputation as nay-sayers in agricultural development circles. We are often put in the position of being critical of development efforts because so many of them have tended to be destructive to the cultural fabric of rural communities. As social scientists become more involved in the *planning and implementation* of agricultural development (rather than just in *evaluation*), it will be up to us to show that development can occur without these destructive effects.

4. Although the six points may seem to apply mostly to biological phenomena, Greenwood and Stini (1977) have argued that biological and cultural evolution are part of the same process. In an ultimate sense, of course, they are correct because culture is the primary means by which humans attempt to adapt to social and natural habitat. Natural selection continues to be operative. On the other hand, social scientists are also interested in adaptive processes that do not necessarily lead to ultimate extinction or survival. Cultures disappear all the time while descendants of their human carriers survive and sometimes flourish.

5. It is not surprising that the evolutionary perspective has been used to good advantage in historical studies. Evolutionary theory in biology is much more useful to account retrospectively for why change has occurred. Predicting the course of change is more difficult.

6. Perhaps the only lesson to be learned from evolutionary theory is that, at least in the long term, variability is a good thing. Contemporary trends that are leading to increasing genetic and cultural homogeneity are probably not for the best—at least in evolutionary terms.

REFERENCES

Adams, Richard N. 1985. Regulation and selection in the micro/macro perspective. In *Micro and macro levels of analysis in anthropology: Issues in theory and research.* Edited by Billie R. DeWalt and Pertti J. Pelto, 5568. Boulder, Colo.: Westview Press.

Barlett, Peggy. 1980. *Agricultural decision making: Anthropological contributions to rural development.* New York: Academic Press.

———1982. *Agricultural choice and change: Decision making in a Costa Rican community.* New Brunswick, N.J.: Rutgers University Press.

Bates, Robert. 1983. *Essays on the political economy of rural Africa.* Cambridge: Cambridge University.

Bennett, John. 1969. *Northern plainsmen.* Chicago: Aldine Publishing Co.

———1976. *The ecological transition: Cultural anthropology and human adaptation.* New York: Pergamon Press.

———1982. *Of time and the enterprise: North American farm management in a context of resource marginality.* Minneapolis: University of Minnesota Press.

Boserup, Ester. 1965. *The conditions of agricultural growth.* Chicago: Aldine Publishing Co.

Bray, Francesca. 1986. *The rice economies: Technology and development in Asian societies.* Oxford: Basil Blackwell.

Brokensha, David, D. M. Warren, and Oswald Werner, eds. 1980. *Indigenous knowledge systems.* Lanham, Md.: University Press of America.

Bulmer-Thomas, Victor. 1987. *The political economy of Central America since 1920.* Cambridge: Cambridge University.

Cancian, Frank. 1972. *Change and uncertainty: The Maya corn farmers of Zinacantan.* Stanford: Stanford University.

———1977. Can anthropology help agricultural development? *Culture and Agriculture* 2:18.

———1979. *The innovator's situation: Upper-middle-class conservatism in agricultural communities.* Stanford: Stanford University.

Cernea, Michael M., ed. 1985. *Putting people first: Sociological variables in rural development.* New York: Oxford University Press.

Chambers, Robert. 1983. *Rural development: Putting the last first*. London: Longman.

Chibnik, Michael, ed. 1987. *Farm work and field work: American agriculture in anthropological perspective*. Ithaca, N.Y.: Cornell University Press.

Childe, V. Gordon. 1951. *Man makes himself*. New York: Mentor.

Cohen, Leonard A. 1987. Diet and cancer. *Scientific American* 257, no. 5: 4248.

Cohen, Mark N.. 1987. The significance of long-term changes in human diet and food economy. In *Food and Evolution*. Edited by Marvin Harris and Eric Ross, 26184. Philadelphia: Temple University Press.

Conklin, Harold. 1957. *Hanunoo agriculture*. Rome: Food and Agricultural Organization (FAO).

DeSchlippe, P. 1956. *Shifting cultivation in Africa: The Zande system of agriculture*. London: Routledge and Keegan Paul.

DeWalt, Billie. 1979. *Modernization in a Mexican ejido: A study in economic adaptation*. New York and Cambridge: Cambridge University Press.

_____1983. Anthropology's contribution to the international sorghum/millet program. *Practicing Anthropology* 5, no. 3: 6, 10.

_____1985. Anthropology, sociology and farming systems research. *Human Organization* 44:10614.

_____1988a. The cultural ecology of development: Ten precepts for survival. *Agriculture and Human Values* 5, nos. 1/2: 11223.

_____1988b. Halfway there: Social science in agricultural development and social science of agricultural development. In *Human Organization* 47:34353.

DeWalt, Billie R., and Pertti J. Pelto, eds. 1985. *Micro and macro levels of analysis in anthropology: Issues in theory and research*. Boulder, Colo.: Westview Press.

Eder, James F. 1982. *Who shall succeed? Agricultural development and social inequality on a Philippine frontier*. Cambridge: Cambridge University.

Epstein, Scarlett. 1962. *Economic development and social change in South Asia*. Manchester: Manchester University Press.

_____1973. *South India: Yesterday, today and tomorrow*. London: Macmillan.

Franke, Robert G., and Dorothy N. Franke. 1975. *Man and the changing environment*. New York: Holt, Rinehart and Winston.

Frankenberger, Timothy. 1985. *Adding a food consumption perspective to farming systems research*, U.S. Dept. of Agriculture, Nutrition Economics Group, Washington, D.C.

Geertz, Clifford. 1963. *Agricultural involution: The process of ecological change in Indonesia*. Berkeley: University of California Press for the Association of Asian Studies.

Gladwin, Christina. 1979. Cognitive strategies and adoption decisions: A case study of nonadoption of an agronomic recommendation. *Economic Development and Cultural Change* 28:15573.

_____1980. A theory of real-life choice: Applications to agricultural decisions. In *Agricultural decision making: Anthropological contributions to rural development*. Edited by Peggy Barlett, 4586. New York: Academic Press.

Gladwin, Hugh, and Michael Murtaugh. 1980. The attentive-preattentive distinction in agricultural decision making. In *Agricultural decision making: Anthropological contributions to rural development*. Edited by Peggy Barlett, 11536. New York: Academic Press.

Goldschmidt, Walter. [1947] 1978. *As you sow: Three studies in the social consequences of agribusiness*. Montclair, N.J.: Allenheld, Osmun, and Co.

Good, Kenneth. 1987. Limiting factors in Amazonian ecology. In *Food and evolution*. Edited by Marvin Harris and Eric Ross, 40721. Philadelphia: Temple University Press.

Greenwood, Davydd. 1984. *The taming of evolution: The persistence of nonevolutionary views in the study of humans*. Ithaca, N.Y.: Cornell University Press.

Greenwood, Davydd, and William Stini. 1977. *Nature, culture and human history: A biocultural introduction to anthropology*. New York: Harper and Row.

Harlan, Jack. 1975. *Crops and man*. Madison: American Society of Agronomy.

Harris, Marvin. 1975. *Culture, people, nature*. 2d ed. New York: Thomas Y. Crowell.

Hill, Polly. 1972. *Rural Hausa: A village and a setting*. Cambridge: Cambridge University Press.

_____1982. *Dry grain farming families: Hausaland (Nigeria) and Karnatka (India) compared*. Cambridge: Cambridge University Press.

_____1986. *Development economics on trial: The anthropological case for a prosecution*. Cambridge: Cambridge University Press.

Hoben, Allan. 1980. Agricultural decision making in foreign assistance: An anthropological analysis. In *Agricultural decision making: Anthropological contributions to rural development*. Edited by Peggy Barlett, 33769. New York: Academic Press.

International Rice Research Institute (IRRI). 1982. *The role of anthropologists and other social scientists in interdisciplinary teams developing food production technology*. Los Banos, Philippines: IRRI.

Johnson, Allen. 1971. *Sharecroppers of the Sertao*. Stanford: Stanford University Press.

Lewis, Oscar. 1951. *Life in a Mexican village: Tepoztlan restudied*. Urbana: University of Illinois Press.

Matlon, P., R. Cantrell, D. King, and M. Benoit Cattin, eds. 1984. *Coming full circle: Farmers' participation in the development of technology*. Ottawa, Ontario: International Development Research Centre.

Mintz, Sidney. 1985. *Sweetness and power*. New York: Viking Press.

Moran, Emilio. 1979. *Human adaptability*. North Scituate, Mass.: Duxbury.

Murray, Gerald. 1987. The domestication of wood in Haiti: A case study in applied evolution. In *Anthropological praxis: Translating knowledge into action*. Edited by Robert M. Wulff and Shirley J. Fiske. Boulder, Colo.: Westview Press.

Netting, Robert. 1974. Agrarian ecology. *Annual Review of Anthropology* 3:2156.

Orlove, Benjamin. 1980. Ecological anthropology. *Annual review of anthropology* 9:23573.

Paul, Compton, and Billie R. DeWalt, eds. 1985. *El sorgo en sistemas de produccion en America Latina*. Mexico: International Sorghum and Millet Collaborating Research Support Project (INTSORMIL-CRSP)/International Corp Research Institute for the Semiarid Tropics (ICRISAT)/International Center for Improvement of Maize and Wheat (CIMMYT).

Pimental, David, and Marcia Pimental. 1979. *Food, energy and society*. London: Edward Arnold.
Pingali, Prabhu, Yves Bigot, and Hans Binswanger. 1987. *Agricultural mechanization and the evolution of farming systems in sub-Saharan Africa*. Baltimore: Johns Hopkins University.
Rappaport, Roy. 1968. *Pigs for the ancestors: Ritual in the ecology of a New Guinea people*. New Haven: Yale University Press.
Rhoades, Robert. 1985. *Breaking new ground: Agricultural anthropology*. Lima, Peru: CIP.
Rhoades, Robert, and Robert Booth. 1982. Farmer-back-to-farmer: A model for generating acceptable agricultural technology. *Agricultural Administration* 11:12737.
Schultz, Theodore. 1964. *Transforming traditional agriculture*. New Haven, Conn.: Yale University Press.
Service, Elman. 1962. *Primitive social organization: An evolutionary perspective*. New York: Random House.
Tripp, Robert. 1984. On-farm research and applied nutrition: Some suggestions for collaboration between national institutes of nutrition and agricultural research. *Food and Nutrition Bulletin* 6, no. 3: 4957.
_____1985. Anthropology and on-farm research. *Human Organization* 44:11424.
van Willigen, John. 1986. *Applied anthropology*. South Hadley, Mass.: Bergin and Garvey.

CHAPTER 5

THE BASIC SOCIAL SCIENCE DISCIPLINES (BSSDs): AGENDAS AND CONCLUSIONS

INTRODUCTION

Following a brief introduction, this chapter has two main subheadings, one for the verbatim report on agricultural and rural agendas for the basic social science disciplines from Peggy Barlett, professor of anthropology, Emory University, and Bonnie McCay, professor of anthropology and ecology, Cook College, Rutgers University, who together coordinated a set of work groups that developed the agendas. Under the second subheading, agendas developed by the editorial group after the Houston meeting are presented with stress on work needed in the basic social sciences in order to remedy their shortcomings and deficiencies for supporting problem-solving (PS) and subject-matter (SM) research in the rural social sciences. It is noted here that the verbatim report touches on needed financial and administrative support for research on agriculture and rural societies by the basic social science disciplines and that although this slightly overlaps work on administrative and funding strategies that was assigned to another discussion area at Houston, it is welcomed and included in this section. Readers, however, are urged to examine Part V of this book where additional administrative and funding strategies are presented in support of basic social science disciplinary work on farming and rural societies.

BASIC SOCIAL SCIENCE AGENDAS FROM HOUSTON

The growing complexity, diversity, and intensity of problems in rural areas presents the basic social sciences with a challenge to broaden and strengthen their contribution. The fundamental knowledge and skills of the basic social sciences and humanities must be harnessed to address the critical issues facing rural areas today. In doing such applied research, scholars do not dilute their enterprise, but rather gather the information needed to test their theories and methods, thus, leading to innovations and improvements in their parent disciplines. Improvements in teaching and extension complement these contributions to research and to the development of each discipline.

The range of relevant disciplines offering theories and methods to understand, explain, and predict real-world phenomena is broad, including: anthropology, economics, geography, history, home economics, philosophy, political science, psychology, and religious studies as well as patently applied fields such as communications and information sciences, regional sciences, management sciences, and demography.

Disciplinary contributions are hampered by three major factors: lack of trained personnel, lack of research funds, and lack of incentives within reward structures for work in the areas relevant to current rural and agricultural issues. Many of the contributions of the basic social sciences could be best realized in a multidisciplinary context, not only among the basic and rural social sciences but also between social sciences, natural and physical sciences, and humanities. Priorities for fostering such interdisciplinary and multidisciplinary applied work have been combined in a final section of this report, rather than repeated for each discipline.

The group that met in Houston developed the following priorities (agendas) for each social science discipline in extensive consultation with colleagues both at the conference and afterwards. The names listed below indicate committee members but do not list the many colleagues who contributed to each statement.

The rest of what is presented here under this main heading is quoted directly from reports originating from SSAAP's Houston meeting, which explains why the terms "priority" and "priorities" are used rather than "agendas" as in the remainder of the book.

ANTHROPOLOGY

Committee:
Peggy Barlett, Emory University, and Bonnie McCay, Rutgers University

Rural studies and food production are a traditional focus of cultural anthropologists who use comparative-research methods and evolutionary theory to understand peasant communities, rural areas of developed countries, and tribal societies. Recent studies have addressed larger regional, national, and international issues of trade, agricultural policy, and foreign aid programs. Other aspects of culture, such as family structure, women's roles, social class, power relations, religion, and ethnicity, can contribute to the study of agrarian systems by providing the full cultural context in which to understand the behavior studied by other disciplines.

Anthropology stresses the holistic aspect of culture, in which all behavior patterns and values are interrelated and interdependent, leading to a broader conception of subject matter than other social sciences. Methodological contributions include commitment to long-term fieldwork in rural and urban communities and to learning about the people being studied in their own terms, as well as in the terms of the scientist.

Topical Priorities

1. Expand research linking *long-term processes of economic and political change*, including national and international trends of world market penetration, to data on household survival strategies and changing community structure. Relevant issues would include causes and consequences of population growth, migration, processes of proletarianization, marketing structures and their consequences, and changes in the nature and conditions of farm labor.
2. Strengthen local-level research on *comparative farm structure*, including industrial-type farms, multiple job holding, and production cooperatives and collectives, to illuminate the internal organization of production units, comparative economic performance, community impacts of structural change, and implications for family structure, gender roles, local and regional power structure and ecological relationships.
3. Expand our knowledge of *indigenous agricultural systems* through research in developing countries, including patterns of multicropping and intercropping, long-term, sustainable ecological knowledge and categories, and mechanisms to maintain common land and water resources, with special attention to locally generated "development," labor-intensive, productivity-enhancing techniques, risk perception and risk-reducing behavior, and the aspects of indigenous systems that affect equity and the distribution of power.
4. Strengthen comparative research on *planned rural change*, including state farms and collectivized agriculture, multinational corporations (MNCs) and plantation agriculture, and development programs concerning credit, extension, and technology transfer that target household-based production. Include the impact of old information technologies as well as new ones and research on effective means of generating local-level participation in design, alteration, and evaluation of agricultural projects.
5. Support research on the *"culture" of agricultural research and development programs*, using participant-observation techniques to study local and national elites, agricultural policy institutions, and priority-setting processes, including how decisions are made and the effects of those decisions. Such studies would also aim to develop better understandings of how to build more effective multidisciplinary teams in the agricultural social sciences.
6. In cooperation with epidemiologists, increase local-level studies of *farm health and safety and rural health issues*, including impacts of farm chemicals and illness patterns.
7. Expand understandings of *values and beliefs* that maintain natural resources through studies of nonagricultural institutions, including religion and the use of symbols and rituals, to reinforce traditional values and beliefs about agriculture, especially those beliefs that support collective goals and long-term decision making. These studies can also determine how to use traditional institutions and the beliefs and values associated with them to support new institutions and values such as sustainable agriculture.
8. Support research in biological anthropology on *human variability in diet and nutritional biochemistry*, including effects of dietary changes on human growth and development.

Methodological Priorities

1. Develop criteria for *minimal datasets* on local-level agricultural systems, including ecological, economic, and political dimensions of food production. Defined methodologies should include rapid assessment procedures as well as more thorough methods to allow good comparison across researchers and locales, as well as to foster more effective communication and collaboration with agronomic scientists.
2. Cooperate with rural social sciences to *develop survey instruments* that are valid and appropriate for diverse ethnic or cultural groups as well as for diverse social classes, localities, and regions.
3. Develop improved methods of measuring exactly what constitutes *agricultural sustainability* and its relationship to reproducing farm families and appropriate cultural systems in a historical/evolutionary context.
4. Develop improved methods for *institutional research*, including studies of elites and governmental institutions, in collaboration with sociologists and other specialists.
5. Improve ability to link findings from anthropological research (qualitative and quantitative) to models and research priorities in other disciplines, including the efforts of some economists and public choice theorists to improve understandings of collective choice and institutional change and the bio-economic models used in resource management.

ECONOMICS AND STATISTICS

Committee:
Karl Fox, Iowa State University, and,
Lester V. Manderscheid, Michigan State University

Economics examines the allocation of scarce (limited) resources among competing uses. Applications of this basic structure have been developed for private-firm decision making, allocation of resources by and among governments, and in situations of market failure. Economists can contribute in many ways to the resolution of rural social science problems and, at the same time, improve the power of economic models to explain real-world phenomena.

Topical Priorities

1. Improve *measures of "economic development"* and the tradeoffs involved in development processes, including

better ways of evaluating development projects.
2. Determine the relationship among rural household *human skills and other resources, employment behavior, and income generation.*
3. Improve *estimations of value* added to raw agricultural commodities in food processing, manufacturing, and marketing.
4. Clarify the *factors influencing critical decisions* by consumers, farm operators, nonfarm business operators, resource managers, and governments.
5. Document the diverse influences on the *flow of agricultural commodities* in local, national, and international markets.

Methodological Priorities

1. Develop means to estimate *indicator functions* incorporating multiple variables, including nonmonetary variables such as gender, ethnicity, and kinship ties, as they affect utility functions. These would allow measurement of progress in development and the benefits of alternative projects. Included would be means of incorporating into utility measures the fact that individual preferences are affected by the utility levels of others, such as other household members.
2. Improve *disequilibria theory*. This would recognize that adjustments to new equilibria are often not smooth. Catastrophe theory and the elaboration of applied mathematical models may provide the mathematical base.
3. Improve the theory of the *effect of time on decisions*. Interest-rate discounting suggests that many long-run benefits are of near-zero value, yet people make decisions assigning significant value to distant events.
4. Enhance the development of *changing parameter models*, including estimation of the path of future parameter change.
5. Clarify *statistical decision theory* and its relation to philosophic value theory and policy analysis. Incorporation of transaction (learning) costs requires special attention.
6. Develop *statistical models not requiring strong distribution assumptions*. In many cases, the true distribution of errors is not known, but is suspected to be nonnormal.

GEOGRAPHY

Committee:
Darrel Napton, Southwest Texas State University, and
Rebecca Roberts, University of Iowa

Geography is concerned with understanding differences in the character of human settlement. The distinctive focus is on the geographic distribution of patterns of resources, places, regions, and routes. Fundamentally underlying the concern with distribution is a concern with how social and natural processes affect the character of places and regions and how, in turn, the economic, political, cultural, and environmental attributes of particular places, regions, and interconnecting flows and routes shape the manner in which social and natural processes operate. Geographic synthesis attempts to capture the interrelationships of social and natural relationships between town and country, region and nation, and between nations without losing sight of the distinctive history and character that different places bring to bear upon the impact of those processes.

Topical Priorities

1. Document *geographic differences in rural land use, land tenure, and production-system dynamics*, including agricultural intensification, abandonment, land tenure and change, and their implication for rural policy and program outcomes.
2. Study the geographic effects of changing world food and fiber markets on *comparative local advantage* of producing regions, commodity transportation, and marketing infrastructure.
3. Clarify the spatial distribution of perceptions and responses to *natural/technical hazards and risks.*
4. Specify the implications of interactions between *rural land use, settlement systems, and international trade* for environmental problems and rural communities.

Methodological Priorities

1. Sharpen the application of *remote-sensing techniques* and geographic information systems for analysis and communication of rural problems.
2. Improve the understanding of *scale and resolution problems* in data collection and management so as to represent the geographic variability essential to solving problems.

HISTORY

Committee:
Sally McMurray, Pennsylvania State University, and
Margaret Rossiter, Cornell University

History entails the systematic study of processes that occur over time, and historians use a wide range of both narrative and systematic social science data-analysis techniques. History provides both a context in which to evaluate contemporary agricultural problems and a perspective from which to weigh potential solutions. Historians examine themes of change in culture, technology, social organization, and thought. One subfield of history, not large but once well established in U.S. Department of Agriculture (USDA), is agricultural history. Those who become involved in or who can expand the focus of agricultural history, as well as forest history and other subspecialties, can contribute to addressing the national agricultural crisis in many ways.

Topical Priorities

1. Document the historical relationships among *agriculture and other productive and extractive activities, society, and the natural environment*, including particular emphasis on the family and women's contributions to rural society and on the differences in agricultural practices and natural resource use among different ethnic and racial groups.
2. Analyze the effects of agricultural sciences and rural institutions on changing agricultural systems, specifically:
   - Major *institutions of U.S. agricultural science*, including land-grant universities, agricultural experiment stations, USDA bureaus, and private units such as foundations.
   - The continuity, change, and cycles in *federal and state agricultural science policies*, their successes and

limitations, and their similarity or dissimilarity to science policy in other sectors (such as medicine and basic sciences).
- The *effectiveness* of public and private agricultural research—its settings, goals, and patterns of funding.
- The rise and development of particular *specialties* (including nutrition and home economics) and their chief participants and clientele and an evaluation of their reward structure.

3. Identify how and why *consumption patterns* have changed over time.
4. Document *past sustainable agricultural systems* such as those of the Amish, Hutterites, and the Amana Colonies.

Methodological Priorities

1. Improve *archival holdings* of documents and artifacts on agriculture and rural life.
2. Generate widely accessible *public exhibits and displays* on the transformation of agriculture and rural life.
3. Survey and preserve the *archival holdings of the state agricultural experiment stations* and of departments related to agriculture, to assure adequate and accessible documentation.

HOME ECONOMICS

Committee:
Steven Jorgenson, Texas Technical University, and Lynda Walters, University of Georgia

Home economics/human ecology encompasses a multidisciplinary approach to the study of individual growth and development within the family context. In turn, the growth and development of families is studied in the context of the family's social, cultural, economic, and physical milieu. The strength of this perspective lies in its holistic approach to family problems and issues.

Home economics/human ecology is eclectic, using methods from a variety of root disciplines (for example, sociology, psychology, economics, biology, and chemistry). Theories, too, are primarily from the root disciplines although home economics has become more creative in this regard in recent years.

Topical Priorities

1. Investigate the relation between changes in the *rural health infrastructure and fertility practices*, patterns, and outcomes. Particular attention should be paid to the decline in numbers of hospitals and private physicians and the effects on fertility patterns, maternal health, early unplanned pregnancy, and infant morbidity and mortality.
2. Identify *food selection and dietary practices* of nutritionally vulnerable groups (both in the United States and in developing countries) and assess the apparent influences of diet on physiological health and well-being. Explore the changes in dietary patterns caused by the U.S. farm crisis.
3. Assess *consumer preferences* in order to strengthen the profitability and competitiveness of agricultural products and industries, with particular emphasis on ways to keep value-added industries within local-producer communities.
4. Assess the role of the indigenous and transplanted *elderly in rural communities*, and their needs in terms of social services, housing, health status, nutritional status, energy consumption, support networks, substance abuse, and relationships with adult children and extended family.
5. Investigate the *multiple effects of technological innovations* on the lives and relationships of rural families, pursuing ways in which technology creates new problems while solving old ones (for example, bovine growth hormone).
6. Investigate the *unintended effects of economic depression and revitalization* on community and family well-being, exploring also the ways that positive effects in one area or family context may be accompanied by negative effects in others.
7. Evaluate the effects of *adolescent employment patterns* (as on-farm work declines) on long-term income generation, consumption aspirations, employment patterns, and the implications for secondary and higher education.
8. Analyze *problems of youth and adolescents* in rural areas, with attention to family stress, changing family structures, decline in viable life choices in recent years, precocious sexual activity, unwanted pregnancy, substance abuse, crime and delinquency, learned helplessness, and "running" from home.
9. Develop theories and methods for studying outcomes of *stress*, recognizing the important role of stress in creativity and the possibility of developing adaptive outcomes as a result of stress, particularly in the current farm crisis. Explore the implications of these findings for service-delivery systems.
10. Develop an understanding of the problems of *Hispanic families* in rural areas, particularly in the burgeoning Mexican-American population, with focus on economic disadvantages, language difficulties, and barriers to receiving a quality education.
11. Evaluate the impact of *laws and public policy* and changes that both have on family functioning. Inheritance laws and tax laws, for example, can disrupt the interdependencies in farm families and the assumption that one or more children will inherit and maintain the farm.
12. Investigate *pesticide residues in farm clothing* and develop safe cleaning processes.

Methodological Priorities

1. Refine theories and methods for studying processes in families in order to be able to *differentiate normative conflict from dysfunctional conflict*. Such conflict has emerged with the farm crisis, but also appears in parent-adolescent and spousal relations.
2. Expand current domestic research to include an *international and comparative perspective*, especially in the area of family, kin, and gender issues.

PHILOSOPHY

Committee:
Edward McClennen, Washington University, and Richard Haynes, University of Florida

Philosophy, one of the humanities, is characterized by two traditions. The foundational tradition is concerned with the critical analysis of transdisciplinary concepts and the basic concepts of the various other disciplines. The synthetic tradition is concerned with interpreting and integrating discipline-based information into one or another coherent world view. The first tradition speaks to essentially normative concerns: developing tools for the evaluation of methods of inquiry and theory for a particular area of research, the private goals and interests that fuel such research, and the ethical issues that arise when such goals and interests conflict.

Topical Priorities

1. Clarify and assess underlying *paradigms and assumptions* in agriculture, and in the agricultural and rural social sciences.
2. Clarify and prioritize *values, goals, and ethical principles* at stake in public-policy problems and explore the normative implications of research-problem selection.

Methodological Priorities

1. Develop tools for the evaluation of methods of inquiry and theory as they relate to policy challenges in agricultural and rural development.

The utility of philosophy to the rural social sciences can come from both traditions in philosophy, but the discipline strengths of philosophy need to be tapped in a manner that provides for an informed exchange in order to avoid disciplinary parochialism or imperialism. Like others who work with the rural social sciences or who are concerned with public-policy issues in this area, philosophers must educate themselves about the related fields. Therefore, it is imperative that any contribution which philosophy is asked to make be fully informed of, and responsive to, the special expertise possessed by those who work in the relevant subject-matter areas and in the social sciences in general.

If effective cooperation between philosophy and the rural social sciences is to be achieved, funding must be provided for internship programs and for cooperative research efforts, and other forms of opportunities and, incentives must be available for philosophers working in this area, including disciplinary and institutional recognition of the value of applied and transdisciplinary research.

POLITICAL SCIENCE

Committee:
William Browne, Central Michigan University

Political science—the study of who gets what, when, where, and why—is divided internally by subfields: international relations, comparative government, national politics, subnational politics, public administration, and political theory. The subfield of public-policy studies has recently emerged, linked with the subfield of public administration. The only two public-policy areas where political scientists have sought specific identities are subfield related: international relations gives rise to foreign policy experts; subnational government brings forth urban political scientists. In other policy domains, political scientists may become part of multidisciplinary efforts. This suggests that political science needs multidisciplinary assistance to play a successful role in contributing to an agricultural and rural agenda. Dominant agricultural social sciences must offer incentives to political scientists.

Political scientists, across the subfields, can contribute to areas affecting agriculture and rural development in at least five matters: policy processes, linkages to the public, the motives of politicians, normative questions about the distribution of resources, and the application of what are essentially multidisciplinary methods of research and analysis.

Topical Priorities

1. Analyze *domestic and international agricultural policy linkage* to better understand domestic-policy processes and their reactions to such international agreements as the General Agreement on Tariffs and Trade (GATT). Studies of agricultural policy institutions and their diversity in each nation can maximize successful cooperation among nations, as each appreciates the hurdles and impediments facing their peers.
2. Measure the impact of *agrarian values on public opinion*, with attention to the use of such ideologies by special interest groups, the farm lobby, policy makers, and the general public.
3. Explore the use of political variables in *reorganizing and revitalizing rural public and policy-making institutions* such as the Cooperative Extension Service.
4. Determine the factors that most influence *congressional decision making* on agricultural and rural issues.
5. Develop recommendations on *restructuring the administrative units of county governments* to deal with the financial stress of diminishing local revenues.
6. Obtain survey data on the *political attitudes* of diverse types of farmers.

Methodological Priorities

1. Develop more complex *econometric and predictive models* of policy outcomes to improve analyses of public choice and general utility.

PSYCHOLOGY

No Committee

Psychology is the study of individual and group behavior in experimental, natural, and clinical settings. Biological psychologists measure the impact of biological processes on individual behavior. Cognitive psychology examines the acquisition, processing, and use of sensory information, including perception and learning. Social psychologists examine the effect of groups and other social phenomena on individual behavior. Developmental psychologists are concerned with change in behavior over time, especially in childhood. Industrial organizational psychology explores implications of organizational design on behavior in businesses. Clinical psychology develops methods to assess individual functioning and change undesirable behavior patterns.

Psychometric and survey-design methods developed by psychologists are used extensively by social scientists, for example, sociologists, home economists, political scientists. Since many of its procedures are needed for multidisciplinary research, psychology can improve its potential for making contributions to the rural social sciences and to rural and agricultural issues in the following ways:

Topical Priorities

1. Clarify the role of individual behavior and its variation in the face of *environmental and economic risk and*

uncertainty, and the implications of this behavior for agricultural policies on income, development, natural resources, and consumer and worker protection.
2. Increase understanding of *stress* and other psychological effects of economic and social change and disruption in rural areas and develop educational and therapeutic programs to help individuals and families adjust to these changes.
3. Strengthen the use of theories and findings on information acquisition, processing, and learning in *management decisions* in the agricultural and rural and private and public sectors on production, marketing, planning, and policies.
4. Apply understandings of *group decision processes* to challenges faced by industry, small businesses, public agencies, and other organizations involved in rural development.

SOCIOLOGY

Committee:
James Christenson, University of Kentucky, and Carolyn Sachs, Pennsylvania State University

Sociologists study the interaction between groups (like farmers) with environmental, institutional, economic, and cultural forces. In short, they want to know why people do things the way they do. They make use of survey, demographic, and ethnographic methods to study social change processes, human values, intergroup and intragroup cooperation and conflict, institutional and community organization.

Topical Priorities

1. Investigate the causes and consequences of *increasing social and economic disparity* between rural and urban areas, national and international. A part of this research will involve longitudinal studies of changing socio-demographic patterns in response to employment opportunities, environments, policies, lifestyles, and institutions.
2. Develop *recommendations to improve the quality of life* in rural communities, including the development of policy to correct for unequal access to employment opportunities, education, and other resources for rural women, blacks, Hispanics, and Native Americans.
3. Examine the relationship between *agricultural production practices, the environment, and the rural population.* Specific efforts should be devoted to exploring the relationship between environmental and economic sustainability of agriculture. The impact of environmental degradation on the rural population should be examined in both the United States and developing countries, including the role of public and farmer perceptions in the development and use of sustainable practices.

Methodological Priorities

1. Develop improved methods to evaluate and predict the *social impacts of technological change and development projects*, including power plants, waste disposal plants, prisons, etc., prior to the introduction of these technologies or facilities.
2. Develop better ways of *combining quantitative and qualitative research methodologies* to resolve research problems, especially through interdisciplinary cooperation with history and anthropology to sharpen theories and methods for understanding social change.

CONCLUSION: GOALS AND STRATEGIES

The fundamental goal of social science disciplinary work in applied contexts is to generate the knowledge, attain the understanding, and help design, implement, and evaluate the programs that will help people achieve societal goals. Concepts reflected in societal goals include the following:

- Sustainable natural and production systems for agriculture, forestry, water use, and fisheries
- Viable communities and institutions
- Social equity in the distribution of costs, benefits, rights, and privileges, goods, and services
- Empowerment of social groups underrepresented in decision-making processes
- Resource stewardship
- Respect for and protection of cultural diversity
- Adequate levels of health, nutrition, and material welfare in human populations
- To help people achieve societal goals, as social scientists we need to know:
- Where are we now? What is happening?
- How did we get here? What processes of continuity and change are taking place?
- Who has benefitted, who pays the costs, and who makes the decisions?
- How can we strengthen movement in desired directions?

The social science disciplines can play major roles in research, extension, and instruction about problems and issues that help us answer these and related questions and achieve societal goals. However, many of these contributions can be made more effectively in a multidisciplinary context. In order to enrich the disciplinary potentials for contributing to PS and SM research as well as teaching and extension in the above areas, changes must be made in reward structures and institutional arrangements.

Funding and Institutional Priorities

1. Support competitive research funding opportunities for the basic social science and humanities disci- plines through the USDA, National Science Foundation (NSF), National Endowment for the Humanities (NEH), and other agencies.
2. Improve the research and problem-solving capacity of social science and humanities faculty through:
   - Joint academic appointments in colleges of agriculture and liberal arts.

- Access to state agricultural experiment station lines for specialists outside the traditional fields.
- Predoctoral fellowships to encourage young scholars to pursue research in agricultural and rural development topics.
- Mid-career fellowships in related rural social science and humanities fields, to develop multidisciplinary familiarity and research strength among established faculty.
- Short-term internships for social scientists and humanists in policy and research centers.
- Fellowships in agriculture-related topics at the major centers for advanced study, such as the Center for Advanced Study in the Behavioral Sciences (Stanford University) and the National Humanities Center (University of North Carolina).

3. Promote multidisciplinary and interdisciplinary research through:
   - Developing requirements for such multidisciplinary efforts within the USDA and other funding institutions concerned traditionally with food, fiber, natural resources, and rural life.
   - Encouraging short-term team approaches to interdisciplinary problem- focused research.
   - Providing funds for consultants for rural social science and humanities disciplines in agricultural and rural development projects.
4. Support new and continued research efforts to address agricultural and rural issues through:
   - Establishing a national center or endowment for the rural social sciences (or rural studies).
   - Expanding the whole, or at least the social science share, of state agricultural experiment stations.
   - Building different and more broadly based constituencies for RSS (rural social sciences), BSSD (basic social science disciplines), and humanities research.
   - Exploring ways to develop incentives within each discipline to reward researchers in pursuing topics that address national needs in the areas of agricultural and rural development.
   - Where appropriate, encouraging international and cross-cultural dimensions of research traditionally limited to the United States.
5. Develop alliances with administrators outside colleges of agriculture and outside universities with such colleges to mobilize support for the applied efforts of social science and humanities researchers addressing agricultural and rural problems.
6. Work with administrators to mobilize support from international agencies for research and extension participation of basic social scientists in international rural development

Teaching and Extension Priorities

1. Encourage the development of a range of new courses (and revisions to the content of existing courses) in both colleges of agriculture and liberal arts that address current national and international issues of agricultural and rural development issues across disciplinary lines.
2. Strengthen coordination of course offerings and course content between basic social science and humanities departments and rural social sciences to better serve students in both kinds of programs.
3. Work with Extension Committee on Organization and Policy (ECOP) and specific institutions to explore contributions of basic social science disciplines to extension work and evaluation.
4. Expand the public awareness of agricultural and rural issues through funding expanded museum exhibits, public television programs, National Park visitors' centers, and other "public education" opportunities.

EDITORIAL AGENDAS DEVELOPED AFTER THE HOUSTON MEETING

As previously indicated, the agendas presented above were developed at Houston under the joint chairmanship of Bonnie McCay and Peggy Barlett. These admirable and appropriate agendas require supplementation for three reasons. *First,* unlike the other two crosscuts dealing with agricultural ethics and databases, the basic social science disciplinary crosscut did not have work groups in the substantive areas to record the concerns of rural social scientists working in those areas about the inadequacies of assistance obtainable by them from the basic social sciences; consequently, the above agendas do not reflect feedback for the basic social sciences from the substantive areas. *Second,* at Houston, one of the four driving forces—human development—was inadequately recognized in the organization of the conference. Since Houston, additional papers have been commissioned and meetings have been held in SSAAP to remedy this difficulty as explained in the introduction to Part III of this book; consequently, agenda items for the basic social science disciplines emerged after the Houston conference as more explicit attention was to the four driving forces (see the four sections of Part IV). *Third,* because the basic social science disciplinarians who developed the above agendas tended to focus on studies they could do regarding farming, agribusiness, rural societies, and consumers in their disciplines, the above agendas center largely on applied disciplinary work in a way that leaves an unmet need for agendas to improve the basic social science disciplines so that they may better serve social, biological, and physical agricultural scientists doing multidisciplinary PS and SM work (see, for example, the last portion of Chapter 2 [Part III, Section 4]). There is some duplication between the agendas presented by the editorial group here and those developed at the Houston meeting. This duplication arises from a desire to preserve the Houston report intact and what the editorial group regards as a necessity to reiterate certain agenda items in the broader contexts of multidisciplinary PS and SM work.

The editorial group presents the following agenda items (arranged by discipline) for making the basic social science disciplines more effective contributors to the capacity of the RSSs to serve farmers, farm families, agribusiness people, and residents of rural communities with PS and SM efforts.

- *Anthropology*—Anthropologists should: Develop more complete and more formal anthropological theories and conceptualizations of the interrelationships of cultural variables with each other and with variables stressed by other social scientists since these variables are important in private and group decision and choice processes.
  - Develop better quantitative and qualitative anthropological techniques for handling cultural variables

that influence responses of individuals and groups to changes in the four driving forces stressed in Part III, namely changes in technical, human, institutional, and natural and manmade resources.

- Develop improved ways of constructing scenarios in time and space for use when important cultural variables are likely to condition responses to public and private projects and programs for agriculture and rural societies.
- Develop improved measurements of cultural and other variables known by anthropologists to be important for PS and SM efforts pertaining to farming, agribusinesses, rural societies, and consumers.
- Explore possible anthropological extensions of the public choice/transaction cost (PC/TC) approach for the analysis of public choices and private decisions.

- *Economics* (including econometrics and mathematical economics)—Perhaps because economics has the most formalized theoretical structure of the basic social science disciplines and, for that matter, among many of the biological and physical sciences, and because parts of economics are highly quantified, its existing theories, techniques, and basic measurements are probably in more obvious need of improvement than those of the other basic social science disciplines. The editorial group of SSAAP judges that the following are important disciplinary agenda items which, if attained, would do much to facilitate the multidisciplinary PS and SM efforts of rural social scientists attempting to assist farming and rural societies. Working in close cooperation with statisticians, economists should improve their theories for dealing with imperfect knowledge and risk regarding the four driving forces for farm and rural development that are treated in Part III. More specifically, economists should:
  - Improve their theories of the economics of learning as part of choosing and decision-making processes in both public and private sectors.
  - Clarify the meanings of risk preference and risk aversion in view of the failure of present risk-preference and aversion theories to deal with how the taking of different amounts of risk affects the value or "utility" of any given attained outcome.
  - Distinguish more sharply in theory between insuring and ensuring.
  - Place additional stress on the taking of chances to attain favorable outcomes.
  - Strive to include risk and chance taking theories more explicitly in extensions of the PC/TC approach to public choice and private decision making considered in Part III of this book.
  - Examine the "new household economics" for needed improvements in it to develop its full potential for analyzing:
    - rural and small town labor markets
    - the demand for social, educational, health and welfare services in rural areas
    - rural demographic change
    - rural self-employment and home-based nonfarm businesses
    - rural/urban and farm/nonfarm income differences
  - Explore and develop a better understanding of the roles of power in "rules of the game" for decision making and choosing.
  - Reexamine frontier production theory; commonly accepted definitions of allocative, price and technical efficiency; and duality. In this connection and more specifically, economists should place stress on:
    - Problems of input and product aggregation as they generate "apparent" solid interiors to "frontier" production functions.
    - Problems of misspecification of the fixed and variable inputs in describing production functions as they again create "apparently" solid interiors for production functions.
    - Reexamining production theory for possible explanations of interior points of production functions in the absence of specification-aggregation errors.
  - Examine the philosophic foundations for the techniques and methods used by economists in doing empirical work. More specifically, attention should be paid to philosophic orientations
    - in which it is acceptable to do descriptive work on the "real values" of conditions, situations, things, and acts and
    - that are more amenable to holistic analyses done cooperatively with other disciplines in a manner that overcomes the shortcomings of positivistic reductionism deplored by McCloskey.
  - Make greater efforts to attain interpersonally valid measures of welfare.
  - Make greater effort to measure intrinsic as opposed to extrinsic or exchange values.
  - Measure the values of acts as well as the values of the consequences of those acts.
  - Stress the disciplinary importance of doing more quantitative work even at the expense of reduced attention to mathematical economics.
  - Expand attention to doing holistic, multidisciplinary systems analyses of real-world systems in such a way that the full power of formal economic theory can be interrelated with theories from other social sciences and the biological and physical sciences to generate holistic, dynamic analyses of the domains of practical problems, issues, and subjects.
  - Explore the mathematic characteristics of systems models and commonly used components thereof to expose inherent instabilities of systems components that are unrelated to "real world" systems and subsystems being modeled.
  - Explore mathematical simplification of both optimizing and nonoptimizing models to save modeling time and computational costs.
  - Extend PC/TC theories to deal with changes in (1) institutions as organizations and (2) the properties, facilities, and staffs of organizations as well as with (3) institutions as "rules of the game." In all three cases, the theory needs expansion to include both *stock* establishment and dismantlement costs in transaction costs. Stock establishment and dismantlement costs need to be related to transaction flow costs for information, negotiation, and enforcement. Also needed are theoretical extensions to *relate* the "values in use" of rules of the game, organizations, and properties, staffs, and facilities *to* their establishment and dismantlement costs *for use* in determining whether institutional changes are advantageous or unjustified.
  - Extend the PC/TC approach to deal more explicitly with the "collection of rents" from fixed institutions

in all three manifestations in a manner that recognizes that opportunity costs can generate
- negative quasi-rents with respect to flow *establishment* costs and
- positive quasi-rents with respect to flow *dismantlement* costs and that
- minimization of negative quasi-rents minimizes losses on fixed institutions while, at the same time, maximizing returns above dismantlement costs, neither one of which is inherently objectionable or universally unethical.

- *Statistics*—The RSSs and BSSDs should:
  - Monitor developments in statistical theory for opportunities to incorporate such developments into
    - the public-choice private-decision theories now being used increasingly in the RSS's and
    - learning and managerial theories.
  - Encourage statisticians to extend their theories about the errors of the first and second kind involved in choosing between two alternatives to the six involved when public and private decision makers choose among three alternatives as they so commonly do.
  - Urge statistical theorists to help extend concepts of ausality (as opposed to mere sequential association) involving values and purpose as *causes* of individual and group behavior.
  - Urge mathematical statisticians, mathematically inclined social scientists, and systems scientists to
    - help develop more efficient models and computational techniques of doing Monte Carlo analysis of
    - complex systems models involving probability distributions.
  - Urge mathematical statisticians, mathematicians, and mathematically inclined social scientists to move in the directions of psychometrics, sociometrics, and anthrometrics.

- *Geography*—The problems and issues that rural social scientists address in doing PS and SM work typically have important, spatial dimensions. Rural social scientists are accustomed to mapping geographic changes. Economists deal with the generation of "place utility" as well as the location of production and consumption activities, while rural sociologists deal with space-occupying communities. Again, economists deal with transportation costs, comparative advantage, and other determinants of the spatial distribution of agricultural and rural activities. Von Thunen's theories have long been used to explain the location of production. RSSs should cooperate with and urge geographers to:
  - Incorporate transaction cost theories in their explanations of changes in the location of industries, people, and their activities.
  - Help build global models of various forms of environmental pollution with particular attention to
    - the mathematical equations used,
    - the estimation of the parameters of those equations,
    - the collection of data for use in estimating parameters, and
    - the validation and verification of such models.

Because time as well as the spatial dimension is important for analyzing such phenomena as global warming, ozone depletion, water contamination, sedimentation, desertification, and the like, it is particularly important that the spatial models of geographers be related to the temporal models of historians.

- *History*—The RSSs should urge historians to:
  - Extend Douglass North's transaction cost approach to history to cover establishment and dismantlement costs and values in use for the institutions (as rules of the game, organizations, staffs, and physical facilities and properties) that influence the four driving forces, namely: technological change; human development; institutions including policies, programs, and social infrastructure; and natural and manmade resources.
  - Help develop techniques and modules to handle the time dimensions of environmental pollution, that is, global warming, resource depletion, desertification, etc., like as multidisciplinary subjects to which social scientists contribute.

- *Home Economics/Human Ecology*—If there is a basic discipline in this area it is taken to be human ecology. The RSSs should recognize that human ecology like the RSSs themselves depends primarily on basic specialized disciplines for theoretical advances, improved disciplinary techniques, and basic disciplinary measurement. The eclecticism and holism of human ecology, however, offer some hope to the RSSs that human ecology may develop an overall approach to the study and modeling of the multidisciplinary domains of practical problems and subjects with sufficient realism to make the results particularly valuable. Such an approach could have widespread applicability and be useful to the RSSs that have responsibility for studying and modeling multidisciplinary PS and SM domains. Particularly needed is more attention to building human ecology variables into multidisciplinary analyses employing the "new household economics" and the PC/TC approach (see agenda items under the economics rubric above). See particularly Part II, Section 1, Chapters 1 and 7, and Part II, Section 2, Chapter 11.

- *Philosophy*—To assist the RSSs, philosophers should:
  - Devote more attention to clarifying what is involved when social scientists accept responsibility for prescribing actions to solve problems such as those involving environmental pollution, racial and gender inequality, drug abuse, hunger and malnutrition, estate management, and agricultural subsidies. It is important that the conflicts among as well as the diversity and constraints different philosophic points of view impose on each other be better understood by rural and basic social scientists who are often dogmatically committed to one philosophic orientation. While this is important for RSS and BSSD researchers and teachers, it is particularly important for RSSs and BSSDs when serving as advisors, consultants, extension workers, administrators, and entrepreneurs addressing multidisciplinary subjects and issues and practical problems.
  - Teach philosophy to agriculturalists either directly or by training rural social scientists and technical agriculturalists to teach modules dealing with the philosophic aspects of
    - research methodology and
    - agricultural ethics.
  - Gain descriptive knowledge of farming, farm families, agribusinesses, rural affairs, and consumers in preparing to teach philosophy to agriculturalists.

- Gain more knowledge of the philosophic orientations that actually structure the agricultural technical sciences, the RSSs, college-level agricultural instruction, extension work, the 4-H and FFA clubs, and vocational agricultural instruction in high schools in preparing to work with such groups.
- Expand their own concern as philosophers with experience and data as a *source of descriptive (synthetic) knowledge of values* without unduly reducing their philosophic concern with analytical knowledge of values and prescriptions.
- Take the lead in reestablishing the close classical relationship between economics and philosophy while including statistics, political science, psychology, and other disciplines concerned with private decisions and public choices with the objective of clarifying and improving our understanding of how contributions of new developments in these disciplines relate to each other and to
  - private and
  - public ethics.
- Contribute philosophic understanding of the processes of acquiring and using knowledge about
  - relatively value-free characteristics of conditions, situations, things, and acts;
  - values (extrinsic and more intrinsic and nonmonetary as well as monetary) of conditions, situations, things, and acts; and
  - "decision or choice rules" for converting value and value-free perceptions into prescriptions.

● *Political Science*—To assist RSSs, political scientists should:

- Contribute to the development of the PC/TC approach around which the so-called "new" political economy is being built. More specifically, it would help the rural social sciences if the approach were extended to deal with:
  - Institutions as organizations and properties, staffs, facilities and equipment, as well as "rules of the game."
  - The roles of power in public choice including military and police as well as market, political, religious, intellectual, and other forms of "social power."
  - Redistribution of the ownership of income (real) producing rights and privileges.
- Coordinate their contributions to PC/TC theory with contributions of historians, philosophers, sociologists, anthropologists, and geographers while obtaining multidisciplinary guidance from the PS and SM work of the RSSs that is, perforce, multidisciplinary.

● *Psychology*—As the social science basically concerned with individual and group behavior, the theories and techniques of psychiatrists and psychologists (including clinical psychologists) have considerable potential for assisting with the multidisciplinary PS and SM work of the RSSs. To assist the RSSs do their work, psychologists could help:

- Provide improved perceptions of the managerial behavior of entrepreneurs, consumers, and agribusiness people for use in multidisciplinary systems models of the domains of important farm and rural problems and subjects.
- Provide improved perceptions of the behavior of public decision makers whose decisions affect:
  - Generation of new technology.
  - Utilization, generation, and/or enhancement of natural and manmade resources.
  - Formation of human capital (improvement of people).
  - Improvement of other governmental and private institutions and policies.
  - Provide improved psychological perceptions for the RSSs to use in dealing with personal problems such as drug dependency, lack of motivation, marital relationships, and teenage pregnancy.

● *Sociology*—To better assist the RSSs, sociology as a BSSD should:

- Recognize that its rather informal theories relate both implicitly and explicitly to theories in other BSSDs and that doing applied specialized disciplinary work while neglecting multidisciplinary PS and SM work deprives sociology of the benefits of interacting with other basic disciplines and the RSSs in problem PS and SM exercises. While disciplinary and rural sociologists interact well with each other, neither reaches out enough to the other social sciences in an effort to better integrate their theories with the theories of other disciplines concerned with the same or related phenomena. The consequence seems to be a tendency to reinvent theories and techniques already used in other RSSs and to ignore interrelationships readily apparent to others doing similar PS and SM RSS work.
- Contribute sociological theories to multidisciplinary systems analysis of problematic and systems domains.
- Develop philosophic orientations to exploit the strengths of pragmatism, various forms of normativism, and pragmatism without being constrained by the weaknesses of these orientations.

● *Multidisciplinary Generalizations to Improve BSSD Contributions to RSS Work to Assist Farms and Rural Society*—The following agendas are important for increasing the contributions of BSSD to RSS efforts to resolve problems and issues important for farming and rural societies. The BSSDs should:

- Provide disciplinary courses for undergraduate and graduate rural social science students that are better coordinated with the more multidisciplinary rural social science courses offered in colleges of agriculture, natural resources, and home economics (human ecology). The rural social sciences need to meet the basic social scientists partway by revising undergraduate and graduate rural social science courses and curricula to coordinate better with curricula of departments outside agricultural colleges so that theory and methods from the basic disciplines can be more fully incorporated into the training of rural social scientists.
- Do disciplinary work as specified under the disciplinary sections included above in this chapter on theoretical and conceptual issues, quantitative techniques, and the measurement of basic phenomena that *are relevant* for the multidisciplinary PS and SM work done by RSSs. Social science theories, concepts, and methods required to permit before-the-fact assess-

ment of the potential social, economic, and environmental impacts of new agricultural technologies need to be improved. Disciplinary social science research of *known relevance* for agriculture and rural societies is needed. More specifically, concepts and theories from anthropology, economics, sociology, history, geography, ecology, and psychology need development and integration to make them more effective for use in helping rural and farm people adjust to the institutional, technical, human, and resource changes now affecting agricultural and rural societies.

A CONCLUSION ABOUT RESOLVING DISCIPLINARY VERSUS RSS STAKES IN IMPROVING THE BSSDs

The two main sections above pose the conflict that now exists between (1) the desires of the basic social scientists outside colleges of agriculture to do applied disciplinary work with respect to farms, agribusinesses, consumers, and rural society, and (2) the crucial need of the RSSs for better basic social science theories, techniques, and data relatable enough across disciplines to be used in multidisciplinary work on problems and subjects important for farming and rural societies.

Resolving this conflict is a matter requiring research on administration (defined to include organization and management) and different funding and administrative strategies. The next part of this book deals with (1) needed research on administration and (2) administrative and funding strategies for the rural and basic social sciences. In that part SSAAP agendas and strategies are presented for resolving this conflict (which is but a small part of the much more widespread similar conflict throughout the agricultural establishment) between disciplinary academicians and those concerned with multidisciplinary PS and SM work as teachers, extension workers, farmers, governmental administrators, agribusiness people, consumers, homemakers, consultants, and advisors.

CHAPTER 1

INTRODUCTION—ETHICS, PRIVATE DECISION MAKING, AND PUBLIC CHOICES

Ethics is viewed herein as evaluative of private decisions and public choices including processes of solving problems and making decisions and choices. Although often implied in this section, ethical codes of professional conduct for social scientists are not stressed herein.

Increasingly, private and public decision makers and choosers in governments, farming, agribusiness, and rural households are held ethically accountable for contributing to the solution of problems involving resource sustainability, the impacts of technical advances, the safety and security of food, rural poverty, the shortcomings of governmental policies affecting agriculture, and the social aspects of agriculture and rural communities, not to mention the shortcomings of market-controlled agricultural economies. Rural and basic social scientists share these responsibilities both when (1) serving as administrators, entrepreneurs, and homemakers and (2) working as educators, researchers, extension workers, advisors, consultants, and the like. They are expected to help resolve such problems and issues. *Sometimes* the demands on social scientists are for what is termed *subject-matter* (SM) work in this book—that is, work on multidisciplinary subjects important to a rather well-defined group of decision makers facing a relatively well-defined set of problems. At *other times*, the demand is for rural and basic social scientists to help in *solving a specific problem* for a *specific decision maker*. In both instances, social scientists encounter value questions and the need to evaluate past and present private decisions and/or public choices concerning actions prescribed to solve problems; in short, they are involved in agroethics.

This chapter first surveys some of the relevant background information available to those participants in SSAAP's Houston work groups that were assigned responsibility for developing agendas relative to agricultural ethics, public choice, and private decisions about farm, rural, and consumer problems. This survey covered concepts used by rural social scientists in working on ethical aspects of private decision making and public choice. Also included is an account of how SSAAP's editorial group has extended the public choice/transaction cost (PC/TC) theory. As extended, this theory contributed substantially to the development by the editorial group of additional agenda items involving values and ethics. The last chapter of this section presents additional agenda items developed since SSAAP's Woodlands Conference at Houston.

BACKGROUND INFORMATION

Serious ethical dilemmas have been created for agricultural and rural administrators, educators, and scientists by three major groups of critics (Johnson 1990). Rural and basic social scientists can contribute to understanding and evaluating these criticisms. The work of agriculturalists and of those concerned with rural life covers a broad spectrum, ranging from solving problems for individual farmers and public decision makers, at one extreme, to disciplinary research and teaching in the basic biological, physical, and social sciences at the other. This work is subjected to increased sharply contrasting criticisms from (1) the biological and physical scientists outside of the agricultural establishment (AE); (2) humanists and social scientists also outside the AE who are concerned about practical, private, and societal impacts of AE activities; and (3) various activists who are also interested in private and societal impacts.

Disciplinary biological and physical scientists outside the AE argue that the large amount of research and extension monies spent by the AE on multidisciplinary problem-solving (PS) and SM agricultural research and extension would produce more for the dollar if devoted to basic research in the biological and physical science disciplines. Some of the relevant references concerning this issue are from the National Academy of Sciences (1972), The Rockefeller Foundation (1982), Marshall (1982), *The New York Times* (1982), *Science* (1982), and Lepkowski (1982).

Humanists, social scientists, religious leaders, and others have criticized the values pursued and/or ignored by farmers, agribusinesses, and the AE. These criticisms were presented at conferences sponsored by the University of

Delaware, July 14–17, 1981; Texas A&M University, March 11–12, 1981; and the University of Florida, March 8–9, 1982, and again in October 18–21, 1982. Rachel Carson (1962), while not a social scientist or humanist, also criticized farmers and the AE on humanistic grounds. The criticisms of humanists, social scientists, and activists also implicate the biological and physical scientists outside of the AE. These critics find the biological and physical scientists outside the AE about as insensitive to humanistic and social issues as those within. The AE is often viewed as being a technocracy controlled, administered, and governed by technical agriculturalists. A dictionary defines technocracy as "government or management...by technical experts or in accordance with principles established by technicians."

Partially as a result of the various national conferences on agroethics, two journals have been established: *The Journal of Agriculture and Human Values*, published at the University of Florida, and *The Journal of Agriculture Ethics*, published in Canada. Both journals publish scholarly articles on agroethics that contribute to objective understanding of the ethical and value dimensions of public and private decision making and choosing with respect to farm, rural, environmental, and food problems and issues. The Kellogg Foundation wisely supported the work on agroethics that led to the establishment of *The Journal of Agriculture and Human Values*. Attention should also be called to a national agroethics project sponsored by both the National Association of State Universities and Land Grant Colleges (NASULGC) and the American Association of State Colleges of Agricultural and Renewable Resources (AASCARR). In addition to developing modules for teaching agriculture in various courses in colleges of agriculture, the project has prepared a book on agroethics. Thus, there was an expanding backlog of experience with agroethics for participants at SSAAP's Houston conference upon which to draw in developing agenda items for agroethics.

Activists have criticized (1) alleged connections among the agricultural research establishment, large farmers, big agribusinesses, and multinational corporations, (2) the development of labor-saving technology that they allege has driven labor out of agriculture prematurely and has led to the early demise of an unnecessarily large number of family farmers, (3) the use of agricultural chemicals and biologicals, (4) the use of exhaustible resources, (5) environmental pollution and food chain contamination, (6) failure to take into account the food and nutritional needs of the poor and disadvantaged (Nelson 1980; Lappe and Collins 1977; Perelman 1978; George 1976; Knowles 1983; Smith 1987; and Comstock 1987), and (7) lack of concern about family farms (Comstock 1987; Berry 1977; Hightower 1973).

Although the complaints of the three groups of critics mentioned above are often in conflict, they are all primarily ethical in the sense that they assert that wrong decisions have been and are being made by the public AE and in the private agricultural sector (often on the basis of values alleged by the critics to be mistaken, incorrect, or ignored) with respect to public and private policies, programs, projects, and market activities.

It would be a mistake to conclude that rural social scientists neglected the ethical dimensions of private decision making and public choice until recently aroused out of lethargy by activists' criticism of the agricultural establishment. While some of the more academic of the rural social scientists have tended to ape the biological and physical agricultural sciences in succumbing to the constraints of logical positivism on working with values, practicing rural social scientists have long worked on public-policy issues and problems of agriculture. Nor should it be presumed that the policy work of RSSs has always supported the status quo and the advantaged. In the "great depression," for instance, rural social scientists contributed to the development of New Deal policies and programs when commercial as well as subsistence farmers were seriously disadvantaged; to the soil conservation movement, programs, and policies of the United States; the cooperative movement; rural zoning; the resolution of land-tenure problems; transportation policies; the development of rural education; balanced farming programs; demographic studies; marriage and the family; rural development programs; international-trade studies and negotiations; home management; etc. Agricultural policy has long been a major interest of agricultural economists, an interest now being picked up by rural sociologists as well.

Sandra S. Batie (1990) and Paul B. Thompson (1990) have recently provided reviews of the impacts of criticisms of the agricultural establishment. These reviews indicate something about the thinking and information that influenced the participants at SSAAP's Houston conference who developed agendas with respect to values and agroethics. An abstract of Batie's 1989 presidential address to the American Agricultural Economics Association is published in this book as Chapter 6 of Section 3 of Part III. Thompson's paper is published in the *Journal of Agricultural Economics Research* (1990). Both Batie and Thompson stress the roles environmental and social activists have played in extending the range of values and other variables beyond those usually considered by neoclassical, modern welfare (post-Hicksian) economists and other social scientists concerned with agriculture and rural society and, for that matter, society in general. As Thompson points out, some of the activists' concerns do not deal with the values of the consequences of actions, but deal instead with (1) the values of acts irrespective of their consequences and (2) ways of viewing nature and man's role with respect to nature. Thompson feels that economists evaluate acts, programs, and policies mainly on terms of their consequences. Of course, evaluation requires attention to all relevant values—both of consequences and of acts. If economists ignore the values of acts and if activists ignore consequences in deciding what ought to be done, both are guilty of incomplete analyses that omit relevant values. Probably neither group omits all of either class of values.

Glenn L. Johnson (forthcoming) has reviewed the philosophic foundation of agricultural economic thought from World War II through the mid–1970s. Although the American Agricultural Economic Association will publish this review in 1991, it was circulated informally and rather widely in agricultural economics circles after the early 1970s and, hence, was available to participants at SSAAP's Houston conference. This article reviews the long, extensive, and continuing interests of general and agricultural economists in not only the philosophy of social science research but in welfare economics, private decision making, and especially the problems involved in working with the ethical and value aspects of policy issues. Logical positivism, various forms of normativism, "conditional normativism," and pragmatism have been consciously followed by the leaders in agricultural economic thought as expressed in their research, education, extension, advisory, consulting, and administrative activities. In this book, Sections 1 and 2 of Part II reflect the long experience of rural social scientists in dealing with public choices and private decisions involving values and ethics.

VALUES AND ETHICS IN SOLVING FARM AND RURAL PROBLEMS

Basically, solving problems involves "correctly" determining "what ought to be done" to solve a problem and then doing it. A proposed solution for a problem is prescriptive. This portion of this chapter examines the nature of PS processes including the processes of choosing and deciding that are inherent in problem solving.

A Diagram of PS Processes—PS processes can be viewed in a number of ways depending upon one's philosophic orientation, past experiences, and academic training. The particular orientation followed herein contains components from many different philosophic orientations and ways of viewing PS processes. While the orientation this view provides is helpful and useful, it is not, of course, the only useful way of viewing these processes.

Figure 1 diagrams six steps in solving a *practical* problem faced by a real-world decision or choice maker (Johnson et al. 1961; Johnson 1977). The diagram also contains two information banks, one of which contains normative information (about values, laws, regulations, prescriptions, recipes, goals, solutions to past problems, and social morés and norms) and the other information not having to do with values. In Figure 1, all relationships among the six steps in the PS process and two information banks are represented by *two-way* arrows indicating that the six steps themselves are highly interrelated, iterative and even repetitive, and that feedbacks are important in problem solving and choosing processes. The two-way arrows from the six steps to the two information banks indicate that PS processes may both draw on existing prior information and store new value and value-free information generated by PS and choosing processes. The over-arching two-way arrow between the two information banks allows for the possible interdependence of value-free knowledge and knowledge about values implied by philosophic pragmatism. The six steps cover learning as is noted below. The knowledge in the information banks is best regarded as imperfect, judgmental and, in this sense, subjective and of varying reliability ranging from near certainty to iterative, judgmental impressions of a sequential Baysian nature. This applies to the information in both the value and value-free knowledge banks.

One step diagramed in the PS process is that of problem definition. Practical problems are defined on the basis of knowledge about (1) the nature of that part of reality that does not have to do with values and (2) values which may or may not be perceived to be part of reality depending on one's philosophic orientation. (See *Equation 1* which is presented subsequently in this chapter.)

Another step in the PS process has to do with learning or the acquisition of additional knowledge by observation and logic or from existing information sources. Both value-free and value information are likely to be so deficient in quantity and quality as to make it advantageous to engage in learning. What is known as the PC/TC approach requires knowledge about transactions costs (both monetary and nonmonetary) in terms of *flow* (information, negotiation, and enforcement) *costs* (values) and *stock* (establishment and dismantlement) *costs* (values).

Another step is to analyze both value-free and value knowledge to comprehend their meaning and usefulness for purposes of solving the problem at hand. Various analytical techniques are used or are potentially useful. Techniques commonly used by rural social sciences (RSSs) include simple budgeting, scenario analyses, benefit/cost ratios, linear programming, the industrial-organization approach, operations research, cohort analyses from demography, the PC/TC, group dynamics techniques, and the like—the list seems almost unlimited as one's mind ranges across the various disciplines.

Still another step involves decision making. Using a decision rule, the problem solver processes value-free and value information into a decision as to "what ought to be done" to solve the problem at hand. Knowledge about what ought to be done is *prescriptive* in nature. Until a prescription is executed, it is a goal in the sense of being the target of an intended effort. Once the effort is made, it is an act. Prescriptive knowledge is different from normative knowledge about goodness and badness. Decision makers often have to minimize losses and prescribe, therefore, that "what ought to be done" is something that is bad. Conversely, decision makers often decide that it would be wrong—"that they ought not"—to prescribe an action with good consequences because another act with still better net consequences can be done (Lewis 1955; Moore 1956). Although economists probably concentrate more on optimization theory (with respect to both monetary and nonmonetary values) than any other social science or any humanity, there are two distinct dangers in labeling optimal choices or decisions "economic." The first is that such terminology may cause noneconomists to avoid optimization while the second is that it may cause economists to focus unduly on simple optimization to the extent of ignoring social, technical, political, and other variables essential for a reasonably complete optimization analysis.

Prescriptive knowledge is derivable from value and value-free knowledge by processing them through a decision rule that makes prescriptive knowledge definitional or analytical although based in part on experiential and descriptive or synthetic knowledge. This at least partially constrains ability to test prescriptive knowledge experientially to reach judgments about its correspondence with reality. This difficulty, however, does not always deprive ethicists of a basis for stating that a given prescription is mistaken. Among other difficulties, the ethicist may find that faulty, inadequately tested value and/or value-free information was used or that crucial information was omitted in reaching the prescription. Common tests include those of *correspondence* with experience, *coherence* (logic), *clarity* or the absence of ambiguity, and the pragmatic test of *workability*. It may also be determined that the decision rule used was misused or inappropriate.

Decision rules typically involve the use of various forms of power: political, military, social, police, market, religious, etc. Some of the most difficult and dangerous decisions to make are institutional ones that change not only the

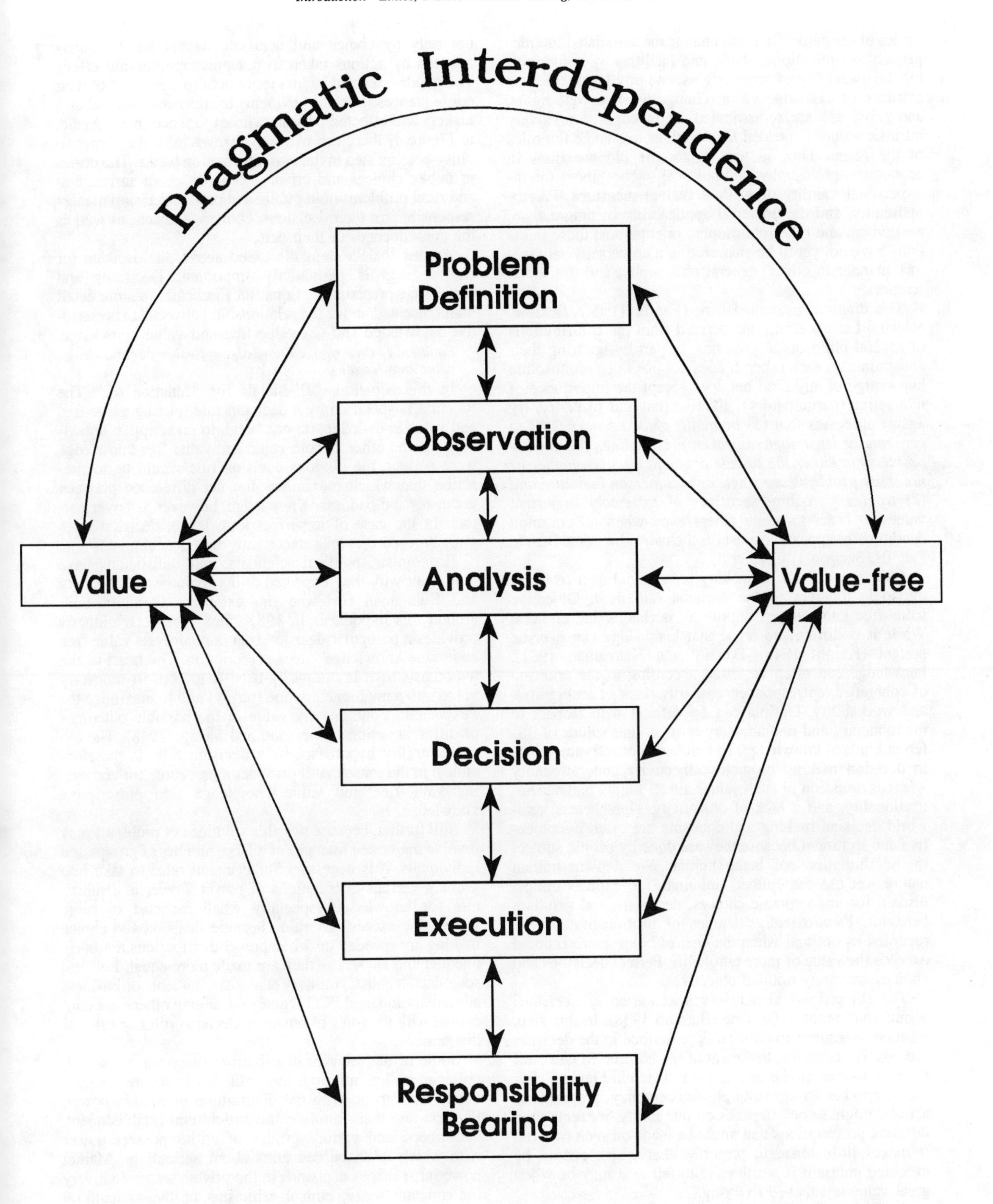

Figure 1. Steps in problem solving related to value-free, and value knowledge.

"rules of the game" but also change the associated interdependent organizations, staffs, and facilities by redistributing the ownership of power, rights, and privileges. Because extrinsic or exchange values change when power, rights, and privileges are redistributed, knowledge of relatively intrinsic values is needed for decisions to change the rules of the game. This, in turn, raises the old questions in economics, philosophy, and political science about the interpersonal validity of welfare (value) measures, Pareto-optimality, and the universal applicability of pragmatism, positivism, and other philosophic orientations; these questions have not yet to be answered in a universally satisfactory manner in ethics, general philosophy, and the social sciences.

The diagram presented here (Figure 1) is a flexible, eclectic, but uncertain one derived from the contributions of several philosophic positions, in part by ignoring their constraints on each other. It does not posit perfect absolute knowledge of any kind but does accept the importance of interactive (participatory), iterative (cut and fit or try, try again) processes that (1) *ironically should be expected to generate at least some mistaken prescriptions for solving problems in either the private or public sector, whether or not those problems are single or multiperson in nature and (2) tragically* require sacrifices of extremely important values in order to attain others even when no common denominator appears to exist for the two values (see Busch, Part III, Section 1, Chapter 5).

Choice and decision making are rational as a result of the logic inherent in the decision rule used. Objective value-free knowledge "improves" decisions and choices. While it is difficult to argue that knowledge can ever be perfect (Knight 1946; Tversky and Kahneman 1981), knowledge can often be tested according to the criterion of coherence, correspondence, clarity (lack of ambiguity), and workability. Optima can be defined with respect to the monetary and nonmonetary costs of and values of different kinds of knowledge. The inclusion of relevant values in decision making promotes objectivity and rationality whereas omission of such values attests to incompleteness, irrationality, and a lack of objectivity. Nonetheless, real-world decision making and choosing are often nonobjective and irrational because they are done by people subject to the limitations of being human. We deplore human nature, yet use the epithet "inhuman" to express utmost disdain for unacceptable choices, decisions, and resultant behavior. Paradoxically, degrees of irrationality can be regarded as optimal when the cost of being more rational exceeds the value of more rationality. Perfect decisions and choices are rarely optimal objectives.

The PS process also involves *execution of decisions* about what ought to be done (Barnard 1938). In this step, an attempt is made to do what is prescribed in the decision process. No complete treatment of the PS process can omit the execution step, the next to the last step in Figure 1. For instance, what an agricultural science policy, program, or action "ought to be" depends on our ability to execute the different prescriptions that might be made on such matters. It makes little sense to prescribe that which cannot be executed unless it is worthwhile to fail as it may be when great value is attached to trying.

An important step in the PS process is that of *bearing responsibility* for the goodnesses and badnesses of the consequences of actions taken. Responsibilities are borne not only by choice and decision makers but by others affected by actions taken to put prescriptions into effect. The goodnesses and badnesses of actions taken and of their consequences become evident to decision and choice makers and affected persons who experience them. Again, in Figure 1, there are two-way arrows from the responsibility-bearing step to the two information banks. The critics of public choices and private decisions about agricultural and rural problems hold public and private decision makers responsible for their decisions, choices, and acts, as well as the consequences of their acts.

Among the PS steps discussed above, the decision (or choice) step is particularly important. Decisions and choices are prescriptive. Equation 1 indicates in more detail than presented above the relationship between (1) prescriptive knowledge and (2) value-free and value knowledge.

Equation 1: Prescriptive Knowledge = f(value-free knowledge, value knowledge)

In this equation, "f" stands for "function of." The function is specified by a decision rule relating value-free and value knowledge, on one hand, to prescriptive knowledge, on the other. If both value and value-free knowledge were perfect, the obvious decision rule would be to prescribe that which maximizes the net difference between goodness and badness. Knowledge, however, is never perfect. In the case of imperfect knowledge, decision rules must be used that take uncertainty into account.

Economists, political scientists, and statisticians have long dealt with the "expected utility hypothesis." Tversky and Kahneman reviewed the extensive literature built around this hypothesis in 1981. This specific hypothesis provides a particular decision rule that converts value-free and value knowledge into a prescription. The heart of the hypothesis as it is ordinarily used is to convert monetary value into a nonmonetary one (utility) and to maximize the "expected" nonmonetary value of the possible outcomes of different actions (Friedman and Savage 1948). The expected utility hypothesis, as a decision rule, is therefore ethical in the sense that it provides a procedure for converting value-free and value knowledge into prescriptive knowledge.

Still further, because possible solutions of problems may involve the vested interests of a large number of groups and individuals, it is necessary for decision rules to take into account various distributions of power. Power is a substitute for knowledge especially when the cost of more knowledge exceeds its value because decision and choice making are speeded up when power distributions are fairly unequal and slowed as they are made more equal. Political scientists, legalists, military scientists, students of business administration, and PC/TC analysts, among others, are concerned with the roles of power in decision rules or rules of the game.

Some of the relevant distributions of power are social, political, police, military, and religious in nature whereas others have to do with the distribution of market power. Farmers and their families, the agricultural establishment, consumers, and various groups of critics possess power with which to shape decisions about agriculture. Market power also shapes decisions in the private sector. In a very fundamental sense, ethical criticisms of the agricultural research establishment, farming, and agribusinesses are from groups of people who hold or think they hold power, and who are dissatisfied with the power they possess in choices and decision making processes concerning agriculture, rural communities, and food. They often feel they have or should be able to exercise power including the power they derive from the knowledge they possess. This brings this chapter to a point where the PC/TC approach needs to be discussed in more generality than discussed in the introductions to Part III and in the four sections of that part.

TRANSACTION COSTS FOR PUBLIC AND PRIVATE DECISION MAKING AND CHOOSING

The PC/TC approach emphasizes the roles of transaction costs in making public choices about institutions. Two academic journals concerned with public choice are *Public Choice,* and *Policy Analysis and Management*. The journal *Economics and Philosophy* is also an important reference.

It was noted in Part IV, Section 1, Chapter 1, that institutional change manifests itself in three interdependent forms: changes in the "rules of the game;" formal organizations; and in the properties, facilities, and staffs of organizations. In this section, attention is focused on the role of transaction costs in private and public decision making and choosing.

At the private level, transaction costs are particularly important with respect to the durable properties, facilities, and equipment of farms, agribusinesses, and households (both farm and nonfarm) as organizations (Williamson 1985). Transaction costs make up the difference between the acquisition costs and salvage value of a durable. This difference consists of the stock costs of putting durable facilities, equipment, staffs, and property in place less the costs of dismantling them when they are replaced or salvaged. Market prices are not applicable for facilities and equipment worth too much in place to be advantageously dismantled or salvaged but not enough to justify expansion. Such facilities and equipment are "fixed" and have to be "priced" according to opportunity-cost or shadow-price principles that provide a basis for allocating the services of such fixed durables precisely because market prices are inapplicable. However, when a resource on hand is worth so little in use that its dismantlement and, perhaps, replacement is advantageous, then the external market provides dismantlement stock costs (salvage price) making it unnecessary to use the opportunity-cost or shadow-price principle in allocating use of the services generated. The same is true for stock establishment costs when acquisition is justified. This simple discussion abstracts from the difficulties in (1) determining the optimum amount of services to extract from fixed durables, (2) converting stock acquisition costs and salvage values into flow values, and (3) dealing with nonmonetary values. Among the flow dismantlement and establishment costs are information, negotiation, and enforcement costs.

When rules of the game, organizations, properties, staffs, and facilities are "priced" on an opportunity-cost basis, ethical questions are often raised about "rent collectors." Those who collect the positive quasi-rent that consists of the excess of opportunity costs (returns) over dismantlement (flow) costs are often disparaged as "rent collectors." SSAAP's editorial group came to see that maximizing such positive quasi-rent is the equivalent of minimizing the negative quasi-rent that consists of the difference between opportunity cost (returns) and establishment (flow) costs; this means that rent collectors may not be so immoral after all because their rent-collection activities allocate resources so as to minimize losses on fixed rules, organizations, facilities, staffs, and faculties put in place earlier at substantial private and/or public establishment costs.

Some of the PC/TC literature treats rent collection as the consequence of unethical manipulation of institutions to create opportunities or niches in which positive quasi-rents can be collected. While institutions certainly can be and are misused in this manner, it would be a mistake to conclude that all institutional changes are made for exploitive purposes. Indeed, public institutions are often changed for the constructive purpose of augmenting each of the four driving forces for agricultural and rural developments that are examined in Part III. As pointed out above, optimizing the collection of positive quasi-rents with respect to the establishment costs of resources overcommitted to constructive institutional change *also* minimizes the loss of negative quasi-rent with respect to establishment costs in a manner more moral and ethical than unethical.

The word "public" is not entirely appropriate in describing the PC/TC approach. For instance, Williamson (1985) used the approach to analyze the institutional structures of private corporations. A better term would be "multiple-person" choices, either public or private. Thus, Part II, Section 1, Chapter 7, contains agenda items to cover opportunities to use the PC/TC approach in analyses of group decisions and choices at farm management, agribusiness, and household levels. Similarly, the word "choice" is not entirely appropriate as the approach applies to decisions as well as choices.

For both public and private decision makers and choosers considering the establishment and the dismantlement of institutions (in all of their three interdependent manifestations), value-free and value beliefs and perceptions are of great ethical significance. (See Figure 1 of this chapter.) It is unethical to make choices and decisions when more knowledge is available through observation and analysis at low cost relative to the costs of wrong decisions and choices. Being dogmatic or ideological—that is, sticking to beliefs that can easily be improved or corrected with observation and analysis—is ethically questionable. Further, there is the unethical possibility that choosers and decision makers may deliberately falsify the knowledge they use in order to "justify" choices and decisions favoring themselves or groups to which they belong. Such questionable self-serving through falsification is particularly tempting to those uncertain about the power and privileges they own and of the justification for such ownership. This helps explain the unethical behavior often observed on the part of "rent" collectors noted by PC/TC analysts to be common in public and private institutions. By contrast, confident holders of power have more reasons to desire accurate rather than false knowledge as accurate knowledge permits them to exploit more fully the advantages of the power and privileges they hold.

A high proportion of public and private farm and rural decisions and choices are made within the institutional constraints of society and the evaluation of such choices and decisions falls within the realm of agroethics. Many but not all of the "goods" sought by decision makers and the "bads" avoided by them are nonmonetary. Ethics and philosophic value theory address questions about how we acquire, verify, and validate knowledge about goodness and badness to use in making decisions and choices.

As was noted in the section above on decision making and choosing processes, prescriptions as to "right" or "wrong" decisions and choices depend on which "rule of the game" is used to derive the prescription. The set of rules from which a particular rule to use can be selected is determined by the constraints society places on its public and private decision makers. In effect, the constraints of institutions (and implementing organizations, facilities, and staffs) define the rights and privileges owned by a society's public and private decision makers and choosers. Even decisions and choices within those constraints that hurt some people while benefiting others can be regarded as pareto-better because those hurt can be viewed as not "owning" the right to not be hurt and, hence, are not deprived of anything they actually own when they are hurt. Serious ethical questions arise about choices and decisions made within the rules a society imposes on its decision makers and choosers—these are questions about the appropriateness of those societal rules.

Beyond the ethical questions that arise about decisions and choices made within the constraints and institutions of society are the still more crucial problems and issues that arise when decisions and choices are being made to change society's constraints and institutions. Such changes were taking place in Eastern Europe, Nicaragua, and South Africa as this was being written. They were also happening as the U.S. Department of Agriculture (USDA), the U.S. Congress, farm leaders, and analysts prepared the various revisions of farm legislation made during the 1932–84 period, rewrote the farm bill in 1985, and revised it in 1990. Changes are also arising in the consideration of a proposed new air pollution act and proposed legislation about drug problems and public support for education. Such changes redistribute the ownership of rights and privileges that determine the power possessed by decision and choice makers in the decision rules acceptable to society—the institutional constraints that determine the set of decision rules from which deciders and choosers select. Although such choices are difficult to make and evaluate, they are of great ethical significance. To the extent that interpersonally valid knowledge of relevant intrinsic values is available, the task is made easier. Exchange or intrinsic values at least partially reflect existing distributions of rights and privileges and, hence, power; therefore, their use in making redistributive decisions is conceptually questionable. However, exchange values are often used because they are so readily available, particularly the monetary ones. Nevertheless, there are important questions about our ability to measure, validate, and verify intrinsic values. In some cases, ethical, religious, and moral arguments are persuasive enough to induce some groups and persons to give up voluntarily the rights and privileges they own and the consequent power they hold. In some cases, the power held is used to resist loss of rights and privileges and, in other cases, to wrest still more rights and privileges from others. The resulting battles for political, military, social, religious, or whatever kind of power are often destructive and costly components of the transaction costs of changing societal constraints. The ethical issues involved in deciding to fight for or against such changes are some of the most crucial in which social scientists become involved. A few phrases will be sufficient to make the point: the drug war, freedom fighters, the cold war, women's liberation movement, "better red than dead," war on poverty, minority rights—the list seems endless.

At a less fundamental level, decisions and choices can be evaluated on the basis of the accuracy of the knowledge—both value and value-free—knowledge including the goodnesses and badnesses of acts as well as the consequences of acts) and of the decision rule used within society's constraints. It can sometimes be argued that a choice or decision is unethical because the knowledge used was not adequately supported by logic and experience, the decision rule used was inappropriate, the action prescribed has good or bad characteristics (as opposed to consequences) which were ignored, or the prescribed act itself was bad in a way that was ignored. For instance, a choice affecting the environment may be ethically criticized even if made within legal and customary social norms because it was based on inadequate knowledge of the badness of nitrate contamination of groundwater or on inadequate knowledge (relatively value-free) of soil hydrological processes. A decision might also be ethically criticized because it imposes damages on those not protected by existing institutional constraints; for example, newborns (ten years ago) who consumed water contaminated with nitrates. Still further, a decision might be ethically criticized when based on a decision rule that is bad because if falsely implies complete protection from risk in a situation where such protection is impossible.

KINDS OF VALUES OF CONCERN IN MAKING PUBLIC CHOICES AND PRIVATE DECISIONS

Before taking up the important question of whether there can be objective knowledge about values, it seems important to discuss more explicitly the different kinds of values of importance for agriculture. Figure 2 graphically portrays four different kinds of values. As indicated in the vertical dimension, some values are *monetary* whereas others are *nonmonetary*. Examples of nonmonetary values include the values of human life, nutrition, and of being justly treated. Monetary values include prices, income, expenses, etc. The horizontal dimension makes a distinction between the *total value* of a condition, situation, or thing and *values in exchange* or instrumental values. Total values are often relatively more intrinsic than values in exchange which are clearly extrinsic. Air, for instance, has great intrinsic value as is immediately apparent to anyone whose supply of air is restricted. Air, however, does not have high exchange value because there is ordinarily so much of it available that people are unwilling to give up money or anything else of value in order to attain a little more of it. By contrast, diamonds have high exchange values, but probably have less intrinsic value than air. Prices are commonly encountered exchange values that are monetary in nature. However, there are probably even more nonmonetized than monetary exchange values. We encounter nonmonetary exchange values when, for example, we sacrifice some of the total value of a wilderness area by permitting the construction of campsites or paths to permit people to experience the value of the remaining wilderness. When something is a means of acquiring something else of value, it can be said to have instrumental value. Conditions, situations, things, and actions can have intrinsic value when they have value in and of themselves irrespective of

	Monetary values	Non-monetary values
Total values (more or less intrinsic and extrinsic)	Cash income	The value of air or of justice
Exchange or instrumental values (always extrinsic)	The price of wheat or the earning of nitrogen in growing wheat	The value of the amount of inequality one will give up to obtain another unit of food

Figure 2. Kinds of Values

their values as means of attaining other conditions, situations, things, and actions of value by trade or as means of production. However, intrinsic values are often sacrificed to attain other intrinsic values in a manner that creates exchange values among intrinsic values. This is done by using the resources that would have been used to attain the sacrificed value to attain the alternative value. In this sense, even an intrinsic value can be instrumental in the attainment of another value since we often have to give up attainment of one intrinsic value to attain another.

It is important to point out here that the commonly encountered dichotomy between economic and social values is a false one. Because there are more or less economical ways of attaining almost any value, it is extremely difficult to identify a single so-called "social" value that is not of economic consequence. The opposite of economic is not noneconomic (e.g., social, technical, religious, or political); instead, the opposite of economic is *un*economic (Knight 1933; Boulding 1981; Johnson 1986) or *wasteful*. There are ordinarily both economic and wasteful ways of attaining a value whatever the nature of the value sought. In common parlance, monetized values are often taken to be economic while the nonmonetized values are mistakenly regarded as noneconomic. For example, the media often strangely reports that the "economic" issues in a labor negotiation have been settled when a wage rate has been agreed upon, but that the "noneconomic" issues involving pensions, health insurance, and working conditions have not been settled, as if the latter were of no economic significance! Confining economics to monetary values would unrealistically eliminate two and part of the third of the three major branches of economics: (1) *consumption economics* which deals with the nonmonetary utility or satisfaction derived from the consumption of goods and services, (2) *welfare economics* which deals with the nonmonetary values of human existence, and (3) the dynamic as contrasted to the static portion of *production economics*.

It is also important to point out that unlike intrinsic values, exchange values always depend upon distributions of various forms of power in the society. The equilibrium market prices (which are exchange values) reached in an economy depend upon the distribution of market power that comes from owning income-producing rights and privileges. Those who own rights and privileges that permit them to have high incomes can bid up the exchange values of commodities they desire while those who own few income-earning rights and privileges are sometimes unable to buy even such basics as food, to say nothing of bidding up its price even when they are starving. For this reason, knowledge of extrinsic or exchange values is much less useful than knowledge of more intrinsic values in making decisions to change institutions in ways that redistribute the ownership rights and privileges and, hence, power among persons.

PHILOSOPHIC ORIENTATIONS AFFECTING RURAL AND BASIC SOCIAL SCIENCE WORK ON AGROETHICS

Three philosophic orientations are reviewed here: logical positivism and reductionism, pragmatism, and various forms of outright normativism. One of the literature-review volumes of the American Agricultural Economics Association has an article on the various philosophic foundations of agricultural economics (Johnson forthcoming).

Logical Positivism and Reductionism in the Rural and Basic Social Sciences—Economics, sociology, psychology, anthropology, and, to a lesser extent, political science, home management and human ecology, and history have all been influenced by the obviously productive logically positivistic, reductionist methods commonly used by biological and physical scientists. The positivistic presupposition that there are no real-world values to be experienced has limited attempts of the basic and rural social scientists to do descriptive research on intrinsic "real" values. Logically positivistic social scientists accept the possibility of doing descriptive work on who assigns how much of what value to what condition, situation, thing, or act, but tend to reject the possibility of describing what "really" has intrinsic value. In economics, those attempting to make economics logically positivistic include John Neville Keynes (1963), Lionel Robbins (1949), Milton Friedman (1952), and Harry G. Johnson (1975), among others. Max Weber attempted to do the same for sociology and, perhaps, anthropology. In Glenn L. Johnson's book (1986) on research methodology, he traces some of the history of economic thought relative to Pareto-optimality and "conditional normativism" as advocated by Gunnar Myrdal (1944, 1969), both of these positions being interpretable as attempts to adapt economics to the dominance of the logical positivism and reductionism in the biological and physical sciences. Donald N. McCloskey's (1982) work on the rhetoric of economics attacks positivism and reductionism in economics. At a more general philosophic level, positivism began to "come apart at the seams," at about the end of World War II. In the *Encyclopedia of the Social Sciences*, A. Kaplan (1968) puts the beginning of the end of logical positivism at about that time. More recently, P. Achinstein and S. F. Barker (1969) treat logical positivism in its past tense in their *The Legacy of Logical Positivism*.

Rural poverty, environmental pollution, food-chain safety, food security, poverty, racial and gender equality, and other similar farm and rural issues have emerged to combine with the general questioning of the logical positivism and reductionism of science by the public and in academic and activist circles to increase the role of alternative and differently oriented methods and techniques in the rural and basic social sciences as well as in society at large. In economics, the inadequacies of Pareto-optimality are now increasingly recognized among researchers (McCloskey 1982; Bromley, Part III, Section 1, Chapter 4; McClennen Part IV, Section 2, Chapter 2). Pareto-optimality and logical positivism had never become very operational among practicing rural and basic social scientists in government and in the private sector. In government and in the private agricultural sector, responsible basic and rural social scientists have had either to avoid reductionism so as to incorporate obvious values in multidisciplinary rather holistic analyses or to suffer the consequences of using inadequate reductionist analyses that ignore such values. In agricultural economics, public-choice theories and private-decision theories now give increasingly explicit attention to descriptions of what "really" has intrinsic value as well as to descriptions of the exchange values different persons and groups assign to various conditions, situations, things, and actions.

Pragmatism—This philosophy has a practical orientation. It is concerned with solutions to practical problems faced by decision makers. In pragmatism, the truth or acceptability of a concept depends upon its consequences for solving practical problems. The pragmatist argues that when one knows all of the differences between the consequences of two competing concepts (including its consequences for purposes of solving practical problems), one knows all the truth there is to be known about the difference between the two concepts (Runes 1961; Dewey 1950). This implies interdependence between value-free and value concepts and, hence, the over-arching pragmatic loop diagrammed in Figure 1. Pragmatism also leads to a complicated holistic, multidisciplinary view of problematic and SM domains. Pragmatists are less willing than logical positivists to subdivide a problematic or SM domain reductionistically into subquestions for different basic academic disciplines and then investigate such specific subquestions in the faith that the results of such fragmented investigations can be added up into a realistic picture of the whole of the domain under investigation (McCloskey 1982). Pragmatic belief in the interdependence of value and value-free knowledge in the contexts of problems requires one to deal with the whole domain of a problem. Pragmatism is an important guiding philosophy for teachers, PS researchers, extension-program investigators of practical problems, the "institutionalists" among agricultural economists, administrators, and resource economists. Part III, Section 1, Chapter 4, by Daniel W. Bromley deals with public choice and pragmatism. Closely related to the Bromley article are the works of Emery M. Castle et al. (1981) that are extensively cited in the introductory Chapter 1 of Part III, Section 1, on institutional improvements. Pragmatism is a major element of modern American education and is reflected in the teaching philosophies followed in primary and secondary schools (Dewey 1950) and in agricultural extension programs, vocational agriculture, and, indeed, in the teaching carried out by such multidisciplinary, SM departments in colleges of agriculture as agronomy, animal husbandry, agricultural economics, and rural sociology (see the Busch and Bubolz and Sontag chapters in this book).

Normative Philosophies—Various normative philosophies are also important for those who deal with the performance of agricultural institutions and people. Utilitarianism is important for agricultural economists (see Chapter 2 of this section by Edward F. McClennen). The Marxist labor theory of value raises its head from time to time, particularly among technocrats and social scientists who develop concerns with social problems (Smith 1987). Frederick H. Buttel (Part I, Chapter 3) indicates some of the impacts of Marx on sociological thought. More recently, an energy theory of value has spawned a technocratic form of energy accounting (Pimental et al. 1973) among physical and biological scientists and engineers.

Not all normative philosophies agree. Some conceive objective descriptive knowledge of values of conditions, situations, things, and acts as based (in the manner of the positivists) on primitive, undefined but experienced concepts of goodness and badness that can then be imbedded in logical or analytical sentences to produce descriptive synthetic knowledge perceived more or less to be about intrinsic values as characteristics of reality (Moore 1956; Lewis 1955; Johnson and Zerby 1973; Johnson 1986). Knowledge about values can, of course, be about both monetary and nonmonetary values as well as about both values in exchange and intrinsic values (see the earlier section in this chapter entitled "Kinds of Value"). There are serious scientific problems involved in measuring welfare (a nonmonetary value) in an interpersonally valid way (Hicks 1937; Arrow 1963; Fox, Part IV, Section 2, Chapter 3). Various forms of normativism permit objective analytic and/or experiential research on the nonmonetary and monetary values so important in setting agricultural science policy, research priorities, and goals; this is their strength. Their weakness is the difficulty involved in measuring intrinsic nonmonetary values as opposed to the monetary exchange and instrumental values so readily observable in or deducible from individual, group, and market behavior.

Thompson (1990) and Batie (Part IV, Section 3, Chapter 6) address the logical status of various value constellations regarded as important by environmental scholars and activists. Some such values are treated (probably unwisely) by some environmental scholars and activists as absolutes—such treatment leads to a willingness to advocate and pay very high opportunity costs for attainment of such absolutes. One can conjecture and even predict that prescriptions based on values perceived to be absolute or near absolute are likely to incur such large consequential opportunity costs (nonmonetary as well as monetary) in terms of foregone attainment of other values that values now perceived to be absolute will be experienced to be less absolute in the future than now perceived.

The Need to be Eclectic—Each of the three major philosophies just discussed has substantial individual strengths and weaknesses. Perhaps it is these strengths and weaknesses that cause at least some rural and basic social scientists to utilize the strengths of all three without being constrained by those weaknesses that preclude exploitation of the strengths of an alternative philosophic orientation. Social scientists rather commonly ignore the constraints of logical positivism on working with values when (1) setting science policies, priorities, goals, and objectives; (2) advising and consulting; (3) doing research on and solving practical problems; (4) researching major practical issues, (5) administering public programs and running private businesses; (6) doing extension work, advising, and consulting; and (7) teaching practical subjects. In other instances, the complexities and holism of pragmatism are avoided by some social scientists in order to exploit the specialized efficiency of reductive logical positivism and various forms of normativism. Also, when some forms of normativism place constraints on the ability to work positivistically with value-free knowledge or pragmatically with interrelated value-free and value knowledge, such constraints on positivism and pragmatism are often ignored (Johnson and Zerby 1973; Johnson forthcoming). As a group, rural social scientists are quite eclectic even though individuals may be strongly, even dogmatically, committed to particular philosophic orientations.

THE DEVELOPMENT OF AGENDA ITEMS CONCERNING AGRICULTURAL ETHICS AT AND AFTER SSAAP'S HOUSTON CONFERENCE

At SSAAP's Houston conference, there were three groups that considered social science agricultural agenda items with respect to ethics, private decisions, and public choices. These work groups, under the coordination of Joseph Havlicek, were concerned with domestic farming, agribusinesses, households, and consumers; international rural development; and natural, human, and community resources. The agendas developed by these work groups reflected the background and some of the thought summarized above as well as the material presented in this section as Chapter 2 on "Philosophy in the Social Science Agricultural Agenda" by Thompson. Also an important source of information about ethics is Thompson's Chapter 5 (Part II, Section 2), "The Bumpers Amendment: AID and Trade Issues for U.S. Agriculture."

Fortunately, in some ways, the substantive area at Houston that was concerned with "natural, human, and community resources" was not well organized; this meant that SSAAP's consideration of the ethical aspects of private decision making and public choices continued to be constructively developed by the editorial group after the Houston conference using Bromley's paper in Part III, Section 1, Chapter 4, that considers the PC/TC approach to institutional change. After the Houston conference, the "natural, human, and community resources" area was broken down by SSAAP's editorial group to generate the four sections considered in Part III on institutional improvements, human development and disadvantaged rural people, technical advances, and enhancements of natural and manmade resource bases. Additional papers were commissioned on disadvantaged farm and nonfarm rural people (Part III, Section 2) that raise fundamental ethical questions. The PC/TC approach was not given adequate attention at Houston, but was given very serious attention by SSAAP's editorial group after Houston; for instance, in Part III that approach is related to (1) institutional change in general; (2) technical change institutions that were almost completely neglected in the formal structure of the SSAAP's Houston conference; (3) human development, including the institutions, such as the family, schools, and medical facilities, that generate human capital; and (4) the institutions that have to do with control of environmental pollution and food-chain contamination, with the enhancement and conservation of natural resources, and with the generation, saving, and utilization of manmade biological and physical resources (capital). Part III, therefore, is central background reading for understanding the developments that have taken place in SSAAP's agendas since the Houston meeting with respect to the ethical aspects of public choices and private decision making. Within Part IV, Sections 1 and 2 are also background for this section. Following Chapter 2 by Thompson, Chapter 3 presents the abridged overall work-group reports from Houston while leaving the more specific agendas pertaining to ethics in the summary chapters of Sections 1 and 2 of Part II, Sections 1 through 4 of Part III, and Sections 1 and 2 of Part IV before presenting additional agenda items developed by the editorial group after SSAAP's Houston conference.

CROSS REFERENCES IN THIS BOOK

PART I: INTRODUCTION

Ch. 4 Agricultural Institutions Under Fire, Lester C. Thurow
Ch. 8 Abridged Work Group Reports from SSAAP's Phase I Spring Hill Conference, June 9–11, 1988

PART II: DOMESTIC AND INTERNATIONAL FARM AND RURAL DEVELOPMENT

Sec. 1, Ch. 5 Integration in Home Economics and Human Ecology, Margaret M. Bubolz and M. Suzanne Sontag
Ch. 7 Farm (Including Home), Agribusiness, and Consumers: Agendas and Conclusions
Sec. 2, Ch. 5. The Bumpers Amendment: AID and Trade Issues for U.S. Agriculture, Paul B. Thompson
Ch. 11 International Rural Development: Agendas and Conclusions

PART III: THE FOUR DRIVING FORCES

Introduction to Part III, and all chapters in Part III, but especially:
Sec. 1, Ch. 1 Introduction to Section on Institutional Improvements
Ch. 4 Economic Institutions and the Development Problem: History and Prognosis, Daniel W. Bromley
Ch. 5 Irony, Tragedy, and Temporality in Agricultural Systems or How Values and Systems are Related, Lawrence Busch
Ch. 7 Institutional Improvements: Agendas and Conclusions
Sec. 2 Ch. 10 Human Development: Agendas and Conclusions
Sec. 3 Ch. 1 Introduction to Section on Resource Enhancement and Growth in Capital Bases
Ch. 6 Abstract—Sustainable Development: Challenge to the Profession of Agricultural Economics, Sandra S. Batie
Ch. 7 Resource Enhancement and Growth in Capital Bases: Agendas and Conclusions
Sec. 4, Ch. 2 Technical Advance: Agendas and Conclusions

PART IV: THREE CROSSCUTTING CONCERNS

Sec. 1 Ch. 3 Social Sciences Agenda for Databases and Information Systems
Sec. 2 Ch. 2 Utility, Utilitarianism, and Public Policy, Edward F. McClennen
Ch. 4 Anthropology, Evolution, and Agriculture, Billie R. DeWalt
Ch. 5 The Basic Social Science Disciplines (BSSDs): Agendas and Conclusions

REFERENCES

Achinstein, P., and S. F. Barker, eds. 1969. *The legacy of logical positivism*. Baltimore: Johns Hopkins University Press.

Arrow, Kenneth J. [1951] 1963. *Social choice and individual values*. 2d ed. New York: John Wiley and Sons.

Barnard, Chester I. 1938. *The functions of the executive.* Cambridge: Harvard University Press.

Batie, Sandra. 1989. Sustainable development: Challenge to the profession of agricultural economics. *American Journal of Agricultural Economics* 71, no. 5 (December): 1083–1101.

Berry, Wendell. 1977. *The unsettling of America: Culture and agriculture.* San Francisco: Sierra Club Books.

Boulding, Kenneth. 1981. *Evolutionary economics.* Beverly Hills: Sage Publications.

Carson, Rachel. 1962. *Silent spring.* Boston: Houghton, Mifflin and Co.

Castle, Emery N., et al. 1981. Natural resource economics, 1946–75. In *A survey of agricultural economics literature.* Vol. 3, *Economics of welfare, rural development, and natural resources in agriculture, 1940s to 1970s.* Edited by Lee R. Martin. Minneapolis: University of Minnesota Press for the American Agricultural Economics Association.

Comstock, Gary. 1987. *Is there a moral obligation to save the family farm?* Ames: Iowa State University Press.

Dewey, John. 1950. The continuum of ends-means. *Ethical Theories.* Edited by A. I. Meldon, 360–66. Englewood Cliffs, N.J.: Prentice Hall.

Fox, Karl A. 1974. *Social indicators & social theory.* New York: Henry Holt and Co.

Friedman, Milton. 1952. *Essays in positive economics.* Chicago: University of Chicago Press.

Friedman, Milton, and J. L. Savage. 1948. The utility analysis of choices involving risk. *Journal of Political Economics* 56:279–304.

George, S. 1976. *How the other half dies: The real reason for world hunger.* London: Cox and Wyman, Ltd.

Hicks, John R. 1937. *Value and capital.* Oxford, UK: Oxford University Press.

Hightower, Jim. 1973. *Hard tomatoes, hard times.* Cambridge: Schenkman Publishing Co.

Johnson, Glenn L. 1976. Philosophic foundations: Problems, knowledge, and solutions. *European Review of Agricultural Economics* 3, no. 2/3: 226.

_____1977. Contributions of economists to a rational decision-making process in the field of agricultural policy. In *Decision-making and agriculture.* Edited by T. Dams and K. E. Hunt, 25–46. Oxford, UK: Oxford Agricultural Economics Institute.

_____1986. *Research methodology for economists: Philosophy and practice.* New York: Macmillan Publishing Co.

_____1990. Ethical dilemmas posed by recent and prospective developments with respect to agricultural research. *Agriculture and Human Values* 7, nos. 3/4.

_____Forthcoming. Philosophic foundations of agricultural economics thought from World War II to the mid-seventies. In *A survey of agricultural economics literature.* Vol. 4, *Agriculture in economic development.* Edited by Lee R. Martin. Minneapolis: University of Minnesota.

Johnson, Glenn L., et al. 1961. *A study of managerial processes of Midwestern farmers.* Ames: Iowa State University Press.

Johnson, Glenn L., and Lewis K. Zerby. 1973. *What economists do about values—Case studies of their answers to questions they don't dare ask.* East Lansing: Michigan State University, Dept. of Agricultural Economics, Center for Rural Manpower and Public Affairs.

Johnson, Harry G. 1975. *On economics and society.* Chicago: University of Chicago Press.

Kaplan, A. 1968. Positivism. *The international encyclopedia of the social sciences.* Vol. 12. Edited by D. L. Sills. New York: The Free Press.

Keynes, John Neville. [1890] 1963. *The scope and method of political economy.* 4th ed. New York: Augustus M. Kelley, Bookseller.

Knight, Frank H. 1933. *The economic organization.* Chicago: University of Chicago Press.

_____[1923] 1946. *Risk, uncertainty and profit.* Oxford: Oxford University Press.

Knowles, Louis L., ed. 1983. *To End Hunger: An Exploration of Alternative Strategies in the Struggle Against World Hunger.* The report of the Church-University Conference on World Hunger sponsored by the Coordinating Council for Hunger Concerns of the National Council of Churches of Christ in the United States of America. New York: Hunger Action Fund, UCBWM.

Lappe, F. M., and J. Collins. 1977. *Food first: Beyond the myth of scarcity.* New York: Ballentine Books.

Lepkowski, Will. 1982. Shakeup ahead for agricultural research. *Chemical & Engineering News* (22 November): 8–16.

Lewis, C. L. 1955. *The ground and nature of the right.* New York: Columbia University Press.

Marshall, Eliot. 1982. USDA research under fire. *Science* 217, no. 4554 (2 July): 33.

McCloskey, Donald N. 1982. The rhetoric of economics. *Journal of Economic Literature* 21:481–517.

Moore, G. E. [1903] 1956. *Principia ethica.* Cambridge: Cambridge University Press.

Myrdal, G. 1944. *An American dilemma.* New York: Harper and Row.

_____[1944] 1969. *Objectivity in social research.* New York: Pantheon Books.

National Academy of Sciences. 1972. *Report of the Committee on Research Advisory to the U.S. Department of Agriculture.* Washington, D.C.: National Academy of Sciences.

Nelson, Jack A. 1980. *Hunger for justice: The policies of food and faith.* Maryknoll, N.Y.: Orbis Books.

Perelman, M. 1978. *Farming for profit in a hungry world: Capital and the crisis in agriculture.* Montclair, N.J.: Allenhold Osman.

Pimental, D., et al. 1973. Food production and the energy crisis. *Science* 182 (2 November): 443–49.

Robbins, Lionel. [1932] 1949. *An essay on the nature and significance of economic science.* London: Macmillan and Co., Ltd.

The Rockefeller Foundation. 1982. *Science for agriculture.* Report of a workshop, "Critical Issues in American Agricultural Research," jointed sponsored by The Rockefeller Foundation and the Office of Science Technology Policy, Executive Office of the President, 14–15 June, held at the Winrock Conference Center, Petit Jean Mountain, Morrilton, Ark.

Runes, D. D. 1961. *Dictionary of philosophy.* Paterson, N.J.: Littlefield, Adams & Co.

Smith, Tony. 1987. A response to Johnson. In *Is there a moral obligation to save the family farm?* Edited by Gary Comstock, 196–9. Ames: Iowa State University Press.

Thompson, Paul B. 1990. Agricultural ethics and economics. *Journal of Agricultural Economics Research* 42, no. 2: 3–7.

Tversky, Amos, and D. Kahneman. 1981. The framing of decisions and the psychology of choice. *Science* 211 (30 January): 453–58.

White House plows into ag research. 1982. *Science* 217 (24 September): 1227–28.

Williamson, Oliver E. 1985. *The economic institutions of capitalism*. New York: The Free Press.

The worm in the bud. 1982. Editorial. *The New York Times* (21 October): 26.

CHAPTER 2

PHILOSOPHY IN THE SOCIAL SCIENCE AGRICULTURAL AGENDA

Paul B. Thompson[1]

The academic discipline of philosophy is most prominently linked to the rural social sciences at two junctures. First, philosophy is crucial to understanding and resolving many important methodological questions in the social sciences. Second, the application of social science knowledge (whether in public policy, extension problem solving, or in private life) often presumes values and goals that are subject to ethical justification or debate. Philosophical ethics and social or political philosophy provide skills of conceptual analysis that are useful in making decisions that apply social science, and the extensive literature on these subjects provides a store of conceptual resources for tackling problems of ethics and values.

In addition to these contributions of substance that philosophy might, under favorable circumstances, bring to agricultural social science, the inclusion of philosophers and philosophically trained social scientists on faculties of agriculture and in subject-matter and problem-solving research projects also promises to broaden the perspective from which agricultural issues are addressed. Philosophers (and professionals trained in the humanities, generally) represent a constituency that includes peoples living in the distant past, as well as the distant future. One task of the humanities is to reflect upon the most universal and enduring traits of human nature, and to arrive at an understanding of the past that enlightens the future. While the balance of this paper will stress the practical and problem-oriented contributions that philosophy might make, the traditional role of the humanities in providing a broad background of meaning for human life should not be forgotten, nor underemphasized.

PHILOSOPHY AND PHILOSOPHICAL RESEARCH

Broadly construed, a philosophy is a set of beliefs or assumptions regarding very general categories of experience including reality and unreality, consciousness or self-awareness, volition, causality, being, and possibility. Philosophies cover the nature of good and evil, the beautiful, the sacred, and the just. The beliefs or assumptions that make up a philosophy may be explicitly held or tacitly presumed by the adherents of a particular view. One might think that disciplinary philosophy involves the study of alternative philosophies, or the construction of a novel philosophy and, to an extent, this is true. Professional training in philosophy, however, places priority upon three skills that underlie the statement or expression of any given philosophy.

First, professional philosophers must be explicit in their philosophical views. They may not allow the crucial components of their philosophy to rest upon tacit presumptions, presumptions about reality, about morality, or about logic. The key elements of a philosophy must be expressed, even if an argument for them is not forthcoming. This stress on full disclosure of one's presuppositions helps philosophers come to appreciate how easy it is to overlook these elements of one's belief system that are most fundamental, most general, and implicit in one's larger philosophical views. Philosophical training imparts skills that are useful in identifying how failure to communicate or to reach consensus can be buried in unstated presuppositions. Philosophical research also requires an ability to be critically introspective in elucidating one's own tacit assumptions, and this can help researchers arrive at novel solutions to problems of theory and practice. The importance of skill in critical questioning of presumptions is evidenced historically in Socrates' method of dialectic, in Descartes' method of doubt, and in Hume's application of skepticism.

Second, students of philosophy are trained to have empathy for the tacit assumptions that underlie the explicit beliefs or views of alternative theories. Although complete disclosure of presuppositions is the goal of philosophical thought, it is an elusive goal, at best, and even the greatest philosophers of times past have left crucial elements of their philosophies unstated. Empathetic reading of opposing philosophies might bring apparently incongruous ideas into harmony; it is an attempt to fill out a set of philosophical beliefs in a way that makes them most plausible, but without violating the integrity of the stated position. Although one constantly risks misinterpretation by investing another person's views with a charitable reading, skill in deducing the unstated premises of a philosophy is a prerequisite to philosophical understanding and analysis. The ability to sympathetically interpret a philosophy is crucial to Plato's recounting of Socratic dialogues, to Spinoza's development of hermeneutics, and to Heidegger's deconstruction of Western metaphysics.

Finally, philosophical research depends upon an ability to derive and state standards of adequacy for contrasting philosophical views. By far the most dominant of such standards is logical consistency, but philosophers are trained to recognize strengths and weaknesses in regard to comprehensiveness, simplicity or elegance, defeasibility, and native plausibility (or common sense) as well. These same criteria are, of course, applied throughout the sciences, and empirical scientists may underestimate the importance of conceptual criteria relative to empirical test in their own disciplines. The process of argument and debate has allowed philosophers to reach remarkable consensus on many theoretical issues that are not readily amenable to empirical test.

These three skills—critical introspection, empathetic interpretation, and argument—are, in effect, key disciplinary values for professional philosophy in the twentieth century. They represent the methodological parameters in which philosophers are expected to work, and research which applies these skills to the broad questions of philosophy, of theology, of scientific theory, or, indeed, of human society is truly philosophical, and would be recognized as such by persons having advanced degrees in philosophy. To call research philosophical is, in this sense, a value judgment akin to that which is made when a given piece of research is dubbed scientific. At one time, the standards for being scientific and for being philosophical may have been identical, but today they are not, scientific values revolving more around measurement, quantification, and prediction. One key to appreciating the unique contribution of philosophers, or of philosophically competent social scientists resides in recognizing the different research values that are accorded to work labeled scientific, on the one hand, and to work labeled philosophical, on the other. Recognition of these values is also helpful for acquiring the patience that is necessary for multidisciplinary work. The philosopher's concern for a complete and logically consistent interpretation of a theoretical or policy position cannot but help strike nonphilosophers as pedantic and fussy on some occasions. Philosophers must strive to do better at confining themselves to essential points when working with specialists from other disciplines, but others must be aware that if philosophers go too far in this direction, they abandon the fundamental disciplinary values that make them philosophers.

One does not need a Ph.D. in philosophy or an academic appointment in a department of philosophy to be capable of bringing these three research skills to bear upon problems of theory and practice. To some extent, these skills are shared with historians and other humanities scholars, as well as many social scientists, particularly anthropologists and social psychologists. These skills are certainly possessed by ethicists trained in theological traditions as well. There is little point in belaboring what distinguishes philosophy from all these other forms of intellectual activity. The word "philosopher" can be presumed to apply broadly to anyone doing the kind of conceptual research and applying the skills of introspection, interpretation, and argument that have been described above.

METHODOLOGICAL ISSUES

Philosophy's contribution to rural social science methodology can be broken down along the lines of a methodological rule that distinguishes disciplinary, subject-matter, and problem-solving research. Glenn Johnson (1987) characterizes disciplinary research as research on the basic theories and methods, the knowledge base, of the respective disciplines. Subject-matter research also creates a knowledge base, but is addressed to topics that are explained and managed through the application of several different disciplines working together. Problem-solving research produces knowledge or information that is needed for direct and immediate decision making. This division of research roles for the sciences is itself subject to alternative philosophical interpretations, but, as a general rule of thumb, it is a useful way of characterizing some of the different tasks performed in the rural social sciences.

DISCIPLINARY RESEARCH METHODOLOGY

Since Newton at least, physics has been regarded as the model of what a scientific discipline should be. Until the late nineteenth century, explanations in physics were thought to consist in theoretical statements of causal laws, such as Newton's laws of motion and gravity, coupled with empirical observations of phenomena (such as mass and velocity) that were specified in the theory. Theory plus data permitted the scientist to perform a calculation that predicts events, and this fact gave physicists both a practical application of theory, as well as a method of empirical test. John Stuart Mill wrote extensively on the applicability of this model to social science research, and concluded that its limitations arose primarily from the sheer complexity of social behavior (which made theoretical coverage more difficult) and from ethical and practical limitations on experiments involving human subjects (Hausman 1984).

Two intellectual modifications to the nineteenth century philosophy of physics proved to have enormous implications for twentieth century social science. One achieved its most extreme expression in *logical positivism*, the philosophical movement associated with the Vienna Circle of 1910–25 (Ayer 1936). The second was *instrumentalism*, a philosophical view that gained popularity as a response to problems in quantum physics. Logical positivism was partly a response to dissatisfaction with the philosophical foundations of cause and effect that had persisted since Hume's *Treatise on Human Nature* (1972). Advances in mathematical logic led many to hope that references to causality could be replaced by purely deductive, logical, mathematical, or statistical relations between variables and theoretical terms. The meaning of empirical statements could, on the positivist view, be specified entirely by the procedures for their verification. Instrumentalism, on the other hand, gained fame with the Copenhagen interpretation of quantum mechanics, and was thought to be required because physicists were universally agreed that quantum mechanics was the best available theory, despite the embarrassing fact that realist interpretations of quantum mechanics were thought to entail logical contradictions. The instrumentalist view was that the concepts and theories of science were convenient fictions that were "useful," but not true in any realist sense. The main criterion of usefulness was in the theory's capacity to produce accurate predictions (Miller 1986).

Although logical positivism and instrumentalism were responses to rather specific problems in philosophy and physics, the widespread dissemination of these ideas created an intellectual climate in which empirical scientists felt unburdened of any need to reconcile philosophical problems or oddities that might be thought to arise from their research. This was in some instances a liberating and highly-productive turn of events that allowed scientists to set aside long-standing philosophical disputes in disciplines, such as biology, psychology, and economics, to lay the foundations for unprecedented progress. The progress was achieved at some cost, however, as institutional and intellectual links among the disciplines deteriorated.

In economics, positivist and instrumentalist ideas were expressed as the view that microeconomics was founded on the formal assumption that individual choice can be represented as a maximization function operating on a set of consistently ranked preferences. The philosophical implications of this view are too numerous to list. The view reflected positivist aims because the classical explanation of market equilibrium, which required the labor theory of value, was replaced by an account in which the deductive power of the theory was thought to reside in formal apparatus, rather than in its faithful representation of causal forces. The view was instrumentalist in that it was not necessarily thought to represent the actual thought process of economic agents, but was rather interpreted as a useful assumption to predicting economic behavior at the aggregate level. This latter view linked economics to behaviorism in psychology, which was positivist in eliminating references to mental causes of action, and instrumentalist in its emphasis upon predicting responses to given stimuli. Both philosophies allowed their respective disciplinary practitioners to set aside questions about how culture influences individual preferences, how property rules and political power affect the formation of expectations, and how changes in these institutional factors might radically restructure preference maps (Boulding 1956; Blaug 1980; Braybrooke 1987; Rosenberg 1988).

A myriad of recent research developments suggest that progress in social science will emerge from renewed attention to these and other neglected areas. Psychologists are using philosophy and computer science to develop computational models of cognitive processes that entail more sophisticated theories of information, expertise, and optimization (Tversky and Kahneman 1975). Economists are using philosophy and political science in the development of rational-choice models for forward contracting to resolve uncertainty, reduce transaction costs, and avoid market failure. There is work underway on political economy, problems in welfare economics, perception of risk, social discounting, and time preferences, to name just a few topics that incorporate insights from philosophy into disciplinary social science (Sen 1986). Not all these developments will turn out to be successful, to be sure, but social scientists who resort to positivist and instrumentalist rhetoric in order to avoid philosophically difficult subjects risk lagging behind on some of the most exciting disciplinary developments of the day.

SUBJECT-MATTER RESEARCH

The rural social sciences consist primarily of agricultural economists and rural sociologists and, of the two, economists are clearly dominant. Papers prepared by the Social Science Agricultural Agenda Project by Frederick H. Buttel, James C. Hite, and Richard J. Sauer make clear the need to bring a wider array of disciplines to bear upon the problems of rural people. One methodological role for philosophy is to help clarify the relative strengths and weaknesses of the various social science disciplines. As noted above, the various social science disciplines have developed differing explanatory strategies and theories, and the respective disciplines reflect this. Research in a broad area such as international trade and development, or even a comparatively narrow subject such as the animal welfare movement requires information from a number of disciplines, but the way that the respective disciplines interact often is complex and even contentious.

While economists and psychologists were developing theories that took individual behavior to be the basic unit of analysis, other social scientists developed historical and functional models of explanation that identified variables and theoretical links not easily reducible to facts about individual behavior. The upshot of this divergence has been a decade or more of divisiveness among the respective social sciences. On one extreme of this debate are economists who are so enamored with equilibrium models that they see no possible dysfunction in social systems save when government interferes in the market-clearing process that produces optimal allocation of resources among individuals. On the other extreme are social theorists who see capitalism as an inherently dysfunctional and unstable organization of society's productive resources.[2]

Researchers within social science have come to recognize their mutual interdependence, yet progress in integrating disciplinary research methods requires a return to some of the philosophical issues that have languished for a half century.

PROBLEM-SOLVING RESEARCH

Problem-solving research produces knowledge that is presumed to be instrumental in eliminating an obstacle to the resolution of some specific difficulty. The strategy of research is to work systematically toward a resolution of the problem. When problems involve conflict among different parties, what counts as the solution to the problem will be determined, in part, by the values of these parties. It will be measured also by the fairness, thoroughness, and sensitivity to outcomes or constraints embodied in problem-solving research itself (Johnson 1987, 14–20). Philosophy plays one role in interpreting the values of parties to the problem situation, and another in eliciting standards of ethical and logical adequacy for the research activity itself.

Problem solving begins by collecting information about the situation at hand. Unlike disciplinary research, where past research traditions set the agenda, or subject-matter research, where the agenda is set by the researchers' shared perceptions of what is at issue, problem-solving research must begin with a survey of circumstances that may be entirely unique to the particular situation. The first stages, therefore, involve description of circumstances, including description of values held by parties to the situation. Description of values is largely a task for traditional social science research, but it can be enhanced by a sensitivity to philosophical value positions, and to their patterns of conflict and harmony.

In order to recommend a solution to a problem, however, problem-solving research must adopt standards that determine what is to count as alleviating the problem, as opposed to worsening it. In short, the notion of solving problems, or helping, in general, involves values in direct application (Dundon 1986, 39–51). If problem solvers ignore this fact, they will apply values that have been implicitly adopted, perhaps by habit, without any direct inquiry as to the larger goals or responsibilities of the problem-solving process. To the extent that problem-solving research hopes to be truly objective in the sense of eliminating undue bias, researchers must undertake direct investigation of what is good, what is beneficial, what is bad, and what is harmful with regard to the specific problem situation (Johnson 1982a).

Problem-solving researchers have traditionally performed normative inquiry in an eclectic fashion, if at all. Researchers have brought values such as honesty, fairness, beneficence, and loyalty to their work, even if they have not always been willing to recognize this fact publicly for fear of appearing unobjective. Values are learned and refined throughout the process of living more surely than they are learned from mere philosophizing, so researchers have learned values in the process of solving problems. Nevertheless, the process of learning and assimilating crucial values into the problem-solving process needs to be made into a less haphazard affair. One of the key needs in a joint social science and philosophy effort is thus to be found in developing models and procedures that will make value-oriented research a more integral and systematic part of the problem-solving process.

Problem solving must recommend a solution; it must move from information about what would be good to a prescription as to what ought to be done. This is a second level of ethical or normative type of information, employing a decision rule (Johnson 1987, 18). Decision theory, of course, has offered a number of strategies for analyzing the consequences of applying particular decision rules in a given context, and has offered help in being able to define rules that maximize the probability of achieving certain definite goals (McClennen 1983). But how are decision rules themselves justified? Are they to be rationalized solely on the basis of the means they help achieve? Are there constraints on how a responsible party may manipulate others? Are there duties that force decision makers to ignore the benefits or harms that might accrue to third parties? On what authority, moral or political, is a given decision made to stand? These are philosophical questions that go to the root of political economy, understood in the grand tradition as a mixture of economics, political science, geography, and philosophy. In order to become applicable in the problem-solving situation, the grand tradition must be particularized to the single case.

CONCLUSIONS

The structural constraints on this paper afford little opportunity to discuss specific philosophical problems. Only a few agriculture and natural resource issues with ethical and philosophical dimensions have been mentioned. Among the topics that have been slighted are agrarianism and family farms, moral obligations to the world's hungry, and the moral imperatives of sustainability and stewardship. The real flavor of philosophical writing on agriculture and natural resource topics, its strengths and weaknesses, is captured better in any of the substantive papers that have been cited than in the survey that has been given here.

PHILOSOPHY AND PUBLIC POLICY

The creation of legislation and the administration of existing law are government activities that have been explicitly founded upon philosophical principles of right, justice, and social benefit at least since the demise of European monarchy, and possibly since the earliest days of recorded history. Notions such as liberty, consent, and community require philosophical articulation in order to become the basis for government operations. Although there are interesting debates over the exact relationship between political theory and government policy, the relevance of philosophical thought for public policy really goes without saying. At the risk of oversimplification, this relevance can be specified in terms of its relation to two interconnected problems: the establishment of social goals and the legitimation of government authority.

ESTABLISHMENT OF SOCIAL GOALS

Public policies are enacted as means to certain ends, but what ends are they to seek? There is, perhaps, no better example of the way philosophical controversies influence the establishment of social goals than the dispute over the family farm. Is the family farm an end in itself, something that public policies ought to preserve, if possible, or is the family farm merely one way of organizing the nation's agricultural production sector? Those who prefer the first characterization have offered eloquent arguments about the family farm's importance for the preservation of democratic liberties (Briemeyer 1965), for entrepreneurial capitalism (Hightower 1972), and for traditional moral virtues of work and self-reliance (Berry 1977). Those who prefer the second characterization have suggested that farm policy should favor efficient conversion of production inputs to consumer commodities on the ground that this makes vitally needed food and fiber available even to the poor, and allows more wealthy consumers to use a greater portion of their incomes for discretionary purposes (Tweeten 1983). Even if one accepts the view that both of these philosophical alternatives have merit, one is faced with the philosophical question of weighing the costs of small farm preservation against the benefits of lower consumer food prices.

Is one of these views "right," the other "wrong?" Is there some common ground, some way of ameliorating the conflict between them? Should the ends of social policy be established by interest-group politics, or should they be established in conformity to some vision of the good society, the good life? Such questions can be asked about a wide range of agricultural policy issues, from animal welfare to ground-water pollution, from famine relief to the relationship between trade and development. While a given individual who has personally answered all these questions to his own satisfaction may feel comfortable in ignoring these questions as he lobbies for one policy option over its competitors, the intellectual ideal of objectivity requires rural social science researchers and policy analysts to have studied and understood some of the major philosophical answers to such questions. When philosophical research proposes new answers, a responsible analyst will give them a hearing, and will offer criticism and comment.

THE LEGITIMATION OF GOVERNMENT AUTHORITY

Legitimation of government authority is the foundational problem for political philosophy. When do governments validly exert power over the citizens of a nation? What actions exceed the limits of justice and right? Historically, this question was crucial to the overthrow of monarchy and the replacement of dictatorial regimes with constitutional governments. Many disputes on agricultural policy become embroiled in disputes over the legitimate use of government power. An early discussion of soil conservation policy, for example, concluded that mandatory conservation practices would be in the public interest but that government's duty to protect rights makes mandatory conservation an unacceptable violation of individual liberties. A mandatory conservation policy would, on this account, be an illegitimate use of public authority, despite the fact that it serves the public good.

Legitimation problems often overlap with those of establishing social goals, but there is an important (if vague) philosophical distinction that mirrors the distinction of legislative and administrative functions of government from those of the judiciary, particularly as the judiciary branch is involved with constitutional questions. The constitutional foundations of government provide a great deal of latitude for the pursuit of social policies that benefit society as a whole, or are supported by a majority of citizens. The philosophical principles that underlie the constitution of a state, however, place limits on government action, and specify procedures that just societies must follow. The nature of these limits and procedures are themselves controversial, of course, but this philosophical debate takes place at a different level from that of establishing policy goals. While standard policy criteria such as Pareto improvement or allocative efficiency clearly have relevance to the identification of social goals, for example, it is less clear that they express principles that distinguish legitimate authority from arbitrary power. Consent of the governed is usually thought to be more fundamental than optimization of benefits in Western political thought, and it is for this reason that economists such as F. A. Hayek (1978), Milton Friedman (1962), or James Buchanan (1987) have preferred libertarian defenses of free markets to the efficiency arguments more frequently advanced by agricultural economists. The intellectual issues here are admittedly deep and wide-ranging, but the difficulty of the issues does not warrant their exclusion from the research agenda of the rural social sciences.

CONCLUSION

This summary of philosophy's relevance to research in agricultural, resource, and rural development issues is necessarily superficial and omits mention of many specific topics where research is needed or has already been initiated. Any attempt at further elaboration of philosophy's potential to help social science researchers attain a better understanding of their primary research topics would become tedious, without substantially correcting the fault of superficiality. Most readers will learn far more about the strengths and weaknesses of philosophical approaches from even a cursory reading of some research articles that have been published in journals such as *Agriculture and Human Values* or *The Journal of Agricultural Ethics.* I shall, therefore, conclude by offering a personal assessment of the prospects for philosophical research on topics of importance to rural social sciences.

Although there is no empirical research to support such a claim, it seems likely that capacity for philosophical research on the rural social sciences declined steadily from the 1930s well into the 1970s, and is still relatively low, but increasing, as we enter the 1990s. The number of researchers holding doctoral degrees in philosophy who work explicitly on agricultural topics has always been low, and may have reached zero with the death of John Brewster in 1967. Philosophical work on topics such as world hunger, environmental preservation, and animal welfare resurfaced in the 1970s, but was not well integrated with ongoing research by agricultural specialists. There are now about fifty philosophers in the United States who have ongoing interests in agricultural topics, and several hundred who have completed research on topics of direct relevance to the broader concerns of the rural social sciences (including the issues noted above). When those philosophers working on theoretical foundations of the social sciences, rational choice theory, and traditional political theory are included, the number grows to well over a thousand. Those with a more theoretical orientation, however, may be reluctant to serve as more than an occasional and informal resource to research on the traditionally applied problems of rural social science.

Of more importance is the philosophical capacity of rural social scientists themselves. Research publications in *The American Journal of Agricultural Economics* often contained a sprinkling of references to philosophical sources well into the 1960s. Today, when one sets aside a few widely recognized (and relatively senior) authors,[3] it is unusual to find published work in agricultural economics that exhibits familiarity with philosophical thought. There are undoubtedly a number of reasons for this. One is certainly to be found in the increased emphasis upon economic models among applied economists, and this trend has, in my view, been a source of strength for the discipline. More disturbing is the fact that the current generation of agricultural economists was educated in an era when it would have been very difficult to find faculty in philosophy departments who would have had interest or competence in the methodological and ethical issues of most relevance to agriculture and to economics. This situation has improved but the decades of neglect have produced a generation of agricultural professionals with little understanding of philosophy, and little inclination to advise their students to do better. The opportunity for today's generation of rural social scientists to complete relevant course work in philosophy varies considerably from one university to another.

Philosophy's role in rural social science research, extension, and resident instruction will continue to be a supporting one. While major agricultural research institutions should have faculty and research personnel specializing in philosophical topics, a cadre of 15 to 20 of such people nationally can (along with the research contributions currently being made by philosophers deriving no support from agriculture and natural resource colleges) meet the major research needs on the current agenda. As such, many smaller institutions will be able to focus on instructional needs utilizing faculty trained in traditional rural social science disciplines or borrowed from philosophy faculty in liberal arts colleges. Several decades of neglect, however, have created a situation in which the short-term need for building philosophical expertise is large and critical. This need can be met through funding of philosophical research and through workshops and short courses designed to increase the capacity of agricultural scientists.

NOTES

1. Paul B. Thompson is an associate professor in the Departments of Philosophy and Agricultural Economics at Texas A & M University, College Station.
2. The problem is discussed in Ruttan (1986).
3. One hesitates to name names. I am, of course, thinking of persons such as James Bonnen, Glenn Johnson, Vernon Ruttan, Luther Tweeten, and Gene Wunderlich, but I hope that my many friends among agricultural economists who are knowledgeable and appreciative of philosophical thought will forgive me for omitting them.

REFERENCES

Ayer, A. J. 1936. *Language, truth, and logic*. 2d ed. New York: Dover Books.

Berry, Wendell. 1977. *The unsettling of America: Culture and agriculture*. San Francisco: Sierra Club Books.

Blaug, Mark. 1980. *The methodology of economics or how economists explain*. Cambridge, UK: Cambridge University Press.

Boulding, Kenneth. 1956. *The image*. Ann Arbor: University of Michigan Press.

Braybrooke, David. 1987. *Philosophy of social science*. Englewood Cliffs, N.J.: Prentice-Hall.

Brewster, John. 1970. *A philosopher among economists*. Philadelphia: J. T. Murphy.

Buchanan, James M. 1987. The economizing element in Knight's ethical critique of capitalism. *Ethics* 98:61–75.

Dundon, Stan. 1986. The moral factor in innovative research. In *The agricultural scientific enterprise*. Edited by Busch and Lacy. Boulder, Colo.: Westview Press.

Friedman, Milton. 1962. *Capitalism and freedom*. Chicago: University of Chicago Press.

Hausman, Daniel M. 1984. *The philosophy of economics*. Cambridge, UK: Cambridge University Press.

Hayek, F. A. 1978. *New studies in philosophy, politics, economics, and the history of ideas*. Chicago: University of Chicago Press.

Hightower, Jim. 1972. *Hard tomatoes, hard times*. Cambridge: Schenkman Publishing Co.

Hume, David. 1972. *A treatise on human nature*. Edited by Selby-Bigge. Oxford, UK: Oxford University Press.

Johnson, Glenn L. 1982a. Agro-ethics: Extension, research, and teaching. *Southern Journal of Agricultural Economics* (July): 1–10.

———1987. *Research methodology for economists: Philosophy and practice*. New York: Macmillan.

McClennen, Edward. 1983. Rational choice and public policy: A critical survey. *Social Theory and Practice* 9, no. 3: 335–79.

Miller, David. 1986. *Fact and method*. Princeton, N.J.: Princeton University Press.

Rosenberg, Alexander. 1988. *Philosophy of social science*. Boulder, Colo.: Westview Press.

Ruttan, Vernon. 1986. Toward a global agricultural research system. *Research Policy* 15:307–27.

Sen, Amartya. 1986. *Ethics and economics*. New York and London: Basil Blackwell.

Tversky, Amos, and Daniel Kahneman. 1975. Judgment under uncertainty. *Science* 185:453–58.

Tweeten, Luther. 1983. *Food for people and profit: Ethics and capitalism*. East Lansing: Michigan State University, Cooperative Extension Service.

OTHER REFERENCES USED BUT NOT SPECIFICALLY CITED

Aiken, William. 1986. Ethical aspects of agricultural research. In *New directions for agriculture and agricultural research*. Edited by Kenneth Dahlberg. Totowa, N.J.: Allanheld.

Aiken, William, and Hugh LaFollette, eds. 1977. *World hunger and moral obligations*. Englewood Cliffs, N.J.: Prentice-Hall.

Arrow, Kenneth. 1951. *Social choice and individual values*. New Haven, Conn.: Yale University Press.

Arrow, Kenneth, and L. Hurwicz. 1972. An optimality criterion for decision making under uncertainty. In *Uncertainty and expectation in economics*. Edited by Carter and Ford. Oxford: Blackwell.

Breimyer, Harold F. 1965. *Individual freedom and the economic organization of agriculture*. Champaign: University of Illinois Press.

Callicott, Baird. 1982. Aldo Leopold's land use aesthetic and agrarian land use values. In *Agriculture, change and human values*. Edited by Haynes and Lanier. Gainesville: University of Florida, Humanities and Agriculture Program.

Caplan, Arthur. 1986. The ethics of uncertainty: The regulation of food safety in the United States. *Agriculture and Human Values* 3, nos. 1–2 (Winter-Spring): 180–90.

Crawford, Mark. 1986. Regulatory tangle snarls agricultural research in biotechnology area. *Science* 234 (17 October): 275–77.

Dewey, John. [1927] 1960. *The quest for certainty*. New York: Putnam.

Diesing, Paul. 1982. *Science and ideology in the policy sciences*. New York: Aldine Publishing Co.

Ebenreck, Sara. 1984. A partnership farmland ethic. *Environmental Ethics* 6, no.1.

Eldridge, Michael. 1985. Theology and agricultural ethics in the state university: A reply to Richard Baer. *Agriculture and Human Values* 2, no. 4 (Fall): 47–53.

Elster, Jon. 1983. *Explaining technical change*. Cambridge, UK: Cambridge University Press.

Emerson, Ralph Waldo. 1904. Farming. In *Society and solitude*, 137–54. Boston: Houghton, Mifflin, and Co.

Fite, Gilbert. 1984. *American farmers*. Bloomington: University of Indiana Press.

Friedman, Milton. 1952. *Essays in positive economics*. Chicago: University of Chicago Press.

Hicks, J. R. 1939. *Value and capital*. Oxford, UF: Oxford University Press.

Johnson, Glenn L. 1982b. Decision making: Consistency between Christian and emerging modern views. Paper presented to the Conference on Transnational Corporations, American Lutheran Church, 19–20 March, Minneapolis, Minn.

_____1984. *Academia needs a new covenant for serving agriculture*. Mississippi Agriculture and Forestry Experiment Stations Special Publication, July.

Kunkel, H. L. 1984. Agricultural ethics—The setting. *Agriculture and Human Values* 1, no. 1 (Winter): 20–25.

Luce, Duncan, and Howard Raiffa. 1957. *Games and decisions*. New York: Wiley and Sons.

Madden, Patrick, and Paul B. Thompson. Forthcoming. Ethical perspectives on changing agricultural technology in the United States. *Notre Dame Journal of Law, Ethics, and Public Policy* 3, no. 1:85–127.

Montmarquet, James. 1985. Philosophical foundations for agrarianism. *Agriculture and Human Values* 2, no. 2 (Spring): 5–14.

O'Neal, Onora. 1986. *Faces of hunger*. Totowa, N.J.: Allanheld.

Popper, Karl. 1959. *The logic of scientific discovery*. New York: Harper and Row.

_____1961. *The poverty of historicism*. 3rd ed. London, UK: Routledge and Keegan Paul.

Posner, Richard. 1981. *The economics of justice*. Cambridge, Mass.: Harvard University Press.

Sagoff, Mark. 1986. Values and preferences. *Ethics* 96, no. 2: 301–16.

Singer, Peter. 1975. *Animal liberation*. New York: A New York Review Book.

Stevenson, C. L. 1944. *Ethics and language*. New Haven: Yale University Press.

Thompson, Paul B. and Bill A. Stout, eds. *Beyond the large farm: Ethics and research goals for agriculture*. Boulder, CO: Westview Press.

_____1986a. Review of Rifkin's *Declaration of a heretic*. *Agriculture and Human Values* 3, no. 3 (Summer): 58–61.

_____1986b. Uncertainty arguments in environmental issues. *Environmental Ethics* 8, no. 12 (Winter): 59–72.

Watson, John B. 1930. *Behaviorism*. New York: W. W. Norton and Co.

Winch, Peter. 1970. *The idea of a social science*. New York: The Humanities Press.

CHAPTER 3

ETHICS, PRIVATE DECISIONS, AND PUBLIC CHOICES: AGENDAS AND CONCLUSIONS

The first main portion of this chapter presents agendas from three of SSAAP's Houston work groups concerned with ethics, private decisions, and public choices. These ethics work groups were parts of three substantive areas concerned with (1) farming, agribusinesses, and consumers; (2) international rural development; and (3) natural, human, and community resources. These three work groups were under the leadership of Bobby Eddleman, an agricultural economist; Paul B. Thompson, a philosopher; and Tom Ruehr, an agronomist, respectively. All three group leaders had previously had group experiences involving agricultural ethics. Joseph Havlicek served as overall area coordinator of the three work groups.

The second portion of this chapter reports agendas developed since SSAAP's Houston meeting largely as a result of subdividing the substantive area on natural, human, and community resources into areas dealing with what SSAAP has regarded as the four driving forces for the development of agriculture and rural society, namely: institutional improvement (includes community institutions); human development, more broadly conceived than at Houston; technical advance, which was formally neglected at Houston; and increases in natural and manmade physical and biological resources, part of which were considered. The four sections of Part III are concerned with these four driving forces. Also since Houston, additional work has been done on ethical information in databases and the basic social science disciplines that are reported in Sections 1 and 2 of Part V. The public choice/transaction cost (PC/TC) approach to institutional change that was stressed at Houston by Daniel W. Bromley has extensive ramifications for agro-ethics. Consequently, the SSAAP editorial group has added substantially to the agenda items produced at Houston under the leadership of Joseph Havlicek. These are found in the second main portion of this chapter.

ABRIDGED WORK-GROUP REPORTS FROM SSAAP'S HOUSTON CONFERENCE

The first part of this section is an abstract of an overall report resulting from coordinating the work of the three work groups previously described. Those parts of the work-group reports specific to domestic and international rural development and to the four driving forces are considered in the final chapters of the respective sections of Parts II and III. Some relevant agenda items are also to be found in the last chapters of Sections 1 and 2 of Part IV.

OVERALL AGENDAS RELATIVE TO ETHICS, PUBLIC CHOICE, AND PRIVATE DECISION MAKING

The rural social sciences should take the lead in expanding efforts of the agricultural establishment to address the ethical dimensions of public choices and private decisions concerning agriculture and rural societies. Unfortunately, this very important area of work is confused, undeveloped, and, indeed, consciously avoided or neglected as unscientific and unscholarly by those with orientations to specialized philosophies of science, particularly that of logical positivism. Researchers and teachers (both resident and extension) can avoid ethics and values and still be productive in generating and disseminating relatively value-free knowledge. Such value-free contributions are important in addressing practical issues and problems and in helping those who must decide on prescriptions to resolve the practical issues and solve the practical problems of agriculture and rural societies in the United States and abroad. However, neglect and avoidance of ethics and values leave administrators, legislators, advisors, and consultants unserved by the objective use of logic and experience to answer ethical and value questions important in resolving the issues and solving the problems discussed throughout this book. In order for the rural social sciences to make their full potential contributions to required value and ethical knowledge, it is important that the rural and basic social sciences cooperate with the humanities to:

- Establish research programs on ethical and value issues in agriculture and rural societies in the colleges of agriculture and the U.S. Department of Agriculture (USDA) that address:

- The value dimensions of specific *practical problems* using experiment station, extension service, USDA, and special funds to mobilize basic social science disciplinarians, philosophers, and humanists, as well as rural social scientists.
- Various (usually) *multidisciplinary subjects* involving ethics such as regenerative agriculture, hunger, resource conservation, gender inequality, energy, poverty, and food entitlements. Again, colleges of agriculture, experiment station, USDA, USAID (United States Agency for International Development), and special funds can be used to mobilize the appropriate basic social science disciplinarians, philosophers, humanists, and rural social scientists. The consequences of alternative courses of action for various groups in society should be stressed in terms of values attained and sacrificed.
- Disciplinary questions relevant for research on values, decision rules, prescriptions, social indicators, conflict resolutions, and the interpersonal validity or lack thereof of welfare measures. This could be done with competitive grant funds from the agricultural establishment to supplement disciplinary research funds now available to the basic social science disciplinarians, humanists, and philosophers within our own administrative units.

- Develop techniques to (1) augment present capacities to acquire, validate, and verify descriptive knowledge of values by using rigorous philosophic reasoning to interpret and analyze past experiences and (2) refine decision-making models and decision rules governing interaction among groups using value knowledge to prescribe private and/or public actions to resolve issues and problems.

- Establish appropriate teaching programs at undergraduate and graduate levels in colleges of agriculture to include, for example:
  - Agricultural ethics modules in regular biophysical agricultural and rural social science courses.
  - A senior-level agricultural ethics course open for graduate students taught at the college rather than the department level.
  - A college-level seminar for researchers, teachers, graduate students, extension workers, and practitioners concerned with values and ethics in agriculture and rural societies.

- Expand the ethics training behind and the ethics and value content of:
  - Agricultural extension programs to improve public understanding of ethical aspects and values important in resolving the public and private problems faced by decision makers in agriculture and rural societies.
  - The advising, consulting, entrepreneurial, and administrative activities of rural social scientists.

- Increase institutional capability of the rural social sciences to deal with ethical questions and values through:
  - Professional upgrading via sabbatical leaves and collaborative research and education (1) among rural social scientists and (2) between rural and basic disciplinary social scientists, on one hand, and philosophers and humanists, on the other.
  - Restructuring undergraduate and graduate teaching programs in the colleges of agriculture to include agro-ethics.
  - Modifying extension/public-service activities to increase public awareness of ethical issues confronting agriculture and to deal more adequately with such issues.

GENERAL AGENDA ITEMS DEVELOPED AFTER THE HOUSTON CONFERENCE

The agendas presented here are related to those for domestic and international farm and rural development in Part II, for the four driving forces found in the four sections of Part III, and for the two crosscutting sections (databases and basic social science disciplines) found in Part IV, but differ from them in that the focus is on the demand that these more substantive areas place on ethics and philosophy. They extend the overall agendas about agro-ethics developed at Houston and presented in the first main section of this chapter in that the agenda items presented here indicate, in a general way what ethicists and agro-ethicists need to do in order to contribute more to the resolution of the important problems for farmers, farm people, agribusiness people, and rural communities. The need for these additional agenda items became apparent within SSAAP's editorial group as a consequence of greater recognition of the potential of PC/TC theory in the resolution of such problems. The agendas presented here were conditioned by continued attention to the important distinctions between problem-solving, subject-matter, and disciplinary work. These general agenda items are not classified according to the four driving forces although problems arising with respect to the four forces are frequently referenced to indicate why an agenda item is important. In general, agro-ethicists and ethicists should recognize that the dynamics of the agricultural system create (1) new multidisciplinary problems to be solved and (2) new multidisciplinary subjects about which knowledge is needed for solving important sets of problems yet insufficient for fully solving any one problem in the sets. This means that specialized disciplinary applications of ethics in agriculture, while useful, should be expected to (1) be overspecialized even when applicable and (2) fail to help ethicists improve ethics at its interfaces with disciplines other than the one being applied. Ethicists and economists should:

- Recognize their common concern with optimality in designing prescriptions to solve problems arising from changes in the four driving forces.

- Recognize that prescriptions to solve problems depend on both value and value-free knowledge (whether regarded as independent or interdependent) and on "rules of the game" or "decision rules" that determine the ownership of the right to decide as well as the ownership of other rights and privileges. This is confirmable by reflecting on such current problems and issues as designing (1) new regulations to control environmental pollution and food-chain contamination, (2) better institutions to educate and improve the productivity of the children of disadvantaged nonfarm rural residents who will be a major part of the U.S. labor force in the next six decades, (3) agricultural science policies and changes in our technical agricultural research institutions to create appropriate kinds of and amounts of technical advances, and (4) changes in the rules of the game for *changing* the rules of the game for making public choices about all four of the driving forces.

- Recognize the inadequacy of the optima defined in static economics and attempt to define more dynamic optima that take into account (1) imperfect knowledge, (2) learning of value, value-free, rules of the game, and prescriptive knowledge about the four driving forces, and (3) all monetary and nonmonetary values relevant for establishing the optimal (or best all things considered) course of action.
- Encourage more attention to preoptimization phases in choice and decision processes.
- Develop better definitions of optimal and then design processes for seeking such optima for use by both
  - public, and
  - private decision makers.
- Be constructive in seeking ways to do descriptive research on the "real" values of conditions, situations, things, and acts. There can be little doubt about the badness of a carcinogenic pollution of a food chain, the goodness of a possible AIDS vaccine, but knowledge is less certain about the badnesses of inorganic fertilizers, ice-minus bacteria, and bovine growth hormones and the goodnesses of fluoridation, saccharine, and some currently approved pesticides. Needed for such research are more extensive uses of:
  - Tests of logic or coherence
  - Tests of experience or correspondence (this implies better measurement)
  - Tests for ambiguity or lack of clarity
- Study decision rules much more intensely with attention to (1) the roles of power in them and (2) the goodness and badness of using various rules irrespective of their consequences.
- Devote major attention to agendas presented in Parts II and III that pertain to use and further development of the PC/TC approach to choosing, deciding, and designing public and private institutions.
- Distinguish between intrinsic and exchange values and between prescriptions and descriptive-value statements.
- Devote more time to the measurement of:
  - Intrinsic values
  - Nonmonetary exchange values
- Explore whether and how the extensions and expansions of the PC/TC approach suggested in Part III, Section 1, Chapter 1, can be built into multidisciplinary, philosophically and technically general, iterative and interactive, participative analyses to *define* and *seek* evolving, changing optima in improving public and private institutions.

INDEX TO PART IV

Part V

Administration and Funding: Needed Research and Strategies

CHAPTER 1

INTRODUCTION TO ADMINISTRATION AND FUNDING: NEEDED RESEARCH AND STRATEGIES

This chapter introduces Part V, which deals with (1) research on administration and funding and (2) administrative and funding strategies needed to make the rural social sciences (RSSs) and basic social science disciplines (BSSDs) more effective and productive in serving farmers, agribusinesses, consumers and nonfarm rural residents. The agendas presented in Parts II through IV of this book will come to little if the work of rural and basic social scientists is not well administered and funded. The last chapter of this part presents agendas for research needed on the administration and funding of the rural and basic social sciences, as well as administrative strategies to increase social science contributions to farming, agribusinesses, households, consumers, and rural societies. Unlike Parts II, III, and IV, Part V has no separate overall introduction or separate sections.

In Part V, SSAAP attempts to present a *legitimate* case for more and different administration and additional funding of the rural and basic social sciences. There is, of course, a fine line between a legitimate case for the rural and basic social sciences, on one hand, and self-serving, unobjective advocacy for the rural and basic social sciences in agriculture, on the other. Part V treads that fine line. There will probably be instances in this part that will cause nonsocial scientists to feel that the line has been transgressed, just as social scientists have sometimes felt the same line has been transgressed in some past agenda-, priority-, and strategy-setting exercises conducted by the physical and biological agricultural scientists.

THREE ADMINISTRATIVE IMBALANCES

Typically, the problems and issues of farmers, agribusinesses, rural communities, and consumers involve the rural and basic social sciences in multidisciplinary ways. However, the agricultural establishment (AE) is so heavily oriented to the technical agricultural sciences and, increasingly, to the biological and physical sciences as basic disciplines, that a major reorientation of administrative effort is now required to put the multidisciplinary problem-solving (PS) and subject-matter (SM) agendas presented in this volume into effect. In turn, PS and SM work requires more attention to questions regarding values and ethics than is typical in the AE. Thus, there are three important administrative imbalances to be considered: (1) a relative overemphasis on technology, (2) neglect of practical problems and subjects (issues) as opposed to academic disciplinary interests, and (3) neglect of the value and ethical dimensions of practical problems and issues.

There is a *current major and severe imbalance* in the AE toward technology. Rural human development, the problems of rural societies, agricultural resources (including manmade resources), and the environment are relatively neglected. They need more emphasis, although for reasons indicated below, technical advance should not be deemphasized. Nontechnocratic problems and issues call for administrative reorganization of the research, extension or outreach, rural instruction, and international programs of the land-grant universities and the USDA, as well as of the non-land-grant colleges and universities that deal with agriculture and rural resources, people, and communities. However, long-term appraisals of the need for agricultural production (Johnson and Wittwer 1984) indicate that the AE should not curtail its investments in technical advance even to address the social science aspects of less technical problems and issues. Technological progress is still needed despite our surpluses of agricultural products, the opposition of dairy producers to bovine somatotropin (BST) as a source of increased milk production, and many other oppositions to high technology agriculture. Even the present neglect of the human, institutional, equity, environmental and food safety aspects of the problems and issues we face in our food and fiber system and in rural societies does not indicate that we should abandon technical advance. Technical advance is a necessary but insufficient condition for progress and increased production. Development and dissemination of new technology need to continue lest technology (like human development, institutional improvements, and natural and manmade resources) become a limiting factor for progress. Almost paradoxically, more investment in social science research, teaching, and extension is probably a long-term guarantor of increased funding for technical advance, rather than a competitor, because continued neglect of social science dimensions of current nontechnical problems and issues by the AE is likely to result in lost support for the AE's technical work. SSAAP's editorial committee is convinced that support for the biological and physical work in the AE will be reduced in the future unless the AE uses the rural social sciences to address the problems and issues involving human development: institutions, programs and policies; the conservation and enhancement of natural and manmade resources; and community improvement. These are in addition to the need to address the social science dimensions of technical change.

The situation is made difficult because past neglect of the social science dimensions of agricultural and rural problems and issues by the AE has now "turned off" important potential supporters of nontechnocratic work in the AE. In mobilizing funds and sponsors for its work, SSAAP's leadership discovered that some philanthropic, federal, state, and activist organizations have simply "given up on" the land-grant colleges of agriculture as effective change agents for rural community development, for human development problems of disadvantaged rural farm and nonfarm people, and even for dealing with environmental pollution and contamination of food chains. Some even regard the USDA and land-grant agricultural colleges as causes of current problems and have opposed the USDA/land-grant system. This alarming situation calls for attention to (1) research on administration and funding of the rural and basic social sciences in the AE and (2) improved strategies for social science administration and funding to help the AE "re-earn" the resources and respect it needs to work effectively on the important current problems and issues of agriculture, rural people, agribusinesses, and consumers.

There is a clear need for a partnership between the social sciences on one hand, and the biological and physical sciences on the other, as they strive to assist farmers, agribusinesses, households, consumers, and rural societies. There is a strong conviction in SSAAP that the AE and the rural and basic social sciences have magnificent, unexploited opportunities to earn resources for what they can do well, and that this can be done without encroaching on the technical advances that will be badly needed, both domestically and abroad, in the world envisioned for the next century. Indeed, lack of attention to the human and societal dimensions of new technology is already resulting in attempts to limit funding for biological research by a public less informed than it could be if more social science research were to be done.

A *second administrative and funding imbalance* was emphasized in Part I of this book. It pertains to the relative neglect (both outside and within the AE) of problem-solving (PS) and subject-matter (SM) work in favor of disciplinary (DISC) work as these three kinds of work are described in Chapter 1 of Part I. Two articles, one by Bloch and another by Palca and Marshal in the same issue of Science (1990), recount Bloch's efforts as Director of the National Science Foundation to reverse the general trend toward disciplinarity in that agency. Administrative units in the AE need to reorient their research, extension, and resident instruction programs more toward the multidisciplinary problems and issues of today's agriculture and rural areas. Promotions and advancement in universities and agricultural colleges now depend substantially on publication of peer-reviewed DISC research in scholarly journals. Although this results from policies put in place by administrators, many land-grant agricultural colleges and, to a lesser extent, USDA administrators now argue that this emphasis is necessary in order to hire and retain high-quality personnel. However unfortunate this is, it is exactly what should be expected when promotion and advancement depend on publication of peer-reviewed DISC research and when the quality of personnel is defined in terms of ability to publish in peer-received disciplinary journals even to the neglect of needed multidisciplinary PS and SM work! The whole system fails to (1) define the nature of PS and SM excellence, both for research and other activities, some of which are as scholarly as research, and (2) determine who are the appropriate peers for evaluating PS and SM research and other work. Much change is needed in administrative practices.

It is worthwhile to consider a line of reasoning encountered among both basic disciplinary and agricultural biological and physical scientists. The argument notes that (1) technological advances depend increasingly on expensive, complex advances in the biological and physical science disciplines, that (2) private industry can best do the developmental work required to convert new, basic scientific knowledge into technical advances, and that, consequently, (3) basic scientific research should be concentrated in a few "flagship" institutions, while much of the applied technological development work should be phased out at "run-of-the-mill" land-grant agricultural colleges and experiment stations that are to be taken over by the private sector. This argument tends to support the observed trends toward DISC work away from PS and SM work in colleges, universities, and governmental agencies.

The above lines of reasoning and observed historical trends, however, raise questions about the development that must be addressed. These include: (1) How can the relevance of disciplinary work be maintained if basic scientists are not in touch with the location, human and institutional specificity of practical problems and issues or subjects? (2) Would the holistic multidisciplinarity of practical problems and issues be adequately handled by specialized disciplinarians in flagship institutions? (3) Can practical problems and issues be adequately handled by the private sector when solutions are *either* socially desirable but privately unprofitable or so privately profitable and prone to monopolization and, in some cases, dangerous that public regulation is required? Such questions are even more relevant for social than for physical and biological work. The neglect of such questions by the AE has been the source of much of the criticism leveled against it. Because the social sciences are concerned with social, practical, and economic aspects of problems and issues, PS and SM efforts are particularly useful in ensuring the relevance of basic disciplinary social science work. Further, institutional and human specificity is even more crucially important in social science work on institutions (policies and organizations), human development, and conservation and enhancement of natural and manmade resources than it is for work on the social dimensions of problems and issues arising from technical change. There appear to be good and compelling reasons for preserving DISC/PS and SM interactions within public AE institutions.

A *third administrative imbalance* occurs because most AE administrators have been selected from the biological and physical agricultural sciences and, hence, bring to their work the logically positivistic reductionist view of science typical of the biological and physical scientists. This view unduly restricts those doing PS and SM research and other work requiring the objective generation and use of value knowledge to reach prescriptions as to what "ought to be done" to solve practical problems. Section 3 of Part IV on ethics, private decisions, and public choices, contains three chapters that address the need to go beyond the reductionist logical positivism of the physical and biological sciences when addressing practical problems and issues in order to correct this imbalance. The need for objective research on values and prescriptions is also considered in this chapter in the section below on agroethics in this.

SELECTED LITERATURE, PAST DISCUSSIONS, AND EXPERIENCES PERTAINING TO ADMINISTRATIVE AND FUNDING STRATEGIES

The three administrative imbalances noted above are examined in the following review of selected administrative and funding literature, discussions and experiences. Much of the "literature" on administration and funding of the AE exists as memoranda, "desk-top" reports, committee reports, unpublished speeches, and the like, although some of it is published in books and scholarly journals. In reviewing this literature, other background material, and experiences, it was kept in mind that SSAAP was created to consider teaching, extension, administerative, entrepreneurial, governmental, and private sector activities, as well as research—i.e., SSAAP is concerned with all the professional activities of social scientists, not just their research. Literature and background experiences relevant for administrative strategies and for research agendas pertaining to administration and funding of the rural and basic social sciences are reviewed here under seven main but somewhat disparate rubrics: (1) the alleged primacy of disciplinary (DISC) versus multidisciplinary problem-solving (PS) and subject-matter (SM) efforts; (2) relative emphasis on the four driving forces: technological advance, institutional (includes policies, organizations, infrastructure, and programs) improvements, human development, and the conservation and enhancement of natural and manmade resources; (3) beyond research to other kinds of work; (4) agro-ethics; (5) administrative relationships among departments, disciplines, kinds of work and kinds of knowledge; (6) funding through endowments, formulas, budget line items, soft money and competitive grants; and (7) USDA land-grant funding and administrative relationships for the rural and basic social sciences.

THE ALLEGED PRIMACY OF DISCIPLINARY (DISC) VERSUS MULTIDISCIPLINARY PROBLEM-SOLVING (PS) AND SUBJECT-MATTER (SM) EFFORTS

Disciplinary (DISC) efforts were described in Chapter 1 of Part I as efforts devoted to improve the measurements, theories, and techniques of a basic discipline such as chemistry, economics, physics, sociology, or biology. Subject-matter (SM) efforts were described as efforts to improve knowledge of a multidisciplinary subject such as energy, environmental pollution, animal husbandry, labor, integrated pest management, agricultural economics, poultry husbandry, agronomy, or sustainable agriculture (the more stable of which have departmental and even institute status), that is important for a rather *definite set of decision makers* facing a rather *definite set of problems* even if inadequate for solving any specific problem in the set. Problem-solving (PS) efforts were described as multidisciplinary efforts intended to solve a particular practical problem faced by at least one specific decision maker. DISC, PS and SM research are considered in substantial detail in Johnson's 1986 *Research Methodology for Economists.* Historically the research, extension, resident instruction, and other efforts of agriculturalists have included all three of these kinds of efforts. After World War II, administrators (both inside and outside the AE) began to give DISC efforts primacy over PS and SM activity. (Bush 1945; Handler 1976; Atkinson 1980; Press 1982) Increasingly, administrators are questioning this development. (Bloch 1990; Palca and Marshal 1990; Johnson 1984; Johnson and Wittwer 1984).

The Pound Report of (1972) was the beginning of a series of administrative and funding discussions and studies in the AE that made a case for more basic DISC biological and physical science research often at the expense of the more traditional multidisciplinary PS and SM research of the biological and physical agricultural sciences. A stream of administrative and funding actions expanded emphasis on basic disciplinary research by the biological and physical sciences at the expense of some of the more practical multidisciplinary SM and PS research on such agricultural subjects as traditional plant and animal breeding, horticulture, agricultural engineering, and poultry science. Although much DISC biological and physical science research and other work of questionable practical relevancy is done, the relevancy of DISC biological and physical science work is more easily understood than is the relevancy of DISC social science work and even, for that matter, PS and SM work with appropriate social science components. Probably, this is partially a consequence of the biological and physical science backgrounds and orientations common among AE administrators.

The rural social sciences also participated in this trend toward the DISC. The *American Journal of Agricultural Economics* has become quite disciplinary and agricultural economics graduate programs have taken on an increased disciplinary orientation in recent years. However, Schuh (1986), Johnson (1986, 1984, 1991), Connor (1989), and Just and Rausser (1989) have deplored what they regard as a resultant overemphasis on DISC work in agricultural economics at the expense of PS and SM work. In this connection, also see Busch (Part III, Section 1, Chapter 5) and Bubolz and Sontag (Part II, Section 2, Chapter 6) in this book. The new journal, *Agricultural Economics*, of the International Association of Agricultural Economists (IAAE) has a specific policy of devoting one third of its space to each of DISC, PS, and SM articles reporting extension, instruction, advising, consulting, administrative and entrepreneurial, as well as research efforts. The American Agricultural Economics Association (AAEA) has recently initiated a publication, *Choices*, for articles dealing with PS and SM efforts that include, but go beyond, DISC economics research to offset the heavy emphasis of the *American Journal of Agricultural Economics* (AJAE) on

DISC economic research. Such general economists as McCloskey (1983, 1990) have also joined the quest for relevance (also see Johnson 1971). Johnson's book, *Research Methodology for Economists* (1986), places equal emphasis on PS, SM, and DISC research and devotes about one-third of its space to differences encountered in administering, funding, conducting, and evaluating DISC, versus multidisciplinary PS and SM research.

The Cooperative State Research Service (CSRS) in the U.S. Department of Agriculture (USDA) recently originated an initiative to identify problems and subjects requiring research attention on the marketing of agricultural products and the activities of agribusiness firms. The results of that effort were presented in Davan's chapter (Part II, Section 1, Chapter 2).

After World War II, a number of rural sociology departments also moved in a DISC direction away from PS and SM work in colleges of agriculture. The consequent loss of financial support for rural sociology from the AE and the AE's own neglect of the social dimensions of emerging problems in agriculture and rural societies have since prompted efforts of rural sociologists to reestablish closer connections with colleges of agriculture at least for doing applied DISC, if not always multidisciplinary PS and SM work. Under the leadership of rural sociologists, a number of initiatives have been developed in the Experiment Station Committee on Organization and Policy (ESCOP) as well in the Extension Committee on Organization and Policy (ECOP). These initiatives have been recognized administratively but have not been given high priority within the sets of initiatives endorsed by the various policy committees (ECOP, ESCOP, etc.). (See Part IV, Section 1, Chapter 1, of this book, for references to these initiatives).

Increasingly, individual research administrators outside the AE in colleges of arts and sciences in land-grant colleges, university-level research units, non-land-grant colleges and universities, and even in the National Science Foundation and Academy of Sciences are recognizing the need for multidisciplinary teams to research multidisciplinary subjects such as environmental degradation, international competitiveness and global warming along with their associated specific problems, to name a few. These efforts spread across the full spectrum of research, from the most basic inquiries to the most practical and applied PS.

A particularly acute administrative problem is that of motivating researchers and teachers to engage in PS and SM activities as contrasted to DISC research and teaching. Within the professions, promotions and other professional awards now go to researchers and, among researchers, to those who publish peer-reviewed DISC research articles. Those who pursue less academic objectives outside the academic worlds of universities, colleges and the more academic units of government and parastatals are often better rewarded for multidisciplinary PS and SM work. As academia becomes more disciplinary, a related administrative difficulty arises—that of motivating university extension workers, advisors, and consultants to engage in PS and SM activities needed badly by farmers, rural community organizations, agribusinesses, and consumers. If it were not for the fact that DISC work benefits from PS and SM and vice versa, the DISC could be left to academia and PS and SM to the private sector and governmental units. However, to do so would be to lose the synergistic effects between DISC research, on one hand, and PS and SM research, on the other.

RELATIVE EMPHASIS ON THE FOUR DRIVING FORCES FOR PROGRESS OF THE FOOD AND FIBER SYSTEM AND RURAL SOCIETIES

Four driving forces were considered in substantial detail in the introduction to Part III and in the introductory and ending chapters of each of the four sections of Part III: (1) technical advance, (2) institutional (including policies, programs, and social infrastructures) improvements, (3) human development, and (4) enhancement of natural (includes the environment) and manmade resources. These forces are viewed by SSAAP as individually necessary but individually insufficient for rural and agricultural progress. A conclusion reached in Part III was that the AE has seriously underinvested in the last three forces relative to technical advance. Literature pertaining to needed research on administration and funding is reviewed by Klonglan in Chapter 2 (Part V). His review also indicates that the AE has been technocratic in the sense of being primarily concerned with funding and administrative requirements for research, extension, and resident instruction to improve production inputs, techniques, and methods for what is often termed "production agriculture."

This technocratic imbalance is also displayed at times in the basic social science of economics and in its rural counterpart, agricultural economics. For instance, both general and agricultural economists have often concentrated on the economics of technical change to the neglect of the economics of human development, institutional change, and the enhancement of natural and manmade resources. The same appears to be true for anthropology, sociology, and rural sociology. Perhaps this is because it is easier for the technocratic AE to finance work on the social dimensions of technical advance than on the social dimensions of the other three driving forces. Social scientists probably anticipated this and, accordingly, focused their proposals disproportionately on technology.

BEYOND RESEARCH TO OTHER KINDS OF WORK

Administrative and funding strategies and research agendas require recognition that rural and basic social scientists engage in much more than research at universities, in public agencies and in the private sector. In universities, they serve as extension workers, resident teachers, administrators, consultants, and advisors, as well as researchers. In the private and public sectors, they serve as entrepreneurs, staff members, administrators, elected officials, consultants, and advisors, in addition to doing research. In order to play these diverse roles effectively, rural and basic social scientists need research to improve their administration and funding for performing all of these functions. They also need better strategies to obtain resources for such work, to provide the administrative services they need particularly for multidisciplinary PS and SM work, to improve their training for such roles, and to allow them the philosophic flexibility required to engage in multidisciplinary SM and PS work.

AGROETHICS

The PS and SM work of agriculturalists (including rural social scientists) has as its objective the generation of prescriptive knowledge to solve problems. For PS work prescriptive objectives are immediate and direct—for SM work they are less immediate and direct but nonetheless central. The multidisciplinary, institute-like agricultural science departments of colleges of agriculture and many administrative units of the U.S. Department of Agriculture (USDA) unavoidably become involved in generating and using both value and value free knowledge to generate prescriptions directly or indirectly to serve decision makers. (Chapter 1 [Part IV, Section 3] contains a rather detailed treatment of public and private decision making, explaining how prescriptive knowledge is generated.) Problems for the AE involving the generation and utilization of new technologies have recently arisen that have made it necessary for AE administrators to improve and use value knowledge in deciding how they ought to resolve their own administrative problems with respect to new technology. Difficulty in solving administrative problems pertaining to technical change is of course but a special case of the general administrative difficulty experienced in doing PS and SM work for clientele of the AE.

Many AE administrators experience difficulties with respect to prescriptive knowledge and value knowledge because of philosophic orientations acquired in the biological and physical science backgrounds common for many AE administrators (Johnson 1986; McCloskey 1983, 1990; also see Part IV, Section 3, on agro-ethics in this book). Those orientations commonly put investigation of value questions and problem solving beyond the realm of objective, descriptive, "scientific" work. For an excellent statement of the reductionistic, logically positivistic, philosophic orientation common among biological and physical scientists, see *On Being a Scientist* by the Committee on the Conduct of Science, National Academy of Science (1989). Also see Chapters 4 and 7 of Johnson's 1986 *Research Methodology for Economists*. For two other philosophic views of science more compatible with doing work on the value and ethical aspects of PS and SM efforts, see Chapters 5, 6, 8, 9, and 17 of the Johnson (1986) reference.

Objective descriptive answers to value questions are fundamental for resolving problems and issues faced in farming, agribusinesses, rural communities, and consuming households. Such questions are also at the heart of many valid criticisms leveled against the AE. Answers to value and ethical questions are also needed by agriculturalists serving as advisors, consultants, administrators, businessmen and as activists or advocates with responsibilities for reaching or helping to reach decisions and often to execute them. If the AE is to make its full contribution to resolving the practical problems and issues of the food and fiber system and of rural societies, it must overcome the limitations of a reductionist, logically positivistic orientation to science.

Figure 1 relates three kinds of knowledge—value free, about values and prescriptive—to DISC, PS and SM research. It is presented here to help persons, with positivistic views of science, see how doing PS and SM research makes it necessary to embrace a wider range of philosophic orientations to science than is common in biological and physical science circles. Because prescriptions to solve problems require knowledge of values—nonmonetary, as well as monetary and extrinsic as well as intrinsic—a logically positivistic orientation is never well suited to PS and is often poorly suited to SM research. The reason for this is simple—logical positivism posits that there can be no descriptive knowledge of real values. It regards perceptions about the badness of such conditions and situations as cancer, food chain contamination, worker displacement, environmental pollution, scientific dishonesty, AIDS, and occupational injury to be matters of emotion rather than of descriptive fact. Logical positivism does the same for goodnesses, such as those of health, a clean environment, honesty, uncontaminated food, justice, and a possible AIDS vaccine. Logical positivism permits scientists to describe the goodnesses and/or badnesses people ascribe to things, conditions, situations, and acts, but it does not permit scientists to describe goodness or badness as a characteristic of reality, whether or not anyone knows of the goodness or badness. Philosophers who conceive of using logic and/or experience to research values include: John S. Mill, John Dewey, Immanuel Kant, and G. E. Moore, none of whom is referenced in the 1989 National Academy of Science report cited above. Value references in that report are more about ethics in science than about the

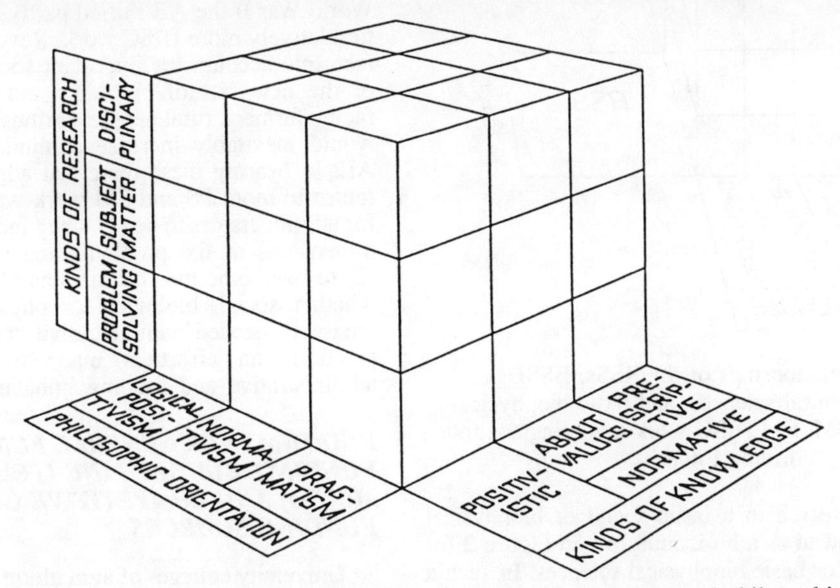

Figure 1. Kinds of research and knowledge produced by agricultural researchers and philosophic orientations

generation of value knowledge for use in reaching prescriptions to solve practical problems and resolve crucial issues. Philosophic flexibility that permits use of experience and logic to generate value knowledge is needed. Such flexibility implies tolerance of pragmatic and normative orientations to science.

ADMINISTRATIVE RELATIONSHIPS AMONG DEPARTMENTS, DISCIPLINES, AND KINDS OF WORK

Figure 2 relates PS, SM and DISC work on the four driving forces to the Rural Social Sciences (RSSs), the basic social science disciplines (BSSDs), the technical agricultural sciences, and the basic biophysical sciences. That diagram, presented below as Figure 2, is useful in envisioning the difficulties administrators face in organizing the three different kinds of work on the four driving forces. As such, Figure 2 does not make a special case for the rural and basic social sciences; instead, it is presented to help clarify the different administrative requirements for doing PS and SM work that inevitably involve the administration of multidisciplinary and multidepartmental efforts. Figure 2 explains and supports SM and PS administration with balanced attention to all relevant disciplines and departments.

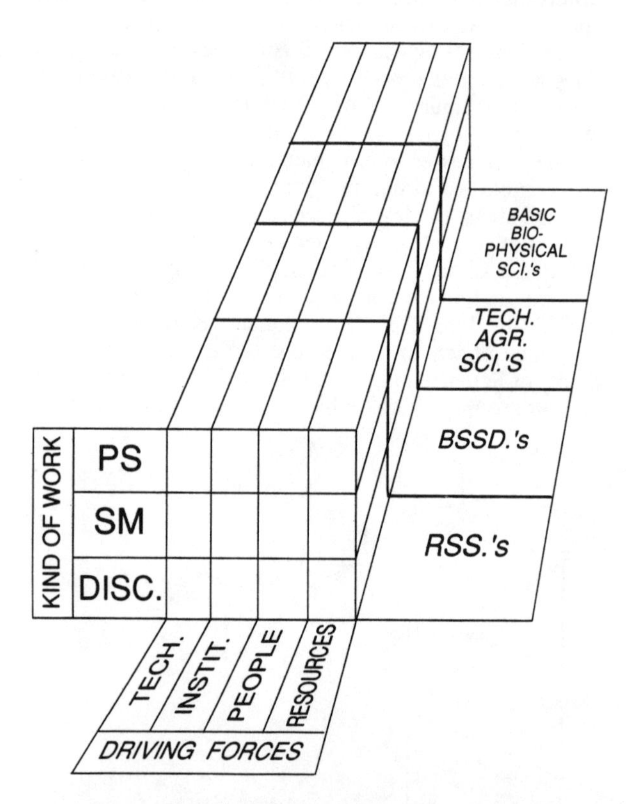

Figure 2. Relationships of the RSSs, BSSDs, technical agricultural sciences, and basic biophysical sciences to PS, SM, and DISC work involving the four driving forces.

Disciplinary research in a basic social or biophysical science can be viewed as a horizontal row in Figure 2 for one of the BSSDs or basic biophysical sciences. In such a row for a biophysical science, work is likely to concentrate on technical change, *physical* human development, or the technical aspects of resources. Specialized applied disciplinary efforts are also likely to be relevant for the broader multidisciplinary horizontal PS and SM slices of Figure 2. DISC efforts by economists, for instance, include applied DISC work on the economics of any of the four driving forces. However, when the focus shifts away from DISC to multidisciplinary PS and SM work, the realms of the subject or problem spread across a PS or SM horizontal slice of Figure 1 to include work on any or all of the four driving forces by basic disciplinarians (biophysical as well as social), by rural social scientists, and by technical agricultural scientists.

Elsewhere, Johnson (1986) has devoted roughly one-third of a book on research methodology for economists to the administrative differences that arise when doing PS, SM, and DISC research. Even larger administrative differences arise when the efforts of rural social scientists go beyond research. For instance, greater administrative difficulties are encountered in conducting PS and SM efforts that cross basic disciplines, the RSS's and the different technical agricultural sciences than in conducting DISC efforts. (Johnson 1986, Chapter 14). The relevant sources of funding for PS and SM work are more complicated than those for DISC work because they include agencies, groups, and persons with practical problems as well as those interested in basic disciplines (Johnson 1986, Chapter 13). In turn, this raises complicated administrative questions about evaluation of PS and SM versus DISC efforts—clearly, funders and those facing the practical problems and issues addressed in PS and SM work have valid claims for inclusion among peer reviewers and on advisory groups, governing boards, and evaluation panels (Johnson 1986, Chapter 15). Persons highly qualified to review DISC research may be poorly qualified to review PS and SM research and even less qualified to evaluate nonresearch PS and SM efforts of agriculturalists, including rural social scientists. Peer review becomes too important in the cases of PS and SM research to be left to disciplinarians!

Serious questions now arise as to whether the AE has enough administrators and the kinds of administrative capacity needed to expand its PS and SM programs. The differences between PS, SM, and DISC work discussed above led to decreased administrative burdens when after World War II the AE shifted partly away from PS and SM to relatively more DISC work. Reversing this shift now, to take into account the important social science dimensions of the new sets of problems and issues (subjects) now facing farmers, rural people, agribusinesses, and consumers would inevitably increase administrative burdens in the AE. In bearing these increased administrative burdens, a return to more PS and SM work would make it necessary for administrators to be (1) tuned increasingly to the ethical dimensions of the problems and subjects addressed and (2) to overcome the chauvinisms of their basic disciplines whether social, biological or physical science. This increase in needed administrative capacity must be anticipated if an effort is made to redress the present administrative and funding imbalance toward the DISC.

ENDOWMENTS, GENERAL FUNDS, FORMULA FUNDING, BUDGET LINE ITEMS, SOFT MONEY, AND COMPETITIVE GRANTS AS FUNDING SOURCES

University colleges of agriculture and other AE agencies receive public support for their work in a variety of complex ways in which the funding of the agricultural and rural work of the rural and basic social sciences is enmeshed. Included in the complex are endowments, general funds, formula funds, line items in budgets, gifts, grants and contracts, and, recently, competitive grants. Administrators, their units, and personnel negotiate, earn, and receive funds in these and other ways.

Although apparently increasing somewhat in importance, *endowments* are relatively rare for the rural social and technical agricultural sciences that depend heavily on formula and general funds. Unless restricted to PS and SM areas of work, endowments are rather well suited to support research and other DISC work. They also provide useful continuity for SM work on enduring issues and subjects and, for that matter, in maintaining capacity to do shorter-term PS and SM work on the ever-changing stream of multidisciplinary problems and issues important for rural farm and nonfarm people, agribusinesses, and consumers. Endowments share these characteristics with the federal and state general and formula funds that are much more common in the AE than endowments.

General funds at universities and institutes (commonly from state sources) provide long-term funding for all kinds of research and instruction. Along with formula funds and even stable line items, they provide much of the continuity for the institutions that make up the AE. Because such funds tend to be committed to departments, salaries of tenured personnel and subadministrative units, they are less useful than grants and contracts for adapting AE institutions, organizations, programs, and projects to the changing problems and issues facing rural areas. However, without endowments and general funds, it is doubtful if society could provide the disciplinary skills and administrative structures to support needed SM and PS work. This becomes more apparent when it is realized that much of the continuity for the basic disciplines is maintained in colleges of arts and sciences outside of the AE.

Formula funding has long persisted for the land-grant colleges of agriculture and the USDA. Donald Holt, Director of the Illinois Agricultural Experiment Station, argues in support of formula funding that it: (1) is important for what SSAAP has labeled PS and SM research which is about 10 times as costly as DISC (basic) research, (2) is necessary to maintain the "public institutional structure" of U.S. agriculture, (3) provides continuity not attainable from short-term funding, (4) helps avoid "capricious" top-down (national) decisions and the "averaging" effected at national levels through consensus-based management, (5) promotes site- and situation-specific PS and SM work, and (6) helps preserve adaptive (PS and SM) research and extension work.

Those who hold basic disciplinary research in high regard disagree about the advantages of formula funding; some from outside experimental stations (and even within) want formula-funded PS and SM efforts in experiment stations reduced so that the savings can be devoted to basic DISC research elsewhere. Part of the antiformula argument is that the more generic, less site- and situation-specific, expensive, advanced, basic disciplinary research should be directed centrally and concentrated at well-financed, more effective "flagship" institutions employing the "cream" of the basic biophysical scientists. With the key to the sequence being DISC research, they also argue that basic DISC research precedes development, adaption, and transfer efforts (SSAAP's PS and SM categories). PS and SM efforts, they argue, can be left to "hewers of wood" doing followup PS and SM work at "run of the mill" institutions and in the private sector. However, Holt (1989), an agronomist, argues that the total process should not be viewed as "wired in series" with basic DISC research preceding PS and SM research; instead, he argues that the process is more accurately viewed as "wired in parallel" so that adaptive adoption and/or transfer efforts may often proceed without the basic research it may stimulate. Sometimes, it is prior PS and SM research that reveals discipline deficiencies not easily discoverable by disciplinaries out of touch with practical problems and issues. Both technical agricultural and rural social science PS, SM, and even DISC efforts are typically so place- and situation-specific that disciplinary relevance often depends on handling variables that differ from place to place and from one situation to another. Johnson (1986), an economist, agrees with Holt. If Holt and Johnson are correct, the case against formula funding is substantially weakened and that for it strengthened. The case for elitist flagship institutions is correspondingly also weakened.

Line items in the budgets of public university and agency budgets provided by state and the federal governments originate commonly with legislative and executive desires to attain objectives and solve problems those branches find important. For colleges of agriculture, state funding is of major importance. It is often of increasing importance when "earned" by PS and SM work that serves the agriculture, agribusinesses, and rural communities of a state. Also, line items sometimes originate in universities and agencies with persons and units that find it important for social, political, disciplinary, bureaucratic, and even personal reasons to fund a particular project, program, institution, activity, or person. Although questionable purposes are sometimes served by line items in budgets, line items nonetheless have, can, and often do provide a means of making academic and governmental units more responsive to the problems and issues of the time. University and agency administrators sometimes resent budget lines as interfering in their administrative prerogatives. In many such instances, administrators seem to feel they are in a position to know social and agricultural needs better than those who originate the line items. On the other hand, administrators somewhat play paradoxically the same game by attempting to finance what they believe to be important work with line items in budgets.

In the past, line items have often been converted into base funding or formula funds as academic and governmental agencies have reoriented their programs and projects to fill the felt needs that prompted the line items. Some legislators oppose such conversions partly because they feel the conversions result eventually in less attention to the problems and issues that are important to both themselves and their constituents.

Funds from public- and private-sector contracts and "purpose-directed" grants from governmental, parastatal, and private agencies are typically short term for use in doing PS and SM work. Such funds are commonly referred to as "soft money." From the standpoint of institutional continuity, about the best such funds can do is provide some "overhead" that can be used to help maintain the facilities and staffs of agencies accepting such funds. A favorable role played by soft money is that of permitting organizations to finance research and other efforts on new problems and subjects not covered by endowments, formula funds, other "hard money," or line items. It has been observed that academic barnacles grow on hard money while soft money assures the practical relevance of academic and institute efforts.

There appears to be little precedence for expecting conversion of soft money to formula funding. After 1961, soft money from outside the USDA/land-grant system played a particularly important role in reorienting rural social science efforts toward international farm and rural development. Such efforts included extension, resident instruction, advising, and consulting, as well as research. When large amounts of soft money went to agriculturalists (including rural social scientists) from the U.S. Agency for International Development (USAID) for PS and SM work, attempts were repeatedly made by university administrators to convert soft, short-term contracts and grants into long-term funding arrangements akin to formula funding, general funds, and even endowments. Included in these attempts were USAID's Title 12 and 211-D programs of which mainly a small strengthening grant component of Title 12 remains in place. Neither the USAID bureaucracy nor those in Congress who funded USAID were very interested in providing long-term funding for departments and basic disciplines of universities. Short-term contracts and grants provided a basis for initiating relevant PS and SM efforts. To the credit of many rural social scientists, they were quick to use USAID money for relevant PS and SM international development work. Such non-land-grant universities as Harvard and Stanford "hived off" similar work into satellite centers such as the Stanford Research Institute and the Harvard Institute for International Development.

Cooperative agreements have been part of the special arrangements between the USDA's U.S. Agency for International Development (USAID) and land-grant-university colleges of agriculture. They are part of the flows of soft money that can be maintained by units that aggressively seek them and deliver the PS and SM results called for in cooperative agreement documentation. Resources are earned on a "produce-as-you-receive" basis.

Opponents of formula funding of agricultural research have argued, partly in accord with the Pound Report (1972), that formula funding for PS and SM work should be reduced with the reduction used to fund *competitive grants*. To date, the competitive grants program has been relatively small and very technocratic. In the spring of 1990, SSAAP cooperated unsuccessfully with the American Agricultural Economics Association and the Rural Sociological Society to support a small competitive grant program for the rural social sciences. In doing this, SSAAP recognized that most competitive grants are for small-scale DISC research projects. Because the rural social sciences, like the technical agricultural sciences, are limited by deficiencies in their undergirding basic disciplines (see Part IV, Section 2), competitive grants for basic social science research do have a role to play in overcoming these deficiencies. Competitive grants large enough to support major multidisciplinary PS projects or SM programs have not been made to date and, if they were to be made, there is a lack of administrative structures beyond peer review panels to relate competitive grants to the different clienteles facing problems and issues. Earlier, Johnson and Wittwer (1984) argued in favor of larger competitive grants to support multidisciplinary PS and SM research—such grants would, of course, require the development of special administrative structures or the use of the existing land-grant/U.S. Department of Agriculture structure that is presently supported with the formula funds some want diverted to finance DISC competitive grants.

U.S. DEPARTMENT OF AGRICULTURE/LAND-GRANT FUNDING AND ADMINISTRATIVE RELATIONSHIP VIS-A-VIS THE RURAL SOCIAL SCIENCES

Beyond formula funding, the special funding and administrative relationships between the USDA and the land-grant universities have been important for rural social science work to serve farm and nonfarm rural people, agribusinesses, and consumers. Extension work and resident instruction (at university and secondary levels), as well as PS, SM, and DISC research are supported and financed in this relationship. Much of the AE's formula and federal matching-funds grants flows through this administrative arrangement. Further, the USDA is an important research agency in its own right.

Historically, the USDA/land-grant relationship has probably been even more important for the rural social sciences than for the technical agricultural sciences. Two reasons for this are: (1) the important roles played by the USDA in developing the national data base for agriculture and in carrying out analyses of national agricultural problems, policies, and programs for Congress, the executive branch and, for that matter, national groups interested in U.S. agriculture, and (2) the site and location specificity of PS and SM rural social science research that make formula and matching grant funding of state programs appropriate.

The database role of the USDA is covered extensively in section 1 of Part IV and is not considered further here except to stress that the collective rural social sciences depend fundamentally on the data collected by the National Agricultural Statistics Service (NASS), the Bureau of the Census, and the Bureau of Labor Statistics (BLS) for the secondary indexes, income, expenditure, commodity supply-and-disappearance tables, and other measures of agricultural performance generated by the USDA's Economic Research Service (ERS). Data produced by USDA action and regulatory agencies are also important. (See Part IV, Section 1, Chapter 1, for a review of the literature and background on agricultural databases.) Since universities or colleges of agriculture are in poor positions to make the sustained effort required to generate and maintain primary and secondary long-term national data and data series, it is strategically important to the rural social sciences that the national database be maintained and updated in the USDA. University people can maintain closer contact with site-specific problems and issues around the country than can USDA personnel, hence, university people are in a better position to criticize and help update the database to prevent obsolescence than they are to maintain it.

The USDA role of carrying out analyses of national agricultural problems, policies, and programs is less exclusively its own than is its database role. The history of the ERS and its predecessor—the Bureau of Agricultural Economics (BAE)—is characterized by a mixture of outstanding accomplishments and frustrations, the latter stemming from administrative difficulties originating in both the executive and legislative branches of the federal government and, at times, a "top down" or "center out" Washingtonian focus of the USDA. In both the pre-World War II years and World War II years, BAE analysts made major contributions to U.S. agricultural policies and programs by working iteratively and interactively with the Farm-Bloc in Congress in close cooperation with such academicians as Galbraith and Black (1938), T. W. Schultz (1945), and Murray Benedict (Benedict and Stine 1956). Yet, all was not well as Charles Hardin pointed out in the chapters on the BAE in his 1955 book. After World War II, some USDA units and analysts started in effect to bypass Congress by doing public-opinion polls on politically sensitive rural and farm programs. Congress reacted by cutting the budgets of such units. After World War II, the executive branch also became increasingly concerned about the political consequences of BAE analyses and the BAE was administratively dismembered (Hardin 1955). Since then, the executive branch has exercised more and more control over rural social science analyses of national policies and programs by the BAE's successor agencies. In turn, rural social scientists and administrators have made attempts to establish more detached, somewhat parastatal agencies and projects, such as the National Center for Food and Agricultural Policy (NCFAP) at Resources for the Future (RFF), the International Agricultural Trade Research Consortium, and the Food and Agricultural Policy Research Institute (FAPRI) which is jointly administered by the University of Missouri and Iowa State University, to facilitate credible analyses controlled less closely by views from either the executive branch or legislative branch. Although these attempts have been useful, they have experienced difficulties stemming from lack of iterative interaction with concerned decision makers and affected persons and agencies, as well as executive and legislative branch sensitivities. To date, NCFAP has not stabilized its financing. This has made it difficult for NCFAP administrators to develop the kind of long-term, national policy-analysis effort that is needed. Thus, there remains the task of obtaining the financing and the administrative capacity to do additional needed objective policy and program analyses in close iterative interaction with national legislative and executive branch leaders and with affected people and organizations at local, state, regional, and national levels, but sufficiently independent from the executive and legislative branches of the federal government to be credible. The relationship between the ERS, the rural social sciences in universities, and centers such as NCFAP and FAPRI needs to be further developed and improved.

Over the years, cooperative agreements between USDA agencies and universities have played a useful role in providing for exchanges of experiences, training, the flow of disciplinary knowledge to government, and the feeding of agricultural information back and forth between Washington and the rest of the country. Originally, cooperative agreements placed USDA funds and personnel in colleges of agriculture for both the social and biophysical agricultural sciences. Site and location specificity are often extremely important for the social sciences. If this were not so, there would be no important regional, state, local, and/or farm-level problems. Although site and location specificity are probably about as important for the social sciences as for the biological and physical dimensions of problems, the USDA has virtually eliminated the placing of its social science personnel in colleges of agriculture under cooperative agreements as ERS's funding has been reduced and its objectives have become more focused on national issues important for the executive branch. The reverse flow however continues as university personnel go to the USDA where they are supported with sabbatical leaves, short-term appointments, and even interagency personnel agreements (IPA's). USDA/land-grant cooperative financial arrangements do continue for the rural social sciences between the ERS and rural social science departments in colleges of agriculture. USDA/agricultural colleges' cooperative agreements to support financial, personnel training, and information exchange arrangements for the rural social sciences are now in need of serious review and reevaluation.

There are many rural social scientists in USDA agencies other than ERS and NASS. When ERS was established in 1961 by pulling economists and rural sociologists from other agencies into a central social science agency, it was envisioned that ERS would serve the analytic (PS) needs of the other agencies. Thus, for many years, ERS staff worked on site-specific as well as national-level problems in collaboration with the Soil Conservation Service, Extension Service, Agricultural Research Service, Agricultural Marketing Service, Farmers Home Administration, and other agencies. Two developments changed the nature of ERS's interactions with other agencies: the steady decline in real funding to ERS during the 1970s and 1980s, reducing the staff by one third, and a major shift in ERS's research priorities from local issues, and micro- and site-specific issues to a focus on making transparent the consequences of alternative approaches to problems of broad national and international significance. As this evolved, other USDA agencies expanded their own staffs of economists, rural sociologists, and other rural social scientists to do the "in-house" analyses and research needed to operate and support their programmatic missions. These now number in the hundreds, and they represent a major body of rural social scientists whose connections to their parent disciplines and academic bases are not well developed; for example, they often operate outside the traditional USDA/land-grant linkages.

It should also be noted that the legislative branch of the U.S. government has created its own analytical capacity by employing rural and general social scientists on the staffs of congressional representatives and senators and in such legislative agencies as the Congressional Budget Office (CBO), Congressional Research Service (CRS), and the Office of Technology Assessment (OTA). Generally speaking, the rural and basic social scientists in colleges of agriculture and land-grant universities have not successfully institutionalized their working relationship with executive agencies such as USAID, the U.S. Department of the Interior, or the Environmental Protection Agency, or with the units and agencies of the U.S. Congress. FAPRI at the University of Missouri and Iowa State University is a very interesting step in the institutionalization of the relationships between two universities and Congress. Similar developments have taken place in state governments and, again, rural and basic social scientists appear to have been slow in developing needed working relationships.

EXPERIENCES OF SSAAP'S EDITORIAL GROUP IN MEETING WITH VARIOUS ADMINISTRATIVE AND FUNDING AGENCIES

At the Houston SSAAP conference, SSAAP's Executive Committee decided, on the advice of its advisory board, that the third phase of SSAAP should not, as originally planned, involve a single, large overall conference to report SSAAP agendas to interested persons, groups, and agencies. Instead, it was decided that SSAAP should arrange to participate in the meetings of various agencies concerned with the administration and funding of efforts to assist farmers and rural society. Consequently, SSAAP meetings were held with the U.S. Agency for International Development (USAID), the Experiment Station Committee on Organization and Policy (ESCOP), the Extension Committee on Organization and Policy (ECOP), the Resident Instruction Committee on Organization and Policy (RICOP), and the International Committee on Organization and Policy (ICOP), and the Joint Council of Food and Agricultural Sciences.

Members of SSAAP's editorial group attended these and other meetings. In doing so, they gained considerable experience and important insights concerning the attitudes and interests of various administrative groups of the AE. This enabled the editorial group to compare SSAAP's then emerging and evolving agendas with various administrative priority, agenda, and initiative statements. These experiences indicated that SSAAP's agendas match the initiatives and priorities of the ECOP better than those of the ESCOP. Apparently, extension service personnel, located in rural communities and in touch with farm people, are more aware of the critical issues and problems now faced in rural America than experiment station personnel. However, SSAAP's editorial group also notes that the extension service has a relatively "poor press" among both academicians and its clientele groups. Perhaps this also appears true to extension's clientele groups because of extension's preoccupations with "process" and the administrative structures of the extension service as contrasted to the "content" and relevance of its program. The mismatch between the problems and issues of rural societies and our food and fiber system, on one hand, and the initiatives of ESCOP, on the other, involves: (1) the neglect of work on human development, (2) disadvantaged farm and nonfarm rural people, (3) agricultural policies and programs, and rural institutional infrastructure, (4) and natural resources, including the environment and the safety of the food chain. All of these are stressed in this book. Experiment stations seem "out of touch" with the problems and issues of agriculture and rural societies and consumers; perhaps this is a result of a tendency to concentrate on basic disciplinary research in the biological, physical, and social sciences, while avoiding the normative and ethical dimensions of the current problems and issues. The Resident Instruction Committee on Organization and Policy (RICOP) seems to reflect the concerns of the AE and is, thus, something of a blend of experiment station and extension service interests.

The SSAAP editorial group met with the International Committee on Organization and Policy (ICOP). The editorial group had a one-day meeting with USAID administrators and others concerned with agricultural and rural development abroad, as well as a two-day meeting with USAID administrators. At both meetings with USAID, substantial preoccupation of the administrators with needed technical advances was apparent, to the relative neglect of needed improvements in policies and institutions, human beings, natural and manmade resource bases, the environment, income distribution, and food-chain safety.

Humanists, social scientists, religious leaders, and others criticize the values pursued and/or ignored by the AE. Such criticisms were made at conferences sponsored by the University of Delaware (July 14–17, 1981), Texas A&M University (March 11–12, 1981), and the University of Florida (March 8–9 and October 18–21, 1982). Rachel Carson (1962), a biologist, also criticized the AE on humanistic grounds nearly thirty years ago. Two scholarly journals now exist: *Agriculture and Human Values* and *The Journal of Agricultural Ethics*. These journals have attained considerable objectivity and are relevant for rural farming communities and consumers as well as academicians and their administrators.

Although AE administrators are becoming increasingly aware of the importance of policy, community, institutional, and human development, and environmental pollution and food-chain contamination problems and issues, they have been slow in translating this awareness into financing and administrative structures to support work on the social science aspects of these problems and issues. It can also be concluded that there has been some increase in the awareness of the importance of ethical issues for the AE vis-a-vis not only the subjects just mentioned, but also biogenetic and nonbiogenetic efforts to improve inputs, techniques, and methods used by production agriculture. Insofar as social science work in universities is concerned, individual social scientists and their departments need to render administrative assistance to research, resident instruction, and extension administrators of the AE who have biological and physical science backgrounds that tend to leave them less than fully equipped to mobilize resources for, understand, or administer the social science aspects of work on the problems and issues now faced by farmers, agribusinesses, consumers, and rural people and societies.

SUBSEQUENT CHAPTERS OF THIS PART

Chapter 2 of Part V by Charles L. Mulford, Gerald E. Klonglan, and Ge Xiao Jia reviews and discusses needed research on the administration and funding of the RSSs and BSSDs insofar as their work is relevant for farming, agribusinesses, rural people and societies, and consumers. Part V also contains a chapter (Chapter 3) by Larry J. Connor entitled "Social Science Knowledge and Tools to Address Problems and Issues: From the Perspective of Both the Rural and Basic Social Sciences." Also included is a chapter (Chapter 4) by Harry O. Kunkel, former dean of agriculture at Texas A&M University, entitled "From the Perspective of Research Administration." Richard G. Stuby, sociologist in the Cooperative State Research Service of the USDA, has written Chapter 5 entitled "Funding Social Science Research: The Problem of Priorities." In Chapter 6, R. J. Hildreth looks at some of the political aspects of research funding and 75 years of cooperative extension administrative experiences. Richard Just and Gordon Rausser, in Chapter 7, present an informative abstract of their presentation at the 1989 meeting of the American Agricultural Economics Association; they dealt with the decreasing relevance of an increasingly disciplinary agricultural economics profession. In addition, there are a number of other chapters in this volume that are relevant for developing appropriate administrative and funding strategies for the rural social sciences. These are listed in the cross references at the end of this chapter.

Chapter 8 presents an abridged version of the administrative and funding strategies and research agendas developed at Houston under the chairmanship of Larry J. Connor. In addition, Chapter 8 extends the Houston reports to include new strategies growing out of the experiences of the SSAAP editorial group since the Houston meeting. Both the Houston and post-Houston agendas include research on the administration and funding of RSSs and BSSDs relevant for agricultural including agribusiness, rural societies, and consumers.

Part V ends with Chapter 9 which summarizes the entire book and challenges both social scientists and their administrators. Chapter 9 is virtually identical to SSAAP's separately published "Executive Summary." Their brief summary nature makes it desirable for readers to consult the portions of this book that are liberally referenced in them.

CROSS REFERENCES IN THIS BOOK

PART I: INTRODUCTION

Ch. 3 Social Science Institutions, Knowledge, and Tools to Address Problems and Issues, Frederick H. Buttel
Ch. 4 Agricultural Institutions Under Fire, Lester C. Thurow
Ch. 7 From the Perspective of Users and Affected Persons, Richard J. Sauer
Ch. 8 Abridged Work Group Reports from SSAAP's Phase I Spring Hill Conference, June 9–11, 1988.

PART II: DOMESTIC AND INTERNATIONAL FARM AND RURAL DEVELOPMENT

Sec. 1 Ch. 2 Identification and Prioritization of Researchable Questions in Agricultural Economics: Where are the Potential Payoffs?, Clarence F. Davan, Jr.
Ch. 7 Farm (Including Home), Agribusiness, and Consumers: Agendas and Conclusions
Sec. 2 Ch. 10 The Relevance of SSAAP's Agendas for Resident Instruction: A RICOP Response, Joseph E. Kunsman

PART III: THE FOUR DRIVING FORCES

Sec. 1 Ch. 7 Institution Improvements: Agendas and Conclusions
Sec. 2 Ch. 2 Human Capital for Future Economic Growth, Wallace E. Huffman
Ch. 10 Human Development: Agendas and Conclusions
Sec. 3 Ch. 7 Resource Enhancement and Growth in Capital Bases: Agendas and Conclusions
Sec. 4 Ch. 2 Technical Advance: Agendas and Conclusions

PART IV: THREE CROSS CUTTING CONCERNS

Sec. 1 Ch. 3 Social Science Agendas for Database and Information Systems
Sec. 2 Ch. 5 The Basic Social Science Disciplines (BSSDs): Agendas and Conclusions
Sec. 3 Ch. 1 Introduction—Ethics, Private Decision Making, and Public Choices
Ch. 3 Ethics, Private Decisions, and Public Choices: Agendas and Conclusions

REFERENCES

Another blast at agriculture's R&D policies and peer review. *Science and Government Report* 17, no. 13: 1–2.

Atkinson, R.C. 1980. Introduction. In *How basic research reaps unexpected rewards*. 3d ed. Washington, D.C.: National Science Foundation.

Benedict, Murray R., and Oscar C. Stine. 1956. *The agricultural commodity programs: Two decades of experience*. New York: The Twentieth Century Fund.

Bloch, Erich. 1990. Education and human resources at the National Science Foundation. *Science* 249 (24 August): 839–51.

Bush, Vannever. [1945] 1960. Science: The endless frontier. Reprint. Washington, D.C.: National Science Foundation.

Carson, Rachel. 1962. *Silent Spring*. Boston: Houghton-Mifflin.

Connor, Larry J. 1989. Land-grant ag. programs: They need revitalization. *Choices* (1st Quarter): 12–16.

Dobbs, Thomas L. 1987. Toward more effective involvement of agricultural economists in multidisciplinary research and extension programs. *Western Journal of Agricultural Economics* 12, no. 1: 8–16.

Experiment Station Committee on Organization and Policy. 1989. *Social science serving rural America*. Madison: University of Wisconsin, College of Agriculture and Life Sciences.

Galbraith, J. K., and John D. Black. 1938. Maintenance of agricultural production during depressions: The explanations review. *Journal of Political Economy* 46:305–23.

Handler, Phillips. 1976. The American university today. *The American Scientist* 64:254–57.

Hardin, Charles. 1955. *Freedom in agricultural education*. Chicago: The University of Chicago Press. (Chaps. 13, 14, & 15 on the Bureau of Agricultural Economics.)

Holt, Donald. 1989. Recapturing the vision: The case for formula funds. Paper read at 1989 annual meeting of the Agricultural Research Institute, Washington, D.C.

Johnson, Glenn L. 1971. The quest for relevance in agricultural economics. Invited lecturer. *American Journal of Agricultural* 53, no. 5: 728–39.

_____1976. Who is a peer? *American Scientist* 64:124.

_____1984. *Academia needs a new covenant for serving agriculture*. Special publication (July). Mississippi State: Mississippi Agriculture and Forestry Experiment Station.

_____1986. *Research methodology for economists*. New York: Macmillan.

Johnson, Glenn L., and Sylvan Wittwer. 1984. Agricultural technology until 2030: Prospects, priorities and policies. Special report no. 12. East Lansing: Michigan Agricultural Experiment Station.

Just, Richard, and Gordon Rausser. 1989. An assessment of the agricultural economics profession. *American Journal of Agricultural Economics* 71, no. 5: 1177–90.

McCloskey, D. N. 1983. The rhetoric of economics. *Journal of Economic Literature* 21:481–517.

———1990. Agon and ag. ec.: Styles of persuasion in agricultural economics. *American Journal of Agricultural Economics* 72, no.5.

National Academy of Sciences. 1989. *On being a scientist.* Washington, D.C.: National Academy Press.

Norman, Colin. 1990. NSF peer review: Under pressure. *Science* 249:1239.

Palca, Joseph, and Eliot Marshal. 1990. Bloch leaves NSF in midstream. *Science* 249 (24 August): 848–51.

Pound, Glen. 1972. Report of the Committee on Research Advisory to the U.S. Department of Agriculture. Washington, D.C.: National Academy of Sciences.

Press, Frank. 1982. Rethinking science policy. *Science* 218:28–30.

Schuh, G. Edward. 1986. Revitalizing land-grant universities: It's time to regain relevance. *Choices* (2d Quarter).

Schultz, T. W. 1945. Agriculture in an unstable economy. New York: McGraw Hill.

Sun, Marjorie. 1989. Peer review comes under peer review. *Science* 244:910–12.

Wolfle, Dael. 1971. The supernatural department. *Science* 173 (9 July).

CHAPTER 2

A SYSTEMS APPROACH FOR UNDERSTANDING RESEARCH ON THE ORGANIZATION AND ADMINISTRATION OF THE AGRICULTURAL SCIENTIFIC ENTERPRISE

Charles L. Mulford, Gerald E. Klonglan, and Ge Xiao Jia[1]

INTRODUCTION

Political leaders, constituents, and administrators need a framework for understanding and making decisions about agricultural-research-enterprise units, including teaching and extension-service activities. These people need to know how to communicate priorities to researchers and other professionals, so they will understand how research and other work should be structured, and know the criteria for evaluating the effectiveness of individual professionals and work units.

We propose, first, that social science can play a key role in understanding the organization and administration of the agricultural scientific enterprise, including agricultural research, teaching, and extension. Second, we propose that a systems approach is appropriate for these analyses. Every system requires input from its environment, conducts work ("throughput" processes), and has output (products, goods, or services) which is evaluated by clients and consumers. Feedback from clients and consumers is used to redesign or develop new projects. Large and complex research units can be analyzed as systems with subsystems. The operations and output of diverse subsystems, such as agricultural production and social science departments, can be compared if a systems approach is utilized. In the subsection that follows, the elements of a system will be described, and examples provided, showing the relevance of this approach for understanding research and other work units.

All systems (except closed and independent ones) require *input* from their environment for survival (see Figure 1). Input consists of information and resources. Input includes demands from constituencies, e.g., their priorities for agricultural research, information about the changing needs of constituencies, changes in the structure of agriculture, and changes in research priorities and funding levels from the government. Resources include funds needed for research, personnel, facilities, and equipment.

It has been noted that the agricultural-research agenda (and we think the teaching and extension agendas, too) is guided by an increasingly complex and dynamic array of influences (the "Government-University-Industry Research Roundtable," 1989). Those in favor of the decentralization of decisions argue that constituencies that are closest to research units, those that are closest to extension personnel, or those that will use the research results, should have more input. On the other hand, those who think that international or national leaders have a broader perspective argue that their priorities should receive the most attention.

With changing and dynamic environments, obtaining adequate information is problematic and administrators may have to make special efforts so that appropriate environmental scanning takes place. Administrators use input, including information, for strategic and operational (short-range) planning. Planning is an important *throughput* activity because it is the most effective tool for reducing environmental uncertainty.

Strategic planning begins with an analysis of the threats and opportunities in the external environment and an assessment by a unit of its strengths and weaknesses. Then, a mission statement is prepared. This statement specifies the research, teaching, or extension unit goals and objectives. At the corporate level in business and at the top administrative levels in large and complex research, teaching, or extension units, appropriate portfolio balance is the key concern in strategic planning. There is a need to identify new promising ventures, assess the needs of stable programs, and identify "dogs" that are sold or closed. Research-unit administrators at the highest level share comparable concerns and must decide which research programs to encourage and which to terminate. Strategic planning at the business-unit level, or lower levels of large and complex research units, is most concerned with the development of effective competitive strategies. Operational (short-range) planning is typically done within a timeframe of only a few months or a year, but with strategic planning, the timeframe may be five years or more.

Debate continues in the planning literature over whether it is best for an organization to have a single competitive strategy or multiple strategies. Some planning experts (Miles and Snow 1978; Porter 1980) state that each strategy is a different approach to gaining a competitive advantage, and firms that try to develop multiple strategies will not, except in rare instances, achieve their goals. This is because utilizing multiple strategies may require inconsistent actions. However, Mulford and colleagues (1990) have found that small and medium businesses do employ multiple strategies and these businesses perform as well, or better than, those that do not. Recent literature on corporate planning, too, suggests that multiple strategies may be appropriate in some environments (Murray 1988; Hill 1988).

Administrators are responsible for structuring the work of scientists, teachers, and extension personnel, coordinating work units, and evaluating individual professionals and work units. Work structuring involves deciding how much professionals should contribute to decisions that are made and the degree to which the professionals must consult their supervisors when choosing research projects, doing research, developing courses, and planning extension projects. Coordination by administrators is needed so that institutional resources, such as laboratories, computers, and clerical staff, are used efficiently and available when needed for the various projects. Evaluation of individual professionals and research units is another administrative responsibility. For this evaluation, administrators may find it helpful to include the perceptions of consumers and consumer advocates.

Of all administrative responsibilities, the appropriate structuring of work for professionals may be most vexing. Scientists and other professionals are highly trained and desire work autonomy and a share in decision making. If they do not have autonomy and share in decision making, they are likely to become alienated. Alienated professionals are disappointed in their careers and professional development, as well as their inability to fulfill professional norms, e.g., be autonomous professionals (Aiken and Hage 1966). Management experts think that alienation may have a negative effect on scientific productivity.

Unfortunately, there have been almost no empirical studies of alienation and scientific productivity (or of teachers or extension professionals). The first studies of alienation and scientific productivity focused upon the importance of personal causal variables and not organizational ones. Typically, personal variables have been minimally correlated with scientific productivity (Gaston 1978). Andrews (1979) reported a positive correlation between age and productivity, but he reasoned that age was a proxy measure for rank, e.g., with rank comes more access

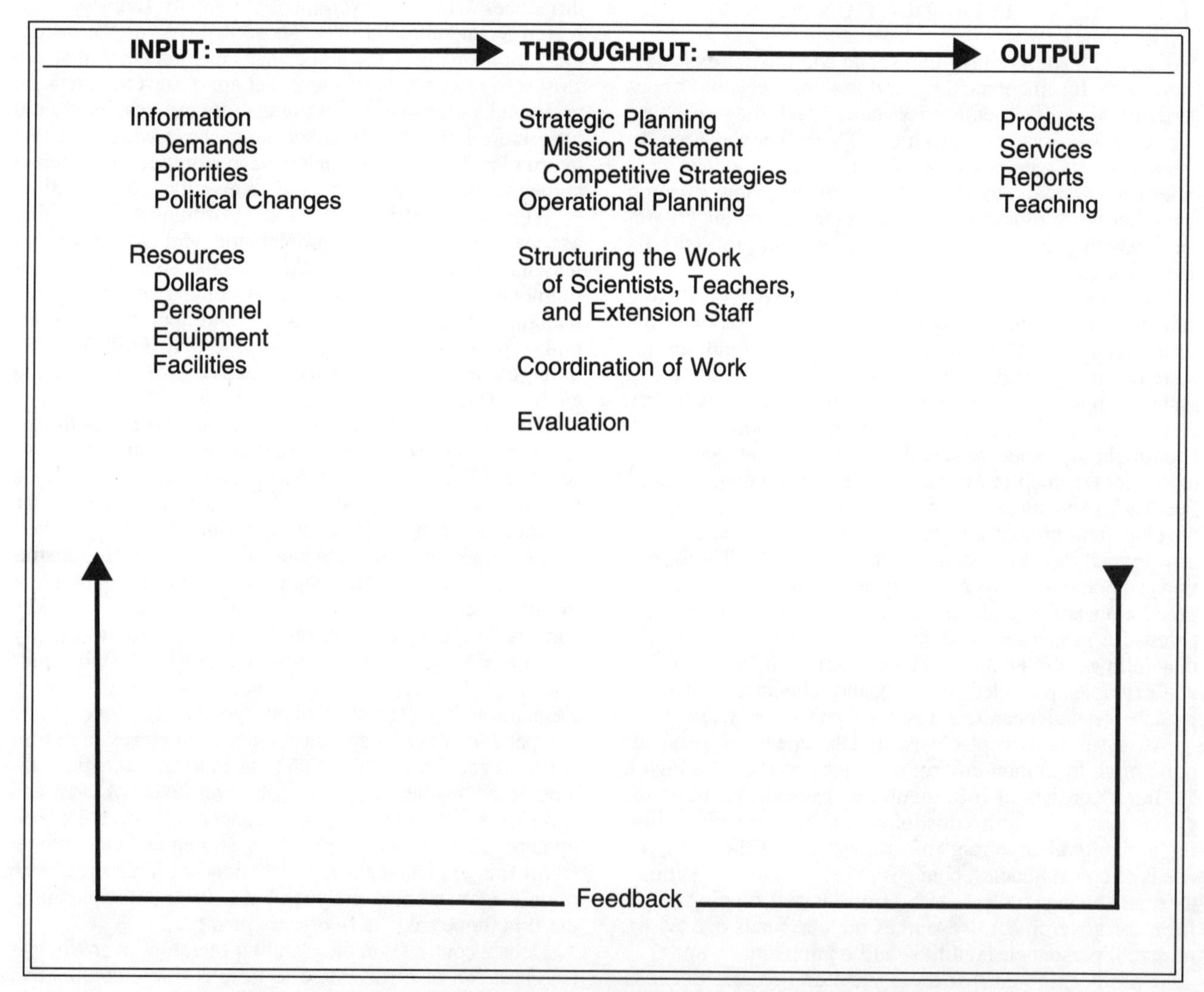

Figure 1. Research, Teaching, and Extension Units as Social Systems.

to resources needed for research and more research productivity follows. Busch and Lacy (1983) and Pelz (1976) and Andrews (1979) found that full-time researchers are not as productive as those who spend only three-quarters of their time on research.

More recently, researchers have shifted their attention to the role that organizational variables play in causing alienation and lowered scientific productivity. Mulford, Waldner-Haugrud, and Gajbhiye (1990) report that the more that agricultural scientists in international research centers feel they lack work autonomy and must take their supervisors' view into consideration, the more alienated they are. Although alienation was negatively correlated with scientific productivity as predicted, the correlation was modest. Other variables, in addition to work alienation, affect scientific productivity; nonetheless, the results suggest that administrators who supervise professionals should provide as much work autonomy as possible and not impose more work hierarchy than needed.

All systems must be concerned that the *products and output* meet the needs of consumers. Systems with multiple constituencies must show concern for a variety of products and services. Effectiveness refers to the number of products that are produced, e.g., number of articles written, number of students taught, and number of clients served by the extension service. The effectiveness of individual professionals and work units should be monitored by administrators. Quality counts, too, because quantity is not the only consideration. Relative efficiency refers to the cost of producing units of output. Quality for a particular professional or work unit may be high, but efficiency may still be an issue because of relative costs.

With multiple constituencies, evaluation of products and output become complex. Criteria of effectiveness will vary from one constituency to another. After their analysis of multiple constituencies, Quinn and Rohrbaugh (1981, 138) concluded that effectiveness should be viewed as "a value-based judgment about the performance of an organization." This means that it is very important for administrators to know which constituencies have a stake in their organizations (including internal constituencies) and what their criteria of effectiveness are. The bottom-line question for administrators is: How can they manage the multiple and conflicting demands of various constituencies? It is regrettable that these issues have received little attention from researchers.

In summary, we think that social scientists can contribute to an understanding of the agricultural scientific enterprise, including research, teaching, and extension activities. We have shown how a social-systems model can aid in this analysis. Three objectives remain for this chapter: First, an indepth analysis will be made of policy issues and research priorities for the 1990s. This discussion will begin with a consideration of the diverse demands and the multiple constituencies that agricultural administrators must take into account, and research priorities will be specified. Second, there will be a discussion of issues associated with the structuring of work for professionals and the design of work units, and research priorities will be specified. Third, issues associated with evaluating the effectiveness of individual professionals and work units will be discussed, and research priorities will be specified.

POLICY ISSUES AND RESEARCH PRIORITIES FOR THE 1990s

It is doubtful if any agricultural administrator can escape being confronted by multiple constituencies and constituencies with changing (and sometimes increasing) demands. However, this is not all bad. Multiple constituencies also mean that administrators can draw support from more points, too. Let us turn to a consideration of constituencies and their demands.

DIVERSIFIED DEMANDS AND MULTIPLE CONSTITUENCIES: THE INPUT SIDE

The public agricultural research system is a successful example of integrated research, education, and extension in a partnership sponsored by the federal and state governments. This system has generated tremendous growth in the agriculture of the United States, but is facing its greatest challenge today. Shrinking sources of public funding and personnel cuts (Brown 1989), social and environmental concerns, new technology development, agricultural recession, rural community disruption, extrusion of smaller farmers from agriculture, and dysfunction resulting from imbalance between basic and "mission-oriented" research and between natural and social sciences constitute a highly uncertain environment within which the agricultural research system now operates (Hadwiger and Browne 1987). Meanwhile, however, the uncertainty and adversity of the changing environment pose a mixture of constraints and opportunities of which administrators should be aware. In this section, we propose that social scientists play a major role in studying the issues and answering the questions regarding the changing environment for agricultural research.

Although the lack of consensus on the nature of the American agricultural research system is not a new phenomenon (Marcus 1986), the demands of the constituencies of the agricultural research enterprises have become increasingly diversified during recent years (Browne 1987). Criticism from the general public, since the publication of the landmark books, *Silent Spring* by Rachel Carson (1962) and *Hard Tomatoes, Hard Times* by Jim Hightower (1973), has been increasingly directed toward issues such as environmental concerns (i.e., changing global climates, water quality, chemical use), negative social consequences unanticipated by agricultural scientists (i.e., family and community well-being, farm-worker protection). Consumer groups also display dissatisfaction with the health consequences, such as food quality and safety, and animal welfare (Friedland and Kappel 1979; Nipp 1988).

Criticism from the scientific community, spearheaded by the "Pound Report" of the National Research Council (1972) and the "Winrock Report" of the Rockefeller Foundation and OSTP (1982), has pointed to the inability of the "island empire" (Mayer and Mayer 1975) to adapt to the future and its neglect of balanced development between basic and "mission-oriented" research activities (Bonnen 1986; National Research Council 1989; Ford 1985; Klonglan 1987). On the other hand, there has been an increasingly heard voice from social science disciplines addressing the long-neglected balance between natural and social sciences (Bonnen 1986; Ruttan 1982).

The nation's changing demographic and economic structures lead the center-of-gravity move increasingly away from agrarian issues to industrial and post-industrial issues. Consequently, the loss of representation and strategic position made the agricultural research system vulnerable in the budget-allocation process (Browne 1987). Thus, public funding, a most important input to the public agricultural system, is experiencing a crisis never before encountered by agricultural scientists (Holt 1989). Federal funding for state agricultural research systems, in real terms, has been stagnant over the past 25 years. The funding levels for some research units are even inadequate for simple system maintenance.

The erosion in financial support for research is coupled with the student-enrollment decline that is being experienced by almost all agriculture-related disciplines. The NASULGC (National Association of State Universities and Land Grant Colleges) data, indicating a major decline in enrollment, has been noted by Manderscheid (1988) and Klonglan (1987). Both addressed the issue at national professional-association meetings. As Manderscheid pointed out, the change in the demographic characteristics of student constituencies (age, family status, ethnic composition, etc.) will present new demands on, and changing interests in, the curriculum mix of our agricultural universities. The career-mobility pattern forces agriculture-related disciplines to reconsider what will be offered to students. An increasing connection with the world market has raised the issue of a more international-related curriculum design. And finally, the rising demands for holistic orientation in agricultural curriculum directs us to pay more attention to the balanced design of production-oriented and impact-assessment-oriented sciences.

The Cooperative Extension Service has been one of the entities more adversely affected by the change. Established by the Smith-Lever Act in 1914, extension programs are currently conducted in 3,150 counties by more than 17,000 professionals who disseminate research results to the general public (Rasmussen 1989). However, changes in the technological complexity of agricultural production practice, increased educational level of the producers, development of communication techniques, reduction in the cost of transmitting information, increased involvement of the private sector in research and delivery systems, and more basic orientation in public research are threatening the very existence of this program (Feller 1986, 1987; Campbell 1989; Holt 1989).

Finally, the expected breakthrough of biotechnology compounds the number of questions agricultural research administrators will have to answer as to social ethics, property rights, and the private sector's involvement (Buttel et al. 1986; Kenney 1986; Kloppenburg 1988). The development of biotechnology will have significant implications for the agricultural academic administration: the effectiveness of booming biotechnology centers on a great numbers of campuses; the possible changes in the traditional partnerships between federal government, state government, and universities with the greater intrusion of the private sector into the public agricultural research arena; and the emerging pattern of sponsorship by federal and state governments and the private sector.

The criticisms from environmentalists, consumer groups, and the scientific community were reflected in the "new definition" of research priority setting (Lipman-Blumen 1987). Congress and executive budget branches, such as the Office of Science and Technology Policy (OSTP) and the Office of Management and Budget (OMB), now require that agricultural research be linked to long-term planning and national goals, and the quality of research be improved by the encouragement of more stringent review processes and competition.

IMPORTANT ISSUES ON THE INPUT SIDE OF THE SYSTEM

The challenges and opportunities faced by the agricultural academic funding structure pose a series of questions for the social sciences about the organizational and administrative issues regarding the input side of the system. Whether the existing agricultural administrative structure for agricultural research is obsolete remains an issue of debate. If it is obsolete, how will the agricultural research enterprise be restructured? If it is not obsolete, what implications will the restructuring have for research management and administration? What administrative and funding structures are more responsive to the increasingly diverse demands from multiple constituencies? What resource-allocation structure will better adapt to future developments?

Ruttan (1982) observed that the development of agricultural research in different countries led to four basic models: (1) the integrated research, extension, and educational model, exemplified by the U.S. land-grant system; (2) the autonomous or semiautonomous publicly or privately supported system, originally developed in the United Kingdom, that is export-oriented and supports large-scale agricultural production; (3) the ministry-of-agriculture model, most easily found in smaller countries, whose major concern is with domestic food production; and (4) the Agricultural Research Council whose major emphasis is on coordinating activities of a system in which two or more of the above models coexist. But, since Ruttan's study, little research has been done by social scientists to assess the relative strengths and weaknesses of the alternative models.

Recently, there has been an increasing voice from the scientific community to restructure the resource-allocation system (National Research Council 1989) and it argues that the competitive grant is more congruent with allocative efficiency in scientific research than formula or institution funding. The land-grant establishment has responded by arguing that research conducted under formula funding has made major contributions to the nation's development. Related to the "funding debate" is a dispute on centralization versus decentralization, and a debate of relative emphasis on basic or "mission-oriented" research. Agricultural academe has been known for its self-contained nature (Mayer and Mayer 1975). This isolation has prevented agricultural researchers from being closely aligned with their disciplinary development. This orientation is largely due to the location-specific nature of agricultural problems and the resultant problem-solving orientation of agricultural research. How to ease the tension between national goals and local divergent demands, and how to reconcile the conflict between disciplinary development and applied problem solving will be major issues facing academic administrators.

A long-time overemphasis on productivity by policy makers led to a lopsided development of biological and physical agricultural sciences, on the one hand, versus rural social sciences, on the other. Johnson (1984) has criticized various "chauvinisms" found in agricultural academia which hindered both healthy intellectual development and practical problem solving. For a long time, rural social sciences were underrepresented in agricultural research, extension, and education. However, the causes and remedies are rarely explored and studied. The unintended "externalities" caused by short-sighted focus on production science to the neglect of impact-assessment sciences, have led to major complaints from the general public. A more balanced approach is needed in future agricultural research priority setting.

Previously, scientific decision has been believed to be the domain of agricultural researchers. However, there have been increasing signs that the political process has been encroaching on the agricultural scientist's territory, which escalates the tension between scientific enterprises and the political process (Lipman-Blumen 1987). Naturally, questions will be raised as to whether comprehensive and rigorous planning and budgeting practices, particularly priority setting, can be applied in the decentralized, autonomous, loosely coupled system.

As Hess (1989, 1113) stated, "Science policy and priorities are not formulated in any pure and solitary test tube. They spring from the messy and often disorderly real world of conflicting demands and unclear choices." The appropriations bill passed by Congress is an outcome of a very intense and complicated process. Despite its importance, very limited studies (Lipman-Blumen and Schram 1984; Lipman-Blumen 1987) have been done to understand the agricultural research input process: research priority setting, planning, and funding allocation at national, state, university, and research-unit levels. Little effort (Britan 1987) has been devoted to understanding the roles played in research priority setting and funding-allocation process by the various agencies, including the USDA (U.S. Department of Agriculture) budgeting agencies, such as the Cooperative State Research Service (CSRS), the Agricultural Research Service (ARS), and the Experiment Station Committee on Organization and Policy (ESCOP); the federal budgeting agencies, such as the Office of Management and Budget (OMB) and the Office of Science and Technology Policy (OSTP); the advisory groups representing both the producers and users of agriculture, such as the Joint Council, the Users Advisory Board (UAB), and the National Association of State Universities and Land Grant Colleges (NASULGC); and the professional scientific associations and scholarly bodies, such as the National Research Council (NRC) and the National Academy of Sciences (NAS).

The institutional responses to the changing conditions will be of great importance to academic administrators. In facing continued student-enrollment declines, strategies, such as modifying curriculum design to include holistic and international approaches and how to adapt academic programs to the demands of future constituencies, were proposed by both economists (Manderscheid 1988) and sociologists (Klonglan 1987). Institutional responses were also proposed to modify reward systems, such as faculty promotion and tenure structure, as well as certification programs (Klonglan 1987). Proactive strategies such as extending agricultural programs to general liberal-arts and social-sciences programs in colleges and universities were also suggested. How do these responses to environmental changes work? Are they effective in deferring or reversing the trend of enrollment decline?

In solving problems facing cooperative extension services, alternative positions can be found in the literature: The first position is to increase productivity through new communication and information technology and associated scale economies to improve efficiency (Brown 1981; Hildreth and Armbruster 1981). The second position can be termed as "support-mobilization strategy" which advocates eliciting support through modified program design and demonstrations to win over the clientele (McDowell 1985; Isreal 1988). The third institutional response emphasizes the organizational linkage between research and extension (Feller 1984, 1987). The fourth position suggests that the key lies in finding new niches for extension and changing the existing program (Holt 1989; Wade 1988).

Some case studies of the successes and failures of change have been conducted. For example, Wade's (1988) study of the University of Missouri at Columbia's "Alternatives for the '80s" demonstrates the opportunities, and difficulties involved in, making change and innovation. Sauer and Pray (1987) studied another institutional response: mobilizing support used by the Minnesota Agricultural Experiment Station. Some microlevel strategies have also been cited: greater use of joint appointments, placement of extension specialists in academic departments, modification of reward (tenure and promotion) systems for faculty, and establishment of regional research centers to strengthen the research/extension linkage (Feller 1987). Since changes have been taking place in almost every extension program, extensive and systematic studies are needed to inform both the public and administrators.

RESEARCH NEEDED ON THE INPUT SIDE OF THE SYSTEM

There are many questions regarding agricultural research administration that need to be answered by social scientists. The following are examples of questions that need to be answered and research that should be emphasized:

1. What administrative structure is appropriate to govern the national agricultural research enterprise?
2. What administrative and funding structures are more responsive to the increasingly diverse demands from multiple constituencies?
3. What resource-allocation structure will better adapt to future development?
4. What are the advantages and disadvantages of the alternative models described by Ruttan (1982) from a comparative perspective? Are there things we can learn from each of these models?
5. Is the existing level of input for agricultural research (money, personnel, etc.) adequate to meet future challenge? If not, what impact will the inadequate funding have on American agriculture in the long run?
6. What is the existing structure of the distribution of expenditures among the various fields of scientific inquiry and along the basic-applied continuum? Are there too many resources allocated to some kinds of research and too few to others?
7. How will the cost of agricultural research be distributed among federal, state, local, and private sectors? How will the long-admired cooperation among federal, state, and local entities evolve in funding public agricultural research?
8. Given the current involvement of the private sector in public agricultural research, what will constitute a

healthy relationship between the publicly funded research units and the private sector, without threatening public interests?

9. How will the three sources of funding—special, competitive, and formula grant—be balanced?
10. What will constitute a creative balance between biological and physical sciences on the one hand, and rural social sciences on the other? What administrative and funding measures are needed to revitalize the rural social sciences?
11. As interest groups that have their stakes in the outcome of the research priority-setting process, how will the above-mentioned agencies interact with one another in this political process? What impact will the interplay have on the outcome of research priority and funding allocation?
12. Which funding structure is more congenial to agricultural research and provides more incentive to researchers? Which is more appropriate as a scientist-rewarding system?
13. Will the existing linkage between research, extension, and education remain feasible in generating and disseminating agricultural knowledge in the future?
14. How can multidisciplinary research be developed and coordinated? What input does multidisciplinary research need? How can the funding structure be improved to better accommodate multidisciplinary research?
15. How can the conflicts between comprehensive planning and structured decentralization, and between rigorous priority setting and scientific autonomy be reconciled? What will constitute an optimum mix of scientific autonomy and social responsibility in those publicly funded research systems?
16. What are used by administrators as strategic responses to the student-enrollment decline? How can qualified students be attracted to the agricultural sciences? How can the academic curriculum be developed for the interests of students? How can academic programs be adapted to the demands of future constituencies?
17. Which strategy is best for extension administrators to respond to the dramatic changes among the four positions mentioned previously? What are the strengths and weaknesses of the four responses advocated for extension services?

STRUCTURING THE WORK OF PROFESSIONALS IN RESEARCH, TEACHING, AND EXTENSION: THROUGHPUT PROCESS

We have observed that professionals desire work autonomy, and experience alienation when this is lacking. Although the correlation is not high, and only a few studies have been done, research suggests that there is a significant relationship between alienation and productivity (Mulford, Waldner-Haugrud, and Gajbhiye 1990). This is enough reason for administrators to be prudent when structuring the work of professionals.

Very little systematic research has been done to determine the characteristics of effective work units in research, teaching, or extension. However, work that has been done in business firms clearly indicates that an administrator is not wasting time when considering this issue. Evidence suggests that the nature of an organization's environment and its members should be considered when deciding upon an appropriate organizational structure.

If the environment is simple and static, with few changes in competitors and constituencies and their demands, a traditional, functional structure is appropriate. With a functional structure, activities are grouped together by common function from the bottom to the top of the organization. For example, with a simple and static environment, a university should use a traditional departmental structure, e.g., there would be an economics department and all economists would work in this department. This form of structure is weak when the environment becomes complex and dynamic.

Firms with more than one product line may emphasize a product structure with divisions that operate almost as self-contained units. A university that places all research under one official, all teaching under another, and all extension service under another is using a product structure.

When the environment is complex and dynamic, and coordination is required to develop the best products and services, a matrix structure is appropriate. The matrix utilizes traditional functional managers and product managers. For example, a university might decide to create an official position responsible for coordinating all agricultural production research across all departments. Persons in departments would still have department chairs to whom they are responsible, but they would also be responsible to the coordinator.

Universities have responded to environmental changes and adopted alternative organizational models to increase their effectiveness in the laboratory, in the classroom, and when working with their extension clients. The University of Missouri at Columbia, for example, restructured its program under the name "Alternative for the 80s" in response to the environmental change (Wade 1988).

Evidence of structural deficiency is relatively easy to detect. When decision making is delayed or lacking in quality, a deficiency exists. This is also true when the organization does not respond quickly and innovatively to changes in demands and opportunities from the environment. In addition, too much rancorous conflict is evidence that the organization may have a poor organizational structure (Daft 1989).

RESEARCH NEEDED ON THROUGHPUT

Since little systematic research has been directed at better understanding appropriate work structures for agricultural professionals in the scientific enterprise, this should be a high priority. Here are examples of important research questions that could be considered:

1. What causes work alienation for younger and more experienced researchers, and what impact does the alienation have on scientific productivity?
2. What are the major causes of work alienation for teachers and extension personnel? What is the impact of alienation on their work?
3. Are researchers more effective when they work alone or on teams? Does this depend upon the age and experience of the researchers?
4. How effective are nontraditional organizational structures compared to functional or product structures?
5. What training needs exist for administrators in the agricultural scientific enterprise?
6. How can universities and other organizations best scan their changing environments?

7. Should universities adopt a single-best competitive strategy or should they use multiple strategies?
8. What are the costs and benefits of having multiple constituencies?
9. How can administrators best respond to constituencies having conflicting expectations?

ASSESSING ORGANIZATIONAL EFFECTIVENESS: THE OUTPUT SIDE

An agricultural research system is concerned with generating, adapting, and disseminating appropriately interpreted agricultural knowledge to its users. Thus, the assessment of organizational effectiveness constitutes an essential part of the organizational studies of the agricultural research administration. Although agricultural research has been commonly recognized as one of the major sources of economic growth in the United States (Evenson, Waggoner, and Ruttan 1979; Ruttan 1982), there has been little agreement on how to assess the contribution of the research system to the agricultural development and public well-being.

The reason for the slow development of effectiveness assessments of agricultural research is related to the general difficulties associated with conceptualizing and measuring organizational effectiveness. Organizational effectiveness is one of the most complex and controversial areas of inquiry in organizational studies. It is complex because of multiple and competing bases for generating effectiveness criteria. For example, Campbell (1977) listed 30 different criteria for assessing effectiveness and Steers (1977), in his review of literature, listed 17 studies in which multiple criteria were derived but with little in common.

Effectiveness assessment is controversial because, at first glance, the various models of effectiveness are favored by different constituents and seem to share little common ground. For example, the goal model defines effectiveness in terms of the formal goals that have been accomplished and in terms of efficiency. The human-relations model defines effectiveness in terms of the job satisfaction of members. Hall (1987, 293) has observed that the alternative models are not just different; they emphasize ends that are sometimes contradictory. Hall has concluded that: "...no organization is effective. Instead, organizations can be viewed as effective (or ineffective) to some degree in terms of specific constraints, goals, and constituent." Fortunately, the competing-values approach to organizational effectiveness was developed by Quinn and Rohrbaugh (1981) and it has brought coherence among the diverse models and indicators of organizational effectiveness. Their combination of organizational dimensions graphically defined four models of effectiveness: human relations, with its focus upon job satisfaction; internal process, with a focus upon the adequacy of planning and coordination; open system, with a focus upon environmental scanning and resource acquisition; and rational goal model, with a focus upon the accomplishment of goals. Quinn and Rohrbaugh have stated that their most important contribution was the realization that organizational effectiveness should be defined as: "a value-based judgment about the performance of an organization." Their competing-values approach delineates the set of criteria upon which effectiveness judgments are often made. It is likely that research funders and consumers of research will favor the goals model and base their judgments of relative effectiveness upon it. However, other constituents may, at the same time, be relating to criteria associated with other models of effectiveness.

The sources for the controversy came first from the different conceptualizations of organization. As Scott (1981) pointed out, the "rational-systems theorists" generally define organization as a system deliberately constructed to pursue specific goal(s). Therefore, a goal model is commonly adopted to evaluate organizational effectiveness. In the literature of agricultural economics, assessment of return on research based on production-function analysis is typical in this respect (Fishel 1971; Evenson and Kisliev 1975; Evenson, Waggoner, and Ruttan 1979; Aragi, Sim, and Gardner 1978). On the other hand, "natural systems theories" assume organization to be social collectives capable of achieving specific goals but simultaneously engaged in other activities to meet organization needs in order to function. Thus, system maintenance is added to the list of effectiveness and system adaptability and assumes an important position. Literature on environmental concerns and "social-impact assessment" studies generally reflected this line of inquiry. Still, the "open-systems theorists" view organizations as highly interdependent with their environment. Whether an organization is effective depends much on its compatibility with its environment. Thus, acquiring information and securing resources become crucial. Yuchtman and Seashore's (1967) "systems resource model" reflects the criteria adopted by this approach.

The diverse conceptualizations of organization often lead to a different importance being attached to the level of analysis. Analysis of organizational effectiveness at the social-psychological level often used individual job satisfaction and alienation as criteria, while analysis at the organizational level stresses the achievement of organizational goals, such as total productivity (publication, student enrollment, number of graduates, etc.). Still others stress the function of the system for the large society as the criteria. The rapidly developed, social-impact-analysis literature generally takes society as its unit of analysis. The study of organizational effectiveness is further compounded by two dimensions: timeframe adopted by the evaluator and multiple constituencies.

Short-term or long-term criteria makes a great difference for evaluating effectiveness in agriculture. Of particular importance to agricultural research is that the outcome of research can only be indirectly measured, and the appropriate time lag must be specified in order to yield meaningful results.

As mentioned above, diverse demands and multiple constituencies compound the issue of criteria even further in studying effectiveness. Various participants and constituents associated with an organization impose different goals and demands on the organization that are often contradictory to each other (Hall 1987). Therefore, which goals should be adopted as criteria? Small farmers? Large farmers? Agribusiness and the private sector? Food consumers? Land-grant universities or the national scientific community? Individual states or the nation as a whole?

Most earlier studies of the effectiveness of the agricultural academe were done by economists (e.g., Fishel 1971; Evenson 1971; Evenson, Waggoner, and Ruttan 1979; Ruttan 1982) and were concentrated on the return to research. The common dependent variables are productivity and profitability while ignoring any other criteria of effectiveness. The common independent variables used are resources in monetary terms, manpower, size, and location in order to determine optimum size, which has scale economy implications, and optimum combinations of manpower and capital, while neglecting structural variables such as complexity, formalization, and centralization, as well as individual variables such as job satisfaction, etc.

About 20 years ago, Heady (1971) warned us about the danger of not including adverse effects in research evaluation and lack of research on solutions to the adverse effects of agricultural research. The unintended externalities or social side effect has drawn more and more attention from the general public. Within academic circles, disagreement remains with regard to how the benefits flow from research to society and how the research benefits and costs are distributed among different sectors and various income groups.

Recently, a more comprehensive scheme was proposed by Bonnen (1986) to understand the four major forces for increasing societal capacity: technological advances, institutional and policy improvement, development of human capacity, and the enhancement and conservation of both natural and manmade resources. We suggest that the four "basic forces" be used as criteria in assessing effectiveness of agricultural academic programs. The effectiveness of a project will mean that it is scientifically excellent, institutionally sound, socially relevant, and ecologically responsible. Therefore, one of the research priorities will be to implement these four concepts and to develop measurements for them.

As many establishments are moving toward restructuring their agricultural programs, questions should be asked as to whether it is more or less effective if research, teaching, and extension are organized by discipline, or along commodity lines (i.e., corn), or by farming pattern (i.e., small, medium, multicrop production), or by ecological regions (i.e., corn belt, dry, region, etc.). Campbell (1989) calls for extensive studies on the relative effectiveness of various types of change made by the Cooperative Extension Service, given that almost all extension programs have modified or restructured their activities. For agricultural-related disciplines, a critical question should be asked: What will be the impact of changing the extension service on the traditional linkage between the agricultural academic community as a whole, and its clientele, as well as constituencies.

The dispute over competitive grant funding versus formula funding has become one of the major issues facing the agricultural academic community today. Their relative merits became the basis of an intense "funding debate." Little empirical research has been conducted, however, and almost all the arguments from both camps are based on speculation and value judgment but have no real, systematic data to support them. As Ruttan (1982) pointed out, each of the two research-management systems has strengths and weaknesses. We suggest that systematic studies on their relative merits be conducted by interdisciplinary researchers so that the arguments about the relative strengths and weaknesses can be grounded on systematic scientific research.

Given the scarcity of resources for research, teaching, and extension activities, agricultural professionals must be held accountable for their activities and the products and services that result. This is also true for departments and other work units where there is a collective accountability. Evaluation is an administrative responsibility. Even though administrators may recognize the desirability of involving peers in the evaluation of professionals, this does not diminish their own responsibility. Evaluation data are needed for counsel with professionals, and to help them plan their future activities. Admittedly, this process becomes even more difficult if the views of multiple constituencies must be taken into consideration when evaluating professionals or work units.

One issue focuses upon the weight given to quality versus quantity. Should all articles written for journals have equal value, or should some carry more value because of the particular journals in which they are printed? If differential weights are used, how will these be determined? Sink (1984) calls for the involvement of professionals in the evaluation process. He warns that the output parameters should be acceptable to the professionals being evaluated. If they are involved in designing the evaluation system, they will be part owners and more likely to accept its legitimacy.

Another issue is the nature of agricultural research which can be focused upon subject matter and problem solving or upon the concerns of a specific discipline. A focus upon subject matter and problem solving usually requires multidisciplinary work. Discipline-oriented research is almost always narrower and may not provide results having immediate value for consumers. It is interesting to note that rural sociology appears to have taken a discipline orientation during the 1970s, but during the 1980s turned again to a subject-matter and problem-solving focus. All agricultural scientists have to confront this issue. Research is needed to determine the relative benefits of each kind of research.

Should efforts be made to determine the actual economic or social impact of products and services delivered? At first glance, this seems desirable. However, it is very difficult. If an agricultural researcher determines that some new or modified technology can have a positive impact on production, should this research be given total credit for any increase in production that occurs when farmers use the new or modified technology? Other factors, such as the weather, the seed quality, the farmer's field and management skills, and the quality of the soil, are also important. Determining the economic or social impact of teaching or extension activities is even more difficult. One compromise approach is to rely upon more than one kind of information. For example, the productivity of researchers can be evaluated by the number of patents, inventions, articles, books, and reports produced, and by the perceptions of consumers who can be asked to evaluate the importance of the various products and services. The perceptions of consumers are no less important when evaluating teachers and extension personnel.

Evaluation is more difficult when the work is completed by teams or work units. How is the credit for success or the blame for failure to be assigned? Evaluating cooperative regional activities may be the most difficult of all. It is desirable that all parties be included in the evaluation process, including the discussion of how credit will be assigned, before the actual work begins.

The evaluation of work done by agricultural professionals and work units has not received enough attention.

Answers to the research questions that follow could make important contributions:

1. What criteria should be used when evaluating researchers, teachers, and extension personnel? How should these criteria be weighted?
2. How can the economic impact of products and services be determined? If it is not possible to determine the economic impact of products and services, and a decision is made to focus upon perceived economic or social impact, which constituencies should be considered?
3. How should the perceptions of constituencies be analyzed if multiple and conflicting constituencies are included in the evaluation process?
4. Which professionals are the most productive: those working alone, those working in teams, or those working on cooperative regional research projects?
5. What is the fairest means of assigning credit when professionals work in teams or on cooperative regional projects?

SUMMARY AND CONCLUSIONS

We have suggested that a systems model can be used to understand agricultural research organizations, including universities and departments within universities. This model can also be used for understanding national and international organizations. A systems model of organizations provides a framework for categorizing and understanding the demands placed upon organizations, that include the issues of multiple and conflicting demands from constituencies, how the work of scientists can be best organized, and organizational effectiveness.

In the past, much evaluation work has been completed by economists. The results from these studies have been helpful, but we suggest that sociologists and political scientists at land-grant universities are especially well suited, because of their training and their understanding of their universities and its constituencies, to help the administrators understand their organizations as systems and to conduct priority research.

Very little research has been conducted on agricultural research units as systems, and a fairly large number of priority-research questions were specified here for administrators to consider. Since funding for this research will no doubt be limited, how can administrators and sponsors of research sponsors best decide which questions should receive attention first? After administrators, constituencies, and research sponsors have been briefed about the questions that were raised in this chapter, we suggest that a survey of stakeholders' preferences be taken. Then, a committee of stakeholders and knowledgeable researchers could be asked to analyze these preferences and specify which research questions should be considered first. In order to meet the needs of more administrators, and for comparative analysis, we would suggest that regional research projects should be given first priority.

NOTE

1. All three authors are with the Department of Sociology and Anthropology at Iowa State University, Ames, Iowa.

REFERENCES

Aiken, Michael, and Jerald Hage. 1966. Organizational alienation: A comparative study. *American Sociological Review* 31:497–507.

Andrews, Frank M. 1979. The international study: Its data sources and measurement procedures. In *Scientific Productivity*. Edited by Frank M. Andrews, 17–50. Paris: UNESCO.

Aragi, A. A., R. J. Sim, and R. L. Gardner. 1978. Return to agricultural research and extension programs: An exante approach. *American Journal of Agricultural Economics* 60, no. 5: 964–68.

Bonnen, James. T. 1986. A century of science in agriculture: Lesson for science policy. *American Journal of Agricultural Economics* 58, no. 5: 1065–80.

Britan, Gerald M. 1987. The politics of agricultural science. In *Farm work, field work: American agriculture in anthropological perspective*. Edited by Michael Chibnik. Ithaca, N.Y.: Cornell University Press.

Brown, George E., Jr. 1989. The critical challenges facing the structure and function of agricultural research. *Journal of Productive Agriculture* 2, no. 2: 98–102.

Brown, Thomas G. 1981. Changing delivery system for agricultural extension: The extension teacher—Changing roles and competencies. *American Journal of Agricultural Economics* 63, no. 5: 859–62.

Browne, William P. 1987. An emerging opposition? Agricultural interests and federal research policy. In *Public policy and agricultural technology*. Edited by Dori F. Hadwiger andWilliam P. Browne. New York: Macmillan.

Busch, Lawrence, and William B. Lacy. 1983. *Science, agriculture and the politics of research*. Boulder, Colo.: Westview Press.

Buttel, Frederick H., et al. 1986. Industry-university relationships and the land-grant system. *Agricultural Administration* 23:147–81.

Campbell, John P. 1977. On the nature of organizational effectiveness. In *New perspectives on organization effectiveness*. Edited by Paul S. Goodman and Johannes M. Pennings. San Francisco: Jossey-Bass.

Campbell, Rex R. 1989. The next 75 years of extension: A call for additional research. *The Rural Sociologist* (Fall): 15–17.

Carson, Rachel. 1962. *The silent spring*. New York: Houghton-Mifflin.

Daft, Richard L. 1989. *Organization theory and design*. Los Angeles: West.

Evenson, Robert E. 1971. Economic aspect of organization of agricultural research. In *Resource allocation in agricultural research*. Edited by Walter L. Fishel. Minneapolis: University of Minnesota Press.

Evenson, Robert E., and Yoav Kisliev. 1975. *Agricultural research and productivity*. New Haven, Conn.: Yale University Press.

Evenson, Robert E., Paul Waggoner, and Vernon Ruttan. 1979. Economic benefit from research: An example from agriculture. *Science* 205:1101–07.

Feller, Irwin. 1986. Research and technology transfer linkages in American agriculture. In *The Agricultural Research Enterprise*. Edited by Lawrence Busch and William B. Lacy, 279–90. Boulder, Colo.: Westview Press.

——— 1987. Technology transfer, public policy and cooperative extension service. In *Policy for agricultural research.* Edited by Vernon Ruttan and Carl Pray, 175–210. Boulder, Colo.: Westview Press.

Fishel, Walter L. 1971. *Resource allocation in agricultural research.* Minneapolis: University of Minnesota Press.

Ford, Thomas R. 1985. Rural sociology and the passing of social scientific chivalry. *Rural Sociology* 50, no. 4: 523–38.

Friedland, William H., and Tim Kappel. 1979. Production or perish: Changing the inequalities of agricultural research priorities. Project on social impact, assessment and values, Santa Cruz, Calif.

Gaston, Jerry. 1978. *The reward system in British and American science.* New York: John Wiley and Sons.

Government-University-Industry Research Roundtable. 1989. *Science and technology in the academic enterprise.* Washington, D.C.: National Academy of Sciences.

Hadwiger, Don F., and William P. Browne. 1987. Introduction in *Public policy and agricultural technology.* Edited by Don F. Hadwiger and William P. Browne. New York: Macmillan.

Hall, Richard H. 1987. *Organizations: Structures, processes, and outcomes.* Englewood Cliffs, N.J.: Prentice-Hall, Inc.

Heady, Earl O. 1971. Welfare implications of agricultural research. In *Resource allocation in agricultural research.* Edited by Walter L. Fishel. Minneapolis: University of Minnesota Press.

Hess, Charles E. 1989. The emerging agricultural research agenda. *American Journal of Agricultural Economics* 71, no. 5: 1113–16.

Hightower, Jim. 1973. *Hard tomatoes, hard times.* Cambridge: Schenkman.

Hildreth, R. J., and Walter J. Armbruster. 1981. Extension program delivery—Past, present, and future: An overview. *American Journal of Agricultural Economics* 63, no. 5: 853–58.

Hill, Charles W. L. 1988. Differentiation versus low cost of differentiation and low cost: A contingency framework. *Academy of Management Review* 13, no. 3: 401–12.

Holt, John. 1989. Managing change in extension. *American Journal of Agricultural Economics* 71, no. 4: 867–74.

Isreal, Glenn D. 1988. Reaching sociologists' clientele in extension. *The Rural Sociologist* 8, no. 4: 341–47.

Johnson, Glenn L. 1984. Academia needs a new covenant for serving agriculture. Special publication by Mississippi State University. Mississippi Agriculture and Forestry Experiment Station.

Kenney, Martin. 1986. *Biotechnology: The university-industrial complex.* New Haven, Conn.: Yale University Press.

Klonglan, Gerald E. 1987. The rural sociological enterprise: A discipline in transition. *Rural Sociology* 52, no. 1: 1–12.

Kloppenburg, Jack R., Jr. 1988. *First the seed: The political economy of plant biotechnology, 1492–2000.* New York: Cambridge University Press.

Lipman-Blumen, Jean. 1987. Priority setting in agricultural research. In *Policy for agricultural research.* Edited by Vernon W. Ruttan and Carl E. Pray. Boulder, Colo.: Westview Press.

Litman-Blumen, Jean, and Susan Schram. 1984. *The paradox of success: The impact on priority setting in agricultural research and extension.* Washington, D.C.: U.S. Department of Agriculture.

Madden, J. Patrick. 1986. Toward an new covenant for agricultural academe. In *Agricultural research enterprise.* Edited by Lawrence Busch and William Lacy. Boulder, Colo.: Westview Press.

Manderscheid, Lester V. 1988. Undergraduate educational opportunities in the face of declining enrollments. *American Journal of Agricultural Economics* 70, no. 5: 985–93.

Marcus, Alan. 1986. From state chemistry to state science: The transformation of the idea of the agricultural experiment station, 1875–1887. *Agricultural Scientific Enterprise.* Edited by Lawrence Busch and William B. Lacy. Boulder, Colo.: Westview Press.

Mayer, A., and S. Mayer. 1975. *Agriculture: The island empire.* Lincoln: University of Nebraska Press.

McDowell, George R. 1985. The political economy of extension program design: Institutional maintenance issues in the organization and delivery of extension programs. *American Journal of Agricultural Economics* 67, no. 4: 717–25.

Miles, R. E., and C. C. Snow. 1978. *Organizational strategy, structure, and process.* New York: McGraw-Hill.

Mulford, Charles L., et al. 1990. Single or multiple competitive strategies for small businesses? *Journal of Managerial Issues* 2(4): 454–68.

Mulford, Charles L., Lisa Waldner-Haugrud, and Hemchandra Gajbhiye. 1990. Variables associated with agricultural scientists' work alienation and publication productivity. Ames: Iowa State University, Department of Sociology and Anthropology.

Murray, Alan I. 1988. A contingency view of Porter's "generic strategies." *Academy of Management Review* 13, no. 3: 390–400.

National Research Council. 1972. Report of the committee on research advisory to the USDA. Springfield, Va.: National Technical Information Service (Pound Report).

——— 1989. *Investing in research: A proposal to strengthen the agricultural, food, and environmental system.* Washington, D.C.: National Academy Press.

Nipp, Terry L. 1988. Congress and the future of agricultural research, extension, and education. *Journal of Productive Agriculture* 1, no. 3: 187–90.

Pelz, Donald C. 1976. *Scientists in organizations: Productive climates for research and development.* Ann Arbor: University of Michigan.

Porter, Michael. 1980. *Competitive strategy.* New York: Free Press.

Quinn, Robert E., and John Rohrbaugh. 1981. A competing values approach to organization effectiveness. *Public Productivity Review* (June): 122–40.

———1983. A spatial model of effectiveness criteria: Toward a competing values approach to organizational analysis. *Management Sciences* 29:363–77.

Rasmussen, Wayne D. 1989. *Taking the university to the people: Seventy-five years of cooperative extension.* Ames: Iowa State University Press.

Rockefeller Foundation and OSTP. 1982. *Science for agriculture: Report of a workshop on critical issues in American agricultural research.* New York: The Rockefeller Foundation (Winrock Report).

Ruttan, Vernon. 1982. *Agricultural research policy.* Minneapolis: University of Minnesota Press.

Sauer, Richard J., and Carl E. Pray. 1987. Mobilizing support for agricultural research at the Minnesota agricultural experiment station. In *Policy for agricultural research*. Edited by Vernon Ruttan and Carl E. Pray. Boulder, Colo.: Westview Press.

Scott, W. Richard. 1981. *Organizations: Rational, natural, and open systems*. Englewood Cliffs, N.J.: Prentice-Hall, Inc.

Sink, John D. 1984. Strategies for the administrative improvement of academic departments. *Agricultural Administration* 16:17–30.

Steers, R. M. 1977. *Organizational effectiveness: A behavioral view*. Pacific Palisades, Calif.: Goodyear.

Wade, Jerry L. 1988. Alternative for the 80s: An experiment in institutional innovation. *The Rural Sociologist* 8, no. 4: 348–52.

Yuchtman, Ephraim, and Stanley E. Seashore. 1967. A system resource approach to organizational effectiveness. *American Sociological Review* 32, no. 6: 891–903.

CHAPTER 3

SOCIAL SCIENCE KNOWLEDGE AND TOOLS TO ADDRESS PROBLEMS AND ISSUES: FROM THE PERSPECTIVE OF BOTH THE RURAL AND THE BASIC SOCIAL SCIENCES

Larry J. Connor[1]

INTRODUCTION

The perspectives of both rural social scientists and basic social science disciplines are important in analyzing problems pertaining to farming, agriculture, and rural areas. With this perspective in mind, the SSAAP conference planners assigned the following objectives for this paper:

- To address this topic from the perspective of all the rural and basic social sciences rather than only from the author's own rural social science area and/or basic social science discipline.
- To place emphasis on the adequacy or inadequacy of theories, techniques, and measurements in the basic social science disciplines relative to the problems and issues resolvable, in part, by the work of rural social scientists.
- To relate potential social science contributions to the improvement of institutions, policies, and programs; technology, human development, and capital growth (biological and physical); and the conservation and development of natural resources needed in food and agriculture, natural and community resources, and the environment—both in the United States and internationally.
- To relate potential social science contributions to the improved knowledge of monetary and nonmonetary values required to solve anticipated problems and resolve issues.

This paper was undertaken by dividing it into two general areas: (1) Social Science Theory, Methods of Analysis, and Tools, and (2) Capacities of Social Sciences to Address Rural Problems.

SOCIAL SCIENCE THEORY, METHODS OF ANALYSIS, AND TOOLS

The need for disciplinary contributions from the social sciences has been well summarized (Johnson 1987, 28):

> Social sciences, like all disciplines, have special responsibilities with respect to disciplinary knowledge. Like the biological and physical sciences, social sciences generate the basic disciplinary advances which, in turn, provide the foundation for application in the form of improved policies, development of rural human resources, and improved agricultural institutions (both public and private), policies and programs. As for the biological and physical sciences, not all disciplinary research in the social sciences is relevant for agriculture....

In order to address problems related to agriculture and rural areas, social scientists fall back on their disciplinary underpinnings. These take the forms of basic theories, paradigms, analytical methods, and tools of analysis. The underpinnings establish the capacity and set the limits of the social science disciplines to address rural and agricultural problems in an applied context and multidisciplinary efforts with other social sciences or applied agricultural fields.

HETEROGENEITY OF SOCIAL SCIENCES

There is a tendency to assume disciplines are relatively homogeneous, and that greater heterogeneity occurs between disciplines. This is hardly the case with the social sciences. In an analysis of variance context, there may be as much variation within some social science disciplines as there is between them. This has contributed to the views of physical and biological scientists that social sciences are basically "soft"—that they lack vigor and powerful, generally accepted methodologies. Social scientists from a given discipline may give totally different responses to problems because of different philosophic and science orientations. Hence, generalizations about the social sciences need to be carefully made and understood.

REQUIREMENTS OF BASIC SOCIAL SCIENCES

To what extent do current problem demands related to agriculture and rural areas expose deficiencies in the basic social sciences? If the capacity of social sciences to deal with rural problems in an applied context (often involving multidisciplinary interactions) is important, the following items appear to be relevant: a dominant or unifying paradigm, deductive analysis capability, empirical orientation, and capacity to handle values. These requirements are applicable in various degrees to social science disciplines, and are important in relating to agricultural scientists (such as agronomists, agricultural engineers, etc.), as well as between rural social scientists. While not applicable to all social sciences for all types of analysis, these requirements are valid for social science research pertaining to agricultural and rural subject matter.

First, are there dominant and unifying paradigms? This is an important requirement inasmuch as it lends credibility within and between disciplines and provides some accepted concepts/methods for problem solving. The social sciences have been vulnerable to attacks from the physical and biological scientists because they do not have established paradigms like some of the physical sciences (such as physics). A major danger of paradigms is that they may produce "cloning" and discourage productive alternative paradigms for dealing with practical problems.

There is a considerable difference among the social sciences with respect to dominant paradigms. Economics probably has the strongest paradigm in its market-price mechanism-choice marginalism emphasis. Sociology also appears to have a dominant paradigm in structural functionalism. The application of general systems theory in sociology has been within this paradigm. Anthropology has a dominant paradigm based on the concept of "culture": an interdependent complex of behavior and beliefs that encompasses economic, political, and ideological realms of human life. The other social science disciplines appear to have less dominant or unifying paradigms. Deductive analysis capability is important in applying or utilizing theoretical concepts.

The ability to generalize with axiomatic reasoning is useful in dealing with certain types of problems. Deductive analysis depends not only on axiomatic logic, but also on inductive tests to validate its value in explaining various forms of behavior (to be able to predict). Of the various social sciences, mathematical economics probably has the most formal deductive analytical capabilities. Other social sciences also have this capacity in varying degrees, although in a more rhetorical base. A major limitation of deductive analysis is the tendency to concentrate on more disciplinary-oriented research questions. Rural social scientists have made outstanding empirical contributions. The development of the agricultural data system is a prime example. On some campuses, the teaching of survey methods appears to be shifting to the social sciences (particularly sociology) as many statistics departments have focused so exclusively on the theory of mathematical statistics that they have ceased to be interested in data, data analysis, or applied statistics. It should be noted that there is a difference between empirical and quantitative-method orientations. University agricultural economists have increasingly become involved in the development and utilization of various quantitative analytical methods (econometrics, simulations, etc.), while decreasing their use of survey methods involving primary data collection. (This is less true with respect to USDA and for agricultural economists working in less developed countries.)

The last requirement relating to basic social sciences is the capacity of the disciplines to handle values (monetary and nonmonetary). The social sciences have always been faced with the problem of integrating positivistic information from the physical and biological sciences with social and humanistic values. Values are crucial from the standpoint of the social sciences, particularly in research on public policy or any kind of public/private decision making.

Social sciences handle values very differently. Colleges of education have long been dominated philosophically by American pragmatism which does not separate values and positivistic knowledge. Other social science disciplines have handled values on a conditional normative or normative basis (see Johnson 1986). Social scientists within individual disciplines often handle values differently. The handling of values by rural social scientists has been a concern to individuals from applied agricultural fields and agricultural administrators. Objective analysis of values is not possible within the logical positivism framework of many of the applied agricultural fields. Hence, social scientists must carefully integrate values and knowledge in dealing with selected real-world agricultural or rural problems.

CAPACITIES OF SOCIAL SCIENCES TO ADDRESS RURAL PROBLEMS

In an applied context, what are the major capacities of the social sciences to address rural and agricultural problems? Alternatively, to what extent can the social sciences link problem sets with social science disciplinary and subject-matter domains?

TYPES AND LEVELS OF RESEARCH

It is useful to identify three broad categories of research (Johnson 1984):

1. Disciplinary research—to improve the theory, measurements, and techniques of one of the traditional disciplines of traditional universities. Examples include the basic theories, measurements, techniques, and tools of the discipline such as techniques for economics modeling, organizational behavior, etc.
2. Problem-solving research—multidisciplinary research having as its objective the solution of a particular problem faced by a specific real-world decision maker or set of decision makers in either the public or private sector. Examples include local community problems dealing with a declining tax base, and management problems associated with a specific cattle feedlot.
3. Subject-matter research—multidisciplinary research on a subject of interest to a rather well-defined set of decision makers concerned with a rather well-defined set of problems. Examples include farming-systems research, community development, food safety, etc.

Rural social scientists engage in all three kinds of research. Some research efforts may be a mixture of these types of research. This does not necessarily detract from the usefulness of the categories in thinking about research. Agricultural research institutions are necessarily concerned with all three kinds of research.

In Figure 1, these three categories of research are illustrated with examples from agricultural economics. As indicated, some research (farming systems, agricultural policy analysis) may contain a descriptive, subject-matter, and problem-solving mixture.

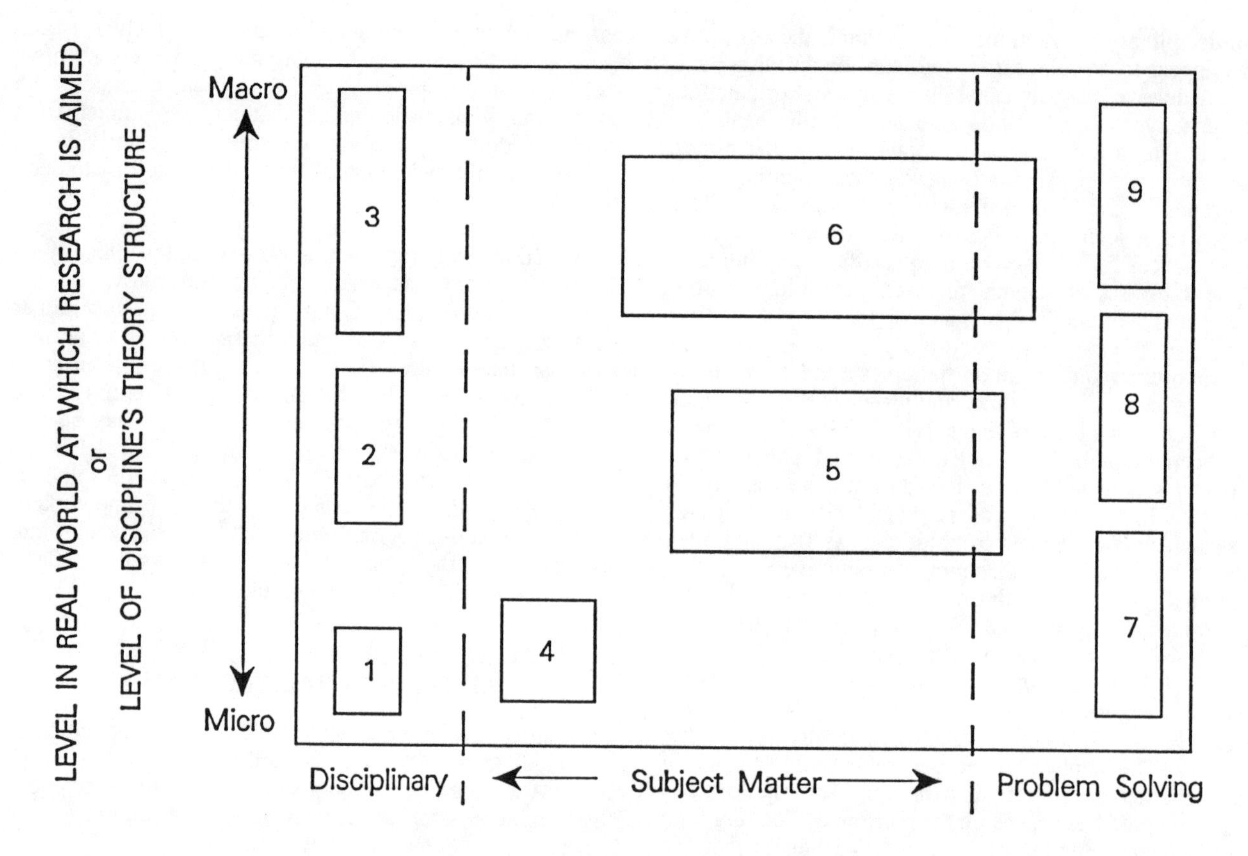

Numbers in the boxes refer to examples of research:
(1) expected utility analysis,
(2) demand analysis models,
(3) macroeconomic models,
(4) soil carbon dynamics and economics,
(5) farming systems,
(6) agricultural policy analysis,
(7) integrated decision-support systems,
(8) community development, and
(9) agricultural sector simulation.

Figure 1: Schematic Example of Various Research in Agricultural Economics.

The level of aggregation or structural level of discipline theory can be a major impediment to multidisciplinary research, particularly in working with agricultural scientists. Entomologists often start with a bug on a particular leaf, soil scientists may be concerned with a cubic yard of soil, and animal scientists may be concerned with only the rumen of an animal. In order for the social scientist to relate to agricultural scientists, the level of aggregation must be on a similar plane. Usually this is at the farm decision-making level. In some cases, social scientists may find it impossible to interact with biological scientists because of the social scientists' inability to deal with the very micro level of analyses at which the biological scientists work and think. Biological and physical scientists may, in turn, often be frustrated in working with social scientists because of their concern with the "big picture," or the long-term consequences of technological change.

A major problem in putting together multidisciplinary teams is the matching of individuals with respect to both disciplinary and applied skills, on the one hand, and the matching of their micro or macro skills, on the other hand. Few social scientists (or other scientists) have the capacity to work across both continuums in Figure 1. Thus, multidisciplinary research is most successful when directed to a very specific problem or subject-matter area. Multidisciplinary research often requires outstanding disciplinary skills particularly for problem identification and developing system structure for analyses.

Multidisciplinary research involving only the social sciences has probably been most pronounced in the area of community development or with the family where economists, sociologists, and human ecology have interacted. Agricultural economists have had the most extensive experience working with the physical and biological scientists in agricultural institutions. Other social scientists have had less frequent interaction in multidisciplinary-research efforts relating to agriculture and rural areas.

In addressing rural problems, what has been the performance of the social sciences with respect to disciplinary, subject-matter, and problem-solving research? The major focus of rural social science research has been in the subject-matter area. Although disciplinary contributions have been made and specific problems researched, funding agencies (such as the Department of Agriculture and Agricultural Experiment Stations) have tended to organize and fund research on a subject-matter basis. Hence, it has had a much greater emphasis. Disciplinary research has not suffered because of peer pressures. Problem-solving research has had the least emphasis because of its strong multidisciplinary orientation. The record of rural social scientists (or biological and physical scientists) in multidisciplinary research has not been outstanding.

MAJOR SOURCES OF CHANGE IN SOCIETAL CAPACITY AND INFORMATION NEEDS

The four prime sources of change in societal change are: technology, human capabilities, institutions, and biological/physical capital. The social sciences have greater relative strengths in dealing with human capabilities and institutions than with technology and biological/physical capital. This is not to say that social scientists cannot make contributions with respect to the latter two areas. Indeed, they can and should. Unfortunately, social science interactions with agricultural, biological, and physical sciences in analyzing questions pertaining to technology and biophysical capital have been much too limited.

The types of information generated by social science researchers have value to private and/or public decision makers. According to traditional informational theory, information is data that has been evaluated in the context of a specific problem situation. The true value of the information is related to the decisions that private or public managers have to make. The relationships between major types of information and prime sources of change in societal capacity are shown in Table 1.

Information can be classified as descriptive, diagnostic, predictive, and prescriptive (Harsh et al. 1981). Descriptive information portrays the "what is" condition. It describes the state of some physical, biological, sociological, or economic aspect of a given entity at a specified point in time. Diagnostic information portrays the "what is wrong" condition. It is utilized for problem identification. Diagnostic information is measured as the disparity between "what is" and "what ought to be." Predictive information portrays the "what if...?" condition. It is concerned with possible outcomes of alternative courses of action. Finally, prescriptive information is directed to decision making and the "what should or ought be done" question.

Social scientists are probably most skillful in providing descriptive and diagnostic analyses. Because of the large number of exogenous variables which cannot be controlled in social/economic/political systems, it is often difficult to predict with precision. (A prime example deals with the difficulties associated with macro-economic forecasting models.) Although physical scientists have similar problems (as evidenced by difficulties in predicting crop yields, livestock production, etc.), rural social scientists must do predictive analyses in such forms as impact, benefit/cost, policy, and political analyses.

Social scientists do not frequently provide prescriptive solutions for private/public decision makers by themselves. In this respect they encounter the same problems as the biological and physical scientists. Social science extension specialists have typically handled values through careful conditional normative prescriptions.

Despite the descriptive and diagnostic capabilities of social scientists research relating to these types of information has been somewhat lacking (Bonnen 1985). As a prime example, our Agricultural Data System still largely reflects the problems of the 1930s. The efforts of various social scientists in generating data pertaining to the recent farm crisis and rural families should also be noted. Surveys of farms, farm families, and other primary collection activities had to be conducted on a crash basis to provide needed information for state legislators, governors, etc. Finally, universities have been happy to leave much of the data-collection work to the U.S. Department of Agriculture, and do less primary data collection today than several decades ago. Unfortunately, some have been discontinued by the USDA in recent years because of budget constraints and increasing pressure to focus only on national-level policy issues, and this in a very short-run context.

IMPACTS OF ALTERNATIVE INSTITUTIONAL MODELS ON RURAL SOCIAL SCIENCES

Are the social sciences properly organized to do effective agricultural and rural research? The answer to this question depends on one's views of the following:

1. What kind of research is important? (Disciplinary, subject-matter, or problem-solving? Descriptive, diagnostic, predictive, or prescriptive? Technology, human capital, institutional, or biophysical?)
2. What are the potential relative contributions of the individual social sciences to agricultural and rural research? The resources available to rural social scientists from various disciplines vary considerably.

The rural social sciences have had varying degrees of success in surviving and prospering over time in academic

TABLE 1: CAPACITY OF RURAL SOCIAL SCIENCES TO PROVIDE SELECTED TYPES OF INFORMATION RELATIVE TO MAJOR SOURCES OF CHANGE IN RURAL AREAS

Types Of Information	Prime Sources Of Change In Societal Capacity[1]			
	Technology	Human Capability	Institutions	Biological/Physical Capital
Descriptive	+	+ to ++	+ to ++	+
Diagnostic	+	+ to ++	+ to ++	+
Predictive	0 to +	+	+	0 to +
Prescriptive	0 to +	+	+	0 to +

[1]Relative Strengths: ++ Strong, + Moderate, 0 Negligible

settings. Agricultural economics has been the most successful. Departments are located in every college of agriculture, and the Economic Research Service is a large component of the U.S. Department of Agriculture. Agricultural economics has probably prospered because of its work on income, which ranks high among human concerns, and its close relationship to colleges of agriculture and the other agricultural disciplines. This has been particularly crucial inasmuch as most agricultural college administrators come from the biological and physical sciences. Family-relations and child-development departments have developed in colleges of home economics (ecology), although they have not enjoyed the same level of funding support as have the departments of agricultural economics. This may be partially attributed to their being in separate colleges. Rural sociology has had mixed success. Some departments of rural sociology have survived, while others evolved within or have been combined with departments of agricultural economics or sociology in social science colleges. Rural sociology's lesser degree of success can probably be attributed to its rural (not agricultural) orientation and lack of a political base. As a consequence, it has had less identification and support from agricultural administrators. A scattering of lawyers, usually in departments of agricultural economics, is also present around the country. Other relevant disciplines—history, political science, anthropology, psychology, etc.—have either not developed or not survived in colleges of agriculture. However, there are individuals in basic social science departments who specialize in such areas as agricultural history, rural development, the politics of agriculture, etc.

Various social science organizational models for relating to agricultural and rural problems and the hypothetical impacts on various types of research are identified in Table 2. The range of organizational models include: private/public universities, such as Harvard, Chicago, and Texas; land-grant universities with various organizational forms; governmental social science agencies; and independent institutes, such as Resources for the Future (RFF), American Enterprise Institute (AEI), and the International Food Policy Research Institute (IFPRI). In interpreting the results in Table 2, it should be emphasized that these are generalizations. Certainly, any organization may have a mixture of professional social scientists with different capabilities. Availability of money to conduct social science research can also influence any organization as to the nature of its research. Nevertheless, there does appear to be some evidence of differences in performance with respect to types of research and organizational models.

The private/public universities have a comparative advantage in conducting disciplinary research. Faculty are recruited on this basis, research funds for this type of research are more readily available internally and from external funding agencies, and faculty generally have less contact with food-system and rural decision makers. The land-grant universities have a comparative advantage in doing problem-solving research, and to a lesser extent, subject-matter research. Government and institutes appear to have an advantage in doing subject-matter research, although organizations such as the Economic Research Service periodically do some problem-solving research for executive and legislative government purposes.

Various land-grant organizational models have been broken down further because of the large number of rural social scientists there. The most disciplinary orientation within a land-grant structure is probably where basic and rural disciplines are in the same department (sociology or economics department). The most applied problem-solving approach is probably where social scientists are separately appointed and located in other departments (such as animal sciences and plant sciences). Where extension specialists are located in departments, their relationships to research specialists and possible joint extension/research appointments also influence the nature of research in universities.

Is there an optimal organization model for land-grant universities? The answer to this question depends on what individual colleges of agriculture wish to accomplish. Colleges of agriculture have a tendency to encounter difficulties when they either overemphasize the disciplinary basis or the more applied subject-matter and problem-solving basis. They also have problems in balancing the capability to address the technological, human capital, institutional, and biophysical dimensions of any problem or subject matter of relevance to agriculture and rural areas. Maintaining a balance is important for long-term survival (both in the context of relating to state-level and disciplinary clientele).

RANKING OF RURAL SOCIAL SCIENCE PROBLEM AREAS

During the 1970s and 1980s, applied agricultural and rural fields increasingly attempted to rank research needs. This was in response to shortages of research funds, inflation impacts, the development of a competitive grant program in the USDA, responding to new pressures such as biotechnology and the farm financial crisis, protecting the market share of the agricultural research dollar, etc. Two major conferences were held for the crop sciences, one for the animal sciences, and various fields have periodically revised and updated their priorities.

The agricultural economics and rural sociology professional associations have ranked research needs in recent years. A 1986 ranking by the American Agricultural Economics Association (AAEA) identified the following critical issues: (1) increasing the profitability of agriculture, (2) organizing to compete in world markets, (3) developing policies to reflect the changing pattern of ownership and control of agricultural and rural resources, (4) improving the linkage between food and environmental concerns and agricultural programs, and (5) developing policies for stressed communities and for the future needs of rural people (AAEA). A 1986–87 national-priorities statement for rural sociology research identified consequences: (1) of technological and economic changes in rural industries, (2) improved methods for predicting the social effects of proposed developments in rural areas, and (3) strategies for enabling people in rural areas to enhance their well-being through increased access to resources of the larger society (Klonglan 1986).

In Table 3, the ranking of research initiatives is shown for the NCT–146 group. This committee was composed of North Central administrative representatives from home economics, agricultural economics, rural sociology, and agricultural education. The NCT–146 ranking is interesting in that it is one of the few collaborative efforts of the rural social sciences to rank research priorities. The committee identified two priority areas and two secondary areas for

TABLE 2: SOCIAL SCIENCE ORGANIZATIONAL MODELS FOR RELATING TO AGRICULTURAL AND RURAL PROBLEMS: RELATIVE IMPACTS ON VARIOUS TYPES OF RESEARCH[1]

Organizational Model	Characteristics	Relative Impacts On[2]		
		Disciplinary Research	Subject-Matter Research	Problem-Solving Research
1. Private/Public University	Basic Disciplines Only	++	0 to +	0
2. Land-Grant University				
A. University Disciplinary	Basic and Rural Disciplines in same department: All applied economics in Economics Department, etc.	+ to ++	+	0 to +
B. College Disciplinary	Rural social science disciplines in College of Agriculture: Ag. History, Rural Sociology, Ag. Economics, etc.	+	+	+
C. School of Rural Social Science	Rural social science disciplines grouped within a school in College of Agriculture: Rural Sociology, Ag. Law, Ag. Economics, etc.	0	+	+
D. College Disciplinary with Salaried Joint Appointment	Same as 2B above except some faculty would have salaried joint appointments in other departments: Ag. Economist located in Animal Science with half his salary appointed in Ag. Economics, etc.	0 to +	+	+
E. College Disciplinary with Independent Appointments	Same as 2B except some faculty would have independent appointments in other departments: Ag. Economist appointed in Fisheries & Wildlife with no appointment in Ag. Economics	- to +	0 to +	+ to ++
F. Center or Institute	Organization independent of departments, with specific charge (tenure, rural development, etc.)	0 to -	+	+
3. Government	Publicly supported (ERS/USDA, etc.)	0 to +	+ to ++	0 to +
4. Institutes	Private Organizations (RFF, AEI, IAPRI, etc.)	0 to +	+ to ++	0 to +

[1]There are obviously various combinations of these models.
[2]Relative Impacts: ++ Strong, + Moderate, 0 Negligible, - Negative, — Very negative

further research. The highest priorities were: agricultural policy in a global setting, and rural family and community well-being. Secondary priorities were: market penetration and efficient marketing of agricultural and forest products, and integrating agricultural technology. At a subsequent meeting of NCT–146, the committee further agreed to recommend to the North Central directors that the initial research initiative be concerned with developing a comprehensive database that was comparable across the region and described the state of well-being of agriculture and rural communities.

The extent or influence this ranking might have on the region's experiment station directors remains to be seen. Of the 21 research areas identified in the 1986 CSRS report, few of the areas in which the social sciences dominate were ranked very high by the North Central experiment station directors. For example, the financial situation of farms, agribusiness, local communities, and families had little impact on most experiment station priorities. Response from cooperative extension services to the farm and rural-family crisis has been much greater. On the other hand, the Experiment Station Committee on Organization and Policy did submit an initiative to Congress for funding on "Agriculture and Rural Viability" for 1988–89. Although not funded, it represented a significant step forward by experiment station directors.

RESEARCH AREAS OF OPPORTUNITY

While the preceding section indicates some of the major research priorities of rural social science disciplines, it does not necessarily indicate major research *areas of opportunity*. The possible long-term nature of major problems and likelihood of funding must be considered along with specific contemporary research needs pertaining to agriculture and rural areas. Broad areas of opportunity which the author believes contain numerous researchable problems include: agricultural competitiveness, rural communities, natural resources, and technology assessment.

Agricultural competitiveness is increasingly a greater concern in the United States because:

1. Expansion of international markets probably provides the major opportunity for enhancing agricultural incomes,
2. The United States is experiencing increasing competition in international agricultural markets (wheat from Canada, France, and Argentina; soybeans and citrus from Brazil; dairy products from Europe; etc.),

TABLE 3: RESEARCH INTEREST IN 13 RESEARCH INITIATIVES BY NCT–146 COMMITTEE (NORTH CENTRAL REGION TECHNICAL COMMITTEE) SEPTEMBER[1]

Research Initiative	Ranking By Representatives Of:[2]			
	NCA–5 Home Economics	NCA–12 AGR. Economics	NCA Rural Sociology	NCA–24 AGR. Education
1. Sustaining Soil Productivity	N	M	H	N-M
2. Maintaining & Protecting Water Quality & Quantity	M	M	H	N-M
3. Rangelands & Pasturelands	N	M	M	N
4. Animal Health & Disease	N-M	N	N	N
5. Improved Management of Crop Pests & Diseases	N	N-M	N	N-M
6. Short-Term Adjustments for Enhancing Economics of Agriculture	M	H	H	M-H
7. Agr. Policy in Global Setting[3]	N	H	H	M-H
8. Market Penetration & Efficient Marketing of Agr. & Forest Products[4]	N-M	H	M	M
9. Rural Family & Community Well-Being[3]	H	M	H	H
10. Interrelationships of Food & Nutritional & Health Status of People	H	N	H	N-M
11. Computer Technology for Agr. Management	M	M	M	M-H
12. Processing & Quality Enhancement	M-H	N	N	N
13. Integrating Agr. Technology[4]	M	H	H	H

[1]Drawn from 21 research areas deemed to have significant social science component in 1986 CSRS Report on "Research Initiatives: A Research Agenda for the State Agricultural Experiment Stations."
[2]H-High, M-Moderate, N-Negligible.
[3]Top two priority research initiatives.
[4]Next two priority research initiatives.

3. National macroeconomic policies have a strong impact upon the competitiveness of U.S. agriculture, and
4. Individual states are increasingly attempting to maintain/expand their agriculture, food processing, etc., at the expense of other states and to find niches in U.S. and international trade.

Researchable competitiveness topics cover agricultural production, input supply industries, food processing, marketing and distribution firms, government infrastructure, etc. Of particular importance is research on national agricultural and rural policies which: (1) provide adequate and stable prices for agricultural commodities, (2) do not disadvantage U.S. products in world markets, (3) do not make unreasonable demands on the U.S. treasury, and (4) do not have degrading environmental and social impacts. Because of pressures from state legislators, agricultural commodity groups, and state economic-development groups, agricultural experiment station directors will increasingly be concerned with the competitiveness of the agricultural industries in their individual states. But without leadership from the social sciences, institutional and human development is likely to be underemphasized compared to research on technology and biological/physical capital.

The impacts of the farm financial crisis of the early 1980s on the health of rural communities are documented. Additional pressure and change will be forthcoming when biotechnology impacts begin to be felt. The continuing decline in farm numbers and corresponding decreases in numbers of input-supply firms will continue to impact small towns, counties, and townships. Changes in nonfarm industries will also impact rural areas. A good example is the decrease in automobile-part suppliers in Michigan and Ohio, and the resultant loss of jobs for rural people. Researchable topics relating to rural communities cover a variety of topics including the family, quality of life, development processes, local governmental financing, community development, provision of local services (schools, roads, etc.), leadership development, etc. Leadership for this research must come from the rural social sciences.

A third general area is natural resources: sustaining soil productivity, maintaining and protecting water quality and quantity, reducing acid rain, minimizing livestock-waste pollution, etc. With the passage of the water act and override of the President's veto, attention is again being focused on environmental quality issues. Public opinion polls show strong and growing public concern for the quality of the environment. In addition, some states are beginning to experience increasing problems involving such issues as ground-water pollution from fertilizers, hog hotels, soil erosion, etc. Social scientists have already done good work in this area. Much remains to be done.

The last area of opportunity for social scientists may seem surprising—technology assessment. To understand its importance, a review of history may be useful. The period prior to World War I up to the late 1940s was basically the mechanical power era in American agriculture. The period from the late 1940s through the middle 1980s has been the chemical-power era (fertilizer, chemical, etc.). Current advances in biotechnology now suggest that the forthcoming several decades will be known as the biological era in American agriculture.

Preliminary analyses indicate major adjustments occurring as the result of adopting biotechnology. For example, adoption of the dairy-bovine growth hormone could result in a great reduction of cow numbers and some corresponding reduction in feed grain use. Various producers' groups are already expressing concerns relative to this technological advance, particularly after the recent dairy-herd termination program (Rauch 1987).

Attempts to do preliminary testing of the growth hormone resulted in negative consumer reaction to the milk produced. As a consequence, the potential of biotechnology may not be fully adopted without adequate social science analyses prior to the release of the technologies. While biotechnology will strongly impact American agriculture, it also will reinforce other existing concerns about technology. These include food additives and dietary impacts on human health, environmental impact relating to water and soils, and issues raised by animal-rights and other activist groups.

To date, there have been limited research opportunities for rural social scientists in this area. Social scientists have been excluded from the Department of Agriculture's special funding of biotechnology. Cornell appears to be one of the few universities that has explicitly attempted to incorporate the social sciences into analysis of biotechnology impacts. Yet, there is little doubt that agricultural technology will come under increasing scrutiny. As it does, agricultural administrators from the biological and physical sciences will increasingly be forced to request social-impact analyses of technological adoptions. This may well place some rural social scientists in difficult situations as they are forced to deal with conflicting views on the value of new technological advances in agriculture.

Finally, the area of information systems should perhaps be mentioned since it has been implicitly included in the other areas. The continuing computer/communication revolution (microcomputers, cable TV, satellites, discs, etc.) will have major impacts on public and private decision makers. Social scientists will be involved in developing expert systems, integrated decision support systems and management-information systems. They will also have to deal with ethical and public-policy issues concerning their use.

SUMMARY

Major needs of basic social sciences as exposed by current rural-problem demands were identified and discussed. These included: dominant or unifying paradigms, deductive-analysis capacity, empirical orientation, and capacity to handle values. Various considerations relating to the capacities of social sciences to address rural problems were elaborated. Types and levels of research, types of information relative to major sources of societal change, impacts of alternative institutional models on rural social sciences, and research areas were identified. The question was raised, but not answered, as to whether the social sciences are organized to do effective research for agriculture and rural communities.

Both the rural and basic social sciences have much to contribute to the solution of problems confronting agriculture and rural areas in America. Rural social science contributions to developing appropriate policies, institutions, programs, and human capacities have not been fully utilized by agricultural research establishments.

The increased need and responsibility for better communications on the part of social scientists should be obvious.

Social scientists clearly need to do a better job of communicating with the agricultural scientists and within the social sciences. Surprisingly, the rural social sciences have done far too little in the way of joint initiatives to build better relationships among themselves. This situation must change on campuses, in government agencies, and within various institutions.

NOTE

1. Larry J. Connor is a professor of Agricultural Economics at Michigan State University. Comments and suggestions of the following individuals are gratefully acknowledged: Consultants—Peggy Bartlett, Sue S. Coates, Don Paarlberg, Glen Taggart, and Thomas Wessell; Michigan State University colleagues—James T. Bonnen, Warren Cohen, Frank A. Fear, James R. Fischer, Carl Liedholm, Warren Samuels, Michael Schecter, and Scott Whiteford.

REFERENCES

American Agricultural Economics Association. 1986. Critical issues facing agricultural America for the 21st century: A statement of economic research and education issues identified by agricultural economists. Ames: Iowa State University, Heady Hall.

Bonnen, James. T. 1988. Improving the socioeconomic data base. In *Agriculture and rural areas approaching the 21st century: Challenges for agricultural economics*. Edited by R. J. Hildreth, Kathryn L. Lipton, Kenneth C. Clayton, Carl C. O'Connor, 452–83. Ames: Iowa State University Press.

Harsh, S. B., L. J. Connor, and G. D. Schwab. 1981. *Managing the farm business*. Englewood Cliffs, N.J.: Prentice Hall, Inc.

Johnson, Glenn L. 1984. *Academia needs a new covenant for serving agriculture*. Mississippi State: Mississippi State University, Mississippi Agricultural & Forestry Experiment Station. Special publication, July.

———1986. *Research methodology for economists—Philosophy and practice*. New York: Macmillan and Co.

———1987. Contributions of the rural social sciences to improvements in the food, fiber, and forestry systems; rural development; and related aspects of general welfare. In *Proceedings of the Eighteenth West Indies Agricultural Economics Conference*. St. Augustine, Trinidad, West Indies: The University of the West Indies, Dept. of Agricultural Economics & Farm Management.

Klonglan, G. E. 1986. National priorities for rural sociology research. *The Rural Sociologist* 6, no. 6: 501–6.

Rauch, Jonathan. 1987. Drug on the market. *National Journal* no. 14: 818–21.

OTHER REFERENCES USED BUT NOT SPECIFICALLY CITED

Bonnen, James T. 1986. A century of science in agriculture. Fellows lecture to the American Agricultural Economics Association meeting, 29 July, Reno, Nevada.

Busch, Lawrence, and William B. Lacy. 1983. *Science agriculture, and the politics of research*. Boulder, Colo.: Westview Press.

———, eds. 1986. *The agricultural scientific enterprise—A system in transition*. Boulder, Colo.: Westview Press.

Buttel, Frederick H. 1985. The land-grant system: A sociological perspective on value conflicts and ethical values. *Agriculture and Human Values* (Spring): 78–95.

———. 1986. Biotechnology and public agricultural research policy. In *Agricultural science policy in transition*. Edited by V. J. Rhodes, 123–56. Bethesda, Md.: Agricultural Research Institute.

Deavers, K. L. 1980. Social science contributions to rural development policy in the 1980s. *American Journal of Agricultural Economics* 62:1021–26.

Kamarck, Andrew M. 1983. *Economics and the real world*. Philadelphia: University of Pennsylvania Press.

Kirkendall, Richard S. See Part I, Chapter 2, this volume.

Lindblom, Charles E., and David K. Cohen. 1979. *Usable knowledge: Social science and social problem solving*. New Haven, Conn.: Yale University Press.

MacRae, Duncan, Jr.. 1976. *The social function of social science*. New Haven, Conn., and London: Yale University Press.

Mayer, Andre, and Jean Mayer. 1974. Agriculture, the island empire. *Daedalus* (Summer): 97–115.

Ruttan, Vernon M. 1982. *Agricultural research policy*. Minneapolis: University of Minnesota Press.

———. 1986. *Cultural endowments and economic development: What can we learn from anything?* Economics Development Center bulletin 86–7. St. Paul: University of Minnesota.

Schuh, G. Edward. 1986. Revitalizing land grant universities. *Choices: The Magazine of Food, Farm and Resource Issues* (2d qtr.): 6–11.

U.S. Congress. 1986. *Technology, public policy, and the changing structure of American agriculture*, Office of Technology Assessment, Washington, D.C.

CHAPTER 4

FROM THE PERSPECTIVE OF RESEARCH ADMINISTRATION

H. O. Kunkel[1]

INTRODUCTION

The perspective of the research administration should not differ much from that of the social scientist. Yet, administrations are more subject to encounters with the constraints of funding agencies, expressions of the clientele who support the institution in the legislatures and the Congress, the expectations of commodity and other groups who take proprietary views of the research institution, the aspirations of the scientists, the understanding of administrators who stand above the research administration—presidents, chancellors, regents—and of advisory councils, and the vision of research administrations themselves. There are also short-term crises and questions such as, "What have you done for us today?"

We sense that the research administration ought to have the institutional responsibility for development of the long-term vision, that is, the strategic perspective and its articulation in persuasive terms. To be sure, the administration should provide the context in which the short-term crises and the external constraints can be handled. But the agricultural research administrator has to lead toward a strategic plan, which must somehow hang on some relevant "nails" that funders can understand, relevant points that administrators of the institution can understand, and relevant objectives for the internal guidance of the research staff. Administration, thus, has to deal with the awkward position of having to filter the priorities of legislators, clientele, and others, priorities that may be different from those of the faculty and staff. The administrator has the responsibility to reconcile the differences and bring accommodation, if not congruence, to the concepts and commitments of the research staff and the requests for public support. In the process, one may begin to feel that the vision of an administrator is too short-termed, too tactical.

Of course, research administration is generally not a single-person job; administration today is likely to be corporate or plural. The advice of staff and disciplinary instincts of various kinds are incorporated into administration. But, the general concerns stated in this paper will surely color the perspective of administration, whatever its form.

PERFORMANCE OF SOCIAL SCIENCES

It is clear that the basic scientific quality of social sciences has improved dramatically in the past decade. Significant amounts of excellent scholarship have accumulated. There is a growing, general recognition that economics and economists, sociology and sociologists, home economics and human ecologists, and, in fact, a whole array of other social sciences and their scholars will contribute even more significantly to the knowledge base and to the solution of important problems. The scientific sophistication of the social sciences is nowhere near its limits. Self-evaluations by social scientists, however, raise fundamental questions: What are the adequacies of the basic science and theoretical foundations? What additional aspects of the basic social sciences, particularly economics, sociology, and psychology, require assessment and use in the rural social sciences? What is the fundamental theory to solve the problem? And, what can be the contributions of philosophy, applied ethics, political science, history, anthropology, and systems science to the rural social sciences?

Sociology, for example, has had an excellent record of doing useful things in group and individual development, community development, and the like, but these may be less important today. Tomorrow, the challenges will be broad and unbounded. There are now emerging questions on the social impacts of technologies in agriculture, of food processing and the marketplace, of the structure of agriculture and further decisions regarding biotechnology, and even of the differences in the goals and values held by different kinds of scientists in the agricultural research institution. A central issue is the industrialization of agriculture. Similarly, the interaction between society and the environment provides issues that have become important. A sociology of agriculture requires construction. Research and scholarly debate should touch on not only the ideologies, the agendas, and the roles in agriculture, but it is critically necessary that they go beyond conventional boundaries.

Born of the need to provide guidance and put sense into the complexities of agricultural production and marketing, agricultural economics has contributed to both policy and innovations in human institutions. Agricultural economists have conceived and described the elements of inputs in a production process: technology, institutional improvements, human capital, and biological and physical inputs and their interrelationships (Ruttan 1984). They built a strong profession around an empirical tradition.

Today, we see the need to turn again to the descriptive, empirical base of agricultural economics, drawing, of course, on the basic science of economics. Technology may be outstripping human institutions. International settings, environmental quality, utility, human health and well-being, racial and sexual inequality, and other quality issues place new imperatives on economics. The tractors, the systems of plant protection, and the management used today, as well as the meat products and the breads appearing in the marketplace today are not the same as they were ten years ago. These are evolving issues that require description beyond quantitative technique. They require the kind of attention that, among economists, only agricultural economists will likely provide.

Home economics has captured the elements of both the natural sciences (nutrition, textile science, etc.) and the social sciences, including psychology, sociology, and economics, as well as human development and family economics. It has done so with particular sensitivity to the problems of people (see Deacon and Huffman 1986). Colleges of home economics, more so than colleges of agriculture, have been forced to deal with the implications of technological development. Through their work with individuals and families, they have directly encountered the problems and crises of community life and rural America. They have had to relate to the cultural and social aspects of eating and how that links to nutrition. Home economists, more than the rest of us, have visualized how consumers enter the marketplace. Colleges of home economics have positioned themselves to deal with the complexities of rural issues by building multidisciplinary faculties. But home economists, too, must look to even wider horizons and seek improvement of their scientific quality, while the required social science base is still developing.

The definition or redefinition of problems, especially the nagging problems, are particular issues of concern to research administrations:

- What, for example, is rural America? What will be its significant elements in the future? If we had truly known the significant issues in the past, would rural America have suffered as much in recent years?

- Many still look at the decentralized market as the economic model for agriculture. Now there are all sorts of institutional arrangements, "deals cut," international agreements, and the like that deny the decentralized market to agriculture. The agricultural market is a structured system, a nonhomogeneous process, the kinetics of which require redefinition.

- Social sciences in recent years appear to focus on those problems in which quantitative techniques are dominant. The trend has been useful, particularly at the microlevel, but the need today is to be useful in the broader policy issues. Descriptions of utility values—why people farm, why people live in rural areas where the services are less than they could gain elsewhere, the effects of agricultural and food technology on humans—may be larger issues in the future. It is not that quantitative methods are not important to the discipline, but another balance may be required.

- The agricultural research establishment is in the business of creating technological opportunities. No one can evaluate better the possibilities and probabilities in the creation of new technology and inherent product quality than the biological/physical scientists concerned. No one else really has that capacity. But, such scientists may be the least capable of evaluating the human values: the impacts on people and the environment, and other negative externalities resulting from the development and adoption of new technologies.

Social sciences have unique implications in agricultural research institutions. They are particularly important in the universities. Technological advance is the mirror of research in all research institutions, but the universities have special responsibilities for consideration of the direction, management, and implications of technological advance. The social sciences have a range of roles for which only they may have the conceptual bases and frameworks, but many of these roles are yet to be adequately undertaken. Obviously, the need for social sciences grows.

ADMINISTRATIVE ISSUES

There may be, on the surface, distinctive problems in managing the work of social sciences in an agenda for the agricultural sciences. There may be problems of integrating the work of social sciences with the work in other areas. There seem to be differences in perspective. There are problems of mutual understandings.

There are differences, also, in expectations of what the social sciences can do as compared to the biological and physical sciences. The predictabilities and the coefficients of variation in the social sciences are large in some instances, and so are the predictabilities of meteorology and climatic studies, the windblown migrations of plant-disease organisms, the response of insects to controls as resistance to insecticides grows, or the relationship of diet to cancer, all of which have resonance in food and agriculture and agricultural research institutions.

Are the social sciences, then, truly different from the hard sciences? Are they more sensitive, more political, more subject to bias, more controversial? My guess is that they are not. There are as much sensitivity and controversy surrounding the results of the experimental and natural sciences. If there are differences, they likely have more to do with the individuals and the problem of the moment than the nature of the sciences.

Boulding (1980) has reminded us that technology can best be applied when there is fundamental understanding. Experimental or observational sciences are intellectually more satisfying when they can be carried out with precision. One can be fairly "secure" in the simpler results of chemistry, sociology, physics, and economics. By contrast, our knowledge of individual human and group behavior and the fundamental particles of matter and molecular genetics is "insecure." The great complexity of the human brain and body and of individual and group human behavior and the difficulties in observing them without influencing them by becoming part of them makes the social sciences more difficult than the simpler biological and physical sciences. Sciences dealing with rapidly adapting biological systems—the human physiology and chronic disease, and climate—may seem more "secure" than those dealing with social systems—national and global economies, and political processes—only because we fail to look at their less secure areas. Yet "less secure" sciences are essential parts of agricultural research. Both the "secure" and "less secure" parts of the social sciences are critical for the whole continuum of agricultural research from the simple to the complex and, hence, from the "secure" to the "less secure."

But, the administrative management of social sciences may yet have distinctive features, some of which derive from the special insights and skills that social sciences bring to research, and some of which relate to what might be termed the "sociology" of the agricultural sciences.

There are issues in the reward system for research scientists. The current research institutions, and the administrators of them as well, have created a market for positivistic research. There has been far less concern with the need to create a market for consideration of values and morals. As a result, quite understandably, social scientists have often tried to emulate the physical scientists. They have seen that it is the more positivistic research that gets rewarded. Some rural social scientists have been captured by the tools of positivism. They seek larger computers, produce more "squiggles," build more models.

There are problems, also, in the reward system for engaging in interdisciplinary work. Two decades ago, Castle (1970) noted that society has permitted and encouraged universities and other social-research institutions to engage in "basic" or "pure" research as one of their traditional and autonomous functions. Castle argued that administrators will ignore this at their peril. The definition of important problems that are researchable calls for first-rate minds who will rebel at inappropriate formulation of the problem. But the issue remains that the multidisciplinary researches—subject-matter and problem-solving research —make important uses of the social sciences. The traditional peer-driven reward system, which has emerged in a logical outflow from the very effectiveness of disciplinary research of the past, is not given to encouraging multidisciplinary research. Thus, the administrator is confronted with a constraint that he/she may not really control.

Much of agricultural science (and also rural social science) operates in a disciplinarian ambience fostered by the conventional and evolving academic structure, peer evaluation, and the indepth education required for research-oriented degrees (see Connor, Part V, Chapter 3). Substantial amounts of disciplinary research, particularly in the life sciences, are increasingly embedded in the multidisciplinary departments of the colleges of agriculture, home economics, natural resources, and veterinary medicine. As a result, a land-grant university may depend on the component units of its agricultural and kindred colleges for its focus on botany, genetics, physiology, nutrition, ecology, biochemistry, or statistics. The issues are qualitatively similar for the social sciences. The basic sciences feeding the rural social sciences are located largely outside of the agricultural and kindred colleges; they are essentially located in traditional settings of the university. But statistical and econometric analyses and other quantitative aspects can take on the colors of disciplines caught up in the belief that academic excellence lies mainly in disciplinary research, even though they are in a multidisciplinary rural social science department. Subsets of social scientists with different theoretical literatures—resource economics, finance, consumer behavior, industrial structures—may behave similarly.

Inexorably, agricultural and rural social sciences are increasingly evaluated on the bases of contributions to disciplinary knowledge and to subject-matter knowledge pointing to new policy, technology, and solution of problems. The dilemma created by the dichotomy of expectations is a significant problem for evaluation of agricultural and kindred scientists at all levels of the university and the scientific community.

The general, desired model would seem to be that the disciplinary sciences be set somehow in a hierarchical arrangement which would allow communication from the relevant disciplines through subject-matter research into problem solving and, in turn, feed back through the system. Administrators have a responsibility for facilitating the access that social scientists need to those outside the colleges of home economics, agriculture, and natural resources, or the agricultural research institution, without casting aside the component staffs of the college. The linkages to other disciplines, including the mother disciplines of statistics, economics, sociology, history, geography, political science, and philosophy, are essential for the vitality of institutions and the agendas of the relevant social sciences.

New divisions of the faculty to work on "lines" of research (subject-matter and problem-solving research) as well as disciplinary problems also are absolutes for the future. That will require groups of scientists from different, once foreign, disciplines working together. And, that obviously includes mixed social science-biophysical science teams as well as teams of wider ranges of social sciences and humanities. Also, there are needs for accelerating the research process; teams of scientists that hold allegiance to the same discipline but provide different skills or interests may be needed to speed the work. Teams are common for work in the physical sciences and are increasingly seen in the biological sciences. It has not been easy to bring together research teams in the social sciences, in part because such operational modes seem alien to those scientists who still tend to work in individualistic settings.

Disciplinary research, particularly that found in traditional universities, requires a minimum of administration (Johnson 1986, 197). The disciplines themselves set the logic and standards for research, and the requirement for direction of the research is minimal. Administrations are uncomplicated; peer administration and review are common. The support base for the research operation is largely external grants. Individualism is dominant, and collective agreement is often difficult to achieve.

Subject-matter researches, relevant to real-world problems and decision making, are much more difficult to administer. Administrations are called for that can overcome disciplinary barriers and traditional structures that constrain important new multidisciplinary synthesis and integrative scholarship and the introduction of nontraditional disciplines. New institutional arrangements and organizations—interdisciplinary models, research institutes, stratified administrative structures, fundings for multidisciplinary efforts, budgetary priorities—have been tested and work if the reward system is adjusted to conform to the task, the unit is removed from the academic setting, or the needed special administrative momentum does not wane. However, in the academic institution, with existent inflexibilities and a certain inertia in funding, such arrangements may be limited in what they can do. The crucial unit is the conventional multidisciplinary department, which, in turn, requires a good deal more cooperation than is needed for a disciplinary department.

The multidisciplinary social science department requires its scientists to be up-to-date for analyses of policy and institutional choices, of rational choices by consumers, and for building management systems. Keeping the faculty holistic in its thinking is expensive. In order to gain the needed capability of analysis, it is required that individual faculty members become sensitive to other disciplines or, alternatively, physically place staff from other disciplines in the department. Despite the apparent constraints related to organization and, perhaps, traditional staffing, the potential for multidisciplinary research and interdisciplinary communication appears to be gaining. The reasons appear to be: the evolution of the integrative and system sciences, the infusion of powerful new scientific tools into a number of departments, and the increased occurrence of informal, on-campus networking among scientists of different disciplines. But, given the fact that scientists' values and personalities intrude into research strategies, the future of social science research may rest, not on administration, but on scientists' intellectual vision and philosophical awareness which go beyond the traditional disciplinary limits.

Those administrators who are not social scientists, and perhaps some who are, often regard the goals of the social scientists and of the physical/biological scientists in agriculture as coincident or, at least, that they ought to be. For most of the history of the agricultural sciences, which reaches back to the early days of agricultural chemistry, the theories of agricultural science have been structured on preconceived and changing human goals and objectives (Krohn and Schafer 1976). Agricultural chemistry and biology are most often carried out not to provide insight into *why* agriculture functions, but *how it ought to* function. Thus, agricultural chemistry and biology become a social science operating with the methods of natural science. The instinctive expectations in such an operative mode is that social sciences per se should serve the same purpose. This view sees the natural science model and the social science model as but analogues of each other, both creative of new methods and insight.

But analyses—be they of social institutions and organizations, of resources, of impacts of technology, or of human implications—tend to be critical. Thus, there is a tendency to label all social scientists as critics. This is particularly true of the image of those scientists generally tangential to the usual agricultural research establishment—anthropologists, political scientists, historians, ethicists—but economists and sociologists may also regard themselves as mainly critics as they analyze the effects of policy, technology, and the political economy. The question is: How can critical investigations be legitimized in colleges of agriculture when such colleges have always generally provided new things rather than criticism for clientele? But it must be done. If not, perhaps the college of agriculture should no longer be the "center" of the agricultural research world.

WORK OF THE SOCIAL SCIENCES

Research institutions and administrations are having to grapple with issues that were largely ignored a decade ago. Not only are there deepening concerns about the vitality of rural America and the viabilities of agriculture and its structure, but there also are the looming aspects of international trade, externalities, the changing boundaries of the research properly assigned to the private and public sectors, and the marketplace, as well as public policy in agriculture. Also, research institutions are having to grapple with these issues using old sets of institutions and, perhaps, old sets of tools. Bonnen (1986, 1077) writes about a now generally accepted perception: The agenda of issues in agriculture today strongly suggests that stronger social sciences are needed. Needs are growing for new institutions or modifications of the old, the development and transfer of technologies, for resolutions of ethical problems, and in the creation of new capital.

Considerable discussion has occurred during the past few years relative to priorities in social science research. Such dialogue has occurred among the leadership of the relevant social sciences, directors and deans, and the Joint Council on Food and Agricultural Sciences, and in hearings of the Congress (see Connor, Part V, Chapter 3). The stated needs for research include efforts to strengthen the rural family and the community economic base. They include analyses of family stress factors, identification and expansion of economic alternatives and opportunities, developments in small-scale and low-input agriculture, and management of the new technologies. They include research designed to deal with the problems of the increasing number of rural and agricultural families facing economic and social crises. Priorities emphasize future needs for human capital in rural America, the development of jobs, and population demographics. They look to strengthening the international competitiveness of rural industries, sources of rural capital, and organization and finance of rural governments, as well as the development of community leadership.

Priorities are stated also for technology assessment: new knowledge on the impact of technological and economic transitions in agriculture, the necessary databases, and strategies for coping with and monitoring the important changes in rural life. They would focus on the interdependence of farms, of agricultural and nonagricultural systems, and of community organization and the larger society. The issues of individual well-being as related to economic policy—emotional distress, decision making, integrity of the family, health and aspirations of families—are matters of special concern to home economics administrators.

These concerns are surely the basic business of social sciences. But, society's support of social sciences' research and education hinges on their contributions to the well-being of society. Serious questions arise with the enormous success of agricultural production, the expanded matrix of society's value systems, and the linkages of issues of science, technology, and society. The ultimate defense for support hangs on our abilities to understand these linkages and deploy the necessary tools to mitigate effects and solve crises.

It is imperative that priorities be set for a *national* agenda for the social sciences. To do so would tell supporters of social science—administrators, funders, legislatures, and the Congress—what is needed, what is missing in the current effort, and what should have added support.

From the perspective of research administration, we must see that everybody's institution is different. The system is not monolithic. Priorities differ for each institution. Special values lie in the multiplicity of institutions conducting research.

Also, it seems to me that the priorities listed above, though comprehensive, are not all-inclusive. The lack of attention of social scientists, other than home economists, to certain issues relating to consumer-food issues is surprising. For example, the pattern of consumption of certain agricultural products is changing substantially in a U.S. population caught up in an overriding flood of "nutritional" information. We use policy principally in the context of agricultural production and the marketing of commodities. However, the use of policy through the marketplace and its attendant advertising also poses a powerful mechanism for agriculture and agricultural science, for the nutrition and welfare of the people, and for the economic base of the community. The marketplace is a harsh, inhuman institutional form, yet with appropriate attention, we can co-opt it, cooperate with it, give it grist for its mill, or provide consumers with the ways to interpret it. We cannot ignore it.

Almost every state agricultural experiment station is now working on the possibilities of value-added aspects of agriculture. Clearly, much of the success of such research will reside in technological research. But, like research on biotechnology, value-adding studies are researches that can soon get ahead of themselves unless we know more about the institutions in which the system is operative. It is easier to modify the product than to reset the production operation. Bringing in communication with the consumer is better than not doing so, because one can see what works and what doesn't. If product design/production/processing/marketing/consumption can be seen as a feedback loop, many stresses on agriculture can be reduced.

There are deep roots in our culture that allow Americans to be experimental. We are a pluralistic nation. Unlike other cultures where the household has enormous power in setting values, the family influence on values appears to be waning or, at least, taking on differing forms. The market will run into lobbies, groups with vested interests, entrepreneurs who are convinced their products will promote greater health, critics, and zealots. Markets are increasingly impacted by many elements in our environment.

We noted earlier that the working environment of the social sciences may see change that will be of great interest to research administrations. Bonnen (1986) states an issue as follows: To practice at the cutting edge of almost any discipline today, requires not only a command of the discipline but also of major components of knowledge from related disciplines well beyond mathematics and statistics. As science grows more interactive, a growing proportion of disciplinary research takes us through multiple disciplines and techniques. To practice a discipline today one must increasingly collaborate with other disciplines. Even as biochemistry has penetrated the ranges of agricultural biology, one or more aspects of the social sciences may become a cohesive factor in a lot of agricultural research.

The center of gravity of research related to agriculture, be it in the social sciences or in the physical and biological sciences, will move toward more integrative scholarship. Call it the systems approach to solving problems, systemics, or whatever, the move may be embodied in the curricula and courses of the academic arena as much as in research thought and in research institutions per se. The reasons for that seem clear. Academic programs in colleges of agriculture have been, for decades, culturally oriented to farming. They took students whose experiences and perceptions were largely conditioned by life on the farm and the rural home. Now the situation has changed. Students with those special integrative abilities, honed by agricultural and rural environment during their precollege days, have greatly diminished nationally and have disappeared in many areas. The rural social sciences must find their new cohorts among students of other demographic origins who initially will have to learn about the many disciplinary dimensions of the rural and agricultural systems in which they will work. Although the change may prove to be an advantage, it is something both scientists and administrators should think about.

Two final statements of caution may be in order: First, the agricultural establishment has generally moved on the signal of science that derives from the notion that science is impervious to politics. But the truth is complicated. Science can be co-opted by any group. It is an instrument, and it can be the voice of anybody. If follows that all who set the course of science—scientists and critics—have significant responsibilities to society. This may have to be the ultimate perception of research administrators. And that, of course, will bother many of us. Second, the struggle that social sciences will wage with a research administration may not be just for greater understanding of the social sciences by the administration, but that very understanding may create greater expectations of the social sciences than they are prepared to deliver. The demands for application of the works of social scientists have an immediacy that can be disquieting to the scholar.

NOTE

1. H. O. Kunkel is a professor of Life Sciences and a former dean of the College of Agriculture, Texas A & M University. The substantial inputs of consultants John E. Lee, John W. Mellor, Barbara Stowe, Ken P. Wilkinson, and Daniel I. Padberg are gratefully acknowledged by Dr. Kunkel.

REFERENCES

Bonnen, James T. 1986. A century of science in agriculture: Lessons for science policy. Fellows lecture to the American Agricultural Economics Association meeting, 29 July, Reno, Nevada.

Boulding, Kenneth. 1980. Science—Our common heritage. *Science* 207:831.

Castle, Emery N. 1970. Priorities in agricultural economics for the 1970s. *American Journal of Agricultural Economics* 52, no. 5 (December): 831–40.

Deacon, Ruth E., and Wallace E. Huffman, eds. 1986. *Human resources research 1887–1987, proceedings.* Ames: Iowa State University, College of Home Economics.

Johnson, Glenn L. 1986. *Research methodology for economists: Philosophy and practice*. New York: Macmillan Publishing Co.

Krohn, W., and W. Schafer. 1976. The origins and structure of agricultural chemistry. In *Perspectives on the emergences of scientific disciplines*. Edited by G. Lemaine, R. Macleod, M. Mulkay, and P. Weinert, 27–52. The Hague: Mouton; Chicago: Aldine.

Ruttan, Vernon W. 1984. Models in agricultural development. In *Agricultural development in the Third World.* Edited by C. K. Eicher and J. M. Staatz, 45. Baltimore: Johns Hopkins University Press.

CHAPTER 5

FUNDING SOCIAL SCIENCE RESEARCH: THE PROBLEM OF PRIORITIES[1]

Richard G. Stuby[2]

INTRODUCTION

Creating and promoting federal funding have become increasingly important activities for those who manage agricultural research. The traditional sources of public funding, including, most notably, Hatch Act formula funds to the state agricultural experiment station system, have not kept pace with changing research needs or inflation. Increasingly, representatives of the experiment stations, under their chartered Experiment Station Committee on Organization and Policy (ESCOP), have engaged in collective activity to promote and protect federal research funding. In concert with the activities of the Joint Council on Food and Agricultural Sciences, they have attempted to focus requests for both ongoing and new research in a system of priorities.

The social sciences dealing with agriculture and rural issues have historically been a minor part of the agricultural research system. Interestingly, in the latter part of the twentieth century, the matrix of problems affecting both agriculture and rural people continues to shift toward social, economic, and environmental issues. That is to say, toward "people problems," not production problems. The research-funding matrix has not yet perceptibly shifted to support these research areas. At least part of the reason for this lies in the nature of the funding process as it is affected by the prioritization of research within the system.

THE FUNDING PROCESS

The funding process referred to here is the totality of the lengthy and torturous activities required to assemble budget requests in the U.S. Department of Agriculture (USDA) and forward them to the Congress for appropriations. There are many elements to this complex process, but primarily there are two intermeshing sets of ideas that directly affect the outcome in general and have particular consequences for social science. These sets of ideas are loosely identified as the *rational* and the *political*. They are not easily separated, but it is important to understand each of them individually as well as the interplay between them.

Funding for all scientific research is premised on justifications that must, at the minimum, have the appearance of reason or rationality. The very nature of empirical, positivistic science demands rationality, and we comply because we are scientists. In the experiment station system, one way to demonstrate compliance with reason is through an exercise called "priority setting." Research managers in several different organizational structures reason together, assumedly under the canons of logic and the ethics of fairness. Emerging from this action is a list of items called "priorities" that are advocated and recommended to the USDA budget process and to the Congress.

Unfortunately for the rural social sciences, however, the emergent priority lists seldom have any social science research at the top of the list where the dollars are hung. Thus, on occasion, one hears the complaint that there is a general bias against social science within the state agricultural experiment station system. Whatever the truth here, it is nonproductive and potentially self-destructive for social scientists to argue the ad hominem case. There are alternative explanations. For example, there are some characteristics of the current priority-setting mechanisms that create inherent, even if unintended, biases against social science. Since these characteristics can be changed, a discussion of them may provide a starting point for moving toward a more equitable funding process.

PRIORITY SETTING

Priority setting is a legitimate part of positivistic, rationalistic science and management. But not all priority setting is rational or positivistic. Nearly any list of items can be arbitrarily hammered into an ordinally fixed set called "priorities." Nearly any person or group can pigeon-hole a list of items.

In democratic political systems, priorities are debated and then ordered according to majority rule. However, in the final analysis, democratic political process demands only representation, not enlightenment, and the weight of debate does not necessarily condition the vote. Political allocation processes shield all sorts of preferences and motives. Within the realm of public policy then, *it is a formidable task to prioritize within the canons of logic and the ethics of fairness.* Even without concern for individual "biases" and philosophical differences, there are generic, systemic problems to be solved. For example:

1. *Complex issues are difficult to prioritize, because it is difficult to reduce them to their elemental properties.* The more clearly a set of items can be defined, delimited, and specified, or reduced to their lowest common denominator, the easier it is to order them in a set. Positivism tends toward reductionism. In particular, a list with both complex and simple items on it often defies rational prioritization.

   This obviously works against any science that deals with complex, system-level, multifactor, real-time issues. Not only does it work against social science, but also against all software-driven, system-oriented sciences. If the complex, interactive, simultaneous nature of the social science subject matter is reduced to its elemental properties, it is often judged to be trivial. We then hear, "Everyone knows that!" On the other hand, if the same subject matter is presented in its systemic totality and complexity, it is said to be "dismally esoteric" and "unresearchable." This "lose/lose" proposition is the result of a particular set of assumptions and a particular methodology, namely reductionism, deeply embedded in our science establishment and all too casually invoked in our priority-setting activities.

2. *Ideally, priorities should be ordered along some underlying dimension, construct, theory, or objective function.* Ideally, the underlying construct should have the characteristic called "unidimensionality." To the extent that there is a single underlying dimension or "factor," the ordinal positioning of items is facilitated.

   The unidimensionality underlying the setting of agricultural research priorities is suspect. There is little commonality or theme among candidate items other than the fact that they all represent activities currently ensconced in the experiment station system. There are vague references to scientific need, economic feasibility, or social importance, but these underlying dimensions are never made explicit, never given empirical weight, and never justified in their own right. One can assume that each person who rates the items does invoke some, or all, of these underlying dimensions, but the outcomes do not indicate whether they all do it in the same way or by the same set of rules.

Thus, even within the realm of rational decision processes, social science has not fared well. This is further compounded by the other set of problems deriving from the establishment of priorities through open, pluralistic, democratic means.

1. *Those who do the priority setting are seldom neutral brokers guided only by reason and logic.* If they were, they probably would not have ascended to the status of "priority setter." Inherently, legitimately, and of necessity, based on the authority of their positions, they have their own agendas, their own vested interests, their own constituencies. They are explicitly empowered to lend voice to those constituencies, interests, and agendas. When participating in public discussions, they are not free from their empowerment. Voice, as well as reason, affects their decisions.

   The problem with social sciences in the experiment station system may well be more the lack of voice than the lack of reason. It is self-serving and excessively smug to think of vested interests, constituencies, and ambitions as opposing reason. The conflict *between* the "politics" and "reason" is not important. However, the conflict *across* the competing voices of the various interests, constituencies, and ambitions is important, and this is the arena where the battle is fought. Most social sciences lack the interests, constituencies, and ambitions that give them voice. This lack of voice is reflected in priority-setting outcomes and, in turn, lack of funding.

2. Those same interests and constituencies that give voice also demand accountability. Because accountability is more easily accomplished with highly tangible and visible products or artifacts, *items that have tangibility are greatly preferred to those that do not.* Mere knowledge or, even worse, "information" is not as usable for accountability purposes as a technological product. One "widget" is worth several thousand pieces of wisdom. Thus, those research activities that result in technology or the potential, therefore, are treated with greater respect than those which do not. Witness the current emphasis on the biological sciences to justify new research that will produce a "biotechnology."

   Social science does not generally produce a tangible technological product, at least not one that promises profitable marketability within the private economic sector. Accountability for its results and performance is difficult to establish. Research managers, particularly those involved in priority-setting activities, generally are reluctant to support research that has a low accountability profile. Risk aversion dictates the subordination of such research in priority lists.

Thus, there are four factors that work against social science in the process of setting priorities for experiment station research. They are: (1) *simplicity*, (2) *dimensionality*, (3) *voice*, and (4) *tangibility*.

"Water quality" has emerged as a high priority for experiment station research in recent years because it benefits from the operational characteristics of the priority process. It appears to fit into a single dimension, even though we know that water-quality issues touch across several dimensions. It neatly encapsulates a complex conglomeration of ideas into a simple notion. The image of "cool, clear water" is something everyone can relate to and no one can oppose. It is tangible. It has voice.

The underlying construct or rationale for many social science issues is not as easily articulated. Contrast water quality with a once popular social science area, "life quality." The latter loses on simplicity, unidimensionality, and tangibility, and currently is not part of the political voice.

The situation would be bleak indeed if the current priority-setting exercises did not have to face a more gestalt reality. Some issues will not go away, regardless of their ordinal placement on the priority list. A germane example is found in the Joint Council report (1987) on priorities for agricultural research in fiscal year 1989. This report has three major sections listed as "significant agricultural issues impacting society." Specifically, they suggest research to: *enhance competitiveness and profitability, increase family economic strength, and revitalize rural America.* Note that these issues are complex, multidimensional, intangible, and, with the exception of competitiveness, currently lack voice in the experiment station system.

However, in the ensuing budget recommendations from ESCOP and the Division of Agriculture, National Association of State Universities and Land Grant Colleges (NASULGC), they were not listed as "priorities," but as "crosscutting issues." The Joint Council report thus defines *two sets of priorities*. One set fits the simple, tangible, unidimensional, with-voice model. The other fits the complex, intangible, multidimensional, without-voice model. There is nothing wrong with admitting this and, indeed, the Joint Council is to be commended for recognizing and publicizing the fact. The critical issue for social science is that the funding recommendations which emerged were assigned to the "priorities" and the "crosscuts" got lost in the shuffle.[3] *Because competitiveness, rural revitalization, and family well-being are complex, multidimensional, intangible, and without vested constituency, they were deflected into a different funding game*. Because the priority process declared two lists, the system had the opportunity to ignore one and fund the other. Social science got frozen out in the process.[4]

One can conclude that the current priority-setting process is not working well for the social sciences. To compensate for this will require some reorganization, adjustment, and reorientation. Part of the adjustment must come in terms of the procedures that determine research priorities, and part must come from action by the rural social sciences.

CHANGES IN PROCEDURES

Both ESCOP and Joint Council deliberations over research priorities have begun to bog down. Positions have become fixed. The decision process has begun to achieve equilibrium and homeostasis; or in more common terms, it has gone into "gridlock." The assumption that the top-priority items will be gratuitously funded by the Congress has not been fulfilled. This has halted the process of "serial equity," in which items float up the list and get funded in due time. Thus, it seems appropriate to suggest that funding strategies depart from the notion of serial priorities to a broader front of critical issues, many of which are tightly interrelated. If a matrix of priorities and crosscutting issues is used, it is imperative that the funding of the crosscutting issues is made explicit.

One way to broaden the front of critical issues is to recognize the unique problems of the systems sciences, including the rural social sciences. The complexity of systems, particularly large-scale, real-world, real-time systems, such as rural economies, weather patterns, and ground-water systems, does not allow them to be easily fractionated and apportioned into "researchable problems." *The problems are problems of the system itself, not its reducible components*. The criteria for weighing the import of these problems cannot be the same as those for weighing laboratory research.

The underlying dimension to which priorities are assigned should be explicitly stated. Without such consideration, emerging priorities are simply an opinion poll across highly selected samples of research administrators. While their opinions are not without merit, there is considerable question as to the congruence of their opinions with those of research administrators in other agencies, in other educational and research institutions, and with members of the Congress. There is a time to listen as well as a time to give voice.

The Joint Council, the ESCOP Planning Subcommittee, and all other groups involved in priority setting need to explore new methods for actuating this important process. Tremendous advances in decision theory, its associated statistical techniques, and computer-based decision support systems, have been produced in the past five to seven years. They offer a wide variety of methods dedicated to explicit, rational, and equitable decision making and planning. Many of these have been created and produced by some of our best social scientists. The best products of the social sciences need to be turned toward the support for them.

WHAT CAN THE SOCIAL SCIENCES DO?

Regardless of the characteristics of the priority-setting process, the social science enterprises within the agricultural experiment station system have the responsibility to cultivate both the tangibility of their research and the voice that speaks for it. To some extent, they have recognized their lack of voice in the councils that set priorities and promote funding. They have sought advice, begged sympathy, and argued the justness of their cause. They have not been ignored. Yet it is equally true that they have not yet been heavily endowed.

For over a period of four years now, rural sociologists, agricultural economists, and family-studies researchers have collaborated to gain voice in the priority-setting activities of ESCOP. The result of this effort was the formation of the ESCOP *Task Force on Agriculture and Community Viability*, which is in the final stages of producing a formal report outlining a research agenda that is highly relevant to current rural concerns (ESCOP). It is noteworthy that this effort is not driven by disciplinary interests; rather, it is driven by institutional and system-related interests and its strength lies in speaking to the system from within the system.

This is a start. What remains is to define more carefully a product in highly tangible terms and to generate an external as well as internal voice. There are tangible products to be delivered. For example, the social sciences have the technical capability to convert abstract analyses into symbols and graphics that people, both lay and professional, can understand. The social sciences have complex models and related databases that can be developed into information and decision-support systems for general use. There is a social science technology that emanates from basic social science research, but social science has not fully exploited it or turned it into justification for funding support.

One must recognize, however, that attention to the rational process is moot if it is not connected to the political process. Ultimately, unless NASULGC, the Department of Agriculture, the administration through the Office of Management and Budget (OMB), and the Congress itself respects and honors the planning activities of the experiment station system, there is some question as to how long anyone will have the will to continue the exercise.

Budget issues are critical at this time. Administration budget requests for the experiment stations have gone to

Congress for several years requesting only modest increases in a few categories, zero increases in many, and major reductions in many, particularly the special grants area. Modesty has not been rewarded. Perhaps it is time to revisit our voice in the congressional arena. Perhaps the time for bold initiatives is upon us. Social science, of all the sciences, should know most about this process. Again, we need to turn the best within our disciplines toward the generation of support for them.

This is a corporate task. There can be no room for disciplinary chauvinism. The Social Science Agricultural Agenda Project and its leadership are to be applauded for their bold efforts toward integration and improved understanding among the social sciences. But, understanding is not enough. We also need an action agenda. Such an agenda has been initiated through the experiment station system. It needs support. It offers hope. The Social Science Agricultural Agenda Project should add its strong voice and support to the task left before us.

NOTES

1. This paper is based on a speech delivered to the "Workshop: Social Science Research in the Agricultural Experiment Station System," held January 25–27, 1988, atthe Rosslyn Westpark Hotel, Arlington, Va. The workshop was sponsored by the Cooperative State Research Service and the North Central Agricultural Experiment Station Directors through Regional Project NCT–146, "Social Science Research Priorities."

2. Richard G. Stuby is a sociologist with the U.S. Department of Agriculture; Cooperative State Research Service; Natural Resources, Food and Social Sciences; Washington, D.C.

3. As a post mortem, in its fiscal year 1990 budget recommendations, NASULGC did include these three categories. The USDA did not support either "rural revitalization" (called "rural viability" in that document) or "family well-being" in the Administration's budget request to the Congress.

4. This is said with all due respect to current attention to competitiveness. The point is that it is assumed that the components of these large issues will appear in the itemized priority list but, for several of reasons given, they sometimes do not.

REFERENCES

Experiment Station Committee on Organization and Policy (ESCOP). 1988. *Agriculture and rural viability: A report of the Task Force on Agriculture and Community Viability*, No. 88–3, U.S. Dept. of Agriculture, Cooperative State Research Service.

Joint Council on Food and Agricultural Sciences. 1987. *Fiscal year 1989 priorities for research, extension, and higher education*, a report to the Secretary of Agriculture, June.

CHAPTER 6

PERSPECTIVES ON THE ADMINISTRATION AND FUNDING OF RURAL SOCIAL SCIENCE RESEARCH AND EXTENSION

R. J. Hildreth[1]

A note from the editors:

From his vantage point as managing director of the Farm Foundation, James Hildreth has accumulated much knowledge and has had many pertinent experiences. Using this knowledge and experience, he has written two papers, one about extension and another about research, that are useful in understanding the administration and funding of the rural social sciences in the USDA/land-grant system. Although clearly not written to be parts of a single presentation, these two papers are published here as two main, but rather independent, parts of this chapter.

AFTER 75 YEARS OF COOPERATIVE EXTENSION—WHAT IN THE WORLD IS AHEAD?[2]

The age of 75 is not old for an organization that has served society well. Consider Rasmussen's statement: "Extension has completed 75 years of service to the American people. It has carried the results of research from the land-grant universities directly to broad segments of the population. It has taught these people how to use this knowledge to improve their lives" (1989, 221). Thus, what will extension service be when it grows up? I attempt to answer this question by discussing the legitimacy and support of extension in a policy-education framework.

The policy-education framework consists of first identifying a set of issues which affect the future legitimacy and support of extension service. Alternative solutions to the issues are then presented. The likely consequences of each alternative are discussed without recommendations.

The legitimacy and the support of an organization are interrelated. No amount of wealth or power can keep an organization alive if there is widespread denial of the legitimacy of its role. The reason is that continued performance of any role requires an acceptance of legitimacy by those who are affected. For example, the ability of the extension service to receive public support depends upon the willingness of the citizens and legislators to provide funding. As Kenneth Boulding (1969) has stated, "To use a rather crude illustration, a bandit can take your money once but anyone who wants to take it every week either has to be a landlord or a tax collector."

POLICY ISSUES

The policy issues regarding extension service are interrelated and complex; issues are nested within issues. Decisions about them can seldom be made individually.

Mission

This issue can be stated in terms of whether or not extension service should have a sharply focused or a broad mission. Should extension respond to the educational needs of farmers or a broad range of citizens? Should extension's mission continue to be fraught with tensions, pluralisms, and ambiguities, or should it be more sharply focused, for example, on technology transfer in agriculture?

Relation to the Land-Grant University

At one time, much of the legitimacy and support for the land-grant university came from extension service, but times have changed. There are considerable unexploited opportunities for positive synergism between the functions of research, teaching, and extension. How can extension provide support for research and teaching, and how can these functions support extension?

While many land-grant universities are seeking to become "public research universities," there is a move toward disciplinary and basic research. The ability of extension service to influence the research agenda has decreased with these shifts. Many extension workers feel they do not have an adequate research base to provide education on the problems in their program areas, and many research workers feel that extension is irrelevant to their activities.

What should (or might) be the relationship of extension service with the various colleges: agriculture, engineering, home economics, arts and science, etc.? While extension is administered in the colleges of agriculture in most states, there are important interrelationships and connections with the other colleges.

The linkages between classroom instruction and extension service have not received much attention. There may be a number of unexplored opportunities for a closer relationship. It has often occurred to me that joint appointments between teaching and extension could lead to improvements in both fields. Very practical scheduling problems might be eased with new electronic technology; for example, AGSAT. There appears to be some growing interest in collaboration between community colleges and extension which might facilitate a useful interaction between teaching and extension.

Who Should Extension Service Serve?

In earlier years, the answer to this question was clear: Farmers and their families, who were all rural, had farms about the same size and, generally, had low income. In fact, one could read the Smith-Lever Act as establishing a "social program" to deal with low farm income and low-quality farm family life.

Now, the answer to the question is not as clear. First, competing sources of knowledge for agriculture are available from the private sector. The extension service has lost its monopoly in the farm market. Second, research-based knowledge is desired by urban residents for horticulture, family economics, nutrition, and youth programs. Community leaders and local government officials also desire research-based knowledge to deal with their problems. The well-being of farm families and rural residents depends on economic activity other than farming.

A decision as to whom extension service should serve impacts other issues, especially extension's management structure. A decision on this issue also affects funding, mission, and extension's relationship to the university. Staff, budget, and campus power are also at stake.

How to Manage the System

A strength and a weakness of the extension service is the system's cooperative nature. A number of groups think they do, or should, manage the system: county workers and their constituencies, state administrators, specialists, Congressmen, and USDA officials. Legitimacy and support has been continued because there is some truth in the perceptions of each group. What would happen to extension if there were less chauvinism and more cooperation among the managers? The extension service in the United States is not a U.S. Department of Agriculture line agency as is the case in most other countries. What are the roles of federal, state, and county offices? What level should take leadership for anticipatory planning and program delivery in the future? What is the role of subject-matter departments, specialists, and field staff in planning and delivery within a state? What is the role of the user versus the extension worker in problem definition and curriculum development? Answers to these questions will greatly impact both the legitimacy and funding support for the service.

While the provisions of the Smith-Lever Act were adopted by all states soon after passage, a number of "who-will-do-what-for-whom" problems had to be worked out, such as the relationships between the state agricultural colleges and the USDA, and the counties and the states. During the New Deal of the 1930s, mission-role problems between extension service and various federal agencies were worked out, but they reappear from time to time.

Funding

The issue of funding involves how much should be provided by federal, state, and local governments, and by other sources. In the 1980s, federal funding decreased in real terms by 25 percent. Few state extension services have escaped significant staff cuts. State funding has increased relative to federal and local support, but financial support has been reduced in those states that are farm, energy, and natural-resource dependent due to state budget constraints. Alternative funding sources include foundation grants, subcontracts from other federal agencies, contributions from the private sector (especially for 4-H), and modest increases in user fees.

ALTERNATIVES AND CONSEQUENCES

What follows is an attempt to provide a set of broad alternative solutions to the issues and some indication of their likely consequences. The alternatives and the consequences are not neatly or clearly defined; each represents a direction that could be followed rather than providing a well-marked road map.

It would be easier to provide an analysis of alternatives and consequences if there was a single decision body. Decisions about the future of extension service will be made by various federal agencies and Congress, various state agencies and state legislatures, county governments, land-grant-university administrations, extension administrations, extension workers, and, finally (perhaps most importantly), by the users of extension. Various points of view, perceptions, and perspectives exist within this list, and, of course, coalitions exist within and between the actors.

Agricultural Technology Transfer

Agricultural technology transfer as an alternative would have the extension service put its major thrust in providing information and education that would increase the productivity of U.S. agriculture. It would focus importantly on farmers, but not be limited to farmers. It would provide both input and processing information for agribusiness. This system would bring scientific and technical findings to site-specific production settings, disseminate these findings, and educate farmers and related firms to the efficient uses of these new approaches. A balance between "technology-push" and "user-pull" strategies would have to be developed.

If this alternative were chosen, a number of decisions would remain. Would the focus be on the relatively small number of commercial farmers who produce the majority of the product? How much attention would be placed on the much larger numbers of small, modest-sized and part-time farmers? Would education efforts be made to increase farm family well-being by increasing off-farm income, or to only increase productivity? In addition, problems of environmental, social, and ethical consequences of modern farm technology call for a broad concept of productivity and efficiency. Technology transfer with a limited and traditional concept of efficiency may not serve society or farmers well, thus reducing support and legitimacy.

A consequence of choosing this alternative would be a change in the structure of the extension service. County staff numbers would likely decline and the number of regional and state specialists would increase. The linkages of the extension system to state experiment stations and federal research agencies would increase. This could take the form of extension's increased applied research to obtain site-specific information, or joint efforts to produce this knowledge. Opportunities to link with the private research systems would need to be explored.

The implications for the extension service's support and legitimacy are not clear. Undoubtedly, commercial agricultural interests would likely increase support if the thrust were done well. But, rural well-being is not determined by farm well-being, thus the support of rural users of extension in the areas of family, youth, and community development could decrease significantly. This could have significant impact on local and state support. Federal support could well increase in the short run. It appears there is considerable support in the general public for assisting farmers, especially if there is understanding that such efforts would increase productivity, lower food prices, and increase competitiveness. However, if attention is not given to small- and lower-income farmers, and the program is viewed as only helping the "big, rich farmers," there could be a sizable decline in support.

The benefits to society that come from increased agricultural productivity as the result of extension-service education are important. Econometric studies cited in *Evaluation of Economic and Social Consequences of Cooperative Extension Programs* (USDA 1980) estimate internal return rates of 30 to 60 percent for public agricultural research and extension as well as indicating that marginal rates of return to research and extension were similar. However, a recent publication by two of the authors cited therein, Huffman and Evenson, estimates the social internal rate of return is 62 percent for public research on grain farms during 1949–74, but was near zero for extension. The authors state, "The poor payoff to extension is puzzling, but evidence on returns to extension have been mixed" (1989, 771). If these results are confirmed by additional studies, will there be public support for the agricultural technology transfer alterative?

Another possible consequence of this alternative is illustrated by the experience of a number of European agricultural advisory services whose programs are limited to agriculture. They are being "privatized," that is, moving to fees for services with the goal of needing no government funds for extension service in a few years.

Initiative Programming

The alternative of initiative programming is the direction in which the Cooperative Extension system is moving. The system selected a set of critical areas for the national priority initiatives. These initiatives were chosen to meet national needs and were developed by an interaction between federal and state concerns through ECOP and Extension Service/USDA. The initiatives provide a framework for programs developed at the local level to meet local needs while "bunching" them in terms of important national needs. The initiatives will change over time as changes in problems at the local and national levels are recognized and identified.

The extension service's constituents would be more diverse with this alternative than the agriculture technology transfer alternative. The constituents would consist of those people needing education on the selected problems. While agricultural constituents would continue to be significant, new constituent groups would emerge.

The consequences for the extension system are unfolding. Clearly, each initiative would cross traditional areas of agriculture, youth, family, and community development. The initiatives are not defined in terms of subject matter. Tensions between subject-matter departments and initiative programs are emerging. More emphasis is placed on the ability of a particular subject matter to make a contribution to a problem rather than being the basis of a program. Also, many extension people, working on specific initiatives, believe they do not have a sufficient research base to deal with the program.

It is too early to determine the impact of this alternative on support for extension service at the federal, state, and local levels. The extension service has plainly made the argument that, by choosing national problems, it is dealing with national needs and, thus, should have increased federal support. At the federal, state, and local levels there are people interested in each of the individual areas. However, coalitions among these supporters need to be further developed and nurtured. The agricultural sector is uncertain if it will lose or gain from initiative programming rather than a focus on agriculture. Extension workers and their supporters within the old program areas are uneasy. But the potential for broad-based support and legitimacy exists for extension with this alternative. This alternative maintains extension's tradition of helping people help themselves with the problems that the people think are important.

Nonformal, Off-Campus Education

The alternative of nonformal, off-campus education would focus extension service's efforts on education rather than knowledge transfer. Extension's mission would be to educate people on how to deal with their real-world problems. Users of extension would learn how to further develop, use, and improve their cognitive skills, that is, how to become better thinkers. In a number of states, cooperative extension is a part of the general extension unit of the university. Selection of this alternative would probably lead to a merger or very close linkages between traditional cooperative extension and general extension functions of the university. It would also likely lead to closer linkages with the community-college systems.

It is difficult to predict the consequences of choosing this alternative. Clearly, the potential for legitimacy and support is very large as extension would develop means of delivering off-campus, nonformal education on a broad range of problems. It is my observation that in most states the support of community colleges is increasing more rapidly than support for large, public-research universities. It is possible to develop a scenario in which, during the next 20 or 30 years, states will not fund their major research universities, but will instead support those educational activities that respond more to the needs of full-time and part-time students.

The role of the county staff would likely be more that of an educational coordinator than that of an educator. This approach would bring closer linkages between the subject-matter faculty and extension-service students in deciding what should be taught. It would lead extension educators to consider each lesson within a broader context of courses and total-learning experience rather than information/technology transfer. While such an approach would establish education rather than organizational maintenance as the major mission of extension, it might lead to renewed evidence for the criticism of extension being all things to all people.

Some Combination of Alternatives

There is always the possibility of some combination of the alternatives listed above. For example, the alternatives of agricultural technology transfer or initiative programming could be combined with a heavier emphasis on nonformal, off-campus classroom education. Agricultural technology transfer could be given a larger role and priority in the issues-programming alternatives. The extension service in the twenty-first century will likely be some combination of the above alternatives and/or those not identified.

The consequences of the combination of alternatives would be a mix of the consequences identified for the alternatives identified. Thus, no specific statement of consequences for the alternative combinations can be made.

Concluding Comments

What in the world is ahead for the extension service and the university? My answer is working hard, making difficult decisions, and having the opportunity to serve the future needs of society. What extension does is important.

THE POLITICAL PUZZLES OF RESEARCH FUNDING

The intent of this presentation is to provide perspective on the intricacies of research funding for social sciences. It includes a naive "primer" on the research funding process and of some puzzles. There is no single puzzle, and puzzles exist within puzzles. An approach for obtaining increased funding for rural social science research is presented.

The funding of social science research in the State Agricultural Experiment Stations (SAES) is the major focus. Clearly, these organizations are not the only ones undertaking rural social science research. The Economic Research Service/USDA, the Agricultural Research Service/USDA, the Agricultural Marketing Service/USDA, as well as other USDA agencies conduct research. Rural social science research is also conducted in parts of the land-grant university other than the experiment station. Non-land-grant universities also conduct rural social science research.

Major funding sources for SAES research can be divided into federal funds and nonfederal funds. In 1984, federal funds accounted for 27.9 percent of SAES funding and nonfederal funds accounted for 72.1 percent (Huffman and Evenson 1987). Federal funds include those administered by the Cooperative State Research Service (CSRS) (17.1 percent), other USDA funds (3.1 percent), and other federal funds (7.7 percent). The nonfederal funds consist of state funds (55.8 percent) and other nonfederal funds (16.2 percent). Federal funding, as a percent of the total for SAES, has declined from 31.5 percent in 1969 to 27.9 percent in 1984. Nonfederal funds increased from 68.5 percent in 1969 to 72.1 percent in 1984.

Social science as a field received 8.6 percent of SAES support in 1984, a slight increase over 7.9 percent in 1969. In 1984, economics received 5.8 percent of total funding, sociology 1.2 percent, and other social sciences 1.5 percent. The major field for SAES was basic and applied biological sciences, which received 77.6 percent. Physical sciences claimed 14.0 percent of total funding.

In past years, most of the federal funding came to SAESs as funds to the states on a formula basis under the Hatch Act. The other USDA funds consisted of cooperative agreements between USDA agencies and SAESs. Other federal funds were grants and contracts from non-USDA federal agencies.

The U.S. Congress authorized a federally funded, competitive research grant program administered by CSRS in the 1977 farm bill. Appropriations for competitive grant funding relative to formula funding are increasing. The competitive grant procedure is similar to that used by other federal agencies, such as National Institute of Health and National Science Foundation. Ruttan (1982) argues that the reason for the interest and growth in competitive grant programs is due to a lack of confidence in the agricultural research decision-making process. The agricultural research establishment is viewed as unresponsive to environmental, distributional, and humanitarian concerns, as well as the growth of new groups interested in such problems as nutrition, rural development, environmental impact, etc.

Competitive grant funding versus formula funding is one of the major issues facing the agricultural research system for the future. Rural social science research has not fared well in either the formula funding or the competitive grant funding arenas.

Ruttan (1982) points out, "Each of the two research management systems has strengths and weaknesses. The system constraints and the reward system in the two programs are very different from each other" (Ruttan 1982, 216). He suggests that the argument about the merits of the two systems should be cast in terms of the relative mix rather than the absolute merits of either system. Marcus (1988, 26), in a historical analysis of the publicly sponsored research system since the 1830s, concludes:

> The 1977 legislative edict and the post–1950 USDA policies have transformed the time-honored USDA-station relationship. The context in which this new rivalry has blossomed also has spawned cutthroat competition for research funds, fragmentation of research funding mechanisms and subordination of agricultural to life science research as well as the explicit pork barrel life science of the 1980s.

It is clear that Congress determines the level of support for agricultural research. The president "proposes" a budget but, as Don Paarlberg has often commented, Congress "disposes" of the proposed budget. The president's budget is developed by the Office of Management and Budget (OMB). Requests are submitted by the various federal departments and agencies. The research agencies within the USDA make proposals to the department.

There are a number of points where the SAES attempts to influence the administration's budget. The Experiment Station Committee on Policy (ESCOP) budget committee is constantly planning two to four years ahead. They receive advice from the Regional Association of Directors and ESCOP. The ESCOP proposals, along with that for extension and resident instruction, are coordinated through the Budget Committee of the Division of Agriculture of the National Association of Land Grant Colleges and State Universities. These recommendations are coordinated through the Assistant Secretary for Science and Education for USDA and on to OMB.

Another player is the Joint Council on Food and Agricultural Sciences. The Council, established in the 1977 agricultural legislation, has the responsibility to coordinate research, extension, and higher education in the food and agriculture sciences, and has impact on the budget process. The Joint Council is made up of representatives from research, extension, and teaching in the land-grant university, USDA science and education officials, the private sector, non-land-grant colleges and foundations. The Join Council issues four reports: a long-term needs assessment, a five-year plan, an annual priorities report, and an annual accomplishment report for the system.

The President's budget is considered by the House and Senate Appropriations Committees. Testimony is given by administration officials. However, ESCOP, the Division of Agriculture Budget Committee, as well as commodity groups, farm organizations, and agribusiness also have attempted to influence the actions of the appropriations committees. Obviously, the appropriations for agriculture research are made in the context of the overall federal budget and are influenced by other issues, such as the growing budget deficit and attempts to reduce it.

The appropriations bill passed by Congress is the outcome of a very intense and complicated political process. The political interests of the individual congressmen on the appropriations committees, as well as influentials in the House and Senate, and the interests of specific commodity and agribusiness groups are important in the process. More recently, the concerns of what Hadwiger (1982) calls the externalities/alternatives coalition of people concerned about the environment, nutrition, etc., and the opinions of the individual scientists have impacted the process. The appropriations bill results from actions in a political marketplace. Entry into the political marketplace is relatively easy so special interests can have impact. Congress is a very responsive institution, and should a large number of voters reach a consensus on needed agricultural research, the consensus would be contained in the appropriations bill. However, there is seldom a sufficient consensus and, therefore, the potential marketplace is very dynamic and fluid.

The pork barrel funding of science is receiving increasing attention. Individual congressmen or senators want to have a laboratory in their state. The desire to place jobs, buildings, and research missions within their state, or to respond to the perceived need for publicly supported research on topics of importance to voters in their states, leads to the pork barrel. Universities have benefitted from the process. An item in Science reports $225 million was set aside in various appropriations bills for projects at specific universities in fiscal 1987 (Byrne, 1988, 1383).

Pork barrel motivation for funding is not new. Formula funding under the Hatch Act was supported by the pork barrel. Hadwiger (1982, 148) states:

> We should instead give considerable credit to pork barrel politics for several fortunate developments in agriculture research. In proliferating research location, for example, Congress has helped unlock high-potential regions such as the High Plains. Moreover, pork barrel politics has sustained experiment stations in poorer states, which in some ways has helped alleviate poverty and malnutrition there, as in the introduction of 'greens' into diets.

Marcus (1988), on the other hand, is more critical of current pork barrel practices, especially as they have supported special interest groups concerned with life science research.

A National Initiative for Agriculture Research has been proposed by an ad hoc steering committee under the leadership of Chancellor Theodore Hullar of the University of California-Davis. The initiative proposes new funding at the level of $500 million per year granted on a competitive basis. The competition would be open to both land-grant and non-land-grant, as well as federal and not-for-profit research units. The proposed initiative places emphasis on opportunities to use the sciences basic to agriculture to augment ongoing agriculture research. It is not intended to substitute for present funding mechanisms or take away from other opportunities for new funding.

The components of the initiative can be conceptualized as a two-dimensional matrix, the elements of which are: (1) output, issue or impact-oriented goals and objectives, such as water quantity and quality; and (2) scientific dimensions, including economics and social science.

The initiative has been endorsed by the Executive Committee of the National Association of State Universities and Land Grant Colleges. The steering committee is in the process of further development of the proposal and obtaining consensus for support by a coalition from academia, farm and commodity organizations, agribusiness, professional and scientific societies, environmental and conservation organizations, and the agriculture community as well as the political system.

The following summary statements by Congressman George E. Brown (1988) in a presentation to the annual meeting of the American Society of Agronomy are instructive:

- Publicly funded agricultural research must be oriented towards meeting the needs of the society, as perceived by the taxpayers, who are supporting that research.
- Sustainability is a useful concept for focusing agricultural research because it captures a diverse set of concerns about agriculture as an economic system, an ecological system, and a social system.
- There are at least four critical challenges facing agricultural research: (1) the need to clearly identify the ultimate objectives; (2) the need to cross disciplinary boundaries; (3) the need to quickly adopt new technologies; and, (4) the need to more closely link research, teaching, and education, making sure there is a good two-way flow of information.
- I stated that agriculture does have some unique characteristics, and thus benefits from unique funding such as the Hatch Act formula funds—however, agricultural research could perhaps be revitalized by complementing certain of the current programs with a diversity of competitive grants such as those funded by NIH.
- I noted that a key question we must address is which priorities to set at the federal level versus the other levels of the research funding system.
- I want to again caution that current political reality means that a continuation of the status quo will result in less research money, and only a cooperative, consensus effort can overcome the tide of deficit cuts.

In conclusion, the actors in the political marketplace are very responsive. If citizens and interest groups could reach a consensus that increased funding of social science would benefit society and themselves, social science would be awash in money. However, very few citizens and interest groups are knowledgeable about the benefits and costs of social science research and, thus, do not give attention to the issue. It seems clear to me that social scientists interested in increased support for their efforts need to be able to communicate clearly the potential benefits of their proposed research. They also need to find groups that are willing to enter the political marketplace to support this research. Social science has not been particularly effective in this kind of activity. It is not sufficient to have good research ideas that will catch the imagination of the members of the social science profession or even of administrators. A number of publics, including other agricultural research professions, must be recruited to support the research and coordinate their efforts. Even though it is my judgment that more social science research is needed as the nation deals with the emerging problems of farming, the food system, and rural areas, that is not sufficient to obtain funding.

NOTES

1. R. J. Hildreth is the Director of the Farm Foundation, Oak Brook, Illinois.
2. Edited version of a speech presented to the Division of Agriculture, National Association of State Universities and Land Grant Colleges (NASULGC).

REFERENCES

Boulding, Kenneth. 1969. The legitimacy of central banks. Paper prepared for the Steering Committee on Fundamental Reappraisal of the Discount Mechanism. Washington, D.C.: Board of Governors of the Federal Reserve System.

Brown, George E., Jr. (Rep. of the 36th Dist. in Calif.) 1988. The critical challenges facing the structure and function of agricultural research. Presentation to the annual meeting of the American Society of Agronomy, 28 November, Anaheim, Calif.

Byrne, Gregory. 1988. Panning pork. *Science* (9 December): 1383.

Hadwiger, Don F. 1982. *The politics of agricultural research*. Lincoln: University of Nebraska Press.

Huffman, Wallace E., and Robert E. Evenson. 1987. The development of U.S. agricultural research and education: An economic perspective. Staff paper no. 169. Ames: Iowa State University, Department of Economics.

———1989. Supply and demand functions for multiproduct U.S. cash grain farms: Biases caused by research and other policies. *American Journal of Agricultural Economics* 71:761–73.

Marcus, Alan I. 1988. The wisdom of the body politic: The changing nature of publicly sponsored American agricultural research since the 1830s. *Agricultural History* 62:4–26.

Rasmussen, Wayne D. 1989. *Taking the university to the people: Seventy-five years of cooperative extension*. Ames: Iowa State University Press.

Ruttan, Vernon W. 1982. *Agricultural research policy*. Minneapolis: University of Minnesota Press.

USDA, Science and Education Administration-Extension. 1980. *Evaluation of economic and social consequences of cooperative extension programs*. Washington, D.C.: USDA.

CHAPTER 7

AN ASSESSMENT OF THE AGRICULTURAL ECONOMICS PROFESSION[1]

Richard E. Just and Gordon C. Rausser[2]

The American Agricultural Economics Association (AAEA) is composed of various groups ranging from industry to government to academia with widely divergent values and interests. This has lead to controversy, sometimes healthy and other times destructive, on the appropriate mode for graduate training and methodologies of research. These differences affect the direction and vitality of the profession and imply both benefits and costs in pursuing the solutions to various problems and issues.

Pressures for day-to-day decision making in industry have led to reliance on methodologies that are often characterized as unacceptable for journal publication. Similarly, the timeliness of analyses in governmental policy-making processes sometimes does not lend itself well to publication in professional journals. In contrast, the research sophistication that has emerged in academic circles has reputedly widened the divergences among various groups within the AAEA.

Does the diversity within agricultural economics enhance or detract from the creation of knowledge? An appropriate degree of diversity creates cross fertilization of ideas and a healthy tension that exposes inferior applications. But has the diversity become excessive? Given the degree of diversity within the AAEA, do the current policies and practices of the association enhance or detract from the creation of useful knowledge? Do the media products of the AAEA promote and encourage new ideas, methods, institutions, theories, data, or articulation of important problems? Do they foster scientific inquiry, dialogue, and debate? What are the research values of our collective organization, the AAEA?

The objective of this paper is to assess the above questions. The paper begins with a review of some anecdotal evidence and reflection upon the current state of the profession. The results of a survey of the views of the AAEA membership conducted in the spring of 1989 are presented in the following section of the paper.

The anecdotal evidence as well as both the quantitative and qualitative responses to the survey presented in this paper imply that the product mix of the AAEA does not sufficiently emphasize problem definition, case studies, and heuristic application or economic principles based on understanding and experience. In the existing portfolio, relatively too much emphasis has been placed on ex poste analysis of historical secondary data using formal frameworks *(American Journal of Agricultural Economics [AJAE])* and on the expression of individual viewpoints (*Choices*). Changing the product mix in these directions would not imply lowering the quality standard imposed by the peer review process but rather would expand the scope of such standards. The criteria currently used in the selection of products have reduced the profession's ability to tackle forward-looking problems and to foster institutional innovations. This is due, in part, to the profession's self-imposed methodological biases that favor historical data analysis and "falsification," an emphasis on linear logic, a presumption of objectivity, and a presumption that economic understanding is a convergent process.

Contrary to many claims that extension, teaching, or industry components are not well related to the profession, the results of the survey show that the profession is highly interconnected through its various media channels. However, the AAEA has a serious problem of balance between inputs and outputs. All major groups in the profession rely upon the AAEA and ASSA (Allied Social Sciences Association) meetings as a major source of inputs in their thinking (probably because of the low transactions costs), but no major groups regard the meetings as an important outlet for their work (probably because of low professional payoff). The same statement applies to *Choices* as well. In contrast, almost all major professional groups place high emphasis on output in the *AJAE* (which provides an incentive given the reward structures for most agricultural economists), but almost no group relies on it as an important source of ideas perhaps because of the time and effort required to read *AJEA* articles).

The experiment with *Choices* has demonstrated that the AAEA Board plays a strong role in influencing the product mix of the profession. This fact, together with the results in this paper, suggests that the AAEA Board should take action to encourage more forward-looking problem definition and heuristic application of economic principles to problems for which adequate data have not yet been generated—not in lieu of the types of products now produced but as an enhancement of the product mix. Changes are needed that will balance the inputs and outputs of the profession by placing higher rewards on those outputs that have the highest impact and reducing transaction costs incurred in accessing the best information the profession has to offer. Some possibilities include introducing a submission and refereeing process for invited papers at meetings (which would give them refereed status), adding a session on forward-looking problem definition (with similar refereed publication status), and broadening the scope of analysis in the *AJAE* by adding sections for brief, highly readable papers on problem definition and heuristic application of economic principles.

NOTES

1. Abstracted version (written by the authors) of a paper by the same name that appeared in the *American Journal of Agricultural Economics*, December 1989, Vol. 71.

2. Richard E. Just is a professor of Agricultural and Resource Economics at the University of Maryland. Gordon C. Rausser is a Robert Gordon Sproul Distinguished Professor at University of California, Berkeley.

CHAPTER 8

ADMINISTRATIVE AND FUNDING STRATEGIES AND RESEARCH AGENDAS

The *first* section of this chapter presents SSAAP's overall administration and funding strategies as they have come into focus within SSAAP's editorial group and in various SSAAP meetings with funding and administrative groups. Following this, the *second* section of this chapter presents specific ideas and results that originated at SSAAP's Houston conference under three subheadings: (1) administrative *strategies*, (2) funding *strategies*, and (3) *agendas* for research on the administration and funding of rural and basic social science work. The *third* section of this chapter, written by the editorial group, relates needed, more detailed administrative and funding changes to the specific agendas found in the final chapters of the nine major sections of Parts II, III, and IV. This chapter then concludes with the *fourth* and final section dealing with a possible long-term rural social science organization that has been suggested by a special SSAAP committee, sometimes referred to as the "short-term committee on the long-term future of SSAAP."

Readers are reminded that SSAAP was concerned with all work done by rural and basic social scientists. Therefore, the administrative and funding strategies and research agendas of this chapter apply to our public, private, and parastatal agricultural institutions and their social scientists with responsibilities for extension, resident instruction, consulting, advising, governmental administration and legislation, farm production, marketing, and utilization, as well as research. SSAAP's concerns go beyond academics and research.

SSAAP'S OVERALL ADMINISTRATIVE AND FUNDING STRATEGIES

It is SSAAP's overall constructive strategy to stress:

- The importance of a partnership role for the rural social sciences
  - *in* our agricultural and rural institutions
  - *with* the agricultural technical sciences
  - *that also involves* the basic social, biological, and physical science disciplines.
- That the following should be expected from the social sciences:
  - Contributions to multidisciplinary problem-solving and subject- or issue-oriented efforts important for farmers and their families, rural society, and consumers, with much more balanced attention than is given at present to problems and issues involving:
    - Technology
    - Human development
    - Institutions, policies, and related organizational infrastructure
    - Natural and manmade resources
  - Applied agricultural and rural disciplinary social science work by individual basic social science disciplines.
  - Work on the deficiencies in the theories, techniques, and data of the basic disciplinary social sciences that constrain practical multidisciplinary work on problems and subjects or issues important for farmers, rural societies, and consumers.
  - Assistance to administrators in the identification of practical problems and issues involving the social sciences and in the design, organization, finance, administration, and conduct of projects and programs to address them.
- The importance of correcting the serious mismatch that exists between
  - the pattern of issues and problems now facing farming, agribusinesses, rural communities, and consumers and
  - the present heavy technocratic emphasis of our agricultural institutions on production methods for agriculture, agribusiness, and consumers.

This technocratic mismatch results less from *overemphasis* on technological advance than from *underemphasis* on institutional, policy, program, and infrastructural improvements; human development; and the social dimensions of enhancing natural (including environmental) and manmade resource bases. What is needed is increased emphasis on the last three, not reduced emphasis on advances in agricultural technology. Even though our agricultural institutions place great emphasis on technology and, more recently, natural resources, the social science dimensions of both are neglected.

- That although some of the above technocratic mismatch can be corrected within our agricultural institutions, at least part of it should be corrected outside those institutions with basic disciplinary and rural social scientists carrying major responsibility for developing, funding, conducting, and administering the needed programs and projects.

- The falsity of the two following common administrative misconceptions concerning the social sciences that are often cited to excuse lack of administrative aggressiveness in funding and using the social sciences:
  - To the dismay of SSAAP's leadership and its editorial group, administrators have asserted to them that the rural and basic social sciences have not demonstrated productivity in the past and that they are less capable of "delivering the goods" than the biological and physical sciences. Such assertions are made despite the two rural social scientists who are Nobel Laureates—one for research on human capital formation (T. W. Schultz) and the other for research on the development of Third World largely agricultural countries (Arthur Lewis). Further, among basic disciplinary as contrasted to rural social science Nobel Laureates are: Kenneth Arrow, for his work on social choices and individual preferences; Wassily Leontief, for his work on national input/output analyses; and James Buchanan, for his work on constitutional theory and public choices. These disciplinary contributions are basic to practical social science work on the problems of farm people, rural communities, agribusinesses, and consumers. Still further, the numerous extensive contributions of rural social scientists to the solutions of real-world problems and the resolution of real-world issues are reviewed in the opening chapters of every section in this book. The perception that the social sciences have contributed little to agriculture is especially ironic when it is remembered that it was agronomic and, to a lesser extent, animal scientists who initially saw the need for the social sciences in our agricultural colleges and experiment stations and, hence, introduced them into their resident instruction, research and, later, extension programs. Administrators and others are respectfully and especially referred to the first chapters of Parts I and V and of the nine sections of Parts II, III, and IV for more details on the practical accomplishments of rural and basic social scientists vis-a-vis farmers and their families, agribusiness people, rural people and communities, and consumers.
  - It is also often stated by administrators of our agricultural institutions that financing is not available to expand social science work for agriculture; agribusiness; rural resources; rural societies; and food, fiber, and natural-resource consumers. This point of view is belied by:
    - The continual criticism of our agricultural institutions for neglecting the social dimension of the crucial technological and nontechnological problems and issues confronting agriculture, rural people and societies, and consumers. These criticisms imply strong potential support for the work of social scientists—neglected, these criticisms threaten present support for all the work of our agricultural institutions.
    - The financing now being given to and obtained by nonagricultural institutions to address the social science dimensions of farm, rural, and consumer problems and issues involving human development, the environment, equality, food-chain safety, and deficiencies in our farm and rural institutions, organizations, and commodity programs, the last of which now need to be redesigned because of our vastly different changing world.

- That the above challenges cannot be met by the mere identification, funding, and successful execution of three or four high-priority, social science initiatives when what is needed is the major reorientation of our agricultural institutions, their administrators, and their social scientists that is called for above. Thus, the SSAAP generated agendas (not priorities or initiatives) presented in the last chapters of the sections of this book for restructured and reoriented institutions, administrators, and social scientists to use in setting priorities across the wide range of new, crucially important problems and issues they face that require contributions from the rural and basic social sciences. The priorities are better set locality by locality, federal agency by federal agency, business by business, organization by organization, state by state, academic unit by academic unit, problem by problem, and issue by issue by those with administrative and funding accountability and responsibility for policies, programs, and projects rather than by a temporary, national organization of social scientists and professionals, such as SSAAP.

- That, if our agricultural institutions can provide no better than in the past for the rural and basic social sciences, their administrators should at least encourage and cooperate with rural social scientists in mobilizing outside financial, administrative, and institutional support. SSAAP notes that going entirely outside our agricultural institutions for social science support could be
  - to the detriment of the constructive partnerships of the basic and technical agricultural sciences with the rural and basic social sciences that are called for above
  - at the cost of much of the present support for our agricultural institutions and,
  - perhaps more importantly, at the cost of lost additional financial, societal, and political support our agricultural institutions could earn by addressing the social dimensions of problems and issues that it is now accused of neglecting.

- That needed work on practical subjects and problems requires attention to values and ethical issues without which
  - practical problems and issues cannot even be defined,
  - let alone be solved or resolved.

- The need for administrators to realize that objective work on the value and ethical dimensions of practical issues and problems requires a broader, more eclectic, and more holistic administrative orientation than is common among biological, physical, and those social scientists who often follow the reductionist, logically positivistic orientations common among biological and physical sciences. See Section 3 of Part IV of this book for more explanation of the nature and limitations of "reductionist logical positivism."

- That it is important for the administrators of our agricultural institutions to recognize the growing importance of what is known as the "public choice/transaction cost (PC/TC) approach" to making administrative decisions to improve the institutions they administer for generating:
  - Technical advances
  - Human capital or improved human capacity
  - Natural and manmade resource-base enhancements
  - Policy, public program, and other institutional improvements

  This approach is readily expandable to go beyond econometrics, induced change, and the industrial organization approaches to become a truly multidisciplinary approach to be used in participative, iterative/interaction of investigators and decision makers with affected groups and persons served by our agricultural institutions.

- With respect to funding of the rural and basic social sciences, the importance of:
  - Funding multidisciplinary subject-matter and problem-solving work requiring social science expertise.
  - Competitive grants for the rural and basic social sciences to do
    - basic disciplinary social science work to remedy the deficiencies of the basic social science disciplines that limit multidisciplinary problem-solving and subject-matter work pertaining to farms, rural people, agribusinesses, and consumers and
    - applied disciplinary social science work
    - while recognizing that much (if not most) of the responsibility for funding the basic social sciences resides outside agricultural colleges in the colleges of arts and sciences and, hence, somewhat outside the main USDA/land-grant system.
  - Making agricultural administrators and administrators of basic social science administrative units outside of agriculture aware:
    - Of the difficulties involved in diverting agricultural funds provided for by farm and rural clienteles to basic disciplinary social science work of questionable practical relevance for those clienteles without endangering political support for existing funds and potential support and funding for new disciplinary, as well as new practical problem-solving and subject-matter work.
    - That the basic disciplinary social sciences should seek funding for their work outside of agricultural institutions *except* when the basic disciplinary work is clearly relevant for practical work important to farm, rural, and consumer clienteles, in which case it should be funded in agricultural institutions as relevant for those problem-solving and subject-matter efforts.
  - Not depending solely on the willingness and ability of administrators of our agricultural institutions to fund the needed social science work either internally or externally; instead, social scientists should also aggressively seek outside funding and be prepared to work outside our agricultural institutions in addressing important farm, rural, and consumer issues and problems. Among the potential "outside" funding sources are state legislatures, state agencies, local governments, foundations and philanthropic organizations (some of which have already "given up" on our agricultural institutions as being likely to address current nontechnocratic problems and issues), non-USDA federal agencies, and the private sector. SSAAP notes that:
    - Activist groups are potential sources of political support for public funding. Because these groups are concerned, in many instances, with "real" problems and issues that require objective rural and basic social science disciplinary work, their support should be sought, rather than disdained as unscholarly because of the questionable objectivity and misinformation that characterize some but far from all pronouncements of such groups.
    - Funding can be more easily "earned" by addressing problems and issues in their realistic, multidisciplinary contexts than by doing more esoteric specialized disciplinary research and teaching that is unrelated to problems and issues.

RESULTS FROM SSAAP'S HOUSTON CONFERENCE

Persons assigned at the SSAAP Houston conference to an area designated as **Funding and Administrative Strategies for the Rural and Basic Social Sciences** included:

Coordinator: Larry J. Connor

Invited members (some of whom may not have participated) W. H. Brown, J. Bruce Bullock, Charles E. Caudill, K. R. Farrell, Mitch Geasler, Don F. Hadwiger, Wallace E. Huffman, C. C. Kaltenbach, Kirklyn Kerr, Gerald E. Klonglan, Lee Kolmer, William Lacy, John E. Lee, Jacquelyn W. McCray, Leo V. Mayer, George Norton, Lynn Pollnow, Vernon W. Ruttan, Richard J. Sauer, Barbara S. Stowe, Richard G. Stuby, Gene Sommers, Kenneth Tefertiller, and James Zuiches.

Three sets of results were developed by this group: administrative strategies, funding strategies, and agenda items for research on administration and funding. These strategies and agendas are presented immediately below. In contrast to SSAAP's overall administrative and funding strategies presented above, these strategies are rather specific as are the agendas on needed research on administration and funding that are to be found in the second set of results presented below.

ADMINISTRATIVE STRATEGIES FROM SSAAP'S HOUSTON CONFERENCE

Over time, new problems, subjects, and issues have emerged for farmers and rural communities that demand new and changing multidisciplinary mixes. These mixes involve important roles for the rural and basic social sciences. The rather detailed administrative strategies presented here supplement the overall ones presented above. These strategies are designed to increase the contribution of the rural and basic disciplinary social sciences to the development of (1) knowledge of multidisciplinary subjects and issues important for farmers and their families, agribusinesses, consumers, and rural communities, (2) solutions to specific practical problems (generally multidisciplinary) of these groups, and (3) the basic, social science disciplines to the end that they may better serve the same groups.

Administrative work requires various types of expertise and support from and the cooperation of different kinds of organizations and persons performing a variety of functions. Governmental agency administrators, university and college administrators, and institute directors, as well as administrators of less academic rural social science activities need to give increased attention to forging administrative strategies and appropriate linkages with new or existing organizations in order to carry out social science programs that are effective, involve necessary collaborators, and reach the intended clienteles. This is necessary to take advantage of present opportunities to mobilize new resources to offset the severe limitations of conventional funding sources. The following administrative strategies are regarded by SSAAP to be important:

- Develop administrative flexibility in public institutions by utilizing a wide variety of organizational models to carry out missions involving the rural and basic social sciences insofar as the work of these sciences pertains to farmers and their families, rural societies, agriculture resource users, and food and fiber consumers. These models include: (1) colleges; (2) institutes; (3) departments, both disciplinary and multidisciplinary; (4) multidisciplinary centers on campuses—statewide, regional, and international—both temporary and more permanent; (5) public and private nonprofit organizations; (6) foundations; (7) governmental divisions and branches; (8) projects; (9) collaborative efforts and projects among universities, disciplines, the multidisciplinary departments of agricultural colleges, between government and/or industry and academia, and between domestic and foreign or international agencies, etc.—both temporary and more permanent; and (10) the use of faculty and staff entrepreneurship in temporary administrative structures to define problems and issues, develop projects, mobilize support, and administer the efforts. The dynamic problems of farmers, agribusinesses, rural societies, and consumers require that administrators, rural social scientists, and basic social science disciplinarians have administrative flexibility in working with widely varying and changing mixes of disciplinarians and organizations.

- As the proportion of an administrative unit's effort devoted to multidisciplinary problems and issues or subjects increases relative to its disciplinary work, more administrative capacity is needed. Proportionally more administrative capacity is needed to:
  - Identify new problems, subjects, and issues.
  - Assemble and administer the changing mixes of disciplines and departments needed to address the particular problems, issues, and subjects at hand.
  - Mobilize political and financial support from appropriate clienteles and agencies for addressing these new subjects, issues, and problems.
  - Develop linkages to other institutions in order to coordinate efforts in addressing multidisciplinary problems and issues.

- Use and encourage entrepreneurially inclined professionals to define problems and issues, develop projects and programs, mobilize resources, and administer short-term multidisciplinary efforts in a manner that
  - avoids establishing long-term administrative structures for short-term efforts, and
  - awards such entrepreneurial efforts while maintaining a long-term departmental or disciplinary home for the entrepreneurs.

- Increase budget flexibility for pursuing critical new multidisciplinary problems and subjects by:
  - Withholding some percentage of a subunit's "hard money" to be "earned" by it and its tenured personnel by addressing current critical problems and subjects.
  - Using proportionally more contractual, nontenured professionals.
  - Seeking "soft money" from and with the support of groups interested in current issues and seeking solutions for current problems.

- Increase planning for research, resident instruction, extension, and public service with stress on important current problems and issues, leaving finance to follow rather than determine plans of work.

- Require administrative training for administrators. This should include training to make them more aware of the administrative differences between multidisciplinary problem-solving and subject-matter projects and programs with respect to
  - accountability and mobilization of political, academic, and financial support;
  - conducting and administering research, resident instruction, extension, advisory and consulting work;
  - review and evaluation; and
  - appropriate philosophic and methodological orientations.

- Recruit administrators with (or train them so they have) enough knowledge of the rural and disciplinary social sciences and humanities to be effective in demanding appropriate performance from social scientists and humanists in the anticipation, definition, and resolution of the problems and issues of agriculture, rural communities, agribusinesses, and consumers that involve human development, institutional improvement, and resource enhancement, as well as technical advance.

- Establish in each governmental unit, college, experiment station, and extension administration that is concerned with farming, farm people, rural societies, and food, fiber, and resource consumers a social science advisory group of qualified rural and basic disciplinary social scientists. This is needed to help ensure that the rural and basic disciplinary social sciences are funded, used, and administered so that they can
  - make appropriate contributions to multidisciplinary problem-solving and subject-matter efforts, and
  - have an opportunity to identify and make those disciplinary advances in the basic social sciences which

are needed for the improvement of farming, family life, agribusinesses, rural societies, and the use of products and services generated with rural resources.

- Communicate research, teaching, extension, consulting, and advising successes and failures to groups, funders, and administrators, making it clear that no one of the following is sufficient, *in and of itself*, to resolve practical issues and solve practical problems of agriculture, rural people and societies, and consumers but that all are essential:
  - Technical advance
  - Institutional and policy improvements
  - Human development
  - Accumulation of natural and manmade resources

  In this connection, case studies of "failures" due to neglecting the social aspects of changes in technology, institutions, policies, programs, organizations, people, and natural and manmade resources are at least as useful as success stories in helping funders and administrators see the necessary appropriate roles to be played by the social sciences with respect to these four driving forces.

- Recognize the important differences that exist between the resource needs of rural and basic social scientists versus those of the technical biological and physical agricultural scientists for office space, assistants, consultants, administrators, computers, secretaries, travel funds, experience in "action agencies," etc.

- Restore promotion, salary adjustment, and recognition credit for (1) agricultural experiment station and extension publications and media reports of multidisciplinary problem-solving and subject-matter efforts and (2) other reports on multidisciplinary problem-solving and subject-matter efforts that are of practical importance to local, state, regional, national, and international governmental units, businesses, individuals, and groups. Problem-solving and subject-matter efforts should be evaluated by users and affected persons as well as disciplinarians. Increased recognition of such work can be attained without reducing absolute emphasis on the importance of publishing practically relevant disciplinary research results in journals whose articles are reviewed and evaluated by disciplinary peers. Such recognition is likely to benefit disciplinary as well as multidisciplinary problem-solving and subject-matter work because of the synergism between the two.

- Develop appropriate consulting arrangements to help rural and disciplinary social scientists contribute to farm and rural societies and consumers and to permit the basic social sciences and the rural social scientists to benefit further from the synergism between disciplinary efforts, on one hand, and multidisciplinary problem-solving and subject-matter efforts, on the other. The importance of this synergism in the long history in the agricultural sciences should not be forgotten or denied today.

- Develop closer research, teaching, and extension linkages (1) between the rural social sciences and the basic social sciences and (2) between them and the basic and agricultural biological and physical sciences.

- Develop closer linkages for cooperative research, teaching, and extension programs involving rural and basic social sciences:
  - Among land-grant universities within regions.
  - Between the 1862 and the 1890 land grants to address the problems of disadvantaged rural farm and nonfarm African-American residents, using scholars from both the 1862 and the 1890 institutions.
  - Among land-grant and non-land-grant universities and disadvantaged Hispanic, African-American, Native American, and Caucasian people and their organizations.
  - Within and among states and between land-grant and non-land-grant universities and community colleges.

- Develop closer professional linkages and scholarly exchanges among the different rural social science associations:
  - Through joint sessions at the individual rural social science association meetings.
  - Through joint meetings of the associations.
  - By having the presidents of the Rural Sociological Society and American Agricultural Economics Association take the lead in organizing rural social science sessions at the annual meetings of the American Association for the Advance of Science.
  - By organizing a rural social science association to provide a network linking existing rural social science organizations with disciplinarians working on agricultural topics in those basic social science disciplines that do not have a rural social science counterpart, such as political science, anthropology, geography, psychology and, in the humanities, philosophy. (See the section entitled "The Long-Term Need For a 'SSAAP-Like' Organization" at the end of this chapter.)

- Develop improved linkages among university social science research and teaching programs, governmental agencies with agricultural and rural missions, and other agencies with substantial social science capability. Improved linkages are needed between universities (land-grant and non-land-grant) and the following sets of institutions:
  - the Economic Research Service (ERS), the National Agricultural Statistics Service (NASS), the Cooperative State Research Service (CSRS), the Foreign Agriculture Service (FAS) in the U.S. Department of Agriculture (USDA), the National Center for Food and Agricultural Policy (NCFAP), and the International Food Policy Research Institute (IFPRI);
  - the U.S. Agency for International Development (USAID) and other parts of the U.S. State Department, IFPRI, the Food and Agriculture Organization (FAO), and the World Bank;
  - state and provincial departments or ministries of agriculture and/or natural resources; and
  - other agencies such as the Soil Conservation Service (SCS), the Agricultural Stabilization and Conservation Service (ASCS) and other agencies in the U.S. government that employ economists, sociologists, and other social scientists without well-developed academic linkages.

- Encourage interactions and partnerships of rural social science departments with the biological and physical agricultural science departments and related organizations and groups such as the professional associations, industry/commodity groups, farm and rural organizations and leaders, natural resource and environmental groups, community organizations, consumer groups, food and environmental activists, and local governments.

- Strengthen the roles of the rural and basic social sciences in international organizations such as the World Bank, FAO, the various regional development banks, and parastatal organizations of other nations.
- Develop improved linkages between the rural social science associations and the national policy- and priority-setting organs of the land-grant system:
  - Extension Committee on Organization and Policy (ECOP)
  - Experiment Station Committee on Organization and Policy (ESCOP)
  - Resident Instruction Committee on Organization and Policy (RICOP)
  - International Committee on Organization and Policy (ICOP)
- Develop improved linkages between the rural social sciences and the relevant committees of the American Association of State Colleges of Agricultural and Renewable Resources (AASCARR).
- Develop improved linkages of the rural social sciences with the primary national-level organizations important to science funding and science policy, including the:
  - Social Science Research Council (SSRC)
  - National Science Foundation (NSF)
  - National Academy of Science (NAS) and its Board on Agriculture
  - Consortium of Social Science Associations (COSSA)
  - Social science foundations, such as the Russell Sage Foundation
  - National Institutes of Health (NIH)

FUNDING STRATEGIES FROM SSAAP'S HOUSTON CONFERENCE

Funding strategies involve far more than a quest for dollars. They involve building the relationships and networks that produce mutual understanding, friendly advice, and encouragement for the rural and basic social sciences and, in turn, give them voice and representation in the agencies and institutions that allocate budgets for research, teaching, consulting, advising, administrative, entrepreneurial, and outreach activities. They also involve interlinkages, communication, and mutual support among the users of knowledge and the knowledge-generating organizations and individuals that produce and extend knowledge to the food, resource, and fiber system and rural societies. While rural organizations have traditionally been served by units located and financed primarily within the land-grant universities and the USDA, the funding base for rural research, teaching, and outreach, has slowly diversified and expanded since the great depression. Other institutions have entered this scene as rural societies, consumers, and farming have changed. In the same period, activities, outlook, and roles of the USDA and the land-grant colleges have also changed. While these traditional institutions are, and will likely remain, important, it is clear that the newer, less traditional sources of funds and kinds of social science education, research, and outreach capability are not only relevant but unique and necessary, in many cases, for addressing the modern-day problems of farmers and their families, agribusiness people, rural residents, and consumers. It is now strategic to expand institutional cooperation among U.S. universities and other agencies so that SSAAP's social science agendas can be better achieved.

- The growing importance of international markets and trade and the critical role that the growth of developing countries will play in any future expansion of U.S. trade makes it strategically critical to fund a linkage of domestic social science capabilities with those in such international institutions as:
  - U.S. Agency for International Development (USAID)
  - Foreign Agriculture Service (FAS) of the USDA
  - Foundations with international programs
  - World Bank, Food and Agriculture Organization (FAO), and other international donors
  - Organization for Economic Cooperation and Development (OECD)
  - Various private voluntary organizations (PVOs), including church-sponsored relief and other charitable organizations
- An organization for doing and systematically funding social science efforts on issues of importance to farmers, agribusinesses, rural societies, and consumers in the less developed countries (LDCs) of the world does not exist in the United States. Such U.S. efforts are now generated and financed in an ad hoc manner using "soft monies" from government agencies such as USAID, foundations, and international organizations. A U.S. system is needed to encourage and fund sustained, coordinated, and carefully evaluated efforts by rural and basic social sciences working with the biological and physical agricultural sciences on problems and subjects germane to agriculture and rural societies in the LDCs. USAID and a few private foundations do a little of this. It should be kept in mind that:
  - The present ad hoc system does focus rather well on problems and issues regarded as important by funders and there is some danger that long-term, more stable, administrative and funding arrangements might move efforts away *from* relevant multidisciplinary problem-solving and subject-matter work *to* disciplinary efforts of lesser relevance.
  - We are rapidly losing part of our present social science capabilities for international work because we are failing, especially in the universities, to replace the retiring cohort of social scientists that has been working on LDC problems and issues.
- At the national level, many governmental and semi-governmental organizations are relevant to the needs of farmers and their families, agribusinesses, rural societies, and consumers and the capability of the social sciences to serve those needs. These include:
  - key congressional and Office of Management and Budget (OMB) staff;
  - national-level science organizations such as the National Science Foundation (NSF), the National Academy of Sciences (NAS), Social Science

Research Council (SSRC), Russell Sage Foundation,. and national institutes of health (NIH) including the National Institute of Mental Health (NIMH);
- National Association of State University and Land Grant Colleges (NASULGC) and the organization and policy committees of its agriculture division (ESCOP, ECOP, RICOP, ICOP);
- American Association of State Colleges of Agricultural and Renewable Resources (AASCARR) schools, other non-land-grant universities, and community colleges;
- national-level professional rural and basic social science associations;
- USDA agencies/councils, including ERS, NASS, FAS, the Joint Council on Food and Agricultural Sciences, and the National Agricultural Research and Extension Users Advisory Board; and the
- National Governors' Association.

- At the state level, several governmental and semi-governmental organizations are important. These include:
  - the land-grant institutions teaching agriculture;
  - community and state non-land-grant colleges teaching agriculture;
  - departments and commissions of agriculture and/or natural resources;
  - county and township governments; and
  - other state agencies concerned with agriculture, rural communities, rural health, aging, etc.

- Among the important nongovernmental agencies are:
  - private-sector firms, especially in agribusiness, general farm organizations, commodity groups, and others;
  - foundations and institutes with various relevant domestic and international programs;
  - non-land-grant universities with relevant research and teaching activities; and
  - private voluntary organizations and church-sponsored organizations having some potential for supporting specific types of social science endeavors in agriculture and rural societies.

NEEDED RESEARCH ON ADMINISTRATION AND FUNDING AS REPORTED FROM SSAAP'S HOUSTON CONFERENCE

Like most agricultural institutions, the agencies and firms in which rural social scientists work are experiencing difficulty in adjusting their work to new agricultural and rural issues and problems. Because important administrative and funding decisions will be needed in the future on how to reorganize and fund agricultural institutions and their rural social sciences for addressing the social dimensions of important issues and problems, much research is needed on organizational and funding alternatives. Ironically, many research organizations fail to research their own administration and funding. Research on administration and funding should be supported by both land-grant and non-land-grant universities, the USDA, USAID, the National Academy of Sciences, the National Science Foundation, private foundations, and industry. There are needs to:

- Conduct research to improve the administration and organization of rural and disciplinary social science teaching. As attention given to traditional subjects is reduced, research is needed on expanding the *scope* of undergraduate agricultural teaching programs to treat the broad food, resource, and fiber system; rural communities; natural resource management; animal welfare; rural people and families; sustainable agriculture; food-chain contamination; international rural development; etc. The research outlined below is viewed as critical for educating students of agriculture, including those in the rural and basic social sciences, to provide better service to domestic and foreign agriculture, rural communities and societies, rural people, and consumers. We need to research:
  - Appropriate mixes of general, disciplinary, and professional education for undergraduate and graduate students.
  - Improved ways of internationalizing courses/curricula.
  - Integration of academic with experiential education.
  - How and what entrepreneurial training should be included in agricultural curricula.
  - Effectiveness of on-campus, extension, and industry leadership-training programs, including the need for continuing education programs relative to rural social sciences.
  - Types and numbers of undergraduate rural social science majors that should be offered in a modern undergraduate agricultural college.
  - How changes in university entrance requirements are likely to affect undergraduate education in food and agriculture, natural resources, rural community development, home economics and human ecology, and international development.

- Appraise alternative graduate education models for the rural and basic disciplinary social sciences. Rural social science graduate education is sometimes praised because of specialization to advance a discipline or an agricultural field; however, it is also cursed when its Ph.D.s fail to do relevant, useful work on multidisciplinary real-world problems and subjects. Four possible alternatives should be researched:
  - a shift to more flexible multidisciplinary and multi-departmental field degrees as opposed to more rigid specialized disciplinary or departmental degrees;
  - a shift to more highly specialized disciplinary degrees in the basic social sciences;
  - mixtures of the above; and
  - various professional masters degrees in the rural social sciences in such areas as agribusiness, resource development, and rural social work.

- Research the combinations of basic social science disciplines needed to address current problems and issues for agriculture and rural societies. Relevant questions include:
  - How faculty can be made more aware of the changing future demands (both applied and disciplinary) that will be made on their students. Strategies and means to keep faculty up-to-date and forward-looking need to be researched. These include:
    - Industry/business/governmental sabbaticals.
    - New, flexible multidisciplinary programs and courses.

- Disciplinary sabbaticals.
- Visiting professors from business/industry and government to interact with and inform faculty of current procedures, policies, working conditions, problems, and issues in the private and public sectors.
- Greater literacy in primary data collection and computers.

▪ How to keep rural social scientists up-to-date, current, and motivated with regard to their basic social science discipline and related supporting disciplines (such as mathematics, statistics, computer science, and philosophy).

▪ How to improve skills for working cooperatively in multidisciplinary teams for addressing practical problems and subjects often in close interaction with public or private decision makers.

▪ How to make faculty members more responsive to new instructional-media approaches to teaching.

● Research improvements in off-campus educational systems. The many technological developments (satellites, down-links, up-links, VCRs, cable television, computer networks, etc.) provide new opportunities to deliver knowledge in many forms to different groups and constituencies. As these new information systems are designed and implemented, research is needed to assess their effectiveness for different audiences. In a more interdependent and global world, the need for off-campus education to help people better understand that world will grow.

● Investigate issues and problems pertaining to agricultural research in direct support of administrators responsible for decisions on research programs and output. We should:

● Research the effectiveness of joint research/extension/resident instruction faculty appointments versus separate research, extension, and resident instruction appointments.

● Determine the effectiveness of alternative organization models and techniques for the administration of multidisciplinary problem-solving and subject-matter efforts versus disciplinary efforts.

● Evaluate the effect of the internal structures of universities (colleges and departments) and government in motivating and rewarding disciplinary versus multidisciplinary problem-solving and subject-matter efforts. For example, we need to understand the effect of alternative ways of recruiting, hiring, using, and rewarding researchers and teachers on their motivations to do multidisciplinary problem-solving and subject-matter as opposed to disciplinary work.

● Determine the appropriate mixes of problem-solving, subject-matter, and disciplinary efforts (both within and across institutions).

● Evaluate alternative methods and standards for assessing the quality and usefulness of social science contributions to multidisciplinary problem-solving and subject-matter research for agriculture and rural communities.

● Establish alternative methods for determining agricultural research priorities for different levels and mixes of resources.

● Research the development and use of feedback systems to help coordinate research and extension work.

● Evaluate alternative systems for interrelating research planning and budgeting.

● Evaluate alternative flexibility strategies with respect to funding and structures for the administration of agricultural research, extension, and resident instruction organizations.

● Assess the impacts of demographic (race, gender, class, age, etc.) factors on agricultural research, teaching, and extension organizations.

● Study processes of research management, including conflict resolution, organizational behavior, resource-allocation strategies, decision-making rules, priority-setting policies and procedures, and evaluation.

● Assess alternative strategies for generating public support for needed problem-solving, subject-matter, and disciplinary research and extension by the rural and basic disciplinary social sciences.

ADMINISTRATIVE AND FUNDING CHANGES NEEDED TO SUPPORT SSAAP'S SUBSTANTIVE AGENDAS FROM PARTS II THROUGH IV

The agendas presented in the last chapters of Sections 1 and 2 of Part II; Sections 1 through 4 of Part III; and Sections 1, 2, and 3 of Part IV reveal needed changes in the administration and funding of rural and basic social work on the problems and concerns of farmers, agribusinesses, rural residents and consumers. The needed administrative and funding changes follow:

● With respect to the *domestic farm, agribusiness, and consumer agendas* of Part II, Section 1, Chapter 7, it is important for administrators to:

▪ Give specific attention to the administrative relationships among subadministrative units for human ecology and home economics, on one hand, and those concerned with farm management, demand analysis, and community development, on the other, to ensure that human considerations involving nutrition, family finances, estate planning, women's rights, and similar problems and issues are adequately handled.

▪ Give specific attention to the need for knowledge of values and the use of ethics in doing all problem-solving and much subject-matter work for farmers, farm families, rural residents, agribusinesses, and consumers.

▪ Recognize that the executive branch of the U.S. government has limited the access of Congress to the ERS for policy and program analyses and that Congress has multiplied its staffs and its own agencies such as the General Accounting Office (GAO), Congressional Budget Office (CBO), Congressional Research Service (CRS), and the Office of Technology Assessment (OTA) to analyze problems and programs. This development makes it necessary for the nonfederal units of our agricultural institutions to relate more specifically to the staff people and agencies of the U.S. Congress.

- With respect to the *international agendas* of Part II, Section 2, Chapter 11, it is administratively important to:
  - Obtain "hard money" funding to sustain long-term capacities for international farm and rural development work by social scientists in the rural social science units of the our agricultural institutions, while seeking and using short-term soft money, contracts, and grants to support problem-solving and issue-oriented work on international development.
  - Engage in international public- and private-sector extension, consulting and advisory work so that the more disciplinary of our social scientists can benefit from the synergisms among problem-solving, subject-matter, and disciplinary work.
  - Provide opportunities for nonadministrative "entrepreneurs" from both the rural social sciences and basic social science disciplines to organize and conduct international multidisciplinary problem-solving and subject-matter projects and work without losing their disciplinary and departmental homes.
  - Actively reward multidisciplinary, normativistic, and public relations activities required for successful international problem-solving and subject-matter work.

- With respect to the *institutional improvement agendas* of Part III, Section 1, Chapter 1, it is important for administrators to:
  - Recognize the institutional deficiencies of our rural, agricultural, and food systems by devoting more resources to the institutional work of rural social scientists in all the roles they play relative to farming, rural societies, agribusinesses, and consumers.
  - Recognize, support, and be part of the development of iterative/interactive, multidisciplinary analyses that incorporate a broad multidisciplinary PC/TC approach to analyzing institutional changes (see the corresponding items of Part III, Section 1, Chapter 7).
  - Encourage attention to the value and ethical dimensions of making changes in farm, rural, agribusiness, and consumer institutions.

- With respect to the *agendas on human development and disadvantaged farm and nonfarm rural groups* in Part III, Section 2, Chapter 10, administrators should recognize this as an area of great opportunity, as well as an area that has been seriously neglected and for which neglect they and their programs and organizations are widely criticized. It is important that administrators:
  - Thoroughly examine their research, extension, and resident instruction programs to ascertain the problems and issues that have been neglected involving disadvantaged male and female African-, Native-, Hispanic-, and Caucasian-American farm and nonfarm rural groups. Among Native Americans in Alaska, attention should be given to Eskimos, as well as Indians.
  - Design and improve their programs for
    - developing the human capacity of members of these disadvantaged rural groups and
    - increasing command over income-earning resources (rights and privileges) by members of disadvantaged groups.

    It must be recognized that the future professional and labor force of the United States will come, in substantial part, from today's disadvantaged parents and families, many of whom reside in rural areas. (See Clifford R. Wharton Jr.'s paper republished as Chapter 3 of Part III, Section 2).

- With respect to the *natural and manmade resource conservation, enhancement and/or growth agendas* found in Part III, Section 3, Chapter 7, administrators need to:
  - Devote more resources to extension, resident instruction, advising, consulting, and research on the social science dimensions of natural and manmade resources, environmental pollution, food-chain contamination, and ecological problems and issues.
  - Recognize far more explicitly than now the social science and humanistic (agro-ethical) dimensions of problem-solving and subject-matter work on natural and manmade resources, and encourage the development of multidisciplinary and multidepartmental teams to handle those dimensions.
  - Encourage the development of iterative, systems-science, multidisciplinary analyses of resource problems and issues done *interactively* with both concerned resource decision makers and those affected by the prescriptions and actions of those decision makers. (See the agendas devoted to the problem-solving/transaction cost approach to resource problems and issues in Part III, Section 3, Chapter 7.

- Although administrators of our agricultural institutions have been doing better with respect to social science work on *technical advance* (see Part III, Section 4, Chapter 2) than on the other three "driving forces," it is important that provision be made to ensure more social science contributions to the design, creation, assessment, regulation, and dissemination of technical advance. Problems and issues related to technical advances are almost always multidisciplinary in ways that involve the social sciences and their close connections to the humanities and ethics.

- With respect to the *database and supporting information agendas* of Part II, Section 1, Chapter 3, a substantial amount of administrative effort is required, including efforts to:
  - Restore federal funding for the National Agricultural Statistics Service's (NASS) capacity for generating data on the U.S. agricultural sector.
  - Expand federal funding for acquisition and improvement of data on rural human development, institutions (policies, programs, organization facilities and staffs) and resources (both natural and manmade).
  - Provide more "bottom up" or "outside in" feedback from states and regions to NASS.
  - Restore and expand funding for the generation by the Economic Research Service (ERS) of secondary measures of activities in the agricultural sector, including modernization of the measurement of variables important for resolving the problems and issues of prospective importance for agriculture, rural communities, agribusinesses, and consumers.

- With respect to the *basic social disciplinary agendas* (Part IV, Section 2, Chapter 5) substantial administrative changes are needed:
  - Better linkages are required among the administrators of the rural and the basic social sciences that are often

located in separate colleges of universities or units of other agencies because
  - work on problems and issues is typically multidisciplinary and often (insofar as the rural social and technical agricultural sciences are concerned) multidepartmental, and
  - is typically synergistic with disciplinary work.
- Administrators should resist attempts to divert resources and funds provided directly or indirectly by various clienteles of agricultural institutions from problem-solving and issue-oriented work to specialized disciplinary work of little or no concern to those clienteles.
- Administrators, however, should use funds provided by agricultural clientele groups for disciplinary work designed to overcome social science disciplinary deficiencies that limit the ability of rural social scientists to serve those clienteles.
- Administrators of agricultural institutions should assist and collaborate with administrators of the basic social science disciplines in the acquisition of resources for general disciplinary work in exchange for the assistance of those administrators in obtaining resources for multidisciplinary problem-solving and issue-oriented work by both rural and basic social scientists.

● Perhaps the most difficult administrative change needed by the rural social sciences in agricultural institutions has to do with *agendas pertaining to agro-ethics, values, and philosophic orientations* (See Part IV, Section 3, Chapter 3). Many administrators of our agricultural institutions need reorientation to consider philosophies of science and knowledge other than the reductionist, logically positivistic philosophy that is (1) more appropriate for disciplinary biological and physical science than for disciplinary social science work and (2) unduly restrictive for multidisciplinary problem-solving and issue-oriented work. Worthwhile beginnings in bringing about this reorientation have been made in over ten conferences and workshops held before SSAAP began it work. These were commonly titled as having to do with agro-ethics, bio-ethics, and human values. They were reviewed in Part IV, Section 3, Chapter 1.

THE LONG-TERM NEED FOR A "SSAAP-LIKE" ORGANIZATION

During the SSAAP advisory committee meeting held after the Houston conference, it was decided that it would be useful to explore the possibility of longer-term institutional followup to the SSAAP to provide a forum and continuity for rural social science interactions and cooperation. To explore these possibilities, the advisory committee appointed a small group, whimsically titled the "short-term committee on the long-term future of SSAAP." The committee was chaired by R. James Hildreth of the Farm Foundation and included James T. Bonnen, Ralph R. Christy, Bobby R. Eddleman, Cornelia Butler Flora, Lee Kolmer, John Lee, G. Edward Rossmiller, and James Zuiches.

If after deliberation, it should be decided that a follow-up organization is needed, the committee recommended the following:

● A "council of rural social sciences" (CORSS) should be formed to continue and expand the activities initiated by the Social Science Agricultural Agenda Project.

● CORSS would complement but not compete with existing rural or other social science organizations by facilitating a host of functions designed to:
- Improve communications and linkage networks among rural social scientists and their institutions and associations.
- Enhance the effectiveness of rural social sciences acting together (as appropriate) to address both common disciplinary/subject-matter problems and practical problems of society.
- Increase understanding of, and support for, the rural social sciences among administrators, legislators, various public groups, and funding authorities.

● It is proposed that CORSS, if established, seek institutional funding from CSRS/USDA, ERS/USDA, and appropriate foundations to facilitate its establishment and to support its activities.

● It is anticipated that CORSS, if established, would consider support of (but not be limited to) activities such as:
- Formation of rural social science "SWAT" teams (modeled after CAST task forces for commentaries) to address urgent multistate farm and rural social problems.
- Joint meetings of rural social science associations (joint annual meetings) and joint sessions at each of these meetings.
- Being a catalyst for interdisciplinary (social science) workshops and/or sessions at rural social science association meetings on specific methodological or social problems.
- More effective participation of the rural social sciences in AAAS annual meetings (especially sections K, O, and X).
- Affiliation with COSSA and work with COSSA and other rural social science associations on special projects.
- Interchange of directory information between rural social science associations and basic social science societies, perhaps using on-line computer technology.
- Possible development of a national endowment for the rural social sciences.
- The international transfer of institutional innovations to and from the United States to deal with agricultural and rural social problems in research, teaching, and extension.

● The classes of membership in CORSS could consist of the following:
- Professional associations
- Rural social science departments of universities
- Affiliates (foundations, government agencies, other organizations)
- Individuals

A schedule of annual dues for each class of membership could be established. CORSS could be governed by a board representing the classes of membership.

● When developing and operating, it is proposed that the CORSS have a staff consisting of an executive director (full- or part-time) and one support-staff member. The staff could be housed in an office of one of the members.

SSAAP recognizes that the formation of CORSS would be a major effort involving:

- Development of initial endorsements from the rural social science associations—rural sociology, agricultural economics, and agricultural history—and persons from political science, human ecology, anthropology, geography, and social sciences without organized rural counterparts who, nonetheless, have interests in the food, fiber, and resource system, and in rural affairs.
- Identification of a small group of individuals willing and able to commit substantial time and energy to the development of CORSS.
- Initial funding of the individuals who would spearhead the formation of CORSS while they establish sponsorship, funding, and a place for CORSS in the agricultural establishment.

This book, its separate executive summary, and a public relations flyer are to be used in conferences, mailings, and other efforts to inform rural and basic social scientists and their administrators and funders about the agendas and strategies SSAAP has generated. During these conferences, an ongoing SSAAP committee, the aforementioned "short-term committee on the long-term future of SSAAP," will continue to operate with the objective of considering and possibly initiating the process of forming CORSS with the help and assistance of members of SSAAP's executive committee and its advisory board. That committee will continue to explore the possibility of convening a conference of public and private foundations to consider and perhaps support efforts to establish the formation of CORSS.

CHAPTER 9

SUMMARY AND CONCLUSIONS: CHALLENGES AND AGENDAS FOR RURAL AND BASIC SOCIAL SCIENTISTS AND THEIR ADMINISTRATORS

Today, agriculture, rural America, and food consumers are concerned about the viability of rural communities, rural health care, disadvantaged minority and Caucasian farm and nonfarm rural groups, food safety, environmental pollution, substance abuse, stress management, family instability, financial solvency, the efficiency of local governments and resource amenities—the list seems endless. The striking thing about the list is that, for the most part, the problems and issues it reflects are not subject to "technical fixes." They all have important crucial social science dimensions that must be addressed before the problems can be solved and the issues resolved.

In general, the relevance and capacities of the rural and basic disciplinary social sciences for addressing such problems and issues are poorly understood in our public agricultural institutions. Even in these institutions, where support for the rural social sciences should be most expected, support is minimal relative to needs.

In attempting to explain the relative neglect of the social scientists, administrators have told SSAAP's leaders that the social sciences are not as productive as the technical agricultural and the basic or disciplinary biological and physical sciences. They have also stated that work on the social dimensions of current problems and issues is difficult to finance. Neither assertion is consistent with the historical record.

- The social sciences have made major academic and practical contributions to farming, agribusiness, rural society, and consumers. These have been:
  - Of an empirical and theoretical nature to (1) our understanding of human development (human capital formation) in agriculture, (2) analysis of agricultural development, (3) input/output analysis, and (4) the development of public choice analysis. *These four contributions have been recognized with Nobel prizes* and have contributed markedly to increased capacity of agriculturalists to solve important problems and resolve crucial issues of agriculture, rural societies and people, agribusinesses, and consumers.
  - To the development of the world's best primary data collection system and secondary measures for agricultural production, prices, product utilization, income, input usage, levels of living, consumption, demographic changes, etc.
  - To the disciplinary development of econometrics, linear programming, and operations research.
  - To the design, establishment, and administration of national, state, and local policies, programs, organizations, and facilities, including, as examples, the production and farm credit administrations, the Bank for Cooperatives, marketing cooperatives, price-support and production programs, the extension of Social Security to farmers, the Soil Conservation Service, the Tennessee Valley Authority, and other resource and development efforts such as the limited-input sustainable agriculture program, etc.—the list is long.
  - To the maintenance, modification, and reform of institutions, policies, programs, organizations, and infrastructural facilities. Like the antibiotics, rust-resistant wheats, machinery, computers, and pesticides developed by the biological and physical scientists, the institutional creations of social scientists lose their effectiveness, become obsolete, and in other ways require maintenance, modification, and redesign. The fact that maintenance is required is not evidence that the original social science work to create them was unproductive.
  - To the management and reorganization of farms, rural households, agribusinesses, marketing cooperatives, agricultural organizations, semigovernmental businesses, and to the design and administration of agricultural programs of national, state or provincial, and local governments.
  - To Third World agricultural development programs, including those of such successful now-developed countries as Japan, Israel, South Korea, and Taiwan, that have done better than countries experiencing only technical "Green Revolutions" without institutional reform, human capital formation, and the enhancement of their natural and manmade resource bases.

- Contrary to common administrative assertions, *financial support* for work on the long-neglected social science dimensions of our farm, rural, and consumer problems *is available* as indicated by:

- The widespread criticism of the USDA/land-grant college system for being too technocratic and neglecting alleged adverse societal impacts of the technologies it has created on family farms, the environment, food chains, depopulated rural communities, food quality, rural health, agribusinesses, farm laborers, the structure of the agricultural sector, etc. *These criticisms need to be, can be, and should be channelled into support* for funding multidisciplinary problem-solving and issue-oriented work on the social and humanistic dimensions of current technical-change problems and issues by social scientists and humanists in our agricultural institutions.
- The growing support for problem-solving and issue-oriented work important for farming, agribusinesses, rural resources, consumers, disadvantaged rural groups, the environment, food safety, etc., that *is being obtained outside* of agricultural institutions *from* local, state, non-USDA federal, and international agencies *for* social science and humanistic work that is being obtained outside of our traditional agricultural institutions. This work addresses various societal dimensions of both technological and non-technological problems and issues faced by farmers, agribusinesses, rural residents and consumers that have been partially or totally neglected by traditional administrators and funders of our agricultural institutions. Institutional change, human development, and improvements in natural and manmade resources, as well as technical changes are studied. If our agricultural institutions do not respond (and quickly), most of the potential funding to address these pressing problems and issues will go elsewhere and important opportunities for our agricultural institutions to contribute will be lost to institutions whose lack of agricultural expertise and knowledge reduces their effectiveness in doing such work. While this book was being published, this point was strongly reinforced in an article entitled "Political Activists Working to Change Land-Grant Colleges," which was published in the *The Chronicle of Higher Education* in its march 20, 1991 issue. This article should be read by all administrators of our agricultural institutions.

SSAAP is a national effort stimulated by neglect of the social science dimensions of problems and issues important for farming, rural people and societies, rural resources, agribusinesses, and consumers. Since World War II, public rural and agricultural investments have concentrated more and more on technology to the benign neglect of rural society and people. SSAAP is responding constructively to the opportunities presented by this neglect.

SSAAP's objectives as stated in its prospectus are:

- Enhancement of the quality and effectiveness of research and related activities in the rural social sciences and in the basic social science disciplines for improving farm and agribusiness productivity, farm and nonfarm rural area development, nonfarm rural resource development, and related aspects of general welfare by:
  - creating a strategic agenda and set of broad priorities for U.S. and international rural social science research, extension, consulting, advising, and related activities, and
  - clarifying the different roles that both rural social scientists and disciplinary social scientists should play to make effective contributions to the agricultural establishment of the United States and the world.
- Development of wide support in funding, administrative, and user communities for the strategic research agenda developed by SSAAP.

All of the work rural and basic social scientists do in the food, fiber, and rural resource system and in rural societies *has been the concern of SSAAP*—resident instruction, extension, advisement, legislation, consultation, activism, administration (both public and private), staff work and entrepreneurship, as well as research.

The rural social sciences, like the technical agricultural sciences, *depend on their underlying basic disciplines*. Agricultural economics, agricultural history, home economics (or human ecology), and rural sociology depend on economics, history, sociology, anthropology, political science, philosophy, psychology, geography, mathematics, and statistics. The individual rural social sciences and individual technical agricultural sciences are more focused on practical problems and issues than the basic disciplinary social biological and physical sciences; this concern with problems and issues makes the rural social scientists more multidisciplinary than their underlying specialized academic disciplines simply because practical problems and issues are multidisciplinary. A capable extension director, Ernest Nesius, observed many years ago that his administrative difficulty was that "farmers have problems whereas universities have departments." SSAAP is concerned with both the rural and basic social sciences and tries to exploit the synergism between their works.

SSAAP's leadership has been acutely aware of the narrow line they are attempting to tread between unjustified advocacy and making the *objective case for the social sciences*. SSAAP's case for the rural social sciences is not made at the expense of the biological and physical agricultural sciences. Because most of the sciences and humanities are necessary (but individually insufficient) for doing multidisciplinary, problem-solving, and issue-oriented work (and even for doing some basic disciplinary work), the social sciences cannot be emphasized at the expense of the biological and physical sciences any more than the biological and physical sciences should be emphasized at the expense of the social sciences. For our agricultural institutions to become unduly "sociocratic" would be as unfortunate as their present undue technocracy.

During the course of SSAAP's work, it became clear that *major reorientations are needed* of the organizations in which rural and disciplinary social scientists work, of the administrators of those organizations and, indeed, of many social scientists themselves before we can adequately address the social science dimensions of problems and issues of farmers; rural people and societies; food, fiber, and resource consumers and users; and agribusinesses. It also became clear that such reorientations call for (1) a set of broad overall *strategies* to facilitate the needed reorientation; (2) rural social science *agendas* that indicate to all the important work the rural and basic social scientists can do effectively in our public, semipublic, and private agricultural institutions; and (3) additional, more detailed strategies for funding and administering the work of rural and basic social scientists.

SSAAP'S BROAD STRATEGIC CHALLENGES

The Social Science Agricultural Agenda Project (SSAAP) holds that the rural and basic social sciences should now strive to forge new, more contributory partnerships throughout the public, semipublic, and private institutions serving agriculture. To accomplish this will challenge both (1) administrators of public and private institutions and (2) rural and basic disciplinary social scientists (inside as well as outside of agricultural institutions). The objective of the partnerships should be that of better serving farmers and their families; agribusinesses; rural societies and people; the consumers of food, fiber, and resource products and services; and, through these groups, all of society.

THE BROAD CHALLENGES FOR ADMINISTRATORS ARE TO ENCOURAGE, FACILITATE, AND FUND

- partnership roles in their organizations for the rural and basic disciplinary social scientists *with*
- the technical agricultural scientists, *involving*
- the basic biological, physical and social scientists along with disciplinarians from philosophy, statistics, and mathematics as needed to *address*
- the social science dimensions of a wide variety of crucial rural, farmer, people, agribusiness, community, resource, and consumer problems and issues that are detailed later in this summary, many of which have long been unduly neglected by our agricultural institutions.

Requirements for Success

Success for the above partnerships requires that:

- The social science dimensions of current and prospective multidisciplinary practical problems and issue-related subjects be recognized and addressed.
- Our agricultural institutions redress their present imbalance toward technology without neglecting the technical advances required in the decades ahead. This will require more balanced attention than in the past to the four primary sources of improved human and societal capacity:
  - Technological advance
  - Human development
  - Improvements in institutions, policies, programs, organizations, and social infrastructures
  - Enhancement of natural and manmade resources
- Our agricultural institutions reverse the post-World War II trend toward disciplinary academic social, biological, and physical science work at the expense of multidisciplinary work on practical problems and issues.

The need is for redressing the current imbalance rather than for elimination or sharp curtailment of disciplinary work. Both kinds of work are essential and there is an important synergism between them.

Satisfying the Requirements

Meeting the three requirements for success listed above will be easier if:

- Work on practical multidisciplinary problems and issue-related subjects is rewarded more adequately, i.e., as compared to disciplinary work.
- Rural and basic social scientists constructively assist their administrators in: identifying problems and issues involving the social sciences, designing and organizing projects and programs to address such problems and issues, and in the funding, conduct, and administration of such projects and programs.
- Philosophic orientations besides logically positive, reductionist views are more widely accepted as legitimate in our agricultural institutions. To date, other philosophies of knowledge, agricultural ethics, and the study of values have been unduly neglected.
- It is remembered that the value of scholarly disciplinary excellence is significantly instrumental as a means of obtaining the problem-solving and issue-oriented output society expects from all of its academic, research, and service institutions and, particularly, from the agricultural institutions in the USDA/land-grant system.
- The productivity of the social sciences is recognized.
- Criticisms of our agricultural institutions for neglecting the social science dimensions of farm, rural, and consumer problems and issues are converted into support for social science work.

THE BROAD CHALLENGES FOR THE RURAL AND BASIC OR DISCIPLINARY SOCIAL SCIENCES AND THEIR ASSOCIATED DISCIPLINES ARE THOSE OF CONTRIBUTING TO

- Multidisciplinary and multidepartmental problem-solving and issue or subject-matter partnership or team efforts important for addressing problems and issues (some long-neglected) for farming, agribusiness, rural people and societies, rural resource users and owners, and consumers.
- Applied, more specialized, disciplinary social science work in individual basic social science disciplines that is relevant to problems and issues pertaining to agriculture, rural societies, rural people and resources, agriculturally related businesses, and consumers.
- Disciplinary work on deficiencies in the theories, techniques, and data of the basic social science disciplines that constrain practical multidisciplinary work on problems and subjects important to farmers, agribusinesses, rural societies, and consumers.

SSAAP has found that *major reorientations* of our agricultural institutions and their social scientists *are needed* to place emphasis on the problems and issues of farmers and their families; rural people and societies; food, fiber, and resource consumers and users; and agribusinesses. SSAAP recognizes the danger that presenting a few simple priority initiatives for social science work would fail to reorient our institutions and social scientists to the significantly greater role that should be played by the social sciences. Thus, *earlier in this summary*, SSAAP called for a broad reorientation of the administrators and social scientists in our agricultural institutions and now presents ten sets of agendas *in what follows*. These agendas should be useful inputs in the processes of setting the priorities of administrators and social scientists as they respond to SSAAP's broad challenges. Priorities should be set federal agency by federal agency, state by state, local government by local government, problem by problem, and issue by issue by those with responsibilities for policies, programs, and projects (including funding) rather than by a temporary, national organization of scientists and professionals such as SSAAP.

TEN CHALLENGING RURAL AND AGRICULTURAL AGENDAS FOR THE SOCIAL SCIENCES

SSAAP's ten rural and agricultural agendas challenge both (1) rural and basic social scientists, and (2) their administrators. The agendas indicate what the rural and basic disciplinary social sciences can effectively contribute in ten areas. All of these agendas should receive major attention in research, extension, resident instruction, advising, consulting, agribusiness, public administration, and legislative efforts, and in the work of commodity, general farm and other rural organizations. The ten agenda sets are only briefly summarized in this executive summary. Much more detail can be found in the references throughout this summary.

In this chapter, SSAAP uses the following outline to present its agendas:

- The first two agenda sets pertain to the problems and issues of *farms (including homes and families), agribusinesses, and consumers:*
  - one set for domestic agriculture and
  - the other set for the agricultures of less developed countries (LDCs).
- The next four agenda sets deal with the *four primary (driving) forces* for improving food, resource, and fiber systems; rural societies; the well-being of consumers; and the lives of rural people. The four forces include:
  - institutional improvements,
  - human development,
  - the enhancement and improvement of natural and manmade resource bases, and
  - technological advance.
- *Four more of SSAAP's agendas* cut across all six of the above agendas. They include:
  - databases and supporting information systems,
  - the basic disciplinary social sciences,
  - agroethics and philosophic orientations, and
  - research on the administration and funding of our agricultural institutions and their rural and basic social science work.

The above ten agenda sets which are briefly summarized below are in addition to the administrative and funding *strategies* developed by SSAAP that (1) were presented in broad form at the beginning of this summary and (2) will be presented in more detail at its end.

TWO AGENDAS FOR DOMESTIC AND INTERNATIONAL SERVICE

Traditionally, rural social scientists have been effective in and have been reasonably well financed and administered when serving *domestic* production agriculture, farm families, agribusinesses, farm organizations, and consumers. More recently, rural social scientists have also earned substantial support for *international* farm and rural development work by, in effect, going outside our traditional agricultural institutions to earn support while doing their own administrative work. SSAAP recognizes the continuing importance of these two areas with separate agendas. These agendas reflect the current circumstances and changes that make it desirable to modify the traditional agendas of agricultural economists, rural sociologists, home economists, and others in these two areas.

Challenging Agendas for DOMESTIC Farming, Farm Families, Agribusinesses, and Consumers

SSAAP's agendas (Part II, Section 1, Chapter 9) for this area include items having to do with:

- Impacts of the globalization of agriculture, shifts in competitiveness of U.S. agriculture, and changes in international monetary and fiscal and trade arrangements on U.S. farms, agribusinesses, and consumers.
- Development of new agricultural institutions and adaptation of old ones for a global market economy in which international agreements on new rules and standards are necessary for the stability and effectiveness of our agricultural sector.
- Finding the delicate balance required between reliance on governmental and parastatal interventions versus market forces in making needed institutional, human, natural and manmade physical resource improvements and technical advances.
- Investigation and design of institutions, policies, and programs for controlling the tendencies for market-regulated agricultural sectors and subsectors to outproduce effective demand at prices that do not permit full recovery of expenditures and investments by either individual farmers or society as a whole.
- A number of new problems and issues to which social scientists should contribute such as environmental pollution, family instability, rural health, local governmental services, nutrition, stress management, the treatment of animals, worker safety, food-chain contamination, teenage pregnancy—the list of new concerns of farmers and their families, agribusinesses, and consumers seems endless.
- Needed changes in U.S. monetary/fiscal, trade, national farm, and other policies and programs affecting these same groups and the impacts on these same groups of

the structural shifts now occurring in the United States because of technical, institutional, human, and resource and environmental changes in agricultural and rural areas.

- The changes needed by farmers, agribusinesses, and consumers in technology, institutions, human capacity, and resources *and* in the institutions that generate such changes (related agendas are found in Part III, Sections 1 through 4, as well as in Part II, Section 1, Chapter 9).
- Agricultural credit as part of a national credit system that is now in crisis.
- The impacts of the bimodalization of farms (more large, fewer medium and more smaller part-time and residential farms) on farming, rural societies and agricultural service institutions.
- Needed improvements in the management of farms, businesses, farm homes, agribusinesses, and urban consumer households. This requires:
  - Better integration of research, extension, and resident instruction work across farm, business, and home activities. (Note: even incorporated U.S. farms are mostly family corporations.)
  - Improvement and further development of managerial theory to deal with the multidisciplinarity of the iterative/interactive, participatory nature of real-world decision- and choice-making processes of farmers, homemakers, agribusiness persons, and public administrators.
  - Further development of what is known in social science literature as the public (really multiperson) choice/transaction cost approach to analyses of farm and home, agribusiness and consumer problems and issues (see Part III Introduction; Part III, Section 1, Chapters 1 and 7; and Part IV, Section 3, Chapters 1 and 3) utilizing:
    - Theories and information from the basic social, biological and physical science and humanistic disciplines (see Part IV, Section 2) as they are relevant.
    - Value as well as value-free and pragmatic knowledge.
    - Less reductionistic, less positivistic philosophic orientations (see Part IV, Section 3).
    - Improved information systems and databases (Part III, Section 1, Chapters 1 and 3).

Challenging Agendas for INTERNATIONAL Farm and Rural Development

In addition to analyzing the domestic impacts of the globalization of international money markets and markets for agricultural products, U.S. social scientists have earned support from outside our traditional domestic agricultural institutions for their direct and indirect contributions to farm and rural development in Third World countries. Important challenges and opportunities continue in this area for social scientists and their administrators that are reflected in SSAAP's agendas (see Part II, Section 2, Chapter 11) that pertain to:

- The impacts of international monetary/fiscal and trade developments on Third World agricultures and international rural development assistance.
- Third World farm and rural development policies including attention to the delicate balance between reliance on governmental interventions versus market forces in making needed institutional, human, natural and manmade physical resource improvements, and technical advances.
- Multidisciplinary work on problems and subject-matter issues important to Third World farm, agribusiness, and home and family managers; natural and manmade resource generators, users, enhancers, and conservers; and nonfarm consumers and users of food, fiber, and natural resource services and commodities.
- Food security and the even more important, closely related problems of low income and poverty in the agricultures of many Third World countries.
- Country- and location-specific resource-sustainability, environmental-pollution, and food-chain-contamination problems arising from structural and technical changes in both Third World and developed countries.
- Meeting Third World agricultural and rural institutional needs such as those for policy development and implementation; research, resident instruction, and extension functions; agricultural production and marketing; regulatory standards; and databases and information systems.
- Needed multidisciplinary team efforts of technical agricultural, basic biological and physical, along with rural and basic social scientists to model and analyze the global *social* as well as the more commonly stressed global *technical* consequences of the structural, institutional, technical, human, and resource changes now taking place in world agriculture. The public choice/transaction cost approach promises to be of increasing value in modeling *such global consequences* in time, space, demographic, income, and other social dimensions of world agriculture. (See the next set of agendas on institutions as well as Part III Introduction and Part III, Section 1, Chapter 7.)
- Important agroethical issues for Third World farmers and their families, agribusinesses, and consumers that cry out for attention from rural and basic social scientists to work on them in close partnerships with philosophers and humanists as well as with technical agricultural and basic biological and physical scientists (see Part II, Section 2, Chapters 5 and 10; and Part IV, Section 3).
- Internationally, Third World agricultural and rural databases remain inadequate and poorly developed for assisting farmers, agribusiness people, and consumers. Meeting these inadequacies demands a wide range of efforts from social scientists working closely with such auxiliary disciplines as statistics, mathematics, and computer science (for more details, see the databases subheading below and Part II, Section 2, Chapter 11).

FOUR AGENDAS ABOUT THE PRIMARY FORCES FOR IMPROVING FOOD, RURAL RESOURCE AND FIBER SYSTEMS; RURAL SOCIETIES; AND THE LIVES OF RURAL PEOPLE

The four forces include: *institutional improvements, human development, the enhancement of natural and manmade resource bases, and technological advance*. Analyses of rural and farm development experiences here and abroad indicate that each of these forces is necessary but individually insufficient for progress. Neglect of any of the four greatly diminishes progress. Since World War II, after decades of keeping the four in reasonably good balance, our agricultural institutions have increasingly stressed one of the four—technology—to the neglect of institutions and people. Even the recent increased emphasis on resources, the environment, and food chains neglects their social science dimensions in favor of their biological and physical science dimensions.

Challenging Agendas for Improving Rural and Agricultural Institutions

The design, adaptation, improvement, and reform of institutions is necessarily a primary domain of the social sciences. As viewed by SSAAP, institutions include (1) organizations and (2) their programs, policies, facilities, and staffs, as well as (3) "rules of the game." The domestic and international agendas presented above consider changes in our international trade and monetary/fiscal institutions and policies; changes in domestic farm price, production control, marketing, and related organizations, policies, and programs; and changes in our agricultural credit institutions. Further, the next three agendas address problems and issues pertaining to our institutions for human development, the enhancement of natural and manmade resources and the generation of technological advanee. Still later agendas treat institutions concerned with databases and information systems, the undergirding basic social science disciplines, and the administration of our agricultural organizations. Thus, the substantive institutional agendas in this set focus mainly on local, state, private-sector, and voluntary institutions, organizations, facilities, and staffs. However, more generic agenda items that pertain to all kinds of institutional change are also considered here. These substantive agenda items are concerned with needs:

- For study of change and development in rural communities and areas.
- To design, evaluate, assess, analyze, and utilize state and local institutions, programs and policies, and the services they create.
- To assist local, state, and provincial governments in making their revenue collection and utilization operations more effective.
- To improve public choices and private decisions concerning institutions with greater attention to the roles of values and ethics (also see Part IV, Section 3, Chapters 2 and 3).
- To research the profound social, economic, and demographic changes that rural society is undergoing and to do this in close participation with relevant decision makers and affected people in order to provide better bases for making appropriate institutional modifications to facilitate the adjustment of farms, agribusinesses, consumers, and rural communities to such changes.
- To help local governments and nongovernmental rural organizations reorganize and operate more effectively in serving different farm as well as nonfarm rural clienteles.
- To better understand and deal with the ethical aspects of institutions used to resolve conflicts. (See also Part IV, Section 3, Chapters 2 and 3.)
- For federal, state, and local governments to develop more adequate databases for rural decision making. (See also Part IV, Section 1, Chapters 2 and 3.)

From a more generic point of view, one of the most exciting and promising current developments in the social sciences is the evolution of the public choice/transaction cost (PC/TC) approach to public and multiperson choices and decisions. For the rural social sciences this development may be as significant as biogenetic engineering is for the technical agricultural sciences. Like biogenetics, the public choice/transaction cost approach is, as yet, quite primitive. It is also unduly specialized on economics. Social scientists need to further develop the public choice/transaction cost approach by integrating and extending its theoretical structure to make it capable of handling induced innovation, technology diffusion, and rent-seeking phenomena as special cases in a more general approach (see also Part III Introduction; Part III, Section 1, Chapters 1 and 7; Part III, Section 3, Chapters 1 and 7; and Part IV, Section 3) by:

- Making it truly multidisciplinary among the social, biological and physical sciences, and humanities so as to be able to work with theories, variables, and data from these disciplines as needed in addressing the relevant multidisciplinary dimensions of the problems and issues important for rural institutions.
- Recognizing the interdependencies of three manifestations of institutional change, namely, changes in: the "rules of the game," organizations, and facilities and staffs.
- Recognizing and estimating both the stock and operating (or flow) costs and returns that are encountered in establishing, elaborating, and dismantling institutions in all of their manifestations.
- Identifying, distinguishing between, and measuring the monetary and nonmonetary worth of existing and possible replacement institutions. This should be done in terms of both flow and stock values and of intrinsic as well as exchange or extrinsic values.
- Distinguishing between institutional changes made for productive purposes and those changes made mainly to create income streams (both monetary and nonmonetary) for noncontributing groups and individuals.
- Identifying better the roles played by losses with respect to replacement costs (negative quasi-rents) and of gains with respect to dismantlement costs (positive quasi-rents) of institutions that are fixed in any of their manifestations because it is not advantageous to change them.

Challenging Agendas for Human Development and the Rural Disadvantaged of the United States

This is the second of SSAAP's agendas pertaining to the four primary forces for farm and rural development.

Human development and the rural disadvantaged are so widely neglected by our agricultural institutions and their rural social scientists that the agendas summarized herein present some of the most challenging and important opportunities identified by SSAAP for serving farming and rural societies. For details, see the agendas of Part III, Section 2, Chapter 10. Those agendas relate to:

- Helping reshape the resident instruction, youth, and adult outreach programs of our agricultural institutions to update the skills and capacities of the rural disadvantaged (including women) without neglecting the rural advantaged whose improved skills and capacities are also needed.
- Helping (again without neglecting the rural advantaged whose skills and capacities are also crucial) improve the focus on disadvantaged rural groups of the K-12 educational system in rural areas by:
  - Researching and, in other ways, addressing the redistribution of educational rights and privileges and the ownership of other property rights and privileges needed to alleviate the poverty of disadvantaged rural groups and increase their contributions to society.
  - Increasing descriptive social science work done on the problems of disadvantaged rural groups. This should include descriptive work on values relevant for defining and resolving the problems of these same groups.
  - Pursuing the more detailed agendas published in this book (Part III, Section 2, Chapter 10) that devote special attention to disadvantaged rural Caucasian, African, Hispanic, and Native Americans. SSAAP's special agendas for rural social sciences' assistance to these groups include:
    - Establishing close, participatory interactions with disadvantaged rural Caucasian (the largest disadvantaged group), African, Hispanic, and Native Americans.
    - Seeking out, doing, and (where necessary) initiating, designing, and leading multidisciplinary and multidepartmental public- and/or private-agency work on the problems and issues of the rural disadvantaged.
    - Using the expanded and improved public choice/transaction cost approach (see the agenda immediately above on improving and using the public choice/transaction cost approach) to do iterative, interactive, multidisciplinary systems analyses of public and multiple-person choices and decisions involving poverty elimination and the promotion of human capital formation among disadvantaged rural groups.
- Remedying those deficiencies in the basic social science disciplines (BSSDs) that constrain the ability of the rural social sciences (RSSs) to address human development problems and poverty of disadvantaged groups (see Part III, Section 2, Chapter 10). With financial and other support from the administrators in our agricultural institutions and elsewhere, rural and basic social scientists should:
  - Develop improved conceptualizations of the roles that social, political, anthropological, psychological, geographic, historical, and economic variables play in the processes of human development and poverty alleviation, so that such variables can be better incorporated into multidisciplinary, interactive/iterative systems models and/or scenario analyses of the domains of problems and issues pertaining to human development and disadvantaged groups.
  - Try to overcome the long-standing difficulties in the social sciences that result from the questionable interpersonal validity and lack of cardinality of measures of values used to define and resolve equality (redistributive) issues vis-à-vis human development and poverty. See the crosscutting agendas below on (1) the basic social sciences and (2) agroethics, and Part IV, sections 2 and 3.
- Improving databases (see Part IV, Section 1) on
  - rural "human capital generating" institutions, activities, and the people served by them and
  - disadvantaged farm and nonfarm rural groups.

Challenging Agendas for the Enhancement, Conservation, Development, and Utilization of Natural and Manmade Rural Resource Bases

This is the third set of "primary-force" agendas developed by SSAAP. Natural and manmade resource agendas interrelate for two reasons. *First*, natural resources are used in creating manmade resources. *Second*, manmade resources substitute for and complement natural resources to increase the productivity of the latter. SSAAP further recognizes that some nonrenewable natural resources are necessarily destroyed by use (examples include coal, petroleum, and fossil water), whereas other natural resources can be maintained at, above, or below their original "natural" levels while still others, such as solar energy, must be used, stored, or wasted. For all three kinds of resources, optimal patterns of use, conservation, and enhancement need to be determined through time, across space, among individuals and groups, and in still other physical and social dimensions. For those natural resources that can be maintained, enhanced and/or renewed, optimal investments and expenditures on their maintenance, enhancement, and renewal need to be determined. Environmental pollution, health risks, and food chain contamination are crucial, associated resource dangers. The following relate to the more detailed important agendas presented in Part III, Section 3, Chapter 7:

- Evaluation of resource policy options.
- Analysis of the effect of market, social, and political elements on the supply and production costs of and demand for widely divergent physical products and services derived from natural resources. Examples of such products and services include: timber, fish and marine products, minerals, wildlife, water, scenery, farm commodities, coastlines, and water and other recreational services, hunting, solitude of wilderness areas, carbon dioxide fixation, oxygenation of the atmosphere, and ozone protection.
- Investigation of the behavior and attitudes of users of natural resources and resource products.
- Investigations of resource degradation, environmental pollution, and food-chain contamination.

- Establishment of better interactions of resource owners and users with public resource agencies to help solve problems and resolve issues at international, federal, state, and local levels, both public and private.

- Determination of optimal rates of depletion, maintenance, and enhancement of a wide variety of natural resources under different relevant circumstances.

- Increased use of an expanded and improved version of the public choice/transaction cost approach that is already being used increasingly by resource professionals in analyzing and designing changes in resource institutions. (See the relevant agenda items above under the heading "Challenging Agendas for Rural and Agricultural Institutions" including the references therein to specific parts of this book.) The needed improvements in the public choice/transaction cost approach are treated there and are presented in more detail below under the heading "Challenging Agendas for Agroethics and Philosophic Reorientations." (Also see Part III, Section 3, Chapter 7, and Part IV, Section 3, Chapter 3.) Multidisciplinary, iterative/interactive, participatory systems analyses are needed of the domains of problems and issues involving natural and manmade resources.

- Disciplinary work on how to model variables from such specialized disciplines as sociology, biology, political science, atmospheric physics, geography, economics, geography, hydrology, economics, geology, anthropology, and ethics in doing iterative/interactive, participatory, multidisciplinary problem solving and subject-matter analysis of natural and manmade resource problems and issues.

- Development of improved databases and information systems for natural and manmade resources, including information on relevant monetary and nonmonetary values as well as relatively value-free data and information.

- More extensive treatment of the ethical and value dimension of natural and manmade resources including environmental pollution, food-chain contamination, and questions of justice and equity both within and between generations.

Challenging Agendas with Respect to Technical Advance

This is the fourth driving force for which SSAAP developed agendas. Despite the fact that our agricultural and other research, education, service, and outreach institutions now place much more emphasis on this driving force than the other three, much social science work is needed in this area because (1) technological advance will continue to be required by farmers, agribusinesses, and households, and (2) social science dimensions of technical change have been seriously neglected. SSAAP's technical advance agendas, which are presented in detail in Part III, Section 4, Chapter 2, support the following summary conclusions.

- Technical advances in farm production, farm product processing, resource management, institutional management, and consumption will continue to be essential. Thus
  - SSAAP does not advocate reduced attention to technical advance by our agricultural institutions, but
  - SSAAP does place high on its agenda increased attention to the *social science dimensions* of generating, disseminating, and using technical advances, while
  - stressing the complementarity that exists between technical advance and improvements in the other three driving forces—institutional improvements, development of human capabilities, and enhancement of natural and manmade resources.

- Improved partnerships are particularly needed *between* the social *and* the biological and physical sciences to focus more attention on the social dimensions of technical change that are important for rural societies and for the food, fiber, and natural resource system.

- The specialized "technology diffusion" studies of sociologists and the equally specialized induced "technical change" studies of economists should be extended into truly multidisciplinary analyses of technical change in farming, agribusiness, rural societies, and rural households. Carrying out this agenda item involves further development of the public choice/transaction cost approach as outlined in the agendas presented under the subsections labeled *challenging agendas for improving rural and agricultural institutions* above and *challenging agendas with respect to agroethics and philosophic reorientations* below.

- The improved and expanded public choice/transaction cost approach called for in the previous item is needed to analyze and solve problems or resolve issues pertaining to the design, implementation, and operation of technology-generating institutions and the consequences of the technical changes those institutions generate. Doing this requires agendas to:
  - Improve databases for technical change (see subsequent subsection on *challenging agendas concerning databases and supporting information systems* and Part IV, Section 1).
  - Use the basic social sciences to assist in specifying, quantifying, and incorporating sociological, political, anthropological, psychological, historical, economic, geographic, and ecological, as well as biological, hydrological, geological, and atmospheric variables in iterative and interactive multidisciplinary public choice/transaction cost analyses of technical changes and in the design, modification and evaluation of technical change institutions.
  - Develop descriptive knowledge of the values pertaining to technical change for use in resolving issues and solving problems concerning technical change and technical-change institutions.
  - Philosophically reorient many administrators and "working professionals" in our agricultural institutions to facilitate the generation and use of the descriptive value knowledge needed in reaching prescriptions to resolve practical issues and solve practical problems about agricultural technology.

FOUR CROSSCUTTING AGENDAS

There are three crosscutting agendas in this book for (1) databases and supporting information systems, (2) the basic social sciences, (3) agroethics and philosophic reorientations, and, in this summary, (4) SSAAP's agendas for needed administrative and funding research are treated as a fourth crosscutting set even if not so treated in the body of this book.

Challenging Agendas Concerning Databases and Supporting Information Systems

This, the first of the four crosscutting agendas presented here, focuses on databases and information systems essential for describing, analyzing, and acting on rural and agricultural problems and issues. To develop their databases, the social sciences must observe and measure phenomena as they occur in the complex, interacting, real social world rather than in the simpler, controlled conditions of a laboratory. In this respect, the social sciences tend to be more like astronomy than chemistry or physics. The care and resources that must go into statistical measurement and into the design of social science information systems, procedures, and institutions are critical to the objectivity, accuracy, and relevance of the analyses and decisions that depend on social science databases and information systems. SSAAP's database and information system agenda (see Part IV, Section 1, Chapter 3) for the federal government, international agencies, and state and local agencies includes attention to needs for:

- Improved coordination of data for decisions on rural problems. Presently, responsibility for collecting, maintaining, and disseminating U.S. data on rural areas and populations is scattered throughout the federal government. A single USDA agency should be given authority to coordinate the planning and implementation of all federal statistical activities relating to food, agriculture, and rural community welfare and development. Coordination is also needed between and within states.

- More systematic input from users in designing and modifying social science databases and information systems at all levels.

- Rural social science work with appropriate national and international institutions to improve the quality of data in Third World countries by:
  - Assessing data and ongoing statistical survey and census programs of less developed countries (LDCs), developed countries (DCs), and international agencies as to their suitability for social science research.
  - Defining data needs according to policy research needs and other objectives of users.
  - Promoting communication and collaboration among institutions, especially between those in DCs and LDCs.
  - Encouraging the planning and implementation of long-term statistical development programs in accord with priorities of individual developing countries.
  - Encouraging the Food and Agriculture Organization and the Statistical Office of the United Nations, through U.S. representation, to organize the evaluation and conceptualization of alternative approaches for improving the development and implementation of food, agricultural, and rural statistics capability in all of their member nations.

- The American Agricultural Economics Association's (AAEA's) Economic Statistics Committee (in cooperation with the Rural Sociological Society and other professional associations, plus the Economic Research Service (ERS) and the National Agricultural Statistics Service (NASS) of the USDA, as well as land-grant university social science departments) to establish a multidisciplinary task force to:
  - Develop a more complete, integrated conceptual base for describing and analyzing the food system and rural society at state, local, agribusiness, farm, and household levels in coordination with national databases.
  - Create operational definitions of relevant social science variables and concepts so that measurements can be made conceptually consistent *from* underlying social science theories *through* statistical data collection procedures *to* the quantitative analyses to be performed. This large, complex task is not quickly or easily done.
  - Develop and apply the above conceptual frameworks in the work of NASS, ERS, the Bureau of the Census, and other relevant government agencies to
    - improve federal data collection, processing and analysis programs and
    - create a coordinated, government-wide, ten-year statistical development program for rural policy.

- More and better descriptive knowledge of values. Some of the values involved are monetary (prices, income, expenditures) while others are nonmonetary. Some values are more intrinsic while others (including prices) are extrinsic or exchange in nature. The following agenda items are important for the work of the RSSs.
  - Expansion and improvement of databases and information systems on such monetary values as input and product prices; expenditures; income (net and gross); the marginal earnings of land, labor, capital, and management; returns to institutional investments and disinvestments; taxation; distributions of monetary and nonmonetized incomes, etc.
  - Development of descriptive data and information systems on nonmonetary values that are important for public choice and private decisions, such as the more intrinsic and nonmonetary exchange values pertaining to the environment, food chain, human health, animal welfare, poverty, disadvantaged groups, justice, equality, participation, and many other conditions, situations, and things of important nonmonetary intrinsic and/or exchange value.
  - Improvement of descriptive data and information about values as to their
    - interpersonal validity and
    - cardinality as opposed to ordinality.

  Though these two measurement difficulties have long hampered such basic disciplinary social sciences as economics, sociology, political science, and anthropology and philosophy, efforts to overcome them must be continued because these data deficiencies seriously constrain problem-solving and issue-oriented work of all agriculturalists including rural social scientists.

- Merging (in our information system) the use of specialized econometric and other disciplinary techniques and methods into broader multidisciplinary, philosophically more eclectic, iterative/interactive, participatory efforts employing an expanded and improved public (multiple person) choice/transaction cost approach as recommended by SSAAP (see particularly the headings above on *rural and agricultural institutions* and the one below on *agroethics and philosophical orientations* and the corresponding sections of this book (Part III, Sections 1 and 3, and Part IV, Section 3).

Challenging Agendas for the Basic Social Science Disciplines (BSSDs)

This is the second of the four agenda sets that cut across the first six more problem- and issue-oriented agendas considered above. Much as the basic biological and physical sciences undergird the technical agricultural sciences, the BSSDs support the rural social sciences (RSSs) with disciplinary theories, basic measurements and techniques. Disciplinary deficiencies of the basic social sciences limit the problem-solving and subject-matter or issue-oriented work of either the rural social or technical agricultural sciences in ways that make disciplinary work to remedy such deficiencies a prerequisite for successful multidisciplinary problem-solving and subject-matter work. Also, the favorable synergistic impact of problem-solving and subject-matter work on basic disciplinary work is at least as important for the basic social as for the basic biological and physical science disciplines. Still further, in both cases, *applied*, specialized disciplinary work makes significant contributions to the multidisciplinary problem-solving and subject-matter work of our public and private agricultural institutions. Both social and biophysical disciplinary skills are commonly needed by multidisciplinary problem-solving and subject-matter teams addressing farm, rural, and consumer problems and issue-oriented subjects.

- With respect to applied disciplinary social science work on the food, fiber, and resource system and rural societies, the desire of disciplinarians to do such work should be encouraged and financed by our agricultural institutions so long as the applications are germane to the problem-solving and subject-matter responsibilities and missions of our agricultural institutions. In financing such work, agricultural administrators should recognize that:
  - Applied disciplinary work seldom has enough breadth to address all of the numerous, relevant disciplinary dimensions of a given practical problem or issue (subject), which leaves responsibility for obtaining such coverage with the administrations of our agricultural institutions rather than with the administrators of specialized basic disciplines such as economics, biogenetics, sociology, physics, or anthropology. If this responsibility is not recognized by agricultural and other administrators alike, there is danger of not fulfilling the problem-solving and subject-matter responsibilities of our agricultural institutions. Our political system will not long allow the problem-solving and subject-matter resources of our agricultural institutions to be used for applied disciplinary work if administrators do not provide the coordination and demand relevance for solving the problems and resolving issues assigned to our agricultural institutions by funders and different supporting clienteles.
  - Disciplinarians often have a greater interest in peer-reviewed (by other disciplinarians) publications than in practical problems and/or issues important in carrying out the obligations our agricultural institutions have to their different clienteles. In this respect, basic social science disciplinarians seem to differ little from their basic biological and physical science disciplinary counterparts.
- Although responsibility for funding basic disciplinary research and training in the social basic sciences resides mainly outside our agricultural institutions, the funds of our agricultural institutions can be appropriately used to
  - Support basic social science disciplinary training of agriculturalists (including rural social scientists) made necessary by the multidisciplinarity of the practical problem-solving and subject-matter responsibilities of our agricultural institutions.
  - Support research to remedy deficiencies in the basic social science disciplines that are known to limit solutions of practical problems and the resolution of practical issues faced by our agricultural institutions. See Part IV, Section 2, Chapter 5, of this book for detailed agenda items that focus on such relevant disciplinary deficiencies.
  - Support participation of disciplinary social scientists in multidisciplinary problem-solving and subject-matter teams in order to exploit the favorable synergistic effects of disciplinary work on problem-solving and subject-matter efforts. (See the next agenda item on problem-solving and subject-matter work by social science disciplinarians.)
- There are continuing *roles for social science disciplinarians to play in the ongoing multidisciplinary problem-solving and subject-matter work* of our agricultural institutions. These include related work in such disciplines as philosophy, statistics, and mathematics as well as roles for
  - disciplinary sociologists, economists, and historians (even though these have rural social science counterparts), and
  - anthropologists, psychologists, geographers, philosophers, mathematicians, systems scientists, and other disciplines without formally organized rural counterparts.

Ways of arranging for such disciplinary contributions include the use of consultancies, contracts, cooperative agreements, and a variety of other arrangements that specify financial and performance responsibilities while making clear the multidisciplinary nature of the practical problem-solving and subject-matter efforts to which disciplinarians will contribute.

- SSAAP's agendas call repeatedly for the development and extension of the transaction cost/public choice approach into a *truly multidisciplinary* approach. Accomplishing this will require theoretical, empirical, and methodological contributions from all of the basic social science disciplines.

Challenging Agendas with Respect to Agroethics and Philosophic Orientations

This is the third set of agendas that cut across the first six agenda sets. Many rural and basic social scientists and administrators of our agricultural institutions are committed to a philosophic orientation sometimes labeled "reductionist logical positivism." Being reductionist, this orientation tends to fragment the quest for knowledge in the conviction that fragmentary bits of knowledge can be assembled into overall bodies of knowledge. As such, this orientation does not serve multidisciplinary teams doing holistic multidisciplinary problem-solving and subject-matter work as well as it serves disciplinarians attempting to improve the theories, measurements and techniques of their specialized disciplines and subdisciplines. Further, since logical positivism presupposes the impossibility of using experience to derive empirical descriptions of values as characteristics of the real world, that orientation makes it difficult for its adherents to perceive of having or even trying to attain objective descriptive knowledge of "real world" values to use in doing problem-solving and subject-matter work. Also restricted by this orientation is a considerable portion of the disciplinary work done on exchange (or extrinsic) and intrinsic values in such basic disciplinary social sciences as economics, sociology, political science, history, geography, and anthropology. Social scientists as advisors, consultants, resident instructors, administrators, activists, extension workers, and entrepreneurs must often deal with nonmonetary values in ways that presume interpersonal, descriptive validity and cardinality of value knowledge. Unfortunately, many administrators of our agricultural institutions bring reductionist, logically positivistic orientations with them from biological, physical, and even social science backgrounds when they assume administrative responsibilities in our agricultural institutions.

In recent years, approximately ten national conferences on agroethics have arisen out of neglect of the social science dimensions of such practical rural and farm problems and issues as those involving institutional changes, animal welfare, poverty, human development, technical change, food-chain contamination, environmental pollution, disadvantaged minorities, rural poverty, gender inequality, and natural resource degradation. These conferences and SSAAP's own work indicate the importance of:

- Establishing research, resident instruction, and extension programs both within and outside of the land-grant/USDA system to deal with the normative dimensions and ethical aspects of the practical problems and subject-matter issues of rural societies and the food, fiber, and natural resource system.

- Encouraging disciplinary work in the basic social science disciplines and humanities on values, public choosing, and private decision making to:
  - Increase the interpersonal descriptive validity and cardinality of our knowledge of values.
  - Improve our knowledge of decision rules for converting value and relatively value-free knowledge into prescriptive knowledge for solving problems.

- Recognizing the various complex roles of optimization in reaching prescriptions.

- Supporting:
  - Further work on the public choice (multiple person)/transaction cost approach to public and private choices and decisions to move that approach beyond its present rather primitive state by participating actively in its expansion and development as outlined in the above subsection called *challenging agendas for improving rural and agricultural institutions.* (See also Part IV, Section 2, Chapter 3.)
  - Iterative/interactive, participatory, multidisciplinary scenario analyses of problematic and subject-matter domains.

Challenging Agendas Pertaining to Research on Administration and Funding

Despite substantial research capabilities, our agricultural institutions fail to do adequate research on their own administrative and funding problems. Crosscutting social science research is needed on important decisions concerning the organization and funding of our agricultural institutions. This research should be done in and funded by both land-grant and non-land-grant universities, the USDA, the U. S. Agency for International Development (USAID), the National Science Foundation, private foundations, and industry. (See Part V, Chapters 1, 2, 5, 6, and 8, much more detail concerning and supporting this set of agendas.) SSAAP's agenda includes research to:

- Improve the administration and organization of rural and disciplinary social science teaching in order, for example, to:
  - Establish appropriate mixes and scopes of general education, disciplinary, professional, and "hands-on" experiences for students.
  - Improve the international dimensions of courses/curriculum.
  - Determine the types and numbers of undergraduate rural social science majors that should be offered in a modern undergraduate agriculture college.

- Appraise alternative graduate education models for the rural and basic disciplinary social sciences involving an appropriate balance between specialization to advance a discipline or agricultural field and the need to provide broader educational experiences for farm and rural professionals who will work on multidisciplinary, real-world problems and subjects or issues.

- Discover more systematic ways to keep rural social and technical agricultural scientists informed about advances in their respective basic disciplines, on one hand, and for improving their skills for working cooperatively with each other in multidisciplinary teams on practical, multidisciplinary problems and subjects, on the other.

- Improve off-campus educational systems to utilize various technological developments, alternative media, and new organizational relationships and partnerships within and outside the university.

- Investigate issues and problems pertaining to administration of agricultural research, including:
  - Evaluation of alternative methods for determining agricultural research priorities for different levels and mixes of resources.
  - Performance of alternative systems in obtaining feedback information from various clienteles.
  - Methods for determining the appropriate mixes of problem-solving, subject-matter, and disciplinary efforts within and across institutions.

- Performance of alternative faculty reward systems in sustaining multidisciplinary subject-matter and practical problem-solving as well as disciplinary research.
- Evaluation of alternative strategies to maintain flexible options in the funding and administration of research, extension, resident instruction, and other activities, and organizations.
- Assessment of alternative strategies for generating public support for rural and basic disciplinary social, biological, and physical science research.

SSAAP'S MORE DETAILED AND SPECIFIC STRATEGIC CHALLENGES

The administrative and funding challenges of the above ten agendas cannot be effectively met by the administrators of the rural and basic social sciences without assistance from the rural and social scientists they administer. SSAAP explicitly recognizes that the multidisciplinarity of practical problem-solving and subject-matter work creates enormous administrative burdens in connection with defining problems and issues, designing multidisciplinary programs and projects, funding, administering, interacting iteratively with clienteles, evaluating problem-solving and subject-matter as well as disciplinary work, and communicating results to users. The rather specific interrelated strategies below supplement the broader strategies stressed earlier in this summary. The detailed strategies fall into two categories, the *first* for administrators and the *second* for rural and basic social scientists.

MORE DETAILED CHALLENGES FOR ADMINISTRATORS:

As indicated in its first pages, this executive summary is structured around broad strategies SSAAP believes are needed to improve the capacity and effectiveness of the rural social sciences in serving farmers, agribusinesses, consumers, and nonfarm rural residents. In this section, administrators are *challenged in more specific ways* than in the broad overall challenges presented at the beginning of this summary. SSAAP believes it is important for administrators to:

- Develop administrative flexibility in utilizing a wide variety of organizational models to carry out missions involving the work of the rural and basic social sciences on the problems and issues of rural societies and agriculture.

- Recognize that administrative needs increase as the proportion of an administrative unit's multidisciplinary problem-solving and subject-matter efforts increase relative to its disciplinary work.

- Use and encourage entrepreneurially inclined professionals to define problems and issues, develop projects and programs, mobilize resources, and conduct short-term multidisciplinary problem-solving and subject-matter efforts.

- Increase budget flexibility for pursuing critical new problem-solving and subject-matter initiatives by
  - aggressively seeking "soft money" for current problems and issues,
  - using proportionately more short-term contractual, nontenured professionals, and
  - even by withholding some percentage of a unit's "hard money" to be "earned" by those in the unit who are willing to address new, critical, multidisciplinary problems and subjects.

- Increase planning for research, resident instruction, extension, and public service, with stress on important current practical problems and issues, while leaving finance to follow rather than to determine plans of work.

- Require the training of new and the retraining of some existing administrators and "working professionals" to make them more aware of the:
  - Important differences between disciplinary and multidisciplinary problem-solving and subject-matter work.
  - Great differences in needs, characteristics, and relevant capabilities of the various disciplines, applied fields, and units for which they are responsible. This includes recognizing the important differences that exist *between* the needs of rural social scientists *and* those of the technical biological and physical agricultural scientists for office space, assistants, computers, secretaries, etc.

- Rethink, reorganize, and rebalance administrative processes so that the priorities coming to the fore are based on careful consideration of not only the biological and physical but also the social science dimensions of problems and issues. This requires that social scientists be routinely involved in the planning and execution of problem-solving and subject-matter programs and projects.

- Establish advisory groups of qualified rural and basic disciplinary social scientists in governmental agencies, colleges, and other primary administrative units of the public, parastatal, or private-sector institutions that are concerned with agriculture and rural society to help ensure that the rural and basic social sciences are funded, used, and administered so that social scientists can
  - make appropriate contributions to multidisciplinary problem-solving and subject-matter efforts while
  - bringing about the advances in the basic social science disciplines that are needed for the improvement of farming, agribusinesses, consumer well-being, and rural societies.

- Restore and increase promotion, salary adjustment, and recognition credit for problem-solving and subject-matter publications in agricultural experiment stations, extension services, and other agencies by recognizing that such work can be of high quality and reflect scholarly objectivity and excellence. Similar recognition should be extended for "quality" television, radio, teaching, oral presentations, advising, and consulting to serve the various clienteles of our agricultural institutions.

- Develop closer research, teaching, extension, and other linkages (1) *between* the rural social sciences *and* the basic social science disciplines and (2) *between* the rural and basic social sciences *and* the basic and agricultural biological and physical sciences.

- Develop closer linkages for cooperation:
  - Among land-grant universities within regions.
  - Between the 1862 and 1890 land-grant universities to address the problems of disadvantaged rural farm and nonfarm African-Americans.
  - Among land-grant and non-land-grant universities and disadvantaged Hispanic, Native American, and Caucasian peoples and their organizations.
  - Among university social science research and teaching programs, government agencies with agricultural and rural missions, and other agencies with substantial social science capability.
  - Of rural social science departments with biological and physical agricultural science departments and related groups, such as professional associations; industry/commodity groups; farm and rural organizations and leaders; natural resource, food, and environmental groups; and national, state, and local governments.
  - Between the rural social science associations and the national policy- and priority-setting organs of the USDA/land-grant system.
  - Of the rural social sciences with the primary international-, national-, and state-level organizations important to science funding and science policy.

- Strengthen the roles of the rural and basic social sciences in international organizations such as the World Bank, the Food and Agriculture Organization (FAO), and various regional development banks.

- Develop a stable U.S. institutional system and program to encourage and fund sustained, coordinated, and carefully evaluated efforts by rural and basic social sciences working with the biological and physical agricultural sciences on problems and subjects germane to agriculture and rural society in *developing nations*. This is necessary because:
  - U.S. efforts are now generated and financed largely in an ad hoc manner using "soft monies" from U.S. government agencies such as USAID, foundations, and international organizations.
  - We are rapidly losing much of our present social science capabilities for international work, especially in universities, because we are now failing to replace the retiring cohort of social scientists that has worked on farm and rural problems of developing countries.

It should be pointed out that the first nine of the substantive agendas presented earlier make still more specific, detailed demands on administrators that are not included here but should not be ignored. In this connection, see Part V, Chapter 8.

SOCIAL SCIENTISTS:

These challenges are for both basic and rural social scientists whose support and administrative help is needed by administrators in defining and clarifying practical problems and issues, in designing multidisciplinary subject-matter and problem-solving programs and projects, in obtaining funding, in evaluating rural and basic social science work, and in communicating results of social science efforts. In order to execute the administrative and funding strategies and ensure effective use of SSAAP's agendas, rural and basic social scientists are challenged to:

- Seek and accept long-term administrative positions in academia, government, parastatals, and the private sector so that the rural and basic social sciences can be better represented in public, parastatal, academic, and private administrative and executive circles.

- Serve on administrative committees in our agricultural institutions to further multidisciplinary subject-matter and problem-solving research, teaching, extension, advisory, administrative, and consultative work.

- Recognize the importance and value of problem-solving and subject-matter work for the many different clienteles of our agricultural institutions.

- Facilitate contributions of basic social science disciplinarians to:
  - The multidisciplinary problem-solving and subject-matter work of our agricultural and rural institutions.
  - Overcoming the deficiencies of their disciplines for the problem-solving and subject-matter work of our agricultural institutions.

- Serve as "entrepreneurs" in developing problem-solving and subject-matter work in such presently neglected areas as human capital formation, assistance to disadvantaged farm and nonfarm rural groups, institutional ("rules of the game," policy, program, organizational, and infrastructural) improvements, natural and manmade resource enhancements, and technical advance.

- Accept temporary administration responsibilities for multidisciplinary problem-solving and subject-matter projects and programs.

- Press for funding of:
  - Work on the social science dimensions of multidisciplinary subject-matter and problem-solving work in our agricultural institutions.
  - Competitive grants for the basic social science disciplines to help them overcome the disciplinary deficiencies that constrain work on farm and rural problems and issues.

- Endeavor to broaden their own philosophic orientations and those of their administrators to facilitate work with values in doing subject-matter and prescriptive problem-solving work for farmers and their families, rural people and societies, agribusinesses, and the consumers of food, fiber, and resource products and services.

MEETING THE CHALLENGES

Social scientists and their administrators have it within their means to meet the challenges presented by SSAAP's agendas and, in so doing, to greatly increase the contributions of our agricultural institutions to farmers and their families, rural people and societies, agribusinesses, and consumers of food, fiber, and natural resource commodities and services.

- The required reorientation will not be expensive to carry out.

- Mobilization of the will to reorient and execute the needed changes need not be expensive.

- Further, attaining some of the agendas presented herein will increase the effectiveness with which present resources are used.

- In turn, greater effectiveness in addressing problems and issues will facilitate the mobilization of additional resources and overall general support for our agricultural institutions.

- Finally, the increase the recommended reorientation will enable social scientists to *earn* more resources and support with which to execute their responsibilities within SSAAP's agendas.

INDEX TO PART V

A

B

I

J

K

L

M

N

T

U

W

Y

Z

Putting the Puzzle Togethe

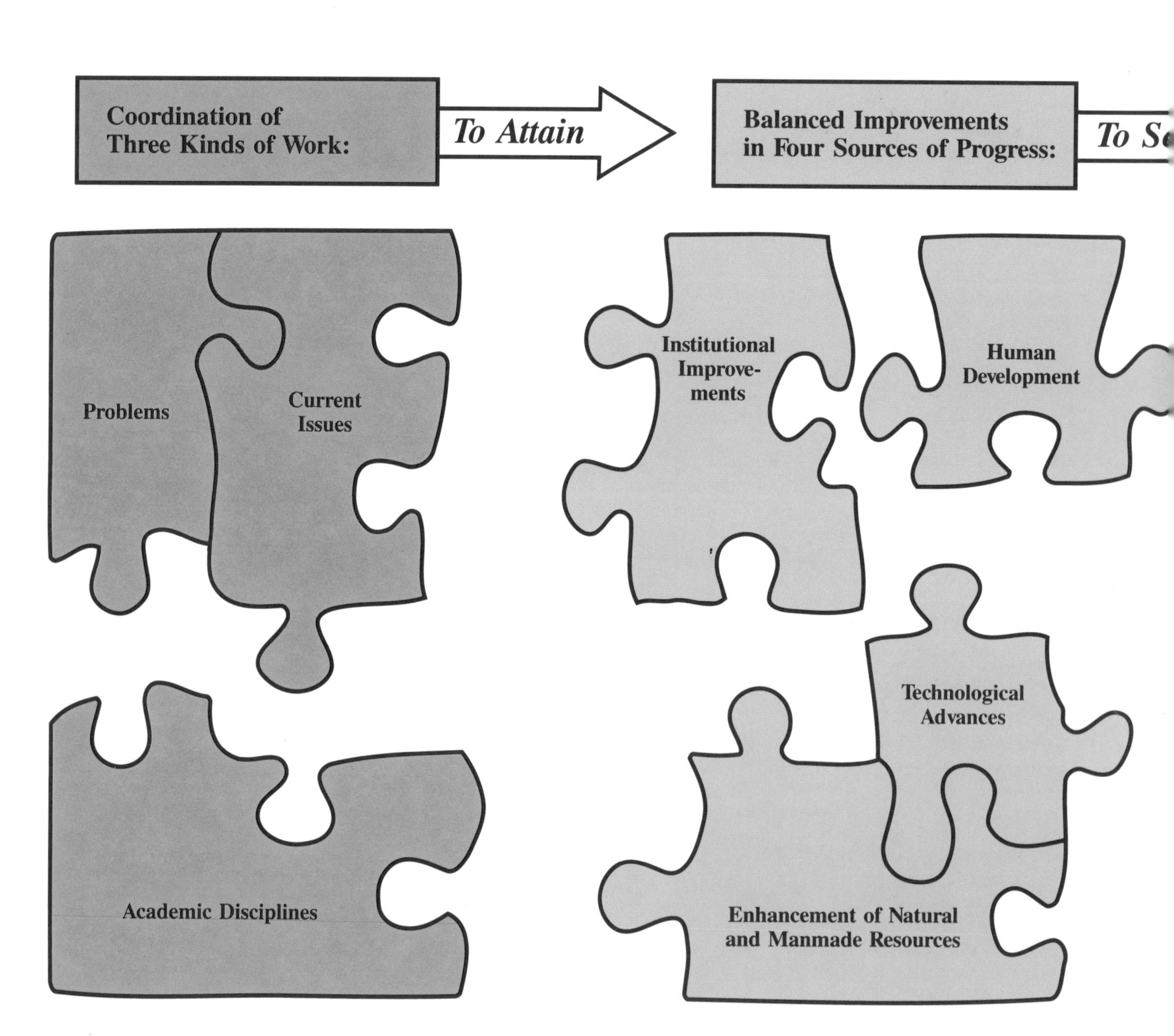